To the Masses

# Historical Materialism Book Series

The Historical Materialism Book Series is a major publishing initiative of the radical left. The capitalist crisis of the twenty-first century has been met by a resurgence of interest in critical Marxist theory. At the same time, the publishing institutions committed to Marxism have contracted markedly since the high point of the 1970s. The Historical Materialism Book Series is dedicated to addressing this situation by making available important works of Marxist theory. The aim of the series is to publish important theoretical contributions as the basis for vigorous intellectual debate and exchange on the left.

The peer-reviewed series publishes original monographs, translated texts, and reprints of classics across the bounds of academic disciplinary agendas and across the divisions of the left. The series is particularly concerned to encourage the internationalization of Marxist debate and aims to translate significant studies from beyond the English-speaking world.

*For a full list of titles in the Historical Materialism Book Series*
*available in paperback from Haymarket Books, visit:*
www.haymarketbooks.org/category/hm-series

# To the Masses

*Proceedings of the Third Congress
of the Communist International, 1921*

Edited and translated by
John Riddell

Haymarket Books
Chicago, IL

First published in 2015 by Brill Academic Publishers, The Netherlands
© 2015 Koninklijke Brill NV, Leiden, The Netherlands

Published in paperback in 2015 by
Haymarket Books
P.O. Box 180165
Chicago, IL 60618
773-583-7884
www.haymarketbooks.org

ISBN: 978-1-60846-635-1

Trade distribution:
In the US, Consortium Book Sales, www.cbsd.com
In Canada, Publishers Group Canada, www.pgcbooks.ca
In the UK, Turnaround Publisher Services, http://www.turnaround-uk.com
In all other countries, Publishers Group Worldwide, www.pgw.com

Cover design by Ragina Johnson.

This book was published with the generous support of
Lannan Foundation and the Wallace Global Fund.

Printed in Canada by union labor.

10 9 8 7 6 5 4 3 2 1

Library of Congress Cataloging-in-Publication data is available.

# Contents

List of Speakers ......................................................................... ix

Editorial Introduction .................................................................. 1
   1. Background to the Congress ............................................. 3
      1a. 1920: Year of Great Hopes ........................................... 3
      1b. Four Historic Conventions ........................................... 9
      1c. The German Party Turns Left ..................................... 14
      1d. The March Action ........................................................ 18
   2. The Third Congress ............................................................ 24
      2a. The Contending Forces Meet in Moscow .................. 24
      2b. Disputes over National Parties .................................. 29
      2c. The Main Congress Debate ........................................ 33
      2d. Profile of a Compromise ............................................. 37
      2e. The Comintern Broadens Its Scope ........................... 40
   3. School of Strategy ................................................................ 45
About This Edition ...................................................................... 47
Acknowledgements ..................................................................... 51
List of Abbreviations ................................................................... 53

*Preliminary Statements*
Provisional Congress Agenda .................................................... 57
Call for the Third World Congress ............................................ 59
Invitation to the Third Congress of the Communist International ........ 67

*Proceedings and Resolutions*
Session 1. Opening Session (22 June) ....................................... 73
Session 2. World Economy – Report (23 June) ......................... 101
Session 3. World Economy – Discussion (24 June) .................. 135
Session 4. Executive Committee Report (25 June) ................... 175
Session 5. Executive Committee Report – Discussion (26 June) ............. 239
Session 6. Executive Committee Report – Discussion (27 June) ............. 271
Session 7. Executive Committee Report – Discussion (27 June) ............. 303

vi • Contents

Session 8. The KAPD; the Italian Question (28 June) ............................... 329
Session 9. Italian Question; Executive Report (29 June) .......................... 355
Session 10. Tactics and Strategy – Report (30 June) ................................. 403
Session 11. Tactics and Strategy – Discussion (1 July) .............................. 447
Session 12. Tactics and Strategy – Discussion (1 July) .............................. 481
Session 13. Tactics and Strategy – Discussion (2 July) .............................. 517
Session 14. Tactics and Strategy – Discussion (2 July) .............................. 561
Session 15. Trade Unions – Reports (3 July) ............................................. 599
Session 16. World Economy; Trade Union Discussion (4 July) ............... 627
Session 17. Russian Communist Party (5 July) ......................................... 651
Session 18. Trade Unions – Discussion (6 July) ........................................ 705
Session 19. Trade Unions – Discussion (7 July) ........................................ 731
Session 20. Youth and Women's Movements (8 July) .............................. 765
Session 21. Tactics and Strategy, Germany, Cooperatives (9 July) ......... 797
Session 22. Cooperatives, Organisation (10 July) ..................................... 809
Session 23. Eastern Question (12 July) ...................................................... 835
Session 24. Closing Session (12 July) ......................................................... 871
List of Delegations ....................................................................................... 897

*Theses, Resolutions, and Appeals*
   Theses on the World Situation and the Tasks of the Communist
      International ........................................................................................ 901
   Resolution on the Report by the Executive Committee of the
      Communist International .................................................................. 921
   Theses on Tactics and Strategy ................................................................ 924
   The March Action and the Situation in the VKPD ................................ 951
   Appeal for Max Hoelz ............................................................................... 952
   Theses on the Communist International and the Red International
      of Labour Unions ............................................................................... 953
   Resolution on Work in the Cooperative Movement ............................. 966
   Theses on the Work of Communists in the Cooperatives .................... 967
   Theses on the Report Concerning the Policies of the Communist
      Party of Russia ................................................................................... 970
   Resolution on the Policies of the Communist Party of Russia ........... 977
   Theses on the Organisational Structure of the Communist Parties
      and the Methods and Content of their Work ................................. 978
   Resolution on Organising the Communist International .................... 1007
   Theses on Methods and Forms of Work of the Communist Parties
      among Women ................................................................................... 1009

Resolution on International Ties between Communist Women
and the International Communist Women's Secretariat .............. 1026
Resolution on Forms and Methods of Communist Work
among Women ........................................................................ 1028
The Communist International and the Communist Youth
Movement ............................................................................... 1030
Forward to New Work and New Struggles (ECCI Appeal) ............ 1034
Addendum: Amendments to Theses on Tactics and Strategy
(Not Approved) ...................................................................... 1041

*Appendices*
1. Before the Congress: The Open Letter .................................... 1061
   1a. Open Letter to German Workers' Organisations,
       8 January 1921 ................................................................. 1061
   1b. ECCI Debate on Open Letter, 22 February ....................... 1063
2. Before the Congress: The March Action ................................. 1071
   2a. Radek to VKPD Leaders in Berlin, 14 March .................... 1071
   2b. VKPD Theses on March Action, 7 April ........................... 1072
   2c. Resolution by Clara Zetkin on March Action, 7 April ....... 1079
   2d. Lenin to Zetkin and Levi on Open Letter, Livorno, and VKPD
       Leadership, 16 April .......................................................... 1086
   2e. Béla Kun Defends March Action to Lenin, 6 May ............. 1088
   2f. Paul Levi Appeals to Third Congress, 31 May .................. 1090
3. The Political Struggle at the Congress: June 1921 .................... 1097
   3a. Lenin to Zinoviev on Tasks at Congress, 10 June .............. 1097
   3b. Lenin on the Theses on Organisation, 10–11 June, 9 July ........... 1101
   3c. German Delegation to ECCI on Zetkin's Role, 10 June ................ 1104
   3d. German Delegation Gives Conditional Support to
       Draft Theses, 16 June ......................................................... 1106
   3e. Lenin Withdraws Harsh Language, 16 June ..................... 1107
   3f. ECCI Debate on French Communist Party and Leftism,
       16–17 June .......................................................................... 1108
   3g. Zetkin on March Action Resolution, 18 June .................... 1132
   3h. Radek on Differences among Bolshevik Leaders, 21 June ......... 1135
   3i. Zetkin on Discussions with Lenin ...................................... 1137
   3j. Zetkin Sends Levi a Congress Update, 22 June ................. 1148
   3k. Zetkin to Lenin on Personal Attacks, 28 June ................... 1151
4. The Political Struggle at the Congress: July 1921 ...................... 1153
   4a. Trotsky Reports to Lenin on Congress Debate, 3 July .......... 1153
   4b. Lenin on Šmeral and Czechoslovak Party, 6 July ................ 1155

| | | |
|---|---|---|
| 4c. | Lenin Reassures Hungarian Delegates, 7 July | 1157 |
| 4d. | German Delegation Meets with Bolshevik Leaders, 9 July | 1158 |
| 4e. | Lenin Speaks to Central European Delegates, 11 July | 1170 |
| 4f. | Zetkin on Taking Leave from Lenin | 1174 |
| 4g. | Lenin on His Final Meeting with Zetkin, 28 July | 1176 |
| 4h. | Lenin on the Outcome of the Levi Initiative, 14 August | 1178 |

5. The Colonial Question ................................................................ 1181
   5a. M.N. Roy: Theses on the Eastern Question ................................ 1181
   5b. Ahmed Sultanzade: Theses on the Eastern Question ................ 1187
   5c. Zhang Tailei: Theses on the Colonial Question ......................... 1191
   5d. Ivon Jones: The Black Question ................................................. 1193
   5e. Against Repression in Palestine ................................................. 1196

Chronology ............................................................................................ 1199
Glossary ................................................................................................. 1203
Selected Bibliography ......................................................................... 1251
Index ...................................................................................................... 1265

# List of Speakers

Session 1. Opening Session
  Zinoviev 73, Kamenev 83, Vaillant-Couturier 86, Frölich 87, Hewlett 89, Kolarov 93, Burian 96, Gennari 97, Tommasi 97, Taguchi 98
Session 2. World Economy – Report
  Trotsky 102
Session 3. World Economy – Discussion
  Brand 135, Sachs 139, Seemann 142, Pogány 145, Thalheimer 150, Bell 151, Zetkin 154, Roy 156, Koenen 157, Trotsky 159
Session 4. Executive Committee Report
  Radek 175, Zinoviev 179
Session 5. Executive Committee Report – Discussion
  Hempel 239, Frölich 242, Roland-Holst 245, Neumann 247, Ceton 249, Michalak 250, Seemann 252, Gennari 254, Heckert 256, Malzahn 260, Münzenberg 263, Radek 265
Session 6. Executive Committee Report – Discussion
  Malzahn 271, Radek 272, Jacquemotte 273, Marković 275, Kolarov 281, Zetkin 283
Session 7. Executive Committee Report – Discussion
  Friesland 303, van Overstraeten 308, Koenen 310, Terracini 316, Javadzadeh 322, Rákosi 323, Smythe 328
Session 8. The KAPD; the Italian Question
  Zinoviev 329, Hempel 330, Radek 330, Bergmann 331, Roland-Holst 336, Lazzari 339, Gennari 344, Lenin 349
Session 9. Italian Question; Executive Report
  Maffi 360, Rakovsky 366, Zetkin 371, Trotsky 374, Loriot 379, Lozovsky 382, Loriot 387, Sachs 387, Radek 388, Heckert 389, Zinoviev 389, Roland-Holst 390, Malzahn 391, Neumann 393, Zinoviev 395
Session 10. Tactics and Strategy – Report
  Lazzari 403, Höglund 404, Radek 406
Session 11. Tactics and Strategy – Discussion
  Hempel 448, Terracini 457, Lenin 465, Michalak 473, Vaughan 476

Session 12. Tactics and Strategy – Discussion
  Heckert 481, Burian 494, Malzahn 499, Bukharin 508
Session 13. Tactics and Strategy – Discussion
  Ballister 519, Friesland 522, Brand 526, Neumann 528, Münzenberg 533, Lukács 536, Thalheimer 539, Zetkin 542, Vaillant-Couturier 548, Bell 551, Sachs 556
Session 14. Tactics and Strategy – Discussion
  Zinoviev 561, Thälmann 569, Trotsky 571, Radek 583, Zetkin 595
Session 15. Trade Unions – Reports
  Zinoviev 599, Heckert 613
Session 16. World Economy; Trade Union Discussion
  Varga 627, Bergmann 637, Earsman 648
Session 17. Russian Communist Party
  Heckert 652, Zetkin 653, Loriot 654, Lenin 656, Sachs 671, Radek 674, Kollontai 679, Trotsky 683, Kerran 689, Hempel 691, Roland-Holst 695, Bukharin 697
Session 18. Trade Unions – Discussion
  Malzahn 705, Misiano 708, Rwal 712, Haywood 715, Brand 719, Lozovsky 719, Marshall 726
Session 19. Trade Unions – Discussion
  Landler 731, Riehs 734, Rees 735, Morgan 737, Hourwich 741, Torralba Beci 743, Kolarov 744, Tommasi 746, Bell 755, Pivio 759, Marković 762
Session 20. Youth and Women's Movements
  Münzenberg 765, Frölich 777, Zetkin 779, Colliard 790, Kollontai 791
Session 21. Tactics and Strategy, Germany, Cooperatives
  Radek 797, Sachs 803, Zinoviev 804, Malzahn 805, Meshcheriakov 807
Session 22. Cooperatives, Organisation
  Koenen 809, Schaffner 832, Zinoviev 833, Vaillant-Couturier 834
Session 23. Eastern Question
  Mann 835, Nuri 838, Dimitratos 839, Aqazadeh 841, Makhul Bey 843, Zinoviev 849, Kasyan 850, Tskhakaia 852, Abilov 854, Roy 855, Zhang Tailei 856, Nam Man-ch'un 857, Yoshihara 859, Kara-Gadiyev 864, Julien 865, Colliard 869, Kolarov 870
Session 24. Closing Session
  Koenen 871, Frölich 873, Koenen 874, Zinoviev 882, Heckert 883, Zinoviev 890

# Editorial Introduction

'To the masses!' – that was the call of the Communist International's Third Congress, held in Moscow 22 June–12 July 1921, to supporters around the world. 'The power of capitalism', the congress appeal stated, 'can be broken only if the idea of communism takes shape in the impetuous upsurge of the proletariat's large majority, led by mass Communist parties, which forge indissoluble ties to the fighting proletarian class.'[1]

This appeal was the heart of a strategy developed by the congress in response to a sharp change in political conditions in Europe: from a time of tumultuous workers' upsurge to a period in which the goal of socialist revolution appeared less imminent. The Communist International (Comintern) sought to develop a plan to prepare for revolution in a period in which it did not appear immediately on the agenda and the working class, although organised and combative, was in retreat.

Prior to the congress, the International's several million members were divided on the nature of this shift and how to respond to it. As the congress convened, with more than 600 delegates from 55 countries in attendance, its outcome was still in doubt, and the majority of its participants favoured a course quite different from what was ultimately adopted. The record of three weeks of congress debates, presented

---

1. Quoted from the post-congress ECCI appeal, p. 1034. See also pp. 234 (Zinoviev) and 269, 417, 442 (Radek).

in these pages, displays a global movement's complex and shifting debate on the questions defining its future course – including many issues still posed today.

The multitude of viewpoints expressed in congress sessions were grouped around two alternative courses of action. A 'leftist' option aimed to galvanise workers into revolutionary struggle through the bold initiatives of a Communist minority. It was expressed most clearly in amendments to the Theses on Tactics and Strategy proposed by the German, Austrian, and Italian delegations. Other forces, led by V.I. Lenin and Leon Trotsky and termed by Lenin as the 'Right', sought to advance toward revolution by rooting Communists in the daily struggles of the working class.[2]

The decisions of the congress laid down a strategic line of march that has guided the actions of revolutionary forces into the twenty-first century. The legacy of the congress includes:

1. A strategy seeking to win to communism a majority of the working class through committed involvement in workers' daily struggles. This course was expressed in the congress call, 'to the masses', and formulated more precisely by Clara Zetkin (quoting Lenin) as, 'Win over the masses as a precondition to winning power'.[3]
2. A campaign to draw together the diverse expressions of anticapitalist resistance in a 'united fighting front of the proletariat'. This approach was expanded, six months later, to embrace alliances with non-revolutionary currents within the working-class movement in what became known as 'the united front'.[4]
3. A proposal to integrate into the International's programme what later became known as 'transitional demands', that is, demands infringing on capitalist property rights and power, as part of 'a system of demands that, in their totality, undermine the power of the bourgeoisie, organise the proletariat, and mark out the different stages of the struggle for proletarian dictatorship'.[5]

---

2. For the amendments, see pp. 1041–58. This introduction avoids the term 'ultraleft', which was not used in the Third Congress, and uses instead the words 'leftist' or 'left' found in the congress text. For Lenin's use of the term 'Right', see his letter of 14 August 1921, p. 1178–80.

3. The concept 'to the masses' was first voiced at the congress by Zinoviev in his opening report: 'The main slogan is to make sure that we attain the majority and reach the masses.' See p. 234. For Zetkin's formulation, quoting Lenin, see p. 1142.

4. See p. 1036; Riddell (ed.) 2011b, *Toward the United Front: Proceedings of the Fourth Congress of the Communist International* (hereinafter 4WC), pp. 1164–73.

5. See p. 936. See also Fourth Congress discussion, Riddell (ed.) 2011b, 4WC, pp. 34–6, 509–15, 631.

4. An analysis of how fluctuations in the capitalist economy can promote anticapitalist consciousness, taking the place of reliance on the expectation of capitalist collapse.[6]
5. In a discussion marked by sharp antagonisms and many missteps, the congress sought, through frank debate and in a spirit of compromise, to promote principled unity of the diverse forces linked to the International.

The congress consisted of not just its plenary discussions and resolutions, fully recorded in these pages, but also a multitude of executive, commission, and special meetings held before it convened and while it was in session. The course of these consultations and deliberations is reflected in this volume by thirty-two appended documents, most published here for the first time in English. The present editorial introduction aims to provide a readers' guide to this diverse material, knitting together discussion inside and outside the formal sessions and supplying necessary context. The introduction also reviews events during the fifteen months prior to the congress that gave rise to the dispute in the Moscow gathering and figured centrally in its discussions.

## 1. Background to the Congress

### 1a. 1920: Year of Great Hopes

The strategic disagreement in the Communist International, perceptible since its foundation in March 1919, emerged and widened because of a contradiction in workers' experience during 1920. Following the Comintern's Second Congress in June–July 1920, hundreds of thousands of revolutionary-minded workers joined its ranks, building a number of mass Communist parties, especially in Germany, France, and Czechoslovakia. Meanwhile, however, the working class as a whole suffered severe setbacks, especially in the Polish-Soviet War and in the two non-Soviet countries closest to revolution, Italy and Germany. The postwar wave of worker radicalism was visibly receding. Communists diverged in their response to this situation. Some proposed launching their newly enlarged forces into an offensive before it was too late, while others favoured policies adapted to a less rapid pace of revolution. The story of the Third Congress must therefore be traced from the moment, fifteen months earlier, when a marked strategic divergence appeared in the Comintern's leadership.

---

6. See pp. 440–2 (report), 919–20 (theses).

## The Kapp Putsch in Germany

Third Congress discussion often referred to disagreements on the Communists' conduct during a March 1920 workers' mobilisation in Germany against a military coup led by Wolfgang Kapp. When right-wing army detachments seized Berlin that month and put to flight the Social-Democratic-led government, the army command refused to defend constitutional rule, while workers across Germany rose up in a massive general strike. Within four days, the Kapp Putsch was defeated, but workers continued their strike, seeking effective measures against rightist violence. Armed workers controlled some areas, including much of the industrial Ruhr region. The army moved against them, and capitalist forces soon regained the upper hand. Revolutionary workers wondered why they had been unable to take advantage of their best opportunity since the German revolution of November 1918. In particular, four actions during the Kapp days by the Communist Party of Germany (KPD) came in for critical scrutiny:

- When the general strike broke out, the Communist Party's central leadership initially refused to support it on the grounds that strikers opposing the coup were defending a repressive bourgeois government.
- In some areas, the KPD took part in or led alliances of workers' organisations, including the procapitalist SPD, that for a time wielded effective power.
- At one point, the KPD expressed conditional support for a trade-union proposal to form a government of all workers' parties and trade unions.
- During the final stage of the struggle, when the army was poised to crush workers' armed detachments in the Ruhr, the KPD favoured a proposed agreement to avert a massacre and pacify the region without an army incursion.

The KPD's conduct during the Kapp episode came under fire from many leaders in the party and the International. Karl Radek, who led collaboration of the Comintern Executive (ECCI) with the KPD, said that both its leadership's initial abstention and its later conditional support of a united workers' government reflected an underlying passivity. Béla Kun, former leader of the 1919 Hungarian soviet republic, denounced the 'model of unity' encompassing all workers' tendencies as 'counterrevolutionary'. Some 'leftist' critics of the KPD reacted by organising the Communist Workers' Party (KAPD); others formed a left opposition within the KPD, represented at the Third Congress by Paul Frölich, Arkadi Maslow, and others.[7]

---

7. See Broué 2005, p. 389 (Radek); *Kommunismus*, 1, 12–13 (3 April 1920), pp. 349–50 (Kun).

Lenin, for his part, expressed critical support for the KPD's response on a united workers' government, doing so in May and again in June 1920. However, the Second Congress (June–July 1920) did not take up the disputed aspects of the KPD's response. A year later, in the Third Congress, the Kapp Putsch was cited by Comintern leaders to condemn the KPD leadership of the time, headed by Paul Levi, for rightist errors, inactivity, and support of the 'workers' government' proposal – the same points made by the KAPD and the KPD's own left opposition.[8]

*The Second World Congress*

Although silent on lessons of the Kapp Putsch experience, the Second Congress took a series of decisions establishing the programmatic and principled framework in which the Third Congress debates took place. Indeed, the Second Congress marked the International's real foundation as a union of parties with tens of thousands of members and deep roots in workers' struggles. Delegates and guests represented diverse currents, ranging from revolutionary nationalists of Asia to anarchists and left-wing Social Democrats of the West. The 1919 founding congress had not discussed the role of Communist parties; by contrast, the 1920 gathering placed the need to build such parties at the centre of the International's strategy. Its resolutions, dealing with the nature and role of Communist parties, participation in trade unions and in parliamentary elections, peasant struggles against exploitation, and anticolonial movements, were often cited in the Third Congress as the framework for its discussions.[9]

The Second Congress also grappled with a challenge posed by the International's new popularity. The Comintern had become 'rather fashionable', one of its resolutions noted, and stood in danger 'of being diluted by vacillating and irresolute groups' – such as the Socialists of France and the Independent Socialists (USPD) of Germany – who were still steeped in the ideology and practices of the pre-1914 Socialist (Second) International. Seeking to challenge the grip of a bureaucratic layer of journalists, parliamentarians, and officials within such parties, the congress adopted twenty-one 'conditions for admission' aimed at enabling Comintern parties to carry out decisions in unified fashion under conditions of intense class conflict.[10]

---

8. Lenin 1960–71, *Collected Works* (hereinafter *LCW*), 31, pp. 109, 166; below, pp. 205–6, 209–10 (Zinoviev), 423 (Radek).

9. For the record of the first and second congresses, see Riddell (ed.) 1987, *Founding the Communist International* (hereinafter *1WC*) and Riddell (ed.) 1991, *Workers of the World and Oppressed Peoples, Unite! Proceedings and Documents of the Second Congress, 1920* (hereinafter *2WC*).

10. See 'Conditions for Admission' in Riddell (ed.) 1991, *2WC*, 2, pp. 765–71.

Congress resolutions mapped out the foundations of a strategy for a protracted struggle for Communist hegemony in the workers' movement. However, another theme was at work in the 1920 gathering: the hope of rapid victory resulting from the impact of war.

*Polish-Soviet War*

The strategy of taking the offensive, which inspired leftist forces heading into the Third Congress, was first formulated in 1920 in a quite different context, that of the Polish-Soviet War. In the spring of 1920, the Polish government had launched an attack on soviet Ukraine, taking its capital, Kiev. The Soviet Red Army repelled the invasion, crossed the frontier, and occupied much of Poland. During the Second Congress, Soviet forces were approaching the Polish capital, Warsaw, while the British and French governments tried to rush military aid to Poland's rulers. Workers across Europe rallied to block imperialist intervention. The Second Congress adopted Paul Levi's resolution calling for destruction of the capitalist state of Poland in the name of an 'independent republic of Polish workers and peasants'. Victor Serge later recalled how Lenin, 'in excellent spirits, confident of victory', discussed the Soviet advance on Warsaw with delegates gathered informally in a sideroom around a map of Poland, while Radek added, 'We shall be ripping up the Versailles Treaty with our bayonets.' Six months later, Radek told the KPD Zentrale that the Comintern Executive had believed German workers were so close to seizure of political power that, 'if [the Red Army] held Warsaw, there would be no further need to advance all the way to Germany'.[11]

A year later, Trotsky spoke of the mood of those days: 'You will recall, the Red Army was then advancing on Warsaw and it was possible to calculate that because of the revolutionary situation in Germany, Italy, and other countries, the military impulse – without, of course, any independent significance of its own but as an auxiliary force... – might bring on the landslide of revolution, then temporarily at a dead point. That did not happen. We were beaten back.'[12]

In the weeks after the Second Congress adjourned, the Soviet forces in Poland were repulsed and withdrew back to near the original frontier. An armistice soon followed, marking the end of a seven-year cycle of war and civil war in European Russia. Nonetheless, the Red Army's Polish offensive inspired an article by Nikolai Bukharin in the Comintern's world journal,

---

11. Riddell (ed.) 1991, 2WC, 1, pp. 134–9; Serge 2012, p. 126; Drachkovitch and Lazitch (eds.) 1966, p. 285.
12. Trotsky 1972a, 2, p. 8.

headlined 'The Policy of the Offensive', which drew on precedents from the French revolutionary wars of the 1790s to make the case that Soviet military advances could spark revolution beyond Soviet borders.[13] In the run-up to the Third Congress, Bukharin's formula was born to a new life in the theory developed by the German party's majority leadership to justify its adventurist policy.

## The Baku Congress

Three weeks after the Second Congress adjourned, the Comintern convened an unprecedented congress of fighters for national liberation from across Asia in Baku, Azerbaijan. The 2,050 delegates, a quarter of whom had no ties with the Communist movement, represented 37 nationalities. The optimism that inspired Bukharin's article on the Polish war echoed through its sessions. When Grigorii Zinoviev, in the name of the Comintern, told delegates, 'Brothers, we summon you to a holy war, above all against British imperialism', he was greeted by thunderous applause, as delegates rose in cheers, brandishing sabres and rifles.[14]

But in Central Asia, too, a cycle of imperialist war was winding down. Over the next two years, Britain withdrew its armed forces, in stages, from Turkestan, Transcaucasia, Iran, and Turkey. In February–March 1921 Soviet Russia signed treaties with Afghanistan, Iran, and Turkey. Most important, on 16 March, Russia and Britain signed a trade treaty, a decisive breach in the imperialist blockade of the Soviet republic, in which the two powers promised not to harm each other's interests in Asia. During this period, pro-Soviet national liberation movements triumphed, with the aid of the Red Army, in most of the old tsarist empire's territories in Asia. Beyond its frontiers, however, national liberation movements in 1920–1, although increasing in scope, were not yet strong enough to mount an assault on colonial and semi-colonial domination.

The enduring achievement of the Baku Congress lay in the impetus it gave to the formation of Communist movements across Asia. It heightened awareness in both the East and West of the role that the peoples of the East could play as a force in a world anticapitalist movement – a perspective summarised in Zinoviev's closing remarks at Baku: 'Workers of all lands and oppressed peoples of the whole world, unite.'[15]

---

13. Bukharin, 'Die Offensivtaktik', *Kommunistische Internationale*, 15 (1920), pp. 67–72.
14. Riddell (ed.) 1993, p. 78.
15. Riddell (ed.) 1993, p. 219. The slogan had previously been highlighted by Lenin; see *LCW*, 31, p. 453.

## Upsurge in Italy

Zinoviev's opening report to the Third Congress devoted extended analysis to events in Italy in the autumn of 1920. Even as the Baku Congress met, workers across Italy, half a million strong, seized factories and began to organise production under the leadership of factory councils. Beginning in the metal industry, the strikes spread to the railroads, other industries, and the countryside, bringing the country to the brink of revolution. Leaders of the pro-socialist trade-union confederation, however, considered the movement to be nothing more than a struggle for immediate union goals, and the Italian Socialist Party (PSI), the Comintern's section in Italy, refused to challenge them to go further. Party and union leaders alike took no steps to intensify the struggle or endow it with broader demands. The government was left free to liquidate the movement through wage increases and a promise of 'workers' control', which was not implemented.

This outcome was demoralising for revolutionary workers. For revolutionary forces within the PSI, the relevance of the Second Congress theses to this disaster was obvious: the PSI had failed to lead because it remained tied to the outmoded structures and practices of pre-1914 socialism. In the view of the PSI left wing, the challenge of revolution demanded a new kind of party of the type sketched out in the Twenty-One Conditions and other Second Congress decisions, a party integrated into a disciplined world movement. In particular, the party's left wing demanded that the PSI expel its openly reformist minority, led by Filippo Turati, which exerted a deadening influence on the party apparatus. Meanwhile, the PSI's central leader, Giacinto Serrati, who had led the PSI into the Comintern, wrote of the world movement with increasing scepticism, finding various excuses to postpone application in Italy of the Twenty-One Conditions. The Comintern Executive argued vigorously for immediate application of the conditions, publishing its debate with the PSI in a hefty pamphlet translated into several languages.[16]

Soon, a revolutionary wing within the PSI coalesced around the former 'Abstentionist' faction led by Amadeo Bordiga, which had long opposed the PSI's participation in elections. Supporters of the Turin newspaper *Ordine nuovo*, whose leaders included Umberto Terracini and Antonio Gramsci, joined in this left convergence; forces breaking from Serrati's current made up a third component. Meanwhile, the Serrati forces, now taking the name 'Unitary Communists' ('Unitarians'), avoided an open challenge to the Comintern and managed to retain the support of most pro-Comintern party members.

---

16. Comintern 1921a, 1921b; For Lenin's view, see 'On the Struggle of the Italian Socialist Party', *LCW*, 31, pp. 377–96.

By the end of 1920, the pro-ECCI forces (the Communist Faction) had taken steps to prepare for a split. Structuring their supporters in branches and federations down to the membership level and functioning through their own publications,[17] they were headed toward a clean break with the Serrati-led majority. Although Zinoviev, on 9 January 1921, said that the Serrati wing would probably vote for the ECCI's positions, Bordiga had already written in his faction's newspaper that, if in a minority, they would defy convention decisions.[18]

## 1b. Four Historic Conventions

During the year following the Second Congress, mass workers' parties in Germany, France, and Czechoslovakia joined the Comintern, while a fourth such party, in Italy, left the Comintern's ranks. These events – and their consequences – were to dominate the Third Congress discussions.

*Halle (Germany)*

In Germany, a convention of the Independent Social-Democratic Party (USPD) in Halle, held 12–17 October 1920, resolved by 237 votes to 156 to accept the Twenty-One Conditions and join the Communist International. Formed in 1917 by members of the Social-Democratic Party who rejected its support of World War I and collaboration with the capitalist class, the USPD in late 1920 embraced eight hundred thousand members and was ten times the size of the KPD. Following the Halle vote, its majority began a fusion process with the Communist Party, while its minority split off, keeping the name USPD. The USPD majority and the KPD joined forces in early December, creating a party of some four hundred thousand members that took the name United Communist Party of Germany (VKPD).

The new party inherited the dispute that had been brewing in the KPD and in its relations with the ECCI since the Kapp Putsch. A new left wing had formed in the KPD in 1920, calling for a more 'active' policy, with bolder initiatives in workers' struggles. Among its leaders were Ernst Meyer and Hugo Eberlein from the wartime Spartacus current; Frölich, who during the War had criticised Spartacus from the left; and Ernst Friesland (Reuter), won to communism as a prisoner of war in Russia. They received encouragement from Karl Radek, responsible for the ECCI's relations with Germany, who accused

---

17. See Terracini's remarks in Session 7, p. 317. In the same session, Rákosi referred to the pre-congress Communist Faction as the 'Italian Communist Party' (p. 324).
18. Spriano 1967, 1, pp. 104–5.

unnamed elements in the German party leadership (presumably including Levi) of 'anti-putschist cretinism' and 'quietism'. August Thalheimer and Heinrich Brandler, also Spartacus veterans, swung toward this viewpoint. At a KPD congress in November, Radek openly attacked Levi, accusing him of 'wanting to do nothing but educate Communists until the party has white hairs on its super-intelligent head'.[19]

At the December fusion convention, a draft manifesto, written by Levi and approved by the provisional Zentrale (Central Bureau), was set aside and replaced by a last-minute text by Radek. Referring to the numerical size and influence of the United KPD (VKPD), Radek's text stated, 'The VKPD is strong enough to go alone into action when events permit and demand this.' The text was adopted, but Levi expressed his reservations publicly: the establishment of workers' rule ('proletarian dictatorship') 'cannot be the task of a small part of that class or of a single, isolated party, but only that of the broad masses of the proletariat, of the class as such'. Communists 'must also be aware that they constitute only a fraction of the proletarian class....'[20]

Leftist pressure on the new party was further increased by the ECCI's decision in December 1920, overriding unanimous and strenuous objections from the KPD leadership, to admit to the Comintern the extreme leftist KAPD as a sympathising organisation, granting it representation on the ECCI with consultative vote along with financial assistance.

*Tours (France)*

Two months after the Halle Congress, Comintern supporters in the French Socialist Party (SFIO) won a decisive victory at its 25–30 December 1920 congress in Tours. The ECCI had set its sights on winning the party almost in its entirety, even offering to weaken the Twenty-One Conditions (the party could keep its name, Socialist Party, for a time; it could preserve neutrality in the trade unions) in order to embrace revolutionary-minded forces influenced by centrism. The Comintern rallied 70 per cent of congress delegates and, after the congress, 60 per cent of the membership. The party was still headed by Louis-Oscar Frossard and Marcel Cachin, who had been distant from revolutionary views during the War; its newspaper was still *L'Humanité*, founded by Jean Jaurès.

---

19. Wilde 2011, pp. 179–84; Radek, 'Die KPD Deutschlands während des Kapp-Putsches', *Kommunistische Internationale*, 12, pp. 164–6; Broué 2005, p. 464.
20. Broué 2005, pp. 464–5. See also Radek's quotation from VKPD manifesto below, pp. 424–5.

Such a decisive Comintern victory inevitably swept into its new French section an ultimately incompatible spectrum of political traditions and outlooks. After the Tours Congress, tensions surfaced in the spring of 1921 around a threat of war. The French government sought to use military force to squeeze greater reparations payments out of Germany, calling up into the army a category of conscripts, 'the class of 1919'. On 8 March, it occupied part of the Ruhr industrial region on the east bank of the Rhine. The French Communists protested,[21] but leftist forces in the party and especially its youth organisation assailed the party leadership for passivity and excessive caution, in terms similar to those used by leftists in their criticisms of Paul Levi. The resulting tensions still riled the French delegation as it arrived in Moscow for the Third Congress.

## Livorno (Italy)

As the Italian Socialist Party approached its January 1921 congress in Livorno, its members were grouped in three factions divided above all by issues posed in the Comintern's Twenty-One Conditions. Alongside the Communist Faction (Bordiga) and the Unitary Communists (Serrati), the right wing led by Turati organised itself as the Socialist Concentration. A fourth, smaller current led by Antonio Graziadei and Anselmo Marabini agreed with the ECCI's stand but sought to reconcile the Communist Faction with the Serrati current, or at least its left wing. The Communist Faction demanded that the PSI immediately expel all participants in Turati's factional conference in Reggio Emilia in October and implement the Twenty-One Conditions fully and immediately. The ECCI fully backed the Bordiga faction's ultimatum. Serrati responded that the PSI would indeed implement the conditions, but in its own way and its own time, and that it was too soon for expulsions. The PSI, Serrati said, was asking only that it be granted the same consideration that the ECCI had shown to the French party; he accused the ECCI of acting in discriminatory fashion.

On the eve of the Livorno conference, Radek, as ECCI representative in Germany, was in agreement with the VKPD Zentrale on the need 'to keep Serrati, but we had definitely to demand of him that the Turati people be excluded'.[22] However, when Levi, as VKPD representative, reached Livorno,

---

21. The French party newspaper *L'Humanité* reported on 9 May 1921 on a party-organised anti-war demonstration of 100,000 held the previous day. Police attacked the protesters, killing one and wounding fifty.
22. Quoted from Levi in Fernbach (ed.) 2011, p. 100; for Radek's confirmation, see Fayet 2004, p. 366, n. 178.

he encountered just-received instructions from Moscow 'stating that the new decision of the Executive was: sharp struggle against Serrati'. Negotiations between Serrati and the ECCI representatives in Livorno (Mátyás Rákosi and Khristo Kabakchiev) and Serrati's discussions with Levi came to nothing. Graziadei proposed to the Communist Faction that it soften the wording of its expulsion ultimatum; this was refused.[23]

The Livorno Congress lasted through a full week (15–21 January) of tumultuous proceedings. When Kabakchiev rose to present the ECCI's message, he was booed by the Unitarians; when he said those not voting for the Communist Faction's motion would be expelled from the Comintern, there were sarcastic cries, 'Viva il papa [pope]'. Kabakchiev argued that the situation in Italy was ripe for revolution; in case of delay, the bourgeoisie would move to attack. By opposing expulsion of the reformists, he said, Serrati was blocking the revolution. Unitarian delegates countered that the ECCI was misreading the objective situation.[24]

The congress vote gave the Unitarians a comfortable majority, with 98,028 mandates; the Communists received 58,783 and Turati's Socialist Concentration, 14,695. The Left thereupon walked out and organised itself as the Communist Party of Italy (PCI); the ECCI immediately recognised it as the Comintern's Italian section. The remainder of the congress pledged its loyalty to the Comintern and resolved to appeal its expulsion to the Third Congress.

The split cost the Comintern most of its proletarian base in Italy. In the trade-union congress held two months later, the PCI's support was 23 per cent. During its campaign for the 15 May parliamentary elections, the PCI aimed its main fire against the Socialists; the Communist vote, however, was less than a fifth that of the PSI. The discrepancy in membership was persistent: in late 1921, PCI membership was 43,000; that of the PSI, 107,000.[25]

Far from advancing to socialist revolution after the Livorno Congress, Italy was gripped by increasingly murderous violence against the workers' movement by Fascist forces led by Benito Mussolini. Starting in the northern countryside and then spreading into the towns, the Fascist attacks were a one-sided civil war, breaking up workers' and peasants' organisations, dissolving socialist municipal administrations, and killing Socialist and Communist activists. Despite widespread unemployment caused by an economic crash, workers often responded with strike action and formed anti-Fascist alliances on a local level. However, Fascist gangs, made up of full-time fighters, financed by leading capitalists, and assured of neutrality or support by the

---

23. König 1967, pp. 144–7.
24. Spriano 1967, 1, pp. 111–13.
25. König 1967, pp. 150–2.

police and army, had military superiority sufficient to beat back such spontaneous and isolated resistance.

The national union organisations failed to respond to the threat, while the PSI relied on the very state agencies that were backing the Fascists. The Communist Party recognised the danger and formed anti-Fascist fighting units, but it took no steps to unite against the threat with workers aligned with non-Communist currents. Bordiga, the dominant voice in the PCI leadership, opposed defence of 'bourgeois legality', which he saw as compatible with fascism. By the time of the Third Congress, workers had independently organised a national anti-Fascist defence league, the Arditi del Popolo (People's Commandos), but the Arditi were opposed by both the PCI and PSI.[26]

*Prague (Czechoslovakia)*

The Comintern's emergence in Czechoslovakia resembled the pattern in France, although it was shaped by a quite different political landscape. Czechoslovakia was pieced together in 1919 by the Versailles Treaty from territories with Czech, German, Slovakian, and Ruthenian populations, each with their own socialist parties. The Czechoslovak Communist Party emerged from a fusion and regroupment process embracing roughly four hundred thousand members.

In 1920, revolutionary forces gained a majority in the Czech Social-Democratic Party, whose right wing responded by splitting the movement. Two-thirds of local organisations sent delegates to the September party congress organised by the Left. The congress gave overwhelming support to the Marxist Left, a current led by Bohumir Šmeral that included both revolutionary and centrist forces. While favourable to the Comintern, the Marxist Left did not endorse the Twenty-One Conditions and stressed the need to guard party unity and continuity with prewar Social Democracy. In early November, the ECCI called on the Czech Left Party to take the name Communist and to unify with pro-Comintern forces of other Czechoslovak nationalities.[27]

The right-wing splitters held their own congress at the end of November, claiming to represent the party's continuity. A legal war ensued over ownership of party property and assets. The rightists called in the police, who on 9 December evicted the Left Party from its headquarters in Prague. Left unions called a protest strike, which grew to embrace about one million

26. Natoli 1982, pp. 67–113. See also Behan 2003. For Zinoviev's December 1922 correction of the Arditi error, see Riddell (ed.) 2011b, *4WC*, pp. 1053–4.
27. Firsov 1975, pp. 350–8.

workers across the country, who seized factories and formed councils in some locations. The strike was broken after a week by military repression.

The strike heightened the impression among many revolutionary-minded workers that the party was ill-equipped to lead in the social confrontation that now seemed imminent. The resulting debate raged on even as the party slowly moved toward Comintern affiliation. Membership discussion of the Twenty-One Conditions began in February; the Central Committee adopted the conditions in March; they were then endorsed by a 96 per cent vote in a party referendum. A 14–16 May 1921 congress in Prague, including representatives from Slovakia and Ruthenia, voted almost unanimously to join the Comintern. The still-separate German-speaking Communists, who organised at a 12–15 March gathering in Reichenberg (Liberec), were a bastion of leftist criticism of Šmeral and his party.[28]

The debate in Czechoslovakia, as in Italy, France, and Germany, focused on objective conditions. All agreed that theirs was a revolutionary epoch, but would its climax come quickly – perhaps in months – or only after longer preparation? Šmeral wrote in April that the party was transitioning from a time of immediate assault to a war of position, a formulation criticised at the Third Congress by Radek and later utilised by Gramsci.[29] Šmeral's report to the May congress elaborated on this theme: he called for drawing the masses into the struggle and avoiding adventures, while criticising the ECCI for harmful interventions in Italy and Germany. The Reichenberg Communists published excerpts from the report in German, a slanted selection aimed at arousing mistrust in Šmeral. It was this version that circulated among Comintern leaders in Moscow and was cited by Lenin in the Third Congress.[30]

The activity of Hungarian emissaries of the ECCI provided a further irritant in the Czechoslovak debate. In March 1921, Béla Kun convened a meeting with reluctant Czechoslovak party representatives in Berlin. Rákosi and Gyula Alpári toured Bohemia urging local leaders to oppose Šmeral, impelling leaders of its party to lodge a collective protest with the ECCI.[31]

### 1c. The German Party Turns Left

The exiled Hungarian leaders, writing in the Vienna-based German-language journal, *Kommunismus*, had emerged in 1920 as the main voice of a leftist

---

28. Firsov 1975, pp. 363–4; Suda 1980, pp. 46–9.
29. See p. 409 and Firsov 1975, pp. 365 and 371.
30. See p. 221 (Zinoviev), including n. 72; p. 409 (Radek); p. 664 (Lenin); Firsov 1975, pp. 371–6.
31. Borsányi 1993, pp. 258–9; Firsov 1975, pp. 366–7.

current within the Comintern. After the Second Congress, when the Comintern began to flesh out the ECCI into an effective apparatus, member parties were reluctant to withdraw central leaders from party responsibilities for a Moscow assignment. The exiled Hungarian comrades, however, were available, and their drive to 'activate' the Central European comrades overlapped with the leanings of Zinoviev, Bukharin, and, to some extent, Radek, the most authoritative Bolshevik leaders carrying day-to-day responsibility for Comintern work. The ECCI's impatience for party initiatives in action was on full display in its response to a major initiative by the German party, its 8 January 1921 'Open Letter to German Workers' Organisations' (see Appendix 1a).[32]

In the Open Letter, the VKPD proposed to join with all workers' parties and trade unions in united action to sustain the incomes of working people, rein in prices for workers' necessities, and secure their supply of foodstuffs, noting that these were immediate and basic demands that all currents in the workers' movement claimed to support. The Open Letter proposal was drawn up by Radek and Levi, but they did not originate it. As Radek candidly admitted to the German leadership, 'If I were in Moscow, this idea would never even come to me'.[33] The initiative came in fact from the VKPD local organisation in Stuttgart, responding to the yearning for unity among non-Communist workers. Late in 1920, a meeting representing 26,000 Stuttgart metalworkers called for joint struggle for a short list of basic demands; the appeal was published 10 December 1920. It was the first formulation of the united front policy that the Comintern was to adopt a year and eight days later.

Leaders of all major German workers' organisations rejected the Open Letter, but the Communists carried their appeal to the ranks, where it gained significant support. The trade-union leadership felt compelled to issue its own list of demands, which the VKPD then supported, demanding concerted action. The Communist initiative was opposed, however, by the KAPD; by Ruth Fischer, Maslow, and their leftist opposition within the VKPD; and – within the ECCI's Small Bureau (its day-to-day leadership body) – by Zinoviev and Bukharin (see Appendix 1b). The Bureau condemned the Open Letter, but the decision was set aside, on Lenin's insistence, and the matter was referred to the Third Congress.[34]

---

32. 'Action' here translates the German word *Aktion*, which often carried a confrontational meaning absent from its English cognate. For Lenin's comment see Appendix 2d, pp. 1086–7; for Open Letter see Appendix 1a, pp. 1061–3.
33. Drachkovitch and Lazitch (eds.) 1966, p. 292.
34. Reisberg 1971, pp. 47–68; Broué 2005, pp. 468–73; Drachkovitch and Lazitch (eds.) 1966, p. 292.

Only two weeks after the Open Letter's publication, Paul Levi and his closest collaborators exited the VKPD leadership. The immediate issue was not German policy but the implications of the split in Italy. Reporting to the German Central Committee on 24 February, Levi criticised the ECCI's conduct in Livorno, insisting that 'it was possible in Italy to separate the right wing from the party without losing the masses'. Even if that meant tolerating Serrati in the International, Levi said, 'the price was not too high'. He also protested that the ECCI should not be carrying out splits in Comintern member parties.[35]

Rákosi, representing the ECCI, rallied a majority of the German party's Central Committee for its Italian policy. Praising the Livorno outcome, he told the German leaders that the German and French parties were too large and needed to be cleansed or trimmed down. The ECCI envoy seemed to be announcing an international Livorno-type offensive against all those with views similar to Levi. Radek, addressing the Zentrale a few days later, conceded that the outcome in Italy had been somewhat unfavourable. The real issue, he said, was Levi's supposedly hostile attitude to the ECCI and its policies. This argument appears to have been decisive in enabling Rákosi to win the Central Committee vote 28 to 23. Levi, Zetkin, and three supporters quit the Zentrale. A new team took the helm, including Meyer, Thalheimer, Eberlein, and Brandler, determined to steer the German party toward bolder initiatives in action.[36]

The events in Germany during the six weeks that followed became the main focus of discussion at the Third Congress. While the new leadership struggled to turn the party onto a more radical course, at about the beginning of March, an unanticipated and unusually authoritative ECCI delegation arrived in Berlin. Its members included Béla Kun; his Hungarian colleague Jószef Pogány; and August Guralsky, a veteran of the Jewish Bund in Ukraine and recent recruit to the Bolshevik Party. All three were identified with the Comintern's leftist wing. This mission, barely mentioned in the Third Congress, had a major impact on the events in Germany debated there.

There is no record of who sent the ECCI envoys or why. The VKPD delegate to the ECCI, Curt Geyer, though resident in Moscow, was unaware of the mission. The decision was likely taken by Zinoviev, perhaps with his close collaborators, although there is no evidence that Lenin or Trotsky was involved. When the envoys departed, Levi's resignation was as yet unknown

---

35. Fernbach 2011, pp. 105, 109.
36. Fernbach 2011, p. 108; Koch-Baumgarten 1986, p. 107; during the congress, Rákosi confirmed his remarks (p. 326), responding to Zetkin (p. 292); see also Drachkovitch and Lazitch (eds.) 1966, pp. 286, 291.

in Moscow. A 14 March letter by Radek reflects his thinking just after the mission departed (see Appendix 2a).[37]

The mission appears to have been an attempt to respond to three simultaneous crises in Germany's international relations:

1.) A threatened French occupation of a sector of the Ruhr region, the heart of German heavy industry, which did in fact take place on 8 March.
2.) Demands by the Allied powers that Germany disarm rightist militias, which were protected by Gustav von Kahr's far-right government in Bavaria.
3.) A struggle between Polish and German militias for control of an industrial region, Upper Silesia, which threatened to escalate into war between the two countries.

Zinoviev may have suggested that the three envoys do what they could to encourage opposition to Levi, a task for which they needed no urging. But, on arrival, finding that Levi had already been replaced, they busied themselves by urging a more active policy on German leaders of all currents. A few weeks later, Levi summarised what Kun had told him:

> Russia finds itself in an extremely difficult situation. It is unconditionally necessary for the burden on Russia to be relieved by movements in the West, and, for this reason, the German Party must immediately step into action. The VKPD now counted half a million members, and this would make it possible to put one and a half million proletarians on the streets, enough to overthrow the government. The struggle should, therefore, immediately begin with the slogan: overthrow the government.

Zetkin confirmed Levi's account. Béla Kun told Lenin that these reports were lies, but his own account confirms them in broad outline (see Appendix 2e).[38]

Kun's insistence on the need for the German party to launch immediate confrontational action is not found in statements by ECCI leaders at that time,

---

37. See Appendix 2a, pp. 1071–2. Koch-Baumgarten quotes an undated letter from Radek to the German leadership, written, she says, a few days after the 22 February ECCI discussion on the Open Letter (Appendix 1a). By her account, after summarising the pressures bearing down on Soviet Russia, Radek wrote, 'It is therefore our duty to intensify the struggle across Europe, and anyone who fails to do all possible to achieve this goal is nothing but a traitor.' Koch-Baumgarten 1986, p. 118.

The Archiv der sozialen Demokratie, indicated by Koch-Baumgarten as holder of this letter, is unable to find it. Inquiries with Koch-Baumgarten and other German researchers in this field have not turned up any trace of the letter.

38. Levi, 'Letter to Lenin', in Fernbach (ed.) 2011, p. 207; Kun, 'Letter to Lenin', Appendix 2e, pp. 1088–90; compare with Radek, 'Letter to VKPD leaders in Berlin', Appendix 2a, pp. 1071–2.

which focus on countering Levi's policies. Kun's initiative most likely reflects the synergy of his encounter with the new leftist VKPD leadership, already inclined toward launching a confrontational action, as well as with the leftist faction led by Friesland, Maslow, and Fischer and with the KAPD. The subsequent March Action disaster was termed by historian Marie-Luise Goldbach 'an industrial accident incidental to factional intrigue in the party, exacerbated by the Moscow emissary'. Pierre Broué suggests, '[T]he most likely explanation is that Kun acted on his own initiative, in the conviction that he would have the support and approval of the ECCI.'[39]

## 1d. The March Action

The new course of the VKPD Zentrale found expression in its statement on the reparations crisis published 4 March. Neither rejection nor acceptance of the Allied demands will help the working class, the Zentrale declared; 'help will come only from a direct struggle to overthrow the German bourgeois government.' The new line was presented to a Central Committee meeting held 16–17 March. Brandler, reporting on party tasks, predicted a rapid escalation of the external and domestic conflicts pressing on the German state, expressed confidence that the VKPD could rally three million workers in struggle for its demands, and called on the party to move into action. He then addressed a just-published announcement by Otto Hörsing, governor of Prussian Saxony, that large police contingents were about to occupy this Central German industrial region, which was a stronghold of the VKPD and revolutionary working class. Brandler suggested that the VKPD might be able to initiate a general strike in the region, perhaps after the 25–28 March Easter holiday.[40]

No specific decision was taken, but the mood of the meeting was suggested by Frölich's statement, reported by Radek to the Third Congress, 'Previously we waited, but now we will seize the initiative and force the revolution.' And even as Brandler spoke, *Die Rote Fahne* had already responded on 17 March with its own appeal calling on German workers to 'emerge from their passivity.... The proletariat must smash the invading forces....'[41]

---

39. For the ECCI's view, see Appendices 1b and 2a, and also the alternative record of its 22–23 February 1921 sessions published in Goldbach 1973, pp. 135–43. Quotations are from Goldbach, p. 91 and Broué 2005, p. 494.
40. Weber 1991, pp. 73–80.
41. See p. 429 (Radek); Koch-Baumgarten 1986, p. 152.

According to historian Sigrid Koch-Baumgarten, publication of this appeal was the first move by a group of Communists acting outside the official leadership bodies and confronting them with one fait accompli after another. The group, convened by Kun, included the three ECCI emissaries; three of the more leftist Zentrale members; two representatives of the KAPD, which had decided to attempt a national uprising; and a member of the syndicalist General Workers' Union of Germany (AAUD). Possessing effective control of the VKPD's main newspaper, *Die Rote Fahne*, through Ernst Meyer and Frölich, the group pressed for a more radical, confrontationist course than that favoured by the Zentrale. In the days that followed, the ECCI team sent Guralsky to Central Germany and, it seems, Pogány to Hamburg to help direct the party's intervention in these major arenas of combat. Another provocative article in *Die Rote Fahne*, several times cited in the Third Congress, was written by Béla Kun and published 18 March. It seized on rightist threats in Bavaria as the occasion to declare, 'Every worker must flout the law and take up arms, wherever he can find them.' Despite a protest from the Zentrale majority, *Die Rote Fahne* continued to write in this vein.[42]

On Saturday 19 March, Hörsing's heavily armed detachments marched ostentatiously into the industrial towns of Central Germany, supposedly to suppress 'thievery'. Although the operation's real and evident purpose was to disarm and intimidate revolutionary workers, police contingents at first avoided confrontation. The regional VKPD's 18 March appeal to workers to strike if police entered their factories thus remained without effect. Nonetheless, local VKPD leaders called strikes beginning Monday, 21 March, and the walkouts spread quickly. On 22 March, Max Hoelz, the leader of a small armed workers' detachment formed during the Kapp struggle and a KAPD member, addressed a meeting of several thousand workers in Eisleben calling on them to begin armed resistance. When workers exited the meeting, police moved in to make arrests. A running battle ensued, and armed resistance continued the next day. Armed or semi-armed contingents of workers embraced some 2,500 workers in total, 400 of them led by Hoelz. However, the insurrectionary movement did not spread beyond the region; within ten days it was crushed by militarised police with murderous brutality.

Meanwhile, the leadership of the VKPD's military wing in Central Germany, headed initially by Guralsky and then by Eberlein, planned bombings and kidnappings designed to expand and intensify the armed conflict. With

---

42. Koch-Baumgarten 1986, pp. 151–6, 222; Angress 1963, pp. 138–9. See also below, p. 428, including n. 26.

the local political leadership opposed and technical means lacking, not much came of these efforts except heated subsequent controversy.

In Hamburg, the VKPD launched its own action, with KAPD support. Several hundred unemployed workers occupied a dock works on 23 March demanding jobs, supported by a demonstration of two thousand workers. The police fired on the workers, killing 22 and wounding 42. By the end of the day, the movement was defeated. That night, the German government declared a state of siege and suspended civil liberties in Prussian Saxony and Hamburg.

The following day, 24 March (Thursday), the VKPD declared a general strike across all Germany. The VKPD appeal focused on the war danger in Upper Silesia and the nationwide threat of repression and counterrevolution. The slaughter of workers in Central Germany and Hamburg received only the briefest mention. The appeal's demands ranged from 'jobs to the jobless' and 'organisation of production by workers' and union committees' to 'obstruct transport of troops and weaponry'. The timing was awkward – the day before the Easter holiday. The strike was opposed by the SPD and the rump USPD as well as by almost all their members.[43]

In the Central German district of Halle-Merseburg, where walkouts were already widespread, the strike was widely observed. Walkouts took place in parts of the Ruhr district. Elsewhere, the strike had little success. In Session 5, Heinrich Malzahn of the German opposition estimated that strikers totalled only two hundred thousand – just over half the party's pre-March membership – a figure not challenged in the congress. Due to the strength of opposition among workers, the strike took on the character of a fratricidal struggle. Indeed, in many instances, Communists battled non-Communists among the workforce; in some cases workers were cleared out of the workplace by force. These fratricidal clashes received one mention in the congress, when the KAPD delegate Sachs, defending the VKPD's strike initiative, said that 'during the March Action broad masses turned against those in struggle, not only with words but by wielding iron bars in the factories to drive out those who called for a strike'. Even the VKPD's own initial assessment of the March Action, adopted by its Central Committee 7–8 April, presented it as a struggle within the working class (see Appendix 2b). By the end of March, the movement was defeated; the VKPD officially called off the strike on 1 April.[44]

---

43. See VKPD Zentrale general strike appeal in IML-SED 1966a, 7, 1, pp. 445–7.
44. See pp. 262 (Malzahn), 559 (Sachs); Appendix 2b, p. 1074.

## Legacy of defeat

The repression that crushed the March Action was sweeping and harsh. Six thousand workers were arrested and four thousand sentenced to jail terms, including eight to life imprisonment; there were four death sentences. About 150 members of the VKPD were killed. Thousands of revolutionary workers were dismissed from their jobs. Social-Democratic union leaders campaigned against VKPD 'putschism', ousting Communists from many of their positions of union influence. Distrust of the VKPD was now widespread even among radical non-Communist workers. Amid the dislocation caused by defeat and repression, the party's membership, as measured by dues payments, fell to about 180,000 in mid-1921, roughly half the level of early in the year.[45]

The VKPD majority leadership, however, hailed the action as a success and promised more of the same. In a pamphlet published by the Zentrale 4–5 April, Thalheimer wrote:

> The March Action as an isolated initiative would be a crime against the proletariat. To this degree our opponents are right. However, the March offensive as introduction to a series of increasingly intense actions is a liberating deed.

The Zentrale's pamphlet also stated:

> The party's slogan must therefore be: Offensive, offensive, whatever the cost, by every means, in every situation that offers serious chances of success.

On 7 April, the Central Committee adopted by a 26 to 14 vote theses that stated: 'Workers have been aroused out of stagnation and idle submission.... The final result has been to deepen and broaden the effectiveness of propaganda for communism' (see Appendix 2b). The theses acknowledged that the March Action represented a conflict within the working class, and insisted that its method must be continued, presenting a theoretical justification that became known as the 'Theory of the Offensive'.[46]

Theses for the minority were introduced by Zetkin at the 7 April plenum (see Appendix 2c). Agreeing that conditions had been present for 'intensified activity' and an 'offensive', she insisted that the proper response lay in the method of the Open Letter and the demand for Germany's alliance with Soviet Russia. Her theses, which strongly condemned the March Action in

---

45. For casualty and membership estimates, see Koch-Baumgarten 1986, pp. 315–18, 446–7; Wilde 2011, p. 218. By September 1922, dues-paying membership had recovered to 224,389. For VKPD Theses on the March Action, see Appendix 2b, pp. 1072–8. See also Malzahn's comments, pp. 504–5.
46. Zentrale der VKPD 1921, pp. 6, 22–3.

its entirety, were defeated by a vote of six for, forty-four against. The party leadership undertook to tighten discipline, ousting many minority supporters from positions of influence. Nonetheless, within a few weeks, even while asserting the Theory of the Offensive and without any encouragement from the ECCI, the party began to return to the method of the Open Letter, urging united action to implement the union federation's official demands, building support for victims of oppression, and seeking unity in May Day actions.[47]

On 12 April, Paul Levi published his condemnation of the March Action as a pamphlet, *Our Path: Against Putschism*. Basing himself on Marx's writings against Bakunin, Levi described 'putschism' as setting the revolutionary nucleus against the working class, in the spirit of 'who is not for us is against us' – a theme found in many articles in the VKPD press. Levi provided many examples where Communists had fought factory workers in order to drive them from their workplaces. He also strongly attacked the ECCI's conduct in Germany and elsewhere, terming it at one point 'a Cheka projected beyond the Russian frontiers'. He omitted a good deal of damning material – Kun's role, for example, and Eberlein's dynamiting initiatives in Central Germany – but still, Levi's pamphlet was a stinging, frontal attack on the party's leadership and conduct. The public nature of Levi's article, as well as its tone, caused outrage among many party members. Three days later, the Zentrale expelled Levi from the VKPD for 'gross disloyalty and severe damage to the party'.[48]

*Reaction in Moscow*

On receiving initial news of the March struggles, the ECCI in Moscow greeted the fact that German workers had gone into battle 'in an attempt to bring to an end the rule of the German exploiters' for the first time since 1919. 'You acted rightly!', the ECCI stated. 'Prepare for new struggles.'[49]

A letter by Lenin to Levi and Zetkin, sent 16 April, struck a different note (see Appendix 2d). While declining to state an opinion on the March Action, Lenin said, referring to Béla Kun, 'I readily believe the representative of the Executive Committee defended stupid tactics, ... [he] is very often too leftist.' Written before receiving news of Levi's pamphlet, the letter urged Levi not to

---

47. For Zetkin's theses, see pp. 1079–86. On the party's return to the Open Letter, see Peterson 1993, pp. 82–6; Reisberg 1971, pp. 137–40; Thalheimer 1994, p. 79.
48. The Cheka was the Soviet security force and revolutionary tribunal. For Levi's view of putschism, see Fernbach (ed.) 2011, pp. 119–65, especially 147–9 and 159–64. Levi refers to Karl Marx and Frederick Engels, 'The Alliance of Socialist Democracy and the International Working Men's Association', *Collected Works* (hereinafter *MECW*), 23, pp. 454–580. Re Levi's expulsion, see IML-SED 1966, pp. 456–8. For a comment by Zetkin on the meaning of 'putschism', see p. 299.
49. Degras 1971, 1, pp. 217–18.

publish his critique but rather to seek rectification through the ECCI and the coming world congress. Delivery of Lenin's letter was blocked by an ECCI representative in Berlin. On Lenin's insistence, it was finally forwarded in mid-May. Meanwhile, a pamphlet by Radek, completed 18 April, gave further evidence of a shift in the ECCI. While directing its main fire against Levi, it made several criticisms of the VKPD leadership's conduct, including its failure to focus the action 'on the demand for withdrawal of Hörsing's measures and for arming the workers' guards'. On 29 April, the ECCI, in backing Levi's expulsion, said this action was correct 'even if he were nine-tenths right'. The statement declined to express an opinion on the March Action and referred the question to the coming World Congress.[50]

On 3–5 May, the VKPD Central Committee drew up theses for the World Congress, reasserting in more guarded form the need to 'move from the defensive to the offensive'. The theses stated that 'despite inadequacies the VKPD's March Action was an initial step to break with the past and...to win the leadership of the masses.'[51]

About that time, Zinoviev announced to the world movement that the World Congress was being held earlier than originally planned, primarily in order to grapple with a right-wing current that had emerged, he said, in Italy (Serrati), Germany (Levi), and Czechoslovakia (Šmeral). In fact, however, the Bolshevik leaders of the Comintern were divided in their assessment of the International's tasks, as Radek explained to the Russian delegation to the congress only one day before the congress opened. The disagreement had arisen, he said, because 'neither Lenin nor Trotsky was in a position to follow the course of this work'. They had objected to the actions of Zinoviev, Bukharin, and Radek, 'demanding that we pay more attention to the left danger' (see Appendix 3h).[52]

Trotsky later explained his and Lenin's outlook as follows:

> There was danger at that time that the policy of the Comintern would follow the line of the March 1921 events in Germany. That is, the attempt to create a revolutionary situation artificially.... That mood was the prevailing one at the congress. Vladimir Ilyich [Lenin] came to the conclusion that, following this course, the International would most certainly go to smash.[53]

---

50. For Appendix 2d, see pp. 1086–7. Radek 1921, quoted in Reisberg 1971, p. 134. Regarding hold-up of Lenin's letter, see Reisberg 1971, p. 133. ECCI April 29 statement in Degras 1971, 1, pp. 218–20.
51. *Die Internationale*, 3, 7, pp. 239–43.
52. Zinoviev, 'Vor dem III. Kongress der Kommunistischen Internationale', *Kommunistische Internationale*, 16 (1921), pp. 1–12; Appendix 3h, pp. 1135–7.
53. Trotsky 1972b, p. 33. See also Trotsky 1936, pp. 87–91.

## 2. The Third Congress

### 2a. The Contending Forces Meet in Moscow

Delegates from abroad reached Moscow during a time of great tension and uncertainty in Soviet Russia. The country was just beginning to recover from a deep trauma of famine, worker unrest, and revolt, while the New Economic Policy (NEP), which authorised a limited reintroduction of a market economy, began to unfold. Those arriving for the first time noted the fresh wounds of civil war and economic dislocation. A Hungarian delegate recalled how a coal shortage forced his train's crew to halt frequently and chop wood to burn in the locomotive. Jules Humbert-Droz wrote that peasants, selling goods in Moscow, would accept only cigarettes as currency, since banknotes were not trusted. Serge, however, who had lived through worse times in Moscow, recalled that 'from one week to the next, the famine and the speculation were diminishing perceptibly'. But the NEP generated talk that capitalism was returning; 'the confusion among the [Communist] party rank-and-file was staggering', Serge stated.[54]

Among the arriving delegates, the prevailing mood was one of support for the line of March 1921; dissent was found mainly among the German 'right' opposition and forces in the Czechoslovak, French, and Yugoslav leaderships.

The Russian leaders held considerable political authority, but initially they were divided. And, even if the Russian delegation rallied against the 'leftist' mood, it could not count on majority support. In a roll-call vote, delegations from Russia and allied soviet republics made up only 13 per cent of the total. The limits of the Russian delegates' voting sway was indicated in the one divided roll-call vote held during the congress. Despite combined opposition by the delegations from soviet republics plus the German delegation and its leftist allies, a motion by the French delegation on selection of the ECCI's Small Bureau succeeded in winning 37 per cent of the tally.[55]

The mood of the congress shifted gradually during weeks of intensive discussions before and during the congress, in corridor discussions, informal gatherings, ECCI sessions, commission meetings, and the congress proceedings themselves. The burdens of Soviet leadership did not prevent Lenin, Trotsky, Bukharin, Radek, and Zinoviev from intensive involvement in the

---

54. Leonhard 1981, p. 245; Humbert-Droz 1971, p. 14; Serge 2012, p. 172.
55. For allocation of votes, see credentials report, pp. 177–8. For the roll-call vote, see pp. 880–2.

congress. Together with three non-Russian Communists, two of whom did not address the congress, they exerted a strong influence on the gathering.

*Seven leading figures*

Lenin played a decisive role in the main congress debate. According to a later memoir by Bulgarian Communist Vasil Kolarov, Radek had predicted before the congress that Lenin would be too preoccupied with Russian domestic issues to concern himself with the congress, and the leftist position would therefore triumph. But, for Lenin, the congress debate assumed supreme importance. Referring in Session 11 to the leftist position, Lenin declared, '[S]omething is wrong in the International.... [W]e must say: Stop! We must wage a decisive struggle! Otherwise the Communist International is lost.' When not in formal sessions, Lenin was often seen deep in discussion with delegates. Both Serge and Alfred Rosmer recall him chasing down delegates unknown to him and ardently explaining his views, so rapt in discussion that he missed meal-time; Radek stepped in to fetch Lenin a plate of food. Lenin's passionate indignation is evident in his 10 June warning to Zinoviev (Appendix 3a), 'You will spoil everything'. Radek 'has spoilt his original draft' of his theses on tactics and strategy by 'concessions to "leftist" silliness'; anyone who does not soon accept the Open Letter policy (so decisively rejected in February by Zinoviev himself) 'should be expelled'; Lenin warns that he is ready for an 'open fight' at the congress. Ruth Fischer later recalled the 'fever of emotional indignation' against Lenin among leftist delegates, who talked freely of his opportunism. Seeking to counter possible personal resentment, Lenin twice during the congress wrote delegates to retract his harsh language (Appendices 3e and 4c). But on the main issues, he was adamant. In comments to the VKPD a month after the congress, Lenin was even more emphatic. 'It *was necessary* to have been on the *right* wing' at the congress, he wrote (see Appendix 4h). Eight months later, he added 'I was on the extreme right flank.... I did all I could to defend Levi.' Subsequent events, Lenin added, had shown that Levi 'took the Menshevik path not accidentally, not temporarily, ...but deliberately and permanently, because of his very nature.'[56]

*Trotsky* wrote 'notes for myself' on the March Action, dated 18 April, that stood midway between Lenin's view and that of the ECCI majority. However,

---

56. Kolarov quoted in Reisberg 1971, p. 162; Lenin, below, p. 467; Serge 2012, p. 161; Rosmer 1971, pp. 139–40; Leonhard 1981, pp. 255–6; Fischer 1948, p. 177; Lenin, Appendices 3a (pp. 1098–9), 3e (p. 1107), and 4c (pp. 1157–8); Lenin, Appendix 4h, p. 1179; *LCW*, 33, p. 208.

at the congress Trotsky fully supported Lenin's views. He provided the factual and theoretical basis to refute the Theory of the Offensive in his 2½-hour opening report (Session 2). His speech on tactics and strategy (Session 14) provided a categorical refutation of the leftist view. Trotsky's report to Lenin on this session reflects the two leaders' partnership during the congress (Appendix 4a). Trotsky was singled out by the Left, both during and after the congress, as having advanced the views with which they most emphatically disagreed.[57]

*Zinoviev* shifted position during the congress visibly and significantly. His opening reports (Sessions 1 and 4) maintained that the congress's central purpose was to combat the Right, a formula used to downplay criticism of leftism in the March Action and elsewhere. In Session 14, however, he acknowledged that he had changed his view, speaking of balanced left and right dangers in terms that Radek had previously identified to the Russian delegates as the Lenin-Trotsky viewpoint. Zinoviev also appealed strongly for reconciliation and avoidance of a further split in the German party. However, while shifting his position on the main political issue, Zinoviev avoided discussion of the ECCI's role in the German calamity.[58]

*Radek* spoke often in the congress, defending the ECCI viewpoint on a wide range of questions, but his role was nonetheless ambiguous. Initially aligned with Zinoviev and Bukharin in support of leftist forces, Radek shifted during the congress to a position intermediate between them and Lenin-Trotsky. Radek continued his campaign against Levi, and he defended the VKPD majority against its critics. Yet Radek also advocated for the course of the Open Letter, which he had advanced jointly with Levi. He also clarified this initiative by explaining the concept of transitional demands, which had arisen earlier in the German mass movement but whose codification was a central political achievement of the congress. Radek also provided the most explicit acknowledgement that the ECCI's position had shifted in the course of the congress.[59]

Three non-Russian Communists also shaped the congress debates: Zetkin, the absent Paul Levi, and the mostly silent Béla Kun.

*Zetkin* was the object of intense personal denigration by some leftist delegates, who sought to undermine her political reputation (see Appendices 2e,

---

57. See Trotsky's 'Zametki dlia sebia' in Drabkin et al. (eds.) 1998, pp. 257–61; speeches in Sessions 2 (pp. 102–33) and 14 (pp. 571–81); Appendix 4a (pp. 1153–5); Leonhard 1981, p. 252; statement by the Left, pp. 597–8; Broué 2005, p. 567 (on VKPD Jena congress).
58. See pp. 81, 233, 562–7 (Zinoviev).
59. On transitional demands, see pp. 421–2, 440–2, 936; on the ECCI's shift, p. 593. On Radek's role, see especially Fayet 2004, pp. 386–91.

3c, 3j, 3k) and even suggested her expulsion. Nonetheless, she held detailed discussions with Lenin (Appendices 3i, 4f) and with Trotsky. Among delegates of the German opposition, she carried the main load in presenting the congress with an indictment of the March Action. According to Friesland, when the Russian leaders ultimately rejected the German delegation's leftist views, the German majority delegates, resentful and embittered, 'placed the blame for this above all on the influence of Clara Zetkin over Lenin'. Zetkin also shaped the congress's brief discussion and adoption of three resolutions on work among women. Harshly assailed during congress sessions, Zetkin was then honoured by a unique tribute on the occasion of her birthday, led off by Heckert, her most vociferously aggressive German opponent.[60]

*Paul Levi*, although absent from the congress, succeeded, through his critique of the VKPD leadership, in setting a framework for the March Action debate that dominated its proceedings. Measures were taken to reduce the impact of Levi's views, such as by pushing through a vote endorsing Levi's ouster, despite opposition protests, before delegates could discuss the actions of the VKPD and ECCI leaders that he had been expelled for criticising. Levi's appeal to the congress demanding reversal of his expulsion (Appendix 2f) was apparently not made available to delegates; it is not found in congress records. Nonetheless, Levi's views were widely known, and the course of congress discussions vindicated the core of his criticism. On this basis, at the close of the congress, Zetkin and Lenin initiated an effort, ultimately unsuccessful, to save Levi for the International, recorded in Appendices 4f, 4g, and 4h.[61]

*Béla Kun*'s prominence among the International's first-rank leaders is reflected in his haughty letter to Lenin defending his conduct in Berlin (Appendix 2e), his role as co-author (with Thalheimer) of the VKPD theses submitted to the congress, his blunt refutation of Trotsky in the precongress ECCI debate on France (Appendix 3f), and his last-minute procedural motion attempting to undercut the impact of Trotsky's summary on the Theses on Tactics and Strategy. He was under sharp attack during the discussions in Moscow, especially from Lenin (Appendix 2d). Lenin dismissed Kun's views with cutting scorn in the ECCI France debate (Appendix 3f), and Lenin's sarcastic references to Béla Kun's blunders (*les bêtises de Béla Kun*), although

---

60. For appendices, see pp. 1088–90, 1104–5, 1148–51, 1151–2, 1137–48, 1174–6. See also pp. 307 (expulsion threat), 283–301 (Zetkin speech); Brandt and Lowenthal 1957, p. 169 (Friesland's opinion); pp. 779–96 and 1009–27 (debate and resolutions on women); pp. 651–5, including 651, n. 1 (Zetkin tribute).

61. See p. 400 (Levi expulsion), 399–400 (German opposition statement); Appendix 2f, pp. 1090–6 (Levi appeal); pp. 392–4, 400–1 (procedural issue); Appendices 4f, 4g, 4h, pp. 1174–80.

toned down in the stenographic transcript, echoed in congress corridor discussion. Aside from one procedural motion, Kun kept a prudent silence in congress debates. There was much to please him in the congress outcome: the criticisms of his conduct were not aired on the congress floor; his role in the March Action debacle was not mentioned; and he preserved his role in the Comintern's day-to-day leadership.[62]

*Debate among Bolshevik leaders*

Although Lenin had expressed doubts about the March Action as early as mid-April (Appendix 2d), his differences with Zinoviev, Bukharin, and Radek remained unresolved as the congress convened. As late as 10 June, Lenin told Zinoviev that Radek had spoilt his initial draft of the Theses on Tactics and Strategy through concessions to the leftists (Appendix 3a). Lenin voted with Trotsky and Lev Kamenev on the five-member Bolshevik Political Bureau to set the line of the Bolshevik delegation against conciliation with leftism. On 21 June, the day before the congress opened, the Politburo decided to publish the Russian leadership's draft theses on tactics and strategy, which incorporated the Lenin-Trotsky position. Nonetheless, Radek's report to the Russian delegation that day presented the Russian leaders as divided into two blocs (Appendix 3h). According to Radek, he, Zinoviev, and Bukharin believed the overriding threat to the International was posed by 'opportunist forces' – the key contention of the leftist wing. Lenin and Trotsky's view that leftist dangers must also be combated rested on insufficient information, Radek said, claiming that he, Zinoviev, and Bukharin had made concessions only to avoid a damaging public rupture.[63]

The Russian leaders carried their disagreement, in muted form, into the congress itself. While giving ground, Zinoviev, Bukharin, and Radek still defended their leftist allies. On 29 June, the day before Radek gave the main report on tactics and strategy, the Russian party's Political Bureau took the unusual step of instructing its delegates to reject the leftist amendments and to speak in the congress along these lines. When the discussion of tactics and strategy concluded on 2 July, the Russian leaders joined in supporting a compromise text worked out with the leftists in commission and designed to win support from the entire congress. Even so, Zinoviev, Trotsky, and Radek

---

62. See Appendix 2e, pp. 1088–90; Reisberg 1971, p. 165 (Kun's authorship); Appendix 3f, pp. 1125–8 (Kun's speech); pp. 582 (Kun's motion); Appendix 2d, pp. 1086–7; Appendix 3f, pp. 1128–32 (Lenin's speech); Serge 2012, p. 163.
63. See Appendix 3a, pp. 1097–1101; Hájek and Mejdrová 1997, p. 310 (Politburo decision); Trotsky 1972b, pp. 33–5; Trotsky 1936, pp. 87–91; Appendix 3h, pp. 1135–7.

presented what were in essence separate summaries of the discussion, and Trotsky's talk, strongly criticising leftist errors, was protested in a written statement by six delegations. The next day, Trotsky reported to Lenin that Zinoviev and Radek had protested his speech as a 'bomb' that violated the agreement among Russian leaders (Appendix 4a). The incident was smoothed over, and the Russian leadership united behind the edited theses, which were unanimously adopted.[64]

## 2b. Disputes over National Parties

The debate took shape in large measure in terms of policy toward four national parties, those in Italy, Germany, Czechoslovakia, and France. The leftist current in the congress sought to rid the Comintern of 'opportunist' leaders in these countries. Much preparatory discussion took place outside formal congress sessions, whose outcome flowed into the congress and shaped its resolutions.

*Italy*

The discussion on Italy was occasioned by the appeal of the Italian Socialist Party (PSI) against its expulsion from the International following the split at the PSI's January 1921 Livorno Congress. On the eve of the congress, Zinoviev responded to this appeal with a flat condemnation of the PSI as a non-Communist, centrist current, and in his opening report, he documented at length the PSI leadership's centrist positions. Egidio Gennari, representing the Italian Communist Party's delegation, spoke further in this vein, demanding the expulsion of the PSI pure and simple. In the discussion on Italy, delegates of the PSI and the Comintern parties largely repeated arguments heard in Livorno. Comments by Lenin, Trotsky, and Christian Rakovsky, however, left open the possibility of reunification, if the PSI expelled its reformist current, and this view was codified in the resolution on the Executive Committee report adopted in Session 9. Zetkin, supporting this proposal, identified it with her controversial stand immediately after the Livorno Congress. Zinoviev's summary on Italy was not entirely in the spirit of the resolution, but its line was strongly presented in the post-congress ECCI appeal.[65]

---

64. Hájek and Mejdrová 1997, p. 310; below, pp. 597–8 (statement by six delegations); Appendix 4a, pp. 1153–5; 'Theses on Tactics and Strategy', pp. 924–50.
65. Zinoviev, 'Vor dem III. Kongress der Kommunistischen Internationale', *Kommunistische Internationale*, 16 (1921), pp. 1–7; below, p. 349 (Gennari), 921–2 ('Resolution on the Executive Committee Report'), 371–2 (Zetkin), 892–3 (Zinoviev), 1037 (appeal).

30 • Editorial Introduction

The Italian CP did not fully agree with the outcome of the congress, creating a discord that was to last for several years. The PSI, for its part, eventually acted on the Third Congress resolution, expelling its reformist wing in October 1922, but the party leadership subsequently failed to win a majority of its members for fusion with the Comintern, and only a minority later became part of the Italian Communist Party.[66]

Much less attention was paid during the congress to the capitalist offensive against Italian workers, the menacing rise of Italian Fascism, and Fascism's violent attacks on workers' organisations. The adopted theses on tactics and strategy made only brief mention of the need to resist Fascism. Zinoviev's closing remarks revealed the Comintern leadership's ignorance of conditions in Italy: he hailed the Communists' leading role in a united anti-Fascist action in Rome, unaware that the Italian Communist Party had stood aside from this initiative.[67]

*Germany*

German delegates, expecting their March Action to be hailed by the Third Congress, were stunned on their arrival in Moscow to be greeted by a torrent of criticism. Their strenuous pre-congress debate with ECCI leaders, and with Lenin in particular, has left few written records. The dispute then moved into the congress, where it dominated the proceedings. Zetkin and other German opposition representatives (who were not part of the official delegation) argued their views strongly, while the German majority drew on support from the Communist Youth International, the Italian CP, and several other delegations. Debate was unrestrained with one major exception: aside from provocative allusions by Zetkin, the ECCI delegation's role in the German debacle was barely mentioned at the congress. Debate centred on the Theses on Tactics and Strategy drafted by the Russian party; the VKPD withdrew its own draft and instead submitted extensive amendments, which were rejected by the Russian delegation as constituting a counterposed political line. To permit comparison, the amendments are printed in this edition alongside the corresponding portions of the ultimately adopted version.[68]

No record is available of the decisive 15 June meeting between the German delegation and the Russian party's Political Bureau. One delegate

---

66. Natoli 1982, pp. 129–33; Riddell (ed.) 2011b, *4WC*, p. 16.
67. See pp. 931 and 894; Behan 2007, pp. 58–69. Compare Lenin's remarks to Central European delegates in Appendix 4e, p. 1172.
68. See Zetkin, pp. 1150, 296–7, 298; 'Amendments to the Theses on Tactics', pp. 1041–58.

subsequently recalled it as 'a godawful battering on every side'. We do have, however, the German delegation's response to this meeting (Appendix 3d), sent the next day, withdrawing its draft theses and proposing the outline of a compromise decision on the German question that resulted from the previous day's discussion. On the same day, Lenin wrote the German delegation's leaders retracting harsh language he had used in the previous day's discussion (Appendix 3e). Amendments to the theses by the German, Austrian, and Italian delegates were presented 1 July; Neumann and Zetkin also submitted an amendment, for which no text is available. Its general thrust was presumably similar to the views expressed by Zetkin in her 18 June letter to Lenin (see Appendix 3g).[69] On 9 July, the delegation met with opposition representatives and with five Russian Central Committee members and worked out the shape of what became known as the 'peace treaty' between the two German factions (Appendix 4d). The congress also adopted a resolution on 'The March Action and the Situation in the VKPD' and a passage on the March Action in the 'Theses on Tactics and Strategy'.[70]

## Czechoslovakia

When delegates of the Czechoslovak Communist Party arrived in Moscow, they faced a barrage of criticism from ECCI members of their party's course. The first draft of the Theses on Tactics and Strategy, drafted by Radek on 15 May, condemned the Šmeral leadership as a centrist current passively awaiting revolution. During the 12–16 June sessions of the Expanded Executive, Bukharin called the Czechoslovak leaders' conduct an expression of pure opportunism and Zinoviev said their duplicity rivalled that of Serrati. In response, Edmund Burian, head of the delegation, informed Lenin that if things continued in this vein, the delegation would withdraw the party's application to join the Comintern. Lenin, while expressing criticisms of Šmeral, sought to halt the drive toward split. On 10 June, he requested documentation regarding Šmeral's role and objected to terming his policy one of passive waiting. Nonetheless, the second draft of the theses preserved

---

69. The 5 July issue of *Moscou*, which published the German-Austrian-Italian amendments, added a note, 'Because of a lack of space, the amendments proposed by the Neumann-Zetkin group in the VKPD cannot be published in this newspaper.' For Zetkin's letter to Lenin, see Appendix 3g, pp. 1132–5.

70. Weber 1991, p. 234; Appendices 3d and 3e, pp. 1106–7; Appendix 4d, pp. 1158–69; pp. 951, 941–2 (texts on March Action).

the condemnation of the Šmeral leadership, which drew a protest from the Czechoslovak delegation.[71]

When the congress convened on 22 June, the Czechoslovak dispute was still unresolved. On 25 June, Zinoviev read into the congress record his polemic against Šmeral given at the 14 June ECCI meeting. The following day, Gennari presented the Italian delegation's call for Šmeral to be barred from leadership positions. Šmeral himself arrived in Moscow 29 June. On 1 July, Burian presented to the congress the protest he had submitted to the ECCI on 16 June. No written records of commission discussions on Czechoslovakia are available, except for a short summary of a 6 July speech by Lenin (Appendix 4b). Following that speech, a motion by Lenin was adopted that removed the critical statement regarding Šmeral and called for a letter to the Czechoslovak party criticising weaknesses of both the Šmeral current and the leftist forces. The congress's decisions on the Czechoslovak Communist movement are found in the resolution on the ECCI report and the Theses on Tactics and Strategy.[72]

*France*

Although conditions in the French party offered ample grounds for leftist criticism, it had been shielded from attack – and its leaders had been omitted from the habitual 'Serrati-Levi-Šmeral' listing of presumed centrists – by the ECCI's policy of dealing with the party in what Zinoviev termed 'a more cautious and conciliatory manner'. Nonetheless, the pre-congress sessions of the Expanded Executive witnessed two tempests of controversy over the French party.[73]

Initially, after Zinoviev's opening report, the French delegates demanded an immediate accounting from the ECCI of its involvement in the March Action. Zinoviev responded that this would be taken up in due course during discussion of this topic. This did not satisfy the French leaders, who pressed their case. A heated exchange took place, in which Radek and Kun made provocative remarks. The French delegation thereupon left the meeting in protest. Zinoviev criticised the walkout as a breach of Communist norms and a relapse into parliamentary manoeuvring.[74]

---

71. Firsov 1975, p. 381; Hájek and Mejdrová 1997, pp. 320–2; Lenin 1958–65, *Polnoe sobranie sochinenii* (hereinafter *PSS*), 52, p. 269. For the Czechoslovak statement, see p. 494, n. 18.
72. See pp. 221–7 (Zinoviev 13 June report); Firsov 1975, p. 384; below, pp. 255 (Gennari); Appendix 4b, pp. 1155–7 (Lenin summary and resolution); congress resolutions, pp. 921–3 and 932–3.
73. See p. 216 (Zinoviev).
74. Rosmer 1971, pp. 127–8; Robrieux 1980, 1, p. 77.

In the 16–17 June sessions of the Expanded Executive, two delegates, Edy Reiland from Luxembourg and Maurice Laporte from the French youth organisation, assailed the French leadership for its allegedly centrist policies. Reiland went so far as to demand the immediate expulsion of Frossard. According to Rosmer, the incident was set up by Kun, who had been seeking to mobilise French-speaking delegates against the Frossard leadership. An extended debate followed, whose highlight was a sharp exchange between Trotsky, Kun, and Lenin (Appendix 3f). Lenin's remarks, in particular, caused a sensation, helping to turn the tide against Kun and his leftist associates. When the congress opened a few days later, the tempest had not entirely blown over, and the dispute over France came up several times during the congress proceedings. In his opening report, however, Zinoviev merely inserted into the record his conciliatory remarks on the French party to the Expanded Executive. The congress resolutions, while making many proposals to strengthen the French party, refrained from any attack on its leadership.[75]

## 2c. The Main Congress Debate

The chief disputed issues facing the main European parties merged into a single debate that occupied the majority of the three-week congress – its first fourteen sessions. During this debate, delegates sought to arrive at a unified appraisal of how economic conditions influenced the class struggle, the state of this struggle across Europe, and the policies needed to advance the cause of revolution under existing conditions.

Trotsky's report in Session 2, 'The World Economic Crisis and the Tasks of the Communist International', set the framework for the entire discussion, starkly portraying the capitalist states' newly won stability and confidence, following three years of upheaval. Workers' 'chaotic, elemental onslaught' had not, as the Comintern had hoped, achieved state power within a year or two, he said; '[T]he situation has become more complicated, but it remains favourable from a revolutionary point of view'. The time needed for world revolution was not a question of months but 'perhaps a matter of years'. Capitalism's current downturn was not a sign of impending collapse but rather a phase in its natural cycle. 'What leads to revolution is neither impoverishment nor prosperity in itself, but [their] alternation... and crisis,' Trotsky added. In the ensuing discussion, his report was criticised for failure to

---

75. See Appendix 3f, pp. 1108–32; Rosmer 1971, p. 127; below, 310 (Friesland), 324–5 (Rákosi), 534 (Vaillant-Couturier), 768 (Münzenberg), 215–20 (Zinoviev). Several sessions of the Expanded Executive were held on the eve of the Third Congress; invited representatives from Comintern parties expanded attendance to about 70.

acknowledge the immediate prospects for civil war. Trotsky and Eugen Varga had drafted theses on the basis of this report, but the German delegation formally requested that there be no vote on them. After a procedural wrangle, the draft theses were approved in principle in a divided vote.[76]

Zinoviev's report from the ECCI introduced a discussion of the Comintern's work in various countries that lasted through six sessions. He presented the slogan 'to the masses', which became the central theme of the congress. Decisions were taken on the extreme leftist Communist Workers' Party of Germany (KAPD) and the Italian Socialist Party. A resolution was introduced by ten European delegations (but not those of Britain, Czechoslovakia, or France) that approved the conduct of the ECCI since the previous congress, including with regard to the VKPD. The absence of the French delegation among the signatories, Fernand Loriot explained, reflected its misgivings regarding the March Action and the ECCI's role in it, and asked that this be frankly discussed in commission. Malzahn noted that the resolution did not mention the March Action or Levi's expulsion and called for full discussion of these points before the vote on approving the ECCI's conduct. Zinoviev then specified that approval of Levi's ouster was implicit in the resolution. Paul Neumann of the German opposition said that it was impossible to vote on the Levi case until the March Action had been considered. He proposed postponement of the vote, but his motion was defeated, and the draft resolution was overwhelmingly approved.[77]

The debate on tactics and strategy, next on the agenda, lasted for five sessions. Radek's lengthy report, given on 30 June, assessed the March Action as a 'step forward', accompanied by mistakes that, if repeated, would lead to 'even greater defeats'. He called on Communist parties to win the masses by participating in and leading their daily struggles. He also proposed the programmatic concept later known as transitional demands. The draft theses were introduced by the Russian delegation only after extensive editing; 'Lenin forced us to rework our theses five times', Radek later recalled. The German, Austrian, and Italian delegations responded with amendments to the draft theses that, among other points, deleted mentions of winning the majority of workers and of the Open Letter, cut out references to combating left sectarianism, and inserted formulations drawn from the now discredited Theory of the Offensive. Sponsors of the amendments canvassed for support,

---

76. See pp. 131, 133, and 165 (Trotsky); 150 (amendment by Pogány), 169 (motion by German delegation), 172–3 (vote), 901–20 (theses).
77. See pp. 234 ('To the Masses'), 921–3 (Resolution on ECCI Report), 387 (Loriot), 392 (Malzahn), 392–3 (Zinoviev), 393 (Neumann), 399–400 (German opposition), 400–1 (vote).

with considerable success. The amendments were presented to the congress by Terracini on 1 July and printed in the German edition of the congress newspaper (*Moskau*) the same day.[78]

The speech by Terracini, followed by Lenin's reply, marked the turning point of the congress. After Terracini's forceful presentation, Lenin countered that the Russian delegation 'must insist that not a single letter in the theses be altered'. He also extended the formula of 'winning the majority' (which Terracini had criticised) to apply not only to the industrial proletariat but to all the 'working and exploited rural population'. 'Lenin clobbered godawfully on all sides,' VKPD leader Wilhelm Koenen subsequently reported. 'This smashing about was justified on some points', but German comrades felt he 'really should have proceeded differently in order to convince comrades'. In the next session, Heckert received shouts of approval when he bluntly told Lenin he should have read the amendments more carefully. The German opposition also submitted amendments, whose text is not available; their spirit may be reflected in Zetkin's insistence that the March Action fell short not merely due to 'mistakes' but to a fundamentally erroneous theory.[79]

Discussion, planned to occupy two sessions, extended over twice that length and beyond. In commission discussions, the Russian delegation did agree to some modifications of wording in the theses in what Trotsky called 'a process of mutual concessions', but the leftist amendments were almost entirely rejected. On 2 July, Zinoviev acknowledged the need to combat the 'left danger' and conceded that he had 'learned a thing or two during the congress' on this point. Although closing statements by Zinoviev, Trotsky, and Radek all advocated support for the proposed theses, Trotsky's remarks stood out as an aggressive restatement of central themes of Lenin's controversial presentation. Six delegations that had sponsored the amendments declared they had reservations regarding Trotsky's speech, thus indicating that, in their minds at least, the dispute was not fully resolved. After further editing by the commission, the theses were adopted on 9 July. Lenin provided

---

78. See p. 436 (Radek). Regarding 'transitional demands', see pp. 436–42 and 935–9. On editing of theses, see Gutjahr 2012, *Revolution muss sein*, p. 485. For the amendments, see pp. 1041–58. Supporters of the amendments included the German, Austrian, Italian, Polish, Hungarian (majority), Czech-German, and Youth International delegations. The French translation appeared 5 July, but Terracini says (p. 457) that the original (German) version was published 1 July.

79. See pp. 457–65 (Terracini) and 465–73 (Lenin); 468 and 472 (Lenin quotations); Reisberg 1971, p. 181 (Koenen); below, pp. 482 (Heckert), 545–6 (Zetkin). A passage from the German opposition amendment was read out in Session 14; see p. 565.

his own summary in a report to a side-meeting of Central European delegates held on 11 July (Appendix 4e).[80]

## The KAPD and its role

Prior to the Third Congress, supporters of the Theory of the Offensive constituted a leftist current deeply rooted in the International's mainstream. The Communist Workers' Party of Germany (KAPD), by contrast, represented a more extreme leftist opposition, which had existed on the fringe of the International since 1919. The KAPD was formed in April 1920 with more than forty thousand members, mainly forces pushed out of the KPD because they refused to take part in trade unions or governmental elections. By early 1921, its membership had dropped to eight thousand. As noted, the ECCI admitted the KAPD 'provisionally' as a sympathising organisation in December 1920, despite protests from the KPD. During the March Action, as Frölich noted, KAPD policies converged with those of the new leftist VKPD majority leadership; a KAPD headline rejoiced, 'The KPD Masses Are Acting in Line with Our Slogans'.[81]

At the Third Congress, however, the KAPD delegation was faced by an ultimatum from the Comintern leadership: either unify with the VKPD or leave the International. The KAPD responded vigorously, submitting draft theses to most commissions and circulating a summary of its history in English and French. KAPD delegates spoke at length under many agenda points. They canvassed left-inclined delegates from Belgium, Bulgaria, Britain, Luxembourg, Mexico, the Netherlands, Russia (Workers' Opposition), Spain (CNT), and the US (IWW) regarding consolidating a leftist current in the International. The response was poor; only the Dutch minority and the dissident Bulgarians were sympathetic to KAPD views. Zinoviev's ECCI report demanded that the KAPD declare in convention, within three months, its willingness to fuse with the official German section. A motion to this effect was overwhelmingly adopted. Following the congress, the KAPD rejected this ultimatum, left the Comintern, and formed a hostile international current.[82]

---

80. See pp. 447 (length of discussion), 572 (Trotsky on concessions), 799–803 (list of changes), 562 (Zinoviev), 571–81 (Trotsky speech), 597–8 (declaration on Trotsky speech), 1170–3 (Appendix 4e). The dispute on Trotsky's remarks continued at the VKPD's 22–26 August congress in Jena, which declared its disagreement with his speech (Broué 2005, p. 567).

81. On the eve of the Third Congress, Lenin stated, 'I clearly see my mistake in voting for the admission of the KAPD.' See Appendix 3a, p. 1099. See also Bock 1969, p. 257; Koch-Baumgarten 1986, p. 156; below, p. 243 (Frölich).

82. Bock 1969, pp. 260–2; below, pp. 329–30, 331–5, 592 (Zinoviev).

## 2d. Profile of a Compromise

The political convergence in the congress resolutions was incomplete. Significant disagreements persisted, within the ECCI and among congress delegates as in the International as a whole. Sponsors of the leftist amendments on strategy and tactics made clear by their statement repudiating Trotsky's closing remarks on this topic that they were far from convinced of the Lenin-Trotsky position in its entirety. This attitude carried over to the VKPD's August 1921 convention at Jena, which endorsed the leftist statement in Moscow of dissociation from Trotsky's summary remarks.[83]

Under these conditions, the congress decisions represented an inevitable compromise, dissatisfying some delegates on both sides of the debate. Its resolutions affirmed a strategic course that rejected the leftist positions, but they left some things unsaid and some issues unresolved. The compromise sought to set out a principled basis on which divergent Communist forces could work together and broaden their area of agreement through further experience and discussion. Zetkin portrayed its dynamics by recounting her initial discussion with Lenin (Appendix 3i), quoting him as follows:

> Now don't give me that puzzled and reproachful look. You and your friends will have to accept a compromise. You must rest content with taking home the lion's share of the congress laurels. Your fundamental political line will triumph, and triumph brilliantly....
>
> The congress will wring the neck of the celebrated theory of the offensive and will adopt a course of action corresponding to your ideas. In return, however, [the congress] must grant the supporters of the offensive theory some crumbs of consolation. To do this, in passing judgement on the March Action, we will focus attention on the way that proletarians, provoked, fought back against the lackeys of the bourgeoisie. Beyond that, we let a somewhat fatherly leniency prevail.[84]

There was another aspect to the compromise, as Zetkin noted during the congress in a letter to Levi. 'The Executive wants the German question to be dealt with, as much as possible, as dirty laundry within the German delegation', she wrote (see Appendix 3j). Her statement suggests that assenting to silence on the ECCI's role was an element in the compromise that ultimately unified the congress around common positions.[85]

---

83. Broué 2005, p. 567.
84. See Appendix 3i, p. 1140.
85. See Appendix 3j, p. 1150.

The congress decisions represented a turn away from the course of the ECCI in the months prior to the congress. The adopted resolutions implicitly broke from the ECCI's previously exclusive emphasis on defeating the 'right danger', modified its wholesale rejection of the Italian Socialist Party, called off its drive to condemn the Šmeral leadership in Czechoslovakia, and repudiated the 'offensive' strategy pursued by its envoys in Germany before, during, and after the March Action. Yet, in a congress notable for candour and controversy, almost nothing was said in criticism of the ECCI's record, including in discussion of the ECCI report (Sessions 4–9). Radek assured delegates that the ECCI was not responsible for the March Action. The unanimously adopted resolution on the ECCI report gave the ECCI's actions – including with regard to Germany – unqualified approval.[86]

Nonetheless, the ECCI envoys' role was raised several times. Zetkin alluded to it on three occasions during the congress, the most explicit of which was her jab at *Die Rote Fahne* for 'publishing appeals and articles whose un-German mode of expression enabled opponents to say, "Not made in Germany"' – obviously a reference to the role of the Hungarian and Polish ECCI emissaries. VKPD leader Fritz Heckert also made a veiled reference to the rebellion of *Die Rote Fahne*'s staffers against the ECCI group's unilateral impositions, while Friesland spoke of the resulting dissension in the Zentrale. Loriot presented the French delegation's request for a special commission on the March Action, discussion of which he regarded as necessarily confidential. The commission could, he said, 'discuss why the Executive was led to act as it did.' In another context, Zetkin reviewed Rákosi's controversial actions as ECCI envoy in January–February 1921 in Italy and Germany.[87]

In addition to the issue of ECCI envoys, two other aspects of its record were of concern to some delegates: the encouragement given by ECCI leaders prior to February 1921 to leftist opposition forces in the German party and the overall leftist bias of its Small Bureau in the months preceding the conference. These topics did not come up for discussion.

ECCI spokespersons repeatedly called for criticism and deplored its absence. Thus the Yugoslav leader Sima Marković, an ally of Levi, was given a special extension to present his criticisms of the ECCI, which he did not do. The two delegates who explicitly questioned the ECCI's record, Zetkin and Loriot, were subject to no condemnation or reprisals.[88]

---

86. See pp. 388 (Radek), 392–3 (scope of resolution), 921–3 (resolution).
87. See pp. 298 (Zetkin on Béla Kun article), 296–8 (other Zetkin references), 312 and 488–9 (Heckert), 523 (Friesland), 387 (Loriot), 292–3 (Zetkin on Rákosi).
88. See pp. 267 (Radek), 395 (Zinoviev), 275–81 (Marković), 296–8 (Zetkin), 387 (Loriot).

The delegates' reticence may have been due to the continued dissension among the Executive's most prominent members. This fact, evident in the differing content of their speeches, was also reflected in the Russian Politburo's special motion giving instructions regarding their interventions, the flare-up of disagreement between Trotsky, Radek, and Zinoviev at the close of the tactics and strategy debate, and Lenin's public chastisement of Radek, a few weeks after the congress, for rupturing the Moscow 'peace agreement' regarding the German party.[89]

The hands-off attitude toward the ECCI's record was also reflected in the membership of the day-to-day leadership (the Small Bureau or Presidium) chosen as the congress closed. In addition to Boris Souvarine from the French party, it was composed of Zinoviev, Radek, Bukharin, Gennari, Heckert, and Kun, all of whom had been identified to varying degrees with the Executive's previous support of leftist currents.[90]

The failure to assess the role of the ECCI emissaries in the March Action, while perhaps an unavoidable component of the compromise with which the congress concluded, had negative results. The focusing of criticism on the German party leadership, while the ECCI envoys' role was passed over in silence, suggested that leadership accountability was not being dealt with in an even-handed manner and, even, that the ECCI itself was above criticism. Ongoing friction over the ECCI's role figured in two splits from the German party in the subsequent year. However, in the period following the Third Congress, there was no further destructive intervention by an ECCI emissary similar to the Béla Kun mission to Berlin, and ECCI representatives played a useful role in promoting Communist unity in many parties.[91]

Quite apart from the handling of the ECCI's record, the broader political compromise at the congress served a necessary purpose. It achieved the central goal of rejecting leftist adventurism and carrying out an agreed-on strategic turn expressed in its slogan 'To the Masses'. While leaving some issues undiscussed or postponed for later clarification, it served a necessary goal – too often neglected in the socialist movement – of preserving the unity of revolutionary forces that was indispensable for further steps forward and providing a principled and broadly agreed basis for their further united action and discussion.

---

89. Háyek and Mejdrová 1997, p. 310; Appendix 4a, pp. 1153–5; *LCW*, 32, p. 516.
90. Comintern 1922a, p. 7; Fayet 2008, pp. 119–20.
91. On the post-congress record of the ECCI, see Riddell (ed.) 2011b, *4WC*, pp. 41–5. Pogány, sent by the ECCI to the US in 1922, organised a faction and took over effective leadership of the US party, but there is no evidence of ECCI involvement in this exploit; see Riddell (ed.) 2011b, p. 42, n. 111.

## 2e. The Comintern Broadens Its Scope

In Session 15, with the great strategic debate finally dispatched to commission, the congress turned to the remaining eight topics on its agenda. Four sessions were devoted to work in trade unions, while seven other topics were squeezed into six sessions.

*Trade unions*

Trade-union reports by Zinoviev and Heckert were heard 3 July, which was also the opening day of the parallel world congress of unionists that went on to found the Red International of Labour Unions (RILU or Profintern). Leaders of the Comintern and its main parties agreed that revolutionaries should work within reformist-led labour organisations and defend their unity. However, they hoped that the RILU could defeat and break up the bourgeois-oriented 'Amsterdam' International in which these organisations were affiliated. Congress discussion focused on differences with revolutionary-syndicalist forces that were strongly represented in the RILU. Debate hinged on the traditional syndicalist contention that unions should have no ties with political organisations like the Communist parties. After a further report from Heckert, the final session adopted a major resolution on the RILU and its tasks.

Jakob Riehs (Austria) found the trade-union debate to be 'sluggish'; Jenő Landler (Hungary) complained of 'disinterest'. Rosmer later wrote that this debate was marked by 'the apathy normal at the end of congresses'. Proceedings of the later sessions do, in fact, show signs of strain, as commissions held extended sittings, racing to complete proposed resolutions. Nonetheless, the trade-union debate was lengthy and full of controversy.[92]

Syndicalist delegates at the Comintern and RILU congresses visited thirteen anarchists imprisoned in Moscow for breaches of Soviet legality. The treatment of Russian anarchists provoked a brief uproar in the RILU congress. In consultation with Emma Goldman and Alexander Berkman, US anarchists then living in Moscow, the syndicalists opened up negotiations with the Russian party leadership; Serge and Souvarine also played a role in this process. A meeting with Lenin took place on 11 July, and the following day, Trotsky conveyed the Russian Political Bureau's reply: the jailed anarchists would be permitted to leave Russia. They were freed and reached Berlin by the end of the year.[93]

---

92. See pp. 734 (Riehs); 731 (Landler); Rosmer 1971, p. 134.
93. Tosstorff 2004, pp. 347–59.

## Russia

Session 17, held on 5 July, was a unique event in Comintern history: a broad and open debate on the internal policies of its Russian party. Lenin's lengthy report focused on the just-adopted New Economic Policy (NEP), which had evoked doubt and uncertainty among many Communists inside and outside Russia. The Russian party's new course was criticised by Alexandra Kollontai, representing the Workers' Opposition within its ranks, as well as by two speakers from the KAPD. Kollontai criticised the Soviet government for insufficiently utilising 'the creative power of the working class'; Trotsky responded that she had presented no alternative course and that the Soviet republic was amply protected by the Communists' firm controls of the levers of economic power. The session adopted a short resolution and a set of theses drafted by Lenin.[94]

In response to the famine then afflicting wide areas of Russia, a decision was taken to launch an international campaign of emergency aid for the Soviet republic. Willi Münzenberg left Moscow to launch this work in Central Europe. Over the next year, these efforts became the Comintern's broadest and most successful international campaign.[95]

## Youth International

Münzenberg's report on the Communist Youth International (CYI) (Session 20) was given the day before the opening of a two-week-long CYI congress. The CYI was undertaking a reorientation: its headquarters was moving to Moscow from Berlin; its national units, many of which had led in founding the world Communist movement, would henceforth be autonomous but politically subordinate to Comintern sections in their countries. While explaining these changes, Münzenberg's report also gave a penetrating analysis of the conditions and problems of working-class youth in Europe. The CYI congress had been preceded by months of contentious internal debate,[96] but differences of opinion had now been mostly resolved. There was time for only one additional speaker (Frölich) on this topic. A resolution was adopted, after amendment, in Session 24.

---

94. See pp. 679–82 (Kollontai), 686ff. (Trotsky), 970–7 (theses and resolution).
95. See 3 July 1921 letter by Münzenberg to Zinoviev in Bayerlein et al. (eds.) 2013.
96. For background on the youth congress, see p. 773, n. 9.

## Women

The Second International Conference of Communist Women, meeting in Moscow on the eve of the Third World Congress, undertook the construction of an international network of commissions for work among women, affiliated to their respective national parties. The conference drew on an appeal and a detailed plan for the women's network drawn up by an initial gathering the previous year.[97] The Third Congress heard reports on this project by Zetkin, Lucie Colliard, and Kollontai, plus a speech by Norah Smythe. The discussion laid bare obstacles: parties had taken steps to organise women only 'with gritted teeth', to which women Communists reacted with 'a measure of bitterness'. Nonetheless, the three adopted resolutions expressed determination to overcome these barriers through systematic incorporation of women in the Comintern's work.[98]

## Cooperatives

At the time of the congress, millions of working people belonged to cooperatives, which made up a third wing of the workers' movement, alongside parties and trade unions. Revolutionaries had previously paid little attention to cooperatives, and the Comintern sought to remedy this situation. When this agenda item came up in Session 21, there was time only for a very brief report and the reading of the theses, after which the session was broken off because of insufficient attendance and the lack of translation. Too many important commission meetings had been scheduled at that time – indicative of the pressures during the final sessions. At the beginning of the next session, the theses were adopted without debate.[99]

## Organisation

The agenda point on party organisation sought above all to grapple with bureaucratic deformations member parties had inherited from the prewar Second International. Parties in Czechoslovakia, France, Germany (ex-USPD majority), Italy, and Norway had joined the Comintern largely intact. They included influential parliamentary, trade-union, and journalistic staffs that were often open to bourgeois influence and unresponsive to party direction.

---

97. For documents of the 1920 meeting, see Riddell (ed.) 1991, 2WC, 2, pp. 972–98.
98. See pp. 779–94 (reports by Zetkin, Colliard, Kollontai), 328 (Smythe), 780 and 781–2 (on obstacles), 1009–29 (resolutions). See also the Fourth Congress reports and resolution, Riddell (ed.) 2011b, 4WC, pp. 837–73.
99. A fuller discussion on cooperatives took place at the Fourth Congress. See Riddell (ed.) 2011b, 4WC, pp. 813–36.

The congress resolution, drafted by Otto Kuusinen, aimed to counter this weakness by involving all members in organised party work ('the duty to be active') and by integrating all in the party's cells, fractions, and working groups into a disciplined, unified structure. Lenin provided extensive input, encouraging Kuusinen to include more detail and insisting that a German comrade (Koenen) replace Béla Kun as reporter (Appendix 3b). (The following year, at the Fourth Congress, Lenin would term the resolution 'excellent' but 'too long' and 'too Russian' in spirit.) Koenen's lengthy report was squeezed into the congress's third-last session, and there was time to hear only three brief comments, each of them critical, before referring the resolution back to the commission for editing. It was adopted in the final session.[100]

The text did not take up financial assistance by the Comintern to member parties, an issue that played a role in a split later that year in Germany. It did, however, propose that Red Aid, the solidarity campaign with victims of capitalist repression, initiated in Germany after the March Action, be expanded internationally. The Fourth Congress returned to this topic, and it became one of the Comintern's most successful broad campaigns.[101]

### Functioning of the International

No agenda point specifically addressed the Comintern's structure. The two resolutions taking up these issues gave blanket approval to the ECCI's activity and called for the Executive and its apparatus to be enlarged and strengthened. Zinoviev protested intimations by Levi and others that some emissaries had acted irresponsibly, and the practice of sending ECCI emissaries to member parties – to gather information but also 'with full powers' – was endorsed.[102]

### Revolution in colonies and semi-colonies

In 1920, the Comintern adopted sweeping resolutions on revolution in the colonies and semi-colonies, worked out in two World Congress sessions and a separate conference on the peoples of the East. For the Third Congress, delegates from China, India, and Iran prepared three draft resolutions that

---

100. See 'Organisational Structure of the Communist Parties,' pp. 978–1006; Lenin's proposals in Appendix 3b, 1101–4; Koenen's report, pp. 809–32 and summary 874–8; Lenin's subsequent comments in Riddell (ed.) 2011b, 4WC, pp. 303–5.
101. See Broué 2005, p. 570 (finances). On Red Aid, see resolution, p. 1001 and Riddell (ed.) 2011b, 4WC, pp. 959–61.
102. See 'Resolution on the Report of the ECCI', 921–3; 'Resolution on Organising the Communist International', pp. 1007–8; pp. 397–8 (Zinoviev on emissaries); p. 1008 (decision on emissaries).

sought to develop strategic concepts for struggle in colonised countries with varying class structures (see Appendices 5a, 5b, and 5c). M.N. Roy's draft stressed the revolutionary potential of the nascent proletariat in the colonies; drafts by Sultanzade and Zhang Tailei called for a revolutionary anticolonial alliance, anticipating what later became known as the anti-imperialist united front.[103]

Perhaps because of the press of business at the congress close, none of these drafts was presented to the congress. A session was scheduled for discussion of the Eastern Question, but it had to be fitted into the final day of the congress, before an organisational commission meeting and the demanding closing session. The commission on the Eastern Question gave no report, and discussion did not address the strategic and policy issues facing Communists in the East. Halfway through the speakers' list, the chair (Kolarov) cut the speaking time to five minutes and dispensed with translation – measures unique in working sessions of the congress. The speech of South African delegate Ivon Jones was omitted from the published proceedings; it is found in Appendix 5d. For a motion by the Palestinian party, not taken up in the congress, see Appendix 5e. Roy spoke out strongly against what he considered the slipshod handling of the Eastern question during the congress. The French delegate Charles-André Julien seconded Roy's complaint, adding that 'the main role [in the session] has been played by cinematography'. The chair, Kolarov, while rejecting Roy's and Julien's protests, conceded that the Eastern question had been dealt with inadequately. At the start of the next and final session, Koenen said that a draft manifesto on the Eastern question was available and obtained agreement for its referral to the ECCI for publication. The manifesto is not otherwise mentioned in the congress; its text was not published and is not found in the congress records. The following year, the Fourth Congress held a two-day discussion on the Eastern question and adopted a comprehensive resolution.[104]

In other congress sessions, delegates heard explanations of the strategic importance of anticolonial struggles by Mir Ja'far Javadzadeh, Roy, Lenin, Zetkin, and Zinoviev.[105]

---

103. Riddell (ed.) 1991, 2WC, 1, 211–90; Riddell (ed.) 1993 (Baku Congress); Appendices 5a, 5b, 5c, pp. 1181–93.
104. See p. 854 (Kolarov); Appendices 5d and 5e, pp. 1193–7; pp. 855–6 (Roy), 865 (Julien), 870 (Kolarov), 872 (Koenen). For the Fourth Congress discussion and resolution, see Riddell (ed.) 2011b, pp. 28–33, 261–5, 649–737, 800–11, 947–51, 1180–90.
105. See pp. 322–3 (Javadzadeh), 156–9 (Roy), 659 (Lenin), 82 and 783 (Zetkin), 63 and 849 (Zinoviev).

## 3. School of Strategy

The Third Congress set in motion a shift in strategy that was extended through: (1) adoption of the united front policy (December 1921); (2) elaboration of this policy with respect to positions on transitional demands and workers' governments and on anti-imperialist struggles (December 1922); (3) development of a policy for united resistance to fascism (May 1923). Although the Third Congress decisions were a working compromise among a still very divided body of delegates, agreement was achieved around a strategic course of going 'to the masses', taking part in their daily struggles, and seeking to win their majority to a revolutionary course, as a precondition for achieving workers' power. The congress manifesto called on workers to join in a 'single unified front'. This crucial step forward opened up a process in which the Comintern developed and tested a wide spectrum of tactical initiatives to achieve the goal of winning mass support through united action. Thus, although the congress endorsed the 'Open Letter' initiative solely in the context of Germany, only six months later, in December 1921, the ECCI proposed it as a generally applicable policy, now termed the 'united front'. Another four months, and Comintern delegates were meeting in a joint conference with representatives of the despised Second and Two-and-a-Half Internationals.[106]

The congress was a practical working meeting, whose outcome was not predictable and not preordained. It was characterised by free and open debate, in which those with unpopular views were not silenced or penalised. Despite the Bolshevik leaders' prestige, there was no reticence about criticising them and no hesitation in opposing their positions. Deep differences were frankly debated, and an area of agreement was defined and widened. Despite shared concern for difficulties experienced by Soviet Russia, there was no subordination of international struggles to Russian national interests.

Despite many difficulties and obstacles, progress was indeed made. Even members of the Italian Socialist Party and the KAPD, whose leaders were openly attacking the Comintern, were offered a credible path to integration into the International. With regard to the mass Communist parties, the congress averted a rupture in Czechoslovakia, nudged the Italian party toward revolutionary reunification, exercised needed restraint in France, and, in Germany, achieved a fragile equilibrium and a new start.

---

106. See pp. 1034, 1036 (manifesto), 928, 933 (Open Letter); Riddell (ed.) 2011b, 4WC, pp. 1164–73 ('Theses on the Workers' United Front'); International Socialist Congress 1967.

The Third Congress took decisive steps in mapping out a strategy for revolutionary struggle in a preparatory period where conditions for revolutionary action were not yet present. Italian Marxist Luigi Cortesi has aptly caught the mood of the occasion:

> The grandeur and representativity of the congress impressed on the world a constantly more tangible reality of an alternative to the capitalist system. There is no evading...a sense of the historic solemnity of this gathering, almost a parliament of humanity.[107]

The congress opened up a two-year period, probably the most creative in Comintern history, of innovative attempts to forge workers' unity in action. It well deserved Trotsky's praise in a 14 July speech to Communist youth, when he termed it 'the highest school of revolutionary strategy'.[108]

---

107. Cortesi 2010, p. 466.
108. Trotsky 1972a, 1, p. 297.

# About This Edition

The Comintern's Third Congress consisted of almost three weeks of intensive, round-the-clock discussion, held in plenary sessions, commissions, and a host of improvised and informal get-togethers. The formal proceedings were led by an elected Presidium. The main working language was German, but delegates often spoke in one of the other three working languages: French or, more rarely, English and Russian. As a rule, each speech was translated after its completion into each of the other three languages.

A stenographic record of each speech was made in the language of its delivery. The secretarial staff prepared a typescript and translated it into the other languages. The German version of each of the twenty-four sessions was then printed for the information of delegates in a printed bulletin, published with only a few days' or a week's delay. Many documents of the congress also appeared in its daily newspaper, *Moscow*, which appeared in several languages.[1] Stenographic records were also kept of many commission meetings, but they remain unpublished.

Less than six months after the congress closed, its proceedings appeared in German in a book widely distributed across Europe and beyond. A Russian edition was published the next year, along with summaries in French and English.[2] The congress resolutions were printed in many languages.

---

1. *Bulletin des III. Kongresses der Kommunistischen Internationale*; *Moscou: Organe du 3e congrès de l'Internationale communiste*.
2. Comintern 1921c, *Protokoll des III. Kongresses der Kommunistischen Internationale*; Comintern 1922b, *III vsemirnyi Kongress Kommuniticheskogo Internatsionala*; Comintern 1921e, *Third Congress of the Communist International*.

In 1933 and 1934, new editions of the First and Second Congress proceedings and of all congress resolutions were printed in Russian in the Soviet Union. Publication of Comintern records was then broken off, however. By the later 1930s, the Comintern had repudiated the key components of its original strategy and ceased to circulate or refer to the records of its early years. The International itself was shut down in 1943. During the next two decades, the Comintern records mouldered in obscurity.

In the 1960s, the rise of Marxist movements independent of Stalinism spurred new interest in the early Comintern documents. In 1967, the Feltrinelli Institute published photographic reproductions of several dozen documentary volumes, including the congress proceedings. An English edition of resolutions from the first four congresses (1919–22) was published by Ink Links in 1980. These texts, which also appear on: <www.marxists.org>, are translated from a Russian text, which is somewhat different in formulation from the German version used in the present work. The following year, a team of Yugoslav researchers published an annotated edition of all seven Comintern congresses (1919–35).[3]

In 1983, New York-based Pathfinder Press began work, under my direction, on an annotated and newly translated edition of the four Comintern congresses held in Lenin's time, along with documentary volumes on the preparatory years. Six volumes were published during the next ten years, ending with the Second Congress and the Congress of the Peoples of the East, both held in 1920.[4] My edition of the Fourth Congress was published by Brill (2011) and Haymarket Books (2012).[5] A forthcoming volume, edited by Mike Taber, will present the record of the three expanded Comintern Executive Committee conferences held in 1922–3.

## On This Translation

The present edition of the Third Congress completes publication in English of the Comintern congresses held in Lenin's time. More than in any other Lenin-era world revolutionary gathering, the course of the Third Congress was shaped by discussions off the congress floor – in commissions or corridors – to the extent that the proceedings alone do not give a complete

---

3. Adler (ed.) 1980, *Theses, Resolutions and Manifestos of the First Four Congresses*; Bosić et al. (eds.) 1981, *Komunistička Internacionala: Stenogrami i dokumenti kongresa*.
4. For a listing of the Pathfinder books, which remain in print, see Selected Bibliography, p. 1249. See also: <https://johnriddell.wordpress.com/>.
5. Riddell (ed.) 2011b, *Toward the United Front: Proceedings of the Fourth Congress of the Communist International*, Leiden: Brill.

picture of how it unfolded. The Editorial Introduction and the appendices in the present work attempt to fill in the record of events outside the congress sessions.

The documentary material comes from three different sources:

1. The proceedings of the congress itself are translated from the German edition of 1921. The text has been compared with the Russian edition in order to correct incongruities and evident errors in the German text. Significant discrepancies between the two texts have been noted. Three preliminary documents found in the German edition have also been included.
2. Theses and resolutions of the congress are translated from a separate German edition of congress resolutions, published in 1921. Reference has also been made to the 1933 Russian version.[6] In the 1921 German editions, some resolutions are printed in both the proceedings and resolutions volumes; they appear here only in the 'theses and resolutions' section.
3. The appendices present thirty-two documents that offer necessary context for the published proceedings. They are translated from archival and published sources in German, Russian, and French. The items are published in chronological order. Most appendices record discussions among delegates present in Moscow during June–July 1921; six come from the preceding five months and one was written in mid-August. Most of the appendices are published for the first time in English; some (including speeches by Lenin and Trotsky in Appendix 3f) appear for the first time in any language.

The Yugoslav edition of congress proceedings and resolutions has been consulted, and its wide-ranging annotation has been utilised throughout, particularly for many references to Lenin-era publications. The records of the congress in the Russian State Archive of Social and Political History (RGASPI) have been utilised, particularly in preparing annotations and the appendix section. A selective check indicates that discrepancies between the archival text of speeches and the version published at the time are minor; such differences are not recorded in this edition.

Where Lenin speeches are available in his English-language collected works (*LCW*), this text has been revised through comparison with the German text in the Third Congress proceedings; the Russian edition of Lenin's writings has also been consulted (*PSS*).

---

6. Comintern 1921d, *Thesen und Resolutionen des III. Weltkongresses der Kommunistischen Internationale*; Béla Kun 1933, *Kommunisticheskii Internatsional v dokumentakh*.

Many names are misspelled in the 1921 German edition of the congress proceedings; these errors have been silently corrected. Paragraphing, erratic and inconsistent in the original, has been modified. Italics in the original text, added during post-congress editing both to indicate emphasis and as a layout feature, have for the most part been retained. Quotations in the proceedings have been sourced where possible, but many were paraphrases for which no original text could be located. Explanatory interpolations by the present editor have been placed in square brackets.

The translation, while remaining faithful to usage conventions within the Communist movement of the time, endeavours to use the vocabulary of today's English, even when Communists of the 1920s would likely have used a different term. For example, *Amerika* is usually translated 'United States'; *England*, most often, as 'Britain'. The German *konkret* is often rendered as 'specific'. No equivalent for 'ultraleft' is found in the original text, and the word therefore does not appear in the translation. In line with the German original, a purification of the Communist party membership is termed a 'cleansing', not 'purge', a word now associated with murderous Stalinist repression.

Two words present special problems. In the 1920s, the German *Taktik* carried a broader range of meanings than its current English cognate, sometimes encompassing what we now call 'strategy'. On occasion, the meanings of *Taktik* and *Strategie* are the reverse of current usage. In this text, *Taktik* is translated according to context, sometimes as 'tactics and strategy', sometimes as 'course of action'. The German word *Aktion* then often carried a confrontational meaning absent from its English cognate. In this case, no way could be found to reflect in English its different usages. It is translated throughout as 'action'.

The chronology focuses on events mentioned in the congress. The bibliography includes major recent works related to aspects of the Third Congress; it does not attempt to encompass journal literature or dissertations. The glossary presents biographical notes for all persons mentioned in the book, with special attention to less-well-known figures in the Communist movement, alongside entries for workers' organisations and newspapers.

# Acknowledgements

Publication of this book was made possible by the help of a wide range of collaborators in many countries.

Mike Taber drafted the footnotes, glossary, and chronology, edited the text, helped shape the Editorial Introduction, and advised on every aspect of the work. Jeff White compiled the editorial style for the book, copy-edited the text, and provided editorial advice throughout the project.

Sebastian Budgen and David Broder of *Historical Materialism* Book Series gave constant support and encouragement, as did John MacDonald of Haymarket Books.

Special thanks are due to Darya Dyakonova, who advised on problems of Russian translation. James Murphy and Jesse Zarley organised access to archival resources.

Gleb Albert, Tom Alter, Bernhard Bayerlein, Marcel Bois, Jean-Numa Ducange, David Fernbach, Sabine Kneib (Archiv der sozialen Demokratie), Lars Lih, Dieter Misgeld, Nancy Rosenstock, Joern Schuetrumpf (Dietz Verlag), Khosrow Shakeri, Peter Thomas, Mete Tunçay, Daniel Tucker-Simmons, Marcel van der Linden, Suzanne Weiss, and Florian Wilde provided valued research, translation, and editorial assistance. Responsibility for errors, however, lies with the editor alone.

Thanks are due to the York University Department of Political Science and York University Libraries for making available research facilities needed for this project. Greg Albo, Jess MacKenzie, Hans Modlich, and Ernest Tate helped put in place the material resources needed to carry out the work.

Heartfelt thanks to Abigail Bakan, Paul Kellogg, and Suzanne Weiss, who took part in the initial decision to undertake this project and thereafter shared in many decisions that guided it to completion.

# List of Abbreviations

| | |
|---|---|
| 1WC | First World Congress |
| 2WC | Second World Congress |
| 4WC | Fourth World Congress |
| AAUD | General Workers' Union of Germany |
| ADGB | General German Trade Union Federation |
| AFL | American Federation of Labor |
| CC | Central Committee |
| CGL | General Confederation of Labour (Italy) |
| CGT | General Confederation of Labour (France) |
| CNT | National Confederation of Labour (Spain) |
| CP | Communist Party |
| ECCI | Executive Committee of the Communist International |
| IWW | Industrial Workers of the World |
| KAPD | Communist Workers' Party of Germany |
| KPD | Communist Party of Germany |
| LCW | V.I. Lenin, *Collected Works* |
| MECW | Karl Marx and Frederick Engels, *Collected Works* |
| PCI | Communist Party of Italy |
| PSI | Socialist Party of Italy |
| PSS | V.I. Lenin, *Polnoe sobranie sochinenii* |
| RCP | Russian Communist Party |
| RSFSR | Russian Soviet Federative Socialist Republic |
| RGASPI | Russian State Archive of Social and Political History |
| RILU | Red International of Labour Unions |
| SP | Socialist Party |
| SPD | Social-Democratic Party of Germany |
| UGT | General Union of Labour (Spain) |
| USPD | Independent Social-Democratic Party of Germany |
| VKPD | United Communist Party of Germany |

*Preliminary Statements*

# Provisional Congress Agenda

Moscow, April 1921

The Third Congress of the Communist International

The Executive of the Communist International has decided to convene the Third World Congress of the Communist International on 1 June 1921. The Executive has adopted the following provisional agenda:

1. Report of the Communist International Executive.

2. The world economic crisis and the new tasks of the Communist International.

3. Communist International tactics and strategy during the revolution.

4. The transitional period (partial demands, partial actions, and the final revolutionary struggle).

5. The struggle against the Amsterdam yellow trade-union confederation.

6. The International Council of Red Trade Unions and the Communist International.

7. Organisational structure of the Communist parties and the method and content of their work.

8. Organisational structure of the Communist International and its ties to the affiliated parties.

9. The Eastern question.

10. The Italian Socialist Party and the Communist International (appeal of the Italian Socialist Party against the decision of the Executive).

11. The KAPD and the Communist International (appeal of the VKPD against the decision of the Communist International Executive).[1]

12. The women's movement.

13. The youth movement.

14. Election of the Communist International Executive and choice of location for its headquarters.

15. Miscellaneous.

*G. Zinoviev*

---

1. When the Executive Committee admitted the KAPD to the Comintern as a sympathising organisation, in November 1920, the German Communist Party (VKPD) strongly protested this decision, including in its press, and appealed it to the Third Congress.

# Call for the Third World Congress

*Letter of the Communist International Executive Committee to all proletarian parties that belong to the Communist International or wish to join it.*

The Third World Congress of the Communist International will convene in Moscow on 1 June 1921. The congress has been called two months earlier than provided for in the Communist International's statutes.[1] Nonetheless, we are convinced that the parties affiliated to the Communist International agree with us that the interests of our cause require this acceleration.

In the nine months since the Second World Congress, a broad discussion has opened up in a great many parties over the principled questions posed at that congress. In a number of countries, this clarification has advanced to the point where an open break has taken place between the Communists and supporters of the Centre. In Germany, France, Britain, Sweden, Norway, Romania, Yugoslavia, Greece, Switzerland, Belgium, and other countries, the split between the Communists and supporters of the Two-and-a-Half International is an accomplished fact.[2] In other countries, such as Czechoslovakia, the

---

1. Point 4 of the Statutes approved by the Second Congress, held in July–August 1920, states, 'The world congress meets regularly once a year.' See Riddell (ed.) 1991, 2WC, 2, p. 697.

2. The term 'Two-and-a-Half International' referred to the centrist International Working Union of Socialist Parties, or Vienna Union, founded at a congress in Vienna, 22–27 February 1921. It was established in opposition to both the reformist Second International and the Communist Third International. The Two-and-a-Half International fused with the Second International in May 1923.

split is posed in the near future. In Italy, the Communists have founded their own independent party. The present Socialist Party there includes recognised reformists and wavering revolutionaries; gradually the healthy proletarian forces will leave it and publicly join the Communist International. In the United States, the unification of all Communist groups is likely in the near future.

The Communist International must take into account the totality of all these developments in the named parties. The Executive Committee of the Communist International had to take extremely important decisions during this period. It must now give an accounting for these decisions before the entire Communist International. The Third Congress must consider above all the degree to which each of the parties affiliated to the Communist International has actually carried out all the conditions established by the Second Congress. An important phase of Communist International activity is coming to an end. Prior to its First Congress, the Communist International traversed its early days, its preparatory period. Between the First and Second Congresses lay a period of initial agitation. At that time, the Communist International was not yet a rounded international organisation; it was only a banner, only a slogan. The period between the Second and Third Congresses is one of intensified and clear division and the formation of genuine Communist parties. The Third Congress will draw the balance sheet of all the accomplished work and will provide the Communist International with a finished organisation and well-honed tactical and strategic policies.

The proposed agenda of the Third Congress has been drawn up by the ECCI and published in its press.

The first point on this agenda is the Executive Committee report. During the nine months that have passed since the Second Congress, the Executive Committee had to become involved in the struggles and splits that took place in several parties. This gave rise, of course, to protests here and there against the Executive Committee. Whether the general policies set by the Second Congress have been applied rightly must be decided by the Third Congress. Above all, however, the Communist International must establish a firm and definite rule: the Executive Committee is always subordinate to the next world congress, to which it must give an accounting. Any decision of the Executive Committee can be appealed to the congress. *But between congresses, the entire leadership responsibility rests in the hands of the Executive Committee.* Its decisions must be carried out. Without this, the Communist International cannot exist as a centralised and disciplined international organisation. The claim of the Communist International to be an International of the deed would be hollow unless this international combat organisation had a general staff and was confident that this staff would be sustained by discipline, not only in word but in deed.

The second agenda point is 'The world economic crisis and the new tasks of the Communist International'. The 'theoreticians' of the Two-and-a-Half International – Otto Bauer, Hilferding, Kautsky, and the like – claim that, with the imperialist war now at an end, capitalism will now succeed in achieving a measure of economic equilibrium. Based on the adjustment to conditions of peace, they say, a renewed 'capitalist' system is entering a period of energetic organisational development. From this, the leaders of the Two-and-a-Half International – to say nothing of the openly traitorous Second International – draw definite practical conclusions. This has led to the shameless defection of all these parties, including the German Independents [USPD] and the French Longuetists [SP], to the camp of open counterrevolution. It is incumbent on the Third World Congress to thoroughly and carefully analyse the economic crisis, with its unprecedented unemployment and mass destitution. On this basis, it must demonstrate to working people around the world that these reformist illusions are a complete falsehood, revealing the impotence of those who believe in the future of a revitalised capitalism and who proclaim this petty-bourgeois policy of global renewal to the international proletariat.

The third and fourth items on the agenda are: Communist International tactics and strategy during the revolution and the transitional period, partial demands and partial actions, and the final revolutionary struggle. In a time of transition such as what we are now experiencing in the revolutionary movement, two tendencies inevitably arise. Some ask why, if the revolution is at hand, we should raise partial demands. Others ask why, if we can raise partial demands, we should then always repeat the entire programme. Some say that we should not squander our energies in partial actions and should gather our strength for the final struggle. Others say that we should seize every opportunity for 'action'. The Third World Congress will have to weigh precisely the specific experiences of the Russian comrades before the revolution, along with those of the German comrades and proletarians of other countries. The Third Congress must determine a precise tactical and strategic course for the Communist parties that steers clear both of sectarianism and of making a grab for transitory successes, while also promoting the creation of a firm link between the Communist parties and the broad proletarian masses and the maintenance of the principled and steadfast character of revolutionary Marxist theory.

Points 5 and 6 are devoted to evaluating the international trade-union movement: 'The struggle against the Amsterdam trade-union confederation' and 'The International Council of Red Trade Unions'.[3] This is one of the most important items on the Third Congress agenda. A struggle is raging within the trade-union movement. *This development will determine the outcome of the struggle between the Second and the Third Internationals, that is, between capitalism and the proletariat.*

Millions of proletarians are now united in the trade unions. The task is to win the proletariat to our side. The policy of forming Communist cells inside the unions, laid down by the Second Congress, has had significant success in Germany, France, Britain, and other countries. The first hard blows have been delivered against the yellow Amsterdam confederation. The yellow Amsterdam leaders are swinging and swaying: one day ready to make concessions, and the next day expelling supporters of the Communist International from the unions. This is a sure sign of their imminent and complete collapse. The Third Congress will draw a balance sheet of the struggle against the yellow Amsterdam confederation and systematise this struggle for the future.

But, above all, the Third Congress is obliged to determine precisely the interrelationship between the Communist International and the International Council of Red Trade Unions. Should we have two parallel international organisations, in which case the Communist International will play the leading role? Or will we have only one Communist International, embracing not only political parties but rather all proletarian organisations that stand with the Communist International, including the red trade unions? In the latter case, the International Council of Trade Unions would be only a section of the unified Communist International. Much can be said both for and against each of these two propositions. How this question is decided will have important implications for the structure of the international workers' movement. All the organisations that belong to the Communist International must consider this question carefully and comprehensively and present their conclusions, precisely formulated, to the Third Congress.

The seventh and eighth items concern organisational questions, namely 'The organisational structure of Communist parties, and the method and content of their work,' and 'The organisational structure of the Communist

---

3. The 'Amsterdam International' was the commonly used name for the social-democratic-led International Federation of Trade Unions, headquartered in Amsterdam.

The International Council of Trade and Industrial Unions was the forerunner of the Red International of Labour Unions (RILU, also referred to as the Profintern, based on its name in Russian). The International Council was founded on the eve of the Comintern's Second Congress in July 1920. The RILU's founding congress was held in Moscow 3–19 July 1921, overlapping with the Comintern's Third Congress.

International and its relationship to the affiliated parties'. Two groups of questions must be considered here.

The first group concerns the question of *how each individual Communist party should be structured.* Among the Communist parties of Western Europe, there are even cases where there is hardly any party organisation functioning in an ongoing way. Only during elections and similar events do all the party's members go into action. These parties do not have regularly functioning, structured Communist cells in the factories and mills, the mines and the railways, the villages and enterprises, the unions and cooperatives. There is no rigorous system for the subordination of these cells to the parties' central leaderships. Moreover, no serious illegal organisation is available to supplement the work of the legal party. We must put an end to this situation, and the Third Congress will take this up.

The second group of organisational questions that the Third Congress must take up concerns the limits of the autonomy of individual parties vis-à-vis the Executive Committee of the Communist International, and how a truly *centralised* international proletarian organisation must be structured, one that is actually capable of leading the international struggle of the proletariat. This must be done in order to improve the ties among the individual parties and between them and the ECCI, so that it is capable of carrying out the constantly growing tasks.

Point 9 concerns an important question. The Communist International can register the first successes of its work among the peoples of the East. The Congress of the Peoples of the East in Baku unquestionably has great historic importance.[4] The congress of peoples of the Far East, now in preparation, will also play no small role.[5] The Third Congress will have to tackle the Eastern question not only theoretically, as was done at the time of the Second Congress, but also in practical terms. Without the revolution in Asia, the proletarian world revolution cannot be victorious. This thought must become the intellectual property of Communist proletarians. Only then will Communist workers have adequate ideological arms to resist the *European opportunism of Hilferding and other heroes of the Two-and-a-Half International*, who can spare only a smile for the subjugated peoples of the East.

---

4. The First Congress of the Peoples of the East, organised by the Comintern, was held in Baku, 31 August–7 September 1920. For the proceedings, see Riddell (ed.) 1993, *To See the Dawn.*

5. The First Congress of the Toilers of the Far East was held in Moscow and Petrograd, 21 January–2 February 1922. For the proceedings, see Comintern 1970.

Point 10 of the agenda, concerning the Italian Socialist Party, is of enormous importance. The Italian SP once belonged to the Communist International. However, influenced by the centrist agitation of the Serrati group, the congress of this party in Livorno declined to carry out the Twenty-One Conditions that the Communist International posed before all parties.[6] The Serrati group, backed by the majority at the congress, wanted to impose on the Communist International such well-known agents of capitalism as the long-standing reformists Turati, Modigliani, D'Aragona, Treves, and company – that is, the Italian Dittmanns, Bernsteins, and Longuets.

In league with these reformists, who had 14,000 votes at the Livorno Congress, the leaders of the Italian Centre, with Serrati at the head, broke with 58,000 Communist proletarians.[7] Serrati was disloyal to the decisions taken by the Second Congress. The true moral victors over the Centre in Livorno were the reformists, with Turati at their head. The Communist workers founded an independent Communist Party. Under such circumstances, the ECCI believed its duty to lie in recognising the newly formed Communist Party of Italy as the only section of the Communist International in Italy and in expelling Serrati's party, which had in fact repudiated the decisions of the Second Congress. The Italian Socialist Party objected to this decision of the Executive and appealed to the full congress of the Communist International. Every party has an unquestioned right to appeal in this way, and the Executive Committee therefore gladly entrusts this decision to the Third Congress.

The Executive Committee knows well the customs and practices of the centrist leaders, who gladly evade clear answers to difficult questions. In a letter to the Central Committee of the Italian Socialist Party, it declared the following:

1.) We demand that you take part in the Third Congress and insist that your delegates to the congress possess all the authority needed to give the congress definitive answers.

---

6. The 'Theses on the Conditions for Admission' approved by the Second Congress – referred to commonly as the Twenty-One Conditions or the Twenty-One Points – can be found in the Second Congress proceedings, Riddell (ed.) 1991, 2WC, 2, pp. 765–71.

7. The Italian Socialist Party's Livorno Congress took place 15–21 January 1921. A left current, which received 58,783 votes, demanded immediate application of the Comintern's Twenty-One Conditions for membership. The majority current led by Serrati, which received 98,028 votes, insisted on the need to apply the conditions flexibly 'in conformity with the context and the history of the country' (Broué 2005, p. 477). The Right led by Turati received 14,695. Representatives of the ECCI demanded that the party immediately apply the Twenty-One Conditions fully, particularly with regard to expulsion of the anti-Communist Right, on pain of exclusion from the Communist International. After the vote, the Left walked out and organised the Communist Party of Italy.

2.) We demand that you *state clearly and precisely* whether you agree to expel from the party and the Communist International the *Critica sociale* group, that is, Turati, Treves, and company, because that is the only issue in the dispute.

The Italian question has assumed international significance. In Germany, the Levi group, which had long sought to create something of a right wing in the Communist International, seized on the Italian dispute, assuring us that the Communist International Executive had committed 'tactical' errors, that the Executive was advocating 'mechanical' splits, and things of that sort.

The Third Congress will achieve full clarity on this question. It will raise the question to the necessary level of principle, cleanse it of all that is petty and accidental, and declare to all that *those who do not carry out the Twenty-One Conditions in life* cannot be members of the Communist International.

The March uprising of German Communists caused severe discord in the VKPD [United Communist Party of Germany]. Levi was expelled from the party, and the Communist International Executive approved this action. The Third Congress will doubtless have the task of taking up the policy issues posed in the March uprising.

Another issue on the Third Congress agenda is that of taking a position on the KAPD [Communist Workers' Party of Germany]. This party must say conclusively whether or not it accepts international discipline.

The Third Congress agenda also includes the questions of the women's movement, the youth movement, and so on.

Finally, the Communist International Executive decided to place on the Third Congress agenda, in one or another form, the extremely important question of economic policy and the general situation in Soviet Russia, the first republic in which the proletariat took power.

We ask all parties and groups that are affiliated to the Communist International, or wish to join it, to immediately hold a far-reaching discussion on the points in the Third Congress agenda, both in their press and in assemblies. We also ask that the question of elections for this congress now be given priority. The ECCI has decided unanimously to propose to all parties that:

1.) The delegations to the congress should contain as many members as possible.
2.) Among the delegates, a third should be members of the central leadership, but two-thirds of the delegates should come from the largest local organisations, who are in ongoing contact with the working masses. We consider this latter point to be very important.

It is essential that the congress include as many workers as possible who can transmit directly the voice of the working masses.

The preparatory work, preliminary conclusions, and the like, are no less important than the congress itself. The decisions of the Third Congress must be prepared and considered in many hundreds of workers' meetings. Little time is left, so let's get to work!

With Communist greetings,<br>
G. Zinoviev,<br>
Chairman of the Executive Committee of the Communist International

*Members of the ECCI*

Russia: *Lenin, Trotsky, Bukharin, Radek*; France: *Rosmer*; Britain: *Quelch, Bell*; Austria: *Steinhardt*; Hungary: *Béla Kun, Rudnyánszky, Varga*; Poland: *Walecki*; Bulgaria: *Dimitrov, Popov, Shablin*; United States: *William Haywood, John Crosby*; Finland: *Kuusinen, Manner, Rahja*; Netherlands: *Jansen*; Norway: *Friis*; Switzerland: *Itschner*; Georgia: *Tskhakaia*; Latvia: *Stuchka*; Iran: *Sultanzade*; International Youth League: *Shatskin*

The Executive asks all parties and organisations to have their delegates bring precise written reports regarding their work during the past year. In addition, it asks all parties to name reporters on the various agenda points and to present draft theses and resolutions on these questions.

# Invitation to the Third Congress of the Communist International

The Small Bureau of the Communist International Executive Committee has decided that the Third World Congress will begin its work in Moscow no later than 2 June 1921.

The Executive is publishing the following preliminary list of organisations invited to the congress. The Executive advises that this list is only approximate and is very incomplete.

Communist organisations that have for some reason been omitted from this list have the right to send representatives to this congress.

*Russia:* Communist Party.

*Germany:* United Communist Party [VKPD]. Communist Workers' Party [KAPD] (with consultative vote).

*France:* Socialist Party of France.[1] The revolutionary trade-union minority.

*Italy:* Communist Party. Syndicalist Union. Railway Workers' Union. Seamen's Union. Socialist Party (with consultative vote).

*Bulgaria:* Communist Party.

*Poland and Eastern Galicia:* Communist Workers' Party of Poland. Communist Party of Eastern Galicia. League of Jewish Workers [Bund] (with consultative vote).

---

1. Presumably the Communist Party of France was meant here.

*Czechoslovakia:* Communist Party of German Bohemia. Marxist Left of the Czech Socialists. Socialist Party of Slovakia (with consultative vote). Internationalist Socialist Party of the Ruthenian people (with consultative vote).

*Britain:* United Communist Party. Independent Labour Party.

*United States:* Communist Party (United). Industrial Workers of the World (IWW).

*Austria:* Communist Party.

*Hungary:* Communist Party.

*Yugoslavia:* Communist Party. Socialist Party of the autonomous region of Fünfkirchen [Pécs].[2]

*Ukraine:* Communist Party.

*Finland:* Communist Party.

*Sweden:* Communist Party.

*Norway:* Labour Party.

*Spain:* Communist Party. Workers' Confederation [CNT].

*Far Eastern Republic:* Communist Party.

*Japan:* Communist groups.

*Argentina:* Communist Party. Communist Workers' Federation (with consultative vote).

*Azerbaijan:* Communist Party.

*Armenia:* Communist Party.

*Georgia:* Communist Party.

*Greece:* Communist Party.

*Belgium:* Communist Party.

*Netherlands:* Communist Party.

---

2. Pécs (Fünfkirchen) was occupied by Serbian troops until August 1921, after which it became part of Hungary.

*Denmark:* Communist Party.

*Switzerland:* Communist Party. Workers' League of Swiss Cities (with consultative vote).

*Romania:* Communist Party.

*Latvia:* Communist Party.

*Estonia:* Communist Party. Independent Social Democracy.

*Iran:* Communist Party.

*Australia:* Communist Party.

*Canada:* Communist groups.

*Cuba:* Communist groups.

*Mexico:* Communist Party.

*Central America:* Communist groups.

*Uruguay:* Socialist Party.

*Chile:* Socialist Party.

*Java [Indonesia]:* Communist Party.

*South Africa:* International Socialist League.

*Lithuania:* Communist Party.

*Portugal:* Communist groups.

*Luxembourg:* Communist Party.

*Ireland:* Communist groups.

*Iceland:* Communist Party.

*Turkey:* Communist Party.

*Khiva:* Communist Party.

*Bukhara:* Communist Party (with consultative vote).

*Palestine:* Communist Party (with consultative vote).

*India:* Communist groups (with consultative vote).

*China:* Left Socialist Party (with consultative vote). Communist groups (with consultative vote).

*Korea:* Communist Party (with consultative vote). Social-Revolutionary Party (with consultative vote).

The Communist International Executive also calls on the following groups that are close to it to send delegations to Moscow to the Third Congress of the Communist International, in order to take part as interested groups, for informational purposes, in the sessions of the Communist World Congress:

Socialist Workers' Party of Finland.

General Workers' Confederation of Italy.

Federation of Russian Workers of South America.

General Trade Union Federation of Greece.

National Workers' Secretariat of the Netherlands.

Federation of Oppositional Trade Unions of Denmark.

Left Socialist Party of Belgium (Brussels Federation).

Netherlands Alliance of Anarcho-Communists.

*Proceedings and Resolutions*

Session 1 – 22 June 1921, 7 p.m.
# Opening Session

*Opening of the Third World Congress of the Communist International in the Bolshoi Theatre of Moscow with delegations of the Moscow Soviet and representatives of the working class. Speeches of welcome by Zinoviev, Kamenev, Vaillant-Couturier, Frölich, Hewlett, Kolarov, Burian, Gennari, Tommasi, Taguchi.*

**Grigorii Zinoviev** (Chair): On behalf of the Executive Committee of the Communist International, I declare the Third World Congress of the Communist International to be in session. (*Loud applause. The orchestra plays the 'Internationale'.*)

Comrades, as at all international proletarian gatherings, our first words here must be devoted to our brothers who have fallen in the struggle for communism. Beside the names of Karl Liebknecht, Rosa Luxemburg, and others that have been entered in the annals of our struggle in recent years, other, no less celebrated names have been added in the past year. We have lost our dear comrade John Reed, the best leader of the American proletariat.[1] Not long ago the Berlin workers buried one of their leaders, Sült, who was killed by the executioners of the German bourgeoisie.[2] A group of Turkish Communists, headed

---

1. John Reed, a leader of the Communist Labor Party and author of *Ten Days That Shook the World*, died of typhus in 1920 after attending the Comintern's Second Congress and the Congress of the Peoples of the East in Baku.
2. Wilhelm Sült was an electrical workers' leader and KPD member. He was arrested on 1 April 1921, and brought to Berlin police headquarters, where he was shot 'trying to escape'.

by our comrade Subhi, who took part in the First Congress of the Communist International, recently fell victim to murder.[3] In the course of the past year we lost a great many comrades in the immediate vicinity of Soviet Russia. During this period, a group of our worthy comrades, among whom Comrades Šilfs and Berce had played a most active role in our struggle, were executed by the Latvian bourgeoisie.[4] Other executions of this type took place in Lithuania.

In Italy, not a single week goes by without the loss by our comrades of one or another of their ranks in the struggle against paid agents of Italian capitalism. In Germany, hundreds of the best German comrades perished in the March Days. Many comrades are missing who were among the delegates at the Second World Congress. You all remember the tragic death of our best French comrades, Raymond Lefebvre, Lepetit, and Vergeat, who died at sea.[5] A group of Greek comrades, including Comrade Alexakis, suffered an equally tragic death while returning from Russia to their homeland.[6] The Finnish comrade Ivan [Jukka] Rahja and a group of his friends also fell for the cause of the proletariat.[7] Our comrade Inessa Armand, who took part so actively in the Second World Congress, also died during this period, and not long ago we also buried Comrade Samoilova.[8] In southern Europe and Yugoslavia, the white terror raging there ripped dozens of comrades from our ranks. Before we begin our work, I ask the Third World Congress of the Communist International to rise in honour of the fallen comrades. (*The orchestra plays the funeral march. All present rise from their seats.*)

## Welcoming Speeches

**Zinoviev** (Russia): On behalf of the Third World Congress of the Communist International, we greet the many thousands – perhaps tens of thousands – now confined behind prison bars in many countries. In Germany we lost hundreds of comrades during the March Days. During recent weeks, four

---

3. On 28 January 1921 Turkish CP president Mustafa Subhi and fourteen other leading Communists were executed by local authorities in Trabzon, Turkey.
4. In early June 1921, twenty Communists were court-martialled by the Latvian dictatorship, which convicted seventeen of them. Nine were shot by firing squad, including Central Committee members Janis Šilfs and Augusts Berce.
5. Raymond Lefebvre, Jules Lepetit, and Marcel Vergeat died at sea during their return from Russia following the Second World Congress.
6. Orion Alexakis and other Communists died at sea in October 1920, while returning to Greece from Russia, when their boat was attacked by pirates.
7. On 31 August 1920 Jukka Rahja and seven other Finnish CP members were killed in Petrograd in an attack on a party meeting by members of a rival Communist faction.
8. Russian Communists Inessa Armand and K.N. Samoilova had both died of cholera.

hundred comrades have been condemned either to jail or penitentiary, and about seven thousand others languish in prison.[9] In addition, we know that the jails of the Hungarian republic are not empty, and the same applies to those of Finland.[10] In the most democratic of bourgeois republics, in the United States for example, thousands of Communists are in prison.[11] In Britain, one of the leaders of our new party is behind bars, as well as many other British comrades who spoke of communism to the British workers.[12] In Czechoslovakia, a considerable number of workers are incarcerated, among them well-known Communist fighters: Muna, Zápotocký, Hula, and a number of others. They are with us in spirit and send us their greetings from behind prison walls.[13]

We are convinced that the hour is not distant when all the capitalist prisons, without exception, will be demolished by the insurgent people, and our brothers and the best sons of the international working class will be free and will take their places at the head of proletarian masses in assault against capitalism.

In the history of the Communist International, this was not an easy year. During this period, in a great many countries, we experienced armed struggle, and, in some of them, this took the form of major pitched battles. As you recall, no sooner had we closed the Second Congress of the Communist

---

9. In 1923 the KPD estimated that 6,000 had been arrested for their role in the March Action. Of these 1,500 were released after a few weeks of confinement. The rest were tried by special courts, which acquitted 500 and sentenced the remaining 4,000 to prison terms. Weber 1993 puts the number of prison sentences at 3,251 (p. 177). Most of those convicted were amnestied in 1922.

10. The Hungarian soviet government, established in March 1919, was overthrown by troops from Romania and other countries on 1 August. A reign of counterrevolutionary terror ensued; an estimated 5,000 were executed, 75,000 jailed, and 100,000 forced to flee the country.
In January 1918 workers in Finland, granted independence from Russia following the October Revolution, organised a Red Army and declared a proletarian republic. The Red Army was able to seize most of southern Finland, but it was defeated by counterrevolutionary forces. The number of victims of the ensuing white terror is uncertain, but some estimates are that 10,000 were summarily shot and over 100,000 were sent to concentration camps, where some 12,000 died of disease or starvation.

11. Between November 1919 and January 1920 over 10,000 suspected Communists and anarchists, primarily foreign-born, were rounded up, in what became known as the Palmer Raids, named after Attorney General A. Mitchell Palmer. More than 500 were subsequently deported.

12. A reference to Albert Inkpin, the CP's national secretary, who was arrested on 7 May 1921 for circulating pro-Soviet propaganda, thereby 'doing, or attempting to do acts calculated to cause sedition and disaffection among the civilian population'. He was sentenced to six months in prison. By the end of June at least seventy leading CP members had been arrested.

13. Following the December 1920 political strike in Czechoslovakia, over 3,000 Communists and working-class militants were arrested; they were released later in 1921.

International than a proletarian mass movement utilising new forms of struggle began in Italy, the country that was then closest to proletarian revolution. The Italian workers demanded the handing over of factories and mills, and held possession of them for two weeks. They organised a red army and were ready to carry their struggle further.[14]

At that moment, the Italian reformists – the very ones who had honoured us with a visit, saying they wanted to belong to the Communist International – turned up in the camp of the bourgeoisie, betraying the cause of the working class. At the decisive moment, the Italian Confederation of Labour, led by experienced opportunists, did everything in its power to disperse the workers' movement. The Italian centrists, with Serrati in the lead – who we still trusted the previous year – found nothing better to do than to portray this great proletarian movement as a peaceful, 'trade-unionist' union movement. The Italian workers had to learn the painful lesson that some of their leaders were no better than wreckers of their struggle.[15]

In December 1920, we registered an uprising of the Czechoslovak proletariat, partially armed and more than a million strong. Inadequately organised, this movement was quickly suppressed. But it toughened the Czechoslovak proletariat and enabled it to obtain the schooling needed to build a mass Communist Party, which is represented among us here for the first time.[16]

---

14. Beginning at the end of August and continuing through the end of September, over half a million workers, led by the metalworkers, seized factories throughout Italy, creating a revolutionary situation in the country. Workers began to organise production under the leadership of factory councils, and in many places workers organised red guards to defend the seized factories. The strikes spread to the railways and other workplaces, and many poor peasants and agricultural workers carried out land seizures. The Italian Socialist Party and the trade-union federation refused to see the movement as anything more than a union struggle, however, and the movement eventually foundered.

15. On 10 September 1920, at the height of the Italian factory occupation, the CGL's directive council declared its opposition to the movement's revolutionary dynamic: 'The objective of the struggle shall be the recognition by employers of the principle of union control over industry. This will open the way to those major gains which will inevitably lead to collective management and socialisation, and thus organically solve the problem of production.' (Spriano 1975, p. 89)

In the end, the CGL leadership negotiated an agreement with the government calling for workers' control and major wage increases, in exchange for workers leaving the factories and going back to work. The promised concessions were never carried out, however. The failure of the movement led to widespread demoralisation within the working class. Fascists stepped up their recruitment and carried out an escalating wave of attacks against the organised workers' movement. They were able to seize power two years later.

16. On 9 December 1920 the government of Czechoslovakia seized the People's House in Prague, headquarters of the Left Socialist (future Communist) Party and its newspaper, *Rudé právo*. A general strike was called in response, observed by one million industrial and agricultural workers, which called for the resignation of the

In the spring of this year, an uprising by the German proletariat embraced no fewer than hundreds of thousands. Although suppressed, it played no small role in the history of the German revolutionary movement. By toughening the proletariat and revealing a new Communist mass movement, it wrote golden words, despite its failure, in the history of liberation struggles.[17] In addition to this great movement, we experienced many smaller uprisings by proletarians in different countries. All of these uprisings hardened our young Communist parties, giving them invaluable lessons, helping them to recognise their weaknesses and, in the future, to avoid the errors that ought not to be repeated. These experiences will also contribute to instilling in our parties a thirst for struggle and the consciousness that we should not rest content with peaceful propaganda. Rather, our parties should lead one struggle after another in an assault against our capitalist foes.

Our enemies point to these mass movements, drawing the conclusion that during the past year the Communist International has suffered one defeat after another. Of course these short-sighted people, who cannot see farther than their nose, view the Italian, Czechoslovak, and German movements as defeats for us. We know that the entire chain of struggles by the international proletariat consists of such defeats. We know that the Russian proletariat also suffered a great many defeats of this kind before it achieved victory. We are also convinced that the struggle waged in Italy, Czechoslovakia, and Germany, although it did not lead to the victory of the international proletariat, nonetheless must be assessed as a giant step forward in the forging of our movement.

When our Second World Congress gathered, it seemed that world capitalism was going through something of an upturn. Now, as our Third Congress assembles, it is commonly believed that world capitalism is experiencing a difficult and lengthy crisis. There are millions of jobless in Europe and America, and many others are working only half-time. We see poverty growing in a great many countries. We see the admirable strike of British miners, unquestionably one of the most important developments in the history of international revolution. This strike displays a marvellous doggedness and heroism. It is all the more magnificent given that, at the decisive moment, the leaders of the old trade unions, as is fitting for these people, betrayed the British

---

government and issued a series of revolutionary demands. In a number of places workers' councils were set up, as industrial workers seized factories and agricultural workers occupied large estates. The government responded by declaring a state of emergency, and workers were fired upon in several centres. After a week the strike was broken.

17. For a description of the March Action, see Editorial Introduction, pp. 18–23.

workers. Yet despite the inadequacy of support from other proletarian layers, beset on every side by enemies, the miners have already hung on for weeks in a strike that is unparalleled in the history of the British workers' movement.[18]

On this, the opening day of our congress, we have received news of the developing revolutionary movement in Italy – the strike of railway, postal, and telegraph employees. It is evident that Italy is entering another period of great struggles. In Germany, still reverberating with the latest verdicts of reactionary courts, a three-day general strike is under way. Bavaria is headed toward renewed revolutionary struggles. In France, a struggle is brewing inside the trade-union movement, one that will lead to the victory of the revolutionary current over the opportunists in the largest union federations.[19]

Our parties have grown enormously during the past year, as you can see by looking at the principal countries. In France, at the Second Congress, we had only a small group of supporters, functioning as propagandists and leaders of the country's first Communist groups. At this congress there are representatives of a party in France that has 120,000 members and has brilliantly defeated the old opportunist party, which has now gone over to the camp of the Two-and-a-Half International. Look at Czechoslovakia. At the Second Congress there was a delegation of a small group of Communist propagandists. Here at the Third Congress, we have delegates of an organised Communist Party that includes more than 400,000 workers, including both the Czech and German comrades. Consider Britain: at the Second Congress we had delegates of eight comparatively small and isolated groups, often embroiled in quarrels; at the Third Congress we have delegates of a party with ten thousand members, who develop their political positions and stand ready to bring a conscious Communist influence to bear on the splendid proletarian mass movement that is now unfolding in Britain.

Consider the United States. At the Second Congress we had only individual groups, weakly represented. During the past year, we united all the

---

18. The British miners' strike began when coal owners locked out miners following expiration of a temporary wage agreement on 31 March. Some 1.2 million miners turned the lockout into a strike to protest the owners' planned wage cuts and extended working hours. Authorities responded by declaring a state of emergency, moving police and the army into the coalfields.

Leaders of the transport and rail workers' unions had promised solidarity strike action. But in a move widely seen as a betrayal, on 15 April ('Black Friday') the leaders of these unions called off the scheduled solidarity strike, leaving the miners in the lurch. The strike lasted until 29 June.

19. A reference to the struggle in the General Confederation of Labour (CGT) between the right-wing leadership and a left wing led by revolutionary syndicalists. The left wing would be driven out later in the year, and would form the Unitary General Confederation of Labour (CGTU).

Communist forces of the country into a unified party. It is persecuted and functions underground, yet it exerts a constantly growing influence on the incipient proletarian mass movement in the United States. So you see, comrades, that our party has been strengthened everywhere, in all countries. The white terror that sought to destroy our party in Yugoslavia did not achieve this, and could not achieve this, despite the aid of supporters of the Second and Two-and-a-Half Internationals.

Yet we also suffered losses. At the Second Congress there was a delegation of a unified and numerous Italian party; at the Third Congress, by contrast, we have the delegation of a new and young Communist Party, which at present, including the youth, includes close to one hundred thousand members. Philistines believe that the Communist International has lost a very great deal in Italy, that it has suffered a great defeat. We have a different view. In Italy we lost some illusions, some negative quantities – forces that belonged to the Communist International only through a misunderstanding. We lost the groups that assumed you could belong to the Communist International without taking on serious obligations. All the better for the Communist International that it has lost this dead weight. We address a passionate appeal to the workers of Italy who have not yet joined the Communist International's ranks, and we are confident that it will not be long before all Italian workers, with their splendid revolutionary temperament, will join our ranks.

But as for the gentlemen who betrayed the Italian workers' movement at a time when workers there had taken possession of the factories and mills, these gentlemen who steal glances with one eye on Moscow and the other on Amsterdam – we have no need of these people. We do not believe it is a defeat for us that the negative quantities have left us. In Italy we have a young Communist Party, composed of devoted members dedicated to the proletarian revolution. To be sure, this young party is not yet large enough. However, we are firmly convinced that the future belongs to this party, and that the time is not distant when this young Communist Party of Italy will draw around it everything that is honest and revolutionary in the Italian proletariat. (*Applause*)

On an international level, the forces opposed to us have now unified. Last year representatives of the right-wing German Independents [USPD] and similar groups came to us, seeking to join the Communist International in order to sabotage the proletarian movement later on, as their co-thinkers do everywhere. We did not admit them.[20] Now they have come together on an

---

20. Prior to the Comintern's Second Congress in July–August 1920, the still-united USPD sent a delegation to Russia to discuss the party's affiliation to the Comintern.

international level, consolidated, and formed the Two-and-a-Half International. We have no reason to regret this development. All the timid, petty-bourgeois, opportunist, and semi-opportunist forces have come together in one spot, united in the Two-and-a-Half International, and freed us from forces that are vacillating, unreliable, and incapable of resistance. The Communist International can only gain by the fact that these forces do not belong to us but rather gather in another place, around another pole.

See what has become of the Second International. A year ago, at the time of our Second Congress, there were still grounds for uncertainty regarding the fate of the Second International. But now, comrades, we can see that the fate of this International is symbolised by that of its worthy president, Thomas. As the miners' walkout began, Thomas, the president of the Second International and the outstanding figure in the Amsterdam International, betrayed them. The betrayal was so disgraceful and the workers' indignation was so fierce that he had to go away for a time to the United States.[21]

Not so very long ago we read that this refugee president of the Second International, this worthy Amsterdam collaborator, was greeted, on leaving the steamer in the United States, with a hostile demonstration by the revolutionary American proletariat. Is that not symbolic, comrades, of the state of the Second International which, rotten at the roots, has become an organisation facing the proletariat with open hostility? We are now waging our main battle against the Amsterdam International, which unites the Second and Two-and-a-Half Internationals. This is where the decisive battle will take place.

After our congress closes, the first world congress of red trade unions will take place here in Moscow. This congress will have enormous importance, because it will bring together, for the first time, unions that want to take up consciously the struggle against Amsterdam and demolish the last bulwark of capitalism. During the last year, the International Trade Union Council, founded during the Second World Congress, has united fifteen million unionised workers. We will endow this organisation with an even firmer foundation at the coming congress.[22]

Comrades, our congress faces an enormous and fundamental theoretical task: it will be called on, once again, to examine the global economic and

---

The delegation consisted of Artur Crispien and Wilhelm Dittmann from the party's right wing, and Walter Stoecker and Ernst Däumig from its left.

21. James Henry Thomas was a British labour leader, treasurer of the Second International, and head of the Amsterdam trade-union International. In May 1921 he travelled to the United States to attend the annual convention of the American Federation of Labor in Denver, held 13–25 June.

22. For the International Council of Trade and Industrial Unions and the Red International of Labour Unions, see p. 62, n. 3.

political situation from every angle. Once again it will consider and test our tactics and strategy, toughen all our parties for a successful struggle against opportunism of every sort, against half-measures, against every form of centrism, which has unfortunately penetrated our ranks even in such tested countries of the classic workers' movement as Germany. In this regard, our congress will find the strength to erect solid barriers against all currents that seek to undermine our solid Communist unity from within.

Our congress will find the necessary strength of purpose to counter decisively all those who try to import the poison of centrism and semi-centrism into our young Communist Party – no matter who they are and how great were their past services.

Our congress will mark out once again, more completely and specifically, a clear and definite line, which must be calculated not only in terms of a more rapid tempo of proletarian revolution but also for one that is slower, if it turns out that the revolution is taking this less desirable path.

Our congress will endow the Communist International with a more finished structure, given that our member parties and the Communist International as a whole face a great many highly important organisational questions. The congress will also draw a balance sheet of the work accomplished during the past year.

The provisional list that I have here shows that forty-three countries are represented at our congress. There will probably be fifty in all. Our gathering today is actually a gigantic world congress of the Communist proletariat. We will have the opportunity to utilise the experiences accumulated by our brothers in many countries. One of the main items on our congress agenda is examination of the internal and international situation of the Soviet republic, until now the only country in which power lies in the hands of the proletariat, which has sacrificed so much in this struggle and experienced such adversity. We are obliged to fully inform our brothers coming from every country about our suffering – and we do this most willingly. We will make known the real state of affairs, revealing both our strong and weak sides, and giving a picture of the heroic and superhuman struggle for power by the proletariat. Comrades from every country know well that the Russian Revolution represents a large part, if not half, of the world proletarian revolution. Everyone understands how important it is for workers of all countries that proletarian power remains inviolable in our country and that now, with the close of the Civil War and demobilisation of the Red Army, we are able at last to go over to peaceful economic construction.

Comrades, even now – before our congress has begun its work – it is encircled by the blind hatred of the world bourgeoisie. The entire bourgeois press is circulating an ocean of lies and slanders about our congress. I have been informed that the Polish bourgeois press has declared with malicious glee that only seventeen delegates have arrived in Moscow. But as you know, almost one thousand representatives are present from workers' organisations of the entire world. Many more fairy tales will be invented. Nonetheless we have the right to affirm that we are sustained by the most advanced, honest, and revolutionary forces in the entire world.

The Second Congress worked out the Communist International's statutes and basic principles of our strategy and tactics. We are confident that our Third Congress, following on this example, will hone the policies and structure of the Communist International. It will aid the sister parties of countries like Britain and the United States, where a strong workers' movement is emerging but communism is still weak in penetrating the masses. Our congress will assist parties that are already supported by broad masses, like those in Czechoslovakia, Bulgaria, and elsewhere, to coalesce their forces for glorious battles. We are confident that our congress will open the eyes of other parties to their errors and weaknesses and help them to rectify their course, cleanse the party of all opportunist forces, and toughen it, so that in every country – just as the Second Congress desired – we will have a section of a unified, fraternal, and Communist world party. (*Loud applause*)

I heartily welcome all comrades present here, and especially the delegations from countries of the Near and Far East. (*Renewed applause and cheers*)

Comrades, in the entire history of the workers' movement there has never been a congress embracing so many representatives of the Near and Far East. Recall the congress in Baku, which took place after the Second Congress. Since then the Communist International has gained increased influence in the countries of the Near and Far East, and this authority grows with every day. The presence at our congress of numerous delegations from the Near and Far East is evidence that our organisation is not merely European; it is an international association of workers not merely of Europe but of the entire world. The presence of these delegations is evidence that the now imminent revolution is not merely European but global – a world revolution in the true sense of the word. That is why the delegates of the advanced proletarian parties of Europe and America must devote special attention to these delegates of the Near and Far East, provide them with the fullest support, join with them in fraternal alliance, and show the entire world that we are capable of uniting not just the advanced proletarians of Europe and America but also the numerous peoples of the Near and Far East.

We welcome all delegations with the cry: Long live the world revolution! Long live the Communist International! (*Enthusiastic, prolonged applause and cheers*)

Comrades, some of the speeches must be translated from different languages. I ask comrades who do not know these languages to be silent, in order not to disturb other comrades. The preceding speech will be translated by Comrade Radek.

**Zinoviev**: The congress will now proceed to the election of the Presidium.

**Paul Frölich** (Germany): Comrades, in order to prepare the work of the congress, the Executive Committee was broadened to include representatives of all the parties present here. This Expanded Executive proposes the following comrades for the Presidium: As chair, our Comrade Zinoviev. (*Loud applause*) As vice-chairs, Comrade Kolarov (Bulgaria), Gennari (Italy), Loriot (France), Koenen (Germany). (*Loud agreement*)

**Zinoviev**: Comrades, this list has already been discussed in the Expanded Executive Committee. Are there any other nominations? Since there are no objections, I declare this list adopted. The comrades in question are elected to the Presidium. (*Enthusiastic applause*)

**Frölich**: Comrades, I ask you to decide on the election as honorary chairs of our congress of our highly esteemed comrades Lenin and Trotsky. (*Enthusiastic applause*)

**Karl Radek** (Russia): On behalf of the Russian delegation's Bureau, I propose that we name as additional honorary chairs the now imprisoned comrades Muna, Inkpin, and Brandler.[23] (*Enthusiastic agreement*)

**Zinoviev**: I give the floor to Comrade Kamenev to bring greetings on behalf of the Central Committee of the Communist Party of Russia and the Moscow Soviet.

**Lev Kamenev** (Russia): On behalf of the Communist Party of Russia I greet the greatest world event at this moment: the World Congress of Communists from around the world. To these greetings from our party, I am glad to add those of the working class and of all working people of the city of Moscow. We are proud that for the third time representatives of the world revolution are gathering within the walls of our ancient city. Here, protected by calloused proletarian hands, you can discuss and make decisions undisturbed. We are happy that the city governed by the Moscow Soviet has become a

---

23. The Czech Communist Alois Muna was jailed during 1921. Heinrich Brandler, who had replaced Paul Levi as VKPD chairman, was arrested and tried for high treason in the wake of the March Action. On 6 June 1921 he was convicted and sentenced to five years' imprisonment. Brandler escaped from prison in November 1921 and went to Moscow. See also p. 1134, n. 46.

symbol of the world proletarian movement and that the struggle against the world bourgeoisie and the opportunists' world betrayal is carried out under the banner, 'For Moscow'.

Comrades, as history would have it, the Communist world congress has gathered in what was formerly the home of evil despotism, of a mighty empire, in a country where 150 million subjugated workers and peasants were governed by a clique headed by the tsar. Soviet power has been triumphant for four years. Foolish people and purveyors of bourgeois influence criticise us for being unable to create a finished communist order. They attempt to undermine the influence of communist revolution and communist ideas by pointing out that in the fourth year that has been granted us since power was placed in the hands of workers and peasants, communism has not yet unfolded in life as fully and entirely as we would wish.

We reply to this accusation, this malicious criticism simply by explaining that no Communist Party, no proletariat, no matter how great its bravery, can create on the ruins of the capitalist order, be it in a year or three to four years, the new world in which there are no exploited and no exploiters. The realisation of this new world, which working people have dreamed of for centuries, will demand unbelievable exertion by the working class. True, we are unable to show the comrades gathered here from around the world a finished communist order. Here in Moscow, in our workers' republic, they will find the ruins of the old order and see how the shoots of a new communist society are springing up from these ruins. We have overthrown and defeated the old tyranny, but we are still struggling to erect a new temple of communist society on the territory wrested from the bourgeoisie.

Comrades gathered here from around the world find us in a time of arduous struggle, in which we face many difficult tasks. We will not prettify the situation. We cannot accomplish the great tasks before us on our own, and we do not propose to do this on our own. Since the moment when the Russian working class became the first in the world to raise the slogan of a republic ruled by the proletariat, of a proletarian dictatorship, we have faced two tasks. Our first task was to demonstrate that the working class that overthrew the bourgeoisie was able to remain in power, even though the entire world took up arms against it. We have carried out this first, preparatory task. (*Applause*) We can say that with pride. Before the eyes of the entire world, of the proletariat and our deadly enemy, the bourgeoisie, we have shown that the working class of Russia, after taking power, defended this power, arms in hand, for three years and emerged from this struggle victorious. It forced the enemy to lay down his weapons. It exists today as an independent, free workers' and peasants' state, pursuing the work of communist construction. We have unified 135 million working people under the Soviet government. We have extended workers' rule from the northern icebound ocean to the Black Sea, from the Baltic Sea to the Pacific, raising the banner of the Communist International. This is what Russian workers and peasants have wrested away from world capitalism.

We now approach our second task. Will we be able to follow up our victory on the military front by demonstrating that the power we have in our possession is capable of transforming economic relations and erecting a communist society on the foundations of the destroyed capitalist order? We were capable of repelling the attack by twelve countries.[24] Will we be capable of dealing with the petty-bourgeois spirit and habits of capitalist property drummed into the people over centuries? We have now exchanged our rifles for hammers, we have gone to our work benches, taken plough in hand, and are setting about a new task: that of showing the entire world how the Russian working class, despite all the destruction wrought by seven years of war – first the imperialist war, then the Civil War – can restore its economy. We will show that the working class understands not only how to tear power from the hands of imperialism, but also how to bring to life a new economic order. (*Loud applause*)

The international congress finds us engaged in this work. We have no judges above or below us. We have only the highest judge of all that the working class of Russia has achieved and will achieve under the leadership of its Communist Party. That judge is the World Congress of the Communist International. (*Applause*) Before this judge, the Russian workers and all the working people of Russia, with the proletariat of Petrograd and Moscow in the lead, can appear with heads proudly raised and say: In the course of four years we have fought in the most advanced battle lines of all humanity. We look forward to assistance, in full certainty that the proletarian masses of the entire world are following our struggle and, at the decisive moment, will raise the same banner that we hold and crown the proletarian world revolution for which the Russian working class has laid the foundation.

Long live our esteemed guests! Through you we greet all the working people around the world, the proletarians of all countries, all humanity, which is taking part with us in titanic struggles extending across the entire world.

Long live the world revolution! (*Applause*)

---

24. During the Russian Civil War of 1918–20, the young Soviet republic faced intervening troops from Czechoslovakia, Japan, Greece, Britain, Poland, the US, France, Canada, Serbia, Romania, Italy, China, and Australia. Different figures on the number of intervening countries are sometimes used due to overlapping relationships with colonial empires.

**Zinoviev**: Comrades, as agreed with the different groups of delegates, we will translate the remaining speeches into Russian only.[25] We now give the floor to delegates who will bring greetings to the Red Army and the workers of our country. I give the floor to Comrade Vaillant-Couturier, speaking for the French delegation.

**Paul Vaillant-Couturier** (France): Comrades, on behalf of the French delegation, I bring to our comrades of the Red Army of the International the greetings of French Communists. (*Applause*) Comrades, like millions of other young Frenchmen, like millions of other people of the entire world, like many of you, I was once drafted into the capitalist army. For months and years we fought for a cause that was not our own. We fought in summer and in winter, in the spring offensives and the winter campaigns. On returning home we discovered that it was we who had been vanquished in this war, while the capitalists everywhere had emerged as victors. The capitalists tear each other to pieces because they think that, through the sword, they can banish from the world the disagreements that divided them – disagreements on the division of the globe. What they have achieved is the awakening of hatred against the bourgeoisie in the hearts of proletarians long lulled by the lure of concepts such as democracy and parliamentarism. (*Applause*) Comrades of the Red Army, you are the first army whose members learn not only to hate but also to love. You love your suffering brothers in every corner of the world. You do not turn back at the border posts. You love all those who suffer in every part of the world, be they French or German workers. They know that your fraternal hearts beat to the same rhythm. They know that you still stand ready to defend them, just as you have defended the revolution month after month, marching barefoot, ill-fed and ill-clothed, just like the French soldiers of 1793, who also fought barefoot in defence of their rights. (*Applause*)

Comrades of the Red Army, you are now soldiers of the Communist International. We greet you as such and tell you all – Russian proletarians, poor peasants, factory workers, now returning after the battle to your work, all of you heroes of the army – you are the great power to which we look in confidence. We call on you to hold firm, for the moment to lay down your weapons has not yet come.

Neither in East nor West is our crop yet ripe. The peoples are only now beginning to stir, to take up arms, to build barricades. You, advanced outposts

---

25. At this opening session held in the Bolshoi Theatre, discussion was addressed primarily to Russian workers who made up most of those in attendance, and the primary language used was Russian. At subsequent sessions, held in the Kremlin Throne Room, Russian guests were present, but discussions were primarily addressed to the international delegates, and the main working language was German.

of the revolution, stand at the ready, alert, finger on the trigger. Be on guard, keep a sharp eye on the capitalist foe who confronts us. We are organising, we are readying ourselves, we will soon come to your aid, but we must first overcome many difficulties that threaten us. We must subdue the pacifism engendered among us by the imperialist war. We recognised pacifism only too well as a weapon of opportunism. We know now what it signified, for one must not say 'let there be peace, let all peoples be brothers' – this is only an illusion of Christian teachings. Pacifism taught us that we can work only with the point of our bayonets, as you have done, and as we too will do. (*Applause*)

Keep a firm hold on your weapons, and if the waiting causes you suffering, endure the suffering a while longer. It is hard to have to tell you this, but we will explain to all our French brothers, 'They are suffering over there'. We will not tell them that everything is outstanding and admirable, and that you have created many superb institutions. They know that already. Rather we will tell them, 'They have suffered. Make haste! Come, come, come, for the Red Army is waiting for you'. At the moment of a new battle, a new revolution, we – children of the first great revolution, of Robespierre, Danton, and Marat – when we are on the point of giving way, then, comrades, we will turn to you, as the red flag waves over our last barricades, saying: 'We are calling for your help, comrades of the Red Army. Come!' And we know that you will come.

Long live the Red Army of Russia!

Long live the Red international army! (*Thunderous ovation*)

**Zinoviev**: I give the floor to the representative of the United Communist Party of Germany – one of the founders of the Spartacus League, whom we met years ago in the first attempts at a new international association, in Zimmerwald and Kienthal[26] – Comrade Paul Frölich.

**Frölich**: Comrades, the German Communists bring greetings to the International. They greet Soviet Russia, the stronghold of revolution, which has held firm through four long years of difficult struggle. They greet the Red Army, the sharp, strong sword of the revolution.

Comrades, we come from the land that once marched at the head of the workers' movement. We come from the land in which socialism suffered its most severe setback, in which, as nowhere else, the banner of the Second

---

26. An international conference of socialists opposed to the social-patriotic position of the leading parties of the Second International took place in Zimmerwald, Switzerland, 5–8 September 1915. Attended by 37 delegates from 12 countries, the conference adopted a resolution and manifesto opposing the imperialist war and calling for peace. A second conference of the Zimmerwald movement took place in Kienthal, Switzerland, 24–30 April 1916.

International was smeared with filth. We come from the land of the old Social Democracy, in which many people who grew tall on the shoulders of the proletariat developed into the bloodiest butchers of the working class.

Comrades, Germany stands today on the verge of a great revolutionary action by the proletariat, which will bring us victory. We come from the country where every shudder of the world market, every clash of peoples on the earth's surface, leads to an inner political crisis. We come from a country that has been shaken for years by terrible civil wars, in which thousands in the working class have fallen victim. What do we expect from the congress of the Communist International? We expect only one thing: that it carry forward the line initiated at the Second Congress.

We can now confirm that the Second Congress had enormous significance for the revolutionary development of Germany. The Second Congress separated the conscious and clear revolutionary forces of the German working class from cowardly, wretched leaders who could not summon up the courage to assume the great responsibility that the revolutionary struggle demands from each of its leaders. Just how correct the Second Congress was became evident in our party's history during our six months as the United Communist Party. It became clear that we could unite all the forces of the German working class who are prepared for great and difficult struggles as the vanguard of the German and international revolution. On the other hand, it became clear that the revolution had to spit out the leaders that had previously headed the Independent Party [USPD]. After the revolutionary forces broke with them, they sank deeper and deeper into the muck of opportunism. That party, which even today declares itself to be the only true revolutionary party, has today become the firmest buttress of the bloodstained German government. Together with the trade unions, now its only prop, this party is the only buttress that keeps the structure of German capitalism erect. A buttress that states plainly: Yes, we are the ones who wish to maintain German capitalism; yes, we commit our strength to supporting the government; yes, we support it even when it throws thousands and thousands of proletarians into the jails and penitentiaries.

Comrades, the outcome of these policies is clear to see. In the unions, above all, things are astir; they are clearly being strongly revolutionised. It could not be otherwise, for one betrayal leads to another.

In order to maintain the capitalist regime, the trade-union bureaucracy is compelled to bear down harder and harder on the working class, betraying it again and again. That means that working-class consciousness, the revolutionising of the proletariat strides forward every day. Economic conditions are driving us into great and powerful battles. Communists in Germany have shown that they are capable of and willing to struggle, and workers in Germany will always find that they must fight together with the Communist Party.

The bourgeoisie senses what lies ahead. It is afraid of the proletariat and seeks to intimidate it through the white terror. This year it once again murdered hundreds upon hundreds. It has adopted emergency laws, created emergency courts that work at a gallop. Already, after two months of work, they have come up with a terrifying record: four hundred condemned to a total of 1,500 years in the penitentiary, six hundred workers condemned to a total of 800 years in prison, eight comrades condemned to life imprisonment, and four comrades whom judges have condemned to death. And that is not enough. They have found new ways of creating martyrs for the proletariat. They shoot our comrades 'attempting to escape' and have developed an entire method for these 'attempting to escape' murders. But if they think they can break the German proletariat in this way, they are mistaken. The German working class has learned to make sacrifices in great number. It will fight on, despite all these challenges, despite the immense losses, and it will fight on until victory. (*Tumultuous applause*)

Russian comrades, you have cried out to us German revolutionaries for help. We understand your suffering, we try to grasp the enormous sacrifices that you have made for the proletariat. We understand how hard it is for you to maintain your present position in the foremost line of battle. We assure you, comrades of Soviet Russia, that we will apply all our strength, we will not grow tired, and together with the entire International we will march forward, link up with your outposts, and from there carry on the struggle with you, shoulder to shoulder, until the world revolution has triumphed. (*Enthusiastic applause and cheers*)

**Zinoviev:**[27] I now give the floor to a delegate of the Communist Party of Great Britain, a miner of its South Wales district, Comrade Hewlett. He recently arrived from the field of battle where the coal miners' strike is raging.

**William Hewlett** (Britain): Comrades, I bring the Third International the heartfelt greetings of the British Communist Party. In the name of British miners, I thank you with all my heart for the outstanding support that you, and especially the Russian miners, have sent during their strike. Although we in Britain probably have fewer opportunities to carry out a revolutionary

---

27. Zinoviev's introduction for Hewlett and, later in this session, for Kolarov and Taguchi, are absent from the German edition and have been taken here from the Russian text.

uprising in the style of the European parties, still, as a Communist Party member, I am very proud of the miners' activity. I promise the Communist comrades gathered at this congress that we will stop at nothing and will leave no stone unturned in order to force to its knees the most dangerous imperialist class of the world. I can say without fear of contradiction that there is no more mighty party in the entire world than British imperialism. We face a contradiction generated by the War. We were told that it would lead directly to the destruction of imperialism but, instead, what we see in Britain is that that imperialism has only been reinforced. This contradiction is evident in the entire British state structure. We are certain that sooner or later Britain will experience the same catastrophe that befell Russian imperialism. Right now, however, the danger that now hangs over our heads is that British imperialism will gather and concentrate its forces until it not merely threatens world peace but destroys it.

I speak of this fact to Russian Communists only with embarrassment and reluctance, because I come directly from a country notorious for imperialist reaction. We recall to this gathering with shame and anger the conduct of Churchill, Balfour, and Lloyd George toward the world's greatest revolution, that in Soviet Russia.[28] Only one fact gives us consolation. Although Britain dictated all the actions taken against the Russian Revolution from 1917 on, I must also note that it achieved a renown that will not be to the imperialists' liking. It involuntarily provided clothing for the Russian soldiers, and for British Communists this is a consolation, although a small one.

For British imperialism, the last three years have been a time of feverish activity aimed at stifling Russia's new life. I concede from the outset that British Communists do not yet anticipate a revolution similar to what you had here in 1917. Still I must note that we were sufficiently competent to be able to prevent British and French imperialism from assisting the Polish war against Soviet Russia. That alone justifies the activity of British Communists.[29]

---

28. British interventionist forces occupied parts of Russia from the summer of 1918 to autumn of 1919 and Britain took part in the blockade of Soviet Russia until 1921.

29. In April 1920 Polish troops launched an offensive in soviet Ukraine. The Red Army was able to push them back into Polish territory and then continued its advance toward Warsaw, where it was stopped. Soviet troops were then forced to retreat. An armistice ending the war was signed in October.

A powerful working-class movement developed in Britain against intervention in this war, as dockers and railway workers refused in May and June 1920 to move weapons destined for Poland. In early August a Council of Action was formed of representatives of the CP, the Hands Off Russia National Committee, and the Labour Party's Executive Committee, launching a direct action campaign to protest British intervention. Hundreds of meetings were held throughout the country. The threat of

I have been asked to say more of the war now under way in Britain and of the general situation there. In 1914 British workers were offered all sorts of castles in the sky. They were asked to clothe themselves in khaki and conduct a war to make the world safe for democracy. When the War ended, the military spokespersons proclaimed, workers would enter into a new world and receive everything that makes life worth living. Class-conscious workers know now that the great promises of those days were exposed as the greatest of the bourgeoisie's lies.

What did the workers see? Did these people construct a new world? Let me sketch it for you briefly. On 31 March the greatest struggle in the history of the British working class began. We had heard before lots of predictions that many of us never hoped to achieve, but even we were astonished when, on 31 March, the British bourgeoisie threw half a million people onto the streets and locked them out of their jobs. They told the country to which they had promised nationalisation – for they had promised the workers everything – that this immense wage reduction was necessary to help capitalism get back on its feet. Comrades, I would like you to know that in Britain there are 2.6 million workers in the mines, which belong to only nine thousand of our forty million inhabitants. Some of you may be interested to hear these figures. At the sessions of the commission to nationalise the mines, it was discovered that the British coal mine owners had scored profits of no less than £260 million during the five years from 1913 to 1918.[30] Despite such huge earnings, these people found it essential to destroy Russia, and they are still attempting to suppress the struggling masses and even to attack the revolutionaries of Germany. Comrades here must understand the worldwide importance of Britain for politics and the revolutionary movement. They must know what a formidable opponent British workers face, and how much we depend on workers of other countries.

Workers of Europe and the entire world must unite and ally more closely with British workers. If they do not, British imperialism will raise its head more boldly and be even stronger than before. To understand this fully, you need only bear in mind that Britain is an island, and that the colonial question is more important for Britain than for any other country. British imperialism has every corner of the world in its grip: India, Ireland, Egypt, Africa,

---

this rapidly developing movement helped convince the British government to back down and refrain from direct intervention.

30. A reference to the Sankey Commission (named after its president, John Sankey), which was set up in early 1919 by the Liberal Party government to avert the threat of a coal miners' strike and industrial unrest. The commission's findings endorsing the principle of nationalisation were rejected by the government.

and we can list all other colonial countries. A review of these international connections enables us to fully understand the importance of a Communist movement in Britain. Britain is an island, and its Communist movement can provide useful service only if it takes into account the colonial question. Just as the British Empire cannot exist without the colonies, the British Communists cannot triumph on their own; they cannot win without the aid of the rest of the world. The British delegates are therefore anxious that this point be given full consideration. Given the nature of the struggle posed globally, we must strive everywhere to bring Communists together in stronger unity.

Let me say something of the Communist Party's activity. It has existed for just twelve months, and during this time many of our comrades have been arrested and are serving jail terms of six months or more. That is not to be compared with what you in Russia had to suffer before the revolution. But considering the short time that the party has existed and the results achieved, we are proud of our activity. One of Britain's great traditions is that its parliament has existed for a thousand years, and that is one of the enormous forces against which the Communist Party must match its strength. Nonetheless, this struggle is nearing a decision.

I will add a few words about the 'great betrayal' [of the British miners' strike]. The Communist Party had a number of members whom it considered its best workers. It had a high opinion of their work and gave them positions of responsibility. They worked at the heart of the great struggle. Some of these comrades, who had been honoured last year in Russia, betrayed us. I will name only A. Thomas, Williams, and MacDonald.[31] I am ashamed to say that they abandoned the miners, leaving them to struggle alone in a losing battle. The latest reports tell us that the miners are still struggling and will continue to struggle. Comrades, I was happy to hear that our American colleagues greeted Thomas very coolly when he was there. All these Mensheviks and social patriots, along with those who betrayed the movement, must be driven from the ranks of the class-conscious proletariat.

To conclude, comrades, I and the British Communist Party vow to take as our most sacred task the preparation of the revolutionary masses for world revolution. We vow that the British Communist Party will work without respite until the battle is won and the proletarian revolution reaps its harvest around the world. Long live the Russian Revolution! Long live the world Communist movement and the proletariat! (*Enthusiastic applause*)

---

31. Robert Williams was part of a British labour delegation that visited Soviet Russia in May 1920. Williams, J.H. Thomas (mistakenly referred to as 'A. Thomas' in the proceedings), and Ramsay MacDonald were among the leaders who in August 1920 publicly opposed threatened British intervention in the Polish-Soviet war.

**Zinoviev**: Comrades, the Bulgarian Communist Party, through its traditions, its history, and its spirit, shows that it stands very close to the Russian Communist Party. I give the floor to one of its outstanding leaders, Comrade Kolarov.

**Vasil Kolarov** (Bulgaria): Across the entire capitalist world the white terror is raging. Not only in Hungary, Finland, and Bavaria[32] – where the brief triumph of the proletariat was followed by defeat – do the embittered magnates and capitalists take their bloody revenge on the working masses.

It is not only in the Balkan countries, where the administration of ruling classes has always rested on despotic and barbarian methods, that the working masses are deprived of any protection under law and the Communist parties are exposed to harsh persecution and mistreatment. Even in countries where 'civilisation' is supposedly on a higher level and 'democracy' more developed – in Italy, Germany, France, Britain, the United States; indeed in all the so-called civilised countries – the ruling bourgeoisie openly tramples on its own laws and hurls itself ruthlessly against the revolutionary movement in order to nip it in the bud.

At one time the bourgeoisie itself was a revolutionary class. It proclaimed the Rights of Man and the Citizen and conducted the struggle against despotism and tyranny in the name of liberty, equality, and fraternity. Its statesmen and philosophers established the theory of political democracy, which was to guarantee political freedom and general progress for all time.

Once the bourgeoisie defeated despotism and took control of the state, political democracy turned out to be the best framework for its exploitative political power. However, in times when its rule was endangered, it seized every opportunity to suspend the rule of law and settle accounts with its enemies in the most barbaric fashion.

The proletariat remembers very well the bloody justice delivered to the Paris Commune.[33]

Today the entire capitalist world is experiencing an acute and incurable crisis. The powerful revolutionary forces born in its womb are multiplying,

---

32. A government of workers' councils was established in Bavaria on 7 April 1919; German Communists held its leadership 13–27 April. Counterrevolutionary forces entered Munich 1 May, and by 3 May had consolidated control, overthrowing the councils. Hundreds of workers were executed and many more were imprisoned.

33. The Paris Commune of March–May 1871 was the first effort to establish a revolutionary workers' government. Following the Commune's suppression, the French president, Adolphe Thiers (1871–3), presided over the counterrevolutionary terror in which more than 10,000 working people of Paris were executed.

organising, and rising, and their impact makes the entire capitalist edifice tremble on its foundations.

The capitalist class is seized with panic. In deadly fear of the rapidly growing Communist ogre, it loses its reason, flies into a frenzy, and with its own hands is overthrowing its centuries-old legal order. Just as Thiers once did, the bourgeoisie of every country now cries out, *La légalité nous tue* – rule of law is killing us. Trampling on its own laws, it organises the forces of counter-revolution.

In Britain, the classical land of law and habeas corpus, the bourgeoisie is conducting a barbaric war against the Irish people, organising enormous forces to settle accounts with the starving and striking proletarian masses.[34] It condemns Communist leaders for their revolutionary activity and ruthlessly throws them in jail.

In France, the homeland of political freedom, the ruling clique of bankers attacks workers' demonstrations to the tune of old revolutionary hymns, mistreats the protesting proletarians, arrests Communist leaders in the name of liberty, equality, and fraternity, brutally invades party offices and trade-union clubs, and makes every effort to avoid the approaching Communist war through acts of violence. The descendents of long-ago fighters against tyranny, who a century earlier carried the foundations of political freedom around the world on the points of their bayonets, now trample on millions of proletarians and peasants and assist sinister forces and black reaction in every corner of the world.

The United States, the land of a broad democracy bequeathed by a revolution and a civil war, is ruled by a powerful and cynical dictatorship of the dollar. The workers' elemental struggle is overwhelmed with blood. Every revolutionary movement, every revolutionary organisation is persecuted, and thousands of Communists languish in jail.

In Germany, home of the most modern and refined republic, which is the true child of social patriotism, the bloodhounds of capitalism continually provoke the impoverished working masses, setting traps for the workers' leaders, arresting them, shooting them down for 'attempting to escape', appointing

---

34. The Irish war of independence of 1919–21, led by the Irish Republican Army, sought to end British rule over the island. The war ended with the Anglo-Irish Treaty signed in December 1921, which partitioned the country. A Free State was created in the south as a self-governing dominion within the British Empire, while open British rule continued in six northern counties. The treaty gave rise to a split in the IRA between supporters and opponents of the treaty, which culminated in the Irish civil war of 1922–3.

special judges, and imposing the rule of the Orgesch and white terror across the whole country.[35]

In Italy, the Fascists are running riot. Protected by the government and capitalism, they are raiding workers' clubs and the print shops of Communist newspapers and burning them down. They kill workers' leaders and terrorise the unorganised and destitute masses in the cities and villages.

In the Balkans, the bourgeoisie has outlawed the Communist parties and revolutionary organisations and is demolishing them. It closes workers' clubs, bans publication of Communist newspapers, and subjects Communist leaders to unprecedented persecution, cruelties, and scandalous mistreatment. In these countries, as in Italy, capitalist dictatorship takes the most cynical and extreme forms. All guarantees for human life are suspended here, while the ruling classes openly proclaim and conduct a barbaric civil war.

In this fashion, cruel and bloody class struggle shatters all democratic illusions, while reformist programmes and theories regarding gradual and peaceful renewal of capitalist societies disappear like a mirage.

Capitalist society is undergoing its death agony. In every country, the betrayers of socialism are rushing to its rescue. Nonetheless, they have not succeeded in halting the revolutionary movement. They have become merely a tool wielded by the bourgeoisie against the working masses fighting for their liberation. Their hands are smeared with blood.

The gulf between the ruling classes and working people is deeper today than ever before. The struggle between them rages more and more furiously. Capitalism is rapidly summoning its forces and placing the entire world under the sign of white terror. But just as quickly, the forces of revolution are mobilising and organising. The masses are rapidly taking their places under the waving banners of the Communist parties and the Communist International.

Unavoidably, there will be clashes. Labouring humanity will free itself from the nightmare of white terror and assure itself of free and harmonious development through the forcible overthrow of the ruling classes and the establishment of the dictatorship of the proletariat.

Proletarian revolution is today the only force for historical progress.

Long live the world revolution!

Long live proletarian dictatorship!

---

35. Group formed in Munich in August 1920 to fight Bolshevism, with a claimed membership of 300,000. Led by Georg Escherich, it was officially disbanded in June 1921, although many of its units remained active, especially in Bavaria.

**Zinoviev**: Comrades, as I said earlier, this is the first congress with representation from one of the most powerful proletarian parties – the Communist Party of Czechoslovakia. I give the floor to Comrade Burian.

**Edmund Burian** (Czechoslovakia): I offer my greetings to the revolutionary Russian workers and the Third International and express the gratitude of the Czech Communist Party for the services it has received. Two great historical phenomena – the Russian social revolution and the Communist International – achieved a miracle in our country. Only two and a half years ago, the Czechoslovak working class, still led by social patriots, assisted the Czechoslovak bourgeoisie in founding the capitalist state.[36] But the Russian Revolution awakened a new spirit among a significant majority of Czechoslovak workers. At present our working class stands as a close friend of the Russian Revolution. We have not yet fought battles similar to those waged by the German and Russian Communists, but the December battle of Czechoslovak workers was a major revolutionary struggle with capitalism. For our working masses, it was the initial baptism of fire.

Even greater was our success in winning the minds of Czechoslovak workers. Their majority is now Communist. We are a large party, comparable in size to the Russian and German Communists. We are proud of this success, greater than in any other country, and will continue to work on the foundation of what has been achieved. We will vigorously advance Communist slogans. We will fill all the struggles of Czechoslovak workers with a Communist spirit and Communist slogans. We are aware of our strength, and our energy is growing. But we want not only to struggle but to triumph. When the decisive day arrives – even if not as soon as imagined by some of our comrades – it will be the day of our victory, the day when we will hurl against our capitalists the great battle cry of the Russian Revolution: All power to the revolutionary Communist Czechoslovak working class! (*Enthusiastic applause and cheers*)

**Zinoviev**: I think that it is not necessary to translate the remarks of Comrade Burian, since the immense majority of comrades understand the spirit and content of our Czechoslovak comrade's speech. I now give the floor to the representative of the Italian Communist Party, which both needs and deserves special fraternal assistance from the Communist International in its just struggle against the betrayers.

---

36. Czechoslovakia was established 28 October 1918 out of a portion of the old Austro-Hungarian Empire.

**Egidio Gennari** (Italy): On behalf of the Italian Communist Party, I bring greetings to the Third Congress of the Communist International. Let us note that at the Second Congress the entire Socialist Party of Italy was represented, including people like Serrati, who became disloyal to the cause of communist revolution and left the Third International.

But the place of Italy has not been left empty. It is now taken by the young Communist Party, ready to throw its full strength into leading the Italian proletariat in the final struggle. The Third International must harshly condemn the Italian betrayers and assist the Communist Party of Italy in ripping the mask from those who deceived a portion of the proletariat. By such a powerful gesture, the Third International will induce the entire proletariat of Italy to turn again to the Communist Party. I am therefore justified in bringing greetings to Russian workers not only from the Italian Communists but from the entire Italian proletariat.

Long live the Third International! (*Enthusiastic applause*)

**Zinoviev**: We observe with great satisfaction all the victories of the French comrades in the trade-union movement. We will now give the floor to one of the best workers of the union movement, a comrade who, with a group of colleagues, was able to win for us the trade-union federation [CGT] of the Seine department [Paris]. Comrade Tommasi has the floor.

**Joseph Tommasi** (France): Comrades, the previous speakers represented organisations that have given proof of their capacity for struggle. We, the French syndicalists, are in a different type of situation. Our history is quite long, but in recent years it has been a sad one for the workers' movement, and we have nothing to bring you but our greetings. We syndicalists have organised in recent times not only against the social patriots of our country but also against the International that unifies renegades from around the world. The Amsterdam International has aroused our hatred. It is like a cruel old mother who so loves her children that – supposedly to spare them grief – from time to time she abandons these children to capitalist robbery, sending them to serve capitalist intrigue on the battlefield and fight for capitalism's interests, which can never be ours.

We must seize our national-syndicalists by the throat. Jouhaux and company must bow out from the stage they have commanded for so long. But they turn to us as workers and say, 'Limit yourself to economic concerns. You did not have a chance to go to universities and gain the education needed for careers in politics. So leave politics for those who grew up in these institutions, and leave them free to act for you. Be confident that if only you stand as a firm, organised mass, that is enough, and we need only raise a finger in order to drive the bourgeoisie into retreat.'

We now have proof that this argument holds no water. For fifty months, blood was spilled in vain for questionable rights, justice, and freedom, which are in fact always trampled underfoot, because they are accessible only to the world bourgeoisie. We have proof that for the working class there is only one road to liberation, and that road is the employment of force.

The bourgeoisie unites in order to strike us down. Our Spanish comrades can no longer walk on the streets without the barrels of revolvers being aimed at them. Our Italian comrades were compelled to retreat and wait for better times, despite the brilliant progress of the past year. In March, our German comrades raised the battle cry on which we had so set our hopes. And you, comrades of Russia, have placed one brick on top of another in order to give form to our work.

The time has passed when it was possible to 'befuddle the workers' brains', as they said during the War. Too long have they been fed with pretty words about democracy and the like.

We face great difficulties. After centuries of slavery we were told that we were free, because the reign of democracy had begun at last, and now we know that the struggle is flaring up anew.

We utilise sources of strength that provide the only arguments that work against the bourgeois clique. We rally around the Moscow International, in order to prepare the unification of the revolutionary masses for the coming revolution. We subdue the old grandmother of the fable, who has outlived her time, and seek to oust her, so that she is not able to link up with our enemies. We will lead our syndicalist party in such a fashion that our 'syndicalist' leaders feel the ground tremble under their feet and will slip more and more to the right. Soon they will appeal to their former rivals, who are our eternal enemies. They will enter into a holy alliance with them behind the back of the revolutionary syndicalists.

We, by contrast, adhere to Moscow and lift high the banner that you have carried for four years with such self-sacrifice. Comrades of Moscow, comrades of Russia, we join with you in the most glorious undertaking, that of revolution. (*Applause*)

**Zinoviev**: Given the events now under way in the Far East, the presence of our Japanese delegation has exceptional importance. Comrade Taguchi will speak on their behalf.

**Taguchi Unzo** (Japan): Comrades and delegates, I speak to you on behalf of the Japanese Communist group.

It cost me great effort to reach the Third Congress of the Third International, which represents proletarians from around the world. I would like now, comrades, to tell you a few things about the situation in Japan. Conditions today in Japan are very bad with regard to our government, the workers' associations, and the masses of Japanese workers. Yet our comrades have succeeded in creating groups of class-conscious workers. At present there are outstanding prospects for broad propaganda in Japan. In recent months, the Japanese Communist Party has established a strong foundation for propaganda and agitation. However, comrades, Japanese capitalism and the bourgeois parties of Russia are hostile enemies of the first Soviet government. Japanese imperialism has advanced not only into Siberia but as far as Central Asia.[37] We Japanese Communists have acted energetically to counter capitalist attacks on the workers of Siberia and we will continue to protest and intervene actively. The Japanese Communists can accomplish little on their own, but our position is clear, and I am confident that our indignant protests will at last be taken seriously by our imperialist government, chiefly because they know that behind us stands international communism.

I will close my speech by bringing greetings to Russia. Long live Soviet Russia, the Soviet government, and the Communist International! (*Loud applause*)

**Zinoviev**: Comrade Heckert has the floor for an announcement.

**Fritz Heckert** (Germany): The Credentials Commission asks that each delegation send one of its number tomorrow at 11:00 a.m. with a list of the comrades who have a mandate. The first plenary session of the congress will begin tomorrow at 6:00 p.m. So far the Credentials Commission has not received many of the mandates; more information is needed from the various national delegations. In order for all comrades to receive their mandates by 5:00 p.m. – without which they cannot enter the Kremlin – they must delegate a comrade to present the necessary information, by 11:00 a.m. sharp, to the Credentials Commission. Comrades who have not handed in their list by 11:00 a.m. will not be able to take part in the first session.

**Zinoviev**: I declare the first session of the Third Congress to be adjourned.

(*The session is adjourned at 10:30 p.m.*)

---

37. A Japanese force, eventually numbering seventy thousand troops, occupied Russia's Pacific coast in 1918 and penetrated as far as Lake Baikal, while Japanese corporations and settlers arrived in an apparent effort to colonise eastern Siberia.

## Session 2 – 23 June 1921, 7:50 p.m.
## World Economy – Report

*Report by Leon Trotsky: The World Economic Crisis and the New Tasks of the Communist International.*

**Zinoviev** (Chair): The second session of the World Congress is now open.

First of all, we must elect a secretariat. In consultation with a number of delegations, the Executive has decided to appoint one secretary from each of fifteen parties. The list will be read, and we ask the congress to confirm it.

**Béla Kun** (*reads the list*): Britain: Smythe. Poland: Kamocki. Finland: Sirola. Yugoslavia: Milkić. Czechoslovakia: Handlíř. Austria: Koritschoner. Hungary: Hajdú. Ukraine: Manuilsky. United States: Marshall. Latvia: Stuchka. Scandinavia: Friis. Far East: Shumiatsky. Near East: Sultanzade. Women: Nikolaeva. Youth: Münzenberg.

**Zinoviev**: If there are no objections, I will take the vote. I ask all comrades who understand German and are sitting beside Russian comrades to translate what has been said. We will now take the vote. Are there any objections to this list? As there are none, the list is approved. I ask the comrades to get together and appoint three comrades for each session.

Comrades, the agenda is known to you all and was approved by the Expanded Executive.[1] The Presidium asks the congress to approve the agenda

---

1. The agenda was approved at the 11 June session of the expanded ECCI that met prior to the congress. The proceedings of that session can be found in the Comintern archives, RGASPI 495/1/35.

without discussion. (*Interjection: 'Let's begin on time!'*) I ask comrades to take this comment to heart, and the Presidium will do so as well. It is therefore proposed to adopt the agenda without discussion. Are there any objections?

**Tommasi**: On behalf of the French syndicalist delegation, I requested in the preceding session of the Executive that the congress take up first of all the question of particular concern to us, namely the relationship between trade unions and communism. And I ask that this proposal not be disregarded. It is of great importance for the French delegation, which must leave for home on 10 July, at the latest, in order to take part in the Lille Congress.[2]

**Zinoviev**: In response to this, we would like to say that the issue right now is to approve the agenda points in their entirety, not to determine their sequence. The French delegation's request is justified, in our opinion, and we will make efforts to take up the trade-union question as one of the first items. In the agenda proposed by us, this question comes right after the question of tactics. It will also be possible to discuss the proposed ordering of points. This matter will therefore not be dealt with too late.

Therefore, we will now vote. We ask the congress to approve the list. Is anyone opposed? No one, so the agenda is approved.

We must now decide on the administration of the congress. The newspaper *Moscow*, which appears in three languages,[3] published today our proposal for administration. We believe that the congress could adopt this administrative framework as well without discussion. Anyone opposed should please raise their hand. The administrative proposal is therefore adopted.

We can now begin our work. The Executive thought that it would be best to start with the question, 'The Economic World Crisis and the New Tasks of the Communist International'. I give the floor to the reporter, Comrade Trotsky.

## Report on World Economic Crisis[4]

**Trotsky**: Comrades, at the First and Second Congresses, we described the world situation in appeals and manifestos, without entering into a more

---

2. The CGT's 25–30 July 1921 congress at Lille was the scene of a heated struggle between left and right. The right wing carried the majority by a vote of 1,556 to 1,348, with 46 abstentions. Within a year the federation split virtually down the middle.
3. Appearing in German, English, and French between 25 May and 14 July 1921, the newspaper *Moskau/Moscow/Moscou* was the daily organ of the Third Congress.
4. This report, printed here as published in the congress proceedings, was subsequently edited and expanded by Trotsky for separate publication. An English translation of the expanded version can be found in Trotsky 1972a, 1, pp. 174–226.

detailed discussion. The task then was to characterise the new situation created by the War in its overall and outstanding features and to impress this on the consciousness of the working class. The question before us now is much more complex. The third year after the War is almost over. Very important economic and political developments have taken place. Capitalism still lords it over virtually the entire world, and we must assess whether our perspective – that of world revolution – is still broadly correct under present circumstances. There has been a shift in the relationship of forces – that is undeniable. The question is simply whether this change reflects some deeper alteration, or whether it is more superficial in character.

If we place ourselves back in the mood that prevailed in 1919 – that was the most critical year for capitalism after the War – and compare the psychological situation, the mood of the classes, the parties, the state power, and so on, with their counterparts today, we must recognise that the bourgeoisie today still feels strong. In the past it was perhaps stronger, but at the very least it feels much stronger now than it did in 1919. I have a folder of material from influential newspapers and the like on the Communist and revolutionary danger around the world, and I will now read a few of these quite instructive quotations.

The *Neue Zürcher Zeitung* is a Swiss bourgeois paper, very conservative and rather clever, which follows the political development of Germany, France, and Italy with some degree of understanding. Here is what it wrote on 26 March about the March Action in Germany. Unfortunately I could not track down this issue and must translate back from my Russian translation. But the sense of it is unchanged.

> Germany in 1921 is quite different from in 1918. Governmental consciousness has been strengthened to such a degree that Communist methods run into resistance in every layer of the population – even though the Communists, who during the days of revolution were only a small handful of determined people, have since become ten times more numerous.

On 28 April, when both camps were preparing for the May Day holiday, we find the following statement in *Le Temps*:

> We need only review the path travelled during the past year to be fully reassured. Last year May Day was to signal the beginning of a general strike that, in turn, was to be the first stage of a revolution. Today total confidence reigns in the nation's effort to overcome all the crises flowing from the War.

*Neue Zürcher Zeitung*, once again, wrote as follows in April about the situation in Italy:

1919: The bourgeois parties, verging on complete collapse, hopelessly fragmented, and in suicidal resignation were giving way before the unified onrush of the disciplined masses of the red forces. 1921: The bourgeois contingents have united in a solid coalition and are advancing into battle, confident of victory, while the Bolsheviks, divided and discouraged, hardly dare to show their face. And all this thanks to Fascism.

Let me take an example from a quite different source, namely a quote from a resolution of our Polish Communist sister party. If I am not mistaken, it had a party conference early in the year, where it was decided to take part in the parliamentary elections. In motivation, the resolution states:

In the winter of 1919 the struggle turned in favour of the bourgeoisie, which then constructed its state apparatus. Thanks to the Polish Socialist Party, the workers' councils were strangled by the government. Given these facts, the party is obligated to utilise the electoral struggle and the parliamentary platform.

There is no suggestion here that the Polish Communist Party intended to alter its stand on principles. It simply evaluates the present situation differently from the way it did in 1919.

Flowing from this, the objective situation of Social-Democratic parties with regard to the state and the bourgeois parties has changed. Everywhere the Social Democrats are being pushed out of the government. When they are readmitted, it is only temporarily – as in Germany, where this happened under foreign pressure. The Independent party [USPD] has executed a complete turn to the right, also under the pressure of this new situation, or of its psychological reflection, for they overestimate its significance. We see the same thing in the trade unions. There has been a consolidation. The Independents of each country and the Social Democrats of each country, who differed so greatly a year or eighteen months ago, have come closer, thanks to the good offices of Amsterdam.

The old Social-Democratic opposition lives today in bigamy with both the Second and Two-and-a-Half Internationals, and these two ladies are not at all upset about it. This triangular marriage provides the best demonstration today regarding the disappearance of the tendencies to oppose the state that were noticeable among the Independents during 1919 and 1920.

These three postwar years were a time of the most enormous mass movements the world has ever seen. Russia, the country that suffered most deeply during the War, was drawn by the March 1917 revolution into the tempest of revolution.

As early as 1917, great mass strikes on economic issues broke out in Britain. At the end of that year, the Russian proletariat took power. I will not try to hide the fact that at that time the road from our seizure of power here to the taking of power in countries of Central and Western Europe seemed much shorter than it turned out to be. This fact also forms part of our evaluation of the world situation. In 1918 there were major strikes in the neutral countries. At the end of that year, military collapse triggered revolution in Germany and Austria-Hungary. A rather chaotic proletarian mass movement for economic goals broadened out more and more. In 1919 we had bloody fighting in January and March.[5] At the end of 1919, in the United States, there were major strikes of miners and railway workers. Then came the raging fury of the bourgeoisie, the destruction of workers' organisations, the arrests, and all that. In 1920 we witnessed the Kapp Putsch in Germany and then the great struggles of armed workers and the campaign of revenge by 'democracy'.[6] For the working class in France, the most critical moment was the May Day celebration and, following on it, the general strike of railway and other workers.[7] In Russia, the Red Army attempted an offensive against Warsaw,[8] which was linked in many ways with many expectations and hopes regarding the international situation. That initiative failed, as did also the great mass action in Italy in September 1920, when the workers occupied the factories but the [Socialist] party failed utterly. That movement awakened the bourgeoisie from its demoralisation; the conduct of the workers' party drove it into an offensive. Turati says that the movement failed because Italian workers were not mature enough to occupy the factories and take charge of production. He's right in one sense: the Italian workers still have not purged Turati and the Serrati people from their ranks.

---

5. The January 1919 events refers to the suppression of the so-called Spartacus uprising in Berlin, during which Rosa Luxemburg and Karl Liebknecht were murdered by government troops. The March 1919 events refers primarily to the Freikorps attack on Lichtenberg, a Berlin stronghold of the revolutionary workers' movement, on 9–12 March, in response to a false rumor published in *Vorwärts* that revolutionaries had stormed a police station and executed seventy officers in cold blood. Between armed battles with revolutionary workers and summary executions, the Freikorps killed up to 1,500 and wounded 12,000 workers.

6. On 13 March 1920, Wolfgang Kapp and Walther von Lüttwitz led a military coup that overthrew the republican government led by the SPD. While the SPD itself offered little resistance, officials of the SPD-led trade-union federation called a general strike that was observed by twelve million workers, virtually the entire proletariat. In the face of the general strike and developing armed workers' resistance, the coup collapsed by 17 March. Subsequently, German army units attacked worker detachments that had led resistance to Kapp.

7. A one-day general strike in France on 1 May 1920 opened a broad strike movement of CGT unions led by the railroad workers, eventually involving nearly 1.5 million workers. In face of severe repression, the railroad strike ended a month later in defeat, with 22,000 workers losing their jobs.

8. For the Polish-Soviet War and the offensive on Warsaw, see p. 90, n. 29.

In Czechoslovakia a general strike took place in December 1920. In 1921 we witnessed the March battles in Germany, the miners' strike in Britain, the general strike in Norway[9] – the greatest struggles that the world has ever seen. But the main thing is the outcome of these struggles: the bourgeoisie remained in control. And Otto Bauer, theoretician of the Two-and-a-Half International, says that the fact that the bourgeoisie is still in power signifies the bankruptcy of the Third International. We had always counted on world revolution taking place in the final phase of the War or immediately after it, he says, and now this estimate or prophesy or hope is shown to be entirely wrong and misplaced. But we did not make some bet with the Second International that obliged us to complete the revolution when the War ended. So we feel under no obligation to pay the wager, that is, to concede the leadership of the proletariat to the Two-and-a-Half International. This was and is not a matter of some purely objective fact, independent of us, that can be foreseen and prophesied, like some astronomical occurrence, except that we made an error in calculation. Rather it is a matter of taking power, which has to be carried out by human beings.

That is the goal for which we are striving, and if we did not achieve it by some specific date, that does not mean the Third International is bankrupt.

All that is required is to examine the world economic and political situation and our fundamental attitude to revolution more precisely. Why was it that during the War, and even before the War, at the Stuttgart Congress of the Second International, we drew a link between international proletarian revolution and war?[10] Because the War, which was then foreseen for the first time, would necessarily disrupt the equilibrium of the entire economic structure of society. We must ask whether this did in fact occur and whether, if that is the case, the bourgeoisie – the ruling class, capitalism – has already been able in the course of three postwar years to recreate that devastated and undermined equilibrium.

---

9. A general strike in Norway lasted from 26 May until 6 June 1921. Called by the Norwegian federation of trade unions in solidarity with a strike by seamen against massive wage cuts, the strike involved 120,000 workers, virtually the entire proletariat of the country.

10. The Second International's Stuttgart Congress, held 18–24 August 1907, was the scene of a debate on war and militarism. A left-wing amendment to the congress resolution, proposed by Rosa Luxemburg, V.I. Lenin, and Julius Martov and approved by the congress, read, 'In case war should break out,' workers must 'intervene for its speedy termination and to strive with all their power to utilise the economic and political crisis created by the war to rouse the masses and thereby hasten the downfall of capitalist class rule'. For the full text of the resolution adopted, see Riddell (ed.) 1984, pp. 33–6.

Comrades, to appraise the economic situation is a very complex matter. Statistics always lag behind. Economic statistics in capitalist society are highly imprecise as a result of the anarchy of the economy itself, and this will surely remain the case. The War did in fact break out, causing not only the economy but the entire state apparatus, including its statistics, to jump clear off the tracks. The figures – and I will cite quite a few – are not entirely precise. I will always indicate which figures that applies to. Well, we will have to use the imprecise figures if we are to obtain even an approximate concept of conditions.

In recent years, we throw around concepts of billions here and billions there, without getting a good grip on what that means in terms of the national or world economy. I will begin with the simplest, most basic facts: worldwide production of goods. Let us start with agriculture. If we compare the total harvest of 1920 with the average of the last five prewar years, we find that the world harvest remains about the same – it is about twenty million quintals [one million tons] lower.

If we set aside America, however, the pattern changes entirely. The harvest in the belligerent countries was 37 per cent lower than before the War. In the neutral countries it was roughly unchanged. In the overseas countries it was 21 per cent higher, not including Russia. Before the War, Russia provided the world market with about 100 million quintals on average. In 1920, after the War, the world market had to do without about 120 million quintals. Even today we find that American farmers are holding rather high stocks of grain, which they cannot sell because of the fall in prices on the world market.

If we take cattle raising, we find almost exactly the same pattern. The quantity of world livestock is almost the same as before the War. The stock of the belligerent countries of Europe has declined markedly; that of the neutral countries has remained at the prewar level, and that of the overseas countries has risen. However, we find that the prices of meat on the Chicago exchange – that is the world's decisive meat exchange – are lower than before the War. So many people were wiped out during the War, and yet the population is nonetheless more numerous than before the War – eighty million more. The marketed harvest is 120 million quintals less than before the War; stocks of meat and grain are available but cannot be purchased. In other words, the world has grown poorer and hungrier. That is an initial simple fact.

If we analyse world production of coal, we find almost the same pattern, but revealed much more sharply. The entire world's coal production in 1920 amounted to 97 per cent of that in 1913, that is, less than before the War. Europe's supply was 18 per cent less; North America's was 13 per cent greater. With cotton and other goods we find a similar ratio. Total production is somewhat or much lower; Europe's has declined; America's has risen.

Now let us take national property – not income, but the property that the nations today possess. In estimating national property, figures are quite uncertain and variable. However, they are adequate to enable us to translate this economy of billions, this economy of astronomical figures, into a solid, material economic framework. Before the War, the national property of the belligerent powers was estimated at 2.4 trillion gold marks, and the national income of these countries at 340 billion gold marks.[11] That was the yearly income at the highest peak of their economic development. What was consumed and destroyed in the War? Different economists offer varying estimates of this amount. But we can roughly conclude that the War destroyed and consumed about 1.2 trillion gold marks. That is not an exaggeration. The amount comes to 300 billion gold marks a year, during four years of war. The prewar national property of belligerent powers was 2.4 trillion gold marks. The War consumed and destroyed exactly half of this amount.

Moreover, the War did not destroy merely a portion of national property, but also much of yearly income. At the peak of development, this yearly income came to 300 billion gold marks, of which not more than a third – that is, 100 billion gold marks – was available for the War. I will not seek to demonstrate that here, but you can take it as an approximation. Society continued to exist and had to consume, and the productive apparatus as well must normally be maintained at a certain level. However, the War used up about 1.2 trillion gold marks, including 800 billion from national property. This means that a third of the former national property of the belligerent countries was destroyed, reducing it from 2.4 trillion to 1.6 trillion gold marks.

Here is another comparison. Europe had invested capital in various forms in other parts of the world, amounting to 150 billion to 200 billion gold marks. So the destruction through war was six or seven times as great as the amount that Europe employed directly in the exploitation of other parts of the world.

Let us consider the circulation of banknotes. Before the War, banknotes in the entire world amounted to 28 billion gold marks. Now their amount is 250 billion to 280 billion or perhaps 300 billion – that is, ten times as much. What does this tell us? This fact has very great importance for what follows. The foundation of capitalist society in the belligerent countries of Europe sank lower and lower. The countries are impoverished. Simultaneously a superstructure of banknotes has arisen, which is also termed capital. For these banknotes and government bonds – all this is called capital. However, this capital represents, on the one hand, a memory of what has been destroyed

---

11. In 1921 a gold mark was worth about US$0.25.

and, on the other, a hope of what can be earned – but it does not represent capital that actually exists. It functions as capital, however, as money, and this distorts the shape of the entire society, the entire economy. The poorer the society grows, the richer it appears, regarding itself in the mirror of this fictitious capital.

However, the creation of this fictitious capital shifts the portions of this constantly diminishing income and property that are held by different classes. National income is reduced, but not in the same proportion as national property. This is explained simply by the fact that the candles of capitalist society were burned at both ends, and that the War and the postwar economy were financed not only from national income but also from national property.

It is understandable that someone facing ruin turns his attention above all to doing what is most immediately necessary, rather than to strengthening the foundations of his private business. That explains why Europe's economy has by and large achieved more in the production of consumer goods – and of current production in general – than it has in raising the real level of the productive apparatus. That means the labour forces devoted to maintenance and expansion of the productive apparatus are insufficient to prevent the impoverishment that has set in from expressing its full impact.

The fact that the productive apparatus was much more devastated than current production is among the most important basic experiences of today's society. It attracts little notice, but no or very few new factory buildings are going up, and the old ones are not being maintained in good condition. This receives little attention because we are now in a severe crisis and unable to fully utilise the existing means of production. In the housing sector, however, this is very evident, because the population continues to grow, even in times of crisis. These people need housing, and the lack of housing is evident around the world. Many billions would be needed for this purpose. I have tried to demonstrate this. But I will not bore you with these statistics. Many billions would be needed to ease the urgent housing shortage. This stands as evidence that the entire productive apparatus – the foundation of society – is devastated and has declined, something that is not easy to assess in terms of statistics.

This impoverishment does not affect all countries in the same way. Among the belligerent countries, Russia is at one pole. We will exclude it, because it is not part of the capitalist world. We will speak of Russia in another context.

We will also disregard Austria, because the Austrian economy also does not lend itself to straightforward analysis.

So let us start with Germany. Germany and Britain are the two ends of the chain of belligerent countries. In describing Germany's economic conditions,

I will utilise the data of Richard Calwer in his rather interesting study, *National Bankruptcy*.[12] The question of national bankruptcy has become rather important for the German economy, and rightly so. Calwer estimates the overall production of goods in Germany. This is hard to determine by quantities alone, because the quality of the goods must also be taken into account. He takes a different approach, which should not be underestimated. On the basis of reasonably plausible calculations, he concludes that the production of goods in 1907 represented the labour of 11.3 million workers. Since then, working conditions have altered fundamentally. The work week is shorter; the intensity of labour has fallen, and so on. And he comes to the conclusion that Germany today has no more than the labour of 4.8 million workers, expressed in 1907 units – that is, only 42 per cent of the previous level.

Calwer arrives at the same results for agriculture. 'Here too', he says, 'I arrive at the conclusion that agricultural production of goods, in terms of quantity and quality, has fallen to well under half the prewar level.'

Germany's national debt stands at 250 billion marks. As for Germany's currency, that's well known around the world. Circulation of banknotes now comes to about 80 billion or 81 billion, of which only five billion is good money.

Thus Calwer arrives at the conclusion that the mark today is actually worth about 6–7 pfennigs.[13] People sought to utilise this fact, saying that Germany was the 'most victorious' country on the world market in 1919 and 1920, precisely because its currency was so bad. I have here a passage from the French newspaper *Le Temps* of 29 April, which says, and I quote:

> Germany ought to have been able to utilise this enormous advantage, caused above all by the depreciation of the mark, to pay off its reparations debt bit by bit.

As I said earlier, impoverishment is reflected in the distorting mirror of fictitious capital, leading society to an entirely false self-conception. And as a result, they arrive at this completely insane notion that Germany has an enormous advantage in possessing a completely devalued currency and is therefore in a position – thanks to the impoverishment of its entire economy and productive apparatus – to sell off its goods at cutthroat prices to the French and the British, at the expense of impoverishing the entire economy, the productive apparatus.

Calwer's analysis leads him to the following conclusion, which I will quote verbatim:

---

12. See Calwer 1921.
13. One hundred pfennigs equalled one mark.

This outcome of disastrous currency and financial policy today can only be violent, given that under present economic conditions a gradual return to orderly conditions on the currency market and in public finances is completely excluded. This catastrophic end, however, is ultimately nothing other than the formal bankruptcy of the government, which gives open expression to what has long been true: the government's inability to pay.

So – national bankruptcy. If we then express that in material terms, we arrive at the following: Before the War, Germany's property amounted to 225 billion gold marks; its income, to 40 billion gold marks. That was the high point. That was the estimate of Helfferich, if I am not mistaken, basing himself on statistical research. Today, German property is estimated at 100 billon marks, and income at 16 billion marks. Of course these estimates are only approximate, but they are sufficient to give us a picture of reality.

Tracing German economic development, we find that during the storm and stress of the final period of economic development, from the middle of the nineties to the onset of crisis in 1913–14, German national income rose by approximately 1 billion marks a year. More precisely, Germany's income in the mid-nineties was 22 billion gold marks; in 1914 it was 40 billion gold marks. Over a twenty-year period, that signifies a yearly increase of approximately 1 billion marks.[14] And today – with of course quite different social results – it has been thrown back into the conditions that preceded German capitalism's time of stormy growth, which created the modern Germany. Under current conditions it is quite clear that Germany will not be able to pay its debts and its so-called reparations requirements. Even such a right-wing economist as Calwer proclaims national bankruptcy to be absolutely inevitable. And now you can read a considerable number of German books on national bankruptcy, written in terms of philosophy, morality, law, and so on. With or without morality, *these gentlemen will not avoid national bankruptcy*.

*France* is, according to its bourgeois newspapers, a country recovering from its wounds. There is no contesting that during the postwar period France can point to several successes. However, it would be a major error to overestimate these successes. It is very difficult to produce statistics on France's economy, since much more is kept secret there than in other countries. The French bourgeoisie does that, and so too does the French government. The capitalist press of France lies more than in most other countries, and that may well also hold true of economic statistics. For example, I have not yet been able to find in the French newspapers any data on the production of cast iron in 1920.

---

14. Both the German and Russian texts here read, 'twenty-eight years' and 'four billion marks'. The translation follows Trotsky's edited text in Trotsky 1972a, 1, p. 186.

But examining the available statistics, we find that French agriculture in the field of cattle breeding is poorer. In 1913 there were approximately 15 million head of cattle; now there are 12.8 million. The number of horses was then 7 million; now it is 4.8 million.

Production of wheat, 86 million quintals in 1913, is now 63 million quintals. In 1913, production of coal was 41 million tons; now it is 35.6 million tons, counting Alsace-Lorraine and the Saar,[15] or – excluding these newly acquired territories – 25 million tons, hardly more than half the 1913 level, and so on. We must bear in mind that France is healing its wounds not by reorganising its economy but, above all, through the pillage of Germany and its colonies. Thus the improvement of conditions in France is due not to a rise in the economy as a whole, but rather to a transfer of goods from Germany to France. In this process – and here is the key point – Germany loses one and a half to two times as much as France gains.

France's trade balance for 1919 shows a deficit of 24 billion francs – that is, a surplus of imports over exports.[16] For 1920 the deficit is 13 billion. Thus during these two years of recovery, of improvement, France ran a foreign trade deficit of 37 billion francs. The significance of this for France's currency is easy to grasp. True enough, in the first quarter of the current year, 1921, France no longer had a foreign trade deficit. There is great rejoicing in the press and parliament over the fact that, in the first three months of 1921, French imports roughly equalled the exports. However, the cleverest French paper, *Le Temps*, had the following to say on 18 May this year:

> The improvement of our trade balance is mainly due to the reduction in imports of raw materials, and this reduction will without doubt result within a few months in an appreciable reduction in the export of manufactured goods.

So it is not the rise of the economy and of exports but the fall in imports of raw materials, that is, a reduction in future production, that has led to a more favourable trade balance. France's national debt is 303 billion, ten times as much as in 1913. Add to that the reconstruction costs, which they are trying to unload onto Germany and which come to 180 billion francs. That makes half a trillion, all told. The circulation of banknotes came to less than

---

15. As part of the Versailles Treaty, Alsace and Lorraine – predominantly German-speaking territories that had been ceded by Germany following the Franco-Prussian War of 1871 – were to be annexed by France. The coal-rich Saar Basin, formerly German-held, was to be administered by the League of Nations for fifteen years, after which a plebiscite would be held there on whether it would belong to France or Germany. During that time, coal from the region was to go to France.
16. In July 1921 one French franc exchanged for approximately US$0.13.

6 billion francs in 1915;[17] in July 1920 it was almost 39 billion francs, that is, seven times greater.

The French budget offers us a picture of total ruin, the hopeless ruin of the French economy. For this year, the regular expenses come to 23 billion francs, plus 5.5 billion francs for the added expenses of occupation and 23 billion francs for war reconstruction, which makes 51 billion francs altogether. How much is contributed by French taxpayers? So far, payments were such that regular revenue is estimated at 17 billion francs.

Fifteen billion francs must be paid from the national budget every year to retire debts, plus 5 billion francs for the army and bureaucracy – 20 billion altogether, just for interest on the debt and maintenance of the state apparatus. And that is covered only partially by 17.5 billion in regular revenue. The regular deficit thus comes to 5.5 billion francs, without counting the notorious obligations for reconstruction. If you pick up the prominent French financial newspaper, *L'Information*, and read the article by its editor, Léon Chavenon, you will find this:

> The financing of the state must be kept closely connected with the issuing of banknotes. In other words, inflation and the pressure of paper money must be promoted.

He does not conceal the causes. He says, 'There is no escape from inflation except through open bankruptcy'.

The alternatives are therefore either to cover expenses by paper money, that is, the state remains a con man, tricking the entire world through counterfeiting and phony money, or to publicly admit bankruptcy and publicly declare, 'There is no escape from inflation except through open bankruptcy'.

France's leading financial writer and a right-wing Social Democrat – I do not know for sure whether he belongs to the right-wing [Socialist] party or not – arrive at the same conclusion: There is no solution except open national bankruptcy or muddling along by printing paper money. That's the situation in victorious France, which now holds the position of undisputed leader of Europe.

*Britain* seemed during the War to be the country that was profiting from it. Comrade Varga's excellent pamphlet,[18] which we are submitting together with the theses, assesses the situation in Britain very cautiously. Subsequently published facts and figures indicate that Britain's situation, from a capitalist

---

17. The German text here reads, 'three billion francs'; the translation follows the Russian text.
18. A reference to *Thesen zur Weltlage und die Aufgaben der Kommunistischen Internationale*, which Trotsky co-authored. See Trotsky and Varga 1921.

viewpoint, is even more hopeless than it seemed not long ago. British agriculture expanded during the War as a result of enormous government subsidies. Now it is falling back to its prewar level. Britain's coal production, where it had a monopoly, amounted to 287 million tons in 1913, and 233 million tons in 1920 – that is, 80 per cent of the 1913 level. Cast iron production was 10.5 million tons in 1913 and 8 million tons in 1920, which is also about 80 per cent of the previous level. As for the situation in 1921, that is well known. Because of the miners' strike and its effects, coal production fell in January to 19 million, in February to 17 million, and in March to 16 million tons.

Coal exports – the most important segment of British exports and the basis of exports in general, amounted to 73 million tons in 1913 and 25 million tons in 1920, that is, 34 per cent – a third – of the prewar level.

During the first five months of this year, exports ran at about 48 per cent of the previous year's level. Foreign trade as a whole, measured in goods rather than in the shadow-patterns of prices, is a third lower in 1920 than in 1913. For the month of May, the current issue of the leading financial publication, the *Economist*, tells us the following:

In May 1920, exports amounted to £119 million; in 1921, to only £43 million. And that is not even expressed in goods but in prices, where it represents a decline of 64 per cent, which has precipitated the general crisis. We see the same phenomenon, although less pronounced, in the British budget, in its national debt. The British national debt, which before the War was £700 million, amounted on 4 June 1921 to no more and no less than £7,709 million, that is, eleven times higher than the prewar level.[19] Merely the expenditure on the army and navy, which was £86 million before the War, is now £237 million, that is, almost three times greater. And if you consult the reports of the corporate chieftains in banking and industry for the months of March and April, you will find the statement that Britain's national income is now a third or a quarter less than before the War. Whether it is a quarter or a third less is hard to determine.

The most evident expression of British decline is its currency. The British pound sterling today is not the pound sterling of old. It no longer corresponds to what is stated in its world passport. We read that it now represents only 76 per cent of what it claims to be.[20] And nothing characterises the instability of

---

19. The German text at this point reads 7,709 billion, an apparent misprint. The Russian text is also garbled. The translation follows Trotsky's edited text, Trotsky 1972a, 1, p. 192.
20. Trotsky's edited text makes clear that Trotsky is comparing the value of the pound relative to its prewar relationship to the US dollar. In July 1921 one pound sterling exchanged for US$3.56.

our times better than the fact that the most stable, absolute, and unquestioned thing in the world, the British sovereign (a word that also means 'ruler') has lost its old position and now represents only a relative quantity.[21] At a time when Germany is so preoccupied with philosophical relativity – I am referring to Einstein's philosophy – we can perhaps conceive German philosophy as a revenge against the British economy, since the British pound sterling has now become relative. The Germans, in times of economic hardship, have always taken their revenge in philosophy.

There are also countries that have made gains: above all the *United States* and in second place *Japan*. We have here a fact of world-historical significance, which must always be kept in view in any evaluation of the world situation. The economic centre of gravity is no longer in Europe but in the United States. Europe has decayed, and by and large it is decaying more and more. During this same period, the United States has developed enormously. The increase in the number of livestock, horses, and cattle is not very significant. For horses, the increase is to 22 million head, from 20 million; for cattle, to 68 million from 62 million. If we consider coal, we find that the 1913 production of 517 million tons rose in 1920 to 580 million tons – a rather significant increase. Petroleum production in 1913 was 248 million barrels; in 1920, 442 million. A huge increase. Cotton and iron remain at about their prewar level.

There is an enormous increase in shipbuilding. The ships built in 1913 had a total capacity of 276,000 tons; in 1919, 4,075,000 tons; in 1920, 2,746,000 tons. Such shipbuilding has made the United States the leading force in this industry. Before the War, Britain possessed more than half the world's tonnage and the United States only 5 per cent; now Britain has only 35 per cent, and the United States 30 per cent. In the automobile industry, as is generally known, somewhat less than 900,000 units were built in 1913, and 2,350,000 in 1920. At present the United States has 8.5 million automobiles, that is, one for every twelve inhabitants. The entire rest of the world has 1.4 million.

Exports are two and a half times greater than before the War. Exports have undergone an internal shift and alteration that is very important for the world economy. Before the War, in 1905, finished goods made up a third of US exports; foodstuffs and raw materials accounted for two-thirds. Now the proportion is reversed: 60 per cent of exports are finished goods, and only 40 per cent foodstuffs and raw materials. That means that the United States has become one of the leading industrial exporters. During the last six years, from 1915 to 1921, the US trade surplus amounted to $18 billion. Now let us look at the US share in the world economy. The United States possesses 6% of

---

21. A sovereign was a gold coin with a nominal value of one pound sterling.

the world's total population and 7% of its land area. In terms of production, it produces 20% of the gold, 25% of wheat, 30% of merchant ships, 40% of iron and lead, 50% of zinc, 45% of coal, 60% of aluminium, 60% of copper, 60% of cotton, 66% of petroleum, and 85% of automobiles.

This is reflected in the American dollar's leading role in the world financial market. Europe's debt to the United States is $18 billion, a sum that increases daily through non-payment of interest and new loans of $10 million.[22] Europe's indebtedness to the United States is one of the most important issues in world politics.

*Japan* has profited a great deal both from war markets and the disappearance of European industrial countries from world markets, although not nearly so much as the United States, because its productive apparatus is much smaller. I will not read the statistics. I will cite only one, namely that coal production, 56 million tons in 1913, was 76 million in 1920, 36 per cent more. Other branches of industry, such as glass production, have grown in hothouse fashion. Now, however, as European countries return to the world market, Japanese capitalists are no longer in a position to maintain the position they captured. There are now no fewer than 2,376,000 workers in Japanese industry, of which 270,000 – 12 per cent – are organised in trade unions. That says a lot in a still backward country where semi-feudal conditions still persist. The significance of this figure will be grasped by all those who understand the role of the Russian proletariat.

Comrades, I must move on to the central issue before us, that is, whether this pattern will be altered by an evolution toward restoration of equilibrium. But first, I would like to make a brief comment. Capitalism's statisticians, economists, and government ministers may well say that Russia's economy has also not advanced during this period. Comrade Lenin will report on the economic situation in Russia. I would like to make a brief comment on this issue in quite another context. The American secretary of state, Mr. Hughes, wrote in a letter to the notorious Mr. Gompers that there was no point in establishing economic relations with Russia, because Russia was now a gigantic vacuum. And the poverty and ruin of Russia's economy cannot be attributed to the blockade and Civil War, according to Mr. Hughes, because there has been a decline even in the branches of industry that were self-sufficient before the War. Moreover, the Civil War armies were much smaller than those of the Great War. Well, the final argument – forgive me, Mr. Hughes –

---

22. By one estimate, US$1.00 in 1921 had the same buying power as US$11.30 in 2011.

is truly ingenious, because mobilisation into the armies is a factor in the ruin of Russia's economy.

But the argument is false in another sense as well, for tsarism, during the great imperialist war, left the most important skilled workers in the factories. It did not require them for the War as we did. It had its aristocracy – trained officers. In our darkest hour, our military apparatus consisted above all of skilled workers, who had to be trained from scratch as soldiers. I can now reveal this secret, since we are now demobilising. During the period when we were fighting on four fronts, our army numbered 5,300,000 men, of which no less than three-quarters of a million were skilled workers. That was an extremely heavy and unbearable loss for the economy.

In addition, Mr. Hughes completely forgets that capitalist Russia formed part of world capitalism and shared in the division of labour of the world market. Even today we suffer from the lack of relatively insignificant and tiny objects that before the War we were unable to produce and whose production we were completely incapable of organising in conditions of blockade and civil war. Our friends who lead the economy have provided a few illustrations of this. For example, we require round and flat cables for our mines. We never produced them here ourselves. Mines in the Donets region suffer enormously from a lack of cables. Everyone knows that metal sieves, essential for paper production, were always imported from Germany and Britain, rather than being made here. Thus branches of industry that were self-sufficient before the War are suffering tremendously. Obviously, it is easy to demonstrate that under those conditions, after the first imperialist war had totally ruined the first army and the capitalist economy, no other government would have been able to conduct a new war for three years, supplying and equipping the army, and so on, without completely collapsing in the process. Only the Soviet government could do that. Obviously I do not intend to deny that we made major errors in this field.

Comrades, we must address the main issue. Even if we come to the correct and indisputable conclusion that, overall, Europe's productive apparatus has deteriorated, despite the establishment of many factories, that the national income of the belligerent countries has declined by a third compared to before the War – so what? Right after the War ended, we saw a return to normal economic conditions. There was an expansion during 1919 and the beginning of 1920. Then a crisis broke out. Well, that in itself is a sure sign that everything is on the right track. The capitalist economy's automatic mechanism came back into play, bringing the economy into equilibrium. That is the main point. First I will briefly describe economic trends in this period, which I already sketched out, without saying so, by describing production over the last two years.

The expansion began in the spring of 1919. The entire capitalist world awaited a great crisis and was in mortal fear of its consequences. Preparations had been made for this crisis. But the transition from the war economy to a postwar boom was made almost without encountering any difficulties. The bourgeoisie was very spirited. Prices rose feverishly during 1919 and 1920. Speculators made big gains. But that was not the case with production. That was clear in Britain, France, and especially in Central and Eastern Europe, where, in a period of so-called boom, the decline of production showed no signs of stopping. Nor did this boom affect all branches of industry in the United States, because war production had to be converted to a peacetime basis, that is, into production of coal, petroleum, automobiles, and ships.

Was there an industrial boom? It was simply a commercial and especially a speculative boom. That can be easily explained. The postwar boom had two causes, one economic and one political and financial. The economic cause was the fact that when the War ended, markets for foodstuffs expanded. Prices increased enormously, and the capitalists, who had profited from war speculation, threw themselves into commerce and speculation and made huge profits.

That was facilitated by the fact that the government, which had been very fearful prior to the transition to postwar conditions, simply maintained wartime practices in peacetime. The government continued in peacetime to issue paper money, fuelling inflation; to pay supplements to workers' wages; to control exports and imports; and so forth. Military censorship and military dictatorship were also preserved after the War. In this way, the speculative wartime boom became a postwar boom, without a real increase in production. On the contrary, in many countries production continued to fall.

As for inflation, it can be best portrayed by the fact that the quantity of banknotes rose in France from 30 billion to 38 billion; in Germany, from 3 billion to 63 billion; in Italy, from 9 billion to 22 billion; and so on. If we consider Berlin, Paris, London, and New York in terms of the economic level before the War, we will find that approximately, purely schematically, in terms of statistics – I wanted to provide you with the statistics, but that would take an enormous amount of time – the level was about the same. Today, after the War and the period of speculative prosperity, we find the following: Germany is poorer; its productive apparatus is much weaker than before the War. France is also poorer, although less so. London, less again. New York, the United States, has become richer.

Turning now to prices, we can perceive the price level in the circulation of banknotes. During the period of prosperity, prices in Germany increased seven times over; in France, the increase was smaller; in Britain, smaller still; in the United States, much smaller. The gap between production and its price-determined superstructure is smaller there, and enormously greater in Germany. The poorer a country is, the richer it appears to be, if we consider its fictitious values to be real – its government debts, its banknotes, and so on. That is the reality of the last expansion, which was a speculative boom. But this fictitious boom, which resulted fundamentally in the impoverishment of the belligerent countries, played a real political role. It has been said by a British professor, who wrote a detailed article about this in the *Manchester Guardian*'s yearly review,[23] that 'our most difficult year' – for the ruling class, that is – was 1919. He says that people returning from the War were quite impatient about the economic situation, 'and the impatience of men fresh from battlefields is dangerous'. And we prepared for this danger, he continues, by setting a large amount of money into circulation, millions upon millions. The government continues to be the largest artificial market. Workers received various governmental supplements to their wages in various forms, and capitalism was thereby preserved through this dangerous period of military demobilisation. Thus this fictitious boom helped capitalism to maintain its ground.

However, we must consider whether the boom achieved this task. It did increase production in various sectors, which shows that it is capable of raising production still further. Must we conclude from this that when a boom begins after attempted or failed revolutions, this signifies that the revolution is finished? Such a claim is based on the well-known exposition by Marx and Engels in 1850–1. In our political life, I believe, the Communist International will soon have to occupy itself a great deal with this question, especially if we now enter another period of expansion, which is far from excluded. I will read the quotation. Engels says here of Marx:

> [It] became absolutely clear to him from the facts themselves... that the world trade crisis of 1847 had been the true mother of the February and March revolutions, and that the industrial prosperity which had been returning gradually since the middle of 1848 and attained full bloom in 1849 and 1850 was the revitalising force of a restrengthened European reaction. That was crucially important.[24]

And in the autumn of 1850, Marx and Engels wrote:

> A new revolution is possible only in consequence of a new crisis. It is, however, just as certain as this crisis.[25]

---

23. The author of the article Trotsky quotes is Edwin Cannon.
24. Frederick Engels, introduction (1895) to *The Class Struggles in France, 1848–50*, MECW, 27, p. 507.
25. From Marx and Engels, 'Review: May to October [1850]' in *MECW*, 10, p. 510. The same quote appears in Marx, *The Class Struggles in France* in *MECW*, 10, p. 135.

Even now, many comrades base themselves on the notion that crisis is the mother of revolution, and that prosperity is, so to speak, the gravedigger of revolution. This viewpoint was expressed in the commission established by the Executive. When a boom begins, the revolution is at an end. Well, comrades, the quotation that I read is extremely important, and it is not quite precisely expressed by these words. As a prophesy, it is false, and Engels himself concedes that it did not come to be. The crisis was not a cause of the revolution, and the crisis of 1847 was mother of the revolution only in a restricted sense. The revolution of 1848 arose from the pressures of capitalism, which collided with the [feudal] estates and combated them. The revolution of 1848 pretty much did away with the guild system and the survivals of serfdom, and thereby gave capitalism new scope for development. Only under these circumstances could the boom of 1848–9 and beyond mark a phase in the revolution's development. The crisis was thus the last push to revolution, which developed out of the social relations and the development of capitalism, which had outgrown the feudal framework. The boom gave the last push to the end of the revolution, after this revolution had accomplished the most important immediate tasks: sweeping aside the guild system, and so on. Anyone who overlooks that will completely misunderstand the quotation.

More generally, capitalist development is not limited to these cycles of boom, then strain, decline, crisis, and gradual easing of the strain, and so on. That does not fully capture the development of capitalism in its entire historical scope; there is more to it than that. For capitalism has two types of motion. The first is the motion seen in the development of productive forces. The curve moves upward, and this ascension takes place through fluctuations and oscillations – namely, the fluctuations of crisis and boom. If we have stagnant development, let us say over a period of fifty years, we will still observe cycles, but they will not be as precise as in a feverishly vibrant capitalist country. If we examine capitalism that is developing upwards, we observe the same fluctuations, but the curve rises upwards. If we examine a decaying capitalist society, the curve points downward, but development still takes place through these fluctuations.

A table published in the *Times* this January displays for us a period of 138 years, from the wars for North American independence to the present day. During this time, if I am not mistaken, we had sixteen cycles, that is, sixteen crises and sixteen booms. Each cycle lasted about 8 2/3 years, that is, almost nine years. That is the zigzag motion.

The table shows an overall upward trend. It begins with £2 [in foreign trade] – that is, twenty-four gold marks – for each inhabitant of Britain. During this period the population increases approximately four times over, but foreign trade rises much more, reaching £30.5 per person in 1920.

This is expressed in gold, not in current money, by which the total reaches £65 for each member of the population. We observe a similar development in production of pig iron. The two lines are more or less parallel through this period. We see that 1851, the year of which we have just spoken, marked the beginning of capitalism's rapid development. Pig iron production in 1848 was 4.5 kilos per person. By 1913 this figure had reached 46 kilos. Then a reverse motion begins.

That is the overall outcome, the overall result of these 138 years of development. If we examine the curve more closely, we find that it consists of five segments. From 1781 to 1851, development is very slow – indeed, stagnant, during entire decades. Then from 1851, from mid-century, there is a movement upwards. We see this in the fact that foreign trade rose from £2 to £5 per person. It then rises, during twenty-two years, from £5 to £21. Pig iron production rose during these years from 4.5 kilograms per person to 13 kilograms. Then, beginning in 1873 – the year of the great crash – a period of depression begins. From 1873 to 1894, we observe stagnation in British foreign trade, even taking into account only real foreign trade, not the political profits, what foreigners left in Britain, and the proportion of capital invested abroad. In twenty-two years, there was a decline from £21 to £17.4. Then an upswing, going £17 to £30 in 1913. Then the War and postwar periods. Here we have the same story. From 1913 to 1917 there was very little increase. But from 1917 to today, it has reached £46. Comrades, this is very important for an understanding of the present situation and the situation that is now beginning.

Capitalist development is thus characterised by a primary movement and these secondary movements, which are always taking place on the foundation of the primary movement. Rise, decline, and stagnation – along this curve there are fluctuations, that is, improvement in the economy or crisis, but they do not tell us whether capitalism is developing or declining. These fluctuations are like the heartbeat of a living person. The heartbeat shows merely that he is alive. Obviously, capitalism is not yet dead, and because it lives, it must inhale and exhale. In other words, there must be fluctuations. But just as the inhaling and exhaling of a dying man is different from that of a growing individual, so too in this case.

It is very dangerous to rely on the quotation from Engels and disregard these fundamental facts. Immediately after 1850, when Marx and Engels made their observations, what began was not an ordinary, normal, usual expansion, but a time of rapid growth, after the 1848 revolution had broadened the basis for capitalism. That is the decisive point.

During this time of rapid growth, periods of prosperity and boom were always very pronounced, and the crises were superficial and brief in character. It was this period that put an end to revolution. The question before us now is not whether a period of expansion is possible but whether this fluctuation in the economy is following an upwards or downwards line. That is the most important aspect of the whole question.

This brings us back to the basic facts that we have discussed: Europe has fallen into decline; Europe's productive apparatus is now on a much lower level than before; the economic centre has shifted over to the United States, not in gradual fashion but through US exploitation of Europe's war markets and its thrusting aside of Europe on the world market. This is a historical situation that never existed before and will not happen again. In the course of four and a half years, Europe lost its entire strength – not only its current, living energy, but what had been accumulated – a generation of workers that were thrown into the War. That entire energy became the basis for the development and expansion of the United States. This fact, in my opinion, is what enabled the United States to carry out a complete about-face in such a short period of time.

However, this event is not something that can be repeated, because Europe, before its decline, had created an entirely artificial market for the United States, a market that cannot be replaced. After creating a market for the United States through its decline, Europe has now collapsed entirely as a US market. Before the War, the European market made up more than half – 60 per cent – of US exports, and this proportion rose higher during the War. US exports rose to three times the prewar level. After the War, it turns out that Europe is a severely impoverished continent, which is quite unable to continue obtaining goods from the United States, because Europe has nothing to offer as an equivalent. It is unable to provide gold or goods in payment.

And that also explains the crisis that began in Japan and the United States. After the brief period of boom, which lasted a year and a half, a very real crisis began, which above all calls out to Europe: 'You are poor, you are ruined; make do with what you have. You cannot import anything more from the United States.' And the same crisis calls to the United States: 'You got rich because you were able to bleed Europe white during four, five, six years of war. But that's all over now. The countries over there are ruined. Their productive apparatus must be rebuilt from scratch and restored; each nation must re-establish its inner division of labour.'

The economies of France and Germany are moving along automatically, propelled by the impulse of prewar years and the War. Germany, however, must move backwards, in order to carry out a rebalancing and achieve proper proportions. Just as scarcity had to be organised in wartime, so it must be done today, unless a revolution takes place. If this process continues, it will be necessary to establish proportion in this impoverishment, beginning with the relationship among the many branches producing production and consumer goods. That means working out the necessary relationship through wars and through partial recoveries, unless revolution intervenes.

The same is true in France, in Europe as a whole, where a readjustment of relations is taking place during a time of economic regression, among the capitalist countries that have suffered most, that are most impoverished. During this readjustment, the United States as well will feel its impact, because what was formerly its most important market is no longer there to its previous extent. This signifies that, for the United States, the crisis is not transitory and normal, but the beginning of a lengthy period of depression.

Let us go back to our chart, where we have defined different periods of time: a period of stagnation, lasting seventy years; then a twenty-two-year period of expansion, from 1851 to 1873. We note that the twenty-two years of stormy growth included two crises and two booms. But the booms were really large, while the crises were shallow. Then from 1873 to the middle of the 1890s, there is another time of stagnation or very slow expansion. Then again an enormous rise. That is adaptation, adjustment. When capitalism in one country bumps up against the limits of its markets' capacity to absorb, it must locate other markets and adapt to them. The character of these segments of time – whether of stagnation, rise, or decline – is determined by great historical events, such as economic crises, revolutions, and the like. That is the most important element in capitalist development.

At present, capitalism has entered a period of lengthy and deep depression. Really, the beginning of this period should perhaps be dated from 1913. That is looking backward; it is very hard to prophesy. It is not excluded that, after twenty years of rapid development that gave us the modern Germany, the world market had in 1913 already grown too narrow for the developed capitalism of Germany, Britain, and North America. And the fundamental truth of that statement is shown by the fact that these gigantic products of capitalist development then settled accounts on this issue. Each one told itself that, in order to avoid this decades-long depression, it would bring on the severe crisis of war, destroy its opponent, and claim a monopoly over this world market, which had grown too narrow. However, the War lasted too long. It brought about a crisis that was not only acute but very protracted, completely ruining the productive apparatus of Europe's capitalist economy. It made possible the feverish development of the United States, bringing about Europe's exhaustion, and thus leading to this great crisis in the US. We now have the very depression that they wanted to avoid, and it has now been escalated to the highest degree by the impoverishment of Europe.

That covers the main features of what I believe must be said, comrades, in describing the economic situation. We have not taken into consideration the entire revolution. Capitalism is still there and continues to develop, whether or not it has potential for growth. It was in 1919, I believe, after the first indications of this boom, that an Englishman – I believe his name is Paish – proposed organising an international loan of £2 billion, that is, more than 40 billion gold marks, in order to carry out reconstruction. It was then considered that if an international loan of this magnitude could be established, and the reconstruction work then undertaken, this would bring about a prosperity unprecedented in world history. In other words, this distorted picture of capitalism led these people astray to such a degree that they thought, 'We have destroyed so much – cities, agriculture, railways – we have sunk so many steamships, that if we print a picture of all that is destroyed on government bonds and write on that, 40 billion to 50 billion gold marks, it will immediately make us immensely rich.' The horrendous mechanism of capitalist society misleads even the capitalists themselves. Then it turned out not to be like that at all. The railways must now be restored on a level that is much lower than before the War, and that must be done in the face of total social devastation.

Now we come to the question of social equilibrium. It is always said – and this is the theme song not only of someone like Cunow, but of Hilferding – that capitalism automatically recreates its equilibrium on a new basis. This concept of automatic development is the most important characteristic of reformism. Of course capitalist equilibrium would be re-established, if only the social expressions of class struggle did not intervene in this cruel game. If the working class of Europe and the world were to submit passively to all capitalism's experiments in re-establishing its normal inner relationships, this would mean that during twenty or thirty years, twenty or thirty million working men and women would be ruined in Europe – for emigrating to the United States is futile now. The United States has five million unemployed and will have even more during the next years and decades. Emigration can no longer serve as a safety valve. As I said, the unemployment question in the United States will remain a constant factor for many years to come. A generation of workers will waste away, and a new capitalist world equilibrium will be established, with the United States as the world's leading power and Europe relating to the United States as Spain formerly did to Britain.

Imagine Europe's shrivelled civilisation in the framework of a new restored capitalism. Theoretically, such a situation is conceivable. The automatic operation of capitalist society will lead it there, provided that we exclude the agency of class struggle. In this regard I have a very interesting statement by a quite clever German reactionary, Prof. Otto Hoetzsch. Writing on the economic situation, he says that we will now have to carry out wage reductions around the world. Workers will not take that lying down and will go out on strike. That is inevitable, whether we call it the automatic functioning of capitalism or capitalist exploitation. However, it is no trivial matter whether we face the automatic functioning of a capitalism as imagined by the opportunists, for whom only the will of the capitalist class is an objective reality. As these gentlemen see it, the will of the revolutionary class does not exist, and thus for them capitalism's entire development proceeds automatically. Hoetzsch tells us we can call this either automatic functioning or exploitation. That means it will be automatic, if the working class is led by reformists, and it will lead to a rebellion against exploitation if the working class is led by a living Communist Party.

This puts a very different complexion on this process of restoring capitalist equilibrium. It is quite significant at this stage that Europe has been thrown back, that Germany is just as poor as it was in the mid-1890s. But Germany's social structure has not been thrown back – quite the contrary. The intensification of social antagonisms during the twenty prewar years has been heightened even more by the course of the War and postwar years, by the period of prosperity and also the period of crisis. So we have a decline in the economic foundation of both national property and income and, simultaneously, a heightening of class antagonisms. That means simply a sharpening of struggle of the classes concerned with their share in this diminishing national income.

And that is the catch in the schematic portrayal of the restoration of equilibrium imagined by people like Heinrich Cunow and others. Everything that capitalism is forced to do in order to take a step in the direction of restoring equilibrium only ruins it even more and drives the working class into even more energetic struggle.

The first task in achieving the new equilibrium is to put the productive apparatus in order. That requires the accumulation of capital. For this accumulation, the productivity of labour must be increased. How? Through heightened and increased exploitation of the working class – since the reduced productivity of labour after the War, during the last three years, is an evident fact. In order to restore the world economy on a capitalist basis, a universal equivalent is required – the gold standard. Without the gold standard, capitalist economy cannot exist. For when prices execute their *danse macabre*, bouncing up or down by 100 per cent in the course of a month, as often happens in Germany, in response to fluctuations in the value of Germany's currency, then production does not take place. The capitalist is then not interested in production because speculation, beckoning from afar, offers greater profits than the slower development of production.

What does it mean to re-stabilise the currencies? For France and Germany, it means declaring national bankruptcy. But a declaration of national bankruptcy entails an enormous shift in the country's property relationships. States that have declared national bankruptcy face a new struggle for shares in the new national property. That signifies a giant step toward class struggle. All this also means the loss of social and political equilibrium, and therefore a revolutionary movement.

However, declaration of national bankruptcy does not bring restoration of equilibrium, but rather brings the lengthening of the workweek, abolition of the eight-hour day, heightened intensity of exploitation. This, of course, runs into immediate resistance from the working class, since – to use Hoetzsch's words – that is capitalist exploitation. In a word, the restoration of capitalist equilibrium is possible, in an abstract, theoretical sense. But it does not take place in a social and political vacuum; it can be achieved only through social classes. Each step toward restoring the equilibrium of economic life, even the smallest, means a blow to the fluid social equilibrium on which these gentlemen are dependent. That is the key factor.

From this we can draw the conclusion that the course of events, whether rapid or slow – we cannot argue about the tempo of events, after history has betrayed us so infamously in this matter – leads to revolution. There is no victorious proletarian dictatorship in Central or Western Europe. But to have the audacity to claim, as the reformists do, that capitalist equilibrium has been insidiously re-established during this period – this is an insolent and ignorant lie. Even the most reactionary of the reactionaries do not say this, if they have a modicum of brains, like Hoetzsch. In his annual review, he says roughly that the year 1920 brought neither revolutionary victory nor restoration of the capitalist world economy. He said it is a fluid and quite restricted equilibrium.

Chavenon, whom I have quoted, says that for now France's only option is to further ruin the capitalist economy through budgetary measures and inflation of banknote circulation, leading to overt bankruptcy. I have made an effort to explain what that means. I have portrayed the most acute crisis that the capitalist world has ever experienced. Three or four weeks ago, you could sense in the capitalist press a hint of an approaching recovery, an approaching period of prosperity. Now this breath of spring has been revealed as premature. There has been a modest improvement in the financial situation, which is under less strain than before. In commerce, prices have dropped, which means no revival of commerce. The stock markets are lifeless, and production is still on the decline. Only a third of American metallurgical productive capacity is being utilised. In Britain, the last of the blast furnaces have been shut down. A downwards trend is still to be seen.

This downwards trend does not signify that things will continue in this fashion forever. That is excluded. The capitalist organism will have to inhale. It will have to inhale some fresh air in the form of a degree of recovery, but to call it prosperity would be premature. A new stage must begin, in order to eliminate the contradiction between this superstructure of fictitious wealth and the poverty that underlies it. The economic body will continue in the future to be wracked by spasms of this type. Altogether, as I have said, this offers us a picture of profound economic depression.

This depression will compel the bourgeoisie to press the working class harder and harder. This can be seen already in the wage reductions that have begun in the buoyant capitalist countries – the United States and Britain – and then spread across all Europe. That leads to major wage struggles. *Our task is to broaden these wage struggles and imbue them with an understanding of the economic situation.* That is quite obvious. But the question is whether these major wage struggles – the miners' strike in Britain provides the classic example – will automatically be transformed into social revolution, the ultimate civil war, and struggles to win political power. To pose the question in that way would be non-Marxist. We have no such automatic guarantee regarding the course of events.

But if this crisis gives way to a transitory boom, what does that mean for our development? Here, many comrades say that if a recovery begins in this period, it will be the undoing of revolution. By no means. For there is simply no automatic linkage between the revolutionary working-class movement and crisis. Rather than an automatic linkage, what we have is a dialectical interaction. It is crucial to understand this.

Let us review what happened in Russia. The revolution of 1905 was suppressed. The workers suffered major losses. The last revolutionary spasms were in 1906 and 1907. In the fall of 1907 a great world crisis began, announced by a Black Friday on the New York stock exchange.[26] A very severe crisis weighed on Russia during 1907, 1908, and 1909. This crisis completely crushed the movement in Russia. Given that the workers had suffered so much in struggle, the depression necessarily had a crushing effect. At the time, we in Russia debated what would lead to revolution: a crisis or a period of recovery, and many of us then advanced the viewpoint that only a new expansion could revive the revolutionary movement in Russia. And that is what happened.

---

26. A reference to the panic of October 1907, in which the New York Stock Exchange fell nearly 50 per cent from its peak of the previous year. The panic spread throughout the country, with many banks and companies going bankrupt.

During 1910, 1911, and 1912, we experienced a recovery and a boom, which rallied the demoralised, debilitated, and discouraged workers. They once again realised their importance for production, and went over to an offensive, first economic and then political. On the very eve of the War, we saw the working class so strengthened by this prosperity that it could have gone over to the attack.

And so today, in a time when the working class is deeply exhausted by the crisis and the struggles, if it is not able to achieve victory – which is quite possible – a change in the economic situation, a spell of prosperity, would not be harmful for the revolution but, on the contrary, would be extremely positive in its effects. It would be harmful only if this boom marked the onset of a lengthy period of prosperity. And the precondition for such a protracted prosperity is an expansion of the market. But this is excluded. The capitalist economy embraces the entire globe. Europe's impoverishment and the lucky rise of the United States in the vast war markets justify the assumption that this prosperity cannot be restored through capitalist development in China, Siberia, and South America – areas where American capitalism finds and secures markets, of course, but to an extent that bears no relationship to the European market. Therefore, we are on the edge of a period of depression; there is no disputing that.

In this framework, a recovery from this crisis would signify not the death knell of the revolution, but rather a possible breathing spell for the working class, in order to resume the offensive on a higher level. That is one possibility. The other is that the crisis shifts from severe to sluggish, and then grows severe again, stretching out for years. None of this is excluded. It is quite possible that the working class, grown astute through experience, will summon up all its strength in the major capitalist countries and win state power. The only variant that is excluded in the years ahead is the automatic restoration of capitalist equilibrium on a new basis and a new capitalist upsurge. Given the overall economic stagnation, that is completely impossible.

However, there is another factor that must be considered: the international situation; the relationship among the capitalist states. I have already taken much too much of your time and will strive to be as brief as possible. In a word, the result of the War in this domain, that of international relations, is the opposite of what the War was supposed to achieve. What did the War mean? The War is armed imperialism, imperialism wielding its weapons. What is imperialism? It is capitalism's drive to eliminate small countries. And 'small country' means not just Switzerland – no, it means France, Germany, and so on. Capitalism strives to create a world imperialism for the capitalist productive forces. That is the nature of imperialist development. Germany gave this tendency its most striking and sharp expression. Germany declared: All Europe under our control! France wanted from the start to partition Germany. The spirit of French capitalism set its stamp on the constellation of European states. We now have small countries in Europe in a manner quite different from before the War. Where Austria-Hungary stood, there are now ten tariff boundaries. To employ a much-used expression, Europe has been completely Balkanised.

These frictions and antagonisms, which led to the growth of militarism, have not been removed. Their effect is much stronger than before. Prior to the War, in 1914, the world's armies (excluding Russia) amounted to 5,152,000 men; now, in the first half of this year, the total is 7,014,000. So militarism has increased. If we include Russia at the time when its armies were at their peak, the second figure is even higher. Even in Central and Southeast Europe, a region that is fully exhausted and impoverished, we see a growth of militarism, precisely as a result of the many new states, each with its tariff barrier, its border, and its army. It is just the same with naval construction. This militarism is also the greatest impediment to economic development. Indeed, one of the most important causes of the War was the concept that Europe's economy could not tolerate an armed peace. Better a horrific end than horror without end. But now it has been shown that the end is no end at all, and that the horror after the end is even worse than before the horrific end, namely, the recent war.

The antagonism between France and Britain grows increasingly acute. We need only follow the semi-official French press. The antagonism between Britain and the United States has, however, has actually been growing in automatic fashion – and here we have a genuine automatic process – bringing closer tomorrow's bloody collision. Everyone knows what the motive forces of this antagonism are; we have seen them in the economic statistics. Britain has been driven out of its position as the dominant economic power on the world market. British industry is decaying. Two American workers produce as much as five in Britain. That has been confirmed by American and British statistics, by the best British economic journal. Two American workers, thanks to better organisation, produce as much as five workers in the highly conservative fabric of Britain's economy.

Britain has been displaced in the field of coal exports. As I have said, the United States produces 70 per cent of petroleum, which has now become the most important factor internationally. Now the Americans are complaining about Britain. In recent years the British have been buying up petroleum resources around the world and now own about 90 per cent of the world's petroleum resources. These resources currently are only a potential; you might say they are underground. Over there, in the United States, the wells produce 70 per cent of the [world's] petroleum, which is then flung at the internal and external market. As for Britain, however, it has located the oil resources geologically, but to exploit them capital must be invested, which is unavailable. If the time comes when Britain possesses 90 per cent of the petroleum reserves and the US wells begin to run dry, if that were the case, this would be one more reason for the United States to hasten the day of a decisive battle. In defence of their claims to Mexican and Mesopotamian oil, the Americans say, 'Within ten to fifteen years our automobile-based economy will be left without any petroleum. We'll be high and dry.' Well, if that were true, it would be just more reason to go to war before that dreadful day arrives. There is nothing more acute, precise, and automatic.

In 1924, the tonnage of the US navy, based on current construction, will be significantly greater than that of the British and Japanese navies taken together. Until now, Britain's guiding principle has been that its navy must be stronger than the next two strongest navies taken together. Now North America is acquiring a navy stronger than those of Britain and Japan combined. Many Americans in the Democratic Party are shouting, 'By 1923, and perhaps even by the end of 1922, we will be just as strong as Britain.' The warning *memento mori* [remember you must die] is now inscribed in Britain's calendar: if you let this moment slip by, you are finished.

Before the War, we had the armed peace. It was said that two railway trains were on the same track, speeding toward each other, and that their collision was inevitable. But just where this would happen was not known; the hour was not marked down in the calendar. Now we have it inscribed on the pages of the calendar of world history. It will happen in 1923 or 1924. Either Britain will say, 'I am being shoved aside and converted into a second-rate power', or it will summon all the strength it has inherited from the greatness of its past, cast this strength into the grisly game, and bet its entire future on this card, within a quite limited period of time.

All relationships, alignments, and groupings among the various second- and third-rank powers are now subordinated to this, the fateful question for the capitalist world. It is hardly a moment suitable for restoration of capitalist equilibrium. That is quite evident from the standpoint of the ruling classes and also for the working classes of not only these two countries but the world. Social development and antagonisms have sharpened to that degree. The economic foundation has fallen, and in the foreseeable future it will not rise again, or its rise will be insignificant. It will necessarily fall in a number of countries and in significant branches of production. Social divisions will be more acute. So too will international relations, simply because the world has grown poorer. That is true in relations among the national capitalist classes and also among the social classes.

Let us consider the social classes. We have the monopolised bourgeoisie, which utilises its monopoly to exploit impoverishment and grow richer out of it, and the non-monopolised bourgeoisie, which is growing poorer both absolutely and relatively. Their profits are declining; they are threatened with ruin; their proportional share of national income becomes smaller and smaller.

As for the peasantry, in the early stages of the War, it seemed to be growing richer. Peasants collected a great deal of paper money and paid off mortgages. It's on this basis that apologists for capitalism asserted that the capitalist economy had become more stable. However, as our theses explain,[27] agriculture consists not of paying mortgages but of cultivating the soil. In this regard, the peasantry has been placed in a most difficult situation by the decay of industry. We see the impoverishment of the farmers in the United States, Canada, Australia, and South Africa. In Japan we see a broad movement of tenant farmers. Across Europe, the broad mass of the peasantry is experiencing increasing difficulties. As for the so-called new middle classes, on whose stability both conservatives and reformists based all their hopes, these new middle classes are decaying more and more as a result of the overall impoverishment and, in particular, the collapse of the currencies. The peasantry is changing from a force sustaining the state to a force for unrest and rebellion.

For the working class, this creates a situation that is on the whole very favourable in terms of revolution but is simultaneously very complicated. We do not have before us the chaotic, elemental onslaught whose first stage was visible in Europe in 1918–19. We then had some historical justification in thinking that, given the bourgeoisie's disorganisation, this onslaught could press onward, rising higher wave by wave, that in this process the thinking of leading layers of the working class would clarify, and that, within one or two years, the working class would achieve state power. It was historically possible. Well, it did not happen.

History, with the help of the bourgeoisie's own good or bad intentions, cunning, cleverness, organisation, and instinct for power, granted this class a rather long breathing spell. There were no miracles. What had been destroyed, burned, and shattered did not come back to life. Nonetheless, in this impoverished environment, the bourgeoisie was well able to get its bearings and restore its state, taking advantage of the working class's weaknesses. Since then the situation has become more complicated, but it remains favourable

---

27. A reference to the 'Theses on the World Situation and the Tasks of the Communist International'. See pp. 901–20.

from a revolutionary point of view. Perhaps we can now say with greater confidence that the situation is fundamentally completely revolutionary. But the revolution is not so obedient and tame that it can be led around on a leash, as we once thought. It has its ups and downs, its crises and its booms, determined by objective conditions but also by internal stratification in working-class attitudes.

After the War and three postwar years, we now have before us an entirely new working class. This is not the prewar working class, which grew up systematically during the prewar expansion and organised itself industrially, in trade unions, and to some extent in parties, with all the prejudices and also the advantages of that epoch. We now have a newly constituted working class, which has grown feverishly out of the ruined petty bourgeoisie, the peasantry, and the working-class women who were previously housewives and are now women workers. The drawing of working-class women into paid labour is particularly significant in France and Japan. This new working class also includes the old layer of trade unionists, the old party bureaucrats, and the skilled workers from before the War, educated by the unions and always careful to pay their dues, in order through the unions to gradually obtain a better life. It also includes the working-class youth, awakened to life by the thunder of war. All these forces have been drawn, thrown, and catapulted into political struggle by these great events. One layer learns lessons at a different time than another. One layer burns its fingers and becomes somewhat more cautious, even as another is eager for struggle without foreseeing the consequences of this struggle. That explains why the situation evolves in so much more complicated a fashion. Of course, if the bourgeoisie had given way right at the outset, we could have educated the workers later on. If we held power, we could have educated the backward layers. But the bourgeoisie has kept the state apparatus in its hands, mounting a fearful resistance, and we collide with this resistance, one layer of the working class after another. And here the most important task of the Communist Party becomes the process, on this foundation, of welding these different layers together, politically and organisationally, in the struggle against capitalism. The most important task is winning and welding together these layers. And in the midst of these complicated class relationships, we must be able to struggle at the head of these masses. The peasantry is a much more favourable milieu for us than it was before the War.

It is possible that when the showdown struggle breaks out, the new middle classes will cling to their mother, to the bourgeoisie. However, in a time of growing struggles, it has become possible to neutralise these middle classes politically, that is, to prevent them from fighting against us. We also see the struggle within the bourgeoisie. We will not seek, as the opportunists do, to become representatives of the non-monopoly bourgeoisie. We must rally the working class around us and, increasingly, gain a foothold in the peasantry and middle class. In this way we will sharpen the struggle between the monopolised bourgeoisies of France and Britain, who are now conducting their decisive battle for power.

To sum up, the situation now, at the time of the Third Congress, is not what it was during the First and Second Congresses. Then we mapped out the broad perspectives and the general line, saying that this line, this direction will enable you to win the proletariat and the world. Is that still true? Absolutely! In this broad sense it is completely correct. However, we did not predict the ups and downs along this line, and we are noticing them now. We notice them through our defeats and disappointments and the great sacrifices and also through our erroneous actions, which took place in all countries, including major errors here in Russia. Only now do we see and feel that we are not so extremely close to the final goal, the winning of power, the world revolution. At that time, in 1919, we thought it was a matter of months, and now we say it is perhaps a matter of years. We cannot say precisely, but we know all the better that development is headed in this direction, and that during this period we have become much stronger around the world.

We do not yet have the majority of the world proletariat on our side. However, we have a much greater portion than was the case one or two years ago. Analysing this situation tactically – an important task of this congress – we must conclude that the struggle will perhaps be prolonged and perhaps will not stride forward as feverishly as one might wish; the struggle will be difficult, demanding many sacrifices. Accumulated experience has made us more astute. We will be able to manoeuvre in and through this struggle. We will know how to apply not only the mathematical line, but also how to utilise the changing situation for a purely revolutionary line. We will also know how to manoeuvre during the decay of the capitalist class, always with the goal of bringing the working-class forces together for social revolution. In my view, both our successes and our failures have shown that the difference between ourselves and the Social Democrats and Independents does not consist in the fact that we said we will make the revolution in 1919 and they responded that it will come only later. That was not the difference. The difference is that, in every situation, the Social Democrats and Independents support the bourgeoisie against the revolution, whereas we are ready and will remain ready to utilise every situation, whatever form it takes, for the revolutionary offensive and for the conquest of political power. (*Thunderous applause*)

**Zinoviev** (Chair): Comrades, before we proceed to a translation of Comrade Trotsky's speech,[28] I'd like to make an announcement regarding the agenda. We believe that today we should limit ourselves to the translations. The French comrades are asked to remain in this room; the English comrades should go to the adjoining room. The next plenary session will take place tomorrow at 6:00 p.m., since a new group of thirty-three delegates is to arrive in the morning.

There are three comrades on the speakers' list: Comrade Brand and Comrades Sachs and Seemann of the KAPD.

**Koenen**: Tomorrow morning at 10:00 a.m. there is a session of the commission on cooperatives.

**Radek**: Comrades, the sitting of the Credentials Commission will begin tomorrow at 11:00 a.m. It will deal primarily with the apportionment of votes. We therefore ask you to send representatives of your delegations. A large number of delegates have not yet handed in their mandates, which therefore could not be checked. The comrades have therefore not been admitted to the congress. We ask all delegations to inform us whether all delegates have received credentials.

**Zinoviev**: This session is now adjourned.

*(Adjournment: 11:20 p.m.)*

---

28. According to the memoirs of Indian delegate M.N. Roy, Trotsky delivered his report in German and then translated it himself into French and Russian, speaking for a total of nine hours. Roy 1965, p. 510.

Session 3 – 24 June 1921, 7:50 p.m.
# World Economy – Discussion

*Discussion on Trotsky's report. Speakers: Brand, Sachs, Seemann, Pogány, Thalheimer, Bell, Clara Zetkin, Roy, Koenen. Summary by Trotsky.*

**Kolarov** (Chair): We will begin with the debate on Comrade Trotsky's report. Comrade Brand has the floor.

**Henryk Brand** (Poland): Comrades, for two years, capitalism has been making one attempt after another to rebuild Europe's shattered economy. Today it is undergoing the greatest crisis of its history. This crisis is accompanied by a powerful offensive against the entire working class. This crisis and this offensive are symptoms of the fact that capitalism today can no longer postpone the task of restoring the foundation of its economy. This restoration faces imposing obstacles.

The very character of these obstacles enables us to see the characteristic features of this crisis, features that differentiate it from all other crises of capitalism. The economy does not dangle in the air; it rests on the ground, in the framework of the capitalist states. And this framework, within which the economy must now be rebuilt, is that of the imperialist Treaty of Versailles. This treaty, as you all know, created a number of artificial states, all of which are unviable and are constantly bickering with each other.[1]

---

1. The Versailles Peace Treaty was signed 28 June 1919 between the Entente powers and Germany. Among its many provisions, the Treaty ceded 10 per cent of Germany's territory to France, Belgium, Denmark, and Poland, and established that Germany

This political framework stands in sharp contradiction to the necessities of reconstruction. It repeatedly leads the requirements of economic reconstruction to clash with the political situation and traditions of the ruling classes. That explains the idiotic imperialist policies of France, Poland, and the like – policies that devastate Europe's economy and prevent reconstruction from beginning.

Last July, the Brussels conference of financial experts solemnly declared that things could not continue in a fashion where 20 per cent of all expenses were still devoted to military ends. The economy could not be reconstructed until there is peace, the conference stated.[2] In November, Lloyd George thundered against people who spread fire and destruction across Europe, running around with a gasoline can and fanning the flames. However, the same Lloyd George is obliged to use force to keep Ireland chained to Britain and to extort interest payments from Egypt, India, and Mesopotamia.[3] Meanwhile, France is compelled to use force to extort reparations from Germany, just as Poland feels compelled to use force to take possession of Upper Silesia.[4] The use of force has become essential to capitalism. The capitalist states cannot survive without force.

All previous crises were overcome by destruction of technically imperfect means of production, placing production on a broader basis, at a higher technological level. This crisis is to be overcome on a narrower productive basis. However, that implies a regression in technology, the economic retreat of Europe. It means that millions of people have no work and no means of survival, that the entire economy withers away. That means that pauperism will be an ongoing phenomenon in Europe for decades. To use Rosa Luxemburg's words, it means a regression into barbarism.[5] The crisis will result not in capitalism's development but its decay.

---

would pay $33 billion ($372 billion in 2011 dollars) in reparations to the Entente powers. It also restricted Germany's military and provided for occupation of German territory west of the Rhine by Entente armies for fifteen years, beginning in 1920.

The parallel treaties of Saint-Germain and Trianon allocated the territory of Austria-Hungary into several successor states.

2. Leaders of the Entente powers met in Brussels 2–3 July 1920 to discuss Germany's war reparations, laying the groundwork for an international financial conference in that city sponsored by the League of Nations. Originally scheduled to begin 23 July, that conference was held 24 September–8 October 1920.

3. Britain was waging a brutal war against Ireland's fight for independence, lasting from January 1919 to July 1921. British troops were also involved in suppressing movements for independence in its colonies of Egypt, India, and Mesopotamia (today Iraq). (See notes on pp. 94, n. 34; 845, n. 17; 846, n. 21; 848, n. 26.)

4. For the events in Upper Silesia, see p. 712, n. 4.

5. In her 1915 article, 'The Crisis of German Social Democracy' (better known as the Junius Pamphlet), Rosa Luxemburg stated that 'Bourgeois society stands at the

The most significant barrier to overcoming this crisis is its social roots. We must understand that the War destroyed value amounting to millions. All this value still exists, however, in non-material form, as demands for interest payments, as government bonds on which interest must be paid. That is the first law of capitalism. The labour of the present generation must not only pay interest on the entirety of capital; it must also pay for the entire War. That is the question of war debts, through which this is expressed.

How can that be done? In order to pay interest on the entire capitalist productive apparatus and all the fictitious capital, the surplus value extorted from the working class must be much greater than before the War. How can that be possible? Britain was able to bear the costs of the Napoleonic Wars because it had developed its technology and, thereby, its productive forces. But there is no technological progress in Europe today, just regression. Perhaps they will try to raise production through increasing the number of workers? No. We see the number of workers diminishing. So they want to achieve this goal by increasing the rate of exploitation. Raising this rate is essential to capitalism's ability to make profits. But what did the capitalists do at the end of the War? They gave workers the eight-hour day – they were forced to. They had to consent to a loosening of work discipline and a reduction in the output of labour, because they had no alternative. In the first months after the War, the German railway administration doubled the number of workers in the railway shops, simply in order to look after the unemployed and avoid creating an even larger army for revolution. In order to save their political and state power, the capitalists were compelled to grant the workers temporary concessions that were incompatible with a profit economy and, over time, could not be maintained.

The entire reform-socialist activity of capitalist governments, their subsidies to the price of bread, the limits on housing rents – measures praised by the reform socialists – is incompatible with the reconstruction of capitalism. That became quickly evident in government finances, in the budget, and it is therefore no accident that the financial experts were the first to recognise that things could not continue like that. The Brussels financial conference, which aimed to take up the currency question, had to address these issues in order to make possible a financial recovery.

The financial situation is an expression, a symptom, of the society's inner mechanics. When the finances are sick, this indicates an illness of the organism. The financial experts wanted to eliminate the symptoms and, quite correctly,

---

crossroads, either transition to socialism or regression into barbarism.' (Luxemburg 2004, p. 321) She returned to this theme a number of times, especially following the onset of the German revolution of 1918–9.

grasped for the most important roots. The Brussels conference addressed all governments with an appeal not merely to avoid arming for war but also to abandon all economic measures that run counter to 'the natural play of economic laws'. That means exploitation of the working class without limit.

As long as the crisis affected only the country's financial sector and national budget, capitalism did not launch an open offensive. Only when the crisis was knocking on the door of every individual capitalist, when they were unable to dispose of their goods, did they realise that it was no longer enough to drive down wages and that sterner measures were needed. Only then were they forced to go over to an open offensive.

This offensive is still only beginning. It is not enough to reduce wages. It is not enough to throw many workers on the street. The workers that remain in the factories must be more intensively exploited. The key goal regarding the workers who produce surplus value is to extract even more from them. That is why it is necessary to lengthen the working day. We will be hit by an offensive against the eight-hour day. They will want to go over to a nine-hour day, perhaps even a ten-hour day. This offensive is imminent. We are headed into a phase of offensive against the working class. They will seek an unprecedented reduction of the workers' entire standard of living and social position. That is the root cause of the crisis.

The question here is not whether capitalism is rebuilding or is headed to ruin. Rather the question is whether we will permit it to rebuild, or whether we will bar its way. There may be defeats in this struggle, but in it we Communists will be standing at the head of the working class. In these struggles we will be seen by the working class as the defenders of their interests.

The Scheidemanns of every country were able for two years to be mediators between the bourgeoisie and the working class. They could do this because the bourgeoisie wanted to appease the working class and was still able to make concessions to the workers. They helped capitalism get through the two most difficult years. During these years, they helped it build a state apparatus, deceiving the workers about these pretend reforms. In Poland, the social patriots themselves created this state apparatus. They played that role, but now, 'The Moor has done his duty; the Moor may go'.[6] The bourgeoisie can still utilise the Scheidemanns but has nothing further to give the workers. The bourgeoisie's axiom is no longer to buy off the working class but to oppress it, to force it to its knees. And if the social reformers now still take the side of the bourgeoisie in these struggles – and they will do it; they have no choice – we

---

6. The quote is from Friedrich von Schiller's play, *Fiesco; or, the Genoese Conspiracy*.

will expose them before the broad masses, as betrayers not only of the workers' historical mission, but also of their immediate needs.

In these struggles, we Communists want to be seen by the broad masses as champions of their essential needs of life. We must be conscious of this task, and it must shape our entire course of action. We must be champions of the workers' basic needs. From these defensive struggles, we will lead the working class to a genuine offensive. That has happened to some extent in Italy. Last year the Italian metal industrialists wanted to reduce wages. The workers responded not only with a strike but with occupation of the factories.

We are now conducting a defensive struggle. We may well encounter more setbacks in this struggle, but a new flowering of capitalism is excluded. Capitalism will offer only its decay, and we must lead the workers out of this decay. Our task is not to predict this development in its details; our task is to intervene in the course of events. Our task is not to show that revolution is needed but to carry it out successfully. And I therefore welcome the fact that the economic report has been given by the leader of the Red Army. That will indicate to our foes, to bourgeois Europe, that the Communist International will combat them not with statistics but with the sword. (*Applause*)

**Sachs** (Alexander Schwab, Communist Workers' Party of Germany): Comrades, the comments I will make deal not only with Comrade Trotsky's speech yesterday but also just as much, or even more so, with the theses that he and Comrade Varga have jointly submitted. It seems to me and my party comrades that these theses are not an appropriate document to explain how the Communist International assesses the economic and the related political situation in the world today. We believe that the theses need to be thoroughly reworked before they are presented to the world in the name of the Communist International and as representing its viewpoint. The starting point of these theses was determined – this must be immediately acknowledged – by the need for a polemic against those who are rebuilding the Second and Two-and-a-Half Internationals. But that does not mean that it is factually justified and polemically effective simply to accept the question as they pose it. This way to pose the question – namely, whether capitalism is entering a reconstruction or a decline and collapse – is incorporated, at least in the introduction to these theses.

It is true that we heard Comrade Trotsky explain yesterday in detail – and I believe we are all in agreement with him here – how the transitory small cyclical crises and periods of expansion are related to the question of capitalism's rise or fall over longer periods of time. We will surely all be in agreement, of course, that the large curve, which pointed upwards, is now headed inexorably downwards, and that within this large curve, both in its upwards and downwards segments, there are also fluctuations.

But what is not stated in these theses, what is not vividly formulated there, is the way this period of decline is fundamentally different from previous periods of capitalist expansion. The presentation and economic analysis in these theses is based fundamentally on national wealth, or global wealth in terms of goods, and the question of productivity. Certainly these are important considerations, decisive for the well-being of humanity and the working masses. But this approach is inadequate for the analysis that we must undertake. It needs to be expanded and, I might say, even superseded by an overriding consideration, namely that the economy today, more than ever before, is organised not for production but for profit. Production is only an accidental outcome, only a means to the goal of profit. The characteristic feature of this period of capitalist decline, taken as a whole and aside from its individual fluctuations, is the nature of the profit economy and the class-struggle character of the economy itself, which is ten times sharper than in the heyday of its development, just as was the case in the past, when capitalism was first being constructed.

We may express this fact popularly, in a fashion that is pointed and exaggerated but nonetheless clearly understandable, by saying that today capitalism is rebuilding itself, salvaging its profits, but at the cost of productivity. Capitalism builds its power by dismantling the economy. This rebuilding of capitalist power is quite different from and even almost directly counterposed to the rebuilding of its economy. This heightening of capitalism's power can only be paid for by the broad mass of the population. For what is being built is only capitalism's firm core – in the last analysis, the big raw-materials monopolists.

In the last analysis, it is the big raw-materials monopolists who hold capitalism's strongest fortress, because all other capitalists, all other industries are dependent, to varying degrees, on their deliveries. What is at stake today for this, capitalism's strongest core, is no longer regular production and the turnover of capital in the slow and regular pace of normal production periods. What is at stake is essentially monopoly profits. That is the second feature of the economic situation during the decline of capitalism. Monopoly profits have become decisive.

It is the proletariat that pays the costs of reconstructing this, the strongest core of the capitalist structure. It is true that these payments, these costs, also weigh on broader layers of the bourgeoisie, those industrialists who are dependent on delivery of raw materials, who do not submit to the raw materials monopolies of Stinnes, Thyssen, and the like, as well as those industries that the raw materials monopolies cannot profitably exploit. As a result, factories are closed or forced to work shorter hours. But if the individual capitalist is often quite unable to avoid ruin and is suppressed, nonetheless we know that capitalism can always escape, as long as the essential features of the capitalist economic system continue to exist. But for the proletariat there is ultimately no escape.

Consider the unemployment statistics in Germany, Britain, and the United States today. We must concede that this is no longer the industrial reserve army of earlier times. Unemployment today has a different character. In earlier times, the term 'industrial reserve army' expressed the thought that these unemployed masses were from time to time reabsorbed into the production process, in large part in order to drive down the wages of the still employed. But given the present extent of unemployment, this concept is absurd. The masses are not unemployed as a reserve army. They are unemployed in order to die off gradually, to starve – not only they but their descendents. That does not take the form of openly letting them starve to death but in the veiled and milder form created by unemployment benefits, which were once presented as a destructive force against capitalism. Unemployment benefits serve today as a means to veil the true situation; they have become a way of protecting capitalism.

With regard to unemployment benefits, I would like to indicate a significant point that is hardly mentioned at all in the theses. That is the role played by government finances, which is greater than in the past. Today, much of the activity of the government's financial administration is directed toward creating a detour or a number of facades that make it harder to perceive the exploitation of the working masses and the broad popular masses in general. Of course, individual taxes cannot be passed along – at least, that was previously the case. It remains to be determined whether the previous theoretical conclusions regarding the passing on of taxes still apply today, in all their particulars, in today's conditions dominated by monopolistic tendencies. Nonetheless, even if there are taxes that cannot be passed on, the fact remains that three-quarters of the purpose of financial administration is to find detours, covers, and disguises to enable the capitalist monopolies to rob the popular masses without resorting to the more difficult direct methods.

Comrade Trotsky says that the most ruined governments will sooner or later have to declare bankruptcy, a perspective very emphatically spelled out in the theses. I believe this is a very serious error. Who would gain from the bankruptcy of the weaker countries in a state of collapse, the countries in the worst financial condition? Who are the debtors; who are the creditors? There are two groups of creditors. First, the individual capitalists who hold government bonds; second, the governments that wish to receive reparations. The individual capitalists have absolutely no interest whatsoever in any government going bankrupt. As the theses tell us, government bankruptcy would unleash a struggle for redistribution of national wealth. The capitalists who govern most of the national wealth, or at least control it, have no interest in unleashing such a struggle; they have an interest in preventing it.

In any case, they find another way to meet their needs, although certainly not to the full extent of the figures entered in the debit and credit ledgers. That is a point on which I disagree with Comrade Brand. It is certainly impossible to pay all the presently existing claims for interest, whether by governments or individuals, down to every nickel and penny recorded in all the account books. That is not the issue here. Capitalism is now no longer at the stage in which it had to go by absolute figures stretching out to infinity. It is at the stage where everything depends on its ability to maintain power and to satisfy its claims, even if only partially, while the claims of the broad popular masses are simply not met.

Thus the capitalists must accept reductions in their claims; accept that, far from receiving everything at this time, they will have to postpone their demands. For the capitalists who keep these ledgers, that is not the issue; they just don't care. What matters to them is simply to survive successfully in the class struggle and in an economy transformed into class struggle. That is why I say that if the individual capitalists have no interest in national bankruptcy – and that will certainly be the case – it will not take place.

And would the ministers and top civil servants perhaps have an interest in bankruptcy? That will not happen. As for the creditor nations, they perhaps do have such an interest. But once again, this decision will not be made by the governments, which from an economic point of view barely exist. It is the capitalists of the creditor nations who will decide if debtor nations such as Germany and Austria will be forced into bankruptcy. It is highly questionable whether these capitalists will have an interest in bankruptcy. The comrade speaking after me will show that the capitalists manage to satisfy their claims in quite another fashion.

I said that capitalism is rebuilding its strength with regard to internal politics by rescuing profits in a concentrated core of capitalist power. I would like to add that governmental authority no longer acts toward capital in its previous manner. Comrade Seemann will have more to say on that, because such matters can be explained better in an international than in a national framework.

**Seemann** (Bernhard Reichenbach, Communist Workers' Party of Germany): Comrades, the remarks of Comrade Sachs and his criticisms of the theses now before us have shown that a new era is unfolding. The question facing the capitalists is very simply this: We are experiencing a catastrophic world economic crisis, such as has never occurred before. How will it be possible to bring this crisis under control, restore stability, and reconstruct the world capitalist economic apparatus? In this situation, the new reality, the reality of new economic relationships never seen before, has also assumed a new form.

It is evident that capitalism has fully grasped the difficulty of this task and the struggle it requires. It is opposing us with new methods of struggle, which we must analyse with precision, in order to do as Trotsky asks right at the beginning of his theses, which read, 'We must decide whether these circumstances require changes in the Communist International's programme or policies.'[7] It is an unfortunate but irrefutable fact, we believe, that capitalism is again in the saddle everywhere, not only on a national level, but also internationally, and in an interweaving of national and international levels. The web of the Versailles Treaty is beginning to unravel and to be scaled down to what can be realised.

So how is capitalism going to undertake this? We know very well that capitalism cannot surmount the impoverishment experienced in the last five years except at the expense of the working masses. This fact is primary in capitalism's course of action regarding reconstruction. Capitalism has understood that it must set aside for the moment all national limitations, all national chauvinism and imperialism – even though these factors are part of its nature – in order to close ranks for combat with the enemy. This enemy is the proletariat, and Communists represent its most advanced and active sector.

Of course it is completely correct and will always remain correct that, sooner or later, the capitalist economy must perish. We do not need to dwell on this obvious truth. Otherwise we would be doing nothing different from the Independents [USPD] and Majority Socialists [SPD]. We do not need a Communist world congress for that. We must deal decisively with the question of how we bring down capitalism. How will we carry out this process in such a fashion that the proletariat takes hold of the reins?

The capitalists have realised that their main enemy is not their competitors but the proletariat. They have realised that the common interests among capitalist states are so great that the capitalists' course of action must be shaped by them. That has already happened internationally through the interweaving of the economy. This begins with the fact that British, French, and American capital has invested substantially in the German trusts, into which national German capital has consolidated itself. Things have already gone so far that

---

7. For the corresponding passage of the theses, see p. 902.

French and British capitalists have an interest, both objectively and subjectively, in the success of Germany's capitalist reconstruction. If you have a 30 per cent or 25 per cent ownership stake in a business, you then have an interest in seeing this business get on its feet.

It is true that there is a fatal flaw in every capitalist process of concentration, whether international or national. This lies in the fact that the foundation of the capitalist economy is the selfish profit motive of every individual enterprise. Even the concentration we see today is based on merging the private self-interest of all the individual capitalists. We agree with Trotsky that the next world-political conflict will probably take place between Britain and the United States. But we do not believe that this is the next immediate stage – and certainly not in the sense that one can predict it with the certainty of a calendar. It remains true that whether or not there will be war depends on imponderables that can intervene at the last moment, and from accidents that cannot be foreseen in advance. But above all, there is quite another reason why this clash is not yet imminent. This should not be the focus of Communists' attention. Rather we should focus on the struggle being waged against the proletariat.

The capitalist economy, which has become interwoven into a community of interest, is guided by the fact that each capitalist wants to earn a great deal of money. This pressure, bearing down on every capitalist and on the united capitalists, seeks an outlet. Among the outlets is Russia. It seems to us that this has not been dealt with sufficiently in the theses. The most immediately available outlet is Russia; that is the challenge facing the countries of Western Europe. Western European capital wants to carry out the reconstruction of Russia. And Russia will represent for a considerable period a welcome outlet, where capitalism's need for markets can be satisfied.

Our task is to examine how Russia can be rebuilt. Russia has the moral right to utilise help from the capitalist states in carrying out reconstruction, if only because the proletariat has left it in the lurch for three years. We must examine how to create a synthesis between Russia's justified vital interests and the task of ensuring that the creation of markets for capitalism in this fashion does not harm the revolutionary cause and does not impede progress. To discuss that here in this plenary, at a large meeting, would be going too far. But we have evidence of the fact that the unified capitalists are tending to pursue this goal. For example, large British industrialists have formed a syndicate, acting with the assistance of the British government. Similarly, leading British capitalists have concluded their negotiations with the magnates of German trusts. The topic of their discussions is already set: it is Soviet Russia. We will discuss that in more detail at another time.

Let me point out that the theses have a task that Trotsky himself referred to at the start but in the end did not discuss: namely, to examine the Communist International's course of action clearly and distinctly from the vantage point of this economic struggle. Granted, this text does not have the job of discussing such policies, but the report should indicate the rough direction. The fact should have been considered that capitalism has found new forms for its struggle against the proletariat, in which it appears to be adapting to the proletariat, such as factory councils and the election of worker representatives onto supervisory boards. Only a few years back, no one even thought about such things. The next slogan of capitalism will be [workers'] control of production. Capitalism's new methods of struggle demand that the proletariat, for its part, adopt new organisational forms, new and powerful forms of struggle, in order to counter the blows directed against it.

We therefore propose that the theses not be finalised here, in today's or tomorrow's discussion, but rather be referred back once again to the commission. Perhaps it will be possible for Comrade Trotsky to take part in a [commission] session, so that we can undertake to expand on this text, which we do not wish to criticise, for it presents excellent material on the overall economic situation. We are well aware how much inspired energy went into writing it. Perhaps the commission on this topic can take up the theses again. I ask you to approve this motion.

**Jószef Pogány** (Hungary): Comrades, the theses presented by Comrade Trotsky in his exemplary report contain, in my opinion, a contradiction and a gap. I would like to read two sentences from these theses. First, on page 4, we read:

> The bourgeoisie nonetheless preserved its ruling position. One of the main reasons for this was the fact that what began a few months after the War was the onset – not of the crisis that seemed inevitable – but of an economic upswing.

Then on page 14:

> During the present crisis, the proletariat has been thrown back by the capitalist offensive. When the economy improves, it will immediately take the offensive.[8]

So the theses note that the proletariat could not take political power in Europe because of the onset of prosperity, an economic upturn, after the War. Then

---

8. For the corresponding passages of the theses, see pp. 903 and 919.

the same theses state that the proletariat is now prevented from taking political power in Europe by the currently prevailing economic crisis. So first the economic upturn and then the economic crisis prevented the proletariat from seizing political power. I have already spoken of this contradiction in the commission. Comrade Trotsky polemicised against my remarks, saying that the connection between the proletariat's revolutionary advance and economic crisis should not be interpreted so mechanically. In general, a crisis has a revolutionary impact, but not always, Comrade Trotsky said.

He cited as an example the history of the Russian workers' movement, where, in conditions of revolution, the proletariat, which had been decimated and shattered by the white terror, was brought back on its feet precisely because there was an economic upturn. Comrade Trotsky wants to apply this example today on a global scale, saying that the proletariat, now forced onto the defensive by the crisis, can go over to an offensive only in better economic conditions. First of all, I believe that this Russian example is not a good one. After all, it is obvious that a proletariat that is decimated when it encounters a crisis and that also stands alone and isolated in the whole world – that such a proletariat will truly need economic prosperity in order to firm up and rebuild its ranks.

I could provide a little example here that demonstrates exactly the contrary. The Hungarian proletariat was struck down by the white terror, and its ranks were decimated. What is going on now with the Hungarian working class? Has it recovered during the prosperity that took hold after the overthrow of the [workers'] dictatorship? No, exactly the contrary. Now, at the onset of the economic crisis, Hungary is again experiencing a new workers' movement that is gaining in strength.

But I do not believe that either example matches present conditions in Europe. The Russian proletariat was defeated in 1905, and the Hungarian proletariat was defeated in 1919, but the European proletariat has not yet been defeated anywhere. It is not true that the European proletariat has been decimated or that its organisations have been shattered. On the contrary, in the time of prosperity the European proletariat built powerful trade unions on a scale never before seen, to the degree that almost the entire working class in Europe is now organised for struggle in different associations. And we also see that, at the onset of this economic crisis, this proletariat has not been humbled or driven back. On the contrary, even as this industrial crisis broke out, powerful mass Communist parties were formed in Germany, France, and Czechoslovakia. It was no accident that the mass Communist parties did not arise during the period of prosperity. Just the opposite occurred: the initial disappointment of economic crisis was needed to enable the previous Communist currents of Germany, France, and Czechoslovakia to grow into genuine mass Communist parties. This enables us to conclude that the crisis does not have a calming effect. It has not brought tranquillity to Europe, such that the working class cannot budge, that it must endure in silence, as the capitalists demand of it.

On the whole, I believe that the theses focus too much on a future world war and not enough on the presently prevailing economic crisis. Within the framework of the great economic crisis, they focus too much on the period of prosperity and not enough on the presently dominant period of crisis, that is, on the crisis inside the greater crisis. I do not believe that the economic crisis will bring tranquillity to Europe. This cannot happen, because the meaning of the crisis is precisely that the bourgeoisie must do everything in its power to defeat the proletariat, to decimate it, and to subjugate it completely once again to capitalism.

Secondly, the crisis does not signify that the proletariat submits willingly. It cannot do this, because there is a Communist Party, and whether willingly or not, this party – so long as it exists – must somehow defend the proletariat in this situation. For this reason, the bourgeoisie is compelled in this crisis to employ state power more and more against the proletariat. I believe that the role of naked, non-economic coercive force receives insufficient attention in these theses.

What is the significance of coercion, of non-economic coercion, in the present situation? It means nothing other than civil war. In my opinion, the role of civil war has also not received sufficient attention in these theses. We can establish that coercion plays as great a role today as it did during the time of so-called primitive accumulation of capital. During a period in which capital is shrinking, coercion plays just as great a role as during the primitive accumulation of capital. What was this role? First, to separate the producers from the means of production; second, to chain the newly created proletarians to the new conditions of labour, to capital. And what is the role of non-economic coercion today? We see the same process. First, the separation of proletarian producers from the capitalist means of production through unemployment, part-time employment, lockouts, and, secondly, the forcible chaining of the proletarian masses to capital. We see the imposition of work discipline and the lengthening of the work week. We see Ludendorff's plans – fantastic and yet realistic – to introduce a universal obligation to work, based on military conscription. We see that the plans of Escherich and the Orgesch in Germany have now been officially adopted.[9]

---

9. For Escherich and the Orgesch, see p. 95, n. 35.

**Kolarov** (Chair): I'd like to point out to the speaker that his time is exhausted.

**Pogány**: Comrades, I would like to request an extension of the speaking time, because I wish to present an amendment. (*Agreement*)

Comrades, I must pose a question regarding the gap in Comrade Trotsky's theses. What will be the results for the proletariat of the economic crisis that we must expect during the coming period? What questions will it pose for the Communist parties and the Communist International? Many comrades may perhaps say that detailed answers to such questions are possible only through prophecy, and that it is always wrong to act as prophets, because we can easily be mistaken. In my view, the crisis itself is its own prophet.

We have already seen the facts and the actions caused by this crisis. I will only mention the two main facts, without discussing them. The first fact is the miners' strike in Britain; the second is the [March] uprising in Central Germany. Leaving the events themselves aside, what was the social content of these gigantic struggles in Britain and Germany? Nothing other than a defensive struggle against a wage reduction by the bourgeoisie. And what form did the struggles take? The form was everywhere the same. The government unleashed violence against the workers.

In Germany, that has been seen before, but in Britain, perhaps never to such an extent. The British government's minister was right to say that Britain had never experienced a crisis similar to the miners' strike. And what was the positive outcome of both movements? We can say without false optimism that the betrayal by the trade-union bureaucracy in Britain created the fundamental conditions for revolution and for a mass Communist Party. And what was the success in Germany? First, that the mass Communist Party became a genuine revolutionary party, and that a so-called left wing developed within the Independent Social-Democratic Party, such that our party is less isolated in Germany today than it was before the great struggle in Central Germany.

There is no need to prophesy in order to see in these struggles, very distinctly and very concretely, not only an expression of the struggles' social content but also of the limits within which they take place. We see that the goal for which the bourgeoisie is really striving in these struggles is to forcibly drive down the living standard of the working class to that of the time before there were trade unions. Thus we see that in Britain, in face of a threatened strike by the so-called Triple Alliance, all trade-union rights were suspended.[10]

---

10. The Triple Alliance was an agreement for joint action between the mine, railway, and transport workers' unions, dating from 1915. The alliance broke down in April 1921 when the rail and transport union leaderships rejected strike action in support of the national coal miners' strike against wage reductions.

We see that after the defeat of the rebellion in Central Germany, not only was the political movement in Germany struck down, but also trade-union rights were diminished and to an extent dismantled.

We can thus affirm that similar phenomena arise both in capitalism's final and initial phases. Both at the beginning of the ascent and during the decline, in times of war and revolution, we see not only robbery, bigamy, and theft; not only the separation of producers from the means of production but also all the violence of the 'bloody legislation' and white terror, which played just as great a role at the capitalist economy's inception as now at its end.[11] If Marx was right in saying, 'Capital comes dripping from head to foot, from every pore, with blood and dirt',[12] then we can say that we now see capital dripping with blood and dirt just as much when it is perishing as when it first appeared.

Comrades, in my opinion, the main goal of the theses is to characterise today's economy. If we examine the present crisis, we see three main features. First, we see the bourgeoisie's offensive against the proletariat all down the line. Then we see, secondly, the proletariat's defensive struggles, namely economic defensive struggles that always and necessarily become political in character. And this is because, third, the bourgeoisie, which reorganised its state power everywhere during the period of prosperity, is now utilising it more often, more generally, and more broadly against the proletariat. And if this is the case, then, in my opinion, the main task of the Communist International and all Communist parties is to draw the conclusions that flow from this. The conclusion, however, is that during this period of crisis we are seeing civil wars, to a greater extent and more intensively than before. We cannot and must not take as our leitmotif either prosperity or a future new, second world war. Rather we must talk of crisis and new civil wars. Radek said that we need an acute political sense of hearing. I say that if we have this politically musical sense of hearing, what we hear in the theses is a new world war and prosperity. I believe that, given the acoustics of this hall and of the current world situation, and after our debates on the Czechoslovak

---

Facing the threat of a general strike in support of the miners, the British government had declared a state of emergency using the Emergency Powers Act of 1920, under which the government could, in face of civil unrest, 'assume such powers and duties as His Majesty may deem necessary to restore order and maintain supplies, or for any other purposes'.

11. A reference to chapter 28 of Marx's *Capital*, volume 1, entitled 'Bloody Legislation Against the Expropriated, from the End of the 15th Century. Forcing Down Wages by Acts of Parliament'.

12. The quote comes at the conclusion of 'Genesis of the Industrial Capitalist', chapter 31 of Marx's *Capital*, volume 1.

question, the situation in France, and the German question, our leitmotif should be not prosperity and a new world war but civil war and crisis.

Based on these considerations, comrades, I would like to move the following amendment. I propose to add only one sentence, which in my opinion is the central point of these theses. At the bottom of page 14, the theses say:

> During the present crisis, the proletariat has been thrown back by the capitalist offensive. When the economy improves, it will immediately take the offensive.[13]

I propose to delete this sentence and replace it with the following:

> The economic crisis has forced the proletariat onto the defensive, as part of which it must carry out massive defensive struggles. These conflicts necessarily become political struggles, because the bourgeoisie increasingly brings state coercion into play. The economic crisis represents a period of intensified political action and civil war. If the proletariat does not carry out these defensive struggles with the necessary spirit, the bourgeoisie will drive down the workers' living standards to the level of the previous period before trade unions were formed. (*Applause*)

**August Thalheimer** (Germany): The theses of Comrade Trotsky unquestionably have exceptional importance for orienting the Communist International's course of action. To a certain degree, they even anticipate this course. It is therefore necessary to examine these theses, and the outlook they express, very carefully, with a critical eye. In this examination, there is a passage in Comrade Trotsky's speech that strikes me as particularly important. He says, 'During 1918 and 1919, we foresaw the onset of a time of revolution.' If I remember correctly, he said that we then believed that the revolutionary overturn in Europe was coming in months, and now we must reckon it in years.[14] I have the impression that if we then set our sights too short, now they are being set too far off. I do not mean this in the sense of wishing to say that it may not require years before the situation in a major country of Europe is sufficiently mature for the conquest of power. There is little purpose in carrying on about dates and deadlines. I mean it in the sense that, as best I can judge, the revolutionary substance of the crisis period in which we find ourselves is not expressed with sufficient clarity, that its critical character is not sufficiently emphasised. The theses very much leave the impression that this time of crisis is a period of – so to speak – capitalism's smooth decay, and that, generally speaking, the main enemy of the world proletariat will

---

13. For the corresponding passage of the theses, see p. 919.
14. See p. 133.

experience a new, temporary upturn and recovery. In my opinion, this viewpoint badly needs a correction. It is true that a degree of social equilibrium might appear to have been established, including on a world level, but this equilibrium is extremely uncertain and unsteady, to the point where it can be destabilised by a relatively small jolt, unleashing a political and social crisis.

Comrade Trotsky has identified the aggravation of British-US relations as likely to cause a world-political crisis in a relatively short time. I see a number of other such causes of conflict. Among the most important is the relationship of Germany and France. As a disruptive force, it appears to me to be much more immediate than that of the British-US factor.

Comrade Trotsky explained in exemplary fashion the economic ways and means that the bourgeoisie was able to utilise to get through the initial dangers after the years 1918 and 1919, prolonging to some extent the methods of war economy: intensified inflation and increased government debt. Comrade Trotsky explained all that in his speech. However, it seems to me that the strategic conclusion he drew from his assumptions regarding the world economy do not correspond to these facts. The conclusions to be drawn here must be emphasised much more strongly, in my opinion, than is done in the theses. Specifically, the period of war in which we live has established an equilibrium that is very unstable. This period of war holds the seeds of sharpened social and imperialist conflict. This is indicated in Comrade Trotsky's theses, but not with sufficient sharpness or clarity. It is true that no one can predict today with any certainty that this period of war will be a time of civil wars – that is, what forms the aggravation of social and imperialist conflicts will take. If we want to be cautious, as we should be, we can say that such an aggravation of social and imperialist conflicts is likely. But we must say it emphatically and clearly. (*Applause*)

**Thomas Bell** (Britain):[15] The problem taken up by Comrade Trotsky in these theses has two parts. First, the question of how international capitalism can restore its equilibrium; and second, how the revolutionary movement relates to these efforts. The speeches seem to focus on these issues, broadly speaking. However, I would like to point out a more general tendency. I direct your attention to the efforts now under way aiming, on the whole, to restore the forms of financial interdependency that prevailed before the War. At that time, there was a widely held view, expressed in Norman Angell's book, *The Great Illusion*, that the financial interdependency of capitalist countries had made wars among them impossible. This notion of financial interdependency

---

15. Incongruities in the German text have been corrected by reference to the English archival record, Comintern archives, RGASPI, 490/1/48a.

of the various capitalist countries had a very important bearing on the international socialist movement. This idea was accepted, in general, by the opportunists of the Second International, and it largely determined their policies and their general political course. But we must not fall into the same mistake by subscribing to a formula that there will soon be war, or increasing prosperity, or even civil war. We should not adopt any formulas that detract from the growth and development of our revolutionary movement today.

Our task is to investigate and analyse social antagonisms and social forces that come into motion from time to time. As war approached, a realignment took place in capitalist relations of every sort. Previously, there were two groupings, the Central Powers and the Entente, and these groupings disrupted the balance of power. But at the same time the War created political instability, and we must keep our eye on this phase of capitalist development. With the peace, there has been a tendency to return to the prewar pattern of interdependency among the capitalist countries, which can be significant for our revolutionary movement. It is vital to our strategic and tactical tasks to recognise the cause of this drift, so that we will be capable of concentrating our forces on the crucial points, thus heading off restoration of the old order.

In Europe, many new methods of stabilising capitalism have been found, beginning with the penetration of American capital. It is said that American capital investment in Europe amounts to $18 billion, of which $12 billion has gone partly to Britain, France, Italy, and another country that I cannot for the moment recall. Another $4 billion has been advanced as commercial credit, and this is having a tremendous effect upon the tendency toward stabilisation of capital going on throughout the whole of Europe. In addition, the quest for reparations from Germany has a similar impact on the condition of European capitalism. The payment of indemnities and the export of coal and iron from Germany has a stabilising effect not only in Germany but, to a certain extent, on capitalism as a whole. It is also important to note how the proletarian standard of living is improved through a rise in production, even if wages are falling.

In addition, we hear that a movement is under way to sell back to German imperialism the merchant ships that were previously taken from it, because of the anticipated effect on the British shipbuilding industry, in which thousands of workers are employed. These reports reflect efforts by capitalism to regain stability. There has been a realisation that the United States, France, and the Entente in general cannot isolate themselves from the Central Powers. These are all important factors in capitalism's efforts at reconstruction, even though it cannot lead to a definitive consolidation. In addition, the development of the Baltic and border countries plays an important role. All these countries are used as a giant police force, in which the British bourgeoisie has become the chief constable.

By their treatment of the German and Austrian proletariat and their operations in the Baltic states,[16] they have imposed on Europe the very Prussianism, the very German militarism, which the War was supposed to kill, in their mad effort to recover the old stable conditions. These attempts to stabilise conditions in Europe have had significant effects on Great Britain. The attempt at reconstruction on the old basis is one of the factors that helps destabilise conditions in Britain.

In this way, the British bourgeoisie is bringing down divine historical retribution on its head. To the degree that capitalism develops in the countries I have mentioned, it causes unemployment, discord in industry, and civil war in Britain. This situation definitely demands our attention and our preparations. The upsetting of world markets and the mutual accommodations made since peace was concluded shifted the commercial balance first from Germany to Britain and then, in reverse, from Britain to Germany.

This development also means the triumph of the policy of the mailed fist in Britain. There has not been a single strike in Britain since 1914 that has not been met by a show of military force, and the bourgeoisie's military basis will be used in every struggle, again and again, to terrorise the workers, so long as capitalism exists. As a matter of fact, police forces have been an important factor in intimidating the trade unions, which Comrade Trotsky accuses of having betrayed the masses. Trotsky said that the leaders had betrayed the masses. In my view, the desire for genuine revolutionary actions was present, but the military show of force persuaded the workers' leaders to make political compromises, running the revolutionary movement into the ground.

It is therefore imperative, in contrast with the past, to concentrate more and more on Britain. As the revolutionary movement in Britain becomes more and more Communist, revolution will also spread increasingly across Europe. Britain will become the focus for all forces seeking to preserve European capitalism, because we are close to Germany and the other Central European countries with their highly developed capitalist economy. I therefore propose to refer this question to a commission for further revision. We should not as in the past rely exclusively on the likelihood of civil war or on other formulas,

---

16. Following the February 1918 Brest-Litovsk Peace Treaty, the Baltic states (formerly part of the tsarist empire) were occupied by German troops. After the German defeat in World War I in November, the Entente powers supported continued German occupation of the region to prevent the Red Army from moving in.

but rather focus on liberating all the social forces that are making for the revolutionary proletarian movement now developing in Britain.

**Clara Zetkin** (Germany): Comrades, Comrade Trotsky's talk and the theses have been criticised for pre-empting to some degree the discussion on tactics and strategy. I cannot share this criticism. My view is that we may be grateful to Comrade Trotsky for having provided the basis for our discussion on tactics in a very careful, comprehensive, and objective way, and for having organised this discussion in the first place. And indeed he did so as a real student of Marx, getting to the bottom of all social events and social struggles.

I do not wish to go into the details of his report; I simply want to emphasise strongly what seem to be the main points of the report, as well as of the theses. I cannot resist the feeling that both Trotsky's report as well as the theses are being considered far too much in terms of the tendency struggle on tactics and strategy rather than according to their purely objective scientific importance and thrust.

What is this thrust? Comrade Trotsky demonstrated and clarified all of the various kinds of tendencies of the current capitalist economy. He demonstrated the fundamental difference between capitalism's earlier crises and the current one. All his analyses culminated in what I believe to be his persuasive conclusion that regardless of whether the capitalist economy develops along this or that path, it is doomed. It is reaching limits that by the capitalist economy's very nature cannot be transcended. It must be smashed; it must be replaced by communism.

Comrade Trotsky emphasised with abundant clarity the role of the state in capitalist society's attempts to rebuild, despite its present state of disintegration. This role is such a striking international phenomenon that no one can ignore the way the capitalists are using and misusing the government in order to rebuild the capitalist economy.

I cannot accept unquestioningly Comrade Thalheimer's view that a French-German conflict lies closer, in all probability, than an English-American conflict. I can see that the possibility of such a conflict certainly exists, but on the other hand I also see contrary tendencies that are working to bring about an agreement at the proletariat's expense in the conflict between the French and German exploitative cliques. At the moment, the latter tendencies seem to have attained the upper hand. In my view, such an agreement between the French and German bourgeoisie is exactly what will do damage not just to the German proletariat, but also to the French proletariat, thereby containing within itself far greater dangers than a quick, acute crisis. The danger of such an agreement demands of the German, French, and world proletariat that it display greater understanding and more activity and proficiency in the struggle.

Comrade Trotsky emphasised quite correctly, in my opinion, that we should not rely on an automatic development of the capitalist economy to lead inevitably to its downfall. No, the social factor, the will of the fighting proletariat, must decisively and increasingly intervene in the course of historical development. But in my opinion Comrade Trotsky also indicated that the Communist Party's revolutionary activity as leader of the proletariat must take place precisely on this economic basis. It would therefore be misguided to expect that a rapid escalation to an acute crisis will be unleashed, so to speak, in a single torrent. Therefore we must not rely solely on the proletariat's enslavement and impoverishment to be the decisive factor. If enslavement and impoverishment could play this role, then the decisive struggle of the proletarian masses would have already taken place during the War. In those days, too, we hoped that an explosive outburst against the predatory imperialist World War would lead to a breakthrough. But that did not happen.

What do we see in Germany with regard to colossal unemployment? Up to now our experience is that, although we have wrestled mightily for the soul of the unemployed in order to turn them into the vanguard of the revolutionary struggle, they have not entered into the struggle to the extent anticipated.

I do not want to speak any further about this question because in my opinion it belongs to the topic of tactics and strategy. Besides, we have one great proof that we should not expect too much from the escalation of impoverishment and enslavement alone. Consider the horrific situation of the proletariat in Austria. Where is the revolutionary outrage? Above all, where is the revolutionary will to act of the broadest masses who suffer this misery? I am the last one to deny that the unemployed can play an outstanding role in the struggle under certain conditions. We must fully appreciate their importance and also actively utilise them. But, comrades, it is also necessary to take into account, as Comrade Trotsky explained, that there may also be temporary periods of improvement in the economy. And we must therefore not be discouraged or afraid, as though we were facing the consolidation of capitalism. Rather, we must then cling to our firm conviction that it is only illusory, and that the task in those periods is to bring to bear the entire revolutionary energy, the entire will, the entire strength of the Communist Party. I understood Trotsky's talk to be a powerful rejection of any passivity of the Communist Party and the proletarian masses. Quite the contrary. Regardless of whatever happens, under all circumstances there is only one road for the proletariat and for the Communist Party: the road that leads directly to the conquest of political power, to the establishment of the dictatorship of the proletariat. This must be intensified to the utmost everywhere through a willingness to struggle at every hour and under all circumstances. (*Loud cheers and applause.*)

**Manabendra Nath Roy** (India): Comrades, when we debate the world economy and the crisis that the capitalist system of production is going through today, we cannot limit ourselves to Europe and the United States. We must leave the borders of these countries behind us, because capitalism, although doubtless centred in the aforementioned countries, is spreading to the most disparate parts of the earth and has subjugated the large non-European countries to its influence. This urge for imperial and colonial expansion has dominated all peoples for a long time and will perhaps play a role for a long time yet, since it offers the capitalist order valuable help in its struggles to survive. Without a doubt, capitalism finds itself in a very dangerous crisis today; and yet, it would be mistaken to believe the supposition that capitalism will give up its position with little resistance. The capitalists are making the greatest efforts to find a way out of these difficulties and free themselves from this crisis. Given that the world proletariat can exploit this crisis in order to bring about the world revolution and destroy the capitalist system, they are forced to mobilise everything they have to find a way out, if there is in fact any chance at all for the capitalist system to restore its stability.

The World War spared two capitalist centres, namely: Britain and the United States. The world today is in fact divided between these two states. The United States has annexed the entire New World, while the entire Asian and African continents are under British influence. The remaining European powers have been reduced to economic dependency on one or the other of these enormous imperial states. Therefore, we have to consider the possibility that both of these large states will solidify their capitalist structures, since they occupy a dominant position in capitalism today. The breakdown of Germany and of German industry had a great impact on British industry as well as on that of the United States. Before the War, Germany supplied Britain, the United States, and other countries with industrial products in enormous quantities. After the War, these markets have been captured by the United States, Britain, and Japan, compensating these countries in large measure for the losses incurred through the economic collapse of Germany.

The large capitalist states are gradually recognising the irrationality of the Versailles Treaty. They have gradually become aware that the conditions of the Versailles Treaty not only destroy Germany, but would probably also entail their own collapse. They are now trying to pull themselves out of this mess that they so short-sightedly got themselves into; they are making efforts to revive Germany's industry and to stabilise it. If Britain were dependent on its own resources alone, it would have been unable to carry out its programme to revive Germany. Britain's current economic and industrial structure bars the motherland from either supporting or reviving Germany without the extensive resources of its enormous colonial possessions. Britain finds the pillars of its power today not only in its own economic structure but also in its extensive colonial and foreign possessions. So in order to revive international capitalism, the drive for colonial and imperial expansion goes hand in hand with world capitalism. Up until the War, it was Britain's policy not to alter the agrarian character of the large colonial countries because it created a receptive market for its industrial products and, on the other hand, was a good source of raw materials. Yet this policy has now been given up because the industrial development of large countries such as India or China opened up enormous markets for Britain's industrial products. The overproduction that at present characterises Britain's industrial system cannot be regarded as a ruinous weakness, at least not under present conditions.[17]

The colonial countries are developing industries, with the result that living conditions of an increasing portion of the population are improving. For as low as wages in all industrialised countries may be, living conditions are undoubtedly better than in the other countries. The industrial development of countries that are now entering the world market is progressing, however, and at the same time, an increase in the buying power of the native population is evident. The industrial crisis is in large part the result of surplus from overproduction, which leaves large sums of capital unutilised. If the capitalists do not find a way to invest this capital usefully the consequences are dire, because the capital must then be invested in other industrial countries. The constant flow of capital from the motherland into other countries takes place in order to participate in their development. For that purpose, large military forces are retained – horrific military forces, which the government uses to terrorise the labour movement. Large profits are used to pay and bribe labour leaders and also to pacify the strong revolutionary forces that slumber among masses of the unemployed by paying high unemployment benefits, pensions, etc. Therefore, I suggest that a clause be added to the theses that refers to the important role that the colonial possessions play in the attempt to stabilise international capitalism. This clause must explain that the task of the International is to make clear on this point that the colonial possessions are resources that can be used by the capitalist system to rebuild its strength.

**Wilhelm Koenen** (Germany): Comrades, it is interesting that the discussion so far has consisted almost exclusively of criticism of the theses, which has

---

17. The translation here follows the Russian version. The German text reads, 'can be regarded as a ruinous weakness'.

gone to the point of quite significant leftist deviations. I do not feel at all obliged to dispute these leftist deviations in any way because we know that Comrade Trotsky will surely take this up with the necessary vigour. But I am surprised that the right deviations, namely the French amendment to the theses, were not publicly motivated. I do not believe that the overriding goal of discussion on this agenda item was to prove that the revolution is an inevitable necessity and to present the Communist Party as an essential tool for that purpose. A far more concrete question for those of us from different countries is: what does the world situation tell us about the next year? The question is: what possibilities does the world situation offer for sudden political, economic crises leading up to the next congress? And that is why we should discuss how the theses can be made more specific. It is important to think ahead broadly to the year 1923 or 1924, which is approximately when, as Comrade Trotsky says, with almost calendrical precision, the next great confrontation will come. But the emphasis on future prospects and on the future struggle between Britain and the United States has led us to get far too distracted from the current struggle. It essential to correct these deviations somewhat because the theses – far from focusing on the future war – address the tasks of the Communist Party next year, as well as working out the economic and political crises that could take place in this time. I agree, by and large, with what Pogány and Thalheimer have said, and I believe that Pogány's amendment is essentially correct.

I also find fault with the fact that Trotsky's talk as well as the theses consider the present situation too much from the Russian-German perspective. They are not sufficiently international in scope. Of course it is correct that a great conflict will develop between Britain and Japan on one side and the United States on the other. But this conflict is too far in the future, and the coming hours and days will show that there are a great many impending economic and political crises. We will even face surprises. The theses fix our gaze too far into the future.

The actual situations have already been debated. The Upper Silesian question is still pertinent; the occupation of the Ruhr is still a threat; the question of disarmament has not yet been dealt with; and the economic question is still not resolved. An abrupt crisis could well break out once more. The previous speaker already made reference to further tensions in the Near East, and, currently, we see that such tensions are erupting in East Asia. What is the nature of the new policy that is being carried out there; how do we orient to that? In recent years, we have lived through vigorous struggles in Poland, in Italy, the backlash on the Upper Silesian question; we experienced difficult struggles in Czechoslovakia, much repression in the Balkans, a large strike in Norway;

the British strike was already dealt with briefly. Other than that, we now see a growing movement again in Italy. We are approaching a most severe crisis. It is important to take a position on these situations. The shifting of power in the Mediterranean – since I am now speaking about Italy – is equally a question of utmost importance. In the Near East, we saw this shift clearly. France with Greece is fighting almost alone against the [Turkish] republic in Asia Minor;[18] the United States is securing great influence over Italy; Britain, which is becoming too weak to keep these countries in line, is being shut out.

Now a couple of remarks on a point in the theses that I think was also not worked out with sufficient clarity. Comrade Trotsky speaks of national bankruptcy, but not in a clear, tangible form. It would be appropriate here, where Comrade Trotsky shows us the declining tendency of capitalism, to demonstrate clearly that the bankruptcy of a state is not the kind of economic event in which various things can be sold off. Indeed a national bankruptcy in that sense is totally out of the question now. National bankruptcy in Germany, for example – that means revolution, and we must prepare ourselves for that when we take a position on these things.

We must prepare for that. I am convinced that if we want to mobilise the workers next year, if we want the current congress report to prepare them, if we want to give them theses, these theses should take a position not so much on the 1923–1924 war, but rather on the current conflicts of 1921. I hope that the commission's work brings us a number of essential improvements so that we can hold our own out there regarding the decisions of the congress better than we can as things stand. (*Loud applause*)

## Summary on World Economic Crisis Report

**Trotsky**: Comrades, the first speaker in the discussion, Comrade Brand, made very interesting remarks that I will not discuss in detail because I am by and large in agreement with them. I wish only to respond to his closing remarks, where – being hurried along somewhat by the chair – he expressed himself in a manner that was too concise, opening the door to

---

18. In May 1919 the Greek army, with support from France and Britain, occupied the region around İzmir (Smyrna) in Turkish Anatolia, against weak resistance, and this territory was granted to Greece in August 1920 by the Treaty of Sèvres. Fighting intensified in 1920 as Greek forces continued to advance. In January 1921 the Greek army launched an offensive into central Anatolia, seeking to overthrow the revolutionary-nationalist regime in Angora (Ankara) that rejected the Sèvres Treaty. The Turkish nationalist forces, led by Mustafa Kemal (Atatürk), repelled this offensive, defeated the Greek armies, and occupied İzmir (September 1922).

possible misunderstandings. Brand said that we will combat the bourgeoisie not with statistics but with the sword, attempting to underline this assertion by the fact that I appeared here as reporter. Well, I must tell you, quite honestly, that I had a lot more to do with the Red Army's statistics than with its sword. (*Laughter*) If Comrade Brand and other comrades imagine that I took part in the struggles of the Red Army, so to speak, with sword in hand, they have too romantic a conception of my functions. I had much more to do with the quantity of boots, trousers, and – with your permission – underwear (*Laughter*) than with the sword.

Generally speaking, I do not believe there is any contradiction between statistics and swords, given that the statistics of swords plays a great role in wars. Napoleon said, '*Dieu est toujours avec les gros bataillons*' – 'God is always on the side of the biggest battalions'. And statistics is also concerned, as you know, with the size of battalions. Comrade Brand will surely recall that we made somewhat of an error in statistics when we advanced too far toward Warsaw, without calculating the distances precisely and without correctly estimating the enemy's strength and resistance. So a well-honed sword, and everything that goes with the sword, fit in well together with good statistics. (*Applause*)

Comrade Seemann took up a remark of Comrade Brand and repeated it in much sharper form, saying that our task is not to demonstrate the inevitability of revolution but to carry it out. That is partly correct but also in a certain sense not correct. We have to show workers that revolution is possible, necessary, and inevitable; and where the bourgeoisie is concerned, we have to carry it through by force. And in my opinion, Comrade Seemann and other comrades that share his point of view are somewhat incorrect to say that the objective analysis of economic development, shows that the revolution will inevitably take place – as I believe Comrade Sachs or Comrade Seemann put it – at some defined point in historical evolution. That was also what we were told again and again by the Social Democrats of the Second International. That doesn't concern us any more. We must set ourselves a goal and reach this goal through appropriate organisation, tactics, and strategy. And so, just as we cannot counterpose the sword to statistics, we also must not counterpose the subjective factors of history – the revolutionary will and revolutionary needs of the working class – to the objective conditions.

The opportunists – the Hilferdings, Kautsky and his followers – convert history into an automatic process by inscribing only the objective factor, the will of the enemy class (which for us is an objective factor) into their great ledger book of historical statistics. They almost entirely exclude the subjective factor – the dynamic revolutionary will of the working class – thus falsifying

Marxism. However, there is another way, methodologically, to conceive of revolution. Specifically, there is a variety of revolutionary thought whose representatives can be closely observed here on Russian soil. These are our Social Revolutionaries, and especially their left wing. They always ridiculed objective thinking, on analysis of economic and political development, on its objective and – to use a philosophical term – immanent tendencies. To this, they – who considered themselves good Marxists – counterposed the free will and the revolutionary actions of a minority. If we detach the subjective from the objective aspect, this philosophy leads logically to pure revolutionary adventurism.

And I believe that we have learned in the great school of Marxism to unite dialectically the objective with the subjective. That is, we have learned to base our action not only on this or that expression of subjective will but also on the conviction that the working class must hew to this subjective will of ours and that the will to action of the working class is determined by the objective situation. Thus we must reach conclusions, to some degree, through economic analysis and also the use of statistics, in order to determine our path precisely, and proceed down this path energetically, wielding the sword.

Comrade Sachs said that the theses were not appropriate for the Communist International because they do not describe the decline and recovery with sufficient precision. I will merely refer you to page 9 of the theses, where this is set out quite precisely. In addition, the comrade says that the proletariat is a subjective, revolutionary factor of history and that the theses do not emphasise this subjective side sufficiently. In my view, Comrade Sachs, whose views differ from most of the speakers, has one thing in common with them: he has not read the theses. In point 34 we say, quite precisely:

> The prospect of reconstructing capitalism on the foundations outlined above poses basically the following question: Will the working class be prepared to make the sacrifices...

That is surely subjective enough!

> ...under these new and incomparably more difficult conditions that are required to re-establish stable conditions for its own slavery, more onerous and cruel even than what existed before the War?[19]

The passage that follows develops the concept of need for accumulation, intensified accumulation, and for stabilising the currency. And a single thought is expressed throughout. Economic equilibrium is not something

---

19. For the corresponding passage of the theses, see p. 915.

abstract and mechanical; it can be restored only through the agency of classes. But the classes rest on the foundation of the economy. During the three postwar years, the bourgeoisie has managed to maintain its equilibrium. That is a fact. For now, the bourgeoisie still holds the tiller. How does it manage this? As I said earlier, by printing money. In Italy, France, and Germany, supplements to workers' wages are paid out of the ruined government finances, in the form of reduced prices for bread and cheaper rents. Every time a German product is dumped on the British market, that means that a portion of a German house that is ruined cannot be paid for, cannot be renovated. Thus, in order to restore class equilibrium, they have to ruin the economy; in order to restore the economy, they have to disrupt class equilibrium. That is the vicious circle that grips the economy and its superstructure. That is the central concept of the theses. I request that those who do not perceive this concept in the theses read them through again attentively.

Comrade Seemann says that Soviet Russia could serve as a safety valve for capitalism and thus, possibly, hinder the development of the world revolution. Well, the situation is not yet so perilous that European or American capital will throw itself on Russia in order to seek rescue from the enormous unemployment into which it has fallen. The situation is by far not so dangerous, and our country is, unfortunately, far too shattered to be able to attract capital in such quantities that it could pose a danger to revolution in Europe and America. That is absolutely excluded.

I now come to the comments of Comrade Pogány. He found both a contradiction and a gap in the theses – on pages 4 and 14. The contradiction, in his opinion, is that we say, on the one hand, that prosperity weakened revolutionary outbursts, but we then say that an artificial prosperity will not halt the revolution but, to a certain extent, promote it. It is quite true that the past and future pseudo-prosperities are evaluated quite differently, and Pogány sees that as a contradiction. But in fact there is no contradiction here, because we assess prosperity in the specific context of the world as a whole and the individual countries. At least on this point, Comrade Pogány's thinking is somewhat automatic and metaphysical, if I may use the old terms, because he says that a crisis always has the same result, as does prosperity. That is quite incorrect.

First of all, such an approach to the theses is quite erroneous. He says that the theses aim at two things: first, wait for the British-American war; second, wait for prosperity. As if it was I who, so to speak, inserted prosperity into our policies, as if I had opened wide the door to prosperity and said, would it please enter in and change the situation. That is not the point at all. What do the theses say? They say that we are undergoing a deep and acute crisis, which has led to a major attack on the proletariat by the capitalist class. The proletariat finds itself everywhere on the defensive, carrying out a defensive struggle on economic issues. Our duty in this regard is to generalise this struggle, to deepen it, to clarify the conditions of struggle through our analysis, to shape it politically, and to broaden it into a struggle for political power. That is our indisputable task.

In addition, I said in my report and also – together with Comrade Varga – in our theses that it is quite possible that a recovery will begin in the next two or three months or half year, provided, of course, that the revolution does not break out in the meantime. If it breaks out, we will join Comrade Pogány in not resisting this development but in taking part in it with all our strength. But, Comrade Pogány, we are addressing the question of what will happen if that does not occur – if what arrives is not a revolution but a recovery? Comrade Varga identified a number of symptoms of such a recovery in his pamphlet. And even if we cannot yet talk of recovery, nonetheless, we must recognise that the pace of decline has slowed down. There's no disputing that. Prices are not falling as precipitously as before. The financial markets are under less strain, and there are indications here and there of quite small, superficial improvements in production. These remain quite insignificant, and it is quite possible that what we observe here is merely a small zigzag, following which things will go down again. But it is also possible that a greater improvement will begin. That does not depend on me, on Comrade Pogány, or on the resolutions of this congress. It is truly something external, independent of our will.

Does this really signify, in terms of policy, the onset of a period of renewed economic development? Not in the slightest. According to Comrade Pogány, if the British markets, exports, and production revive in three months' time, we must abandon hope that the revolution will develop immediately, that political power can be won. We do not believe that to be the case. There is a great difference between prosperity right after the War and the prosperity that is now approaching. After the War, the working class had many illusions. It was disorganised, as was the bourgeoisie as well. All the classes were disorganised. Within the bourgeoisie, only a small minority was aware of its goal, and the same was true in the working class: only a small minority, the Communist group, was aware of its goal. The broad masses were vacillating, and in such a situation, it was crucially important whether the workers returning from the War were jobless or whether they immediately received a reasonably respectable wage, whether their bread was cheap or expensive, because they weighed all these circumstances against their exertions and sacrifices on the battlefield.

Meanwhile, the bourgeoisie made great financial sacrifices and at the cost of further ruination of the basic economic situation created circumstances that stabilised, for two years, the confused moods of the broad masses. Of course, entire layers of workers broke away, again and again, but still the government was able to hold on up to the present. Today, however, unemployment has caused deep impoverishment among the masses. The Communist Party has taken shape, disillusionment and disappointment among the masses have grown enormously, and we are now struggling in the framework of this crisis and will continue to do so. It is by no means excluded that in the course of these struggles and this crisis we will succeed in achieving power in one or another country. Should this struggle, however, not lead to a successful outcome, to victory, then – as the theses say – a pseudo-prosperity will by no means have a pacifying effect on the workers. Quite the contrary. At the first sign of prosperity, every worker will recall all the disappointments he has suffered, all the sacrifices he has made, and will demand compensation for everything – including the wage reductions and the crisis. There are historical, economic, and psychological reasons for this. As for the melody that Comrade Pogány heard in my speech, to the effect that I am waiting for a new war and prosperity, I do not know whether my voice is not musical enough, or Comrade Pogány's ear is insufficiently musical, or perhaps the acoustics here are poor. (*Laughter*) In any case, between my organ of speech and Comrade Pogány's organ of hearing there is a misunderstanding. I am not telling anyone to wait for a war between Britain and America.

Had I known that the date 1924 would lead anyone into temptation, I would have abstained from mentioning the accursed date. It plays no role in my analysis; I mentioned it only by way of illustration. Addressing the issue of economic equilibrium, I asked: what is the state of equilibrium in the international relations among states? And I said that, just as we had an armed peace before 1914, preparations are now under way for war. But no one was thinking of such a rapid tempo; no one was banking on the certainty of an unavoidable clash within two, three, or four years. And this inevitable conflict is not a mathematical point in historical development; it influences the present groupings of states in Europe.

Comrade Thalheimer repeated the same charge that I wished, if you will, to hold in reserve the proletariat's revolutionary energy until war should break out in 1924. This sounds a bit peculiar. Then he said that my viewpoint implies capitalism will disintegrate along a peaceful path. He plainly stated that the theses are oriented to a peaceful collapse of capitalism. I direct your attention to point 34, which says the exact opposite. It says, with regard to the automatic disintegration of capitalism, that if an equilibrium is re-established, this would take place through the class struggle, and for that very reason equilibrium cannot be restored. That's what it says.

The question of reparations also came up in this regard. It was said that Germany's reparations serve as a means to stabilise capitalism in the Entente countries. *Quite correct – except that the reparations must actually be paid.* In order for them to be paid, the German proletariat must produce not only for itself, for the profits of its bourgeoisie, and for its state, but also for these reparations. That means intensified exploitation, which means a sharpening of the class struggle – and by no means the establishment of an equilibrium.

Many comrades ask in a quite abstract fashion whether it is impoverishment or prosperity that leads to revolution. Posed in this way, the question is quite wrong, as I have tried to demonstrate in my report. A Spanish comrade told me privately that it was the prosperity of Spanish industry brought about by the War that produced a revolutionary movement on a grand scale, since earlier there had been stagnation in Spain. So, not a Russian example but a Spanish one, at the opposite end of Europe. Comrades, what leads to revolution is neither impoverishment nor prosperity in itself, but the alternation between prosperity and impoverishment and crisis. It is instability, the lack of constancy that drives revolution forward.

What is it that has made the bureaucracy in the workers' movement so conservative? After all, these are mostly modest folk, who do not enjoy any great luxury but are accustomed to stability in their lives. They need not fear unemployment, so long as they stick within the framework of normal party and union life. That has an impact on the psychology of a broad layer of the better-off workers and these bureaucrats. But now the glories of these stable conditions belong to the past. Price levels leap up and double, and wages shift in pace – or not in pace – with the value of the currency. So there are the leaps in the value of currency and in wages, and then the alternation of a feverish pseudo-expansion with deep crises. This absence of stability, of any security in the private existence of a worker, is the revolutionary factor in the period we are now going through. And that is also said very precisely in the theses, which refer to both crisis and prosperity. On page 13 we say:

> The instability of living conditions, reflecting the general instability of national and world economic conditions, is now one of the most important factors in revolutionary development.[20]

And that is just as important for times of crisis as for times of prosperity. It influences the political conditions in which the working class lives. Before the

---

20. For the corresponding passage of the theses, see p. 917.

War, the working class had become accustomed to Prussian government. True enough, it was a rigid framework, but a secure one. You knew what you could do and what you could not do. Now this framework of Prussian stability has disappeared. Before the War, you received only three marks a day, but these coins had a clear ring; you could buy something with them. Now you receive (I don't know exactly) twenty, thirty, forty, or fifty marks a day, but they buy very little.[21] Yes, previously there was the German Kaiser to deal with, but you knew that you would not be killed on the street. If you went on strike, in the worst case you would be jailed. Today, however, when you walk down the street as a free citizen of the republic, you don't know – you might get shot. This absence of security shakes the most imperturbable worker out of equilibrium. That is the driving force for revolution.

What has been said here about me and the theses focusing on the conflict between Britain and the United States and disregarding other conflicts is completely wrong. What Koenen says about the relationship between Germany and France is quite fully discussed there. Even the latest capitulation and everything connected with it is discussed on page 10. There it is stated:

> Nonetheless, German's surrender in May on the reparations question represents a temporary victory for Britain, assuring the further economic decline of Central Europe without, however, excluding France's occupation of the Ruhr region in the immediate future.

Everything said by Comrade Koenen has been stated in principle in the theses. Obviously, we cannot concentrate our attention on international politics only on the year 1924. We must be alert to every possible eventuality, studying each day's events, and preparing energetically. In my opinion, it is precisely the international issues that offer the best prospects for winning the proletariat, which is our key concern. Before we achieve power, we must win the proletariat.

What is the position of the Second International and the Two-and-a-Half International on these issues? Let me call your attention to a small example: a polemic between *Vorwärts* and the Belgian newspaper *Le Peuple*. I don't know whether this controversy has been sufficiently publicised in Germany. This polemic between two official publications of parties that belong to the same Second International, concerning the most immediate and crucial question, that of German reparations, is highly instructive for every German, Belgian, and French worker. At the moment when Briand was threatening to occupy

---

21. In June 1921, US$1.00 exchanged for 63 to 75 marks, with the mark's value falling rapidly.

the Ruhr region, *Le Peuple*, this scandalous Belgian Socialist paper, asked the German comrades the following questions:

> We saw how bravely the German workers conducted themselves during the Kapp events. Why are they silent now? Why do not worker organisations from one end of Germany to the other give unmistakable expression today to their desire to avoid an occupation of the Ruhr region, bringing with it labour under military supervision?

This means: My Belgian government, along with the French regime, is going to strangle you German workers, if your government does not pay reparations in the amount demanded. It is therefore your duty as German workers to carry out a revolution against your bourgeoisie and compel them to pay reparations, so my government will not be compelled to strangle you. (*Laughter*) That amounts to playing around with revolutionary duty like clowns at a circus. Your duty is to subjugate your bourgeoisie to mine, so that I will not be obliged to fight against your bourgeoisie. (*Applause*)

In response to this, *Vorwärts* wrote:

> We send every one of these questions back to the Belgian workers' organisations. After all, it is not our armies that must be kept from advancing.

That is said by the same *Vorwärts*, the same Social-Democratic leadership, that earlier supported the Peace of Brest-Litovsk.[22] One can talk of these people before the Belgian, French, and German working class only with horsewhip in hand.

Comrades, the revolution flows along three channels, and Comrade Roy has reminded us of each of these channels. The first great channel of revolutionary development is the ruined Europe. The social equilibrium of Europe – of Britain above all – was always based on Britain's and Europe's world supremacy. This was founded on Britain's position as the world's dominant power. But all that is gone. There may be fluctuations, but the dominant role of Europe is finished, and with it the dominant role of the European bourgeoisie – and the European proletariat too. That is the first broad channel of the revolution.

The second channel is the feverish development of the United States, its enormous and feverish rise, created by conditions that will never become stable and will never be repeated: a massive upsurge followed inevitably by a great crisis and depression. These unprecedented ups and downs of a great

---

22. The Brest-Litovsk Peace Treaty between Soviet Russia and the Central Powers headed by Germany was signed on 3 March 1918. Under its terms, Soviet Russia ceded a quarter of the population of the old Russian Empire as well as nine-tenths of its coal mines.

nation, a great society, are a powerful factor for revolution. It is not excluded that the revolutionary development in the United States of America may now proceed at an American tempo.

The third channel is the colonies. During the War, when European countries were excluded from the world market, the colonies developed strongly in a capitalist direction. That has no great economic impact on the world market, where Indian, Chinese, and even Japanese capitalism play no decisive or significant role. But for the revolutionary development of these countries, capitalist development, and the degree of its development, is decisive. In India we now have a backward proletariat. But the potential role of such a proletariat in a land with half-feudal agricultural relationships can be seen in the entire recent history of Russia. The proletariat will play a role there that is out of all proportion to the level of capitalist development and to the number of workers. For the peasantry of India or China has no prospects, no conceivable focus of attention other than the young proletariat, ready for struggle.

The struggle in the colonies is therefore the third important channel of the revolutionary movement. These channels should not be counterposed. The movement flows in the three channels in parallel fashion, each influencing the other, and there is no predicting whether at any given time the movement will press more strongly in this or that channel. Everything is set up in such a way that objective conditions – the automatic factor in history – are working excellently for us. I hope that my comments have not restrained the subjective factor, as some comrades fear, but rather that both objective and subjective factors for revolution will work together and accomplish splendid achievements.

It was proposed that the congress refer the theses back to the commission. It is certainly necessary for the theses to be reviewed again by the commission on the basis of this discussion. However, I ask the congress to approve the theses in principle, as a foundation, before they go back to the commission. (*Loud applause and cheers*)

**Koenen** (Chair): Delegates are asked to remain here, so that after the translations we can vote on the theses in principle.

**Kolarov** (Chair): We will now proceed to the vote.

**Radek**: Comrades, I propose that we adopt the theses of Comrades Trotsky and Varga and refer them to the commission to serve as a basis for the amendments that have been proposed. My second proposal is that the congress recommend to the commission the drafting of a manifesto on the coming struggles that the working class across all Europe and America will have to wage against the capitalist offensive.

In motivation of these two motions, I would say that no objections of principle were raised here against the theses. We need to register this fact by accepting the theses, because only minor corrections are called for here. As for the second motion, I would point out that the reporter had the primary task here of providing an objective analysis of the situation. This analysis provides the starting point for our political, tactical, and strategic decisions. The first decision that we must take after such a report is to call the working class to struggle against the capitalist offensive that is now under way.

**Trotsky**: I support both of Comrade Radek's motions, but with a small modification. In my opinion, the appeal or manifesto should be referred not only to the Economic Commission but also to the Commission on Tactics and Strategy, since this is also a policy question. And I must share a little secret. The theses have been criticised for containing nothing about tactics and strategy. Originally, they did. But Comrade Radek, who is reporting on questions of tactics and strategy, pointed out to me that I had wandered into foreign territory. My character is not at all inclined in that direction, despite everything that has been written about me in this regard. (*Laughter*) I therefore omitted all policy issues from my report. I propose that the drafting of this manifesto be undertaken by both these commissions. (*Applause*)

**Radek**: I agree with Comrade Trotsky's proposal and withdraw my original motion.

**Frölich**: On behalf of the German delegation, I ask the congress not to vote on the theses in principle. We consider that such a vote would be binding on the commission, and we cannot favour that. We regard it as an entirely unnecessary formality. Dangers could arise with regard to interpreting the theses, since it could be said that the congress agrees with the line of the theses. There could be a dispute regarding what the line of the theses means. We ask that the commission have complete freedom in dealing with this material.

**Radek**: Comrades, although I am not the reporter on this question, permit me to note that the German delegation, in criticising Trotsky's report, has not revealed any principled issue that they could hold against Comrade Trotsky. What we have heard was a criticism – justified or not – of specific portions of Comrade Trotsky's report. It only makes sense to refer the theses to the commission – after a discussion that has lasted the entire evening – if the congress gives the commission a clear line. Otherwise the entire debate will be repeated in the commission and then again in a second plenary debate. So I can only conclude that Comrade Frölich is unclear regarding the meaning of the word 'principle'.

The motion by the German delegation makes the following procedure necessary.

Since the motion calls into question all the work that has been done, we must therefore vote by delegations.[23] For this reason I ask that, if the motion goes forward, the general debate should be immediately interrupted, since we must receive the report of the Credentials Commission before taking the vote.

**Trotsky**: Comrades, the motion by our friend Frölich is quite strange. For there are only two possibilities. Either there are differences of principle or there are not. If they do not exist, as Comrade Radek suggests – and there are grounds for this view based on what comrades have said here – then there are absolutely no grounds not to approve these theses. If, on the other hand, there are principled differences, the case for voting on the theses is ten times stronger. Because, if two tendencies are contending here at the congress, referring the theses to the commission achieves nothing. If the congress cannot sort this out, how will it be possible in the commission? Would that not mean that the congress is declaring itself incapable of resolving this principled question?

Comrade Frölich's proposal is also peculiar because he is a member of the commission that drafted these theses, and in the commission he raised no principled objections. Other comrades did, but Comrade Frölich sat there quite contentedly, and he took part diligently in editing the text. Now he says we should not bind the commission. If there are members of the commission that first draft a text and then say they cannot vote for it, then I ask that these members be firmly bound before they are sent into the commission. (*Laughter and applause*)

**Frölich**: We do not want to have a dispute in the commission over whether a question raised there should be regarded as principled or not. We want the commission to conclude its work rapidly. There is much room for doubt as to what constitutes a principle. If it is a matter of recognising the correctness of the line of economic development outlined in the theses, of making a decision in principle regarding a line that demonstrates how capitalism's attempts at

---

23. Beginning at the Second Congress and carrying over to subsequent congresses, a weighted voting system was adopted that allocated votes to delegations on the basis not only of the size of a party's membership but also the weight of the country and its working class in world politics. Thus the delegates from the very small Communist groups in the US held ten votes, just as did the much larger Russian Bolshevik Party. Such roll-call votes were to be held on request by three delegations. For a roll-call vote during the Third Congress, see pp. 881–2. The normal procedure, however, was for all seated delegates to vote individually, using their red voting cards. See Riddell (ed.) 1991, 2WC, 1, p. 16; and 2, pp. 839–43.

recovery can only fail, then we are in agreement. As for the tactical conclusions that have been drawn from this, quite a number of critical remarks and suggestions have been made during the debate here. And so we say that the commission must be fully free to deal with this question. That is the decisive question, and nothing else. (*Applause*)

**Erwin Schaffner** (Switzerland): Comrades, I agree with what Comrade Frölich has just said. For it has become clear during the discussion that on at least one point there is a principled difference of opinion, namely point 39, which states: 'The proletariat, driven back by the capitalist onslaught during the present crisis, will go over to the offensive as soon as the economy revives.'[24] I believe that on this point the amendment of Comrade Pogány is correct. In any case, the original text can be utilised by the social patriots of the Second and Two-and-a-Half Internationals against the congress and the Third International. We therefore have every reason not to refer the text to the commission for final editing based on this formulation.

I agree entirely that we should approve Comrade Trotsky's theses in general and as guidelines. But we must then demand of the congress either that it take up these questions again, after the commission – which previously really had no chance to do the job thoroughly – has sorted things out on the basis of these theses, or we must vote here on the amendments right away. I propose that we adopt the theses, but also that when the commission submits its text, the congress consider them once again – which will not take long. For the theses cannot go out to the world as the work of Comrades Trotsky and Varga and the commission; they must be presented as the work of the Third International.

**Radek**: A commission is established, and it prepares the basis for a plenary discussion. It does not yet express the relationship of forces in the congress; it prepares a basis, and the matter then goes to the plenary to be motivated. If fundamental disagreements arise in the commission, then they are expressed through counterposed sets of theses.

The commission met. The comrades say they did not do the work thoroughly. The principles expressed at the congress resulted from thorough work, to be sure, but not from the work of a commission. The principles are presented to the congress.

Comrade Frölich and other comrades of his delegation took part in the commission. They did not present there any fundamentally different assessment of the situation. They spoke here – we heard Thalheimer and Koenen.

---

24. Compare the final text, point 40, p. 919.

Their comments related to certain policy issues that Trotsky did not contradict. The congress did its work, determining that there were no disagreements of principle. Now this matter goes to the commission, in order to give the resolution its finishing touches. The motions made here will either be included or excluded, based on the plenary discussion and congress vote on the theses in principle. If that is not the case, we must continue the plenary discussion until Frölich comes up with principles that he counterposes to the theses. Let us have no fiddling about here. I hear a proposal that we should adopt the theses not in principle but as a basis, because no other theses are available. Either you have other theses or you do not – there is no third option. I therefore ask that the question be called.

Comrade Schaffner said that there was a principled difference between Trotsky and Pogány. Trotsky said that when there is prosperity, the workers will go over to the attack. Pogány has the opposite view, saying they can take the offensive right now.

The congress has asked Trotsky to draft a manifesto, and he has accepted. Comrades, at an international congress, things should be taken a bit more seriously. (*Applause*)

**Kolarov** (Chair): Discussion is closed; no one else has asked for the floor.

**Radek**: We are in a difficult spot. Votes on principled questions have to be taken not by raising cards but by delegations, with each delegation receiving a specific number of votes. The distribution of votes has just been decided in the Credentials Commission, but not yet by a plenary session. I propose that we take a straw vote with cards. If the outcome is doubtful, we will have to take the next step. If the result is clear, the card vote can be accepted as sufficient. (*Applause*)

**Kolarov** (Chair): We will proceed to the vote. First we must decide whether we will accept the motion that we vote today with our voting cards. All those in favour of voting by raising the voting cards, please raise your hands. (*Vote*) Very well, we will vote by raising cards.

Now we will take the vote on Comrade Radek's motion that the congress agree in principle with the theses of Comrades Trotsky and Varga and refer them to the commission. All those in favour, raise your cards. (*Vote*) I see that an overwhelming majority is for the motion. (*Calls: 'All those opposed!'*) I will take those opposed. All those opposed, raise your cards. (*Vote*) A minority.[25]

---

25. A report from the editing commission on this resolution is discussed in Session 16.

We will now vote on the second proposal, namely to issue a manifesto to the workers of the world that calls on them to rise in struggle against the capitalist offensive – including, of course, Comrade Trotsky's amendment that the manifesto should be referred for editing to both commissions.[26] (*The congress adopts the motion.*)

**Koenen**: The Presidium proposes that the commission set up by the Executive to carry out this task be confirmed to continue this work, but that the delegations be authorised to replace individual members of the commission by others. In addition, all delegations not already represented in the commission are asked to send a representative to it. (*Adopted*)

**Kolarov** (Chair): Before we adjourn, I will announce the agenda of tomorrow's session. It will begin at 11:00 a.m. sharp with Comrade Zinoviev's presentation of the Executive's report to the congress.

(*The session is adjourned at 1:00 a.m.*)

---

26. The Third Congress manifesto, issued as an appeal by the Executive Committee, can be found on pp. 1034–40.

# Session 4 – 25 June 1921, 12:25 p.m.
# Executive Committee Report

*Radek: Report of the Credentials Commission. Zinoviev: Report on the Activity of the Communist International Executive Committee. Appeal for Max Hoelz.*

**Koenen** (Chair): Comrade Radek will report on the decisions of the Credentials Commission.

## Credentials Commission Report

**Radek**: Comrades, the Credentials Commission has not yet been able to check all mandates, since they have not yet all been submitted. So far we have recognised 291 mandates with decisive vote, 218 mandates with consultative vote, and 100 guests from abroad, who have received guest cards. The delegates come from forty-eight countries, and there are also delegates from the international youth organisation and the women. The Poale Zion and also the Jewish Workers' League, which works in Poland, have been admitted with consultative vote. We also have granted consultative vote to the Near and Far East Bureau.[1]

The Credentials Commission had to dispose of a number of questions that were not purely of a formal nature, on which I must report. First, we rejected requests by two groups in *Bulgaria* to be admitted to the congress with consultative vote. These are the so-called Communist Workers' Party of Bulgaria

---

1. For the Near East and Far East bureaus, see p. 869, n. 56.

and a second current called the Group of Left Communists. In both cases, the Credentials Commission was able to establish that the groups have no significant following. The first group, the so-called Communist Workers' Party, arose from a current within the social-patriotic party that split away in 1919. They appeared here in Moscow, accusing the Communist Party of Bulgaria of not being radical enough. But their newspaper printed excerpts from Kautsky's book *Terrorism and Communism*.[2] This fact alone enabled us to determine that this was not a left group. The majority of this group now belongs to the Communist Party of Bulgaria. The second group, the so-called Left Communists, cannot demonstrate any activity, and we do not consider it appropriate, in a country where there is a large Communist Party, to reward attempts at a split by granting them consultative vote. The group protested that we had rejected their application without giving them a hearing.

The Executive Committee of the Communist International reviewed the charges against the Bulgarian party. Based on all the submitted materials and lengthy memoranda from all quarters, a commission of the Executive Committee adopted a resolution before the congress began. This resolution formed the basis for the decision of the Credentials Commission; we also consulted the Communist Party of Bulgaria.

Our second report concerns *Romania*. As you know, the Romanian party was not a member of the Communist International. There are substantial groups of Communists working underground in this party for its affiliation to the Communist International, while carrying out their own independent Communist agitation and propaganda. These organisations were headed by the 'Coordinating Centre'. Shortly before the congress, the *Romanian party declared it was affiliating to the Communist International*. But after doing that, the party leadership and several hundred leading Romanian comrades were arrested right out of the congress on government orders.[3] We have received a report of a Bulgarian comrade who went to Bucharest after these arrests. The comrades said that their party would not be in a position to send an official delegation to the congress. However, they hoped that individual comrades, working in the underground, would succeed in getting to the congress. And representatives of the underground organisation did in fact come; they are all members of the party. So the question for us in the commission was whether

---

2. Karl Kautsky's *Terrorism and Communism: A Contribution to the Natural History of Revolution* was published in German in 1919, with an English edition the following year.

3. The Romanian Socialist Party's congress of 8–12 May 1921 voted to join the Comintern and change the party's name to Communist Party of Romania. Before the congress concluded, however, the police surrounded the building and arrested the delegates.

recognising a small segment of the Romanian comrades as representing the party would perhaps be perceived as overstepping our authority, as giving representation not to a party but to a group. The comrades from the Balkans said that this was not the case. We have recognised the representatives of the Romanian party on a provisional basis, without in any way infringing on the rights of the Romanian party. We did that out of solidarity with the jailed Romanian comrades.

A third group of questions concerns the *presence of parties with consultative vote*, parties that do not yet belong to the International but have begun negotiations with it. Examples are the Estonian Independent [Socialist] Party, the Jewish Workers' League in Poland, and the Poale Zion world federation. The Credentials Commission states that admitting these organisations to the congress with consultative vote in no way implies their admission as parties. It will be up to the congress, its commissions, and the Executive to determine, in discussions with these parties, to what extent they conform to the requirements for admission to the Communist International, and the extent to which new requirements may be needed. We believe that these parties should be handled in the same fashion as the German Independent Party [USPD], to which we granted the right to be present here [at the Second Congress] and put forward its point of view, as long as it was still negotiating with us. I ask that you approve the decisions of the Credentials Commission. (*Applause*)

**Koenen** (Chair): Discussion is open on the report of the Credentials Commission. Does anyone wish to raise any type of objection against the commission proposals?

Seeing that no objections have been raised to the commission proposals, I declare the report and its proposals to be adopted.

We now come to *determining the basis for voting*.

**Radek**: We have decided to propose to the congress that the delegations be divided into five groups. Of course, we did not arrive at a single unified principle that could serve as a basis for this division. The size of the parties' membership cannot alone be decisive. We have parties that, although quite weak, will over time play a decisive role, because of the overall situation of their countries. Therefore, we cannot allocate such parties to a group based solely on the size of their membership. We have therefore combined *the number of members, the country's political importance, and, thirdly, the prospects for development of the workers' and Communist movement in that country*.

We propose to establish four groups. The *first group*, which will have *forty votes* each, consists of Germany, France, Italy, Russia, Czechoslovakia, and – finally – the youth association, which has 800,000 members. The *second group*, which will have *thirty votes*, consists of Britain, the United States of North America, Poland, Ukraine, Norway, Yugoslavia, and Bulgaria. The two English-speaking parties are unfortunately not yet large mass organisations, but they're convinced that – given the situation in their countries – they will become so in short order. Given the importance of the movement in their countries, we have allocated them to the second group, with thirty votes. The *third group*, with *twenty votes*, consists of Spain, Finland, Romania, Latvia, Switzerland, Hungary, Austria, the Netherlands, and Belgium. The Belgian party remains small, but as you know, following the split of the Jacquemotte group [from the Belgian Social-Democratic party] we have every prospect of a good Communist Party there. The *fourth group*, with *ten votes*, consists of small countries with an old workers' movement, and imperialist countries where a Communist movement already exists. Included in this group are Azerbaijan with Baku, where a fine workers' movement has existed for twenty years, Georgia, Lithuania, Estonia, Denmark, and Luxembourg. Also Persia [Iran] and Turkey.

The *fifth group*, with *five votes*, includes the South African organisation, Iceland, groups in Mexico, Armenia, Argentina, Australia, New Zealand, and the group in the Dutch East Indies [Indonesia].

We granted *consultative votes* to a number of countries where the movement is not yet at all consolidated, such as in China, where we see the beginnings of a workers' movement but the Communists are not yet organised except in trade unions.[4] Other such countries, where the movement is more revolutionary than political and Communist, are Turkestan, Khiva, Bukhara, and Mongolia.

As for Japan, where there is a strong workers' movement, it must have a decisive vote. The Japanese comrades present here have told us in all modesty that they represent only a portion of the Japanese workers' organisations of Korea and Japanese workers in the United States, and that they therefore have no claim to a decisive vote. Later, we received word that a proper delegation had left Japan. When they arrive, they will of course receive a decisive vote. The Japanese representatives here now have come on a personal basis and have a consultative vote.

These decisions of the Credentials Commission were adopted unanimously, and I ask you to adopt them as well.

Now a word about *how we will vote*. We took last year's voting method as a basis, with one change. We propose that voting be done by having the elected

---

4. The Communist Party of China was formed in July 1921 by a congress with fifty-three participants that convened in Shanghai.

representatives of delegations deliver the votes of the delegations on all politically decisive questions. If there is a difference of opinion within the delegation, it can either decide how to divide the votes or, in particularly difficult cases, come to an agreement with the Presidium. A number of comrades have been invited specifically because they have alternative viewpoints. They will be given an opportunity by the Presidium to take the floor, independently from their delegation. They do not have the right to vote. (*Applause*)

**Koenen** (Chair): Comrade Radek has reported on voting procedure. Since the commission voted unanimously to present this proposal to the plenary session, and no objection has been raised here, we take it that the congress is also unanimously in agreement with this proposal. We move on to today's agenda. I give the floor to the chair of the Executive Committee, Comrade Zinoviev, for the report on its activity.

## Executive Committee Report

**Zinoviev**: Comrades, our Communist International is now already in its third year. The Executive, by contrast, has been functioning as a genuine international body for only a year, since the Second Congress. From the First to the Second Congress, the leadership of the Communist International was recruited, by and large, only from a group of Russian comrades. It was not easy, at the close of the Second Congress, to convince parties to send their representatives to the Executive for an entire year. Comrades who took part in the Second Congress will recall how the German party's representative, for example, and other parties as well were opposed to choosing delegates of the different parties to come here to Moscow for the Executive and to having these delegates work here during this entire period. There was an inclination to simply leave the management of affairs, as before, in the hands of the Russian comrades. Only when we protested and insisted categorically on our demand did the congress decide to send delegates from the non-Russian parties.

Ten of the sister parties did in fact send their delegates. Nonetheless, we must say that during this year, *not all parties carried out their duty to the International*. Several parties met their organisational obligations only inadequately, and ties were therefore rather loose. In this regard, no one is less content with the work of the Executive than the Executive itself. We demand that the Third Congress take all the needed measures so that we obtain an Executive that is genuinely *international* in composition, an Executive that looks after all the daily work and organises the whole political leadership in a genuinely international fashion.

We must discuss the Executive's activity clearly and unsparingly. There have been inadequacies in the work of the Executive. Errors have been made, and we will follow the discussion intently and accept the parties' instructions.

On the organisational side – we must tell you this at the start – the work was rather inadequate and sometimes even bad. Still, comrades, I believe we can note with satisfaction that, despite everything, this year the Executive provided, for the first time in the history of the modern workers' movement, a *genuinely international leadership*. In the Second International, the International Socialist Bureau was not a political leadership, nor was it a body that carried out practical daily work. The Bureau gathered every three months, mostly for show. In the Communist International's first two years, its leadership was not yet fully international. We can say with satisfaction that only this year did we see the beginnings of an institution, composed of representatives of at lest ten or twelve parties; one that, based on this composition, at least *attempted* to lead the Communist workers' movement in an international fashion. Comrades, I believe this is a great step forward for the international workers' movement. And if we all agree that our International should continue to evolve along these lines, we will shrink from no sacrifice and will all help out with the best forces at our disposal. In this way we will soon have a really good international leadership.

We convened this congress somewhat earlier than required by the Statutes, aware of the great responsibility borne by this first genuinely international Executive. During this period, in many of the countries most decisive for the modern workers' movement, very important processes of development have been and still are under way. The Statutes state that, between congresses, the Executive of the International has decisive authority. We believe, however, that when major questions arise and if it is in any way possible, our Executive should always appeal to a congress, which is the source of all our decisions. And given that we faced very important problems in a number of countries, and especially given that it was possible, we considered it our bounden duty to convene this world congress as rapidly as possible, in order to let the congress itself make these crucial decisions.

I will now share with comrades some *statistics regarding our Executive's activity*. Not quite eleven months have passed since the Second Congress. During this period, the Executive met in 31 sessions, which took up 196 questions – 128 of them purely political, and the others organisational in character.

We had the strongest ties with Germany. It was also in Germany where developments in the workers' movement were the most important. During the year under consideration, the Executive's sessions took up Germany 21 times, Italy 12 times, the United States 12 times, Britain 9 times, Romania 12 times, Czechoslovakia 10 times, France 7 times, Bulgaria 7 times, and the Near and Far East 10 times. Then there are other countries that were dealt with two, three, or four times in Executive sessions. In this regard, I must note that – as almost all of you know – in addition to the Executive there is also a smaller Bureau, made up recently of seven comrades and holding sessions more frequently, roughly twice as often as the Executive itself.[5] We received a large number of visits during this year, from the most varied countries. We had less cause for complaint in this regard than we did the previous year. It was much easier to travel to Russia, and many parties took full advantage of these opportunities.

What was the *political content* of our work during this year? It was determined, of course, by the decisions of the Second Congress. So what was achieved, in broad terms, at the Second Congress?

We said at the time that the Second Congress was essentially the first, founding congress of the Communist International. What we call the First Congress was in fact only a gathering of a quite small number of groups. The Second Congress was thus the real founding congress. It developed the Statutes of the Communist International, provided us with basic resolutions on the role of the parties, and defined the Communist International's policies in rough, general terms.

What was the line of the Second Congress? We conducted a battle on two fronts there. We had to contend with those of our comrades who – like some of the British, Italian, and American comrades – considered themselves as a so-called 'left' opposition to us. Recall, for example, the question of the British comrades' participation in the Labour Party. The Second Congress spent two days on that question, and our British comrades were almost unanimously opposed. They considered participation in the Labour Party to be opportunist. The American comrades – the late John Reed and his friends – supported them in this regard. We opposed them. Britain is a country where the mass movement is developing magnificently but where the Communist Party's influence has increased only very slowly. Precisely in such a country, we believe, we have a great responsibility to take part in the mass organisation that embraces hundreds of thousands and millions of proletarians, to organise our forces there, form cells, and in this way win influence in it. Here the

---

5. Established to exercise day-to-day leadership of the Comintern's work, the ECCI's Small Bureau (Engeres Büro) was elected following the Second Congress. It consisted of Grigorii Zinoviev as chair, with Ernst Meyer, Nikolai Bukharin, Endre Rudnyánszky, and M.V. Kobetsky. Added to it shortly after were Béla Kun, Alfred Rosmer, Wilhelm Koenen, and Karl Radek. In September 1921, following the Third Congress, the body was renamed the ECCI Presidium.

Second Congress gave us a clear directive to take part in these mass organisations and to oblige all our new Communist groups to take part in formations like the Labour Party and in the trade unions. We told the comrades, 'You have to organise there and struggle *within* the trade unions *against* the trade-union bureaucracy and reform-socialist politics. You must succeed in winning influence in these organisations for communism.[6]

We also had to contend with the so-called Left during the Second Congress on the question of *parliamentarism*. As you recall, Comrade Bordiga – whom we can now confidently term one of our best and most sincere revolutionaries in Italy and the entire Communist International – Comrade Bordiga and his group launched a struggle in this very room against parliamentarism. They had support from a number of Swiss and Belgian comrades. We combated this point of view and obtained adoption of a decision that Communists should not reject revolutionary parliamentarism. Our point of view here was similar to that in the question of activity in the Labour Party or the trade unions. That was one of the congress's directives.[7]

The second directive took the form of the celebrated *Twenty-One Points*. This second decision has had a much greater impact on our activity over the last year. It was directed *against opportunism, against centrist and half-centrist forces*.

On the left, we faced not enemies but friends who were inclined to sectarianism, who lacked understanding of many of the concrete conditions of revolution. On the right, by contrast, we faced an entire array of dangerous enemies. As you will recall, general conditions in Europe and the United States at the time of the Second Congress were such that it became the fashion then to join the Communist International. Every centrist with a modicum of wits wanted to belong to the Communist International. We even received a delegation from Hillquit's party in the United States[8] – roughly speaking, the same current as the right USPD or the Scheidemanns [SPD] in Germany. This delegation was quite astounded not to be admitted in hospitable fashion. You will recall *Dittmann* and *Crispien*, who are now taking part officially in

---

6. The debate on the Labour Party took place during Sessions 2 and 16 of the Second Congress; see Riddell (ed.) 1991, 2WC, 1, pp. 141–78 and 2, 733–44. The debate on trade unions and factory committees was held in Sessions 11 and 12 (pp. 589–634).

7. The debate at the Second Congress was over participation by Communists in bourgeois elections and parliaments, and the policies to promote this activity. The topic was discussed in Sessions 9 and 10 of the congress; see Riddell (ed.) 1991, 2WC, 1, pp. 421–79. The resolution approved, 'Theses on the Communist Parties and Parliamentarism', appears on pp. 470–9.

8. In March 1920 the centrist-led Socialist Party of America, which had expelled the Communist majority several months earlier, formally applied for admission to the Comintern. The delegation referred to may be M.A. Schwartz and Jessie Molle, leading members of the SP from California who were in Russia during the summer of 1920.

bourgeois governments – they were here and demanded to be admitted to the Communist International.[9] You will also recall the presence here of D'Aragona and other Italian reformists, who have now proved to be quite open saboteurs of the proletarian struggle. They too considered it obvious that they should belong to the Communist International.

On the other hand, the situation was then still so unclear and relationships so inadequate that even we Russian comrades, shut off by the blockade, had very little information. We were so naïve that, initially, we welcomed gentlemen like D'Aragona as brothers. I am still ashamed to recall that I was responsible for the fact that tens of thousands of magnificent Petersburg proletarians literally carried these gentlemen on their shoulders through the streets of Petrograd. We thought that genuine brothers had come to us.

The situation became much clearer during the course of the Second Congress itself. The congress adopted a tough and unambiguous stance toward the right wing. We faced genuine enemies on our right. We were all well aware that these clever people would go to any ends simply to sneak into the Communist International, which they would then sabotage from within. Our struggle with the centrists resulted in the Twenty-One Points. And these directives shaped our entire subsequent activity.[10]

The situation in Germany after the Second Congress was that the Communist International's only affiliate was the Spartacus League, an organisation with a glorious past that was, however, not a mass party at that time. In addition, we had in Germany the USPD with its left wing, whose worker forces were also revolutionary. The congress charged the Executive with the task of drawing the best and genuinely Communist forces out of the USPD and unifying them with the Spartacus League.[11]

We received similar tasks regarding other countries.

Comrades, looking back today, after a year of activity, to the Second Congress decisions, we must ask who was correct in the issues disputed with our friends on the left and our enemies on the right.? Consider the question of British Communists' participation in the Labour Party. As you know, the Labour Party itself decided, on the initiative of the Hendersons and MacDonalds, not to admit our comrades to the Labour Party.[12] In my opinion, that is the surest

---

9. The USPD was not part of a national governmental coalition during the Third Congress. It did join with the SPD in certain state governments.
10. For the Twenty-One Points, see p. 64, n. 6.
11. At the time of the USPD's Halle Congress in 1920, the KPD (referred to here as the Spartacus League) had some 80,000 members, while the USPD numbered around 800,000.
12. Following the formation of the Communist Party of Great Britain in August 1920 the party immediately sought affiliation to the Labour Party. This was rejected

indication that it was we who were right, and not the British comrades who feared that they would lose their Communist innocence if they entered the Labour Party. The opportunists sensed the danger at once. They noticed that when Communists organised within the Labour Party and sought to exert influence within it, this represented a great danger to them. Serrati, of whom we will have much to say, was with the lefts on this question. He said then, 'How can we join a Labour Party?' Now he writes, 'See how inconsistent the Communist International is. In Italy it demands that Turati be expelled, and in Britain it insists that Communists go into the Labour Party.' Serrati is by no means so innocent a child as to be incapable of perceiving here that there is a minor difference. He has tried deliberately to mislead the Italian workers. I believe the British comrades will now admit that it was not they but the Second Congress that was right in this matter when it said: Not out of the Labour Party, but into it, in order to struggle for communism and expose the traitorous leaders from the inside. (*Applause*)

As for *parliamentarism*, we did not achieve any great success during the past year, and that must be stated frankly. All the splits have revealed that the most vacillating, moderate, and worst elements are to be found in the parliamentary fractions. We have seen that in France, Italy, Germany, and also Switzerland. That was the situation wherever there were splits during the past year.

And if you ask me which of the Twenty-One Conditions was carried out the worst this year, I must say it was the condition *that the parliamentary fraction be completely subordinated to the party and that it carry out genuinely revolutionary parliamentary activity*. Although we did not yet achieve much in this field during the past year, I nevertheless still believe that it will now be quite clear to every comrade that the majority at the Second Congress was correct here. We were still able in this way to achieve closer ties with the masses. Revolutionary parliamentarism has brought us initial successes in several countries, and we will press the Third Congress to do everything necessary to drive our party forward in this area.

So, comrades, *what was the legacy, the slogan that the Executive received from the Second Congress?* The slogan was that the British and American comrades, indeed comrades in all countries where communism was still weak but where there was a massive workers' movement and working class, must come into contact with the masses and establish firm links with them. We had to do

---

by the Labour Party's National Executive Committee on the grounds that the CP's stance was inconsistent with Labour's goal of 'the achievement of the political, social and economic emancipation of the people by means of Parliamentary Democracy'. Many CP members joined as individuals.

everything possible so they would not remain on the sidelines and become a sect, but would rather take part in the mass movement.

Our other task was this: Given that belonging to the Communist International was in fashion, the Executive had to do everything possible to *denounce these super-intelligent diplomats in the centrist camp*, draw the best forces away from them, and win them for the Communist movement. These were the great tasks – political and also, quite significantly, organisational – that the Second Congress passed on to us. Today we must judge to what degree the Executive has fulfilled these tasks.

As events unfolded during the last year, the convention of the *German Independents* in Halle was the most important milestone. However, for the Communist International, it was not so much the German but the Italian question that was politically decisive. This was true not only with regard to the difficulties we had to overcome but also because we saw here the first indications of a degree of crisis in the Communist International. I will therefore deal at length with the *Italian question*.

As I said earlier, when the Italian delegation came to Moscow, communications were still so poor that we did not know that those who came were reformists. At that time, we had *full confidence in Serrati* and also in those he brought with him. Our view at the time was that these forces were not entirely clear on the issues, but that they were honest in their intentions toward the proletarian revolution. And here we experienced a bitter disappointment. It is only now that the proceedings of the Second Congress have appeared in German, unfortunately only after much delay.[13] I hope that the technical apparatus will now function better, so that we will have the proceedings of the Third Congress after about a month. At least the German comrades will now be able to read the proceedings of the Second Congress. Anyone reading these proceedings today and considering the stance of Serrati and the Italian comrades must ask how we could still have any illusions, how could we still hope to win over Serrati?

The proceedings include a list that indicates how often the speakers took the floor. Serrati spoke four times on matters of principle: on the national question, the agrarian question, the Twenty-One Conditions, and the Communist International's basic tasks. As you see, all four of these topics figure among the most important issues before the congress. On all four of these topics Serrati made a statement indicating that he was opposed or would abstain on the vote. He would take ten minutes to relate anecdotes, but the content of

---

13. An abridged German-language edition of the Second Congress proceedings, Comintern 1920, *Der Zweite Kongress der Kommunistischen Internationale*, was published shortly after the congress in July–August 1920. A more complete edition under the same title appeared the following year; see Comintern 1921f.

his remarks on these four decisive issues was hostile to the congress. We considered at the time that it was perhaps merely a matter of misunderstandings, and we did all that we could to convince him. The course of events showed us that we had been sorely mistaken.

We had to put out a special book on the Italian Socialist Party's relations with the Communist International.[14] The book consists in the main of articles, statements, and resolutions by Serrati himself. That is what makes the book important. We are very sorry that we must discuss these matters today *in the absence of representatives of the Italian Socialist Party*. We did everything possible to bring them here. We issued our invitation to them three and a half months ago and asked them to come here on time. When the first group of Italian comrades arrived in Moscow two weeks ago, we once again sent off a telegram asking them to come on time. Members of that party have not yet arrived, although three weeks have passed since 1 June, the original date on which the congress was to open, and about a thousand delegates have arrived from every conceivable country. That means that *the Italian comrades do not want to come*. I am therefore compelled to try to explain the Italian problem in the absence of representatives of the Italian Socialist Party.[15]

The first article that Serrati published in *Avanti*, immediately after his return, consists simply of an attempt to *discredit the Communist International congress*.[16] I will have to read many quotations, and I ask those present to be patient. But in my view the Italian question has been decisive in the Executive's activity over the past year. So Serrati writes in this, his first article:

> The Second Congress began in conditions where most delegates came to Russia before the Twenty-One Conditions had been made known in their countries, and their mandates were therefore only general and personal in character.

That is Serrati's first point and *his first untruth*. He then continues, second:

> Many points on the agenda were not examined ahead of time in the individual parties, which were unfamiliar with some far from unimportant issues.

---

14. See Comintern 1921b, *Le parti socialiste italien et l'Internationale: recueil de documents*.

15. The PSI delegation to the Third Congress, consisting of Costantino Lazzari, Fabrizio Maffi, and Ezio Riboldi, arrived in time for the seventh session two days later.

16. The article by Serrati that Zinoviev quotes from, 'Il secondo congresso della Terza Internazionale: Alcune osservazioni preliminari', was published in issue 24 of the PSI publication *Comunismo*, not in *Avanti*. A comparison with the printed Russian translation of Serrati's article (Comintern 1921a) shows Zinoviev's quotations to be accurate although somewhat abridged.

I must explain that a comparison of preparations for the Second and Third Congresses will show that those for the Second Congress were far more carefully done than for the Third. The theses were ready weeks in advance, and we had carried out sweeping discussions with the USPD on all significant issues months earlier. So the second sentence is *the second untruth*. Third:

> The site of the congress was far distant from countries with a proletarian movement. Communications were difficult, given the very protracted blockade. There was almost no supervision by workers, who ought to have been present, and by the press, which could have reported promptly to a broad public. All these circumstances gave to the sessions the character of closed meetings, lacking any connection with the outside world.

Serrati wrote this only a few days after the congress, a few days after he had taken his place in the congress Presidium. No supervision by workers or the press. It was a secret conspiracy. Fourth:

> Delegates at the congress did not know each other well...

True, at least we did not know Serrati well.

> ...They were not familiar with the movements, with the forces actually represented by this or that delegate, with the resources at their disposal. We did not know what influence they held in international politics.

It's obvious that this statement by Serrati also does not correspond to reality. Fifth:

> The congress met *under the protection* of a great revolutionary government...

Was this perhaps not to Serrati's liking?

> ...at the very moment when its armed forces were engaged in a life-and-death struggle with the forces of reaction, and when the Communist government was required – as it is to this day – to carry out both defence and offense against international and national capitalism.

Here is where Serrati begins his *vile insinuations*. The fifth point continues:

> Policies that assist the Soviet republic will indisputably be of assistance to the proletariat as a whole, but they may not correspond to the tactical needs of a country that is undergoing a critical period of its own still latent revolution.

I suggest to the comrades of the KAPD that they might be interested in Serrati's fifth point here, because on this topic Serrati anticipated the views of leftists from the KAPD who are now publishing the writings of Herman Gorter. Sixth:

> There was an obvious discrepancy in the qualities of different delegates, to a greater degree than ever before at an international congress. This was a significant cause of very understandable difficulties, vacillations, and concessions during the discussion.

Understand that if you can, and if you care to. For my part, I do not understand what this is supposed to mean. 'Discrepancy in qualities at an international Communist congress': I think he is trying to say the same thing as Crispien, 'What kind of Communists are these?' Seventh:

> The votes allocated to each country did not correspond to the real and genuine importance of the different parties, in political and moral terms, but rather to the capitalist importance of the countries they represented. Thus France received the same number of votes as Italy, even though the French delegates represented only an entirely insignificant minority both of the party and the [trade-union] confederation.

Serrati leaves no stone unturned in discrediting the Second Congress. Then, eighth:

> The remoteness of the congress site and the difficulties of communication obstructed the reporting of its decisions to an even greater degree than during its preparation. It is sufficient to note that two months after the congress, some parties have not yet been able to receive a single report on it, since the final text of the decisions taken there were only made known more than a month after the congress closed.

And so on, and so on. As we see, no more than a few weeks after the Second Congress closed, in September 1920, Serrati was already doing everything in his power – and beyond his power – to diminish the congress in the eyes of Italian proletarians and to present matters as if the congress had been neither communist nor international. Unfortunately, we ourselves were then insufficiently cautious, and we still cherished the hope that Serrati was someone whom the Communist International wanted.

Given conditions in Italy, Serrati had to make the best of a bad situation. Regarding the Twenty-One Conditions, he said, as he had to say, that he was for them. In the article I have quoted, he states:

> We accept the Twenty-One Conditions, even though they have been presented to Socialists internationally in much too harsh a form. However, we set two conditions.
>
> 1.) First, no unnecessary concessions should be made to those who were infected by the nationalist fever during the War and most disgracefully betrayed the proletariat, but now declare, in the same shameful fashion,

that they submit to the harsh discipline prescribed by Moscow. Tomorrow they will betray us again. Along the road the proletariat is travelling we meet far too many Pauls to be able to believe they are all truly honest.[17] True, a moral verdict on a person's past actions in revolutionary struggle is not all so important. Nonetheless, there is a political criterion that must be applied to the immorality of certain transformations, and the proletariat must apply it without fail, in order not to breed traitors in its own ranks.

2.) Parties belonging to the Communist International must preserve the right to carry out, on their own responsibility, the actions necessary to cleanse their ranks, in order to avoid damaging in any way the unity of the proletarian movement and of the revolution that is believed in Moscow to be so close.

Thus Serrati, draping himself in the toga of a man of the left and a revolutionary, declares as his first condition that we should be *more stringent toward the right, especially the French comrades*. Overall, Serrati seems to have some special hatred for the French comrades. I have no idea why. He has attempted to portray himself to Italian workers as a pillar of orthodoxy, demanding stern measures against the Right. To this end, he proposed a twenty-second condition. He said that a twenty-second condition was adopted *against the Freemasons*. But although this condition was adopted, he said, Zinoviev stuck it in his pocket, and it no longer existed. That is the kind of fairy tale that Serrati is peddling around Italy in all earnest. What is the story with these Freemasons? There was a motion of the Italian comrades. We regarded it as obvious that the motion should be adopted, but we said that it was impossible for the Communist International to print such a motion. And Serrati, in all seriousness, is presenting the matter to the Italian working class so as to suggest that I am probably a Freemason and the majority [of delegates] are also inclined in that direction.[18]

The second condition set by Serrati is posed in an indistinct manner. There is to be a *cleansing*, but in such a way as not to injure the unity of the proletarian movement. Later he found other formulations, such as 'cleansing but with autonomy', which means that the cleansing should be left in the hands of the party in question. The Italian party's Central Committee held thorough

---

17. The reference is to the biblical story of the Apostle Paul's conversion on the road to Damascus.

18. Serrati's motion stated: 'Parties belonging to the Communist International are urged to expel from their ranks members of the Freemasons, which is a petty-bourgeois organisation.' Riddell (ed.) 1991, 2WC, 1, p. 308.
The Comintern's Fourth Congress in 1922 was to adopt a resolution barring Freemasons from membership in Communist parties. See 'Political Resolution on the French Question,' in Riddell (ed.) 2011b, 4WC, pp. 1128–30.

discussions on these issues. Two resolutions were presented there, one by Comrade Terracini and the other by Comrade Baratono, a friend of Serrati. Terracini demanded unconditional acceptance of the Twenty-One Conditions. Baratono demanded their acceptance, but the party must reserve the right to interpret them. The Central Committee voted, and Comrade Terracini received a majority; Serrati was defeated.

In order to intimidate people, Serrati had stated that he would resign as editor of *Avanti*. Our Italian comrades, instead of greeting this resignation with enthusiasm, said that this was unacceptable and Serrati must stay put. Our comrades have now learned their lesson, on their own, and we do not want to rub salt in their wounds. But they did make the error and left Serrati in his position as editor, under the condition, of course, that he carry out the decisions of the Central Committee. Serrati retained editorship of *Avanti*, a large and influential newspaper with a circulation of two hundred thousand copies, but he did everything other than carry out the decisions of the Central Committee. He began to conduct an *unprecedented polemic against the Executive, which gradually developed into a vicious polemic*. Later, I will read you the most significant passages.

Then came the reformists' convention in Reggio Emilia, where they united in a 'Concentration Faction'.[19] They concentrated themselves. Turati and D'Aragona took part in the conference. These are clever people, and they are aware that you cannot tell the Italian workers flat out that you are against the Communist International. Their resolution therefore says the following:

> The differences in assessment of the current historical period are insufficient to justify a split in the party. There have always been different schools of socialist thought in the party. Their coexistence was never, in the past, an obstacle to its powerful development and will not, in the future, obstruct fraternal common work. This work will be all the more fruitful to the degree that different sectors of the party hold each other in mutual respect and display a common will to maintain freedom of opinion, whatever the situation, while observing stringent discipline in the manifold forms of development of the class struggle.[20]

---

19. The reformist wing of the Italian Socialist Party, the Socialist Concentration faction, held a conference in Reggio Emilia, Italy, on 10–11 October 1920.

20. The resolution proposed by Socialist Concentration leaders Gino Baldesi and D'Aragona concerning the PSI's ties to the Comintern ('La concentrazione socialista in cerca di un programma') was published in *Avanti*, 12 October 1920.

This is the summit of reformist diplomacy, in which Turati, Treves, and D'Aragona are past masters. They will make outstanding government ministers. What did they do? They passed the following motion:

> The Concentration Faction approves the party's affiliation to the Communist International, as well as a consistent application of the Twenty-One Points in keeping with conditions in each country. It declares categorically that anarchist and syndicalist groups and the forces of Freemasonry must be excluded from sections of the International.

They thus simply repeated what Serrati had whispered in their ear. They are for carrying out the Twenty-One Points, but the Twenty-One Points aligned with conditions in the country; for a united party, but against the syndicalists and anarchists. But our Communist comrades were derided by them as syndicalists and Freemasons. That cost them little.

The decision of the Concentration Faction could not avoid saying something about the dictatorship of the proletariat. Here is what they said: 'The dictatorship of the proletariat, understood in a Marxist sense…' – Turati and D'Aragona, parading as interpreters of Marxism – '…is not an obligatory programmatic demand but a transitory measure rendered necessary by special circumstances.'

They are crafty. They say they do not oppose 'the dictatorship of the proletariat, understood in a Marxist sense'. It is quite true that the dictatorship is not eternal but rather a temporary necessity. But they look at matters as if the dictatorship were liquidated entirely. They therefore assert that if revolution in Italy is carried out forcibly and destructively, and if the soviet order as in Russia is introduced immediately, as the extremist forces propose, this will lead rapidly to its collapse, unless it receives active economic and political support from the proletariat of some more developed state during the unavoidable time of economic collapse.

Here you see the teachings of these reformist gentlemen: *they do not want the revolution in Italy to take a violent and destructive form.* They are also against immediate establishment of a soviet government on the Russian model. Well, actually a soviet government on an Italian model would have been just fine. (*Laughter*)

This short declaration was made together with the long-winded resolution on Freemasonry.

So much for the credo of the reformist group in Reggio Emilia. That is the true face of the group, under a magnifying glass. We had to take action here and expel these elements. The whole quarrel concerned only this group, which is against the dictatorship of the proletariat and against revolution and against the soviet order 'on the Russian model'. After all these declarations, Serrati had the effrontery to say that there are no reformists in Italy. He wants to expel the reformists, wants it even more than us, but someone should please tell him who these reformists are. Poor Serrati has no idea where to find reformists in Italy.

As you recall, Comrade Lenin sent Serrati an open letter that included, of course, the demand for expulsion of the reformists. Serrati responded with an article entitled, 'Reply of an Italian Communist to Comrade Lenin'.[21] In this article we read:

> 'Can reformists be tolerated in the ranks of the party?' Permit me to respond to this question with another question, 'Who is a reformist?' If, as your letter indicates, reformists are those who strive for class collaboration, who wish to share power with the bourgeoisie, who engage in counterrevolutionary activities, and who might at any moment transform themselves into the Scheidemanns and Noskes of our country, then you are quite right, and I join you in favouring their expulsion.

Serrati then seeks to demonstrate that Turati, Treves, and company are not reformists. He says:

> These are people who two months ago were asked by one of your government's representatives in Italy, Vodovosov, to exert pressure on Giolitti on behalf of the parliamentary fraction in order to obtain concessions.

That is Serrati's method. When you talk of principled questions, he responds with petty gossip about money for the *Daily Herald*, and so on. But he does not tell us plainly whether he is with the reformists or against them.

In an article in *Avanti* on 24 October, Serrati states:

> What are we supposed to do? There are only two possible paths: Either achieve power by legal means or make the revolution. Achieve power in whose interests? And how? And why? Given the present devastation, the only result of taking power would be to transfer the responsibility now weighing on the bourgeoisie to the Socialist Party.[22]

---

21. Lenin's article was published in the 10 December 1920 issue of *Avanti* under the title 'La lotta delle tendenze del Partito Socialista Italiano'. It appeared originally in *Pravda*, 7 November 1920, and can be found as part of 'On the Struggle of the Italian Socialist Party' in *LCW*, 31, pp. 377–91.

Serrati's reply appeared in *Avanti*, 11 December 1920, under the title 'Risposta di un comunista unitaro al compagno Lenin'.

22. 'Il dovere dell'ora presente', in *Avanti*, 24 October 1920.

That was written in October 1920. What kind of statement is that? It is just the same as what Dittmann and Crispien said: We are afraid to take power, even if we could, because we do not want to take responsibility for the economic devastation caused by the War. The only possible conclusion is simply this: We must wait until the economy improves, until we have helped capitalism become strong once again, and only then can we make the revolution. Previously it was only Kautsky who said this. His position is that first we must increase production, and the struggle for power comes later; otherwise it can only be a consumer socialism. And Serrati, the 'communist', advances this Kautskian viewpoint quite openly in October 1920.

Comrades, this is actually the crux of the matter. During the Second Congress, there was general agreement that Italy was closest to proletarian revolution. Serrati too had to concede that. But if there is an example anywhere in history where a party has missed a situation and thus directly damaged the movement, it is the example of Italy. It is an incredible error for a party to have missed a situation the way this happened in Italy.

A year ago, the Italian working class was enthusiastic, prepared to struggle, and better organised than anywhere else. The bourgeoisie was dejected. Both the soldiers and the peasantry, in great number, were sympathetic to the proletariat. Then came the magnificent movement in September, in which the Italian workers discovered a new form of struggle by occupying the factories.[23] The bourgeoisie was completely disorganised. Giolitti himself said that in September there was nothing he could do. When he was asked, why did you not send in the army in September in order to clean out the factories, he responded: It was not in my power to do that. I had to start by utilising homeopathic remedies; only later could I resort to surgery. With the help of Serrati and his comrades, he first suppressed the movement with homeopathy, and now he has switched over to surgery. The Fascists are excellent surgeons. They are butchering the Italian working class very conscientiously and thoroughly.

The party, and especially Serrati, are to blame for having allowed a favourable conjuncture in the struggle to pass them by, objectively delivering the working class over to the bourgeoisie. The bourgeoisie was granted a year of time in which to recover its health, organise itself well, and make the transition from homeopathy to surgery. During this time, the working class was corrupted and broken apart.

---

23. For the September 1920 occupation of the factories in Italy, see p. 76, n. 14.

Then came *the Italian congress* [in Livorno].[24] Comrades, as you know, the Executive tried to send Bukharin and me to the congress. We did not receive visas, and the Italian party – Serrati in particular – did not lift a finger to facilitate our presence at the congress. We had to reorganise the delegation, with the Bulgarian comrade Kabakchiev and the Hungarian comrade Rákosi as our representatives. A great deal of gossip and nonsense has been written in the international press about the actions of these two comrades. It was Serrati who started this; that is his method. There are good comrades who believe Livorno would perhaps have turned out much differently if Kabakchiev and Rákosi had acted more shrewdly and diplomatically. An attempt has been make to portray Kabakchiev as a fierce dictator. Anyone acquainted with him knows that is pure invention. He is one of the most cultured Marxists, a very quiet comrade who is not swept away by passions in the manner depicted by Serrati. He is a comrade who worked for many years in the Bulgarian party as a theoretician. There is nothing but good to be said of him.

Comrades who were in Livorno will themselves relate what happened there. It is no exaggeration to say that the congress was turned into a circus. When Comrade Kabakchiev took the floor, there was an uproar, with shouts, 'Long live the pope!' Someone released a dove, and there were various displays of outrageous chauvinism. And after all that, they say that Comrade Kabakchiev was to blame.

After all of Serrati's statements in September and October, no one here can have any further doubt. What's at issue here is not what was said by Comrade Kabakchiev. Rather what we have is the *degeneration of a left revolutionary party, or at least of its leading layers, into a simple, ordinary Social-Democratic party*. That is what we see in Italy: a degeneration under the pressure of a whole number of factors, a degeneration of the leadership into simple Social Democrats. I must say that in Halle, the right-wing Independents – and I owe it to them to say this – conducted themselves far more properly toward the Communists than Serrati and his people did in Livorno.[25]

Serrati and his group came to the congress with their own special resolution. He proposed that the party take the name *Socialist-Communist Party*, that it adopt the Twenty-One Conditions, but that it keep its hands free. There was no mention of any split. Turati was the only one to make a principled speech, and he received an ovation.[26] Turati is actually the leading figure in the party. He said quite frankly that he was against the use of force and that everything

---

24. For the Italian Socialist Party congress at Livorno, see p. 64, n. 7.
25. For the Halle Congress of the USPD in Germany, see p. 204, n. 42.
26. Turati's speech can be found in PSI 1962, pp. 319–35.

should be done by peaceful means. Yet people are trying to shove the blame for the split onto the Executive.

What alternative was there for the Executive? Surely it is quite clear. It was *the first collision between the Communist International and the reformist forces*, the first test of strength. If the Communist International had given way in this situation, at that moment – I must say frankly – we would no longer have had a Communist International, we would have lost all moral and political authority. If we had given way on this point, it would have meant that the Communist International had got down on its knees before Turati and the other reformists. It would have perished, or, if it continued to exist with large parties in its ranks, it would have been morally defunct. It was the first test of strength, and we emphasise that the Communist International must be proud that at this moment it did not waver, but rather said firmly and decisively that even if we lose a large number of Italian workers for a period of time, that cannot be avoided, and we will win them back again. But *not a step, not a single step backwards*, for otherwise the Communist International is lost. What was at stake was the clarity of the Communist International and the principles of communism. And we are indeed sorry that some groups of leaders, such as a segment of the German comrades who had otherwise provided great services, did not perceive clearly at the time what was at stake. But by and large the Communist International, as an international association of the working class, grasped very quickly that what we were shedding was a major illusion. We were absorbing a loss, but we had to hold firm all the way, for the sake of the principles of communism.

Serrati began to sing in a different key. Before it was the hard line, demanding no concessions to the Freemasons. Now it was different. Serrati came up with a theory about equal rights, demanding equality between Italy and France. Why have more concessions been made to the French comrades than to the Italian comrades? I will take up the French party later. It was our bounden duty to deal with each party according to the specific conditions of the relevant country, considering the history of the workers' movement, the degree of revolutionary maturity, and so on. We could not deal with the French, American, Italian, Latvian, and Czechoslovak parties according to a formula.

The internationalism of our Executive consists of basing our judgements of every party on the specific circumstances and defining our attitude on that basis. Our approach to the French party was developed accordingly. It is quite clear that a genuine Communist cannot come and say: Because the French party is still backward, you must treat the Italian party that way too, so that it too will be backward. That is not internationalism.

Serrati initiated a quite personal and sordid campaign against us. Thus, in an article printed on 24 December, he wrote the following, and I quote:

> If it is not out of place to take up Amsterdam, we would like to ask Zinoviev why the Russian government, so irreconcilably opposed to opportunists, gave £72,000 – as all Europe knows – to the *Daily Herald*, which supports the policies of opportunist socialism in Britain. And why did the Communist International take a stand that Communists should join the Labour Party, which belongs to the Second and Amsterdam Internationals?

Comrades, this quotation alone will be enough to demonstrate to every genuine revolutionary comrade what kind of person appears before the forum of the Communist International. We say that Turati and D'Aragona are reformists and we had to expel them. That was decided by the Second Congress.

Serrati goes on to say that Chicherin and his government paid £72,000 to the *Daily Herald*, a claim – first made by Lloyd George – that was used as the pretext to expel our comrade Kamenev from Britain.[27] Serrati simply makes a denunciation. The Communist International is well aware that the Russian government must negotiate with various individuals and forces. The International also knows why such dealings are necessary: simply because the working class in all these countries is still too weak. We, the only proletarian government in the world, must still negotiate with bourgeois governments. But what connection is there between this fact and the question whether Turati and other reformists have to be expelled from the party?

As I have already said, Serrati nurses a particular hatred for the French section. In one article, 'A Few Other Considerations', which appeared in *Avanti* in January 1921, he writes:

> In France, for example, the majority of the Socialist parliamentary deputies, who only yesterday were for the 'fatherland' and the 'sacred union', went over en bloc to the Communist International.[28]

And, in another article, he said that fifty-five deputies had gone over to the Communist Party. That is a flagrant lie. There were sixty-seven deputies in the Socialist fraction, of which only twelve or thirteen went over to the Communist Party, while fifty-five stayed with Longuet, that is, with Serrati's friends. He is deceiving the Italian working class, utilising his post in *Avanti*

---

27. Lev Kamenev, who was heading a Soviet delegation to Britain, was ordered to leave the country on 10 September 1920 on charges of having used the sale of Russian crown jewels to give £72,000 to the *Daily Herald*, a Labour Party newspaper.

28. Serrati's article, 'Di alcuni altre nostre raggioni' was published in *Avanti* 1 January 1921. The term 'sacred union' (*l'union sacrée*) is a reference to the class-collaborationist policy of the majority of the French SP and CGT during the War.

to tell a lie. He says that fifty-five deputies came over to us. If that were the case, it would be very good. But it is one of Serrati's *impudent falsehoods*.

The same goes for the German party. Serrati says, in one of his articles, 'The split of the Independents in Germany is to be explained more by national factors than by those of international doctrine and practice'. So the split in which half the party went over to communism took place for national reasons? What is that supposed to mean? That is *chauvinism, plain and simple*. He is trying to persuade Italian workers that the German workers belong to the International for national reasons, not international ones. That amounts to *baiting the German working class*. These are the tools Serrati uses to work against the Executive and against the most important section of our International. Further, Serrati writes – and permit me to quote:

> As for anonymous sources of information, a few comments are in order. The Executive of the Communist International sends representatives from Moscow to every country, chosen from among the Russian comrades and known to the Russian comrades on the Executive. Whether a representative has the qualities needed for such a mission, and whether he can carry out the work in an appropriate way – this is up to the Executive alone. And such an *éminence grise* sends reports to the Executive that are entirely unknown – or may be unknown – to the party leadership in the country where the supplier of this information is active. This flow of information is subject to no criticism, no supervision.[29]

Comrades, as I demonstrated earlier, Serrati is Levi's forerunner. Serrati coined the term, *éminence grise*, and Levi, the word Turkestaner.[30] I believe

---

29. From 'Di alcuni altre nostre raggioni', *Avanti*, 1 January 1921.
30. 'Turkestaner' was a term used mockingly by Paul Levi in his pamphlet *Unser Weg* to refer to Béla Kun, one of the ECCI's envoys to Germany during the March Action. Later in the congress, Karl Radek uses the term ironically as a synonym for ECCI emissary (p. 584).

The origin of the term is unclear. According to some accounts, based on Victor Serge's *Memoirs of a Revolutionary* (Serge 2012, p. 164), it refers to Lenin's exile of Kun to Turkestan as punishment for atrocities committed by Kun during the Soviet conquest of Crimea in 1920. This explanation is effectively refuted by György Borsányi. Anti-Soviet exiles and the capitalist press did claim Kun to be responsible for reprisals in Crimea, but without convincing evidence. They habitually blamed 'foreigners and Jews' for alleged Soviet misdeeds, and Kun was the most prominent potential target, Borsányi notes. (Borsányi 1993).

Jean-François Fayet, who drew on the Serge account in his biography of Radek, now believes the epithet 'Turkestani' was current in Comintern parties before the March Action, as does David Fernbach (communications to the editor; compare Fayet 2004, p. 368 and Fernbach (ed.) 2011, p. 18). Fayet recently wrote that '[i]n several parties, acerbic comments were [then] increasingly to be heard regarding "Turkestanis" or

I may say that the air in this room is somewhat fresher because these two gentlemen are not present with us this year. (*Applause*)

Comrades, I could present many more quotations, but you have the book, and in addition, I believe the examples I have read out are fully sufficient. I would like merely to read the resolution by Bentivoglio that was adopted in Livorno after our comrades left. It reads:

> The Seventeenth Congress of the Italian Socialist Party has discussed and confirmed the resolutions on the basis of which it joined the Communist International and has endorsed its basic methods without any reservation. Nevertheless, the congress protests the statement of the Executive Committee representative, which declares it to be expelled on the basis of a difference regarding the judgement of local and incidental issues. Such issues could and must be resolved through amicable statements and fraternal agreements. Reaffirming fully the party's affiliation to the Communist International, the congress refers the dispute to the upcoming congress of the Communist International, to be dealt with there. The party commits itself now, in advance, to accept the decision of the congress and to carry it out.[31]

Comrades, in formal terms, here is the situation: after the Communists left, Serrati's party adopted this decision. It appeals to our Third Congress and declares in advance that it will accept our decision. That is the resolution it adopted unanimously. And what happened then? Several months went by, during which Serrati did not show any intention of accepting congress decisions, but rather, through various machinations, managed to ensure that the party has no delegates here. I ask you comrades who have seats in the French or some other parliament to help me find a parliamentary expression for this conduct. Serrati and his friends decide, after the Communists have left, that they will accept the decision of the congress. And when the congress meets, there are no delegates here. It is obvious to any thinking person that they are unwilling to submit. After the resolution was adopted, Serrati stated, and I quote:

> It is quite possible that the statements (of the Executive representative) were composed in Livorno; nonetheless, the Communist International will never *repudiate* them. In addition, Levi told me yesterday that they in Germany are

---

"Moscow's leather boots"; shadowy figures allegedly conspiring behind the backs of national party leaderships in the executive's name'. (Fayet 2008, p. 113)

According to Stefan Weber, Levi, in using the epithet, based himself on Kun's dark complexion (Weber 1991, p. 72).

For Kun's own comment on the term, see his speech in Appendix 3f, p. 1125.

31. The Bentivoglio motion can be found in PSI 1962, p. 417.

also being treated without respect. It is enough to note that the KAPD, which has a nationalist orientation and supported the Kapp-Lüttwitz Putsch, has been accepted into the Communist International as a sympathising party.[32]

That's the kind of thing you find in *Avanti*. And that's continued right up until the convening of this congress. That's the formal side of the question.

Comrades, we must be clear about the situation. Since the Livorno Congress, the party has degenerated even more. Here is some evidence. In the *Avanti* of 11 May there is an article entitled, 'International Solidarity'. It is full of enthusiasm and internationalist feelings. Why? An organisation sent fifty thousand lire to the trade unions. Certainly a fact that could have international significance. But what organisation sent the money? The Amsterdam trade-union International.[33] And that gives rise to an enthusiastic article, which states:

> The Amsterdam International Federation of Trade Unions, which has sent us the expression of solidarity and sympathy announced here, is not entirely in agreement with us regarding the necessary requirements of the proletarian movement. Some of its leaders are, in fact, far removed from our political ideas. If this were the moment for a personal polemic, we could reproach several of them regarding the solidarity they expressed during the War for those who today are the most outspoken representatives of capitalist reaction, both here and in other countries.
>
> But we do not wish to diminish the importance of this internationalist gesture, which moves us deeply. Regardless of the names of those who stand at the head of the Amsterdam secretariat, it is indisputable that the international proletariat united under its banner, many millions strong, is bound by common interests with the oppressed of the entire world. And we are bound to it and to them by the same ties. And there can be no doubt that every honest and sincere expression of internationalism speeds on the proletarian unification of workers of every country.[34]

Comrades, as you know, every vulgarian, every revisionist, every centrist is constantly shouting about Moscow gold, although it is quite natural for the victorious working class of Russia to provide help to workers in other

---

32. The quote is from an abbreviated account of remarks by Serrati at the Livorno Congress, published in the 22 January 1921 issue of *Avanti*. A more detailed version can be found in PSI 1962, pp. 417–18.

33. Fifty thousand lire were given by the Amsterdam International to the CGL under the guise of helping its struggle against Fascist reaction.
In July 1921, one lira exchanged for approximately US$0.05.

34. 'Solidarietà internazionale' (unsigned), in *Avanti*, 11 May 1921.

countries, and that is generally understood. But when the Amsterdam trade-union federation, which has relations with the League of Nations through its International Labour Office headed by [Albert] Thomas, sends the Italian Serratis fifty thousand lire, they tell us that it is no disgrace to accept the money and write about it. And Serrati does not notice that by doing this he dirties his hands. He does not consider the money he has taken from these traitors to be a red-hot coal. He writes about international solidarity. As you see, truly the dead ride swiftly,[35] and this man who is dead for the Communist International has excelled himself in this regard.

I have here a booklet entitled, *Il Bolscevismo: guidicato dai socialisti italiani* [The Italian Socialists Assess Bolshevism], written by a bourgeois.[36] This booklet was distributed even more broadly than the one by Levi. It consists of quotations by the gentlemen who Serrati brought here and whom we welcomed so hospitably. They have pulled together everything that happened and that didn't happen in order to show how terrible things are when the working class is in power.

I would like to give you a bit more information, comrades, on recent developments, for example the elections. In *Sowjet*, a publication edited by Paul Levi which still enjoys the collaboration of several members of the VKPD, there is an article by Comrade Curt Geyer on the Italian elections. According to him, the election results are as follows: Serrati's party obtained 1.4 million votes, and the Communist Party about 450,000 – which he says means that the masses are with Serrati and this is an obvious defeat for the Communist International. Indeed he asserts that the setback of Italian Communists is a defeat not only for communism but for Zinoviev and the Executive.[37]

So when a new party gets 450,000 votes, this is a defeat. On the contrary, when Scheidemann, after he and his gang had murdered Rosa Luxemburg and Karl Liebknecht, still received millions of votes, that was a genuine and painful defeat for the working class. (*Loud applause*) It shows that many workers and petty bourgeois still vote for these murderers.[38] But where is the defeat in Italy?

---

35. The expression is from Gottfried August Bürger's ballad, *Lenore*.
36. See *Bolscevismo* 1921.
37. Curt Geyer's article, 'Über den italienischen Wahlkampf', was published in *Sowjet*, 3 (1 June 1921).
38. The German elections of 19 January 1919 – the first held after the fall of the Hohenzollern monarchy – took place four days after the murders of Rosa Luxemburg and Karl Liebknecht. The SPD received 37.9 per cent of the vote, almost double the total of any other party.

Here is an article from *Le Populaire* [*de Paris*] of 4 June, written by Cesare Alessandri. He is an Italian deputy who appears to be close to Serrati. He writes about the elections – and I will report only the figures:

> The new Socialist Party parliamentary group consists of 123 deputies, of which three are not party members; they were elected as a protest against their jailing. So of 120 Socialist deputies, 48 belong to the Right, 42 to the Left, and 30 to the Centre.[39]

So Cesare Alessandri, a friend of Serrati, says that the new group consists of 120 deputies, of which 48 are with the Right, 42 with the Left, and 30 in the Centre. You have to consider, comrades, what it means in Italy when Cesare Alessandri refers to the 'Right'. It means simply Scheidemann-Noske. Supposedly, Alessandri is on the Right, and on the Left are Lazzari, Maffi, and others who could not or did not want to come here. Lazzari, who during the War was an outspoken pacifist, like Bernstein, is on the Left. On the Right is someone like Dugoni. Yesterday, I was given a newspaper reporting on a trade-union congress in Mantua, where this man made a speech and got a resolution adopted that reads as follows:

> Having examined the situation that recent events have created for the trade-union and cooperative movement, this congress protests any violence, wherever it comes from.

So, at a trade-union congress, Serrati's friend introduces a resolution in which the congress protests against any use of violence, regardless of whether it comes from the bourgeoisie or the proletariat. So here we have an entirely neutral point of view.

That is the situation. I want to read you one more quotation. Serrati is still for a coalition with the bourgeoisie, for collaboration with it – that goes without saying. During the electoral campaign,[40] Turati himself wrote an appeal to workers in the chemical industry, which was printed in the French paper *La Vie ouvrière*. In this manifesto, Turati says:

> Do not give way, brothers. Do not accept defeat. Do not strike out wildly. I pledge to you that violence will bring no gains to those who use it. When the tempest has passed, you will be the stronger. Do not be provoked; provide them with no pretext. Do not respond to their curses. Be good; be patient; be holy. You have been so for a thousand years; continue on this

---

39. Cesare Alessandri, 'Lettre d'Italie. Le Parti socialiste ne change pas sa politique', in *Le Populaire de Paris*, 4 June 1921.
40. An apparent reference to the November 1920 elections to the Italian Chamber of Deputies.

course. Be tolerant, good-natured, and also forgiving. The less you think of revenge, the more will you be revenged. Those who have deployed terror against you will tremble at what they have done. The war remains, it refuses to die, it persists in its hateful existence, and yet it is in its death agony. You, peasants of Italy, represent work and peace. You are, therefore, the enemy, but you also represent the victory that is certain; you are the future.

To that, Comrade Frossard commented simply, 'As you can see, these people are the most obvious and unambiguous reformists.' That is certainly the least that one can say. It is with such electoral manifestos that the Socialists triumphed – that is how Serrati's party has evolved in 1921. Given these facts, comrades, I believe it will truly be a simple matter for us to come up with a fully unanimous decision on this question.

There are the first signs of rifts in Serrati's party. Baratono has spoken up, demanding that at least those who most blatantly violate discipline should be expelled.[41] Serrati immediately opposed this. Baratono tried to publish an article about this; Serrati forbade it. Baratono persisted, however, and got the letter published after the elections. He says, 'If it is really the case, Serrati, that you and your associates have concluded that the party must turn to the right, then you must find a way to call a congress and propose to the party that it pursue different policies.'

Serrati, of course, replied as always with anecdotes and gossip, casting suspicion on Baratono. Serrati said quite plainly:

> Yes, we must learn from the election results. It is in fact true that we must steer the party toward the right. That is not something we – or Turati – have thought up; it is a historical necessity. Even Lenin is at this moment turning to the right.

You can also find this line of argument in Levi's notorious journal, *Sowjet*, where his most recent article states: What are the Bolsheviks doing now? They are making concessions to the workers, to the peasants. It is essential to maintain contact with the masses. But I, Levi, have proposed the same thing in Germany.

So in a country like Russia, where the working class is in power, a country where the workers and peasants have the majority, the party makes concessions to the masses in order to maintain the dictatorship of the working class.

---

41. A member of the left wing of Serrati's Unitary Communist current, Adelchi Baratono had taken a more critical stance toward the reformist Turati wing. At the Livorno Congress, he advocated a more conciliatory approach toward the Comintern and the Communist Faction.

And in Germany? A minor detail is overlooked: namely, what prevails there is the dictatorship of the bourgeoisie, not the working class. And this distinction is decisive. Serrati is no child. He must understand that, and in fact he understands it very well.

So, comrades, that is the situation in Italy. We must not harbour any illusions. Time will be needed to bring the revolutionary workers of Italy fully over to our side. We must turn to these workers. For us, Serrati is nothing; these workers are everything. *We must turn passionately to these workers*, on behalf of the entire congress. We must have patience in order to win them over to our side. The more quickly we expose Serrati before the whole world, the faster this will be achieved. (*Loud applause*)

In my view, the example of Italy highlights the whole situation inside the International. It also clarifies the general political situation. As I have already said, after the Second Congress, a wonderful movement started up in Italy, in which the workers occupied the factories. It was a new form of proletarian struggle. In many localities, the workers held on for two weeks. A beginning was made in organisation of a red army. Then the trade-union federation stepped in and *stabbed the workers in the back*, betraying the movement. After that, in response to Lenin's open letter, Serrati declared that this movement had not been revolutionary but rather a simple trade-union matter. The factory occupations were not evidence, he said, that a revolutionary uprising was taking place. Rather it was a broad and deep trade-union movement, he said, which had proceeded quite peacefully, aside from minor incidents.

*That marked Serrati as a Judas.* Everyone understood that this was not a peaceful trade-union movement, but rather the beginning of a genuinely revolutionary struggle. Under Serrati's leadership, the party did everything possible to let the struggle fizzle out and deliver over the working class, helpless, to the bourgeoisie. And the bourgeoisie understood Serrati and was able to utilise his betrayal very cleverly. We must never forget this lesson.

*Offensives should not be undertaken lightly, but it is also wrong to let opportunities for such offensives pass us by.* Missing this opportunity set back the movement in Italy for many years. The working class will now have to wait patiently and make many more sacrifices than would earlier have been necessary – all because its leaders were on the side of the bourgeoisie, not the working class, and because they were a straitjacket on the workers during their revolutionary movement. That is the lesson for the Italian party. And there is also a lesson for us in our internal relationships, which can be summed up in a proverb: 'All that glitters is not gold.' Not everything that looks like real Communist gold is so in fact.

Comrades, in the future, we have to be mistrustful. We have experienced too many examples of betrayal similar to that by Serrati. We must test every party ten times before concluding that we can trust it. Genuine Communists will have no objection to this. This example shows that the main enemy is on the right and nowhere else. (*Applause*) Italy provides an example of how we have succeeded in educating our friends on the left. I have already referred to Bordiga, who stands at the head of the Communist Party. He has dissolved his faction and has abandoned any personal or factional attitudes from the old party. Here is a soldier of the proletarian revolution. We need forces like this, and we must develop friendly relations with them – up to a certain point, of course. In the case of the KAPD, they went beyond this point. But the real enemy is on our right, lying in wait for us and seizing on our weaknesses, poised to creep through every hole in order to sabotage us from within.

Serrati stated, not long ago, 'We now stand *devant l'église* – in front of the church door. Well, we are Christian comrades. We will wait until the door opens and then go in.' That is well put. But in reality he is not standing in front of our Communist church. *He is lying with his nose in the manure pile of bourgeois ideology.* (*Loud applause*) We have proceeded decisively on the Italian question. We were fully aware, of course, of the responsibility we assumed, and we now confidently await the verdict of the Third Congress, a verdict on whether we were right to slam the door in the faces of these people and call out to them: 'Either communism or reformism. Whoever is not with us is against us, with the bourgeoisie.'

I now turn to the *German party*. Obviously, I can only take up the most important experiences, which had a real impact on our policies. The Halle Congress was our first great success following the Second Congress.[42] The ground had been prepared during the Second Congress. I believe that our conduct in Halle showed that we know full well that what the Communist International needs is not sects but large revolutionary mass parties. We exerted ourselves to build such a mass party in Germany, and we believe that in this we have largely succeeded.

There were two urgent questions in Halle. The first was whether the Spartacus League should continue to exist, in one or another form, somewhat as a precaution, a guarantee, a supplementary organisation. On behalf of the

---

42. At the Halle Congress of the USPD ('Independents'), held 12–17 October, 1920, a majority of the delegates voted to accept the Twenty-One Conditions and join the Comintern, against strenuous opposition from a right-wing minority. The left wing subsequently fused with the KPD; the right wing split off and kept the name USPD. Zinoviev gave the main speech in support of Comintern affiliation. For Zinoviev's speech, see Lewis and Lih 2011, pp. 117–58.

Executive I spoke out against that, and I believe we were right. We have had a lot of experience in Russia with organisations of that type. In our opinion, such organisations have an inner logic. If there is a danger that the party is going to be watered down, it is better not to unify. If you unify, however, you must do it in loyal fashion, without maintaining separate organisations. I must point out that all leading comrades in the Spartacus group held basically the same view, and the question was therefore resolved quite readily and smoothly.

The second question concerned the tempo of development that the party should have in view. The political atmosphere in Germany was then such that even people like Ledebour were talking about the existence of a central bureau for murder.[43] The bourgeoisie was attempting, together with the Social Democrats and the right USPD, to provoke the party as quickly as possible and involve it in a big struggle, in order to deprive the party of the opportunity to organise itself solidly. On behalf of the Executive, I advised the leading comrades then not to be drawn too rapidly into decisive struggles. Of course, we were not so doctrinaire as to think this depended on us alone, rather than also on the overall situation and the stance of our opponent. We considered that the party should be allowed as much time as possible for its consolidation. There was no difference of opinion among us on this point. It was obvious that the unification of two parties, embracing 100,000 and 400,000 members, would not proceed completely smoothly. There would be frictions, backward steps, and centrist or half-centrist ailments.

Bearing in mind the entire history of the German movement, it was obvious to us that, here too, the danger threatening this party came mostly from the right, not the left. (*Applause*) We saw how the Spartacus League even before the fusion let such situations pass it by, for example during the Kapp Putsch.[44] That was an indication that our party was insufficiently engaged in the historical movement. This was even more true of the USPD. Tracing back the party's history, we saw that we should expect ailments of this character. We told the German comrades during the Second Congress that we did not understand why, when there is a movement that suffers defeat, you immediately come up with a shibboleth, saying that it is a putsch. We said, do not keep raising this concept of 'putsch'.[45]

---

43. Right-wing political assassinations were becoming more frequent in Germany at the time. During the summer of 1921, prominent victims included politicians Karl Gareis (USPD) (see p. 524, n. 10), and Matthias Erzberger (Centre Party).
44. For the KPD's record during the Kapp struggles, see pp. 4–5.
45. Zinoviev is referring to opinions he and Radek expressed to Paul Levi at the Second World Congress in July–August 1920, particularly with regard to Levi's

We told them not to be thoughtless, not to get involved in struggles that are unprepared. But looking back on the course of the German working class, we can say that it has not carried out a single putsch, let alone that this course is strewn with putsches and putschists, as one might well conclude to be the case from publications criticising the revolutionary course of the German proletariat. It is so easy to accuse every movement that does not succeed right away of being a putsch. We suffered dozens of such defeats in Russia, before we triumphed. If we had viewed all these struggles at putsches, we would never have won! (*Applause*)

When the VKPD was formed, we feared the emergence within it of centrist currents. Unfortunately, our fears all too quickly became reality. I have already discussed the Italian question, saying it was international in nature and linked with Germany. The Executive wrote a resolution and took disciplinary action against leading German comrades, with our esteemed comrade Zetkin at their head. We did not do that gladly. We considered twenty times over whether we should take this action. We were well aware that such resolutions should only be adopted in extreme circumstances.

I have explained to you the Italian question. It gave rise to the conflict in Germany. What was at issue? Levi was in Livorno as a representative of his party. He conspired there with Serrati against the Communist International. That is proven by everything that transpired in Livorno. Levi returned to Germany; a resolution was adopted; then there were amendments. Then five or six members of the Zentrale [Central Bureau] resigned from it because they were not in agreement with the Executive on the Italian question.[46] They said that the Executive had made errors and wants artificial splits, sects, and the like. Serrati went to Berlin and found his way to Stuttgart.[47] He wrote in *Avanti* – in boldface type – that the German party was with him. Our new Italian sister party thus received a stab in the back from the German comrades.

I asked the German comrades to imagine that after the split in Halle, a Russian comrade, like Lenin or Trotsky for example, had said, 'I do not agree with this split. I resign from the central leadership in protest against the Executive.' Everyone came to the conclusion that the action by some German comrades

---

criticism of Communists' assumption of governmental power in Hungary in 1919. See Broué 2005, pp. 432–5.

46. At a meeting of the KPD Central Committee on 22 February 1921, Paul Levi, Ernst Däumig, Clara Zetkin, Otto Brass, and Adolph Hoffman announced their resignation from the Zentrale, following the CC's repudiation, by a vote of 28 to 23, of Levi's stance on the Livorno Congress. A March 1921 ECCI resolution condemning these resignations was published in *Kommunistische Internationale*, 17. It can also be found in Degras (ed.) 1971, 1, pp. 211–12.

47. Clara Zetkin lived in Stuttgart.

represented just such a stab in the back against the Italian party. (*Shouts of 'Very true!'*)

As we said, you had to be blind not to recognise that Serrati had evolved backward to reformism. I have presented quotations showing how he acted on all the major issues, how all his articles besmirched the French and German parties, how he betrayed the party in the September movement. So it was quite obvious that we were dealing with a typical reformist – and then they stab us in the back and resign from the Zentrale. Writing on this matter, Radek asked whether members resigned their posts so quickly in the old Social-Democratic Party when they disagreed on a specific question. Even if we had been wrong in Italy – and in fact we were only too right – even in that case it was necessary to act more cautiously. Not a word was said to the Executive in advance; it was confronted with the *fait accompli*. That is why we concluded that something was rotten here. It is not merely the Italian question. We are all great internationalists, but we know that there would not be such nervousness in Germany if only the Italian question were at stake. Mostly, people get nervous when their own party, their own movement is at stake. People sensed that there was a connection.

Comrades, if it turns out that Serrati acted cleverly, wisely, and with talent, and that comrades who are reasonably experienced in politics were in error, and that all this is a misunderstanding, so much the better. But comrades, let's not get our hopes up.

That is why we had to intervene in this question, and we ask the congress to tell us frankly if it was an error on our part, so the Communist International can learn something from our errors. Or was it an error by the comrades who resigned? You must speak frankly on that too, so the Communist International can learn something from that, and so that we finally begin to feel we are an international party.

The *March Action* will be dealt with in a separate report. I will not say a great deal on that. When we began to receive news about it, Comrades Brass, Geyer, and Koenen were here. On hearing the news, we all felt that finally things were on the move, finally the movement in Germany had begun, finally there was a fresh breeze. After the defeat, when we wrote our first appeal, Comrades Brass and Geyer judged the matter in the same way as all of us. (*Radek: 'Hear! Hear!'*) *We dictated the statement, and Comrade Curt Geyer wrote it down.* ('*Hear! Hear!*') He acted as stenographer. The German comrades did not make a single amendment. Why did they act in this way? Simply because they had the feeling, as any revolutionary would have, that there had been a struggle, one that was forced on us, and it had been lost. We must absolutely not stab the workers in the back. Comrades then judged the matter objectively. So I am saying here for the record – and I am convinced both comrades will confirm this – that this is how the initial appeal came to be, one in which we all said that we defended the action.[48] (*Commotion*) You have read our resolution on tactics and strategy. As you see, we do not engage in the usual gushing praise. We take up the errors of the March Action clearly and precisely. The congress is not being held so we can pay each other mutual compliments.

Much too much has been said about the revolutionary offensive.[49] God save us from wading through these stupidities all over again. We are completely in agreement with what Comrade Brandler said in his pamphlet:[50] *It was not an offensive; it was a purely defensive struggle.* The enemy took us by surprise. There is no need to bewail the concept of a wrongly understood offensive. Many errors were made, and many organisational weaknesses came to light. Our comrades in the German Zentrale are not ignorant of these errors; they wish to correct them.

The question is: *can we assess these struggles as a step forward, as a revolutionary episode along the painful road of the German working class, or must we brand it as a putsch?*[51] In the Executive's view, *the March Action was no putsch.* It is absurd to talk of a putsch when half a million workers took part in the struggle. That is not a putsch, that is a struggle that was forced on the German working class in that situation. We must speak plainly of the errors and learn from them. We hide nothing; we are not engaged in factional politics; this is not secret diplomacy. Our opinion on this struggle is that *the German party, by and large, has nothing to be ashamed of.* Quite the contrary.

I will not conceal the fact that the fate of the International is tied in with this question. We must say plainly, without diplomacy, that there is a danger of premature movements. When Comrade Terracini gave his report in the Executive Committee,[52] I had somewhat the impression that the Italian

---

48. A reference to the 6 April 1921 ECCI proclamation, 'An das revolutionäre Proletariat Deutschlands', published in *Die Kommunistische Internationale*, 17, pp. 413–15. A translation can be found in Degras (ed.) 1971, 1, pp. 215–18.

49. The 'theory of the offensive' was advanced by majority leaders in the KPD after the 1921 March Action to justify their policies in launching the action and their proposal that such policies continue. It was rooted in previous texts by Béla Kun (1919) and, in another context, by Bukharin (1920). The theory called on Communists to radicalise their slogans and initiate minority actions that could sweep the hesitant workers into action.

50. Brandler 1921b, *War die Märzaktion ein Putsch?*

51. A reference to Paul Levi's characterisation, presented in his pamphlet, *Unser Weg: Wider den Putschismus*. Published in English as 'Our Path: Against Putschism', in Fernbach (ed.), 2011, pp. 119–65.

52. A reference to Terracini's 20 June 1921 report to the expanded ECCI meeting held prior to the Third Congress. The text can be found in Comintern archives, RGASPI 495/1/39/3–46.

Communists too believed that now they were out of the swamp party they had to launch their attack. No, you cannot draw such a conclusion just like that. Twenty times more caution is needed at this time; everything must be carefully prepared and thought through twenty times before you launch the struggle. In this regard, Comrade Trotsky was right to be critical regarding the French question.[53] We must perceive this danger, even exaggerate it a bit – that will not cause us harm.

I will now take up the *KAPD*. As you know, this question has also taken on international importance.

At the Second Congress, we made concessions to this party and permitted it to speak here to this international forum. The party's representatives here decided that it was better for them to hit the trail ahead of time. That is what Otto Rühle did, and as you know, he has now covered quite a distance.[54] Although he believes he has the most left-wing position, actually he is now in the counterrevolutionary camp. We had many discussions with the VKPD comrades at the Halle Congress and afterwards. Almost everyone believed that we should not admit the KAPD into the Communist International, even as a sympathising party. The Executive had a different view. On behalf of the Executive, I presented this view to the comrades in Berlin. Of course it is awkward to have to go against the decision of the party on such an important German issue.[55] Nonetheless, comrades, the Executive certainly had the right – formally, morally, and politically – to take this action in such circumstances.

We believed it essential to admit the KAPD as a sympathising party for the following reasons. We believed that *no stone should be left unturned* in efforts to educate the genuinely revolutionary proletarian forces in this party and win them to us. We believed that the record of our German party, its lack of activity, its great errors – for example in the Kapp Putsch, which it has itself conceded – could well have provided fertile ground for the KAPD. We believed that the sickness lodged in the KAPD could most readily be cured through international influence. Even though the party is not large – indeed it is only

---

53. Trotsky's speech on the French question at the meeting of the expanded ECCI on 16 June is printed in Appendix 3f on pp. 1114–25.
54. The KAPD had two representatives in Moscow for the Second Congress, Otto Rühle and August Merges, but they declared the congress theses to be opportunist and declined to attend. Rühle was expelled from the KAPD in late October 1920 and helped found a German syndicalist union.
55. The KAPD was admitted to the Communist International by the ECCI as a sympathising section on 28 November 1920. The KPD leadership strongly and publicly opposed this decision. Speaking about this decision on the eve of the Third Congress, Lenin stated, 'I clearly see my mistake in voting for the admission of the KAPD'. See Appendix 3a, p. 1099.

a very small party, a sect – we had to do everything possible, through the International, to win the best of these workers. The entire international workers' movement underwent such a dreadful crisis during and after the War, so it is only too understandable that the different parties and groups suffer from many ailments. That is why we had to be patient with these forces, who are fundamentally revolutionary.

The Executive was almost unanimous in deciding to grant this party sympathising status. After a fundamental discussion in which Comrade Gorter presented the KAPD position, while that of the Executive was presented most fully by Comrade Trotsky,[56] the Executive resolved to admit the KAPD with consultative vote. Giving the summary on behalf of the Executive, I said the following:

> There are only two logical ways out of this situation. Over time we cannot have two parties in a single country. Either the KAPD will develop into a genuine Communist Party and then become an integral part of the Communist Party of Germany, or the KAPD will cease to belong to us, even as a sympathising party.

That is the question we face today, and I believe that the Congress cannot avoid taking a decision on this question.

Unfortunately, I must say that the leadership plays a greater role in the KAPD than is the case in any of the other parties. (*'Very true!'*) With regard to this leading layer, we observed a regression during the past year. Allow me to demonstrate this. I have here a pamphlet, *The Path of Dr. Levi – the Path of the VKPD*, published by the KAPD. No author is listed, but clearly this is written by Gorter.[57] The KAPD comrades really do Gorter a great service in printing everything he writes. It would be better if Gorter had left much of what he has written recently lying on his desk, in order not to damage his reputation as a great Marxist, which he once was.

Now, comrades, listen to how this sympathising party speaks of the International. Chapter 3 carries the title, 'What Are the Preconditions for the Proletariat to Win State Power, and How Is State Power Won?' Gorter explains it to you in detail for three pages. He has considerable experience in winning state power, experiences gained in the Netherlands. (*Laughter*) He says:

> Levi answers these questions on pages 18 to 42. These are central questions of revolution, the very core of revolution. And here we see most clearly

---

56. Trotsky's 24 November 1920 speech to the ECCI in response to Gorter was published in *Die Kommunistische Internationale*, 17 (1921), pp. 186–202. An English translation can be found in Trotsky 1972a, 1, pp. 137–52.
57. See KAPD 1921.

the stupidity of the author, the stupidity of the VKPD, the stupidity of the Moscow Executive Committee, and the stupidity of the Communist International.

I have heard that in Dutch, the word *stupidity* does not mean the same thing as in German. Gorter continues by accusing the Executive of crimes against the international revolution. In Russia, the peasantry was a revolutionary class, but in the rest of the world, it is a *counterrevolutionary* class. In Western Europe there is only one revolutionary class, the proletariat. But this revolutionary class, the Western European proletariat, is itself counterrevolutionary, as we see in the trade unions. And so on. Therefore we must make the revolution tomorrow. These are Gorter's postulates. He believes there is only one revolutionary class, the working class, which is itself counterrevolutionary. And therefore, we should not proceed slowly and carefully with these masses and these stupid trade unions, but rather make the revolution tomorrow. That is his entire argument. And all that is cleverly mixed together with a jumble of abuse toward the Communist International, Soviet Russia, and the largest party in the International.

Comrade Gorter continues: 'And now look at Levi – and with him, the VKPD, the Communist International, the Executive Committee, and all the national parties with one exception...'. Who the exception is remains a puzzle. I don't know – is it perhaps the Dutch school?[58] Or the KAPD? I am not sure whether Gorter would give up on the Dutch party so readily. I do not think so. Take a look at *Proletarier*, published by the KAPD with the modest subtitle, 'The Dutch Marxist School'.[59] In this little pamphlet you will find the entire school. It consists of three articles: 'Party and Class' by Gorter, 'Marxism and Idealism' (the most burning question of social revolution) by Pannekoek, and 'The Rise of a Mass Communist Party' by Henriette Roland-Holst, of whom I truly must say, 'It long has been a grief to me that I see you in such company.'[60] With her outstanding abilities, she really should have been able to do better in the Communist International.

Joking aside, comrades, the KAPD, in its literary publications, has developed into an enemy of the Communist International. Gorter says in one spot, 'But in the past, the spirit of Levi has also been that of the VKPD, of the

---

58. The 'Dutch school' refers to a leftist current in the international Communist movement led by Anton Pannekoek and Herman Gorter. Allied with the Bolsheviks in the Zimmerwald Left during 1915–19, these Dutch Marxists led an ultraleft opposition in the early Comintern and quit the International with the KAPD after the Third Congress.
59. 'Die Holländische Marxistische Schule', in *Proletarier*, 4 (1921).
60. The quote is from *Faust* by Johann Wolfgang von Goethe, referring to Faust in the company of the devil.

Executive Committee, and of the Communist International. For how did they act in Tours, in Halle, in Livorno?'

So, you see, we acted wrongly in Halle, wrongly in Tours, where we expelled the French centrists, and wrongly also in Livorno, where we embraced too many of the masses.

In Gorter's opinion, the fact that we are admitting too many of the masses is shown by his statement that 'you only want numbers, not quality'. So the entire International does not represent quality; only Gorter represents quality. Then Gorter says, in the manner of Cicero, 'How long will they continue to pursue the politics of leaders, rather than of the masses? Are Russia, Bavaria, Germany – or just Russia alone – not enough of an example...?' What does this mean, comrades? This sounds very similar to Dittmann. What does it mean to say that Russia is an example of the politics of leaders? If so, he should say clearly how this is expressed. Who are these leaders? What are the policies? Who are the proletarians that have fallen in vain? What is the politics of leaders that these people are condemning? That must be said plainly. Gorter continues:

> How long will they continue to support the pseudo-struggle of the trade unions, these pseudo-realities, while boycotting the struggle of the factory organisations? How long will they continue to sabotage new *scientific Marxist policies*?

So are the trade unions, which today represent the genuine starting point of the entire *social revolution*, pseudo-realities, because they do not adhere to our policies? Noske, Scheidemann, Thomas, Ebert, Hörsing – they are all pseudo-realities. Only Gorter is not a pseudo-reality.

This is not the situation at all. Yes, the trade unions today are ultra-reactionary, but if we do not win over the unions and their weapons, the proletarian revolution is finished. Anyone who tries to teach that trade unions are pseudo-realities is at best a thoughtless phrase-monger, rather than a leader of the combative working class that aims to overrun the bourgeoisie. Elsewhere we read:

> The objection that the VKPD failed this time because it was not yet strong enough is invalid, because *so long as it is a mass party* it will never have sufficient inner strength. (The emphasis is in the original in the boldest possible type.)

So they do not want a mass party, and yet they demand mass politics. Understand that if you can. In my opinion, comrades, what I have quoted from the Dutch school's pamphlet will be enough for now.

However, I must say that this is not as harmless a matter as it may seem. The KAPD comrades are going over to exactly the same methods as Serrati. Here is an issue of *KAZ* [*Kommunistische Arbeiter-Zeitung*] dated 1 May, that is on a holiday when we make special efforts to stress international solidarity and all that unites us. This is what we read there:

> Moscow must grasp the lessons of the March struggles this year. If that does not happen, if there is no last-minute decision to place a review of the Twenty-One Points on the agenda of the next congress, we will be compelled to draw the only possible conclusions.

To which I must reply: Go right ahead; we have no objections. Gorter then continues:

> We will then be justified in drawing the conclusion that the main reason why we are being dragged ever deeper into the swamp is a complete lack of understanding regarding the problems of revolution in Western Europe, combined with an inclination to serve the particular interests of the Russian Soviet government.

To that, there is nothing to add beyond what I said in Halle. We told the right-wing USPD people in Halle, 'Gentlemen, today you are for Soviet Russia, but tomorrow you will be in the camp of the enemies of Russia.' They cried out, 'Never'. But already today they are open and outspoken opponents of Russia. Today I say the same thing. *These politics, half childish and half criminal, will turn you into enemies of the proletarian republic.*

**Radek**: Gorter is already defending Kronstadt![61]

**Zinoviev**: The same article continues:

> But if we want to be true to the needs of the Western European revolution, the goal for which we must strive is to break the Communist International free, politically and organisationally, from the system of Russian government policy.

Although expressed somewhat diplomatically, the meaning is clear. We said at the Second Congress, and we repeat today in the name of our party, that

---

61. Soviet soldiers and sailors in the Kronstadt fortress, on an island close to Petrograd, mutinied on 2 March 1921, at a moment of grave economic crisis and widespread discontent in Soviet Russia. The revolt was forcibly suppressed by 18 March. Bolshevik opponents such as Mensheviks, Socialist-Revolutionaries, and anarchists pointed to the fate of the Kronstadt rebellion to bolster their opposition to the Soviet regime, as did openly counterrevolutionary and imperialist forces.

*we will be overjoyed by the victory of the proletarian revolution in Germany or elsewhere, which enables us to move the centre of the Communist movement to Berlin or to another location.* Of course it fills us with pride that the workers of the most diverse countries give us this honour at present. We have made efforts to follow the specific problems of international revolution in each country, to study conditions in every country, and to learn from them, and we will continue to do so. You know that better than we do. However, this May article makes it quite clear that the KAPD comrades are following in the footsteps of Serrati, which will drive them into the arms of Dittmann.

I received by telegraph a decision of the expanded Central Committee of the KAPD, taken on 5 June 1921.

> The expanded Central Committee of the KAPD resolves that the party's membership in the Communist International, whether with sympathising or full status, is conditional on the inviolability of the party's programme.

What a great International this is! The KAPD's programme must be inviolable. Why not then also the programmes of the French, Italian, and Czechoslovak parties? What kind of childishness is this? Is it Gorter's childishness? There cannot be an International in which this or that party is inviolable. The Central Committee continues:

> As regards fusion with the VKPD, any ultimatum is to be rejected. The delegates are mandated, if appropriate, to declare the KAPD's *immediate resignation from the Communist International.*

Comrades, if this situation arises, if the KAPD comrades really believe it is useful for them to leave the International – and I hope they will think that over carefully – if the decisions of the international Communist proletariat have no weight for them, if only the Dutch school is authoritative in their eyes, well, then they should leave. But in my opinion, we in this congress should not regret having gone through this experience. We have demonstrated to every revolutionary worker in the KAPD that *our intentions are to work with them honourably and fraternally*, that we have given them time and made concessions to them. If they leave now, they will leave at a time when we in Germany have a mass party, tested in struggle. Perhaps it has made major errors, but we all make errors. We are nonetheless a large revolutionary party, tested in fire, which has a completely different moral weight in the eyes of the working class than the KAPD. If we now suffer the misfortune that Gorter and his close friends leave us, we will find some way of coping with this misfortune. We are convinced that sooner or later the large majority of workers who still support the KAPD will recognise these errors.

These workers will not say they are inviolable. They will say, 'Of course none of us are inviolable, and the Communist International will be authoritative for us all.' That is what I have to say about the KAPD.

To wrap up our comments on Germany, I will take up the *Levi case*. Paul Levi wrote us a letter asking that his expulsion from the German party be reversed. The Presidium will present a motion to the congress on this question. As you all know, the Executive approved the expulsion.[62] Since Levi's pamphlet discusses policy questions, we maintain that they should be discussed under our agenda point on tactics and strategy. As for the other questions – the talk about Turkestaners and all the other gossip – I believe, and you will surely agree with me, that it would do the pamphlet too much honour for me to speak of these matters any further here. (*Applause*) That settles the matter.

I now come to the other parties. First of all, the *French party*. We gave an exhaustive report on this in the session of the Expanded Executive.[63] It is true that we handled the French party differently from the other parties, because we were aware of the situation in that country. In our opinion, we had to proceed more cautiously with this party. We had to consider that there were still elements in this party like the Longuet people, and we therefore had to allow the party time for clarification. We are well aware of the weaknesses of this party.

Comrades, permit me to place in the congress proceedings the stenographic transcript of the speech on the French question that I made to the session of the Executive, and then move on to the other parties, because otherwise we will lose too much time.

*Speech in the Executive Committee session of 12 June 1921 on the French question*[64]

Comrades, first of all, I would like to motivate to Executive members our conduct toward the French party. Actually, the old Executive, with its old composition, took a decision to admit this party, which was then explained in a large number of statements. As you know, Serrati complained about the Executive and about me, asserting that, in his view, we had made excessive concessions to the French party. A collection of articles and resolutions is

---

62. The KPD Zentrale expelled Levi on 15 April 1921, a decision upheld by the ECCI on 29 April. The ECCI statement can be found in Degras (ed.) 1971, 1, pp. 218–20. For Levi's appeal, see Appendix 2f, pp. 1090–6.

63. See Appendix 3f, pp. 1108–32 for excerpts of the debate on the French question at the expanded ECCI meeting held prior to the congress.

64. According to the ECCI minutes, Zinoviev's speech on the French question was given on 17 June, not 12 June. See Comintern archives, RGASPI 495/1/38/57.

available, explaining our conduct toward the Italian Socialist Party. In this collection the reasons are laid out why I, as the Executive's representative, have acted differently toward the French party than I have toward the Italian one, why I made a special agreement, so to speak, with the French comrades. Serrati has written a large number of articles demanding that we should act toward the Italian party in exactly the same way as we did toward the French party. I consider it my duty here to explain the attitude we took toward the French comrades and the reasons for this approach.

It is true that we intended to act toward the French party in a more cautious and conciliatory manner than toward the Italian, which already belonged to our International. This was for the simple reason that the situation in the French party, in our opinion, was different from that in Italy. When Cachin and Frossard were in Moscow,[65] we faced a party in France that had not yet undergone its first split. Thomas and Renaudel, the French Scheidemanns, were still inside the party. We had to reckon with the fact that the Communist group inside the French party was rather weak, and almost all of its leaders were in jail. For this reason, we favoured taking a softer line toward the French party than toward the Italian party, which already belonged to the Communist International, which had taken part officially in the Second Congress, and which had made commitments that it unfortunately did not carry through.

The agreement with Renoult included a point that if it should turn out that Longuet accepted the conditions of the Second Congress, we were ready to propose to the next congress making an exception for him.[66] Renoult asked for that in the name of Loriot, and we agreed. There is no reason to regret that now. Longuet soon made his famous speech. That made it clear he could not conceivably agree to the Twenty-One Conditions. Still, the French comrades insisted on this point. They wanted to make plain for the French working class that we were prepared to make an exception for Longuet. I believe that we handled this case correctly. And Serrati is completely wrong to claim that he too should have been able to stay in the International.

---

65. Marcel Cachin and Louis-Oscar Frossard were in Moscow during June and July 1920. While there, they attended the Comintern's Second Congress as representatives of the French SP, but without decision-making authority. At the congress they declared themselves in favour of the Comintern's Twenty-One Conditions for Admission.

66. During his stay in Germany to attend the October 1920 Halle Congress of the USPD, Zinoviev met with Daniel Renoult, a leader of the pro-Communist forces in the French Socialist Party. They agreed that if Jean Longuet's supporters submitted to the majority, they would be permitted to remain in the party and would receive one-third of the places on the party's leadership bodies.

Longuet did not accept the Conditions, and the party broke with him. At the last moment, when Longuet had already said that he was not willing to accept the Conditions, Frossard asked him not to leave the party. Comrades who took part in the Tours Congress will no doubt remember that the Executive sent the congress a last-minute telegram, coming out very strongly against Longuet. It branded him as a reformist, that is, an agent of capitalism, and demanded his expulsion.[67] Frossard made an attempt to excuse this telegram to Longuet, saying that the Russians were given to strong language and that this should not be taken too hard. The telegram was formulated rudely, he said, but Longuet should stay in the party just the same and fight together with the party. I do not know if this telegram ended up playing the deciding role, but we believed it had at least made a major contribution. Frossard was obviously wrong in continuing his efforts to convince Longuet to remain in the party.

After the decisions made at Tours, we faced the question of our future conduct toward the French party. It was quite clear that this was not yet a Communist Party, not fully, at least. Various forces remained in the party that are even now still centrist or half-centrist, giving expression to these traditions everywhere – in the party, in its press, and in parliament. Nonetheless, our opinion was still that we had to act differently in this case than toward the Italian party, which had already belonged to the Communist International for two years. We made a tacit agreement with the comrades in the Communist group within the French party: We would grant them a number of months to enable them to reorganise and carry out organisational work within the party. We did not put pressure on the party. Yesterday, Loriot quoted an article in which I am supposed to have said that the French party had acted correctly. I confirm that. This refers to a telegram that the Executive sent to the last administrative congress of the

---

67. The Tours Congress of the French SP (25–30 December 1920) voted by a 75 per cent majority to accept the Twenty-One Conditions and affiliate to the Comintern, giving birth to the CP of France. The minority ('Dissidents') split away, preserving the SP's name.

The ECCI's telegram to the Tours Congress stated: 'The resolution signed by Longuet and Faure shows that Longuet and his group have no desire to be exceptions in the reformist camp. They were and are outright conductors of bourgeois influence into the proletariat. Their resolution is unmistakable, not only on the points it deals with, but even more on those about which its authors keep silent. On the world revolution, the proletarian dictatorship, the soviet system, Longuet and his friends prefer to say nothing, or to utter the most banal ambiguities. The Communist International can have nothing in common with the authors of such a resolution.' Published in *Die Kommunistische Internationale*, 16 (1921), pp. 451–2. Translated in Degras (ed.) 1971, 1, pp. 207–8.

French party.[68] In the telegram, the Executive states that it still welcomes the French party and that at our next congress we will negotiate with its representatives about what needs changing in the party's policies.

We must size up the party and its organisation accurately. Our discussion here yesterday and today has done this. I believe that the Executive has acted correctly in displaying extreme caution and toleration toward the French party over the last half-year. That does not mean, however, that we should refrain from saying here what we believe needs to be said. In my opinion, the so-called 'leftist stupidities' are not so dangerous for the French party. Sizing up the overall condition of the French party as it is today, everyone will agree that the dangers threatening the party do not come so much from the left as, rather, from the so-called opportunist elements. (*Applause*) The youth movement is very weak in France. If it commits blunders, we must point this out. Obviously, when the party is opportunist, the youth, as a vanguard, must not be opportunist. The conduct of the youth will promote the party's recuperation. I believe that precisely in the French party the old traditions, brought with them by some parliamentary deputies, are very dangerous and must be consistently combated.

As was said here yesterday and repeated today, *L'Humanité* is not an entirely Communist paper. Comrade Kun has already been put through the wringer today, and I certainly do not want to make his life more miserable.[69] His assertion that *L'Humanité* is worse than *Freiheit* is contrary to the facts. *Freiheit* is an outright counterrevolutionary paper, while *L'Humanité* is at worst a paper that is not yet consistently revolutionary. *L'Humanité*'s evolution is positive; *Freiheit*'s is negative. Frossard makes progress, slowly and with vacillations and relapses. *L'Humanité* deals honestly with Russia, while *Freiheit* carries out concealed, sordid propaganda against the only proletarian state, engaging in strike-breaking.

Nonetheless, we must insist that *L'Humanité* must become a strictly revolutionary paper, developing in a revolutionary direction. Comrade Trotsky, in his speech yesterday, provided a glaring example of such a failure.[70] There are a dozen such questions that *L'Humanité* has not taken up. What is more, the French comrades acknowledge this both in their official reports and in private discussion. Even Loriot said today, 'We are quite well

---

68. A reference to the French CP's Administrative Congress held 15–17 May 1921.
69. Lenin's speech polemicising with Kun at the expanded ECCI meeting, to which Zinoviev refers, can be found in Appendix 3f, pp. 1128–32.
70. For Trotsky's remarks at the expanded ECCI, see Appendix 3f, pp. 1114–25.

aware that our paper and our [parliamentary] fraction are opportunist. We are well aware that there is much that we do badly.' The Executive believes that the time has now come to intervene and say forthrightly and frankly what we expect of the French party.

Comrade Lenin was right in saying that things are going well in the French trade unions, and that some steps forward can be noted there. When he adds that this is an achievement of the French party, however, I must say that he has not followed this question well. Even the French comrades do not say this. Loriot himself said that the party's work in the trade unions is not good, and that it is pursuing an unclear political course. If the syndicalists obtain a majority at the next congress, neither they nor the party will know what to do with this majority. True, we note the progress in the trade unions, despite the party's vacillation and confusion on this question. (*Applause*) The party does not yet have a clear line on this question, and for that reason, the syndicalists do not have one either. And that is exactly why the present situation arose, in which the syndicalists consciously want to establish their own political party.

And here I want to say a few words regarding the comments by Comrade Sachs. He said that the example of France teaches us that the Second Congress decisions on the trade unions were not advisable. On the contrary, it is precisely the example of France that shows how right it was to propose building cells in the trade unions. If we had followed the advice of the KAPD, where would we be today? We would be even further removed from our goal, and we would merely have brought grist to Jouhaux's mill. Our advice was Communist. Despite the bad conditions in the party and the bad situation generally, a number of trade unions are with us. Although conditions in France remain somewhat chaotic, there are grounds to hope that the party will find a path to the syndicalists and the unions. It is precisely the example of France that shows how right the Second Congress was in calling on the party to turn its attention to the trade unions.

I maintain that, despite all the weaknesses, and despite the bad practices that Cachin has brought from the old party, we must have confidence in the French party. During the War, there were no grounds for confidence in the party, and – as we know – the workers themselves displayed great mistrust in it. But precisely because there is a group of Communists in parliament and in the trade unions, we can now state confidently and without exaggeration that trust in the banner and the idea of revolution has reawakened in France. Today we have a party in France that already has more than 100,000 members. This party is shaped by a different spirit than that of the old French party, even though it also has many weakness and imperfections. Our main enemy is the opportunist current. Still, we must concede that we have taken a great step forward in regaining the confidence of workers in France. In the French parliament there is a small, weak, but nonetheless internationalist Communist fraction. Conditions today are not entirely satisfactory, but they improve daily. Our French comrades themselves acknowledge their errors and are therefore glad to accept the advice of the Communist International Executive.

The Executive must convey its opinion to the party frankly, in a resolution or a letter. Of course it is quite excluded that we would make a proposal to expel Frossard. Such a proposal cannot even be posed for serious discussion. A positive evolution is under way in France, but opportunism is still present, and that is the enemy we must overcome. We must tell the French workers what is at stake here. It is possible that there will be split-offs; indeed, if major struggles arise, the party may face not only split-offs but a major crisis. This is confirmed by the French Communists. Still, we want to help the party now and support it, so that it remains a mass party. Developments in the French party have shown that we had a correct policy on this question at the Second Congress. It was correct against left blunders, as explained today by Comrade Lenin, and especially against opportunist blunders. The line adopted at the Second Congress should be reaffirmed at the Third Congress.

The Czechoslovak question was also very important for us, and was also discussed very fully in the Expanded Executive. I hope that this material will also be inserted into the proceedings. I will restrict myself here to a few words. We have polemicised against the Šmeral current. We hope that he will still arrive here, so that all these differences of opinion can be discussed in his presence. Information received from Comrade Burian and others indicates that the Czechoslovak party is developing into a real revolutionary mass party. And given that we have demonstrated to the Czech comrades, in comradely fashion, the weaknesses of their party, I believe we will soon experience the existence in Czechoslovakia of a tested Communist Party. It is possible that at first there will be some reformist forces in this party, just as in the German sister party – indeed given the entire context that is rather to be expected. But we believe that such a genuine proletarian organisation, built with solid proletarian timber, will be able, with support from the International, to overcome readily any possible opportunist or centrist elements. We do not yet have a unified Communist Party in Czechoslovakia; that remains to be created. We must have *a unified and well-organised Czechoslovak party, led and consolidated across natio1nal divisions*. That is the goal that the Executive formulated and that I would like to stress once more.

*Speech in the Executive Committee session of 13 June 1921 on the Czechoslovak question*[71]

I have been asked to motivate the resolution on the Czechoslovak question drafted by the Small Bureau and distributed to the Executive Committee. First of all, I would like to express my regret that Comrade Šmeral is not present. At the party's congress in Prague, he launched a political struggle against the Communist International.[72] In our view, it was his duty to come to the congress and conduct this struggle here. Therefore, after consulting with the Czech comrades present here, we decided to send a telegram to Šmeral, requesting him to come to the congress in Moscow, if at all possible, and defend his position here. So far, we have not received an answer, but we have still not given up hope that Šmeral will appear here in person.[73]

I would like to discuss above all the *national question*, which plays such an important role in Czechoslovak affairs. We must exercise great caution here. To start with, I note that a few weeks ago *Právo lidu* attributed to me a very stupid assertion. I am supposed to have stated in the Executive that I absolutely do not recognise the Czechoslovak state. (*Laughter*) *Právo lidu* makes a big deal out of this fictitious statement. How could anyone imagine that the Executive or one of its members would not recognise an established fact? For our part, we will not object to an assertion by the Czechoslovak comrades that they intend to struggle in the framework of this state, which is a product of the War and of historical development. But at the same time we do not say that world history has yet spoken the last word on all these territorial questions.

We consider that these questions will be definitively resolved only when soviet governments exist everywhere. The boundaries established by these soviet governments will be definitive. I hope that when Czechoslovakia is a soviet state, its representatives will join with us in taking the offensive in a war to the end against all monarchical and [bourgeois] democratic republics. As early as the First Congress of the Communist International, we stressed

---

71. According to the ECCI minutes, Zinoviev's speech on the Czechoslovak question was actually given on 14 June. See Comintern archives, RGASPI 495/1/36/150–7.
72. At the 14–16 May 1921 congress of the Czechoslovak Left Social-Democratic Party that founded the Communist Party of Czechoslovakia, the main report was given by Šmeral. In his report Šmeral contended that conditions were not ripe for revolution and that there was no prospect for immediate revolutionary action, an implicit criticism of ECCI policy. He called for avoiding putschist adventures and drawing the broad masses into struggle. He also advocated tolerating diverse views within the party, provided that members maintain discipline; he cautioned against rapid unity with the German-Czech party. Firsov 1975, pp. 371–4.
73. Šmeral did arrive in Moscow on 29 June to attend the Third Congress.

that the existing national boundaries are very fluid and provisional and will be rather quickly overtaken by history.[74] That has been the position of the Communist International since the moment it was born, and I hope that the Czech comrades too will approve it. In this regard, the Czech comrades need to constantly stress an internationalist viewpoint. We do not deny the existence of the Czechoslovak bourgeois state. But as internationalists, we must declare that the Czechoslovak comrades need to deal with all national issues, which are quite acute now and will become more so later on, with proletarian policies and from an internationalist point of view. (*Applause*)

Now as regards the *mass party*. We certainly need to express appreciation for the fact that the Czechoslovak comrades have come to the Communist International with a party of 350,000 members. The Czechoslovak comrades deserve great credit for this. It is obvious that we have taken a great step forward in Czechoslovakia, handing Social Democracy a humiliating defeat. That is a great achievement, and we must not overlook it. We are more committed to the concept of a mass party than gentlemen like Levi who are constantly making the case for it. In fact, we note that it is precisely those who really favour sects who always talk more about mass parties than others, like us, whose politics have nothing in common with sectarianism.

We gladly concede that the Czechoslovak party is a genuine proletarian mass party. That is our starting point and the foundation that determines our policies on this question. However, there are mass political parties that are neither socialist, nor communist, nor revolutionary. Unfortunately, such mass parties exist. We know that the Social Democrats in Germany are still quite a substantial mass party. We know that the Labour Party in Britain is a very large mass party. We know that the working class in France is fashioning a large mass party. But is that enough? If there were no Social-Democratic mass parties, the entire world would long ago have been swept by revolution. (*Applause*) We can well imagine that there are mass parties that pay homage to bourgeois or half-bourgeois ideology. But in Czechoslovakia, this is not the case. The Czechoslovak party is certainly not based on bourgeois ideology. But a layer of the masses is still quite susceptible to centrist influences. We must keep this fact in view and reckon with it. We want this to be a mass party in line with the Communist International's conditions. We have not set Comrades Muna, Zápotocký, and Šmeral on a fixed line of march; on the contrary, we said that they should not proceed

---

74. The themes of national boundaries and antagonisms were taken up at the First Congress in the 'Theses on the International Situation and the Policy of the Entente' and the 'Manifesto of the Communist International to the Proletariat of the Entire World.' See Riddell (ed.) 1987, *1WC*, pp. 211–19 and 222–32.

too quickly in launching the Communist Party. They should wait for the right moment. But we also told them, *if you do found a Communist Party, then it must be a genuine Communist Party.* (*Loud applause*)

As for the Czechoslovak comrades who are continually saying that if we oppose Šmeral that will result in a new Livorno, I must ask what that means? Does it mean that these comrades are forced to admit that the Czechoslovak party is currently centrist? (*Loud applause*) What was Livorno? I do not wish to pre-empt the discussion of Livorno, and will speak of it only briefly. What we saw in Livorno was a split in a mass party with about 200,000 members. The majority went to the centrists; the minority to the Communists. Our blame in this matter consists solely in the fact that we trusted Serrati too much and too long, that we failed to build a strong opposition against Serrati.

If comrades are saying that the Czechoslovak party will quickly split and only a small minority will remain Communist, what does that mean? It means that they have a large mass party, in which the Communists are still only a minority. If the outlook is really so gloomy, you must have no illusions. I only hope that it is not in fact so gloomy. We know that there is a group in the Czechoslovak party that has perceived all the political and organisational problems very clearly. We have seen the letter that Comrades Muna and Zápotocký wrote from prison. Everyone should study this letter conscientiously; it is a very important document. They explain exactly what we are saying here. It is true, unfortunately, that they do not mention Šmeral by name; I do not know why. But they analyse the situation just as we do. The fact that no one dared protest their letter shows that these comrades have support in the party. At the very least, the Communist International must declare its solidarity with the statements of these comrades in prison.[75]

However, we must go further and quite frankly make all the criticisms of Šmeral that are in order. We do not want to tell the comrades, 'Make the revolution now.' Do not think that is our view. We also do not want to say, 'You must launch your attack tomorrow, or a month from now.' What we do want to say is that *agitation and propaganda must be revolutionary and not centrist in character.* When I listened to Comrade Taussig's speech yesterday,[76]

---

75. The letter referred to was read out to the founding congress of the Communist Party of Czechoslovakia on 14 May 1921. It was signed by A. Zápotocký, A. Muna, B. Hula, B. Stadnik, and M. Mičoh, all prominent Czechoslovak Communists who were in prison at the time. It assailed the 'deviational and vacillating tone of several of our newspapers and a lack of clarity in the central leadership' and called on the congress to elect 'firm and resolute communists' to the leadership. Quoted in Firsov 1975, p. 369.

76. Taussig's remarks to the ECCI meeting of 13 June 1921 can be found in Comintern archives, RGASPI/495/1/36/135–38.

I could only think that these are the words of someone from the Two-and-a-Half International. Among other things, he said – and Comrade Bukharin has already taken this up in detail – 'We are surrounded by ruined states. Therefore we cannot make a revolution.' What does that mean? Are we supposed to wait until capitalism has regained its strength, and only then strike out against a capitalist system in full bloom? That is the same theory that Kautsky advances. I also heard an interjection from Comrade Taussig. When a speaker said that the Czechs should not wait for other states, Comrade Taussig called out, 'Then there must be a strong movement in Poland as well.' I too believe that a strong movement is needed in Poland. Indeed, this movement exists, despite the white terror. However, is not what Comrade Taussig says exactly the same as what we hear from the Second International? The Second International also says, 'I am ready to launch the attack, but my neighbour must do so too, at the same moment.' How do they imagine that this is going to happen? Perhaps they think that one fine day the leaders will come together and adopt an agreement setting down the exact day on which the revolution will break out everywhere. That would be truly ideal. But revolutions cannot be carried out so neatly as to permit us to simply sign agreements with each other and then, one fine day, launch the attack. Launching the attack depends on numerous factors. Going by this theory, we must ask why backward Russia came first in line, rather than the capitalist United States? (*Loud applause*) We must really have done with these theories of the Second and Two-and-a-Half Internationals. Under no circumstances do we want to propose to any party that they launch the attack on such and such a day. The Executive will never make such a proposal. Obviously, such a question must be weighed a thousand times before a decision is taken.

Something quite different is at stake here. Must we accept that a party convention elects leaders who then simply spit in the face of the International? (*Loud applause*) There are a thousand delegates here [for the World Congress]. Comrades may wish to divide into groups in different rooms and carefully read Šmeral's speech [at the Czechoslovak CP congress]. I am convinced that every comrade will say that Šmeral's speech is half-centrist. In this speech we see the same tone, the same method, the same insincerity as with Serrati. And this speech was given at a moment when the party had already declared that it wished to join the International. The party should have protested immediately against Šmeral's speech. That would have created a much different situation. Now we have to speak against Šmeral's speech.

The resolution proposed by the Czechoslovaks states two or three times that they accept all of the Twenty-One Points and will implement them. Why all these repeated solemn assurances? Would it not be better to set about, finally, implementing these conditions? What is the point of swearing such an oath, when the party leaders argue in the newspaper against the Twenty-One Conditions? How can they claim to be carrying out the Twenty-One Conditions? Šmeral talks against the Communist International; many of their leaders speak against affiliation and against the Twenty-One Conditions. Šmeral is now even beginning to talk of collaborating with other parties in the country, saying that we are such a large party that we can exert real influence on the present government. Anyone familiar with the history of socialism up to 1921 knows full well the meaning of such words from a man as skilled as Šmeral.

What happened during the December strike?[77] Everyone coming from Czechoslovakia confirms that if there was anyone who was helpless as a baby in the face of these events, it was Šmeral. Everyone confirms this, including the press. Šmeral simply wanted to float around for a few more years in capitalist waters, watching and waiting, and only then taking a stand. That is why we believe, comrades, that we must take a clear and explicit position. As to whether we should admit the party, we must say yes. What should be done with Šmeral? We do not call for him to be expelled or immediately removed from his posts, but we do wish to assert our right to say what we have to say to tell Czechoslovak workers, and warn them against, such speeches and actions. We must not forget that Šmeral's three-hour-long speech was not off the cuff. It was worked out in advance, and every word was carefully chosen.

We call on the Czechoslovak working class to develop further and not slip backwards. The Czechoslovak comrades tell us that the bourgeois press will greet our resolution with a shout of joy.[78] I am not sure that this joy would be justified. We know that the bourgeois press will attempt to utilise this unedifying polemic for its own purposes. Once again it will chatter idiotically

---

77. For the December 1920 strike in Czechoslovakia, see p. 76, n. 16.
78. A reference to the original draft of the theses on the tactics of the Communist International submitted by Radek, which openly attacked Šmeral as follows: 'Seeing that the Communist International wishes to create only truly revolutionary mass parties, they are making a big noise about the Comintern falling into sectarianism. This is what the Levi group in Germany, the Šmeral group in Czechoslovakia, etc., are doing. The nature of these groups is quite clear. They are Centrist groups; who cloak the policy of passive waiting for the revolution with Communist phrases and theories. The Šmeral group put off the organisation of a Communist Party in Czechoslovakia at a time when the majority of the Czechoslovak workers had taken a Communist stand.' *LCW*, 42, pp. 570–1. On Lenin's proposal, this paragraph was deleted. See Appendix 4b, pp. 1155–7.

about Moscow's diktat and the Hungarian comrades.[79] I am well aware that even party members are susceptible to such insinuations and ideology. But to concern ourselves with such stupid prattle is not true internationalism. It will not have the slightest influence on our decisions.

We have to speak honestly to the Czechoslovak workers. We have nothing against Šmeral as a person. He came here a year ago and bared his soul to us, saying, 'I was a social patriot and now I am here.' We did not place a single obstacle in his path. We gave him a fraternal welcome, and for a whole year we have supported him in every way possible. Even today, we have no reason for personal hostility to him. He is without doubt a person who wishes to serve the proletarian class selflessly. But we must note his political errors. Comrade Kreibich was right to remind us that when we discussed Šmeral's conduct with him a year ago, we were in favour of taking action against Šmeral. Kreibich argued persuasively against this, saying that it was only a matter of minor differences of opinion regarding Šmeral's policies. However, recent events have convinced Comrade Kreibich otherwise.

We ask the Czech comrades to set aside all national considerations in this matter. I am well aware that we are all human, fostered on bourgeois ideology, who absorbed national sensitivities with our mother's milk. But what is at stake here is not a national question, not a German or Czech question; it's a matter of consistent communism as against vacillating half-communism. Why is Šmeral now raising the question of superstructure and federalisation? How can we conceive of the Communist International in any way other than as a unified party in each country? How can that issue still be an object of debate in a Communist Party? It is simply necessary to establish a commission to carry through with centralisation rather than putting it off.[80] For these reasons, comrades, we must tell the delegation of the Czechoslovak party plainly what we think about the situation in their party. It is no accident that the delegates of the Bulgarian, Italian, German, Russian, and Polish party have said this too. We are following the situation very closely indeed. We are compelled to do this by the attempt that has been made to create a crisis in the Communist International. This is positive. I am convinced that there will not be another Livorno. I am confident that when the majority hears what the Communist International has said, not only the

---

79. Hungarian CP leaders in exile were among the most prominent ECCI envoys during this period and had been active in discussions with Czechoslovak Comintern supporters.
80. A reference to the structure of the Czechoslovak Communist movement, which was still divided into separate national units. A congress uniting all national Communist parties within Czechoslovakia into a single organisation was held 30 October–4 November 1921.

majority, but also those who have friendly relations with Šmeral, will say that although Šmeral is our friend, the Communist International is a greater friend. I am convinced that a large majority of workers in Czechoslovakia will accept our decisions, and I hope this will be true of most comrades in other countries. Let Šmeral think what he wants. In submitting our resolution to the Executive, we are confident and fully convinced that it will greatly assist the development of a genuine Communist Party, a genuine party of struggle, inside the Czechoslovak working class. (*Loud, prolonged applause and cheers*) Comrades, I ask you to adopt the resolution that Comrade Karl Radek will distribute on behalf of the Small Bureau of the Executive.

I want to say a few things about the Scandinavian parties. In Sweden and Norway, we have quite different parties. In *Sweden*, there has been some progress from a half-pacifist party to a genuine Communist one, but this evolution is not yet completed. In *Norway* there is a mass party that must still be freed from certain centrist influences.

In the Swedish party, much must still be accomplished organisationally. For example, in Clause 2 of this party's statutes I read:

> The parliamentary fraction and other party members who receive any kind of official governmental task must receive the approval of the Central Committee and, in important matters, the party council, before accepting such tasks.

I must say that I simply do not understand this. Nor do I understand Clause 3, which states:

> The activity of the parliamentary fraction must fully conform to the party programme and party convention decisions. During the interval from one convention to the next, the parliamentary fraction is obligated to carry out proposals and adopt the viewpoints expressed by the party council or the Central Committee.[81]

What tasks would a bourgeois government give to Communist deputies? I do not get that at all. The same applies to the discipline applied to the parliamentary fraction. They say that the fraction is subordinate to the general line of the party congress, and, between congresses, Central Committee decisions are binding. That has a far too innocent ring.

---

81. A reference to the statutes adopted by the May 1917 founding congress of the Left Social-Democratic Party of Sweden, which came out of a split in the Swedish Social-Democratic Party. The new party decided to join the Comintern in June 1919, and its May 1921 congress voted to adopt the Comintern's Twenty-One Conditions by a vote of 173 to 34, changing its name to Communist Party.

There is also something less than full clarity in Sweden on the question of arming the proletariat. Branting says, 'My Communists are good; they are good people'. But I know very well that our opponent says such things with a purpose, and I do not take it seriously. We must judge matters more objectively than Branting, who has been harmed in many ways by our Communists. Nonetheless, we must note that the party newspaper, *Politiken*, is not yet a fighting, inspiring proletarian paper. The paper has failed to take a completely clear position on issues that are crucial for the Communist International.

As for the *Norwegian party*, we have reached a degree of agreement on collective tasks. We have made certain concessions to this party. Nonetheless, we consider that this state of affairs cannot be more than transitory, and that this party too must be organised on the same basis as has been done in the other parties.[82]

Comrades, during the past year we have not only carried out splits but also worked for unifications, namely in Britain and America.

In *Britain*, at the time of the Second Congress, we had eight small currents, more or less Communist, which were fighting with one another. Now we have a single, unified party.[83] That is the result, to a considerable extent, of pressure from the Executive.

The same is true in the *United States*. We said that we would not admit any of the factions in the United States until they unified. We must advise our American friends not only to learn to work in the framework of an underground party but also to organise – in the teeth of the white terror – a movement that is legal or semi-legal and can work parallel with the party to win broader layers of the working class.[84]

For the American and British parties, it is a matter of life and death to stop being sects. The soil in Britain and the United States has been very well

---

82. In 1918 the left wing won the majority of the old social-democratic party, the Norwegian Labour Party, and the organisation affiliated to the Comintern in 1919. However, the party retained its previous organisational norms, particularly regarding inclusion of membership through affiliated trade unions alongside individual membership. The majority of the party left the Comintern in 1923.

83. For the unification of Communists in Britain, see p. 553, n. 39.

84. In 1919 the US Communist movement, divided between the Communist Party of America and Communist Labor Party, was driven underground by a wave of government repression. The Communist forces reunified through fusions in May 1920 and 1921. By late 1921, following easing of the 'Red scare' and unification of the movement, the majority of the US leadership took steps to found a legal organisation – the Workers' Party of America – existing alongside of and controlled by the underground party. This plan was approved by the ECCI in November 1921, and the party was founded in December.

prepared, and our party must be able to sow the seed. In our opinion, the main slogan for these two parties must be: *Closer ties with the masses; more legality.* (*Loud applause*)

As for other countries, I note that in *Denmark* there has been a split among the syndicalists, and that some of them have joined the Communist International.[85]

In *Austria* too, the left wing of the Social-Democratic Party split away and joined the Communist Party.[86]

The situation is similar in *Belgium*, where the Jacquemotte group broke away. The Belgian [Workers'] Party press was very upset over that split, but our Communist comrades do not consider it to be an important development. I believe they are mistaken. We consider the split to be quite significant. And in my opinion, the International has an interest in unifying this group with our Belgian sister party as rapidly as possible.[87]

A similar development took place in *Switzerland*, where the left broke away from the Social-Democratic Party and joined the Communists, who expelled Nobs in the process.[88] During the debate with us, Nobs made reference to a letter from Clara Zetkin. I believe we should keep this experience in mind and not be so quick to write letters to such people. I too have written a letter to Nobs, and he has printed it, but only as evidence of my bad manners. (*Laughter*) But Nobs tried to use Comrade Zetkin's letter against the Communist International. That is a bad business.

The movement in Switzerland is making good progress. Our comrades in French Switzerland have enjoyed good success, and the influence of the Social-Democratic Party is diminishing day by day. Grimm, the celebrated leader of Swiss Social Democrats, has turned into a mere agent of the bourgeoisie.

---

85. A reference to the syndicalist Union of Oppositional Trade Unions (Fagoppositionens Sammenslutning – FS). In early 1921 the majority of the FS decided to formally ally with the Communist Party of Denmark, leading to the creation of the Communist Federation.

86. A reference to the group led by Josef Frey, who had been expelled from the Social-Democratic Party in late 1920. He and his supporters joined the Communist Party in January 1921.

87. Joseph Jacquemotte led an organised left wing within the social-democratic Belgian Workers' Party, known as the Friends of the Exploited. Expelled from the Belgian Workers' Party, this group decided to found a Communist Party in May 1921. In September 1921 Jacquemotte's group fused with the already existing Communist organisation in the country to found the Communist Party of Belgium.

88. At the 10–12 December 1920 congress of the Swiss Social-Democratic Party in Bern, right-wing and centrist forces defeated a left-wing motion to join the Comintern by a vote of 350 to 213, after which the Left walked out. In the process of the split, the Left broke with centrist forces in the party led by Ernst Nobs. The Communist Party of Switzerland was founded 5–6 March 1921 by a fusion of this Left with members of the Swiss Communist Party (Old Communists) formed in 1918.

In *Spain* we see a similar evolution toward unification of the Communist groups.[89] Something quite interesting took place there. A delegation from the old [Spanish Socialist Workers'] party came here. One delegate, a worker, was a Communist; the other, a professor, was a reformist. This professor was naïve. He told us frankly: 'I do not want to join the Communist International, but the Spanish workers who sent us do want to join, and I have to do their bidding.'[90] (*Laughter*)

We get many visits of this sort. A certain Mr. Flueras, a former government minister, came to us from Romania. He was quite surprised when Comrade Bukharin told him, with his characteristic courtesy, 'Mr. Flueras, given that you are a bourgeois minister, and that in our opinion you ought to remain so, we ask you to please leave the room.' (*Laughter*) He was appalled by our lack of international hospitality. We had quite a few rather peculiar visits of this type during the last six months.

In *Romania* the split has now taken place, and we can report to the congress that our Comrade Cristescu, and others who previously were often termed centrists, have loyally carried out their responsibilities. As supporters of the Communist International, they have all been sent to prison. We have too little information about the situation in Romania, but we must say that so far the negotiations are producing good results.[91]

Our *Yugoslav party* is now underground. It was a large party with about eighty thousand members. The centrists have been so contemptible as to publish a legal newspaper in which they utilise their monopoly of legality to attack our Communist comrades. This centrist wing has been expelled and is now back in the Two-and-a-Half International. I cannot say whether centrist remnants remain in the party, of course, because I have no close knowledge of the underground party's composition. We hope that this is not the case. But if such centrist forces exist, we ask the Yugoslav delegation – which has come here in good number – to take up the struggle against them immediately in the name of the old Executive Committee.

---

89. The two Communist groups, both represented at the Third World Congress, were the Spanish Communist Party (PCE) and the Communist Workers' Party (PCO). The two groups fused in November 1921.

90. The reference is to Fernando de los Rios.

91. At the 8–12 May 1921 congress of the Romanian Socialist Party, the majority voted to join the Comintern and change the name to Communist Party of Romania. A centrist and right-wing minority split off and formed a separate social-democratic party. For the arrest and imprisonment of Romanian CP members, see p. 176, n. 3.

Reformist socialism is a poison with a special purpose. Comrade Barbusse wrote a brilliant article about reformist socialism,[92] which I showed to Comrade Gorky, saying: Barbusse understands very well what you do not yet understand. Barbusse says, *reformist socialism is a poison designed specifically for the proletariat*. Even a few drops of this poison in our body can cause it to break out in gangrene, just when it is locked in a most difficult struggle. We must keep our attention fixed on this poison and always have the antidote at the ready, in no small quantities.

Our *Bulgarian party* is one of the few that – like the Czechoslovak party – seems to enjoy the support of almost the majority of the working class. The most recent reports indicate that this party as well may possibly be driven underground and may suffer greatly from the white terror. We do not know if these reports are correct.

The party has been charged with a failure, on occasion, to launch a mass struggle at the decisive moment. Investigation has shown that this is not correct. We have been following the party's history since 1913. It has experienced a considerable number of splits. We believe that, despite some weaknesses, we have a good, strong Communist Party in Bulgaria. When this party makes the transition from preliminary propaganda to action, it will show what it has been preparing for during twenty or twenty-five years. We cherish the hope that in the decisive hour, our party will not disappoint the Communist International in any way.

Let me speak briefly of the *Finnish party*. It belongs to the Communist International as an underground party. But despite the white terror, the entire underground Finnish workers' movement is Communist, heart and soul. From what we hear, this underground movement has twice as many members as the old Social-Democratic one, which has been absolutely demolished. When we meet ordinary Finnish workers, they always tell us, 'In Finland, communism is no longer a question of agitation but of weapons, of technical preparations.' (*Loud applause*)

Comrades, if I failed to mention one or another party, that was not because there was nothing to say, but because I have to end at some point.

Now let's take up our important contingents in the *Near and Far East*. The propaganda council established by the Baku Congress is active in the Near East.[93] There is much organisational work still to be done there. In the Far East the situation is similar.

---

92. Henri Barbusse's article, 'Le devoir socialiste' was published in *L'Humanité*, 24 October 1920. It subsequently appeared in *Kommunistische Internationale*, 15.

93. The First Congress of the Peoples of the East held in Baku in September 1920 established a Council for Propaganda and Action, which was to work under the aegis

It is absolutely necessary to develop closer ties with Japan, where we must establish a firm foothold. The situation in this country is roughly similar to that in Russia in 1905. A powerful revolutionary mass movement is developing there. You should see the materials being published there. The first and second volumes of *Capital* have been translated into Japanese and have already been printed. Many trade unions have been formed there spontaneously by workers acting alone, without leaders. These unions have great sympathy with the Communist International, but, unfortunately, our communications with Japan are very poor.

Given that we wish to be a global International, the Executive has the duty of devoting more attention and resources to the *women's and youth Internationals*. (*Applause*)

The *women's conference* has taken place, and we have followed its work. We founded an international women's publication, *Die [Kommunistische] Fraueninternationale*. We believe that the work among women must be promoted by every means. It is indisputable that without the women, the proletariat will never triumph. We must have the women; without them the proletarian republic in Russia could never have survived.[94] (*Loud applause*)

The *Youth International* is even more important. It will be holding a world congress here. We have done everything possible during the past year to support the Youth International. Comrade Trotsky is entirely right to say in this regard that the youth means even more for us today than we previously thought, because the working class has been so exhausted by the War. *We must devote a hundred times more work to the youth and support them a hundred times better than before. This is one of the most important questions.* We therefore hope that this congress will reinforce the youth movement, and we will support the world youth congress in every way possible.

Some persons have tried to foment conflicts between the youth and the Executive. They tried to stir up the youth against the Executive through articles in Levi's *Sowjet*. But this will never succeed. In my opinion, the political leadership of the youth must be located in the same place as that of the

---

of the ECCI. It lasted until early 1922, when its responsibilities were transferred to the Comintern centre in Moscow.

94. Zinoviev is referring to the Second International Conference of Communist Women, held in Moscow 9–15 June 1921, on the eve of the Third Congress.

In August 1920 the ECCI had established the International Communist Women's Secretariat as a section of the Comintern, with Clara Zetkin as its secretary. This secretariat was sometimes referred to as the Communist Women's Movement. The Communist Women's Secretariat published a journal, *Die Kommunistische Fraueninternationale* ('Communist Women's International') from 1921 to 1925 and coordinated the work of women's committees and bureaus in each Communist Party. The secretariat was dissolved in 1926.

International as a whole.[95] If we have two parallel leadership bodies in different countries, the directives of these bodies will sometimes unintentionally be at cross purposes and in contradiction to each other. This is twice as dangerous in the youth movement. Therefore, I believe that we should overcome all the organisational difficulties in order to have a *common political leadership* – today in Russia, tomorrow in Germany or France, depending on how the world revolution evolves. But no matter what happens, we must support the youth everywhere much more generously than in the past. The youth have carried out outstanding work; they have always been in the lead in Czechoslovakia, France, and other countries where a struggle against social patriots and centrists is required. The task is very great, and much more work must be carried out in this field than before. We must support the youth movement with all our energy. (*Loud applause*)

Implementing an initiative of our Executive, the Second Congress formed the red trade-union International. At the time, this was an entirely new task, but now we have achieved a great deal. Comrade Lozovsky drew up a table showing that more than fifteen million organised workers now belong to our trade-union International. We started by publishing a manifesto opposing the Amsterdam International,[96] and we will take a new and important step forward at this congress. In my opinion, we all understand the importance of this trade-union congress very well, because we must carry through the battle against the Amsterdam International – the bourgeoisie's last bulwark – to the finish. That is why trade unions now stand as the most important issue before us, to which the congress must pay the closest attention. After the congress, this question must be given top priority in every sister party.

That is the report, in rough outline, on the work carried out by the Executive during the past year. *What should be done next?* What line of action should we continue to carry out? I believe that the line of the Second Congress was, by and large, correct. During the congress, there were leftist deviations by the British and American comrades. We must overcome this; we need a consistent line. The struggle against the Right, however, is far from over. Indeed, it has not yet begun, if we consider that Amsterdam still represents a trade-union International with twenty million workers. *The struggle against the Right is the main issue.* The struggle against the trade unions and against the centrists is

---

95. The Moscow session of the Communist Youth International's Second Congress, held in July 1921, voted to transfer the CYI's headquarters from Berlin to Moscow. See also p. 773, n. 9. For a comment by a Levi supporter, see *Sowjet*, 3, 3, pp. 48–50.

96. Presumably a reference to the ECCI proclamation adopted 14 January 1921, 'Dem Bürger Jouhaux, und den Bürgern Fimmen Oudegeest, Amsterdam' [To Citizen Jouhaux and Citizens Fimmen, Oudegeest of Amsterdam], in *Die Kommunistische Internationale*, 16 (1921), pp. 441–5.

a policy question. Only the fact that we had set down sound policies enabled us to achieve these gains in different countries. Our tactics and strategy were correct, and this course will bring us victory. In countries where, in the third year of our struggle, we do not yet have a majority, the main slogan is to make sure that we attain the majority and reach the masses.

So far, we have almost never had an *international action plan*. I heard many comrades ask, 'Well, what does international strategy mean exactly? Carry out obstruction in parliament? Organise international demonstrations and strikes on specific days?' Yes, comrades, that is part of it, and I must say that we have not done even that. We have not organised a single international demonstration. We must recognise these weaknesses and frankly acknowledge them.

We must make that good by organising international actions during the coming year. We must hold international demonstrations, act internationally in parliaments – and this will happen even in France. We must start with such small efforts. We have not yet been able to open up a breach in one country in order to support and deepen the struggle in a second country. We were too weak; our foundations were too weak. Our present task is to make up for that.

Now I will say a few words about centralism. An attempt has been made to claim that we impose a dreadful pressure, a dreadful centralism. The opposite is true. Our organisation has been far too loose. We are well aware that many important questions are of such a nature that they must be resolved by the parties directly concerned, in the framework of national conditions. We have thoughtlessly proposed slogans to resolve on an international level issues that are inherently capable of resolution only on a national level.

However, there are issues where international guidelines must be established. We must have a much more centralised organisation, and we must build connections that are much tighter and more effective than has previously been the case. There has been a great deal of stupid uproar about *decrees from Moscow*. In reality, however, the only reproach that can be held against us is that *we were not centralised enough; our forces were insufficiently unified*. ('*Very true!*') The bourgeoisie is much better organised than us. We must emulate it; we must grasp the need to build *a united international party*.

Comrades, do not be shy in passing judgement. We ourselves recognise the errors. You must assign the best forces from every country to the next Executive. You must not choose on the basis that so-and-so is not needed at home; he can be sent to Moscow. We will commit twenty times more blunders if we do not have a leading comrade from the country in question on whom we can rely. It must be understood that having an Executive is not a luxury. Do not say that everything is already set up – the party, the trade unions, the organisations – why do we also need an Executive? It's not like that at all. The work of the Executive must be taken seriously!

If you want a competent International, a competent Executive, a genuine international proletariat, you must contribute your best forces. We are reproached for our errors; it is said that communication is too weak. But let me turn that around, comrades, and ask the parties what you have done to organise all this? Almost nothing. Your criticism is welcome, but we also demand self-criticism. We need the best forces for the Executive – numerous forces, backed up with sufficient technical staff – and this requires major sacrifices by all parties. If you give us that, then we will have an Executive during the coming year that can rightly be termed a *general staff of the proletarian revolution*.

Previously, for us to use this term glossed over reality; we had not earned it. We lagged somewhat behind the parties, but by and large we did not deviate from the Second Congress line, applying it in specific conditions. In the coming year this must be done better; we must construct a genuine international Executive. When the Executive is built in this fashion; when our policies have been tested once again; when we have withstood the ordeal of fire; when we have seen the main elements of our tactics and strategy confirmed in the struggle to win the masses – only then will the genuine international work of the Executive and the Communist International begin. At that point, the Executive will genuinely be the highest authority between congresses. Its word will be law. There will be no inviolable parties or inviolable programmes any more, but rather iron discipline, international proletarian discipline in struggle against the bourgeoisie. (*Loud, prolonged applause*)

**Koenen** (Chair): Before we hear the translation, we wish to make a decision on a declaration drafted by the Small Bureau regarding Comrade Max Hoelz, who has been condemned to life in prison.[97] Comrade Radek will distribute and motivate the Small Bureau's declaration.

## Appeal for Max Hoelz

**Radek**: Comrades, Max Hoelz was condemned yesterday in Berlin to life imprisonment. His name is familiar only to our German comrades. Only they

---

97. Max Hoelz, a KAPD member, led an armed workers' detachment in Central Germany organised in 1920 to fight the Kapp Putsch. Subsequently, Hoelz reformed his unit, and it functioned during the March 1921 conflict as an independent armed detachment engaging in guerrilla attacks. Captured following the March Action in 1921, Hoelz was convicted and sentenced to life imprisonment. Following an international defence campaign, he was amnestied in 1929.

know something about Max Hoelz as a person, for he is not a member of a Communist Party. (*Interjection: 'Not so. He is a member of the KAPD.'*) Comrades from other countries know of Max Hoelz only from what the bourgeois press reports about him. At this moment, when the German bourgeoisie has condemned *this brave and honest revolutionary as a common bandit and thief*, we consider it our duty to take our stand for Max Hoelz as a revolutionary and a Communist. (*Loud applause*)

Hoelz's course of action was not ours. As early as the March struggles in 1920, Hoelz went his own way. At that time, disregarding the party's discipline and advice, Hoelz launched a campaign of retaliation against the bourgeoisie. Even now, in the March struggles [of 1921], Hoelz did much that was not appropriate from the standpoint of Communist tactics and strategy. But one thing is certain. Before the War, Hoelz was not a socialist. He was a railway employee who enlisted during the War and was put in charge of a prison in the rear. There, in this prison, he learned the meaning of communism, in broad outline. I believe he has been driven to communism far more by everything he saw during the War than by theoretical teachings and writings. He perceived the bourgeoisie's ruthless struggle against the popular masses.

And when German imperialism was shattered by the stronger imperialism of Britain and the United States, when the masses rose up, Hoelz saw it as his task to lead the proletarian struggle. He did this in one of the most backward regions of Germany, where the proletariat was wasted away by five hundred years of exploitation. He gained the workers' sympathy, but the emaciated textile workers of Vogtland did not have enough strength to build a large organisation. So this energetic man, who had seen in the War what energy means, took the leadership of the masses, seeking through energy, self-sacrifice, and dedication to lead them further. As I said, much that he did was not appropriate. But we stand with Hoelz in his integrity, and we share his hatred of the bourgeoisie. The Small Bureau therefore proposes the following declaration addressed to the German proletariat.

[*Radek reads the declaration. For the text, see p. 952.*] (*Loud applause*)

Comrades, we are convinced that Hoelz will not have to serve out his sentence. We are convinced that the bourgeoisie's hand, if it does not reach for a murderous revolver, will be stayed by the German proletariat's struggle. During these times of turmoil, Hoelz was not able to find his place in the ranks of the proletarian masses, who were not yet fully united. However, we are firmly convinced that the day will come when we will greet him as ours, a fighter in our ranks, who, subordinating himself to the general will, struggles in our ranks with the same enthusiasm that he previously displayed while following his own path. (*Loud applause*)

**Hempel** (Jan Appel, KAPD): Given that this telegram is being sent to the world on behalf of Comrade Hoelz, who is a member of our party, I want to express our joy over the fact that the Communist International stands at his side. But we must also point out that this telegram also insults Max Hoelz. (*Commotion and objections*) The telegram states that Comrade Hoelz was motivated only by a desire for revenge against the bourgeoisie. That is not the case, as is made clear by the Berlin trial itself and by subsequent reports of it. Every one of Comrade Hoelz's actions and deeds in the March struggles took place in the framework and in the interests of proletarian revolution. It is therefore wrong to speak of Max Hoelz's actions in the manner of this telegram. If your goal in this matter is to combat the German bourgeoisie, then you should be fully consistent and not back off. You have every reason to be happy with the results of Max Hoelz's conduct; he represents and has carried out the policies of the KAPD. (*Commotion and objections*)

**Koenen** (Chair): I must express my regret that this declaration by an international congress of support for Max Hoelz, who is so important for proletarians in every country, cannot be adopted without discussion. Given that the KAPD has seen it appropriate to debate even this point, Comrade Radek will respond.

**Radek**: Comrades, I too regret this disturbance. I attribute it to the fact, first, that the KAPD did not hear correctly what the declaration says, and, second, they do not even know what Hoelz himself has said. Our declaration reads, 'his deeds flow from his love for the proletariat and his hatred of the bourgeoisie'.[98] That describes a comrade and a Communist who acts from love for the proletariat and hate against the bourgeoisie. And we share with him this hate against the bourgeoisie and love for the proletariat.

As for the political side of the KAPD's tactics and strategy, I prefer not to take that up now, for a number of reasons. I will say only that in a letter we received from Hoelz, which he wrote in prison, he himself says that a great many of these actions were inopportune and that it would have been better if they had not occurred. As regards our attitude to individual terror and to guerrilla warfare carried out without any link to the party, without the party's leadership, all of us here have a common view. If the comrades of the KAPD do not share this opinion, they should keep their views to themselves and, so long as we tolerate them, they must subordinate themselves to our point of view. We will not trouble them about their private opinions. We only want to say that we are not hysterical women but men, who say quite frankly what

---

98. For the corresponding passage in the resolution, see p. 952.

it is that divides us from Hoelz. This just confirms the sectarianism of the KAPD, which stops at nothing when it serves their needs.

We will go our way and fight our fight. If the KAPD comrades do not want to take part in this, that is their responsibility. (*Loud applause*)

**Koenen** (Chair): We will now take the vote. All those in favour of the appeal, please so indicate. (*The vote is taken.*) I can therefore say that the declaration has been adopted unanimously.

Please take note that the next sitting of the congress will take place tomorrow afternoon at 6:00. The agenda point for this session is discussion on the Executive Report.

*(The session is adjourned at 4:30 p.m.)*

## Session 5 – 26 June 1921, 7:45 p.m.
# Executive Committee Report – Discussion

*Discussion of Zinoviev's report. Speakers: Hempel, Frölich, Roland-Holst, Neumann, Ceton, Michalak, Seemann, Gennari, Heckert, Malzahn, Münzenberg, Radek.*

**Koenen** (Chair): Comrades, the discussions that took place in adjoining rooms have already taken up a considerable part of the time for today's session. I will therefore be all the more strict regarding the speaking time, which is fixed at ten minutes. During this discussion, which promises to be extensive, we will make very sure that the ten-minute limit is respected. After nine minutes, I will ring my bell and will allow the speaker time only to complete his thought and not to begin a new one.

**Seemann** (KAPD): We must protest against the chair's statement that he will closely observe the speaking time, given that it is already so brief, and that several hundred comrades were here at the scheduled time.

**Koenen** (Chair): I would have emphasised the need to observe the speaking time precisely in any case. My introductory remarks were intended only as a gentle warning to the delegations in future not to take up the session's time with such consultations.

The discussion on the Executive report is open. I give the floor to the first speaker, Comrade Hempel of the KAPD.

**Hempel** (Jan Appel, KAPD): Comrades, we are in agreement that the question of the Communist Workers' Party of Germany should be taken up in a separate agenda point. However, the comments of Comrade Zinoviev in his report yesterday cannot be left unchallenged. Comrade Zinoviev has a well-known habit of comparing us to opportunist elements like Serrati, Dittmann, and the like. We energetically protest against this accusation of opportunism. Our entire history and the development of our party speak against such a charge.

To demonstrate this, I will refer only to our stance during the Kapp Putsch in Germany and also on 20 August last year, when Russia's red soldiers stood at the gates of Warsaw, near the German border. On the latter occasion, only the KAPD expressed solidarity in action.[1] The others, including the Communist Party of Germany of that time – the Spartacus League – wrecked active solidarity in action with Soviet Russia. Further, let me point to our stance in the Berlin electrical workers' strike, a stance that was recognised as correct by Comrade Radek.[2] We could point to many such facts and examples. Not a single fact can be cited that shows us to have lapsed into opportunism. That is our real position, our course of action, and also our principles. They vouch for the fact that we have not lapsed into opportunism.

We will have occasion to discuss our tactics, strategy, and principles under other agenda points. We hoped that this would give us sufficient opportunity to demonstrate our line quite clearly and distinctly. It is not possible for me to go into these matters at great length in the ten minutes at my disposal. All I can do is protest against us being lumped together with Serrati, Dittmann, and other opportunists.

Comrade Zinoviev also saw fit to attack a pamphlet published by our party, entitled *The Path of Dr. Levi – the Path of the VKPD*. Comrade Zinoviev says that the pamphlet was written by Gorter. Let us be clear: this is a pamphlet of the KAPD. Gorter worked on it, but we assume full responsibility for this pamphlet.

What is being held against Gorter and our party here? That we say, with regard to the Third International and its policies, 'You are seeking only the masses, and not quality.' Yes, that is certainly what we say. We will say it under other agenda points as well and explain how we see matters. But Comrade Zinoviev passes over these matters so flippantly, simply saying, 'Here you claim that in Germany we do not have the Russian peasants, but

---

1. As the Red Army advanced through Poland toward Germany in mid-August 1920, the KAPD and anarcho-syndicalist forces made plans for uprisings in a number of German cities and towns. Most of these plans were cancelled as the Red Army retreated, but in Velbert and Köthen on 20 August the local KAPD went ahead anyway. The actions were quickly suppressed.

2. A reference to the 7–12 November 1920 strike by electrical workers in Berlin. The ECCI criticised the KPD for not having tried to extend and generalise the strike. The KAPD denounced the SPD and KPD's role in the strike, which it termed a betrayal.

rather only the proletariat, and this proletariat is counterrevolutionary.' And then you go further, saying, 'The revolution could begin tomorrow.' Comrades, you cannot fathom such questions of revolution in this fashion. We strongly regret the use of polemics of this sort.

We will demonstrate that we intend to carry out the revolution with the masses, not without them, one way or another, as proposed in the theses adopted at the Second Congress of the International. We have a perfect right to point here to the lessons that the German revolution has provided to the international proletariat. And it is wrong of Comrade Zinoviev to pass over this so lightly.

Comrade Zinoviev also said that the KAPD calls for unity but will quite soon be counted among the enemies of Soviet Russia. He refers to this year's May Day issue of *Kommunistische Arbeiter-Zeitung*. He read a few lines from this paper. I will read you some other lines, and will then speak directly to the point that Comrade Zinoviev has touched on. It says here:

> The notion that mass Communist parties can be deployed to carry out parliamentary and trade-union – that is, bourgeois – methods of struggle has been exposed as a giant bluff. Such mass parties are good at demonstrating for Soviet Russia on Sundays and holidays, but they are completely useless for revolutionary struggle.

That is our assessment of the policies advocated by Comrade Zinoviev. And we must tell you that we cannot continue like this. We also say that this is rooted in the policies of the Russian state. Therefore we add:

> This does not imply calling for struggle against Soviet Russia in the fashion of Rühle. We commit ourselves to use every means to ensure, through action, that Russia continues to exist as a proletarian power. But the goal that we must strive for, in order to do justice to the requirements of revolution in Western Europe, is to detach the Third International, politically and organisationally, from the policies of the Russian state.

That is the point Comrade Zinoviev is taking up when he says, 'If you continue like that, you will be outside the Third International.' He refers to the telegram we have received from our party empowering us to leave the Third International. He then concludes, 'If you leave the Third International, you will be fighting against Russia.' Not at all, comrades! We tell you that we are fighting for the proletariat of Soviet Russia, and we will not let ourselves be led astray in this work. If you no longer want us in the Third International, if you want to continue down the opportunist path, we will still stand up for Soviet Russia anyway. But we will denounce the opportunist actions of the Communist International. I will now read a statement of our delegation on this particular point, which we have written and will read, so that our words cannot be misinterpreted and distorted.

> We protest most energetically against the use of quotations taken out of context in an attempt to liken our political line to that of Serrati and Dittmann. Not for a minute do we underestimate the difficulties caused for the Soviet government by the delay of the world revolution. But we also see the danger that this delay, these difficulties, are producing a contradiction between the interests of the revolutionary world proletariat and the immediate interests – apparent or genuine – of Soviet Russia.
>
> It was stated in a commission meeting that the Third International should not be seen as a tool of the Soviet government, but rather the Soviet government should be seen as the strongest outpost of the Third International. We agree that it should be so. But in our view, when contradictions arise between the vital interests of the Soviet government of Russia and those of the Third International, a duty exists to subject this to a frank and fraternal discussion inside the International.
>
> We have always carried out our evident duty of expressing solidarity in action with Soviet Russia. For example, we celebrate the October Revolution through demonstrations; we participate energetically in the care of interned Red Army soldiers; we prepared support actions in August 1920, which were thwarted thanks to the USPD and KPD. When our party decided to affiliate to the Third International, despite our grave reservations regarding the International's reformist policies, one of the decisive considerations was to give expression to our solidarity with Soviet Russia.
>
> We will hold firm on this course. However, we will resist most vigorously, whenever and wherever we see that Soviet Russia's policies find expression – mistakenly or through misunderstanding – in the Third International taking a reformist course, all the more given our conviction that such a course contradicts the true interests of Soviet Russia just as much as those of the world proletariat.

**Frölich** (Germany, VKPD): Comrades, I agree with Comrade Hempel on one point. We cannot deal thoroughly with this question now. This must be done under the agenda point where the question of the KAPD's affiliation to the International is to be decided.

When the Executive admitted the KAPD as a sympathising party, it did so, as has been clearly stated, in the belief that this party was imbued with revolutionary activity, and that this would serve to spur along the KPD. At that time, we [in the KPD] protested against their affiliation. We thought this action revealed an overestimation of this party's strength and activity. We considered that the party's activity was hindered by its pronounced sectarian character. This judgement has been confirmed again and again, even though the party sometimes – abruptly and unexpectedly – flares up in activity.

It is not just organisationally that the party's sectarianism is expressed. It has been evident from the start in the basic issues that distinguish them from us – parliamentarism, work in the trade unions, and other matters. After the party joined the International as a sympathising member, it became clear that its overall character had not changed in the slightest. In our experience, the party's sectarianism prevails on all major political issues. We saw this in the party's stance toward the issue of limited actions. The party stated that it was opposed in principle to policies seeking to engage the proletariat around its immediate vital interests. It denounced as opportunist any policy seeking to revolutionise the working class, to draw it into a movement, and drive it forward. It therefore opposed our Open Letter initiative and did its utmost in struggle against it,[3] thereby condemning itself to be completely ineffectual.

In addition, we noticed that the party's narrow-minded outlook utterly blocked it from forming a correct judgement of the political situation. We noted this on the reparations question, where it had absolutely no feeling for how acute the situation was and for how important this question was for the entire proletariat. Its newspaper declared that this matter did not concern the proletariat at all, but rather only the bourgeoisie of the different countries. It said there are no grounds for us to be drawn into these disputes, and that our sole task is to carry on propaganda for the final struggle. Here too, we see the party's utter incapacity to link up with the given situation and to draw revolutionary strength out of it, to whatever extent possible.

After the Executive made its decision, we pursued efforts to approach the party and join with it in common work. And in the March Action, such common work did turn out to be possible. We showed that when we negotiate over practical matters, talking through the issues together, we are able to get this party to adopt quite specific policies in current struggles.[4] But, comrades,

---

3. On 8 January 1921 *Die Rote Fahne* published an open letter from the VKPD to other German workers' organisations, calling for united action around the immediate demands of the workers' movement, including defence of workers' living standards, self-defence against violent rightist attacks, liberation of workers in political detention, and renewal of trade relations with the Soviet Union. For the text of the Open Letter, see Appendix 1a on pp. 1161–3.

The KAPD attacked the Open Letter for being 'opportunist and demagogic'.

4. During the first stages of the March Action, the political course of the most radical VKPD leaders converged with that of the KAPD. On 30 March, the KAPD reacted to published remarks by Frölich with the headline, 'The VKPD masses are carrying out our slogans.' Béla Kun, the senior ECCI emissary, appears to have convened leaders of the KAPD and Frölich's more radical wing of the VKPD majority in a joint committee that took initiatives independent of the official VKPD leadership. Koch-Baumgarten 1986, pp. 151–2, 156.

the hopes that we placed on this joint work were cruelly betrayed. The KAPD displayed a complete lack of understanding of the action that it had itself participated in. The pretty pamphlet by that great Marxist, Gorter, 'demonstrates' in minute detail that the March Action was a putsch.

**Seemann**: Not so!

**Frölich**: Please, that is written in the pamphlet, *The Path of Dr. Paul Levi – the Path of the VKPD*. Dear Comrade Seemann, if you wish I can show you the documentary proof afterwards.

In this regard, the KAPD is fully aligned with Paul Levi. It is very peculiar to denounce as a putsch an action in which you yourself participated and to raise this argument against the VKPD, especially when your history includes quite genuine putsches. Comrade Hempel referred a while back to the great action that the KAPD carried out during the offensive against Warsaw. What did this action consist of? The conquest of the towns of Velbert and Köthen in order to declare a soviet republic. (*Interjection by Hempel*)

But dear Comrade Hempel, the issue here is the tactics and strategy of the KAPD and the International. This is not about denunciation at all. You have admitted that you carried out this action –

**Hempel**: But other actions too.

**Frölich**: And given that the big action in this case consisted of establishing council republics in two towns, we must say that we cannot understand why you describe our own action, which you carried out together with the VKPD, as a putsch.

Comrades, we drew a great many important conclusions from this action. With respect to organisation, we concluded that we need to strengthen discipline and centralisation of the party and its actions. It is significant that the KAPD has drawn exactly the opposite conclusion. It explained that centralisation and discipline was shown in this action to be thoroughly counterrevolutionary. It has drawn narrow-minded and sectarian conclusions from this action. It calls for the free development of the individual through actions, and takes care that the party remains as pure as distilled water. Thus they deliberately push away the masses and abandon strict organisation and discipline.

A party with this attitude will never be able to carry out a truly revolutionary struggle. Instead, if it remains on this path, it will only promote disorganisation.

And now, after this united action, we continued our ties with the KAPD. We believed that it might provide us with a stimulus. And indeed we did receive a huge, powerful political stimulus from the KAPD just before we left

Germany. This did not consist of the KAPD stating that there was a perspective for new actions. Rather what they said was that we must do something particularly clever. We must proceed to undermine the capitalist state, which has essentially become Stinnes's state, his economic apparatus, through passive resistance. We have to say that this political insight is a direct result of the party's sectarian outlook. We do not believe that it is possible for such a party to be recognised indefinitely as an affiliate of the Third International.

But there is more that must be said. During the March Action and on other occasions, we have noted that the workers who belong to the KAPD are to a large extent energetic revolutionaries who are ready to struggle together with us. We are convinced that the best forces will come to us if the International puts the question to them: Do you want to belong to a mass revolutionary party, or to a party withdrawn into a sectarian shell? If the theorists who head up the KAPD persist in their false orientation and try to block off the masses from taking the road to the mass Communist Party and the International, then, in our opinion, the road must pass right over them. If the International adopts the correct decisions, we believe that those who now talk of the Communist International's stupidity can find salvation in their own stupidity; they can then do without the masses, some of whom still follow them today but will come over to us tomorrow. (*Loud applause*)

**Henriette Roland-Holst** (Netherlands): Comrades, I am sorry to say that I must take a few moments to speak of disagreements and other circumstances in the Netherlands. However, Comrade Zinoviev spoke in his report of the 'Dutch Marxist school', sharply attacking Comrade Gorter. I feel obliged to say something in this regard. With respect to this school of Marxism, which has been called the Dutch school, I make no claim to belong to any specific national variety of Marxism. In my view, there is no such thing as national Marxism, since Marxism is international. However, if there is something national about Marxism in the Netherlands, I believe that must be attributed to the specific conditions of our country, and there is no reason to rejoice at that.

Marxists like Pannekoek and Gorter, in my view, count among the best minds in the Communist International. But the fact that they live and work in a country that unfortunately lacks a mass movement, where our party still has no ongoing, living relationship to the masses, can easily lead to the emergence of a certain one-sidedness of outlook. That is why it is such a shame that these two outstanding representatives of Marxism are not present in Moscow at the congress. Comrade Pannekoek is delayed for professional reasons, and as for Comrade Gorter, I know that he definitely wanted to come. From what I know, he has set out for Moscow, but has not yet been able to complete the trip. I certainly hope that he will still come and defend his point of view in person.

However, given the possibility that he will not reach Moscow, I would like to say this: a year ago, a pamphlet by Comrade Pannekoek was translated and distributed here at the congress.[5] All comrades present there were able to familiarise themselves with his views. That was a very generous way of treating Comrade Pannekoek, and I wish that Comrade Gorter had been dealt with in the same way.

Comrade Zinoviev said yesterday that it had been proposed to translate his most recent short pamphlet and also the KAPD pamphlet on which he collaborated. Comrade Zinoviev said that there was no point in this. Well, in my view, it would be unjust to judge Comrade Gorter on the basis of this pamphlet. If you want to know his viewpoint on these issues, I would say that the essential points are already found in his open letter to Comrade Lenin. If this letter has not yet been translated from German to other languages, I hope that this can still be done.[6]

In addition, I have located in issue 17 of *Die Kommunistische Internationale* the stenographic report of the speech by Comrade Trotsky, responding in the Executive Committee to the speech of Comrade Gorter. Among Comrade Trotsky's many outstanding and profound qualities, he is a brilliant polemicist. Reading this speech, one is readily convinced that one of these talents is to pinpoint all the weaknesses of his opponent. Nonetheless, Comrade Gorter's speech is not found in *Die Kommunistische Internationale*, and it seems to me it would be appropriate to learn the views of Comrade Gorter not only from the brilliant, psychological speech of Comrade Trotsky, but also from his own words.[7]

I would like to add a few words regarding my collaboration on the KAPD publication, *Der Proletarier*. Comrade Zinoviev gently reproved me for this yesterday in the form of a sugared pill, but even in this form, the criticism must be answered. As far as I know, there is not as yet any blockade against the KAPD publication, and I am just as free to collaborate with it as with any other international party publication. I would like to add in this regard

---

5. A reference to Anton Pannekoek's pamphlet, *Die Entwicklung der Weltrevolution und die Taktik des Communismus* (Pannekoek 1920). An English translation ('World Revolution and Communist Tactics') can be found online at: <http://www.marxists.org/>.
6. Gorter's open letter was first published in the KAPD's *Kommunistische Arbeiter-Zeitung* in August–September 1920. An English translation can be found at: <http://www.marxists.org>.
7. Gorter's 24 November 1920 speech to the ECCI can be found in the Comintern archives, RGASPI 495/1/21.

that I do not share Comrade Frölich's point of view and believe it is absolutely my duty to collaborate on KAPD publications, and not just those of the VKPD. I do this with pleasure, first, because I agree with some of the programmatic and tactical viewpoints of the KAPD, and, second, because I prize their honest revolutionary intentions, which have been demonstrated in action. Comrade Trotsky said that we also prize these same revolutionary intentions in the so-called French Left. In my opinion, this French Left does not yet exist. So I believe I may continue my collaboration with the KAPD publication with confidence.

However, I hope that this will not be necessary for very long. I hope that the KAPD will find it possible to bring itself to fuse with the VKPD within a certain time period. I am against the existence of such parallel parties, perhaps because I have seen in the Netherlands on a small scale how much harm this can cause to a party, and how difficult it then is to hold to a correct path.[8] I believe that when you are in disagreement on major policy issues, you have a better chance of bringing the party onto a correct path if you work within it rather than standing on the sidelines. I am convinced that we of the 'Left', we who want to remain part of the 'Left', should be the quickest to submit to international discipline in such cases, because for us unity in action and unity of proletarian policy is a matter of principle. (*Loud applause*)

**Paul Neumann** (Germany, VKPD opposition group): Comrades, the sharp criticism that Comrade Zinoviev directed yesterday at the KAPD was just as justified last year, at the Second Congress, as today. Yet even though the Executive was familiar with the positions of the Communist Workers' Party, and could not have had any doubt regarding the KAPD's theory and practice, the Communist Workers' Party was accepted into the Third International as a sympathising party against the wishes of the German [KPD] Zentrale. Admitting the KAPD had two results. I am well aware of the Executive's lines of reasoning, but none of this was correct. The activity of the KAPD did not drive forward the revolutionary work of the VKPD in any way, because the Communist Workers' Party was really not needed for that. Secondly, following the [December 1920 VKPD] fusion convention, the KAPD lost almost all its importance. What we then saw was that the admission of the KAPD as a sympathising party seemed to revive it artificially. Everywhere we observed that in the factories and wherever workers came together in large numbers,

---

8. The Dutch Communist Party originated as a tendency in the Social-Democratic Workers' Party (SDAP), grouped around the newspaper *De Tribune*, which was founded in 1907. In 1909 the *Tribune* group was expelled from the SDAP and formed a small left-wing group that took the name Social-Democratic Party. In 1918 it changed its name to Communist Party.

the revolutionary sectors of the KAPD were inclined to join the VKPD, and in many cases significant sectors of the Communist Workers' Party simply transferred over from KAPD to VKPD. This process came to an end almost automatically when the Communist Workers' Party was admitted as a sympathising party.

In addition, admission of the KAPD had another effect. As a result of their fifty years of trade-union organisational work, German workers saw in the Communist Workers' Party not only a political party but also a factory organisation that is almost automatically linked to the KAPD. And the workers who belonged to trade unions immediately perceived that there must be a sympathy for the other form of KAPD organisation, the factory organisation.[9] And the sympathy perceived by the workers had significant negative results for our work in the trade unions and factories. The trade-union bureaucracy drew immediate advantage from this mood among uncommitted workers. This mood affected the ranks of the VKPD as well. Thus the question of factory organisation, the ongoing propaganda of the VKPD, and the KAPD's status as a sympathising party all had an impact on workers in the United Communist Party.

Today, comrades, we observe that the KAPD's propaganda with regard to smashing the trade unions has won not only sympathy but a degree of support in sectors of the VKPD. And that has happened because the Executive admitted the KAPD, rather than continually emphasising the attitude of the KAPD to the [factory] organisations. The KAPD's attitude to the VKPD was in reality anything but sympathetic. If you read its newspapers, you will find that there is no greater gang of villains in Germany than the VKPD. You can read that every Monday in their newspaper. When the Executive took that decision to admit the KAPD to the International, they should have kept in mind how this would obstruct our work.

When you hear the KAPD comrades speak – and this applies especially to delegates from other countries – you are astonished by the vast influence the KAPD enjoys. If the Communist Workers' Party enjoyed one-third of the

---

9. In the early stages of the German revolution factory councils were organised widely, often meeting the hostility of the SPD-led trade-union officialdom, which sought to harness them to union structures under their control. This reality led many within the KPD to counterpose the two and call for workers to leave the unions. Many supporters of this view joined in 1920 in forming the KAPD, which advocated replacing trade unions by factory councils. At their peak in 1920–1, syndicalist unions in Germany had more than two hundred thousand members.

For the KAPD's perspective on the relationship between trade unions and factory organisations, see the discussion in Sessions 18 and 19. A Comintern resolution on the topic can be found in Riddell (ed.) 1991, 2WC, 2, pp. 625–34.

influence that it claims to possess, the party would truly be very well situated. But that is not the case. And these [factory] organisations actually assist the trade-union bureaucracy, which now lumps together the factory groups, the VKPD, and the KAPD, to the detriment of the United Communist Party's work in the unions to overcome the union bureaucracy. It is hard to talk the workers out of this.

We therefore believe that the Executive and the congress must take a clear position regarding our future attitude to the Communist Workers' Party. It will not do that a party belongs to the International that – while sympathising with it – still fundamentally denies the International's programme everywhere and in all its newspapers. And the Third International is supposed to be grateful for such sympathy. That is the question posed to the congress for a clear decision.

Listening to the comrades who have spoken before me, saying that the KAPD should come to an understanding with the VKPD, I must say that such attempts have been made not once but five, seven, and twenty times. And the KAPD says there is no way it will change its positions. That is why we say that its acceptance as a sympathising party was wrong. We in Germany knew full well that their affiliation would have the results that we see today. If some sectors of the party then had a different opinion, they will be in agreement now that what we said back then was correct.

Finally, I would like to say that the congress should make the Executive conform to the congress's guidelines, so that there will be no future incidents complicating the work of the national sections, and that in the future we are spared such experiences. (*Loud applause*)

**Jan Cornelis Ceton** (Netherlands): Comrades, a brief explanation is needed on our part. So much has been said here about the Dutch school that it can give the impression that the Dutch party represents the KAPD current. This is not the case at all – not now and never in the past. Quite the contrary. There is perhaps no party on the continent that equals ours in such a degree of conscious agreement with the tactics and strategy of the Russian party and the Executive. From the very start, we have continually defended the Russian Revolution, and we have existed for a considerable time. Is it really true that the KAPD university is located in the Netherlands? Not at all. This current has very, very little significance in our country.

When Comrade Roland-Holst, speaking for the minority in our party, says that Pannekoek and Gorter are the best minds in the International, we can only reply that this was once the case but is no longer so. Comrade Roland-Holst excuses these two comrades by saying they live in a country without a mass movement, where a connection with the masses is lacking. But this is not entirely correct. These two comrades do not have the right to say this, because they have never taken part in agitation. We do this work; they do not. Neither Pannekoek nor Gorter. They never write articles for *De Tribune*, our daily paper. Can these two comrades, who call themselves members of our party, be excused by saying there is no mass movement in the Netherlands? That is not entirely correct. It is true that we do not have a mass movement with the scope of those in Russia and Germany. But we do indeed have a revolutionary movement in the Netherlands, in which these two comrades do not take part. That explains why these two comrades, Pannekoek and Gorter, so readily go astray. If you work out a policy course while outside the movement, then we can certainly say that this course is likely to be wrong, because such a course can be determined only in connection with the masses and their movement. And it is therefore important for us here at the congress to know that these two comrades, who represent the KAPD's university, do not do so in any connection with the Dutch workers' movement. (*Loud applause*)

**Michalak** (Adolf Warszawski, Poland): Comrades, before speaking to the Executive report, I first want to say a few words about the ties between our Polish Communist Party and the Executive. Until a few months ago, the ties between the Polish Communist Party and the Executive hardly existed. We live in a country that has become an armed camp, with hostilities on almost all its borders, which bristle with weapons. That is why it became almost impossible for our party to maintain ties with the movement outside Poland.

Our party was founded at the end of 1918 and was thus the first Communist Party formed after the founding of the Russian Communist Party. As a result, we had to resolve questions regarding our party's policies and organisation not only on our own, but also without any input from abroad, without any collaboration with the outside world. We take up, of course, all the issues that the Executive has to address, such as work in the trade unions. We decided that question at the very start in the same manner in which it was resolved a year and a half later by the Executive and the International. We always sought to be a mass party, and we always worked in the trade unions. Before the War, we had so-called party trade unions, but starting in 1919 we built unified unions.[10]

Our work and our achievements in the unions are so good that, despite the difficult conditions in which we work, we can show positive results. That will be discussed in another connection. I only want to inform you that in

---

10. In July 1919 the Polish trade-union movement, previously fragmented along political and national lines, merged into a unified federation. By 1921 the federation numbered one million members.

this field, as in that of the mass party – given the difficult conditions in which we exist – we still function as an underground party, just as we did in tsarist times. Given that fact, the task of becoming a mass party is more difficult for us. However, it is so important for us to become a mass party and to work in the trade unions that we have committed all our forces to this task. I can say, therefore, that we were always in agreement with the International in this regard, even though, as stated, we had no organisational or political connection with it.

Now as regards the other question that Comrade Zinoviev addressed, that of the Italian party. As soon as our central leadership and party received the necessary material and was informed about the affair, not only the Central Committee but also the party conference declared its agreement with the Executive on this question. Just as on other issues, we were very glad to hear of the split in the French Socialist Party and of the appearance of Comrade Zetkin at the French party convention.[11]

We faced a special policy question, however, regarding which you, comrades, were probably quite uninformed. Poland shares a border with Soviet Russia and soviet Ukraine. We therefore had to address the question of how we would respond to a possible war between Soviet Russia and bourgeois Poland. At the beginning of 1919, in January or February, our social patriots were shouting, 'Here comes Bolshevik imperialism, here comes the Red Army, invading Poland.' So it was not just a theoretical question for our party whether the Red Army had the right to come to us. We answered this question in February 1919 by concluding that yes, the Russian army has the right to come to us; the Polish proletarians have the right to demand support from the Russian Red Army in their struggle against bourgeois Poland. We presented that position in public meetings. After giving such speeches, our comrades were often arrested. Nonetheless, they courageously raised the question in the Warsaw workers' council,[12] which still existed at that time, arguing along the lines of what I have said here.

Later, the following year, this issue was posed during the advance of the Red Army. All units of our party without exception – I must stress this point – considered the Red Army to be our own army, and the Polish army to be that of our enemies. There were no disagreements on that point in our ranks.

---

11. As a representative of the ECCI, Zetkin crossed illegally into France in order to attend the French SP's December 1920 congress in Tours. Her keynote address is found in Parti socialiste 1921, pp. 369–77.

12. Workers' councils emerged in Austrian Poland in early November 1918, during the revolutionary upsurge that accompanied the defeat of the Austro-Hungarian Empire in World War I. By the end of the month, these councils had spread to Warsaw and all of Poland.

The same is true with regard to the question raised here by a KAPD comrade. With regard to counterposing Soviet Russia, as a state, to the international, Western European revolution, we view Soviet Russia in the same way as we do the Red Army. We make absolutely no distinction. Our workers do not understand how one can counterpose Soviet Russia, the Russian party, and its tasks, to the tasks of any party in Western Europe. Our workers do not draw that kind of distinction. Soviet power in Russia is our power. There is no distinction, no contradiction between Soviet Russia and its tasks as against the tasks of the International. Anyone who sees the matter otherwise is not a Communist. That is, in brief, what I wanted to tell you.

I must add that we will later submit a statement explaining our view of the Executive Committee's activity. However, I can tell you now that we are in full and complete agreement with it. (*Loud applause*)

**Seemann** (Bernhard Reichenbach, KAPD): Comrades, the previous speaker referred again to a point regarding which Zinoviev also earlier criticised us, when he termed our criticism of Russian government policy as being aligned with that of Dittmann. I will not go into this further; that will be done later.

However, I must once again protest the method of simply branding every criticism that is raised as counterrevolutionary. This method amounts to choking off all opposition. It indicates a lack of any understanding of the need for opposition, without which an organisation as vast as the International is simply condemned to stagnation. Allow me to give you an example. Clemenceau and Karl Liebknecht both maintained that the War did not have a defensive character [for Germany]. However, I do not believe that anyone here in this room – including Comrade Zinoviev – would consider the two positions identical, based on this similarity. It is just as absurd to liken us to Dittmann. I will demonstrate what an opposition means and what purpose it serves, and why such methods should not be used against it, simply in order to conceal every error.

We have been reproached for speaking so sharply. We did not think that we were in a ladies' finishing school here. We learned this approach from the Russian comrades, who always act sharply and energetically when they believe an error has been made. They slip in the word 'fraternally' here and there, while using the same sharp words.

I must also demonstrate the character of our opposition. I will give an accounting to show that the question of the Third International is not a simple matter for us, and that we do not take it lightly. We have demonstrated how useful the opposition is; unfortunately the Executive does not make any use of this fruitful opposition. Instead, great care has been taken to prevent delegates to the Executive here in Moscow from seeing our publications.

Let me cite some examples. Before the March Action, we carried out a sharp struggle for several months against the way in which the VKPD carried out education of proletarian public opinion. We pointed out that the broad masses are not capable of reversing course so quickly, when their publications have been pounding away in quite another spirit. Here the Executive had an opportunity, for it had publications from which it might have learned, for they portrayed the disastrous path that the VKPD had taken before it was too late, as during the March Action. What we said back in January was repeated later, in April and May, by Comrades Zinoviev and Radek. They said precisely what we had told the Executive in advance. When Levi still had his party post, we wrote an article entitled, 'Does the VKPD Belong to the Communist International?'[13] This article stated what was later confirmed by Zinoviev and Radek, namely that the VKPD press, because of its opportunist stance during the months before the action, was itself to blame for the fact that, during the March events, broad sectors of the party sabotaged the action. It is wrong to introduce a method that, over time, simply cuts out any opposition.

Unfortunately, Comrade Frölich has not read our newspapers any more attentively than the Executive, although he had more opportunity. He comes up with the most blatant stupidities. You claim that we are naïve fools and that our entire attitude to current political issues has been wrong, and that this was expressed particularly strikingly with regard to reparations. We are said to have written that this was not of concern to the proletarians. No, we did not write that. Granted, we did not refer to a looming conflict between Germany and France, because – as is now obvious to everyone – no such conflict exists. Instead, the bourgeoisie is about to achieve a far-reaching agreement. We said that this was what deserves the proletariat's vigilance, rather than waiting for a conflict with France.

The main thing is not to block criticism that must necessarily be present in an organisation that includes so many different types of workers from every country. Even if such an opposition now and then makes a mistake, that will cause no harm. Recall the last congress. It was that congress's shame to have as its two honorary chairs, sitting next to Zinoviev, Serrati and Levi. Take care that the present congress is not shamed by the fact that the KAPD is compelled to leave the Third International.

**Radek**: And where is Rühle?

**Seemann**: Not in the KAPD.

---

13. 'Gehört die VKPD noch der Kommunistischen Internationale?' (unsigned) in *Kommunistische Arbeiter-Zeitung*, 178 (undated, 1921).

**Egidio Gennari** (Italy): Comrades, the Italian delegation will later have occasion to address matters of special concern to the Italian proletariat. The Italian delegation agrees completely with the way the Executive has handled the Italian question and other issues. What has been said so far about the Italian Socialist Party's activity, however, is only a small part of what could be said. The time will come when we have to use new arguments in dealing with this party. If it asks to be admitted to the Third International, you will have to consider this. Serrati's errors caused great harm to the Italian Communist Party and damaged its organisation. It has lost all its illusions in Serrati. Given its experiences with Serrati and the centrists, our party is obliged to warn Czechoslovak proletarians of the dangers they and proletarians of every country face if the policies previously employed toward Serrati are now used with Šmeral and other centrists.

The Italian party has the duty to speak of this here. We know the Czechoslovak proletariat. We know its revolutionary spirit and the reasons why this proletariat has sent its leaders to Moscow. But we need guarantees against the opportunism of centrists of the Šmeral variety. The Czechoslovak delegation's report is reminiscent of some of Serrati's articles and reports, as where they say that there are no centrists or opportunists in the Czechoslovak party and demand that a resolution to this effect be presented to the congress. It is inexplicable why the Executive had such trust in Šmeral. During the War, he defended Austrian imperialism. He sent a delegation to Budapest for the coronation of Emperor Karl [in 1916]. After the battle on the Isonzo he sent a telegram to Borojević.[14] After the War he came to Moscow at a time when the entire Czechoslovak party had lost confidence in him and he no longer enjoyed any popularity in Czechoslovakia. He came to Comrade Zinoviev and asked for financial support. It is unfortunate that he received this support. What use did he make of it?

Šmeral's claim to be a Communist amounts to no more than remaining a Social Democrat and believing in the goals of communism without any intention of realising them. Concessions by the Executive gave Šmeral every possibility of dragging out the formation of a Communist Party in Czechoslovakia. He asked that the party retain the name Socialist Party. The Executive's

---

14. As head of the Czech Social-Democratic Party during the war, Šmeral advocated federalisation of Austria-Hungary, rather than independence of its component nationalities, and was criticised for his pro-Austrian stance.

From June 1915 to October 1917 there were twelve battles between Italian and Austrian troops along the Isonzo River. General Svetozar Borojević was commander of Austrian troops in that sector.

decisions demanding reorganisation of the Czechoslovak party were hidden from the masses, the proletarians. We have no idea why.

After the December strike, an editor of *Rudé právo* wrote an article against Soviet Russia and the Communist International. Another editor had spoken against Soviet Russia. Communist comrades in Czechoslovakia took a stand against these people, demanding that they be expelled. Šmeral defended them. We hope that the experiences we have had with Šmeral, Levi, and Serrati will be instructive for the Executive and this congress. We want to avoid experiencing other such disappointments. We therefore ask, first, that Šmeral be removed from his leadership position; secondly, that the Executive write an appeal to the Czechoslovak proletariat, alerting it to all the weaknesses and dangers of Czechoslovak opportunism; and, thirdly, that an appeal be made to proletarians in every country demanding a struggle against centrists and opportunists. I present the following statement on behalf of the Italian delegation.

> In view of the Czechoslovak delegation's statements, the Italian delegation proposes approval of the statement adopted by the meeting of the Executive Committee, and notes in addition:
> 1.) The International should not just dissociate itself from Šmeral's activity but in addition should bar him from holding a leadership post in the party.
> 2.) An appeal should be made to the Czechoslovak proletariat, which has entered the great family of the Communist International and has been accepted by it with full confidence. This call should summarise all the opportunist deviations by Šmeral and his friends and demonstrate the danger to the party if they should continue to hold leadership posts.
> 3.) The International should continue and if possible intensify the struggle it has undertaken against centrists and opportunists of every type who have gained a foothold in our party. We must counter the danger of repeating once again all the disappointments and defeats of our struggle for proletarian revolution.[15]

---

15. Three days after Gennari's speech, as discussion on the ECCI report concluded, the Italian delegate Umberto Terracini wrote his party leadership as follows on Gennari's resolution: 'With regard to the admission of the Czechoslovak party, around which a fierce battle is raging,... the speeches by Radek and Zinoviev and the resolution proposed by the Executive also...seem to us to be far too broad and liberal.... Regarding admission of the Czech party, the Italian delegation initiated a motion, supported by many delegations including those of Switzerland, Germany, Britain, Bulgaria, etc., expressing grave reservations as to admission of the opportunist Czech leaders in the International.' Natoli 1982, p. 131.

**Heckert** (Germany): Comrades, the Italian question triggered a crisis in the German party. Here is why this happened. A segment of the party leadership considered that the split that took place at Livorno, where the Communist forces in the Italian Socialist Party broke from the Serrati forces, was provoked by the Executive. In their view, the Executive intended to abandon the course adopted at the Second Congress and to convert the mass parties back into sects. And because the Communist International's Executive Committee supposedly intended to convert these mass parties into sects through a cleansing [of the membership], the comrades said that the Livorno split was indicative of the future that lay before the International as a whole. They said that this policy must be opposed. The debate in the German Communist Party led a group of leading comrades in the Zentrale to declare that they agreed with the Central Committee majority in taking a view of the Italian question different from that of Paul Levi and some of his friends. They said that they could not go along with such a disastrous policy.

What was the situation? At the Second World Congress, of which Serrati was a chair, it was assumed that as an honest revolutionary he would return home and lead the Italian workers to communism. But here Serrati let us down. He began right after the World Congress to sabotage the decisions made here. He did not bother with them. Even after receiving a slight nudge in the ribs, he did not come to his senses and fulfil his Communist duty. Instead, he wrote letters and articles taking positions directly opposed to the Communist International. An article by Serrati appeared on 18 December 1920 in the supposedly scientific-socialist publication of the German Independents, Breitscheid's *Der Sozialist*, which stated that the revolution here in Russia was not sustained by the broad masses of working people. Rather, he said, a criminal Soviet bourgeoisie is leading a depraved existence on the backs of this tormented and apathetic people. This rude attack on the Communist International and Soviet Russia was just as impudent and explicit as anything said earlier by Crispien and Dittmann.[16]

These comments by Serrati had a purpose that he soon revealed, namely to show what an upstanding revolutionary Turati was, speaking out against the Soviet bourgeoisie, which was carrying out such horrendous policies against the tormented Russian people. And then he recounted the fine speeches that Turati was making in the Italian parliament – speeches so touching that even someone who later joined the Communist Party embraced Turati. If Turati acts in this manner in the Socialist Party, one cannot possibly ask that we

---

16. Serrati's articles in *Der Sozialist* during this time, included 'Eine Anklageschrift gegen Moskau', 12 (1921), pp. 269–80; 'Der Opportunismus der III Internationale', 14 (1921), pp. 321–6; and 'Die französische Kommunisten', 18 (1921), pp. 423–9.

break with him, Serrati said; the Communists in the Italian Socialist Party were demanding something unreasonable.

Then came the Livorno convention, to which Comrade Levi travelled on assignment from the German Communist Party. Paul Levi is a leader who knows his way around in the International. He must have been aware of these statements by Serrati in Breitscheid's *Der Sozialist*. But during the Livorno negotiations, as the Italian comrades have again assured us, Levi did not oppose Serrati with sufficient firmness. Instead, his conduct supported the tendencies represented by Serrati. Encouraged by Levi's failure to attack him, Serrati grew bold and turned against the left forces in the Italian party. He was unwilling to discuss with them the expulsion of Turati and Treves. Instead, when our Communist comrades posed at the convention the need to choose: either communism and the Third International or Turati and Treves, Serrati thought it proper to turn away from the Communist International and take the reformist path. According to Levi and some of his friends in Germany, the fact that Serrati had taken this path was the fault of the representatives sent by the Executive to Livorno. The line had been drawn in the wrong place. It was bluntly asserted that this split in Livorno concealed a conscious intention to convert a mass party back into a small party.

Then, at a Central Committee meeting, the majority of the party representatives stated that they could not accept that Levi was correct, but rather, based on reports of what had happened in Italy, it must be concluded that the Serrati leadership was playing a shameful game with the workers, and that a split was therefore necessary. And when they wanted to determine whether the Executive was in agreement with the conduct of the two representatives it had sent to Livorno, Levi found it necessary to mock the party Zentrale, from which he had just resigned, and the Central Committee as a whole. He said:

> We cannot take the path of the Central Committee majority or lend it even limited support. It turned to the Oracle of Delphi, in order to learn from the mouth of the Pythia the real meaning of the events in Italy.[17] We believe we are man enough to draw conclusions regarding the underlying principles from the events themselves. For even if the Central Committee majority were to receive the desired answer from Moscow, what would that prove? Merely that the Executive Committee is mistaken in its assessment of the specific conditions and their inevitable results.

---

17. In ancient Greece, the Oracle of Delphi was a shrine where Apollo's priestess Pythia answered petitioners' questions regarding the future.

Paul Levi goes on to say in this article, referring to himself and his friends who resigned from the Zentrale:

> We decidedly reject either being identified with Serrati or condemning him. We reject basing our judgement on opinions we have formed on Italy as foreigners; rather we base our criticism of what happened there and of the Executive's conduct on the same facts upon which the Executive reached its conclusions.[18]

Although a large quantity of documents incriminating Serrati were available, Paul Levi said, 'We reject condemning Serrati.' But Serrati does not stand *alone* in the Socialist Party; there is not just the *Serrati* case. We must recall another case that is even more striking. In this Italian Socialist Party, a member of the Third International, we find D'Aragona. As a member of the Third International, he went to London to the congress of the Amsterdam trade-union bureaucrats and took part there in the writing of a manifesto in a commission together with Thomas and Fimmen and other Amsterdam criminals. This manifesto said that they turned their backs on Moscow with disgust and remained loyal to the Amsterdam International.[19] These were the leaders of this Italian Socialist Party who – in Levi's opinion – we could not break from.

Comrades, perhaps the Italian Communist Party, and the Executive comrades who supported this party in its course, were wrong in their judgement of the Italian Socialist Party. Perhaps it is still a party that wanted to remain a member of the Third International and work in its framework. Well, it is quite significant what was written in *Avanti*, the official publication of the Serrati people – or rather of the Turati people, since Serrati has now sunk from the first to the second category of leadership. *Avanti* is the newspaper of the Serrati party, whose delegates, Comrades Lazzari, Maffi, and Riboldi, are coming to us here – I believe they are here already. In order to repudiate the Communists who separated from them, they wrote about the Moscow Congress on 16 June 1921 as follows:

> The delegation does not have the great hopes of last year, and it does not bring with it our party's unreserved and enthusiastic approval for the international movement's leadership.... Events not only in Italy but in many other countries have shown us and our viewpoint to be correct.

---

18. Paul Levi, 'Wir Anderen' in *Die Rote Fahne*, 1 March 1921.
19. The London Congress of the International Federation of Trade Unions was held 22–27 November 1920. For the resolution attacking the Comintern, see International Labour Office 1921, pp. 23–4.

In France, the Communist movement stands rather more to the right than the Socialist Party of Italy. In Germany, serious errors by Executive Committee delegates brought about a severe crisis in the party, for which there had been great hopes.

Even in Russia, if our information is correct, there is a reaction against stubbornness and lack of understanding. Of course, this will not be noticeable at the congress. Comrade Zinoviev is too skilled and dextrous at organising congresses for his viewpoint ever to lack broad and secure support. But there is already evidence in the International of far-reaching weariness with his personal dictatorship, which is no dictatorship of the proletariat but is rather its caricature. (*Loud objections*)

Despite the difficult circumstances, our comrades will say what is necessary, alongside Clara Zetkin, Paul Levi, and many others. We hope that this message will be heard by those who need to hear it. The Communist International cannot be the monopoly of any individual. It must live and develop and struggle with full understanding of every situation and with a sufficient analysis of all proletarian activity.[20]

That appears in the issue of *Avanti* that also contains a picture illustrating the Italian Socialist Party in its struggle against Giolitti. Giolitti appears as a bomb-throwing Fascist. Beside him is a man holding a ballot, which is supposed to mean that it is through the ballot that the struggle against the bourgeoisie and the Fascists is to be conducted. (*Gales of laughter*) These are the brave comrades that Levi wanted to save for the International, and for whose sake he and some other comrades demonstratively resigned from the party leadership, thus converting the Italian question into a German and international question, while initiating direct support to counterrevolutionary elements.

Comrades, we must learn from this experience that the International must avoid such an outcome in similar situations, come what may. We therefore fully support what Comrade Gennari has said regarding the Czechoslovak question. We emphasise that the Communist International Executive must devote very close attention to the Czech Communist Party, so that we do not experience a repetition of Livorno there, and so that Šmeral does not become a new Serrati. The kind of disruption that the International went through after Livorno is not exactly what we need in order to move forward. I ask the Executive to direct that all similar questions be handled in the same way as in Italy. (*Loud applause*)

---

20. 'Verso il Congresso di Mosca', unsigned editorial in *Avanti*, 16 June 1921.

**Malzahn** (Germany, VKPD opposition group): Comrades, I will limit my remarks to the March Action, since Comrade Zinoviev has dealt with it in his report. In speaking of the March Action, he began as follows: 'We tell you frankly that major errors were made. The theory of the revolutionary offensive was stupid; it was a weakness. God protect us from this theory.'[21] Let us emphasise this insight. Back in March, we of the so-called opposition, who are often denounced as opportunists, drew the same conclusions as Comrade Zinoviev. We saw the danger in the German Communist Party, in the Communist movement. Because we saw the danger, we pointed it out forcefully, and in this way opened up a struggle against this approach. Comrades, the Zentrale and almost all the party press held firm to this theoretically false approach, emphasising with all energy the theory of the revolutionary offensive.

As for the Executive's point of view, you have heard it stated explicitly in the words of Comrade Zinoviev. And I must tell you that as revolutionaries, seeing the danger as we did, we considered it our duty to draw attention to it. Moreover, I believe that if Comrade Zinoviev had been in Germany, he could not have acted differently from the way we did. He would not have judged the question in any other way. Given the limited time at my disposal, I cannot discuss the run-up to the March Action and tactical approach. We will go into that fully when we take up the question of tactics and strategy.

Comrades, at this point, I would like to say that all delegations have the duty not to deceive each other and not to exaggerate one way or the other. Rather, here we must speak the truth, open and unadorned, so that the lessons and results can be drawn from all actions and struggles that have taken place in one country or another. I say that because Comrade Zinoviev stated that half a million workers took part in the March struggles in Germany. I believe that Comrade Zinoviev and the Executive have received false information on this point. We, the German delegates, the Zentrale, and all of us here, now have the task of determining as precisely as possible what was the scope of the struggle in Germany. I will limit myself today to making this correction; later, in the discussion of tactics and strategy, we will examine the approach and the assumptions that led to this action.

What then was the scope of the movement? What was the movement like outside the region of struggle, across the rest of the country? To begin with, let us note that in Silesia, East Prussia, West Prussia, Pomerania, and Mecklenburg, there was no trace of a general strike. The same is true across all of

---

21. Malzahn is probably summarising an aspect of Zinoviev's remarks on pp. 208–9.

southern Germany, in Bavaria, Württemberg, and Baden. Nor was there any sign of a general strike in Frankfurt/Main, Magdeburg, Anhalt, or Hanover. What is then left of Germany? To start with, there is industrial Saxony with its millions of proletarians. Here, we have to note that only small groups in isolated factories took part in the struggles in industrial Saxony – perhaps a few thousand workers in all. (*Commotion and objections*)

And how did things look in Berlin, the centre of industry and the seat of the German government? After the November 1918 revolution, the Berlin workers in their millions demonstrated again and again that they are capable of carrying out great revolutionary struggles. This is where the United Communist Party, strong with 350,000 to 400,000 members, held its founding congress. How did things turn out in Berlin? Between 4,500 and 5,000 workers took part in the strike. (*Commotion*)

Comrades, these are facts that we, as Communists, must not conceal. We must understand the situation clearly, in order to avoid drawing conclusions from false assumptions. As to why the struggle could not work out, we will deal with that fully under tactics and strategy. We are guided, in our opposition to the Zentrale and our attitude to the action, by our honest proletarian feelings, wishing the best for the revolution.

How did things turn out in Rhineland-Westphalia? In the Ruhr, the coal region, the most important industrial centre of Germany? Here there was no strike whatsoever in the big factories. Only a portion of the coal mines were struck, and we can estimate this as 20 per cent of the mines. And even in the mines, the strikes were partial, except for a few mines where it was solid. But even there, comrades, you could not call that a general strike. Workers walked out of the mines and then, the next day, they resumed work. Especially in the Ruhr and also in other areas this division in the working class led to a struggle of worker against worker. Already on the Wednesday after Easter [30 March], the regional leadership in Rhineland-Westphalia saw itself obliged to give up the struggle and drop the slogan of general strike.

What was the situation along the coast? In Bremen and Bremerhaven there were some partial strikes embracing a few hundred workers. In Stettin, Kiel, and Lübeck there were no strikes. As for Hamburg, the regional leadership there issued an ultimatum to the Hamburg government, demanding the disarming of the local police, the national police, and the militia within three days; otherwise there would be a general strike. Individual shipyards and factories were occupied, and demonstrations followed that ended in bloody clashes. Within a very short time, two days, it was all over in Hamburg.

Comrades, I believe it is important for comrades from abroad to know the scope of the March Action movement in Germany, of which so much has been said, in order in our subsequent discussion of tactics to come to a clear understanding of how we must act in the future.

We are now left with the actual region of struggle, Central Germany, where the provocation was made clear to the workers by Hörsing's invasion.[22] Here, we must note that the Leuna Works, with 22,000 workers, and the copper mines, with about 40,000 workers, joined the struggle – but, comrades, once again it was not universal. Those who know the facts must know and admit that if there was shooting in one place, in another place in the same district work continued and the workers had to be taken out by armed bands. These facts must be registered. In Central Germany, the number of participants in the strike can be estimated as 120,000 workers.

Adding in all the other figures, and estimating participation on the high side, we can say that 200,000 to 220,000 workers took part in the strike. That, Comrade Zinoviev, is an objective presentation of how things stood in Germany. Let someone from Berlin come and dispute what I have presented; let someone from Königsberg, East Prussia, or other regions present a different picture. We, from our honest proletarian point of view, want to drive forward the revolution in Germany – (*Commotion*) – we want the Executive and the congress to see things clearly and to realise that our Zentrale let itself be guided by false assumptions. That must be stopped. I ask you to judge the situation from this point of view. That was the extent of the March Action.

The crucial point is that things were rushed into, there was no time for events to build, and the fight was begun before the brutal provocation by this Hörsing was widely known among the workers.

Finally, one more thing. In a radio broadcast to Germany, the Executive told German workers that they had acted rightly. I can understand that, because even if the Executive had been fully informed of all the details, there was nothing else it could do. But we do criticise members of the Zentrale and party functionaries for having taken the Executive's opinion and used it within the party in the theoretical debate regarding the correctness of their theory [of the offensive].

That was really not the Executive's intention. Of that we are firmly convinced.

We must talk about these things, about the lessons of the March Action, so that we in Germany will be able to resolve the important issues before us in a revolutionary manner and in the interests of the Communist International. (*Applause*)

---

22. Otto Hörsing, an SPD member, was governor [Oberpräsident] of Prussian Saxony. On 16 March 1921 he ordered the Prussian police to occupy the province, ostensibly to combat strikes, looting, and acts of violence.

**Willi Münzenberg** (Youth International): Comrades, people like to reproach youth for pushing ahead too vigorously. We therefore hesitated to ask to speak this evening, in the hope that representatives of the party – particularly those whose parties were attacked rather strongly in the report – would put their names on the speakers' list. We are thinking here of the Swedish and Norwegian parties and the Italian Socialist Party, whose delegates are now present here in the room. Since this did not happen, the youth will be again in the front rank in taking the floor.

Comrades, we must say at the outset – as Comrade Zinoviev has already indicated – that we of the Youth International, along with our component youth leagues, fully and completely endorse and approve of the policies of the Communist International Executive Committee during the last year, policies that we ourselves have implemented. Above all, we approve of the Communist International's conduct with regard to Italy. This was expressed most clearly a few days after the Livorno Congress at the national congress of the Italian youth, where 40,000 of the 42,000 members took a stand enthusiastically and unanimously against Serrati and for the Communist International and the Communist Party.[23]

We also approve of the Communist International's conduct with regard to Germany. To start with, I must say that Comrade Malzahn has a curious way of bringing clarity to the March Action. If Malzahn was really trying to clarify this issue, then he would have known just as well as the youngest member of any youth branch that, in evaluating policies and the March Action in general, it is not so much a matter of how broad were the layers involved in it. Rather the point is that the party was obliged in that situation to issue a call for struggle, and the question is not so much how many took part in it, but rather, why the scope was not larger– (*Loud applause*) Therefore, dear Comrade Malzahn, as other speakers in this discussion will quite soon demonstrate, a large part of the blame and responsibility rests with the old policy of passivity advocated by Levi and his group. That is the issue. (*Interjection: 'Where were you?'*)

Where was I? I was then in Berlin, where we were preparing the international [Communist youth] congress, and I placed myself at the disposal of the German Zentrale. That is what is at issue here.

We also consider that the KAPD question would not have become such a long drawn-out crisis if the VKPD's parliamentary fraction had earlier carried out emphatically the Second Congress decision to make use of parliament in a revolutionary fashion. We are convinced that the KAPD would have

---

23. The congress of the Italian Socialist Youth Federation was held in Florence, 29 January 1921.

dwindled away earlier if the VKPD had really been what it is now in the process of becoming. (*Applause*)

Comrades, let me also tell you that the Youth International is also demonstrating its full and unanimous support of the Executive's policies in the new arrangements for the relationship between us and the Communist International. The time is past when the Youth was compelled and had the opportunity to play an independent political role of its own. Our new proposals and theses explain that, in all parties where genuine revolutionary Communist parties exist, the task of the youth is to subordinate itself to the political slogans of these parties.[24] (*Loud applause*)

But at this point we would like to stress a weakness that Comrade Zinoviev conceded in his report, namely, the weakness of organisational ties. We are sure this will be taken up later, as per the agenda. However, we would like right now to point out how important these ties are. The organisational question is a political one, and many blunders in Central Europe would have been avoided if it had been possible to come to agreement more quickly with the Executive Committee. Ties with the Executive Committee and its representatives, the newspaper – in short, the entirety of this question is for us not only organisational in character but also political. We do not want to go into this question, but rather just indicate it.

One more thing. At the end of his speech, Comrade Zinoviev referred to the fact that attempts had been made in several quarters to bring the Communist Youth into factional opposition to the Executive Committee and the Communist International. He said that the Executive was convinced this was not the case. I can only underline that. Whatever the resolution of the different organisational issues between the Youth and the Communist International, one thing is clear: the youth were the first to stand steadfast at the side of the Communists, the Bolsheviks, in the turbulent times of Zimmerwald and Kienthal, and they have never been and will never be separated from the Communist International. (*Loud applause*)

I would like to say one more thing. We recognise that the call, 'Break from Moscow, break from Moscow's decrees', is now the rallying cry of the opportunists. In this difficult time the Russian Communist Party, and it alone, sustains the Russian Revolution and assures its forward march. The fact that the Russian Communist Party is forced by our passivity to struggle alone, under very difficult conditions, only makes our hearts beat more strongly, with even greater enthusiasm, for this party. We must say this plainly to our friends of

---

24. For the Third Congress resolution on the Communist Youth's political subordination to the Party, see pp. 1030–3.

the KAPD. We will never have cause to betray and sell out our comrades. We will never resort to the methods that, according to the KAPD, represent democratic socialism and who knows what.

In this difficult situation, we state emphatically, as the Communist Youth of the entire world, that we belong to Moscow, we belong to the Communist Party, we belong to the Communist International. (*Loud applause*)

**Radek** (Russia): Comrades, as a member of the Executive, I listened to the debate on the report with growing amazement and no little relief. After all I had heard about harmful actions by the Executive, I was expecting that one comrade after another from Western Europe, Central Europe, and other countries linked with Western Europe – even if they are in the east (*Laughter*) – would take the floor, enumerate the Executive's sins, parade all its errors here before the congress, and declare that they wanted to have nothing further to do with this monstrosity, this den of wolves. (*Laughter*) Instead of that, comrades, the debate has temporarily been bobbing around the naughty boys of the KAPD, who say we are bad while warding off our blows. Two comrades of the VKPD opposition spoke here. They came here by special request of the VKPD opposition in order to call the Executive Committee to account for its misdeeds, namely, for instigating putsches in Western Europe and, secondly, for imposing an outrageous dictatorship – nothing other than a Cheka-style special commission, to use the words of our former comrade Levi.[25]

I have heard nothing about any of these accusations. Comrade Neumann has the mistaken impression that those he represents sent him to Moscow to discuss the KAPD. Comrade Malzahn tells us that he was right to say, after the 'Bakuninist' putsch: 'You were wrong.' In this situation we must tell you of a Russian proverb, which states, 'You can't get away from this business so easily'. Since you do not criticise, we will ask questions. Comrades Neumann and Malzahn joined Levi in claiming that it was a Bakuninist putsch. We ask them today, was it really a Bakuninist putsch or was it a class struggle – if not of half a million, then still of two hundred thousand workers? That was the figure mentioned to us today.

The German delegation may wish to dispute this figure with them. I am simply asking, was this a Bakuninist putsch or not? And if it was not, what were they doing when they lent their names to protect Levi as he excommunicated the German party and trampled on the Executive's reputation before

---

25. The Cheka (Special Commission) was the security force and revolutionary tribunal established in 1918 to defend the Soviet republic. In his 'Our Path Against Putschism', Levi wrote: 'The ECCI works more or less like a Cheka projected beyond the Russian frontiers – an impossible state of affairs.' See Fernbach (ed.) 2011, p. 164.

the workers of Western Europe, when he presented the Executive as a handful of unscrupulous adventurers? It is not the Executive that is at stake here. The charges by Levi, a man who never fought in the trenches for the proletarian revolution, do not harm the Executive Committee. But you are proletarians, comrades. You want to remain members of the Communist Party. So I must tell you that you cannot take the easy way out. For months you stood with Levi, through thick and thin, in this kind of struggle against the International and your own party, and then you come here in order to say in friendly tones that the Executive made an error on the KAPD question and there were only two hundred thousand workers. That just won't do. That won't do, Comrade Malzahn. (*Loud applause*)

**Malzahn**: I could not cover every question in only ten minutes.

**Radek**: Comrade Malzahn, your responsibility was above all to say that you had committed a political error in declaring your agreement with Levi. That was your first responsibility. (*Applause*) Comrade Malzahn tells us that even Zinoviev said the theory of the offensive was stupid. That is what the Executive said to the bleeding German workers, who were defeated not during an offensive but as they were defending themselves against an ambush by Hörsing. It was our duty then to say that the theory of the offensive is wrong. But dear Comrade Malzahn, here is the resolution that Comrade Clara Zetkin presented in the Central Committee plenum on 7 April, a month after the struggles. What did she say about the offensive? Here is what she said:

> Both the economic conditions as well as domestic and international political relations called for the VKPD to undertake intensified activity as well as for its offensive and action. The possibilities for such an initiative were also there.[26]

So, comrades, there it is. You had a chance to address this, Comrade Malzahn. If it was a sin, an error, to advocate an offensive – which I never did for a single day – well, I just established the fact that Comrade Zetkin sinned in the same way. You reproach us, who did not carry out an offensive, for not having reprimanded the German Zentrale. Our reply is that we must reprimand other comrades as well. Today neither the comrades who resigned from the Zentrale nor Comrade Zetkin believe that the policy of the offensive can be definitive. Well, that is no cause for joy. Comrade Malzahn, who spoke here on behalf of this current, has no cause to peck away at Comrades Thalheimer

---

26. Zetkin's resolution was published in *Die Rote Fahne*, 10 April 1921. For the full text, see Appendix 2c on pp. 1079–86.

and Frölich for being the devils of the theory of the offensive. This theory was adopted by you all.

We will address these things specifically in the debate on tactics and strategy. But we must get this straight. We must hear what you say about the call in the Executive report for Levi's expulsion. Where do you stand on that? For Levi was quite right in his speech to the Central Committee when he said:

> Comrade Pieck told us that the facts of the March Action will not be taken up because it is solely and purely a question of 'breach of discipline'. And I tell you that what is at stake here is solely the question of whether the March Action was correct. If it was, then I deserve to be thrown out. If, however, as I and many of my friends believe, the March Action was an error, then the others should be thrown out.[27]

We hear nothing from your side now about the Bakuninist putsch. Please, dear comrades, that just won't do. You must speak plainly here. A decision must be taken here on the Executive report, which approves Levi's expulsion. Yes or no?

Comrades, in dealing with this report, there are many questions to be discussed. Many comrades will be speaking, and I must ask them to please be specific on their view of the *Italian question*. Delegates of the Socialist Party of Italy are with us here. It is very important that they hear from us what we think about this question. It is here, on the Italian question, that a decision must be made on the entirety of the politics we pursued during the previous year.

In his speech, Zinoviev demonstrated that our course is toward the masses, but that does not mean that we want mass parties at all costs. Scheidemann's party is a mass party, as is the Labour Party in Britain. We want revolutionary mass parties. And the comrades who say the Executive showed in Livorno that it has taken a sectarian path – and five comrades left the German party's Zentrale under this slogan – these comrades now have a duty. Given all the documentation presented here regarding Serrati's party, its course of action, and its development from Moscow to Amsterdam, they must say here what is the sectarian policy that we followed toward the Italian party. Choose: it's either us or Turati. Did we not act in Livorno in accord with the decisions of the Second Congress, which pointed the way to mass revolutionary parties?

---

27. A reference to Levi's speech to the Central Committee on 4 May 1921, appealing his expulsion. It was published subsequently as a pamphlet under the title, *Was ist das Verbrechen? Die Märzaktion oder die Kritik daran?* (Berlin 1921). For the English text, see 'What Is the Crime? The March Action or Criticising It?' in Fernbach (ed.) 2011, pp. 166–205.

If we acted wrongly in Livorno, then was that not also true in Halle? (*Loud applause*) Then didn't we have the duty in Halle to accept Hilferding and Dittmann, who led much broader masses than Serrati and his group?

Comrades, we face a wide range of issues that have not yet been even touched, such as the policies of the French Communist Party, the situation in the Balkans, and the parties there. The Executive and the Presidium separated the discussion on its report from that on strategy and tactics deliberately, in order not to create the impression that we in some way feared to take responsibility and sought to evade criticism. What the Executive did was the minimum of what we wanted to do. We had very poor communications with the individual parties, but still, the discussion here of what the Executive did should not be general but rather specific, point by point. Give us or do not give us your approval, for the Executive intends to follow the same path in the future as in the past. And that means a struggle against all centrist and half-centrist tendencies in the International, disciplining the Communist parties into united parties of struggle, and, simultaneously, a struggle against every attempt to launch the mass Communist parties into premature actions that would diminish their mass character. (*Loud applause*) The congress must take a stand on all these questions.

Finally, a few words on the KAPD, which has taken up a disproportionate amount of time in our discussion. We were witness here to quite an amusing spectacle. Comrade Roland-Holst, featured by the KAPD in an issue of *Der Proletarier* on the 'Dutch school', rejects that title, while pleading on behalf of the school's founders, Pannekoek and Gorter. We have a small country with no great revolution, she says, and it is therefore no surprise that the comrades sometimes write things that have a curious ring. Comrades, we could cite other reasons. One of them is an astronomer, gazing only at the stars, and never at a living worker, while the other is a philosopher and, what is more, a poet. (*Laughter*) When Comrade Ceton took the floor to make a statement on behalf of the Dutch party against the Dutch school, my heart was with him. And when we see the KAPD comrades take the floor here with a sectarian fury that speaks only to the issues of their sect, we realise how great is the damage caused in comrades' minds by such a Dutch production. The fact that we have to polemicise here against a large number of speakers indicates that a tendency finds expression in this Dutch school that will crop up wherever there are beginnings of a Communist movement.

We must fight out a battle here, in this congress, in this room, over whether the Communist International was right to follow the course pursued during the last year. Is it right to say now, after a waiting period: no more fooling around; you have to choose now between the Dutch school and the Communist

International. Comrades, your decision on the Executive report is also a decision on all the other points. If the decision is made here as it must be made, then under the other points we will simply apply the finishing touches. All our past work took place in this framework, on the path indicated here, namely: to the masses and with them into the revolutionary struggle. (*Loud applause and cheers*)

**Koenen** (Chair): Tomorrow's session will begin at 11:00 a.m. Commissions will meet tomorrow evening or early the following day. Whether we will hold a plenary session or commission meetings tomorrow evening will be announced tomorrow at 5:00 p.m.

In any case, the discussion will be continued tomorrow; today's sitting is now adjourned.

(*The session is adjourned at 12:00 midnight.*)

## Session 6 – 27 June 1921, 12 noon
## Executive Committee Report – Discussion

*Continuation of discussion of the Executive Committee report. Speakers: Malzahn, Radek, Jacquemotte, Marković, Kolarov, Clara Zetkin.*

**Loriot** (Chair): Comrades, now that the Italian Socialist Party delegation has arrived, the Presidium is unanimously in favour of combining the last two points on the proposed agenda, the Italian and German questions, together with the present discussion on the Executive report. The Presidium also believes it necessary to ask delegations not to repeat what has already been said. It proposes to give the floor first to the Italian Socialist Party and then to the Italian Communist Party, and to other delegations only if they ask to speak on particularly important questions.

**Koenen**: Comrades, it has been proposed that further discussion should deal with the Executive report together with the German question and the resolution of the Italian question, because there is no way to separate them out. We ask that the comrades of the Italian Socialist Party be prepared to speak about their case early tomorrow morning, so that we can dispose of the Italian issues tomorrow together with the report of the Executive. The Presidium asks the congress to approve this change.

The discussion continues. Comrade Malzahn has the floor to make a statement.

**Malzahn**: Comrades, in his comments yesterday, Comrade Radek tried to create the impression –

**Radek**: I protest the fact that the Presidium has given the floor to Comrade Malzahn for this statement, which does not figure in the agenda.

**Malzahn**: Comrades, in his comments yesterday, Comrade Radek tried to create the impression that we of the German opposition wished to evade a debate on the March Action. In response, I wish to point out that when I placed my name yesterday on the speakers' list, the chair asked what topic I wished to discuss. I said the March Action, to the extent that it was covered by Comrade Zinoviev in his report. The chair responded that he did not consider that necessary, because the March Action would be taken up during the discussion of tactics and strategy. I then clarified that I would deal with the issues only to the extent that Comrade Zinoviev did in his speech. I will address tactics and theoretical issues under the question of tactics and strategy, as I stressed at the outset of my remarks. I went into the theoretical issue only to the extent that Comrade Zinoviev did in his remarks, that is, giving an assessment of the action, since that is agreeable to the Executive. It is therefore clear that we have no intention of evading a debate. I want to stress that during the action we carried out our responsibilities fully. (*Shouts: 'Hear! Hear!'*) The Zentrale will confirm that. (*Commotion and objections. Cries: 'Comrade, that is not a point of order.'*)

The opposition represented here carried out our responsibilities fully during the March Action. The Zentrale will confirm that, and we will speak to the other questions later.

**Radek**: Comrades, Comrade Malzahn has made a statement defending himself against charges that were not made against him. No one accused him of failing to present his theoretical views of the March Action. I criticised him because neither he nor Comrade Neumann, as representatives of the opposition, had the courage to defend the outrageous attacks on the Executive made by the group they represent, namely that the Executive had, through its representative, instigated a Bakuninist putsch in Germany. Nor did they have the courage to withdraw this insinuation. I note that Comrade Malzahn has used the occasion to make a statement regarding the opposition's heroic activity during the March Action, but has said not a word on the issue that is decisive for this group's relationship to the International.

So we are left with the fact that despite an opportunity to state whether it still stands in agreement with Levi's attacks, which assert that the Executive provoked the March putsch, the group has said nothing on this point. As for Malzahn's statement regarding the group's participation in the action, I note that no charges have been made that Malzahn, Neumann, or Zetkin sabotaged the action, as were made against Richard Müller and Däumig. And as for Comrade Däumig, he himself confirmed that charge by a letter to the Zentrale in which he stresses that his conscience would not permit him to take part in the March struggles. (*Applause*)

**Joseph Jacquemotte** (Belgium): Comrades, the Executive Committee invited the left wing of the Belgian Workers' Party to this congress in its capacity as a sympathising member of the Third International. Since we received this invitation, which we accepted, the left wing of the Belgian Workers' Party has left the old party. We therefore strongly hope that we will take part in the sessions of the next congress of the Communist International as an affiliated section.

Given the very important questions before the congress, I do not intend to take up its valuable time with a detailed presentation of the difficulties facing us in Belgium or of the battles we had to wage with the Social-Democratic party. Let me just say that Belgium is the homeland of the most brazen representatives of the Second International. I often hear comrades' complaints regarding the social patriots whom they have to combat in their country's movement. I cannot avoid saying that it is really we who must speak on this point, because we have the unfortunate merit of having the Second International's most shameless leaders in our country, including Vandervelde, former president of the Second International; Huysmans, secretary of the Second International; de Brouckère; Anseele; and Hubin. Mentioning these names is in itself an admission of the political backwardness of Belgian workers, who still today tolerate such unworthy figures in their leadership.

With Vandervelde as Belgian minister of justice, the Belgian police carry out raids on the dwellings of members of the Belgian Workers' Party and its left wing, with the curious result that Vandervelde submitted to the Workers' Party's general council a resolution of protest against the court-ordered searches arranged by his own staff of prosecutors.

Camille Huysmans declared in a plenary session of parliament that, for political reasons, the passport system had to be maintained, even while putting an end to all restrictions that hindered resumption of commercial relations among merchants and industrialists.

De Brouckère plays the same role in Belgium as Boris Sokolov's itinerant circus, which recently visited Belgium peddling faked photographs of a new revolutionary movement in Russia.

Hubin, a longstanding parliamentary deputy and party member, made the statement that the imperialist war had been ended too soon, and that if it had been continued for another four weeks, a durable and just peace could have been achieved.

I have mentioned these facts only in order to stress the need for us in Belgium to make the most serious and forceful efforts to suppress the influence that Social Democrats possess even today, and to create a powerful Communist Party in Belgium. To this end it is absolutely necessary to be able to count on the support of the International and also to be able to maintain enduring and regular communications with neighbouring parties. Without wishing to give any kind of advice to the congress, we believe that it is not enough for the different national parties to meet yearly in a congress. It is not enough for them to be in ongoing contact with the Executive. Rather it is indispensable that neighbouring parties maintain uninterrupted and close relations. I was very happy to learn that the French comrades, represented by Vaillant-Couturier, and the German comrades, through Clara Zetkin, have undertaken to use their moral authority to support the young Communist Party of Belgium.

I insist that closer relationships among neighbouring countries are urgently necessary, all the more so where there are industrial regions that extend across several countries, or at least across the borders of several countries. This is the case, for example, with the industrial regions of Belgium and Luxembourg, the French basin of Briey and Longwy, and the Ruhr district. The Communist International must pay close attention to these regions, which include a very dense industrial population. In my opinion, they deserve special treatment in agreement with the affiliated parties of the relevant countries. All this should be done, of course, under the supervision of the Communist International, in agreement with the parties of these countries.

There is another question that, in my opinion, must absolutely be raised at this congress, because it can pose obstacles to the development of the Communist movement in Belgium. This question arises from the existence of a group already affiliated to the Communist International. We hope to be able to unite with it, if the Communist International Executive Committee is willing to lend its enormous moral authority in the interests of the Communist cause in Belgium. There are profound differences of opinion between the already affiliated group and the left wing of the Belgian Workers' Party that is now in the process of splitting away. In one of the recent issues of *L'Ouvrier communiste* we read the following passage. The author of the article, 'What Divides Us', while discussing the left forces splitting from the Belgian Workers' Party, says in passing of his own party, the Communist Party affiliated to the Communist International:

> We reject parliamentarism, because it can only be harmful to revolutionary action. We reject the formation of a mass party, because such a party, just like Social Democracy, will be inevitably condemned to reformism and betrayal.

You will understand, comrades, that under such conditions it will be difficult for us to bring to life a Communist movement in Belgium that would conform both to the potential for Communist action in Belgium and to the theses of the Communist International.

I do not want to prolong these remarks and take up more of the congress's time. I hope that the Executive Committee will very soon issue its directive and instructions on this issue. It is quite enough that I have expressed here our firm hope that, with the support of the International's parties in neighbouring countries, we will be able to reduce the scope for action by opponents within the country itself. We are firmly convinced that we will succeed in building a powerful Communist Party in Belgium. The Belgian workers are revolutionary. In the past, they have utilised the weapon of the general strike for exclusively political goals. They will do so again. Vandervelde said that the War killed ideals. In fact, the War killed the ideals of those who had sacrificed the future of the proletarian movement to their thirst for power under bourgeois rule, but not of truly Communist workers. I am firmly convinced that by the next congress we will be an army, representing a powerful group within the Communist International.

**Sima Marković** (Yugoslavia): Comrades, I would be very happy to take the advice that Comrade Radek gave us yesterday by expressing a position on all the important questions presented in the Executive's report. However, I must say at the start that it is completely impossible to speak to all these questions in ten minutes. Shortening the speaking time only makes sense if it is possible to have a very detailed discussion in the commission. (*Shouts: 'Very true'*) It is not possible to state a position on every important question in ten minutes. That is not our fault, but the Executive's, for not having made it possible for us to have a detailed discussion in the commission.

**Radek**: I propose to extend the speaking time.

**Marković**: First of all, I must return to two aspects of Zinoviev's speech that affect the Communist Party of Yugoslavia. Comrade Zinoviev recalled his speech at the Second Congress, where he said, among other things, that the Communist Party of Yugoslavia, although large and strong, has a right wing that should be lopped off.[1] Comrade Zinoviev has confirmed that the Communist Party of Yugoslavia did in fact lop off this right wing. Comrade Zinoviev added that he could not guarantee that the party will not contain

---

1. See Zinoviev's comments in the Second Congress, Riddell (ed.) 1991, 2WC, 1, p. 307.

some opportunists in the future. He gave no reasons for his reservations regarding the Communist Party of Yugoslavia, and he cannot do so.

In the face of Comrade Zinoviev's unwarranted reservations, I am therefore compelled to present a number of facts. The Communist Party of Yugoslavia stands on the twenty years of irreproachable revolutionary conduct of the Serbian Socialist Party, which was well known to the entire International. There may well be no party in the International that from its foundation was so fully and hermetically sealed against reformism as our party. Anyone familiar with socialism before the War can confirm that. The Communist Party of Yugoslavia is the successor of the Serbian Socialist Party. When Austria-Hungary collapsed, and Serbia then became Yugoslavia, the Serbian Socialist Party became the Communist Party of Yugoslavia.[2]

The Serbian bourgeoisie inherited great riches from Austria. That is not true for us, the Serbian Socialists. What we inherited from Austria was the worst opportunism and reformism and – even worse – Hungarian reformism. We therefore had to wage a difficult struggle against the survivals of Austrian and Hungarian Social Democracy. We had to wage this struggle from the very start, and in a very short time we achieved complete victory over reformism, so that there can be no serious talk of reformism in the proletarian ranks in Yugoslavia.

In April 1919, at our first postwar congress, a resolution for affiliation to the Third International was adopted unanimously. We were therefore the first large European party to join the Communist International. At the very outset of our new life as a revolutionary party we were put to the test. We had the soviet republic of Hungary on our border, and intervention against Hungary was on the agenda.[3] The Yugoslav bourgeoisie was under pressure internally by nationalist hate-mongering and also by France, on whose financial support the Yugoslav bourgeoisie was completely dependent. It stood ready to take

---

2. Yugoslavia was formed in 1919 by annexing to Serbia Austro-Hungarian territories that included the present Slovenia, Croatia, Bosnia, and Montenegro. The Social-Democratic Party of Serbia changed its name to the Socialist Workers' Party (Communist) of Yugoslavia at its congress of 20–23 April 1919 and voted to join the Communist International. It changed its name to Communist Party of Yugoslavia in June 1920.

3. A soviet republic was established in Hungary 21 March 1919, consisting of representatives of the Social-Democratic and Communist parties, which fused into a single party. The new government adopted a number of revolutionary measures including establishment of a red army and workers' councils, nationalisations of industrial enterprises and banks, and introduction of the eight-hour day. It also implemented a series of ultraleft measures that increasingly isolated it, such as refusing to give expropriated land to poor peasants and overhasty collectivisation. The soviet government was ousted by troops from Romania and other countries on 1 August.

part in the strangling of the Hungarian soviet republic. However, thanks to our party's strength and its influence on the broad masses, such an intervention by the Yugoslav bourgeoisie was out of the question. The brilliant general strike of 21 July made this intervention impossible.[4] Not a single [Yugoslav] soldier took part in the strangling of the soviet republic of Hungary, while thousands of Yugoslav workers marched in the front ranks of the Hungarian Red Army. (*Loud applause*)

During the past two years, we have carried out three splits in our party, cleansing it completely of all centrist or half-centrist forces. We did not shrink from any sacrifice when the Communist purity of our party was at stake. We expelled our former comrade, Lapčević, who had been the leader of our Serbian Socialist Party for twenty years. He was no Cachin. The entire International knows him for his revolutionary stand not only before but during the War. Nonetheless, the moment he tried to divert our Communist Party from the revolutionary path of the Communist International, we expelled Comrade Lapčević. Comrades, I have had to present these facts in order to liberate Comrade Zinoviev from his strong reservations. I want to show all comrades that our party's irreproachable revolutionary conduct, including toward the centrist and half-centrist forces in our party, provides a sufficient guarantee that in the future, too, we will not tolerate any opportunist tendencies in our party.

I now turn to the second point that I must address. Zinoviev said he was not informed about Yugoslavia. Who is to blame for this? At the end of last year, the Communist Party of Yugoslavia was outlawed.[5] During the last five months, we in Yugoslavia sent three detailed written reports to the Executive, one of which appeared in the most recent issue of *Die Kommunistische Internationale*.[6] If Comrade Zinoviev says he is not informed regarding Yugoslavia, I can only conclude that the International's chair does not read its official publication. Implausible as that may seem, it nonetheless appears to be the

---

4. The 21 July 1919 general strike in Yugoslavia was called in solidarity with the Russian and Hungarian revolutions. The successful strike, involving workers in all industries, was led by the united trade unions and the Socialist Workers' Party of Yugoslavia (Communists) and Communist Youth League.
5. In the context of a massive strike wave, the Communist Party of Yugoslavia was banned during the night of 29–30 December 1920, under the pretext that it was preparing a coup d'état. Its offices and printing plants were seized and several thousand members were arrested or fired from their jobs. Also closed down were 2,500 trade unions affiliated to the Central Workers' Trade Union Council, as well as consumer cooperatives, workers' centres, and reading rooms. The ban lasted until December 1921.
6. 'Die wirtschaftliche und politische Lage Jugoslawiens' in *Die Kommunistische Internationale*, 17 (1921), pp. 452–68.

case, for otherwise he would not have said that he was uninformed about Yugoslavia.

Let me add to that. The outlawing of Yugoslav Communists at the end of last year is a very significant event, all the more since the Yugoslav bourgeoisie is following the example set by the bourgeoisie of Romania and, it seems, Bulgaria. Comrade Zinoviev's report paid almost no attention to this development. However, it is of the greatest importance, because it opens a new period of politics in the Balkans. The Yugoslav bourgeoisie has proclaimed a ruthless and open dictatorship. It is telling us, 'Yes, you Communists are absolutely right. You pose the issue correctly: dictatorship of the bourgeoisie or dictatorship of the proletariat. *Tertium non datur* [there is no third option].'

The Yugoslav bourgeoisie has opted for the first of these choices and proclaimed a ruthless dictatorship. It thus demonstrated that it too has abandoned all illusions in bourgeois democracy. Would that this were also true of the proletariat in Western Europe! Even the Yugoslav bourgeoisie has abandoned all illusions in bourgeois democracy and parliamentarism, saying openly, 'Laws and the constitution serve only to secure our class rule. The moment that democratic methods prove inadequate, we will resort to force.' And the Yugoslav bourgeoisie has resorted to force in order to secure its class rule. In our opinion, this will happen in every country, the moment the bourgeoisie feels the earth trembling under its feet, as was the case with the Yugoslav bourgeoisie.

It carried out a coup d'état against the Communist Party, on the pretext – as the government's decree states – that the Yugoslav Communist Party stood ready at that time, five months ago, to carry out a brutal revolution on the Russian model, seizing total control of state power. Unfortunately, this was not the case at that time. The Communist Party was not then strong enough to launch the final struggle to win power. It was strong enough, however, to instil in the Yugoslav bourgeoisie a great fear of revolution. Afraid of imminent revolution, the Yugoslav bourgeoisie resorted to force. The Romanian and – it appears – the Bulgarian bourgeoisie have followed this example.

It seems to us, comrades, that the dictatorship of the bourgeoisie must precede that of the proletariat in every country. In many countries, the bourgeoisie is demonstrating that it has unfortunately learned more from the Russian Revolution than the proletariat has. The bourgeoisie is saying that it does not want to play Kerensky's role. Statements by the Yugoslav minister of the interior found an echo in Romania and Bulgaria, and I fear that they will be echoed in other countries as well. This is without doubt a very important fact, which should be stressed in the Executive's report.

Since my time is very limited –

**Radek**: [Proposes extension of the speaking time]

**Zinoviev**: I propose to extend the speaking time to twenty minutes. I would like to make a personal request of Comrade Marković that he present his position on the Serrati and Levi issues.

**Marković**: I would be glad to. I still had a great deal to say about our party's activity in this time of illegality. However, I must turn to other questions, so that Comrade Zinoviev will not have the impression that I am evading them.

Let me turn to the Italian question. As I have said, the Communist Party of Yugoslavia carried out three splits during the last two years. We cannot be reproached for being afraid of splits. And precisely because we have much experience with splits, our opinion on the split in Italy is not without interest. We were able to follow developments in the Italian party from up close. We were quite well informed. What Comrade Zinoviev said against Serrati was well founded. The articles by Serrati that Zinoviev quoted from reveal many centrist and half-centrist tendencies. One thing I must say: the first of Serrati's articles that Zinoviev criticised was written a year ago, but Zinoviev took that up only at this congress. We in Yugoslavia were forced much earlier to take a stand against Serrati and his centrist tendencies.

I must tell you that, during the splits with our centrists and half-centrists, I kept bumping into Serrati, because our centrists referred to him and his articles. And given that Serrati then enjoyed the Executive's full confidence, the centrists confronted us with the assertion that Serrati and the Executive – which was in fundamental agreement with him and did not speak against him openly – were the real Communists, while we were not Communists but anarchists. So we were forced to speak out against Serrati more than a year ago. We did this at the risk of thus becoming embroiled in a struggle with the Executive, since we had no idea whether the Executive agreed with our statements.

No one can reproach us, therefore, for defending Serrati and the opportunists, centrists, and half-centrists, when we note that the split in Italy was in a sense an error. We consider it an error because it was not prepared. We have a lot of experience in such splits. In Yugoslavia, we have considered every split to be an important party action, which like every other such action must be prepared not only through ideas but also organisationally. This did not happen in Italy.

Who is to blame for this? Both the Communist comrades in Italy and the Executive. The Executive has the right and duty to combat centrist and half-centrist tendencies in every party, as soon as they are apparent. It had no right to tolerate Serrati as long as it did. The comrades in Italy vacillated with regard to Serrati and his centrist tendencies. From our Yugoslav vantage point, the split in Italy came too late, not too early.

**Radek**: And that is why you oppose it? (*Laughter*)

**Marković**: No, I am saying that the split was not prepared. It should have been prepared earlier and carried out earlier. But the Italian comrades and the Executive failed to do that. It was not sufficiently explained to the revolutionary masses in Italy that Serrati is a Communist with centrist and half-centrist tendencies. Who is to blame for that? The Communists in Italy, who did not speak out strongly enough against Serrati and were too lenient toward him. The split was an error only in the sense that it had not been sufficiently prepared. Again, in order to avoid any misunderstanding: the split with the centrists is not an error, but the split in Italy was an error because it was insufficiently prepared. If Comrade Zinoviev had spoken out strongly when the first Serrati article appeared, the Italian masses would not have gone with Serrati in Livorno but would have stayed with the Communists. Serrati should have been exposed and unmasked before the Italian masses during the last year, when he became an opportunist. The Italian comrades failed to do that. This is where the error in the Italian split lies. I believe, comrades, that I have presented clearly enough our stand on this split in Italy.

I will now turn to the German question. The March Action brought to light two important factors: first, the German workers' strength of will and readiness to sacrifice; and, second, poor leadership. Even during the March Action, when we knew nothing of Paul Levi's pamphlet and the stand of the Executive Committee, the Central Committee of our party in Belgrade took a position on the March Action. Even then, we saw clearly that the March Action's leadership was marked by enormous error. We were convinced then that the Communist Party of Germany's March Action was a brilliant opportunity to develop a struggle against the German bourgeoisie on as broad a front as possible. Unfortunately, this brilliant opportunity was let slip as a result of both a false theoretical attitude and also a number of serious tactical errors committed during the action. Nonetheless, the March Action is a step forward. (*Shouts: 'Hear! Hear!'*) We approve of the March Action as a struggle by workers who were attacked by Hörsing. Nonetheless, we must strongly emphasise that the leadership of this action was afflicted by very serious errors. As a result of this poor leadership, the action, which could have become a great struggle for power, represents something of a fiasco for our Communist Party in Germany.

That is our position on the March Action.

As for the Levi case in particular – Comrade Radek is very curious regarding my opinion of the Levi case – in my opinion Levi made a big mistake in publishing his pamphlet. It is possible that he made not only one but several errors. (*Commotion*) However, the German leadership of the March Action also made many errors. If Paul Levi is to be expelled for his errors, and if the leadership of the March Action is to be judged by the same standard, then the responsible (or irresponsible) leaders of the March Action should perhaps receive even more severe punishment. (*Loud commotion. Shouts: 'Lay charges!'*) That is my opinion on the Levi case.

**Radek**: Comrade Marković, make a motion presenting your charges.

**Marković**: I believe that we will have a chance to speak later on about the strong and weak points in the March Action.

**Radek**: The Levi case is being decided now.

**Marković**: I hope this will be taken up by a commission before we come to the vote.

A few words more, to wrap up. I must stress a major defect in Comrade Zinoviev's report. I expected the report to present a wealth of statistical data. Comrade Trotsky spoke fittingly of the importance of statistics as a weapon. We should never lose sight of the fact that that in our revolutionary work the weapon of statistics plays as great a role as the statistics of weapons. That is without a doubt a great defect in Comrade Zinoviev's report.

In closing, I want to fully endorse Comrade Zinoviev's final demand, namely that all Communist parties send their best forces to the Executive, so it can become a true general staff of the world revolution. (*Applause*)

**Loriot** (Chair): Comrade Sirola of Finland now has the floor. He is absent. I therefore give the floor to Comrade Kolarov.

**Kolarov** (Bulgaria): On behalf of the Bulgarian delegation, I wish to express its full and complete agreement with the Executive Committee report delivered by Comrade Zinoviev.

However, I am not taking the floor just to make that statement. I wish to make further remarks on one question raised in the report. This concerns how the Executive actually leads the international Communist movement.

We have always spoken out for the idea that the Communist International needs to be centralised organisationally and in its leadership. We repeat that today. This is an essential precondition for the victory of the international revolution. We do not shrink before the charges of the bourgeoisie and the social patriots, who call us vassals of Moscow. What we need is a clear-sighted and active Executive, full of initiative.

We fully approve of the Executive's clear and decisive conduct with regard to splits in the German, French, Italian, and Czechoslovak parties, as well as to Levi's breach of revolutionary discipline. But we also note that in certain cases it has failed to take a clear position in good time, as was the case recently when a crisis broke out between the Entente and Germany regarding reparations.

At the critical moment, the German Communists raised the following slogan: the gates to the West are closed for us, but the East stands open. Let us conclude an alliance with Soviet Russia. The French Communists, however, did not find it possible to take a clear, public position against the machinations of French imperialism. It was the Executive's duty at that moment to issue a clear slogan and to do everything to support the actions of the Communist parties in both countries by issuing authoritative guidelines for both of them.

It is unfortunate that this was not done at that decisive moment, and that the two parties committed the error of not acting according to a common plan.

The German Communists took the right path in proposing an alliance with Soviet Russia, but they were wrong in telling the German proletariat that the gates to the West were closed to them, since behind these gates is the proletariat of the Entente countries, to which they must find their way. But it was particularly galling to see the conduct of the French party in such a vital matter, where they got entangled in a net of ambiguities.

The Executive acted correctly toward the party of French proletarians, but it did not do enough. I am putting special stress on the conduct of the Executive toward France because of the important role of French imperialism in the European counterrevolution. I also do this for another reason. The rulers of France are the real masters of our country, dictating to the Bulgarian government the laws enacted to suppress the Communist Party. For this reason, we Bulgarian Communists have the right to regard the French Communist Party somewhat as our own and to take a greater interest in its activity and development. Well, we recognise that developments in France are favourable for our views, and we rejoice in the progress of the French Communist Party. However, we do not want to conceal the great difficulties that the French party must still overcome in order to become a true and genuine Communist organisation.

Consider how parliamentary activity is conducted in France. Previously, it was the parliamentary weakness of the Socialist Party that bred syndicalism and drove the workers to anarchism. Now that the French proletariat sees a powerful movement gathering around the Communist International, it is absolutely necessary to break with the old parliamentary traditions and finally take the new road of revolutionary parliamentarism.

In this regard, a comment on the press is appropriate. In line with the traditions of the old French Socialist Party, the workers never saw the position of the party expressed in its publication. Instead, they learned there of the various opinions of currents within the party, usually quite different from each other. It was left to the workers to make their own judgement and form an opinion, according to their taste. Has the French Communist Party now broken with this tradition? Has it succeeded in creating a true party publication? The answer to these questions is 'no'. *L'Humanité* does not yet present an overriding, clear, and open Communist point of view. Even a scholar like Comrade Paul Louis sees French imperialism's counterrevolutionary conquests only as errors and deviations, to which he responds merely that they should be avoided.

The Executive discussed relations between the Communist Party and the trade unions. We must point out again to the congress that the French Communists do not take a clear and unequivocal position regarding the role of Communists in the trade unions, a fact that could lead to a serious and dangerous crisis in the French revolutionary movement.

With respect to revolutionary mass struggle, we must note that the party is still only in its very beginnings. It has not yet gained authority as an organiser and recognised leader of the masses. I must stress in particular that the party has not yet found it possible to develop vigorous agitation for mass actions against French capitalism, which reveals its reactionary and counterrevolutionary character around the world.

I do not mention these things to reprimand the French party. On the contrary, I acknowledge the efforts and good will of the French comrades in creating a genuine Communist Party, and the marked progress already achieved in this regard. Our task, however, is to help the French comrades in every way possible, and this is among the most important tasks of the Executive. Let us hope that it will devote more activity to this task in the future. It is the task of Communist parties in every country to strengthen the Executive's initiatives and render them more enduring by organising for them more effectively and assigning to them the best forces.

**Clara Zetkin** (Germany): Comrades, the day before yesterday, Comrade Zinoviev unfurled the Leporello List of my sins,[7] and Comrade Radek continued in that vein yesterday. I assume that, as the principal defendant, I will receive a longer speaking time, for in ten minutes it is impossible even to touch on the questions that I must cover. First of all, as to my transgressions,

---

7. An allusion to a comical scene in Mozart's opera *Don Giovanni*, in which the servant Leporello attempts to console one of Don Juan's seduced lovers by displaying a list of thousands of his master's romantic conquests.

I must emphasise that I have never in my life corresponded with or conspired with Comrade Nobs in Zürich. This claim must be based on an error.

Now as to the Italian question and my position on it, which was a decisive factor in my leaving the German Zentrale. Here is what I have to say: Based on Comrade Zinoviev's report, and the speeches of Comrades Heckert, Radek, and others, I have the impression that this matter is being dealt with too much as the Serrati case rather than as a question of the masses of Italian proletarians who, to our regret, have not yet taken a clear and solid ideological stand in the framework of communism. Much has been said here about Serrati's ambiguity, treachery, and evasion, when faced with a specific decision. Well, comrades, I cannot bring myself to make a decision on the Italian question based on arguments that always wind up by saying that Serrati is a bad egg, that his politics are never fully clear, indeed are vacillating and undefined. Comrades, if we are to base decisions solely on moral criteria and on a consistently applied political line that makes a political figure's positions fully evident to both friends and opponents, then I would say – and I stress that I am far from wishing to criticise – I would say, Comrade Radek, that I see 'a man who isn't there' because his positions are often vacillating, changeable, and indefinite.

Comrades, I set aside all personality issues. I am truly not among those who, as Comrade Zinoviev said, are full of regret that the Presidium's table is not adorned with D'Aragona's handsome beard, which, by the way, I have never seen. No, comrades, I tell you truly that my aesthetic sensibility is fully satisfied by the internationally renowned curly locks of our friend Zinoviev. (*Laughter*) If I were to judge in terms of personal feelings, then I must state frankly that I am drawn not to Serrati but rather to Turati, who is really quite a fine fellow, even though I consider his politics abominable and deserving of the most vigorous opposition. But for me, the decisive factor has always been to take the broad masses into consideration, and, unfortunately, they are still with Serrati. I will say this: If Serrati was really the kind of man portrayed in the quotations read out by Comrade Zinoviev, then I do not understand why he was on the Presidium at the Second Congress. Why was there not an effort much earlier and in more decisive fashion to break from him and achieve a clear-cut decision?

Nonetheless, comrades, I understand full well why the Executive hesitated to intervene forcefully in the development of Italian party relations. The Italian party was among the first large parties to commit itself, without reservations and in a difficult moment, to the Third International. Nonetheless, we should have been warned by events not to overestimate this fact. The September [1920] events showed that the Italian party was incapable of grasping the situation and evaluating the revolutionary possibilities for a massive political struggle to win political power or at least to make a big push in that direction.

Comrade Terracini told us here that the party leadership debated for two days whether to call the revolution or not. In my opinion, what was more appropriate in this situation was for the party leadership to decide immediately to commit all its resources to launching a political struggle. That would have revealed how much progress had been made along the road of revolution. But the fact that this decision was not taken cannot be laid solely at the door of Serrati, who was then not in Italy but on his way home to Italy from Moscow. And even now it seems to me that the blame cannot be placed exclusively on the Serrati forces, because the Maximalists had the majority in the party leadership, and, nonetheless, the decision was taken to place the matter in the hands of the opportunist trade unions.[8] For me, this fact demonstrates two things. First, the Italian party, which we regarded with pride and admiration, was not what we thought it to be, either ideologically or organisationally. And in addition, the insurgent masses themselves in Italy had not progressed further than their leaders. Because otherwise, comrades – I have always held this view and still hold it today – if the masses had truly been imbued with revolutionary understanding and will-power in that situation, they would have rejected the decision of their vacillating trade-union and political leaders and would have taken up the political struggle regardless.

**Heckert**: This is the same excuse as the one offered by the Scheidemann people for their betrayal in 1914. (*Commotion*)

**Zetkin**: Pardon me, but this is not an excuse, merely an estimate of the historical facts – namely, that there is always a relationship between the level of the leaders and that of the masses. Certainly, the leaders' conduct is often decisive, but, in other circumstances a truly mature revolutionary proletariat in certain decisive situations will generate leaders from its ranks that replace the old leaders. I do not say that to diminish in any way the guilt of the political leaders but for another reason, namely, to demonstrate how great was the Executive's responsibility to make all efforts toward the emergence in Italy of an ideologically and organisationally united party. Such a party could take in hand the education of the still-confused masses, imbued only with their revolutionary instincts, and provide them with leadership.

---

8. Since before the War, the majority in the PSI had been known as 'Maximalists' because of their insistence on the importance of the 'maximum' demands in the Social-Democratic programme, which dealt with the achievement of socialism.

I have always viewed the Italian problem from the vantage point of creating a party of this type. I was therefore totally in favour of the Executive's decision that if the Italian party wishes to belong to the Third International, it must break from the Turati forces immediately and in public. I emphasise the last words: immediately and in public. In my opinion, permitting the so-called Unitarian group[9] to continue its reformist, Turati-style policies garbed in Communist phraseology was totally excluded. What made this break difficult was the existence of a middle force, which indisputably included broad proletarian masses. These masses had shown in the past and still show that they sincerely sought a path to communism and the Third International. They were striving to find it, and not only through lip-service; they were prepared to take action.

I considered it extremely important to win these masses for a Communist Party in Italy. Why was that? Not, as has been suggested here, because I am attracted in any way to centrist politics. No, I had other reasons. I knew that among these masses were workers, organised in trade unions and cooperatives, who could carry the struggle against reformist and opportunist policies in these organisations and who must play that role. And I had another reason, which will show you how distant I am from any half-centrist, pacifist impulses. I have been told – and I cannot confirm that this is true; our Italian friends will correct any error here – that in Italy the municipal governments, the mayors and town councillors have control over the political police in a situation of civil war that, in my opinion, has broken out in Italy. Under these conditions, I hold that it adds considerably to the Communists' strength that in thousands of municipalities they have control of an armed force – at least, over the armed police – obviously not so that armed police can serve as honour guards at demonstrations but so they can intervene in conflicts on behalf of the revolutionary struggle.

These were the considerations that led me to emphasise the need not merely to break away from the Turati forces at once but to make an attempt, so far as possible, to bring into the [Communist] party a significant part of the so-called Unitarian Communists, if possible without Serrati – I say that frankly – but also with Serrati, if there was no other way. After all, even in politics, when the need is great, sometimes the devil must dine on flies.[10] I was convinced that further developments in a strong Communist Party would force Serrati to

---

9. A reference to the Unitary Communist faction led by Serrati, whose national conference was held in Florence 20–1 November 1920. That meeting voted against a break with the reformists, but called for adherence to the Comintern.

10. A reference to the German proverb, *In der Not frisst der Teufel Fliegen*. It is roughly equivalent to the English expression, 'Beggars cannot be choosers'.

show his true colours, either to carry out an honest policy or to expose himself in such a way that not a single worker could have any doubts regarding him any longer. I advanced the opinion that the Executive was right in demanding expulsion of the Turati forces, which was the *sine qua non*, the precondition on which we must not give way. On the other hand, for the reason just given, I thought that after such long hesitation in carrying out the split – not out of sympathy for Serrati but out of concern for the masses – an effort was necessary to draw a significant portion of those masses over to us. It therefore seemed to me that the Executive's representatives in Livorno should have sought to achieve an agreement with our friends of the left wing and also with the Serrati forces that would have permitted us to bring thousands and tens of thousands of workers into the ranks of the Communist Party. In my opinion, the motion presented by Graziadei did not yet represent this path, but it could have served as a basis on which to agree on a formula that would have enabled us to bring the genuinely Communist workers to a Communist Party.[11] In this way, the split would not have taken place in such a straight, smooth line way off on the left, as it now has. Instead, it could at least have been a split within the Centre.

This is the point of view advanced in the resolution that I submitted to the Zentrale, and by and large it coincided with the resolution presented by the Executive's representative.[12] I modified it only on one point, in saying that the door should be left open to permit a large segment of the workers following Serrati to find their way to the Communist Party.

What did the resolution say? It gave unreserved support to the Executive's demand that the Turati forces be immediately expelled, without any argument. Secondly, it reproached Serrati for having made two major errors. First, during the six months since the Second World Congress, he had not made a single proposal to carry out the split in any other manner. And then, in Livorno, he had chosen unity with the 14,000 Turati forces as against unity

---

11. Graziadei's formula was, 'All those who refuse to freely declare their adherence to the theses and conditions of the Third International and will not commit themselves to applying them following the congress, thereby, regrettably, render themselves unacceptable as members of the Party and the Third International.' See PSI 1962, p. 67. Graziadei and Anselmo Marabini led a current within the PSI that attempted to reconcile Serrati's Unitary Communist Faction with the Communist Faction led by Bordiga.

12. Zetkin's resolution on Italy took the form of an amendment to a resolution by the Executive representative, Radek, calling for unification with 'the communist elements' that remained in Serrati's group, the PSI. The Zentrale approved the amended motion unanimously on 1 February and published it the next day in *Die Rote Fahne*.

with the Communist Party and its 68,000 proletarians.[13] Then the resolution explained that there were doubtless proletarian forces supporting Serrati who honestly wanted to embrace communism, and the door should therefore be left open for them to come to agreement with the Communist Party and join in a unified party. The Executive was asked to look into whether anything further could be done along these lines. In addition, the resolution said that obviously in Italy there was only one legitimate Communist Party, namely the Communist Party of Italy, and all sister parties had to support this party and it alone. Comrades, the fact that this resolution was free of centrist leanings was confirmed when the Executive, in a later session, unanimously adopted this resolution. So if I am accused of centrist leanings because of this resolution, I am certainly in good company.

Let us continue, comrades. I was then carrying out agitation in the countryside, and was uninformed. As they say, 'I simply didn't have a clue.' When I returned for a meeting of the Zentrale, I learned to my very great surprise that another discussion was planned on the Italian question. I asked why. I was told, 'Well, first of all, Levi spoke at a meeting of Berlin functionaries, interpreting the resolution in manner favourable to Serrati. In addition, a representative of the Executive has come here from Livorno, and he says that the adopted position is inadequate and must be changed.'[14]

With regard to Levi's statement, I expressed the humble opinion that, however much I valued his abilities, an individual figure cannot, by expressing an opinion, reverse the decisions of an entire leadership body. It would be sufficient for the Zentrale to state that Levi, in giving such-and-such an interpretation to the resolution, had not been speaking on our behalf.

Another resolution was presented by Comrades Thalheimer and Stoecker. Let me add one point. If memory serves me right – my documentation was unfortunately seized at the German border by the solicitous German police[15] – the Zentrale adopted the first resolution unanimously, with one abstention and one member absent. Now the resolution was raised again for reconsideration together with the Thalheimer-Stoecker resolution, of which I will speak

---

13. An error by either Zetkin or the stenographers; the Communists' vote at Livorno was 58,000.

14. The Berlin meeting took place about 10 February. The Executive representative coming from Livorno was Rákosi.

15. The Thalheimer-Stoecker resolution, reflecting Rákosi's viewpoint and calling for a broad ideological struggle against the PSI as a whole, was presented to a Zentrale meeting about 15 February. The 'solicitude' of the German police consisted of seizing Zetkin's personal papers when she arrived at the German border on 5 June. The documents included testimonies of participants in the March Action, many of which were published by the SPD late in 1921 in its newspaper *Vorwärts*.

later. The Thalheimer-Stoecker resolution was rejected by a majority of the Zentrale, and the original resolution was again adopted by a large majority, after I had sharpened it considerably so that it could not possibly be interpreted in a manner favourable to Serrati. My view of this is confirmed by the fact that the Executive's representative, as I am told, said that the old resolution was adequate after it had been made sharper.

Comrades, there is a lot of talk here about the requirements of discipline and of the minority giving way to the majority. It was expressly decided in that session of the Zentrale that the sharpened resolution would be submitted to the Central Committee in the name of the Zentrale as a whole. It was not considered important to forbid individual members from bringing in their own resolution, as would be required by a strict interpretation of the concept of discipline. Why did I oppose the Thalheimer-Stoecker resolution?[16] I said that I supported this concept of discipline. I merely pointed out that it had been decided to present the resolution of the Zentrale as a whole, and none other. And adopted by majority decision, at that!

**Heckert**: The opposite was decided.

**Zetkin**: Comrades, it was decided that this would be the resolution of the Zentrale as a whole, but afterwards it was stated that individual members had the right, if they wished, to submit resolutions as individuals. Incidentally, I would like to say that this is a trivial question that does not affect the heart of the matter. In my opinion, the concept of discipline is applied too strictly.

I opposed the Thalheimer-Stoecker resolution for the following reasons: First of all, it motivated the expulsion of the Serrati forces – quite apart from their other errors, which have already been stated – on the basis of the Italian party's position regarding nationalities, the trade unions, and the agrarian question. Now these three questions had been taken up by the Second Congress,[17] and, in my opinion, using positions on these questions as the basis for expulsion is a violation of the authority of that congress. The question is posed: Why, if the position of the Italians on such matters was so different from that of the Communist International as a whole, was it not the duty of the Second Congress, even then, to expel the Italian party from the International? And there is another factor. Even now there are disagreements on

---

16. Despite the Zentrale's decision not to carry its disagreement into the Central Committee, the Thalheimer-Stoecker resolution on the Italian question was reintroduced into a Central Committee meeting on 22 February 1921 and adopted, by a vote of 28–23.

17. See Serrati's statements in Riddell (ed.) 1991, 2WC, pp. 234–5 (colonial struggles); 623–4 (trade unions); 653–4 (agrarian question).

these three questions, in terms of both theory and practice, in almost every country, in almost every Communist Party. I recall that there were intense struggles in our Russian sister party quite recently on the agrarian and trade-union questions, regarding not only theory but practice.[18] It therefore seemed to me that if this was to be the standard for membership in the Third International, there was hardly a single party at present that could belong to it.

There was another reason why I was opposed to the Thalheimer resolution. It stated that a vigorous struggle had to be waged against the Serrati current. I have no objection to a sharp struggle against Serrati, but not against the Serrati current, because that was a general term that in my opinion was also aimed at proletarians who wanted to come to the Communist Party.

This declaration of war seemed to me particularly unwise at that moment for a specific reason. As you know, I have been accused of carrying on diplomacy with Serrati. I can confirm that Serrati, after travelling to Berlin, was also in Stuttgart, doubtless because of the simple fact that it is much easier to get to Berlin and Stuttgart than to Moscow. But what is this about my diplomacy? It is important for me to clarify this.

I had heard that Serrati had been in Berlin and had consulted with members of the German Zentrale. The Zentrale had decided to send the Moscow Executive a proposal or request that it consider whether a special commission should be sent to Italy that, in collaboration with the Communist Party and the proletariat, would seek a formula for the immediate expulsion of the Turati forces and for a split. Given this fact, I thought that I should not be more Catholic than the Pope, and if the Zentrale has done this –

**Radek**: The Pope was Levi.

**Zetkin**: There was no way I could know that. I was told that I should be cautious in discussions with Serrati and that, immediately after the discussion, I should write down the results and send it off special delivery to the Zentrale, so that Comrade Curt Geyer could take it with him to Moscow. I held strictly to this advice.

When Serrati came, I was not at all diplomatic. I gave him a sharp dressing down because of his letter to Lenin and his letter to Longuet after the split at

---

18. A debate on the place and tasks of trade unions in Soviet Russia took place in the Russian Communist Party from December 1920 to March 1921. Significant divisions arose within the leadership, with Lenin on one side and Trotsky and Bukharin on the other. The Russian Communist Party's Tenth Congress in March 1921 adopted Lenin's view.

The discussion on the agrarian question referred to here probably concerns the introduction of the New Economic Policy, considered at the Tenth Congress, which approved the tax in kind of peasant crops as a centrepiece of the NEP.

Tours. I explained that this was an error, and he admitted this. He excused his conduct as that of a man under pressure, attacked from every side, from left, right, and centre, who had therefore been clumsy in defending himself.[19]

This carried very little weight with me, but I thought of utilising this situation to promote a split and clarification in the Italian [Socialist] Party. I told Serrati, 'If you are serious about coming to an agreement with the Communist Party and the International, I believe it is not adequate that you make your proposal through the intermediary of the German Zentrale. It will be more honest and politically astute if you direct the Italian Socialist Party leadership to make the same proposal directly to the Executive in Moscow.' After much discussion back and forth, Serrati accepted that, and I thought that I must push him further.

'In your position, that is not enough,' I told him. 'You must have your party leadership send a copy of this request immediately to the leadership of the Communist Party of Italy, and you must add to it, 'Dear Comrades, we are enclosing a copy of a request to the Executive of the Third International. We ask you to take note of our initiative and, if possible, to express support for it.' Comrades, Serrati agreed to that as well. As for what I hoped would come of this, we did not discuss that.

What did I hope to achieve? I wanted to force Serrati into a corner, where he would either have to honestly carry out his promise to me – I considered that to be in the interests of coming to an agreement and clarifying the situation in Italy – or, if he did not hold to it, then we would have a weapon for use against him. We could then demonstrate that his professed adherence to the Third International and loyalty to it was only lip service, and that he lacked the will to act on it.

In that context, I considered it unwise to vote for the Thalheimer-Stoecker text. Why was that? Because it provided an easy pretext for Serrati to break with his undertaking and to do nothing to arrive at an understanding with the Communist Party of Italy and the International. Of course I made inquiries with our friends in Italy: Serrati had done nothing to carry out his promise. (*'Hear! Hear!'*) He could readily point to the fact that the German Central Committee had adopted a resolution that declared war on him. I must say that if I had been in Serrati's shoes, this threat of war would not have shaken me in my opinion that I must find a path to the Third International and the Communist Party of Italy. All the more, after that resolution, I would have declared my honest intention to join the Third International. (*Applause*)

---

19. Serrati's visit to Berlin and Stuttgart took place earlier, close to the beginning of February. For Serrati's open letter to Lenin, see p. 192, n. 21.

Comrades, along with this Central Committee resolution, the decisive factor in my resignation from the German Communist Party Zentrale was the intervention in our debate of the International's representative in Italy, Comrade Rákosi.[20] I have not the slightest criticism of the conduct of Comrade Kabakchiev. The most I could say is that, in my opinion, he did not do enough to bring about an additional split, a reproach that I also directed at Paul Levi. In my opinion, given that no initiative had been taken elsewhere, he ought to have taken the initiative. So as I said, when I now refer to the Executive's representative in Italy, I mean only Comrade Rákosi.

Anyone who has read attentively what he said in his first speech, and then in speaking to the Central Committee, will see that he did not provide a single new fact, but rather just expressed the familiar arguments with new words. He intervened in the Central Committee debate, advancing the opinion that the split in Italy must stand as an example. In the French party too there were undesirable forces that should be cleared out. He referred to Lafont and Cachin, saying that perhaps the party will have to be split ten times over. He advanced the view that what the Communist International needs is not a mass party but a pure, small party. He said explicitly that the Communist Party cannot and should not bring in new recruits. It should be limited to members who are well educated and can take the lead in any situation. This concept ran into immediate opposition, and the comrade later claimed that he had never made this statement.[21]

Comrades, this comrade had earlier made the same statement to me, in a private conversation, and had expanded on it, saying: 'Comrade Zetkin, your party in Germany has become much too large; it must be made small again.' At that I laughed in his face, saying, 'Excuse me, I can only laugh at this claim. In our opinion, the party is still much too small for its tasks, and we must devote all our energies to making it larger, not only quantitatively, of course, but also qualitatively. It's not just quantity that concerns us, but the quality contained in that quantity. The Communist Party's task is to create that kind of a quality in the quantity of proletarians organised in the Communist Party.

Comrades, based on the statements of the Executive's representative in Italy, I concluded that the old question must be raised once more for debate: do we want a mass party or a small, pure propagandistic sect? I admit my

---

20. Zetkin is referring to Rákosi's remarks in the Central Committee meeting of 22 February. After the adoption of the Thalheimer-Stoeker resolution at the 22 February meeting, Zetkin, Levi, and three others resigned from the KPD Zentrale.

21. Rákosi spoke first to a meeting of the VKPD Zentrale in mid-February and then to the Central Committee 22 February. Zetkin is referring here to the latter meeting. For Rákosi's reply to her remarks, see p. 326.

mistake in assuming that a representative of the International, of the Executive, could not make statements such as those made in that session on his own responsibility.

**Interjection**: But what do you have to say about the declaration?

**Zetkin**: The declaration contradicted what had been said earlier. It was said in the Central Committee that the comrade in question stood by what he had said.[22] I was naïve enough to assume that the representative had acted in the Italian situation on behalf of and according to the instructions of the Executive. It never entered my head that the Executive's representative, in a situation as challenging and delicate as that in Livorno and then at our Central Committee meeting, could have acted on his own in making such statements and then repeating them. I admit my error, and I am glad to see that the Executive sharply rejects this point of view.

But there is something else I must say. Given the position taken by the Executive's representative, it seemed to me that the decision on the Italian question had raised a fundamental issue for every section of the Communist International. This may be an erroneous view. Comrades, I am not one of those lofty theoretical intellects who derive the right to their theory from the fact that they are terrible political practitioners. I simply judged on the basis of the situation as it appeared at that time. I thought that in such a difficult situation I could not assume responsibility.

I frankly admit that I was influenced by another factor that I did not want to throw into the debate in order to avoid giving rise to personal antagonisms or bitterness. I had observed that a large proportion of the Zentrale's members had changed their view on the matter. I do not criticise the comrades for this fact. I stand ready to change my view twenty-four times in a day and to admit that the twenty-third time I was an ass and was ignorant of the facts. But what I could not understand was that a decision was overturned without the presentation of any new factual material, simply because it was argued in a different way.

**Interjection**: What about Levi's conduct?

**Zetkin**: Please, for the majority of the Zentrale, his conduct was not decisive. I must admit that I would never impute to the Zentrale such a mark of weakness and incompetence as to allow Levi's conduct to determine their own.

**Interjection**: And the rest of us?

---

22. Presumably a statement by Rákosi clarifying his remarks at the 22 February Central Committee meeting.

**Zetkin**: Whether you were influenced by Levi's conduct is your business. I have never let myself be influenced by whether Levi or Müller or Schulze favoured a position, but rather only by whether it seemed to me to be right or wrong.

Comrades, we were in a situation that could lead the proletariat to engage in intense activity and, perhaps very quickly, to unleash a massive advance, or risk a political and moral disaster for the party and severe danger for the proletariat. In such conditions, I could not in good conscience work together with comrades who – despite my great esteem for them – changed their minds in a fashion that, judged according to my old-fashioned concepts, was much too hasty.

Comrades, let me say one more thing. No one can say of me that I ever feared to be in a minority. I have almost always been in a minority. Allow me to recall that for a long time I was almost alone in conducting a struggle for the utilisation of parliament.[23] Even the members of the Zentrale who agreed with me did not come to my side. They said that they were convinced it was necessary to take part in parliament, but given the mood in the party, we could not challenge the mass sentiment. I call on you all to testify as to whether in my forty years of work in the party I have ever resigned from a post because I had a difference of opinion, betrayed those who elected me, or stalked off in a sulk. And that is why I thought that if I resign from a post in such circumstances, it will be a signal, a kind of warning, which I regarded as very necessary.

Now my resignation from the Zentrale has been censured as a breach of discipline. I do not want to quarrel over words, but let me say this. Despite everything, I would not have resigned from the Zentrale if I had thought that the party was so unstable that my action, which took place without consultation with Levi or anyone else, could have caused any damage to the party. And I must add that a party post is not a sweet chocolate bonbon handed out for political good conduct. No, comrades, it involves entrusting someone with a post in battle, in the conviction that the right person is being placed in the right role. And I thought that under these circumstances I was simply no longer the right person for this position. Rather than a factor strengthening the Zentrale and the party, I had become a disruptive factor and was thus damaging the party.

Comrades, that is why I acted in this way. And I believe that here I can count on the benevolent understanding of the chair of the Executive. He

---

23. An intense debate occurred in the KPD in 1919 on whether it was correct for Communists to participate in bourgeois parliaments. The issue was finally resolved in October 1919, when the anti-parliamentarian tendency was defeated, leading to its exit from the party and the later formation of the KAPD.

knows well from his own experience that, in certain political circumstances, comrades are placed in a situation where, despite all loyalty to the party and discipline, their conscience faces the question: What is one's duty to the party, to the proletariat, and to the revolution? Is it to remain in the post or to resign while continuing one's work? I recall the events in the Bolshevik Party on 10 October and 4 November 1917. In October 1917, Comrades Kamenev and Zinoviev felt compelled to resign from the Central Committee of the time.[24]

**Radek**: And they got a sound drubbing for that, too. (*Laughter*)

**Zetkin**: Well, comrades, so did I. (*More laughter*) They believed they were required in good conscience to resign from the Central Committee. They certainly got a drubbing for it, and they said publicly that they were wrong. Comrades, in situations where I was in error, I have never shied away from publicly admitting this. As soon as I am convinced that I have gone wrong, I will do that too. But I can assure you that in the situation as it was, I considered it necessary, in the interests of the party and the proletariat, to act as I did. And I must say, in addition, that if in the future my convictions lead me to see matters as I saw them then, I would do the same once again, because for me loyalty to the proletariat always comes before party discipline. But if I recognise that I am wrong, comrades, I will be the first to say not only that I was wrong, *mea culpa*, but that I was grievously wrong, *mea maxima culpa*. However, as I said, I must first be convinced. That is what I have to say regarding a breach of discipline. I have never felt humiliated when I was censured for an error, real or imagined. By contrast, I would feel not only humiliated but unworthy to stand before you if I had done something against my own convictions. I accept the reprimand without any protest and I confidently await the decision of the congress.

I have a few more things to say about the Italian question. In my opinion, the policies followed by Serrati and his party since the Livorno Congress have revealed unambiguously their reformist and opportunist character. (*Applause*) I recognise that fully. That is revealed fully by their stand on the question of the White Guards, the struggle against Fascism.[25] Can this really be a communist party – indeed I will say more – can this be a political party at all, when it tries to combat the civil war represented by Fascism with sermons

---

24. On 23 October 1917 (10 October by the old Russian calendar), Zinoviev and Lev Kamenev voted in the Bolshevik Central Committee against Lenin's proposal to organise an insurrection for Soviet power. After the motion was adopted, they continued to express their opposition in the party at large and the non-Bolshevik press and resigned from the Central Committee.

25. The PSI's stance of accommodation toward the Fascists would be illustrated a few weeks later, on 3 August 1921, when it signed a 'pacification pact' with the Fascist Party.

about morality; by saying that Fascism must be overcome by the methods of Christian ethics? (*Laughter*) No, I must say that in proletarian struggle my opinion has always been to return every blow twice over. Force must be broken by force. And Fascism in Italy cannot be overcome by the soft flute-like tones one finds in *Avanti*, but rather only through the armed struggle of the proletarian masses. (*Loud applause*) Moreover, the Serrati forces' entire approach to political problems reveals to me their unambiguously opportunist character. Many comrades say that this confirms the correctness of the split in Livorno. Comrades, it is possible to disagree. It can also be said that the split by the left wing drove the Unitarians [Unitary Communists] almost forcibly into the arms of the Turati forces.

**Radek**: Like Hilferding into the arms of Scheidemann. (*Laughter*)

**Zetkin**: Well, comrades, there are two sides to everything. I greet this development, to the extent that it is a matter of exposing uncertain, wavering leaders. I regret it, to the extent that hundreds of thousands of proletarians still remain under their spell. And I wonder whether it will not be easier to break this disastrous spell more readily if we could draw them as quickly as possible into the orbit of the Italian Communist Party. I will leave it to the scholars to dispute over whether the development of the Italian party proves the split at Livorno to have been correct, or whether it has been harmful. I hold to the fact that the [Socialist Party] policies are opportunist, and in my opinion this compels the Communist International to take a position. In my view, it is no longer enough for the congress simply to demand the strict application of the Twenty-One Conditions. Anyone who wants to belong to the Communist International must break unequivocally from the Turati forces. And the congress must also reject unambiguously all policies that are in any sense opportunist and directed at confusing the masses. Comrades, in my opinion we cannot resolve this matter until we have heard representatives of both currents. But on the basis of the documentation before us, my opinion stands as I have just expressed it.

I would like to make a few comments, if you permit, on the Levi case, so that I will not fall under suspicion of trying to avoid the question. I say once again that we do not fault the Executive for having insisted on a break, a clear break from the Turati forces. The question is only whether it might have been possible to carry out the split earlier, to prepare it better, and above all to seek to divide the Serrati forces and win the best workers for the Communist Party.

In addition, I criticise the Executive openly and vigorously that they have not taken more care in choosing their representatives abroad. That applies to the representative in Italy that I heard [Rákosi]; I cannot speak of the other

[Kabakchiev] whom I did not hear. Moreover, it also applies to the Executive's representative in Germany, a question we will take up in discussing the March Action. I must also say that Comrade Zinoviev, through his general comments on the character and tasks of the Communist parties and the Third International, has already fully repudiated the disastrous activity of that irresponsible representative.[26] For that reason, there was no reason to unleash a sharp struggle against the Executive.

**Radek**: Levi did that, and you did not disavow him.

**Zetkin**: We will speak of that shortly. Please be patient. On the Levi case: In my opinion the Levi case is not primarily a simple case of discipline (*'Very true!'*); it is primarily and above all a political matter. It can be judged and evaluated correctly only in the framework of the entire political situation. I am therefore of the opinion that it can really be dealt with only in the framework of our debate on Communist Party tactics and strategy and especially on the March Action. If it is desired to deal with the Levi case now, as a disciplinary matter, I will not oppose that – on the condition, however, that we immediately take up the March Action as part of this debate, because otherwise the entire historical background is missing. Otherwise we miss the entire atmosphere that makes the disciplinary case comprehensible.

In addition, Comrade Radek yesterday posed the case against Paul Levi very personally when he called out, to great effect, 'When did Paul Levi ever lie in the revolutionary trenches?' Comrade Radek, if I am to take that literally, then I must ask, did the originators of the March Action, who justified it theoretically and organised it, did they all in the literal sense of the word lie in the revolutionary trenches? (*Commotion; shouts of 'Yes, of course'.*)

And something else. Comrade Radek knows as well as I do that Comrade Paul Levi is truly not among those cowards who flee from the battle. During the dangerous January and March actions of 1919, he did not abandon his post in the struggle, even though after the events in Lichtenberg a price of twenty thousand marks was placed on his head.[27] He shared with Comrade Thalheimer the dangerous life of underground struggle, sleeping here today and there tomorrow. In my opinion, these are also actions in the revolutionary trenches. I just want to mention that here, without going into it more fully. I want to stress this one point: it is only in the framework of the March Action that we can reach a correct decision regarding Paul Levi's positions and conduct.

---

26. Presumably a reference to Béla Kun.
27. For the events in Lichtenberg, see p. 105, n. 5.

I have always stated my agreement with the broad and fundamental political line of Levi's attitude to the March Action. I have said that in assemblies attended by many tens of thousands of workers. I have always said that I do not agree with every word in the pamphlet and that I certainly am far from agreeing with all of its opinions. If you want to know what I really think, I must say that I would not have written the pamphlet, and if I had written it, it would have looked much different. But it was then a life-and-death matter for the party that there be a sharp criticism. Why was that? Because the Zentrale declared that this same policy was going to be continued in the future.

That was decisive, comrades, and I will say no more about this question unless it is decided that the March Action will be discussed together with the Executive report. Only by clarifying the March Action can we establish an objective basis to pass judgement on the Levi case.

As for the question that Comrade Radek raised, I will say just one thing. In my opinion, the Executive is in no way to blame for the fact that its decision was used to instigate a putschist initiative. But the fact remains, as we will demonstrate in the March Action discussion, that representatives of the Executive certainly carry a large part of the responsibility for the way this action was carried out.[28] They bear a large part of the responsibility for the incorrect slogans and the incorrect political orientation of the party or, more correctly of the Zentrale. And no one knows this better than Comrade Radek.

**Radek**: How so? I was not in Germany.

**Zetkin**: A few days ago, you said in front of witnesses that when you were given a report, you immediately told the Executive's representative that his slogan – I am not going to employ here the unparliamentary word that you used, but rather a gentler word – was stupid. My position is that if anyone has grounds to complain about Paul Levi's conduct, then it would be we of the opposition – we, whose criticism was directed not at the March Action as a struggle, but at the incorrect orientation and the poor execution by the central leadership. Because, instead of a discussion of the Zentrale's politics, we had a broad debate on the Levi case. In my opinion, this is grounds for the Zentrale to erect a monument to Comrade Levi. (*Laughter*) He became the whipping boy on whom all the disappointed proletarians could let off

---

28. Among the Comintern's envoys in Germany during the March Action were Béla Kun, József Pogány, and August Guralsky. According to the Serbo-Croatian edition of the Third Congress proceedings, the ECCI's representatives also included, in addition to Kun, Poganyi, and Guralsky, the Hungarian Communist leader Ferenc Münnich plus two ECCI officials resident in Berlin, Thomas (Yakov Reich) and Felix Wolf. Bosić (ed.) 1981, pp. 772–3, n. 161.

steam regarding an action marked by an incorrect orientation and erroneous leadership and execution.

**Heckert**: That's a cheap shot.

**Zetkin**: We will present other arguments soon enough, when we discuss the March Action, and I do not wish to go into the question, given that that it is not yet decided whether it is to be discussed here or under the point on tactics and strategy.

**Chair**: Under tactics and strategy.

**Zetkin**: I have only one more thing to say here. Comrade Marković said quite correctly that if Paul Levi is to be severely punished because of his criticisms of the March Action and for having undisputedly made them the wrong way, what will the punishment be for those who committed the errors in this matter? When we attacked putschism, we were not referring to the actions of the masses in struggle. No, comrades – and here Comrade Gorter is quite right – the putschism existed in the thinking of the Zentrale that led the masses in struggle in this fashion. It existed in the fact that order was followed by counter-order, and finally everything dissolved into disorder, chaos, and disorientation.

I have no objection to the congress making a decision now on the Levi case. But only, as I said before, after a debate on the entire factual framework, for Comrade Levi acted from sincere conviction that he was doing the party a service.

Comrade Paul Levi can raise in defence of his breach of discipline the same grounds that were once used to defend Russian comrades who broke discipline. He acted out of the sincere conviction, in order to save the party and be of service to the proletariat.

**Radek**: Of service to the prosecution.

**Zetkin**: That is a very flimsy argument, Comrade Radek, given that the evidence for the prosecution does not, in fact, come from Levi's pamphlet, but rather from the appeals and articles in *Rote Fahne*. (*Commotion*) It played only a trivial role in Brandler's trial.[29] I say it is not very intelligent to refer to that trial, because in it the complete or partial uncertainty of the leading individuals came to light so clearly. ('*Very true!*')

**Radek**: What about the offensive?

---

29. For Brandler's trial see p. 83, n. 23.

**Zetkin:** I will not speak about the question of offensive or defensive, Comrade Radek, until we take up the matter as a whole.

When you make use of sentences ripped out of context, Comrade Radek, you are following an age-old procedure, which you did not discover but are merely imitating: give me twenty lines someone has written and I will bring him to the gallows.

I will explain soon enough how I view the question of offensive and defensive. (*Interjection from Heckert*) Comrade Heckert, I will do that whether or not I have your blessing. So far you are not yet my political father confessor.

Comrades, in the Levi case we have to pay heed to the factual and political context, along with the motivations for writing it and also the effects that it had. Comrade Radek tried to minimise these factors by saying that the pamphlet provided evidence for the prosecution. *Rote Fahne* did that to a much greater extent. It also greatly nourished the myth that the action was instigated from outside, by publishing appeals and articles whose un-German mode of expression enabled opponents to say, 'Not made in Germany'.[30]

But what is far, far more painful, comrades, is the fact that Comrade Levi's pamphlet caused grief to many workers, holding them back from objectively and critically assessing the situation and the Zentrale's conduct. I fully appreciate the indignation and anger ('*Hear! Hear!*') that echoed back from the workers' milieu. But I must also say that I regret the inability of trained Communists to reply to the way the pamphlet was utilised by our enemies. For if we take as a criterion the way our opponents utilise the written or oral statements that we make as Communists, we must never write a line or open our mouths, because our opponents will twist everything and suck honey from every blossom.

I am sincerely convinced that without Levi's criticism, it would have taken us longer to come to grips with the theory and practice of the March Action, and we would have done so less thoroughly than was actually the case. The Communist Party and the proletariat would have been exposed to the danger of being launched into renewed ill-advised undertakings.

Comrades, the reason why I have taken such a forceful stand in this entire complex of questions is because I consider – then and now – that it is absolutely necessary under present circumstances for the German proletariat to engage in intensified, vigorous action. My concern is not that the workers engaged in struggle, not that the slogan was incorrect and the leadership deficient. What concerns me is that now, at a moment that cries out for action,

---

30. Zetkin is probably thinking in particular of the article, 'Kahr Is Flouting the Law', apparently written by Béla Kun. It is discussed on pp. 428, 488, and 523. The quoted words are in English in the original text.

the Communist Party is incapable – is too weak to undertake the necessary action. (*Cries of protest*) I am calling on the congress to undertake a searching and conscientious examination of both theory and tactics during the March Action. And I do this out of the conviction that our debate must lead to preparing ourselves for intense struggles, without regard for whether they lead to defeat or victory. For defeats can also bear fruit, if they are defeats in which the proletarian masses face an enemy whose strength is greater, defeats in which the proletariat can say with pride that it has lost everything but not its honour, defeats in which it fought and drove forward in revolutionary fashion. (*Loud applause and cheers*)

(*The session is adjourned at 3:40 p.m.*)

## Session 7 – 27 June 1921, 8:30 p.m.
## Executive Committee Report – Discussion

*Continuation of discussion of the Executive Committee report. Speakers: Friesland, van Overstraeten, Koenen, Terracini, Javadzadeh, Rákosi, Smythe.*

**Friesland** (Ernst Reuter, Germany, VKPD): The comments that representatives of the German opposition made here today and, in part, yesterday on the portion of the Executive report dealing with Germany have, with great skill, evaded the main question under debate and the decisive considerations. Even Comrade Clara Zetkin, whose detailed speech sought so passionately to justify her position and her specific actions in the German party; even her great passion cannot blind us to the fact that her memory, her political memory falls somewhat short of her passion, and that her statements here on a whole number of political questions were different from what we experienced in Germany.

As for the level of debate expressed by Comrade Malzahn, this requires no comment. He considers it appropriate to demonstrate the correctness or incorrectness of his friends' policies by presenting statistics. I am well aware that the comrades associated with him had ample time at their disposal to busy themselves in Germany with statistical material. I am well aware that his friends in Berlin found it possible to drive by automobile from factory to factory, not to summon the workers to struggle but to tell workers that the strike was not occurring in this or that place (*'Hear! Hear!'*) and to hold the workers back from struggle. I see that the atmosphere here in

Moscow has brought about certain modifications in Comrade Malzahn's point of view. He is now talking about two hundred thousand participants, as against the figure in his earlier statements in Germany, in which the figure was somewhat smaller. There is also a minor change in his assessment of the March Action. No longer does he speak of it as a great putsch, no longer is it a horrendous crime; now it is a struggle forced on the Communist Party, which he says it carried out courageously.

I must tell you that if this question is to be taken up at all in the discussion of the Executive's report, that can only be in the context provided by Comrade Zinoviev. From the German point of view, the decisive aspect of the question is: *how did the Communist Party develop prior to the struggle, and how did the Communist Party conduct itself in this struggle?* And we consider that whatever the errors in this action may have been – and they were gigantic – we are the last to conceal these errors in any way. *But we will talk about these errors with comrades who struggled by our side,* and not with those who sabotaged the proletarian struggle, who systematically opposed the action. We will discuss the errors with comrades who stand together with us on the present battlefield and with no one else. (*Loud applause*)

We know well that there is not a single party that does not make errors in such struggles – not the Communist Party in Germany or any such party elsewhere. And if we are going to talk about errors, then let us start with this: *What was the main error?* The main error was committed by the old leadership, which resigned because Comrade Zetkin and the others found Comrade Rákosi displeasing, and because Comrade Zetkin had the impression that Rákosi had been sent to split the Italian party. It is indisputable that the leadership prior to the fall of the old Zentrale was not suitable for transforming the party into an organisation of struggle. In her lucid moments, even Comrade Zetkin emphasised that she was very well aware that there were *great dangers of passivity and inactivity* among her friends in the Communist Party. I well remember this statement by Comrade Zetkin.

Comrades, what is the decisive factor in the German party? It is the fact that, following the Second Congress of the Communist International, it was systematically organised for the conduct of a struggle against the Executive. What was at stake here was obviously not Comrade Zinoviev's handsome 'curly locks', which would perhaps have been untouchable for us. This struggle carried out against the Executive challenged the political methods and principles of the Russian Revolution and the Communist International as a whole. And anyone who has followed the situation in the German party knows that, from the moment he returned from Moscow, Comrade Levi made systematic efforts to undermine the reputation of the Communist

International and its Executive. And whenever a question came up in the German party, no matter what it was, we were always able to perceive efforts at work to strengthen Western European influences in the Communist International, as against those of 'Asiatic Bolshevism'.

I remind you of the entire way that the KAPD question was handled. I ask you frankly: Do the comrades of the opposition still consider today that the KAPD was dealt with by the German party Zentrale of the time in a political fashion, or do they consider that the way it was perceived and treated showed touchiness and hysteria? It would be much appreciated if you would state your views on the disputed questions. Do these comrades now agree, at last, that this matter was dealt with by Comrades Levi and Däumig in a way that demonstrated a desire to cause conflict with the Communist International?

It is interesting that Comrade Marković of the Yugoslav party was able, even during the course of the March Action, to report to his Central Committee on the situation in Germany and to have it adopt decisions on the matter. I am surely not wrong in assuming that the Central Committee of his party, located in Vienna, was in contact with Dr. Levi. We certainly recall that Dr. Levi strongly emphasised that he, thank god, had his connections in the International. And we maintain that from the time of the Second Congress a behind-the-scenes campaign was organised in Germany and the International. Levi was very touchy at that time about the formation of factions and secret 'Turkestaner' relationships in the German and other parties.[1] Those familiar with the methods of this political figure can only find this fact amusing. We believe that these methods were applied quite systematically in our movement. And we add that German workers and the German revolutionary proletariat have a clear and distinct sensitivity for the political meaning of these methods and the goals of this struggle. And, when it is a matter of choosing between the leadership that evaded the revolutionary struggle when it broke out in Germany, when it is a matter of utilising all the burning revolutionary issues in order to prepare the struggles of the proletariat and the Executive's leadership, then the German workers certainly know well whom they have to choose.

Comrades, I am almost finished. Unfortunately, it is impossible to say in ten minutes all that needs to be said. I ask you to give special attention to the March Action and to the specific errors of the German party in this action. I also ask that those who claim to speak here as trained Communists should be somewhat more careful in what they say. For they know that those against

---

1. For 'Turkestaner', see p. 197, n. 30.

whom they lay these charges have rejected these errors much more thoroughly, not in the framework of solidarity with Levi but of solidarity with the masses in struggle. I ask them to cease their evasion in this discussion. And I must add that everything said by Comrade Zetkin and other comrades has been perceived here – despite all our respect for Comrade Zetkin – as an *evasion of certain questions*.

Comrade Zetkin said here that she had never expressed solidarity with Levi in any way.[2] Perhaps Comrade Zetkin will not dispute this: I remember well that she did indeed express solidarity with Levi. I recall that *Rote Fahne* published a report stating that Comrade Zetkin said, after a district meeting, that *it would be cowardly and contemptible for her not to give full support to Levi*. And I ask – apart from the errors of the March Action – *do the comrades today still stand in solidarity with Levi's shameless slanders, with the talk about Turkestaners, with his assertion that the Executive's representatives were behind all manner of bomb attacks, and were using Russian money to organise factions with the aim of breaking apart the German party?* Do any of the comrades seriously consider Comrade Rákosi's perhaps incautious statements in our Central Committee to be grounds for concluding that the Executive had changed its position with regard to building mass Communist parties? Let me remind you that when this claim first cropped up, the entire Central Committee emphasised that if anyone held that position, we as the German party would not approve it. It was said then that there were perhaps certain tendencies to make the party bigger than it actually needed to be. Such tendencies may have been present then, here or there. *But there were no tendencies to turn the party into a sect.*

We expect participants in the discussion to frankly state their view on this question, rather than remaining silent and leaving us in Germany with the same calamity as before. The Russian party representative who was hounded by the police, denounced by Comrades Däumig and Düwell in the opposition documents, denounced in a shameful fashion, this representative officially asked the Central Committee, 'Tell me please, what terrorist act did I participate in? Please do tell me.' And there was silence. We say that we do not want to see again this spectacle, in which such things are evaded. We expect comrades to speak plainly. We want to return home with a frank statement. We do not want to witness again the spectacle where it is said that Levi is a

---

2. It is unclear what Friesland is saying here. On p. 298, Zetkin said, "I have always stated my agreement with the broad and fundamental political line of Levi's attitude to the March Action."

fine fellow and he recognised the errors of the March Action. Rather, *we want a fully unambiguous statement by these comrades and by the congress.*

We consider that people who express solidarity with Levi, who asked him not to resign from his parliamentary seat until the congress had taken its decision, that people who have stabbed the party in the back in this fashion, who have systematically undermined the political and moral reputation of the Executive, cannot be allowed in the ranks of the Communist International unless they very clearly repudiate these slanders. Comrade Zetkin says that she would probably have written the pamphlet somewhat differently. That may be true. But the eight opposition comrades cannot evade political responsibility for the publication of this pamphlet. It is clear that proofs were read in advance and that advice was given. (*'Hear! Hear!'*) That is one of the decisive questions in the German party, and it is not merely a matter of discipline, as Comrade Zetkin believes.

The Executive devoted all its activity to the task of creating a mass revolutionary party, and this was one of the decisive questions for the German movement. After the masses of the former USPD came to the Communist International, the old sloppiness ended. Let me tell you, *the expulsion of Levi was an action that won enormous respect for us in the eyes of the party comrades.* (*Loud applause*) That was something German workers had never experienced before. They had Scheidemann, Ebert, and Noske, and were betrayed by all these leaders. There was no one who took a stand against these leaders. And here, for the first time, there was an International that insisted on discipline and that forced leaders to stand with the masses. Our entire organisational and political activity teaches us that when the entirety of the worker masses stood solidly with the party on this question, it is no accident. Even Comrade Zetkin, whose reputation among the working masses stood higher than Levi's, was unable to win over her district, where she was well established, to her political position. In my view, this fact alone is proof that at decisive moments the revolutionary proletariat has a better understanding for the party and the International than is sometimes the case with some of its best and most highly placed leaders. (*Loud applause and cheers*)

**Loriot** (Chair): Before going further, the congress must again make a decision on the speaking time. If we are providing every speaker with extended time, we might as well decide on a longer time right now.

**Radek**: I propose to leave the speaking time at ten minutes. It was pointed out that Comrade Zetkin spoke for an hour and a quarter. When lengthening the time of a speaker on the list is called for, we can always do that. We need simply to make a motion for an extension. (*Applause*)

**Loriot** (Chair): Since there are still fourteen speakers on the list, I ask the congress if the speakers' list should be closed.

**Delagrange**: If there are still fourteen speakers, no one should speak for more than ten minutes.

**Souverine**: Ten minutes should be the limit for everyone.

**Loriot** (Chair): I ask everyone who believes that fourteen speakers is enough and that the list should be closed to please raise their hands. (*The vote is taken.*)

The list is now closed. The speaking time is ten minutes. Comrade Javadzadeh of Iran has the floor.

Since he is not present in the hall, I give the floor to Comrade Overstraeten of Belgium.

**Edouard van Overstraeten** (Belgium): Comrades, I am obliged to correct some of the statements made by Jacquemotte, the delegate of the left wing of the Belgian Socialist Party. Jacquemotte cited some of the difficulties encountered in forming a Belgian section of the International. In particular, he said that Belgium is a den of former leaders of the Second International. However, figures such as Vandervelde or Huysmans and other representatives of the Second International are not the only obstacles. They are actually the pinnacle of an entire reformist system, which has developed more fully in Belgium than elsewhere. The Workers' Party in Belgium unites in its ranks political, trade-union, and cooperative organisations. This magnificent centralisation has brought about an extremely flourishing bureaucracy, which suppresses the best revolutionary impulses arising in the workers' organisations.

After the armistice [1918], we immediately realised that the political organisations cannot exist without support from the trade unions. We said to the comrades who were then conducting a more or less confused and lacklustre opposition in the [Workers'] Party that they should not limit themselves exclusively to criticism of the political party's measures but should carry out agitation and propaganda in the unions. People in the [Workers' Party] minority then told us that this approach was quite illogical. 'If you leave the political organisations, you must simultaneously leave the trade unions,' they said. We replied, 'No, although it is possible that there is a logical error here, we want to carry out agitation and propaganda precisely in the organisations where there is genuine life among the workers, that is, in the trade unions.' Nevertheless, we encountered truly formidable obstacles.

Jacquemotte thought it proper today to describe the outlook of the Communist Group of Belgium, which last year formed a small Communist Party and rejected some theses of the Third International, particularly those on parliamentarism. Last year, I defended the theses proposed by Comrade Bordiga.[3] When I returned home from the congress, the comrades still stood by the anti-parliamentary theses, but the congress had decided that the party had to submit to the Executive's discipline.

On the other hand, Jacquemotte also felt compelled to say that the [Communist] Party systematically resisted forming a mass party. It is true that the painful experience of the Belgian working masses led to strong hesitation on this point in the still weak Communist Group that had arisen in Belgium. We believed that we stood in very great danger of letting ourselves be overrun by a mass of petty-bourgeois elements, but that we could not lose a moment, in order not to lose contact with the working masses in the trade unions. And, during the last year, the party has concentrated all its forces and agitational activity in the unions.

Jacquemotte did not take up something that would have been much more interesting, namely, an aspect of the conduct and activity of the minority in the party that – at least so far – contradicts all principles of the Third International. The minority, of course, accepts parliamentarism. But, when we saw how the minority defended parliamentarism during the last elections, we grasped that what was involved was a parliamentarism that was not revolutionary but purely reformist in character. One of the best arguments of the minority at that time was to utilise Lenin's *'Infantile Disorder'* and some passages from Comrade Zinoviev's speech in the cause not of revolutionary but of opportunist parliamentarism that consisted of winning control of the municipalities, step by step, through a series of successive reforms.[4]

In various cases, and we could list quite a number, the minority gave proof during the last year of timidity as well as opportunist and centrist tendencies – even though at their most recent congress they adopted the Third International's programme. We definitely do not reject a unification with the minority, but we doubt that it can succeed. The objective conditions do exist in Belgium to call into life a mass party that will be revolutionary in character. Our main task is therefore to strive for the creation of subjective factors, which will soon be urgently needed. In truth we have an industrial class whose spirit is revolutionary, as it has demonstrated decisively on various occasions. But

---

3. Bordiga's minority theses on parliamentarism at the Second Congress can be found in Riddell (ed.) 1991, 2WC, 1, pp. 440–3. For the approved resolution, see 2WC, pp. 470–9.

4. Lenin's *Left-Wing Communism: An Infantile Disorder*, published prior to the Comintern's Second Congress in 1920, can be found in LCW, 31, pp. 17–118. 'Zinoviev's speech' presumably refers to his four-hour speech at the Halle USPD congress (see p. 204, n. 42).

these revolutionary feelings must be supplemented by clear and secure political convictions. That is the task to which we in Belgium must above all else apply our energies and which must be the main object of our efforts. We had neither a Marxist nor a syndicalist-revolutionary tradition in Belgium. There was no Belgian Marxist tradition apart from the Marxism of Vandervelde, and no syndicalist-revolutionary tradition either. During this preparatory period, which we had no choice but to traverse, all our efforts had to be aimed at clarifying our positions, in order to be able to create the subjective factors and the clear-sighted workers' cells within the working masses.

This morning, Jacquemotte called the French comrades to his aid. However, I must frankly confess that, in terms of the revolutionary education of the masses, our French comrades are at present able to provide very little assistance. All our French comrades say with one voice that they need all their resources, indeed, that these resources are insufficient to achieve what Comrade Trotsky recently demanded of them. I believe that if you read *L'Humanité* and study the French party's various efforts, you will perceive that, at this time, the French comrades truly do not have sufficient forces.

During the last two years, *L'Humanité* has been read extremely widely in Belgium, and we certainly do prefer *L'Humanité* to *Le Peuple*. But, whenever we gave *L'Humanité* to workers, we did so with regret, because we knew quite well that it was not a revolutionary newspaper. We work more with *La Vie ouvrière*, although we do not share its ideology, because this newspaper has a much more distinct revolutionary line. Thus our French comrades can be of great service to us by working in their country to create a good revolutionary publication that we can take to the masses and utilise confidently and securely, without encountering points of disagreement as we have until now in the French press.

I cannot take up the time of the congress by discussing the question of unification. Let me repeat that we are absolutely not opposed to unification. But we are thoroughly convinced that Belgium will in the future be the scene of great conflicts. We must aim all our attacks on the reformist tendency that has penetrated deeply inside the new Communist Party and against the incredible timidity that was manifest from the start. Let me repeat: the possibilities before us are great, and we will take advantage of them energetically.

**Koenen** (Germany): Comrades, the question that Comrade Zetkin took up in a lengthy speech cannot possibly be dealt with by noting in passing an error or mistake by this or that leading comrade. No, the conduct of this group is in the truest sense of the word *the martyrdom of a new mass Communist Party*. This tragic martyrdom, brought about through this group of leaders, must be made clear to the international congress. The upsurge of the Communist movement in Germany began when, after the Kapp days [March 1920], the workers realised that they needed a unified, united party. On that occasion, they entered battle and shed their blood without achieving anything. They were defeated because they lacked a unified leadership. They aimed to continue the struggle and set about creating a unified party. The workers, reorienting their thinking on the basis of these struggles, broke free from the leaders that had until then directed them, from Crispien and the aged Ledebour, with whom they had traversed many struggles, to Louise Zietz and the like, and sought a new leadership. They broke with the old leadership and sought to find a new and better one. They then perceived this leadership in the United Communist Party and in the new Zentrale, of which they were proud, because it included figures with international prominence and experience in struggle with the proletarians. This Zentrale enjoyed a strong reserve of trust on the part of such workers, who really wished to struggle.

From the two million workers organised in parties, a body of about half a million had crystallised, each of whom was determined to commit body and soul to the German revolution. Most of them had already demonstrated in one struggle after another, in political movements and strikes, that they were genuine fighters. For them, there was only one question: *how to struggle?* They looked up to their new leadership, which was to resolve this one great question that still remained for them in Germany. And behind these leaders, who had a reputation in Germany, stood of course the Russian leadership, the general staff of the world revolution. And this great reserve of trust that had accumulated among the true proletarians, tested in struggle, was *shamefully squandered and destroyed by the Group of Five and their eight or ten followers*. (*Loud applause*) Not only did Levi and his followers in the Zentrale seek to sow mistrust in the Communist International, but also, after their resignation and the events that followed, they dealt blows to the party that it could hardly have survived had it not been a genuine party of fighters. (*Loud applause*)

Everyone looked to this leadership, and there was a certain pride in having such figures in the party. We did not thoughtlessly jump into premature opposition to this group. In the very Central Committee session where these comrades resigned and where a struggle against the so-called leftist forces was organised, these comrades received full support on the four most important questions: that of organisation, the trade unions, the KAPD, and the alliance with Soviet Russia. Their position was fully endorsed. And then came the final question, that of Italy, and only here were they placed in a minority. These leaders, who talk of conscience, responsibility, revolutionary spirit, and other fine things, even though they had received support on all other questions, now felt it proper to take the one remaining question and arbitrarily convert it into an issue of personal conscience. They walked out and left the masses and the party in the lurch. As if that were not enough, they dealt a hard blow to the new Italian party, the new United Communist Party, the Executive and the entire International. They took responsibility for all that; their conscience permits all that. Then they step back and, after such deeds, talk about conscience. (*Loud applause*)

But that was not enough. After the old leaders had left, and after the masses had undoubtedly been thrown into a certain confusion, the new leadership then tried to reorient the party in a few weeks toward more vigorous activity and greater readiness for struggle. This reorientation, of course, requires time. After the old Zentrale had failed to carry it out, and while the new one had not yet completed its preparations, it was suddenly faced with Hörsing's provocation, which forced it to take up active struggle in the middle of its preparations. That was when errors were committed about which the people of conscience and responsibility make such a big deal. The blame rests with those who did not join in the preparations for activity. (*Loud applause*) The new Zentrale demonstrated that it wanted to prepare. It cannot be held responsible for the fact that it was taken by surprise midway in its preparations. It was not an easy transition, and the new Zentrale had to undertake it regardless. And it is very wrong for those who left the party in the lurch then to now pontificate about errors.

The party went bravely into struggle. It was not enough that these five comrades dealt it those blows; they simply left the party in the lurch. I recall Däumig, Müller, Wolf, Anna Geyer, Sievers, Düwell, also the rebellion in the *Rote Fahne* editorial board and the debates that had to be conducted in the different departments.[5] Everywhere we were held back by influences flowing from the ideology of this group. Now there is talk of errors, but it was their conduct that made these errors inevitable. And nonetheless, after all these errors, when the Central Committee meeting took place, where this group received only four votes, they have the nerve yet again to strike blows from behind at the party and the International. The Levi pamphlet appeared with their agreement. It was not enough to use that pamphlet to upbraid the party,

---

5. The 'rebellion in the *Rote Fahne* editorial board' resulted from an appeal published in that newspaper on 16 March, which called on workers to take up arms against the rightist Orgesch militia on a national level. The appeal, written by Béla Kun in an 'un-German form of expression' (Zetkin, p. 300), ran counter to the Zentrale's line of refraining from armed actions until they became unavoidable. Many *Rote Fahne* staff members protested against the article's publication as well as against the paper's editorship by Meyer and Frölich, who were working closely with Kun but independently from the Zentrale. Koch-Baumgarten 1986, pp. 152–5.

bleeding as it was from a thousand wounds and burdened by persecution and repression. After that, they trampled on the wounded body of the party, which they themselves had brought into this sad state by their resignations and their anti-party statements, making every conceivable attack on a party that was wounded so badly it could hardly stand. All of that they justify with reference to conscience and world revolution. I am simply astounded by the way they treat their consciences.

It is also established that during this entire process they repeatedly spread false reports – again and again. Despite their journal, *Sowjet*, despite widespread propaganda, they have not succeeded in gaining a foothold anywhere. Only tiny minorities vote for them; not a single district supports their viewpoint. Even Frankfurt, Levi's district, produced a two-thirds majority for the Zentrale. They have absolutely no backing in the party. Their support, their reputation, their standing in the party has crumbled since the very day they resigned – and still they continue their struggle against the party. It is incomprehensible how they can still talk about conscience and responsibility to the proletariat when they abuse the party in such fashion. This is not a question of accidental mistakes by individual comrades, but of the martyrdom of a newly formed mass party. And yet this mass party has been able in only three months to be done with these tribunes of the people – Comrades Zetkin, Däumig, and Levi – and has also withstood the March struggles. So I ask you, *the fact that the party has stood up to all this and is still drawing new forces from its ranks – is this not a sign of good health?* (*Loud applause*) After having borne all this, after losses in the thousands, the party has demonstrated that it is rising once again, as we will demonstrate statistically in our report on the March Action.

We now come to the question of the underlying causes advanced today for this mistreatment of the party and the International. What does Comrade Clara Zetkin say? That the resignation from the Zentrale was for the sake of the not-yet-Communist masses in Italy. The revolutionary masses in Italy would have driven out their leaders, and we should have waited for that. What is perfectly clear here is that when a revolutionary movement is under way, as in Germany, the masses have certainly driven out their leaders, but only in the course of a process that severely damages the party. Is this the example that Comrade Zetkin proposes for the new Italian party? Must it, too, suffer blow after blow, before it finally settles accounts with these leaders? No, it was correct to shorten the process.

It was right for the Executive to say: *Draw a line between the leaders and the masses.* As for the argument about the Communist police administrations utilising their forces and their structures for the class struggle, that is obviously an illusion, and there is really no need to discuss it in this congress.[6] (*Applause*)

The other motivation – and it is the most substantial one before us today – is that Serrati made some promises to Comrade Clara Zetkin, and she uses this as the basis for saying that the German Zentrale should not take any further decision, because to do so would give Serrati an excuse to back away and not come through on his promises. Well, comrades, I really am not sure whether Comrade Clara Zetkin has more confidence in the German party or in Serrati. It is very significant that she cited this today as one of the major, substantial factors that led her to resign from the Zentrale. We always suspected that the discussion with Serrati influenced Comrade Zetkin in some way. The promise was not supposed to be altered, and because it was altered, Comrade Zetkin had to resign. Well, is his promise then of more worth than the Central Committee decisions? That is not a sign of conscience.

Rákosi, too, is supposed to have said something. First of all, I maintain that the report given of his statement is inaccurate. I made that clear in the Executive. However, given that the comrades could possibly utilise these statements, it must therefore be said that to utilise a remark by a single representative, who was sent to Italy with a special mission, a special task, in order to justify resignation from the German Zentrale, is a poor excuse indeed. No serious person in the International believes that; it is believed only by those who have their own factional reasons for crediting it. Comrade Clara Zetkin's argument can therefore be characterised as an excuse, manufactured after the fact.

Comrade Zetkin now maintains that no new factual data is available, when in fact it has been presented to the Zentrale in great quantity. First we had Comrade Levi's report, in which factual data was sparse.[7] After Levi's article came the one by Comrade Bordiga, which told us how much damage had been done by Levi's position.[8] We concluded there must be some mistake here. Then came Böttcher's report – for we had another representative in Livorno, who was very close to us and was strongly linked with the Communist masses. He presented different facts than Levi did. Then came Serrati. Is it not also a fact, that there were discussions with Serrati? I myself also talked to him for an hour. It was easy to sense that when he began a sentence, it would

---

6. Regarding Italian police, see p. 286.
7. The text of Levi's report to the Zentrale on the Livorno Congress is not available. His viewpoint is explained, however, in his 20 January report to the ECCI (Drachkovitch and Lazić (eds.) 1966, pp. 275–82), and his 24 February speech to the VKPD Central Committee (Fernbach (ed.) 2011, pp. 92–112).
8. A letter by Bordiga protesting the attitude of Levi at Livorno was published in *Die Rote Fahne*, 4 February 1921.

wind up with the words of a Crispien or Dittmann. After one discussion in the railway station, that was really enough. These were facts that led us to suspect that Levi had given a false report.

Then Rákosi arrived. He passed on a very great deal of additional information, which I can convey to comrades who have not heard it in four or five main points. A great deal of this information had an impact on us. Of course, anyone who does not want to listen and has a different viewpoint will not be impressed. Those to whom Serrati has made promises will not be influenced by Rákosi. Finally, after we had adopted a resolution of the Executive's representative, came Paul Levi's speech to a meeting of functionaries.[9] He spoke not just as any member but as party chair. That led to new debates. Despite all the new facts, Levi spoke again against the resolution along the lines of his initial remarks. An attack on the Executive. That launched a discussion, and the majority in the Zentrale approved the resolution, saying that it finally achieved clarity. We owed it to the new Italian party to immediately make amends for what we did to it through Levi's actions. That was our duty, and that is why we introduced a more pointed resolution, which took sides in favour of the new Italian party. Comrade Zetkin and Levi did not think that we were obliged to assist the new party in its bitter struggle against the opportunists, the Fascists, and the government, which shows that they have not grasped the meaning for Communists of international solidarity. And that, I believe, is the crucial point.

In conclusion, comrades, Comrade Clara Zetkin says that she never acts contrary to her convictions, and that her conscience does not allow her to do this or that. We have had quite enough of that now in Germany, and I believe we must speak plainly about it in the International. It is obvious that one must act against one's convictions, when that is in the interest of the party. (*'Very true!'*) And there are circumstances where pangs of conscience can be resolved only by saying, *for the party or leave the party!* That is the only solution. The International cannot permit anyone to play around with concepts in the party. You have to make that clear for all the parties. When people start to play word games in the party, something is wrong and you must call a halt to it. (*'Very true!'*)

Now here is a warning for the International. Earlier you were told to keep a close eye on your leaders. I would say: Do not let your leaders become too arrogant. Do not elevate them too high. For if they become arrogant, they will get the idea that they can abuse the party. They will elevate the leadership above

---

9. The motion by Radek, amended by Zetkin, was adopted on 1 February; the meeting of Berlin functionaries was held about 10 February.

the party. That is disastrous for the party; we learned that in the debates. This should be a lesson for the International. Of course we need leaders, but in Germany we have lost so many leaders, and the party has developed regardless. There is no place here for sentimentality or special consideration, but only for clear, decisive, and ruthless decisions. We recommend that to all parties who want to avoid receiving blows from such leaders in their ranks. I suggest to the Czechoslovak and French parties that they learn the lessons of the German party's experience and make sure that they demand ruthless defence of the party's principles and discipline, especially where leaders are concerned. Party discipline comes first! That is what must be learned from these struggles in the German party. They are prattling about conscience and responsibility, when party discipline calls. (*Loud applause*)

**Umberto Terracini** (Communist Party of Italy): The Second Congress of the Communist International adopted conditions for the reorganisation of a Communist Party, along with an explanation, in the form of an appeal specifying that all Communist parties had to reorganise within three months along the lines of the Twenty-One Conditions adopted by the congress as a whole. At the time when these conditions were adopted, there was a Socialist Party in Italy that belonged to the Third International. This Socialist Party wanted to renew its membership in the Third International but for that it had to be reorganised.

The viewpoint advanced by Comrades Marković and Zetkin this morning can be summarised as follows. True, they say, the Twenty-One Conditions should have been applied in Italy, but it would have been more expedient and better to postpone applying them strictly for a time. Comrade Marković also said something that totally contradicts this statement. He said this morning that the split in Italy should have been carried out before Serrati, the Unitarians, and the opportunists in the party were able to carve out for themselves the position that they later gained in the Socialist Party of Italy. Comrade Marković added that, even before the Livorno Congress and the Second Congress of the Communist International, he had anticipated what Serrati's position would be.

He thus confirms that it was good to carry out the split in Italy and eliminate not only the reformists but the opportunists as well, given that he, too, had foreseen what the opportunists were planning to do.

He also said that preparations for this split had not yet been completed, and Comrade Zetkin also states that preparations by both the Italian comrades and comrades of the Executive were insufficient. I do not understand how these two facts can be reconciled. And we also saw that these two statements were made by precisely the comrades who always spoke against the established fact, against the split in Italy and the policies applied there. We can therefore see clearly that there is no agreement on this point in the opposition, but rather significant disagreement.

I now ask Comrade Zetkin, who claimed that the split in Italy was not adequately prepared, that she indicate exactly what measures were necessary before the Italian situation could be viewed as being sufficiently ripe. The Executive Committee sent personal letters to both the Italian Socialist Party and Serrati. Comrade Zinoviev addressed appeals to the Italian proletariat and the Italian Socialists in which he said that the Executive Committee was not in a position to intervene more directly in the affairs of the Italian Socialist Party.[10] He had full confidence in the Italian Communists and considered that the entire preparatory work for expulsion from the party of the reformists could be confidently placed in the hands of the Italian Communists. I therefore call on Comrade Marković to indicate how the split in the Italian Socialist Party could have been carried out before the Livorno Congress, that is, before February.

We could not carry out this split because the Second Congress convened only in July last year. Many months passed before the decisions of the congress were known in Italy. Only in October did the Twenty-One Conditions come to the attention of the Italian Socialist Party and of other Socialist and Communist parties. That means we were certainly unable to prepare the expulsion of the reformists before October. It is absolutely impossible to improvise a split of this type, without thorough preparation. Preparations had to be undertaken then, and this work toward excluding the reformists, done solely by the Italian Communists, required no little time for its accomplishment. If Comrade Zinoviev has read *Avanti* and *L'Ordine nuovo* and the entire Italian weekly press, he will have seen that during three months, from October 1920 to the Livorno Congress, not a single issue of the Socialist press appeared in which the Twenty-One Conditions were not discussed, enabling the viewpoints of the Communists, the Unitarians, and the reformists to be made known to the broad masses in Italy.

We can certainly affirm that the situation in the Italian Socialist Party was already known before we arrived in Livorno. Every faction was united in a strong organisation, and the Communist Faction already had its own sections and federations as well as its own press. There is no basis for saying that preparations were not carried out in Italy for the expulsion of the reformists.

---

10. An appeal by Zinoviev, on behalf of the ECCI, to the PSI was published in *Avanti*, 24 December 1920. Two personal letters by Zinoviev to Serrati were published in the 4 November issue.

But there is one word that has been wrongly understood by the delegates present here. In the session of the Communist International's Expanded Executive Committee and again here in this session of the congress, we have spoken of the Italian split. We have spoken of the preparations for the split of the Italian Socialist Party, and never once did I hear mention of expelling the reformists. I assume that no one thought that the Twenty-One Conditions approved by the International's Second Congress would result in a split of the party. Certainly, it was necessary to exclude all opportunist and reformist comrades from the party in Italy, and the Communists worked for the expulsion of the reformist faction. Comrades of the Executive Committee also always spoke in their letters and their appeals to the Italian workers of the expulsion of the reformists. Why then did we have a split in Italy? The split was caused by Serrati's refusal to expel the reformists and his ardent desire to remain united with them. That was the way the split was instigated. Only then, after the congress in Livorno, did people begin to speak of a split in the Italian Socialist Party. Previously, we never tried to instigate a split in the Italian Socialist Party, because our firm intention was to retain it, fully and entirely, in the Third International.

Some comrades have suggested that consummating the split in Italy could have been postponed until some time after the Livorno Congress.

These comrades say that if we had waited for a time, many of the workers who stayed with the Unitarians, many Italian Socialists who were still under Serrati's influence would have realised what a great error it was to remain in the same party with the reformists, with the result that more workers would have gone with us than we have with us now. In this regard, I would like to propose that to have waited longer after the Livorno Congress would have made it impossible to create a Communist Party in Italy. Even before the Livorno Congress, the Socialist Party was falling into disorganisation. As we have seen, the Socialist Party was already no longer a strong organisation. It had no programme of any kind and could do no more than retain the two hundred thousand workers who already belonged to its sections. If we had waited longer, the Socialist Party would have become even more disorganised. If we had tried then to form a Communist Party, we would no longer have been able to do it.

Comrade Zetkin also mentioned Comrade Rákosi this morning, stating that many of the errors made in the split of the Italian Socialist Party were his fault. In addition, she assured us that the VKPD Zentrale immediately realised what Comrade Rákosi was aiming for and what was the deeper meaning of his work in the Communist Party. Comrade Rákosi certainly does not need anyone to defend him. Still, it must be noted here that this comrade did not commit the crime of provoking a split in the Italian Socialist Party. He only arrived in Livorno, where Comrade Kabakchiev was already present, after the congress had begun. Comrade Rákosi worked together with Comrade Kabakchiev and the executive committee of the Communist Faction. He did not impose his opinion on anyone. He presented his proposals to the congress in the form of a statement, and the comrades of the executive committee of the Communist Faction had every possibility to introduce changes to the proposal formulated by Comrade Rákosi.

I cannot understand, therefore, how Comrade Zetkin can claim that the mistake made in the Italian split should be blamed solely on Comrade Rákosi. Comrade Zetkin approved of Kabakchiev's statement and disapproved Comrade Rákosi's. Kabakchiev and Rákosi always worked together, and it follows that one must either agree with them both or condemn them both. But in any case there is no need to defend the work of Comrade Rákosi. I understand that he will speak and make a statement regarding why he acted in Italy as he did and why he spoke as he did when he was with the VKPD Central Committee. Comrade Zetkin also said that the split in Italy could have been carried through in September, referring to the occupation of the factories. If the delegates of the Italian Socialist Party had had the opportunity to hear Comrade Zetkin's comments, I do not think they would be particularly heartened, given the fact that this party considers the occupation of the factories to have been an unanticipated misfortune.

Comrade Zetkin said: 'However, when the Italian workers in various localities had forcibly occupied the factories, the leadership of the Socialist Party met in Milan. The majority of this body was made up of Communists, Maximalists, indeed the same comrades who now attend the congress of the Third International as delegates of the Communist Party of Italy.'[11]

Actually, Comrades Turati and D'Aragona then belonged to the Italian leadership. In addition, it is imperative that all delegates have a close understanding of the situation in Italy at the time when the factories were occupied. You must understand how it was possible for the reformists, who dominated the CGL, to sabotage all the work of the party and of the workers who had occupied the factories. The CGL comrades chose this moment to submit their resignation to the Socialist Party leadership.[12]

---

11. Terracini is probably referring to Zetkin's remarks on p. 285.
12. The offer to resign by D'Aragona and other leaders of the Confederation of Labour (CGL) was made at a 9–10 September joint meeting between the leaderships of the two organisations.

They motivated this as follows: 'In our opinion, it is impossible to expand the factory occupations any further. In our opinion, what we have here can be viewed only as a purely trade-union movement, which cannot be broadened into a political movement. However, comrades of the party leadership, if you wish to expand the scope of the movement, if you wish to change the trade-union movement into a political one, then we submit the resignation of the trade-union council and ask you to replace us with other comrades.'

Comrade Zetkin and many other comrades have asked us, 'Why then did you not accept their resignation? What did you not name other comrades to take their place?' Well, let me ask comrades this: Suppose that on some occasion the Soviet republic sees itself compelled to enter into struggle, let us say with Poland. Suppose that the head of the Red Army, Comrade Trotsky, is against launching this struggle and opposes the view of those comrades who are in favour, and the comrades nonetheless reach the decision that the struggle must absolutely be begun. Suppose, further, that Comrade Trotsky says, 'Fine. I will leave my post, I resign, and I hand over the command of the Red Army to another comrade whom you will appoint.' I ask you: would not the comrades who still wish to take up the struggle in such a situation find it necessary to wait? Is it possible to launch the struggle when the main leader, who has prepared the masses and the army and directs the entire organisation of the struggle and the battles, is virtually convinced that the struggle will lead to a defeat? That is exactly the situation in which the Executive Committee of the Italian Socialist Party found itself during the occupation of the factories. When the comrades who held the leading posts in the CGL submitted their resignations, the party leadership had no one available and no possibility to replace them. It was Comrades Dugoni, D'Aragona, and Buozzi who held the reins of leadership in the CGL and who spoke on every occasion as the genuine representatives of the masses.

**Loriot** (Chair): In your reply to Comrade Clara Zetkin, you are going into too much detail on the Italian question and exceeding the allocated time. Is the congress in favour of permitting Comrade Terracini to continue?

**Terracini**: Only a few more minutes. I told Comrade Loriot that I am speaking on this subject only because Comrade Zetkin touched on it this morning, and it is possible that some of the delegates may not yet understand it adequately. This question has no other major relevance for tomorrow's discussion, because the occupation of the factories is only a component of the much broader and more general question of the expulsion of the reformists, which the Communists were demanding, and the split that then followed in Livorno. However, I can come back to this question later. I simply wish to fully explain to delegates why the leadership of the Socialist Party, and the Communists who belonged to this Socialist Party leadership, did not dismiss the CGL leaders from their posts. It was not appropriate for the Italian proletarian movement to launch a struggle precisely at the moment when this was rejected by the leadership that had prepared this movement and was fully in charge of it.

Returning to the arguments that I made at the outset, I would like to stress that the split in Italy was a direct result of the decisions taken at the Second Congress of the Communist International. The Second Congress had stated that it was absolutely necessary to drive the reformists out of all parties affiliated to the Third International. The congress also made a statement that all parties that do not carry out this expulsion will themselves be expelled from the Third International. The question was thus posed very clearly, and in Italy a choice had to be made: either an organisation of proletarians outside the Third International or within it. Had the split not been carried out in Livorno, the entire Socialist Party, still tolerating the reformists in its midst, would have been expelled from the Third International.

I would like to pose a question that I hope the congress will discuss and decide on. I am speaking of the Zionist organisations that have representatives here at the congress with consultative vote, but that are actually in the same situation as representatives of the Communist parties in every country.[13] If the Third International continues to allow the Zionist organisations to be represented in the congress, if they do not immediately take decisions to transform themselves from organisations of a nationality into organisations of the workers and Communists, then I fear that in the future the Zionist organisations, which are in contact with Communist parties in every country, will cause us a great deal of trouble.

The policy applied to the Bund in Russia is the only policy that can be used toward the Zionist organisations.[14] The policy applied in Russia, however, has not been followed in other countries. True, the Executive Committee has sent statements to some countries, but not with sufficient force. This was the case in Poland, where the Third International Executive Committee

---

13. Terracini is referring primarily to Poale Zion, a wing of which had been given consultative vote at the congress. A socialist Zionist organisation formed beginning in 1897, Poale Zion had split in 1919, with a left-wing minority attracted to the October Revolution and moving toward communism.

14. The Bund (or Jewish Workers League) refers to the General Jewish Workers Union in Lithuania, Poland, and Russia. An opponent of Zionism, the Bund split in 1919, with the left-wing majority of the organisation inside Soviet Russia forming the Communist Bund, most of whose members joined the Russian CP in 1920 and 1921.

demanded that the Polish Bund unify with the Communist Party of Poland or else join with it in close alliance. However, we know that the delegates of the Polish Bund have not yet formed such an alliance, because they consider that such a combination is no easy matter and cannot be achieved for a considerable time. When I raised this question in the Credentials Commission, Comrade Radek responded that the Bund is not a Zionist organisation. However, in my opinion, the Bund differs from Paole Zion only in appearance. In reality, they are similar, because both organisations include only Jewish workers. They are organisations that demand that their members be Jewish either in nationality or religion. I do not believe that Jewish workers must pursue their struggle in a manner different from that of Christian workers or workers of other religions. In my opinion, Jewish workers will not succeed in freeing themselves from every form of oppression by the bourgeoisie and the state until it is possible for all workers to free themselves from bourgeois rule. We saw this in Russia, where Jewish workers did not achieve their freedom until after the communist revolution had broken out and workers had seized power. I therefore believe that this organisation must be asked to unify with the Communist Party. I would therefore like to pose, as a condition for this Jewish party, that it unite with the Communist Party that already exists in its country. This will avoid a situation in which these organisations, which are workers' organisations that nonetheless want to separate off from other workers of their country, could once again be invited to the next congress, and ensure that delegates of these organisations no longer enjoy the right to take part in discussions of the Third International.

**Mir Ja'far Javadzadeh** (Iran): On behalf of a number of comrades from the Near East, I would like to stress our agreement with what Comrade Zinoviev said in his report on behalf of the Communist International Executive. Comrade Zinoviev said that we have developed broad agitational and political work in the East but that in organisational terms we have achieved very little or even nothing.

That is quite true. At present there is a great deal of agitation in the East in order to acquaint the masses with the nature of the Communist Party and the Communist International. But this developing agitation is not backed up by an organisation that would be able to unite all the forces sympathising with the Communist International, in order to utilise them for the aims of the world revolutionary movement. The national question was very carefully examined by the Second Congress, which called for energetic support to the national movement in every country of the East.[15] However, even in this area,

---

15. A reference to the discussion and theses on the national and colonial questions at the Second Congress. See Riddell (ed.) 1991, 2WC, 1, pp. 211–90.

the relationship between nationalists in various Eastern countries and the Communist International is exceptionally loose. Under other circumstances, this movement would contribute in natural fashion directly to the struggle against world imperialism. But at present, given the character of the existing Communist organisations, it cannot be conducted in such a fashion as to serve the interests of the Communist International.

In the East, sympathy for communism and its influence is so strong that, in many countries where there are not yet strong Communist parties, a crisis is already perceptible within the Communist movement itself. That sounds somewhat strange but is a fact. In Turkey, for example, there are thus three Communist parties.[16] In Iran and Korea there are also several Communist parties.[17] This has happened because, in Turkey or Iran, any nationalist leader may come upon the idea of founding a Communist Party in order to increase his influence and make use of communism. To do that, he promptly sets up a central committee, of which he is the chair, and there you have it: a Communist Party. That is how parties were founded in Turkey, in Angora [Ankara], and also two parties – neither of them influential – in Iran. That has happened because the Communist International Executive and the Communist Party are not in close contact and because there is no leading body that could prevent the formation of such ephemeral, pseudo-Communist parties.

Nonetheless, we hope that in light of the revolutionary energy amassed by Communists in the East, the incoming Communist International Executive will devote more attention to the peoples of the East, who expect so much from it, and will fulfil their hopes and expectations.

**Mátyás Rákosi** (Hungary): Comrades, the Executive has been reproached for sending bad representatives on very responsible missions. I was one of these bad representatives. Some comrades in Germany and Italy have already stated their opinions of me. I have very little to add to that.

---

16. In addition to the Turkish Communist Party represented at the Third Congress, there were two other self-proclaimed Communist parties. One of these was the People's Communist Party of Turkey, organised in November 1920 within Anatolia; sympathetic to Soviet Russia, it promoted Islamic precepts, such as in family life. The third 'Communist Party' was one set up in October 1920, on instructions of Mustafa Kemal (Atatürk), as a way of channelling the energies of more radical elements to serve his own Turkish nationalist movement.

17. A division had arisen among Iranian Communists between a 'national-revolution' faction that emphasised the struggle against British imperialism and alliance with nationalist forces, and a 'purely Communist' faction that emphasised the fight for a soviet republic in Iran; rival central committees reflecting the two factions were formed.

The Korean Communists were divided into rival exile groups based respectively in Irkutsk and Shanghai.

I acted in Italy in full agreement with Comrade Kabakchiev and the Executive of the Italian Communist Party.[18] There was no disagreement among us. Indeed, I had very little to add, because we all judged the situation in the same way. Disagreements arose only when the former comrade Dr. Paul Levi got involved. As comrades know, the main issue at the Livorno Congress was to remove the reformists and Turati supporters from the Italian party. We could have received a good deal of help in this work from representatives of the large Communist parties that had already gone through a split. Above all, we were hoping for help from the new French Communist Party, which had carried out a split only a few weeks earlier. The defenders of Serrati had based their arguments above all on the weaknesses of this party. But although invited by the Italian Communist section [faction], the French party sent no representative to this congress. It is possible that this letter of invitation went to the wrong address, just like the request of the Luxembourg comrades, and that, as a result, the leadership of the new Communist Party did not consider it necessary to appear uninvited at the congress. As a result, we had to do without the help of the French comrades.

However, we hoped that the German comrades, who had experienced all the pain and agony caused by opportunists within the party and who had several splits behind them, would be helpful. All the greater was our consternation, therefore, when Paul Levi, after a two-hour discussion with Serrati, came to us and said more or less the same thing that we had heard repeatedly from Serrati. We told him that perhaps this was his personal opinion, upon which he most confidently produced a letter which, as he put it, he just happened to have with him. This letter was from Comrade Zetkin, and in it were pretty well the same views that Serrati and Levi put forward at the congress. In the letter, Comrade Zetkin said that she considered Serrati to be a good revolutionary and had a very negative opinion, by contrast, of Bordiga, Bombacci, Graziadei, and company. In her opinion, Serrati would build the Communist Party much better than the just-mentioned comrades. We were of course even more unpleasantly surprised by this, and we asked Levi at least to refrain from expressing his opinion at this congress. Naturally our request came somewhat late, because Serrati had made no secret of Levi's and Comrade Zetkin's opinion.

Such support from the two leaders of the largest Communist Party did much to strengthen the backbone of the Serrati group and made our work that much more difficult. We asked Comrade Levi to express our view. He

---

18. Rákosi is referring to the Executive Committee of the Communist Faction within the PSI.

made a rather insipid statement and then took off, the following day, despite our request that he remain until the congress concluded. We had hoped that if Comrade Levi took part in the congress right through to the end, he would change his opinion.

Comrades know the results of the congress vote. The Communist International and its Executive – which we are told function so poorly – received the news via radio telegraph and immediately told Serrati categorically that it recognised *only the newly founded Italian [Communist] party* as belonging to the Communist International. The Executive in Moscow could see very clearly from Moscow that Serrati wanted to keep the masses under the influence of the Turati group, for he tried to persuade them that, one way or another, they still belonged to the Communist International. The Executive in Moscow perceived that and took immediate preventive measures. Serrati, of course, was clever, and when the telegram arrived,[19] he said that this was merely the opinion of the Executive, which they would appeal to the Third Congress.

We hoped that, after hearing the arguments, the parties that would be attending the Third Congress would then express their views categorically in opposition to those of Serrati. The French party did take an official position, but its official publication printed an article by Jacques Mesnil that said in black and white that *Serrati could belong to the left wing of the Communist Party of France.*[20] That, of course, was a juicy morsel for Serrati. He was even more pleasantly surprised when Levi's celebrated article appeared in the 22 January edition of *Die Rote Fahne*.[21] That naturally placed the Italian comrades, who after the split in the organisation at Livorno were carrying out district congresses, in an enormously difficult position, because Serrati could say that not only Levi but the two largest Communist parties were of this opinion.

When I was in Berlin, I learned about the resolution that the United Communist Party [VKPD] had adopted on the Italian question. I immediately saw passages in this resolution that could offer new grounds for Serrati to pursue his scandalous conduct. I therefore immediately asked the party leadership to adopt a resolution that would leave no room for doubt. Based on my report,

---

19. Two days before the Livorno Congress, *L'Ordine nuovo* published a telegram from the ECCI signed by Zinoviev and Bukharin. The telegram featured an attack on Serrati's faction and stated: 'He who refuses to effect this schism [with the reformists] violates an essential decree of the Communist International, and with this act alone puts himself outside the ranks of the International.' Cammett 1967, p. 143.

20. Mesnil's article was published in the 25 January 1921 issue of *L'Humanité*, under the title 'Après le Congrès de Livorno. La scission du parti'.

21. Levi's unsigned article, 'Der Parteitag der italienischen Partei', dated 22 January 1921, appeared in the 23 January issue of *Die Rote Fahne*.

such a resolution was in fact drawn up.[22] Meanwhile, quite independently of us, the Executive in Moscow also spotted the error in this resolution and also asked the German party to modify the resolution in such a way as to exclude any erroneous interpretation. I took part in sessions of the party Executive and the national committee, in which I portrayed to comrades the situation in Italy. The comrades, including above all Comrade Brandler, were outraged, because Paul Levi had informed them that the genuinely Communist masses in Italy were with Serrati and that the masses calling themselves Communist were in reality gathered from syndicalists, anarchists, and confused forces.

It was in this report that, according to Comrade Zetkin, I made three errors. I am said to have considered the VKPD to be too large; to have said with regard to the French party that it is sometimes necessary to split a party ten times; and also to have said that we wanted to use the Italian question to set an example. I will reply briefly on these points.

In a private discussion with Comrade Clara Zetkin,[23] I spoke of the fact that when a party suddenly obtains four hundred thousand new members, a portion of these new members will certainly drop away, either in the course of actions or through the cleansings [of the membership] that we at the Second Congress declared to be obligatory for Communist parties. That is what I meant when I said the VKPD was too large. I also spoke of the fact that there are cases where a party must be split ten times. That came up with reference to the French party, where I said that if we had to choose between paying for the mistakes of opportunists through the loss of tens of thousands of proletarians – which was the fate of the Hungarian proletariat under the leadership of opportunist forces[24] – or of splitting the party ten times, I would opt for splitting. (*Applause*)

I also spoke of the fact that we had to set an example. I said that with reference to the Italian party. As we know, when it was in fashion to join the Third International, there were opportunist forces who came into the International solely in order to maintain their positions of power, so that they could use the revolutionary halo of the Communist International to continue their reformist game. Nowhere did this mischief flourish as luxuriantly as in the Italian party. And I said that we must make an example of the Turati and Modigliani and Treves people, in order to show that it is not only easy to get into the Communist International; it is also easy to get thrown out. (*Applause*) Those

---

22. Rákosi is referring to the Thalheimer-Stoeker resolution, summarised by Zetkin, pp. 288–90.
23. For Zetkin's account of Rákosi's remarks, see p. 292.
24. Rákosi is presumably referring to the treacherous conduct of opportunist leaders in the overthrow of the 1919 Hungarian soviet republic.

were the three things that Comrade Zetkin held against me. I raised them and other points at the [Central Committee] meeting.

As a doctor of law, Dr. Paul Levi has the ability to seize on these matters with skilled lawyer's tricks, saying that I had used the experience of the split in Italy to preach the necessity of a split in Germany. Of course I immediately denied his assertion, making an energetic statement that was presented in that same session and printed verbatim in *Die Rote Fahne*.[25] As comrades know, a resolution was adopted at that session, although Comrade Zetkin summoned up all her skills to thwart it, giving categorical support to the Italian Communist Party. This was not worth much, however, because the resignation of six members of the party leadership fully robbed it of authority. Quite the opposite: their resignation once again handed the Serrati people a strong weapon.

That is the role I played in the Italian split. We did everything possible to organise the Communist masses within the framework of the Communist Party. Comrade Zetkin's activity, by contrast, was designed in every respect to cause confusion among these masses, who were on the road to the Italian party. Those are the facts. Now, five months later, Comrade Zetkin, wiser by virtue of massive evidence, admits that she misjudged Serrati. Unfortunately she has only corrected a small fragment of the enormous mistakes she made regarding the Italian party and the Italian revolution. I can only add that, given Comrade Zetkin's so erroneous assessment of the Italian split and the Italian party in general, this incorrect assessment will necessarily lead to equally wrong judgements regarding the future policies of the VKPD. In my opinion, these consequences will turn out to be just as bad as her hopes and her opinions on the Italian question. (*Applause*)

As for the Executive's report, I would also like to say on behalf of the Hungarian party that *we are fully satisfied with every facet of the Executive's activity*. We are well aware that there were some technical shortcomings, especially with regard to communications with the national sections. But we must also say that inadequate communications – as we know from experience – is also partly the fault of the national sections. The sections are glad to leave the task of organising communications to the Executive alone and are glad to complain about bad communications instead of improving them.

On behalf of the Hungarian party, I would like to ask that you, enriched as you are by the experiences of the split in Italy, keep a close eye on the parties within the Communist International that still contain centrist or half-centrist

---

25. Rákosi is apparently referring to his speech to the VKPD Central Committee on 22 February. A report of his speech appeared in *Die Rote Fahne* on 26 February.

tendencies, so that at our next congress we will not have to busy ourselves with Serrati issues in the French or Czech parties. (*Loud applause*)

**Norah Smythe** (Britain): Comrades, the British delegation has decided not to speak at this time about the British question, because it will be taken up in the report on tactics and strategy. I do not want to take up your time with continuous repetition. But I would like to touch on another question. Comrade Radek said yesterday that our remarks should take up the activity and organisation of the Executive, and I would like to deal with one such point.

I was quite surprised that Comrade Zinoviev dealt so briefly with the Women's Secretariat. Indeed, that he said nothing about it, even though the Women's Secretariat is part of the International Secretariat, and its activity forms part of that of the Secretariat as a whole. I have the impression that the Executive has not carried out its responsibilities in this regard. Otherwise, it would have made some comments about it. Comrade Zinoviev said that it is important to organise women, and I am fully in agreement with him. He spoke of the great importance of the youth organisation, and there too I agree with him. One of the reasons why the woman question is important is the influence and effect of women on children and youth.

The fact that last year's theses still exist only in German shows again that the Executive has not carried out its duty in this regard.[26] Other countries have not yet been able to read these theses, and it is therefore not surprising that they have not done much work in this field. The woman question will be discussed later in this congress, and I will therefore not deal with it in detail. However, I call on the delegates to impress upon the Executive the importance of the women's secretariat and to make clear to the Communist parties in each country that in future years work among women must be conducted more energetically.

(*The session is adjourned at 12:30 a.m.*)

---

26. Smythe is presumably referring to the 'Theses for the Communist Women's Movement' prepared by Zetkin for the Comintern's Second Congress. The document was subsequently adopted by the ECCI. See Appendix 6b in Riddell (ed.) 1991, 2WC, 2, pp. 977–98.

# Session 8 – 28 June 1921, 7:30 p.m.
## The KAPD; the Italian Question

*The Communist Workers' Party of Germany. Speakers: Zinoviev, Hempel, Radek, Bergmann, Roland-Holst. The Italian question. Speakers: Lazzari, Gennari, Lenin.*

**Kolarov** (Chair): Comrades, the general debate on the Executive Committee report is now ended. According to the decision taken yesterday, the questions of the Socialist Party of Italy and the KAPD are to be dealt with separately. We will now take up these two questions. Yesterday evening we said that the session today would begin with discussion of the Italian question, but the Italian comrades are not yet here. It is therefore appropriate that we begin with the KAPD question. The Presidium proposes to give the floor to only one representative of the KAPD and one of the VKPD, and to have no further discussion, because this question has already been sufficiently addressed in the general debate. Of course, a representative of the Executive Committee will also speak. I have been informed that the VKPD does not wish to speak on this question.

**Zinoviev**: Comrades, before the congress begins this discussion, I would like to state very precisely the motion that I have already presented in general terms in my report. The motion is that the congress should decide to grant the KAPD a period of two or, at most, three months, so that the comrades can call a convention. At this convention, after an examination of the decisions of this congress, the party is to state whether it is prepared to submit to international discipline and is willing to join the VKPD. If the answer is yes, the matter is resolved; if no, the Executive will have the right to consider this party as having been expelled from the International.

**Kolarov** (Chair): The VKPD delegation informs us that it is in full agreement with the proposal by Comrade Zinoviev.

**Hempel** (Appel, KAPD): Comrades, I wish to speak to a point of order. The question of the VKPD appeal against the Executive decision admitting the KAPD as a sympathising organisation of the Third International was previously considered a separate congress agenda point. This point was to be taken up after the principled and tactical questions had been dealt with. That was the right procedure. We prepared for that. Then the day before yesterday – or was it yesterday? – the Presidium told us curtly that the question of the Italian delegation and our question would be taken up at the same time as the Executive report. The Presidium had previously agreed on this with the delegation of the Socialist Party of Italy, which had arrived, but not with us. We faced a fait accompli. We said nothing about the matter at the time, hoping that if we agreed to what the Presidium proposed, this would lead to a favourable outcome. We submitted the following statement to the Presidium, seeking to reach agreement on this basis. I will read it:

> We have just been informed by the Presidium, five minutes before the beginning of the session, that the KAPD question is to be resolved by permitting us to speak for half an hour.
>
> This proposal is not in keeping with the importance of the question, which is far too complicated to be dealt with in a brief contribution to the discussion. We must have a report or supplementary report of at least an hour, along with the right to a summary in rebuttal.
>
> The Presidium has decided against this proposal. We regard this as a manipulation of the agenda, directed against us, and we protest it. We do not want to be complicit in an illusion that the congress was adequately informed, so as to be able to take a decision, and we will therefore not take the floor on this question.

We submitted this statement, and five minutes ago we received a response, namely that we will be allowed a speaking time of half an hour, and that is that. In response, we say that this is being done to keep us quiet, and we are not going along with it. If judgement is to be passed on us, we cannot explain our position clearly in half an hour. Do what you will. I submit this statement and ask that you take note of it. (*Commotion*)

**Radek**: Comrades, first of all, I must correct the version of the facts just presented by Comrade Hempel. It was not five minutes ago but five hours ago that the KAPD delegation was informed by my secretary that the Executive was placing the KAPD question first on the agenda today, and that representatives of the KAPD and the Executive would each receive half an hour to present their point of view. The KAPD representative did not protest this. He merely insisted that the KAPD speak for an hour. That is the first fact, and it is not insignificant.

The KAPD delegation completely misunderstands the meaning of Zinoviev's motion. If the KAPD wishes to learn about the work of the congress and inform us of its point of view, there will be an opportunity for this under all the other agenda points. What is now at stake is to inform the KAPD regarding our position. And after that is done, the KAPD will continue on as part of the congress. No one is asking that it communicate any decision to the congress now. All Hempel's talk about shutting the mouth of the KAPD, after these comrades have gratified us by using their mouths so freely (*Laughter*) is just childishness, and we hope that the KAPD continues to make abundant use of this most useful part of the body. We would be very sorry to see the KAPD leave our congress. We would then have to be satisfied with studying their books. We have the sacred works of the 'Dutch school' and their press and will have to rely on these sources exclusively for our information. (*Laughter*)

**Bergmann** (Fritz Meyer, KAPD): Comrades, the question now under discussion is crucially important for the KAPD. We stated earlier our agreement with the Executive's proposal to take up this point separately and after dealing with all the principled questions. That was sufficient accommodation from our side. When Comrade Radek asserts here that 'we have decided this', he is referring to the entire congress, thereby pre-empting the decision of the congress as a whole. The congress is to decide here regarding the KAPD question and the position on it taken by the Executive. That is what is up for discussion here. Given that our ideas and writings have not been circulated among the masses as much as they should have been, and that they are not known to all the comrades, it is necessary to have a thorough discussion here on this question. We therefore demand that we receive speaking time of an hour on the present agenda point, and of course a summary after the discussion. We take that as a matter of course. If a different decision is made, allowing us speaking time of only half an hour, and if the discussion is broken off and shut down, we absolutely refuse to speak. We tell you: Go ahead and pass judgement on us and lead us to the gallows like a convicted murderer.

**Zinoviev**: Comrades, we have yet to discuss the trade-union question, which the KAPD considers to be the most important one. The comrades will obviously be able to take the floor on that point. The same holds for the discussion of tactics and strategy. The question before us now is whether a party that has not accepted discipline and refuses to do so can remain in the International, and if so, under what conditions. That is the only question now before the congress. The KAPD comrades have spoken on all questions and will do so from here on in. Only one issue is before us now for decision: should the congress insist that the party declare, within three months, whether it is a party like all the others or, by contrast, is inviolable – as stated in their well-known resolution.[1] That is the only question before us now for decision.

I think it is truly outrageous that the KAPD comrades have given us an ultimatum. Procedurally, the congress has acted quite properly. A motion was made yesterday morning to take together the report on the Italian question plus that of the KAPD, since they are interrelated. The KAPD comrades were here in the hall but said not a word. The congress made a unanimous decision on this yesterday, and everyone can see that this is only logical, because these questions are interrelated. And the Italian comrades, who have significant disagreements with us, understood that this is procedurally correct. The only thing we can do is to take the speaker from the Executive first and then let the KAPD comrades have the last word.

The question that we must now decide is simple and clear: Should the International continue to accept in its ranks a party that declares, after a year of experiences, that it is inviolable. We can confidently decide on this without long-winded discussion, given that we have already heard a number of KAPD speakers. I therefore ask the congress to make the decision that is objective and correct and flows from what has happened here. If the KAPD comrades decline to speak, they are simply repeating in a milder form what Otto Rühle did in 1920.[2] (*Applause*)

**Kolarov** (Chair): I believe we can end the debate on procedure. (*Applause*)

**Radek**: Comrades, the Executive's motion on the Communist Workers' Party, which has been a sympathising member of the Communist International for six months, provides for a specific period of two or three months within which it must decide if it will submit to the Communist International decision and thus, in the framework of this decision, carry out a unification with the VKPD.

To explain the Executive's position, some remarks are needed on the history of relations between the Communist International and the KAPD. The present

---

1. This resolution is quoted by Zinoviev on p. 214.
2. See p. 209, n. 54.

disagreements between the KAPD and the Communist International have existed from the very moment of the KAPD's formation. The KAPD based its perspective not on the mass movement but on forming small and pure Communist parties. On the trade-union question, they denied that our task was to win the trade unions from inside through the struggle of Communists within their ranks, in order to transform them from tools for 'civil peace' and 'collaboration' to tools for the class struggle. Instead, they held that Communists must separate themselves off from the broad masses of workers in struggle, and that separate organisations are needed, formed mainly of workers who stand for a proletarian dictatorship. With regard to parliamentarism as well, the KAPD stands in opposition to the Communist International, which regards this only as a means, like other means, to arouse and organise the workers to revolutionary struggle.

The conflict between the KAPD and the Communist International was thus obvious from the time of its founding congress. Even so, the International sought to build bridges to this party, not as part of an all-inclusive policy seeking to merge Tom, Dick, and Harry, but from an understanding that a position such as the one advanced by the KAPD will also find expression in errors within the revolutionary Communist movement of the proletariat in every country. Wherever new revolutionary layers awaken and enter the arena of political struggle, clearly these layers will not always and not everywhere have a fine sense of what is politically necessary. And since we are dealing here with errors of revolutionary proletarians, the Executive said that everything must be done to win these proletarians for the International. At the Second Congress of the Communist International the Executive removed every obstacle in order to enable the KAPD delegates to take part in the congress, to express their views there, and to acquaint themselves with the positions taken by the overwhelming majority of Communist proletarians of every country. The Executive went so far as to offer the KAPD representatives decisive vote, even though they said in advance that they would not accept the congress decisions. The KAPD delegates considered it preferable to flee, in order – as they said – not to be present at the congress when it demonstrated its opposition to their policies. That is how Rühle later justified his absence from the congress.

After the congress, the situation in the KAPD clarified to some degree. The KAPD separated off from its National Bolshevik wing, led by Wolffheim and Laufenberg.[3] Then it separated from Rühle as well. And when the

---

3. The National Bolshevik current in the KAPD, led by Fritz Wolffheim and Heinrich Laufenberg, contended that Germany as a whole had been proletarianised and called for a national alliance of the German nation to wage a revolutionary war against the

KAPD decided to send delegates to Moscow for consultation, the Executive decided – against the advice and opinion of the VKPD – yes, we want to make another attempt, we want to open a path once again by which these mistaken proletarians come to us. It decided to accept the KAPD into the Communist International provisionally as a sympathising member. In so doing, the Executive said frankly to the KAPD representatives: you will soon have to choose between the path toward fusion with the VKPD and the Communist International and being outside the International. There is no third choice. With due allowance for a certain period of transition, there must be only one section of the Communist International in each country. In admitting the KAPD, the Executive required it to strive for fraternal agreement with the VKPD on all questions posed for action and to support the VKPD in all its action initiatives.[4]

Comrades, we now have half a year of the KAPD's development behind us. We must note that the KAPD's evolution has not been on the path from a sect to a mass party, but rather the reverse, toward becoming a sect that is more and more prone to adventurism. Since its founding, the KAPD has always opposed the Executive's policies, but only recently did it begin to brand these policies in its official writings as a crime against the international proletariat. Thus Gorter, for example, writes, 'If the Russian policy of party and leadership dictatorship is pursued further, after the disastrous results it has had so far, that is no longer a matter of stupidity but of a crime against the revolution.'

The KAPD hardened its position of principled opposition to the formation of mass Communist parties. In its pamphlet, *The Path of Dr. Levi – the Path of the VKPD*, it states on page 26: 'The March struggles have shown that such a mass party cannot exist, or more precisely, that it cannot exist as a mass Communist Party.' The KAPD's international policies have evolved to the point where it stands arm in arm with the entire Menshevik press against the Communist International and Soviet Russia. I am not referring merely to articles in *KAZ* that accuse the Communist International of being a tool of the Soviet government's foreign policy. Gorter's pamphlet, published by the KAPD, even stands in defence of Kronstadt.[5]

---

Entente powers. Along these lines it urged cooperation with right-wing nationalist forces on an anti-Versailles programme. The Wolffheim-Laufenberg current was expelled from the KAPD in August 1920.

4. See 'On the Policy of the KAPD', Trotsky 1972a, 1, pp. 137–52.

5. For the Kronstadt revolt, see p. 213, n. 61. *KAZ* refers to the KAPD's organ, *Kommunistische Arbeiter-Zeitung*.

> The proletariat has risen up against you, the Communist Party. You have had to declare a state of siege in Petersburg directed against the proletariat (which was a necessity for you, just as are all your policies). Given these facts, has it not occurred to you that it would indeed be preferable to have a dictatorship of the class rather than of the party?

That shows just how disastrous your evolution is. We are convinced that this evolution reflects not the KAPD workers but rather a small clique of leaders. We base this conviction on the fact that the KAPD tries everywhere to keep its workers from joining with VKPD workers in common struggle. Let us recall that when the VKPD's Open Letter appealed to all workers' organisations in Germany to form a common front, the KAPD rejected a common struggle on principle. Let me remind you of what happened in recent weeks in Hamburg, where the KAPD leaders, after uniting with the seamen's alliance and the VKPD, withdrew at the last moment in order not to confuse the masses. The same thing happened in Berlin.

Given this evolution, the Communist International must pose an alternative to the workers in the KAPD: either go with a handful of confused leaders, or go with the Communist International. Either force these leaders to join the Communist International, or, together with these leaders, leave the International.

There are other facts to consider. Recently, an adventurist current won the upper hand in the KAPD, a current for which we can take no responsibility. This current is attracted to acts of individual terrorism. It elevates illegality into a principle and utilises it as an excuse to call on workers to do things that have nothing in common with Communist International politics. The Communist International will not take any responsibility for this. Either the KAPD will submit to the decisions of the Executive in all matters, including tactics and strategy, or it will not. If it does submit, the decisions of the Communist International will provide it with a path to the VKPD and it will struggle together with this party and under the overall leadership of the Communist International's principles. Otherwise, it will be deprived of the opportunity to carry out its policies under the banner of a sympathising organisation of the Communist International.

Comrades, we ask the congress to adopt our motion unanimously. We are convinced that we will not lose a single proletarian who wishes to struggle for the ideas of communism. The VKPD has shown the masses through its March Action – however many errors it may have made – what a lie it is to say that, as the Communist International's section in Germany, it is unwilling to struggle. It has shown its will to struggle, thereby making it possible for the broadest masses of impatient proletarians, above all the unemployed, to join its ranks.

Before the VKPD's action, it was possible to fear that we were losing touch with the impatient working masses. However, subsequent evidence, taken from life, shows that this is no longer to be feared. In the Hamburg elections among the unemployed, after the March defeat, the VKPD obtained almost as many votes as the USPD and SPD combined. (*'Even more!'*) Comrades, that shows we have succeeded in penetrating every sector of the proletariat. And if the KAPD does not fall in step, then it will be the disruptive force. What we demand of the KAPD is that it submit, that it act with discipline in the ranks of the Communist International, as we must require of forces on both right and left.

Today we are to decide the case of Italy. We will put the question to the wavering forces in Italy: Do you want to go with the Communist International or with the reformists? And we are simultaneously putting the question to the KAPD workers: do you want to go with a few poorly written publications of the so-called Dutch school and the tiny handful of those defending these views, or with the millions of proletarians who stand with the Communist International and who join as an army in common battle, carrying out the struggle against capitalism.

Comrades, we do not willingly relinquish even the smallest group of class-conscious workers, workers who wish to struggle. At this moment, when it is unambiguously clear what the congress is going to decide, we propose that the Executive simultaneously write a fraternal letter, on behalf of the congress, to the workers who still support the KAPD, presenting this decision as what it is – an attempt to integrate them into one unified army of the proletariat, which we are building. (*Loud applause*)

**Kolarov** (Chair): I give the floor to the representative of the KAPD. (*No one rises to speak*) It appears that the comrades wish to grant themselves the pleasure of a petty demonstration against the Executive. Does anyone else wish to speak against the Executive's decision on the KAPD question?

Comrade Roland-Holst has the floor.

**Roland-Holst**: Comrades, the minority of the Dutch delegation has adopted the following declaration, which I will read:

> The minority of the Dutch delegation regards the decision of the congress not to lengthen the speaking time of the KAPD representatives to one hour as an act of intellectual violence, against which it vigorously protests. (Signed:) *Roland-Holst, I. Jansen, Varkel* (delegate of the Communist Party of the Dutch East Indies).

Comrades, I have no intention of trying to address the factual issues with regard to keeping the KAPD in the Communist International as a sympathising organisation. It was up to their representatives to do that. But I cannot avoid pointing out that they have been hindered from doing so by an act of intellectual violence. It is impossible to separate the question of discipline from the principled and tactical issues on which the KAPD has a distinctive position inside the Communist International. It is equally impossible for its delegates to deal with these issues thoroughly in only an hour – and certainly not in half an hour.

It seems to me that the KAPD motion to take up their case only at the end of the congress was completely correct, given that the congress's position on their points of view obviously may be influenced by the arguments that they advance on all the agenda points that have yet to be addressed. The KAPD would have been able, under these points, to present their views rather fully. The fact that they have not been permitted to do this puts them in a very difficult situation. Their speaking time has been systematically reduced. Consider how much time was given yesterday to Comrade Clara Zetkin for the presentation of her personal view of the Italian question. One can only conclude that two standards are being used here. I must add that this has not happened just today, not just now. This approach has been evident in several past incidents, but in this case it is especially blatant. I am convinced that it would hardly occur to the congress and the Executive to limit the speaking time of the Serrati party in Italy to half an hour. What is right for some should be right for the others. I cannot limit myself to justifying this statement in formal terms; I feel obliged to take a few moments to go into the essence of the matter.

In sessions of the Executive, leading comrades have repeatedly stated that the danger on the left is no less important than the danger on the right. Well, we on the left cannot agree with this view. We consider the danger on the right to be infinitely greater and more threatening than that on the left. Given the delayed unfolding of the revolution, given the hesitation and uncertainty of broad masses of workers, both inside our parties and outside the Communist International, I consider it essential for the International's healthy development that the Left and the Far Left have an opportunity to develop. Comrades, there is not yet a Left in the Communist International. Only its first beginnings are starting to take shape. No decision has yet been taken [here] on the different issues and items: parliamentarism, the trade unions, supercentralism, and so on – there are other points as well.

But this Left can unfold together only with the struggles of the parties and the development of communism. If the Far Left is cut away, and this decision is already the beginning of cutting it away, if the framework for agreement is removed, this entire development is weakened. Whether intentionally or not, this strengthens the tenacity of the right wing. I fear, therefore, that this decision, adopted almost without words, almost without discussion, can have serious negative results for the Communist International. If the KAPD is eliminated, this will lead to the formation of small parties in different countries – a considerable number of them. We want to have these parties inside the International, even if they do not immediately submit to discipline. Patience is needed, along with confidence in the development of the revolution and in the dominant forces in these parties. There are other forces, smaller in number but of high quality, and these forces everywhere have similar traits: those who are the greatest idealists, those who perhaps focus excessively on the distant goal and are not sufficiently able to carry out realistic policies. How are we to carry out policies that are both realistic and revolutionary: that is the great and difficult art, the great and difficult science, that we wish to learn and must learn. That is why we have gathered in this congress, and that is what we wish to learn from the Russian comrades, especially from Comrade Trotsky. And it is therefore painful for us that Comrade Trotsky is now dealing with this Far Left in much more critical fashion than the right wing.

**Trotsky**: I have not yet had an opportunity to talk about the right wing. Just wait and be patient.

**Roland-Holst**: I will wait, and wait gladly. In my opinion, however, the way that Comrades Lenin and Trotsky intervened in the Executive regarding the errors and weaknesses of the French party, and the way they spoke to the young French comrades, represented a course that I feel was set too much toward the right.[6] I would like to add that these small groups contain unyielding personalities and strong-willed fighters. They include personalities and minds that, while somewhat dogmatic, are, like Comrade Gorter, very good at keeping the overall perspective in view, even if they sometimes neglect the immediate situation. That is why I asked the KAPD to overcome its limitations. We do not want to do violence to them; we want them to go beyond their limitations. If they split away, it will only cause harm to the International – perhaps contrary to its wishes, but that is what will happen. There is an iron necessity in this business. And so we say to the entire congress that we cannot and do not want to do without these forces. We do not want to be deprived of their pure idealism. There are many good and excellent political figures in the Third International who, however, have their weak sides. In addition, we want to have comrades whose feel for politics is perhaps

---

6. See Lenin and Trotsky's remarks in Appendix 3f on pp. 1114–25 and 1128–32.

insufficiently developed, but who have a strongly developed revolutionary will, revolutionary determination, and revolutionary idealism. That is why I and the minority of the Dutch delegation consider this decision to be ominous. Nonetheless, I hope that the KAPD comrades will take part fully in the rest of the proceedings, that their points of view will influence the congress, and that it will be possible at the end of the congress to overturn this unfortunate decision. (*Applause*)

**Kolarov** (Chair): That concludes the speakers' list. The debate on this question is ended.

We will now take up the Italian question. Comrade Lazzari of the Socialist Party of Italy has the floor.

**Costantino Lazzari** (Socialist Party of Italy): Comrades from every land! This is not the first time that relations between the Italian Socialists and the International have been strained. I recall – as will other comrades here – the disputes we had with the International of Huysmans and Vandervelde, whom we regarded as persons from a 'small country' and as a factor unworthy of any great attention.

We are present here before representatives of the Third International in an unpleasant situation: we are regarded as representing traitors! We have always done the utmost and spared no effort to carry out our national and international duty. We have never been guided by personal interests, thinking always and only of the movement that we represent. Since the time of Judas, traitors have always been those who focused solely on their own interests. We have always served our cause with selflessness and self-denial. We therefore protest that we must appear here after having been morally belittled. We have been belittled in a number of different ways, including, for example, by an article in the newspaper *Moscow* signed by an Italian, Gennari.[7] This article states in disparaging terms that only my stand on the Turati question speaks in my favour, making no mention of the fact that for forty years I have carried out a stubborn struggle against the Italian bourgeoisie, a struggle in which I sacrificed my family, my health – in a word, sacrificed everything. In addition, he said that my policy toward the Great War was ambiguous. I remind this article's author and you all that my policy resulted in my arrest and conviction,[8] while the author of those lines, despite the perfection of his politics, encountered nothing of the sort.

---

7. Gennari's declaration appeared in the 6 July issue of *Moscou*.
8. As PSI secretary, Lazzari was arrested in January 1918 together with deputy secretary Nicola Bombacci and charged with disseminating defeatist anti-war propaganda. Lazzari and Bombacci were tried and convicted on 26 February; they

We are submitting a written statement explaining the reasons for the mandate we are carrying out here. It rests on objective and specific grounds that everyone should acknowledge. We had the misfortune to arrive late, although I must note that the fault was not ours. You all know the great barriers obstructing freedom of travel and also the difficulties of our situation. This delay prevented us from hearing Comrade Zinoviev's report. I waited in vain for the French translation and therefore had to use the English text, which shows that the report's discussion of the Italian Socialist Party ranged far and wide. We still hope to see, with bitter satisfaction, the Italian movement receive more respect and recognition from comrades of the International.

We are pleased to see that Comrade Zinoviev's information office has pulled together all the documents relating to the situation in which the Italian movement finds itself. We thank him for having collected all the documents that he thought to be of interest in such an objective fashion.[9] This collection lacks certain items, the need for which we did not foresee, and which are of sufficient interest to lay before the congress. By the way, we Italians make little use of written documents, since we are accustomed to acting against the bourgeoisie with deeds. Nonetheless, I must note that Zinoviev has used some material wrongly. The appendix to this volume attributes to the Italian Socialist Party some wretched personal writings, which were neither supported nor defended by any party organisation, and in any case did not have any influence on the political conduct of our party.

The representative of the Italian Communists has come here in order to assure us that the Communists did not seek a split at the Livorno Congress. He neglected to mention, however, that the Communist Faction decided in Imola to leave the party if it did not have a majority.[10] He also forgot to mention that with regard to the failure of the factory occupations, it was the representatives of Turin, themselves workers and Communists, who recognised that it was impossible to continue the struggle and the occupation.

The statement we are submitting gives the reasons why we believe that we have the right to be admitted to the International.[11] We affiliated to it before any party in another country did. At the beginning of 1919, a comrade came from Russia to Italy – he was arrested and we were able to free him – bringing the first manifesto and first appeal of the Communist International, tucked

---

were sentenced, respectively, to 35 and 28 months imprisonment and were jailed until November 1918.

9. See Comintern 1921b.

10. The Communist Faction within the Italian SP met in Imola, 28–29 November 1920. The conference united together Bordiga's Communist Abstentionist current, the *Ordine nuovo* group in Turin led by Antonio Gramsci, and Left Maximalist forces.

11. For the PSI statement, see p. 356–7.

into his shoe. As soon as I received these, we – the Italian Socialist Party – declared our unconditional affiliation. From the outset of the Russian Revolution we had been imbued with a sense of admiration and sincere gratitude. We felt something akin to envy regarding the heroic efforts to give Russia a government of labour and freedom. We always maintained our affiliation, because we urgently needed international connections, not only to be true to our ideals, but also because our nation is the greatest source of emigration, and it is urgently necessary for Italian workers in every country to be welcomed with solidarity and fraternity.

In keeping with these aspirations, we have never spared any effort, both in times of peace and of war, to carry out our duty with all the means available to us. Even during the War we unfurled the banner of the International, as at Zimmerwald and Kienthal[12] – Comrade Lenin knows this very well – and we need only repeat what we said then: as Italian Socialists, we cannot promise to do great deeds, but we do promise this: always to do our duty. Imbued with these feelings, in a poor and ignorant country, we have built a movement that has forced even the bourgeoisie to reckon with us as a serious factor, a movement that has succeeded in summoning the working classes of Italy – farmers and workers – and in unifying them into a significant force. It is thus truly irritating to see ourselves treated here as traitors.

For this reason, quite apart from our movement's errors and weaknesses, we have always sought eagerly to preserve political unity in action. We seek to defend this unity from one end of Italy to the other, against the class unity of the bourgeoisie. It is our ardent wish for the Third International to be a powerful organisation, not a weak one. When the Communists split away, this weakened us. We deplore the fact that it was the Third International, of all things, that pushed through the split in Livorno. And here we are, together with comrades who treat us so cruelly. We have no intention of responding to unjust criticisms by making others. Certainly we have used harsh words against our opponents. Nonetheless, we hope that the response you will give to our application to affiliate will include a proposal that I can transmit to the French comrades. The same holds true for the German and British comrades, who also know us, and who are also embraced, as in the words of Comrade Frossard, in 'neither complete subordination nor absolute independence'.[13] This formula is adaptable and adroitly phrased –

---

12. Lazzari and Serrati were among the Italian delegates at both the Zimmerwald (5–8 September 1915) and Kienthal (24–30 April 1916) socialist conferences, which affirmed an internationalist policy against the War.

13. These were the words of a mandate given by the French CP's Central Committee [Comité Directeur] to the party's delegates to the Comintern's Third Congress.

**Loriot**: Please note the scope of the adjectives.[14]

**Lazzari**: – and our delegates intend to propose it for the Communist International. They will be guided by this concept during the debate that will surely take place regarding the German and Italian questions. We hope that when you examine our written statement, you will keep this concept in mind, instead of passing sentence on us as demanded by the Italian Communists, who are currently our opponents and competitors.

In addition, we have stated that we are prepared at any time to accept the decision of the international congress. It would be unjust to condemn us, but that would not hinder us from carrying out our international duties, in accordance with our means, and continuing to defend the reputation, the freedom, and the honour of the Russian Soviet republic, as we have done in the past and will do in the future. Very recently, we defended the integrity and the interests of your diplomatic mission in Rome. We have maintained relations with its head, Comrade Vorovsky, and we succeeded in making up for the hostile reception that nationalist and bourgeois forces prepared for him.[15] We are happy to know that we are able to contribute in this way to supporting and defending the heroic efforts of Russia's revolutionary government.

As for you, French comrades, who have always been so well informed in matters touching on us, we would like to remind you that we never lost sight of the integrity of our movement, even when the French comrades who are now such good friends of the Third International came to Rome and treated us there as people who had 'sold out to the Kaiser'.[16] I then had the opportunity to defend the integrity of our movement on the occasion of a speech that I made in the Palais Bourbon to the French parliamentary fraction, in the presence of Sembat, Thomas, and Guesde, all government ministers, who responded by pounding their fists on the table. The time has come to prove that you have a correct assessment of the situation we face in our country and in the international organisation.

I know that in this discussion of Zinoviev's report, we represent only a small minority. We are not recognised as a section of the International, we have no voting rights, and enjoy neither the rights nor the means to influence you toward an appropriate decision on the Executive Committee's report. If

---

14. In the German edition, this sentence is attributed to Lazzari. The text follows the Russian edition, which states it to be an interjection.

15. A reference to the first Soviet diplomatic mission in Italy headed by V. Vorovsky, which had arrived in May 1921.

16. During World War I the French SP majority, which included future Communist leader Marcel Cachin, actively supported the Entente powers' war effort and attempted to mobilise international support for it.

the congress wishes to adopt a resolution on the Italian question, we would be pleased to be able to discuss it and contribute to drafting it. We arrived here burdened by the odium of moral inferiority created by the split that you yourselves brought about in our party. We are surrounded by opponents who even occasionally become our enemies. Nonetheless, we are still imbued today with the same feelings of solidarity and brotherhood. Moreover, the love we feel for the unity of the movement in Italy leads us to hope that you will meet us half-way and accept us as brothers. We are well aware that our movement has a great many weaknesses, but that will not prevent us from perfecting our organisation and activity – even if you fail to spur us on and give us the effective means to fully carry out the necessary cleansings. We hope that you will provide us with a solid political foundation that will enable us to force the reformists in our party to take a stand, one way or the other, in a fashion that excludes any suggestion that this is about personal considerations.

In drafting your resolution, you must not think that our party is a collection of groups formed around personalities like Turati and Serrati. In our party, when personalities no longer represent the interests of the organisation and the masses, they no longer have any significance. They then have no importance at all. We are not here for the sake of one or another grouping but to defend, independent of personality, the rights of the entire movement as a whole that we represent against the Italian bourgeoisie. We fully understand that your Executive Committee faces an urgent necessity of shaping perfected and solid revolutionary forces and driving them forward as rapidly as possible, especially in our country. We do not refuse to eradicate our reformists, but it is nonetheless necessary for you to grant us the capacity and responsibility to choose the appropriate moment and to maintain the party's influence on the masses.

Comrade Lenin, we understand that different measures are appropriate in the different phases of a revolutionary movement. In Italy, we find ourselves at present in a preparatory period. But when we encounter the period of revolutionary action, you may be sure that we will not hesitate to take all necessary measures to safeguard the dictatorship of Italy's proletarian class.

Comrades of the congress, in your task of acquiring a sufficiently clear understanding of the Italian question, we recommend that you read and study the document that you will find on page 135 of the book that has been published about us. This is the manifesto that our party's leadership issued after the split at the Livorno Congress.[17] You will find there a summary of our

---

17. A reference to 'Manifiesto al lavoratori d'Italia'. It can be found in Comintern 1921b and also in PCI 1922, pp. 7–20.

party's contributions. You will also find there an indication of the forms and spirit that have guided us in breathing life into our movement in the unfavourable situation created by the conduct of the Communists in our country. It is true that we consider ourselves far too weakened to carry out successfully the revolutionary policy that we have always defended heretofore. Nonetheless, we are certain that the party and the masses in economic organisations will not be taken in by illusory reformist policies, and will always refuse the collaboration and participation of those whom we have always combated.

I would like to say in closing that, regardless of the resolution that you adopt concerning our application to be admitted to the Third International, this will not result in any change in our conduct. We have never sought any other satisfaction in life save the fulfilment of the duties placed on us by our conscience. That we will always do. It is both an honour and a duty to uphold policies capable of securing for the Russian revolutionary government the possibility of utilising its wonderful example to spread unforgettable rays of light to proletarians the world over. We are certain that the day will come when you will recognise what we already stated in our written declaration: that the Italian Socialist Party has worked for revolution, not counterrevolution.

I have just read the theses on tactics and strategy that the Executive is proposing to the congress. This is a precious gift that we will utilise to better define our movement's policies and also to keep clear of anarchist fantasies and reformist illusions. We hope that experience will show the fruits of this congress to have been not entirely wasted for the Italians. You must understand that even though we accept full responsibility to implement the decisions that you will take, we cannot disregard the duty to spare the Italian proletarians, to the degree that it is humanly possible, the horrors of defeats suffered in the history of proletarians in Germany, Finland, and Hungary. We seek in this way to serve the cause of world revolution and to earnestly prepare for the emancipation of labour in our country.

**Gennari** (Communist Party of Italy): When the Executive Committee sent an invitation to representatives of the Italian Socialist Party to attend this congress of the Third International, it should have included two conditions.[18] First, that the delegation have sufficient authority and should not attempt to evade responsibility by referring to an inadequate mandate. Second, that the delegation include not only Central Committee members but also forces who are close to the masses.

---

18. Both the Russian and German texts refer here to the 'Italian Communist Party'; the context makes clear that the reference in fact was to the Socialist Party.

The delegation should have stated clearly whether it considers permissible participation in sessions of the Third International by individuals who took part in the notorious meeting in Reggio Emilia.[19]

And now the delegation has come, and Lazzari has spoken, and we must repeat the same questions.

My task is to demonstrate, using documentary proof, that the assertions of Italian Communists, which Lazzari has attempted to dispute, are indisputable. That will not require of me any eloquent turns of phrase or emotional appeals.

Above all, I maintain that the Italian Socialist Party embraces in its ranks pronounced reformists who are no better than a Thomas or a Scheidemann. We are assured that the Italian opportunists were always against the War. That is not correct. I can point to the article by Ciccotti and others. In addition, the party's slogan, 'neither to support the war nor to sabotage it', provided scope for a display of social patriotism.[20]

It was only the Maximalists, among whom I was active, that brought the party onto a correct path. At that time, Lazzari himself, together with Serrati, called us the 'Florence lunatics'. Serrati is lying when he claims that there are no veteran fighters in the Communist Party of Italy.

At the moment of our sharpest struggle against the War, people like Bellini and Soglia published manifestoes with a strong patriotic coloration. Everyone is also familiar with the heroic patriotic exploits of the lawyer, Mazzoni, also a party member.

Turati refrained from that, but his restraint gave way when the Italian army met catastrophe at Caporetto.[21] Both Turati and Rigola, head of the labour federation, expressed themselves then in an outrageous fashion. In articles by Turati and Treves we read:

> The fatherland is in danger! Only now, as the jubilant, barbaric victor has invaded our country, we realise that our fatherland is not identical with other fatherlands. As Marxists, we are also realists in our emotional life. We cannot conceivably ignore an objective fact such as the love for country.

---

19. For the Reggio Emilia conference of the reformist Socialist Concentration Faction of the PSI, see p. 190, n. 19.

20. The Italian SP campaign against the War was waged under this formula (*'né aderire né sabotare'*) raised by Lazzari in May 1915.

21. At the Battle of Caporetto in October–November 1917, German and Austrian troops broke through Italian lines, forcing a retreat to the south. Some 40,000 Italian troops were killed and 280,000 were taken prisoner.

In the wake of the battle, Turati, a prominent member of the PSI's parliamentary fraction, publicly associated himself with the perspective of national defence, leading to calls within the PSI for his expulsion.

We do not proceed from humanity to Italy but from Italy to humanity. For the sake of duty and love of country we must break the bonds of petty formalities within which the party has confined us.[22]

The bulletin distributed by the labour confederation was written in the same spirit. Milan's Socialist municipal government took a similar stand. This approach, warped by patriotism, shocked Serrati, and in order to straighten it out he called on us, the Maximalists – myself, Bordiga and others. When Lazzari was put on trial, the prosecutor cited Turati as an example of the praiseworthy patriotism of sensible Socialists.

Then came the events connected with the fighting near Monte Grappa,[23] which evoked a new outburst of patriotism from Turati. After his speech in parliament, everyone wanted to embrace him, including its most sinister forces and Leonid Bissolati, expelled from the party as a social patriot.[24] The parliamentary caucus stood in full solidarity with Turati. As a result, the Central Committee held a special session where it expressed its extreme disapproval.

The proletariat was shocked to learn that Turati was embraced in parliament at the same time as other Socialists were thrown in jail. The Central Committee threatened to expel Turati, Belori, and others. But Turati took no note of the Central Committee. Parliament had barely begun its session when Turati made another speech, in which he said, ironically: 'After my speech here, which was imbued with the spirit of nature and love, the temple priests came to me, brandishing outdated phrases and rules and trying to beguile me once again'. And still Turati has not been expelled from the party!

Lazzari claims that the Socialists never voted for war credits. Quite right. Given the proletariat's mood, such a performance was dangerous, but Mazzoni, Zibordi, Belori, and Soglia, in affectionate union with a bishop, published an appeal to the proletariat to commit all their savings to the purchase of patriotic loans, pointing out, among other things, that such an act of patriotic morality has distinct monetary advantages. Would it not have been

---

22. F. Turati and C. Treves, 'Proletariat e la Resistenza', in *Critica sociale*, 1 November 1917.

23. This refers to a series of battles between Italian and Austro-Hungarian troops that took place around the Monte Grappa mountain in the Alps from the summer of 1917 to October 1918.

24. A reference to Turati's speech to parliament on 12 June 1918, after which the entire house erupted in cheers and he was embraced by minister Bissolati and a number of deputies. For excerpts from Turati's speech, see Turati 1955, pp. 223–4.

Bissolati, a minister without portfolio in the Italian government during World War I, had been expelled from the PSI in 1912 along with a number of other reformists for supporting the Italian war against Libya. He then helped form the Reformist Socialist Party.

more honest to vote openly and unambiguously in parliament for the war credits?

I must also point out that there are many pacifists in the party. True, Lazzari himself took a strong stand against Wilson, but Caldara, the mayor of Milan, extolled Wilsonism, along with many others. At the Rome Congress – my dear Lazzari, you were not there because you were then in prison – Turati made a speech that stood as his credo.[25] He said that we must not confuse defensive with offensive wars, and that a war begun to defend a small, wronged country is morally justified.[26] He said that the internationalists were splitters, called on all classes to rally in national solidarity, and showed that this is in the interests of the proletariat, which would otherwise be oppressed not only by its own domestic capital, but by foreign capital as well.

Lazzari claims that the Italian Socialists never desired to collaborate with the bourgeoisie. Quite true! The mood of the proletariat made any open attempt of that type impossible. But the reformists waited for an opportunity. And it appears that such an opportunity has now presented itself. Back in 1918, Turati and some others joined the so-called 'State Commission on the Postwar Period'. The Central Committee wrote Turati, telling him to withdraw from it, but he did not do so.[27]

In addition, I maintain that there are marked Social-Democratic tendencies in the party. Their chief representative is Modigliani. Was it not he who claimed that the bourgeoisie would accept a half-Social-Democratic coalition government, in order to block the rise of communism?

Clearly, outright counterrevolutionary tendencies are present in the party. At the Bologna Congress, Turati spoke of Russia in such a fashion that he was interrupted by an uproar and whistling from the entire audience.[28] In the debates on reconstruction in Italy, Turati spoke of his hope that the party would finally have done with senseless issues of conquering power through force and would heed the voices calling for organised participation in the government together with the bourgeoisie.

Since then, Serrati and his friends have begun to slander Russia.

---

25. A reference to the Fifteenth Congress of the Italian Socialist Party held in Rome 1–5 September 1918.
26. Germany's attack on Belgium in the early days of World War I was utilised by propagandists for the Entente powers, with stories of 'poor little Belgium'.
27. Turati and Claudio Treves had been appointed to a commission to address postwar problems raised by the conflict. Both had to resign under pressure from the PSI's Maximalist leadership.
28. A reference to the Sixteenth Congress of the Italian Socialist Party held in Bologna, 5–8 October 1919.

There are outright enemies of the Third International in the Italian Socialist Party. Lazzari is proud that the party responded to the initial call for affiliation to the Third International. But I remind him that he himself, along with Comrade Bacci, spoke against this, claiming that it was a premature step.

And what are we to make of Turati? Did he not publish articles by Martov and Sukhomlinov[29] against revolutionary Russia? Here is what he wrote:

> In a few years the legend of the Russian Revolution will have been forgotten. The Russian Bolsheviks draw their strength from their distinctive nationalism, whose significance lies in its opposition to bourgeois imperialism – and yet it is itself a kind of imperialism. Bolshevism faces a dilemma: either it must die or it must be transformed, and now they cling to us. It calls into being the Third International, in order to prolong its death agony. But we will not become the tool of eastern imperialism. We will affiliate to a civilised International.

Turati published Bauer's book, *Dictatorship and Democracy*, with a foreword in which he states his full agreement with the author. He praises the Two-and-a-Half International and claims it is governed by the same spirit as the Italian Socialist Party.[30]

The reformists have always understood and have never concealed the fact that they cannot coexist with Communists in a single party. Turati stated that the difference between these two tendencies is not one of detail but concerns principle and fundamental world outlook. Why then do the reformists wish to remain in the party, at all costs? A candid and naïve opportunist explained this fully and completely. First, he said, we give voice in the party to criticism and imbue it with a spirit of moderation, which has a marked effect on the party and an even stronger effect on the masses close to it. Second, leaving the party would separate us from the army that we strive to lead and would rob us of our political significance.

After all that, Lazzari feels able to say that the breach was artificial and took place on orders from Moscow. No! It came too late. It should have taken place much earlier. We were all convinced of its necessity, and from Moscow we received confirmation.

Unity, he says. But for us it is only unity of the revolutionaries that counts. Does unity imply that we must tolerate enemies within our ranks? It was

---

29. Presumably a reference to Vasilii V. Sukhomlin, a Russian Socialist-Revolutionary who had been a correspondent for *Avanti* during the War.

30. The Italian edition of Bauer's book, *Bolscevismo o democrazia sociale?* was published in Milan in 1921.

purely in the cause of this latter form of unity that Serrati separated all the Communists from the party.

The break resulted in a shift of the Socialist Party of Italy to the right. The party shows absolutely no resolution in the struggle against Fascist attacks. Things have gone so far that *Avanti* repeats the words of Christ about taking blows on both the right and left cheek. Not long ago the party published an election manifesto. Turati is quite satisfied with it, writing that there are remnants of revolutionary phraseology in the first part, but the second part could have been taken entirely from his works. 'It is simply stupid', he said, 'to cling to the fantasy of the Third International'.

My dear Lazzari, it is for the sake of such people that you broke with us. And yet we must drive these people from our midst, for the very reasons that lead them to want to stay with us. If we drive them out, they are officers without an army and will necessarily lose their political influence.

The delegation of the Italian Communist Party demands that the Italian Socialist Party be expelled from the Third International. The International must launch a serious struggle against them, and publish a manifesto severely criticising their policies. Our party demands that the Third International call on the Italian proletariat to leave the ranks of the Italian Socialist Party and rally under the banner of the Communist Party. (*Enthusiastic applause*)

**V.I. Lenin** (Russia):[31] Comrades, I should like to reply mainly to Comrade Lazzari. In his speech, he said: 'Cite concrete facts, not words.' Excellent. But if we trace the development of the reformist-opportunist trend in Italy, is that merely words; does it not concern facts? You lose sight, not only in your speeches but in your entire policy, of a fact that has great weight for the Socialist movement in Italy: namely, that not only this trend, but an opportunist reformist group has existed for quite a long time. I still very well remember the time when Bernstein started his opportunist propaganda, which ended in social patriotism, in the treason and bankruptcy of the Second International. We have known Turati ever since, not only by name, but for his propaganda in the Italian party and in the Italian working-class movement. Since then – over the past twenty years – he has been the disrupter of the Italian socialist workers' movement.

Lack of time prevents me from closely studying the material concerning the Italian party, but I think that one of the most important documents on this subject is a report, published in a bourgeois Italian newspaper – I no longer recall whether it was *La Stampa* or *Corriere della sera* – of the conference held

---

31. The translation is based on *LCW* 32, pp. 462–7 and has been edited to conform with the German text.

by Turati and his friends in *Reggio Emilia*.[32] I compared that report with the one published in *Avanti*. Is this not proof enough? After the Second Congress of the Communist International, we, in our controversy with Serrati and his friends, openly and definitely told them what, in our opinion, the situation was. We told them that the Italian party could not become a Communist Party as long as it tolerated people like Turati in its ranks.

What is this: political facts, or again mere words? After the Second Congress of the Communist International we said publicly to the Italian proletariat: 'Don't unite with the reformists, with Turati.' Then Serrati launched a series of articles in the Italian press in opposition to the Communist International and convened a special conference of reformists. Was all this mere words? It was something more than a split: it was the creation of a new party. You had to be blind not to have seen this. This document is of decisive importance for this question. All those who attended the Reggio Emilia conference must be expelled from the party; they are Mensheviks – not Russian, but Italian Mensheviks.

Lazzari said, 'We know the Italian people's mentality.' For my part I would not make such an assertion about the Russian people, but that is not important. 'Italian Socialists understand the spirit of the Italian people very well,' said Lazzari. Perhaps they do, I will not argue about that. But they do not know Italian Menshevism; that is evident from the facts and their persistent refusal to eradicate Menshevism. We are obliged to say that – regrettable though it may be – the resolution of our Executive Committee must be confirmed. A party which tolerates opportunists and reformists like Turati in its ranks cannot be affiliated to the Communist International.

'Why should we change the name of the party?' asks Comrade Lazzari. 'The present one is good enough.' We cannot agree with this view. We know the history of the Second International, its decay, decline, and bankruptcy. Do we not know the history of the German party? And do we not know that the great misfortune of the working-class movement in Germany is that the break was not brought about before the War? This cost the lives of twenty thousand workers, whom the Scheidemanns and the centrists betrayed to the German government by their polemics and complaints against the German Communists.

And do we not now see the same thing in Italy? The Italian party was never a truly revolutionary party. Its great misfortune is that it did not break with

---

32. This report was published in *Corriere della sera* of 11 and 12 October 1920 as well as in *Avanti* of 13 October 1920. Lenin gave a detailed description of this conference in 'On the Struggle within the Italian Socialist Party' (*LCW*, 31, pp. 377–96).

the Mensheviks and reformists before the War, and that the latter continued to remain in the party. Comrade Lazzari says: 'We fully recognise the necessity of a break with the reformists; our only disagreement is that we did not think it necessary to bring it about at the Livorno Congress.' But the facts tell a different story. This is not the first time that we are discussing Italian reformism. In arguing about this with Serrati last year, we said: 'You won't mind us asking why the split in the Italian party cannot be brought about immediately, why it must be postponed?' What did Serrati say in reply to that? Nothing.

And Comrade Lazzari, quoting an article by Frossard in which the latter said, 'We must be adroit and clever', evidently thinks that this is an argument in his favour and against us. I think he is mistaken. On the contrary, it is an excellent argument in our favour and against Comrade Lazzari. He will be obliged to explain his conduct and his breaking away to the Italian workers. What will they say? What will you tell them if they declare our tactics to be clever and adroit with regard to deviations and to the pseudo-Communist Left – the Left which at times is not always Communist and more often falls into anarchism?

What is the meaning of the tales told by Serrati and his party about the Russians only wanting everyone to imitate them? We want the very opposite. It is not enough to memorise communist resolutions and use revolutionary phrases on every possible occasion. That is not enough, and we are opposed in advance to Communists who know this or that resolution by heart. The first requirement of true communism is to break with opportunism. We will be quite frank and open with Communists who subscribe to this. We will tell them boldly and with justification: 'Don't do anything stupid; be clever and skilful.' But we shall speak in this way only with Communists who have broken with the opportunists, something that you have not yet done. Therefore, I repeat: I hope the congress will confirm the resolution of the Executive Committee.

Comrade Lazzari said: 'We are in the preparatory period.' This is absolutely true. You are in a preparatory period. The first stage of this period is a break with the Mensheviks, similar to the one we carried out with our Mensheviks in 1903. The sufferings that the whole of the German working class have had to endure during this long and arduous period in the history of the German revolution after the War are due to the fact that the German party did not break with the Mensheviks.

Comrade Lazzari said that the Italian party is passing through the preparatory period. This I fully accept. And the first stage is a definite, final, unambiguous, and determined break with reformism. When that is done, the masses will side solidly with communism. The second stage will by no means consist of a repetition of revolutionary slogans. It will be the adoption of our wise and skilful decisions, which will always be such, and which will always say: 'Revolutionary policy must be adapted to the specific conditions in the various countries.'[33]

The revolution in Italy will run a different course from that in Russia. It will start in a different way. How? We do not know yet, and neither do you.

The Italian Communists are not always Communists to a sufficient degree. During the occupation of the factories in Italy, did we see anything resembling communism? No, at that time, there was as yet no communism in Italy; there was a certain amount of anarchism, but no Marxian communism. It still has to be created, and the masses of the workers must be imbued with it through the experience of the revolutionary struggle. And the first step along this road is a final break with the Mensheviks, who for more than twenty years have been busy collaborating with the bourgeois government.

It is quite probable that Modigliani, whom I was able to observe to some extent at the Zimmerwald and Kienthal Conferences, is a sufficiently astute politician to keep out of the bourgeois government and to keep in the centre of the Socialist Party, where he can conveniently be quite useful to the bourgeoisie. But all the theories of Turati and his friends, all their propaganda and agitation, signify collaboration with the bourgeoisie. Is this not proved conclusively by the numerous quotations in Gennari's speech? What is this? Merely words? No, it is the united front that Turati has already prepared.

That is why I must say to Comrade Lazzari: speeches like yours and like the one which Comrade Serrati made here do not help to prepare for the revolution, they disorganise it. (*Applause*)

You had a considerable majority at Livorno. You had 98,000 votes against 14,000 reformist and 58,000 Communist votes. As the beginning of a purely Communist movement in a country like Italy, with its well-known traditions, where the ground has not been sufficiently prepared for a split, this vote is a considerable achievement for the Communists.

This is a great victory and tangible proof of the fact that the working-class movement in Italy will develop faster than our movement developed in Russia, because, if you are familiar with the figures concerning our movement, you must know that in February 1917, after the fall of tsarism and during the bourgeois republic, we were still a minority compared with the Mensheviks. Such was the position after fifteen years of fierce fighting and splits. No right wing developed among us, and it was not so easy to prevent one from

---

33. The quotation is a paraphrase of the last sentence in point 16 of the Twenty-One Conditions; see Riddell (ed.) 1991, 2WC, 2, p. 770.

growing, as you seem to think when you speak of Russia in such a lenient tone. Undoubtedly, development in Italy will proceed quite differently.

After fifteen years of struggle against the Mensheviks, and after the fall of tsarism, we started work with a much smaller number of adherents. You have 58,000 Communist-minded workers against 98,000 united centrists who occupy an indefinite position. This is proof, this is a fact, which should certainly convince all those who refuse to close their eyes to the mass movement of the Italian workers. Nothing comes all at once. But it certainly proves that the mass of workers – not the old leaders, the bureaucrats, the professors, the journalists, but the class that is actually exploited, the vanguard of the exploited – supports us.

And that proves what a great mistake you made at Livorno. This is a fact. You controlled 98,000 votes, but you preferred to go with 14,000 reformists against 58,000 Communists. You should have gone with them even if they were not genuine Communists, even if they were only adherents of Bordiga – which is not true, for after the Second Congress Bordiga quite honestly declared that he had abandoned all anarchism and anti-parliamentarism. But what did you do? You chose to unite with 14,000 reformists and to break with 58,000 Communists. And this is the best proof that Serrati's policy has been disastrous for Italy.

We never wanted Serrati in Italy to copy the Russian Revolution. That would have been stupid. We are intelligent and flexible enough to avoid such stupidity. But Serrati has proved that his policy in Italy was wrong. Perhaps he should have manoeuvred. This is the expression that he repeated most often when he was here last year. He said: 'We know how to manoeuvre, we do not want slavish imitation. That would be idiotic. We must manoeuvre, so as to bring about a separation from opportunism. You Russians do not know how to do that. We Italians are more skilful at that sort of thing. We will see what happens.'

And what is it we saw? Serrati executed a brilliant manoeuvre. He broke away from 58,000 Communists. And now these comrades come here and say: 'If you reject us the masses will be confused.' No, comrades, you are mistaken. The masses of the workers in Italy are confused now, and it will do them good if we tell them: 'Comrades, you must choose; Italian workers, you must choose between the Communist International, which will never call upon you slavishly to imitate the Russians, and the Mensheviks, whom we have known for twenty years, and whom we shall never tolerate as neighbours in a genuinely revolutionary Communist International.' That is what we shall say to the Italian workers. There can be no doubt about the result. The masses of workers will follow us. (*Enthusiastic applause*)

**Kolarov** (Chair): That ends the session. The next session begins tomorrow morning at 11:00 a.m. with continuation of discussion on the Italian question. Please arrive promptly, so that the session can begin at the announced time.

*(The session is adjourned at 12:00 midnight.)*

# Session 9 – 29 June 1921, 12:15 p.m.
## Italian Question; Executive Report

*Continued discussion of the Italian question. Declaration of the Italian Socialist Party. Speakers: Maffi, Rakovsky, Zetkin, Trotsky, Loriot, Lozovsky. Resolution on the Executive Committee report. Speakers: Loriot, Sachs, Radek, Heckert, Zinoviev, Rakovsky, Roland-Holst, Malzahn, Neumann, Zinoviev (summary). Statements by the Austrian and Yugoslav delegations. Statement by Comrades Malzahn and Neumann.*

**Kolarov** (Chair): On the agenda for our session today is the Italian question. The Presidium believes it must specify that it will hold strictly to the decision to limit speaking time to ten minutes. The speakers, too, should adjust to this rule. Comrade Maffi of the Italian Socialist Party has the floor. First, however, we will hear a statement by the delegation of the Socialist Party of Italy.

### Statement of the Italian Socialist Party

*Statement by delegates of the Italian Socialist Party to the Third Congress of the Communist International*

In accordance with the decisions of the Second World Congress, the Italian Socialist Party – one of the first to adhere to the Communist International and also earlier one of the founders of Zimmerwald and Kienthal – gathered in January 1921 in Livorno to examine the Twenty-One Conditions, which must be adopted in order to retain membership in the Third International.

This gathering adopted the following resolution by an absolute majority:

> The Italian Socialist Party (PSI) resolves to strengthen its unity, to introduce a greater uniformity in its organisation and membership, and thus to achieve a centralisation so strong that every party member and organisation subordinates its actions to the common interest and directs them toward the ultimate goal. Every other activity, such as propaganda, must also be subjected to supervision.
>
> To this end, the conference resolves to take all necessary measures so that political goals and political thinking will extend into the trade unions and prevail over temporarily opportunist or seemingly trade-unionist goals. In this regard, the leadership bodies of the economic and trade-union movements remain subordinated to the political party.
>
> The conference resolves that it is absolutely essential to preserve the party's complete unity, in order to speed the winning of political power. This goal should be pursued using all means, provided they are consistent with absolute class intransigence and the goals of the communist revolution. This requires that political work be extended into the economic work of the trade unions. The legal or illegal organisation must therefore use every means that promotes education and progress of the masses, every means that can contribute to success or to the founding of organs that can replace those that presently exist.
>
> As for the discussion of the relationship between the PSI and the Communist International, the congress confirms once again its original and voluntary decision to join this international association and simultaneously accepts the decisions of the recent Moscow congress. Consequently, the PSI declares that it incorporates the Twenty-One Conditions into its programme, adding to it the freemasonry clause.[1] As for implementing the Twenty-One Conditions, this is to be left to the country in question, as provided for in the Communist International decision, points 16 and 21, as well as by the procedure applied to other countries.[2]
>
> Everyone who submits to the Third International's conditions must do this with firm conviction to translate this into reality. As regards point 17 of the conditions, the congress must reject the charge that its conduct was irresolute during the accursed war. The congress also proposes that, contrary

---

1. Both the German and Russian texts read, 'omitting the freemasonry clause'. The text follows the version subsequently published in PCI 1921, p. 81. The Comintern's resolutions on freemasonry are discussed in p. 189, n. 18.
2. The Italian version of this sentence begins: 'The Twenty-One Conditions will be interpreted in the framework of existing conditions and historical needs of the country where they are applied, as provided for...'. PCI 1921, p. 81.

to the conditions, the PSI retain its name, at least temporarily, because it links up with many glorious memories in the workers' movement, without however making this an essential condition.

After the Executive Committee stated that the PSI, by adopting this resolution, had placed itself outside the Third International, the congress unanimously adopted the following decision:

> The Seventeenth Congress of the PSI confirms again the decisions that declared its affiliation to the Third International, accepting its principles and methods without reservation. The congress protests against the statement of the Communist International announcing the expulsion of the PSI from the Third International.[3] This action can only be based on differences of opinion regarding the Italian party's activity, and these can be eliminated through fraternal honesty.
>
> The PSI reaffirms its stand for the Third International and accepts the decision of the upcoming international congress, which will clarify the differences of opinion. The PSI states its readiness in the future to submit to the decision of this, the highest body.

Based on clause 9 of the International's Statutes,[4] the [PSI] delegates present to the Third Congress the reasons why these decisions were taken by the majority of the Livorno Congress:

1.) Given that the PSI congress completely accepted the Twenty-One Conditions, there has been no infraction of international discipline. The resolution states that the Twenty-One Conditions are accepted fully and entirely.

   The PSI congress merely presented three questions to the Executive and asked that they be discussed. This concerns the expulsion of the reformists, an action that gives us the right to call ourselves Communists.

2.) As regards the expulsion of the reformists, the Livorno Congress permitted no exceptions. The PSI can refer here to its traditions, which go back further than those of the Communist International. In 1912, the reformists Bissolati, Bonomi, Cabrini, Podrecca, and others were expelled from the

---

3. The original motion reads, 'statement of the Communist International Executive Committee representative.' PSI 1962, p. 417.

4. Section 9 of the Comintern's statutes states, in part: 'The Executive Committee of the Communist International has the authority to demand of its member parties the expulsion of groups or individuals that breach international discipline as well as the authority to expel from the Communist International any party that contravenes the resolutions of the world congress. Such parties have the right to appeal to the world congress.' Riddell (ed.) 1991, 2WC, 2, p. 698.

party because they had violated the PSI's discipline and policies. In 1914, the decision was made to expel the Freemasons, who, it was shown, were pressing the party to ally with the Left Bloc. In 1915, it treated those who supported the War in the same way.[5]

The majority of the party was well informed of the fact that many elements were violating their promises to accept party discipline unconditionally and were continuing to pursue a policy of compromise. That is obviously damaging for the party and puts its future in danger. It is absolutely necessary to eliminate this danger, but we must choose the right moment for this hazardous operation. This was the only point on which there was a difference of opinion at the PSI congress. A group of comrades, calling themselves the 'Pure Communists',[6] advanced the view at the Livorno Congress that the reformist forces must be expelled. The majority, however, considered that this was not yet the right moment and, in particular, that the working masses could not be won to support such a sudden expulsion.

Looked at this way, the situation certainly could arouse discussion, but it cannot be considered as a violation of discipline. The difficulties that stood in the way of convening the First Congress of the Communist International[7] clearly showed that the expulsion of reformist and centrist elements is unavoidable and necessary when the struggle has reached a certain phase, but this point can be determined only by carefully examining the attendant circumstances. That was what the First Congress decided in its theses regarding socialist movements in different countries, which read:

> The organisational split is an absolute historical necessity. The task of the Communists in every single country is to determine the moment for this break according to the level of development of the movement in their country.[8]

---

5. For the expulsion of Bissolati and others in 1912, see p. 346, n. 24. The Fourteenth Congress of the PSI in Ancona, 26–29 April 1914, on a motion from Giovanni Zibordi and Benito Mussolini, voted to exclude Freemasons from party membership. After the onset of World War I, Mussolini became a strident advocate of Italy's entry into it, and he was expelled for this reason.
6. The Communist Faction in the PSI frequently referred to itself as the 'Pure Communists' to distinguish itself from the Unitary Communist Faction led by Serrati.
7. Attending the First Congress in 1919 was difficult both because of the Entente blockade and internal repression by the capitalist governments of Europe.
8. See 'Our Attitude toward the Socialist Currents and the Bern Conference', in Riddell (ed.) 1987, 1WC, p. 201.

This approach to Communist tactics was confirmed by the Second Congress. Indeed point 16 of the Twenty-One Conditions states that consideration must be given to the varied conditions in which each party works and struggles.[9]

The PSI holds that it was in the interests of the Italian proletariat not to carry out the break immediately. The party and the working masses were still feeling the impact of the September events, when the factories were occupied with the full agreement of party bodies. We did not seek to overturn the government, not because of differences of opinion, but because we did not have sufficient military forces available to take the offensive against the police and army contingents mobilised by the government.

That was the conclusion of the national council of the General Confederation of Labour, and this opinion was shared by many delegates from Turin, the city where, from a technical point of view, the struggle had been best prepared.

The party leadership, composed in its majority of men who logically belonged in the ranks of the 'Pure Communists', was revealed to be indecisive and not at all prepared for the struggle. During the entire period of unrest, they displayed uncertainty, even after the reactionaries had burnt the offices of *Avanti*, even after the revolt in Ancona; later, the Bologna events (November 1920) took them by surprise.[10] During the factory occupations, despite the PSI executive's authorisation, this Communist leadership did not venture to support extending the movement and did not protest when it was brought to a peaceful end.

It must not be forgotten that among the masses, who have no understanding of theoretical debate, the leaders of the PSI's right wing are popular. They opposed the War; they were among the Zimmerwald delegates; they belong to the Communist International; they defended the Russian Revolution enthusiastically; they supported the workers' takeover of the factories. To be sure, they did not approve of extending the movement, but that was a point of view shared by many Socialists. They assumed leading positions in

---

9. The final portion of point 16 reads: 'In all their activity the Communist International and its Executive Committee must take into account the diverse conditions under which each party has to struggle and work, adopting universally binding decisions only on questions in which such decisions are possible.' See Riddell (ed.) 1991, 2WC, 2, p. 770.

10. The *Avanti* offices in Milan were burned down by Fascists on 15 April 1919.
The revolt in Ancona, an anarchist stronghold, took place on 26 June 1920, after a mutiny by troops being sent to Albania precipitated a popular uprising. The revolt was suppressed by the following day, with twenty-five people killed.
The 'Bologna events' refers to a large Fascist attack there on 21 November 1920 that assaulted and deposed the Socialist-led town council and destroyed the offices of working-class organisations.

the trade unions and enjoyed the complete confidence of those who elected them. Replacing them is no small matter.

These 'Pure Communists' who felt strong enough to take on the leadership of the entire political and trade-union movement have so far come up with no more than big promises. In the political and economic arena, however, they either do nothing or plunge into unwise adventures.

All these facts influenced the majority at the Livorno Congress and brought about their decision. These facts were submitted to the Communist International Executive. They are submitted now to the congress in order to show that we are dealing not with principled deviations regarding theory and tactics, not with petty fears concerning the life of individuals or groups, but with quite sincere political considerations that led us to postpone the final breach.

Delegates to this congress from other countries have criticised our Livorno congress in unambiguous terms. Most of the trade unions in Italy were on the side of the majority, and those few that were with the 'Pure Communists' recently returned to the PSI. This shows that the majority at Livorno was correct.

We believe we have presented the disputed issues to the congress with sufficient clarity. It is up to the congress to resolve them.

As regards the position of the Livorno Congress, this is quite clear. The accusations made by the Third International against Livorno are not relevant to the PSI. During the entire War the PSI maintained an unparalleled position. If it is to be accused of social patriotism, then there is no party in the entire world with a right to membership in the Communist International.

The PSI has made its position absolutely clear. It remains in the Third International. It does not permit any deviations from the principles of class struggle, and it condemns any coalition with the bourgeoisie. The PSI leadership has already decided to call a new congress, which will take place in an exceptionally difficult and decisive epoch of Italian politics. This problem will be raised at the congress. The PSI is and will always be with the revolution, and never against the revolution.

**Fabrizio Maffi** (Socialist Party of Italy): Following what Comrade Lazzari said yesterday; following Lenin's so simple, clear, sound, and strong speech; and especially following our statement, which constitutes part of the question discussed here in its entirety yesterday, it seems almost superfluous to speak about this again. Only for this reason do I not insist that the statement be translated before my speech. As the accused party, however, we cannot let the congress think that we are running away from the petty charges levied by Professor Gennari.[11] We have the duty and the right to respond. For my part, I hope that the Presidium will proceed with generosity, as is always done to the accused party, and allow us full freedom in answering the charges brought against us, not for personal reasons but because these charges themselves contain evidence that speaks entirely in our favour.

Comrades, I must say that I myself would have dispensed with any discussion. In my opinion, we are not at the congress of a district, a region, or a province, but in the Kremlin of the proletariat – and not in Livorno. That was the appropriate place, Comrade Gennari, where your petty charges should have been presented. (*Commotion, shouts*) All this could have been done in Livorno (*Commotion, interjections*) where the accused would have been in a position to answer them. One does not bring this kind of material to a world congress, thousands of kilometres away. That is a very simple method of distorting the truth: dispense it to your audience in small doses by extracting unrelated sentences from a speech and isolated facts while obscuring the general line that governs the party's work. I protest against these small doses of truth, which are simply an incarnation of deceit. (*Shouts, commotion*)

We do not defend Turati – no, not at all. The reformists' activity is governed by their understanding, which Comrade Turati has never sought to conceal. In addition, we must express to you our astonishment at the personal way that the so-called Serrati question has evolved. We know only the invitation to the Socialist Party of Italy to attend the Third International congress. The charges that Gennari has just levied against the Italian Socialist Party rebound on him and his comrades. Unless I am mistaken, during Gennari's term as consul, *Critica sociale* did not cease to appear. Turati wrote his articles, which were read by two thousand intellectuals, but which remain until today unknown to the peasants and workers. They are known to the bourgeois press, which is always ready to utilise the speeches of Gennari and Turati. ('*Never!*') Even the words of Lenin have been used to deceive the world proletariat. This is a well-known game and is only too simple.

Professor Gennari was playing exactly the same simple and transparent game when he made use of Turati in his remarks directed against us and the Italian Socialist Party, offering us Turati's words and ideas. But these are games. There is much that speaks in Turati's disfavour. He has caused much harm and is more of a literary than a political figure. As we have always said, he has done too many things that caused harm to the party. From time to time

---

11. Gennari had worked as a mathematics teacher.

we made efforts to draw the necessary conclusions with regard to the party. I personally recall Turati's speech after the defeat at Caporetto. During his speech, I felt that I could foresee Bissolati coming to embrace him, and I shed bitter tears over that. Well, which of you took the occasion to disavow Turati? Was it perhaps the parliamentary leader? Or was it Graziadei, who was then one of the most blatant patriots? (*'Give proof!'*)

No proof is necessary, and in any case it is already available in printed form and there is therefore no need to produce it now. (*Commotion*) Yes, we are dealing with the printed word, and it would be stupid to repeat all that. (*'That is a lying, distorted triviality!'*) Yes, a two-hundred-page triviality that is well known, and you would admit that if you had the courage. Turati wrote his political credo before Bologna, and Gennari was then party secretary.[12] (*'He was secretary after Bologna.'*) Please wait and let me speak. Gennari was party secretary a month later, when the list of candidates was drawn up, and Turati was duly confirmed as one of the candidates for Milan. (*'No! No!'*) Who was the secretary then? Perhaps Bombacci? Yes, my friends, Bombacci. Is there a big difference between Gennari and Bombacci? The current already existed that is now pledged to a cleansing. Turati was the candidate chosen by this current in the 1919 parliamentary elections.[13] (*Interruptions, commotion*) There is no need to draw conclusions at every turn. (*'No! No!'*) The conclusions will follow quite well on their own. Have patience and wait. After the tragedy in Bologna,[14] Turati made a speech that won strong applause from some among us.

**Gennari**: We protested strongly against it.

**Maffi**: What use are protests? It was necessary to negotiate. Protests –

**Kolarov** (Chair): Please allow the speaker to conclude. He still has two minutes left to speak.

**Maffi**: I am only now getting to the enormous errors of the men who are now reckoned among the so-called Pure Communists. For in today's Communist Party, you find the pure and the purified, right? Gennari with his reformist past in the National Bloc, if I am not mistaken. (*'This is absurd'*) You are too impatient. Just wait for the conclusions that I will draw for this.

---

12. The reference here is to the Bologna PSI congress, 5–8 October 1919.
13. A reference to the first postwar elections in Italy, which were held 16 November 1919. In these elections the PSI received 32 per cent of the vote, twice its total in the previous election in 1913, emerging as the strongest political party in parliament.
14. The reference is to the Fascist assault in Bologna of 21 November 1920.

I have only two minutes of speaking time left, and obviously in two minutes I cannot say everything that ought to be said. I therefore ask the congress for an extension. (*'Keep on speaking for a few minutes more.'*)

**Kolarov** (Chair): Our decision was that the speaker has only 15 minutes speaking time. The proposal to adopt this rule was adopted by the entire congress.

**Maffi**: Very well, I will dispense with going further into the details. But let me tell you this: I would be very well able to lay against Gennari many of the same accusations that he makes against others. But let me say that this is not my intention. I only wanted to show that both during and after the War, the Italian Socialist Party, regardless of who was secretary, did everything that was possible. Granted, this statement is quite banal, but still there is great truth in it. During and after the War, the Italian Socialist Party did what it could. Thus Lazzari, for example, expelled [from the PSI] the mayors of Verona and Sampierdarena. He was not able to expel the mayor of Reggio, because the mayor said he was ready to obey and submit and because special conditions were present according to which the conduct of various secretaries at different times was roughly the same.

For this reason, I wanted to tell you about some very delicate and questionable points that could easily lead to errors. Professor Gennari, do not be so harsh with others, when you are so lenient toward yourself. For it is very easy to make mistakes when you are working, and very easy to avoid this simply by not working. Now, what conclusions can we draw from discussing all these petty details in the life of the Italian Socialist Party? We learn from this discussion that in Italy we have had quite a number of secretariats and leaderships – a litany of them – feeble, vacillating, and insecure. The imperious demands of necessity were beyond the party's capability; they went beyond the limits of the party's real strength. Conscientious Socialists cannot refuse to recognise that this is a way of assessing reality. A great mass of words go pale in face of reality. (*'The reformists'*)

**Kolarov** (Chair): Your speaking time is exhausted.

**Maffi**: I ask you to grant me another five minutes. I remind the congress again that I am speaking here as a defendant.

**Kolarov** (Chair): We cannot treat the Italian question as if it were the only item before the congress, when we have on the agenda another fifteen questions that must still be discussed.

**Maffi**: Yes of course, but I would like to point out that I will be finished in ten minutes.

**Kolarov** (Chair): But then you will ask to speak in order to respond. We cannot –

**Maffi**: For my part, I wish to say that I am not going to insist on individual cases. Everyone will discuss my comments, because the conduct of different secretariats and leaderships is pretty much the same. It is a matter of the interplay between necessity and possibility. We really should have a full discussion on this point. Such a discussion would indeed be what you could call a favourable opportunity.

**Interjection**: What about driving out the reformists?

**Maffi**: Please wait, comrade, there is still time for that.

**The same voice**: I've been waiting too long already.

**Maffi**: So give me another ten minutes.

**Kolarov** (Chair): You have been speaking for twenty minutes.

**Maffi**: I have been constantly interrupted.

**Kolarov** (Chair): But that's just your way of doing things.

**Maffi**: It is my duty, not my manner. I have no intention of disobeying the Presidium. But I still need another few minutes in order to conclude. I am quite able to respect authority, and especially socialist authority, but I protest against having my speech broken off before I have finished.

I still need about eight minutes, and I ask not to be interrupted, because that is my right.

In the early months of the year there was a shift in the Italian political situation. It neared maturity. At present there is every indication that the Italian bourgeoisie is armed, or at least is in the process of taking up arms. The bone of contention, over which people and groups are taking their orientation, is quite different. Every member of the great, broad masses can now see clearly that we must consider the arming of the proletariat, and it is equally obvious that it would be extremely dangerous to permit having forces in the party that we were previously compelled to tolerate.

Given the present state of affairs, I ask whether you think it makes more sense, in terms of the interests of the Italian and world proletariat, for a decision of this magnitude to be taken in conditions where the entire proletariat is obeying a command from Moscow, a congress resolution known to our peasants and workers only in rough outline? For my part, I contend that it would be much more expedient to allow this quickly progressing process of maturation to be brought to completion by the already indicated forces. This is how we must respond to those who demand an answer from us in the manner proper to a bourgeois court. We are not obliged to give them any such answers.

The situation created in the Italian Socialist Party by the Livorno Congress is clear-cut. After the vote on the Baratono resolution, Kabakchiev made his statement,[15] and then the congress adopted the Bentivoglio proposal, which stated: 'We hereby declare that we will submit in disciplined fashion to all the decisions of the Third Congress of the Third International.'[16] What more can you ask for? So, we are telling you – (*Interjection*) – I have the right not to be interrupted, comrades, because otherwise I will lose the few minutes still at my disposal.

As I was saying, there will be a congress in a few months, at which the situation will be a bit more complicated. The next congress of the Italian Socialist Party will probably – (*Interjection*) Another half-minute gone. The next congress will probably be forced to disavow the Livorno decision –

**Interjection**: The parties are sovereign over themselves and their congresses.

**Maffi**: – and thus the next Italian Socialist Party congress will simply have to carry out what the Third International decides. That is clear, and it is also included in our statement. That is the fact of the matter.

My friends, if we have come together in order to reach agreement, then there cannot be the slightest doubt about what I have just explained to you. It does not lack the slightest particle of clarity. But if this is – how shall I put it? – a political spectacle, well, that is another matter. We are telling you, comrades, that we commit ourselves to the necessity of a cleansing. [*Interjection*] The congress will pass judgement, but as delegates we must tell you that we have no cause to respond to your cries of 'Out, out!' – for which there is no justification. We need only sincerely direct your attention to the decisions of the Livorno Congress. In addition, we demand that you maintain an ongoing communication with our party, so that the responsible bodies of the Third

---

15. The Baratono resolution adopted by majority vote at the Livorno Congress was based on the motion of the Unitary Communist faction, formulated at its November 1920 conference in Florence. It called for adherence to the Comintern and its Twenty-One Points, while insisting on party unity and maintaining the name Socialist Party. For the Florence resolution, see PSI 1962, p. 441.

Kabakchiev's subsequent statement, read out to the congress, announced that the Serrati current would be excluded from the Comintern. He stated that all factions that 'do not accept the thesis of the International are excluded from the Communist International'. This statement can be found in PSI 1962, pp. 394–7.

16. Maffi is paraphrasing the Bentivoglio resolution, whose text is found on p. 198.

International will be in a position, in fraternal collaboration with us, to study the conditions we face and to understand the meaning of expediency, as Comrade Lenin remarked so aptly. That is what we ask. At the next congress we will propose the adoption of the Third Congress decisions. But we are not children to whom you can say, 'But no, you must answer just so, because that is what was decided.' It is not words that are decisive, but our free opinion, our will, and our convictions. We did not come here to play word-games or carry out diplomatic tricks. Comrades of the Third International, help us through your heartfelt and ongoing sympathy, through your wise and upstanding advice, through the overwhelming power of your experience, which freed the Russian people and provided the world proletariat with countless examples. There is nothing we desire more ardently, and we assure you once again that we stand ready now and always to carry out our duty.

**Kolarov** (Chair): Comrades, with regard to the proposal concerning the agenda, the Bureau states that it will insist that speakers not go beyond the allotted time. We must exercise Communist discipline in our work.

Comrade Rakovsky has the floor.

**Christian Rakovsky** (Ukraine): Comrade, no one can miss the great significance of the events in Italy. Before us is a proletariat that split in two, just at the moment that the Italian bourgeoisie – which during the previous year had so well concealed its true face – threw off its mask and went over to a vigorous offensive against the proletariat. Listening to the speeches of Lazzari and Maffi, I wondered what motives they might have had to carry out this split in the Italian proletariat. For there is no doubt that this split resulted from the Socialist Party of Italy's refusal to comply unconditionally with the decisions of the Second Congress. Responsibility cannot possibly be foisted on the Communist minority that remained true to the instructions of the world proletariat gathered in Moscow. I wondered what political motives lay behind the paradoxical fact, which Comrade Lenin highlighted here yesterday, that the Socialist Party of Italy preferred to follow the 14,000 reformists rather than the 58,000 Communists.

I listened closely to the speech by Comrade Lazzari. I must add that I have been in Italy and have some knowledge of the events there. I know Italy. Anyone who has followed the socialist movement during the last thirty years knows that not only did reformism in Italy really exist, but also that it was actually a precursor of reformism in Germany. Turati was a predecessor of Bernstein. After the Zurich international Congress in 1893,[17] Turati never attended another such event.

---

17. The Second International's Zurich Congress was held 6–12 August 1893.

I recall how he left the Zurich Congress in 1893 together with Comrade Anna Kulisciof, protesting as he exited against German hegemony. This hegemony was then represented by [Wilhelm] Liebknecht and Bebel. When I went to Rome in 1915, invited by the Italian party to take part in their initiative for neutrality,[18] the same attitude prevailed there. I met Turati and Treves then, and they told me, 'The fact is, we have put an end to German hegemony.' They were pleased that the former revolutionary movement had been poisoned by opportunism and had freed itself from international hegemony in general.[19] Moreover, the traditions of the *Risorgimento*[20] found expression more than once in *Critica sociale*. This old social-patriotic tradition is expressed in Turati's conduct as a whole.

Anyone familiar with the history of Italy's socialist movement knows very well that reformism has always existed in Italy. The party leadership could not conceal it. I would like to ask Comrade Lazzari: how much diplomacy did you engage in over the last twenty years to hide the scandalous character of Turati's politics? We can be sure that the Entente took fewer diplomatic initiatives to draw Italy into the War than the party took to keep the scandal of Turati's activity in parliament well hidden. *Avanti* always ran *Critica sociale*'s advertisements, claiming it was a journal sponsored by the party. When you asked the party leadership how they could tolerate that, they replied using the same words that we have just heard spoken by Maffi: 'It is read only by a few thousand intellectuals, and the workers do not even know about it.'

After Caporetto we had the famous embrace between Bissolati and Turati.[21] But Turati – let us give him credit for this – never denied his past. He has remained a reformist and a nationalist. He is an enemy of the Russian Revolution. Yesterday the opinion was expressed that Turati's foreword to the book of the two delegates who slandered the Russian Revolution is not an important matter.[22] No, comrades, it is not a petty matter. What is at issue

---

18. Beginning in the fall of 1914 with a conference in Lugano, Switzerland, the PSI and the Swiss Social-Democratic Party had taken the initiative in campaigning to convening a conference of socialists in different countries who opposed the War. Meanwhile, the Italian Socialists campaigned to preserve Italy's neutrality in the conflict. Italy went to war the following year.

19. Prior to World War I, the German SPD was considered the principal bulwark of Marxist orthodoxy within the Second International, restraining reformist currents in each country. With the SPD's betrayal of revolutionary internationalism in August 1914, these right-wing currents were given free rein.

20. The *Risorgimento* was a nineteenth-century national movement for Italian unification, which led to the establishment of the Italian kingdom in 1861.

21. This sentence has been edited in comparison with the Italian text in PCI 1921, p. 97.

22. Gregorio Noffri and Fernando Pozzani, *La Russia com'è*, preface by Filippo Turati. The preface was also published in *Critica sociale*, 2 (1921), pp. 16–30.

is not the Russian Revolution, which towers above the things said by Turati and his friends. (*Applause*) The Russian Revolution does not need to justify itself in face of the reformists' slanders. Nonetheless, to present the proletarian revolution as a whole as a wedding, free from terror, hunger, and war, is to administer poison to the Italian proletariat, drop by drop. This recalls the way revolution was presented, in the style of Montecitorio[23] and the reformists. (*Applause*)

Theories have been devised ad hoc to defend Turati – in the press, in Italian socialist literature, in Serrati's newspaper. We even heard them expressed here last year. These theories sought to demonstrate that the Italian centrists, even Comrade Serrati, are much more advanced than the Communists of the Third International – all this merely in order to keep Turati within the Italian Socialist Party. A web of true Communist metaphysics was spun on the agrarian and national questions as well as the Communist parties' policies in Britain and the United States.[24]

Serrati, one of the Italian party's leaders, succumbed to abstract formulas, which take no account of context with respect to time or location. He imagines that a Communist Party that holds power is the same thing as a Communist Party in opposition. He and his friends say, 'We are against the Communist International's revolution on the nationalities question because we are opposed to nationalism. We are opposed to the entry of the British Communist Party into the Labour Party because this stands in contradiction to what the International asks of the General Confederation of Labour.' Serrati fails to understand the most elementary concept, namely, that the tactics and strategy of the Communist Party are not dogmatic but dialectical, and they must adjust to circumstances. What is appropriate for Britain and the United States, where the Communist movement is not yet solidly on its feet, is not appropriate for Italy, where the Socialist Party declared for communism last year and where it must stand ready to take hold of power and point out the road forward for the trade-union movement. Yes, the Italian proletariat has been poisoned, and is poisoned even today by these false teachings. And all this is being done purely in order to defend Turati and the reformists.

I see a psychological problem here. You exhaust all of Italy's reserves of lime in order to whitewash Turati; why do you find him so indispensable? Because the Italian comrades of the Socialist Party have placed all their hopes – not on the working class – but on an intellectual elite of specialists.

---

23. Montecitorio is the palace in Rome that houses the Italian parliament.
24. Serrati's disagreements on the agrarian question at the Second Comintern Congress can be found in Riddell (ed.) 1991, 2WC, 2, pp. 653–4. His disagreements on the national question can be found on pp. 234, 235, and 276–7.

They are saying, 'The Italian workers are not mature enough; they are not sufficiently politically developed. That is why we need specialists.'

They say that Turati is a very poor Communist but a marvellously skilled parliamentary strategist. Rigola is a reformist.

**Lazzari**: He was overthrown.

**Rakovsky**: Yes, he was overthrown, but only to be replaced by another reformist, D'Aragona. They are popular in the General Confederation of Labour. They tell us, further, 'We are doing all this in order to preserve the unity of our party and avoid splitting our forces. We control three thousand municipalities.' I am not saying anything here that cannot be found in the official Italian documentation. 'We need collaborators; we need competent trade unionists, people who have practical experience in trade-union work; we need political figures who have a grasp of parliamentary strategy.' The Italian party clings to this illusion of unity. 'We need unity at any cost', they tell us, 'even at the cost of revolution'. Comrade Lazzari, one must be true to oneself. In Bern, in Kienthal, in Zimmerwald, you helped deal the death blow to this doctrine of unity.[25] If this doctrine was not an abstract principle but a force for revolution, you would have remained true to it and not destroyed the infamous Second International bureau led by Vandervelde and Huysmans in Brussels. You would not have approved the split among the Social Democrats and later between the Communists and the Independents in Germany. If you find the policy of splitting unacceptable, you would not have approved of it in other countries. And now you claim that this policy of splitting applies to other countries but not to Italy. That is a contradiction. Are there then no reformists in Italy? Your reformism is more consistent. It is tied by a thousand strings to the Italian intelligentsia, who play a quite special role in the life of your party. Where does this Communist nationalism come from – this ambition, which claims that everything in Italy must be done differently than in other countries? That is an argument that all opportunists have made use of.

The French opportunists say that the German opportunists are nationalists, while Renaudel, by contrast, is said to be continuing the best traditions of French socialism. The German opportunists said during the War that the French socialists were nationalists, while they, by contrast, were students of

---

25. Bern was the site of the 5–8 February 1916 meeting of the International Socialist Commission elected at the Zimmerwald conference of September 1915. For the Zimmerwald and Kienthal conferences, see p. 771, n. 5. These and other international meetings during the War registered the deepening split in the world socialist movement.

Marx. That is an old story. You created a theory of specialists. Your deputies, Montecitorio, and all that – they may be the best strategists and with them you can form an excellent government, but you will never carry out a revolution. Together with Rigola and D'Aragona you are able to sabotage the marvellous metalworkers' movement, but you cannot carry out a revolution. With a party leadership that attempts to hide its internal disagreements from the workers, that heeds the principle that dirty linen should be washed indoors, you can formulate the best of intentions, but they will simply remain platonic, because you cannot carry out a revolution with such leaders.

You forget that the Communist Party must be a mass party. You do not place your hopes on the forces arising from the depths of the working masses, workers organised in trade unions, or members of the party sections. You have your traditional core, men who have remained in their posts unchanged for twenty years. You have Turati, Treves, and so on. But now this question has been disposed of, once and for all. The attempt to defend the Italian reformists has resulted only in making the charges against you all the more serious. The question that concerns us at this time is what will you, Italian Socialists, do now? How will you conduct yourselves? Will you follow the revolutionary proletariat, the Communist International, or will you turn back to Vienna, to Amsterdam? Do you perhaps want to found a Two-and-Three-Quarters International? No, you yourselves have protested too vigorously against the Scheidemanns, the Independents, and the French opportunists. If you propose to the Italian proletariat some day to go back to the betrayers, the proletariat will turn away from you.

Comrades, you have been given a period of grace, and I will utilise it to say that for me, you are not yet outside the Communist International. You are here; we are listening to you; and we extend all our personal friendship to the comrades who play an important role in the Socialist Party of Italy. The interjection, 'Out, out!', of which Comrade Maffi spoke, did not refer to you or even to your party. No, we would be very happy if you would come to us as individuals, as Frossard and Cachin did last year, but you must tell us that you promise to accept unreservedly the International's conditions; that you will, if necessary, oppose your party; that you will support these conditions within it as well.

Fusing the parties is a technical question. When I learned that the recent Livorno Congress decided to accept unconditionally the [Second] Congress resolutions, I thought, 'There is no need to call a new congress. All that is needed is for the party leadership to submit to the decisions of the International.' But let me return to my theme and reiterate that the question is posed not to you personally or to the party but to the proletariat, to the conscience of every Italian worker, who must ask, 'Whose side am I on? Am I for the revolutionary world proletariat, or for the International that has become disloyal to my cause?' You have no other choice. You must state here, before the best representatives of the proletariat, that you, as Italian Socialists, will submit unconditionally and unreservedly to the decisions of the Third International, of the world proletariat gathered in Moscow. If you want the Italian proletariat to gather its forces and stride forward toward the victory of communism, you must make a decision without delay to restore to the Italian proletariat its organisational strength and its belief in the revolution.

**Zetkin**: Comrades, surely there is no one among us who does not feel the gravity and responsibility of the decision that we must take on the Italian question. What is at stake here is not the fate of a few leaders – regardless of whether or not we like them, regardless of whether or not their policies provoke us to sharp protests and passionate struggle. What is at stake is not merely the political fate of thousands of workers belonging to the Socialist Party of Italy. This decision involves an element in the fate of Communist parties in every country, of the International as a whole, and beyond it, of untold millions of exploited and oppressed the world over. For it is the speed and unity with which workers around the world rally to the Communist International that will determine how long proletarians will be exploited and enslaved by capitalism, or whether they will finally achieve full humanity through communist liberation.

Comrades, this situation demands – not only in Italy but the world over – that a strong, united, and cohesive party take the leadership of the revolutionary proletariat. In the name of unity, the Italian proletariat has been prevented, until now, from deploying in united fashion against the bourgeoisie. And yet this unified advance is even more urgent than ever. The Italian bourgeoisie no longer parades in the glittering attire of democracy. In Italy, too, it has been shown that all the liberal phrase-mongering of the ruling and exploiting class is nothing but lies and deceit. In Italy, too, the ruling class speaks with the voice of military might, striking the masses with bloody violence. And this might must be broken by the unity of the revolutionary proletariat. But comrades, unity of the proletarian front must not be achieved at the expense of revolutionary clarity, revolutionary energy, and revolutionary action. Unity must never be won at such a price. That is why it is necessary to draw conclusions not only through fine resolutions but through living and forceful deeds.

We face a situation where, since the Livorno Congress, there is no unity of the party, no unity in the revolutionary battle lines. I am still of the opinion that it is supremely important for the Communist Party and the valuable forces that unquestionably are still to be found in the Unitarian camp to unite in a single mass party – but not by giving up the principled foundation and the tactical programme of struggle.

We have just heard Comrades Lazzari and Maffi assure us, with honest conviction, that the Italian Socialist Party is determined to take this path. But I must say frankly, comrades, that we have the right at this time to raise before the party as a whole the same question, to lay the same accusation that we put to Serrati before Livorno, namely: what has the entire party done since Livorno in terms of action to take the path to the Third International? I do not wish to list here the individual facts indicating that nothing has been done to carry out a firm Communist policy. I only want to highlight a single incident that brightly spotlights the failure until now to act as one must act in order to belong to the Third International now and in the future.

The fifty thousand lire that the Amsterdam International gave to the Italian trade-union federation: the Socialist Party of Italy did not call this gift by its right name, did not denounce it as it should have done from a Communist point of view.[26] What was the situation? These fifty thousand lire came from the hands of the same betrayers of the workers, the same social patriots who had waded for four years with the bourgeoisie of every country through the bloody ocean of world war. This money came from people whose hands dripped with the blood of twenty thousand slaughtered German proletarians. In reality, the fifty thousand lire were not an expression of fraternal international solidarity. They were something different: Judas's piece of silver with which the red Moscow trade-union International was betrayed and sold for the benefit of the yellow Amsterdam trade-union International.

Comrades, the acceptance of this money did not arouse any storm of protest from the ranks of the Italian party. On the contrary. *Avanti* was pleased, greeting this event as an expression of international solidarity. In my opinion, this fact alone suffices for the International to declare: 'This far, and no further!' The Socialist Party of Italy has now arrived at its Rhodes, where it must jump.[27] The facts speak strongly. The party's policies show one thing clearly now: As long as there has been no clean separation from the Turati forces, the Unitarian party in Italy will not be a vanguard force against the bourgeoisie; it will rather be a protective wall between the bourgeoisie and the revolutionary proletariat. (*Applause*)

---

26. For the Amsterdam International's donation of 50,000 lire to the Italian CGL, see p. 199, n. 33.
27. A reference to one of Aesop's Fables, in which an athlete boasts that he once made a colossal long jump on the isle of Rhodes. One of his listeners challenges him to do so on the spot: 'Here is Rhodes, jump!'

The intentions may be good, indeed they are certainly good and even, in my opinion, outstanding. But political logic has its own laws. At this time there is no intermediate reformist camp between the bourgeoisie and the proletariat. Anyone who covers up for and endorses Serrati's reformism is hindering the proletariat from massing together with full revolutionary understanding and readiness for action. I have said expressly that the same judgement must now be made of the party's policies that was made earlier of Serrati as a person. By this I mean that *the present congress of the Third International must arrive at an unequivocal decision. It must begin by stating that the break from the Turati forces must be carried out immediately, ruthlessly, and without evasions.* Not in the way that one throws out individual leaders, one after another, who have been caught in the act, so to speak, stealing from the proletariat's revolutionary cash box. No, the party must finish off with the opportunist current as a whole, or more properly, with the entire reformist policy.

Our congress must build a firm wall between the proletarian army and this pernicious current. Given how things stand, I do not think it advisable to present a harsh and deeply felt critique of the policies that our friends in Italy have carried out recently in an honest attempt to find a path to communism. But the congress must state unambiguously, in a fashion that permits no twisting or turning, what the practical policies are that we demand of the Socialist Party of Italy from this moment on, in order to be integrated organically into a unified Communist Party of Italy.

Comrades, in my opinion, the congress is not offering a pittance, as our Italian friends of the Socialist Party believe, when it provides these comrades with the opportunity to take part in working out this resolution. On the contrary, this is an action of self-evident fraternal fairness. But I must also say frankly that I consider it to be the fraternal, international duty of our comrades Lazzari and Maffi to make a contribution from their side to clarify the situation and promote understanding. We know that they are not authorised to make any statement here or to agree to anything.

We know that their coming congress will decide the question. However, we must ask one thing of them. Comrade Lazzari, Comrade Maffi, and all of you are present here as flesh and blood of the Italian proletariat, as witnesses, as a personification of its best traditions and its struggle. You must act as the honest, conscientious, and passionate translators of this congress's decisions for your party and for the Italian proletariat. It is up to you to dispel the misunderstandings that have arisen among the masses and in your party during this debate. Given your laudable past, you will play the role of honest and reliable mediators in this situation. We have confidence that when you arrive back home, you will explain to your friends, the Italian workers, that the Communist International is acting not out of any petty motives, not out of dogmatism, not because we take pleasure in condemning, let alone in splitting. The Communist International carries out splits only in order to forge unity on a higher and more solid level. Workers of Italy: Learn from the situation! Learn, and draw the right conclusions! If you genuinely want to come to communism, separate yourselves nationally from forces with whom you no longer can nor should be united. And unite internationally with forces that ought to be united. You must choose! (*Loud applause and cheers*)

**Trotsky**: Comrades, I shall not dwell on the past of the Italian Socialist Party. Enough has already been said on this subject.

The fundamental reality is the great crisis of last September, which produced the present state of affairs. Even a review from afar of the political situation leaves one with the impression and even the conviction that in the years following the War the Italian proletariat entered on a decidedly revolutionary course. The broad working masses understood everything written in *Avanti* and everything stated by the speakers of the Socialist Party as a summons to the proletarian revolution. This propaganda struck a responsive chord in the workers' hearts and awakened their will, resulting in the September events.

Judging the party from a political standpoint, one can only conclude – for this is the only possible explanation – that the Socialist Party of Italy conducted a policy that was revolutionary in words, without ever taking into account any of its consequences. Everybody knows that, during the September events, no other organisation became as flustered as the Socialist Party of Italy, which had itself paved the way for these events. Now these facts are proof that the Italian organisation – and we should not forget that the party is not only a continuity of ideas, a goal, and a programme but also an apparatus, an organisation, which through its ceaseless action creates a guarantee of victory – in the month of September this organisation was the scene of a gigantic crisis for the proletariat and the Socialist Party of Italy itself.

What conclusions did the Italian proletariat draw from these events? It is very hard to estimate this, given that a class that breaks with its party immediately loses its sense of orientation. But the party: what conclusions has it drawn from this experience? For three years following the War, each and every comrade who came from Italy would tell us: 'We are ripe, indeed overripe for revolution.' Everyone there knew that Italy was on the eve of the revolution. When the revolution broke out, the party proved bankrupt. What lessons were drawn from these events? What was done?

Did they say, 'We were unprepared because our organisation was composed of elements that were completely incompatible and that acted to paralyse each other. To create certain conditions, insofar as this depends on our will, one must have the will to create them'? This, Comrade Lazzari, is the crux of the matter; one must have the will to revolutionary victory. Only if this will exists can one then engage in discussion and undertake to analyse, because strategy is indispensable, and it is impossible to gain victory through a powerful will alone. Strategy is indispensable, but above all else one must have the will to revolution and to its victory. Turati and his friends are in this sense honest, because they declare daily, openly, and unambiguously that they do not want the revolution. They do not want it and yet they remain members of the Socialist Party, indeed a significant part of this party.

You lived through the September experience. But what course did you pursue after this tragic month? You moved further to the right. In your new parliamentary fraction, the reformists – that is, people who don't want the revolution – constitute the majority. Your central organ *Avanti* has turned the helm sharply to the right. That is the present state of affairs. It is impermissible to boast about the past when the present situation is so clear and unmistakable. There is a contradiction between lip-service to the revolution and the cruel demands of the revolutionary situation, as we saw in your conduct in September. Out of this contradiction flows one of two things: either you will renounce the portion of your past that was revolutionary only in its lip-service, and become truly revolutionary; in other words, you will break with the reformists who hinder revolutionary action. Or, on the other hand, you must say: 'Since we did not want the September events we must likewise reject the methods that called them forth.'

Turati will not fail to make use of the lessons of September; he is shrewd enough to single out the obvious contradiction that it makes evident. So far as you, your party, and your Central Committee are concerned, you are only preserving the confusion that prepared and predetermined in advance the failure of the September events and that has produced the Socialist Party of Italy's shift to the right. Serrati's idea lay in bringing forces together. He wanted to keep the Communists, the centrists, and the reformists together within a single party. There was a time when this idea of concentrating forces could be justified by a hope of preserving the maximum of revolutionary forces in the party. That is what he wanted to do. He wanted to unite these three groups in order to be able later to say: 'Here are the genuine contours of our party; whoever stands outside is hostile to us.'

You have gone through extremely bitter, clear, and tragic experiences. Only afterwards did this idea of 'concentration', which is somewhat abstract in and by itself, take on a definite political form.[28] This idea became utterly reformist

---

28. For the PSI reformists' Socialist Concentration Faction, see p. 190, n. 19.

and not centrist, because the party's development has now definitely swung to the right.

Turati has declared: 'In September the proletariat was not yet mature enough.' Yes, it was not mature. But have you properly explained to the proletariat why the party was not mature? Did you say to the proletariat: 'Yes, Turati is correct in this sense, that you, Italian workers, were not mature enough, before engaging in decisive action, to cleanse your party of all the elements that paralyse the party's work. Turati is correct in this sense, that the Italian proletariat by its failure to expel him from its ranks has thereby demonstrated that it was not mature enough for the decisive September actions.'

What is the present situation of the Italian proletariat? I am certain that it has become much wiser after it was involuntarily betrayed by the party in which it had placed its full trust. Comrade Lazzari tends to interpret such expressions in a moral and personal sense. He said: 'We are accused of treachery, but what did we get for it?' But it is not a question of betrayal by corrupted individuals. It is a question of the bankruptcy of the party. And, in political terms, this is nothing else but a betrayal of the interests of the proletariat. I ask myself: what can the Italian proletariat possibly think? The party surely stands terribly discredited in its eyes. A new party has arisen – the Communist Party. We are certain that it will continue to grow even were it to remain as isolated in the future as it is today. This party turns to the proletariat and offers it its revolutionary communist programme. Are you not afraid that the Italian proletarians will say after listening to you: 'But we've heard this melody before, we've already been duped in September.' Thus you have created quite a difficult situation in Italy for a period of time that, let us hope, will be a brief one.

Through energetic and audacious work, the new Italian party must conquer anew genuine revolutionary trust, which is indispensable not only for parliamentary activity – which is something else again – but also for a new assault against capitalist society. It is necessary to conquer anew the revolutionary reputation that the party squandered through its activity, or better said, through its inactivity in September.

You tell us that the followers of Turati submit to party discipline. Yes, it was quite correct to say that a plea had been delivered on behalf of Turati; it was a plea constructed in accordance with all the rules of juridical defence. What is the meaning of party discipline? There is formal discipline, and there is real discipline. Either I act in a certain way because circumstances leave me no choice or because I act of my own free will. In my opinion, there is a clear distinction between these two options. We submit to the discipline of the capitalist state, we submit to capitalist legality – but how? Only to the extent we are compelled to do so. But, at the same time, we mock bourgeois legality, we create underground organs to circumvent such legality, and we utilise every avenue to break through bourgeois legality or to extend its framework. And what is Turati's attitude to your discipline? It is exactly the same attitude, Comrade Lazzari. He submits to your discipline as we submit to bourgeois legality. He creates his own illegal organisations, his own faction in your party. He instigates a conspiracy with the government, naturally on the sly and behind your backs. He does everything to extend and to break through the framework of this discipline and, above all, he mocks your discipline in his speeches and in his newspaper. He is therefore our conscious, systematic, and methodical enemy, just as we are the enemies of bourgeois society and its legality. This is the true state of affairs.

You say: 'But Turati has not given us any real grounds for expulsion. We need facts; we have not got enough facts.' Yes, it can be flatly stated that even if we continue to wait indefinitely we shall still lack these facts, since Turati knows exactly what he wants. Turati is no run-of-the-mill careerist, eager to become a minister in a capitalist government. Insofar as I can make him out, he has a policy of his own which he wants to carry through. He is not chasing after a ministerial portfolio. I can clearly visualise an interview between Turati and Giolitti. Giolitti says to him: 'Here is a portfolio that you deserve.' But Turati replies: 'Haven't you listened, my dear colleague, to the fiery speeches of Lazzari? The instant I accept this portfolio, I shall supply him with the pretext he has been waiting for. I will be expelled from the party, and once expelled I shall lose all political importance so far as you and the preservation of the capitalist state are concerned. Since what is at issue is not so much the installation of one more Socialist minister but the support of democracy, that is, the support of capitalist society, I cannot accept your portfolio; for I do not intend to play into the hands of my severe colleague Lazzari. In the interests of bourgeois society let us leave things as they are.'

You say: 'Aren't we paying too much attention to Turati, his speeches, his books, his prefaces? Isn't this rather an isolated incident? It is a *quantité négligeable* [a trifle]! If that is the case, if so far as you are concerned all that's involved is a loss of one or more individuals, the loss of a *quantité négligeable*, then why are you so intransigent? Let us imagine, dear comrades from Italy, that, while we are discussing here, Giolitti rings up Turati on the telephone to inquire: 'Is there not a danger that Lazzari has left for Moscow to assume some obligations there?' And Turati answers: 'No, no! This is purely an isolated incident.' As you know, capitalist society holds to the principle of division of labour; and by breaking with the Communist International for the sake of safeguarding Turati, you are doing a great service to that society.

You say that you are becoming extremely enthusiastic about the Russian Communist Party and about Soviet Russia. Permit me in this connection to speak somewhat freely, for the benefit not only of the Italian comrades but of all parties. When it comes to talking about us, it happens all too frequently that a very delicate tone is employed, as if to avoid picking a quarrel with us. As all of you know, our situation is extremely difficult. You were present at Red Square and you have seen not only our soldiers and our armed Communists who are ready to come to the defence of the Third International;[29] you've also seen our youth, our children, most of whom go around barefoot and undernourished. On visiting our factories each of you observes our economic and material breakdown, more severe than any other form of poverty.

Whoever arrives in Russia with the hope of finding a communist paradise here will be cruelly disappointed. Whoever comes here with the aim of gathering impressions for eulogising Russia is not a genuine Communist. But whoever comes here in order to collect facts pertaining to our poverty in order to employ them as evidence against communism is our open enemy. (*Applause*) And here, comrades, is what Turati, a member of your party, has to say about Russia: 'The Russians have invented the soviets and the Communist International for their own profit and to further their own national interests.' This is what he told the Italian worker who was dragooned into the War to defend supposed national interests and who was duped like all the others. Today another national bogey is being dangled before him – Soviet Russia, which is seeking to further her own national interests through the Communist International.

Go through the German press for the period of the March events, and you will find there the selfsame thought expressed about the condition of the soviets. It says there that the soviets found themselves terribly discredited at the time, and in order to save herself, Soviet Russia issued, through the Communist International, a command to launch revolutionary action in Germany. Today our perfidious enemies are spreading a legend – and one of its most fervent disseminators is your Turati – to the effect that to bolster up our domestic situation we are demanding of all other parties that they engage in revolutionary actions that have no connection whatsoever with the political and social development of the respective countries. If we permit people who

---

29. A parade was held in Moscow's Red Square on 17 June to honour the delegates to the Third Congress.

spread such ideas to remain any longer in our International, we can very well bring it into a very difficult situation.

Yes, comrades, we have erected a bulwark of the world revolution in our country. The country is still very backward, still very barbaric. It offers a picture of poverty. But we are defending this bulwark of the world revolution, given that at present there is no other. When another stronghold is erected in France or in Germany, then the one in Russia will lose nine-tenths of its significance; and we will then stand ready to go to you in Europe in order to defend this other, more important stronghold. Comrades, it is absurd to believe that we consider this Russian stronghold of the revolution to be the centre of the world. It is absurd to assume that we believe it is our right to demand of you to make a revolution in Germany or France or Italy, whenever this is required by our domestic policy. Were we capable of such a betrayal, then all of us would deserve to be put against a wall and shot, one by one.

Comrade Lazzari, how can we remain in the same International with Turati who is a member of your party and who calls our International a 'preposterous International'? These are his very words. Karl Liebknecht and Rosa Luxemburg are dead, but for this International they remain eternally alive. How can we combine within the ranks of our International Karl Liebknecht, Rosa Luxemburg, and Turati? Turati says that our organisation is preposterous. And just think of it, yesterday even he himself was still a member of it. Well, that episode in the life of the Third International is truly preposterous. (*Loud applause*)

**Loriot** (Communist Party of France): Comrades, during his remarks, Comrade Lazzari was unable to resist the temptation to justify the position of the Italian Socialist Party by attacking the French Socialist Party.[30] However, Comrade Lazzari restricted his critique to certain members of the French party; he did not go as far as Serrati did at the Livorno Congress, where he built his entire speech on this critique. Although Comrade Lazzari's reference to Comrade Frossard was quite discreet, still we cannot pass over it in silence, since it has given rise to utterly wrong conclusions.

The French delegation will not say anything that could diminish the reputation of the Socialist Party of Italy. It will not say anything that could dull the halo that surrounded the Socialist Party of Italy during the War. It will not investigate the degree to which the wartime course of the Italian Socialist Party was influenced by the experience of the war in Tripolitania [Libya] and by awareness in the working class of the imperialist character of the

---

30. The French CP is clearly meant here.

intervention that Italy was dragged into.[31] We in no way disregard the services that your party, Comrade Lazzari, has rendered to the cause of communism.

We certainly do not forget that after Zimmerwald you became a guiding star, especially for us. I personally have a particularly strong reason to keep this in mind. I was staying in London as the sole representative of the French party's Far Left. No one but the Italian comrades would support my initiative; no one but Comrades Lazzari and Modigliani was willing to support our motion.[32] However, Comrade Lazzari, this motion related to a very specific situation that is fundamentally different from what we face today.

Similarly, Zimmerwald, to which you refer so often, was certainly a historic event of indisputable importance, but now, after all, it lies in the dead past. Merrheim and Martov were present in Zimmerwald. Does this then mean that they are right today? Can their present activity be judged by referring to their earlier services? Parties, just like individual militants, cannot nourish themselves from their past. They must always be judged on the basis of the present. When you draw a parallel between the French Socialist Party and the Socialist Party of Italy, you forget to take the present into account. That is why you are unable to come to a correct conclusion.

If you would reflect on the current situation, you would recognise that you do not have the right to condemn the French party as Serrati did. We are pleased to welcome the aspects of your critique that are justified. We know that our party is not yet entirely Communist, and that it embraces in its ranks comrades who are not yet fully imbued with a Communist spirit and sometimes are guilty of petty-bourgeois and opportunist conduct. Be that as it may, and regardless of whatever criticisms could be directed at the French party, it is nonetheless apparent that the party is on the road to revolution. True, again and again along this new and thorny road, its feet are take a bruising. It is still too young not to stumble over the barriers that it must overcome. But it is aware that it is on the right road and is firmly resolved to attain its goals – and that is the most important thing.

The situation in the Italian party, by contrast, is quite different. It is on the road to reaction and is in the process of being absorbed by the bourgeoisie.

**Interjection**: Did you discover that on your own?

---

31. In 1911 Italian troops began a war of colonial conquest in Libya, attempting to seize it from the Ottoman Empire. By the following year Turkish forces sued for peace, but Italy then faced a war of resistance by the local population. Italian troops occupied the country into World War II.

32. An apparent reference to the Second Inter-Allied Socialist Conference, held in London 28–29 August 1917.

**Loriot**: It is not a discovery, but rather a conviction I have formed based on the parties' history and my observation of their development. I have attempted to show you that my estimation is correct. When the indictment of Turati was read out here, the Italian comrades protested, saying 'We are not here to plead Turati's case.' Whether you admit it or not, Comrade Lazzari, it is still Turati's case that you are pleading here, even as you believe that you are speaking for your party. Have a look at what is happening all around you, for example, what took place in the French party when it was faced with a split, which took place in your party just as in ours.

There will always be forces that remain in the old party but feel they are close to the forces that exited – and sometimes they are in fact very close to them. It even happens sometimes – and this was in fact the case in France – that precisely these forces are leading the party at the moment of the split. This creates the impression that the French [Socialist] party, with Longuet and Paul Faure, and the old Italian party with Serrati are still basically the same as they were when the split took place. This is erroneous. The split always reinforces the influence of the right wing, since they are no longer confronted with a counterweight. The left forces, to the degree they do not bitterly attack the new [Communist] party, are bound hand and foot – or rather compelled in the criticisms, on which they are increasingly dependent, consciously or unconsciously, to go beyond the limits they had earlier observed. And so they slide down the slippery slope and gradually merge with the right wing.

What was the role of the supposed revolutionary forces in the French [Socialist] party, when they turned away from us after the split? What happened to Paul Faure, to Pressemane, to Longuet, who had assured us that they would never change? When the split took place, it seemed as if they would continue to exert control over their party. But what role are they now actually playing? Since the split, the party is no longer under their influence, and they have been pushed into the background. Just have a look at *Le Populaire*. What political principles have the splitters maintained since they broke away? Where do they find inspiration? From the men on the Far Right. Léon Blum is today the guiding spirit of the splitters' political orientation; the supposedly revolutionary forces now have no influence. What has this party of splitters come up with now? It wants to re-establish the Left Bloc.[33] It wants the party to unite with the French Radicals. This is the policy now being advocated by Paul Faure, Longuet, and people who take their revolutionary phraseology seriously. This policy may be resisted – at least verbally – by one

---

33. The Left Bloc was formed in 1899, led by the bourgeois Radical Party and including some Socialist forces in parliament.

or another individual, here and there. However, their resistance lacks force and conviction and wins no response outside the party.

*Le Populaire* simply reflects the majority point of view. People who have retained a revolutionary outlook to some degree and who still claim to want to remain socialists – if there still are any people like that among the splitters – will be forced one fine day to take the step they could not bring themselves to take at Tours. They will have to leave this party, whose activity is more and more traitorous, and return to the Communist Party.

You yourselves have a striking example of the errors that you will be drawn into – errors that lead directly to collaboration with the government. Consider Serrati. Since his return from Russia, he allows his position to be utilised by that well-known renegade, Merrheim. Take Comrade Alessandri. What French paper does he write for? For *Le Populaire*, a newspaper that a few days ago, when Lafont was attacked,[34] sank so low as to defend bourgeois politics.

The future belongs to the Left, Comrade Lazzari. If there are still genuine revolutionaries in your party, sincerely striving for the full liberation of the proletariat, they must not remain in a party of which Turati is still a member. They must either expel from the party Turati and the reformists that follow him, or themselves leave the party. By doing so they will serve the cause of revolution not only in Italy but rather of all the Western European peoples, that is, the world revolution.

**Solomon A. Lozovsky** (Russia): Comrade Maffi said that the Italian reformists' activity gives expression to their opinions. That is absolutely true. We are anxious to learn about the Italian Socialist Party's conduct. Its activity shows that it is not just the Italian reformists whose work expresses their opinions. Rather the entire party takes its direction from the reformists' opinions – a much more significant phenomenon.

I have taken the floor in order to give an example. At the Livorno Congress of the Italian General Confederation of Workers (CGL), it was decided to establish very close ties between the CGL and the [Socialist] party.[35] The nature of the two organisations' unification was to be determined by the party's Central Committee and the CGL. Italian comrades are familiar with this. Comrade Lazzari will confirm that the policies of the CGL are generally the same as those of the Socialist Party of Italy. At the [CGL's] Livorno Congress a resolution on the Red International of Labour Unions was put to a vote. Here is the text of this resolution.

---

34. Ernest Lafont, a member of the French CP, was beaten by police at a demonstration at the Père-Lachaise Cemetery in Paris on 28 May 1921.

35. The Fifth Congress of the General Confederation of Labour (CGL), held in Livorno from 26 February to 3 March 1921, a month after the PSI Livorno Congress.

1.) Affiliate wholeheartedly to the initiative to found a red trade-union International, subject to the condition that the ties between the Labour Confederation and the Socialist Party remain in place and that the principle of unification of the Italian trade-union movement in the Confederation be recognised.

2.) Break from the Amsterdam trade-union alliance, in accord with the decisions to be taken by the Moscow congress.

Comrades, when the congress states that it is breaking with Amsterdam and will accept the decision of the Moscow Congress, this quite obviously means that relations between the Italian CGL and the Amsterdam trade-union alliance will no longer be so close. But what we see is that since the Livorno Congress the Italian CGL has moved closer to the Amsterdam alliance and further away from the red trade-union council. In April, the national CGL council decided to turn to the Amsterdam International regarding the question of Fascism. The Italian CGL is thus turning to an organisation that, as it very well knows, is unwilling and unable to do anything, an organisation whose role is to sabotage the world revolution. I am sure there is not a single comrade who does not grasp the nature of the actions by Jouhaux, Huysmans, and company – the leaders of this 'International'. And nonetheless, the Italian CGL turns to the Amsterdam trade-union International, which responds with a friendly letter, in which it announces a contribution of fifty thousand lire for the struggle against Fascism. What could that possibly mean? And how did the CGL respond? It sent the Amsterdam trade-union alliance an affirmation of friendship, which states, 'We thank the trade-union International that has come to the aid of our movement at a difficult moment, thus demonstrating that the international proletariat stands in solidarity with us.'

The Italian comrades know very well that the very gentlemen who sent them fifty thousand lire take part in the International Labour Office side by side with Italy's industrial magnates, such as Alberto Pirelli, and Michelis, who represents Italy's monarchical government. They act as good neighbours in the International Labour Office with those who are organising Fascism and its pogroms in Italy. With their left hand they send the Italian proletariat fifty thousand lire, while their right hand reaches out to those who organise pogroms in Italy. This exchange of courtesies between the CGL and the Amsterdam trade-union bureau shows that the CGL has gone much further than was intended by its Livorno Congress.

What did the party decide on this matter? A declaration on this show of solidarity appeared in *Avanti*, which read:

> The Amsterdam trade-union International, which recently sent our Confederation the message of solidarity printed below, is not in complete

agreement with us regarding the urgent needs of the proletarian movement. Some of their leaders are, indeed, quite distant from our ideals. If this was an appropriate time for polemics, we could reproach some of them for having solidarised during the War with forces that were then and still are among the most unrepentant representatives of reaction. Still, we are far from wishing to minimise the importance of this expression of international solidarity, which has touched us deeply.[36]

Is it possible to reproach the people who lead the Amsterdam trade-union bureau for their traitorous and perfidious activity during the War? No. But we can reproach them for what they are doing now in France, Britain, and Germany. We must reproach those who lead the trade-union movement for the fact that they are the worst enemies of the revolutionary movement. Did they not contribute to strangling the March Action in Germany? Why does the party's official publication write that they can be reproached only for their activity during the War? Well, what are they doing now? When they send money to the CGL, does that make their activity beyond reproach? Is this perhaps an isolated case? Not at all. When the party carries out reformist policies, it pushes the CGL closer to the Amsterdam trade-union alliance.

In order to demonstrate the spirit that prevails among the CGL leaders, let me give you another example. A few days ago, we received a telegram from the Italian CGL that reads as follows:

> The CGL proposes holding the [red trade-union] international congress in Stockholm or Reval [Tallinn] and postponing its date to August, so that the resolution of the Third International congress can be placed before it. After taking up the general questions, the congress must deal specifically with the international position of trade unions as well as with their programme and that of the Communist International.

We responded that we stood ready to hold a congress not only in Stockholm but in Italy itself, but the congress we had already called could not under any circumstances be cancelled. It was a mystery to us what they wished to achieve by moving the congress to Stockholm or Reval. However, just then we received a letter from D'Aragona dated 25 May. The telegram had been sent later than the letter, which contained an explanation of the proposal to shift our congress to Stockholm. D'Aragona wrote as follows:

> In order to ensure that all delegates are able to maintain unbroken contact with those they represent and to enable their mandates to be carefully

---

36. This statement is also quoted by Zinoviev, more fully and with a slightly different German translation, in Session 4. See pp. 198–9.

> scrutinised, we consider it desirable that the congress take place in a city suited to these purposes. In order to also do justice to your interests, we would propose Stockholm or Reval.

It is questionable whether the Swedish government would permit the holding of such a congress. Could we be certain that the government would not throw the delegates in jail? And what is the meaning of this ambiguous sentence stating that the validity of mandates can be better scrutinised in Stockholm or Reval? They are suggesting that here in Moscow representation could be faked and that we could arrange for phony delegates. In order to permit 'scrutiny', you want to meet in Stockholm, under the patronage of a bourgeois government. What is that supposed to mean, Comrade Lazzari? Well, this is certainly a dexterous form of politics, but I do not consider it to be very wise. It seems to me that the comrades in the CGL leadership are manoeuvring here with the intention of going through a different door.

The money received from the Amsterdam trade-union bureau, the cordial exchange of letters between the CGL and the Amsterdam bureau, and finally the ambiguous letter sent to us, which carries a distinct odour of diplomacy – this entire procedure tells us that the Italian CGL is preparing to enter the Amsterdam bureau through the back door.

I can hardly believe, comrades, that the Italian workers will permit their leaders to carry out this ambiguous policy. The resolution adopted in Livorno is reasonably clear. It says that they will remain with the Red International of Labour Unions. But what do we see? Instead of moving toward the RILU or turning to us, they are turning to Amsterdam, which is morally linked to the people organising pogroms in every country. These facts give us a clear indication that the Italian Socialist Party has become caught up in the mechanism of reformism.

There is a logic in this conduct. You cannot break free of all the facts. If you fight against the Left, you cannot avoid moving closer to the Right. You cannot always dance on the tightrope, you will fall either on the left or the right side. What did the Italian comrades do during the Livorno Congress? They shifted to the right in every field of activity. I am focusing on the trade-union movement. Now, Comrade Lazzari, what do you make of the Italian CGL's proposal to move our congress to Stockholm? Can the CGL guarantee us that we will be able to hold our sessions there? From a diplomatic point of view, the proposal is a clever move, but it is Machiavellian, to use an Italian term. Hundreds of delegates have already arrived in Moscow, and those from America and other distant points had to leave their homeland two months before the congress, in order to arrive on time. Given knowledge of that fact, such a proposal is impermissible from both a class and a revolutionary point of view. In my opinion, this proposal, and the attempt to move away from the international trade-union organisation, show quite clearly that the Italian party is trying to enter through the trade-union door of the Amsterdam bureau in order then to return through the political door into the Two-and-a-Half or the Second International. It is not possible to separate off the trade-union movement from politics.

Take care, Comrades Lazzari and Maffi. Together with other loyal comrades, you want the party to turn left. You need to examine these facts closely. They are not isolated incidents but rather an overall political course showing that since the Livorno Congress the Socialist Party of Italy has shifted right in the trade-union movement and in its activity as a whole. This is an extremely great and urgent danger for the Italian proletariat.

The Fascists are demolishing labour halls,[37] carrying out pogroms, destroying trade unions, and murdering militant proletarians. This is happening because the comrades of the Italian Socialist Party are not carrying out effective resistance. I have read a report on a socialist meeting that took up the question of resistance against Fascism. The speeches made there had a Tolstoyan colouration. But this is no time for Tolstoyism, no time for passivity. In order to combat Fascism, the Italian party must expel the reformists from their midst. Failing this, you will be driven to the right, while the Italian proletariat will move to the left and make the revolution without you and against you.

**Rakovsky**: Comrades, on behalf of the Ukrainian delegation, I propose that the discussion be closed. The question has been sufficiently discussed, and I do not believe that further debate serves the interests of the congress. (*Applause*)

**Kolarov** (Chair): Is there any objection to Comrade Rakovsky's proposal? I see none. I therefore declare it to be adopted. Comrade Koenen has the floor in order to submit a resolution on the report of the Executive Committee.

**Koenen**: Comrades, a large number of delegations have submitted a signed resolution summarising the discussion on the Executive's report, which we now recommend for the delegations and propose for adoption.

The resolution reads as follows:

*[For the text of the Resolution on the Report by the Executive Committee of the Communist International, see pp. 921–3]*

---

37. The labour hall (*camera del lavoro*) was a local union centre that played a large and militant role in the Italian labour movement, going back to the 1890s. These centres became a major target for Fascist attacks. Between January and May 1921, 243 labour halls were attacked, with 202 workers killed and over a thousand wounded.

This resolution was proposed by the following delegations:

Signatories for the delegations: CP of Italy: *Terracini*; CP of Bulgaria: *Kolarov*; CP of Poland: *A. Michalak*; CP of Germany: *Thalheimer, Frölich*; CP of Norway: *Scheflo*; CP of Czechoslovakia (German section): *Kreibich*; CP of Hungary: *Szántó*; CP of Austria: *Frei*; CP of Switzerland: *Rosa Grimm*; CP of Romania: *A. Badulescu*; Communist Youth International: *Willi Münzenberg*.

**Loriot** (France): Comrades, the French delegation did not sign this resolution. In our opinion, the Italian question has been discussed as a whole, but this is not true of the German question, which actually consists of two different issues: (1) the March Action; and (2) the question of the KAPD. We understand quite well why it was that the congress decided to take up only the question of the KAPD in the just-concluded debate. The French delegation is of the opinion that the March Action cannot be taken up in a plenary discussion of the congress. Nonetheless, the delegations must not be left fully in the dark regarding this matter.

The French delegates therefore propose that the congress immediately establish a special commission to take up this question. The congress also refrained, for the same reasons, from discussing why the Executive was led to act as it did. This commission could also deal with this question.

Before the Executive is authorised to decide on the fusion of the KAPD and the KPD, the delegations should be informed regarding the measures that it intends to take. These measures need to be discussed by the delegations. We therefore request that the debate be closed and the voting postponed until the commission we are proposing has finished its work.

**Boris Souvarine** (France): We do not insist absolutely on a special commission. It would be sufficient if the commission that has already been chosen would begin its work.

**Loriot** (France): It is not so vital that a new commission be created. It is more important that the already existing one take up the tasks of which I spoke.

**Sachs** (Schwab, KAPD): Comrades, I wish to speak on a point of order on behalf of the KAPD delegation. We ask, first, for the adoption of the French delegation's motion to take the vote on the resolution now before us at the end of our deliberations.

Secondly, we ask the congress to specify now that the vote on this resolution will be taken in sections, that is, that the different issues should be separated out and then, of course, that another vote be taken on the resolution as a whole. Regarding the separate vote, we present a counter-motion to the passage in the resolution that takes up the KAPD. I would now like to read this motion:

1.) The Twenty-One Conditions of the Second Congress will in the future be even less able than now to provide any guarantee against the reformist swamp.
2.) After having created and admitted mass parties shot through with centrism and reformism, the Third International needs even more than before to encompass a purely proletarian and revolutionary opposition.
3.) Such an opposition can be effective only if it is not oppressed by the apparatus and the voting strength of a party devoted to recruiting the masses whatever the cost, which necessarily leads to opportunism.
4.) The VKPD, in particular, is based even today, in its tactical principles, on the ideas of Paul Levi. Even its left wing is at best trapped in disastrous self-deception.
5.) Finally, currents related to the KAPD are now being formed in almost all the parties of the Communist International. But they will be able to evolve in a manner favourable to the interests of proletarian revolution only if the KAPD remains within the Communist International as a separate party.

For all these reasons, we propose that the congress decide to maintain the KAPD's affiliation as a sympathising organisation. If it is decided to discuss this matter further in commission, we are agreeable to referring this motion there. If a discussion of this question in commission is rejected, and the congress wishes to take the vote now, we would like to motivate this motion briefly.

**Radek**: Comrades, I ask that the motion of the French delegation be rejected for the following reasons. Comrade Loriot cited a number of questions that we have discussed and that form part of the Executive report, such as the Italian question, the KAPD, and so on. He conceded that these questions have received sufficient discussion. The only question which he believes has not been clarified – and for the sake of which he asks that the vote be taken only after the work of a commission – is the significance of the March Action. But the resolution on the Executive report says nothing about the March Action. So if Comrade Loriot and the French delegation believe they have not yet received sufficient information – and I believe they are right in this – that should not prevent them from expressing their opinion on the Executive's activity. (*Applause*) It was not the Executive that carried out the March Action. So a lack of information on this matter does not prevent you from expressing an opinion on the Executive's activity as a whole.

As for the question of a commission, we have a Commission on Tactics and Strategy. This commission's task is to examine that issue, not to review the past. There is not a single question touched on in the report that would not benefit from further review in a special commission. As for the reasons why the Commission on Tactics and Strategy has not met, this is straightforward. After the first session of this commission, we found out that only the Russian delegation's theses were available. It was decided that every delegation should submit a written report on its tactical and strategic course, in order to provide a basis for further discussion. Since the commission's chair did not receive new resolutions or a report by the French delegation, it was not possible to convene the Commission on Tactics and Strategy. For these reasons, I propose that Comrade Loriot's resolution be rejected, despite the support it has received from the KAPD.

As for the KAPD's motion to divide the resolution into separate parts, that is a technical matter. If there are groups here that wish to vote in favour of one part but against another, it is appropriate to divide the motion. Then we have the KAPD's demand that it receive special status because it is the bottle containing revolutionary spirits to warm and cheer us (*Laughter*), the discussion up to this point is sufficient to enable us to decide if you have a special liking for these spirits. The KAPD statement demands, further, that it receive a revolutionary plural vote on the grounds of its high quality. We have the opportunity to decide on that now. I therefore propose that the resolution of Comrade Loriot be rejected, but that the KAPD's motion to divide the vote be approved.

**Heckert** (VKPD): Comrades, the German delegation interprets Comrade Loriot's motion as signifying that the March Action must be discussed in a commission because it is not possible to say everything to the congress. If that is the reason why Loriot made his motion, then I urge the German delegation to reject it, because we have no intention of introducing private confessional in the Communist International. ('*Very true!*') However, if it is desired that the March Action be taken up in a special commission before the plenary session, then the Commission on Tactics and Strategy is sufficient for that. As for the rest, we agree with the comments by Comrade Radek. (*Applause*)

**Zinoviev**: I have not had the opportunity to speak to all members of the Executive about the present situation, but I am convinced that I am expressing the opinion of almost every member – in fact, probably all of them – in saying the following:

I hope that what we have in the motion by comrades of the French delegation is perhaps based only on a technical misunderstanding arising from insufficient knowledge of the language. In our opinion, the March Action must obviously be addressed in the next point, the discussion on tactics and strategy. That is the right time to do this thoroughly. We agree with the French comrades regarding the need to examine this question thoroughly. If that is what the French comrades are asking for, it is rather easy to agree with them. If that is not the case, then I must say, as the reporter, that I view this as nothing other than a somewhat disguised motion of non-confidence in the Executive. We ask our French friends to say that openly and clearly.

Of course they have the right to be displeased with our activity. But then that should be stated openly in a resolution. That is much better and much less likely to poison our relations. But simply putting off the vote is clearly impossible. We have had four days of political discussion, and after that, can we not say, 'For or against'? The entire world is watching our deliberations. If we do not vote today, that can only be taken as a vote of non-confidence against the Executive. Let me repeat that our French comrades have every right to say that we were not sufficiently revolutionary, not sufficiently Communist, that we applied the Twenty-One Conditions badly, that we carried out the Second Congress decisions badly, but that must be stated in a clear resolution. Otherwise the comrades are placing a big question mark over the Executive's entire activity.

If this is a misunderstanding, I ask the French comrades to withdraw their motion. If it is no misunderstanding, but rather a desire to express opposition to our activity, then as Communists we must say clearly and openly whatever there is to be said. If the motion is not withdrawn following this statement, we regard this politically as an attempt to put a motion of non-confidence in the Executive's political activity. (*Applause*)

**Rakovsky**: Permit me, for my part, to add a few words, directed especially to the French comrades. You are doubtless experienced in parliamentary procedure as well as in the procedures of the congress and of the commissions that give an accounting of their activity. When a committee reports to the congress, and the vote of approval is postponed until later, then for the committee that constitutes an expression of non-confidence. That is why, in order to keep our deliberations in normal bounds, I turn to you with the request that you withdraw your motion. After four days of debate, it is absolutely necessary that we say something regarding the activity of the Executive, which during the past year has represented the revolutionary proletariat of the world. We must state whether we accept its activity or not. Obviously, changes can be made in the wording of the resolution, but the meaning of our collective vote should not be left in doubt, and it must express approval. We must say that the Executive Committee has indeed earned the trust of the Communist parties of every country.

**Roland-Holst**: Comrades, the minority of the Dutch delegation and the delegation of the Dutch East Indies [Indonesia] Communist Party present a motion to postpone a vote on the KAPD question until this party has been able to express its views on the tactics, strategy, organisation, and other questions. I can motivate this motion in two minutes.

Comrades, in my opinion no small number of those present at the congress had the feeling yesterday that something about the way the KAPD matter was handled was not correct, and that the KAPD was dealt with roughly.

**Interjection**: We were too considerate.

**Roland-Holst**: I believe this because various delegates spoke to me along these lines and told me – irrespective of their political views, for that is not the question here, for it is an issue of elementary justice – that the KAPD should have simply been given time to present its views.

I am sure that it will be said in reply that even after the vote takes place, delegates will be able to take part in the congress deliberations. I do not question that at all. I am merely saying that the congress should be more accommodating in this matter. A psychological atmosphere is being created that is unfavourable for these comrades. There are many comrades here – excepting of course those of the German and Dutch East Indies parties – comrades of parties in other countries and even other continents, who are poorly or not at all informed regarding the KAPD's overall positions. I believe it is a simple matter of fairness to enable these comrades to be informed without creating an unfavourable atmosphere around the KAPD. I appeal to the sense of justice of all of you who were ever in a minority in your national parties or the Second International.

**Malzahn**: Comrades, we note that the March Action is not mentioned in the resolution. Therefore we too ask the congress to reject Comrade Loriot's motion that the March Action be taken up by a commission. But we hope that the March Action will be taken up thoroughly in the discussion on tactics and strategy, so the entire congress can draw the lessons and conclusions of these events.

In addition, I would like to take this opportunity to stress that we have not yet received any submissions in the Commission on Tactics and Strategy, although the March Action falls under these theses.

**Radek**: Comrades, I wish to say only a few words in reply to Comrade Roland-Holst's appeal to the feelings of justice of all those who have ever been in a minority or have been suppressed. I was often part of minorities, and I was often suppressed, but, comrades, that did not inspire me to delusions of grandeur. The delegation of a small party appeared here, and on every agenda point so far at least two of its delegates have spoken. Yesterday this party permitted itself the luxury of giving up its right to speak. And now Comrade Roland-Holst comes and appeals to all the noble feelings that I know are present in the breast of every delegate. Comrades, do not give way to provocation! (*Laughter*) Save your noble feelings for a better occasion, when we can apply them, perhaps, to protect Comrade Roland-Holst and the comrades of the Dutch minority from being suppressed by a solid majority of a mass party. (*Laughter*) We are dealing here with a question that requires no understanding of either the KAPD's viewpoint nor of philosophy in the Netherlands or Berlin. What is at issue is whether the Communist International should contain parties that pay no heed to the International's programme. Quite apart from this consideration, one thing is clear: as an international association, we can establish a certain transitional period during which a party is linked with us only loosely, but the moment comes when we pose the question whether it is going with us or not. Perhaps it will take not six months but nine months before the question of the KAPD's affiliation to us has fully ripened and can be decided according to the laws of philosophy. (*Laughter*) I request that the congress not be confronted with such tearful argumentation.

**Heckert** (VKPD): Comrades, following the comments by Comrade Malzahn, we feel the need to make a statement, so that the picture is not distorted when this resolution is adopted. The Executive approved Levi's expulsion. By adopting this resolution, which takes up the Executive's conduct in German matters, the congress expresses its expectation that in the future the Executive will conduct itself in the same way as in the case now before us.

**Malzahn**: Every attentive participant in this congress will have noted, when the resolution was read out, that nothing is said in it about either the March Action or the Levi case. Comrade Heckert says it is indeed present in the resolution; I can only respond that we are hardly in a position after all the editing to form an opinion on this matter. One thing is certain: nothing is said about the Levi case. If the Presidium interprets the matter in the same manner as Comrade Heckert, we ask that the vote and the decision be postponed until the question of tactics and strategy has been addressed. And I tell you, if Comrade Heckert's interpretation is adopted by the congress, the German issue and also the Levi question are thereby dealt with (given that the German issue also includes the March Action) we then have good reason to ask the Presidium to explain whether a decision is to be made today on the March Action. We ask this without any lack of confidence in the Executive, because if a decision is to be made today, this would deprive the congress of the possibility of discussing the March Action. If that is in fact the case, we ask that the decision be postponed until after the question of tactics and strategy.

**Zinoviev**: Comrades, as reporter, I wish to say that I regard it as obvious that this resolution approves Levi's expulsion. (*Tumultuous applause*) The March Action will be taken up as part of the question of tactics and strategy. As for the case of this gentleman – regardless of whether he is right or wrong on this or that tactical issue – he wrote a renegade pamphlet, saying that the Communist International Executive (which previously enjoyed the confidence of the entire Communist proletariat and will continue, I hope, to enjoy it in the future) is nothing but a bunch of wire-pullers and Turkestaners, and who presented matters as if irresponsible elements had staged a putsch, giving all the prosecutors and bourgeoisies, including in America, the chance to attack the Executive. So it is quite obvious that Levi must be thrown out of the Communist International. (*Enthusiastic applause*) Of course we took full responsibility for our action in approving this gentleman's expulsion. If the congress is of a different opinion, so be it. But if it expresses its confidence in us, it will be joining us in saying that Levi does not belong to the Communist International. (*Loud applause*)

**Neumann**: Comrades, in my opinion a very strange method is being applied here. The section on the March Action in the [draft] theses on tactics and strategy states, in the final paragraph, that the congress approves Levi's expulsion.[38] Of course I leave it to you to judge the Levi case. The Levi case was regarded initially as purely a disciplinary matter. But Comrade Zinoviev says that a portion of the criticisms in Levi's pamphlet may be correct. In that case, this review of the Levi expulsion would relate to whether his criticism of the March Action is right or wrong. If the opposite is true, then the review will obviously have to concern itself with Levi's expulsion alone. It is therefore extremely strange to address and judge the Levi case before having considered the entire complex of issues that led to it. We were convinced that the Levi case must be dealt with together with the March Action. That is why I say that in our opinion the vote must be postponed until the March Action has been discussed. If you do not do that, and give in to the [German] majority, you will not yet have demonstrated that your judgement of this question is correct. Comrade Loriot is right, and when the March Action is examined we will– (*Objections*) – if you please, the question has already been decided, already judged. That is why I say that to vote on the question now is wrong. I agree with Comrades Malzahn and Loriot that the vote on this question should be postponed.

**Radek**: Comrades, the entire congress here has witnessed the fact that from the beginning Comrades Neumann and Malzahn, who represent the Levi group here with consultative vote, have been openly provocative. We have told them not to tell us about their relationship to the KAPD or to the cosmos, just tell us *what is your position on the Levi case?* What is your position

---

38. See section 7 of the completed resolution, pp. 941–2.

on the Levi case now that you have come here and stated that the March Action was not a putsch.

**Neumann**: We will certainly do that.

**Radek**: The comrades have been dodging giving an answer to the question.

**Neumann**: That is not true!

**Radek**: You just said –

**Neumann**: Even if you repeat it ten times, it is still not true!

**Radek**: You just said that you would speak about the March Action.

**Neumann**: Certainly!

**Radek**: We responded to that, but the question before us now is whether the Executive acted rightly, at a moment when seven thousand German proletarians were sitting in jail, when the party was bleeding from all its wounds, and a man throws a bomb against this party (*Loud applause*) – whether it acted rightly in expelling this man. We have said that you, Neumann and Malzahn, are proletarians who carried out your duty during the March Action, even though you believed it to be an error. Now that you have retracted the charge that the March Action was a putsch instigated by the Executive, have you the courage to say that a man who raged against the party in such a situation, without trying to influence it through the party structures and through the International, is a renegade. We said that to you. You kept silent, and now, unfortunately, you have the gall to stand before the congress and demand that the congress should be just as much a weakling as you and not have an opinion on whether a renegade is a renegade. He can write books that are philosophically correct and still be a renegade. I propose to close the discussion. (*Tumultuous applause*)

**Kolarov** (Chair): We will proceed to the vote. First of all, the motion by Comrade Roland-Holst to postpone the vote on the KAPD until all questions before the congress have been dealt with. Who is in favour of this motion? Six delegates – a minority. The motion is therefore defeated.

The second motion, by Comrades Malzahn and Neumann, states that the decision on the resolution should be postponed until after the question of tactics and strategy has been dealt with. Who is in favour of this proposal? No one. The motion is defeated.

Before we take the vote on the resolution itself, I give the floor to the reporter for the Executive, Comrade Zinoviev.

## Summary on Executive Committee Report

**Zinoviev**: Because of illness, I will speak only quite briefly and limit myself to a few remarks. That will be all the easier for me given that – despite a very extensive discussion – in my opinion there was far too little criticism of the Executive itself. You should criticise us more than you did. And since you refrained from that, it will be easier for me to be brief.

On the Italian question, after the speeches of Comrades Gennari, Rákosi, Lenin, Trotsky, Rakovsky, and others, I have nothing to add. I am fully in accord with them. I am pleased to note that Comrade Zetkin also, at least on this question, spoke in approval of the Executive's conduct. In this regard I'd like to draw Comrade Zetkin's attention to the following quotation. In the journal *Sowjet*, issue 3 of 1 June, published by Paul Levi with the aid of a number of comrades, we find the following on Italy on page 84:

> Well, the election results indicate a defeat of the Communist Party of Italy and an overwhelming victory of the Socialist Party of Italy: 121 seats for the Socialist Party; 16 for the Communists. Such a defeat can only be termed catastrophic. But it is a defeat not only for the Communist Party of Italy but also for the Executive, the Communist International, and the VKPD.

As you see, there are entirely too many defeats in this little quotation, but nonetheless –

**Interjection**: The article is by Curt Geyer!

**Zinoviev**: Yes, by Curt Geyer, who regards himself as part of the Communist International, who resigned from the Zentrale together with Comrade Zetkin and the other comrades, and who is still in solidarity with this group. I hope that Comrade Zetkin will succeed in convincing Curt Geyer that he is mistaken. When a new Communist Party receives four hundred thousand votes and sixteen seats, surrounded as it is by enemies, that is in no sense a defeat. And it is no more a defeat for the Communist International than when, after the murder of Karl Liebknecht and Rosa Luxemburg, Scheidemann receives millions of votes. Clearly, such judgements represent a stab in the back of the Communist Party of Italy. It is also clear that after this congress, this kind of thing will definitely not be tolerated. Of course I cannot speak for how the new Executive will address this question. But in my opinion, after this congress takes a decision on the Italian question, which I hope will be unanimous, no member of the Communist International will be permitted to publish articles like that. (*Applause*)

Comrades, I believe that on the Italian question, more than on any other, the Executive enjoys the unanimous support of the Third Congress. We are very pleased to note this. *As has been said, the Italian question was the most important political issue this year.* It turned out that Comrade Zetkin was wrong in her evaluation of this question, and the Executive was right.

I must stress this all the more given that in her speech Comrade Zetkin insisted that she was right when she left the Zentrale because of the Italian question. As you will recall, she said that the Executive's representative, Comrade Rákosi, made this or that statement about Livorno. He is supposed to have said that Livorno was an example for other parties. Comrade Zetkin could not stand for that and had to draw attention to the danger, and she did so by resigning from the VKPD Zentrale.

In my opinion, this position is untenable. First of all, there are ways to draw attention to the danger without having to resign from the Zentrale. Comrade Zetkin did not send a single letter to the Executive, although she was a member of it. I believe she was in Moscow much later than Rákosi and took part in all the Executive discussions, and still we never encountered great, principled differences. It was at her insistence that I went to Halle. When I returned from Halle, if I am not mistaken Comrade Zetkin was still here. So she knew very well that the Executive is not at all for sects but for mass parties.

If Comrade Rákosi really said what has been attributed to him, Comrade Zetkin is still wrong, because when she and an entire group left the Zentrale, this threw the party into a severe crisis. And that is why we say that the Executive was right to disapprove of this step, especially as it turned out that we acted quite correctly on the Italian question. I do not know what Rákosi may have said, but I would like to remind you of a sentence spoken yesterday by Lenin: fifty-eight thousand Communist workers in a country like Italy is not at all too few and is a very good start toward a mass party. Of course you could seize on this sentence as well and say that Lenin, too, is a man who wants a sect. Comrade Zetkin is quite wrong in this regard, and I hope that she now recognises this herself.

As for the KAPD, I would like to add this: the KAPD comrades say that it no easy matter for them to decide whether to leave the Communist International. We believe that, and the decision in this matter is not easy for us either. However, we must demand that the KAPD, just like every other party, submit to international discipline. That is the only issue here. The comrades tell us we must tolerate opposition, but they conduct themselves as if they are unwilling to tolerate any opposition from the International. They want to impose their position on the Communist International. That is the only possible meaning of the statement that their programme must remain 'inviolable'. That is to say, 'Do whatever you want, decide whatever you want; we could not care less about your decisions'. Over time, such a situation is untenable. We have shown rather a lot of patience in this matter. We want the comrades to stay in the congress and, moreover, we want to grant the party at least two to three months' time so that all the workers in the KAPD can come to a decision. But we consider it to be our absolute duty to pose this choice to the KAPD workers in the name of the International.

I also owe Comrade Marković a few remarks, since he polemicised rather vigorously against my report. He said I was wrong if I had reservations about centrist remnants in the Yugoslav sister party, and he referred to this party's past. We are familiar with the glorious past of this party and of many of its leaders, most of whom have fallen, unfortunately. We never doubted that for a moment. I must explain what induced me to make those statements. When the delegation of the Yugoslav sister party arrived here, I had a discussion with them. About fifteen comrades were present. After this discussion, it was clear to us that Comrade Marković, who is, I believe, chair of the delegation, did not share our point of view on either the Italian or the German question, but rather opposed it. Mind you, Comrade Marković said in his speech to the congress that he now considers the March Action to have been a step forward. However, in our first discussion he took Levi's position. I am very glad that on this issue Marković, too, has 'taken a step forward'.

My previously mentioned statement, which perhaps seemed incomprehensible to some comrades, was based precisely on the fact that Comrade Marković had quite serious reservations regarding the Executive's conduct on these two important issues – Italy and Germany – and made no secret of it. Of course he has every right to express a different point of view, but it was also my right to say that I feared that on these so decisive questions the party still lacked clarity on principles. If this is not the case, I can only congratulate the Yugoslav sister party. I have always considered it to be one of the best proletarian parties, and I hope that it will continue in the future to struggle in the front ranks of the international proletariat.

I cannot avoid saying a few words about an issue on which Comrade Zetkin maintained silence in her speech, namely that of our representatives abroad. In her opinion, we did not always make a good choice of representatives, or rather, we always chose them badly. In this regard, she coined the phrase, 'irresponsible' representatives. Comrades, given the present situation, in which our friends, whom we send on missions to various parties, are being abused and denounced – by Levi as 'Turkestaners', by Serrati as 'éminences grises', and Turati also comes up with various compliments – I believe it is my duty to make a statement on behalf of the Executive. Obviously, we do not have at our disposal any infallible representatives, and we ourselves are poor sinners and are not completely infallible. All of us, including our representatives, have made various blunders and errors. But *there is no basis for speaking of irresponsible representatives.* Here I must express myself in parliamentary fashion: I am saying that this kind of statement should not be made. The comrades whom we sent out to various countries did all that they could for the party. They ran various risks, and obviously they acted according to their conscience as revolutionaries. We never received a single official protest, either from a party, or a group, or an individual – not even from Comrade Zetkin. After we have suffered a defeat, it is easy to come forward and say, 'You acted irresponsibly'. It is easy to posture after the event as the wisest of men. Obviously, the Executive takes responsibility for the representatives that it sends abroad. The Executive is responsible, just as the International is responsible for the Executive. We ask all the parties to be so good as to allocate better forces to the future Executive than are presently available. This may improve the quality of its envoys in countries abroad, and also of its administration and political leadership. But we must protest that the hurling of abuse of this kind in the present period, as Levi did, is truly irresponsible. In such a situation, such language should not be used against *veteran, tested revolutionaries*, who may make errors as we all do, but who have repeatedly demonstrated that they would put their hand in the fire for the proletariat.

Comrades, I have come to the end of my remarks. Because of the incident with the French comrades, I must once again state explicitly that the March Action will be taken up thoroughly in the discussion on questions of tactics and strategy. The German questions on which you are now asked to express your confidence in us concern three important factors. The first is, Halle – the split of the USPD and the unification of the Communist Party. The second is the expulsion of Levi. The third is the March Action and the political turmoil. This third factor will be taken up mainly under tactics and strategy. The issues posed now for a vote relate to the second point, the split and the consolidation of the party; Levi's departure and our expulsion of him; and the reprimand of the Zetkin group.

I believe we have shown that we have done everything possible in the given situation to avoid aggravating the conflicts. In our opinion, the comrades of the German opposition should not stamp about so much in the past but should think more of the future. We of the Executive have done everything possible to give these comrades, who do not have decisive vote at the congress, the opportunity to present their point of view here, which they have done and will continue to do. But we strongly urge the comrades to grasp something that the KAPD comrades must also understand. They must realise that *Levi was perhaps their friend, but the Communist International and the proletarian revolution must be for them a greater friend*. That is why we are convinced, comrades, that the German party will return home strengthened from this congress. It will shake off those who, like Levi, broke discipline and stabbed the party in the back. We will all learn from the mistakes made in struggle in Germany, where perhaps the fate of world revolution will now be determined. We hope to have a unified revolutionary party in Germany, marching in step with the Communist International, and recognising the binding character of everything decided here. (*Loud applause*)

**Kolarov** (Chair): We will now proceed to the vote. The Presidium has meanwhile received three statements, one each from the Austrian and Yugoslav delegations and one from Comrades Neumann and Malzahn. First of all, these statements will be read out.

**Koenen** (Chair) reads the following three statements.

## Statement of the Austrian Delegation

The Austrian delegation rejects the KAPD's politics and strongly disapproves of Comrade Gorter's pamphlet. The delegation considers that the proper place for the revolutionary fighters of the KAPD is inside the revolutionary ranks of the VKPD. Nonetheless, the delegation voted for the Roland-Holst resolution in order to dispel even the slightest suggestion of doing violence to this party.

*Franz Koritschoner, Josef Frey*

## Statement of the Yugoslav Delegation

The Yugoslav delegation endorses the statement of the French delegation. It will vote for the resolution now before us while strongly rejecting the repeatedly voiced suspicions regarding the revolutionary purity of the Communist Party of Yugoslavia.

For the Yugoslav delegation: *S. Marković*

## Statement of Comrades Malzahn and Neumann

Radek said in a speech to the congress that the case of Levi was not about discipline but rather relates to the March Action – that is, a political question. This was not an accidental faux pas by Radek; it is the Executive's point of view. That is shown by the theses signed by Radek, Zinoviev, Lenin, and Trotsky, in which the Levi case is discussed in connection with the March Action – granted, from the angle that Levi did not observe the necessary limits in his criticism of the March Action and was therefore correctly expelled from the party.[39]

We do not approve of everything in the way Levi presented his criticisms, which obstructed distribution in the party of his correct ideas. However, we have held from the start that to do justice to Levi's stance, it must be examined in the context of the party's mistaken policies in the March Action. The Executive has recognised close to nine-tenths of this incorrectness. For these reasons, we favour postponing the vote until after the discussion of the March Action.

**Kolarov** (Chair): Two motions are now before us: that of the Executive and also that of the KAPD, calling for postponement of the vote until the end of the discussion on tactics. The vote will take place by delegations, and I therefore ask comrades to take the place designated for them.[40] The Presidium proposes that the vote be taken separately on each point. (*Applause*) There will therefore be separate votes on the Italian, German, and KAPD questions. Then we will vote on the other points and, finally, on the resolution as a whole. Is anyone opposed to voting in this way? No one. The vote will therefore be taken in this manner.

So we will first vote on the *Italian question*. Delegations opposed to the passage of the resolution dealing with the Italian question, please so indicate. No one. *The passage on the Italian question is therefore unanimously adopted.* (*Enthusiastic applause and cheers*)

We will now take the vote on the *German question*. Delegations that are opposed to the passage on the German question, please so indicate. No one. Are there any delegations that wish to abstain? No one.

**Interjection**: Yes, yes! The Yugoslav delegation.

**Kolarov**: I therefore rule that *all delegations except the Yugoslav voted in favour of the passage on the German question.* (*Enthusiastic applause and cheers*)

Now we have the vote on *the passage relating to the KAPD*. As you know, the KAPD representatives have distributed a resolution on this question. Does anyone want this resolution to be read out once more? ('*No*') So we will now take the vote. I note that if the resolution is adopted in its original text, the KAPD resolution is thereby defeated. I therefore ask that those opposed to the original text raise their hands. No one. Now, will the delegations

---

39. The 29 April 1921 ECCI resolution endorsing the expulsion of Levi was signed by a large number of ECCI members when it was published in *Die Kommunistische Internationale*, 17. In addition to the four Russian signatories named by Malzahn and Neumann, the statement was signed by Bukharin.

40. For the procedure on voting by delegation, see p. 170, n. 23.

abstaining from this vote please so indicate. (*The vote is taken*) I therefore rule that *the resolution on the KAPD question is approved by all delegations except that from Mexico.* (*Applause and cheers*)

I now inform you that the delegation from the *Near and Far East* has distributed an amendment. I ask Comrade Koenen to read out the amendment.

**Koenen**: Reads the following amendment of the Far and Near East delegation.

## Amendment on the Near and Far East

Reviewing the Executive's work in the Near and Far East, the congress welcomes its initiative in launching extensive agitation. The congress considers it necessary to undertake even more intensive organisational work in these countries.

**Kolarov** (Chair): I ask all delegations opposed to this amendment to please so indicate. No one. Is there any delegation that abstains? None. I therefore rule that *the amendment is adopted unanimously.* (*Applause*)

Now we will take the *vote on the other points in the resolution*. Delegations opposed to the other points, please raise your hands. No one. I now ask that delegations that are abstaining please so indicate. No one. I therefore rule that the *remaining points in the resolution are unanimously adopted.* (*Loud applause and cheers*)

We will now vote on the *resolution as a whole*. Delegations in favour of the resolution as a whole, please raise your credentials cards. (*The vote is taken.*) Who is against the resolution as a whole? No one. Who abstains? No one. I therefore rule that *the entire resolution is unanimously adopted.* (*Prolonged applause*)

(*The session is adjourned at 8:20 p.m.*)

# Session 10 – 30 June 1921, 12:30 p.m.
# Tactics and Strategy – Report

*Statement of the Italian Socialist Party delegation (Lazzari). Statement by Comrade Höglund, delegate of the Communist Party of Sweden. Statement by the Czechoslovak delegation. Karl Radek: Report on the tactics and strategy of the Communist International.*

**Koenen** (chair): The congress is now in session. The delegation of the Socialist Party of Italy has requested to be permitted to present a statement on the resolution that we unanimously adopted yesterday. Comrade Lazzari has the floor.

**Lazzari**: Dear comrades of every country, permit me to submit the following statement on behalf of the Italian Socialist Party delegation.

## Statement of the Italian Socialist Party

As delegates of the Italian Socialist Party, we must take note of the resolution relating to us, all the more in that it is in full accord with the Bentivoglio resolution adopted by our congress in Livorno.

Nonetheless, we cannot conceal the painful impression on us of several particulars in the motivation that you have linked to your decision, which in our opinion do not correspond to the real situation in Italy after the Second Congress. However, we promise you that we will do our best to secure the adoption of your resolution by the next congress of our party. We are fully convinced of the necessity for revolutionary unity in the organisation of the Communist International's different sections.

*Costantino Lazzari, Fabrizio Maffi, Ezio Riboldi*

**Koenen** (chair): We take note of this statement and anticipate that the Communist Party of Italy will do everything possible to clarify the issues within the Socialist Party in the interests of the Third International.

We also have a statement by Comrade Höglund of Sweden on yesterday's decision. The Presidium has been asked to make this statement known as well. The statement reads:

## Statement by Höglund

In his report, Comrade Zinoviev made some critical remarks regarding the Swedish Communist Party, which I wish to set straight. In order to understand our party's present situation, you must bear in mind how the party was formed and how it developed. The party was formed in March 1917 as one of the first that broke from the old Social Democracy. Three distinct opposition currents united in the Left Social-Democratic Party of Sweden. First, there was the revolutionary Marxist current, which developed primarily out of the youth league. Second, there was the humanist-pacifist current of the well-known mayor, Lindhagen, who wavers between Lenin and Christ. There was also the centrist current that was based in the parliamentary fraction. Obviously this created a degree of unclarity about the party, its programme, and its tactics. Nonetheless, in the most recent congress, the Twenty-One Conditions were approved by a large majority. Lindhagen and the centrists left and formed an independent party. Our party then took the name Communist Party of Sweden and adopted the Communist programme.

Comrade Zinoviev says that the programme does not contain the demand for arming the proletariat. That is not correct. This demand is advanced explicitly, and the party has carried out propaganda along these lines both among the masses and in parliament.

Comrade Zinoviev's comment about the party's position on the governmental commission is based on a misunderstanding. The situation is that members of certain parliamentary commissions are formally named by the government. The decree criticised by Comrade Zinoviev aims to assure the party of the right to determine when the party will delegate members to such commissions and who it will name.

As for our newspaper, *Politiken*, I do not deny that its editing has shortcomings and contains errors. But the comments heard about it in the Swedish party are of quite a different character. There it is said that the paper is insufficiently theoretical and too focused on popular agitation.

What Branting writes about our party cannot, in our opinion, damage our party's reputation in the Communist International. If it could, there would be not much left of the reputation of our Russian comrades, who are daily insulted and ridiculed in Branting's newspaper.

[Karl Zeth] Höglund

**Koenen** (chair): I submit Comrade Höglund's statement for the record. We also have a message from the Czechoslovak delegation, which I will read out before we turn to today's agenda point. The declaration reads:

## Declaration of the Czechoslovak Delegation

In view of the negotiations that the Czechoslovak government has been conducting for some months with the Horthy government,[1] and in view of the treaty announced at the beginning of this month between the Romanian and Czechoslovak governments, the Czechoslovak delegation submits the following statement to the Executive of the Third International:

The Little Entente created through Entente pressure and consisting for now, officially, of Romania, Yugoslavia, and Czechoslovakia, obviously pursues the goal of setting up defences against the political and military influence of the Soviet government.[2] Recent reports make clear that, in addition to the officially listed members, Horthy's Hungary and Poland are joining in this chorus, in order to promote the capitalist strategy against communism. In addition to the published provisions of the Romanian-Czechoslovak treaty, accords were made for the named governments to proceed together against communism. That is evident in the increased persecution of the Communist movement. Shortly after the treaty between the Romanian and Czechoslovak governments was signed, the Romanian comrades' congress was broken up and its participants arrested.

Class-struggle strategy must take into account the capitalists' secret and public diplomacy. Based on this principle, the undersigned delegation proposes that in view of the moves by their bourgeoisies, the delegates present at the Third Congress of the Third International from the proletariats of Czechoslovakia, Romania, Yugoslavia, Hungary, and Poland should hold a meeting to develop their policies, particularly with regard to propaganda among the

---

1. Miklós Horthy was regent and dictator of Hungary from 1920 to 1944.
2. The Little Entente was a mutual defence arrangement formed 1920–1 involving Czechoslovakia, Yugoslavia, and Romania.

soldiers of these states. Representatives of the Little Entente at this congress should issue a manifesto to the proletariat of Romania, Yugoslavia, Czechoslovakia, Hungary, and Poland.

For the Czechoslovak delegation
Chair: *Burian*. Secretary: *Handlír*

**Kolarov**: Comrades, I propose that we forward this statement without discussion to the Executive and the Small Bureau for implementation. The Presidium and the Small Bureau will convene these delegations to a discussion of this question.

Comrades, we now take up the agenda point on tactics and strategy, which includes the various subordinate points enumerated in points 3 and 4 of the agenda.[3] The two agenda points have been joined, and Comrade Radek has been chosen to give the report. Comrade Radek has the floor.

## Report on Tactics and Strategy[4] by Radek

1.) *The overall world situation*

The question of the Communist International's tactics and strategy cannot be separated from the facts regarding the period of time in which it is functioning. In determining its tactics, the Communist International must begin with a specific analysis of the present epoch. That is why we sought, through the report by Comrade Trotsky at the beginning of the congress, to provide as objective as possible a presentation of the forces now at work, a presentation that would enable us to say whether the world revolution as a whole is now rising or declining.

Beyond any question, the Communist International will exist and function even if the world revolution suffers defeat. If there is a lengthy breathing spell in capitalist society, we simply have different tasks than we do in a situation in which we perceive *a general rising tendency of revolution*. It would then not have the task of preparing proletarians to confront all the eventualities of civil

---

3. Points 3 and 4 of the agenda were 'Communist International policies during the revolution' and 'the transitional period'. Under the latter point were 'partial demands, partial actions, and the final revolutionary struggle'.

4. The title of this agenda item in the German-language proceedings is 'Taktik der Kommunistischen Internationale'. The German term *Taktik* then had a broader connotation than the English word *tactics* does in contemporary usage, closer to 'course of action' and embracing strategic as well as tactical issues.

war. Its principal task would then be to carry out organisation and agitation and to build armies for the coming battles.

Well, comrades, Comrade Trotsky's report demonstrated that, in our opinion, *there are not yet any visible forces* that would lead us to think that the development of world revolution has been interrupted by forces that are building up and consolidating capitalism. It was noted in Trotsky's report and the discussion that when we say events are headed toward world revolution, this does not at all mean that we dogmatically exclude the possibility that an interval will occur, and that the world economic crisis could give way to a transitory economic recovery. But the fundamental direction, the general course we are following, is based on this fact: *the forces of world revolution continue to unfold. What lies ahead is not a decline of world revolution but a gathering of revolutionary forces for new struggles.* This is not just our opinion. I imagine that no one in this room considers Martov to be particularly oriented, as a theoretician and political figure, to world revolution. Nonetheless, this Martov wrote the following in the May issue of *Freiheit*:

> The strengthening of counterrevolution by no means indicates that capitalism has overcome the results of the economic crisis caused by the War or has normalised the process of production and trade. On the contrary, more clearly than ever before we see *capitalism's incapacity* to restore world production on the scale of the prewar period and to assure its well-ordered continuation. Enormous and unprecedented unemployment, the systematic shutdown of factories or shortening of working time in every branch of the economy, an acute shortage of goods in some countries, while in others warehouses are overflowing with goods for which there are no markets – that is the pattern of present world production.
>
> *There is no basis at present for a counterrevolution of the type that began in 1849, when the crisis that had afflicted the popular masses was overcome by an economic upswing.* If capitalism cannot succeed, through overcoming national conflicts and planned international regulation, in establishing an economic equilibrium – and so far there is no evidence that might indicate that competition between national capitalisms is being overcome in this way – then after the present ebbing of the revolutionary wave the crisis will necessarily set loose *a new flood-tide of revolution.*[5]

Martov's comments lead me to the question of how much validity there is in the objections raised against the Communist International by the Two-and-a-Half International, especially in the remarks by Friedrich Adler at their

---

5. Martov, 'Von Niederlagen zu Siegen' appeared in *Freiheit*, 1 May 1921.

Vienna conference.[6] They say that although the world revolution has not ended, we placed our bets on a rapid victory, while they, as political realists, reckoned with the world revolution developing at a slower pace. Comrades, I will not tire you with a series of quotations from the Russian Communist press in 1918, which I could bring by the bucketful, pointing out that given the relationship of forces in Western Europe and the strength of the bourgeoisie there, it was unlikely that capitalism could be swept aside by an uprising of the popular masses. There is no need for me to remind the German delegates that since 1919 we established as the starting point for our policies the fact that *the world revolution would develop at a sluggish pace*, and that we must therefore struggle with all our energy against revolutionary impatience. The Second Congress took place in a situation where we seemed to be on the verge of a mighty collision between the forces of world revolution and world reaction. Nonetheless, all the resolutions of that congress were oriented to preparing the Communist International for an extended struggle.

The difference between us and the Two-and-a-Half International was not that they, as political realists, understood that good things take time, while we wanted to gobble up the cake right away. Rather the difference was that we have an entirely different understanding of the slow process of world revolution than they do. When the Two-and-a-Half International speaks of the slow development of world revolution, what they mean is that this period will be one of preparing the parties, quietly, peacefully, and gradually. Once they are large and strong, then the day will have come, and then even Adler and Crispien will fight on the barricades. When we, on the other hand, talk of the slow pace of revolution, we mean that it is an extended process of great struggles. Parties of communism will have no opportunity to structure themselves quietly and by stages, entrenching themselves, and working slowly and peacefully while waiting to see what time will bring. *There will be ups and downs in the struggle.* One need only take a look at what this slow process, this slow development has been like so far.

After the tumultuous struggles of 1919, did we enter a period of slow and peaceful development? No, a period began in which uprisings by the popular masses gave way to the *white terror of the bourgeoisie*, and the party was forced

---

6. A reference to Adler's report to the Two-and-a-Half International's February 1921 Vienna Congress on 'Methods and Organisation of the Class Struggle', stressing the centrists' differences with Communists. Communists, he said, regarded the War as 'a lever of the revolution'. But experience had shown that 'with the present strength of the working class, victory of the proletariat cannot by any means be assured.' Zagladin et al. 1984, p. 414.

to go underground. And then a new wave of revolution enabled the party to emerge once more and move again onto the attack.

This process, which has taken place without interruption in Central Europe, is only now beginning in the Western European countries. But even there the Communist parties are not able to develop quietly and peacefully while preparing for future struggles. Instead, they prepare while under persecution and through confrontations. I must therefore say that when voices are audible in the ranks of the Communist International – as in the speech of Comrade Šmeral – talking of this gradual development, and when metaphors are used like the one about transition from a war of movement to trench warfare, in my opinion this represents a *false conception of the pace of development*.[7] What we are experiencing is not the transition from a war of movement to trench warfare, but rather the *formation of great armies of the world proletariat*.

What happened in Czechoslovakia? Did you leave behind the period of war of movement? That is not true. You have experienced only the awakening of the Czechoslovak proletariat. All we saw in the December strike [1920] was the contingents of the Czechoslovak Communist proletariat beginning to take shape. And does the enemy permit you now to prepare yourself quietly for the coming struggles? He is trying to strike you down before you become strong. Let me call your attention to the struggles of metalworkers in Czechoslovakia. This is not trench warfare, where you order the troops not to shoot off their ammunition and to sit quietly and wait. No. We see two armies marching against each other, the finished capitalist armies and the proletarian forces, still forming up. Capitalism is trying to disrupt us during our deployment, to defeat us before we are in position. That is the general pattern.

As we advance toward coming struggles, we have no cause to give up a single one of the basic ideas around which we rallied and entered into action. The Two-and-a-Half International made strenuous efforts at its congress to squeeze out a programme that they could counterpose to ours. The Two-and-a-Half International was founded on the thought that 'Communists are imposing the Moscow course of action as a template, converting the experiences of the Russian Revolution into a universal dogma. That is why they favour the dictatorship of the proletariat and the soviet system. We, however, the Western European party –' As you know, Western Europe begins in

---

7. In his speech to the May 1921 Czechoslovak CP congress, Šmeral said, 'We now find ourselves in a time of organisation and of gathering revolutionary forces. We are not on the eve of decisive offensive.' See also p. 221. Šmeral's newspaper, *Rudé právo*, wrote on 24 April that the party's line of march was shaped by the proletariat's transition 'from an immediate assault to a war of position'. Firsov 1975, pp. 365, 371.

Russia, with the Mensheviks. (*Loud laughter*) 'we want to adapt our policies to the needs of each country'.

At the risk of exhausting your attention, I must not fail to show you what pathetic results the Two-and-a-Half International came up with, after such extended efforts of great theoreticians such as Bauer, Crispien, and Robert Grimm – and please do not take that as irony. They arrived at the following result, which is worth immortalising in the proceedings of our congress, as evidence of what brilliant minds can achieve through diligent effort. The resolution of the Two-and-a-Half International reads as follows:

> As soon as the class struggle has reached a level of development in which democracy threatens to be converted from a means of bourgeois class rule to a means of proletarian class rule, the bourgeoisie will in general seek to forcibly put a stop to democratic development, in order to prevent democratic state power from passing into the hands of the proletariat. Only in countries where the bourgeoisie does not possess the necessary and above all the military instruments of power, and therefore cannot risk challenging the weapons of political democracy with open civil war – only in such countries can the proletariat achieve political power by democratic means. But even there, when this happens, the bourgeoisie will as a rule use its economic power to sabotage the functioning of the democratic state that has fallen into the hands of the proletariat. Even in this case, the proletariat will be compelled, after winning political power, to take dictatorial measures to break the resistance of the bourgeoisie. The proletarian dictatorship takes the form of dictatorial rule by a democratic state that has been won by the working class....
>
> On the other hand, where the bourgeoisie disposes of sufficient force to maintain its rule against the mass rebellion of working people, it will destroy democracy and – holding its means of coercion at the ready – challenge the proletariat to open struggle. This struggle will be decided not at the ballot box but by the economic and military strength of the struggling masses. The working class will then be able to establish its rule only through direct mass action (mass strikes, armed uprisings, and the like) and maintain it only by dictatorially holding down the defeated bourgeoisie. The dictatorship of the proletariat must be exercised through workers', peasants', and soldiers' councils and through trade-union and other proletarian class organisations.[8]

Where is there such a land, where the bourgeoisie does not possess the military instruments of power? The resolution does not say!

---

8. The resolution 'Der Kampf gegen die internationale Konterrevolution' (The Struggle against the World Counterrevolution) can be found in International Working Union of Socialist Parties 1921, pp. 114–15.

What does this mean? As a rule, the proletariat must break the bourgeoisie's resistance with coercive means. As a rule the proletariat must establish its dictatorship in the form of soviets or based on trade unions and other proletarian organisations. What other proletarian organisations could this be? Certainly not parties. For as we know, the Two-and-a-Half International is against the dictatorship of a party. Not consumer cooperatives. That leaves only trade unions and workers' councils. But if trade unions are merged as instruments of government, then workers can no longer organise by branches of industry, because you cannot govern through ten competing branches of industry. They must be combined locally and nationally. What does that leave you with? Workers' councils based on factory organisations. So we see that despite the efforts of the Two-and-a-Half International to somehow come up with a new theoretical idea, and after all their talk about our theoretical bankruptcy, they have found nothing other than the banner of the Communist International, the banner of communism, the dictatorship of the proletariat and the soviet system.

But wait: they say that a different situation can arise when the capitalist state stands defenceless, without any soldiers. The Communist International would be happy with a situation where it faced an opponent that could only capitulate. It would not find it necessary to repress this opponent by force. We do not break down open doors, but doors to bank vaults are not normally left open.

To close my introductory remarks, I would like to refer to the new refrain being sung in recent months against the Communist International and its principal strategic and tactical thinking. This is the assertion that the situation in Russia proves the dictatorship of the proletariat not to be the path to victory. The same people whose fundamental resolution identifies the dictatorship as the only way forward are now beginning to whistle another tune. Confident that they are now under less pressure from the masses, they say, 'Look at Russia! Concessions to foreign capital; concessions to the petty bourgeoisie! What then is the point of the dictatorship? Russia shows that the dictatorship does not lead to communism.' I would like here to make only one general point. If Russia demonstrates anything, it is this: *It is extremely difficult for an isolated and moreover predominantly agricultural state to enter into a transition to communism.*

I must also ask this: in 1919 Otto Bauer wrote a pamphlet saying that the only correct path to socialism is via democracy.[9] It is now possible for us to review the results of this path. The Two-and-a-Half International can now refer to the

---

9. An apparent reference to *Der Weg zum Sozialismus* (The Road to Socialism). See Bauer 1919. The text in German can be found online at: <http://www.marxists.org>.

fact that this path was blocked in Austria by economic collapse and was also impassable in Germany, indeed, that the path led from Renner to Schober and from Scheidemann to Wirth and not from democracy to socialism. But let us consider the *leading, victorious capitalist countries*. Consider Britain, a country whose working class exerts such a great influence on governmental politics and whose social weight is so great that the government is compelled to take into account the attitude of this class. During the three years since the War, we do not see a single step toward either a state capitalism that would show some consideration for workers' interests or toward the guild socialism that Otto Bauer holds forth as such a brilliant perspective.[10] Not even a single social reform worth mentioning.

Russia has shown that a solitary and isolated country must employ its energies primarily in the struggle for its independent existence. Russia has shown that the transition to socialism is difficult in a petty-bourgeois country. But Britain and France have shown that the democratic path, pursued without any pressure of blockade, leads to undisguised domination by the plutocracy and by reaction. In Britain, the land of democracy, the government is now deploying machine guns against peaceful striking miners.

These comments are sufficient to motivate what is said in the theses. The tactical questions are limited in scope. The issue they address is that *we must carry out the struggle in order to enable the proletariat to achieve victory along the path laid out for it in the founding manifesto of our International*.[11] What is at issue is not our goals and our path forward but our form of organisation, the direction of our activity, and the stages along this path.

2.) *The theory of the Dutch school*

Comrades, the main task that the Communist International posed from its very inception for the new Communist groups and parties was to win the broad masses of the proletariat for the goals of communism and to assemble the working-class forces that play a decisive role in social and political life, the most active forces, as a proletarian, revolutionary vanguard formed up in the ranks of the Communist parties and the Communist International. This path was challenged even within the ranks of the Communist International. It was challenged by a layer of comrades who consider themselves as standing to the left of us. The challenge was posed theoretically under the leadership

---

10. Guild socialism, advanced primarily in Britain in the early twentieth century, advocated worker self-government of industry through national worker-controlled guilds.

11. A reference to 'Manifesto of the Communist International to the Proletariat of the Entire World' in Riddell (ed.) 1987, *1WC*, pp. 222–32.

of Gorter and Pannekoek. Our present debate on tactics and strategy is the right place for me to clarify briefly our position regarding this theory.

I will not wear you out with quotations. You will find these ideas expressed with Dutch conciseness in two pamphlets, *The Tactics of World Revolution* by Pannekoek, and *Open Letter to Lenin* by Gorter.[12] You could not find a more flat-footed presentation.

These pamphlets present the road to communism, with the same starting point as ours. World revolution is understood and presented as a time of long and difficult struggles. In Western Europe, they say, the basis for proletarian dictatorship must be much broader than in Russia, because the bourgeoisie is much better organised there. The peasantry, more enlightened and conservative, rallied behind the bourgeoisie in decisive numbers from the start. Finally, the proletariat is more active and has a higher cultural level than that in Russia.

I do not know why Pannekoek and Gorter believe that they have made any kind of point against us here. We fully share this opinion, and we have made plain to the Dutch comrades that the basis for proletarian dictatorship must be much more substantial in Western Europe and other countries of developed capitalism than it is here in Russia, where we were able to hold out with a narrower base. The disagreements begin only when these theorists address the question of how to win the proletarian masses for the ideas and goals of communism and for the coming struggle. Here they arrive at a concept that can be explained and understood only in historical terms; it is completely unacceptable for a Marxist. Here is how they conceive of the movement: a small group of Communists is formed, which then plays the role of prophet to the workers' movement, criticising all non-Communist organisations and proposing to them the goals of communism. This group does not struggle together with the masses for necessities of life, for that would be reformism. It does not set about to organise the masses, for it would be betrayal to coexist in an organisation with the counterrevolutionary trade-union bureaucracy. It forms a small, pure, and lucid Communist Party and also a small but pure factory organisation of workers who already agree on the need for dictatorship. And these forces provide the masses with an example.

What kind of example? They cannot launch an uprising, because that cannot be done by a small minority, except through a putsch, which they reject. An uprising must be carried out by the popular masses. They cannot conduct mass strikes, because that too requires the masses. What then does their example consist of? Propaganda. It is characteristic that in all the output of

---

12. For the pamphlets by Pannekoek and Gorter, see 246, nn. 5 and 6.

Dutch activity in this field we do not encounter a single slogan for action, a single plan for action, or a single idea concerned with action.

This propagandistic course is understandable given that this theory comes from a country in which there has not yet been a revolutionary mass movement. It comes from individuals of Communist purity. One of them is a highly esteemed theoretician who from his astronomical observatory studies the heavens, not the turmoil of poor, sinful people who are not pure Communists. The other is a classical philologist and, besides that, a poet.

Why do these teachings find support among proletarian forces like those in Germany? Here we must say that, in reality, these proletarian forces pay no attention at all to this theory. The KAPD was not formed because they said, 'The Spartacus League is storming into battle, while we believe that the period of struggle will be extended.' On the contrary, they left the KPD because they were more impatient and were pressing to launch the attack prematurely. Their starting point was different from that of the Dutch school.

The theoreticians and wise men from the Netherlands say we must not get involved in the petty struggles for a crust of bread. The workers must be told, 'communism – nothing but communism'. But the factory organisations exist in order to demand more in this struggle and fight with more vigour than the trade unions. This stands in total contradiction to the Dutch theory! The KAPD uses this theory as the Blacks in Africa use suspenders – as ornaments for their poor bodies. (*Laughter*)

In these circles, only one aspect of this theory finds a response. These groups of workers fear contact with the socialist and communist workers who are not yet pure. They hold parliamentarism and the trade-union bureaucracy in contempt. This provides them with a bridge to the theorists of inward-looking communism. The Communist International must reject this concept on theoretical grounds, based on a Marxist understanding of the course of development and all the experiences of the struggle. Never has the workers' movement taken so much as a single step forward on the basis of the theory they are proposing. The hundreds of thousands of German workers who are now on the side of the Communists do not do this because the Communists have separated themselves off, telling them that communism is the only solution. Rather they have done this because communism was present where the working class was struggling and bleeding, because the Communist Party was present even when the working class was struggling merely for wages.

We criticised inadequate slogans, but we went with the masses. It is only in struggle, in broad proletarian organisations where these masses gather together, in the trade unions, which may have counterrevolutionary leaders but still gather workers for struggle – that is where we have won a portion of the proletariat that now stands with us. And the supporters of the theory of communism as a distilled liquor have remained a small propaganda group. We would have liked to take them into our ranks, because they have produced many outstanding proletarian fighters, devoted body and soul to communism, but these forces are unfortunately squandering their revolutionary energy in isolation from the masses.

3.) *Experiences in mass struggle*

Comrades, the main task before us is to *win the broad masses of the proletariat to the ideas of communism*. The First Congress established this as our central task.[13] At the Second Congress, we took positions on specific political issues through several sets of theses. We mapped out a path forward, and that is the path we wish to follow. But in order to do this, we must provide an overview of our experiences in this field to date. Zinoviev already did this, in part, in his speech giving the Executive's report. Nonetheless, his topic restricted him to the relationship of the parties with the Executive. He could not thoroughly examine the record of the struggles we have experienced. The most important question we must now answer, comrades, is *how the Communist parties can generalise, sharpen, and exert Communist influence on the spontaneous movements of the proletariat*, transforming them into a struggle for power. This overriding question can be answered only if we examine the lessons provided to us by the practice of our movement and by all the significant struggles.

a.) *The British miners' strike*

Let me begin with one of the smallest Communist parties in a big country that is now the scene of mighty class struggles. Permit me to start off this survey with *the conduct of British Communists during the present great miners' strike*.[14] Comrades, I am beginning this way because I want to lead off my comments on *specific policies* with the proposition that there is no Communist Party outside the mass movement. No matter how small a Communist Party may be, it has the task of marching at the head of the mass movement in its country. During such struggles, it must concentrate all its forces on this mass movement. And in my opinion, the British example demonstrates that our new and small Communist parties are still failing to do the most important and simplest things that must be done in this regard.

---

13. Presumably a reference to the First Congress 'Theses on Bourgeois Democracy and the Dictatorship of the Proletariat' and Lenin's report on this topic. In Riddell (ed.) 1987, *1WC*, particularly pp. 163–4.
14. For the British miners' strike, see p. 78, n. 18.

During the entirety of this strike, I followed very carefully the British Communist Party's publication, *The Communist*. It must be granted that the British Communist Party has been able to shape this publication for agitation, in contrast to its earlier paper, *The Call*. The present paper thus gives the impression of having some relationship to the real life of the proletariat, rather than of having been published on the moon – the impression given by publications of many Communist parties.

However, it is significant that this paper does not carry any reports of what the party is doing in the mining districts. This fact alone aroused my suspicion. I asked our friend Borodin, who wrote an excellent study of the British strike for the Executive,[15] to make inquiries with the delegations that have just arrived from Britain about the facts of the miners' strike. And I would hope that a large number of comrades will familiarise themselves with this report. What we learn from this report is that meetings did in fact take place in the mining districts, but they were not organised systematically by the party's central leadership. These meetings were organised by individual Communist groups.

I asked what slogans the comrades raised in the meetings, what they said to the masses, what their stand is on nationalisation and on the specific demands that the workers are raising. One of the comrades answered, 'When I go to the podium to address the meeting, I have no more of an idea than the Man in the Moon about what I will say, but as a Communist I work it out in the course of my speech.' What does that tell us? The party, caught up in an enormous, tumultuous proletarian struggle, *is not planning the allocation of its forces*. That is the first point: the smaller the forces are, the more expediently they must be allocated. And that is not all. The forces they have allocated do not advance slogans for the struggle. Comrades are not informed what to say about today's struggle, nor about what to say with regard to tomorrow.

And there is more. In many localities, the party operates in the guise of 'worker committees', so that to the degree that its agitation meets with success, the masses do not associate this with the Communist Party.

Comrades, we believe it is our duty to tell even the smallest Communist parties that they will never become large mass parties if they focus on propaganda concerning Communist theory, or on Communist theory itself, or if they approach such a movement with only the slogan, 'Do not trust your leaders,' which the British Communists were right to popularise. They must assist the proletariat, fighting by its side in the front ranks. They must become

---

15. Presumably a reference to Borodin's article 'The Strike of the British Coalminers and Its Lessons', later published in *Communist International*, 18, October 1921.

known in the movement as the Communist Party, and help the workers, through their struggles, to learn the lessons of the struggle. If they fail to do this, they will never stand at the head of the working masses.

So we repeat the general slogan: *Go to the masses.* Every day in which this does not happen is a lost day for communism. And the smaller the size of the party, the more exclusively it must direct its energies to this task.

b.) *The Italian struggle*
Comrades, during the year covered by this report, we experienced *three big mass struggles of the proletariat*, which posed major tasks to Communists. These were the struggle in *Italy* to occupy the factories, the struggle in Czechoslovakia, and the German March Action. Let me examine the lessons of these three struggles, for only by examining their interrelationship can we correctly analyse the mistakes that were made and point the general path forward that we must follow.

I will begin with the Italian experience – the great September movement last year – and its lessons.[16] Let me briefly call to mind the course of events. The movement began in the Italian metal factories. It embraced the broad masses of metalworkers, and the metalworkers' union felt compelled to set itself at the head of the movement. The movement expanded to encompass factories that deliver semi-finished goods or raw materials for the metal industry. It leaped over to the chemical industry and to a large number of other industries, creating a climate in which the most deprived layers of the proletariat came into action. The metal, textile, and chemical workers occupied the factories, throwing the factory owners out on the street. The masses of homeless proletarians came into motion, and a movement of the homeless, linked to that of the workers, occupied the villas and palaces of the rich, housing their wives and children there. And the movement jumped off into rural districts from Sicily to southern and central Italy. The peasants set out with red banners, occupied the great estates, and formed red guards. And in such a situation, where the working class is advancing into a major struggle, where the villages are stirring, the initial and decisive question for us to ask is: what is the nature of this movement? Based on these facts alone, we can only conclude that this is a great revolutionary mass movement. The workers are seizing capitalist society by the throat. They are laying hands on what is most holy to capitalism: its factories, its moneyboxes.

Serrati, on the other hand, said that this was purely a trade-union movement. Think it over, comrades: was this a purely trade-union movement,

---

16. For the September 1920 occupation of the factories in Italy, see p. 76, n. 14.

given that hundreds of thousands of workers occupied the factories, sought to raise the productivity of labour – and there are hundreds of examples of that – and succeeded in organising the sale of what they produced? Was it a trade-union movement when it broke open the capitalists' cash boxes, gathering these resources into a common fund, which in turn was used by the metalworkers' union to issue currency and by the consumer cooperatives to distribute food? Was it a trade-union movement, given that it involved nothing less than the workers' attempt to take possession of the roots of capitalist power, the factories? The situation thus created cannot be better portrayed than through the words spoken by the Italian prime minister, Giolitti, on 26 September. He said:

> And so the factories were occupied. According to the government's critics, two courses were possible. Either I should have prevented this, or, if I did not act promptly enough to prevent it, I should have had the factories cleared by force.
>
> Prevent it? We are talking about *six hundred metalworking factories*. In order to prevent the occupation, assuming I had acted with such lightning speed as to arrive before the occupation, I would have had to post garrisons in the factories, about a hundred men in the small ones, and several thousand in the large ones. In order to occupy the factories, I would have had to employ the entirety of the armed forces at my disposal. And now, who would have kept watch over the *five hundred thousand workers outside the factories*? Who would have protected public safety in the country?
>
> I was being asked to exercise unattainable foresight or to take an action which, if I had carried it out, would have placed the state's armed forces in a situation where they were besieged and would no longer have any freedom of movement. I felt able to set aside this option.
>
> Was I then supposed to use armed strength to clear the factories? Obviously, I would then have to launch a struggle, an open battle, in a word, launch a civil war. *And this after the General Confederation of Labour had given a solemn undertaking that it renounced any political goals for the movement, that this movement would be kept within the framework of an economic struggle. I trusted the General Confederation of Labour then, and it showed itself to be worthy of this trust*, because the broad masses of workers adopted its proposals.
>
> If we had taken refuge in violence, if we had sent in the army, the Royal Guard, and the gendarmes against the five hundred thousand workers – do the critics have any idea of what I would then have been leading the country into?

This statement by Giolitti – a very clever representative of Italian capitalism, perhaps their most clever – tells us everything. Five hundred thousand workers were engaged in revolutionary struggle; the government was powerless; and the trade-union bureaucracy, trusting the government and trusted by it, broke off the struggle and began negotiations in full knowledge that everything they would achieve thereby would be no more than a piece of paper, once the workers had given up the factories.

Comrades, the Italian confederation is headed by people who came here as Communists and were, until recently, members of the Communist International. And this confederation concluded an agreement with the Italian Socialist Party. They acted jointly. So what happened? The syndicalist and anarchist workers took part in the struggle. The Italian party knew that the trade-union bureaucracy would strangle the struggle, but that these workers wanted to struggle. It did not insist that representatives of these workers be invited into the joint negotiations. The large organisations of railwaymen, seamen, and dockworkers were outside the confederation. The party did not insist that representatives of these organisations be drawn into the struggle. It wanted to win the majority. It proposed to continue the struggle. The trade-union bureaucracy responded, 'We will halt the struggle and gain workers' control of production.' The party let itself be voted down, submitted, and gave up.

What was the result, comrades? Today I asked the Italian comrades what happened with workers' control of production in Italy. Even though the government had signed a promise to introduce control of production by law if the workers would give up the factories, it did not introduce a single piece of paper about this in parliament. Comrades, when the struggle was broken off, the reformist papers celebrated this granting of workers' control as a great victory. They said that finally the two forces of labour and capital would work together: labour would supervise capital, to ensure it does not steal; the capitalists would supervise the workers, to ensure that they work. That would even re-establish the value of the currency, which was very low.

But, once the workers went back into the factories, the whites began their savage campaign against the workers. They began to attack workers' organisations, one after another. The editorial offices of party papers in Genoa, Milan, Rome, and Brescia were destroyed one after another. In Bologna they fired on the workers. Thousands of workers were jailed. The government proceeded intelligently, singling out those whom the Socialist Party had left outside the family of those in struggle – the anarchists and syndicalists, whose leaders were arrested en masse.

The great struggle of the working class ran aground because, in the face of this great revolutionary tide, the Italian Socialist Party had only one thought: may God let the cup of leadership in a revolution pass from my lips. Comrades, we do not know whether it was possible to win power in this struggle, but we know that a great deal could have been won. Two things, to begin with: genuine control of production, not in order to strengthen the capitalist state's currency, but in order to weld the workers together solidly in a broad proletarian organisation against the capitalist state; and the arming of the workers. If the Italian working class, in struggle for these goals, did not succeed in winning power, it would nonetheless have carried out a great battle against capitalism under the leadership of the Communist Party. During this battle, it would either have won important positions for future struggles, or, in the worst case, if it were defeated in this battle, it would have emerged enriched in experience and in knowledge about how to struggle.

The Italian party evaded the struggle. It excuses this by saying that its influence has grown nonetheless, and that in the elections it still received a great many votes. Yes, the revolution, the maturing of conflicts drives the workers to us, even if we make enormous mistakes. But when we make such mistakes, the workers do not win either insight in the road forward or confidence in their strength. They vote for you, because who else is there to vote for? The capitalists? But the proletariat's sense of power is diminished. Important opportunities go to waste, in which victory or partial victory might have been possible. And what is the result? Capitalism consolidates. Before the Italian elections, Oda Olberg, an Italian-German reformist, who has been commenting attentively and astutely on the Italian movement for decades in *Vorwärts*, wrote, 'The bourgeoisie feels quite differently now, because the Italian party has shown that it fears the struggle.'

c.) *The December strike in Czechoslovakia*
Let us now consider the December strike in Czechoslovakia.[17] It began when Černý's capitalist government, in order to protect the Social Democrats, invoked all the clauses of the thieves' code that bourgeois society calls civil law in order to steal the House of the People, property of the Czech proletariat, and turn it over to the traitorous leaders. The workers responded to this by striking, and persisted even when the government reacted to the first clashes by declaring a state of siege, and even a state of emergency, which was termed – using the old language of king-and-kaiser – *statarium* [martial law]. The government cut telephone connections and arrested the couriers of the Left Socialist Party, but even so, the movement jumped from one city to another. After only a few days, the territory of Bohemia, plus Moravia – in which Ostrava used to be a right-wing city – and Slovakia was in struggle, and the German workers of northern Bohemia joined with the Czech workers. The struggle varied in character. In one city the strike was waged with the slogan, 'Give us back the People's House and free the prisoners'; in

---

17. For the December 1920 strike in Czechoslovakia, see p. 76, n. 16.

others, wage demands were raised; in others, the demand was raised to form workers' councils; elsewhere, workers were called on to occupy factories and estates and to take up arms.

Nonetheless it was clear – and the leadership of the Left Socialist Party admitted it frankly – that this spontaneous movement caught them completely by surprise. They had not thought that there was so much revolutionary energy in the working masses. Since its founding, after all, the party had based all its politics on the notion that the masses had not yet progressed far enough to make it possible to launch an openly Communist Party or to openly join the Communist International; that the masses were not sufficiently mature to take up our slogans, if these were stated openly. Suddenly the masses were there, in struggle, more mature than their leaders.

I obtained a copy of the party paper, *Rudé právo*. There is not a single appeal in it to show the workers what the stakes really were and what lessons should be drawn from the movement. And when the struggle was called off, the leadership of Levice – the Left Socialist Party – published a manifesto that took note of only one single fact: that for the first time this magnificent Czech proletariat, which had been encased in nationalism, had risen like a lion into struggle, that nationalist illusions fell to the ground like broken pieces of glass, and that the Czech proletariat had made its appearance on the field of battle. But why did the struggle end in a defeat? What did the Czech proletariat need to do in order to be able to struggle more effectively in the future? Neither the appeal nor the next two editions of *Rudé právo* had anything to say about that.

The first lesson of the movement was this: you suffered a defeat because you had not formed a unified party, because the Czech, Hungarian, Slovakian, and German workers, although living in the same country, oppressed by the same state and the same government and exploited by the same bourgeoisie, are organised in several different parties. So the first organisational lesson was, 'Proletarians of all nations in Czechoslovakia, unite in a single party.' This conclusion was not drawn. The second lesson was political in character: What kind of party should it be; what forces should it break with; what forces should it unite with? The concept of forming a Communist Party came inevitably to mind, but this concept, too, was not presented to the workers.

The Czech party could not do this because their leaders were not yet resolved to accept the lessons that the masses had in reality already accepted. The masses had already adopted the framework of militant communism, and the leaders were not even limping along behind them. It took another four months before they decided to do, politically and intellectually, what the proletarians had already done in action.

And there was a further lesson. This movement in Czechoslovakia raised the question, 'What slogans should we raise when workers awaken and enter into struggle, but where the situation as a whole is not yet so advanced as to enable us to take hold of power? What transitional slogans should we raise?' The Left Socialist Party had nothing to say about this question either. It had thus surrendered, not only organisationally but also politically, the leadership of a movement that was rushing into its arms. So what we have here is a harsh and typical example of how a great mass party can let a spontaneous movement run aground, rather than influencing it and leading it in a communist direction. Later, I will define and examine the inner causes of the error that we see here. For now, I will say just this: it is a passive policy, which is the essence of the half-centrist currents that we still have with us. It is what these currents have in common with the centrists outside the Communist International.

### d.) *The March Action*

I will now take up an opposite case, which is a classic example of exactly the opposite kind of error: the German March Action. Before portraying the events, I must first say that we must speak both very frankly and fraternally about the meaning of the March Action and the mistakes it entailed – in the VKPD and in all Communist parties. It is necessary to understand the essence of this struggle and of the mistakes made during its course, especially because we do not regard these mistakes as a transitory aberration. The late and lamented Levi presented this episode in his pamphlet as something that was slipped into the worthy and thoughtful German movement by a few muddle-heads, leading thoughtless people like Brandler to suddenly begin thrashing about. There are very few lessons to be drawn from this approach. You would just have to say that the muddle-head should stop muddling worthy people. The lessons that flow from such an analysis are as flat as a sanded floor. Apart from that, it is nonsense to think that a new party, whose leadership has no authority, and whose members have seen how great and respected figures could fade away, that in such a party, the pressure of a single comrade could set the masses in motion and launch them into struggle.

I would also like to add another comment, by way of introduction. When we talk to you frankly and fraternally about mistakes, we do not do this because we assume the Executive to be wisdom incarnate, and that if we had sent Zinoviev instead of another comrade, everything would have gone like clockwork. We are convinced that the transition to action is extraordinarily difficult for every party, and that difficult and important lessons must be learned through struggle before the leadership has a sure instinct to think through every aspect of the party's relationship with the masses. Of course, we understand that it is much easier for us now to spot all your errors than it was for you yourselves in the heat of the struggle. But that is precisely why we gather in international congresses – in order, after the battle has been fought, to learn from it. We are not teaching you, we are learning together with you. There are now seven thousand proletarians behind bars in Germany, and some are telling them that they fought in vain. We testify on their behalf and yours that this is not true, because the proletariat learns only from its mistakes and from its clumsy steps. The losses that we suffer in order to gain these lessons are the price of our future victory.

So permit me, comrades, to speak of these matters now with complete frankness. I must review the history of the VKPD. It arose from the Spartacus League, which took the lead in the first upsurge of proletarian struggles in Germany. When the masses rose up for the first time, and it seemed that they would overrun the capitalist state, Spartacus stood in the front ranks of these struggles. Then came the period after the conclusion of the bourgeois revolution – for the November revolution was only the conclusion of the German bourgeois revolution – a period in which the army of German proletarians was gradually drawn together for future struggles.

Robbed of its great leaders, the party consisted of a few thousand proletarians. It had to take care that its strength was not frittered away in skirmishes over outposts, that it did not get tangled up in struggles before it had gathered a body of workers around the banner of communism. The Spartacus League had to play the role of a force holding the proletarians back from unneeded clashes, organising and educating them, in order to lead them into large struggles when there was no longer a danger that they could be isolated and struck down.

This was the prime need in 1919, a year of deployment, and it shaped the ideology held by a portion of the leadership, which led the struggle against putschist impulses that were then very real. This anti-putschist tendency viewed every movement with anxiety, fearing the possibility of violent and dangerous clashes. This outlook led to the failure of the Spartacus League [KPD] leadership during the Kapp days. Communists across the country fought brilliantly during the Kapp days, but at first the leadership was inactive. A few hours before the outbreak of the biggest general strike in Germany's history, they said that the masses were not yet ready. And later, when they corrected this position, they were still unable to play a leading role in the struggle. They lapsed into the stance of a loyal opposition, which effectively castrated communism.[18] When a genuine workers' party carries out opposition,

---

18. For the March 1920 Kapp Putsch, the general strike against it, and the KPD's initial stance, see introduction, pp. 4–5.
After the defeat of the putsch, the general strike continued, as workers sought effective measures against the rightist threat. On 17 March, the head of the Social-Democratic unions proposed a 'workers' government', made up of workers' parties and the unions. The KPD Zentrale declared on 23 March that in its opposition to the Kapp Putsch, it would support a broad workers' government that would include the

this has to be tied to the goals of communism. Our conduct toward our enemies must never be what is called, in bourgeois jargon, 'loyal'. When we make compromises, we do so, in the words of the *Hildebrandslied*,[19] 'spear against spear', rather than giving pledges of loyalty.

I call this episode to mind because it shows that part of the Spartacus League leadership was not a force pressing for action. And the leaders of the Left Independents [USPD] who then came to us consisted in their majority of people who had earned their spurs in the trade-union movement and as parliamentary representatives of their party. Through sincere effort, these comrades had made their way to Communist ideas. But it is easier to accept forty-eight conditions on paper than it is to carry out a single condition of Communist struggle in life. (*Loud applause*) It was difficult for these comrades to make the transition to activity.

When the party met in congress and we discussed its future and its tasks in the Zentrale, the general opinion was that this was a mass party with 500,000 members. In fact, this figure had not been checked, and in my opinion we never had more than 350,000 members. A party of this scope cannot limit itself to what is sufficient for a vanguard of 50,000 workers. It cannot content itself with peddling the idea of revolution. It has much greater specific weight in the overall relationship of class forces. When struggles arise spontaneously, it has the capacity to seize the leadership. Where masses are in ferment, it has the responsibility of attempting to launch actions. No one in the Zentrale or the congress opposed the paragraph that was quite consciously written into the party's manifesto, which reads as follows:

> As a small party, the KPD sought to get into the big workers' organisations in order to demonstrate to the masses in practice, through its proposals for action, the meaning of communism as, in Engels's words, the 'doctrine of the conditions for the emancipation of the proletariat'.[20] But it could not undertake mass actions, because it did not have any mass following. Unless it succeeded in winning the USPD's support for its action proposals, it was limited to critical propaganda. *The United Communist Party is strong enough,*

---

unions and the other workers' parties. It stated: 'The Party declares that its work will retain the character of a loyal opposition as long as the government does not infringe the guarantees which ensure the freedom of political activity of the working class, resists the bourgeois counterrevolution by all possible means, and does not obstruct the strengthening of the social organisation of the working class.' Broué 2005, p. 369.

The negative view of the KPD position Radek presents here contrasts to Lenin's opinion from May 1920, 'This statement is quite correct both in its basic premise and its practical conclusions.' *LCW*, 31, p. 109.

19. The *Hildebrandslied* was a ninth-century Old High German heroic poem.
20. The quote is from Engels, 'Principles of Communism', in *MECW*, 6, p. 341.

*where circumstances make this possible and necessary, to initiate actions on its own.* It seeks to draw together its members and, beyond that, its hundreds of thousands of supporters in fractions in trade unions and factory councils. It seeks to establish very close ties with the conscious masses through its press and its appeals. It seeks to give expression to their suffering and to enable the broadest popular masses to achieve consciousness of this suffering and how it will be overcome. It will be capable of initiating actions by the proletariat or of placing itself in the leadership of actions that arise spontaneously.[21]

Comrades, in my opinion, this passage mentions all the conditions for the party to play a leadership role. First, it must be tied to the broadest masses through its press. It must give expression to their suffering. It must encompass hundreds of thousands of workers in the trade unions. It must watch for situations that make mass action possible or necessary. Only then will it have an opportunity to lead spontaneous movements of this character or to initiate them. But the party had not absorbed what was said here, on a general level, as a living experience. Every German comrade will confirm that the party before March did not have a press linked to the broadest layers of the masses, and does not have one to this day. The circulation of our press is not even as large as the party's membership. (*'Very true!'*) Our press is still, to a great extent, focused on theoretical enlightenment. It does not speak with the passionate voice of a tribune of the people that participates in all the suffering of the population. It publishes mile-long articles that are educationally and theoretically very sound, but you do not hear from our press the cry of the masses.

I would like to ask comrades to take a look at the photographic reproductions of *Pravda*. That was the totality of our *Pravda*, our central publication in Russia, when we were struggling for power. It was just four pages, half of which were taken up with short reports from the factories. Whatever was alive in the masses was expressed in this paper. Your press is not like that yet, and that shows that the party has not yet carried out the preparations for great struggles.

Some say that actions cannot be prepared in the same way as a parade on Red Square in front of the Kremlin. Of course it is hard to manoeuvre in struggle with unorganised masses, but the party's preparatory tasks lie above all in the period before the struggle. The party's tasks of preparation encompass

---

21. The KPD's manifesto, 'Manifest an das deutsche und das internationale Proletariat', was written following the fusion of the KPD and the USPD left wing in December 1920 and addressed to the German and international proletariat. The manifesto was drafted by Radek. Published in IML-SED 1966a, pp. 356–72.

everything that it does in practice in every possible form – in meetings, in the factories, in the press, in the trade unions, in associations for proletarian sports, in the proletarian pubs – everywhere, on the streets and among the masses, to prepare for action.

The party set about its preparatory work, and here, I must say, it encountered what I talked of earlier: the legacy of its past, the passivity of its bureaucratic apparatus, which earlier had been dedicated to recruitment rather than to preparation for the clash of struggle. It was not possible to get good and intelligent comrades to write agitational articles and to organise campaigns. The party lacked the concept of a political campaign. One day they would start writing about a question of concern to the workers, and three days later no one cared two hoots about it.

The most important question facing the party was: *how will we reach the masses?* In Germany the masses are not unorganised; they belong to trade unions that have ten million members and to parties with millions of members. So the first question is how we reach these masses. The party chose the correct approach. It said that those who favour the dictatorship of the proletariat and communism are already in the party or close to it. After Halle it was no longer possible, for a while, to attract new layers of the proletariat around the slogan of the final struggle. We had to undermine our opponents. Where was that possible? We had to demonstrate to the masses that the Social Democrats, the Independents, and the trade-union leaders are lying when they say that although they do not want the dictatorship, they struggle for a crust of bread. We have to show the masses that the SPD, USPD, and trade-union leaders have absolutely no desire to struggle, even if the proletarians are dying of hunger.

It was this line of thinking that gave rise to the Open Letter, the decision of the party to initiate a broad campaign bringing the party closer to the masses and separating them from their trade-union and Social-Democratic leaders.[22] Comrades, we all understood that this could not be carried out through agitation alone. When it was decided to take this step, it seemed that major struggles were likely. You recall the struggles of the railway workers, the postal workers, and the unemployed.[23] Our concept at the beginning of January

---

22. For the VKPD Open Letter of January 1921, see pp. 1061–3 and p. 243, n. 3.

23. Fighting for wage demands, railroad workers called a strike at the end of 1920. In January 1921, the union leadership and the government reached a deal averting the work stoppage.

In early December 1920 postal workers and other civil servants throughout Germany held protest rallies to publicise their demands for a cost-of-living allowance. Following a Reichstag strike ban and threats to fire civil servants if they struck, on 12 December some sixty thousand civil servants demonstrated in Berlin. Unemployment rose in Germany during the economic downturn of 1920–1, and its effects were harsher due

was to compel the Social Democrats and trade-union bureaucrats, through our pressure, either to whip up the masses and initiate a unified movement, together with us – in which our task would be to increase our influence on the masses through this struggle and to heighten the demands – or, if the bureaucracy rejected this, to achieve a clear field for battle. We wanted the masses to understand, before the struggles began, how the Social Democrats and trade unions would conduct themselves. The government made concessions to the working class that divided it and derailed the movement.

I will now take up the situation in the party at that time. Some of the comrades who are now raising a hue and cry about sectarian dangers – Geyer, Brass, and the others – were against this concept. And so we lost a precious week, which was very costly to us later on.

We then carried out the campaign. I ask the speakers here who advocate close ties with the masses: where were the meetings that Communist trade-union leaders organised in the districts, when we were winning hundreds of thousands of workers in many places? Where was their attempt to pose the issues in a broad political campaign at a higher level, in which we could make the transition from agitation to public congresses of the Communists and the groups sympathetic to them? Not only did you do nothing of this nature, the left current did not do anything either.[24] We did not succeed in linking things together, and that revealed how difficult it was for the party to make the transition. But one thing must be said. If the left current displayed clumsiness, a good part of the party officials showed an indisputable fear of broad campaigns.

Then we had the struggle in the party over the Italian question. A right wing took shape in the party. I note that this wing later raised the charge that nothing had been done to initiate an action to prepare for a struggle. When Levi led the Zentrale, he did not once make any proposal, apart from that for the alliance with Soviet Russia – but that could not serve as a proposal for mass struggle.[25] The left-wing comrades were left alone in the party executive,

---

to the impoverishment affecting all workers. See the demands on unemployment in the KPD's Open Letter of January 1921, Appendix 1a, p. 1062.

24. In late 1920 and early 1921, a left-wing faction within the KPD coalesced in Berlin, led by Ernst Reuter (Friesland), Ruth Fischer, and Arkadi Maslow. This current viewed the Open Letter as opportunist.

25. Paul Levi had proposed the slogan of an alliance with Soviet Russia in August 1920. This demand on the German government was presented to the working class as a way of alleviating the effects of the economic crisis. On 2 February 1921 the demand was the centrepiece of a speech Levi gave in the Reichstag, and in early March the KPD began organising mass meetings around it. Although opposed by the Friesland-Fischer-Maslow 'Berlin Left', the slogan was supported by Levi's team, the Zentrale that replaced him, and Radek, and it figured among the slogans of the KPD's general strike appeal during the March Action.

and now they had to undertake the task of activating the party. And here I come to the basic error that they made in this process.

You say that we saw the sky overcast with dark clouds, such as the Upper Silesia question, the danger of sanctions, and the Bavarian question. Every tension was exacerbated. When serious threats arise, the first thing to do is to intensify agitation in order to alert the masses to the danger. During the first days after the outbreak of the March Action, as I sorted through the German papers, I gave Comrade Trotsky two packets, one containing the *Rote Fahne* before 17 March, and the other *Rote Fahne* after 17 March. Up to 17 March – and all the papers were like this – we were stuck in the same old rut. Then, from 18 March on, we pounded our fist on the table, shouting 'Kahr is flouting the law'.[26] This was the main mistake. You say that the mistakes were made in the past. Yes, you are right to blame the old organisation and the right-wing leaders, who did not gear up the party organisationally. Agreed, they carry most of the blame. But in the three weeks leading up to 17 March, when you were on your own, where is there the slightest indication of a change? It did not take place. You did not understand that *if you want to struggle tomorrow, you must prepare for the struggle today and put yourselves on a battle footing.*

On 17 March the Central Committee met. I want to portray briefly the errors that were made there, because they were fundamental. Anyone who does not grasp the mistakes of that 17 March meeting will be incapable of properly preparing future actions. I will not tire comrades by reading quotations. I will simply ask the question: what was the central idea of the 17 March meeting? What was the party saying to representatives of the districts? First of all, it showed them the great dangers from a proper perspective. What conclusions did it draw from these dangers? The first conclusion for a revolutionary Marxist was that we were entering a period in which broad struggles were very possible. For this reason, the party had to prepare the masses for these possibilities through its agitation and orient the organisation accordingly. And then the party had to address the question whether it was in its interest to bring the conflicts to a head as rapidly as possible. I maintain that the party was not ready for broad struggles either politically or organisationally and had no interest in forcing the issue.

You refer to the dangers of sanctions, to Upper Silesia, to disarming [the workers], but is there not a difference between the way these dangers are

---

26. The article beginning 'Kahr is flouting the law' was published in *Die Rote Fahne* 18 March 1921. Gustav Kahr was the right-wing governor of Bavaria during 1920–1. The article, written by Béla Kun, included the words, 'Weapons will be decisive... Every worker must flout the law and get hold of a weapon, wherever he can find one.' See Clara Zetkin's comments on p. 300.

perceived by the party's political leadership and by the masses? The political leadership of the International had to also take into account the danger of a British-American war, which may not come to pass. But suppose we were to tell the American comrades, 'Begin the struggle, because the British-American war is coming' – that would not be a mass-oriented policy. The masses do not respond to dangers that are still to come; rather they act under the pressure of events bearing down on them immediately. Since the party was not prepared for this struggle, your sole task consisted of doing this, of intensifying the organisational work, and transforming the organisation.

Was the party content with that? No, Brandler said in his report, 'We are headed into massive struggles and we must be ready to enter into struggle immediately after Easter.' It was seven days before Easter. What was his line of argument? He sought struggle and examined the question whether we should perhaps force the issue and provoke the enemy to take the initiative. And then my friend Frölich spoke up like a cavalry lieutenant, saying, 'Today we are breaking with the party's tradition. Previously we waited, but now we will seize the initiative and force the revolution.'

The representatives went back to their organisations with the general perspective that the sooner we engage the enemy, the better. Before they left, the party had to discuss with them what they should do if Hörsing invaded Central Germany. And what did the party tell them? After the bugle call announced a charge came misgivings, and the Zentrale provided the organisation with this orientation: 'Attempt to avoid the struggle for the moment; Easter [March 25–28] is not the right time. Wait until the enemy occupies the factories – that's when we should rouse the workers.' I expressed objections to one of the comrades from Central Germany, saying, 'You were directed to wait, and still on 19 March you began armed struggle.' When I said this, comrades, he responded, 'Had I not started it up then, we would have been in real trouble. *You cannot follow up with the bugle call for a charge by signalling a truce.*' The party cannot make out when things are meant seriously. When *Die Rote Fahne* calls on every proletarian to take up arms, no proletarian is going to think the party is saying that in order to stock up weapons for the long run. Such words mean struggle; they are the signal for struggle.

If a major error was made, it was that the party was not told, 'We are headed into great struggles. We are still too weak and unprepared. But if Hörsing invades Central Germany, we must struggle. We cannot leave our comrades in Central Germany in the lurch.' *But how to struggle?* With or without technical and military methods? If the party had posed this question, it would have given instructions as follows: 'If Hörsing invades Central Germany, we will stand by the Central German workers and proclaim a mass strike. We will mobilise the entire party around the slogan of defending the

Mansfeld workers from Hörsing's bloodhounds.' And it was duty-bound to tell the Mansfeld workers, 'You are a minority. If you try rough stuff with their battalions and machine guns, you will be defeated.'

The party did not do that. It did not raise the slogan, 'Launch the struggle with arms in hand,' and it also did not raise the opposite slogan. The party's position was unreal. And when the struggle began, as was unavoidable, the party no longer had a grip on what were the slogans under which the struggle was to be conducted.

Comrades, let me stress that we defend the March Action, and we consider it was the party's duty to hurry to the aid of the Central German workers. Why? Not for sentimental reasons. There will be many cases where the party is unable to provide assistance to proletarians who are under enemy attack. We here in Russia, when we held state power and the Red Army was being formed, looked on while our Ukrainian and Finnish brothers suffered martyrdom at the hands of White Guard governments after their dictatorship was overthrown. We stood by, tight-lipped, and said no, we cannot run to their aid now, because that would mean defeat for both them and us. When the Hungarian revolution was threatened on all sides, we did not come to their aid, because we were locked in struggle with the main enemy, Kolchak's large armies, and we knew that if we divided our forces, both we and the Hungarian comrades would be defeated. We saved the main army of world revolution, in Soviet Russia, and let its advanced post in soviet Hungary go down to defeat.

But I say to you that *in this case the party was duty-bound to act on behalf of the Mansfeld workers*, and here is why. Not the Zentrale in Berlin but the Mansfeld workers were the Communist centre of Germany. This concentrated mass was the centre of the German proletariat. There was also a second reason. The German revolution saw one party after another go downhill. It saw how the masses were addressed with revolutionary phrases, and then these phrases vanished into thin air. The Communist Party must earn the trust of the masses in the front-lines of struggle. That is why I say that anyone who claims that this or that was done badly but does not express an opinion on how the party should have responded to Hörsing's attack shows that he has nothing to say, that he is criticising the party's struggles but does not want to learn anything from them.

Now, comrades, we come to the central element. On 24 March, we called for a general strike across the entire country. It turned out that the forces we had gathered around us were much smaller than we had hoped. The statistics are hard to establish. When the comrades of the Right say two hundred thousand, that is obviously inaccurate, because no fewer than two hundred thousand workers were in struggle in Central Germany alone.

But that is not the point. The party had gone through a great struggle and had to draw lessons from it. How did the party do that? In the following manner. The party should have said: it is a slander to assert that the struggle was a Bakuninist putsch. A putsch is a struggle by a small minority aimed at taking power. We went into struggle to defend the proletarians of Central Germany. We did not do this as a conspiratorial group but as a proletarian party. We have made mistakes, we did not strictly limit our methods and our goals. Instead of saying this, the party proposed the theory of the offensive.

Comrades, let me first establish a few facts here. When we criticise the *theory of the offensive*, we must recognise that with the exception of Levi there was no one who opposed this theory. As I previously noted, Comrade Zetkin said on 7 April, in a resolution put before a session of the Central Committee, that she accepted the concept of the offensive.[27] I have that resolution here. It says, 'A large party is obligated to take the offensive.'[28] Comrade Zetkin rejected the March Action because she considered it to be a putsch rather than an offensive, but still, in theory, she accepted that framework. The criticisms advanced by Comrade Zetkin cannot, therefore, stand as a correction of this error. Why is that? The most important factor is missing from her criticisms. Comrade Zetkin did not say what should have been done when Hörsing invaded Central Germany; she said of a great movement that it was a putsch. And when she simultaneously said she was for an offensive, what was she proposing for the future? She proposed an offensive under conditions that were even less promising than at the time of the March Action.

When is it, according to Comrade Zetkin, that we are obliged to take the offensive? It applies, she said, in the framework of the slogan, *alliance with Soviet Russia*. If it is impossible to draw broad masses into struggle for fear of the effects of sanctions that might be felt over the course of a year, it is just as impossible to mobilise them in broad struggles around the slogan of a diplomatic alliance with Soviet Russia, whose favourable effects will be fully evident only over time. It is a completely utopian idea, which creates the impression that Comrade Zetkin supports the concept of the offensive but rejects the March Action, and has spoken in favour of an offensive out of thin air because she is trying to say, in diplomatic fashion, that she rejects the action.

---

27. For Zetkin's resolution, see Appendix 2c, pp. 1079–86. Further comments by Radek on Zetkin's statement can be found on p. 266. See also responses by Michalak (pp. 473–4) and Zetkin (543–4).
28. Radek gives here a rough rendering of the opening paragraph of Appendix 2c, p. 1079.

This impression is strengthened by the fact that Comrade Zetkin and the group associated with her carried a small detail along with them, which they shoved into the lead, namely Paul Levi, who denounced this proletarian struggle as a putsch, imposed from the outside. Paul Levi uttered the following pearl of wisdom:

> It is not my view however that *every partial action is a putsch*. We were *against partial actions in 1919*, when the revolution was on the decline and any armed movement only gave the bourgeoisie and Noske the hotly desired occasion for drowning the movement in blood. In declining revolutionary situations, partial actions are to be avoided. *In rising revolutionary situations, however, partial actions are absolutely necessary*. Despite the extensive revolutionary training of the German proletariat, it still cannot be expected – that would need a rerun of a miracle like the Kapp Putsch, but this time not misconstrued by the Communists – for the proletariat to leap into readiness in a single day, when a button is pressed, as a Social-Democratic party secretary, or Rudolf Hilferding, understands it.

What does this mean? For now, no partial actions; only when the curve of world revolution rises. In other words, the situation is not revolutionary. How, then, can the revolutionary wave take shape? Levi continues:

> *If the revolutionary wave rises again in Germany, then, just as before 1918, there will be partial actions, even though the greater maturity of the German proletariat compared with that time will find expression in such partial actions being more powerful and more solid than previously.* But, by a partial action, we understand only one thing – the proletarians rising up in struggle in one part of Germany, or a large city, or an economic region. We do not mean that, in one part of the Reich, or in the Reich as a whole, Communists strike or take action. Partial action should always be interpreted in a *vertical*, not a *horizontal* sense.[29]

At the end of his pamphlet, Levi says that if it is not possible to save the party – and only Levi could save the party – this would mean that the forces of counterrevolution had triumphed and it would be the end of the International. If the revolution comes, then fine, we are not against partial actions. Partial actions then mean simply that today Halle is in struggle, tomorrow Frankfurt, Berlin the day after tomorrow, and so on. Partial actions thus mean that the German proletariat forgets every lesson of its history and permits itself to be defeated one piece at a time.

---

29. Translation of Levi quotations is from Fernbach (ed.) 2011, p. 160. Emphasis is by Radek.

Comrade Zetkin's group struggled against the Zentrale, accepting the offensive, but only for some fine day when the Scheidemanns go on strike for an alliance with Soviet Russia. Meanwhile, Levi says when the revolution comes we will begin the whole routine all over again. This is no alternative to the unrealistic and unworkable theory of the offensive that the left wing of the party proposed in the heat of the moment, elevating its mistakes into a theory.

Comrades, why is this theory of the offensive so distant from reality? First of all, it is playing games with military concepts. Now it is true that my friends in the party have never imagined me to be a Napoleon, but still, from time to time, I read military books. When I was trying to understand the theory of offensive war, I decided to turn not to one of our German lieutenants from the cavalry reserve but to a really outstanding military intellect. I reread Clausewitz's chapter on offence and defence right through. While reading it, I realised how useful it is for a political figure to pay attention to military matters, and how dangerous it is when one does not give due regard to the peculiarities of the circumstances. Clausewitz makes the brilliant statement that 'defence is parrying a blow and its characteristic feature is awaiting the blow,' Then he says, 'What is the strong side of defence and the strong side of offence, in a military sense? In defence,' he says, 'I cling to the territory that I know well and let the enemy come to me. In offence I have the advantage of surprising the enemy.'[30]

What is the analogy here? In political defence, what is the territory that you cling to, which is better known to you than to the enemy? And where is the possibility in offence of surprising the enemy with millions of proletarians, who obviously cannot be mobilised in secret? Playing with this thought is utterly absurd.

But there is a thought in Clausewitz that can be utilised here. He says that defence is a strong means of struggle because I am defending what I possess. When I read that, I saw in my mind's eye the entire history of the working class, all its great struggles, unroll before me. What was the Chartists' struggle?[31] The defence of the proletarian masses against the effects of youthful capitalism. And the awakening, the great struggles of the seventies, and the creation of the First International? The youthful working class was defending itself against capitalist development. The great struggles of the last decades of the nineteenth century, the big strikes, the creation of big trade unions – what did that represent? The proletariat's struggle against capitalist oppression, which gathered new force at the end of the nineties. What is social

---

30. Karl von Clausewitz, *On War*, book 6, chapter 1.
31. The Chartists were a mass working-class movement in Britain from 1838 to the 1850s, which demanded universal manhood suffrage and other democratic reforms.

revolution today? Its development represents the uprising of the suffering working masses, whom capitalism drove with cannon fire into war for four years and decimated there, and whom it seeks to decimate today through famine-level wages, and against whom it is now taking the offensive.

We cannot triumph without the striking power of the broad, united masses, without their offensive. By and large, we will creep up on the enemy. We will succeed in instilling in the working class, down to the last man, the thought that they must save their skins if they are not to be reduced to the status of slaves. And because that is the situation, the idea that the party is committed to an offensive, as the main method to be used in every situation of struggle, is erroneous and unworkable. Comrades need only ask: how can we as a Communist Party initiate the offensive? Can we as a Communist Party, representing only a minority, organise mass strikes? Mass strikes can exert a measure of influence only when they embrace the broad masses. Uprisings and decisive struggles require the broad masses of workers. So an independent party has only a very limited scope for manoeuvre.

We must not close our eyes, of course, to the possibility of an offensive taking shape independently. Assuming that, as in the Kapp days, the enemy is divided in wings that begin to fight each other, then, given the general mood aroused by such struggles in the ranks of the enemy, an advance by a resolute minority may carry the masses forward in taking another step that drives a breach into the enemy camp. Or it may happen, if the trade unions continue to crumble away – this has already begun, and for now this is just a symptom, one that is not yet positive or revolutionary, because many of those who leave the trade unions remain on the sidelines – however, this shows that they have lost their confidence in the traitorous leaders. If this process continues, it is possible that a situation will often arise in which we are in a position to lead broad masses, united by their suffering, into struggle against all other organisations. But in such a situation it is the party's duty to examine carefully every situation of struggle and all the possibilities for struggle. When the party sees a possibility to drive forward, it must seek to prepare its shock troops by arousing the masses and linking the party with the broadest masses. We must always remember that although we should keep a step ahead of the masses, the gap between the vanguard and the broad masses, who are the heavy artillery of civil war, should not be so great that we risk being struck down in an isolated struggle.

Comrades, let us identify *the main lessons* of the March struggles. The *first* of these is that it is not easy to carry out the transition from agitation to propaganda for action. Even very good Communist parties, mass parties, of which we have no cause to suspect that there is anything dubious, should not rejoice, for *only in struggle will we see what is truly Communist gold*. Only then will it be evident which members are really with the party and capable of struggle. Only then will it be clear what is the real nature of the various shadings of opinion within the party.

The *second lesson* is this: the forces in the party that seem passive can emerge quite readily, in real struggles, as a clearly defined opportunist current, perhaps a half-centrist one. It is quite a stretch from Comrades Zetkin and Malzahn to Levi, and when the Zentrale was struggling with them intensely we had to act toward them in a more protective fashion. When the Executive approved Levi's expulsion, it simultaneously asked the German Zentrale to hold off until the heat of battle had dissipated and we were able to speak to these comrades.

It was not so much through his arguments but through the way he acted that Levi showed there was no organisational tie between him and the party, and that he was capable of throwing a bomb at the party when it was bleeding. If he really believed what he wrote, namely that the party was struck down and would remain so for some time, then there was no danger of the mistakes being repeated in the near future, and he had time to get in touch with the party and the Executive. If he did not believe that, why did he write it? Levi says, 'Group after group responded and went into battle under the Zentrale's slogan,' but at the same time he calls it a Bakuninist putsch. He is just showing here that he will employ any argument that can be utilised against the party. The other comrades expressed agreement with Levi but also showed, by their active participation in the struggle, that they were tied to the party. We considered these comrades as forces that the party needed, because they, as trade unionists, have a connection with the masses that provides ballast, keeping the ship from making sharp turns that could destroy both captain and ship. As for drawing organisational conclusions, we say to the German party: 'We have discussed the mistakes here so that they can be avoided in the future and so you can work together with all those who fought with you in the struggle, shoulder to shoulder.'

Comrades, the lessons of the March Action also demonstrate that we have an apparatus that is not yet battle ready. Organisations were formed for the struggle – military-political detachments – but they were shown to be illusory. They did not yet exist in reality, and if they were present here or there, their weapons existed only on paper. The little that was available was undisciplined. They wanted to give orders to the party rather than carrying out its instructions. The party's organisations, taken as a whole, were shown to be an apparatus that is not yet capable of conducting a struggle.

We must draw important lessons from this. Comrades, the March Action, despite its mistakes, is a step forward. But we say this, comrades, not to bandage the wounds perhaps caused by our criticism, but because we are convinced that *you are heading into struggles where you will suffer even greater defeats unless you learn to avoid such mistakes*. Moreover, in our opinion, the party's will to struggle, its capacity to unite masses in struggle, has shown that despite the numerical losses, which have been much exaggerated by the opposition, *the party has emerged from battle hardened and steeled*. It will be ten times stronger if you fully draw all the lessons of this struggle. We welcome the fact that you have begun to recognise these mistakes. If we compare what is stated in the 7 April resolution with the resolution at the international congress, we see a sobering up.[32] The fact that the German delegation has not submitted theses fundamentally opposed to ours is evidence that *the great although still young German party stands ready to draw the lessons from this struggle that will enable it in the future to conduct all its struggles, whether offensive or defensive, more successfully, in both political and organisational terms, and through these struggles to lead the proletariat to victory*.

4.) *Slogans for the coming period*

Comrades, I am not able to take up here all the questions that are outlined briefly in the theses, questions that you will be able to develop critically and pursue further in the discussion. Allow me to turn, in this last portion of my report, to the slogans for partial struggle, for actions that are approaching and that we will work for – the slogans we will utilise in working through these struggles. That is a field where we need only formulate what we have very often said in our theoretical discussions and our activity. The task here is to work out clearly the *differences between the minimum programme of Social Democracy, the action programme of the centrists, and the slogans of the Communist International*.

Comrades, you all remember very well the old programme of Social Democracy. It counted on capitalism existing for a long time. It worked out a system of demands for this period that were to improve the lot of the working class and protect it against capitalism's tendency to drive it downwards. Rosa Luxemburg once characterised the true function of the Social-Democratic pro-

---

32. The VKPD Zentrale's resolution adopted on 7 April, entitled 'Leitsätze über die Märzaktion' (Theses on the March Action), can be found in Appendix 2b, on pp. 1072–8. For theses prepared by Zentrale for submission at the Third Congress, see p. 490, n. 14. For the delegation's confirmation of their withdrawal, see Appendix 3d, pp. 1106–7.

gramme in a polemic with Sombart by saying, 'Actually, we are only struggling to ensure that labour power, as a commodity, is sold for its real price, and that the worker receives a wage permitting him to reproduce his labour power.' Karl Marx put it this way in his 'Critique of the Gotha Programme':

> Between capitalist and communist society lies the period of the revolutionary transformation of the one into the other. Corresponding to this is also a political transition period in which the state can be nothing but *the revolutionary dictatorship of the proletariat*.
>
> Now the [Gotha] programme deals neither with this nor with the future state of communist society.
>
> Its political demands contain nothing beyond the old democratic litany familiar to all: universal suffrage, direct legislation, popular rights, a people's militia, etc. They are a mere echo of the bourgeois People's Party, of the League of Peace and Freedom. They are all demands which, insofar as they are not exaggerated in fantastic presentation, have already been *implemented*. Only the state to which they belong does not lie within the borders of the German Empire, but in Switzerland, the United States, etc. This sort of 'state of the future' is a *present-day state*, although existing outside the 'framework' of the German Empire.[33]

What Marx says here with regard to the Gotha programme applies to all Social-Democratic programmes. Of course, certain characteristic features are unique to the Gotha programme, but basically this applies to every minimum programme of Social Democracy. It advanced demands that could be realised within capitalist society. Their revolutionary effect arose from the fact that even these demands, which were realisable and essential to the working class, were rejected again and again by capitalist society. Social Democracy today still rests on the foundation of this programme. It is poking about in the ruins of the capitalist world economy, while the forces that push the proletariat toward the abyss, threatening every day to shove it over the edge, are trying to awaken the impression that they are working diligently to shore up this collapsing shack. The German historian Dahlmann once said, in his history of the English Revolution, that the reform of a collapsing house is its collapse.[34] *But Social Democracy is deliberately trying to trick the proletariat with its game about reforms*. German Social Democracy tries to sanctify all its betrayals and deceit through clauses of its programme, just as the German general staff uses clauses of its regulations to sanctify the horrors of war.

---

33. *MECW*, 24, p. 95.
34. A reference to *The History of the English Revolution* by the German liberal historian, Friedrich Dahlmann.

The centrists try to create the impression that they do not accept the Social-Democratic approach to programme, and so far they have not proposed a minimum programme anywhere. They claim to stand for social revolution and to advance only action demands that can be achieved in the process of social revolution. What is the centrists' real position? This can best be seen in two countries, Germany and Britain – in Germany, through the action programme of the Independents [USPD], and in Britain, through the stand of the ILP [Independent Labour Party] on the question of the mines. Here is what these two parties proposed.

In the sixties, Lassalle told the proletariat, 'You should concentrate your energies on a single point of attack. Do not look left or right, but rather ask every party and every individual where they stand regarding universal suffrage.'[35] Now the centrists tell us that democracy has been achieved, that the issue is not the universal right to vote, for the burning issues are now economic in character. The question is how we can tear the factories and mines out of the capitalists' hands. Now they tell us that the most important area is heavy industry, which in turn is based on the question of coal. And so they draft a seemingly revolutionary plan to concentrate proletarian action on nationalising the British coal mines and on socialisation in Germany. This plan specifies how the proletariat can win support from layers of the petty bourgeoisie that suffer from the rising price of coal and even from the manufacturing industry that suffers from the private monopoly in coal production. They plan how the proletariat will launch the struggle to socialise the coal mines. They say that if this struggle leads to major clashes, these clashes will be the starting point for revolution.

You can find this silliness in Rudolf Hilferding's pamphlet, and of course the USPD press talks about it interminably. Considering this proposal, we find that it involves nothing other than *fleeing from the genuine struggles into the blessed land of well-laid plans*. Why was Lassalle able to focus workers' energy on the issue of universal suffrage? The working class was gagged, and the first thing that could help release it from these restraints was the right to vote. Whether they were beaten by policemen, mistreated by judges, or exploited by capitalists, the right to vote provided a lever with which to better their condition. Lassalle linked this question to issues affecting workers' stomachs and with the financing of cooperatives, which, it was then supposed, would be the salvation of the petty-bourgeois proletariat. Today the working class is bleeding from a thousand wounds. It is completely utopian to think

---

35. Ferdinand Lassalle was a champion of universal manhood suffrage at a time when German liberals preferred a limited, property-based suffrage that excluded the working class.

that the proletariat can be focused on a struggle for socialisation – in reality, the nationalisation – of the coal industry, even if only for a few months. The example of Britain shows how impossible this is.

In 1919, the British coal miners' union, led by Smillie, carried out an excellently conducted large-scale campaign to draw the attention of the British working class and British public opinion to this issue. Let me remind you of the coal commission's public hearings in which Smillie conducted a war against the coal barons – a war before a commission of inquiry, aimed at teaching the British working class the basic concepts of political economy.[36] Let me remind you that the coal miners' union carried out an agitational campaign in exemplary fashion, and even so it was not possible to keep workers, assailed as they are by a thousand other issues, focused on this campaign. The struggle for nationalisation in Britain has now retreated to the background of political struggle. It did not play the same role in the big strike that it had in 1919. The centrists pretend to be planning the organisation of the revolution, but in reality they are setting up a screen behind which they bring in the old Social-Democratic programme.

As Communists, our position on slogans is different from what it was in 1918. I recall the speech of Rosa Luxemburg on programme at the founding convention of the [German] Communist Party. Here is what she said:

> Comrades, that is the general foundation for the programme that we are adopting officially today and whose draft you have of course read in the pamphlet 'What the Spartacus League Wants'. It is deliberately counterposed to the conception that underlay the old Erfurt Programme,[37] that is, the division between immediate, so-called minimum demands for political and economic struggle and, on the other hand, the ultimate goal of socialism as the maximum programme. In deliberate contrast to that, we are settling accounts with the last seventy years of development, and of the World War's immediate outcome in particular, when we say *we no longer have a minimum and maximum programme. Socialism is both at the same time – it is the minimum that we have to accomplish today.*[38]

---

36. In September 1919 the British miners' union secured the near-unanimous backing of the Trades Union Congress for a mass campaign around nationalisation of the coal mines. For the Sankey Commission on coal, see p. 91, n. 30.
37. The Erfurt Programme, adopted by the SPD in 1891, was viewed as a model for parties of the Second International. For the text, see: <www.marxists.org/history/international/social-democracy/1891/erfurt-program.htm>.
38. Translated from Luxemburg, 'Unser Programm und die politische Situation', available at: <http://www.marxists.org>, together with an English version. For 'What does the Spartacus League want?' which became the programme of the Spartacus League, see Luxemburg 2004, pp. 349–57.

And what did Rosa Luxemburg propose as a minimum? *All power to the workers' councils, arm the proletariat, cancel state debts, seize ownership of the factories*, and so on.

What was the situation when this programme was adopted? The workers' councils were the supreme power in Germany. Formally speaking, the working class held power. The task of the Spartacus League consisted precisely in telling the workers' councils what is the nature of working-class power – nothing more than that.

Obviously we are not in such a situation today. The bourgeoisie holds power. The first onslaught of the working class, during the period of demobilising the army, was beaten off. The proletarian revolution is only now growing again. And we cannot promote this proletarian revolution, we cannot organise it, if we advance only the bare programme of the dictatorship of the proletariat. When workers are striking, because they have nothing with which to feed themselves tomorrow, we cannot come and tell them, 'Take the factories'. If they were able to do that, they would already be engaged in a struggle for power. We have to point out to them, of course, that they cannot gain any lasting improvement in their situation unless we win power and take possession of the factories. But we must link up with what they are struggling for right now.

Here we must say that the Communist International is not capable of adopting a programme whose various clauses speak to all these needs. The Communist International can only give its parties the following thoughts on method, which they must then translate into demands, based on their specific situation. The first of these thoughts is that when we say that there can be no enduring improvement in working-class conditions without the taking of power, it is absurd to *counterpose* this to the actual struggles of the proletariat.

In response to our Open Letter, the KAPD writes: 'You lame brains! First you sit down at a table with scoundrels like Scheidemann, and then you advance reformist slogans. Do you not know that even if workers now earn forty to fifty marks, the prices will rise again tomorrow? You are deliberately raising unrealisable demands.'

Our answer to this is: 'You can never win a single worker for communism in this fashion. If the worker is able to give his children a little piece of meat tomorrow, or the next day, because his wages have been raised by five marks, then we must fight together with him for these five marks. Rather than worrying that we may be reforming the capitalist state, we should focus instead on the fact that we are helping the worker in this struggle, and we will lead him beyond this struggle to other, heightened struggles.'

Here is our second point: of course we have many demands that we try to achieve when conditions are favourable, and around which we group all our other demands. These are demands that the working class advances in struggle in order to organise and stimulate this struggle. First of all, we must seek to lead all these struggles around wage increases, working hours, and unemployment toward the intermediate goal of control of production. By this we do not mean the system of production control that the government has introduced through a law setting down that from now on the proletariat must take care that the capitalist does not steal, and the capitalist must take care that the worker works. Control of production means educating through proletarian struggle, establishing elected *factory councils*, and linking them in struggle locally and regionally by industry.

If we succeed in seeing to it that the working class forms such organisations in these struggles in an autonomous, independent fashion, or transforms the bogus organisations granted them by the government, it becomes possible to unite the workers organisationally for major struggles. Those who wish to restrict the organisations only to workers who are already conscious and revolutionary are quite mistaken. When the need is posed to end capitalist sabotage and to get an entire industry functioning again, such slogans can unite broad masses who are not Communists, whom we need, and whom we will lead, through this unity, to further struggles.

The second slogan that we should always keep in mind and that we should try to realise in every crisis is *arming the proletariat and disarming the bourgeoisie*. We do not mean arming the proletariat only in a secret combat organisation of a small minority. In every field where we are active, we need to urge the masses to demand disarmament of the white bands. We must instil in the masses a determination to have arms. We must pose this demand to the government in every struggle.

We could name many such slogans. I will not do that; they arise from the struggle itself. What I am saying and what we propose as a slogan and a general guideline is that *in all the struggles of the proletariat we must not counterpose ourselves in doctrinaire fashion to what the masses are fighting for. Rather we must make the struggles of the masses for their immediate needs more acute and broaden them, teaching the workers to develop a greater need – the need to take possession of power.*

Comrades, we realise that the parties need to compare what they are doing in this field and exchange their experiences. So far, this has not been done. So far, the parties have not forwarded their programmes to the Communist International, and the exchange of agitational and organisational experiences among us has been quite limited. When this exchange takes place, this will enable us to create a specific system of actions and transitional demands. Their characteristic feature is that they aim not at refashioning capitalism but at heightening the struggle against capitalism. This is not the minimum programme of the social patriots. Nor is it a specific programme regarding what our dictatorship will do on the day of its victory. It comprises all the demands that mobilise the broad masses for the struggle for this dictatorship.

*Conclusions*

I have reached the end of my report, and I wish, at the close, to stress some of the conclusions that flow from it.

I said at the start, in full agreement with all comrades of the Executive, that we are *headed into major struggles*. If a discussion develops here regarding the passage of Trotsky's resolution that takes up the meaning of prosperity, this could happen only because some faint-hearted radicals are afraid of having an accurate insight into reality. Such a discussion could arise only from a boastful self-deception that the revolution must triumph because capitalism is crumbling more and more every day. They do not understand Trotsky's point of view, which is that *capitalism is decaying, but the decay does not follow a straight line*. The revolution advances, but with ebbs and flows, even in this time of great struggles. In noting this possibility, we are preparing ourselves not for a lapse into inactivity but for every type of situation in which we will have to lead actions. *We do not believe that agitation and propaganda should be counterposed to action.* Effective revolutionary agitation and effective revolutionary propaganda lay the basis for action. And given that we are headed into major struggles, we say to you, above all, that *you should be the bell that summons the living to struggle*. But at present we are still only a very small bell. If we in the Communist International today represent a significant force, it is not because we, the International, have carried out good agitation, but because *the Russian proletariat and the Russian Red Army agitated well, with their blood and their hunger. Their struggle, the Russian Revolution, was the great bell that summoned the Communist International.*

Everywhere our agitation is only just beginning. Nowhere does it reach the broadest masses of the people. When we say that we are headed into great struggles, we must also tell ourselves, *above all, use every means to go to the masses*. We do not know what tomorrow will bring. Perhaps tomorrow we will already be locked in great struggles. That is why we must tell ourselves, secondly, that our task is to prepare these struggles. The revolution cannot be organised. You can command an army, but the revolution is a spontaneous process. However, within this process we have the task of raising the masses to political consciousness regarding what is at stake. Organisationally we must assemble the proletariat's shock troops, its front lines, which – borne forward by the wave of revolution – can lead the masses in a gallant advance into struggle.

*Preparatory work is not counterposed to the period of agitation.* To those who say that we want to wait and carry out propaganda and agitation as before, we respond, 'Do not wait. If tomorrow you can carry out broad actions, all the better.' Passivity is the organisation's greatest enemy, but the opposite of passivity is not taking the offensive. Its opposite is, in the struggle, *to respond to every situation with the means appropriate to it.* Struggle is revolutionary agitation, revolutionary propaganda. Struggle means organising underground and training the proletariat militarily. Struggle is the party's schools, demonstrations, and rebellion. Our slogan must be to get the most out of *every* situation.

Comrades, there are some who believe that this is a shift to the right, because while we are combating opportunism, we are also talking about errors committed by the good left forces. That is mistaken. *The good left forces are not to the left of us.* The left forces in the Communist International are those who are preparing to conduct struggles. The right-wing forces are those who use opportunist theory to obstruct preparation for the struggle. And anyone who hampers efforts to conduct struggles with success by taking too little account of the realities of the struggle, anyone who has no feel for the need for preparation, he is not an opportunist, to be sure – he is an unopportunist. He does not perceive what is opportune and necessary. The Communist International, which arose as a broad organisation of struggle of the revolutionary proletariat against the falsification and betrayal of socialism by the right-wing socialists, does not need to defend itself against the charge that it has right-wing leanings. We have already taken decisions at this congress that stand as evidence regarding the Executive's course. There is our decision on the Italian party, our decision on the half-centrist tendencies in the Czechoslovak sister party, and our decision on the German question – the expulsion of Levi.

And because, comrades, we are carrying out a ruthless struggle against all tendencies that might obstruct our struggle from the right, we have the duty to tell you, a thousand times over, 'Prepare thoroughly for the struggle.' I recall the outstanding comments made by Trotsky twelve years ago in *Die Neue Zeit*, that impatience is the common ground of opportunism and verbal radicalism.[39]

Opportunism seeks to avoid the final goal, which is distant. Radical revolutionism tries to leap over the obstacles. The mother of both these deviations is impatience, if you consider the matter psychologically rather than socially.

---

39. Trotsky, *Die Neue Zeit*, 12 March 1909. An English translation, 'The Collapse of Terror and Its Party (On the Azef Affair)' was published in *The Militant* (New York), 1 February 1974.

And precisely because we have deep confidence in the advance of world revolution, because we have confidence that we will soon see the formation of broad mass parties, we tell you not to demand of today what only tomorrow can bring, but rather to do each day the work that this day demands.

Prepare yourselves, prepare the proletariat for the struggle. Organise it, lead it in the struggles that history sets before you. We do not need to hunt for struggles; they will come to us. And we will fight our way through them much better if we prepare for them. The mistakes that we make always represent a setback, and there is no doubt that we absorbed a setback in Germany and then had to overcome it. The lessons of the March Action will help us in this. When we speak in this fashion, we do so on the basis of what we have learned in our struggle. Zinoviev has already spoken of how often we warned against attacking too soon. And how often we insisted, 'Now is the moment; attack now!'

Comrades, we all admire Lenin's tactical genius. I say that not as a member of the Russian party but as one who followed a rather difficult path to full recognition of Lenin's tactical genius. Consider the contradiction between two tactics: the Brest-Litovsk Treaty and the advance on Warsaw. When the party saw great danger, it proceeded like a mule at the cliff's edge, feeling its way with its feet, for it was weak. But when there was a chance of victory, it rushed forward into battle. It set off for Warsaw, in order to carry the revolution further. It was defeated in the process. But this defeat is just as significant for a revolutionary as the victory at Brest-Litovsk. It showed that *tactical flexibility* does not cause the party of the revolutionary proletariat to be tied into knots or buffeted like a rubber ball. It may make mistakes, but it always acts with great caution.

Comrades, if the left-wing comrades made mistakes, specifically in the March Action, I say that these mistakes are evidence in their favour. They demonstrate a will to struggle, and that is why we stand with them, despite every mistake. But it is better to win than to demonstrate a will to victory. And that, comrades, is why *our tactical and strategic line is oriented to world revolution*. The path to world revolution, in our view, is the winning of the broad masses. We want to lead these masses into the great struggles posed before us by history. We will lead them all the better if we examine what is possible and take the maximum advantage that revolutionary energy and clear insight permit us to take from every day – even days when reveille is not sounded, awakening the masses and welding them together. If we act in this fashion, our victory is assured.

The struggle in Western Europe will be more difficult than the one that brought us to power [in Russia]. If we suffer defeats and have endured a protracted ordeal, that is because the broad proletariat must first learn from these defeats what is needed for victory. Our victory in 1917 was possible because we already had thirty years of revolutionary experiences behind us and because we were defeated in 1905. History *gives the Communist International the possibility of shortening the proletariat's ordeal*. We stand before a historical turning point, and there is no power – at least, we do not perceive any power – that can save capitalism. We wish to hasten its death, and that can happen only if we bring the broad masses together under the banner of communism.

*We are only the awakeners and organisers.* It is the proletariat that will carry capitalism to its grave. The proletariat will be the great hammer that drives nails into its coffin. The proletariat, with its broad and ponderous masses, which develop only slowly, harbouring a thousand doubts, is nonetheless the unshakable foundation on which we will struggle and win. (*Tumultuous, prolonged applause*)

**Koenen** (chair): I would like to make a few important announcements. Several proposals have been made regarding how to proceed with the agenda, and how to open the discussion on the question of tactics and strategy and on Comrade Radek's report. The Presidium will consider these proposals and then make a specific motion to the congress. We will hold our next session tomorrow morning, and the agenda point will be the discussion of Comrade Radek's report.

(*The session is adjourned at 4:20 p.m.*)

# Session 11 – 1 July 1921, 12:40 p.m.
## Tactics and Strategy – Discussion

*Discussion on Radek's report. Speakers: Hempel, Terracini, Lenin, Michalak, Vaughan.*

**Koenen** (Chair): The session is now open. Many comrades have asked the Presidium to speed the pace of the discussions. In particular, the trade-union delegates pressed us to bring our discussions to a close rapidly, so that they will be able to hold their congress of the red trade-union International. The Presidium considers it appropriate to be stricter in allocating time for future agenda points. There was much discussion under the first agenda point of a wide variety of questions, which could have been held over for later agenda points.

In our opinion, it should be possible for the discussion on tactics and strategy that is now being opened to be essentially concluded in two sessions. We want at least to try. Then, of course, the written material, the theses, and the motions, will be turned over to a commission. Perhaps it will be possible, after the commission discussions, to devote a half-day to these questions. But we want at least to make the attempt to deal with this question in two sessions. Comrades who wish to speak are requested to make their request.

We will now begin the discussion on tactics and strategy. The first speaker is the representative of the KAPD, Comrade Hempel, who has extended speaking time.

**Hempel** (Appel, KAPD): Comrades, after listening to Comrade Radek's report on the tactics and strategy to be adopted by the Communist International, we can say that we agree with a portion of his initial comments: namely, the assertion, based on examining the economic situation, that we are witnessing the collapse of the capitalist economic system, which will lead necessarily and unconditionally to proletarian revolution. However, as soon as we come to the question of how this proletarian revolution unfolds, how the revolutionary proletarian masses form up in struggle, differences become apparent.

I will attempt to go into this quite briefly, since I have been given little time. Let us consider the period of the revolution in Russia, in 1917. We observe revolution in Germany and Austria, and all the revolutionary struggles of this period, and we note that the proletariat in Russia formed up for struggle in soviets. In Germany we call them councils. That is how the proletariat formed up; that was the organisational form of the masses.

We also observe this in the smaller revolutionary struggles that took place in Italy during the occupation of the factories. The proletariat has its councils, or at least the form of councils. The proletariat in Britain had factory councils, and they are forming now in the great miners' strike – the genuine revolutionary leadership of the shop stewards.[1] In all the revolutionary struggles of the German proletariat after 1918, ranging from the very small to the very large, the struggle was structured by councils, factories, and workplaces. That is what we observe in the revolution.

We should reflect on this. We should conclude that if this is how the proletariat forms up in revolution, then that is how we as Communists, who wish to be the leadership in this revolution and must be that leadership, should undertake to organise the revolutionary proletariat. That is what we of the Communist Workers' Party say. And this is not something cooked up, as Comrade Radek believes, in the brain and test tube of Comrade Gorter in the Netherlands. It arises from the experiences of the struggle that we have fought since 1918. We workers are not great theoreticians; we have only the experiences of our struggles. We have learned to separate off revolutionary workers who really want to fight from the old structures of the workers' movement and give them support in the new forms in which the revolution is taking place.

---

1. Shop stewards committees, elective organs of workers' struggle that developed in Britain before World War I, expanded rapidly during the War. Centred in the Clyde Valley industrial district, these committees spread throughout England and Scotland. After 1917 the movement took on an increasingly political character, actively opposing British military intervention against Soviet Russia.

That becomes fully apparent if you consider the tasks assumed by the old workers' movement – or more precisely, the workers' movement before the period of outbreak of direct revolution. Its tasks were, first, to utilise the political organisations of the working class – the parties – to send deputies into parliament and other institutions made available by the bourgeoisie and the bureaucracy for working-class representation. That was the first task, and that was done. And for that time, it was correct.

The economic organisations of the working class, for their part, had the task of improving the status of the working class in capitalism, through struggle, and when struggle was no longer possible, through negotiations. I must be brief. Those were the tasks of workers' organisations before the War. But when the revolution broke out, new tasks became apparent. The workers' organisations could no longer focus on the struggle for wage increases and content themselves with that. They could no longer set their primary goal as merely being represented in parliament and pushing through improvements for the working class. That is reformism. Now we are told, 'But we don't want that', and we reply: we believe that you do not want it, but when you take the same path as the old workers' movement, you will be swept along down this path. You cannot avoid it, and no number of resolutions will protect you from that. This is shown by experience.

The old workers' movement had good reason for its specialised organisations. After all, what do you need in order to be represented in parliament? You do not need revolutionary fighters. You need education regarding conditions in this state plus people who know how to negotiate – parliamentarians – who send you reports. That is all.

What is needed for the economic struggle? You need a unification of workers. You elect union representatives, able workers, who can negotiate with the employers and their organisations. Such organisations need leaders, and the masses follow them unquestioningly. You collect money in order to be able to carry out a strike. You set up support organisations – the trade unions – which are tools of the working class for a quite specific purpose, namely, to find a place within the capitalist order. And if Communists then believe that this tool, incapable of conducting revolutionary struggles, and this leadership and these organisations can be utilised to carry out revolutions – they are wrong and they will be crushed.

Again and again we experience that the workers' organisations following this path fail in the decisive battles, despite all their revolutionary speeches. That is the great lesson that we draw from these experiences. That is why we say that the proletariat must keep focused on the goal, which is to demolish capitalist power, demolish state power. It is only for this purpose that the proletariat must create organisations. The proletariat creates them itself. We see this when in a factory, let us say in Germany, workers raise demands that the employers cannot accept in this period. What do the workers do? They elect as representatives people who they know, people from their factories, their workplaces. They must conduct this struggle, from its earliest beginnings, against the will of the trade unions. That is demonstrated by a lengthy history – from small struggles and small strikes right up to the recent massive struggles.

So the working class is forced to organise itself in the revolutionary struggle in the economy, and is doing so. We say that we, as Communists, should recognise this. We should recognise that the path of the old workers' movement is wrong. We have something new – the revolutionary struggle. That is why we say that workers should organise in a manner consistent with the development of the revolution to this point, and we Communists should be in the leadership when they go into battle. That is why we say that Communists must get the proletariat to organise by factory and workplace with a quite specific goal and purpose, namely to take over production, the productive forces, the factories, and all the rest, and take all this in hand. With this in view, the proletariat must organise on such a basis, for these are the things for which its struggle is waged.

Comrades, I am not able to go into these matters in more detail. It is up to Communists to recognise and come to grips with these tasks.

We now come to the next point. The methods of proletarian struggle flow from its tasks and the way it forms up and organises. Its methods, which must be revolutionary, are determined by analysing the situation of the economy and of our opponent at this time. At present the enemy is taking countermeasures. That did not begin now, but it is more intense now. These countermeasures are designed to maintain its power – the power of its state and also the profits generated by the economy. They are incapable of getting the entire economy working. That is not possible. What they can do is to consolidate one segment of the economy, its core, at the cost of the other. That is taking place today in every country of the world. We Communists must analyse this and examine what the further effects will be of this start-up by these very conscious capitalists.

The result for the proletariat is that a segment of it is being sustained – those in the factories that are being maintained, in the economic sector that is kept viable. And we see that this core, these cartels, these super-cartels in every country are joining together and are dominant. However, if one segment of the proletariat is engaged and sustained by these cartelised factories, another segment is ejected. And this extremely large mass of unemployed, who cannot find a job in the present system, are condemned to extinction. In this way, the working class is divided in two and split economically. The worker in the factory, who is still able to get by, is anxious not to lose his job. And the worker who is already outside the factory is the enemy of those that still have a livelihood. Capitalism strives consciously to achieve this split, while the bourgeois press fans the flames. That is how capitalism is being reconstructed today.

We do not say that this reconstruction of capitalist rule is permanent. It is a temporary reconstruction built on the corpses of starving proletarians. We must recognise this situation, which determines our policies in struggle and the methods we utilise to move forward. We Communists must, with the aid of the proletariat, prevent the consolidation of this one segment of the economy, the proletariat, from taking place. For that would be a defeat for the proletariat. We have to take up the struggle in all its phases, wherever the slightest opening exists. We have to use every means – I agree with Comrade Radek; use every means – to prevent the economy from being reconstructed in line with the capitalists' plans.

To this end we must utilise the enormous and constantly growing mass of the unemployed and starving workers. We must unite them. We do not unite them so that they can elect members of parliament or vote for resolutions. Our appeal to them must be based on their immediate needs. We must organise them in councils and bring them into contact with other councils and with union stewards from the factories. That is how we create the proletariat's organisation; that is how we unite the proletariat in life. We will have to engage in consistent struggle. The platform for the unification of the revolutionary proletariat is not, as Radek suggested, the speeches, the decisions, and the open letters. The platform is the ongoing struggle.

Comrade Radek spoke of offence and defence. At the beginning of this year, we saw how things in Germany were developing. We saw how bourgeois democracy was being maintained, using every means, from the Social Democrats to the Independents, using all parliamentary parties and organisations. This process was advancing at a crawl, and capitalism required this crawl. It had to be stopped. We called for every conflict in every factory to be utilised and driven forward, for defying the individual capitalists at every opportunity, for the establishment of ties from one factory to another, for intensifying the struggles.

Comrades, as we have seen, this process led to a sharpening of the situation in Central Germany, and then the March Action happened. Hörsing launched his attacks, and the torpor in Germany was banished. This was an offensive, as we conceive of it, and it had to be carried out.

But ordering the offensive quite suddenly, without preparation, is nonsense. Let me refer to our conduct on 20 August 1920, when the Red Army troops were on the border of East Prussia and near Warsaw.[2] That must also be considered in judging offensive and defensive. We of the KAPD had prepared across the country for many weeks, through public meetings, leaflets, propaganda in the factories, and by utilising the mood regarding the presence of Red Army troops at the borders. Then when troops and munitions from France started rolling across Germany, the question was posed of what to do. We decided then to drive things forward toward a rebellion. We began preparing for that systematically in every field of work.

During the evening before 20 August and on the day itself – only now can we speak of these things, because previously this would have landed our comrades in prison – *Die Rote Fahne* and *Freiheit* and all the provincial newspapers carried an appeal: 'To the proletarians of Germany: Beware! Provocateurs, spies, and unscrupulous elements want to draw you into a bloodbath', and so on. We now concede freely that if we ever made a mistake, it was on this day. Our mistake lay in bending every effort to hold back the action that was to break out in the most important sectors of Germany.

We were successful in many localities. Today people sneer at us because our comrades in Velbert and Köthen proclaimed a soviet republic. We say: let them jeer, it does not bother us. But it was the duty of Communists to launch an offensive at that moment. We regard that as an offensive in Germany, and internationally it was not an offensive but simple solidarity with the struggles of the Russian brothers, who had been placed under great pressure by the deliveries of war materiel. These are things that must be said in passing judgement on offensive and defensive.

Now let us consider partial demands. I already touched on this. We have the Open Letter and workers' control of production – these are partial demands. And Comrade Radek has said very clearly how partial demands should look and how they should not look. The Open Letter in Germany, supported by the trade unions and the parliamentary parties, this Open Letter was opportunist and could only be opportunist. An Open Letter based on economic and revolutionary organisations offers what Comrade Radek finds lacking in the VKPD. Where do we see meetings of the action committees that were needed to create the foundation for the struggle that the Open Letter was supposed to call into being? Yes, we rejected it, because we knew these people, we knew it could lead to nothing but negotiations with the government; it was all just

---

2. For the KAPD's participation in the 20 August 1920 uprisings in Velbert and Köthen, see p. 240, n. 1.

talk. That is why we rejected it. We are always in favour of launching a struggle, but you must also consider how that is done. You can't just produce it out of thin air. Revolution requires preparations, which must be undertaken. These preparations would have been made if there were revolutionary organisations, and they would have existed, if the Spartacus League Zentrale and the Third International had not for two years been calling for using the old trade unions [*Gewerkschaften*] rather than building factory organisations and syndicalist unions [*Unionen*].[3] You must see things as they are. Ask the fighters permanently engaged in struggle; they will tell you where things stand. They will show you how to struggle. However, I do not have time to go into this in detail.

There has also been discussion of partial actions. Our position is that we never reject partial actions. Every action, every struggle – for they are actions too – must be developed and driven onward. We cannot say that we reject this struggle and that struggle. Struggles that arise from workers' economic deprivation must be driven forward by every available means. Especially in a country like Germany, or like Britain and other countries with a bourgeois democracy, who have experienced bourgeois democracy for forty or fifty years and felt its effects, the workers must first of all become accustomed to struggle. Slogans must correspond to these partial actions.

Let us take an example. Suppose that a so-called general strike breaks out in a factory, in several factories, and sweeps across a small region. In such a case the slogan cannot be, 'Struggle for the dictatorship of the proletariat'. That would be nonsense. The slogans must conform to the circumstances, and to what can be achieved there. The slogans must also be brought into line with the nature of the struggle that is to sustain this movement. Let us assume that a generalised uprising is taking place in a country. In this case, the slogans should be for a struggle for our basic goals.[4]

Now I would like to take up the March Action, in order to show briefly what have been the effects of your teachings in this case, given that this has not yet been touched on here. The March Action, in itself, was not an action that could bring about the overthrow of capitalist power. Everyone now agrees on that point. We saw it too. But it was nonetheless necessary to raise the slogan, 'Down with the government!' This slogan was required because otherwise

---

3. *Gewerkschaften* is the standard word in German for trade unions. Anarcho-syndicalist and Left Communist forces began after the War to create a new type of workplace organisation, termed *Unionen*, which combined party and union functions and were counterposed to the conventional unions. To reflect this distinction, *Unionen* is translated as 'syndicalist unions'.
4. The translation here follows the Russian text; the German text inverts the meaning.

proletarians in Germany can no longer carry out a genuine struggle. However, it was also necessary to raise this slogan because overall, in Germany, proletarians have no alternative. The existing social order means that millions and millions of proletarians will die of hunger, that larger and larger portions of the population will die. Accordingly, the working class, facing this emergency, has no option but to set itself the goal of overthrowing this social order. That is what the slogan had to be in Central Germany. That slogan was needed in order to show the German proletariat for the first time how it could get out of this emergency.

I would like to cite an example from Germany in January 1918. War, together with all its consequences, weighed down on the proletariat. In January 1918 the munitions workers and the dockworkers succeeded everywhere in rising up against the straightjacket of war, against hunger, want, and poverty. They launched a general strike.[5] What was the result? The proletarians in uniform did not yet understand the workers. Some did, but the ice was not yet broken. And how did this struggle develop across the country? How did the smear campaign against the workers take shape? As they were being persecuted in every nook and cranny, news of this strike, of this working-class movement, penetrated everywhere. Everyone knew of it. And when conditions had developed to the point where the militarised economy and the so-called German Empire was beyond salvation, the workers and soldiers acted as they had been taught to act by the pioneer fighters of January 1918.

That is how things are in Germany today. The March struggles of 1921 showed the proletariat in Germany the only way it can escape collapse. Everyone in Germany now knows this. We do not have sufficient means and propaganda tools to take this message into every corner of the country. We must leave that task to the bourgeoisie, and the bourgeois do it in a different way than we do. They stir up hatred against us, curse us as criminals and miserable dogs, and they persecute us. And today the proletariat joins in cursing us. They join in the curses. And when conditions grow more acute and urgent, then will the proletariat be ready to follow the same path – and to recognise this path. That is how the revolution forces its way through. That is why it was necessary to raise the slogan and to orient the struggle toward the overthrow of capitalist power and of the existing social order. That is the great lesson for the German proletariat and the International that witnessed the March Action. This lesson is greater than all the petty matters that people here are stressing so much.

---

5. A general strike of four hundred thousand workers took place in Berlin 28 January–3 February 1918.

Comrades, I still have to explain briefly how the struggling proletariat should be organised. Earlier I only touched on this. The proletariat should no longer organise itself in order to achieve political and economic representation in the capitalist state. It should no longer organise in order to utilise bourgeois democracy. Instead, the proletariat should organise for the revolution. The proletariat should absorb the lessons of revolutions – those of the Russian Revolution, of the German and Austrian revolutions – and should organise itself accordingly. That is why we say that the Communists must act right now to create a nucleus and a framework that the proletariat can fit into when conditions draw it into struggle. This framework is provided by the factory organisations set up in different industries, sectors of the economy, and regions. Today such organisations are still few.

**Interjection**: Fewer and fewer.

**Hempel**: They are the organisations that hold their banners high and provide a framework. And when struggles flare up, as will happen more and more, the proletariat will be compelled to grasp hold of this framework, because it cannot any longer struggle through and with the trade unions. We must recognise this. This understanding must guide the policies of the Third International – that will enable us to advance. In order to maintain these organisations, to lead them, and to provide ongoing education for the class organisation as a whole, the proletariat needs a Communist Party. Not a Communist Party that is unable to take the lead through its every individual unit and has to be led by directives issuing from a central leadership. Instead, the proletariat needs a thoroughly educated party of cadres. That is how it should be. Every single Communist should be fully competent to play a leading role at his post. That should be our goal. Whatever the circumstances, whatever the struggle in which he is engaged, he should stand his ground, and the force that enables him to stand firm is his programme. What forces him to act is the decisions taken by the Communists. He is governed by the strictest discipline, based not on forgiveness but on expulsion or other forms of punishment. In other words, a party that is a nucleus; that knows what it wants; that stands firm, tested in battle; that no longer negotiates but rather is constantly engaged in struggle.

Such a party can arise only if it really throws itself into the struggle, breaking with the entire heritage of the trade-union and party movements, with reformist methods – which include the trade-union movement – and with parliamentarism. Communists must break with all that. Instead they have barred off their own road with such obstacles, and not only that, but through collaboration and participation at the points left open by the bourgeoisie in order to serve as a trap that captures and transforms revolutionary energy. Communists must banish all that from their ranks. Only when they have been reformed in this way can they take up their tasks and undertake revolutionary activity.

I have thus explained very briefly, to the degree that time permits, the course that the Communist International must follow in order to play a leadership role.

Viewing these matters from an international standpoint, we see that we will find the forces to sustain this structure, the materials from which to construct this revolutionary workers' organisation, this revolutionary International. In France, Spain, Italy, and also in the United States we encounter syndicalists and anarchists. Perhaps someone will cry out, 'Yes! You are an anarchist, a syndicalist!' Let us pause to consider these matters. It must be conceded that for many years, this is where the most revolutionary forces of the working class have been located. We realise that they do not understand the class struggle, the organised class struggle. Well, comrades, they were living too early in history. Their tactics and strategy were premature by many decades. The methods of the old workers' movement in Germany and elsewhere were then correct, but, now, in this time of collapse, we need the methods of direct struggle. These anarchists and syndicalists of the world have not experienced the organisation of the working class and its cohesiveness. Here is where the Communists should step forward and teach them to conduct the struggle and unify the forces, while offering them an organisational form they can unite with and fit into.

To be sure, these forces demand that the break with all bourgeois traditions be carried out in such a manner that there is no going back. All the workers who went into the anarchist and syndicalist camp have been disoriented by the betrayal of the parliamentary leaders. They recognised just how grave were the errors of the parliamentary workers' movement. The task is to yank them out of this camp, and Communists must take care not to fail in this task.

Rejection of parliamentarism and the trade-union movement are not principled questions for Communists. They are practical issues that are on the agenda today. If we view the matter in this fashion, we see that precisely in the United States and the Western European countries there are large workers' organisations that demand anti-parliamentarism and a break with the trade-union movement. So the question today is what this congress will now decide. If it adopts the line of the old workers' movement, it will also follow the course of the old workers' movement. And if it resolutely follows the path and resolutely takes the step of joining with the left-wing forces that are here today in Moscow, and recognises that there is some good in them, then the Third International congress will give new impetus to the revolution. Any other course will run it aground. It is up to this congress to take its decision. That is also how we view the question of our affiliation to the Third International.

**Koenen** (chair): The discussion continues. The next speaker is Comrade Terracini.

**Friesland** (*point of order*): Comrades, Comrade Terracini is motivating amendments to the theses proposed by Comrade Radek that have been moved by a number of delegations. I would therefore like to move, on behalf of the German delegation, that he be granted a longer speaking time. As you have seen in the newspaper *Moscow*, the amendments were submitted by the German, Austrian, and Italian delegations.[6] They have now also received support from the delegation of German Bohemia and from several other delegations, which have stated that they will probably join in supporting these amendments. Enabling Comrade Terracini to speak at greater length will promote a smoother discussion. I therefore move to grant him a speaking time of one hour.

**Koenen** (chair): Comrade Terracini says that he will need about half an hour, or forty-five minutes at the most, in order to motivate the basic points in these amendments. I believe that we can approve this proposal. Is there any objection? There is none. Comrade Terracini has the floor.

**Terracini** (Communist Party of Italy): Delegates have already read this morning in *Moscow* the amendments that the German delegation, together with those of Austria and Italy, wishes to propose to the congress delegates. We have now been informed by the Communist Youth that they wish to join with the Italian, German, and Austrian delegates in expressing their opinion on our proposal.

Let me say right from the start that we do not wish to alter the theses that Comrade Radek proposed yesterday at the close of his report – at least, not as regards their fundamental principle. In our opinion, Comrade Radek's theses are actually linked to the theses and report by Comrade Trotsky on the world situation. When Comrade Trotsky spoke on this topic, he also noted that Comrade Radek had protested that Trotsky had deviated from the question under discussion and taken up aspects of the Theses on Tactics and Strategy. In his summary, Comrade Trotsky said he was pulling back somewhat in order to

---

6. For the text of these amendments, see pp. 1041–58.

leave the entire topic of these theses to Comrade Radek. This incident shows that there is in fact a relationship between the reports of Comrade Radek and Comrade Trotsky, and that you can move from one report to the other without presenting new principles and adding new explanations.

All delegates, including those from Germany, Austria, Italy and the Communist Youth, have given general approval to the theses proposed by Comrade Trotsky. That signifies that they have also declared their agreement with the theses of Comrade Radek. They would be contradicting themselves if, having approved Comrade Trotsky's theses, they were now to reject those of Comrade Radek.

In our view, the theses of Comrade Radek can serve only as a foundation for the debate, unless they are first modified by fundamental amendments. You read the amendments today in *Moscow*. Comrades, they fill almost a full page. All these amendments rest on general principles that I will now propose. Each individual amendment will then be explained and clarified by other comrades, who – like me – can convey news on the situation in specific countries and on specific conditions that bear on the theses.

One of the sections in Comrade Radek's theses deals with the situation in each country and the developments in different parties. These theses on the current situation should give us the key to the tactics that must be carried out by each party and country. The expression, 'events in individual parties' must therefore be altered, in our opinion. Take the situation in Italy, for example. What is said here on Italy does not correspond to the true situation in the Socialist Party and among the proletarian masses of the country. These assertions can easily give our enemies a weapon to use against us. In point 4, we read:

> The politics of the Serrati current, while strengthening the influence of the reformists, also strengthened that of the anarchists and syndicalists, in which the masses sought to find leaders for the struggle against capitalism. They also generated anti-parliamentary verbal-radical tendencies within the party itself.[7]

The claim that the Italian masses sought leadership for the struggle against capitalism among the anarchists and syndicalists does not, in our opinion, correspond to reality. The anarchists and syndicalists in Italy have never had an organisation. It is not true that the proletarian masses turned to the anarchists and syndicalists to find other leaders of the anticapitalist struggle, after the Socialist Party had shown itself to be weak. Many opponents of communism and the Communist Party in Italy did in fact claim that the

---

7. For the corresponding passage in the theses, see p. 930.

masses sought leaders among the syndicalists and anarchists after the Third International appraised the Socialist Party in disparaging terms. From what I hear, Comrade Zetkin told the VKPD Central Committee that the Communist Party of Italy is largely composed of syndicalists and contains many anarchists. Serrati, too, has asserted more than once in the columns of *Avanti* and in his speeches that those who split from the Socialists in Livorno were merely anarchists and syndicalists. He tried to arouse the belief that the Third International's organisation in Italy, like all its parties in other countries, was nothing other than an organisation of anarchists who had previously belonged to the Socialist Party and had now left it. Therefore, he said, the Socialist Party did not want to tolerate any anarchists or syndicalists in its ranks in the future.

The proletarian masses will have to make the choice between the anarchists, on the one hand, and the reformists and centrists on the other. The reformists today represent a rather large organised force. We are convinced that the proletarian masses will follow the Communist Party. In Italy, too, after the period of confusion following the Livorno Congress, these masses sought a new focus for organisation and found it in the Communist Party of Italy.

We therefore propose that the sentence regarding the masses' efforts to find new leaders among the anarchists and syndicalists be amended as follows:

> In moments of confrontational action, the centrist attitude of these leaders resulted in a situation where the Communist parties either failed to take the lead of the mass actions with sufficient energy or where centrist or half-centrist elements attacked them from the rear.[8]

There is no doubt that this danger is now behind us, and that there is now in Italy a genuine Communist Party that leads the masses in struggle against capitalism and the bourgeoisie.

We must raise a principled question: that of the radical current within the Communist Party. There has already been a sharp struggle against the radical tendency in debates within the Executive and here at this congress. When we in the Executive discussed the question of the Communist Party of France, the delegate of the Communist Youth of France attempted to demonstrate how strong opportunism is, even today, in the Communist Party of France. He cited examples and cases where the Communist Party of France, in his opinion, had not taken a truly revolutionary position.[9] On this occasion, many comrades heatedly attacked the delegate of the Communist Youth of

---

8. Compare point 7 in the published amendments; see 1053–6.
9. For Laporte's remarks to the pre-congress expanded ECCI meeting, see Appendix 3f, pp. 1110–14.

France. We certainly do not hold that the proposals of the French Youth comrade must be adopted here. It is not our view that the Communist Party of France should have carried out the revolution and resisted the French army's invasion of Luxembourg arms in hand.[10] We do not believe that, when the class of 1919 was conscripted,[11] the French Communist Party should have issued the order not to respond to the call, or that, when the guards came to fetch the young French comrades, they should have resisted arms in hand. However, we do not believe that every radical tendency must be rejected in such ruthless fashion. In our opinion, the statements in Comrade Radek's theses about radical tendencies in the French party and in other countries are too strong. (*Interjection*) No, they are too strong, not too weak.

The Third International still has a major struggle to fight today, a struggle against the rightist tendencies, against the centrists, half-centrists, and opportunists.

We expelled Levi from the Third International and the VKPD and refused to admit Serrati into the Third International. But we cannot yet conclude that the Third International is now free from all centrist tendencies and from the threat of opportunist tendencies. The full challenge of the struggle against centrist and opportunist tendencies lies before us now. Strong centrist tendencies, which still exist in the Third International and many of its member parties, must be combated energetically. On the other hand, the proposals that we adopted yesterday in the Executive, the proposal regarding the Executive's conduct, speak of certain parties affiliated to the Third International that still display centrist tendencies. We explained that these tendencies must be wiped out. We spoke of certain parties that joined the Third International because the masses wanted it, even though this was against or almost against the will of their leaders. These leaders belong to the Third International today only because the masses wanted to join it. The possibility now exists that these leaders, who entered the Third International only because the masses wanted them to, will now make an attempt to switch over once again to centrist or reformist policies. The Executive must keep a close eye on these party leaders and take care that no new Serrati or new Levi crops up, who would represent a danger not only for the revolutionary movement in their country but for the Third International as a whole.

---

10. For the French invasion of Luxembourg, see p. 1109, n. 21.

11. On 3 May 1921, the French government remobilised the conscription class of 1919, some 200,000 men who had reached draft age in 1919. It did so to meet its manpower needs for occupying the Ruhr Valley in order to force Germany to pay war reparations.

We therefore consider that it is not the struggle against radical tendencies, but rather above all the struggle against the rightists that must be taken up – especially in the paragraphs dealing with the situation in the Communist Party of France. Specifically, all the references in these paragraphs that crudely target the tendencies referred to here as 'impatient and politically inexperienced forces'. Instead of that, we should add advice to the radical forces. We can advise the Central Committee of the French party to work to prevent the radical forces, in the words of Comrade Lenin in the Executive, from 'committing stupidities'.[12] However, it must be emphasised that the Executive of the French party must direct its attention and its work above all toward the right tendency.

In his report on the Executive, Comrade Zinoviev spoke quite fully against the right tendencies. If we now adopt the amendment to the Theses on Tactics and Strategy, we will be only reaffirming the statements of Comrade Zinoviev. We do not expect Comrade Radek to raise any objections to our amendment. When the Executive discussed the question of the French party, Comrade Radek spoke not against the radical tendency but against the rightists.[13] Our amendments aim at nothing more than to stress in the Theses on Tactics and Strategy the same points that Comrade Radek has already made in the Executive with regard to the French party.

When we come to the situation in Czechoslovakia, we encounter a second principled question, which is mentioned quite often, in a general sense, in Comrade Radek's theses. However, I would like to speak specifically of the situation in Czechoslovakia. The question here is how large mass parties should be organised. In his theses, Comrade Radek seems very concerned to prevent the Communist parties in different countries from devoting themselves to any task other than the organisation of larger and larger masses of proletarians and workers. So we read, for example, in point 1: 'it's a matter of the tactics and strategy to be applied in our struggles...'. Well, in our opinion, the words regarding the need to win a majority of the working class to Communist principles can lead to misunderstandings in the parties and the other workers' organisations.

Yes, we must strive to organise the majority of the proletariat in the Communist Party, we must make efforts to bring ever broader proletarian masses to the organisations of the Communist Party. As for the words, 'winning the masses', all we can say is that we must strive to win the sympathy of the

---

12. A reference to Lenin's speech to the expanded ECCI on the French Party. For the text, see Appendix 3f on pp. 1128–32 and p. 1128, n. 39.
13. Radek's speech to the 18 June session of the expanded ECCI can be found in Comintern archives, RGASPI 495/1/38/116–21.

vast majority of the proletariat for revolutionary struggle. Comrade Radek's theses contain the notion that we must win the majority of the proletariat for communism. In point 4 – page 9 in the French version of the theses – we read that in Czechoslovakia there is already a party with 350,000 organised members, plus another 60,000 in the German party in that country. As a result, when the two parties fuse, there will be a total membership of 400,000. It follows from this that the Czechoslovak party faces the task of attracting and educating the majority of the working class of this country through a truly Communist agitation.

In our opinion, the Communist Party of a country as small as Czechoslovakia, a party that already counts more than 400,000 members, faces yet other tasks, namely those of winning the remaining workers who are still outside the party. You cannot halt propaganda work; you cannot close the gates of the Communist Party to the workers who wish to join it. That lies beyond any doubt. But there is still another task, namely the Communist training of the 400,000 workers who are already organised in the Communist Party of Czechoslovakia. The workers that heretofore stood under the influence of reformist and democratic leaders, who always instructed them in a reformist and opportunist spirit, must now be educated as Communists. The statement that the Czechoslovak party has the task of winning even broader working masses, and moreover not merely through propaganda, thus signifies that the Communist Party must also be expanded through action.

We now wish to explain what we can expect from revolutionary struggle and what it will look like. It must truly be a struggle of the entire proletariat, or almost all of it. In our opinion we must not postpone revolutionary action until the majority of the proletariat is organised and acknowledges the principles of communism. We have heard often enough that the Russian Revolution was carried out and triumphed while the Communist Party of Russia was still a small and relatively unimportant organisation. So when it is said that the majority of the proletariat must be organised in the party, that can only mean that the majority of the proletariat must be involved in the revolutionary struggle.

When I read the theses of Comrade Radek, I had the impression that he was saying that the majority of the proletariat must be organised before the revolutionary struggle begins. We do not share this point of view. On the contrary, we believe that the working class cannot be won over otherwise than through action by the party. The workers who now belong to the democratic and reformist parties are more likely to be convinced by action than by our propaganda that the principles of communism are correct. Only then will they quit the reformist parties. In my opinion, a Communist Party will always consist of only the most active workers, until it launches itself in struggle – and, what is more, until it has almost triumphed.

The workers who now belong to the majority and reformist parties and are won by our propaganda will not join the Communist Party but will remain outside, forming a party of those without affiliation. That happened in Russia, where the unaffiliated workers are only now, after three years of revolutionary struggle, joining up with communism – indeed, without for the moment having any clear conception of what it is.

The theses should therefore not assert that the main task of the Communist Party consists of winning the majority of the proletariat for the principles of communism. It would be much more correct to say that the majority of the proletariat must be drawn into the revolutionary struggle. We must not, however, propose the notion that the majority of the proletariat must be organised in the Communist Party. That statement would give the reformists a sharp weapon to use against us. The reformists have always claimed that the revolutionary struggle must not begin until the majority of the proletariat is organised in the Communist Party. What we have here is a democratic principle that people want to use against the Communist Party. However, this is suitable only for the reformists and not for the theses proposed for the Third International.

We find this assertion again in the passage that takes up the tasks of the German party and the position of the KPD with regard to the Third International (page 9). There we read:

> The VKPD was formed from the fusion of the Spartacus League with the working masses of the Independent [USPD] left wing. Although already a mass party, it faces the major task of increasing and strengthening its influence on the broad masses; winning the proletarian mass organisations, the trade unions; and breaking the hold of the Social-Democratic party and trade-union bureaucracy.[14]

From this it follows that the VKPD also has the task of strengthening its influence on the broad masses. In our opinion, however, a party like the one in Germany, which has a large number of members, has another much more important task, namely that of placing itself at the head of the masses in the coming struggles of the German proletariat. We can be sure that the revolutionary movement in Germany is not yet over. On the contrary, the future struggles of the German proletariat will be more significant and more bitter precisely because the German proletariat was defeated in the March Action.

---

14. See the corresponding passage of the theses on p. 933.

I was in Germany when the struggle broke out. I stayed there for several days and then returned to Italy. I must say that I saw how the influence and popularity of the German party in Italy was significantly greater after the March Action, when there was no longer any hope of victory, than before. The Italian comrades and the workers with whom I spoke asked question after question about the struggle of the German proletariat. There is no way that I can portray to you how great was the sympathy of Italian workers for the German party, which had the courage to take up the struggle to defend the German proletariat under the most difficult conditions imaginable. The Italian workers displayed greater sympathy for the KPD after the March Action in Germany than before. They demonstrated greater admiration, greater trust in the party than there was in Germany itself. In Germany there now exists a true mass party. Before, the Italian workers could not be convinced of that. Comrade Trotsky shakes his head. It appears that he does not quite believe what I am saying.

**Trotsky**: I am not just referring to what you are saying right now.

**Terracini**: I thought as much. However, I can definitely say that my statement reflects the true feelings of the Italian proletariat.

Moreover, the March movement in Germany was useful to the VKPD in many regards. It contributed to tearing the mask from the face of numerous opportunists. The German party learned in the March struggle how discipline is expressed in action. We have always spoken of discipline but we never had the opportunity to apply it. During the March struggles, however, the German comrades learned to apply discipline. They have now achieved a competence in struggle that was lacking before the March Action, and which we ourselves still lack to this day.

Comrade Radek and others spoke sarcastically about the theory of the offensive. It is true that this is a poor choice of words. It is adopted from military language. It seems that Comrade Radek has read quite a bit regarding military tactics, such that he now feels able to speak sarcastically of the policy of an offensive that found its theoreticians in Germany after the March Action. Nonetheless, the words 'theory of the offensive' have a certain meaning, which we must clearly understand. We are convinced that this will be of significant benefit for the revolutionary struggle. We should not reject this theory; rather we must try to understand its meaning.

When comrades talk of the theory of the offensive, they mean a tendency toward expanding the activity of the Communist Party. The term aims to stress that a dynamic tendency will now replace the static one that has until now struck deep roots in almost all Communist parties of the Third International. The formula 'theory of the offensive' signifies the transition from a period of inactivity to a period of action. In our opinion, the theory of the offensive can be accepted only in this sense and this spirit. If we interpret it in the fashion that I have laid out, then the Theses on Tactics and Strategy must not reject, out of hand, the statements of comrades who speak of the theory of the offensive; rather we must correct the exaggerations in their statements.

The main principled changes that we are proposing to congress delegates are these: first, we must not deal with the Left too sharply while abandoning the field to the rightists in the Communist parties and the Third International. On the contrary, in our view the Right must be combated, for it represents a much greater danger for communism. The Left, on the other hand, will only pose a danger to the party if it fully develops its activity. Also, it must be stressed that it is not absolutely necessary that the Communist Party have already organised and won the majority of the working masses. What is important is merely the capacity of the Communist parties, at the moment of struggle, to draw the masses with them.

As I said earlier, other comrades will take up additional questions raised by the theses. For my part, I am limiting myself to the two questions that I have just discussed.

**V.I. Lenin** (Russia):[15] Comrades! To my deep regret, I must confine myself to the defensive. (*Laughter*) I say 'to my deep regret' because, after hearing Comrade Terracini's speech and reading the amendments introduced by three delegations, I had a very strong desire to take the offensive. For faced with views such as those defended by Terracini and these three delegations, it is really essential to take the offensive. If the congress is not going to wage a vigorous offensive against such errors, against such 'leftist' stupidities, the whole movement is doomed. That is my deep conviction. But we are organised and disciplined Marxists. We cannot be satisfied with speeches against individual comrades.

We Russians are already sick and tired of these leftist phrases. We are people of organisation. In drawing up our plans, we must proceed in an organised way and try to find the correct line. It is, of course, no secret that our theses are a compromise. And why not? Among Communists, who are already holding their Third Congress and have worked out definite fundamental principles, compromises under certain conditions are absolutely necessary. Our theses, put forward by the Russian delegation, were studied and prepared in the most careful way and were the result of long arguments and meetings with various delegations. They aim at establishing the basic line of the Communist

---

15. The translation is based on *LCW*, 32, pp. 468–77 and has been edited to conform with the German text.

International and are especially necessary now after we have not only formally condemned the real centrists but have expelled them. Such are the facts.

I am obliged to defend these theses. Now, Terracini comes up and says that we must continue the fight against the centrists, and goes on to show how it is intended to wage the fight. I say that if these amendments aim to indicate a definite trend, then a relentless fight against this trend is essential, for otherwise there is no communism and no Communist International.

I am surprised that the German Communist Workers' Party has not put its signature to these amendments. (*Laughter*) Just listen to what Terracini is defending and what his amendments say.

They begin in this way: 'On page 1, column 1, line 19, delete the word "majority".' Majority! That is extremely dangerous! (*Laughter*) Then further: 'instead of the word "principles", insert "goals"'. Principles and goals are two different things. Even the anarchists will agree with us about goals, because they too stand for the abolition of exploitation and class distinctions.

I have met and talked with few anarchists in my life, but still enough. I sometimes succeeded in reaching agreement with them about goals, but never as regards principles. Principles are not a goal, a programme, a tactic, or a theory. Tactics and theory are not principles. How do we differ from the anarchists on principles? The principles of communism consist in the establishment of the dictatorship of the proletariat and in the use of state coercion in the transition period. Such are the principles of communism, but they are not its goal. And this is the first mistake of the comrades who have tabled this proposal.

Secondly, it is stated there: 'the word "majority" should be deleted'. Read the whole passage:

> The Third Congress of the Communist International is undertaking its review of tactical questions at a time when the objective conditions are ripe for revolution. A number of mass Communist parties have appeared, but there is not yet a single country in which they have actual leadership of the majority of the working class in genuinely revolutionary struggle.[16]

And so, they want the word 'majority' deleted. If we cannot even agree on such simple things, then I do not understand how we can work together and lead the proletariat to victory. Then it is not at all surprising that we can no longer reach agreement on the question of principles. Show me a party that has already won the majority of the working class. Terracini did not even think of providing an example. Indeed, there is no such example.

And so, the word 'goals' is to be put instead of 'principles', and the word 'majority' is to be deleted. No, thank you! We shall not do it. Even the

---

16. For the corresponding passage in the theses, see p. 924.

German party – one of the best – does not have the majority of the working class behind it. That is a fact. We, who face a most severe struggle, are not afraid to utter this truth, but here you have three delegations that wish to begin with an untruth, for if the congress deletes the word 'majority' it will show that it wants an untruth. That is as clear as it can be.

Then comes the following amendment: 'On page 4, column 1, line 10, the words "Open Letter", etc., should be deleted.' I have already heard one speech today in which I found the same idea. But there it was quite natural. It was the speech of Comrade Hempel of the KAPD. He said: 'The "Open Letter" was an act of opportunism.' To my deep regret and shame, I have already heard such views privately. But when, at the congress, after such prolonged debates, the Open Letter is declared opportunist – that is a shame and a disgrace. And now Comrade Terracini comes forward on behalf of the three delegations and wants to delete the words 'Open Letter'. What is the good then of the fight against the KAPD? The Open Letter is a model. This is stated in our theses and we must absolutely stand by it. It is a model because it is the first step in a practical method to win over the majority of the working class. In Europe, where almost all the proletarians are organised, we must win the majority of the working class. Anyone who fails to understand this is lost to the Communist movement; he will never learn anything if he has failed to learn that much three years after the great revolution.

Terracini says that we were victorious in Russia although the party was very small. He is dissatisfied with what is said in the theses about Czechoslovakia. Here we have twenty-seven amendments, and if I had a mind to criticise them I should, like some orators, have to speak for not less than three hours. We have heard here that in Czechoslovakia the Communist Party has 300,000–400,000 members, and that it is essential to win over the majority, to create an invincible force and continue enlisting fresh masses of workers. Here Terracini is fully ready for battle. He says: if there are already 400,000 workers in the party, why should we want more? Delete that! (*Laughter*) He is afraid of the word 'masses' and wants to delete it. Comrade Terracini has understood very little of the Russian Revolution.

In Russia, we were a small party, but we had with us in addition the majority of the Soviets of Workers' and Peasants' Deputies throughout the country. (*Shout: 'Very true!'*) Where do you have that? We had with us almost half the army, which then numbered at least ten million men. Do you have the majority of the army behind you? Can you show me such a country? If these views of Comrade Terracini are shared by three other delegations, then something is wrong in the International. Then we must say: Stop! We must wage a decisive struggle! Otherwise the Communist International is lost. (*Animation*)

On the basis of my experience I must say, although I am on the defensive here (*Laughter*), that the aim of my speech, and also the principle of my speech

(*Laughter*) consists in defence of the resolution and theses proposed by our delegation. It would, of course, be pedantic to say that not a letter in them must be altered. I have read many resolutions, and I am well aware that very good amendments could be introduced, perhaps in every line of them. But that would be pedantry. If, however, I declare now that, politically, not a single letter can be altered, it is because the amendments, as I see them, are of a quite definite political nature and because they lead us along a path that is harmful and dangerous to the Communist International. Therefore, I and all of the Russian delegation must insist that not a single letter in the theses be altered. We have not only condemned our rightists elements – we have driven them out. But if, like Terracini, people turn the fight against the rightists into a sport, then we must say: Stop! Otherwise we will be in very grave danger.

Terracini has defended the theory of the offensive. In this connection the notorious amendments propose a formula two or three pages long. There is no need for us to read them. We know what they say. Terracini has stated the issue quite clearly. He has defended the theory of an offensive, referring to 'dynamic tendencies' and the 'transition from passivity to activity'. We in Russia have already had adequate political experience in the struggle against the centrists. As long as fifteen years ago, we were waging a struggle against our opportunists and centrists, and also against the Mensheviks, and we were completely victorious, not only over the Mensheviks, but also over the semi-anarchists.

If we had not done this, we would not have been able to retain power in our hands for three and a half years, or even for three and a half weeks, and we would not have been able to convene a Communist congress here. 'Dynamic tendencies', 'transition from passivity to activity' – these are all phrases the Left Socialist-Revolutionaries used in battle against us. Now they are in prison, defending there the 'goals of communism' and thinking of the 'transition from passivity to activity'. (*Laughter*) This is no way to discuss. The amendments do not contain any trace of Marxism, any trace of political experience, or of reasoning. Have we in our theses elaborated a general theory of the revolutionary offensive? Has Radek or anyone of us committed such a stupidity? We have spoken of the theory of an offensive in relation to a quite specific country and at a quite specific period.[17]

---

17. This may be a reference to the article by Nikolai Bukharin, 'Über die Offensivtaktik' [On the policy of the offensive], that appeared in *Die Kommunistische Internationale*, 15 (1921). Justifying the Soviet invasion of Poland, Bukharin called to mind the French Revolution of the eighteenth century. Attacked by counterrevolutionary powers, revolutionary France succeeded in moving beyond France's borders, shifting from defence to a military offensive and initiating revolutionary changes in the conquered territories.

From our struggle against the Mensheviks we can quote instances showing that even before the first revolution there were some who doubted whether the revolutionary party ought to conduct an offensive. If such doubts were raised by any Social Democrat – as we all called ourselves at that time – we took up the struggle against him and said that he was an opportunist, that he did not understand anything of Marxism and the dialectics of the revolutionary party. Is it really possible for a party to dispute whether a revolutionary offensive is permissible in general? To find such examples in this country one would have to go back some fifteen years. If there are centrists or disguised centrists who reject an offensive in principle, they should be immediately expelled. There is absolutely no basis for a dispute on that point. But for us to argue even now, after three years, about 'dynamic tendencies', about the 'transition from passivity to activity' – that is a disgrace.

There is no argument on this point between us and Radek, who drafted these theses jointly with us. Was it not an error to begin talking in Germany *about the theory* of the revolutionary offensive when in fact no actual offensive had been prepared? Nevertheless, the March Action was a great step forward, despite the erroneous way it was led. But this does not matter. Hundreds of thousands of workers fought heroically. However courageously the KAPD fought against the bourgeoisie, we must repeat what Comrade Radek said in a Russian article about Hoelz. If anyone, even an anarchist, fights heroically against the bourgeoisie, that is, of course, a great thing; but it is a real step forward if hundreds of thousands fight against the vile provocation of the social traitors and against the bourgeoisie.

It is very important to be critical of one's mistakes. We began with that. If anyone, after a struggle in which hundreds of thousands have taken part, comes out against this struggle and behaves like Levi, then he should be expelled. And that is what was done. But we must draw a lesson from this. Had we really prepared for an offensive?

**Radek**: We had not even prepared for defence.

**Lenin**: Indeed only newspaper articles talked of an offensive. This theory as applied to the March Action in Germany in 1921 was incorrect – we have to say that. However, the theory of the offensive in general is not false.

We were victorious in Russia, and with such ease, because we prepared for our revolution during the imperialist war. That was the first condition. Ten million workers and peasants in Russia were armed, and our slogan was: an immediate peace at all costs. We were victorious because the vast mass of the peasants were revolutionarily disposed against the big landowners. The Socialist-Revolutionaries, the adherents of the Second and Two-and-a-Half Internationals, were the major peasant party in November 1917. They demanded revolutionary methods but, like true heroes of the Second and Two-and-a-Half Internationals, lacked the courage to act in a revolutionary way. In August and September 1917 we said: 'Theoretically we are fighting the Socialist-Revolutionaries as we did before, but practically we are ready to accept their programme because only we are able to put it into effect.' That is what we said and what we did. The peasantry was ill-disposed towards us in November 1917, after our victory, and sent a majority of Socialist-Revolutionaries into the Constituent Assembly. But we won them over, if not in the course of a few days – as I, for my part, mistakenly expected and predicted – at any rate in the course of a few weeks. The difference was not great. Can you point out any country in Europe where you could win over the majority of the peasantry in the course of a few weeks? Italy perhaps? (*Laughter*) If it is said that we were victorious in Russia in spite of not having a big party, that only proves that those who say it have not understood the Russian Revolution and that they have absolutely no understanding of how to prepare for a revolution.

The first step of our movement was to create a real Communist Party so as to know whom we were talking to and whom we could fully trust. The slogan of the First and Second Congresses was 'Drive out the centrists!' We cannot hope to master even the ABC of communism, unless all along the line and throughout the world we make a clean break with the centrists and semi-centrists, whom in Russia we call Mensheviks. But the creation of a genuinely revolutionary party and the break with the Mensheviks is only the first step. It is only a preparatory school. We are already holding the Third Congress, and Comrade Terracini keeps repeating the task of the preparatory school: hunting out, pursuing and exposing centrists and semi-centrists. No, thank you. We have already done this long enough. Already at the Second Congress we said that the centrists are our enemies. But now it is really necessary to move on a bit.

The second stage, after forming the party, consists of learning to prepare for revolution. In many countries we have not even learned how to assume the leadership. We were not victorious in Russia solely because we had an undisputed majority of the working class on our side. During the elections in 1917 the overwhelming majority of the workers were with us against the Mensheviks.[18] Immediately after our seizure of power, half the army was with us. And in the course of some weeks, nine-tenths of the peasants came over

---

18. During the late November 1917 elections to the Constituent Assembly, the Bolsheviks received 23.5 per cent of the vote overall. But in most cities and major industrial regions, the Bolsheviks received an absolute majority, as they did in elections to the All-Russian Congress of Soviets held in October 1917.

to our side, because we adopted the agrarian programme of the Socialist-Revolutionaries instead of our own, and put it into effect. Our victory lay in the fact that we carried out the Socialist-Revolutionary programme; that is why this victory was so easy.

How can you in the West possibly have such illusions? It is ridiculous! Comrade Terracini and all of you who have signed the amendments, just compare the concrete economic conditions! Although the majority came over so rapidly to our side, the difficulties confronting us after our victory were very great. If we nevertheless won out, it was because we kept in mind not only our goals but also our principles, and did not tolerate in our party those who kept silent about principles but talked of goals, 'dynamic tendencies', and the 'transition from passivity to activity'. Perhaps we shall be blamed for preferring to keep such gentlemen in prison. But dictatorship is impossible in any other way. We must prepare for the dictatorship, and this consists in combating such phrases and such amendments.

Throughout our theses, we speak of the masses. But, comrades, we need to understand what is meant by masses. The KAPD, the left-wing comrades, have all too often misused this word. But Comrade Terracini, too, and all those who have signed these amendments, do not know what is meant by the word 'masses'.

I have already spoken too long, and I will limit myself to a few words about the concept of 'masses'. The concept of the masses changes in line with the changes in the nature of the struggle. At the beginning of the struggle it sometimes takes only a few thousand genuinely revolutionary workers, a few thousand workers, to warrant talk of the masses. If the party not only draws into the struggle its own members, but also succeeds in arousing non-party people, it is well on the way to winning the masses. During our revolutions there were instances when a few thousand workers represented the masses. In the history of our movement, and of our struggle against the Mensheviks, you will find many examples where several thousand workers in a town were enough to indicate that our party had assumed a mass character. When several thousand workers, ordinary workers who are politically unaffiliated and drag out a miserable existence begin to act in a revolutionary way – that is the masses.

If the movement spreads and intensifies, it gradually develops into a real revolution. We saw this in 1905 and 1917 during three revolutions, and you too will have to go through all this. When the revolution has been sufficiently prepared, the concept 'masses' becomes different. Several thousand workers no longer constitute the masses. This word begins to denote something else. The concept of 'masses' undergoes a change so that it implies the majority, and not simply a majority of the workers alone, but a majority of all the exploited.

Otherwise you are not a revolutionary at all; you have no understanding of the word 'masses'. It is possible that even a small party, the British or American party, for example, if it initiates a movement at a favourable time, if it has carefully studied the course of political development and become acquainted with the life and customs of the unaffiliated masses (Comrade Radek has pointed to the miners' strike as a good example) if it intervenes with its slogans at a favourable moment and succeeds in getting millions of workers to follow it – these are the masses.[19]

I would not altogether deny that a revolution can be started by a very small party and brought to a victorious conclusion. But one must know how to win over the masses. For this, thoroughgoing preparation of revolution is essential. But here you have comrades coming forward with the assertion that we should immediately delete the word 'majority'. We must struggle against these comrades. We need a decisive struggle against these comrades. Without thoroughgoing preparation you will not achieve victory in any country. Quite a small party is sufficient to lead the masses. At certain times there is no necessity for big organisations.

But to win, we must have the sympathy of the masses. An absolute majority is not always essential for victory; but what is essential in order to win and retain power is not only the majority of the working class – I use the term 'working class' in its Western European sense, i.e., in the sense of the industrial proletariat – but also the majority of the working and exploited rural population. Have you thought about this? Do we find in Terracini's speech even a hint at this thought? He speaks only of 'dynamic tendency' and the 'transition from passivity to activity'.

Does he devote even a single word to the food question? The workers want to be fed. They can put up with a great deal and go hungry, as we have seen to a certain extent in Russia. We must, therefore, win over to our side the majority not only of the working class, but also of the working and exploited rural population. Have you prepared for this? Almost nowhere.

And so, I repeat: I must unreservedly defend our theory, and I hold that this kind of defence is obligatory. We not only condemned the centrists but drove them from the party. Now we must deal with the other aspect, which we also consider dangerous. We must tell the comrades the truth in the most polite form – and in our theses it is told in a kind and considerate way so that no one feels insulted – we are confronted now by other, more important questions than that of hounding the centrists. We have had enough of that sport. It has already become somewhat boring.

---

19. The translation of this sentence follows the text in German, the language probably spoken by Lenin. For a translation based on the Russian text, see *LCW*, 32, p. 476.

Instead, the comrades must learn to wage a real revolutionary struggle. The German workers have already begun this. Hundreds of thousands of proletarians in that country have been fighting heroically. Anyone who opposes this struggle should be immediately expelled. But after that we must not engage in empty word-spinning but must immediately begin to learn, on the basis of the mistakes made, how to organise the struggle better. We must not fear revealing our mistakes to the enemy. Anyone who is afraid of this is no revolutionary. On the contrary, if we openly declare to the workers: 'Yes, we have made mistakes', it will mean that they will not be repeated and we shall be able better to choose the moment. And if during the struggle itself the majority of the working people prove to be on our side – not only the majority of the workers, but the majority of all the exploited and oppressed – then we shall really be victorious. (*Prolonged, loud applause and cheers*)

**Koenen** (chair): Comrade Michalak has the floor.

**Michalak** (Warszawski, Poland): Comrades, the theses of the Second Congress actually already took decisions on all the questions that concern us here. It could appear that what was said and decided at the Second Congress and set down in its theses should really be enough with regard to the questions that we are now again debating. Nonetheless, it turns out that an old lesson has been confirmed again: that theses alone are not enough to make a party, a movement, and an action. It turns out that with good theses you can carry out a bad action. It turns out that if you do not have the necessary experience and schooling, you will not understand, even given the best theses, how the principles of these theses are to be implemented.

That is why we are again quarrelling over the question of the mass party, which was so thoroughly discussed by the Second Congress, and on which it took decisions, as regards principles, policies, revolutionary parliamentarism, and discipline. And that is the basis, that is the meaning of the question that now stands at the centre of our discussion, namely the March Action. For it provides a classic and typical example of how difficult it is to implement the theses. This example shows that what stands on paper must be understood in the process of struggle and growth.

First of all, comrades, let me make a few personal, quite personal remarks. A few days ago, Comrade Radek, in one of his speeches, accused Comrade Zetkin of having spoken of an offensive, of having had a theory of the offensive in that situation.[20] I then took the liberty of shouting that this concerned something quite different. And because Radek tried again yesterday to

---

20. For Radek's comments on this point, see pp. 266 and 431.

demonstrate that Comrade Zetkin has a theory of the offensive in that situation, you must permit me to take up the matter briefly.

First of all, frankly – and Radek will surely not resent this – this is a verbal quibble. Read the theses, the first resolution of Comrade Zetkin after the March Action.[21] What do you find there about the offensive? We find expressed there, in terms both of form and often of content, expressed much more clearly and concisely, exactly what Radek and we all are now trying to say. Comrade Zetkin takes up in these theses the conditions and tasks of the party before and after the action. However, instead of the word 'action', she sometimes uses the word 'offensive'.[22] One has the impression that she was probably making a verbal concession to the Zentrale. She even speaks of a 'partial offensive' – that is, of the partial actions that we are discussing here.

Moreover, comrades, in a preliminary draft written by Radek and a couple of German comrades, we read 'the preparation of the offensive', and later the talk is of 'actions'. And even more, comrades. Comrade Radek says in the present theses that we should be a party of assault against capitalist society. What does the word 'assault' mean other than an offensive? I am not as familiar with books of German strategists, but I recall that Kautsky, writing many years before the War in response to both Rosa Luxemburg and Radek, once attempted to muddy somewhat the waters of strategy by writing of a strategy of attrition.[23] This word from the lexicon of the military experts, a word taken from quite another domain, really has very little to do with the determination of the tasks that are before us now and with our cause.

And another thing. The comrades, my German friends, who are so afraid of being the object of cutting remarks, love it greatly when Comrade Zetkin is dealt one blow after another. (*Commotion*) Comrades, if I may once again give you my personal impression, young men sometimes behave like old women, and the only man in the German delegation is Comrade Zetkin. (*Laughter. Shouts: 'You yourself don't believe that.'*)

So, comrades, what is at issue is not the word 'offensive' or 'defensive'. There is a good saying in German that the best way to parry is to strike a blow.

---

21. For Zetkin's resolution of 7 April 1921, see Appendix 2c on pp. 1079–86.

22. 'Action' here translates the German word *Aktion*, which carries a confrontational connotation absent from its English cognate.

23. In April 1910 Karl Kausky wrote an article 'Was Nun?' [What now?] for *Die Neue Zeit*. Replying to Rosa Luxemburg's call for political mass strikes to win universal manhood suffrage in Prussia, Kautsky's article counterposed a 'strategy of attrition'. Luxemburg responded to Kautsky in a series of articles entitled 'Ermattung oder Kampf?' [Attrition or struggle?].

The German-language texts of both articles can be found at <http://www.marxists.org>.

Our theses, too, say that in certain conditions one should go over as quickly as possible to striking a blow. The main thing is that the March Action was a workers' struggle, an armed encounter, one in which the leaders used very bad tactical concepts. But comrades – and I say this against the opposition – the Paris Commune was led by men, as we all know, who had concepts of tactics that were very naïve, much more naïve than the German comrades. They carried out many stupidities. And still, after their fight, Marx extolled the Paris Commune, the armed encounter, and all the battles. I recall how in December 1905 there was an armed encounter of the workers against tsarism. The workers were defeated in struggle. The Menshevik Plekhanov said at the time that is was stupid to have taken up arms. But Lenin said it was good, and we should extol this lost battle as part of the tradition of the Russian working masses.[24]

So, first of all, we have the Paris Commune, which as a result of the enormous losses it incurred killed the workers' movement for many years. (*Commotion and objections*) Nonetheless, we extolled it. That was also the case with the 1905 December struggle of Russian workers in Moscow. That is how every Communist must regard the German March Action. Much has been said of the many errors made by the Zentrale. In my opinion, however, beyond all the errors there was an overriding error. Not that the action was badly prepared. Not that the moment for an offensive had been poorly chosen. For me, the greatest error – regardless of whether it was offensive or defensive – was that they did not have any understanding of the conditions and the tasks of the party in this action. (*Commotion*) This great error demands more discussion than all the other small ones.

And there is more. We had a criticism of the errors, but for a long time, unfortunately, only criticism by an opportunist. The great error of my friend Clara Zetkin is that she did not perceive this. Levi's criticism is two-sided. One side is that he stated openly what had been said to him in private. That in itself is a fact for which he deserves to be expelled, at the least. Radek and Lenin say that your attitude to the party is the main issue. Well, comrades, I tell you, Levi made known conversations that really took place in confidence. That was no accident.

Basing himself on the pamphlet by Comrade Lenin on the conditions for victory in Russia, Levi limited himself to saying things that in this context were absolutely irrelevant. But he did not point out a revolutionary path for the party; he did not indicate its immediate tasks. Instead, because he could

---

24. During the 1905 revolution, workers in Moscow staged a general strike and armed uprising. The revolt was crushed by tsarist troops, with over one thousand killed. For the assessment by Lenin, see *LCW*, 11, pp. 171–8.

not provide a revolutionary analysis, he had to reach for a dirty weapon, and blurt out things that he had heard. In this regard, it can be said that the German party made a major error in waiting until the opportunist pamphlet describing the revolution appeared because it did not want to provide a revolutionary criticism. (*Commotion*) I would like to read a statement of the Polish delegation. However, I will limit myself to saying that, in my opinion, this congress is dominated by a mood that is not entirely appropriate. It seemed as if many comrades were saying that Lenin spoke for forty-five minutes against the Left and only fifteen minutes against the Right.

Based on this impression, many comrades have said that Lenin is taking a rightist course, and that Trotsky is doing the same. The reason for this is that the comrades from abroad, in particular, are not familiar with the record of the Bolsheviks' past struggles in Russia. Otherwise, they would have known that this party grew in struggle against both the Right and the Left. It is not a change of course, but rather the old path of Bolshevism, in new conditions and with new tasks. But it is the same path, not a change of course. When I read the stenographic transcript of Comrade Lenin's speech in the Expanded Executive, I immediately concluded that the faster this speech is printed, the faster will the false impression held by many comrades disappear. The main thing that he and also Trotsky said is that we must warn against the leftists, in the same way that the Russians do, and then fight against the Right: there is no contradiction here.[25] Now, comrades, Comrade Lenin has spoken against the amendments to the theses. The Polish delegation has also proposed amendments, and I have been instructed to read the following declaration:

> The delegation from Poland supports the thrust of the amendments introduced by the three delegations and reserves the right to make further proposals along these lines in the commission.

**Shouts**: 'Your speech was completely different.' (*Laughter*)

**Joseph J. Vaughan** (Britain): Comrades, with regard to the criticisms raised against Radek and his theses, I would like to start by emphasising that none of the parties belonging to the Third International places a greater value on criticism than the British. But we insist that criticism of a party must have two goals. First, it must be useful to the party being criticised, so that this party can learn from the criticism, which will be of value not only for this party but for the entire International. Secondly, Comrade Radek, before he

---

25. For the remarks by Lenin and Trotsky to the expanded ECCI, see Appendix 3f, pp. 1114–25 and 1128–32.

begins to criticise a party, must have obtained reliable information about the party's actions.

In his speech, Comrade Radek refers to the British Communist newspaper. He reproaches it for not having carried out its duties during the recent strike of the Triple Alliance and the miners. Apparently, Comrade Radek did not read the articles in *The Communist*, for otherwise he would have seen that the party's official newspaper fully and correctly evaluated the meaning of the events in Britain. I have read *The Communist*, and I know what it drove home to all workers in Britain not only during the miners' dispute but long before the strike broke out.

As early as 5 March, *The Communist* alerted workers to the employers' conspiracy, which was then taking shape, regarding a wage reduction. The articles in *The Communist* pointed out that the employers' action against the miners was only the first round of attacks against the entire working class of Britain. The newspaper continued by making clear to the workers the stakes in the approaching struggle. When the strike broke out, *The Communist* gave workers the slogan, 'Keep a close watch on your leaders!' And this call sunk root across the country as a whole, drawing the mineworkers' attention to their leaders and helping them to remain true to their principles during the many negotiations with the government and the mine owners. One article after another made this point.

*The Communist* made it plain to the workers that they themselves should take over the leadership of the pits, for otherwise the mine owners would withhold their wages. The newspaper pointed out that the miners had to undertake something in this unprecedented struggle that could have an effect on the working masses of Britain. During the coal strike, all the efforts of the Communists were directed toward work among the miners. The Communists' newspaper took the leadership of the strikes and gave the miners every assistance that was possible. That is shown by the call, 'Keep a close watch on your leaders', which took root across all the country. That is why I maintain that Comrade Radek's severe criticism is not rooted in fact.

Secondly, Comrade Radek attempted to convince the congress that the Central Committee of the British Communist Party did not fully and entirely understand its responsibilities in the great miners' strike. I will demonstrate to Comrade Radek that the British Communist Party Central Committee fully understood its responsibility and directed its entire attention to this struggle by the miners. The Central Committee was convened, and this gathering considered what was the surest means of influencing the workers of Great Britain in the interests of the striking miners. And all the energy of party members, from agitators to the staff, was concentrated on the miners' strike. In addition, the Central Committee ordered all its sections, all its branches to build district committees to link up with the strike. In regions where such miners' committees already existed, the Communists were told to place themselves at these committees' disposal.

But the Central Committee of the British Communist Party went even further. It considered how the entire working class of Britain could unite with the miners and use the revolutionary situation to achieve the best results. Comrade Radek holds it against us that the party did not act openly and energetically enough and left the miners' committees to do work that we should have carried out ourselves. The British Communist Party is only a small organisation. If Comrade Radek is familiar with the history of the British trade-union movement, he must know that this movement is imbued with powerful traditions. He must know that it would be simple idiocy for the Communist Party to have attempted to influence or give advice to the miners, who have one and a quarter million members in their union.

When we realised that we in Britain could use only the most effective means of propaganda that were available to us, we instructed our members, who were simultaneously members of various trade unions, to see to it that their unions prepared for the coming general strike of the entire working class of Britain. We utilised the workers' committees, because we were aware that the trade unionists of Britain listen more readily to workers of their own branch of industry than to the Communist Party of Britain.

What were the results of this policy? The results were those that Comrade Radek would have most desired. Under our leadership, the workers' committees, in line with our instructions and directives, went on the attack and achieved an unprecedented success among the British miners and other workers. It was through us that these millions of workers perceived the need to stand together and to declare a general strike, by calling on all workers to show solidarity with the miners. We distributed leaflets to the transport workers and to workers of every single section. We sent propaganda workers into the mining districts, the industrial cities, and everywhere, in order to appeal to workers to support the miners. That was what the British Communist Party did.

Comrade Radek contends that none of this took place. Nonetheless it is a fact that it certainly did occur, and his criticisms demonstrate that what happened is exactly what he would have advised us to do if he had come to Britain at that time. That is what we must conclude from his report, in which he says that we should focus only on the present and not gaze at the dark and distant future.

We assisted the working class of Britain in their struggle and sought to lead them to their ultimate goal of revolution. That is our task in Britain. I believe that the conclusion of Comrade Radek's report, where he describes a correct course of conduct, is in line with reality. But I maintain that under the given conditions, the methods we employed were correct. I cannot say that the Communist Party made no errors at all, or that improvements were not in order, or that we utilised every opportunity. But certainly the critical remarks of Comrade Radek, to the effect that we failed completely to utilise the available opportunities, were unjustified. The British Communist Party stands blameless before the Third Congress of the Communist International; it has done everything possible to bring the revolution closer.

*(The session is adjourned at 5:00 p.m.)*

# Session 12 – 1 July 1921, 8 p.m.
## Tactics and Strategy – Discussion

*Further discussion on Radek's report. Speakers: Heckert, Burian, Malzahn, Bukharin.*

**Koenen** (chair): The session is now open. The first speaker on the list is Comrade Heckert of the VKPD. The Presidium agreed to grant the request of the VKPD to lengthen his speaking time, in order to enable him to present a coherent account of the March Action. Half an hour has been proposed. We hope there is no objection. Hearing no objection, we give the floor to Comrade Heckert.

**Heckert** (VKPD): Comrades, before I defend our position during the March Action, I wish to make two preliminary remarks, one with reference to the speaker from the Polish fraction and one regarding Comrade Lenin.

Comrade Michalak, who spoke on behalf of the Polish delegation, stated that the German delegation must take some blows. He said that we should not be sentimental, like old women, when we get some blows aimed at giving us a lesson. He then spoke of the errors that we made, and he wanted to speak of them. No one in the German delegation could make any sense of what he tried to say. However, we were thoroughly astounded that Comrade Michalak attacked the amendments we had introduced, since the comrades of the Polish delegation had told us that they approved our proposals. We heard at the conclusion of Comrade Michalak's remarks that the Polish delegation identified with our position. It is indeed strange for one speaker of a delegation to speak against another, and then at the end he cancels out both himself and his delegation. If another delegation feels the need to put on such a show, I can say on behalf of our delegation that we are prepared to absorb these blows.

Now to Comrade Lenin. He criticises our amendments, and in our opinion he is too quick in his judgements. He held things against us that are not found at all in our amendments. If Comrade Lenin had read them attentively, he could not possibly have said what he did, unless he had aims quite different from those he expressed. (*Commotion. Shouts: 'Hear, hear!'*) He said, for example, that we wish to delete the words 'Open Letter' from the theses. If Comrade Lenin had read this passage accurately and right through, he would have recognised that the two words 'Open Letter' had to be deleted, because in the theses the statement is made that it is through this Open Letter that the German Communist Party became a mass party, and that the Open Letter was published in 1919. In fact, no Open Letter was written in 1919, and the Communist Party became a mass party through the fusion convention on 5 December 1920. The Open Letter was written in February this year.[1] It was thus two months after we became a mass party that the Open Letter was written. So it is impossible to refer to the Open Letter at this point in the theses. We left it unchanged in the one other place where it is cited, because we all agree that the policy of the Open Letter was absolutely correct, and that it must be continued in similar fashion. Thus Comrade Lenin's argument against us is invalid.

**Trotsky**: You are not taking the matter seriously.

**Heckert**: I do indeed take it seriously.

Comrade Lenin then criticises us because, on page 2 of the theses, we have deleted the two words 'the majority' of the German working class, as if we were trying to slip in something particularly reprehensible. But when the wording is changed from 'the majority of the working class' to 'the working class', the concept is not narrowed but broadened, and I do not understand how this blow applies to us. I simply cannot grasp it.

One place where Comrade Lenin's criticism would apply to some extent is the first change regarding winning the majority of the working class for the principles or the goals of communism. Comrade Radek told us yesterday that he could accept the word 'goals'. I agree with Comrade Lenin that it is better to let the word 'principles' stand. The principles of communism signifies something different from the goals of communism, if we accept Comrade

---

1. The VKPD's Open Letter was published 8 January 1921.

Lenin's argumentation. It is probably correct, in light of the use of these terms that is prevalent in other countries. Communism is not only a social order or a science; it is a movement aimed at achieving a specific goal, a specific social order. It thus refers to methods of struggle. From this point of view, the principles of the communism here encompass the methods of struggle. And so I believe it will be better to let the word 'principles' stand and not replace it with 'goals'.

Now as regards 'winning the majority'. Our comrades were of the opinion that 'majority' should not be used here because it could be interpreted in the sense that the workers in their majority must be won for the organisation. That would signify reinforcing the opportunist forces in the Communist International, who take fright at every movement because, as they always say, the organisation is not strong enough. The remarks of Comrade Terracini show clearly that nothing further was intended than what I am saying now. For he said very clearly that the main task of the Czechoslovak party is not to further expand its ranks but to turn the four hundred thousand organised members into true Communists, that is, for them to become active.

But in view of that, then I do not know what remains of Comrade Lenin's criticisms that is particularly severe. I believe that in large measure he has been breaking down open doors. And we must assume that something else is involved here. And since we would like all those present at the congress to understand this, it would be good if Comrade Trotsky – since Comrade Lenin is not here – would make some comments on this. We would welcome that gladly, because we are not a party that believes it is the fount of all wisdom. We would truly like to learn. We can provide evidence that we have learned from the history of our party and of the revolutionary movement that we have experienced. We want to learn from our errors, because that is the best form of criticism of the opportunists in our ranks.

Comrades, the Communist Party was born in its present form in Germany not so very long ago – only last year, in December. And the connections among all the workers who now belong to the VKPD were not forged in struggle, where theories right or wrong could have been put to the test. Instead, they were based on a marriage contract. In Halle an agreement was made with leading comrades of the USPD that the party would be structured in such and such a manner. It was more a matter of fitting the two organisations together than of testing the revolutionary power and courage of the comrades, for that was not a time of struggle. So we understood from the start that the party would not retain the number of members that it had at the time of fusion. Rather the first serious test would result in a realignment of forces.

That is what happened during the March days, and that cancels out a good part of the criticism, which focuses on the party's loss of members. Comrades may be right that, in this or that branch, people joined without understanding that we are a party of serious struggle. But that is no reason for us to defend ourselves to the Russian comrades. Indeed, Lenin made the best speech for the defence today when he said that hundreds of thousands of workers were in struggle, and that anyone who acts against them, as Levi did, is a criminal.

The Communist Party (Spartacus League), which was one part of what is now the VKPD, led an ill-fated existence for an entire year. After the revolutionary movement had receded, and the putschist anarchists and other non-Communist forces had been driven out of the party at the Heidelberg convention,[2] we experienced the departure of a significant number of Communist proletarians along with those who had been driven out, because they did not understand the meaning of the split and of communism itself. Then we were hit by the Kapp Putsch. We had not been able to prepare ourselves, because we had been thrashing about in a thousand meetings with the KAPD.[3] There were times during this struggle with the KAPD when a large portion of the proletariat simply did not want to have anything to do with us.

The Kapp Putsch took place, and our party did not exactly play a very fortunate role in it. To be precise, it was actually only the Zentrale and the capital city that played an unfortunate role, not the districts.[4] The comrades in the districts battled in exemplary fashion. But as Radek said earlier, a party that is not able to formulate clear slogans in the first moments of an emergency will lose its capacity to struggle. That launched a bitter struggle in our ranks, and I must say that comrades were right in criticising our conduct. I believe it was Lenin who said that through our incorrect conduct at that time we missed a chance at revolution.

Possibly that went too far, but the criticism does contain a certain kernel of justification. However, comrades, we were not able to draw the conclusion from the Kapp Putsch that we should become more active, because there were forces in the party that were always of the opinion that any move against the enemy would mean a defeat and would pose the danger of a putsch. And the leader of these comrades, who were always warning that the party would blunder into a putsch, was Comrade Levi. There is no need for me to demon-

---

2. At the KPD's Heidelberg convention of 20–24 October 1919, Paul Levi led the majority in rejecting ultraleft positions on the trade unions and on participation in parliamentary elections. The convention resolved to exclude forces who did not accept these decisions.
3. Following the Heidelberg convention, the KPD conducted an extended discussion with forces both inside and outside the party opposed to the convention decisions, ending at the party's 25–26 February 1920 convention at Karlsruhe. The KAPD was formed on 3 April 1920. Bois and Wilde 2007.
4. For the KPD's stance during the Kapp Putsch, see Introduction, pp. 4–5.

strate that. I recall all the articles he wrote on tactics in the Hungarian soviet republic, and also his criticism of the Munich movement.[5] In this way our party, the Spartacus League, became somewhat rigid.

The revolutionary proletarians of the Left USPD were pushing their way toward us – not, of course, because they had understood the laws of motion of a revolutionary period but because they were driven onward by their feelings. And we, too, were watching the barometer of those feelings – their rise and fall. The strongest motion in Germany during those times was among the Independents when the Russians stood before Warsaw. Everywhere, in the streets, the cities, the villages of our country, the workers said: we do not want to make a revolution now, because the Russians will soon come. Just as they marched up to Warsaw, they will also come to Berlin. These were not forces who joined the Third International from inner conviction, who were determined to commit themselves to revolutionary struggle with all their strength. Rather they were hoping to be liberated from without, by outside forces.

Then came the great defeat, and it had a sobering effect. In Germany, the highpoint of the revolutionary upheaval among the broad popular masses was now far behind us. The Left in the USPD was a big majority, but it was clear that it had taken with it hardly anything of the party apparatus. Fewer members came over to the United Communist Party than our comrades had expected. No sooner had we unified, no sooner had we said that our mass membership gave us greater responsibilities, than the great movement of electrical workers broke out.[6] During this movement the party went through major vacillations. It did not have the strength to develop this struggle into a generalised movement. As a result, the Executive reproached us for our failure to achieve more, for our party was not yet active enough.

A struggle developed in the party, with one wing striving to activate it, while the other always insisted that we were not in a position to do anything. I recall the speech that Paul Levi made in his defence before the military court during the Kapp days in Berlin, where he stated that there was no chance of a revolutionary movement during the next two to three years. The offensive that the trade-union bureaucracy conducted against us and the immense pressure bearing down on us made the comrades inflexible.

---

5. Levi's article on Hungary, 'Die Lehren der Ungarischen Revolution', was published in *Die Internationale*, 24 (24 June 1920), pp. 32–41. An English-language translation can be found in Fernbach (ed.) 2011, pp. 70–8.

Levi's article on Munich, 'Die Kehrseite' was published in *Die Internationale* 1, 9/10 (4 August 1919), pp. 9–13. A partial translation can be found in Gruber (ed.) 1967, pp. 185–90 and Fernbach (ed.) 2011, pp. 47–53.

6. For the Berlin electrical workers' strike, see p. 240, n. 2.

Then we encountered the Italian question, and I must review it briefly in a few words. Comrade Radek asked what did the new Zentrale do, the Zentrale that had now been freed of its right wing, during the three weeks between the departure of the five comrades up to 17 March – had it issued any active slogans? Anyone who has read the articles in *Die Rote Fahne*, who has followed our appeals and our rallies, knows that the Italian question was not disposed of simply because the five comrades took their leave. The party was deeply shaken. In thousands of meetings we had to explain and demonstrate to comrades that Clara Zetkin, Levi, Däumig, Brass, and the others were wrong, and we met mockery from many comrades. That was the situation in our party. It lacked any unity. The Zentrale was not yet firmly grounded in the masses. And at that point an event occurred: the referendum in Upper Silesia.[7] The referendum took place at a time that was not quiet but marked by profound disruptions. Gangs had been fighting in Upper Silesia for weeks, and there were grounds to fear that the referendum could well give rise to an immediate explosion.

Every Communist understood that problems of this type are not resolved by referendums. The uprising raging there at present is evidence that we were right. In addition, the disarmament question flared up. On 16 March the Entente gave the German government an ultimatum, telling it to take legal measures to secure the disarmament of Bavaria.[8] A strict deadline was set. Given that the Entente had occupied Düsseldorf, Duisburg, and Ruhrort only a few days earlier and had set up a new tariff barrier along the Rhine, it was clear to us that this was no bluff.[9] The Entente was serious about applying sanctions. In addition, Germany was ordered to deliver the gold held in the Reichsbank. The German bourgeoisie stood opposed to that. Things came to the point where the miners rejected the coal agreement and refused to carry out overtime work.[10] They balked at carrying out the agreement, because they saw that because of it the miners in Britain, France, and Belgium were bound

---

7. For the Upper Silesia referendum see p. 712, n. 4.
8. To carry out the disarmament clauses imposed by the Versailles Treaty, on 19 March 1921 the German government passed a law calling for general disarmament within Germany, removing the question from the jurisdiction of each federal state. The law called for the dissolution of armed right-wing groups, which were particularly strong in Bavaria.
9. The French army, with 130,000 troops, occupied the Rhineland cities of Düsseldorf, Duisburg, and Ruhrort on 8 March 1921, after Germany failed to meet an ultimatum on reparations payments. They withdrew in September.
10. Coal miners in the Ruhr, Silesia, and elsewhere in Germany were refusing to carry out overtime work as instructed by an Inter-Allied Commission. In the Mansfeld area, ten thousand miners went on a protest strike during February 1921, with demonstrations by thousands of workers.

hand and foot. In addition, there was great ferment in German agriculture. Wage contracts had been shattered by the assault of the Junker landowners, and a general rising of the agricultural labourers seemed very possible.

We did not imagine these movements; they were real. We did not know whether they would begin immediately or only after a period of time. There were comrades in the party Zentrale who claimed we were wrong, that there would be no uprising in Upper Silesia, that sanctions would not be imposed. The Zentrale was right to say that the party had to be activated; we could not let ourselves be surprised by events and wash our hands in innocence like Pontius Pilate. We are no longer the Spartacus League with its 50,000–60,000 members. We are a party of 400,000 Communists, which swore an oath on 5 December to break with passivity and resolve the problems posed before us.

On top of all that was the movement of the unemployed. On 23 March there was to be a generalised demonstration of the unemployed in every major city and economic region. The jobless wanted to enter the workplaces, identify with the workers, and force through the hiring of the unemployed. We could have said that this was crazy. We would then have been totally discredited, and rightly so. The level of unemployment had doubled. We could not simply fold our hands as in 1920, when Paul Levi came up with a theory of the lumpenproletariat, thinking that this would dispose of the issue.[11]

Well, comrades, then we had Hörsing's provocation. He marched in. The critics say, and Levi asserts it flat out, that there was a connection between sending in the Russian emissaries and Hörsing's provocation[12] – (*Shouts:* 'Hear, hear!*'*).

I do not know what Levi meant by that, but perhaps his friends here in the congress can clear up the issue. The leadership of our party in Halle cautioned the workers regarding the grave situation. But a segment of the workers in Mansfeld did not heed this slogan. That is understandable, because two months earlier the workers there had been involved in a defensive movement. The employers brought in the factory cops, without consulting the shop stewards or the legally constituted factory councils. The workers defended

---

11. In a speech to the Fourth Congress of the KPD on 14 April 1920, Levi spoke about how the bourgeoisie was increasingly relying on the lumpenproletariat as a force to be used against the working class. A translation of this speech can be found in Fernbach (ed.) 2011 as 'The World-Situation and the German Revolution', pp. 79–91. Levi returned to the theme in more detail in *Our Path: Against Putschism*. However, Levi stated that the unemployed were workers, not lumpenproletarians. (Fernbach (ed.) 2011, p. 153).

12. In *Our Path: Against Putschism*, Levi states that ECCI pressure helped prepare the ground for the March Action but whether the ECCI bore direct responsibility cannot be determined. See Fernbach (ed.) 2011, p. 138.

themselves, and everyone said, 'Well done! Follow their good example.' Then the trade-union bureaucracy stepped in, calling it a wildcat strike.

The Mansfeld workers had won payment for their days on strike and, further, the abolition of the factory police. But with the aid of the trade-union bureaucracy and the miners' federation, three-quarters of the payment for strike days was deducted on the next payday. So all the workers' hope was dashed, leading to a menacing ferment across the district. The workers wanted to lash out immediately in response.

We went to them and said they should not do that. The trade-union bureaucracy has succeeded in driving a wedge into your ranks. You will not be able to conduct the struggle in the way you did two weeks ago. You must wait until another favourable occasion arises and unites you workers once again.

But, comrades, what use is there in telling an aroused working class that they should not let themselves be provoked. We told them that many times, but it had no effect; they took up arms regardless. And, comrades, when the Mansfeld workers entered into battle, something else happened. The entire bourgeois press in Germany mobilised those who were fearful and insecure, writing that the Communists were cutting off their ears and gouging out their eyes. The entire bourgeois press was full of war atrocity stories.

Our comrades saw this as blatant fraud. Our Hamburg comrades, the unemployed, wanted to demonstrate on this issue, to defend the Communist Party. The party had not called them into action, but they had mobilised to defend it. They said: if our Mansfeld workers are in battle, it's our responsibility not to leave them in the lurch. The comrades were cut off from the Zentrale, and there was no quick way to restore communications. So here we were, the German Zentrale, on Maundy Thursday [24 March], with battles in Mansfeld, battles in Hamburg, and a raging white terror. At that point, we had no alternative other than to call the general strike that had been forced on us, and to issue that as a slogan.

We knew that the holidays were close upon us and that the movement was being launched at a bad time. But a party that is forced into such a situation cannot say that since it is Easter, for the moment you should just let your comrades be massacred. If we had not called a general strike, we would have thrown away all our credit with the German working class. They would have said – and rightly so – that this is a party like the SPD: a big talker that does not want to fight. What was the attitude of the different districts? The comrades – especially our Communist comrades – simply could not have accepted the party remaining passive.

It is now said that the movement was launched by the fact that *Die Rote Fahne* published an article, 'Kahr Is Flouting the Law; Take Up Arms.' I will tell you frankly that we were not all happy with the publication of this article. And it is true that comrades who are familiar with the entire situation only from *Die Rote Fahne* will get a bad impression.[13] Our comrades said it is necessary to give a signal so that workers would realise what was actually taking place. Because it was not just a matter of Hörsing's assault; there were also the events in Upper Silesia that were also headed toward an explosion. We had to sound the alarm. If there is a dispute regarding whether or not this article was appropriate in the given situation, I believe we will quickly come to agreement in the German delegation and the German party. But if it is claimed that this article is to blame for the movement, that is not true. Even without this article, it would have broken out.

But that's the way it is with the movement's critics. They do not investigate the causes of the movement, and they do not pose the question of what the party should have done. Instead, they criticise a number of errors committed during the movement, errors that were criticised more sharply in the party than by Comrade Zetkin and her friends. I will use a document to demonstrate that. In its theses on the tactics of Communist mass movements, which assesses what has been learned through the March movement, the German Communist Party writes the following:

> Communists must go into all proletarian mass movements with the goal of intensifying them as much as possible and taking their leadership. The initial slogans of partial actions must link up with the understanding of the masses who are to be set in motion, or who are in motion, as well as with the given situation. As the struggle grows in scope and energy, the slogans of the struggle must be intensified.
>
> Conversely, when the development of an action is blocked, the Communist parties must also be able to limit their slogans and, if necessary, openly break off the struggle and lead the masses in united fashion out of the struggle.
>
> While maintaining close contact with the working masses and responding actively to their suffering, Communist parties cannot always orient their actions toward the most backward and passive layers of the working class. They cannot limit themselves to mere propaganda until the moment when these masses come into action on their own.
>
> In tense situations, where vital interests of the proletariat are threatened, Communists must step out ahead of the masses and attempt to lead the struggle through their initiatives, even if at the risk of bringing only segments of the working class along with them. Never should important positions be surrendered without a struggle.

---

13. See p. 428, n. 26.

The statement takes a strong stand against acts of terror that had taken place. It reads:

> Individual acts of violence are effective in the period of transition as a necessary component of military actions. Such actions must be rejected if they replace mass actions or are designed to call them into being.[14]

These are only a few quotations from what we learned, and what we thought it necessary to present to the International. In many, many other passages of these theses, the conclusion is drawn just as forcefully regarding the need to stay with the masses and ensure that slogans are adapted to them. But some situations are so grave that they require us to step out ahead of the masses. I believe that is something that every comrade will do and will consider to be responsible. That is entirely consistent with the line adopted last year, one that the Russian comrades have followed.

Well, comrades, as I said, our critics in Germany remain stuck on the errors made during the movement. Acts of individual terror occurred that could not be understood as being necessary to the struggle but were individual acts aimed at spurring on or replacing a movement. We strongly rejected such actions. We told the KAPD that we condemned such actions, regardless of the circumstances, and that we would not take part. We had that argument with the KAPD back in the Kapp days, and above all when it was time to draw the lessons from the struggle. The comrades have a theory different from ours. We believe that they are not Communist. Now we are told that the Communists too made mistakes. What is the basis for this? The material published by a pseudo-Communist, Düwell, which was subjected to thorough examination in a meeting of the Central Committee. When comrades were asked to document their accusations, they were silent. It was Koenen who presented this, and the Central Committee could only laugh at how ridiculous it was – it proved absolutely nothing.

Now we come to the question of why the March movement had to commit so many mistakes. These errors did not arise solely from our lack of knowledge of laws of motion or from the incompetence of the Zentrale. Rather the errors were caused in no small measure by the passivity of the forces that represent the opposition at this congress. They carried out deliberate sabotage. They said that they could not do this in good conscience and played themselves up as great heroes. They published a declaration right here in *Moscow*,

---

14. From the VKPD's resolution of 7 May 1921, 'Leitsätze zur Taktik der Kommunistischen Internationale während der Revolution' [Theses on the tactics of the Communist International during the revolution], printed in *Die Internationale*, 3, 7 (1 June 1921), pp. 239–45.

the newspaper, saying that it is not appropriate to drive up to factories in an automobile.[15]

When the general strike was called in Berlin, we gathered the factory shop stewards' representatives and asked the comrades who had become critics to come along and state their opinion. For this or that reason they were unavailable, except for Malzahn, who was the only one to go along. In this meeting it was not the Berlin leadership but one of the opportunists who said that if workers did not go out on strike, it was necessary to go into the factories with clubs and hit them on the head. It was we from the Zentrale who explained that this would be wrong, because it would not forge ties with the masses but isolate you from them. Some of these comrades did try on Monday [28 March] to enter the factories with clubs, and then came the isolation from the masses.

The group supported by Malzahn and Neumann said that the Berlin organisation had given a directive to go to the meetings with clubs. Perhaps they are even now still spreading that lie. I want to stress that it was the party Zentrale, not the critics after the fact, that forbade members from doing anything so foolish.

And comrades will also be interested to know that Anna Geyer, Brass, and so on were part of the party's Zentrale, and they took part in the decision for a general strike. They were under discipline to say nothing in the Zentrale, but then they went to Levi's circle and disparaged the Zentrale, accusing it of every conceivable offence. It was proposed to cut the electrical power lines. It was Brandler and I who explained to the comrades that it was totally crazy to cut the power line; in two hours it will be working again. And when we received word that in Bremen they wanted to blow up the electrical power plant, we said they must not do that. We sent a telegram to Bremen forbidding it, because we knew that, in a movement in which the masses are not with us, they would only be repelled by such an action.

Paul Levi maintained that he was unable to establish contact with us, and the other critics also said that they were not in a position to unburden themselves. We asked Däumig to come, and he did not come, but rather wrote his well-known letter.[16] We invited others, but they did not come. They came later on with all their fine comments. Paul Levi could have come to us if he had wanted to, but he did not want to. It was part of his plan that we should stray

---

15. A reference to a statement by Richard Müller in the 30 June issue of *Moscou*, denying that he had driven up to a factory by automobile to urge workers not to strike during the March Action. The statement was in reply to remarks by Ernst Reuter (Friesland) on p. 303.

16. A reference to Ernst Däumig's letter to the VKPD Zentrale of 28 March 1921. In it Däumig stated that the KPD's role in the March Action put at risk the 'fate of communism in Germany'. *Sowjet*, 3, 1 (1 May 1921), pp. 9-10.

from the path, so that he could give us a jab that would shove us out of the Communist Party. He wanted to carry out not a Communist policy but rather the policy that he laid out in issue 4 of *Sowjet*, namely that his path is the one that must be followed single-mindedly. We stated immediately that, with the movement in such a situation, it was unacceptable not to offer objective criticism within the organisation. What happened then? On Wednesday during the action [30 March], Levi came to Berlin with a manifesto in his briefcase, and Clara Zetkin prevented this manifesto from being published while the movement will still under way.

It was Wednesday, and on Friday the struggle was broken off. I know that Levi had already sought to link up with some friends, who got busy working with the party's money outside Berlin. It was clear that during this period they found support in the regions, at a time when all Communists were being hunted down by the police and the Orgesch.

During this period, the manifesto was taken out of the briefcase, in order to save the party, because its jewels had been besmirched in the pigpen, as the pamphlet tells us. There were already some thoughtful forces among the opponents who recognised where this path was leading. It is interesting to make reference to these opponents, because our goal here, in this discussion, is to deal objectively with the March Action. Levi pulled off an arithmetical trick in his pamphlet, in order to show that we only had one-sixteenth of the vote in the elections and an influence extending to only one-eighteenth of the trade-union membership, and so on. At this point, it was someone from the ranks of our opponents who said, 'This is where we draw the line. If this revolutionary struggle of the proletariat, now under way in Germany, is to be criticised, it must be done with different material. One cannot carry out such arithmetical conjuror's tricks.' And then a portion of the comrades in opposition turned away from them and are now with us.

The comrades speaking after me on behalf of the German opposition should say something regarding their own conduct during the March movement. They should not, as yesterday, wander down every byway. They should stride right through the movement and explain what they were doing, including the business of automobile rides to the factory gates and their tours across Germany in order to organise a bloc in the party to put the others down. The congress will greatly enjoy hearing how active they were, how they made themselves useful, and how they displayed a spirit of the offensive. We were not dismayed as we saw all that. We know the comrades in our movement. We know that there are individual comrades who need a back brace, because they are not capable of giving clear leadership in difficult situations.

Comrade Zetkin, I must say something about you. You know that you did not join the Spartacus League in its early days. You know that you said, when you were not with us, 'Those idiots, asinine resolutions'. Your reputation did not permit you to take part in something like that.[17] Later, you identified with us, even though you vacillated at times. And I believe you are once again on the road to identifying with us and moving away from Paul Levi, given what you have said here at the congress. Perhaps you are still reflecting on the matter. We in Germany would have raised more criticisms of the March movement, but what happened when we spoke out against the comrades? What happened then? They immediately brought down on us a new calamity in the party. When we told the 'League of Explainers' to write an article showing that it was a Bakuninist putsch –

**Malzahn**: It was rejected.

**Heckert**: It was not rejected. I must stress that when the statement appeared, saying that the March uprising was a Bakuninist putsch, Comrade Malzahn was told to prove it on behalf of the national trade-union commission. He did not write the article and could not write it, because he does not know what Bakuninism is. (*Laughter*)

Paul Levi played a great trick on us. When we declared that his parliamentary mandate was invalid, because the party had revoked it, he wrote a letter to the Reichstag speaker saying that he was not relinquishing his mandate – not by his own decision but because his friends had told him not to do so. The Communist Party of Germany became the laughing stock of the bourgeois Reichstag.

Comrade Clara Zetkin, it is said that you personally went to the speaker and told him you also would refuse to relinquish your mandate.

**Zetkin** (interjection): That is based on false information. Let me correct that here at once. I was informed that White Guards had discovered a large number of documents, including our statement, at the party headquarters. I then went to the Reichstag speaker and said that if any unknown person presented this declaration, it should first be presented to me, so that I could determine whether it came from the party or not.

**Heckert** (continuing): If the rumour is untrue, then that is positive. But it is a fact that Paul Levi declared that he would relinquish his mandate only

---

17. Zetkin replies to this claim by Heckert in her statement read out to Session 14, on pp. 595–6.

in agreement with his eight friends. When the Chemnitz electoral district declared that he was no longer their deputy, he referred to his eight friends, just as he referred in Frankfurt to the eight friends who supported his pamphlet. Read the statements: again and again they identify with Paul Levi; again and again they bar the door to criticism of the March Action by the Zentrale. And what is worst about Comrade Zetkin is that she has used her international reputation to cover up the breaches of discipline and betrayals by Levi and his friends. (*Loud applause*)

That is the worst thing. Comrades, I maintain that, without Clara Zetkin, Levi would not have changed his course; without Clara Zetkin there would not have been any declarations, and without Clara Zetkin we would not be arraigned as defendants at this international congress, because we would then be permitted to demonstrate with our party documents and the newspaper articles we have written that we have learned where mistakes were made in the March Action. For we certainly do not intend to keep our errors secret. We want to recognise our errors and learn their origin, so that comrades in other countries will not commit blunders like ours. Levi deliberately tried to prevent us from following this course, which is in the interests of the party, and Clara Zetkin assisted him in following a course against us.

And now we expect from our opponents here in this gathering an objective criticism of our action, as well as an acknowledgement of what they have done. They should explain all that they did, including the fact that they incited Levi to publish this pamphlet, because he declared publicly in Frankfurt am Main that they had prevailed on him to maintain his parliamentary mandate, against the will of the party. He declares that he will only relinquish it if his eight friends want him to do so. We ask the congress to stop these comrades from pussyfooting around. They should give an accounting for their actions, just as we have done for ours. (*Loud applause and cheers*)

**Burian** (Czechoslovakia): Comrades, first of all, I must present two statements of the Czechoslovak Communist Party.

The first explains our vote on the report of the Executive. We have voted for the resolution as a whole. Regarding the passage dealing with the Czechoslovak Communist Party, however, we hold to the position that we presented in the Executive. We insist in particular on the declaration that we submitted there.[18]

---

18. The Czechoslovak CP's statement, which Burian read out to the 16 June session of the expanded ECCI meeting, was published in *Moscou*, 23 June 1921: 'In the Executive's resolution certain of our comrades are characterised as centrists and semi-centrists. In our view no comrades in our party can be characterised as such. The varying opinions that exist or may exist in our party are those of Communists, just

Our second statement concerns the theses of Comrade Radek and his report. We are fully in agreement with the theses of Comrade Radek and will vote for them. We are also in agreement with his report, with the exception of one passage, which I must now address – the passage on the Czechoslovak Communist Party. We propose the deletion of one or several sentences that speak of the existence of two currents in our party, a Šmeral current and a current led by Muna, Hula, and Zápotocký. We propose deletion of the words, 'as they still find expression in the politics of the Šmeral current' and also of the words, 'their best imprisoned comrades Muna, Hula, Zápotocký', so that the text will read as follows:

'The Communist Party in Czechoslovakia will accomplish these tasks all the more quickly if it overcomes all the centrist traditions and ideas in a clear and determined fashion and follows the advice it receives from the Communist International...' and so on to the end.[19]

We propose the deletion of these words for the following reasons: Nowhere in the theses is there discussion of a specific party and its currents. Nowhere are names cited – not Cachin or Frossard. Only Serrati and Levi are named, but otherwise there is no mention of anyone who is in the right wing in any of the Communist parties. Let's put it this way: the same rule for everyone. We ask for the Czechoslovak party what is granted to the Communist Party of France. I believe that these grounds alone are adequate to enable the serious forum of this international congress to deal with us in the same way that it treats the other sister parties.

There is a second reason. I state here formally, on behalf of the entire delegation of the Czechoslovak Communist Party, that there are no such tendencies in our ranks. Specifically, I tell you that our delegation's representative from our working class in Kladno called me to declare here, in his name and the name of the Kladno comrades, that there is no Šmeral current and no other current in their ranks. Various opinions have been voiced, but for now we do not have any tendency struggle of this kind. And the absence of any such

---

as happens in other Communist parties. For that reason we regard the characterisation of our comrades as centrist to be incorrect. We are accustomed to not discussing decisions made at our congresses other than inside the party, and, if necessary, to amending those decisions at the next party congress. We would desire the same thing for the International as a whole. We declare that we are not in agreement with the Executive's resolution, but at the same time we are opposed to splitting with the Third International. We will remain with the cadres of the Third International, and we will endeavour to make the Communist character of our party clear to the whole world, and at the next International Congress we will ask that the opinion adopted with regard to our party be revised.'

19. For the final text of the section on the Czechsolovak CP in the 'Theses on Tactics and Strategy', see pp. 932–3. For Lenin's comments, see Appendix 4b.

tendency struggle in our party is best demonstrated by the fact that the comrades who, not long ago, could be counted among adherents of the Šmeral, Skalák, and Vaněk current, together with Zápotocký, Muna, and Hula, not long ago sent a common letter to the International's Executive. In other words, they acted together. The letter to the congress was not written to contradict anyone in our party or to permit it to be read as representing any tendency.

I tell you emphatically that, in speaking here, I speak on behalf of the entire delegation. I am not presenting my personal viewpoints and evaluations. Rather I am called on to present what we have discussed through together, and I am simply carrying out the will of our comrades. In listening to me, comrades, you must size up the situation as it actually is. We here are a delegation of nineteen comrades. Only two among us are intellectuals; some of the others are former workers, but many of us are workers still active today in the factories. We are governed by the type of discipline that Comrade Koenen spoke of here. We take this unconditional discipline for granted, and leaders do only what our comrades ask of them. When I speak to you here, it is the same as if our entire delegation were addressing you; as if representatives of our working class in Kladno and Prague, in Brünn [Brno] and Moravian Ostrau [Ostrava], and other important industrial regions were speaking to you.

As I told you, there is not at this time any tendency struggle in our party, and given what we have seen here at the international congress regarding the tendency struggles in various parties, we would consider very carefully before having a tendency struggle in our ranks in the future. We have a firmly established party, held together with iron bonds of discipline, and we will remain in the future a party with iron discipline. That at least is what we are striving for, and it is urgently necessary.

Comrades, I will not say anything further here about Šmeral. What our delegation has to say about this was already presented to the Executive. I only want to make it clear to you that we here are acting solely in the interests of our party and the International as a whole, since the interests of our party, of course, now coincide with those of the International. These interests begin with the need to maintain a unified party and to bring our entire large, unified party into the ranks of the Communist International.

I explained to the Executive that incautious conduct can threaten even the best party. This statement was met in the Executive by some scepticism. However, I will demonstrate this point through a quotation from *Červen*, the first newspaper in our country to declare for the Communist International. It is published by a group of workers who founded Communist groups in our country and quite often criticised our party or individuals within it. Šmeral too was often criticised in this newspaper. On 20 May, this paper wrote an article on putschist policies, which reads:

> No sooner had the possibility appeared of a consolidation of the Communist movement in Czechoslovakia into a definitive international party, than there appeared phenomena and influences that threatened this consolidation, in a manner very harmful to the proletariat. The reverberations of the conflict in the Italian and above all the German party, along with disruptive efforts promoted by hidden figures who enjoy great influence but have relatively little responsibility, threaten to create conditions here that are not at all conducive to a definitive unification of the revolutionary proletariat.

This article was written by people who work primarily with our German Communist comrades and share their positions. So I am citing this only to show that we here really have defended the unity of the party, here in the Executive and also earlier.

And, comrades, this danger has now been fully overcome. However, we demand that those sentences be deleted for another reason – namely the interests of our party. To be exact, the refrain that we hear about Šmeral has two verses. We always hear only one verse; the other is not written or spoken to us, and yet we still hear it – or, to put it in other terms, this verse is simply a complement to the other. One verse goes that that Šmeral is an opportunist, a centrist, a half-centrist politician, but the other asserts that our party is therefore poor in quality. What is really involved here is an attack not on Šmeral but on our party. Or, on the other hand, the second verse is that Šmeral is a bad politician, but the first verse is that our party is of very poor quality, is too inactive, too passive, and all this is because of Šmeral. Thus in calling for the deletion of these sentences, comrades, we are protecting our party. We maintain that the quality of our party is by no means poor, and it is by no means passive.

Well, comrades, I do not consider it necessary to dwell too much on our quality. It is not necessary for our workers in Kladno – a stronghold of communism that stood firm in a hundred hard struggles – to demonstrate their quality to anyone. I have witnessed their proud bearing in court. I know them to be absolutely fearless. They are under no obligation to demonstrate their fine Communist qualities to anyone. They demonstrated all that a long time ago. The Communist workers of Brünn dominate the party, the trade unions, the cooperatives, and the entire workers' movement. It is not necessary for our workers in Ostrau to demonstrate their quality. Not long ago they were a tiny minority; now they probably have with them a massive majority of the Ostrau working class and are educating the Polish workers, until now nationalists, as Communists.

Comrades, the quality of our working class is the quality of our party. Our working class would not have this party unless our party in the past had been of good quality, unless its character had been good and – if I may say – robust, just like our working class, as Comrade Zinoviev pointed out correctly in describing it.

Comrades, I am not aware of any passivity in our party. We are engaged in uninterrupted, continuous, incessant struggles. In September the earlier Social-Democratic Party was torn apart, and now there are two parties. Just last December we were in a great struggle. It was not just the working class that entered into struggle in such numbers; the party also issued a call. The German comrades are complaining here that in their March Action, of their 500,000 members only 200,000 took part in the struggle. Everyone in Czechoslovakia knows that, together with the [ethnic] German comrades in the country, we have 420,000 Communist worker members, and about one million workers took part in the December struggle.[20]

Comrades, our party is of the same quality as the workers, and there is nothing passive about us. In Pilsen [Plzeň], there are twelve thousand workers in the Skoda Works, and we have only three hundred Communists there. That is our weakest spot in the country. And in the December struggle these three hundred Communists carried out their simple duty, even though they knew that they could well lose their jobs. They went on strike, and probably they are even now still on the sidewalk. In our country, it does not happen – as in Germany – that only 200,000 of 500,000 members join the struggle. When our party gives the call, every party member responds, simply carrying out his duty in every spot and in every locality. And this is the way our party always functions, comrades. It was explained here that the Bulgarian Communist Party is an outstanding, excellent party. I do not have a thorough, complete knowledge of this party, but I am convinced that everything this excellent Bulgarian Communist Party achieves – in its press, in assemblies, in struggles, in parliament; in struggles of every type – our party achieves all this as well. Without any doubt. And if we have to catch up in some respect, we will definitely do so.

I am familiar with conditions in Germany. We do not say that you carried out a great struggle but did it badly; we do not condemn this struggle. We admire your struggles and your revolutionary activity. We have not condemned any aspect of your struggle. But I must say this: What you have accomplished – with the exception of the machine-gun battle – is of course enormous. And we are well aware that, with this exception, you have still other achievements to carry out through your press, in your organisation, in the struggle with the trade unions. And everything that your outstanding and

---

20. For the events of December 1920, see p. 76, n. 16.

exceptionally good Communist Party achieves in Germany is also being done by us. I can track that very closely and say a thing or two about it.

As you see, we are not at all passive. And that is why we call for these sentences to be deleted. I ask you to criticise all you want, criticise abundantly, indeed criticise like the Man in the Moon, who observes conditions on the Earth without documentation, without evidence – which has indeed happened. Criticise responsibly or irresponsibly: that is up to you. But it is our right to demand this as a party, not as Šmeral the individual. We regard these sentences, as advanced here and elsewhere, as a condemnation not of Šmeral but of our party. Comrades, we reject this condemnation. We do not want to return home and be greeted by scornful cries that we disgraced ourselves. 'You shouted until you were hoarse, "Long live the Communist International," and then it condemned you.' That is how our delegation sees it, and you can think of it what you will.

In conclusion, permit me to express a judgement about you as well. You have had little patience with us. Without any documentary evidence – please, Comrade Radek, I am not speaking of you, because you know our situation well. There were other critics who spoke here. Comrades, you have had little patience with us. Please permit me to tell you now what is our – or, rather, my – opinion of a good number of the Communist parties in the International. You have no patience with us. You said that our quality is poor. We exercise much more patience toward you. It seems to us that many parties are not all that strong, do not represent that large a proportion of the working class. And yet we have unlimited patience with all these Communist parties. But we can tell you that we have not worked poorly, we know it, and we will show it again and again and a hundred times. There is still a great deal that we can show you regarding how well we have worked. Confident that we have worked well, extremely well, we have only this to say: Comrades, you can judge us as you will, and we too have the right to pass judgement. And we can only tell you this: Work and struggle as we do, and then you will be just as we are. (*Applause*)

**Malzahn**: Comrades, I will certainly follow the advice given by Comrade Radek in his report that we speak to the disputed issues in objective fashion. I will not at all be influenced by the provocative statements of Comrade Heckert. But I would like to stress that if the tone adopted by Heckert persists, particularly in Germany, it will be very hard to come to agreement and to common action. We came here to the World Congress as an oppositional group within the VKPD, in order to take up the disputed issues, to put the Communist movement back on a solid foundation, and restore the possibility of working together.

What did Heckert say, in remarks that lasted almost an hour? He strongly attacked Comrade Paul Levi, whose case, at the express request of the German delegation, had already been dealt with in the [Executive] report. Heckert also strongly attacked those who had identified with Levi and attacked Clara Zetkin. We know Comrade Heckert. We know that his tone has often done great damage to us in the German movement, if we are not mistaken, going right back to the Spartacus League. But I would like to say this of Comrade Heckert: he can see here the value that the congress places on his remarks. He made accusations against Comrade Levi (*Interjection: 'Comrade?'*) in 1919 and 1920, with regard to the Kapp Putsch. We are not fully familiar with what took place in the Spartacus League. But so much is clear: right before the fusion convention, Levi was petitioned by Heckert and Brandler to take the chairmanship.

**Radek**: That was an ultimatum coming from the USPD.

**Malzahn**: If everything that is now held against Levi is true, then we cannot understand how the Spartacus League comrades could have proposed such a person to us as chair. That gives some indication of how Heckert's attacks should be evaluated. I regret the fact that he abuses Comrade Zetkin – who has truly won a reputation in the international Communist movement – as a traitor, and the like. We know Heckert, and that is why what he said leaves us cold.

In our opinion, we should not content ourselves with hollow phrases at the World Congress. We should not tell it untruths or mislead it, but rather present the facts objectively.

Combine Trotsky's report on the world economic situation with Radek's report, and you have the two fundamental elements needed to judge the situation. We must recognise that these two reports lay out a line of march for the Communist International into the future. I and my friends are in general agreement with Radek's report.

**Interjection**: You were also in agreement with the offensive.

**Malzahn**: Without any doubt, it would be a sign of weakness for us at this Communist congress to conceal in any way the difficulties that will confront us in every country or to be silent regarding the errors that have been made. It is through an understanding of the errors that we must come to a decision.

**Shouts**: What about Clara's errors?

**Malzahn**: People are portraying things here in such a way as to protect themselves. I do not get that at all.

What was the situation in Germany immediately before the March Action? When the Spartacus League and the Left USPD came together at the fusion convention, it gave us, without a doubt, a great lift, and we all solemnly promised to bend every effort in the interests of the revolution and to do everything possible to drive the situation forward. We of the opposition – we were prevented from sending any comrades here other than Neumann and myself – we are members of the national trade-union committee, a subdivision of the Zentrale responsible for carrying out trade-union work in the country as a whole.

**Interjection**: That is typical.

**Malzahn**: As representatives of the national trade-union leadership, we had travelled to the regions of Germany in order to oppose the trade-union bureaucrats in conferences and assemblies and also to give our trade-union functionaries and factory committees instructions for their work. As you can see, we were in close contact with functionaries in the factories and are able to form an opinion.

You must understand that comrades, unfortunately, are very much of two minds. In demonstrations and rallies they are enthusiastic, but at the workplace they see matters more realistically, because they face obstacles there. Building the party; fusing the two groups, Spartacists and USPD; fitting together their intellectual outlooks – all this caused great difficulties. Nonetheless, it was possible to win a powerful influence before the March Action, especially through the work in the trade unions and the factories. This was helped along by the employers' offensive. They provoked strikes in specific districts, lockouts, and the like, in order to worsen the wage and working conditions. That was when the VKPD turned to the other parties and organisations with its Open Letter. This Open Letter, together with the slogan of a workers' and employees' united front against the employers' general offensive, won for us the trust of the working class. The best measure of the extent of our trade-union influence is the fact that the union bureaucrats felt that their power was threatened and responded by dismissing union staffers and expelling Communists. That did not harm us, but rather contributed to increasing the party's reputation and influence.

The trade-union bureaucracy was more and more exposed. In addition, the strikes and lockouts in Hamburg and in the dye factories of Leverkusen contributed to bringing the trade-union bureaucracy, which was committed to *Arbeitsgemeinschaft*,[21] to the point of open betrayal. So our influence grew,

---

21. The term *Arbeitsgemeinschaft* (working group) was used in postwar Germany to refer to the policy of class collaboration between trade unions and capital in order to achieve economic reconstruction.

even though the party apparatus was not yet in working order. In addition, in the Prussian elections, we achieved 1.25 million votes, 250,000 more than the USPD, even though we utilised this opening not to collect votes but to call for the activation of the masses.[22]

So Heckert is quite right to say that the conflicts within the economy were more and more coming to a head. He gives a portrait of the provocations in industry and the increasing army of unemployed. The miners had renounced the agreement on overtime. We had oriented our whole apparatus to push the miners onward in their struggle. There were also sharp conflicts in the potash industry, because there too the employers were not willing to carry out the wage agreements. In addition, there were struggles in Central Germany about six weeks before the March Action, plus the movement of agricultural workers in Pomerania and East Prussia. All these economic conflicts were developing. A situation was developing in Germany that was favourable to us. In addition, there was the worsening international situation, the Paris ultimatum, the occupation of Düsseldorf, the business about disarmament, and so on.[23] It can truly be said that storms of conflict were threatening on every side.

And now, comrades, it was our view that at such a moment, given a confrontation between two power blocs – the bourgeoisie with its counter-revolutionary accomplices facing the proletariat led by the VKPD – the party Zentrale had to watch the situation very closely, like a general staff.

**Friesland**: We will name you as chair.

**Malzahn**: Friesland is better at that. It was necessary, of course, to note that the government, the German bourgeoisie's executive body, with its satellites Hörsing and Severing, was closely watching the unfolding of events. They too saw that if these conflicts came to a head simultaneously, there would be no way to halt the advance of history. That is why Hörsing and Severing cooked up a plan for the troops to march into Central Germany as a conscious provocation, in order to bring about a premature explosion of the conflicts in that region. Something like this happened once previously in Germany. I recall the battles of January 1919, when the dismissal of Eichhorn, head of

---

22. A reference to the Prussian Landtag election of 20 February 1921. The VKPD received 1,211,749 votes, while the USPD received 1,076,498.

23. The Paris conference of Entente powers met 24–30 January 1921. Britain and France threatened to expand their occupation of the Rhineland unless Germany continued to comply with disarmament and reparations.

For the French occupation of Düsseldorf, Duisburg, and Ruhrort, see p. 486, n. 9.

the [Berlin] police, drove the Berlin working class into struggle.[24] The goal then was to prevent Berlin workers from joining forces with the struggle in Central Germany and in the Ruhr.

Meanwhile, other events were in motion. Five members resigned from the Zentrale. On 17 March the Central Committee met and heard the presentation of the well-known theoretical position of the so-called offensive.

**Interjection**: What did you say to oppose it?

**Malzahn**: Comrades, I will get to that. The session took place, and Brandler's report was open to every conceivable interpretation – whatever you wanted to think of it.

The report by Brandler, which was to introduce the new general line, was extremely vague. I have already drawn Comrade Radek's attention to this, and he has stated his view about all this. But there was a putschist orientation in the minds of some members of the Zentrale. What did Paul Frölich say then? He said we must break with the past and force the revolution into being. (*Shouts: 'Very true!'*) What? Could he really force it into being? Oh, if only we had such brilliant minds in the Zentrale capable of forcing the revolution into being. Certainly, such brilliant spirits have been little in evidence up to now. And Comrade Friesland, too, said in the Central Committee meeting that we must take action even if only the Communists were taking part.

We did not remain silent, comrades. Granted, there was no possibility in the Central Committee agenda of 17 March to take a proper position on these questions. I took the floor, and used the available time to explain that Brandler's speech should be interpreted as meaning that no approval is given in advance for a coming action. In addition, I said in reply to Comrade Friesland that in practice it is completely impossible to launch a general strike or a struggle if only the Communists are taking part. Anyone who understands matters from practical experience in factory and trade-union life knows that in a factory of, say, a thousand workers, with a fraction of fifty or sixty Communists, it is simply madness for these Communists to leave the factory, separating themselves from the mass of workers.

So that was the situation. Comrades, I have already portrayed the scope of the action during the discussion on Comrade Zinoviev's report, and no one spoke to that, including Comrade Heckert. The figures I cited were not

---

24. Emil Eichhorn was a USPD member and Berlin's chief of police following the November 1918 revolution. On 4 January 1919 the Prussian government, led by an SPD member, dismissed Eichhorn as part of an attack on the revolutionary workers' movement. An upsurge of protest developed that became known as the January 1919 'Spartacus uprising'. See Riddell (ed.) 1986, p. 244.

contested – and cannot be contested. Comrade Heckert presents it as if the working class could no longer be held back, and gives Hamburg as an example. What happened there? Hamburg is a city with about one million inhabitants. And according to information from Comrade Thälmann, ten thousand Hamburg workers went on strike.

**Thälmann**: Yes, dock workers!

**Malzahn**: I informed you regarding the extent of the struggle in Berlin. We regret that the movement did not take place on a larger scale.

But are we going to fool ourselves through a lot of hot air? Comrades, let us examine the results of the action. The fact is that unfortunately, through these battles, we as a party lost the confidence of the workers. Even during the struggles, in almost every industrial region where the struggle took place, it was evident that workers were battling against workers. And further, of course, this led to the active element in the factories, the functionaries, being dismissed. As for those who were not dismissed, this false position and the events as a whole resulted in their adopting a passive stance in the factories, so that we have lost our strong points in the factories and the trade unions. The trade-union bureaucracy, the Dissmanns and Grassmanns, took advantage of this situation to struggle against the Communists with renewed vigour.

Immediately after the action, as a result of all the confusion, the party was very close to dissolution. In that context, comrades, one would have expected that the Zentrale would at least have created the conditions for containing the situation. Instead, *Die Rote Fahne* declared again and again that it had been a revolutionary offensive, that the struggle was being continued, and so on and so forth. This empty scolding and raging almost whipped the workers over to the Menshevik leaders. Did you not yourselves condemn the writing style of *Die Rote Fahne*? Looked at from this angle, a confusion was generated where all of us had good reason to shove these things to the side and to make every effort to bring the party and the movement back to a sensible basis.

**Interjection**: Through your statement.

**Malzahn**: And through the fact that the report of Comrade Radek on the March Action fully and completely confirmed all of our criticisms.

**Radek**: That is not true!

**Malzahn**: It is significant that you say it is not true. You are adopting here a curious position, and your interjection will not improve your reputation at this congress. You had the same opinion of the false position as we did. When we arrived in Moscow and had a meeting with you, you told us, 'Yes, that is how we too judged the matter.' If you do not have the courage today to hold to your words, then please do not accuse us of cowardice, but attend to your own cowardice.

**Radek**: What an outrage! I will never discuss with you again.

**Malzahn**: You reproached us for finding it too difficult to make the transition from propaganda to action. You compared our ideas with those of Robert Dissmann or Grassmann. But the reality is that we are the ones – we of the opposition group – who stood in the leadership of the struggles during the War and in the struggles after the November revolution.

**Radek**: And where were you during the revolution and in the January battles of 1918?

**Malzahn**: I was on the action committee [in Berlin], but immediately after the January battles I was conscripted and sent to Thorn [Toruń]. And if you would like to know the details, once there, as soon as I had the first opportunity, I deserted, in order to place myself once again in the leading ranks of the proletariat. You are not going to make an impression on us with that kind of stuff. Our representatives here, Malzahn and Neumann, are not pedantic pen-pushing theorists.[25] Our past is an open book. During the War, in the Executive Council, in the factory councils, we held our own and more. We arrived at this world congress with respect and feelings of exultation. And when Comrade Zinoviev says that our friendship with the Third International must be stronger than to Levi, I must respond, 'Certainly, our friendship with the Third International is ten times greater than to any individual.' We came here determined to create a firm foundation for the German party and for a great revolutionary movement. (*Applause*)

Comrade Zinoviev said that we should not linger too long on the past, but should rather say what is to be done in the future. Yes, that is what we want.

**Interjection**: If you do not turn to sabotage once again.

**Malzahn**: Comrades, in response to these constantly repeated interjections, I must state that when the Zentrale proclaimed a general strike on Thursday [24 March], I immediately travelled on behalf of the Zentrale to the Ruhr district, where the miners' forces were used in action, and during the action I carried out my duty fully and completely.

---

25. The term 'pen-pusher' could have been applied to several leaders of the KPD's leftist majority with little practical experience in the workers' movement, but in Session 13 Friesland takes it as referring to him personally. See p. 522.

**Friesland**: You know very well that we are not talking about you but about your group.

**Malzahn**: As regards Neumann, Franken, and Comrade Clara Zetkin, they all carried out their duty.

**Interjection**: Müller, Däumig!

**Malzahn**: None of these comrades engaged in sabotage. (*Interjections*) When the Zentrale crept away somewhere, I don't know what hole it was, it was Comrades Geyer and Düwell who went to the press office of the Zentrale and provided the necessary information for the party's press.

**Interjection**: But how?

**Malzahn**: That was their work, and they carried it out. There is no basis to talk of sabotage here. The structure of lies that you have constructed will not get you far. You are trying to drag in something by the ears in order to escape the real consequences.

**Heckert**: You were so agile that you already had the German party in your pocket.

**Malzahn**: Here is how things stand: the way things are developing in Germany, we believe that, through common work and through the struggle, we can overcome our present disagreements in the context of the constantly escalating employer offensive. For, despite everything that has been said here, I do not believe that matters in Germany can be long postponed. In my opinion, the employers' measures are more and more pronounced. In a few months we may already be compelled to take up the struggle on all fronts, to head off the absolute impoverishment of the working class. The situation is that the working class is so boxed in by the fragmented condition of the German party, that only our intensive work in the factories and trade unions can liberate them from the disastrous influence of the trade-union bureaucracy. All struggles that we have carried out since the revolution in Germany failed to achieve their goals or were defeated because the trade-union bureaucracy maintained its ideological and organisational grip on the masses. As for me, I understand Comrade Radek's comments and support them in the sense that we as Communists must never permit ourselves to be separated from the masses, but must rather seek, in close collaboration with the masses, to win their confidence. But that cannot happen if we utilise our party press for appeal after appeal, when one slogan chases after another –

**Interjection**: But what about the statements?

**Malzahn**: – and when empty abuse is constantly hurled at the trade-union bureaucrats. That only drives workers who still lack political understanding into the arms of these leaders. We must strive to win the workers through active work in the factories and trade unions. I only hope that there is an end to the hairsplitting and speculation that have taken root in our party, and that the great theoreticians – Thalheimer, Frölich, and Friesland – will come along now and then to trade-union meetings, will confront the Dittmann people from time to time. That would free them from their sickly condition, hunting for opportunists here and there. For that has truly become a sickness in the life of our party. That is why we say we have come with determination and resolve with the goal of enabling the German party, the Communist movement to heal. We can only regain unity through work and through struggle.

**Interjection**: If you are with us!

**Malzahn**: We will not talk about the Levi case any more because, on the insistence of the German delegation, it has been decided by the congress and that settles the Levi matter for us.

The question of *Sowjet* has been raised here, and Heckert said that Malzahn should have written an article on the March Action, and you all broke into laughter – you, as proletarian representatives.

I wrote such an article and sent it to the press office. It forwarded the article to the Zentrale, which rejected it. Comrade Radek says here in Moscow, 'You wrote an article for *Sowjet*; why did you not, you idiot, publish the article in the party press?' I responded to him that the Zentrale had rejected it. Then he said, 'I'm not aware of that.' Yes, that was the situation. I gave the article to Comrade Walcher, because Heckert had gone away on a trip, and Walcher was his replacement in *Kommunistischer Gewerkschaftler*. The article was entitled, 'The March Action and Our Trade-Union Work'. In the article, I presented the issues in my upright, honest, and proletarian manner. Walcher did not accept the article. *Sowjet* and similar matters are not an issue for me now. The issue for me is the forum of the World Congress. And for me, what the World Congress decides is binding. (*Interjection*: 'Very true!')

Comrades, as I said earlier, we came to Moscow with true, proletarian feelings and a sense of exultation. We saw how things were, and we also see the dark sides here in Russia. We are determined to drive the German revolution forward as quickly as possible, in order to help our Russian brothers. But I ask you: is a loudmouth who uses the party newspapers mostly for debates between one leader and another – is he a true leader? No, this approach only repels the workers. We have the best intentions, and I do not want the tone adopted by Heckert to continue. We have presented our position. The comrades who will speak after me will go into the details of what Heckert presented. However, I want to decisively reject the assertion that we engaged in sabotage. We want the best outcome, and we ask the congress: help us create healthy conditions in Germany! (*Applause*)

**Nikolai Bukharin** (Russia): Comrades, the comrade who spoke before me, Comrade Malzahn, objected to the tone adopted by Comrade Heckert. However, Malzahn himself spoke in a similar tone. As a result, I am obliged to be as meek as a little lamb. (*Laughter*) In the present discussion of different positions and problems, in my opinion, we have quite often spoken of things that are truly obvious. So, for example, when Comrade Hempel of the KAPD spoke here of new methods of mass action, that is a quite obvious matter for us here. We discussed this theme in some detail even before the War. It is just as obvious that, as regards what has been said here about offensives in general, even Comrade Lenin recognises that there is no Marxist who could speak against offensives in general. It would therefore be perhaps desirable, to include that sentence by Comrade Lenin in the theses.[26] (*Laughter*)

**Trotsky**: But only using the wording of Comrade Lenin: 'Only asses could believe the contrary.'

**Bukharin**: In discussing the world situation as a whole, we must keep in mind that it is not at all excluded for the relative temporary equilibrium that seems to prevail in Europe to be suddenly disrupted, and for the situation in this or that country to suddenly change. In this regard, Comrade Lenin spoke of a number of things, and his remarks need to be interpreted somewhat – of course, to be interpreted strictly in the fashion of Lenin. Let me provide some examples.

In the first phase of our revolution, the Central Committee of our party sent instructions to all our agitators to protest against the shameless lies of the bourgeoisie, who claimed that we, the Bolsheviks, were for civil war. Those were our own instructions. And in the situation at that time, these instructions were entirely correct. Now if we take quite a different situation, for example, just before the October Revolution, this sentence and these instructions would be not only completely wrong but completely criminal. At that time, of course, we gave all our agitators instructions to carry out an uprising and engage directly in civil war.

Let us take a second example, which comes from after the winning of political power. During the [1918] Brest-Litovsk Peace, our party and Comrade

---

26. A reference to Lenin's remarks on pp. 468–9.

Lenin, the recognised leader of our party, were for the Brest-Litovsk Peace, as you all know. Later, during the [1920] Polish events, the same Comrade Lenin was for the offensive, for a military policy. That was absolutely correct, of course. These examples show that *the tactical line is something that is not fixed but is absolutely in motion, always determined by the specific position, specific conditions, and the specific conditions.* If we can grasp that, we will be able to deliver a warning to comrades who find Comrade Lenin's speech to be undialectical. (*Laughter*)

We all know very well that the future Executive, however it is composed, must heavily upbraid any party that, under certain circumstances, does not take the offensive. In other words, the general tactical line proposed in the theses by the Russian delegation *cannot be used as justification for all conceivable future vacillations committed by opportunist forces inside the Communist Party.* (*Loud applause*)

Now a few words about conditions in Germany. A certain entirely undialectical contradiction exists among the different comrades. On the one hand, it is said that we must study our errors very carefully, and, on the other, that we should talk only of the future. In my opinion that is not a contradiction but an absurdity. We must, should, and will talk about the conditions. Despite the various remarks of Comrade Malzahn, I will say a few words about the Levi affair, because it is by no means a personal matter but concerns a current. And we know very well that there is sill a certain political affinity between certain forces in the German party and Paul Levi. To continue to speak about the March Action now and going forward would be quite strange, since a great deal has been said already. Nonetheless, I would like to analyse certain passages of Levi's most recent article, passages showing us that Levi has now developed into a quintessential Menshevik.

I will start with the question, 'sect or party,' which as you know plays a major role. When we look back on the past and recall what Levi did during the Second Congress, it is clear that during the congress he said that the Communist International should be pure, that it would be a crime against the Communist International to admit syndicalist trade unionists. If we do that – these were his very words – that action will amount to burying the International. (*Shouts: 'Hear, hear!'*) That is what Paul Levi said during a session of the Executive. Now he has turned around completely. Now Levi is claiming that we were against mass parties and mass organisations of the proletariat. That is no dialectical contradiction. Rather it means that Levi is seizing hold of any argument in order to break free of the party. In the question of the relationship of masses to leadership, Paul Levi spoke out quite sharply against the KAPD, and rightly so, referring to this group's lack of understanding of the role of leadership in a mass party. Now, however, an article by Levi expresses solidarity with a group within the Russian party, namely the so-called Workers' Opposition, which is the embryo of the tendency that is fully developed in the KAPD.[27] This appears in black and white in Levi's last article. That tells us, once more, that Levi grasps at any tool to destroy the big workers' party, the Communist Party. (*Loud applause*)

Let us take a third question, 'the struggle for the dictatorship of the proletariat'. For us, this struggle is of course self-evident. Even Levi could not think otherwise. Taking his most recent article, we find the following on conditions in Russia:

> It seems to us that creating the possibility of political struggle is all the more urgent, given that Russia has entered the phase of granting concessions.[28]

What is that supposed to mean? The text of the article as a whole indicates what it means. Levi says that the situation in Russia is not yet sufficiently clear. In his view, Russia today is undergoing a political and social crisis. The Communist Party needs to make a correction in order to find the right path. From what side will this correction come? From the side of the Social Revolutionaries, of course, from the side of the Mensheviks, that is, against the dictatorship. That is clearly specified here. Of course this signifies a blow against all the policies of the Russian party. This also has a certain relationship with what Levi said earlier against Moscow and Moscow's dictates. Aside from that, these are psychological considerations. From a logical point of view, what we have here is the embryo of a conception that is directed against the dictatorship of the proletariat as such. (*Loud applause*) Of course, this is a fully Menshevik conception. To express it differently, this is *the transition from the concept of the dictatorship to that of free democracy*. There is no other way to interpret it.

Then we have, in addition, the question of the dictatorship of the party. We Marxists – at least, we orthodox Communists – have always maintained that the dictatorship of a class can be expressed only through the dictatorship of the vanguard of that class; that is, the dictatorship of the class can be realised only through the dictatorship of the Communist Party. We have always rejected the entirely absurd concept that counterposes the dictatorship of the class to the dictatorship of the party. That is nonsense. And Levi was

---

27. For the Workers Opposition, see p. 679, n. 22.
28. Levi, 'Von den Konzessionen', published in *Unser Weg (Sowjet)*, 6 (15 July 1921), pp. 167–72. 'Concessions' here refers to Soviet Russia's willingness, under the New Economic Policy, to permit limited foreign investment projects, subject to government control.

with us completely on that point. Now we find, in his most recent pamphlet, ideas regarding Russian affairs, but there are also conceptions that attempt to generalise the Russian experience. We read there:

> Every dictatorship of the proletariat is a dictatorship of Communists, but not every dictatorship of Communists is a dictatorship of the proletariat.[29]

So if there is a rift between the proletariat and the Communist Party, then the dictatorship of the Communist Party is not the dictatorship of the proletariat. In response, I would ask: how do we determine in this case the classes in the party? Is it possible, from a Marxist standpoint, to form a classless party? Yes or no? Obviously, as Marxists, our answer to this question must be 'no'. There is no classless party. It follows that if the Communist Party is at the helm, it represents the interest of some class. What class? If it is a Communist Party, it represents the interests of the proletariat.

So what can be the meaning of this sentence of Levi's? The sentence has and can have only one meaning, namely, a concept hostile to the party dictatorship. From a purely theoretical point of view, the following situation may arise: The proletariat becomes demoralised. The party governs. The party does not have the support of the entire proletariat, and perhaps not even the majority of the proletariat. Now tell me please, in such a situation, where a part of the proletariat has been declassed, does the ruling party not represent the interests of the proletariat? In such a case, who does represent the real interests of the proletariat? The party, of course, the ruling party. What then is the point of all this talk? The goal of this chatter is simply to develop the embryo of a line of thinking opposed to the dictatorship of the proletariat as such and *therefore for bourgeois freedom, for democracy*. This line of thought is absolutely clear.

We can observe that the embryo of such liberal concepts is also found in the KAPD. I have touched on this question deliberately because I consider this ideology and these symptoms very dangerous. In my opinion, *this signifies the road to the Mensheviks and the road out of the Communist Party*. (*Loud applause*) We must therefore draw the following conclusions: An energetic battle must be waged against such tendencies, or the remnants of such tendencies, in all parties, including the German party. Every formation, every group that crystallises out of such conceptions must be immediately dissolved. In my view, we must put an end to the opposition faction, as such, within the German party. (*Loud applause*)

---

29. Levi went on to develop his ideas on the nature of Soviet power in his November 1921 introduction to Luxemburg's 'The Russian Revolution'. See Fernbach (ed.) 2011, pp. 220–56.

I will now move on to another question, that of the KAPD. Comrade Hempel declares that we do not need leaders or theoreticians. This statement, in my opinion, stands as evidence that hatred of leaders is so strong in this party that it has made a poor choice of leaders. (*Laughter*) This party publishes various educational pamphlets and propaganda articles. Among the pamphlets we find one by their main theoretician, Herman Gorter, *Class Struggle and the Organisation of the Proletariat*. This pamphlet presents the KAPD's line of thinking and ideology much better than the speech of Comrade Hempel today. Gorter is not such an adroit diplomat as Hempel, although Gorter is a man of letters and Hempel an ordinary worker. By the way, we heard another ordinary worker today, Comrade Burian. Now let us listen to what Gorter says in this pamphlet.

> The greatest weakness of the German and world revolution and one of the main causes of its defeats is the fact that it is not guided by a policy that is scientific, that is, historic-internationalist.

As we shall see, Gorter writes like a good Christian cleric. He continues:

> In determining tactics and strategy, the question of productive and class relations in Germany, Western Europe, and America was not given priority and perhaps was not considered at all. The main responsibility here lies with the Russians – Lenin, Zinoviev, Radek, etc. – and the entire Third International.

The idea expressed in this sentence is then developed in the pamphlet along various lines. That was from page 1. At the end of the pamphlet, Gorter writes as follows:

> The Kronstadt proletariat revolted against you, against the Communist Party. You proclaimed a state of siege in Petersburg that was also aimed against the proletariat. (Given all your policies, you had no choice in the matter.) After doing that, did it not occur to you that it might be better to have a dictatorship of the class rather than one of the party? And that it would perhaps be better in Western Europe and North America to have a dictatorship not of the party but of the class? And that the 'Lefts' are perhaps right after all?

To wrap up, he writes:

> If the Russian policies of party and leader dictatorship are still pursued here, after the disastrous results they have already produced, that is no longer a matter of stupidity but a crime. A crime against the revolution.[30]

---

30. See Gorter 1921.

So first Gorter says that for agrarian Russia the only correct policy is a dictatorship of the party. Naturally that does not apply to the developed capitalist countries of the West. Consequently, it is a crime against the International and the revolution to mix up these two different things. Then, on the last page, he says that mistakes have been made in Russia, and that KAPD policies must be applied in Russia as well. (*Protests from the KAPD representatives*) Dear comrades of the KAPD: it's written here in black and white. Let me cite a Russian proverb. It says, 'The crocodile is as long from tail to nose as it is from nose to tail.' (*Laughter*) That goes for politics as well.

The final page of Gorter's pamphlet refutes completely what he said on page 1. So there is no difference between Russia and North America, and vice versa. Then Gorter tells us about the trade unions, and that to impose the relationships of agrarian Russia on distant countries is a bankrupt policy. The trade unions are outmoded institutions and are therefore of no use.

**KAPD representatives**: That is not true.

**Bukharin**: Dear comrades, that is written here in black and white. Tell me, why should we not apply exactly the same policy to the parties? The parties, too, arose previously; they too arose in an earlier period. You respond that this is why Social Democracy is of no use. That means, it follows, viewing the question by analogy, that the old trade unions were also useless. What has happened to the parties must also have happened to the trade unions. Either the one or the other. And if you apply the line of reasoning you have developed for the parties to the trade unions as well, the picture becomes quite clear. The old trade unions really had quite different functions, which by no means justifies the entire theory of the trade unions presented by Comrade Hempel in his speech today. We carried out a theoretical and practical struggle with the trade unions in Russia and in other countries. We always fought against those views on the trade-union question. We said that the unions are mass organisations of the proletariat, which must be educated toward the final struggle together with the party, together with the other party organisations. You have not offered any counter-argument.

Gorter relies here on quite a curious argument. Completely distorting the matter, he declares:

> Our modern Western European and American world is cartelised, imperialist, and based on banking capital. In such a world, capital is no longer organised by trades but rather by enterprises.

So, not by trades but by enterprises. That is completely wrong. It is not a matter of enterprises, or even branches of production, but by various combinations of production branches. What Gorter says is complete nonsense. Suppose it were true, what would that tell us, according to Gorter? It would mean that we should also consolidate our trade unions. Gorter provides no other evidence, and neither does Comrade Hempel. You cannot say that new epochs demand new organisations. New organisations are all very good, but experience teaches us that the old organisations should not be given up. The sentence about organising by enterprise is wrong, factually speaking. All you can conclude from that is simply that the trade unions should be organised in the same fashion as production is. If you are satisfied with such generalities, why not apply this to the party as well?

The arguments about the relationships among the parties and between the leadership and the masses are just as weak. Gorter says that the party was able to win in Russia because the proletariat was small. In other countries, capitalism is enormously large and the enemy is much bigger and stronger, and therefore we do not need any leadership or party in the strict sense of the word, but rather entirely different organisations. I must reply that the entire argumentation is completely wrong. The party and the leaders cannot be counterposed one to the other. If we have a large party, it must have a central committee. What does 'central committee' mean? It means simply the leadership.

The [chair's] bell has given me a signal. So in conclusion I will say only this to the comrades of the KAPD: you maintain that you are good Communists, as stated by your theoretician, who considers himself a representative of a proletarian party that is better than us. Any halfway intelligent person tries to establish the social causes of the crisis [in Russia]. How did this crisis find expression? Simply through an attempt at a peasant *vendée* aiming to overthrow the proletariat.[31] You do not want to recognise that, and still you say, 'We are a more proletarian party than you.'

**KAPD representatives** (*raising objections*): That's a slander!

**Bukharin**: That is no slander. It's written here in black and white. What other sense could these words have?

**Radek**: No sense at all. It's nonsense. (*Laughter*)

**Bukharin**: In my view, we must tell the comrades that these goals and these ideas unite the KAPD fully with its most hated enemy, with Paul Levi. You stand on the same theoretical foundation as Paul Levi.

---

31. Vendée is a department in northern France that was a centre of royalist and peasant insurrection against the French Revolution from 1793 to 1795.

**KAPD representative**: And what about in practice?

**Bukharin**: Given that your practice is rather different from your theory, that shows you to be *complete muddle-heads*. That is why we call on the KAPD comrades not to let themselves be led astray in this fashion by their leaders. Their leaders must not write such things, otherwise we will have to finish off with the entire party. (*Loud applause*)

**Koenen** (chair): I would like to inform comrades that in addition to the German, Czech, and Polish delegates, the majority of the Hungarian delegation has also taken a stand, through a statement to the Presidium, in favour of the amendments that have been distributed. In addition, I adjourn the continuation of the discussion on tactics and strategy until tomorrow at 11:00 a.m.

(*The session is adjourned at 11:30 p.m.*)

## Session 13 – 2 July 1921, 12:30 p.m.
## Tactics and Strategy – Discussion

*Statement by the Communist Party of Czechoslovakia – German Section. Statement of the Hungarian Delegation – Majority. Statement by Gennari. Further discussion on Radek's report. Speakers: Ballister, Friesland, Brand, Neumann, Münzenberg, Lukács, Thalheimer, Zetkin, Vaillant-Couturier, Bell, Sachs.*

**Koenen** (chair): The session is now open. I have before me a statement with personal comments from Comrade Gennari, which he submitted regarding the previous agenda point after it was over. We will enter it in the record.

In addition, we have a statement of the Communist Party of Czechoslovakia and another by the majority of the Hungarian delegation. Here are the statements.

> The delegation of the Communist Party of Czechoslovakia (German Section) supports the amendments to the theses on tactics submitted by the German, Italian, and Austrian delegations.

The statement of the Hungarian delegation is as follows:

> The majority of the Hungarian delegation approves the position of the amendments submitted by the German, Italian, and Austrian delegations and supports them in the commission.

Here is the statement by Gennari:

> Since the debate on the Italian question has been closed, I did not have the opportunity to refute

Maffi in the congress session. I therefore ask that the proceedings record that I very strongly protest the lies against me introduced by the delegate of the Italian Socialist Party. I declare that:

1.) He lied in claiming that I have a reformist, compromising past behind me. On the contrary, during the entire twenty-four years that I was a member of the Socialist Party, I have belonged to its far-left wing. From 1910 until the present day, I have combated reformism and compromising policies in all their forms.

2.) He lied in claiming that, as the party's secretary, I could have done much and in fact did nothing when Turati was proposed in 1919 as a Socialist Party candidate in the parliamentary elections. This is not merely a lie; several lies are contained in what he stated here. The fact is that:

a.) I was not Socialist Party secretary at that time.

b.) At the Rome Congress of 1918, as part of the Maximalist faction, I favoured removing Turati and his friends from the Socialist Party.

c.) Before the Bologna Congress [1919], given that there was opposition to a split, I advocated in a meeting of the party leadership the need to remove from the party's list of candidates for parliamentary and municipal elections all those who did not accept the programme adopted by the congress. You can read this in the report that was printed in *Avanti*. The majority of the party leadership and the Bologna Congress decided, on the contrary, that even reformists could be proposed as party candidates. They merely established that the number of candidates from the different party factions had to correspond to a given proportion. However, I stated that this was a serious mistake, representing a major danger for the party. I found no one willing to support me in this.

Prior to the 1917 elections, Turati, Modigliani, and other reformists who had been proposed as candidates by the provincial federations declared that they were willing to be elected to parliament but only subject to certain exceptions regarding party discipline. In response, I formulated and submitted, together with Bombacci, who was then party secretary, a statement to the Secretariat, in which I opposed granting any of the exceptions that these people wanted to set up as a precondition. Maffi is very familiar with all of this.

3.) Maffi said that I should have presented my charges to the Livorno Congress. Yet he knows very well that in Livorno, despite all the confusion sowed by his friends – that is, the reformists and the Serrati people – I presented my charges and explained the urgency of expelling the reformists in a three-hour speech.

4.) He said that, after the Fascists' violent actions in Bologna,[1] I had approved Turati as a representative of the Socialist group in parliament. Maffi is well aware that on this occasion the Socialist parliamentary fraction met suddenly without informing me, and that for this reason I was unable to take part in the meeting. Maffi knows that as party secretary I did not fail to submit my protest to a subsequent session of the parliamentary fraction leadership. Maffi also knows that at the meeting of the Communist Faction in Imola,[2] I rebuked Bombacci with regard to the congress preparations as well as his conduct in this matter.

Maffi knew all this very well. He lied, and did so quite deliberately. He merely wanted to provide the Communist International congress with an example of the abusive and slanderous methods always utilised by the Italian reformists and opportunists. Indeed, Comrade Lazzari could also testify to the reformists' methods of struggle. He need only recall the shameful campaign by Turati and company against him, when he was not a defender but a prosecutor of Italian reformism.

**Koenen** (chair): We will now continue the discussion on yesterday's agenda point, the tactics and strategy of the Communist International. The Presidium decided to grant some speakers, as an exception, extra speaking time. All the speakers in question have already taken the floor. There are no more such decisions for today's session. The speakers who take the floor today must absolutely abide by the speaking time – otherwise we will never finish. I will proceed as I did a few days ago: after nine minutes, I call on the speakers, by ringing my bell, to conclude their remarks. There are twenty-three speakers on the list. We must absolutely conclude this point today. I therefore ask you to please support the Presidium's strict policy.

The first speaker is Comrade Ballister from the United States.

**Ballister** (Robert Minor, United States): The delegation of the Communist Party of America declares its agreement with the Theses on Tactics and Strategy proposed by the Bureau of the Russian delegation. We unconditionally approve everything related to its principles and unreservedly accept the underlying fundamentals.

As for working in the trade unions, we must stress that the demands presented in the theses fully correspond to the needs of the Communist movement in the United States. We have already begun to carry out in our country

---

1. For the Fascist attack in Bologna see p. 359, n. 10.
2. For the Imola conference of the Communist Faction see p. 340, n. 10.

the principles set down in the theses. We also agree with the point in the theses that calls on us in the United States to create a political organisation through which we can have contact with the masses and carry out Communist propaganda. It has unquestionably become necessary to have in our country, alongside the illegal party, an additional, open political organisation. However, we must continue our illegal work, chiefly because of the white terror in the United States, which is no less severe than that in Poland, for example.[3]

Let me emphasise once again, comrades, that we accept the theses as a whole. There are a few minor, technical points that we wish to improve. However, the proposals that we wish to make do not alter the spirit of the theses in the slightest. The three points that we wish to raise relate to issues of fact. We are well aware that the small errors made by the authors of the theses must be attributed to the conditions in which they were written, before news of the most recent events in the United States reached Russia.

The theses reveal that the authors were not aware that the unification of Communist forces in the United States had finally been achieved.[4] The two delegates who have just arrived from the United States were present at the important political congress that took place there. The Communist Party of America and the United Communist Party of America fused fully and entirely. Now there is only one Communist Party in the United States. The theses speak of the United Communist Party. It no longer exists. We have all adopted the name, Communist Party of America. There can therefore not be the slightest doubt, of course, that the congress will decide to adopt this small technical change. No discussion is needed either here or regarding the other technical points. The matter can be readily dealt with in the commission, which, we are confident, will adopt our proposals without further ado.

In the comments of the theses on the parties in the United States, we find the assertion that American Communists have yet to begin the most elementary and simple task of building a Communist nucleus. Given the fact that all the Communist forces in the United States have now come together, the commission will no doubt agree to alter that passage in order to indicate that we have just concluded the constitution of a Communist nucleus and now face the task of bringing this nucleus into contact with the working masses of the United States. As you see, we are modest enough to admit that we have actually only just begun to establish this linkage of the nucleus with the masses through real political agitation.

---

3. For US Communists and the legality question, see p. 228, n. 84.
4. On 15–28 May 1921 a Joint Unity Convention was held between the United Communist Party and the Communist Party of America, forming the Communist Party of America (Section of the Communist International).

As for the second point, here too our proposed change arises from the fact that the authors of the theses were not acquainted with the most recent events in the United States. The theses tell us, 'the Communist International draws the attention of the Communist Party of America to the need to create a political organisation'. In fact the Communist International does not need to draw our attention to this point. We have already turned our undivided attention to this demand. Our programme, which we will submit to the commission, provides clear evidence on this point. The paragraph of the theses taking up the formation of a political party as the legal organisation of the Communist Party of America is somewhat unclear, and is not as comprehensible in the English translation as in the German and Russian versions. We must therefore ask that the English translations be edited somewhat more carefully. But even in the other translations – and that is the only reason why we are raising this – there should be a minor clarification regarding the Communist Party's legal and illegal organisations.

We are compelled to function illegally because the white terror in the United States rages at such a pitch that anyone carrying a Communist newspaper runs the risk of being condemned to ten years of forced labour. We are compelled to function illegally. I assume you agree with us that all Communist parties in countries where the bourgeoisie holds power must do this, and that an illegal party must exist even in cases where the party has the possibility of having a legal organisation. No doubt we are all agreed on this point. We must merely formulate it more precisely. Together with our entire delegation, I support the sense of the theses, but the formulation must – at least, for American conditions – be made somewhat more precise, so that there are no grounds for doubt that the legal organisation should only be an addition to the illegal organisation and must always be subject to the latter's unrestricted control. This is merely a question of formulation, however; we agree fully with the authors' intentions.

The third and final point that I will mention here also relates to a question of formulation. The word 'sabotage' has a different meaning in English, and particularly in American usage, than it has in Europe. In order to avoid major misunderstandings in the United States, we must replace this word with something else. We insist that in terms of US usage it is impossible to refer to sabotage as 'winning strategic positions in the course of direct struggle'. We therefore ask for a small improvement.[5]

Comrades, we of the American delegation have closely studied the theses, for we know that we cannot adopt them unless they provide the necessary

---

5. See point 8 of the Theses on Tactics and Strategy, p. 944.

guidelines for our colossal historic task: the overthrow of the most mighty, wealthy, and arrogant capitalist state of the world. We have checked the theses closely, and we must tell you that they fully meet our needs. The American delegation will not fail to cast its vote in favour of the theses.

**Koenen** (chair): Comrade Friesland has the floor.

**Friesland** (VKPD): Comrades, how we judge the theses proposed by Comrade Radek is naturally linked to a factual presentation of the theses' foundation: the struggles of the Communist International and the lessons it has learned, particularly through the March Action. It is to be welcomed that Comrades Neumann, Zetkin, Franken, and Malzahn today presented an amendment that clearly opens the road toward coming to a so-called understanding.[6] I am happy to see in this amendment formulations that completely contradict the things that played an important role for us in Germany and contributed to confusion among the sections in the International.

But when the comrades say there that an incorrect approach of theoretically leading comrades on the question of the offensive played a disastrous role, I must inform the congress of the facts. From Comrade Radek's large trunk I retrieved the proceedings of the Central Committee. The 'pen-pusher' [Friesland][7] explained that the comments of Brandler were not intended to mean that the Communist Party of Germany was supposed to overthrow the government on 15 or 16 March, but rather that the party must orient itself so that it is ready and willing to initiate a struggle against the government on a very broad scale. He continued that we must link up with all the economic and political conflicts, that we must struggle under all circumstances, even if with only our own forces, that we must abandon the attitudes that were previously dominant in the party, and avoid small partial actions, so that the Communist Party could finally become a party of struggle. We must even link up, he continued, with the demands of the Open Letter. Comrade Malzahn, the honest worker that immediately saw through the pen-pusher's theorising, said the following:

> And now I too can say what Comrade Friesland explained earlier: even if we Communists launch a movement with our forces alone and we thereby suffer a defeat, this can only strengthen our party. And here I am thinking of the entire Ruhr district.

---

6. A passage from the amendment by Neumann et al. was read out by Zinoviev in Session 14, p. 565. The full text is not available.
7. 'Pen-pusher': See comments by Malzahn, p. 505.

So the honest worker and the pen-pusher were in complete accord on this question. The next day *Die Rote Fahne* carried the ominous appeal, 'Kahr Is Flouting the Law'.[8] This appeal is now cited as proof of our criminal and idiotic position. The honest worker Neumann said in the action committee that this was a brilliant statement. And the pen-pusher, Friesland, said that he thought this appeal was wrong, and he went to the Zentrale and said there that he did not consider these methods to be correct, because the action had to built slowly and systematically.[9] My viewpoint was approved, even then, and it was recognised that such a transition was too abrupt.

Mind you, I was then in disagreement with Comrade Neumann. The difference between majority and minority then consisted – as it still does today – only in the fact that we did not elevate our errors into slogans. We did not struggle against the party at the decisive moment. We carried out a superior and more thoroughgoing criticism of the errors within the party, to its benefit, and on the foundation of the working masses in struggle. That was the basic difference between us and these comrades.

The comrades now tell us that they want to come to an understanding. They say that the theses of Comrade Radek provide an appropriate basis. That may well be. The amendments we are proposing relate to specific points that need to be worked up with more precision. But if you want an understanding, comrades, you can obtain it quite readily and at no great cost. You have of course made a great many statements, indeed you have truly shown yourselves to be masters at making statements. Why do you not tell the congress clearly and precisely and with the courage that we expect of you that you have made a serious error in the course of the party discussion, namely the error of having strayed outside the framework of the party in the course of this discussion, identifying with people who had taken up arms outside the party and against it? Why do you not affirm, clearly and precisely, that our task is to rally the party's forces, to bring the party together again, and to prepare it for new battles? Here in Moscow – and Moscow air works wonders for some people – you discover that it was not a Bakuninist putsch. Here in Moscow you discover that the party engaged courageously in the struggle. Here in Moscow you discover that the March Action was a step forward. Why is it that you cannot be so honest as to also discover, here in Moscow, that at the decisive moment of the German Communist movement you committed a very serious error?

---

8. 'Kahr Is Flouting the Law': See p. 428, n. 26.
9. Friesland was a leader, together with Fischer and Maslow, of the leftist opposition in Berlin, which was not represented in the Zentrale and was critical of Kun's provocative appeals.

You talk about how the Communist movement in Germany lost influence. Our response is that this is utterly untrue. We did not lose any influence with the German working masses; on the contrary, our influence is growing from day to day, despite the errors, despite the poisonous campaign that you have carried out, despite the fact that everywhere you held the working masses back from preparing for new struggles. Despite all this, the Communist Party's ties with the working masses are growing.

You have recounted magical fairy tales with all your statistical information. You have a lot of time for statistics; I wish that we too had time for that. But we can also make use of statistics. You told comrades at this congress that *Die Rote Fahne* is done for. *Die Rote Fahne* had a press run of 38,000 on 1 January; now its press run is 45,000. You are all welcome to decide for yourselves whether our *Rote Fahne* is done for. When you consider that *Die Rote Fahne* is banned a couple of times a month, then everyone will understand that our party has not collapsed; on the contrary, our influence has grown. Comrade Clara Zetkin said that the membership of our organisation has decreased. On 1 June, the membership records of our Berlin organisation showed that 26,000 members had paid their dues. If you add to that all the jobless, that shows there is no basis to talk of any decline in membership.

In the most recent railway workers union elections, the party trailed the USPD and SPD by only seventy votes. In the metalworkers' union the bureaucracy was compelled to make concessions to the USPD and SPD, and only in this way were they able to maintain a majority. In the combat zones, our entire organisation was destroyed and our press was banned for months. In Mansfeld, for example, we previously had a newspaper circulation of 10,000. After eight weeks, the newspaper was again allowed to publish, and circulation has already reached 8,000. Anyone familiar with the facts knows full well that there can be no talk of any loss of influence. In Halle, before the action, our party was the strongest. According to Levi, it was shattered by the action. When [Karl] Gareis was shot, the SPD and USPD organisations felt compelled to co-sign an appeal with the VKPD.[10]

This appeal demands the overthrow of the old bourgeois government and calls on the working class to engage in resolute struggle against the blood-soaked system. And yet we had people who did not want to hear the words, 'overthrow the government'. Recently we have seen that even the vacillating

---

10. Karl Gareis, head of the USPD's fraction in the Bavarian assembly, was assassinated by rightists on 9 June 1921. The VKPD called for a united working-class struggle for self-defence and against government repression, and initiated a campaign that was able to involve the SPD and USPD. A two-day general protest strike in Munich took place, and there were protest actions in many other cities.

USPD leaders, like Rosenfeld, have advanced this position, namely that the working class can have only one goal, that of overthrowing the government. Comrade Lenin says that every revolutionary party must favour offensives, and you have to be an ass not to favour offensives – (*Interjection by Trotsky*) – excuse me, Comrade Trotsky, but we unfortunately still have asses like that in Germany.[11] Have a look at conditions in Germany: you will see the asses there, always crying, 'Hee-haw, hee-haw'. (*Laughter*) They carry on just like Buridan's ass.[12]

The point for us is not that these comrades must sign another twenty-four conditions and theses. The point for us is that all forces in the Communist movement must function in a party framework, and do so not merely in words but in deeds. Only such comrades have the right to reproach us for the errors we have made. (*Applause*) In our view, only such a party is capable of winning the majority of the proletariat. And since there is discussion here about the majority of the proletariat, let me point out that no one is so naïve as to say that we do not need the majority of the proletariat. We knew that back at the outset of the revolution. The problem is how to win the majority of the proletariat. That has not been addressed.

And there are parties that, instead of winning members and carrying out propaganda, merely churn out revolutionary verbiage. The workers in the USPD experienced that on more than one occasion. For our party to win the majority of the proletariat, it must show that it is determined to intervene in all circumstances for the interests of the proletariat as a whole. That is why it is by no means dogmatic on our part to insist so stubbornly at the congress on the fact that *the comrades who had a different viewpoint on various questions should state here categorically that they will no longer go along with the politics of smashing the party, and that they break with the past*. For us that was not dogmatism but the decisive question of the revolution. They may well say that we are pen-pushers and they are ordinary workers. In response, we can say that we pen-pushers express the feelings of the working masses better than you ordinary workers do, because you have fully lost your connection with the working class. We expect the congress to take a stand that is fully in our framework. (*Loud applause*)

**Koenen** (chair): The French delegation has asked that we strictly enforce the agreed limit on speaking time for all those who take the floor.

---

11. See Trotsky's remark on p. 508.
12. 'Buridan's ass' refers to a philosophical paradox often attributed to fourteenth-century French philosopher Jean Buridan. In it, a donkey standing equidistant from two identical stacks of hay cannot decide which one to eat, and starves to death.

**Brand** (Poland): Comrades, the Polish delegation stated that it supports the line of the amendments and that it will make other proposals to the commission in this spirit. I wish to motivate this proposal.

**Radek**: Michalak already did that yesterday.

**Brand**: What is the sense of these proposals? Is it putschism, is it KAPD-type thinking? Not at all. We want the theses to be a tool for educating the Communist parties of Western Europe to be genuine Communist parties of struggle. We want the theses to be a tool for taking up the struggle, without the help of the Executive Committee, against everything in our parties that Comrade Bukharin yesterday referred to as 'opportunist idiocies'.[13] Comrade Lenin maintained that the opportunist danger no longer exists, that we have thrown the centrists out the door and we must now struggle against leftist blunders. In my view, it is not so easy to finish with the centrists; it is not just a mechanical action of heaving some centrists out of the party in order to make it a genuinely revolutionary mass party. We know that a mass party can remain revolutionary only if it is constantly subjected to revolutionary criticism, and if there is a continuing struggle against all opportunist tendencies. That is the only way a mass party can remain a revolutionary party. On the other hand, here in the theses we find a great number of formulations that are insufficiently sharp and that the opportunists have an opportunity to interpret in their own fashion. The point is this: the opportunists always haul in statistics and say not only that we are not strong enough to make the revolution, but that we are not strong enough to fight.

**Trotsky**: That is why you were against statistics and for the sword![14]

**Brand**: The opportunists say we are not strong enough to fight. That is not our opinion, and that is also not the point of view of the theses. There are a great many excellent paragraphs in the theses where the idea is clearly expressed that the Communist Party can develop only in struggle. But beside these passages are others that confuse the issue and give the opportunists leverage to oppose us. That is why we believe it necessary to propose a number of amendments. But that is not the end of the matter. The theses display an exaggerated fear of putschism. I believe that the Russian delegation has conjured up a devil, which it is now combating. In my opinion, the danger is really not so great. But to fight so strenuously against this devil, with such

---

13. The record in the published proceedings of Bukharin's speech in Session 12 does not include this remark.
14. A reference to Brand's remarks under the world economic crisis agenda point. See p. 139.

extended paragraphs, only provides grist to the mill of the opportunists. That is why we believe that the long paragraphs directed against adventurism can hardly remain in the theses, or that they must be reduced to brief sentences.

Now for a few more comments on the Open Letter. Comrade Lenin believes that the danger is now so great that, in his view, the Communist parties in Western Europe, particularly the German Communist Party, refuse to pose specific demands, refuse to recognise the Open Letter, and therefore want to delete it through the amendments. He considers the danger to be very great.[15] That is a misunderstanding. The German party is not proposing to delete the Open Letter. It is only to be removed from the spot in the text where it does not belong. The amendment begins where the theses read, 'Thanks to the policies of the Communist International, the Open Letter, and revolutionary work in the trade unions, the German Communist Party has become a revolutionary mass party.' But we must note that the Open Letter did not have this effect. It could not have this effect.

Here is another example of this exaggerated fear of putschism. Comrade Trotsky even accused the Polish party of putschism. That is contradicted by the course of events. I maintain that although we are a small, illegal party, we have always exerted ourselves to maintain ties with the masses. Not only have we made such efforts, but we have also succeeded in launching broad mass actions, which drew into the struggle large sectors of the non-Communist workers, including even those in Christian trade unions. The struggles were waged for specific demands, for political freedom, against the payroll tax. That is why we do not deserve this reproach. We say that the danger is not so great, and that the struggle is being waged against a devil that does not exist.

**Trotsky**: Against a devil that is now trying to make itself look very inconspicuous.

**Walecki**: Good tactics indeed!

**Brand**: That is the negative side of what we want to delete. But there is also a positive side that needs to be deleted. After discrediting tendencies that have found expression – tendencies toward revolutionary action that we learned from you – the theses alert the proletariat to 'voices' that indicate the difficulty of action. Of course we have to take difficulties into consideration, and I believe this point is made frequently, in every session. But for us to establish in the Communist parties a special post of those who sound

---

15. For Lenin's comments on the Open Letter, see pp. 467, 1086–7, and 1098–9.

the alarm, voices that we should listen to with special attention, that is quite ambiguous – or perhaps not ambiguous at all.

Who are these voices that always see nothing but difficulties? Serrati, Levi, and others. If we leave that in the theses, we will have such voices in great abundance. Then we have comrades like Comrade Malzahn, who say that we can count on only two hundred thousand workers who go with us. If we had acted in this manner, we would not have initiated any movement at all in Poland during the last two years. But that is not what we have done. We appealed to the workers against the war, although the majority of workers did not understand why they should fight against the war.[16] We did that in the most difficult moments of 1920. That is little known, just as there is little knowledge of any of our political movements. We called for a general strike in the entire country, but only the miners in the Dombrova [Dąbrowa Górnicza] region came out, and even then not all of them – I believe it was ten mines. The workforce was arrested and the movement suppressed, but it saved the honour of the Polish proletariat. Had we not done that, we would not be Communists. We did that and we would do it again in similar circumstances, and we will not listen to the voices of those who warn us against action. There were no such voices among us in Poland.

We are for deleting these special 'voices'. On the contrary, we ask the congress and the Russian comrades to listen to the voices of the undersigned comrades and the delegations that support them, who are telling you that the theses need to be improved. (*Loud applause*)

**Neumann** (opposition group, VKPD): I am unfortunately not in the happy position of having access to Comrade Radek's mysterious documentary suitcase. If I were, I would perhaps be able to find material that would not exactly be gratifying for the defenders of the March Action. But let me take up another question, comrades. It has been claimed here again and again that we were quite cowardly, yet Comrade Heckert said yesterday that he regretted having to do battle with Neumann and Malzahn, because it was others who were the main offenders, and they would not come. Well, comrades, he made that claim although he had knowledge of a fact tells us a great deal about certain comrades. I have before me here the text of a telegram, one sent to the VKPD Zentrale. The telegram reads:

'Do everything necessary to prevent the departure of Brass and Anna Geyer.' (*Shouts: 'Hear, hear!'*) 'For reasons of party tactics.' (*Commotion. Shouts: 'Hear, hear!'*) 'It must not appear that they have the support of any forces. (Signed) August.' (*Commotion. Shouts: 'Hear, hear!'*)

---

16. For the Polish-Soviet War, see p. 90, n. 29.

Who is this 'August'? It is August Thalheimer. And at the same moment, just after we arrived and had a discussion with Comrade Zinoviev, he told us that he would send a telegram to Germany saying that everything should be done to make it possible for Comrade Anna Geyer to come to Moscow. Comrade Koenen signed it as well, which is significant, because he was aware of the other telegram.

**Koenen**: No, I knew nothing of it.

**Neumann** (continuing): That is characteristic of you and the Zentrale, and it is characteristic that we German Communists in Moscow must learn of the content of this telegram from Menshevik newspapers, from *Freiheit* and the *Leipziger Volkszeitung*.

**Maslow**: How does it get into those newspapers?

**Neumann**: Friesland told us about it, and today you can read in *Moscow* how *Freiheit* got hold of this document.[17] On behalf of our delegation, I must say that we cannot check that out, for the simple reason that we could not have any knowledge of a telegram addressed to the Zentrale. Greater caution is needed in making such assertions. We have no interest in making such documentation publicly available. One can only conclude that others would do this in order to pin it on us and then raise their eyes piously to heaven and say, 'I give thanks to you, God, that we are not like other people.'

Given what Comrade Friesland said here about the appeal in *Die Rote Fahne* just before the March Action, I must provide an explanation. When the *Rote Fahne* appeal was discussed in a session of the Berlin-Brandenburg action committee, I said that I was pleased to see a more cheerful tone prevailing at last in *Die Rote Fahne*. Nonetheless, one can have another opinion about the style and content of what was stated in the appeal.

**Friesland**: I have no recollection of that.

**Neumann**: I'm aware of that; you can never remember disagreeable things. I recall how the idea of the revolutionary offensive was constantly broadcast to the masses. In meetings called to discuss the March Action, Comrade Maslow spoke as the offensive's main defender, always stressing this revolutionary offensive. And Comrade Friesland never took the opportunity to speak against Maslow's point of view and reject the revolutionary offensive.

---

17. The 2 July 1921 issue of *Moscou* printed a brief article reporting that *Freiheit*, *Vorwärts*, and other Social-Democratic newspapers were utilising the bourgeois media as their main source for news on Soviet Russia.

And, comrades, when the action was over, the emphasis on the revolutionary offensive continued.

We said that if this is the revolutionary offensive that is always being talked about, then we say, 'No, thank you.' Previously the question of an offensive was discussed in the party in a different fashion, namely in terms of the party adopting an orientation to action, of becoming capable of action – but not of jumping blindly into the traps set by Hörsing. Comrade Thalheimer, the theorist, published a collection of materials.[18] In one article in this collection, Thalheimer had this to say:

> The March Action, taken alone, would have been a crime – our opponents are quite right about this. But the March Action is the first in a sequence of actions, which constitute the revolutionary offensive.[19] ('*Very true!*')

When you shout 'very true', that confirms what was emphasised in Berlin: we are going to continue actions of this type. But Comrade Friesland told us, 'Comrades, you really must admit your errors.' We are completely innocent. And they say that they themselves admit their errors. I must reply that they learned this only here in Moscow; they did not do that in Berlin. And I will provide evidence. In the 7 April Central Committee session, the German Zentrale and Central Committee had ample opportunity to lead the March Action discussion down a different path. But you know very well that the Central Committee did not concede that the March Action was wrongly begun and wrongly conducted. Rather, the reality of this error was contested in the Central Committee, which decided that by and large the March Action was a good thing. And then, on my third day in Moscow, to my astonishment, I heard members of the Zentrale say, 'What? The March Action was an offensive struggle? Nonsense, it was defensive in nature.'

Yes, Comrade Radek, if the March Action was a defensive struggle, then the discussion about the Bakuninist putsch goes in an entirely different direction. And if you, Comrade Radek, as leader of a faction in the German section, dispute that, I must point out that, on the putsch issue, it was said that Brandler certainly did not mean it that way when he spoke about overthrowing the government. It was just that the Central Committee was so stupid as to misunderstand him. Comrade Brandler, it is said, meant it entirely correctly: to move forward by stages to the overthrow of the government.

Let me specify that already on the Wednesday following Easter [30 March], that is, two days after it was possible for the struggle to take effect, the German

---

18. *Taktik und Organisation der revolutionären Offensive: Die Lehren der März-Aktion*, Zentrale der VKPD 1921.
19. Zentrale der VKPD 1921, p. 6.

Zentrale faced the following situation: Comrade Franken from Rhineland-Westphalia came to Berlin and gave a report on the state of the movement. He demanded that it be broken off. Then Comrades Brandler, Heckert, Thalheimer, and Stoecker spoke up right away and called for breaking off the struggle. And then a Zentrale member jumped up, pounded his fist on the table, and said that we can still expect an escalation, that the agricultural workers in East Prussia and Pomerania may still go on strike, and in any case things are still generally advancing. The comrades I have named then all gave way. This member of the Zentrale then said that in three or four days the worst will be over in central Germany; we can keep the movement in a holding pattern and carry on a guerrilla war.[20] Following this statement in the Zentrale, Comrades Heckert, Brandler, Thalheimer, and Stoecker declared themselves in agreement with allowing the struggle to continue. Comrade Thalheimer, who already wanted to draft the statement breaking off the struggle, said, 'Let's complete the statement but not publish it for a few days until the struggle is actually broken off.'

**Thalheimer**: That's a complete fabrication!

**Neumann**: I am sorry, but Comrade Franken is here as a witness, and he will confirm what I said. But comrades, when you write an appeal in this way for the breaking off of the struggle, you demonstrate that you have very little connection with the masses. Of this I am sure: it just will not do to write an appeal to break off a struggle and then leave it lying around for a few days like a cheese, which when aged tastes better and better.

Comrade Radek, you say that we have now declared here in Moscow that the struggle was a step forward. I have read many writings by Rosa Luxemburg. She was of the view that every workers' struggle can be a step forward, if it awakens a spirit of struggle.

**Radek**: Why did you forget that?

**Neumann**: But when it is asserted that the entire March Action was a step forward, I must say no.

**Interjection**: Our amendment refers to the March Action as a 'struggle' and not the March Action 'as a whole'. (*Laughter*)

**Neumann**: Well, comrades, that is a distinction that needs to be made. In my view, the March Action as a whole consists not only of the struggle but of

---

20. Thalheimer later identifies the Zentrale member in question as Hugo Eberlein. See p. 539.

its inception, conduct, and conclusion. It was not a step forward but a step backward. Comrade Radek, I too am just an ordinary worker, not one of the notorious cobblers of theses that we have here in Berlin and whose outstanding representative, Comrade Maslow, is with us here. I look at everything from a practical and revolutionary point of view, and I tell you once again: as a struggle the March Action signifies a step forwards, but the action as a whole was a disastrous error.

Comrades, I will now speak briefly regarding the future. As Comrade Malzahn said here yesterday, we are convinced the situation in Germany will come to a head. The imposition of sanctions is forcing the German employers to intensify enormously the exploitation of the workers, through wage reductions and extension of the working time, which will in turn produce even more unemployed, and so on. The task of the Communist Party is, as much as possible, to utilise this escalating situation in order to drive the masses onwards. Not, as Comrade Maslow says, *to drive forward every movement*. We have often disputed that; we say rather every movement to the degree possible. But if we want to do that, we must attempt to place the industrial sectors in the centre of the struggle and, as much as we are able, drive the trade-union bureaucracy forward.

But in order to carry out this work, we must return home with a clear and principled programme. For this it is essential that the personal struggle within the party cease – this *personal enmity and morbid search for opportunists*. In my opinion, it took a certain amount of courage for Malzahn and me to come here and defend a viewpoint, when we know that the entire German delegation will use all its connections in an attempt to put us in the wrong. (*Commotion*)

But we were pleased to see that representatives of the Executive grasped what was at issue. Thus we can say that the report of Comrade Radek corresponded generally to the situation in Germany, and so too the reports by Comrade Trotsky, Comrade Lenin, and Zinoviev. And Comrade Radek, if the report you gave yesterday had been delivered in Germany on 17 April, there would not have been a pamphlet by Levi. Instead, we were branded everywhere as criminals who did not want to fight. I say to comrades who are taking the floor again here with the assertion that we did not and do not want to fight, without any evidence for this assertion, that they are engaged in shameful slander.

As for Däumig, well, Comrade Radek, Däumig's letter is signed by Däumig, and Neumann's letter would be signed by Neumann. But Comrade Däumig will take responsibility for his own letter. Writing letters is a tricky business, for I have no control over what Comrade Friesland writes to Moscow. Letters should be defended by those who wrote them and not by us. Let us put an end to the whole sorry plight of the party and to conditions like these. If we are successful in this and in making the party ready for battle once again, that will please us indeed. We will wait and work and demand that others do the same. (*Applause*)

**Münzenberg**: Comrades, I hope that it will not be perceived as disruptive if I speak once more of the theses and amendments, which have not been addressed since yesterday morning. Comrades, we in the Youth International delegation have considered the proposals of the Russian party and also the German amendments. We have come to the conclusion that we are unanimously in agreement with the general line of the Russian party's proposals, but that they must absolutely be corrected as indicated in the German proposals. We therefore approve in principle of the German amendments.

Comrades, we believe that the Russian proposals, as presently formulated, hammer much too heavily on the Left and are much too gentle and weak in dealing with the failings and shortcomings of the so-called Right. We now see, in the history of the proletarian revolution over the last three years, that the so-called misdeeds and blunders of the Left have not caused even a tenth as much disaster and ruination as blunders of the Right. In our view, a correction is absolutely necessary.

I believe that Comrade Lenin is wrong to present matters as if the Left intended to form a small party, with few comrades, which would then make a revolution with hand grenades and machine guns, and that the Right consists of comrades who want to build the mass movement with broad principles and political perspectives and with model actions. That is not how things are in reality. All the parties denounced here as bad, like the French and Czechoslovak and others as well, deserve the criticism that Comrade Lenin delivered so strongly in his remarks yesterday – at least to the same degree.

To be sure, Comrade Burian said yesterday that more had been achieved in organisational and trade-union work in Czechoslovakia than in Germany and by the other parties. I believe that is not quite true. We are the ones who take our stand on the basis of the party's activity, and for us that means activity in propaganda and organisation. Of course, we go much further and explain that this is not enough for a Communist Party. It is also quite impossible for a Communist Party in Western Europe that is engaged in an intense daily struggle against the centrists and social patriots to limit itself essentially to propaganda. Doing so would lead in a very short time to a complete collapse of mass work. The problem of unemployment, of underemployment – in a word, the problems unleashed by the sanctions, are not enough to sustain us in political life, as they do the social patriots and the USPD. Rather it is also necessary to replace and complement such propaganda with genuine actions. (*Applause*)

When the class of 1919 was called up, none of us ever demanded that the French party launch the revolution or try to forcibly halt the mobilisation. Our demand was that the French party conduct vigorous propaganda, carry out actions corresponding to the forces available, hold rallies and demonstrations that might develop into a generalised strike, and attempt to utilise the crisis in the country and thus possibly prevent the occupation of the Ruhr region. The ultimate result would have been to support the Communist Party of Germany at a difficult moment and stand by this party. And I could well say that the present theses, and the speeches made so far against the so-called Left, should be turned against the rightist parties to at least the same degree and with the same vigour. We do not deny the need for a mass party.

Comrade Burian said yesterday that when the Czechoslovak party so decides and gives the call, more than one million will respond. Comrade Šmeral, who has yet to speak, says that they could make a revolution in Czechoslovakia if they wanted. To this we reply that it is not enough to have a mass movement and a mass party. How is this any different from the previous mass parties? The difference is that we say our mass party and mass movement should be revolutionary. To this end, the theses must absolutely be expanded. Comrade Lenin said that the theses of the Russian comrades arise from the vital needs of the entire world. The Left, however, is very severely criticised in the theses. The Right is treated much more leniently and in a kindly fashion. I will briefly criticise only the part of the theses dealing with the French party and its policies. The text there reads:

> Impatient and politically inexperienced revolutionary forces attempt to apply extreme methods – inherently more appropriate to a decisive revolutionary proletarian uprising – to isolated questions and tasks. Such efforts contain elements of highly dangerous adventurism and, if put into practice, can set back for a long time genuine revolutionary preparation of the proletariat for winning power.[21]

I must point out that no one in France proposed to respond to the call-up of the youth with a revolution. What did the French youth want? The French youth called on the French party to utilise the critical situation against the French bourgeoisie and against imperialism, and the youth crowded forward into rallies against calling up the conscripts. Well, in a session of the Executive Committee, a youth representative told this story in a somewhat awkward

---

21. For the corresponding passage of the theses, see pp. 931–2.

way, resulting in an attempt in the theses to thrash the French youth with all these blows.[22]

Such severe treatment is not meted out to those who carry out the worst adventurist policies, namely the Right. A correction in the theses is absolutely needed here, so that the right danger receives at least the same degree of emphasis. What is the left danger, now that the KAPD question has been disposed of? I recall that we warned at the Second Congress of the dangers threatening us from the right. In his summary, Comrade Lenin portrayed leftism as a crime. The danger from the Left is absolutely not present to the same degree as was the danger from the Right a year ago. If we consider merely the speech by Burian and the conduct of Šmeral and the French party, *the danger from the Right is much greater, and we must therefore insist that this danger be identified to a much greater extent in the guidelines on tactics and strategy.* (Loud applause and cheers)

**Koenen** (chair): Comrade Lukács has the floor. With regard to this speaker, we have a statement by the majority of the Hungarian delegation, which states that it is not proposing a speaker in this discussion. Comrade Lukács, it says, is speaking on behalf only of the minority of the Hungarian delegation. The delegation's minority has submitted a statement, which reads as follows.

> In yesterday's congress session, the Presidium read a statement of the 'majority' of the Hungarian delegation, which gave its support to the German amendments. This statement needs to be corrected. In recent months, disagreements arose in the Communist Party of Hungary between the majority of the Central Committee and, on the other hand, Béla Kun and some of his followers. On the Central Committee's initiative, the matter was brought to the Communist International's Executive Committee for decision. The Executive Committee ruled that the question should be dealt with during the congress. The Presidium of the Executive recognised Béla Kun and his supporters as an independent faction. The Hungarian delegation is therefore divided into two parts. In addition, representatives of the Pécs-Baranya district were also included in the delegation with consultative vote. The supporters of the Béla Kun group then resident in Moscow formed a numerical majority of the Hungarian party's representatives. No protest was registered against forming the delegation in this manner, because it was agreed that both factions would have the same number of votes. Under such circumstances, it is not possible to speak of a majority of the Hungarian delegation.

---

22. Maurice Laporte's speech to the expanded ECCI meeting appears on pp. 1110–14 in Appendix 3f.

The undersigned delegates of the Communist Party of Hungary are in principled agreement with the Russian theses. However, they will work in the commission to ensure that the passages directed against centrists and half-centrists and those emphasising the role of the party in the revolution are expressed in a fashion that excludes any possible misunderstanding.

*Jenő Landler*, chair of the Hungarian delegation

*Janos Hirossik, Albert Király, Georg Lukács*, delegates.

**Georg Lukács** (Hungary): Comrades, the submitters of this statement – representatives of the Communist Party of Hungary 'Minority Faction' – are in fundamental agreement with the theses presented by the Russian party. However, we are of the opinion that there are certain passages in these theses that – although not lending support to centrist or half-centrist currents – could possibly be reinterpreted by such tendencies in that fashion. We will address this issue through our own amendments and by supporting other such proposals. This does not mean that we reject all of the amendments now before us. It means simply that we cannot give these amendments our full support.

We want to define our position above all with respect to the role of the party in the revolution. That is the most significant problem of tactics and strategy, and it is closely linked to the March Action. Therefore, it is not surprising that almost all the comments here, whether approving or disapproving, have turned on the March Action. However, there are two issues at stake in the March Action, which can be distinguished in terms of principle, theory, and also tactics. First, there is the genuine essence lodged in the March Action, which we can learn from. Second, there is the way that the March Action was carried out and defined by its initiators.

We must here take note of an unusual phenomenon. Elsewhere, we see cases where putschist undertakings have been justified in Marxist terms after the fact. But in this case, a great revolutionary mass movement, which represented a significant step forward, was presented as if it was a matter of a putsch. This theoretical aberration arises from the theory that was constructed around the March Action. I will read a few quotations from the anthology that demonstrate a one-sided military and entirely putschist approach, which however is quite unrelated to the March Action itself. One passage in the anthology reads: 'When the proletariat takes the offensive, the reactionaries do not have time to arm their scattered masses and bring them together in time.'

Comrade Pogány says here that unemployment today corresponds to the separation of the producers from the means of production in the period of primitive accumulation. This is complete nonsense. The factory worker is just as separated from the means of production as the jobless worker.

The spirit of this putschist outlook is most clearly expressed in the following passage: 'Therefore, the party's slogan can only be, "Offensive, offensive at all costs, using every means, in the present situation, which offers significant possibilities of success."'[23]

**Pogány**: You are quoting incorrectly.

**Radek**: That is from Lukács's article in *Die Internationale*.[24]

**Lukács**: I will continue. This same article asserts that it was a question of a partial action, and the goal of this partial action is defined in the following way: 'So it poses the final goal not as taking power but simply as disarming the bourgeoisie and arming the proletariat.' This completely obscures the most important problem posed by the March Action. What was at stake in the March Action? What is different about the situation in Germany compared to all other countries? First, that there is a Communist Party in Germany that is a much more consolidated mass party than those of other countries. That imposes great responsibilities on this party. On the other side, there are the counterrevolutionary workers' organisations.

The theses put the trade unions, controlled by a counterrevolutionary leadership, almost on the same level as the counterrevolutionary workers' parties, although the function of the workers' parties is in fact considerably different and much more dangerous than that of the counterrevolutionary trade unions. This distinction is expressed by the difference in our attitude toward them. In a word: we want to wrest the unions out of the hands of the Social Democrats and the centrists, while in the case of the right-wing and centrist parties, we want to shatter and destroy them. So the stakes in each of these two cases are quite different.

The essence of the difference lies in the effects. The counterrevolutionary effects of the trade unions are expressed in a tendency toward depoliticising the movement, making the working masses politically disorganised and

---

23. The quotation is from the article, 'Vom Kapp Putsch zur Märzaktion', Zentrale der VKPD 1921, pp. 22–3. The article is signed 'I. Heyder', whom Lukács identifies as Jószef Pogány, one of the ECCI emissaries in Germany during the March Action.

24. *Die Internationale* published two articles by Lukács on the March Action: 'Spontaneität der Massen, Aktivität der Partei' [Spontaneity of the Masses, Activity of the Party] (no. 6, 15 March 1921, pp. 208–15) and 'Fragen der organisatorische revolutionärer Initiative' [Organisational Questions of Revolutionary Initiative] (no. 8, 15 June, pp. 298–307).

amorphous. This enables them, very often, to hold back the masses from spontaneous action. But their most important function is to lead astray and sabotage actions that have already broken out. The counterrevolutionary workers' parties, by contrast, provide their supporters with a definite and politically clear reactionary course. They are thus able to prevent even the possibility of spontaneous mass actions, even the possibility that a ferment could develop within the proletariat that the Communist Party could then utilise to press the revolution forward.

In Germany, even before the revolution, there was a certain differentiation among the workers' parties. This became more pronounced during the revolution, and significant sectors were activated, especially among those most interested in politics – not only in a revolutionary direction, not only in the Communist Party, but also in the USPD and SPD. This differentiation has become much more pronounced in recent times and is expressed ideologically and organisationally in the parties. Among the masses organised in trade unions, on the other hand, or in areas where the struggle over ideas and lines of action has not yet penetrated so deeply, we do not observe a hardened differentiation of this type. We observe this difference in individual sectors where, despite the counterrevolutionary trade unions, powerful spontaneous actions sometimes break out. That creates the specific challenge that now confronts the VKPD.

It is not enough to carry out propaganda and even to issue appeals for action in such a situation, because we are no longer addressing an amorphous political mass, no longer merely trade unions that seek to depoliticise the working class, but rather counterrevolutionary workers' organisations with specific political programmes. Here the VKPD had to employ actions, because only initiatives in action can organisationally tear loose the masses that are ideologically and politically tied down. That is what partial actions are for.

However, the term 'partial action' cannot possibly encompass actions whose purpose is, for example, to disarm the bourgeoisie and arm the proletariat. That is a slogan that we must hold in view as a goal posed at the end of the struggle. We must work toward the goal that the movements will culminate in the arming of the proletariat. But we cannot start off actions today with that slogan, because it cannot attract masses who have grown counterrevolutionary. We must link our partial actions to issues of the day. This involves taking initiatives, that is, going on the offensive to set the working masses in motion, in ferment. This requires not just education but initiatives and actions by the VKPD. If such a movement comes into being, if the masses are torn loose from the counterrevolutionary workers' organisations, it is then possible to propose other and more advanced slogans. The great error consisted of beginning the action with what might have been its ultimate demands. As a result, we did not achieve what was possible. Behind the action lay an incorrect theoretical approach of a sector of the leadership, which did not understand this problem. In this regard, we will propose amendments, which will be distributed. (*Loud applause*)

**Thalheimer** (VKPD): Comrades, to start with I must establish a few simple facts relating to the March Action. With regard to its effects, it is perhaps sufficient to cite a few facts. We now hold the leadership of the unemployed movement in Berlin. We hold the majority in the Hamburg unemployed council. In the elections among railway workers in Berlin, we received about 4,900 votes, compared to just over 5,000 votes for the USPD and SPD taken together. In the bindery workers' union, where the SPD and USPD made common cause, we won a majority. A few more facts: In the federation of salaried employees, a meeting of officials decided by a vote of 69 to 63 to expel the Communist officials. This decision was reversed the following day by Leipart, the chair, because they were not strong enough to carry it out. Something similar happened in the shipwrights' union. A motion against the Communists was rejected by a 75 per cent majority.

As regards what Neumann said here, a few corrections. What he said about the telegram concerning Anna Geyer is correct.[25] I have no intention of dropping the matter. The situation was that Anna Geyer committed a gross breach of trust. She took part in what happened in the Zentrale without protest and then passed on documentation to Paul Levi. (*Shame!*) She repeatedly carried out gross breaches of discipline. In my opinion, a Zentrale that lets itself be led around by the nose in this fashion is not worthy of leading the party. Comrade Neumann would have done better to keep quiet about the way *Freiheit* exploits such matters, for the question inevitably arises of how *Freiheit* gets hold of such documents and why they are useful to *Freiheit*. (*Loud shouting*) Caution was in order, because this is not the first such case.

As regards how the movement was brought to an end, Neumann is spreading reports that we have heard quite often, but which do not gain in accuracy through repetition. He claims that the majority of the Zentrale was for breaking off the struggle and let itself be terrorised by Eberlein. Here are the proceedings from 30 March, according to which Comrade Brandler spoke as follows:

> Just as the action was begun in united fashion, so too it must be brought to an end in unity. There appears to be a misunderstanding that I am advocating an end to the struggle as early as today. That is not the case. Although the decision on this question will be communicated only in two or three days,

---

25. For Neumann's comments, see p. 528.

nonetheless we must clarify the issue no later than today, so that we will be able to adopt an appropriate orientation to our comrades and districts.

Then comes Thalheimer, the 'theoretician':

> Given that a majority is against calling off the action, I will not oppose giving these comrades one or two days to arrive at a common approach regarding the position taken here on the need to end the movement, in order to be able to carry this out in a unified and concerted manner.

Our opinion was that even though there was strong disagreement, calling off the action had to be carried through by the party in a unified fashion.

**Radek**: Very true!

**Thalheimer**: Neumann also recounted another myth about an appeal that was drafted in advance. I do not need to speak to that, because it is truly pure fiction.

Now, as regards amending the theses. Comrade Lenin went after the amendments with all the energy that we so admire, but I had the impression that he was energetically bashing down open doors. The general position of the German delegation is that *we are in agreement with the basic thrust of the theses*. That is expressed in the fact that we have not introduced any counter-theses. However, we consider that in a number of cases the emphasis and balance must be shifted. Specifically, the balance between right and left must be shifted toward the left, because *we do not see any serious left danger in the International*.

Comrade Lenin said that we have settled accounts with the Right, that there is nothing further to be gained by struggling against the Right, and it is time to begin another chapter. Unfortunately, we have not yet disposed of the Right. We have not yet achieved that even in the Russian party. The overall situation in the International is and will probably remain such that it will be necessary to wage an ongoing struggle against both right-opportunist and left aberrations. The question is which danger is the greater and which is the lesser. Comrade Lenin said that we have approved the expulsion of Levi, and that is a political fact. Serrati is outside the International, and that is also a political fact. We have given the KAPD an ultimatum, with a deadline, and that also is a political fact. And we have defeated the anti-parliamentary current in the Italian movement,[26] and that also is a political fact. We can only conclude that the left danger cannot be particularly great.

---

26. A reference to Bordiga's Communist Abstentionist faction, which was one of the components that united together in the Communist Faction at the November

Now, as to the basic thrust of the amendments we are proposing. As Comrade Lenin sees it, their basic thrust is that we have reservations regarding the viewpoint that we must form large revolutionary mass parties and that the majority of the working class and of all layers of working people must be for communism in order to launch the assault against bourgeois society. But that is not the situation.

The programmatic point of view of the German party, as advanced in the past and also here, can perhaps be explained with reference to the way it is already set down in the Spartacus League programme. I will read this passage. In the programme of the Spartacus League, adopted at the end of 1918, we read:

> The Spartacus League will never take over governmental power except in response to the clear, unambiguous will of the great majority of the proletarian mass of all of Germany, never except by the proletariat's conscious affirmation of the views, aims, and methods of struggle of the Spartacus League.[27]

Thus we never opposed this programmatic position. Rather we have demonstrated in action that we thoroughly agree with the viewpoint presented here in the Spartacus League programme. Our criticism of the draft was based on concern that its text would give opportunist forces an opening to develop an assessment of the possibilities for struggle in purely arithmetical, statistical terms. That is why we proposed to take out the term 'majority' and in its place say simply 'working class'. What does that mean? It means nothing less than half of the working class, and, in fact, a good deal more.

Now another passage. In the section on Czechoslovakia, we did not delete the reference to the party's task of attracting still broader masses. Rather, here too we sought to shift the balance, to make an adjustment, by saying that the party indeed has this task, but above all it has the task of educating the broad masses that support it and, through its propaganda, to have an impact on them and lead them into the coming struggles.

That is the general point of view underlying our amendments, a point of view that we believe needs to be taken into account. Indeed, it must be taken into account, given that a number of parties and delegations have given us their support. Comrade Lenin was quite right in saying that the theses now before us are a compromise – in a Communist framework, of course. Now we have a range of additional forces that do not want to shift the line out of this

---

1920 Imola conference. Bordiga's current dropped its abstentionist position after the Comintern's 1920 Second Congress.

27. 'What Does the Spartacus League Want?' in Luxemburg 2004, pp. 356–7.

framework but rather seek, within this framework, to adjust it. In my opinion, therefore, the final outcome must definitely take into account this relationship of forces. (*Loud applause*)

**Zetkin**: Comrades, first of all, some clarifications. As regards the documentation concerning the effects of the March Action that I and my colleagues have made known, I would say this: these materials were turned over to us by the party's editors. Given that these materials are nonetheless being contested, I have made a request of the Executive that it summon one or another of these editors to come here with the factual evidence underlying their work, so that the material can be checked over objectively and conclusively. Later on, there will also be much to learn about the documentation introduced here by the other side.

It is not my intention to respond to all the personal attacks that have rained down on me yesterday and even earlier. Regarding some of the assertions that seem to me important, I have made a written statement for the proceedings, which you will hear at the end of this session.[28] As regards another assertion, I said the essential thing yesterday in an interjection,[29] but I forgot to add one thing. Regarding Comrade Heckert's claims that I had clung to my parliamentary mandate, he could have taken instruction from the columns of *Die Rote Fahne*. Following a consultation with me, the matter was put right, but only after *Freiheit* had the previous day served up this tasty duck to its readers for quite transparent reasons.

As regards the Levi case and my supposed guilt in this regard, I will not speak of that here. In all Comrade Heckert's attacks yesterday, the only thing missing was that Comrade Paul Levi was not born of his mother but rather that this hellish sulphurous political monster had been brought into the world by me. (*Laughter*) Over my objections, the Levi case was disposed of for the congress and thus for me as well under the Executive report. It is true that, in my opinion, it is up to Paul Levi himself to say the last word in the matter, if he – as I hope – remains despite everything a Communist who shares with us a common principled framework and works and struggles in the future on the same line as the Communist Party.

Comrades, you have been told that, since the Communist Party was founded, I have been a wavering and uncertain figure. I will make several comments about this later in my statement, but for now I will just say this. I felt greatly consoled, after Comrade Heckert's testimony as to my weaknesses and inadequacies, when I realised, after Comrade Lenin's remarks yesterday,

---

28. For Zetkin's statement, see pp. 595–6.
29. For Zetkin's interjection, see p. 493.

what outstanding educators and what strong theoretical and practical support I possess in the person of the members of the German Communist Party Zentrale.

I object to the fact that a *Zetkin case* is now being cooked up, in order to be handled following the Levi case. In my opinion, it was very harmful to a thorough discussion and clarification of the disputed issues in Germany and here as well that instead of taking up the bankruptcy of the Zentrale's theory of the offensive and their retreat into a defence of the March Action, we have a wide-ranging discussion of the Levi case. I do not wish to contribute to the Zetkin case now playing the same role for the congress.

On the substance of the matter, I will say this. I concede, and in fact I declare categorically, that I have made not just one but two errors – very great errors indeed. The first of these is that during the March Action I did not differentiate with enough emphasis and clarity between the struggle waged by the proletarian masses and the leadership given by the party Zentrale. Second, I did not distinguish sufficiently between the party's will to advance from propaganda to action, which was definitely honest and positive, and the Zentrale's completely inadequate theoretical and political outlook regarding the action. So you see, I have not shied away from affirming that I have made a mistake and learned from the events.

Now to be sure, Comrade Radek has reproached me, saying, 'You too also talked about a revolutionary offensive and thus contributed to the emergence of the false theory.'[30] Yes, Comrade Radek, sometimes things happen in a quite unforeseeable way. But if, because I spoke of a 'revolutionary offensive', I was guilty in this way of contributing to the emergence of the Zentrale's false theory, then you, Comrade Radek, are my accomplice. In the 15 March issue of *Die Internationale*, after characterising the VKPD's previous position, you wrote:

> These facts certainly provide sufficient proof of just how hard it was for some of the Spartacus League's leading comrades to emerge from the defensive stance forced on us during 1919 and to go over to the escalating offensive that became possible in 1920 following the radicalisation of the working masses in the USPD.[31]

Comrades, I am quite in agreement with Comrade Radek about the 'revolutionary offensive', but neither he nor I meant by these words anything like the political position of the Zentrale at the critical moment. Rather we were

---

30. For Radek's remarks, see p. 266.
31. Radek, 'Die Krise in der V.K.P.D.', in *Die Internationale*, 3, 3 (1 June 1921), p. 72.

referring to greatly increased activity by the party, which could lead – in close contact with the masses – to revolutionary action. And in this sense I am ready even today to use the term 'revolutionary offensive', although I know that it is not quite accurate to apply technical military terms to politics and to the terrain of class struggle. Like all comparisons, this one is imperfect. Comrade Michalak has already spoken excellently to the substance of the matter. For proletarians there is only revolutionary struggle, because defensive turns into offensive, and offensive immediately becomes defensive. And neither the one nor the other is possible without the constant, sure-footed activity not only of the party but of the broad masses outside the party.

It is in this sense, comrades, that I spoke of how a revolutionary offensive was not only possible but indeed necessary. But my attitude to the proposed offensive was quite different from that of the Zentrale. I defined precisely the conditions that were, in my opinion, required for such an offensive. This included, first of all, a precise assessment of the entire economic and political situation. That also entailed clarity on what stand the trade-union leadership and membership would take in the given conjuncture. And there was the need for the party to have intimate and close contact with the masses. In addition, the goals of the struggle had to be derived – and note this well – not from the Communist Party's list of general propaganda slogans, but from the specific goals of proletarian mass struggle. And let me add that these goals grow naturally out of the situation, are felt by the broad masses to be essential to their survival, and therefore have the capacity to unleash and animate their understanding, determination, and intense energy. Finally, there is also the necessary organisational orientation of the party.

In my view, the revolutionary offensive, as conceived of by the Zentrale, violated these elementary preconditions. Rather than evaluating the actual situation as a whole, the Zentrale started with one-sided theoretical speculation about economic and political possibilities, which were indeed possible, perhaps even close at hand, which could have materialised, but against which countervailing tendencies were at work. They evaluated these specific tendencies of economic and political life as already existing facts – and, what is more, as facts of life that were already living forces in the thinking of the masses, strengthening their determination. Focusing on what might happen, they lost sight of the real situation. They thought that they could force the situation by a decision, cooked up in the test-tube by the party's leading bodies, a decision that would bring about an immediate reorientation of the party masses, which had not been prepared inwardly, intellectually, and politically.

All this was quite clearly expressed in the main slogan: overthrow the government. It has been objected that the slogan was never raised. However, there is ample evidence of it. The slogan was also raised in the Reichstag speech by Frölich. In it, he made a remark – a very bold remark, I think – that the situation in Germany was the same as on the eve of the proclamation of a [workers'] council dictatorship in Hungary. Frölich closed his speech by saying, 'We call on proletarians to struggle for the overthrow of the government.' Really, overthrow of the government! I would be the last to shrink back from doing just that. But what was at stake then was not our wishes but something else: Did the broad masses at that moment recognise overthrow of the government as their next immediate goal?

(*The chair rings the bell, as a sign that Zetkin's speaking time is exhausted.*)

Comrades, could I be permitted to speak somewhat longer? I have taken such a beating here that I cannot possibly respond in ten minutes.

**Zinoviev**: I propose that Comrade Zetkin be granted another fifteen minutes' speaking time. (*Applause*)

**Zetkin** (*continuing*): Comrades, I will conclude rapidly. In my opinion, the orientation was –

**Vaughan**: I am against an extension of the speaking time.

**Zetkin**: Then I will have to conclude that I have been prevented from putting forward my point of view.

**Koenen** (chair): Is there any objection to extending the speaking time? I will hold a vote on whether Comrade Zetkin should be granted, on request of the Presidium, another fifteen minutes' speaking time.

(*The motion is adopted.*)

**Koenen** (chair): Comrade Zetkin may therefore speak for another fifteen minutes.

**Zetkin**: Comrades, here is my position: Because the Zentrale had an incorrect political orientation to the revolutionary offensive, it came to a false position regarding the March struggle and was not in a position to carry out the struggle in the necessary fashion. How it should have been done has been portrayed by Comrade Radek. I will not elaborate on that. I only want to stress the aspects in which my view of these matters differs from his.

In my opinion, the errors of the March Action were not mistakes like those that take place in every struggle and are to some degree unavoidable. Rather the mistakes were organically rooted in the erroneous theory of the offensive itself. And resolving the disputed issues would have been much easier and more painless if the defenders of the revolutionary offensive had undertaken an impartial review and criticism of the action. Instead of that, what did we see? Instead of objective and calm criticism of the movement, what we saw in *Die Rote Fahne* was its one-sided glorification and justification. And this was done in terms not of the March Action as a defensive action by proletarian masses, but rather of the theory, a deceptive and harmful theory, in my view. It was stated that this theory must be definitive in activating the party and the masses for future revolutionary struggles. The Zentrale's anthology, *Tactics and Organisation of the Revolutionary Offensive*, states, and I quote:

> The March Action as an isolated step by the party would have been a crime against the proletariat. Our opponents are right at least on that point. The March Offensive as a prelude to a mounting series of actions is an act of liberation.

So you see, comrades, that is the situation that gave rise in Germany to an intense and passionate atmosphere of criticism and debate.

**Thalheimer**: I have never heard of this book.[32]

**Zetkin**: It was not published, but praise for this theory continued in *Die Rote Fahne* day after day. That caused deep concern, from which arose the struggle against the theory, and the actions that it justified. In the future, actions will be required that are a question of life or death for the party. If they are conducted according to the schema set up by the new theory, that means destruction for the party, and the revolutionary proletariat of Germany will thereby lose the leadership it requires.

I must add one more point. In our view, the false theory of the revolutionary offensive that is condemned in the theses of our Russian friends arose not as the result of but as the point of departure for the practice of which the March Action – and the manner in which it was conducted – provided the first living test. This conviction has led us to propose our amendment to the appropriate paragraph of the Theses on Tactics and Strategy.

There is also another way in which our opinion differs from that of our Russian friends. I will express this opinion of ours frankly, although it will encounter vigorous resistance. Along with many comrades in Germany and other countries, I firmly believe that criticism of the errors and mistakes must

---

32. The anthology, *Taktik und Organisation der revolutionären Offensive. Die Lehren der März-Aktion* (Zentrale der VKPD 1921), was produced by the Zentrale under Thalheimer's direct guidance. It was published 4–5 April 1921, but was rapidly withdrawn from circulation. The quotation Zetkin read out is from p. 6 of the introduction to that book, presumably drafted by Thalheimer himself.

not be restricted to the party organisation and the party press. This criticism should properly be presented to the broadest public and the masses themselves. We understand the contrary opinion of our Russian friends, given the history of their party and the situation in Russia. But in Western Europe our conditions are different. Let us suppose that we go to a mass meeting, and the Scheidemanns and Dittmanns attack us, asking, 'What is your position regarding this or that action of your party?' Will we then say that we only discuss such matters with people who can produce a membership book proving that they belong to our party? That would destroy our public credibility. But there is something more important. Our workers themselves would not tolerate that. They demand that the errors and weaknesses of the party be openly discussed, because such debates, if conducted objectively, are educational and enlightening for them as well. The proletarians have a right to this in another sense as well. They must pay for our policies and our errors through their sacrifices, their liberty, and their lives. (*Applause*)

As regards the Theses on Tactics and Strategy now before us, in my opinion many passages will benefit from more robust formulations, so that the will to struggle and to vigorous attack is expressed more precisely and powerfully. That, however, is a matter of minor stylistic corrections by the editing commission. I believe it is objectively important to add a paragraph on page 16, requiring the parties in France, Germany, Belgium, and Luxembourg to work together systematically and over time to mobilise for the revolutionary struggle the working masses in the large centres of coal and iron mining of Central Europe. A similar requirement should apply to the Communist parties of Germany, Poland, and Czechoslovakia regarding the eastern centres of coal and iron mining. I believe these are demands that require no motivation and no further remarks from me. I can provide the motivation in the commission.

In closing, I do not believe that we should engage in efforts to reconcile individuals with each other or to hush things up. All of us, as individuals, count for nothing compared to the revolution. What is at issue is to *create a principled foundation from which the Communist Party of Germany can look forward to its great future battles*. This principled foundation was established, in my opinion, by the theses of Trotsky and of Comrade Radek. Both belong together and form an inseparable whole. Together, they present an immense challenge to the proletarians of the world: whatever the situation, you are obligated to summon up all your energy for revolutionary struggle. The theses, taken together, appeal to all Communist parties to imbue their tactics with the necessary flexibility in order to be ready for every situation. You must win the power to advance and to be prepared at any moment to engage in the final struggle. For we do not know whether any given event will bring this about, like a thief in the night. But you must also preserve the capacity to endure, if the final struggle does not arrive so quickly.

I welcome the fact that the theses, which join together as a unity, have come from the ranks of our Russian comrades, imbued by their theoretical insight and, above all, by their revolutionary experience. We thank our Russian brothers, we thank the Russian proletariat, for more than just an understanding of the methods and paths of struggle in this period, when the old world is collapsing amid the thunder and flames of world revolution. We thank our Russian brothers above all because their example has shown *what an important and ultimately decisive power for revolutionary struggle resides in the revolutionary will*. A will that clear-sightedly registers every available opportunity, a will unalterably directed to the final goal or, more correctly, to the next stage toward the goal of winning political power and establishing a proletarian council dictatorship as the great door through which the world revolution is striding. (*Loud applause and cheers*)

**Vaillant-Couturier** (Communist Party of France): Comrades, it is truly unfortunate that in this debate, which was supposed to deal only with the report of Comrade Radek, his report and the Theses on Tactics and Strategy have become mixed in together. This resulted in some degree of confusion. I would now like to present to you the position of the French delegation with regard to Radek's report as well as the theses as a whole.

The French delegation is in agreement, by and large, with the theses proposed by the Communist Party of Russia. It asks only that some modifications be made to specific points and regarding certain formal issues. It wishes to propose taking some facts into account that were entirely overlooked. The commission will have to deal with these issues as soon as it convenes.

The French party believes it is desirable that the paragraph dealing with parliamentarism be formulated somewhat more precisely. I will set aside entirely my personal views and simply present here the position of the French delegation.

With regard to parliamentarism, by the way, it would be desirable that our comrades in parliament receive more precise instructions. In France, forms and habits of courtesy have become well entrenched in parliament, and you know full well the danger that this presents. You yourselves say that our comrades in parliament readily commit certain infractions. That is why we must explain our position on this issue in the commission.

As for the question of the so-called Left, which is taken up in the theses with great firmness, we agree that, so far, one cannot say that there exists a left wing in our party with its own doctrine. All we can say is that there are – as you know – some centrist tendencies in the party. We are a Social-Democratic party. I must say that, even though I do not wish to compliment Comrade Radek for his derisive comments. We are a long-standing Social-Democratic party that is now making its way to communism. Nonetheless, there is in the party a certain spirit that holds us back to some extent. Some forces in our majority are being attracted to the so-called left wing, and the theses, referring to these forces, speak of adventurism.

In our opinion, we must deal a sharp blow to the right wing. On the other hand, it would not hurt to deal the left wing a cordial but sharp smack.

Comrades, I will not take up the events cited in the theses – that is, the calling up of the class of 1919, and so on. The text here is quite muddled. As regards the Luxembourg events, in my opinion there is a misunderstanding. As Comrade Overstraeten has said, this issue simply does not exist.[33]

The German theses that I saw contained an imprecision with regard to France.[34] They present certain facts, but, with regard to the reparations crisis, they are guilty of an imprecision. We of the old party majority wish to clarify our position on this question. In our opinion, what was at stake was not merely justified claims, as the German text states; we were anxious to come to agreement with the German comrades. We took the position that it is not a question of reparations here; rather the task is to make the revolution and to lead it to victory.

There is no response that French and German capitalism can give that will induce us to raise the question of reparations.

We have heard many speeches here. I am very anxious to learn German, and I find the German speeches quite wonderful. Much has been said about the March Action – without any doubt, a fundamental and extremely important question. Nonetheless, we should proceed somewhat differently. We will then have a better chance of getting to the root of certain issues. That is my personal opinion.

The French proletariat followed the March events with keen interest. We honour the memory of the militant workers who fell during the March Action. Certainly, errors were committed. Important lessons can be drawn from these struggles as well as from the doctrine that provided their starting point. Of course, lessons can be drawn from every struggle and every battle. As for the

---

33. For the call up of the class of 1919 and the French intervention in Luxembourg, see pp. 460, n. 11 and 1109, n. 21. See also Appendix 3f, pp. 1108–32.
34. The VKPD Zentrale prepared theses on tactics and strategy for presentation to the Third Congress (see p. 490, n. 14.). The German delegation withdrew the text after a meeting with the Russian delegation (see Appendix 3d) but presented many of the ideas in these theses anew in the amendments submitted together with the Austrian and Italian delegations and printed on pp. 1141–58.

special features of the Levi case, as stated, the Executive decision has resolved that matter.

I will conclude my discussion of the theses by returning to the question of France. The theses explain that France is a colonial power. They contain a warning to the French party to keep in mind its tasks with regard to coloured troops.[35] For my part, I would have preferred that the theses had developed the colonial question and taken it up in detail. In light of the theses of the Second Congress, it is surely necessary to deal with the colonial question fully.[36] We are far from agreement with certain forces that have roused movements in the Near or Far East whose goals are quite distant from communism. However, even if we do not at all agree with these forces, we have the task of committing our full strength to supporting them in their struggle against world imperialism. The International must pay them close attention. We have aroused great hopes among these oppressed peoples, who bear the double yoke of their capitalists and the great landowners, on one hand, and the big capitalists of the West on the other. We must not give them the impression that they have been deserted; we must really commit our full strength and stand by them.

Comrades, Comrade Radek's report dealt with our international relations and bringing our forces together. In this regard, we can only hope – and I am speaking here to the German comrades, in view of the misunderstanding that arose with them – that the ties among large parties in neighbouring countries will become increasingly effective. The misunderstanding arose precisely from the fact that our relations with other parties were too infrequent and insufficiently close. But this is surely only a passing phenomenon. When this is overcome, we will be all the better able to work for the good of the revolution.

Certainly, as regards the Communist International, we all agree that it should organise large international demonstrations. In this way, we will be able to display to the bourgeois world, in action, the International's viability and power.

Finally, I believe we all agree that the International should, by selecting appropriate personnel for the large parties, demonstrate that its work is serious, strict, and carefully thought out.[37]

In conclusion, I must say that we fully agree with the content of the theses when they explain that we must have an International of communist action

---

35. During and after World War I, many troops from France's African colonies fought in the French army, numbering some 200,000 by the War's end. Some 125,000 were used in combat.

36. For the Second Congress 'Theses on the National and Colonial Questions', see Riddell (ed.) 1991, 2WC, 1, pp. 283–90.

37. Vaillant-Couturier may be referring here to the choice of ECCI personnel to act as emissaries to the large parties or coordinate relations with them.

and not merely one of empty talk and theory. In France, we are now entering a period of persecution. Until now the bourgeoisie has restricted itself to small actions, to minor attacks against this or that revolutionary group. They are preparing laws in parliament now and intend to enact others in the future for use in a broad general offensive. Consequently, in my opinion, we in France are obliged to summon all our forces, including those who are termed left-wing, who can do good work in action, provided they are kept under discipline –

**Trotsky**: Agreed!

**Vaillant-Couturier**: – and also those who only yesterday were part of the right wing but are increasingly aware of the need to find an arena for common agitation and propaganda so that, with ranks closed and in disciplined fashion, we can advance forward to victory. (*Loud applause*)

**Bell** (Great Britain): Comrades, in my opinion we have devoted too much attention at this congress to the affairs of the German party. True, it can be fruitful to draw general lessons from the German party's mistakes and experiences. Nonetheless, I hope that Comrade Radek's summary will not deal solely with the German issues, but will keep in view that the Anglo-Saxon and other countries are of equal interest. They impatiently await the International's leadership in questions of tactics and strategy as well as those of overall international policy.

Yesterday evening, Comrade Bukharin said that the question of mass action – or rather the dispute over whether it is 'offensive' or 'defensive' in character – is out of date. I am inclined to agree with the interjection by Comrade Trotsky, when he said that we should add to the theses that 'anyone who does not take this matter seriously is an ass'. No doubt there are still some Communists, some members of the Communist International, whose ears have grown a bit too long. It is therefore essential that we establish, once and for all, what we mean by a mass organisation, a mass party. The congress is far from having digested this question. It is far from clear what exactly we mean when we speak of a mass party.

This relates particularly to Britain and the United States, where we so far unfortunately do not have a mass organisation or mass party. This is an especially important issue for the Anglo-Saxon countries, and I must say that the Communist Party of Great Britain is by and large in agreement with the theses proposed to us here. The Communist Party of Great Britain is very well aware that if the international Communist movement is founded on sectarianism, it cannot triumph. This movement must reach out and encompass broader and broader layers of the working masses, layers that do not yet accept communism in its every principle and doctrine. There were quite a large number of such sectarian groups in Britain, and they doubtless carried out worthwhile propaganda and educational work, but they never succeeded in fully winning over the workers. We must finally recognise now that we can no longer limit ourselves to educational and propaganda work. We have now entered a period of struggle for the seizure of power across the entire world. Our educational work must be developed in harmony with the demands placed on us by a struggle for power. Our work will be utterly without value unless it is developed along lines that pave our road to victory. This question is of special interest to us in Britain, because Britain is the classical country of compromise. The British bourgeoisie is the classical advocate of compromise in world history, and the Labour Party is an opportunist and compromising organisation *par excellence*. The Communist Party of Great Britain can learn in two ways. We have seen sectarianism and its results. We have also become familiar with the Labour Party's opportunism. The Communist Party seeks to find a middle way between the left wing's ossified doctrines and the Labour Party's pliability, a suppleness that is at its root nothing other than pure bourgeois opportunism.

As for our ultra-revolutionary delegates here, their methods may well suit the needs of their own organisations and guarantee the purity of their principles. However, I must point out something they must learn: in Britain such methods will never help them to attain the leadership and influence over the working masses that is absolutely necessary for our movement's revolutionary development. In addition, I must stress that it would be pointless for us to steer too far to the right and follow the opportunists along this path. We must not let ourselves be carried away by the concept of a mass party as a simple numerical accumulation of forces; otherwise the unhappy day will arrive when we discover that we're dealing with a large number of opportunists living at the expense of the workers' movement.

The Communist Party of Great Britain supports the Executive's decisions on the Czechoslovak, Italian, and French questions. In our opinion, we can confidently leave it to the bulk of the workers to track down on their own the Šmerals, the Turatis, the Serratis, and all other supporters of the Second International. We have to rely on their common sense; they are well able to expose their own opportunists. The Communist International can confidently leave this question to the workers.

The Communist Party of Great Britain supported the International on these three issues because we are convinced that the logic of events in present-day struggles will teach the working masses what they must know, giving us an opportunity to cleanse the movement of the Šmerals, the Levis, the Serratis, and the Turatis.

Our friends on the left fear that if the party takes on mass proportions, it may grow too large and become an essentially opportunist party devoid of any revolutionary enthusiasm. We must establish once and for all how we can best prevent our movement from deviating too far to the right or the left. We have been asked what test should be established for this purpose. We possess an outstanding touchstone. We do not judge on the basis of proclaimed dogmas, theories, formulas, or doctrines, or on the grounds of abstract theses and fine articles like those of Levi and other bourgeois intellectuals. The touchstone that we use is deeds. That permits us to readily identify opportunists who slip through the working masses into our organisation. That is how Levi was exposed. Had there been no March Action, Levi might well still be here today, playing a major role among us. The same holds true for Czechoslovakia. They claim to be able to exert a very great deal of influence on the masses, yet they are held back by their leaders. That is the way things were in the Italian section. The touchstone of the deed not only reveals who is an opportunist but also who among the leaders is inclined too much to the left. In this regard, I believe that the left wing is no less dangerous than the right.

I will now take up Britain. The section of the theses dealing with Britain, in the English text, is quite unclear. The passage in question should surely read: 'The *British* Communist movement too has not yet succeeded in becoming a mass party, even though it has brought its forces together in a unified party.'[38] At present the party consists of ten thousand members, and as I recall, Comrade Zinoviev's report mentions that the danger of sectarianism exists in Britain and the United States.

To be sure, the British party is still small. This is not at all because we do not want to carry out the wishes of the Communist International Executive. Rather, the cause lies in the prevailing political and psychological conditions in Britain. In addition, the party is actually only three months old, although the first Communist Party was formed last August. In line with the wishes of the Communist International, we did not undertake any steps until we had won over the other Communist forces. Thus, the Communist Party has really only existed since the Leeds conference, that is, since 31 January.[39] We have thus done much more to enlarge the party than is assumed in Russia.

There has never been a large political party in Britain. The Liberal and Conservative parties are quite small. They are nothing more than electoral machines, which manipulate the masses, setting them in motion for the parties'

---

38. For the corresponding passage of the theses, see p. 929.
39. On 31 July–1 August 1920 a Communist Unity Convention in London united the British Socialist Party, 22 Communist Unity groups, and more than 20 other small groups. A second convention in Leeds 29–30 January 1921 completed the unification process, bringing in the Workers' Socialist Federation, Communist Labour Party, and other organisations. Pro-Communist forces in the Independent Labour Party joined in April.

own purposes. Even the Labour Party, which is regarded as representing the British working masses, is not a mass party in the sense that the term is used on the European continent. Indeed, it is not really a party at all, but rather merely a coordinating force in the industrial and political arena. True, it has 4.5 million members, but they do not really form part of a political party in the way we think of it. They cannot be relied on to accept any form of discipline. So we see, for example, that members of this so-called party of the British working masses vote in elections for Liberal, Conservative, and other bourgeois candidates. For this reason, the British workers' organisations cannot be measured by European standards.

Inquiring about the Labour Party and the trade-union movement, Comrade Lenin says, 'How many members are there in the Communist Party? Only ten thousand! How is it possible that millions of workers take part in an uprising and yet do not belong to the Communist Party?'

It will probably never be possible to organise a big political party in Britain. The Labour Party in Britain is simply a reflection of the discontented working masses, who lack any political consciousness. The Communist Party is the largest revolutionary party that has ever existed in Britain. Before this party was formed, there was not a single revolutionary group that could claim more than 2,000 or, at most, 5,000 members. The old Social-Democratic Party, the spoiled child of Huysmans, never had more than 2,000 active members. The British Socialist Labour Party never had more than 500 members, and other groups never had more than 200–300. So the Communist Party, with its 10,000 members, represents a great step forward. We should not undermine its courage by calling it a sectarian party. Instead, we should be doing all we can to assist it.

The revolutionary spirit of the British Communist Party cannot be compared with that of the German party, which has 300,000 members, or the Czechoslovak party, with its 400,000 members. It has been shown that numerical size is not the main thing. That is why we too in Britain have not tried to build the party on the basis of a large number of members. We have not let ourselves be carried away by the desire to recruit 500,000 or 600,000 members, only to then see the international congress forced to spend most of its time discussing our internal disputes.

I therefore propose for adoption the following amendment:

Page 6, column 1, at the bottom, should read: 'The *British* Communist movement too has not yet succeeded in becoming a mass party, even though it has united its forces in a unified party.'

As a result of the historical, traditional, and political background of the British workers' movement, the British Communists face a difficult task.

Nonetheless, however, they must proceed without further delay to structure themselves as a real party.

Independent of whether they are Conservative, Liberal, or Socialist, political parties in Britain have never had a large number of members. Even the Labour Party developed only thanks to the fact that the trade-union bureaucracy placed their bets on the electoral loyalty of trade-union members. The political parties were always distant from the masses. They were nothing more than sectarian groups or parties, content to leave it to other organisations to lead on their own. The British Communists must therefore struggle against the conditions created by sectarianism and sharp attacks in the press. They must combat the notion that economic and political struggles should be separated from each other, and all that. Nonetheless, they enjoy a significant advantage: even if the workers have lagged behind politically, they are accustomed to organised economic mass actions.

We must take care that the Communist Party is protected from the old traditions.

It is not enough to go into the other workers' organisations and urge them to take actions. This course would water down the party to the point where it did not possess independent strength to lead the struggle of the working masses. The party must do everything possible to attract revolutionary workers to the party in greater and greater numbers. It must become a true mass party, a true instrument of struggle. It must demonstrate to the workers, once and for all, that economic and political goals are inseparable. It must strive with all its strength to lead the economic struggles and to bring to the fore the political problems and goals that arise from these struggles.

On page 6, column 2, in the middle of paragraph 3, in place of 'no influence of the party', it should read, 'Abstract criticism by the party can never win it influence among the masses comparable to what it can gain from stubborn, incessant work of Communist cells in the trade unions, exposing and discrediting the social traitors and the trade-union bureaucracy, which has become a political tool of capitalism to a greater extent in Britain than in any other country.'

However, we agree completely that, as stated in the theses, every Communist must take part in all industrial, social, and political activity that affects workers' welfare for good or ill. This is how workers must be won to communism.

In conclusion, I would like to say that we agree with the spirit of the proposed theses. We ask you in the future to devote more attention to the British Communist and workers' movement. This will convince you that the British movement will respond with loyalty to the Communist International beyond what has yet been demonstrated by any other movement.

**Sachs** (Schwab, KAPD): Comrades, my remarks link up with what has just been said by Comrade Bell from Britain. For it appears to me that on a quite significant point, namely that of the party's size, he has borne out the correctness of our point of view. But I will come back to this point further on.

I prefer to first take up the remarks of Comrade Heckert yesterday. I note that he has conceded something that is undeniable: the old KPD failed in the Kapp Putsch in Germany. However, he skated in polite silence around the failure of the KPD, the official section of the Communist International, in August 1920, when the Russian army was advancing toward Warsaw. That silence may help his party but does precious little to inform the rest us about the situation at that time. Third, he conceded the party's dangerous and disturbing vacillation during the Berlin electrical workers' strike.[40]

What is more, who was responsible for this vacillation; who was it that actually brought about the party's failure, its inactivity, during the electrical workers' strike? That was not the fault of Paul Levi. It was Comrade Brandler, now the left-wing revolutionary chair of the VKPD, new and improved edition. We all have the pleasure today to deliberate, some with decisive and some with consultative vote, under his honorary chairmanship. I did not elect him. It was Brandler – and a lot more could be said about him (*Commotion*) – Brandler, who imagines that the revolution and the dictatorship of the proletariat as a system of workers' councils can be carried out with due respect and within the framework of the German constitution. (*Commotion*) He said that at his trial. Here is the newspaper where this appears.[41]

Perhaps the day will come when Comrade Heckert and others of his party will admit that, this time too, during the run-up to the struggles of the March Action, this very same improved edition of the KPD failed again. That happened – despite everything that has been said so far – regarding something that has not yet been mentioned, namely that the party issued its call for a general strike only on the Friday before Easter [25 March].

Heckert thought it necessary to apologise at length for the fact that the party issued its call for a general strike on Friday, although it knew full well that Easter would follow, when the workers are not in the factories. It did not occur to him that, in Halle, on the Tuesday before Easter [22 March], in the absence of any call, gas, water, and electricity workers had gone on strike in support of the workers of Central Germany. These workers were left on their own, receiving no help either from the Halle district leadership (heading the

---

40. For the November 1920 Berlin electrical workers' strike, see p. 240, n. 2. During that walkout leftist elements within the KPD criticised the Zentrale for not issuing a call for a general strike.

41. For Brandler's conduct at trial, see p. 1134, n. 46.

VKPD's strongest district) or the national leadership. They returned to work in order not to be left alone in struggle. We had pressed in every city across the nation for quick action, so that the general strike would start up before Easter and could be maintained through the Easter holiday. Nonetheless, it was only on Friday that they finally managed to issue the call for a general strike.

I tell you, Comrade Heckert admitted three instances of failure. Perhaps he will admit a fourth instance some day soon. Now is it not quite remarkable that in all these cases the only genuine and patented Communist Party of Germany failed, while in each case, through a remarkable coincidence, the KAPD – or rather the former opposition that gave birth to the KAPD – always did the right thing? The districts that took up the struggle during the Kapp Putsch immediately were formerly districts of the opposition. So were those who tried to utilise the month of August [1920] but were blocked by resistance from both you and the USPD. Those who did not take part in the vacillations over the electrical workers' strike but rather tried with all their strength to provide the workers with solidarity and support – once again, that was the KAPD. I tell you, either this comparison results from a strange series of coincidences or there is some deeper cause at work here.

**Rogalski**: Sheer fantasy!

**Sachs**: Comrade Rogalski, I took part in all this; there is no fantasy here.

Well, the underlying factor in this comparison, in these remarkable occurrences on both sides – this factor cannot be of interest solely in a German framework. It is of concern to the entire International. It must be of importance for you. Fundamentally, it is simply the fact that the KAPD – even if it has developed clarity only slowly and with difficulty – that the KAPD's programme, organisation, course of action, and its fundamental positions provide from the outset a guarantee that the party taken as a whole cannot fail in such situations.

Yesterday, Comrade Lenin spoke, surprisingly, in much the same terms as Comrade Bell of the potential of a small party. To our astonishment, he explained that even – he said 'even' – a small party could well be in a position to initiate revolutionary struggles and, indeed, the decisive and final revolutionary struggle, and to carry it through to victory. So what became of the principle of a mass party, which had previously been defended so frantically? Where did it disappear to? For Comrade Lenin said that even a small party can do this, provided – and he is right here – that it wins the majority of the proletariat and of the working population as a whole for its policies. Very good indeed! Here we are in complete agreement with him, and we do not understand why, with regard to this point, he is still so disturbed about our leftist blunders. We ask him this: if even a small party can do this, could he please say where he stands on the following proposition: In our view, a small party can do it, but if a mass party tries – a mass party in the sense that has been proclaimed as dogma – in all likelihood, it will fail. What does he say to this point?

In our view, such a mass party, formed as it is according to the principle of encompassing as many as possible and then battering them into shape, so that under the battering and pressure of its leadership it becomes properly revolutionary – such a party, battered into shape in this way on the model of the VKPD, carries within it, in its entire structure, a high probability of failure. For these masses are not just lifeless figures in account books and lists. They are living workers, who come to meetings, send the delegates from their branches to the local leadership and from the locality to the district, and the influence of their intentions and outlook makes itself felt. Perhaps it is possible, elsewhere in the world, to build a party in this fashion, led and commanded in military fashion by a leadership with a sergeant's swagger stick in hand, reckoning the members as so many heads or digits. But this will no longer work today in Germany, France, Italy, Spain, and Britain.

Certainly we too are well aware, we too explain that broad masses are necessary for the victory of revolution in the industrially advanced countries. Of course the Communist Party must win these broad masses. But now we hear the 'Open Letter' published in Germany being recommended as an exemplary method of winning the masses. I hope that comrades abroad are familiar with the Open Letter, which is a conglomeration of everything conceivable. Well, here we must say that of course the Open Letter was written with good intentions to win the masses and thereby help them advance.

Nonetheless, there are evil souls who claim that the Open Letter's real intention was to carry out electoral propaganda. I will not get into an argument about that right now, but I will say that the Open Letter's method is unworkable and undialectical. It is a method of attracting the masses as they are, without dwelling on their suffering and oppression, but rather just linking up with the thinking of the masses such as it is. Of course, the final sentence says, 'We are well aware that this is not adequate, but nonetheless we demand', etc. The masses do not understand this contradiction, but they do know that it cannot be done that way. Or on the other hand, they are still blind and do not yet see the truth. And so they conclude that if even the Communists are saying that we must demand this, then it must be a good thing. In short, the masses are reinforced in their opportunist illusions. If we want to win the masses, then we must say that the recent March Action, taken as a whole, with all its errors and weaknesses, represents a much better method of winning the masses than the Open Letter.

It is true that hundreds of thousands, perhaps millions, raised their hands in support of the Open Letter. But this did not win them to the cause of communism. Further, it is also true that during the March Action broad masses turned against those in struggle, not only with words but by wielding iron bars in the factories to drive out those who called for a strike. But that is simply how the dialectical process takes place. Initially, we unite those who are ready and able to struggle, so that they can advance. Then, after a certain time, the masses who were against the action will understand and learn. 'We were against this struggle', they will say, 'We thought things would get better, but they did not, and we see now that you were right, you whom we then hit over the head with iron bars'. By and large, that is the right way to win the masses.

Comrades, for us of the KAPD, neither the theses presented here nor the amendments are the main issue. I have no mandate and am not able to take a position for or against the one or the other, for the very simple reason that these theses, as a whole, are obviously based on the previously existing foundation of the Second Congress decisions. They are a continuation, and in some respects they are no doubt an improvement, and we may find that very welcome, but it is not the main issue. We still believe that the main task is to modify the basic decisions of the broad tactical and strategic guidelines adopted by the Second Congress. We therefore present the delegations and the Presidium with our Second Congress theses, which deal with the trade-union movement, the factory councils, and workers' control of production, and our theses on proletarian revolution.[42] We do not believe that these theses are arriving too late, and if they arrive with some delay, that is your fault, because you did not pay heed to us sooner. We hope that many delegations will take these theses home with them, so that they can become seeds of a discussion that can lead us to victory more quickly and more surely than the theses adopted by the Second Congress on these themes.

I would like to take up briefly Comrade Bukharin's attacks on us yesterday. Comrade Bukharin attacked us quite harshly, but with arguments that were bookish in the extreme. He quoted some sentences from a pamphlet by Comrade Gorter, believing he could hit us over the head with these passages. In the process, he did read one decisive sentence, but most of his listeners no doubt missed it. The sentence was as follows: 'The Kronstadt proletariat revolted against you, against the Communist Party. You proclaimed a state of

---

42. For KAPD resolutions, see Comintern archives, RGASPI, 490/1/5, and the KAPD publication *Proletarier*, 1, 7.

siege in Petersburg that was also aimed against the proletariat...'![43] This is the inner consistency of events, with respect both to the Russian course of action as to the forms of resistance that arise against them. Gorter always recognised and emphasised that this was inevitable. This is the sentence that you must read in order to understand that neither Comrade Gorter nor the KAPD was taking the side of the Kronstadt rebels. Rather they were saying that these difficulties are inherent in the situation here. And when Comrade Bukharin says that Comrade Gorter is our best theorist, well, that may be true. But he has learned a very great deal from our practice, and we from him. Thus I am in a position now to say that if Gorter were to deviate from the party's line in his theoretical writings, and he has not done that so far, nonetheless the party's line prevails, not that of Comrade Gorter.

Let me say again that Comrade Bukharin took us on yesterday with purely bookish arguments. He did not advance any arguments taken from life – neither ours nor that of the VKPD – and he cannot do so. The kind of word games that Comrade Bukharin employed against us yesterday can perhaps have some effect at a congress, for those who do not and cannot know the facts, but not in Germany, where we will go to report just what it is that many comrades here are denouncing as 'leftist blunders'.

**Koenen** (chair): Comrades, it is now somewhat late. We still have fourteen speakers on the list. Only two speakers have set a good example by declining their right to speak. Earlier, there were sixteen speakers. The Presidium hopes that a number of other speakers will follow this example. We must consider whether the debate should be closed at an appropriate moment. If we all aim for that, then it may be possible to conclude this agenda point with a session of about two hours. We propose to end the session at this point and to resume at seven o'clock. The next speakers are Comrades Zinoviev and Trotsky.

*(The session is adjourned at 5:00 p.m.)*

---

43. See p. 512.

## Session 14 – 2 July 1921, 8:45 p.m.
# Tactics and Strategy – Discussion

*Further discussion on Radek's report. Speakers: Zinoviev, Thälmann, Trotsky. Summary by Radek. Statement by Clara Zetkin. Statement by the Italian delegation. Statement by the Youth International. Statement by the German, German-Austrian, Polish, Hungarian, Czech (German Section), and Youth International delegations.*

**Zinoviev**: Comrades, there has been a good deal of argument here over whether our policies have been oriented correctly regarding left and right. I have the feeling that this question is being judged too simplistically. It has been said that if we are carrying out a policy aimed against the Left, then we should immediately and much more energetically apply a policy against the Right. It is like an urge to place the matter on the scales of justice, as if it is a question of justice, or courtesy, or convenience.

If the question is posed as whether the Left poses a great danger because it really represents a significant force, then of course we must say that, compared to the centrist parties and half-centrist groups, the so-called Left, as an organisational force, is insignificant in size. But the question cannot be posed so simplistically; it does not concern organised strength. We cannot claim that those who are to the left of the Third International represent an enormous force and an enormous danger – if it is even possible to refer to a Left outside of the Communist International.

The question must be posed in terms of a tendency, and here I must go back once again to the Second Congress. During the Second Congress the so-called left danger did not represent a large organised force, but yet this tendency posed a major danger for the International.

Recall the trade-union question, where a group of comrades, headed by our late comrade John Reed and other British and American comrades, wanted to commit us to rejection of the trade unions. As an organised force, this danger represented hardly anything at all. But this was the most dangerous tendency. Where would we be today if we had given way on this question in 1920? Where would the Communist International be today? We would have helped Jouhaux and the other gentlemen of the Amsterdam International. It is wrong to say that we are threatened on the right by great dangers from half-bourgeois ideologies, but on the left only from small groups that are not organised. The question is whether this tendency is dangerous, if it gains a foothold in our ranks. In the course of events, a moment may arrive when it is much more dangerous for our movement.

Personally, I have learned a thing or two during this congress regarding the need not to underestimate this tendency. We must keep our eye on it, just as we did during the Second Congress. It is easy to explain the historical origin of this tendency. During the Second Congress we perceived a distinct sectarian danger. Comrade Bell was annoyed with my speech because I said that this danger still exists in Britain and the United States.[1] The danger is created not by a desire of our party to be sectarian but by the broad historical developments that have brought it into being. Great economic factors are involved, such as the state of British industry, its monopoly position, and so on. But this issue also has much to do with our party's understanding, and we must remind the British and American comrades of the continuing danger that they are still too far removed from the masses. That is shown by various experiences, as in the miners' strike, and elsewhere. Here the party was not yet in a position actually to stimulate the movement politically. Given that Britain is certainly just as important as Czechoslovakia and Bulgaria, how can we forget this danger? The Second Congress did all it could to bring comrades closer to the masses. During the last year, we have made some gains in this regard. But the Third Congress cannot avoid stressing its urgency once again.

Then there is the second danger, which also has historical roots. After the debates in the Executive and then the report on the Italian and German questions, can anyone deny that there is a danger that the clever bourgeois will provoke our new party into premature struggle? Looking at the Italian question, I can well understand why our Italian friends are so very sensitive.

---

1. See pp. 551–5 for Bell's comments.

The blame lies with the Socialists and centrists, with Serrati. Terracini's bad defence of the rather bad amendments flows from Serrati's conduct. In 1920 Serrati and the entire Italian delegation was fully convinced that the situation in Italy was ripe for a great revolutionary movement. We asked Terracini, 'Do you have the support of the majority of the army and of the peasants?' Unfortunately, that was not yet the case. But it was precisely in Italy that we experienced events showing just how impregnated the party was with centrism.

In 1920, however, Serrati and the entire Italian delegation believed that we had the support of the majority of proletarians plus a large proportion of the peasantry and the army. That was the view of all the Italians, including Serrati. Now, however, the situation has changed, and we must start all over again. The working class must go through this crisis and undertake to redeploy its forces. That will probably take more than a year. There has been a regression in Italy. Considering this situation, I understand full well why the new Communist Party is now subject to another danger. In explaining this, we certainly do not intend to justify it. The danger must be looked in the eye. There is a danger of leading the party into striking a blow prematurely. It is centrism that has accomplished this – that we should now have such a danger in a movement like that in Italy.

Among the Germans we see something similar. Consider the Kapp Putsch. What was the situation? When the counterrevolution surfaced, this acted as a spark for the entire working class. The working class took a united stand against the counterrevolution, prepared to struggle, and was on the very edge of taking power. Suddenly the trade-union bureaucracy, the old Social Democracy, and the Independents [USPD] acted to ruin the chances of the working class. The counterrevolution was saved, and Scheidemann and the bourgeoisie were once again in the saddle. The proletarian party had missed its chance.

Certainly, when the core of the revolutionary German workers see this situation and experience such a crisis, it is quite understandable that even there a portion of the working class will resort to an attempt at launching the struggle somewhat too soon and will grow somewhat impatient. To repeat: the responsibility for setting these events in motion lies basically with the social patriots, the real betrayers of the working class. We, the Communist Party, must recognise who is mainly to blame. But we must then not overlook this danger that, although created by the centrists, places us in mortal peril. That is the heart of the matter.

We cannot judge the situation simplistically in terms of 'Are you for the Right or for the Left'? Of course, the rightists are our true enemies. They are the bourgeois agents in our camp; it is their aid that enables the bourgeoisie to hang on. If the Amsterdam International were not on the side of the bourgeoisie, we would have victory sewn up by now. The working class must overcome this obstacle. The enemy is the rightists. But that does not mean we should underestimate the danger posed by the leftist tendency. We do not say, like Comrade Roland-Holst, that since the leftists are revolutionaries, ready for any sacrifice, imbued with ideals, good comrades ready at any moment to give their life for the proletarian revolution, therefore this danger is not so great. It is precisely because they are our friends and comrades, because they work and labour at our side, that any error they make – any major, significant error – can be extremely dangerous for the Communist International.

That is the reason for the passionate polemic against the so-called left wing. You must understand that this is done as an expression of love. There is a Russian saying: I love you from the bottom of my heart, and that is why I will shake you the way one shakes fruit down from a pear tree. (*Laughter*) That must be our attitude when Lenin or other comrades speak against comrades who have committed 'leftist blunders' – and that has the ring of a parliamentary understatement. This is not like measuring gold on a scale, saying, 'You have spoken a quarter of an hour against the Left and only five minutes against the Right, which proves you are guilty of a rightist deviation.' It takes only half a second to say that the entire Right is made up of bourgeois agents. A great deal more time and effort is needed to patiently examine the mistakes that our movement makes out of inexperience and because of the difficulties we face in this transitional period. We must keep that firmly in mind.

I heard, for example, that the comrades of the Italian Socialist Party are now saying that Lenin has provided them with new arguments against the Communist Party of Italy. In fact, we confirmed the expulsion, saying that for now you do not belong to the Communist International and that you must fulfil your duty to drive out the bourgeois agents. The Italian Communist Party is a full member of the Communist International. We discuss with this party in friendship, sometimes perhaps with passion, regarding errors that are in the air, errors that can be made if you are not sufficiently on the alert and fall for the provocations of a very clever and well-organised bourgeoisie. How can this possibly serve the centrists? When advanced by comrades who fought against centrism, who are real Communists, such accusations carry great weight. When advanced by Serrati or one of his supporters? It is mere hypocrisy for one of them to assert that they are sticking with Turati because Terracini has made some errors regarding the movement's tempo.

I will now take up the German question. First, let me note with regard to the March Action that we are rather close to a solution that can perhaps be adopted unanimously. Let me quote a passage from a motion presented over the signatures of Franken, Neumann, Malzahn, and Zetkin:

> Despite the erroneous outlook underlying the March Action and the flawed manner in which it was conducted, the Third Congress of the Communist International assesses it as a struggle that demonstrates a will to action and, thereby, is a step forward. The congress expresses its conviction that the VKPD must devote its full energy, through intensified and consistent activity in every field of work, to leading the struggles that arise out of present conditions inside and outside Germany and that may well break out at any moment.

Comrades, we can take satisfaction in noting that we are close to a unanimous decision in this heatedly disputed question, whose clarification was the goal of this congress. We must recognise this fact. Compare our Russian theses with the Zetkin amendment and even with the amendments proposed by the VKPD delegation: there are still some disagreements, but we are close to our goal. That has to be recognised. It would be pointless for me to try to determine who made concessions in this process. We came here for the purpose of analysis, not to prove who was right or to aggravate even more the situation in Germany. We are in fact quite close to a unanimous decision, and that will be a most important outcome of our congress.

Comrade Malzahn complained yesterday that Comrade Heckert had spoken somewhat too harshly. I heard only one part of Heckert's speech, but it is clear that he spoke with some vehemence about the situation in Germany. And I must say that Comrade Malzahn too was not gentle in this regard. But it is not really that important who was harsh or gentle. The question is how we go forward from here. Malzahn referred to a statement by me that our task was not to wallow in the March Action but to determine what comes next. That is the question now before the congress. There is only one possible answer: under no circumstances must we have yet another split in the ranks of the German Communist Party. I really do not know whether our party can bear yet another split. There are truly no grounds for that, after we have come to the point where we are able to unanimously adopt the theses proposed by our Russian delegation. That is why the congress must strive for agreement.

The German question is not national but to the highest degree international in character. The ailments in Germany are international ailments. That is why we have every interest, on behalf of the congress as a whole, to strive for agreement. True, we are well aware that nothing is achieved by empty words about unity. If conditions were such that unity was impossible, empty words about unity would be pointless. But is the situation in Germany really such that unity is impossible, and that there are disagreements that cannot be bridged? Based on the entire discussion, I say 'no'. The fact that we are now demanding unity of the German delegation reflects not pacifist delusions but the dictates of internationalism that must be and will be carried out by both groups.

This is not mere talk about unity. On the contrary, we are also providing the foundation on which this unity can be based. The theses that we have placed before you and that almost all delegations have approved in principle provide this foundation. We therefore propose to the German comrades who adhere to this foundation a unity that is not just formal but genuine, not just a unity in words but a genuine unity, and we are convinced that this unity will be carried through in life. The Zentrale has recognised, in many regards, the errors that it made. The opposition has stated, through Comrade Zetkin, that it now recognises the great historical significance of the struggle. That is the most important thing.

I would now like to take up Heckert's speech. You will recall how the conclusion of his speech was received here – with much appreciation. Why was this? Do you really believe that the entire congress agreed with Comrade Heckert in his sharp polemic against Comrade Zetkin? I do not think so. The congress agreed only in part. Why was the entire congress, with all its heart, on the side of this comrade, when the main issue, the March Action, was at stake? Because behind this comrade there is a proletarian struggle that was a great struggle; because despite all the serious errors, we are convinced that it was a great struggle, in which broad masses took part, hundreds of thousands of proletarians; because the best proletarians of Germany linked up with this struggle with great sacrifices of life and limb. That is why we all feel that, despite every error, there is something here that we must support with all our soul. If that has now been understood by both sides, then I believe we have overcome the main obstacle. It is clear that there can be no talk of a Bakuninist putsch here. It's a question of serious errors. We must stand by this experience and put an end to taking a certain pleasure from seizing on everything that supposedly shows the weakness of our party after the March movement. Certainly our party has many great weaknesses. They should not be concealed. But still they should not all be self-righteously collected, both what was true and what was untrue, in order to show that the party is finished, as Levi's pamphlet does from its very first line. All that is over.

It was a movement whose weak points must be recognised, but the strong sides of the movement must be cherished and supported and not portrayed as if the party were finished. Then we will have built a bridge that makes unity possible.

The International must have certain organisational assurances that the majority of the Zentrale will carry out the congress decisions conscientiously, that it will recognise the mistakes not only on paper but in life and will attempt to overcome them. We are convinced that the comrades will do this. We also demand organisational guarantees from the opposition group. A faction has been formed, and it must cease to exist as a faction. There must be no party within the party. It is absolutely excluded that we would tolerate something like this in the Communist International. If the comrades really want to conscientiously carry out the decisions of the Communist International, their first decision must be to dissolve this group and put an end to factional war.

I must now inform you that one of our representatives delivered a letter to me yesterday that informs me that Däumig is organising meetings of the opposition. I do not know if that is true. I am aware that accusations are often made in the heat of battle that prove, on closer examination, not to stand up to scrutiny. So we must take this with a grain of salt. But after you have recognised your errors before the congress and it has come to a conscientious decision, we must have guarantees that there will be no ongoing factional war.

Now a few words on the Czechoslovak question. Comrade Burian said that there was no tendency struggle within the Czechoslovak party. That is correct in the sense that our Czechoslovak sister party is not yet organised in a fully distinct fashion, and the tendency struggle is therefore somewhat indistinct. Comrade Bell's sectarian statement here that Šmeral is a bourgeois opportunist only shows Bell's inadequate knowledge of the Czechoslovak movement. We have many criticisms of Šmeral, but it is quite obvious that to describe comrades like Šmeral as bourgeois is an exaggeration. Such exaggerations do not strengthen the struggle against the centrist current; they weaken it. So I must say that we will perhaps have a few issues to discuss with Šmeral. For it is quite true that the Czechoslovak party, although a good proletarian mass party, is still only beginning the process of clarification – in the Communist sense of the word – within the party itself. (*Objections from delegates of the Czechoslovak party*)

I believe, Comrade Burian, that my judgement of the situation is accurate. But perhaps I am mistaken, and that the party's consolidation will soon be complete. You have now truly carried out the first stage of this consolidation. You have broken free from the Social Democrats and the overtly centrist forces. Only two months ago, you were still in a common Central Committee with the Social Democrats.[2] You should not be blamed for that; it is the peculiar way that the Czechoslovak party developed. The first stage, breaking free from Social Democracy and the overtly centrist forces, has been completed. Now we enter a new stage. We join with you, Comrade Burian, and with

---

2. Zinoviev is probably thinking of the convention of Czech Comintern supporters held in May 1921, which changed their party's name from Left Social-Democratic to Communist, adopted the Twenty-One Conditions, and applied to join the International. The split from the reformist faction had taken place earlier, however, in September 1920.

Šmeral and the other Czechoslovak comrades, in wishing with all our heart that this stage goes as smoothly as possible, without calamities and without new splits. But we are convinced that you still have a great deal to go through in the party.

And, actually, this tendency struggle is now expressed rather distinctly. Yesterday, Comrade Burian said there is no tendency struggle. But here I have an issue of the Vienna ROSTA,[3] in which I find a resolution adopted on 12 June at a mass meeting in Komárno. The resolution reads:

> This assembly demands the immediate convocation of a unification congress in order to found the united Communist Party of Czechoslovakia. It expresses its mistrust of all those who through a policy of postponement are compromising the party's capacity for action, and we demand their exclusion from the party. The task of cleansing the party must be carried out with all speed, regardless of personal considerations. Only in this way can the Czechoslovak CP function as a section of the Third International and lead an energetic and successful struggle for the liberation of the proletariat.

So, comrades, a large mass meeting of more than ten thousand workers took up this question and adopted the resolution that I just read to you. We cannot just say that Czechoslovakia is a heaven with angel choirs and no tendency struggle. The tendency struggle is merely not yet fully defined. We hope to work out, together with the Czechoslovak delegation, a series of measures that will enable this magnificent mass party to become a genuine proletarian party. We hope that the party succeeds in taking to heart the experiences of other parties and in overcoming as quickly as possible, with as few calamities as possible, everything that has to be overcome. This does not involve more political heat, but there is still much in the party that needs to be surmounted. Our Czechoslovak delegation will recognise that themselves. The more resolute and determined you are in recognising these weaknesses, the easier it will be for you to surmount everything that must be surmounted.

Comrades, it goes without saying that we must not return in our congresses to the habits of the Second International. We must not seek unanimity at all costs; we must not put on a show or congratulate each other. We must say openly and clearly the way things are. Nonetheless, in my opinion, we must do all we can in an attempt to reach unanimity in our Communist ranks.

Based on the entire debate we have carried out here, I believe that a unified line can be perceived even in the most difficult issues facing the movement.

---

3. A reference to the publication of the Russian Telegraph Agency's Vienna branch. ROSTA was a precursor of Soviet news agency TASS.

Some will ask: is this really a shift to the right, as many here have said? That is stupid stuff. Anyone who was present at the Second Congress will remember that at this foundational event we had much to criticise with regard to the so-called Left. Nonetheless, what we worked out at the Second Congress was by and large a blow against the Right and against centrism. And I believe that our decisions here at the Third World Congress will also be a deadly blow against these gentlemen. (*Loud applause and cheers*)

**Thälmann** (VKPD): Comrades, I am extremely sorry that I did not succeed in speaking after the address by Comrade Trotsky, because I understand that he intends to deliver a sharp attack against the amendments proposed by the German delegation. I have no choice but to take up Comrade Zinoviev's remarks. He said that statements were made here that the Left was being dealt with harshly while the Right was treated gently. And in his view, the discussion revealed that the left wing's outlook enables the clever bourgeoisie in many countries to lure the party out of its lair. He gave special attention to that issue.

I believe that if there are two currents in the International, it may be that they are being glued together artificially. Zinoviev says that we must now undergo extraordinarily difficult struggles in Italy, that we are compelled to awaken the masses who still have the idea that Serrati, even today, has sympathy for Soviet Russia. The Italian workers have seen that when the struggles broke out, the Serrati forces, who formerly enjoyed their trust, withdrew to the sidelines. They did not encourage and support the workers in such a way as to have launched them into a struggle to win political power. There is a danger that the centrist currents will have an opportunity, with the bourgeois foes on the attack, to give expression to the same tendencies, saying that we should take up the struggle only if the majority of the proletariat is with us.

Let me take up the notion that the bourgeoisie will lure the new Communist Party out of its lair. As has been said, the March Action is a step forward and a battle that was forced on us. That means that the Communist Party, when this battle was forced on it, had to choose whether to respond with a show of protest, or whether to support our brothers fighting in Central Germany. The masses in Germany would not have understood if we had abandoned the Central German brothers to their cruel fate. As early as 17 March, many districts were demanding that the party finally go beyond a policy of demonstrations. That was not just the view of the Zentrale.

Among the masses there was a revolutionary impatience, which reflects both the social decay and the masses' will to struggle. Conditions in Germany cannot be analysed as Trotsky did during the first agenda point. I am convinced that a time of general prosperity would have quite a different character in Germany. We will not have increased production here. Rather, given the obligations to the Entente, we will have a shrinkage of production, increased joblessness, and a ferment in the working class. The German party will then face the difficult task of determining whether it has the sympathy of the proletariat in its majority. We have taken the approach in the trade unions and other bodies that a general strike means an armed insurrection because, when the party calls for a general strike, the bourgeoisie will unleash all its forces against the proletariat.

If the Communist Party had left the elite of the revolutionary proletariat in the lurch in the March Action, that would have meant splitting the revolutionary wing from the Communist Party. That was the most important factor, and we recognised it in that situation.

But we must also recognise something else: men in the party who previously advanced the view that the March Action was a Bakuninist putsch have come to the conclusion during this congress that this view is false.

But consider this: at a moment when attacks were raining down on the Communist Party, which was engaged in a life-and-death struggle, comrades in the party moved to stab it in the back, just as Kautsky did to the Russian Revolution in 1918. And these comrades had already clearly shown on another question that they were displeased with the party's course. You have to imagine yourself in such a situation. Such a criticism can perhaps be understood by men who are in the party and carry out theoretical work there. But how are the masses to respond when they see such currents in a party that is supposed to be ruled by strict discipline? Such differences can be expressed inside the party, but not publicly. That is the crime committed by the comrades. All the comrades had to do was to submit to the party's discipline.

Zinoviev says that we cannot endure a split in Germany. That is quite true. But we have evidence that efforts are already under way in the party to organise a split. Comrade Däumig has already held meetings in Berlin with the goal of establishing an organisational apparatus aimed at destroying the party. This danger does not arise from the Left. I must tell you that the entire working class organised in the VKPD, in all its districts, stands with the party, and Comrade Clara Zetkin and the others have the support of only a small minority, perhaps 5 to 7 per cent. Nonetheless they are trying both publicly and here at the congress to show how powerful they are. It is therefore dangerous to treat them with consideration while deploying the heavy artillery against comrades who may soon be forced by the economic situation as a whole to bring the proletariat into action. In Hamburg, we have already held membership meetings in which the major errors, organisational weaknesses, and false theoretical positions were discussed, along with the lessons of this struggle that we have learned for the future. This struggle is therefore a defeat not for the party but rather for the proletariat. For the party, it was a victory in the sense that it emerged from the struggle strengthened by the masses.

As early as February and March, the proletariat itself was saying that we always relied on demonstrations and similar actions and evaded the struggle, even when what was posed was major struggles over wages. We in Germany hold that, given the struggles within the country and the increasing international tensions, we must develop along the lines laid down in the Second Congress. The March Action proved that we were right in this regard. One should not say, as Lenin did, that an intense struggle should be waged against those who moved the amendments to the Russian theses. Every comrade in the Communist Party has the perfect right to add to the theses what is essential in order to reflect the economic conditions of a country. In addition, Lenin's harsh attack was also unwarranted because, at the end of his speech, he said that a small Communist Party is capable of leading broad masses, even millions, in the achievement of political power. That is exactly the idea that the amendments introduce.

Comrade Zetkin has made it clear that she does not in any way commit herself not to speak publicly in the future about the errors and weaknesses of the March Action. Simply imagine the situation this creates for the Communist Party. Everything is lined up against the Communist Party: the Majority Socialists [SPD], the bourgeois press, and so on. They are trying to present us as hangmen. Are we then to show the public – through meetings, editorials, and the like – that there are currents in the party that say the party brought about a bloodbath? No, we must be against public criticism. I am against that for another reason as well: comrades who do not abide by discipline do not belong in the party. Within the party, one can talk about anything, but to go outside the party and speak to the broad public – that is something I must condemn. Our opinion is that the path adopted today is one fraught with crisis.

I am disciplined and centralist, though it has cost me a struggle. I am so centralist that I carry out decisions. But I must point out that the Communist Party of Germany has a different point of view, and these differences, given the amendments to the theses, take on a scope that is extremely serious, in view of the crisis-ridden conditions in Germany. We will be faced with a difficult struggle against the parties to our right. They will rub our face in it and say that the differences between them and us are not so very great. I have told you frankly what we really face given the present economic conditions in Germany. (*Loud applause*)

**Trotsky**: First, a very brief formal comment. Comrade Thälmann, whose impassioned speech we just heard, complained that he was not allowed to take the floor after me. But after all, the order of speeches is determined by the speakers' list. Comrade Thälmann also said that he is a very disciplined comrade. As such he must abide by the discipline of the speakers' list; he really had no grounds to complain about this objective fact.

Comrade Thälmann also complained – once again unjustifiably – about Comrade Lenin, portraying matters as if Comrade Lenin had said that we are proposing Theses on Tactics and Strategy here and the other delegations do not have the right to present amendments. This was not what he meant, and Comrade Thälmann's viewpoint on this matter is quite wrong. Lenin said: 'The theses we are proposing were not concocted and produced by the Russian delegation by gathering in some small office and spending a brief hour writing them up.'[4] On the contrary! Comrade Thälmann can make the necessary inquiries among the members of his own delegation: he will learn that we conducted lengthy, exhaustive, and at times impassioned negotiations and discussions over the theses, including with members of the German delegation. Various proposals were made, including by the German delegation, in a process of mutual concessions. Our theses are the result of this rather laborious process. I do not claim that these theses were approved by every party, group, and tendency, but I do say that from our point of view, the theses were viewed as a compromise in the sense of a modification to the left. I will take up later just what this term 'left' signifies. For now I want only to stress emphatically that we view the theses as the limit of the concessions to the current represented here by many comrades, including Comrade Thälmann.

Comrades, many delegates have expressed to me privately their impatience with the fact that the German delegation is taking up rather a great deal of time for such an extensive discussion of its internal affairs. In my opinion, the impatience of these comrades is unwarranted. This involves above all the March Action. Of course it is simply human, all too human, that this very political question is mixed in with personal concerns, personal frictions, and passions. Certainly, some comrades have needlessly sharpened the personal and emotional side of the question, as did Comrade Heckert, whose speech was otherwise very interesting. But I believe we must identify here the main issue, focus in on the main question, and this question is not a German one; it is eminently international. The German party is the first in what we, from our Russian geographical point of view, regard as Western Europe that has developed into an independent, firmly defined, large party and has, for the first time, led a major independent action. And because the new, very new Italian party and the larger French organisation that is also very new as a

---

4. See p. 465.

Communist Party confront conditions that are very similar in this respect, I believe that every delegation, and especially those I have mentioned, have a great deal to learn from this question.

I shall begin my discussion of the March Action with an analysis of the proposed amendments. The congress must choose here between two tendencies. I will, of course, not take up the editorial and factual changes to the first draft of the theses. We have to choose between two tendencies. Between the tendency represented here by Comrade Lenin, Comrade Zinoviev and particularly by the reporter Comrade Radek, and now defended by me; and then the amendments and proposals that give or seek to give expression to a different tendency. It is therefore important to analyse these amendments. I will limit myself to the passage that deals with the March Action. Our proposals say in this regard that we view the March Action 'as a struggle forced on the VKPD by the government's attack on the Central German proletariat. We recognise the courageous action of the VKPD, which has demonstrated that it is a party of the revolutionary proletariat of Germany.' Then we identify the major errors committed during these actions and, in conclusion, provide the following advice:

> In order to carefully weigh the possibilities for struggle, the VKPD needs to take into account the facts and considerations that point up the difficulties of a proposed action and work out carefully how they may be countered. But once the party leadership has decided on an action, all comrades must abide by the party's decisions and carry out this action. Criticism of an action should be voiced only after it has concluded, and then only within the party structures and in its newspapers, and after taking into consideration the party's situation in relationship to the class enemy. Since Levi disregarded these self-evident requirements of party discipline and conditions for party criticism, the congress approves his expulsion from the party and considers any political collaboration with him by members of the Communist International to be impermissible.[5]

Now Comrade Brand was flatly opposed to making any reference to a cautionary voice to which the party should pay heed. We will perhaps return to Comrade Brand, who takes exception to cautionary voices, statistics, and a great deal more. What is being proposed with regard to these passages by the German and other comrades who signed these amendments? They propose that the Third Congress of the Communist International recognise the VKPD's March Action as a step forward, saying:

---

5. For corresponding text in the theses, see pp. 941 and 1052.

The strongest mass party of Central Europe made the transition to effective struggle. It made an initial attempt by the Communist Party to achieve a leading role in the struggles of the German proletariat, a role which the party identified in its initial programme. The March Action defeated the Independent party [USPD] and the centrist forces hidden within the VKPD itself, exposing their plainly counterrevolutionary character.[6]

And so on and so forth.

So the congress is being asked to state that the March Action was more than a mass struggle, a mass action forced on the working class and thereby on the party, and that the party conducted itself courageously. The congress is also being asked to recognise that the Communist Party made the attempt to establish its leadership role in these struggles. In that case, the congress must also be granted the right to say whether this attempt was successful or unsuccessful. When we say that the March Action was a step forward, we are referring – at least I am – to the fact that the Communist Party was no longer an opposition inside the USPD or a Communist propaganda group but a solid, unified, independent, centralised party, and that it is capable of intervening independently in the proletarian struggle, which occurred for the first time in the March Action.

At the Second World Congress, I had many discussions with French comrades concerning the situation in the trade unions and in the party. I told them, 'Yes, you are together with the syndicalists, anarchists, and socialists, and still you represent only an opposition.'[7] As a result there are certain tendencies and nuances, and even perhaps potential blunders. You will take a great step forward the moment you break free of the old organisation and take the stage as an independent force.' That has now been fully accomplished.

That does not mean, however, that this initial action, this attempt to play an independent leading role was successful. It is said that we have learned a great deal from this, including from the mistakes. That is what the amendments say. I will not read them out. But it is said there that the great merit of the March Action was that it made possible the identification of errors that had been committed, in order to correct them later on. Well, to seek merits in this fashion is certainly a very bold approach. I told Comrade Thalheimer privately that this reminded me of a Russian who translated an English book in the 1870s and wrote in the preface that he had translated the book so that the whole world could see how completely worthless it was. (*Laughter*) One does not launch an action simply for the sake of seeing what errors one will

---

6. See point 7 in the amendments, pp. 1053–5.
7. During the Second Congress in July–August 1920, French Communists were still an oppositional, although growing, minority within the Socialist Party.

commit in order to correct them later on. These amendments are written in a defensive spirit, not one of analysis.

In his interesting speech, Comrade Heckert portrayed the March Action by showing that conditions were extremely acute at that time. There was the question of reparations, the occupation of the Ruhr, Upper Silesia, the economic crisis, unemployment, and major strikes. In this broad framework of the world-historical movement, contradictions were intensifying even more, and then the movement of the Central German workers gave, if you will, the last impulse for the party's offensive. This is truly a fine, honest, economic picture. But another comrade, defending the same action, gave us quite the opposite picture. If, thirty years from now, Comrade Thalheimer – by that time old and grey – takes in hand Mehring's pen in order to write the history of the Communist Party,[8] he will come upon documents and books –

**Radek**: In my magic suitcase...(*Laughter*)

**Trotsky** (*continuing*) – documents and books that present quite a different picture of the movement. Specifically, the international situation was somewhat confused, and it was by and large moving in the direction of compromise. The Upper Silesian question was hanging fire, and in any case it could not exert any revolutionary influence. As for the disarmament question in Bavaria, *Die Rote Fahne* consistently declared, contrary to Heckert's speech yesterday, that it was increasingly clear that this question would be resolved by a compromise at the expense of the revolutionary workers of Bavaria and of all Germany, and that this would take place without any major clashes on an international scale or between the German and Bavarian governments.[9]

What is more, thirty years from now, Comrade Thalheimer will find articles showing that the crisis in Germany had and still has quite a different character from that in the United States or in Britain. In Germany this crisis did not become as catastrophically acute as in those two countries. Given that Germany's entire economic life is in a state of decay, under the prevailing economic conditions the crisis did not have the power to erupt in that fashion. The number of unemployed in Germany is insignificant in comparison to the United States and Britain.

As for the internal situation, the Social Democrats are partly in the government, partly in the opposition. The same applies to the Independent party, which moves closer and closer to the Social Democrats. The trade unions and

---

8. A reference to Franz Mehring's 1,500-page *Geschichte der deutschen Sozial-demokratie* [History of German Social Democracy] (Mehring 1960), covering the years from 1830 to 1891.
9. For the disarmament question in Bavaria, see p. 486, n. 8.

their bureaucratic leadership are all against us. What conclusion should be drawn from this? After all, the same comrade tells us that a wall of passivity prevailed among the workers, and the task was to break through this wall through the revolutionary initiative of a resolute minority. Heckert, on the contrary, said that everything was in uproar, everything was stirred up. Much storm and stress. And then came the events in Central Germany. The other comrade says, 'We were mired everywhere in a swamp. There was a wall of passivity. We had to break through it at any cost.' Each of these pictures is splendid as a finished, logical portrayal, but I hardly think they fit together.

Then again, another comrade – it was Comrade Koenen – stated that there was an open insurrection in Central Germany, while passivity reigned all around. Activity encased in passivity. From all this we get the impression that members of the German delegation still regard this experience in terms of defending it at all costs, rather then investigating and analysing it. Everything we hear is, so to speak, just a means to an end – namely the goal of defending the March Action at all costs before the International. That is hardly likely to succeed. The main issue for me, therefore, is what Comrade Thälmann referred to. He said that if the theses and even the amendments are adopted, 'we will carry out a reorientation in our country'. I believe that our brave and dogged Comrade Thälmann is quite correct. He must have a very close feel for the masses.

**Thälmann**: Indeed, a very close feel.

**Trotsky**: I do not doubt that in the least, especially when I consider the state of mind in which many comrades arrived from Germany, which is reflected in the many articles and pamphlets they wrote in Germany. They had a rather long and uncomfortable journey to Russia, during which they could take a cooler view of the situation. Then the theses appeared, which encountered stubborn resistance. Later, there were discussions with other delegations, including the Russians, in which the German comrades could not help noticing that comrades of the International did not view matters through German spectacles. At that point they began to carry out something of a strategic retreat.

There is no denying that the proposed amendments are dangerous, not so much in what they say plainly and directly, but because they seek to express in a somewhat concealed and confused fashion the concepts that were advanced on behalf of the Zentrale among German workers and in the German Communist Party apparatus during the most intense days of struggle and the period that followed. And Comrade Thälmann and other comrades think, 'We must return home with theses that do not disavow us.' Well, we do not want that either. We certainly do not want to disavow the party, because the German party is one of our best. But the entire conception of the March Action and the conditions of struggle and victory are presented here and are expressed to its members through many of the German Zentrale's articles, speeches, and circulars in a fashion that can only be regarded as quite abrupt and dangerous.

That is the main issue. They want to influence the situation in such a fashion that the resolution adopted here will be not precise but confused and open to gradual and imperceptible reinterpretation later on to give it a different meaning reflecting something of their viewpoint. That is the main issue. This is impermissible. In our opinion, the danger is far too great to allow so much scope for this spirit of offensive to die away gradually and imperceptibly. We will never accept this; that is excluded. True, you can overwhelm us with a majority decision of this congress. In that case, we will struggle within the framework permitted us by the congress – and only within that framework.

But I hope that the outcome with the resolution on tactics and strategy will be the same as with that on the economic situation. In that case as well, the comrades of our German delegation's left wing wanted to stage a demonstration. They voted for the theses in principle, but also introduced a resolution that contained outspokenly contrary views. But it then turned out that they no longer dared to stand by what they had previously sought to introduce. And, in the commission, nothing was left of their position but a few insignificant remnants. In my opinion, that is exactly what will happen regarding the tactical and strategic questions.

I know from my own experience how extremely unpleasant it is to be disavowed by a congress of the party or the International. However, comrades, the best thing for your situation in Germany is to introduce clarity on this question. I do not believe what Levi said about the party being destroyed by this. But the congress must tell German workers that it was an error, and that the party's attempt to play a leading role in a great mass movement was unsuccessful. We must establish that this attempt was unsuccessful, in the sense that if there should be a repetition, this excellent party really could be destroyed.

**Thalheimer**: You know very well that this is excluded.

**Trotsky**: Excluded for you, yes, but not for the thousands of organised workers who thought the congress would cheer enthusiastically for what we in fact view as an error. (*Loud applause*) The same is true for our young French friends. The Executive took up the question of the calling up of the class of 1919, questioning whether the French party should have issued the slogan of refusing to obey the call-up order.[10]

---

10. For the 1921 call-up of the conscription class of 1919, see p. 460, n. 11.

At that point I asked our young friend Laporte what was meant by that: should those who were called up have offered armed resistance or merely resisted passively? And the comrade replied emphatically, 'With revolver in hand, of course'. And he thought that in this way he was demonstrating his full agreement with the Third International, his great revolutionary enthusiasm, and his sense of duty. And he was quite serious about it, fully prepared to fight against the call-up with revolver in hand. Of course we had to throw a bucket of cold water on him, and I am sure that the comrade has learned from this. He came into a new milieu here, one he does not encounter just any day, and some of his rough edges were smoothed out.

During these two to three weeks that we spend together here at the congress, our thinking changes in many ways. But what has changed during these two to three weeks in Germany, France, or Hungary? What has changed in these countries? Nothing whatsoever.

This celebrated philosophy of the offensive, which is completely non-Marxist, has arisen from the following curious outlook: 'A wall of passivity is gradually rising, which is ruining the movement. So let us advance, and break through this wall!' I believe that an entire layer of comrades in the German party leadership, or close to it, were educated for a stretch of time in this spirit. Now they are waiting to see what the congress will have to say. Should our response be that, while throwing Paul Levi out the window, we speak of the March Action only in the most confused fashion as the first step, a step forward – phrase-mongering to muffle our criticism? That would be a betrayal of our duty. We are obliged to say frankly to the German working class that we regard this philosophy of the offensive as the greatest of dangers, and that to apply it in practice is the greatest of political crimes.

I am in complete agreement with Comrade Zinoviev and, like him, cherish the hope that we will be united in expressing our opinion at this congress. I believe that we cannot make any significant concessions to the so-called Left in this overriding question of policy. Many comrades, including, I believe, those from France, were somewhat concerned that a struggle was being waged against the Left. Comrade Zinoviev spoke to this issue. Fortunately, it is precisely in the French language that the term *gauche* has two meanings: *gauche* refers to what stands on the left, and *gauche* also means 'clumsy, awkward'.

**Interjection**: *Linkisch*.

**Trotsky**: Yes, *linkisch* in the negative sense of the word. In German it comes to much the same thing. Well, I believe that in struggling against the so-called Left, we do not at all feel that we are to the right of these 'Lefts.'

We see no party to the left of us, because we are the International, the Communist, Marxist International, the most revolutionary party possible. That means we are a party that is capable of utilising all situations and all possibilities, not only to conduct struggles but also to achieve victories. That is our true goal. It is sometimes forgotten that we learn the art of strategy, precisely and soberly estimate the enemy's power, and analyse the situation, rather than rushing into battle to break the wall of passivity or, in the words of another comrade, 'to activate the party'.

And here, obviously, statistics have a role to play. This is true despite the fact that, as Comrade Brand says, opportunists also make good use of statistics. In his speech, he counterposed statistics and the sword, and in a second speech the charge of opportunism was flung at us. Such an outlook is dangerous for our Italian comrades, who will in the future have a great deal to do with statistics. If I were to talk about Italy in the style of Heckert and Thalheimer, I might have said: 'Here is a country in which the workers occupied the factories, the Serrati forces betrayed them, the Fascists have assaulted the workers' print shops and burned their offices. The party's call must be: Forward against the enemy with all our strength. A party that fails in this is cowardly and will stand utterly condemned before the court of history.' But let us examine the situation not with such phrase-mongering but with a sober assessment of conditions. Then we can say only what Zinoviev said here. You must win the confidence of the working class anew, because betrayal has made workers much more cautious than they were previously. They will think that they heard much phrase-mongering from Serrati. He said pretty much the same thing and then betrayed them. What guarantee is there that the new party will not also betray them? They will want to see the party in action before they go into decisive struggles under its leadership.

We have three rather well-defined tendencies at the congress, three groups that have taken shape temporarily as tendencies. Without examining them, there is no way to size up accurately the forces at play in this congress. First of all, there is the German delegation, which came here straight from the fires of the March Action and expressed their outlook most sharply in the philosophy of the offensive. Many German comrades have, of course, pulled back from that now.

Then there are the Italian comrades, who are following the same path – unsurprisingly, because the party is on the rebound from the centrists. The Italian comrades say that now they finally have a free hand, now they can carry out their duty, launch revolutionary mass actions, and thus be revenged for Serrati's betrayal.

And now, comrades, as you know, it has been said not only by Levi but also by the capitalist and Independent [USPD] press that the March Action was ordered by the Executive and that Levi was expelled because he was not willing to obey the order. Many a comrade in the French and Czech parties wondered whether they too would receive such orders given in the name of the Executive, and, if they then refused to carry them out, they would then be expelled. Such a view may well indicate that these comrades are not that familiar with the spirit of the Executive, but there are many comrades in the Communist International who have such fears. So we have these two points of view here.

There is also a third point of view, expressed, we hope, in our theses. This viewpoint states that it would of course be absurd for the Executive to adopt this tactical philosophy of intensifying struggles through more or less artificial mass actions, sending off orders to this country and that. Quite the contrary. We have now grown strong and thus face the responsibility of leading the mass movement as an independent, centralised party. This places on us the responsibility to analyse the situation in every country quite precisely, with a cool eye, and then – when it is possible and necessary – attack with passionate determination. That is exactly what our proposed theses say.

A comrade tells us that there are no leftist comrades in France. That is quite true. The French party is going through a period of moulting. Read its official publication, *L'Humanité.* You will perceive in its agitation and in the speeches a rather confused and vague tone. Thus you find in *L'Humanité* the 'swinishness' – to borrow a term from Comrade Bukharin, associated with the writings of Longuet and his close associates. The newspaper is sustained by a Communist resolve, but this resolve is not effectively harnessed. Communist thought is not precise and clear enough. The resolve required to drive the situation forward and clarify it does not shine through. Given that we do not find this in the official publication, it is excluded for me that the party can acquire overnight the capacity to initiate and lead broad revolutionary mass actions. The first precondition is that a clear, revolutionary thought and resolve take shape in it and find expression in all its agitation and propaganda. It may take two, three, or six months or possibly a year for this process of crystallisation to take place. That depends on the conditions. Many comrades will find that it does not take place quickly enough.

They do not take into account the inward state of this process – the revolutionary metamorphosis of a large party. They want to skip over that, and it seems to them that the only thing lacking for a revolutionary action is a pretext. So they say, 'Frossard and the others just won't do it. Here we have the perfect occasion. This is where we can make a start.' The call-up of the class of 1919, for example – and precisely in France, where anarchists and syndicalists are so strong. Given French temperament and the Paris working class it is possible that a good segment of this working class, an excellent segment, which can have decisive weight in major struggles, can be drawn by younger, less experienced, and impatient workers into an action that could be disastrous for the movement in France for many years. That is the situation.

Of course it can be said that this is an attack on this or that comrade who made a bad speech, but that is unimportant. Well, comrades, if everyone could form an opinion on their own, then we would have no need for an International. Our task lies precisely in perceiving a danger even if it is very small, expressing it clearly, drawing attention to it – even, if you will, exaggerating it. For me or you to exaggerate a danger – delivering a warning in a loud voice – is no great problem. But the opposite danger, that of missing such an error, allowing it to grow to the point where it collides against a provocation, leading us into a perilous adventure – that is a great danger indeed. That explains the passion with which many comrades have spoken on this issue.

Let me tell you, sometimes, when I talk privately to this or that comrade, I notice that he does not understand me. He thinks that I am older, while he is younger. I already have some grey hairs, while he is more determined. He considers it to be a matter of temperament and says, 'You are too cautious.' Then I say to myself that the greatest danger lies in the fact that certain comrades do not understand the nature of danger. He is politically inexperienced in a revolutionary sense. He does not understand that this warning, while very real, is also limited in character. He thinks we are moving to the right. No, that is not the case.

You have broken with the opportunists and you are remaking this movement from within. But look around you: there exist in this world not only opportunists, but also classes, capitalist society, the police, the army, definite economic conditions. Some are for you, others against, still others rather neutral. It is a big, complex world, and it is quite a task to figure things out. You must learn this when you answer me. You want me to fight the centrists? But all the resolutions of the First and Second Congresses remain in full force. And the entire activity that we will be engaged in is, after all, nothing else but a frontal blow at opportunism. But our task does not lie solely in always condemning opportunism theoretically. We have to overcome capitalist society in practice, pin the bourgeoisie to the ground, and destroy it. That is the task. And for this task, I must repeat, we have to unify the cold language of statistics with the passionate language of revolutionary force. We will learn to do that, and we will triumph.[11] (*Loud applause and cheers*)

---

11. For Trotsky's comments on the heated reactions to this speech, see his letter to Lenin printed in Appendix 4a on pp. 1153–5.

**Koenen** (chair): Comrades, we have received a motion by the American delegation to close discussion after Comrade Trotsky's speech and to take the summary by Comrade Radek. (*Commotion, objections*)

**Béla Kun** (on procedure): Comrades, I move that we close the speakers' list, but we should not end the debate. Comrade Trotsky's hour-long speech has just delivered an attack on the so-called Left, and he has done this in a tone that absolutely requires that we give a response. This is why I believe that closing the debate in these circumstances would mean suppressing discussion. In my opinion, this American motion, pulled out of the air at a favourable moment, is political manipulation, and I strongly protest it. I move that the speakers' list be closed but that the debate continue.

**Koenen** (chair): First of all, a correction. There is absolutely no manipulation here. We received the motion before Comrade Trotsky began to speak, and we read it out only after his speech, which was the appropriate moment, because that was when the end of the debate had been requested.

I cannot present a motion if the request is to present it only after Trotsky's speech. But I ask the comrades to speak up regarding closure of the debate and vote on it. By no means has the Presidium taken a position on this; we are presenting you with the motion of the American delegation.

**Frölich**: I note that the Presidium, without consulting the congress, permitted Comrade Zinoviev to speak against the Left for forty-five minutes, and then Comrade Trotsky for a full hour. I note that the American delegation's motion had already been made when Comrade Trotsky took the floor. In my opinion, unless the congress wishes to say that the Left is being steamrollered here, it must absolutely permit the debate to continue.

**Marshall** (Bedacht): Comrades, I would like to point out, on behalf of the American delegation, that there was absolutely no intention, then or now, to gag anyone. The American delegation, and so too the British, were of the view that the entire debate that has gone on today, after that of yesterday and those in the Executive, have not added anything essentially new. And neither Trotsky's hour-long speech, nor a subsequent speech from the other side, will alter the opinions in this hall. We would like to put an end to this now and not have to listen to the same arguments over and over again.

**Koenen** (chair): In this type of procedural debate regarding ending a discussion, it is customary to hear a speaker for and a speaker against the motion. We have already heard several speakers for and against the motion, and we already have before us a whole number of other requests to speak. So in my opinion, we have no other option but to take the vote.

**Friesland**: The German delegation asks the congress to adjourn the session for two or three minutes, so that the delegations can consult on the matter. To end debate at this point might have decisive importance.

**Zinoviev**: I propose that we have a break of ten minutes and then take the vote. I believe that will be the most effective way to proceed.

**Koenen** (chair): Is there any opposition to that proposal? There is none. The session will therefore reconvene in ten minutes.

*(The session reconvenes after a ten-minute break.)*

**Koenen** (chair): The session is again open. We will now take the vote on the motion to close the debate.

**Zinoviev**: In my opinion, the debate should be closed. In the event that a member of the commission presents a motion that touches on principle and that is rejected by the commission, then we will propose to the congress to let this comrade speak in a plenary session. (*Applause*)

*(The congress decides accordingly.)*

**Koenen** (chair): Comrade Radek has the floor for his summary.

## Summary to Report on Tactics and Strategy

**Radek**: We have had two days of discussion in which, repeatedly, we have had speeches that were in fact summaries. (*Laughter*) So permit me, comrades, to present a summary on behalf of the Executive recommending adoption of the theses we have presented. I will do this in light of all the evidence presented in this debate and the outcome of a discussion that was not just an exchange of personal opinions but was fruitful in bringing a great many facts to light. First, comrades, permit me to summarise what has been said by representatives of a number of different delegations.

Comrade Lazzari was the first to take a position on the theses, even before the theses had been fully motivated here. He was in complete agreement with the theses, except for what was said there about Italy. The comrades of Czechoslovakia then stated that they were in complete agreement with the theses, except for the passages referring to Czechoslovakia. The British comrades then declared their full love and affection for the theses, except for the fact that with regard to Britain they were quite wrong. (*Laughter*) These statements remind me of a Polish poet, who said, 'You are confessing to the sins of other people.'

When the sins of the Czech comrades were openly attacked, Lazzari said, 'You are too gentle: to the gallows with them!' The Czechs were not so harsh in calling for the Serrati people to go to the gallows, but they gave their approval. (*Laughter*)

This shows that our assessment of the state of the International must start with the fact that we have not yet overcome the opportunist danger in the workers' movement. We face the Amsterdam trade-union International, and we face strong opportunist parties in every country. In the Communist International too, the danger of opportunism has not been overcome, and it will become even greater if the movement proceeds at a slower tempo. I see it as a dangerous symptom of opportunism that representatives of parties are taking the floor here to say that everything in their party is just fine. Comrades, we have certainly spoken of the situation of our youngest child, *our Czech sister party*, in quite different terms than we intended to at the beginning of the congress. We have spoken in a most gentle fashion because we have been convinced that although its development is quite slow, it is nonetheless developing to the left. But consider: in my report I made clear that the December strike took the party fully by surprise, the party did not lead it either organisationally or politically, and after the struggle the party did not in any way impress upon the workers the lessons of the strike. Then Comrade Burian gets up here and says, 'Our party is in excellent shape, and if its leadership calls it to struggle, the party will respond.' We can only answer: '*That is the way things are done in the Second but not in the Communist International.*'

Of course we would be very happy to be able to say that each of our parties was carrying out its tasks to perfection. But we know that the road to revolution is difficult, and a thousand errors are made along its course. And when we hear assurances that 'everything in our party is just fine' coming from a country in which only a year ago the Communists belonged to a common party with Němec and Soukup, we are more uneasy than when the worst Turkestaner sends his worst warnings to the Executive. For this shows us that a spirit of criticism is lacking in the Czech party. We therefore have to say to the Czech comrades, 'You will not build a sound and supple party if you persist in praising everything it has done in the past rather than trying to learn from your errors.'

Consider the case of the British comrades. I stated that it was impossible to learn anything from the party press about the real activity of the party during the miners' strike. I had to ask the comrades what they had done. They gave me quite a sad picture. Yet the first representative of the British delegation to take the floor protested against this. I have here an issue of the British party paper of 11 June. Besides the pictures, the front page contains a political analysis, the second an economic analysis, the third a call for liberation of the prisoners, and then the next three pages have pictures again. I have nothing against using pictures for agitation, but a party can find ways to report on actions other than speaking through symbols as one would to the deaf and dumb. It is very bad for a new party, which has played a minimal role, to come here and say that everything is just fine; the Liberal Party is also quite small. My dear comrades, if you achieve power, we will see if you can do it with a party as small as that of Lloyd George. Meanwhile, the fact is that the Liberals and Conservatives are in power. You have a weekly paper, with three-quarters of its pages devoted to illustrations, and a small membership. And when we say, 'To the masses', you reply, 'Lloyd George also has a small party.' That is not the way to respond when we say we need to go to the masses.

Comrades, we have said almost nothing of the other parties – the *French party*, for example. We made only a few comments about it. I must say that the participation of the French party in the congress has not given us a sufficient basis to form a clear picture of its politics. But if the French comrades believe that our relationship in the future can consist of us not bothering them and them not bothering us, we disagree. The Executive's approach toward the French party has been to allow the situation to mature somewhat. However, we believe that in the future we will have to give close attention to whether the French party, which has not spoken against the theses, actually carries them out.

Comrades, it was the *German party* that has been most discussed here, and that has been most harshly taken to task for its errors by both us and you. The German party has given us a large number of presentations that have provided factual material on which to judge the situation and our policies. And I am convinced, comrades, that this lively exchange on the German question will have immense importance not only for the German party's own development but for the Communist International. Through great struggles and unprecedented suffering, the German proletarians have constantly provided us during the last three years with lessons that go beyond those of the Russian Revolution. It is the fate of the German working class to be the bearer of the first great revolutionary movement outside of our half-agrarian Russia and in an industrial country. This fact makes the German working class a pacesetter for the international proletariat, a role previously played only by the Russian workers. The experiences of the Russian Revolution have given the international proletariat the slogan of the dictatorship and the slogan of soviets. But the road that led us to victory in Russia could well be shorter than the road the proletariat will travel in all the capitalist countries. And the German proletariat's suffering, the slow pace of events, the struggles and the defeats, provide the outstanding source of our new experiences, which we wish to make accessible for the international proletariat. True, we have argued a great deal with the VKPD, on the one hand, and the KAPD on the other, but we have done this not because they have made errors while other parties are exemplary, but because the Communist movement of Germany, through its errors, defeats, and victories, allows us to shield other parties from such errors.

Comrades, I grouped three examples together: the Italian party during the occupation of the factories, the Czechoslovak party during the December strike, and the VKPD during the March struggles. I did this not accidentally or for chronological reasons, but because a comparison of these three movements enables us to evaluate the potential of these actions, the requirements and duties of the party, and the dangers that threaten it. The Czechoslovak and Italian movements provide us with an example of how parties faced with broad, spontaneous movements were incapable of leading them, because they were insufficiently Communist and still carried the poison of opportunism in their veins. The German movement showed how a new Communist organisation, eager for action and battle, did not allow the situation to mature sufficiently and, in addition, made a number of errors in directing the struggle that threatened to loosen its ties to the broad proletarian masses.

Comrades, I simply cannot grasp why no one during the debate went into the Czechoslovak and Italian examples, and that interest was focused instead on the errors of the German March Action. The errors committed in Italy and Czechoslovakia signify the party's complete breakdown, its nonexistence, a deadly sin against communism. Some half-centrist forces respond to our discussion on the March Action by exclaiming, *nostra vittoria!* [We have triumphed] We consider it our duty to point out that we struggle against the errors of the Left because these errors can reinforce opportunism, which is our deadly enemy and is the overriding target of our struggle. If the fact that we have struggled hard here against the Left in the German or Italian parties and alerted them to their errors leads the opportunists to believe *nostra vittoria*, then we must tell them, 'You are rejoicing prematurely!' We are convinced that these discussions, drawing on everything achieved in the struggle, will assist good Communist parties in carrying their struggles through to victory. And then these Communist parties will destroy opportunism, not with the weapons of criticism but in the struggle itself.

Comrade Lenin said here that the First Congress took up the struggle against opportunism, and the Second Congress did likewise. That does not mean that we give the opportunists carte blanche for the Fourth Congress.

Rather it is a challenge to the Communist parties to learn, through carrying out mass politics, to pull the rug out from opportunism in the proletariat. It is not through words but through its entire activity that the party will heighten the masses' trust in its strength and future victory. In this manner, it will pull the rug out from under opportunism. Now that economic forces have demolished the labour aristocracy, the only breeding ground left for opportunism is the proletariat's lack of trust in its own strength.

Now let us take up the balance sheet of the German discussion. What did it show us? First, that the party acted correctly, when the German Communist government assaulted the strongest contingent of the German Communist proletariat, by rushing to assist this proletariat. The party was quite right to do this. It was no putsch carried out on orders from above, but a revolutionary action by hundreds of thousands of proletarians. In addition, the debate has shown that the party leadership made a series of errors in carrying through this mass action. Later, a portion of the comrades, convinced that new actions would soon take place, created the false theory that under present conditions the party is obliged to take the offensive.

I have already said in my report that we cannot triumph without an offensive, without an assault on capitalism's Bastille. A party must carry in its breast the spirit of offensive. It must be capable of arousing in every proletarian an awareness that liberation can come only from direct toe-to-toe combat, in which it can prevail only by straining all of its strength. A party that cannot do this is not worthy of the name Communist. And you have heard from the lips of our unquestionably most level-headed leader, Comrade Lenin, that anyone who rejects in principle taking the offensive does not belong in the Communist International.

In addition, comrades, we have established here that this theory was false because, in the given situation, conditions were not sufficiently acute, were not assessed with enough cold calculation. The party ran out ahead of the pace of events and was not capable of gathering around it the broad proletarian masses outside its ranks. But at the same time, comrades, our resolution, our theses, our proposal on the March Action said that the German party was itself beginning to recognise these errors. Why did we say this? Merely in order to make it easier for the German party to make the transition? No, there were material reasons to do this. Specifically, one need only compare the resolution of 7 May with that of 7 April – the resolution on the March Action and the theses adopted by the party Central Committee for the international congress, to see how the party began to understand its most important error, namely the danger of a loosening of its contact with the masses. This is shown also by Brandler's pamphlets and the letters written us by Stoecker, vice-chair of the party.[12]

There has been mention here of the theses presented by two comrades, Comrade Kun and a comrade from Germany [Thalheimer], which we rejected. As one of those who talked with them, I'd like to point out that after the very first discussion the comrades said, 'We exaggerated the issue because we feared you would be so intimated by our defeat that you would put too much stress on the other side of the question.' In further discussions with the German comrades, it became clear that they were not advancing anything counterposed, in principle, to what we were proposing. This gives us the right to assume that when the German comrades return home, having worked out the Communist International's tactics and strategy together with us, they will carry out these commonly achieved policies as something arrived at together with us through common intellectual endeavour.

Comrades, the delegate from Hamburg, Comrade Thälmann, spoke here quite bitterly about the need to make certain changes. Anyone familiar with the situation in Germany and the history of the party's evolution will fully understand Comrade Thälmann's fervour. Thälmann came to us, along with many other comrades, from the USPD. Some organisers, editors, and trade-union officials came to us because they did not want to be in a minority in their organisations. Such comrades like communism best when it is advancing slowly and does not require such strenuous efforts. But hundreds of thousands of proletarians also came over, and they had perceived how one struggle after another was defeated or betrayed by the USPD and SPD leaderships. Proletarians came to us whose will to struggle had been heightened. Having disposed of the Hilferdings, these proletarians were eager for struggle.

When the proletariat in Halle rose up and, without the Zentrale's knowledge, decided on a mass strike, because Comrade Stern had been fired, this was not a policy of the offensive. What happened in Flensburg?[13] Events there demonstrate that the will to struggle was growing among the advanced layers of the proletariat. This was the main factor that impelled the party into the

---

12. The VKPD Zentrale's resolution adopted on 7 April, titled 'Leitsätze über die Märzaktion' (Theses on the March Action), can be found in the Appendix 2b on pp. 1072–8. The VKPD 7 May resolution was titled 'Leitsätze zur Taktik der Kommunistischen Internationale während der Revolution.' (Theses on the tactics of the Communist International during the revolution) and was printed in *Die Internationale*, 3, 7.

The pamphlet by Brandler consisted of court transcripts from his treason trial in June 1921; see Brandler 1921a.

13. The Flensburg events began on 29 December 1920, when KAPD member Paul Hoffmann was arrested by police and then shot 'attempting to escape'. Fifteen thousand working people attended Hoffmann's funeral on 4 January 1921. The protest was attacked by police, with ten killed.

struggle, so that it engaged in struggle in March quicker and with less preparation than was perhaps necessary and advisable. Now we are saying to these proletarians: bind up your wounds, you have fought valiantly, and prepare better next time. These proletarians, who have listened to much revolutionary talk and have often seen their leaders give way, are disquieted. Comrades wonder what the workers will say if we talk in this manner. Our response is: 'You will tell them that given the enemy's strength, it is necessary to prepare for struggle. Our task is not to demonstrate our courage; our task is to defeat the enemy.'

I am convinced that Thälmann and other comrades will not merely carry out our policies because they have a sense of international discipline. Rather they draw on their experience of struggle. They will understand that the revolutionary energy of this segment of the workers must be engaged in confident, calm, calculated proletarian struggle, and, when it is necessary and possible, also in all-out attack. That is why we stand here in support of the March struggle, despite its errors. It has been said that we do not go into struggle in order to learn from our errors. Well, I must respond, 'If we must engage in struggle, we must then examine our errors, so that when the next struggle comes – and we will likely not choose the time or circumstances – we will come out victorious.'

For we are not dealing with a Red Army here, but with masses, who get organised while assembling and in the struggle, and whose enemy often dictates the terms of the struggle. And there is something else. We Russian Communists suffered a defeat a year ago, although we commanded armies and were more capable of estimating the contending forces than when the armies only take shape in the course of the struggle itself.[14] We made errors, and our relationship to these errors is not one of people who believe that errors arise from erroneous philosophy. We regard this erroneous philosophy of the offensive as the result of an extremely complex conditions of defeat. In addition, we regard struggle itself as the means to overcome these errors.

Our Russian comrades are the most vehement in criticising these errors because they perceive these errors as elements in the ideology that in Russia inspired the adventurous policies of the Social Revolutionaries. However, we must not forget that there is no objective basis in Germany for a party like the Social Revolutionaries. This party was based on the petty-bourgeois intellectuals and the peasantry, and it only struck root in the working class to a very limited extent. We see no reason to think that such conditions exist in Germany. There is no basis in Germany for policies like those of the Russian

---

14. A reference to the Soviet defeat in its advance on Warsaw in 1920.

Social Revolutionaries. We are opposed to the erroneous theory of the offensive and will struggle against it, but these theoretical errors must not blind us to the great struggles of the masses.

Comrades, the situation is somewhat different in Italy and France, two countries where petty-bourgeois traditions are very influential. And we see how the French comrades adopted a position akin to Hervéism,[15] when we examine how the trade unions fell into the hands of syndicalists who sail without any Marxist compass. Here the dangers may well be even more acute. That is why Comrades Lenin and Zinoviev were so sharp in their criticisms of our friend Terracini.

If I may return to the German situation, for us the errors committed there are not the main issue. The main issue is the struggle itself. And in drawing a balance sheet we must not disregard the fact that a portion of the leadership flatly sabotaged the struggle. I will name only Levi, who betrayed the struggling masses right into the hands of the bourgeoisie. I must also note that a considerable number of worthy comrades, whom we wish to have in the party, stated their agreement with Levi. These comrades now regard Levi's expulsion as an accomplished fact, but they have not yet said anything that significantly dissociates themselves from him.

Taking this fact into account, we say to the German party: you have fought and you have made mistakes in this fight. The struggle you waged proved that you are a good Communist Party. And we say to the other German comrades: You have not only established that the leadership made mistakes. You have solidarised with a man who, at a moment when seven thousand proletarians had been jailed – and I stress that this is the decisive factor for me – this man presented the struggle as a surprise coup by a few party leaders and denounced the Executive. So we tell these comrades: we need you for the movement and we want to have you in the movement. But one thing you must know: if you do such things again, the Communist International will not forgive you.

And we have something else to tell these comrades: in the amendments proposed by Comrades Zetkin, Malzahn, Neumann, and Franken, there is a passage at the end about freedom of criticism. The comrades are proposing this amendment to replace the portion of our resolution that speaks of breaking with Levi, discipline in the party, and stimulation through criticism in the party press and in its structures. There is not a word about the break with Levi in their resolution. Not a word about Levi's expulsion or the ban on collaboration with Levi's publication. Instead of that, they demand unlimited freedom

---

15. Gustave Hervé was a French Socialist Party member known before 1914 for ultraleftism. He then adopted a patriotic, pro-war stance, and by 1921 he had swung over to a pro-fascist position.

of criticism. We tell you frankly and openly: after Levi's expulsion, you wrote articles for Levi's journal, *Sowjet*. We leaned on the German party Zentrale, urging it to hold off taking action on this in order to enable all these questions to be discussed with you here at the congress, so that you could clarify your stand on the harsh March struggles.

We well know that in the heat of battle, the actions of many comrades were judged unfairly. I admit that I was misled regarding Malzahn's role in 1918 by an article of Barth. However, what has been proposed here regarding freedom of criticism is absolutely unacceptable. Of course Thälmann is wrong to assert that no criticism should be permitted in the party's press because the enemy could learn something from it. No, we believe that criticism of our actions is necessary. We leave it to the good sense of every comrade to decide whether public criticism is called for in the given conditions.

Situations may well arise where the party leadership must say that such criticism is not possible for the moment. When we suffered defeat in the Polish campaign, there were quite strenuous disagreements among us, and even so none of us wrote any articles about that. And the comrades in leadership positions who were critical of the campaign – I was among them – considered after the defeat that it was not at all so important to establish for history's sake that I was right and the other comrades wrong.[16] We could dispense with public criticism because all of us understood the reasons for the error and were able to take them into account.

But by and large, every member of a party, although expected and obliged to abide by discipline, has the right to take part in the working out of the party's line. This right encompasses expressing differences of opinion in the press, because only a segment of the comrades take part in the party's meetings, and the others do not learn what takes place within the confines of the meeting room. Comrade Zetkin asks, 'What should I say when Crispien asks me what is my position on the March Action?' She should answer, 'I do not discuss with people who helped strike down the Mansfeld movement.' (*Loud applause and cheers*) Here is where we draw the line, and here is where concessions stop.

Comrades, we are in favour of the German party thinking now of the future, not the past. It should do justice to the lessons of the past but now orient to the new struggles that will come, whether we want them or not. To that end it is necessary to bring into play all the forces at the party's disposal. In order to achieve that goal, we demand the dissolution of every separate group or

---

16. One biography of Radek cites a pamphlet by him on the Polish-Soviet war, written before the Red Army advance into Poland: *Voina polskikh belogvardeitsev protiv Rossii* (Moscow, 1920). Gutjahr 2012, p. 429.

separate faction within the party. And if Däumig tries to violate this, then we respond that simply on the basis of his letter to the Zentrale Däumig deserved to be expelled. (*Applause*) If Däumig tries anything like that again, we will not lean on the Zentrale. We are telling the comrades who make up the immense majority in the party that the struggle was necessary, and the party's involvement in it was it was to its credit. Errors were made, and many comrades went much too far, but now we call a halt to personal recriminations and put the past behind us. We must be vigilant. What happened cannot be erased from the party's consciousness. But now all forces that belong together must come together in the common work. In this way, after the transitional difficulties in Germany, we will have a large, strong, active, and revolutionary party.

Comrades, I now come to the question of the KAPD. As I said earlier, the KAPD is a small party that has pretentions to being the nucleus of a new International. Based on its actual strength, there is no reason why we should do it any favours. But it represents a current, and that is why we have concerned ourselves with it. Sachs says here that, according to Lenin, a small party can lead millions in a country where the masses are still amorphous. In response, we must say that this can happen when the masses are not organised in broad historical formations. In order to destroy these formations, you must yourselves construct large organisations. And how can you construct them? How can a small party win the confidence of the masses? Only if it conducts struggles for their immediate vital interests. If you say that it is opportunism for the party to fight for the necessities of life, you will certainly remain a small party and will never win the trust of the broader masses.

Comrades, don't get carried away by ideas of good proletarians who cannot see real life because of their mistrust of parliament and the trade unions. If you get set on such ideas, we will part company and you will chase, cursing, after the working class's wagon. You have already set out on this path. Every time a struggle arises, you will stand in its path, in sectarian fashion. We call on you, for the sake of all that unites us, to go into the party. It may not be an ideal party, but it showed in the March Action that it is willing and able to struggle.

Comrades, I do not want to impose too much on your time. We will have ample opportunity in the commission to refine our theses, and if there are still principled differences, we will come back to you and you will make the decisions.

Now let me take up the proposed amendments. It is quite wrong to conclude from what Lenin said that *Roma locuta est, causa finita*.[17] – that the Russian delegation has presented its view and the matter is settled. That is not

---

17. 'Rome has spoken; case closed.' From sermon 131.10 by St. Augustine.

our intention. The theses are the outcome of lengthy deliberations. There was talk here of a compromise, and it was said that the theses reflect concessions to the Left. As a rule, any compromise has two sides. If anyone feels that the theses reflect concessions to the Left, there are others who believe they contain concessions to the Right. Surely you noticed that before the congress we were waging the struggle mainly against the Right. But it reflects no opportunism for me to say now that I have seen indications that there is a danger on the left and the struggle must be waged against the Left. The first draft of the theses took up factually all the errors but did not contain a passage on the March Action. I do not regard it as a compromise to have voted for this passage; in fact, I wrote it. Based on discussions with the German delegation, I became convinced that it was necessary to speak openly of our mistakes. Nothing was changed as to the content.

Certainly, if the German comrades had not committed their errors, and nonetheless an opposition to the March Action took shape, this opposition would be ripe for expulsion. The errors made it necessary to show more tolerance to this opposition, because it is not clear whether they are all opportunists or whether they are delivering a warning. That required concessions to the Right.

We will examine in the commission whether these amendments are really matters of formulation or whether they affect the basic line. The Russian delegation will not agree to a modification of the basic line. That does not mean you cannot change it; you can vote us down.

A struggle against opportunism; a struggle against the Right and warning against errors on the left: that is our line, and we are not willing to change it. As for questions of wording, we will try in the commission to find the appropriate formulations, and we will find them.

Comrades, the discussions at this congress do not give a complete picture of what the Communist International represents. A number of delegations have had very little to say on these matters. I personally have the impression, which is shared by some other comrades in the Executive, that the speeches of some comrades have been understood in a different way than they were intended. When people who have personally experienced major revolutionary struggles get up here and warn us about ill-considered actions and mistakes on the left, we must all understand that this is said by soldiers who bear the scars of battle and have a right to deliver warnings. And if opportunists conclude that these are warnings against struggle, then we must tell them, 'You resemble the spirit you can understand, not me.'[18]

---

18. The quote is from Goethe's *Faust*. The idea is that Faust's imagination cannot rise higher than his own limitations.

The Russian Communist Party is aware of the great responsibility it carries as a party that has traversed the longest revolutionary path. When it delivers a warning, this is not because things are going so well in Russia that it can wait another twenty years before your gradual triumph. None of you think that way. We had every reason to sound a different note here, because no proletariat can long remain isolated in struggle. When the Executive warns you of your errors, it does this with feelings of responsibility, feelings that we are at the first stage of the world revolution, and the world revolution is not advanced unless a passionate heart is paired with a chilly head. Warnings were delivered here out of a feeling of responsibility to the workers' movement in every country. But Comrade Bukharin was a thousand times right to tell you, 'Anyone who thinks that these words of warning mean you can let situations that demand struggle pass you by will perhaps hear us speak with a different voice.'[19]

When we warn you, we do this as an advanced post of the world revolution, aware that if we had gone into the decisive struggle in July 1917, we would have been defeated,[20] but had we not taken the decision in October 1917 to launch the struggle for power, the peasants would have left the front, bourgeois Russia would have signed a separate peace, and the historical situation in which the proletariat could make a bid for power would perhaps have passed us by for many years. Based on our experiences, we call on you to strengthen the party's actions, we call on you to direct all the impulses of the working class toward the struggle. But at the same time we call on you to bear in mind that the enemy is clever, organised, and determined to defeat us by taking advantage of our inexperience.

That is the meaning of the Executive's warning. It does not mean that the parties should call things off for a long period, during which we will read and explain not the Communist Manifesto but the pamphlets of Lenin and Trotsky. It does not mean founding libraries for the study of the revolution so that our grandchildren can carry out the revolution. Our line is oriented to battles that may well come sooner than most of us think. But it also tells us that the enemy is strong, and the Communist International must be firmly organised and must calculate with care so that the impending great struggles can be carried through to a victorious conclusion.

---

19. The stenographic transcript of Bukharin's speech in Session 12 does not include a statement along these lines.

20. A reference to the July Days of 1917 in Petrograd, where many revolutionary-minded workers and soldiers sought to have the soviets seize power from the Provisional Government. Given the unfavourable relation of forces within Russia as a whole, the Bolshevik leadership tried to prevent the movement from becoming a decisive conflict and to turn it into an armed but peaceful demonstration.

In this sense, comrades, our struggle against opportunism is a precondition of victory. Every one of our errors benefits the foe. The errors that we made in March will help us to win more surely tomorrow, but right now they are helping the Scheidemanns and the Crispiens. This is why we say we must struggle against opportunism, while at the same time ensuring that our struggle is conducted in the best way to draw the masses under our banner. We still have a lot to do in this regard. I repeat: our line is to win the masses for the Communist International, to lead the masses into the revolutionary struggle, to prepare the masses for this struggle, and to utilise every situation that makes it possible to take a step forward. At the same time, we must take care to avoid every sacrifice that can be avoided, by counterposing our battle plan to that of the bourgeoisie. (*Loud applause*)

**Koenen** (chair): Before we take the vote, we must receive two personal statements. Comrade Zetkin has given the Presidium the following statement to be read to a plenary session.

## Statement by Clara Zetkin

1.) Comrade Heckert accused me yesterday of having known on Thursday, 31 March, that Comrades Däumig, Levi, Geyer, and others intended to issue a manifesto criticising the conduct of the Zentrale during the March Action. I must point out that I heard something regarding their intentions only on 2 April, when I arrived in Berlin, from Comrades Walcher and Hauth. What is more, I immediately used every means at my disposal to dissuade the opposition comrades from issuing the manifesto. I considered that subjecting the March Action and the Zentrale's conduct to harsh and ruthless criticism was a life-and-death question for the party, and it was precisely for this reason that I rejected the path that many opposition comrades wished to take.

2.) In addition, Comrade Heckert claimed that my attitude to the Communist Party had been vacillating and indecisive from the start, since I did not immediately join the party when it was founded. Regarding this assertion, I have the following to say:

The founding convention of the Communist Party took me by surprise. Comrade Luxemburg had just informed me that she, and even more Comrade Leo Jogiches, were strongly of the opinion that we should break from the USPD only at its convention and only then constitute ourselves as the Communist Party. Due to a combination of circumstances, I received no word of a change in plans and that a founding convention was being held.

Just before she was murdered, Rosa wrote me that I should not insist so impatiently on coming to Berlin and declaring officially that I was joining the Communist Party. After discussion with Leo, she felt it would be more useful to our cause if I remained a member of the USPD up to its convention. She promised to write me soon and explain this at greater length.

The brutal blows of the cowardly, bemedalled murderers prevented her from sending that letter. Shortly thereafter Comrade Leo wrote me that he was aware how pained I was by this awkward situation, but I should stick it out until the USPD convention. First, as editor of the women's supplement to the *Leipziger Volkszeitung*, I was occupying an advanced post in enemy territory. Secondly, this post could well lead the USPD to commit a political error by taking action against me. Thirdly, I should not give up the opportunity to take part in the USPD convention and present there our point of view by criticising the party's theory and practice and then announcing my resignation. This could well break off a portion of the left opposition and lead them to us. Utilising this opportunity was all the more important, in his opinion, because he was still of the opinion that the Communist Party had been founded prematurely and that we ought to have waited for the USPD convention.

I acted accordingly.

Clara Zetkin

**Koenen** (chair): The Italian delegation also wishes to make a statement. The statement reads as follows:

## Statement by the Italian Delegation

The Italian delegation declares that the amendments it is supporting should be understood only with the meaning intended by their movers and certainly not in the manner indicated by Comrade Lenin in his speech. The Communist Party of Italy has never supported a putschist theory and has no intention of supporting one now. The best proof of this is the struggle that the party carries out on a daily basis against the anarchists and syndicalists. Contrary to Comrade Lenin's apparent interpretation, the Italian delegation does not oppose organising the proletarian masses on a constantly widening basis. This is assured simply by the broad recruitment work carried out by the Communist Party of Italy among the working masses. The Italian delegation does not deny the need to lead the workers in struggles or limited actions. And, indeed, the Communist Party of Italy does lead them in all their movements and risings.

In his interpretation of the proposed amendments, Comrade Lenin ruthlessly battles the nightmare of putschism, which – where it exists – is truly dangerous. But this danger is not present in the Communist Party of Italy. Comrade Lenin is thus, without wanting to, providing the opportunist and centrist tendencies, with which we have been engaged in prolonged struggle, with a weapon and a means of struggle against us. The Italian delegation explained at the beginning of the debate, on behalf of the others proposing the amendments to Comrade Radek's theses, that the delegation would vote for the theses and accept them in their broad outline before sending them back to the commission.

## Statement of the Youth International

**Luigi Polano**: In accord with the explanation given by Comrade Münzenberg and after hearing the debate, the Communist Youth International delegation states that it accepts the theses proposed by the Communist Party of Russia with the following reservations:

1. The commission must still correct certain inaccurate evaluations of the Youth's actions against the centrist and opportunist tendencies that still exist in some parties affiliated to the Third International (France).
2. In the commission, the Youth will join other co-signers in supporting the amendments proposed to the congress.

*Polano, Laporte, Tranquilli, Köhler*

**Koenen** (chair): Comrade Heckert wishes to make a statement.

**Heckert**: I make the following statement on behalf of the German, Polish, Hungarian (majority), German-Austrian, and the German part of the Czechoslovak delegation as well as the Youth Executive.

## Statement by Six Delegations

The undersigned delegations state that they accept in principle the Theses on Tactics and Strategy proposed by the Russian delegation, but they express strong reservations with regard to the explanation of these theses in the speech by Trotsky.

*Brand*, Communist Party of Poland

*Thalheimer*, United Communist Party of Germany

*Köhler*, Youth International

*Kun*, Hungarian delegation (majority)

*Kreibich*, German Bohemia [Czechoslovakia]

*Koritschoner*, German Austria[21]

**Koenen** (chair): We will proceed to the vote. We will do this in the same way as with Comrade Trotsky's theses. The vote will be taken on whether the congress accepts the theses as a whole, in principle, as a basis for discussion in the commission. It goes without saying that the amendments will also be forwarded to the commission. The commission will then present a report on the outcome of their discussion. Those in favour of these proposals, please so indicate. (*The vote is taken.*) Those opposed? I declare that the congress has adopted the Presidium's proposal.[22]

Now, as regards the congress's schedule, let me inform you that the next session will take place tomorrow at 1:00 p.m. This sitting will take up points 5 and 6 of the agenda, which concern the trade-union question. Tomorrow we will hear the reports of Comrades Zinoviev and Heckert. The discussion will take place on a subsequent day. Tomorrow at 5:00 p.m. we will have the ceremonial unveiling of the monument to our late comrade John Reed. In the evening, the trade-union congress will hold its first sitting.

(*The session is adjourned at 2:00 a.m.*)

---

21. German Bohemia refers to the mostly German-speaking portions of Czechoslovakia, also known as Sudetenland. German Austria refers to the other large ethnically German portion of the pre-1918 Austrian Empire, now known simply as Austria.

22. For the commission's report back to the congress in Session 21, see pp. 797–802.

Session 15 – 3 July 1921, 2:00 p.m.
# Trade Unions – Reports

*Zinoviev and Heckert on the trade-union question. 1. The relationship of the Red International of Labour Unions to the Communist International. 2. The struggle against the Amsterdam yellow International.*

**Koenen** (Chair): The agenda today is the trade-union question. (1) The relationship of the Red International of Labour Unions to the Communist International. (2) The struggle against the Amsterdam yellow International. Comrade Zinoviev has the floor to speak on the first agenda point. After him, Comrade Heckert of the German delegation will report on the same question.

### Report on RILU Relationship to Communist International

**Zinoviev**: Comrades, the Second Congress of the Communist International adopted Communists' basic position on the trade-union question. I believe there is really no need to alter in any way the theoretical foundations of the position established by the Second Congress. In our opinion, a year of struggle has certainly confirmed the correctness of the Second Congress decision. In several countries – Britain and Germany, France and the United States – the trade-union bureaucrats have moved to expel Communists and Communist cells. This fact alone, in our opinion, is sufficient proof that the decision we took was correct, and that we hit the nail on the head during the Second Congress.

Now we have a new task. It is no longer a matter of formulating our position on the trade-union question theoretically – that has already been done. The task is rather *to better organise the struggle against the yellow Amsterdam International*. The task is to *specify the practical relationship between the Red International of Labour Unions and the Communist International*. The congress must address this task.

Comrades, we already said a year ago that the Amsterdam International was a yellow bourgeois organisation. This assertion of ours was met by a great deal of bitter abuse, and even some of our somewhat confused friends considered that we were exaggerating out of polemical zeal when we called the Amsterdam International a yellow International. I recall what we experienced in Halle, when we stated there, on behalf of the Executive, that the Amsterdam International was a yellow organisation, whose leaders did more harm to the working class, in many respects, than the gentlemen of the Orgesch organisation.[1] The task at our congress is to establish that such an assessment of the Amsterdam International is not at all an exaggeration and was not merely a polemical turn of phrase.

Unfortunately, it is a plain, firmly established fact that the Amsterdam organisation really is a tool of the bourgeoisie. I have here a passage from an article by Albert Thomas, one of the leaders of this organisation. In a report on the trade-union International's first year of activity, printed in the journal *Internationale du travail*, he tried to explain how this International came to be founded.[2] He said that, after the War, the working class felt great stress and a great need to organise. But this factor alone was not enough. At the same time, the bourgeoisie felt the need to create an organisation. He said:

> On the other hand, the governments, who bear responsibility for public safety, were concerned by the grave problems posed by demobilisation and disturbed by revolutionary propaganda carried out everywhere by Bolshevik Russia. They too had no choice but to seek, for their part, an orderly and methodical resolution of the immense social conflict and the wartime suffering.

In other words, the governments – the bourgeois governments – were also quite disquieted after the War by the crisis and by the revolutionary propaganda carried out everywhere by Bolshevik Russia, and they found them-

---

1. For Zinoviev's remark at Halle, see Lewis and Lih (eds.) 2011, p. 125.
2. An English-language version of Thomas's article was published as 'The International Labour Organisation – Its Origins, Development, and Future', in *International Labour Review*, 1, 1 (January 1921).

selves impelled, for their part, to regulate this movement, to support it, and so on. So you see that reality is just like what Albert Thomas is saying here.

The Amsterdam yellow International was born from the efforts of the trade-union bureaucrats combined with those of bourgeois governments. It now truly represents the strongest bulwark of the international bourgeoisie. I will not report in detail about this organisation's activity; that would not be fruitful at a Communist congress. I will only provide a few facts. First, we must note that Jouhaux, one of the Amsterdam International's leaders, took part in the Versailles Conference as a technical aide to the French government, a fact of considerable importance.

Or consider a statement made by Fimmen, another leader of the Amsterdam International, during the Hungarian boycott.[3] He declared in so many words that based on his discussions with representatives of the Horthy government, he has concluded that the white terror in Hungary was organised not by the government but against its will. The government – that is, the Horthy government – is doing all it can to prevent the white terror! But this poor white government simply did not have the power to prevent the white terror.

I can finish by quoting what Thomas said about the 'Labour Office' – a hybrid standing between the Amsterdam International and the League of Nations – that this Labour Office has unified the working class with the reasonable bourgeoisie, and that the sensible wing of the working class, together with the reasonable wing of the bourgeoisie, would attempt to surmount the crisis.

Oudegeest said the following about Italy: 'The Amsterdam International took a great interest in the movement experienced in Italy last autumn. It immediately sent a large number of agents and delegates to Italy.' And, Oudegeest observes, right from the very start this struggle took on the character of an absolutely normal trade-union movement – the very same assertion made by Serrati and D'Aragona. Let us note in passing that in the same account Oudegeest states that he had a discussion with D'Aragona, who told him that despite all the crises now being experienced by the Italian party, the Italian [trade-union] confederation's affiliation to Amsterdam is more secure now than ever before. We will soon have a chance to find out whether D'Aragona is really in a position to come through on his promise. We received a telegram yesterday saying that two delegates were on their way here on behalf of the

---

3. In March 1920 the Amsterdam International appealed for a worldwide boycott of goods to Hungary to protest repression following the fall of Soviet Hungary. In response, the International Federation of Transport Workers called for a boycott on loading, discharging, and transporting goods to Hungary, to begin 20 June. Only partially observed, the boycott was called off 8 August after seven weeks.

Italian trade unions. So in a few days we will have the pleasure of meeting these two outstanding representatives of the Italian trade-union movement and of finding out the degree to which these gentlemen are in a position to hold to their agreements with Oudegeest and other leaders of the Amsterdam trade-union International.[4]

It is enough to cite a few statements by the last president of the Amsterdam trade-union International. As you know, earlier Appleton was the chair. Then he was deposed because his betrayal was simply too blatant.[5] That was the first switch of presidents. Soon, however, the Britisher [J.H.] Thomas had to be ditched. But before that, he wrote in the *Manchester Guardian*, where he had previously printed gushing praise of the British king, explaining the Amsterdam programme, to this effect:

> If better and healthier relations can be established between capital and labour, along with a closer working partnership, this will be the most effective means of restoring complete trust between the employer and the employee. Many of our difficulties arise simply from the fact that we do not have a sufficient understanding of the employer's point of view. Given that we have no opportunity to acquaint ourselves with this point of view, it is not surprising that we make mistakes.

So it is enough that the workers have a good understanding of the employer's point of view, and then everything will turn out just fine.

That is the real face of this organisation! It is no exaggeration: *this organisation is truly the international bourgeoisie's last barricade.* Only through the support of this organisation is the international bourgeoisie still able to hang on.

Consider the latest developments. What assignments are being given to the trade-union International in Amsterdam? When a treacherous struggle is launched against – let us say – the British miners, who does the dirty work? Thomas, the president of Amsterdam. When a bloodbath, a bloodletting of

---

4. The two CGL delegates, Giuseppe Bianchi and Carlo Azimonti, arrived in Moscow 13 July. They explained to the trade-union congress that they were present as observers, and that the CGL's relationship with the Comintern was dependent on the status of the Italian Socialist Party. The congress unanimously adopted a resolution condemning the conduct of the CGL leadership and expressing the hope that its members would soon secure its affiliation to the RILU. A few months later, the CGL definitively ended its relations with RILU. Tosstorff 2004, p. 322.

5. William A. Appleton, secretary of the British General Federation of Trade Unions and closely linked to right-wing US labour leader Samuel Gompers, was elected president of the International Federation of Trade Unions (Amsterdam International) in July 1920. Facing growing criticism within the Amsterdam International and the Trades Union Congress in Britain, Appleton resigned as IFTU president in November 1920. He was replaced by J.H. Thomas.

the working class is needed in Germany, who does this? Hörsing, a trade unionist and member of the Amsterdam trade-union International. When wage reductions are desired in France – a declaration of war against the working class – who receives the honoured assignment to carry that out? Jouhaux and the other gentlemen who are firm pillars of the Amsterdam trade-union International. The international bourgeoisie has now begun a broad economic and political offensive against the working class in a number of countries, in which the Amsterdam yellow International is playing the leading role. For the working class, that is a serious fact, unfortunate but very real, and every trade unionist must take it into account. Unfortunately, it must be said that a great many of them have not perceived it yet. Many conduct themselves toward Amsterdam as if it were a quarrel within socialism between one faction and another faction. In reality, it is not a struggle between tendencies inside the trade-union movement but a *class struggle*, even though the social composition of the Amsterdam trade-union International is proletarian.

We cannot deny that, formally speaking, millions of proletarians belong to Amsterdam. But the question is not so simple as just defining an organisation in terms of its social composition. That would be un-Marxist. We know that the Christian trade unions unite workers, as do the Liberal trade unions. We also know that even now, millions of workers vote in elections for the bourgeoisie or the petty bourgeoisie. But that tells you nothing. There is still a class struggle, and understanding this is the order of the day. It is not a struggle of tendencies or of factions. It is a class struggle, taking a form that for us is quite peculiar, difficult, and strenuous. It is the last bastion of the bourgeoisie. When we have overcome this obstacle, we will have overcome nine-tenths of the barriers in our path.

The bourgeoisie is no longer able to hold on against the will of the great majority of the working class. It can maintain itself only with the support of a portion of the trade unions, which thereby become a mainstay of the bourgeoisie. It can maintain its power only because of betrayal by part of the working class. The transitional period after the War threw the entire international workers' movement into a crisis, of which Amsterdam is a current expression. That is the most important question before us. *Hic Rhodus, hic salta!*[6] This is where the dice of our movement will be cast.

That is why I maintain, comrades, that there is no more important question in the life of the Communist International and of the proletarian revolutionary movement as a whole than revealing the nature of the Amsterdam International to the broad masses of the working class.

---

6. See p. 372, n. 27.

We have had important successes during the past year. Comrade Lozovsky, secretary of the International Trade Union Council, gave me a list of the organisations that belong to the Red International of Labour Unions. The table reads as follows: Russia, 6.5 million. Germany, about 2 million, perhaps more. Austria, 35,000. Switzerland 90,000. Czechoslovakia, 290,000. Poland, 250,000. Romania, 90,000. Bulgaria, 65,000. Yugoslavia, 140,000. Greece, 50,000. Turkey, 20,000. France, 300,000. Belgium, 10,000. Italy, 2 million to 3 million. Spain, 900,000. Portugal, 50,000. Sweden, 85,000. Norway, 140,000. Netherlands, 93,000. Denmark, 50,000. Finland, 60,000. Latvia, 30,000. Britain, 300,000. United States, 300,000. Mexico, 119,000. Argentina, 214,000. Australia, 400,000. Altogether, somewhat more than 18 million. Let us not be fooled; these figures must be regarded with caution, and we do not want to deceive ourselves.

Looking at this table, we must also recognise the magnitude of the tasks before us now. In Czechoslovakia, for example, we have 290,000 trade-union members who belong to the Red International of Labour Unions, at a time when there are 400,000 members of the Communist Party in that country. What does that tell us? It shows us that there are countries in which our party, despite its strength, has not yet been able to win over the trade-union movement, which is so important to the proletarian revolution. I have here a leaflet from Czechoslovakia directed to the textile workers and women workers, attacking the bureaucracy of the textile workers' union. The struggle in Czechoslovakia is only beginning. But right in Czechoslovakia, which has quite an impressive organisational tradition, and where we have a large party, we find the same phenomenon as in all the other countries. Our parties do not yet have sufficient forces in the trade-union movement, and they have not yet devoted sufficient attention to this question.

The first demand that this congress must place before all the parties is to devote much more, a hundred times more attention to the trade-union movement than before, and to bend every effort toward winning a majority in these trade unions. That is the primary arena for our struggle, where the decisive battles of this epoch of proletarian revolution will be fought. The decisive battles will be fought there. And we still have a situation where we have half a million party members in a country where there are only a quarter-million unionised workers in the Red International of Labour Unions. There are surely other examples as well. For example, there is Spain, with a movement that is syndicalist but nonetheless clearly revolutionary, with about one million members, and beside it is a Communist Party which, counting both its wings – the Communist Party and the former Left of the Social-Democratic Party – has only about fifteen thousand members. Obviously, in Spain, there is no way yet that our party can fully and intellectually lead the trade-union movement, given that we still have a new party with only fifteen thousand members alongside a million good, revolutionary proletarians, organised in trade unions.

We also have a distinctive and quite complicated situation in Italy. There is a new Communist Party, a splendid revolutionary mood among the workers, and a syndicalist movement, the *Unione Syndicale [Italiana]*. The latter is marked by a somewhat confused revolutionary mood without any theoretical clarity or solid foundation. At the same time there is the Confederation [CGL], with two to three million members. Led by reformists, it is now cleverly manoeuvring between the Socialist and Communist parties, seeking in this way to keep the leadership in the reformists' hands. Our new Communist Party in Italy succeeded in winning almost half a million votes at the first trade-union congress after the split, but that is only a small beginning of what needs to be done.

In Norway we have an unusual situation. The party has worked its way through to becoming a good Communist party, with the support of a large majority of the country's working class. Meanwhile, the leadership of the trade unions remains in the hands of centrist forces who are members of the Communist party, but in their hearts belong to Amsterdam. The Norwegian comrades will concede that without hesitation. They cannot contest the fact that many leading figures in the Norwegian movement, in their hearts, are not with us but with Amsterdam. This situation imposes immediate and weighty tasks on our party.

We admitted syndicalist forces to the Red International of Labour Unions on the Communist International's initiative, and I believe that was correct. Syndicalism went through a major evolution during and after the War – a crisis similar to that of socialism. After such an enormous revolutionary crisis, it was our bounden duty to discuss with the radical syndicalist forces, while trying to follow carefully their evolution. Now, however, we can draw a certain balance sheet of this evolution.

There are three varieties of syndicalism with which we have to reckon. First, the blatantly reformist variety that is best represented by Jouhaux. That is syndicalism as it was, and during the War it went bankrupt, in the same manner as Social Democracy. It is a markedly petty-bourgeois movement, just like the leadership of Amsterdam. The second form of syndicalism is expressed in Sweden and Germany. These groups are not numerically large, but they want to belong to us. We must examine the nature of this syndicalism. If you read the publication of German syndicalism, *Der Syndikalist*, you often have the feeling that you are reading a quite ordinary Social-Democratic newspaper of the Scheidemann variety. The evaluation these syndicalists made of the March movement in Germany was despicable and bourgeois Social-Democratic. There is no other way to put it. They did not express criticisms from a proletarian point of view, as has been done by some at our congress, where an attempt has been made to examine, from a Communist point of view, whether the movement was led correctly, whether it was premature, and so on. No, it was not criticism of the type carried out by various speakers here. No, their criticism was malicious, dogged, banal, petty-bourgeois, and counterrevolutionary, of the type we encounter with our class enemies.

We find the same thing with the Swedish syndicalists, who say they are for the dictatorship, but do everything they can to compromise the first state of the proletarian class. This is the style of the syndicalist Centre, which tries to mediate between Jouhaux and the truly revolutionary syndicalists, with one foot in Moscow and the other in Amsterdam.

And then, comrades, we have a third variety of syndicalism, which is for us the most important, and with which we must carry out an earnest and friendly discussion. I am referring to the truly revolutionary syndicalist current, which is now recovering from the wartime crisis and is most clearly expressed in France.

And the most important question for us, and also for the congress of the Red International of Labour Unions that is opening today, is how we will relate to this syndicalist current, which is truly revolutionary, or at least revolutionary in a great many respects. That is a major question for us, both theoretically and practically. I must tell you, comrades, that if you follow only the press of the revolutionary syndicalists in France and not their practice, you get the impression that great difficulties stand in our way in this respect. But I hope that the ideology reflected in the press is not a fully adequate expression of what is now brewing among the masses of ordinary syndicalist workers.

Rather what we have here is an obsolete ideological quarrel, whose implications for the movement's practice are not so great. This is now a rather old, yet in a certain sense always new quarrel between us and the anarchists and syndicalists about the meaning of political struggle, the role of parties, and whether trade unions should be politically neutral. You have already heard mention here of the modern banner of revolutionary syndicalists: the 'Amiens Charter'. I will read you the complete text of this document, so that you know why it is that this piece of paper, although somewhat obsolete, is nonetheless playing a major role in our struggle. The following resolution, written by Griffuelhes, was adopted [by the French CGT] in 1906. I want to refresh the German and French comrades' memory of it, so that they can judge whether it is really worthwhile to conduct such vehement struggles over this obsolete piece of paper. Here it is:

*Amiens Charter*
The Amiens Congress affirms article 2 of the CGT's statutes, which say:

The CGT includes, independently from every political current, all workers who are aware of the struggle that must be waged to abolish wage labour and the employing class.

The congress views this declaration as a recognition of the class struggle, which brings workers, in the economic framework, into strong opposition to all forms of exploitation and oppression, whether of a material or moral nature, that is employed by the capitalist class against the working class.

The congress applies this theoretical insight through the following points.

In its daily work for specific demands, the trade-union movement strives to coordinate the workers' efforts to improve their well-being by achieving immediate gains, such as reducing working time, increasing wages, and so forth. These efforts, however, are only one side of the trade-union movement's aims. It is preparing for full emancipation through a general strike and an uprising, as its main weapon. It considers that the trade unions, which today are instruments of resistance, will in the future be organisations for production and distribution and the foundations for social reorganisation.

The congress declares that this double task, in the present and the future, flows from the status of wage-workers that weighs on the working class and that compels all workers, whatever their opinion or their political or philosophical tendency, to belong to the essential organisation represented by the trade union.

As a result, the congress assures to all union members the right to take part, outside the union framework, in any form of struggle that corresponds to their philosophic or political conceptions, *reserving only the right to ask, in return, that they not introduce within the union the opinions that they profess on the outside.*

As for the organisations, the congress declares that, in order to achieve the maximum success, the trade-union movement must carry out action directly against the employers. *The confederal organisations, as union bodies, should not concern themselves with parties and sects that, outside and on the side, enjoy full freedom to strive for social transformation.*[7]

As you see, comrades, what you have here is neutrality, outspoken neutrality. Do not bring politics into the union! You can be active anywhere else with communism, as a Socialist or Communist, but the union must be a

---

7. The translation has been checked against the original French text. Emphasis by Zinoviev.

place where all unite on neutral ground. That was said in 1906, before the bankruptcy of the Second International and of anarchism. And now this intellectual beggar's soup – pardon the expression – is brought to the Third International Congress and an attempt is made to persuade us that we can still stick with this position. Many years ago, Kautsky explained – he was then still a Marxist – that we cannot accept neutrality because it is impracticable. That is the great weakness of neutrality: it is impracticable.[8] And Kautsky was completely right about this. Take France. When the question of – for example – calling up the conscripts comes up, trade unionists cannot just say, 'That does not concern me. It is a political question, so I will remain neutral.' For a trade unionist to make such a statement would be counterrevolutionary. The parties had different attitudes to the calling up. The Communists were against; the Socialists are petty-bourgeois, so they vacillated. The CGT had to say either it was against the mobilisation – thus supporting the Communists – or that it remained 'neutral', thus supporting the bourgeois parties.

Take the miners' strike in Britain, at first glance a purely economic struggle. But is this strike really of concern only to the trade unions? And not to the party, too? Obviously, it is simultaneously also a major political issue. Now, after the War, class antagonisms have become so acute that there is hardly a single significant question before the working class that is not simultaneously political and economic. Neutrality is a phantom, a fantasy, and not reality. In reality, no mass organisation can be neutral, and the notion of neutrality is in reality a tool of the bourgeoisie. When an idea is rightly applied and takes root among the masses, it becomes a force – and if it leads the masses astray, as in this case, it becomes a reactionary force. Neutrality is one of the ideas that are expertly utilised by the bourgeoisie in order to suggest to workers that they should stay on the sidelines.

Consider the situation of the bourgeoisie. In many countries, it rules with the bayonet, but it would be wrong to claim that it rules only through force, only through the bayonet. That is not true. In most countries it rules through the bayonet and through deception. And deception has played just as important a role as the bayonet. Deception must be well organised. If the bourgeoisie acts too blatantly, too crudely, it will not win the workers.

The bourgeoisie cannot come to the French or German workers and say, 'I ask you, please, to join my bourgeois party.' That will not work; the worker will not do it. If he joins, goes to the meetings, and sees the bankers and so on sitting there, he will recognise that these are not his people and he will not

---

8. A reference to Kautsky's 1900 series of articles in *Die Neue Zeit*, 'Die Neutralisierung der Gewerkschaften' [Trade union neutrality].

stay there. So the bourgeoisie cannot call on the workers openly to join the bourgeois ranks. However, it can tell the workers that they should have nothing at all to do with politics, which have no value for the workers. They should remain 'neutral'; politics is not for them but for educated people. Workers should concern themselves purely with economic issues and remain 'neutral' with regard to all parties. The bourgeoisie has had success along these lines.

The notion of neutrality is an extremely sophisticated bourgeois idea, which it uses to entrap many of our brothers. They say that you should remain neutral in politics and limit yourself purely to economic questions, that your concern is only a small increase in your wages, etc. But we know that a trade union – even a syndicalist one – that remains neutral is objectively on the side of the bourgeoisie. Any trade union that takes as its starting point the false notion of neutrality, that declares itself to be neutral, will become an objectively counterrevolutionary factor in the decisive struggle. Just as the bourgeoisie needs the idea of the hereafter and of God Almighty, it needs the idea of trade-union neutrality. Just as the bourgeoisie needs priests, informers, lawyers, bourgeois parliamentarians, and bourgeois journalists, it also needs bureaucratic trade-union leaders who delude the trade unions with this neutrality.

It has even come to the point that many fine revolutionary forces, like the revolutionary syndicalists and anarchists in France, have fallen into this trap. When all Social Democracy was opportunist, the syndicalists' mistrust of all parties was easy to understand. In 1906, the Amiens Charter could be readily comprehended. One knew where it was coming from. But now, in 1921, after the War, the birth of the Communist International, the Russian Revolution, after the struggles of the Russian trade unions, which have played so important a role in our revolution, this is really deplorable.

Take an ordinary revolutionary-syndicalist worker. He will feel offended by my contention that he is objectively a prisoner of the bourgeoisie. But that is simply the fact. Someone who still holds to neutralism, who comes to workers and tells them that the trade unions must be neutral, is objectively a prisoner of the bourgeoisie, a tool of the bourgeoisie. In politically developed countries like France, there is quite a long list of political parties. They have there a register of several dozen parties, almost all of which call themselves 'socialist'. But by and large, we know that in the entirety of modern Europe there are only three groups of parties. The first is those that are decidedly bourgeois, even if they carry the label 'socialist'. The second is the petty-bourgeois parties, the Social Democrats. The third group is the proletarian parties, or better, the party of the Communists. And when the bourgeoisie demands that our trade unions declare their neutrality with regard to all parties, what does that mean? What does it mean when a proletarian organisation declares that it is 'neutral'? It means in reality doing what is useful to the first and second groups.

That is the reason why the entire Second International favoured neutrality. For the Second International, the Amiens Charter was in many respects acceptable. But the notion of neutrality was abandoned on 4 August 1914.[9] The same Legien – of blessed memory – who was for neutrality on 3 August 1914 had to take a stand on 4 August for 'his' bourgeoisie. During the War, the concept of neutrality was dropped. But when efforts began to organise the Amsterdam International, the notion of neutrality popped up again, and Amsterdam was built around this idea. The idea of neutrality was reborn. Note that carefully. This idea was born a second time in Amsterdam.

During the War, the situation was too clear. The bourgeoisies were fighting among themselves, and the social patriots of every country served their 'own' bourgeoisie.

But when a new attempt is made to deceive the working class and to construct yet another so-called International, the concept of neutrality appears again. The leaders of the Amsterdam trade-union International have even taken it to the point where, in the same breath, they speak in favour of neutrality and of accepting ministerial posts in government. Hörsing is for trade-union neutrality; Noske is for trade-union neutrality; Dittmann, Vandervelde, Jouhaux, and all the others, all of them socialists, are simultaneously ministers, technical advisors, secretaries, and so on in the bourgeois governments. That is a striking expression of this 'neutralist' con game. And even though this policy is really so blatant and so flagrantly obvious, comrades, the working class is as yet so lacking in intellectual maturity that such tricks still succeed, and many honest workers still advance the notion of neutrality as if it were something new.

That is why on this point, comrades, we must tell the French syndicalists and all the syndicalist comrades quite frankly what must be done. They may be offended by what we say, but with every day that passes the course of events will convince them more and more that we are right. The Amiens Charter must be overturned *as rapidly as possible*. At one time it was perhaps a step forward, comprehensible as a move against opportunism, as it was at

---

9. On 4 August 1914, the SPD fraction in the German Reichstag voted in favour of the government's request for war credits, marking a sharp break from the traditions of the SPD and the international workers' movement. Leading parties of the Second International in other countries rapidly followed suit, supporting the war effort of their respective bourgeoisies. In left-wing and revolutionary circles, 4 August became synonymous with the Second International's betrayal of socialism.

that time. But anyone who advocates this now is trying to throw the movement back fifteen years rather than leading it forward.

That is how things stand in France and also in other countries. What conclusion do we draw? It is certainly *not our conclusion that trade unions should simply be subordinated to the party.* There is a discussion under way on this in France, and it is quite lively, with articles appearing in *L'Humanité* almost daily. Previously, we must concede, the stance of our sister party in France was not yet entirely clear; it contains a good deal of unclarity. At first, the comrades had a distorted picture of the matter and felt somewhat uncomfortable about it. This distorted picture has it that we really demand that trade unions be directly subordinated to the party. That is not the case. In Russia we had the clearest evolution on this issue, and we must say that the trade unions as such are not subordinated to the party. For years we fought for influence in the unions. Even during the October Revolution we represented a minority within them – perhaps 40 per cent. Only after the October Revolution did we win a majority.

Your ideas can only be influential if you first win a *majority* in the unions. The challenge is for the ideas of the party to gain political leadership, and the party can win that only through long, hard work – not through decrees, and not through resolutions. For fifteen years we contended with the Mensheviks for influence in the trade unions. That requires time. And we always told our comrades that they must win influence in the unions through their daily work, so that the Communist is viewed in all everyday matters as the best, wisest, the most self-sacrificing. Through this everyday work, during fifteen years, we won decisive influence in the trade unions. And even today we do not subordinate the unions as such to the party. Instead we view the Communist cells (fractions) in the unions as branches of our party structure, so that these branches carry out the will of the party. That is something quite different from simply mechanically subordinating the trade union to the party.

So the French comrades need make no apologies to the syndicalists. They need not believe the distorted picture that we simply subordinate the trade unions to the party. What the Third Congress must demand of our trade unionists is *one hundred times more everyday work in the unions, wherever the masses are to be found.* Not only during major movements but also in everyday union struggles, however limited they may be – everywhere the Communist should point out the way, persistently struggling, year after year, to increase his party's influence. And, of course, where that has been won, the party's influence must be asserted. Even if we have only three Communists, they must immediately form a cell. The French Communists must draw only on efforts of our own party members. We can form alliances with other forces, but we can rely only on our own members. That is what the party's relationship to the trade unions should be: persistent, extended struggle for party influence; organisation of the party's forces; participation in all everyday struggles; *no mechanical subordination*.

To repeat, the major challenge is: how do we win a majority in the trade unions?

In my opinion, we can also talk of trade-union autonomy, in a certain sense. But the meaning of autonomy should not be understood in the way you might imagine. Of course, there is autonomy and 'autonomy'. We learned from the struggle with the reformists that these gentlemen understood autonomy to mean that the trade unions are one thing and the party quite another. We are against autonomy in that sense, against that kind of independence, which boils down to neutrality. But we are certainly in favour of the trade-union movement having considerable leeway. The party should not get involved in all the minor details but should set only the overall line and should intervene only when something politically important comes up – and then only through the Communist cells (fractions). We have no objection to this kind of autonomy.

And that is how the relationship of the Communist International to the Red International of Labour Unions should be decided. The Red International was founded on the initiative of the Communist International. It has existed for only one year and is only now beginning its struggle. At first we were almost a fully unified organisation. Now that the Red International of Labour Unions has grown, a certain differentiation must take place; the Red International must be granted a degree of independence. True, the ideal situation would be to have a *unified International* embracing every branch of the workers' movement. But we must now say that the Communist International as a whole should not be merely an arithmetical sum of different party leaderships. It is something more. We are here not only as forty central committees; *we want to embrace all the movement's needs*. We want to provide orientation to the entire proletariat that is struggling for its liberation. We want to lead the struggle – in the soviets, the trade unions, the educational institutions, the cooperatives, and so on. All that must be drawn together in the Communist International. It is the head of the entire movement, leading the entire liberation struggle of the proletariat, and not merely its political struggle, in the narrow sense of the word.

The Red International of Labour Unions must have a degree of independence. First of all, this must be structured so that there is reciprocal representation, and gradually this will grow into something closer. We must do that because we need to be cautious; the pattern of the trade-union movement globally is too multi-coloured, too diverse. Compare Italy and Norway, Czechoslovakia and Britain, Germany and France: entirely different situations;

entirely different stages of development. That is what we must reckon with. That is why we have to find an organisational structure that is flexible enough to enable us, as quickly as possible, to gradually become a common, unified organisation, which is what the Communist International ought to be.

So what we are proposing is that, along the path to a broad, unified International, we will differentiate to some degree and not worry about it. We must meet the movement's needs. Rather than stubbornly resisting them, we need to understand the organisational difficulties. We must proceed flexibly in each country, because we face significant difficulties. We should utilise every available means in order to tear the unions away from the yellow leaders, because achieving that is the nub of the matter, the main factor in the struggle for proletarian revolution.

That does not mean that we should have two parallel Internationals. It would be quite perilous to create two Internationals, standing jealously side by side. There must be a degree of autonomy and self-evident flexibility on organisational matters. This demands that the Communist International must absolutely retain political leadership, with daily consultation and reciprocal representation, so we can help each other, step by step, to overcome the movement's weaknesses. *We must do everything possible for the two Internationals to work together, linked together like two arms.*

That is our line of march. We are convinced that this will enable us to overcome our difficulties. We must impress on the comrades that there is no task more vital than winning the majority in the trade unions. When we have that, we have everything. When we have destroyed the last bastion of the bourgeoisie and raised the red banner of the Communist International, then we will be able to say that the greatest difficulties are behind us and our victory is now secure.

The decisions taken by the trade-union congress will have very great international significance. We must make every effort to come to common decisions, to do everything to hold the two organisations together. If we succeed together in overcoming the movement's weaknesses and advancing together against the Amsterdam International, social patriotism, and social pacifism, our victory will be absolutely secured, and very soon. (*Loud applause and cheers*)

**Koenen** (Chair): Comrade Heckert has the floor.

## Report on the Struggle against the Amsterdam International

**Heckert**: Comrades, in order to approach the task of defining what the Communists have to achieve in the trade unions and what the unions themselves must do, it is necessary that we clearly pose the tasks that the unions have faced and, secondly, ask what unions can do in the present period in order to carry out these tasks. When the trade-union associations were founded, the question of the unions' tasks was unambiguously and clearly posed. Carrying out the workers' struggle for better wages and working conditions: that was the task, the goal, that the unions wished to achieve. Improved wages and working conditions – some thought that this could be achieved within the capitalist order, and others held that achieving these goals within the capitalist order was not possible. That is why there were, from the outset, two currents in the unions, one that came to terms with the existence of the capitalist order, within which the union struggle was to be carried out; and the other, which explained that a genuine improvement of wages and working conditions within the capitalist order was not possible, and that we must work for the capitalists' overthrow.

We must keep all that in mind during our present deliberations on the unions' tasks. Is it possible to achieve the goal of those who said that better wages and working conditions can be achieved within capitalism, or is it not possible? Furthermore, if it is not possible to achieve better wages and working conditions within the capitalist order, what should the unions be doing? We Communists therefore study the prevailing economic situation on the planet today. That has already been done at this congress, and the discussion has been rich. There is no need to say more.

We know that when the World War ended, the capitalist economic order was shaken to its foundations. The only remaining question is how long it will take before the disintegration process within the capitalist order leads to a catastrophe, even without the organised assault of the worker contingents. The capitalist economy is in dissolution. This economic order has given rise to immense unemployment, combined with a colossal hunger for goods. But this hunger cannot be satisfied, because the broad population of consumers does not have the means to acquire these goods. So given this situation, we ask: what must the trade unions do in such a period of crisis? Should we wait for some kind of miracle that could revive capitalism, enabling the unions to carry out a struggle for better wages and working conditions within the capitalist order for another fifty or sixty years? Or is it not also the unions' task to take advantage of this crisis of capitalism, which is prolonged rather than transitory, to overthrow the capitalist system? Our policies must be based on our evaluation of the capitalist order's condition, that is, whether we think capitalism is viable and capable of reconstruction or whether, on the other hand, it must absolutely be replaced right away. So we have two distinct tendencies. The Communist tendency states that capitalism is rotting; if it survives, it can bring only death to the working class. We call for rapid, organised struggle to create a new social order. But the social patriots say that we must first make capitalism viable again.

In his speech, Comrade Radek already pointed out that the trade-union and social-patriotic leaders disseminate the myth that socialism and communism can exist only if the capitalist order bequeaths an overabundance of wealth. However, there is no such overabundance today, and in our opinion this abundance of wealth can be created only for a minority of people. Moreover, to create this overabundance, millions of workers must pay with their lives, their happiness, their entire existence. We therefore reject the notion of labour partnership, which has it that the capitalist mechanism must first be repaired, so that there is something there to socialise. I will not speak of the struggle that Communists have carried out against this labour partnership notion – there is no time for that. Many things can only be referred to in passing.

What must we do in the present period? In our view, even if the trade unions can only struggle to defend workers' existence, they must carry out a revolutionary struggle. Given the decay of the capitalist order, it is no longer possible to maintain workers' basic living standards. Therefore we, in our struggle to defend our existence, can no longer limit ourselves to the methods used in the prewar period. We must consider how to utilise other methods of struggle. And here we Communists say flatly that all methods that serve to destroy, dissolve, and do away with capitalism, in order to open the road for a new social system – all such methods should be employed by the trade unions. They can carry out their task only by intensifying actions to destroy the capitalist system. Thus, the trade unions should strive to advance from a conventional wage struggle against a single employer to a general strike against a country's capitalist employers as a whole, with demonstrations, and ultimately with an armed insurrection against the economic and political authorities. But let us examine our trade-union organisations. Can we say that these organisations are adequate in their present form to carry out this task? We must concede that their present form is not appropriate, indeed, it is a form inherited from the period of capitalism's emergence.

It is true that as the capitalist system has grown, unions of individual trades, which at first were local in character, became more and more centralised and now exist as national organisations. Capitalism experienced an evolution such that the employers transformed a country from an agrarian to an industrial state and brought the different industrial branches more and more into interrelationship. But that is not all. We have seen gigantic enterprises created in this capitalist economy, in which workers of many varied crafts, twenty to thirty of them, are found in a single factory. And if the workers of such a huge enterprise – Armstrong, let us say, or Stinnes – launch a struggle to improve their standard of living, we find the workers divided into a wide variety of different craft organisations, and it is hard to unite these workers in a concerted struggle.

This demonstrates that the present form of trade unions has not evolved as far as the structure of the capitalist order confronting us. The trade unions must therefore undergo a new process of concentration, regardless of how they are at present. The attempt must be made to bring together all the workers employed in a workplace. When our Russian comrades faced the challenge of creating trade-union federations appropriate to modern conditions, the organisations they created were not small and local but large and centralised, built in each branch of production. Workers were united in the factories and workplaces where they were active. The workplace was the basic unit, and the different factories and workplaces of a single branch of production were unified in a countrywide central organisation. In the opinion of the Communists, that is the trade-union form that we need in order to carry out our tasks in the present period of capitalism. So we see that the question of direct struggle to overthrow the capitalist order determines not only the content of the trade union but also its form.

But let us note that the organisational form must be able to take on a content that corresponds to actual conditions in the capitalist order and the requirements of the workers' class struggle against capitalism. The capitalists have enormously consolidated their power. Just think of capitalists like Stinnes. This example proves at once that such power cannot be challenged by a collection of small federated organisations.

It is the centralised power of capitalism that compels us to centralise trade-union forces. It would be idiotic to try to argue against such hard facts. If we are unable to oppose them with the similarly centralised power of the trade unions, we will always be defeated, and that is the death sentence against any form of federalism. What the German syndicalists preach, and the line of reasoning of many syndicalists in France and other countries, will never work. Trade-union centralism is a precondition for our victory.

In the last few days, we have read in the newspapers that the Entente is discussing with Germany how the Versailles Peace Treaty is to be carried out. It was openly stated that Walter Rathenau – earlier it was Stinnes – is to get together with Loucheur and, uninfluenced by other forces, exchange opinions on how Germany – that is, the German working class – can possibly carry out the obligations of a defeated German capitalism to British and French imperialism. How absurd it is to assert that when two giants of capitalism – two individuals – can work out the solution to this problem in Germany and France, the workers would be able to resolve the issue in their favour without centralising their forces, whether in Lyon, Brest, or some obscure one-horse town, to the task. How absurd it is to preach, as Otto Rühle does, that the autonomy of small factory organisations must be preserved in every workplace. There is no cause for any further debate over such absurd impossibilities. We must apply our energies to convince revolutionary workers that it is an error for them to think we can do without centralism and that there is some way to do away with capitalism other than through the workers' concerted power.

When we say that it is no longer possible to achieve improvements in wage and working conditions within the capitalist order, this could suggest the conclusion that there is no longer any need to struggle for such gains and that all efforts should be focused on the day and the hour when capitalism can be overthrown. There are still considerable forces in Germany, France, and the United States that imagine such a line of thought to be revolutionary. Alas, capitalism cannot be overthrown in an hour. Surmounting the capitalist system of production depends on conditions that we must all take into account. During the period in which working-class forces are being assembled for the final assault against capitalism, we find that many a day and hour passes in which workers endure their everyday sufferings. Here the task is to firmly place in the masses' consciousness the daily struggle to alleviate these sufferings. In this way the workers can undertake not only the struggle to ease their daily woes but also, simultaneously, the struggle to organise the forces that will centralise the entire strength of the proletariat in order to overcome capitalism.

During the present period, even the smallest struggle can actually have immense effects. As a result, Communist trade-unionists do not merely have the task to show that we must destroy capitalism. They must also take part in all the small struggles to ease suffering, in all the small-scale work required to gather the working masses and imbue them with confidence. We face a problem. The process of capitalist decay has expelled millions of workers from the production process, rendering them jobless. Must the unemployed wait for the moment when capitalism is overthrown before other workers concern themselves with this suffering? All must join in answering, 'No!' And that gives us as trade unionists the task of struggling to incorporate these jobless workers into the production process, so they can live.

This is a harsh and difficult struggle. Harsh and difficult, because this struggle cannot be conducted by the jobless alone. In this struggle to reincorporate the jobless into the production process, the unemployed themselves are to some degree a limiting factor. We must consider the fact that the capitalist order no longer requires these workers. And the many millions who are still engaged in production are fearful that one day they too may be thrown out. The employers are able to bring pressure to bear on them through a standing reserve army of workers. They threaten to reduce wages, because thousands of workers stand in front of the factory gates, ready to be utilised. In order to resolve the unemployment problem, therefore, we must go to those who are still engaged in production and tell them that there is no struggle more important for us as workers than that of incorporating the jobless in production, because it involves defending our livelihood. If you do not help the jobless, no one will help you when you are out of work, and you will have nothing to eat. The jobless will be utilised to drive down wages. The first task that we must carry out is the struggle for the jobless brothers.

This struggle must be carried out in the workplace. That is absolutely certain. In the workplaces, where the workers are located – that is where they must be made aware of this. There is another reason why this must be done, namely that the economy is what sustains us, and when the economy stalls and no longer goes forward, we will have nothing more to eat, or, at least, much less to eat. Workers must reject the possibility of unemployment not only because it is bad on a personal level but because it also signifies destruction of the economy. That is why workers must oppose with all their strength the shutdown of factories and layoffs of workers. Given the current shortage of goods, every fall in production worsens the conditions of life and makes it even more impossible to carry on a more or less healthy existence.

It is true that the problem of unemployment will not be resolved until the social revolution has won and the proletarian dictatorship has been established. But it is in the living struggle for the interests of the working class that this will become clear to millions of workers who do not want to hear about the dictatorship of the proletariat and have understood nothing about social revolution as an urgent necessity in order to maintain the economy and sustain the working class.

Comrades, we see that the unemployment problem is not of concern to us alone. The Amsterdamers have had to occupy themselves with it for some time. Let me provide two examples of how they think to deal with this problem. About two months ago, the trade-union editor of *Vorwärts*, Dr. Striemer, spoke about the unemployment problem at a meeting in Spandau. Everything the Communists say about this is nonsense, he said. There would not be any unemployment if the jobless were settled in the countryside, and if such settlements were promoted. It is absurd, of course, to propose such an idea. But people who have been saying for two years that only they can help the jobless, and have nonetheless failed to do so, must now recommend something as a measure against unemployment, and so they come up with absurd nostrums like that proposed by Dr. Striemer.

A member of the General German Trade Union Federation, Ernst Schulze, disrupted the trade unions in Halle, because the Communists were the leading force there. He said that the cause of joblessness at present is that people have not been sparing in procreation. They have multiplied like rabbits. We must therefore take prudent measures with regard to procreation. He says this after a World War that has consumed the lives of sixteen million people. And before the War there was a shortage of workers in the capitalist states. This socialist has forgotten everything that we learned and how things were before the War. He has forgotten that the War slaughtered sixteen million people. His comments are simply a justification for a new war in which another sixteen million people will be slaughtered, a justification for people like Professor Gruber and company, who stated that there are fifteen million too many inhabitants in Germany, and they must emigrate or die, because otherwise capitalism will not survive.

Among the Amsterdamers, too, the top leaders are thinking about how we can save the economy from ruin, and how we can make it so that we are no longer under pressure from the unemployment question. They come to the same conclusion as the capitalists: either emigrate – except they do not know where to go – or die, because there are too many people. The old ideas of Malthus are being rewarmed and served up as the newest additions to Marxist thought.[10]

However, the employers are closing the factories right now not only because their economy is in a rut but in order to free themselves from revolutionary forces among the workers in the factory. What is their purpose? They know full well that the War has delivered a death blow to their social system, and that capitalism will not recover if a wave of Bolshevism rolls over the earth and revolution becomes a reality. The capitalist therefore thinks, 'I will arrange matters so that those who give the workers courage – telling them not to go down without resistance – are driven out of the factory.' And he throws them out.

And so the crisis dogging the capitalist economy and creating unemployment is worsened by the actions of capital. It closes factories in this great crisis in order to clean out the revolutionary forces, separate them off from the working class, and drive them into the lumpenproletariat through poverty and suffering. And when the jobless respond by taking to the streets, they use machine guns to shoot them down. It is not only in Spain where that happens; it is their procedure in every country. Comrades, what methods should we

---

10. Thomas Malthus contended that food supplies increase arithmetically while population grows geometrically. Unless measures were taken to limit population growth, he prophesised, humanity would be condemned to hunger, wars, and disease.

use to prevent capitalism from doing something like that to us? We have to make use of the trade-union forces at our disposal, use them not only when the danger reaches its highest point, but right away. When the employers are up to something, we must attempt immediately to carry out a counterstroke. What is more, we must try to strike such counterblows not only when the employers want to hit us but constantly, preparing for struggle, so that the employers are forced back onto the defensive and no longer have the initiative in acting against us. And that has a precondition: we, as workers, must unite our forces.

I would like to mention two factors that make it necessary to wage a united struggle against the employers. In Germany, for example – and this has also happened in Austria and other countries – when the capitalists could no longer continue production, they turn to demolishing the means of production as a source of profit. The capitalist produces not in order that people have the means to live, but in order to make profits. If production is no longer worthwhile, perhaps there is gain in destroying the means of production. Countless brickworks in Germany have been demolished. The German sugar industry is operating at far below the prewar level. What is the result? A large number of workers have lost the possibility of employment in this branch of production, because the German economy has been deprived of the chance to recover from this crisis, even if we do away with capitalism. What use is there in a victory over capitalism if capitalism has previously destroyed all the means of production?

We have to prevent it from doing such a thing. But to prevent that, we need to use the strongest force available to the working class: active struggle on every front. In Italy, for example, we have seen what workers do in such situations, when the employers are simply sabotaging production, and this has happened in other countries as well. I am referring to occupation of the factories, through which the working class tries to prevent the employers from stopping production, destroying the means of production and selling them abroad, and making a selection among the workers, and so on.

But can occupation of the factories be conceived of as a means of struggle limited to one locality and to a fixed length of time, as advocated by the Italian trade-union bureaucracy, for example? That is something absolutely impossible. The moment workers set about occupying factories and workplaces in order to defend them against the capitalists, the need arises for the entire working class to defend these workers. It is more than just a minor trade-union struggle that can only be maintained for a few days. What is the result of a factory occupation on a local basis? If it is a local occupation, we must be prepared for the arrival of the police with machine guns to drive the workers out of the factory. Production can be maintained for a week, but then it stops, because there is no supply of raw materials, the banks provide no money, and, therefore, the workers receive no wages. A local factory occupation can be maintained for a few days on this basis, but it amounts to the workers protecting the employers' factories, and surely there is no need for the workers to commit themselves for that.

We must explain to the workers that if measures are to be taken to defend their existence, greater use must be made of this power, in order to provide the workers with money, to pay wages, to obtain raw materials and fuel; links must be set up between the city and the countryside, to make possible an exchange of agricultural and industrial products. So we see that if the workers act to protect production, this develops immediately into a class struggle as powerful as anything one can imagine. This is inconceivable as a purely local movement, because machine guns and prisons are brought into play in order to crush the workers.

Comrades, we must stir up the working-class struggle as a whole, in order to achieve gains in wages and working conditions from the capitalist order in which we live. Many will tell us this cannot be done. To be sure, it is impossible; capitalism cannot accept that. That is what the Amsterdamers tell us. We hear this on a daily basis in Germany, including from the Social-Democratic Independents, who say it is not possible to conduct a strike, the employers cannot pay because productivity is not high enough, and so on. And we have just received a significant historic document showing the complete bankruptcy of the Amsterdamers, who want to quarrel over improvements in workers' conditions within the capitalist order. On 30 April this year, the leaders of the Amsterdam trade-union International met in London to discuss how the different countries could carry out the obligations of the Versailles Peace Treaty without resort to arms.[11] The French and British trade-union leaders declared there that the Germans should commit their entire strength to ensuring that the German government carried through punctually on all its obligations. The German trade-union leaders said that the others should commit themselves to preventing their governments from sending troops into Germany, and if this was done, the German workers would carry out their obligations. That is how the Amsterdamers serve the bourgeoisie and assist it in beating down the working class.

---

11. This meeting was held alongside the Entente powers' conference in London on the reparations question.

But things like that have results. This was evident in the Spa agreement on coal.[12] The German miners were subjected to extortion. Jouhaux, the envoy of the General Confederation of Labour, came to Germany and told the German miners, 'Work hard, work the overtime, and the French people will thank you'. The German miners were lured into working the overtime, and what was gained by this? Miners in France and Belgium were thrown out of work, mines were shut down. The workers lost the capacity to defend their standard of living. Miners in Britain were placed in the worst possible situation. By getting the trade-union leaders of these countries to impose overtime on the German workers, the employers of these countries were able to oppress their own working class.

There is a vital interdependency here, which the trade-union movement must not ignore, and which compels us to deal with the consequences. What are the lessons of the coal agreement for us as Communists? The German, French, British, and Belgian miners must link up for united defence of their living standards. That breaks right through the limits of national autonomy. To recognise the right of national union bodies to do whatever they want will lead in this period to the downfall of these groupings of workers. We must therefore say that the time has passed in which workers can be organised only on a national basis, while international solidarity remains only a promise made at congresses. It is an urgent necessity that we link up internationally in the struggle to maintain workers' standard of living.

There is more to say on this. To the degree that the capitalist economy is shattered in this or that branch of production, the capitalist class will utilise this in an attempt to split the working class, driving one segment down to a low level and playing it off against the other segment. We see an example of this in the textile workers. There is a deep crisis in a number of countries. People are unable to buy clothing, and as a result textile workers lose their jobs. The crisis is so profound that they are not in a position to resist successfully. From this flows a lesson that must be explained to the workers: they must go into struggle united; they cannot protect themselves on their own. Such far-reaching solidarity is not a humanitarian issue. It is a way of ensuring that when they are in a similar situation and need the help of others, this help will be forthcoming and will protect them. If the conditions of textile workers, construction workers, and so on is declining, it is possible for the capitalists

---

12. The conference of the Entente powers held in Spa, Belgium, 5–16 July 1920, took up the reparations payments that, under the terms of the Versailles Treaty, Germany was to make each country, with the conference allotting 52 per cent to France. It was decided that for six months after 1 August Germany would deliver up two million tons of coal per month as reparations.

to drive down the living conditions of the other workers as well. Here we see the full meaning of the crime that took place on the notorious Black Friday in Britain.[13] The employers targeted a layer of workers, in order to worsen their living conditions and break their capacity to struggle. Their goal was to then try out the same methods on other layers and in other countries. It was urgently necessary for the transport and railway workers to join the struggle, not to help the miners but to help themselves.

So every workers' movement in a county must be broadened, both to defend the movement itself and to defend the workers who are not yet in motion. That is what we must learn from this period. The capitalists, as Comrade Zinoviev quite rightly said, are clever people. They employ not only violent methods but methods of another kind aiming at tearing the working class apart. Here I must again cite some examples from Germany, because I know it best, because the workers in this country have already made a revolution and then, in their ignorance, threw it away, and because these examples provide the richest lessons. The miners in Germany were always the best weapon of the German working class. When the miners went out, we were in a position to beat any power that the employers used against us. What was done by capitalism in our country and by Entente capital? It gave the miners a so-called 'gold bonus': it gave them bacon and sausage. The food was taken from another category of workers and given to the miners. The miners were satisfied. The other workers, who had been deprived of food, were bitter at the miners, and in this way the workers were forced apart. It is therefore necessary that every honest trade unionist help prevent such things from happening.

Another method used to boost production is to give a worker a specified bonus if he works hard, telling him, 'You are receiving a share of the profits from production.' There are many workers who believe that this is proposed in all honesty. We Communists must prevent something like this from taking place. What is at stake in this period is not to get a share of the profits. Not enough is being produced to meet people's needs. It's a matter of destroying the capitalist impulse for profits. That is the task we have to carry out.

Now some people from within the working class, comrades, are coming up and saying they want to resolve problems in a peaceful way. They talk about socialising, about nationalising. There's no need for me to discuss this.

---

13. On Black Friday, 15 April 1921, two weeks after the onset of the coal miners' strike (see p. 78, n. 18), leaders of the transport and rail workers' unions that were part of the Triple Alliance (see p. 148, n. 10) broke their pledge of support to the coal miners and called off the solidarity strike scheduled for that day. The miners were forced back to work in July 1921, with a substantial wage cut.

It has already been pointed out in other reports that this is nothing more than a sordid swindle aimed at deceiving the working class with the ultimate goal of safeguarding capital and giving it a guarantee, while the workers get new shackles.[14] If you want to conduct a real struggle for socialisation, this cannot be done peacefully and it cannot be limited to one branch of industry; it has to be done all down the line. The most powerful struggle for socialisation is therefore a struggle for power, to fight against the economic power of the bourgeoisie. That means a struggle to win state power, to make this power secure in the hands of the workers, so the road is open for reconstruction.

No matter how we conduct a trade-union struggle in the present period, it has political results. Communists must explain this to the workers. The capitalist is dying, and in the process dragging down the working class into poverty. The workers must turn against the employers, using all means at their disposal. They must use methods of struggle that every worker can grasp – methods that every worker understands and believes will serve to protect his existence. These methods are not always those that will dispose of capitalism overnight, but rather methods that unite the working class and that, when utilised, show that even the most limited struggle to defend the working class is a struggle for power. Such methods show that you cannot safeguard production through labour partnership and such things, but rather only by chasing away the employers.

So the workers must be united in broad, national organisations, according to their branch of production. International ties must be based not on promises but on the possibility and desire to conduct strikes internationally and to extend the economic struggle into the countryside. And there is something else we must not forget. If we carry out such a task of the revolution, the proletariat will not stand still. We have seen what the employers are doing in every country. In Germany they set up the Emergency Technical Assistance, in Italy the Fascist gangs, while in the United States there are the Pinkertons.[15] Everywhere capitalism relies not just on its organs of state power but on other, special bodies to defend its property and to oppress and disperse the working class.

---

14. Socialisation schemes are discussed in Radek's report on tactics and strategy. See p. 439.
15. Emergency Technical Assistance (Technische Nothilfe) was an organisation of strikebreakers formed by a German government decree of 30 September 1919 with the stated purpose of maintaining essential services.
The Pinkertons are a US detective agency, established by Allan Pinkerton in 1850. Beginning in the late nineteenth century, they were used primarily for strikebreaking and to disrupt labour activity.

We too, as workers, must set up self-defence organisations in our trade unions, so that we can hold off the Pinkertons, combat the Fascist bands, and make it impossible for capitalism to use them in its defence. You see how workers' leaders everywhere are cut down like mangy dogs by the bourgeoisie. That is why we need self-defence organisations to protect our own leaders. For nothing weakens the working class more than when one top leader after another is cut down by the White Guards. In addition, the proletarian defence organisations should be deployed in the struggle that the employers wage against workers, locking them out, throwing them on the street, clearing out the factory, and sending in the Emergency Technical Assistance, the factory police, and the Pinkertons. Workers' organisations must defeat these efforts wherever possible. I recall how, in Germany, when the employers shut down production on a sweeping basis, and the workers could not defend themselves against that because they had left the point of production, the workers rose up and said, 'We want control of the goods coming in by railway; we want to see if the workers agree with shutting down production.' That put a spoke in their wheels. It is only the embryo of a new method of workers' struggle against capitalism, which must be extended.

Comrades, I am coming to the close of my report. I would like in summary to repeat the following: the capitalist economic order has been shaken to its foundations. In order to defend the working class and maintain its present living standards, the proletarian forces organised in trade unions must be firmly unified. This cannot be done in small, local organisations, separated off from one another in federated organisations. It requires the creation of broad, national, production-based organisations. Defence is possible only in harsh struggle against capitalism, only when we do not evade the struggle. We must not remain on the defensive but rather go onto the attack against capitalism. This is the same struggle that the Communist International is conducting, and we should not be separated off from it; we must proceed shoulder to shoulder, in unity. We must draw the lessons, just as we did from the Second World Congress.

I will close by saying that the task of Communists is to intervene in the broad trade-union struggles in order to make the unions into organisations of class struggle, to centralise their strength everywhere, and to spur them onward, so that the battle can be led forward to victory. Wherever comrades are present together in an organisation, they must form a cell, in order to spread our ideas there, and so that, in close unity with the Communist International, we will defeat the enemy. (*Loud applause and cheers*)

**Koenen** (Chair): Delegations are requested to choose their representatives for the Trade Union Commission.

The Commission on Tactics and Strategy meets at 11:00 a.m. tomorrow morning in the Continental Room.

Following today's sessions, all congress participants are asked to go to Red Square for the unveiling of the monument to John Reed, who died last year in Moscow.

This evening, at 6:00 p.m., the trade-union congress will open in the House of Trade Unions.

The next session takes place tomorrow, 4 July, at 6:00 p.m.

*(The session is adjourned at 5:20 p.m.)*

Session 16 – 4 July 1921, 7:30 p.m.
# World Economy; Trade Union Discussion

*Varga: Report of the Economic Commission on the economic situation. Discussion of the trade-union question. Speakers: Bergmann, Earsman.*

**Kolarov** (Chair): The next point on the agenda is the report of the Economic Commission on the economic situation.

### Economic Commission Report

**Eugen Varga**: Comrades, the commission established by the congress for final editing of the theses has completed its work. After rather detailed discussions, we succeeded in dealing with almost all the objections that had been raised by various delegations regarding specific points of the theses – partly by convincing the comrades that what they proposed was already covered by the theses, and partly through compromises, in which we encompassed suggestions of the different delegations.

Looking over the long list of proposed amendments to the theses, we can readily identify four groups. The first group consists of amendments whose goal was to better portray the specific conditions of a given country. We had very little scope to encompass amendments of this type, comrades, because the theses obviously take up the capitalist world in its totality. It was impossible to draft theses of this type that would reflect the specificity of each country. The commission rejected almost all the amendments in this category.

The second group of amendments related to economic conditions in countries of the European Entente. Here we resolved the problem by completely redrafting the point on this question.

The third group of amendments dealt with the condition of peasants in Europe and agrarian relations. Comrades are generally aware that peasant and agrarian conditions vary widely, and it is difficult to formulate a text that will apply equally to agrarian conditions in Britain and Western Europe, and to those in Central Europe and in the Balkans. Therefore, we rewrote these paragraphs as well, and I believe that the new text does what is required. Above all, we attempted under this point to analyse the political divisions among the possessing classes, the differences among the peasants of Central Europe, as found in Hungary, Poland, Bavaria, and Bulgaria. As comrades know, the situation in these countries is that the bourgeoisie is locked in struggle with the proletariat. In this struggle it requires the support of the peasants in the form of the various armed bodies. The peasants are, in general, prepared to lend armed support to the bourgeoisie against the proletariat. On the other hand, the peasants want to be freed from the burdens of reconstruction. Specifically, they do not want to pay taxes. Where obligatory deliveries of foodstuffs are still in force, they do not want to make these deliveries. In this way, they are sabotaging the efforts of the bourgeoisie to rebuild the capitalist economy. This point of view, put forward chiefly by Comrade Brand, is encompassed rather effectively, in my opinion, in the new version of this paragraph.

Finally, the fourth group consisted essentially of a continuation within the commission of the debate on tactics and strategy. Here is the question that came up: as comrades know, the question of a policy of offensive has dominated the congress to this point, and it was posed in these theses as well, because they are actually the foundation for the Theses on Tactics and Strategy. In the commission discussions on this question, the following became clear. First, the only way we can speak about a working-class offensive against capitalism in general terms is in a historical framework. This is the type of offensive that Comrade Lenin and Comrade Radek were referring to when they said that the proletariat cannot possibly seize political power without going on the offensive. However, within this broad offensive of the proletariat, there are two types of offensives. One is economic, in the form of economic strikes within the bounds of capitalism, seeking to improve the conditions of proletarians. Obviously, given the ruined condition of capitalism at present, the revolutionising of broad masses of workers, and purposeful leadership by the Communist Party, such struggles are always transformed from an economic to a political basis, to a struggle for political power. And then there is a political offensive, separated from trade-union demands, a political armed struggle for power: that too can be called a policy of offensive.

Well, the debates in the commission turned on the following question: are conditions for a political offensive more favourable in a time of economic crisis or a time of economic expansion? Comrades know that Marx and Engels were always of the opinion, and this is recorded in many of their writings, that the masses can more readily be drawn into political revolution in times of crisis than in times of prosperity. And the comrades who favoured the policy of offensive in this third sense considered that the present economic crisis offers the best opportunity for a political offensive aimed at launching the final struggle. Given that they hold this view, they are also of the opinion that the present economic crisis will continue for a very long time. They attempted to insert into the theses a passage that would advance such a view energetically. I will read the proposed change and the change actually adopted by the commission. These were the main topics of discussion, the main considerations. Now for your information, comrades, I will take the liberty of reading you the changes that were adopted.

The text of point 11 is new, and it reads as follows:

> France, Belgium, and Italy were economically ruined by the War beyond any cure. The attempt to restore the French economy at the cost of Germany is crude robbery combined with diplomatic extortion. It heightens Germany's devastation (coal, machines, cattle, gold) without saving France. The entire economy of continental Europe is severely damaged by this effort. France receives far less than Germany loses. Even though French peasants, through a supreme effort, have restored considerable parts of the ruined landscape, even though certain industries (chemical, armaments) experienced new growth during the War, France is headed for economic ruin. The national debt and government expenses (militarism) have reached unbearable heights. At the end of the last upswing, the French currency had lost 60 per cent of its value. Restoration of the French economy is hindered by the severe losses of human life during the War – which, given the low rate of population increase, cannot be made good. The economies of Italy and Belgium, with some variations, are in similar condition.[1]

That is the text, which takes into account the wishes of the French delegation as much as possible.

The next change is in point 18. It expresses in more concise fashion the thought that ongoing currency fluctuations obstruct normal capitalist trade,

---

1. For the corresponding passage in the theses, see pp. 905–6.

thus posing an obstacle to a revival of capitalism. In point 18, paragraph 3, after the sentence, 'Gold has been destroyed as a world currency', there is an addition:

> Devaluation of the currency of European countries (up to 99 per cent) poses very serious obstacles to the exchange of goods on the world market. Incessant and sharp currency fluctuations transform capitalist production into chaotic speculation.[2]

In the same point, a change was made to stress more strongly the fact that all countries are withdrawing from the capitalist world economy through export bans, import bans, and increases in tariff rates. It is in the fifth paragraph of this point. After the first sentence, 'Europe is still a madhouse', we have added the following: 'Most countries are enacting export and import bans and multiplying their tariffs. Even Britain is introducing tariffs.'

In addition, some small changes have been made in the final paragraph of point 18. Instead of the words, 'Paris speculation', it now reads, 'Entente – especially French speculation'. In the passage, 'controls German exports and all of German economic life', the word 'German' is replaced by 'Central European'. And the term 'Versailles Treaty' has generally been replaced by 'peace treaties'.

The following change is really intended only to improve the transition from point 18 to point 19. The new version of point 19 thus begins, 'The elimination of Soviet Russia as a market for industrial goods and source of raw materials has contributed greatly to disrupting global economic equilibrium.' The rest of point 19 is unchanged.

In point 20 there was just one quite minor change affecting only a few words. In the passage that takes up the concentration and impoverishment of workers, we added the words, 'Stinnesisation on the one hand,[3] proletarianisation and pauperisation on the other', in order to make the point more precise.

Then comes point 21, which is entirely rewritten. The new text begins as follows: 'The increase in prices of agricultural products, which seemed to enrich the villages as a whole, enabled the large peasants to achieve a genuine increase in income and property.'

---

2. For the corresponding passage in the theses, see p. 908.
3. 'Stinnesisation' or the 'Stinnes question' refers to the growing trend toward concentration and monopolisation under capitalism. Starting from his extensive ownership in the German coal and steel industry, Hugo Stinnes had moved into other areas of the economy such the media and public utilities.

The original text spoke only of an apparent enrichment of the entire village; now it states that the large peasants really did become richer. I am sure the congress will agree that this reflects reality more accurately. Let us continue:

> The peasants succeeded in paying off with depreciated paper money, which they had accumulated in large quantities, the debts they had contracted in undepreciated currency. But agriculture involves more than simply paying off mortgages.
>
> Despite the enormous increase in the price of land, despite unscrupulous abuse of the monopoly in foodstuffs, despite the enrichment of large landowners and large peasants, the decline of European agriculture is unmistakable. It is seen in the frequent regression to more extensive forms of cultivation: tilled land converted to pasture, disappearance of livestock, three-field crop rotation. This was caused in part by the shortage of labour, the shrinkage of herds, the lack of chemical fertiliser, high prices of manufactured goods. Also, in Central and Eastern Europe, production was deliberately reduced in reprisal against attempts of the government to take possession of agricultural products.[4]

This is a reformulation of the fact that, as you know, across all Central and Eastern Europe, where prices are fixed or were in the past, the peasants have deliberately reduced production in order not to be forced to deliver goods at these low prices. I will now read out the portion of this point that takes up politics:

> Large and, to some extent, middle peasants are creating strong political and economic organisations to defend themselves against the burdens of reconstruction. Taking advantage of the bourgeoisie's distress, they are imposing on the government, as the price of their support against the proletariat, a one-sided pro-peasant tariff and tax policy that restricts capitalist reconstruction. A division between the bourgeoisie of village and city has arisen that saps the strength of the bourgeois class.
>
> At the same time, a large segment of the poorer peasants are proletarianised and pauperised. The village has become a breeding place for discontent, and class consciousness is growing among the agricultural proletariat.

The final portion is unchanged.

In point 38, the portion dealing with Britain was rewritten. It was the British comrades who wanted to express more strongly the fact that the

---

4. For corresponding passages in the theses to this and the following quotation, see pp. 909–10.

trade-union leaders there responded like cowards to the use of police power and the armed power of the state. This was done in the following passage, which is rewritten:

> In Britain, the powerful strike movement of the past year was repeatedly repulsed by the government's ruthless imposition of military force and the resulting intimidation of the trade-union leaders. If the leaders had remained loyal to the cause of the working class, the trade-union machinery, despite its defects, could have been utilised for revolutionary struggles. The recent crisis of the Triple Alliance provided the occasion for a revolutionary confrontation with the bourgeoisie, which was prevented by the conservatism, cowardice, and betrayal of the trade-union leaders.[5]

I will now take up, comrades, the opening points in the political and tactical portion of the theses: points 39, 40, and 41. An addition was made at the end of point 39 as proposed by the German delegation:

> The re-establishment of capitalism requires, as a precondition, an enormous increase in exploitation, the destruction of millions of lives, the reduction of the standard of living for millions below the survival level, and the perpetual insecurity of proletarian existence. As a result, the workers are driven again and again to constant strikes and rebellions. These pressures and struggles build the masses' determination to overthrow the capitalist order.

Now I come to the final change. Because it is closely related to the issue of tactics, I would like to read out first the amendment that Comrade Pogány submitted and then modified and, second, the text proposed by Comrade Trotsky and adopted by the commission. The change proposed by Comrade Pogány reads as follows:

> The economic crisis has now driven the proletariat onto the defensive, which will require it to wage major defensive struggles. These struggles will lead naturally to political conflicts, because the bourgeoisie will respond to them by greater and greater use of force. The economic crisis presents us with an epoch of intensified proletarian actions and civil wars. If the proletariat fails to carry out this defensive struggle with the necessary offensive spirit, the bourgeoisie will drive down the standard of living of the working class to the level achieved by the trade-union movement in a bygone era.

Comrade Pogány himself later modified this amendment somewhat. An amendment proposed by Comrade Trotsky was then adopted by the

---

5. For corresponding passages to this and the remaining amendments quoted by Varga, see pp. 918–19.

commission unanimously, that is, with the agreement of Comrade Pogány and the German delegation. It comes at the beginning of point 40 and reads as follows:

> A Communist Party's basic task in the present crisis is and remains to lead, broaden, deepen, and unite the proletariat's present defensive struggles and, in pace with the developing situation, *turn them into decisive political struggles for power*.

As comrades see, the disputed point here is whether to elaborate more fully the tasks of the Communist Party in the economic crisis now before us, which I think will be short in duration, but Comrade Pogány believes it will very likely last a long time. In order to further accommodate this point of view, the beginning of the remaining text of point 40 was modified. What was said explicitly in the original text is, in the amended text, merely assumed. The change is as follows:

> Should the pace of these developments slow, and should the present economic crisis be followed in a greater or lesser number of countries by a period of expansion…

So it is mere supposition. And the second paragraph of point 40 will read as follows:

> In the event that the proletariat is thrown back during the present crisis by the capitalist offensive, the beginning of an economic upturn will see it move back to the offensive.

As comrades can see, we were successful in bridging the gap between these two positions so that both sides can view the compromise as consistent with their viewpoints and adopt it. That concludes what I have to say on the substance of the commission's deliberations. There are also some small, purely stylistic changes and textual corrections, and I see no need to read them out. I believe that these changes can be adopted by the congress without further discussion. (*Loud applause and cheers*)

**Kolarov** (Chair): Comrade Frölich has the floor for a short declaration.

**Frölich**: Comrades, before submitting the statement of the German delegation, a brief remark. I believe that comrades who took part in the work of the commission will be surprised to hear that we debated the policy of the offensive there. I also consider it quite unjustified to criticise comrades who wished to leave point 40 unchanged for supposedly having let their particular political goals influence their assessment of economic developments. The fact is that the theses, as submitted to us, presented a line of march for future conditions of economic expansion, but said not a word about the present crisis. This could give rise to the idea that we had abandoned any expectations that the crisis could lead to revolution. That is what was at issue. I believe that quite a successful solution was found during the commission discussions.

On behalf of the German delegation, I declare that we agree with the theses in their present form and will vote for them. (*Loud applause*)

**Kolarov** (Chair): Comrade Trotsky has the floor for a short statement.

**Trotsky**: Only a small correction. In the original text of point 40, the following is said about workers' offensive and defensive struggles. In a situation of renewed prosperity, it reads, '[Workers'] economic offensive will display the same tendency to be transformed into open civil war as does their present defensive war.' So this took note of the defensive war, and, in addition, of its tendency to develop into a civil war. Thus no one could think that the defensive war and its tendency to revolution was being ignored here, or that only the war of attack in a time of prosperity was being considered. This is established here concisely in a formulation taken from the Theses on Tactics and Strategy that was also previously in the theses before us now. This brief review is just to clarify the text that previously formed part of point 40.

**Kolarov** (Chair): No one has asked for the floor, so the debate is closed. We will now take the vote. We are voting on the theses as presented by Comrade Varga in the report of the commission, including its amendments.

*The theses are unanimously adopted.*

*[See text of theses on pp. 901–20]*

We will now move on to the next agenda point and make some arrangements for the commissions. First of all, the Commission on Tactics and Strategy. The Presidium proposes that the commission be composed just as established by the Executive, and that it meet to consider the Theses on Tactics and Strategy under the leadership of Comrade Radek. Thus the commission will meet only as originally set up for the tactics and strategy discussion. Members of the commission that were added later will not form part of the next stage of discussions on tactics and strategy.

Since no other proposal has been made, and there is no objection, the proposal is adopted. The delegations that previously had no representative in the commission are asked to name them immediately and send them to its sessions. The Presidium proposes that Comrade Radek, the reporter on this item, be named chair of the commission. Is there any other proposal? Is there any objection? Since neither is the case, the proposal is adopted.

We now propose to establish a commission to prepare the agenda point on cooperatives. All delegations should choose a delegate for this commission. The Presidium proposes that the reporter, Comrade Khinchuk, act as leader of this commission. Is there any other proposal, or any objection? No. The proposal is adopted.

We propose to establish a commission to prepare the agenda point on the Eastern question. For this commission, as with the others, the delegations should now choose their representative. It is left to the Small Bureau to convene this commission, since the Presidium has not yet received any proposal regarding its leadership. We ask the Small Bureau to choose the leader of this commission. Is there any other proposal or any objection? Since that is not the case, the proposal is adopted.

**Kolarov** (Chair): We propose Comrade Heckert as chair of the Trade Union Commission.

**Gota**: The commission should choose its own chair.

**Shouts**: Rosmer.

**Kolarov** (Chair): We must be certain that the commission can function, and that is why we propose a comrade to convene it. Obviously, the commission is empowered to change its chairperson.

**Radek**: Given that we are not dealing merely with technical questions, I propose that we choose a German and a French comrade.

The Presidium is in agreement with this proposal.

**Kolarov** (Chair): So Comrades Heckert and Rosmer have been proposed. There has been no objection; they are elected.

The leaders of both commissions – on tactics and strategy and on trade unions – are asked to have their commissions meet here in the adjoining rooms tomorrow evening at 6:00 p.m. in order to begin their deliberations.

**Radek**: As regards the trade-union question, I propose that we leave it to the commission to decide when it should convene, since this must be coordinated with the sittings of the trade-union congress.

**Kolarov** (Chair): The commission on the trade-union question will hold its discussions jointly with the parallel commission of the Red International of Labour Unions congress, when that is possible and necessary. It is essential that a jointly agreed statement of principle on this question be arrived at by the sessions of the political and trade-union congresses.

Comrades, now that we have heard the reports on the trade-union question, do you wish to open the general debate on this agenda point, or do you prefer to wait for the report of the commission?

**Radek**: Comrades, in my opinion it is much more appropriate to hold the general debate now, for the following reason: if divergent opinions are expressed for the first time only in the commission, and then we take up these opinions only after the commission is finished, we will then have to refer the matters right back to the commission again for final treatment. For this reason, I think it is appropriate to begin the general debate now.

**Kolarov** (Chair): Is there any other proposal? It seems that is not the case. Now that the congress has decided to start the general debate, I must tell you, on behalf of the Presidium, that this debate cannot take place until Wednesday morning [6 July], because Comrade Zinoviev has been suddenly called to Petrograd, and he cannot return here until then. In addition, we do not yet have the theses, and it is possible that we may receive them by Wednesday.

**Radek**: It is certainly quite inconvenient that Comrade Zinoviev is unable to be here today. But he will have an opportunity to read the stenographic report of the discussion before the summary and before the decision. In the meantime, what is at issue is not the reporter or the report but enabling us here at the congress to listen to and clarify the different points of view. We can dispense for now with a vote on the theses, for example. The broad line was presented in the report. So if it now turns out that there are no great differences of opinion, we can leave it to the commission to hold the vote. In any case, what the congress must know in this important organisational question is whether we have common ground; whether there are major differences of opinion or not.

For this reason, I propose that we begin the discussion today, unless the Presidium proposes another important topic for discussion this evening. We have to save time. The delegates are rested today, and I therefore propose to utilise the time for discussion on this question.

**Kolarov** (Chair): Is there any other proposal? Then Comrade Radek's proposal is adopted. The Presidium wishes to inform you that, as already agreed, Comrade Lenin will give his report tomorrow on the economic and political situation in Soviet Russia. We will begin the discussion on the trade-union question today, then interrupt it tomorrow and continue it only on Wednesday. Is that agreeable?

**Radek**: Comrades, based on what we know from newspapers and the positions of the parties regarding the different currents, it is clear that there is only one viewpoint that objects to our position on the trade-union question on a principled basis, namely that advanced by the KAPD. Secondly, the most significant existing differences of opinion are those arising from the situation of the French Communist Party with regard to syndicalism and the French trade unions. I therefore propose that we give the KAPD comrades and also those from France an opportunity, if they wish, to present their viewpoint here – for these are the most important issues – and the discussion can then proceed.

**Kolarov** (Chair): The KAPD has submitted a motion to grant it a counter-report on this question. The Presidium is agreeable to granting the KAPD an extended speaking time of half an hour on this agenda point.

**Seemann** (Reichenbach, KAPD): It seems that the Presidium considers a speaking time of half an hour to be sufficient. We protest against this and ask the congress to give us a real counter-report. I can certainly agree with Comrade Radek that we will present a viewpoint on this question that is different in principle. I hope that at least on this important and principled question we can take the floor with a genuine counter-report. We appeal to your interest in this important question and ask you not to accept the Presidium's proposal to fob us off with half an hour, while the French and other comrades receive a much longer speaking time.

**Radek**: I propose that rather than losing half an hour in a debate on procedure, we grant the KAPD an hour's speaking time. (*Applause*)

**Kolarov** (Chair): We will take the vote on Comrade Radek's proposal. Those in favour of granting the KAPD an hour's speaking time, please raise your hands. The proposal of Comrade Radek for an hour's speaking time is adopted.

## Discussion on Trade Union Question

**Bergmann** (Meyer, KAPD): Comrades, yesterday Comrade Zinoviev stressed in his report the decisive importance of our position on the trade unions for the development and conduct of the revolution. As we know, the assumption of political and of economic power must proceed hand in hand. Indeed, far more is at stake than merely the assumption of political and economic power. Even now we must prepare for the fact that taking power in itself achieves nothing unless we have created the preconditions for reinforcing and maintaining this power. That is the problem for which we must now find a solution.

In the previous phase of the revolution in different countries we have seen that certain segments were setting about to seize power, but they did not understand how to reinforce and secure this power, once it was in their hands. That was the case in 1918 when the German revolution broke out, and the task was then to secure economic power. Comrades, we must look into the causes of this. Comrades must examine what must be done to prevent such errors and to find the ways and means to prevent any future repetition of them.

In the highly developed capitalist countries, we cannot and must not depend on accidental occurrences and give way to the delusion that everything will turn out for the best. Concretely, insofar as this is possible within capitalist society, we must attempt to create bodies that can spring into action when the occasion arises for them to carry out their task. Comrade Heckert's report yesterday provided us with an analysis showing us the tasks that the old trade unions undertook and attempted to carry out within capitalist society. Comrade Zinoviev showed clearly and distinctly what trade unions must do in the revolution and how they – as I have just explained – must then secure and help construct economic power.

Let us consider the task and structure of trade unions under capitalism. Everywhere in the highly developed capitalist countries, their task was to improve the living conditions of the working class. This task assumed by the trade unions can no longer be carried out, can no longer be accomplished. On that there is no disagreement among us here. Nonetheless, we see that many trade unions are still attempting, even today, to carry out these old tasks, which were appropriate and correct in prerevolutionary times. But the facts now make it evident that these tasks can no longer be accomplished. These trade unions have now become an auxiliary weapon of the capitalist state.

Comrade Zinoviev said yesterday that capitalist states are now holding down the working class not only with the sword but also by means of deception. And this state apparatus of deception that permanently holds down the working class is now the old trade unions. That is what they are today. We see this above all in Germany. They have turned into nothing less than an instrument and bulwark of the capitalist state.

Comrades, some think that such organisations can be won over today and transformed into instruments for revolution. On this point, the opinion of the KAPD – and not it alone, as was stated here – is quite different from that of the majority of parties affiliated to the Communist International. As I said, the KAPD is not alone in this view, because the shop stewards in Britain, the IWW in the United States, and the syndicalist organisations in France, Spain, and Italy also hold an alternative view, namely that it is impossible, by winning the counterrevolutionary trade unions, to convert them into instruments of revolution and with their help revolutionise the working masses.

We can see quite clearly in Germany how this pattern is developing and progressing. Until now, comrades of the VKPD have stood for winning the trade unions. But yesterday we heard for the first time, in the speeches of Zinoviev and Heckert, even if not explicitly, that the trade unions must be smashed.[6] If that's the way these matters are addressed, if you are talking about smashing the trade unions, then perhaps there is common ground between us and the majority. We are categorically for clearing the old counterrevolutionary trade unions out of the way. Not because we take any pleasure in destruction, but because we see that they have become genuine agencies of the capitalist state, which it utilises for suppression, in the worst sense of the word, of the revolution.

In 1918 the collapse of the German army seemed to have brought about the moment for the conquest of power. We seemed to be only hours, minutes removed from having power in our hands. It was then that the German trade unions and their leading bodies – which during the War had preached 'holding out' from the first moment to the last – stitched together a state that had collapsed. It was trade-union leaders, Noske and others, who, with the help of an officers' clique, reconstituted the shattered bourgeois bands and thus blocked revolution in Germany.

Today the whole array of old trade unions are united around this viewpoint. Comrades, they are trying to replace the open struggle of the working masses with mock battles. In 1918, following the example of the Russian Revolution, the German workers set about creating workers' councils. The idea of workers' councils found expression again and again among the German proletarian masses. This concept refused to be buried and suppressed. Meanwhile, the trade-union leaders twisted and turned right up to April and May 1919. At first they strongly opposed the idea of workers' councils and suppressed them harshly, with bayonets. But this concept popped up again and again. So these trade-union puppets helped to create the law on workers' councils, which supposedly assured the working masses of some influence on production, consumption, and the economic process as a whole.[7] Large masses of workers were fooled by this, thinking that the law on councils would really give them

---

6. No implication that trade unions should be smashed is found in the stenographic transcripts of Zinoviev and Heckert's reports on the trade-union question in Session 15. Bergmann appears to be referring to what he later states to be the inevitable results of the establishment of Communist cells in the unions. See p. 641.

7. Presumably a reference to the German law adopted 2 February 1920. The existence of workers' councils was also recognised in Article 165 of the Weimar Constitution.

influence over future developments. Bit by bit, however, it has become plain that the law is cleverly crafted to serve as nothing other than a club against the revolution. Today we see that the working masses who fell for the bait of the council law, when it was tossed to them, have turned away from this idea.

This does not mean that all workers have already seen through this blatant deception. However, today we see that large segments of the revolutionary workers have taken up arms in a vigorous struggle against this seemingly revolutionary but in reality reactionary law. The councils that were elected and set up at that time are not instruments of revolution for the masses but nothing less than instruments of reaction. We say this in every struggle, large or small. Let me take just one example. In March, when the struggle began and unfolded in Central Germany, in the largest factory in this region – the Leuna Works – confidence in these councils had sunk so low that the first action of the twenty-five thousand workers there was to overturn the legally constituted council and elect, in its place, a revolutionary action committee.

**Heckert**: That is simply nonsense.

**Bergmann**: Well, Comrade Heckert, I'm more familiar than you with the situation at the Leuna Works, and I know what happened there. One comrade of the VKPD and one from the KAPD overturned this council, after a struggle, and on Tuesday morning [22 March] the factory workers elected a revolutionary action committee.

That was the situation almost everywhere the workers moved into struggle. Comrades, we must now assess whether developments can and should continue on this path. We see that the workers have no confidence in these factory councils legally established according to the law on councils. So we must attempt to draw workers together in a different way, to give them different councils, which will then, on the morrow of the victorious revolution, really enjoy the trust of the broad masses of the industrial proletariat. How can that come to be? Is it or is it not possible inside the current trade-union movement? We say that this is not possible. The old trade unions have shown in life that they have become a segment – and indeed a strong segment – of the capitalist state itself.

Not only in Germany but everywhere the trade unions have developed in this manner. We see it in the United States with the big trade unions led by Gompers. We see it again, quite recently, in recent weeks in Britain, in the giant strike in Italy that was defeated with the help of the reactionary Socialist Party. Everywhere we see the old trade unions and the old Social-Democratic parties joining hand in hand. They work together hand in hand, in order to bridge class antagonisms, while we as Communists have the task – which we must fulfil – of making these more apparent. The development and the entire structure of the old trade unions makes them bodies that function inside capitalist society and are adapted to it.

The initiative and determination of individuals or even quite large minorities could not find living space in these trade unions. It was simply an impossibility for significant minorities to make headway against the will of the leaders of the individual unions, given their thickly webbed laws, statutes, and regulations. Everywhere we see that a substantial majority of members active in the union are assaulted and must submit against their will to the dictatorship of the leaders, who have a firm grip on the reins of the organisation, indeed its entire apparatus, including its finances. For this reason, these large masses of members are absolutely unable to be active in a revolutionary fashion. They are condemned to subjugation and forced against their will to collaborate in maintaining the present capitalist trade unions. In our view, it is not possible to revolutionise such trade unions.

There have been many attempts of this kind, and we can now observe how the first and most emphatic of them is developing in Germany. The comrades of the VKPD undertook such an effort to revolutionise the trade unions by forming cells in them, Communist cells. But the logic of such cells is to disrupt and destroy the unions. Deny it as you will, wherever such cells have been set up, what we see in reality is a destruction of the fabric of the national trade union. It is evident everywhere that the formation of cells does not change the unions' character and does not break the leaders' grip on the membership. Rather, what we observe is that so long as the masses are tied organisationally to these counterrevolutionary union leaders, they are inclined to follow the slogans of these leaders more than those of the Communist parties.

We have experienced typical examples of this in Central Germany, where broad masses who are members of the VKPD did not follow the slogans of their party because, as members of the union, they followed its slogans against the strike. And so it is, wherever you look. Comrade Zinoviev told us here yesterday that the trade unions must be bodies that undertake the construction of the future society, that have as much influence as possible in building the communist society. Look at the past of the unions, the tasks they took on previously, and their present struggle for the revolution. What we see is the opposite of the way they are utilised in a revolution and what they must be made into today.

In Germany, even during the War, a strong aversion developed against the trade-union movement, even a splitting away of large segments of workers from the old unions. When the revolution began, in its first weeks, we believed that the trade-union question was not so urgent. At the founding convention of the Spartacus League [KPD] this question was not resolved in the way that is necessary today.[8] At that time we believed that the wave of revolution would advance rapidly. (We were not alone in this belief. Other comrades too, including the Russian comrades, were wrong about the pace of the revolution.) We thought the pace of revolution in Germany and other countries would be quicker, and the trade-union question would not play the decisive role that it has in fact played in the course of the revolution. To repeat, even during the War, significant portions of the workers left the old unions, because their betrayal was more evident than before the War. That is why, in the very first months of the revolution, the Spartacus League slogan to the working masses was, 'Out of the trade unions!'.

This slogan received a strong response, above all among the working masses in the Ruhr district. Here, in the German miners' federation, the betrayal had been so blatantly obvious that a large portion of the miners took up this slogan and founded their own factory organisations. Later, of course, the best leaders of the revolution – Rosa Luxemburg, Karl Liebknecht, Leo Jogiches, and thousands and thousands of unknown proletarians – fell to the ground. Levi and his clique won the upper hand, and this slogan was transformed, indeed reversed, because they feared the struggle. They wished to evade the struggle against the reactionary trade-union bureaucracy. They adopted the slogan of going into the trade unions and revolutionising them from within, of winning them over.

That was carried further in the course of the revolution. They went over to forming cells. Wherever that was done, it soon became evident that the trade unions could not remain unified in their previous form. Indeed not only members of the cells but entire units of the organisations were expelled from the German federations. Today, in Germany, there are cases where all former members of cells and indeed entire segments of the organisation have been expelled from the federations. So, in reality, the result is a wrecking of the trade unions. The old trade-union bureaucracy claims that this has wrecked and split apart the unions, and I say that too. The comrades of the VKPD, on the other hand, claim that this is not the case, and that they form these cells to build the unions. They believe that they can breathe a revolutionary spirit into the unions, which have become firm bastions of reaction.

Comrades, as was said yesterday, the working class is subjugated by sword and revolver and by deception, by both the army and the trade-union

---

8. At the KPD founding congress, 30 December 1918 to 1 January 1919, participation in the trade unions was a point of contention, with some delegates calling for boycotting the unions. The congress avoided taking a position on the question. See Riddell (ed.) 1986, pp. 186–91.

bureaucracy. You cannot breathe a Communist spirit into the standing army; there is no dispute about that. Just as you cannot convert the standing army into an instrument for revolution, so too you cannot do this with the instruments of deception, the trade unions. That is how things are developing everywhere. That is why the Communists' slogan must be not to win over the trade unions but to destroy them and, simultaneously, to build new organisations.

Comrades, we must today recognise and clearly define the form needed by the proletariat in order, once it is victorious, to maintain and secure its power. That is why even today it is necessary, especially in the highly developed Western European countries, that we bring the masses of the proletariat, as far as possible, to create organs whose task is to take control of production. Heckert said yesterday that the cells to be established in the factories must develop beyond them into industry-wide organisations. We are striving for this same goal, but in a more distinct form, through the *Unionen* [syndicalist unions] of different types established during the German revolution.

The old workers' syndicate of miners, which I referred to earlier, displays in its entire being and direction a different character than the old organisations of the earlier period. It stands in fierce struggle with reaction, with the Amsterdamers, and it shows that it can build organs capable of taking control of production. Granted, these organisations are not yet free of weaknesses, but they will become purer and more solid in the course of the revolution. For example, in the miners' syndicate, they still believe that the legally established factory councils are a tool for revolution. But even the miners' workplace and industry-wide organisation will come to understand, in the course of the revolution, that this law on factory councils is a blatant means of deception.

The General Workers' Union of Germany [AAUD], which works closely with the KAPD, declared from the start and recognised that the trade unions are today going down another path, that they must be built in a different manner, and that other methods must be found to struggle and fight. The AAUD rejects wholesale the methods of struggle previously practised in the trade unions. The AAUD statutes specify as a precondition of membership in the factory organisation that the member must support the dictatorship of the proletariat. Its statutes also state that members must reject the old rotted-out weapon of political action, namely participation in parliamentary elections. Out of its ranks and its factory organisations it creates the councils that will be the organs exercising power when the day of struggle comes. On that day, the masses of the proletariat will support these organs.

These councils, comrades, are not like the fake councils we saw arise in Germany at the beginning of 1919. They are not councils anchored in the laws of the capitalist state, constituted and elected on the basis of the law on factory councils, and charged with ensuring that factory production rises and that law and order reigns on the shop floor. Rather, these are councils formed by the working masses themselves, who are themselves working at the carpenter's vice and bench, leading the factory workers in their daily struggle, and giving expression to the will of the comrades working in the factory. These are councils rooted in the masses, showing them the path of struggle. These councils, comrades, these organs, will truly have the working masses with them on the day of battle.

We must establish the preconditions so that we will not see – even in Germany – conditions like those of 1918, when the working masses and soldiers created councils. At that time the German proletariat did not understand the concept of councils. They knew nothing of them except the few crumbs of information that had come our way from Russia. And if we do not build these councils today, in the present revolutionary epoch, and thus show the masses in action the way forward, then there is an urgent danger that in a coming revolutionary upsurge the proletariat will be once again be betrayed, and that it will once again find that we do not have the organs needed to secure our victory. That is why we are obliged to create these bodies everywhere.

It is not only in Germany that we see developments taking this path. This is true in a number of highly developed capitalist countries. In Britain we see a current, the shop stewards, conducting a vigorous struggle against British trade unionism. We see that their influence today is numerically small, because these workers' organisations have to struggle not only against the trade-union bureaucracy but simultaneously against the full power of the government. In almost every country, the old-line trade unions have become arms of the government. They enjoy very broad governmental protection. After the battles in Central Germany, we observed that in the giant factories the workers are now obliged to join the old trade-union organisations. The employers exert pressure on them to do that if they wish to work again in the factory. Everywhere we see events developing in this fashion. And these comrades still insist that it will be possible to win over these trade unions from the inside and imbue them with a Communist spirit. This is such a delusion that we can make no concessions to it. We believe that this is not possible, and we see this belief confirmed in life. We must create organs today that can take up the struggle against these bulwarks defending the capitalist state.

Comrades, the international workers' movement, the international Communist movement must focus its attention on this. To avoid a mistake, to perceive the course of events in the capitalist countries, it must take this path, in order to be in a position, when it is able to win power in the capitalist countries, to maintain its grip on this power. As we can see today, the old trade unions even now have the task of masking the class antagonisms that are growing more and more acute, of bridging them over, and of deluding and tricking the workers. All the more, therefore, is it our task to show the workers in life that it is possible now to create working organs that show the working masses another path. These organs will show the workers in life what a council system must be. This cannot be done in the old trade unions. Our conception of trade unions is to build them as factory organisations at the point of production, where the great masses of workers are together, where they form a great unity in the workplace. Here each worker must be drawn into activity as much as possible, in the shaping of their organisation, so that he gains an interest in the broad course of development and activity.

Comrades, we must not create national trade unions in which a dictatorship at the centre rules from the top down. That must not be. On the contrary, the will of the masses, the highly developed industrial working masses, must find expression from the bottom up. The source of this power is in the factory itself. Here in the process of production we must educate and school the workers to truly become instruments of revolution. So centralisation from the top down cannot be the basis for shaping the trade unions; indeed, quite the opposite. In the factories, we unite the workers in factory organisations. The workers in the factories elect their councils, their institutions, which represent their interests.

Comrade Heckert said yesterday that we, the Communist Workers' Party [KAPD], refuse to take action on issues of the day; that we always keep our focus solely on the overriding goal. It is not our task as Communists to throw the slogans of daily struggle at the working masses. Rather, these slogans must be raised by the working masses themselves in the factories. We must always point out to these working masses that resolving these daily issues will not improve their conditions, let alone bring about the downfall of capitalist society. Rather we, as Communists, have the task of always bringing home to these broad masses the overriding goal, the overthrow of capitalism and the construction of a communist society. We Communists have the task of fighting alongside them and leading them forward in these daily struggles. So, comrades, we do not reject the daily struggle, but, rather, place ourselves at the head of the masses in these struggles and always show them the road to the great goal of communism.

That is the task of Communist parties in these workers' organisations.

We are well aware that these economic organisations can only too readily decay into opportunism. Everywhere we perceive the danger that they will fail to understand the goal. We see this not only with the German trade unions, but with unions everywhere that have broken free from the old confederations and are struggling in revolutionary fashion. We saw this in Italy with the occupation of the factories, and also, in part, with the IWW [Industrial Workers of the World], which rejects political struggle in principle. Everywhere we see that this leads to the organisations losing their depth.

The task of Communists is to fill these trade unions with a revolutionary spirit, the spirit of communism, so that they do not stray onto the path of opportunism. So we take part in all these struggles. Wherever struggles arise, Communists have the bounden duty to forge ahead. Comrades, in founding these factory organisations, we can and must not forget to link them together on a broad scale into a block, which forms a unified whole. These factory organisations are unified locally, regionally, and nationally, such that we see the foundations of a council system developing inside capitalist society. It is possible at least to constitute and hold on to the council system in broad outline and familiarise the working class with this concept.

We will conduct the struggle and school the working class along these lines, educating them so they become instruments to tear down the capitalist state and build a communist one. If we do that, comrades, we will have already created the preconditions, within capitalist society and, when the revolution comes, we will not stand there with empty hands. We will have familiarised the working class with the concept that we absolutely have to instil in them. We must promote and help shape the development of these organisations and fill them with the spirit of communism.

**Schulz**: What percentage of Dittmann is there in this concept?

**Bergmann**: I don't understand why you would compare this with Dittmann, Comrade Schulz. Today we see organisations of many countries coming together for the congress of the Red International of Labour Unions, all imbued with the idea of driving through the world revolution, filling the masses with a revolutionary spirit, and overthrowing capitalist society. So we must find ways and means of uniting these masses, as much as possible, around a common fundamental line, uniting them in such a manner that as much scope as possible is accorded to the individual countries, in a manner appropriate to their structure. The movement is not identical in every country; there are diverse tendencies and possibilities for development. In the United States, IWW members belong simultaneously to the old trade unions, and we recognise that they perhaps have no choice in the matter right now. But if they go into these trade unions, at the same time they have another organisation. They build a new organisation, and that is the core of their movement.

But that is not the present situation in Germany. If the VKPD comrades would recognise – as they must, in our view – that winning the trade unions is nonsense, that it will not work, then they must take other paths. Three million or two and a half million trade-union members in Germany have now decided for affiliation to Moscow. However, this fact means nothing for us unless they simultaneously break from the spell of their leaders. This programmatic statement, this sympathy with Moscow means nothing. Unless the attempt is made to break them free from the old trade unions, we will see that even though these members have opted for Moscow through a ballot or by raising their hand, when the battle breaks out they will follow the call of their old trade-union bosses and leaders. We see that in Chemnitz, Comrade Heckert, where you live. And if you have a different point of view, produce evidence to sustain it.

Comrades, events are moving quickly. If we believe that revolution is developing, we must absolutely move into action. Otherwise the revolution will take us by surprise. We do not think that a simple declaration in favour of affiliation, made by a segment of trade-union members, constitutes evidence that the cell policy is revolutionising the masses. More evidence is needed.

It is nonsense to project revolutionising the trade unions in countries where they have become firm pillars of capitalism. To think this can be done is a false start. The nine or ten million German trade unionists, if they were revolutionary, if they were organs of the revolution, could actually seize power today. If they were on our side, they could on any day, at any hour, utilise the situation to overthrow capitalist society and kindle revolution in Germany and thus drive the world revolution forward. We see these bodies failing everywhere, as they must, and that is why we demand and insist, in the interests of the revolution, that they must be destroyed, before we can arrive at the victory of the revolution.

Comrades, it is true that the decay of the trade unions in the highly developed capitalist countries is not yet that far advanced, the struggle within them is not yet that intense, and we on our side have not yet given it sufficient emphasis. The reason for this is that the beginnings of revolution in these countries are more political than economic in character. We see today that the economic question has perhaps moved somewhat more to the foreground, and that the economic basis of the struggle is more clearly defined. As a result, the decay and destruction of the trade unions is proceeding apace. In Britain and in Germany we see that, although the trade-union bureaucrats were guilty of at least as many sins during the War as the political parties in prerevolutionary times, the trade unions did not decay at a comparable pace, because demands were not made on them in a forceful manner. However, comrades, by this I do not mean to say and to maintain that the political organisations have now fulfilled their task. That is not how this should be interpreted. Rather, what we are seeing everywhere, as I have said, is that the economic question has now risen to a higher level and pressed its way to the fore. The trade unions from the prerevolutionary period cannot resolve this task of the revolution, and that is why they must be destroyed.

Comrades, on the trade-union question we stand in sharp opposition to the majority of comrades present and represented here. The fact that we have come to this conclusion and hold to it more firmly every day is not because it is our own idea, an idea with no foundation. Rather, it is because we have recognised, through the revolution's course in Germany and other countries, including now in Britain, that we must now create bodies capable of taking over production. We take this stand in the interests of the revolution and its development, and we must cling firmly to this position in order to avoid obstructing the revolution in these countries. We recognise the way things are developing with regard to the economic situation in each country; we draw the appropriate conclusions; we will act on that basis. Only if we see and understand the situation clearly and draw appropriate conclusions will we be able to perform genuine services to the revolution and create genuine preparatory bodies that will serve, on the day of revolutionary victory, as the bulwark on which the dictatorship of the proletariat can be constructed. There is no other way to do it. It cannot be done by leaving the old counterrevolutionary organisations in place and trying to undermine them from within. Rather, we must create new bodies to tear down capitalism and simultaneously build communism. Only then will the victory of the revolution be secure.

**William Earsman** (Australia): Comrades, I was very pleased to hear, in Comrade Zinoviev's speech, that the Third Communist International has no intention of attempting to take control of the trade unions. We, in Australia, could not have supported any concept in which the Third International did not afford the trade unions adequate scope for their development. In saying this, I do not mean to imply that we should not influence the trade unions; this should be done but in a different way. Let me explain to you what we have achieved in Australia. Please note – especially the German comrades – that, in terms of the level of trade-union organisation, Australia is probably the most highly developed country outside Russia. I say that in full understanding of what has been achieved in other countries to this end.

This morning I received news that the first trade-union congress in Australia, which met during the first week of June, resolved to affiliate to the Red International of Labour Unions.[9] I believe this is the first country where such a thing has happened.

When I left in March, the Communists expected that they would receive approximately 45 per cent of the votes at the congress. Now, however, we

---

9. The All-Australian Trades Union Congress, representing 700,000 workers, met in Melbourne, 20–25 June 1921.

learn that in the last three months they have won over another 40 per cent and have now received a vote of 85 per cent.

Our situation in Australia differs from that of many other countries in that we were able – and I believe we can demonstrate this to our friends of the KAPD – to achieve something in the old trade unions.

The old 'craft unions', as we called them, have agreed, after about three years of propaganda, to accept fully the proposal to merge into industrial unions. In other words, they have formed red trade unions, and in doing so, they have not only adopted mere resolutions and written books on it, but have carried it out in life: the Australian workplaces and factories, of which there are two hundred thousand, are now a firm component of the so-called OBU.

But the OBU, or 'One Big Union', is not syndicalist, in the way the word is understood in many countries. Far from being syndicalist, it fully recognises the principles of the trade-union International. Even though we had engaged in the process of imbuing the trade unions with Communist ideas for only a short time, the leaders of the unions during the last eighteen months have been more honourable in nature.

And now, comrades, I must explain to you a situation that will please some of you and displease others. Parliament served as the means to cleanse the trade unions in Australia. Here is how it happened. We have about fourteen parliaments in Australia, two in each state and one for the entire country. In every state other than Victoria, there was a Labor government. Not just once or twice, but for a whole number of years. You will find that during the last twenty-five years the Labor Party was in power more often than the National Party.

What does that mean? It means that if you are a leading official of a trade-union movement, you automatically climb up from the trade-union ranks into parliament. The result was that our leaders tried to remain close to the masses, because they knew that they could advance to an easier and more pleasant occupation than they had enjoyed as trade-union representatives. But, from 1917 to 1920, the trade-union movement in Australia declined. It did not perish, but it displayed no vigour. This was chiefly because a major strike broke out at the end of 1917, which spread from New South Wales to Victoria, and ended with the persecution and jailing of a large number of leaders.[10]

During the next few years, the task was to free the leaders. There was really no revolutionary movement in the country during this period. When

---

10. A strike by railway workers in New South Wales began on 2 August 1917 to protest speedup. It soon spread to other industries and states, involving some 100,000 workers. Confronted by the use of scabs backed by employer and government repression and victimisation, the strike ended unsuccessfully on 15 October.

these men were freed, we were compelled to catch up with the movement in Europe, and the trade-union leaders understood developments in Europe and were well aware that if they stood by the Labor Party, as it was at that time, their days were numbered.

They understood that the tide of the revolutionary movement in Australia was rising, and if they had trust in this movement and wished it to grow, then their place was within it, that is, in the Communist movement. These were the leaders that founded the Communist Party in 1920, and the message I received this morning indicates that they did their job well. They succeeded in winning a majority of votes at the first congress of trade unions held in June.

We should note that this congress was convened not by the revolutionaries within the trade unions but by the Labor Party, which realised that it was collapsing and tried to win the masses over again by seeking to unite the unions and proposing a programme that would bind them to their past.

But the Communists were alert and understood the value of the trade unions. As for the IWW, despite its agitation and the considerable influence it enjoyed, it had no support in the unions. On the contrary, the Communists utilised this influence with good results and for their own purposes, as I have described. I hope that, when the congress takes its decisions on this question, it will do so in accord with the theses of Comrade Zinoviev.

I will close by taking up one other issue: the question of [trade-union] neutrality. In my opinion, this should be categorically rejected. Such a proposal is completely impossible. I will go further: those who favour neutrality do not understand the situation. Surely they must grasp that sooner or later they will be driven from this stance and have to confront the question of which way to turn – right or left? Why not make that decision straight away? Why put off the evil day when they will be driven from their posts?

Today the workers stand on firm ground. Their position is just as clear today as it will be at a time of unrest or possible social revolution. Given this fact, I hope that our friends of the KAPD and the syndicalists themselves will understand before this congress ends, before it is adjourned, that their place is within the old trade unions. There is great scope for work there that will be fruitful and lead to the goal for which we all yearn.

**Kolarov** (Chair): The next session of the trade-union congress convenes tomorrow evening at 7:00 p.m. in the trade-union building. The next session of our congress will begin tomorrow morning at 11:00 a.m. On the agenda is discussion of the Russian party's policies. The reporter is Comrade Lenin. This session is now adjourned.

*(The session is adjourned at 12:00 midnight.)*

# Session 17 – 5 July 1921, 12 noon
## Russian Communist Party

*Tribute to Comrade Zetkin: Heckert, Zetkin, Loriot. Lenin: Report on the policies of the Communist Party of Russia. Discussion on Lenin's report. Speakers: Sachs, Radek, Kollontai, Trotsky, Kerran, Hempel, Roland-Holst, Bukharin. Resolution on the Russian Communist Party's course of action.*

**Loriot** (Chair): Before we proceed to the agenda point and give the floor to Comrade Lenin for his report on the situation in Russia, I wish to inform the congress that today is the sixty-fifth birthday of our dear comrade Clara Zetkin. (*Enthusiastic applause*) For this reason I give the floor to a member of the German delegation, Comrade Heckert.[1]

---

1. July was in fact Zetkin's sixty-fourth birthday. Heckert later explained the circumstances as follows:

Clara Zetkin bitterly attacked us. That was why we, especially I in my speech, retaliated in kind. But it happened that the day following these attacks Clara was celebrating her sixty-fourth birthday. Of course, at the congress it was necessary to hail the old revolutionary who was in the vanguard of our struggle. A large bouquet of roses was brought for her.

But then the question arose as to who was to present the flowers to her. I was chosen. Of course, I tried to shun that assignment and used dozens of excuses, but Lenin took me firmly by the arm and said:

'Comrade Heckert, you pursued a wrong policy in Germany, for which you have good reason to be angry. Clara merely told you the truth about your policy; maybe not all her words were appropriate, but yesterday you, too, attacked her bitterly and unjustly. Make up for it with a bouquet of roses today.'

I tried my best to do it. Clara accepted my bouquet with gratitude. When I left the rostrum Lenin said to me jokingly, 'Here you are, everything has turned out fine.'

Bezvesel'nyi and Grinberg 1968, pp. 228–9.

**Heckert**: Comrades, the German delegation is fulfilling a joyful duty. Among us is an old combatant for socialism, our comrade Clara Zetkin, who is today celebrating her sixty-fifth birthday. And for the workers' International, the name Clara Zetkin represents a programme. Clara Zetkin did not wait for her later years to come to the socialist movement. While still young she joined the workers' movement with a burning spirit and has remained until this day its loyal and self-sacrificing soldier.

Clara Zetkin has behind her an extraordinarily rich life of struggle, during which she has been persecuted and slandered by the tyrannical bourgeois states and also slandered by many who struggled together with her for many years. When, for many years, the Anti-Socialist Law weighed down on the German working class and the layer of that class that led the way in struggle against the old Prussia, the old Germany, Clara Zetkin, our old comrade, stood firm in the front ranks.[2]

After the Anti-Socialist Law was overturned, and right-wing currents became evident in the party, Clara Zetkin took her stand with the left wing of the party. She was one of the most vigorous opponents of revisionist ideas. Together with Rosa Luxemburg, Franz Mehring, and a few others, she put her pen at the disposal of the radical current in the International. She contended against the ideas of Bernstein with fiery words.[3] During the long period in which Karl Kautsky was still in the radical wing of the German Social-Democratic Party, she stood protectively at his side. When a genuine left wing took shape in German Social Democracy, just before the War, she joined it.

Her heart was always with the proletarians engaged in genuine struggle. She was fully committed to this militant layer of the proletariat. She rejected half-measures. And when the War broke out, it was Clara Zetkin, as editor of *Die Gleichheit*, who stood firm against the German Social Democrats, against jingoistic patriotism, against social chauvinism. When the proletarians were

---

2. The Anti-Socialist Laws were passed in 1878 by the German government of Chancellor Otto von Bismarck. While not banning the Social-Democratic Party outright, they outlawed the propagation of its views through the press and public meetings and banned its local organisations and all Social-Democratic-led trade unions, allowing only parliamentary activity. Through its underground activities and taking advantage of legal openings remaining to it, the SPD was able to grow greatly in membership and influence. The laws were repealed in 1890 under pressure from the rising working-class movement.

3. In 1896–98 Eduard Bernstein, a prominent member of the SPD, openly rejected Marxism's revolutionary goals and put forward the view that capitalism's contradictions were abating. These positions, codified in his book *Evolutionary Socialism*, were labelled 'revisionism' and became the subject of an intense debate in the world socialist movement. Bernstein's views were rejected by resolutions of the 1901 and 1903 congresses of the SPD and by the 1904 congress of the Second International.

driven apart, it was she who helped open the road toward reconstituting their movement, in order to prepare for the victory of proletarian revolution. It was also she who, during the War, when a left wing came together and separated off from German Social Democracy, associated herself with these forces, even while arguing with them.[4]

And, after the War, during the revolution, Clara Zetkin came to the Spartacus League [KPD] and was among its best minds. She was a leader, a fearless leader of the small Spartacus movement in Germany. And then, when we created the United Communist Party, she joined its Zentrale and became one of its most important figures.

As we have seen at this congress, there are disagreements between the present Zentrale of the VKPD and Clara Zetkin. Yet these differences over facts never led – not for a single hour – to any personal spitefulness. That cannot and will not be, because we have such high respect for our old fighter. We know what she has contributed to our movement; we know that she will always stand with the proletarian masses. And we hope – no, it is not merely a hope, it is a certainty – that she will be with us again. We know that the dispute that arose between us out of objective circumstances will not last beyond this congress. And so I believe that the International and the German delegation will long have in Clara Zetkin a worthy fighter on the left wing of the workers' movement, a red general of the great proletarian army, who will assist us in striding forward to victory. And it is in this spirit that we convey our birthday congratulations to her and ask the entire congress to join us in these greetings. (*Loud and prolonged applause and cheers*)

**Clara Zetkin**: Comrades, your recognition and praise takes my breath away. When you deal blows against me, I feel quite satisfied in the conviction that in all these struggles I am serving the cause, the achievement of clarity in driving the revolution forward. But when you praise me, I am humbled. I feel everything that I strived for and could not achieve. I feel everything that life and the idea of revolution have given me, and everything that I unfortunately still owe the revolution because I could not do more than my strength permitted.

Comrades, what I did could not have been more natural and obvious. I always obeyed my inner nature and do not deserve any praise for that. I cannot be anything other than what I am; I could not have done other than what I have done. Should the river be praised for flowing down the valley? Should

---

4. A reference to the 1917 split in the SPD that led to the formation of the USPD. Up until the formation of the KPD in December 1918, Spartacus League cadres, including Zetkin, also belonged to the USPD as a way to gain members and influence.

the bird be praised for singing? It was only natural. And so I served the revolution out of an inner necessity to serve the revolution.

I will not dwell on all the fine things that Comrade Heckert has said about me. But there is one thing that I am duty-bound to say to you: I am profoundly indebted, for my development and for what I have accomplished, to German theory and practice; I also learned from the history and example of our French and British brothers. However, the sense of determination that I have placed at the service of the revolution and – let me say this without any bourgeois flavour – for my revolutionary moral sense I am eternally indebted to the example of the Russian revolutionaries, the Russian Social Democrats, and the Bolsheviks. For what I have become in a moral sense and the measure of energy that I have committed to the revolution, I must thank my long and intimate association with the Russian Revolution, from the 1870s onwards.

There is something else that I must say here. I cannot stand before you here without being overcome by the memory of a person who was part of my being and will always remain so: Rosa Luxemburg. Everything that I was, everything that I achieved, was done in common with Rosa Luxemburg. And I cannot restrain expressing my pain that she today no longer stands beside me and is no longer among us. All these flowers here: my spirit lays them on her grave.

Comrades, I am too moved to give you a fine speech. My heart has only one desire – and you can all contribute to its achievement – namely that I will not go to the grave without first having witnessed the revolution in Germany and, if possible, in other countries as well. (*Loud applause*) My work and struggle is imbued with only one resolve: to contribute to the proletarian revolution, to the victory of the revolutionary proletariat. (*Prolonged, enthusiastic applause and cheers*)

**Loriot** (Chair): Dear Comrade Clara Zetkin, I am happy to have the honour of joining with the German delegation in expressing the fraternal solidarity of the entire congress.

Dear Comrade Zetkin, I cannot find any great words. I would rather exert myself to speak simply, and I am convinced that I can best express the feelings of us all if I let my heart speak for me.

Today is a holiday for the Communist family gathered here. It is interrupting for a moment its difficult labour of readying the fields of revolution for cultivation and is gathering around you and celebrating your beautiful and noble life. The German delegation and Comrade Heckert have portrayed in broad strokes the stages of this glorious life. But you alone, dear comrade, know the cost in suffering hidden in these forty-three years of harsh struggle, full of constant effort, pure and profound joy, but also bitter tears.

You have just called to mind the death of your dear comrades Rosa Luxemburg and Karl Liebknecht. Truly you alone can tell us the meaning of all these memories, linked to the efforts of forty-three years – the efforts in Stuttgart and Copenhagen, where you were present.[5] Today all this lies so far in the past. Without neglecting your struggles as part of the revolutionary movement's Far Left, against currents in the old Social Democracy, for me it is your work during the War that is above all memorable. You belong to the international proletariat, which can only follow your work during these tragic years with admiring recognition. The proletariat cannot forget that it was you who convened the Bern congress, in face of almost universal collapse – the international women's conference that said what the deluded proletariat was not able to say.[6] I will not evoke every stage of this struggle during the War. I will only remind you of something that is very dear to us, the Communists of France.

Before the Tours Congress (1920), we knew that you wanted to bring us the glow of your authority, but we were dubious regarding the outcome of such an attempt. We were aware that the French police knew you far too well to let you through. I knew they would never permit you to make this trip. But we also knew that a women like you would triumph over the police. Imagine our joy and the bourgeoisie's dismay as it was learned that you had succeeded in crossing the border, so we could greet you at our congress.[7] Dear Comrade Zetkin, the cause of revolution, which you have done so much to promote, is now to a considerable extent a reality. The Russian Revolution and the development of the revolution in Germany – signs of which are already evident, together with the efforts of our other comrades – give us confidence that it will be granted you, Comrade Zetkin, to see your work crowned with success. The revolution is under way, and you will live to see the fruits of your labour: the full and final liberation of the world proletariat.

That is all that we desire. (*Ovation*)

**Loriot** (Chair): I give the floor to Comrade Lenin for his report on the policies of the Russian Communist Party.

---

5. For the intervention by left-wing forces at the 1907 Stuttgart Congress, see p. 106, n. 10. The Second International's Copenhagen congress, held 28 August to 4 September 1910, saw a continuation of the struggle by left-wing forces. See Gankin and Fisher (eds.) 1940, pp. 69–78, and Riddell (ed.) 1984, pp. 69–71.

6. As secretary of the International Socialist Women's Bureau, Zetkin initiated and chaired the International Conference of Socialist Women in Bern, 26–28 March 1915. The conference, held less than a year after the collapse of the Second International in August 1914, voted to call for mass resistance by proletarian women to World War I. For its appeal, see Riddell (ed.) 1984, pp. 277–9.

7. For Zetkin's trip to France in 1920, see p. 251, n. 11.

## Report on Policies of Communist Party of Russia

**Lenin:**[8] Comrades, strictly speaking I was not in a position to prepare a proper report. All that I was able to properly prepare for you was the translation of my pamphlet on the tax in kind and the theses on tactics of the Russian party.[9] To this I merely want to add a few explanations and remarks.

*The international situation*

I think that to explain our party's tactics we must first of all examine the *international situation*. You have already had a detailed discussion of the economic position of capitalism internationally, and the congress has adopted a resolution on this subject. I deal with this subject in my theses very briefly and only from the political standpoint. I leave aside the economic basis. But I think that in discussing the international position of our republic we must, politically, take into account the fact that a certain equilibrium has now undoubtedly set in. Of course, this equilibrium exists only in quite a limited sense, between the forces that have been waging an open, armed struggle against each other for the supremacy of this or that leading class. It is an equilibrium between bourgeois society, the international bourgeoisie as a whole, and Soviet Russia. It is only in respect to this military struggle, I say, that a certain equilibrium has been brought about in the international situation. It must be emphasised, of course, that this is only a relative equilibrium, and a very unstable one. Much inflammable material has accumulated in capitalist countries, as well as in those countries which up to now have been regarded merely as the objects and not as the subjects of history, that is, in the colonies and semi-colonies. It is quite possible, therefore, that insurrections, great battles and revolutions may break out there sooner or later, and very suddenly too. During the past few years we have witnessed the direct struggle waged by the international bourgeoisie against the first proletarian republic. This struggle has been at the centre of the world political situation, and it is there that a change has taken place. Inasmuch as the attempt of the international bourgeoisie to strangle our republic has failed, an equilibrium has set in, and a very unstable one it is, of course. (*Loud applause*)

We know perfectly well, of course, that the international bourgeoisie is at present much stronger than our republic, and only the peculiar combination

---

8. The translation is based on *LCW* 32, pp. 478–96 and has been edited to conform with the German text.
9. Lenin, 'The Tax in Kind (The Significance of the New Policy and Its Conditions)' in *LCW*, 32, pp. 329–65. The theses on the tactics of the Russian Communist Party can be found on pp. 970–6 of the present volume.

of circumstances is preventing it from continuing the war against us. Even in the last few weeks we have witnessed fresh attempts in the Far East to renew the invasion,[10] and there is not the slightest doubt that similar attempts will continue. Our party has no doubts whatever on that score. The important thing for us is to establish that an unstable equilibrium does exist, and that we must take advantage of this respite, taking into consideration the characteristic features of the present situation, adapting our tactics to the specific features of this situation, and never forgetting that the necessity for armed struggle may arise again quite suddenly. Our task is still to organise and build up the Red Army. In connection with the food problem, too, we must still continue to think first of all of our Red Army. We can adopt no other course in the present international situation, when we must still be prepared for fresh attacks and fresh attempts at invasion on the part of the international bourgeoisie. In regard to our practical policy, however, the fact that a certain equilibrium has been reached in the international situation has some significance, in the sense that we must admit that, although the revolutionary movement has made progress, the development of the international revolution this year has not proceeded along as straight a line as we had expected.

When we started the international revolution, we did so not in the belief that we could leap ahead of the revolution's development, but because a number of circumstances compelled us to start it. We thought that either the international revolution will come to our assistance, and in that case our victory will be fully assured, or we will do our modest revolutionary work in the conviction that even in the event of defeat we shall have served the cause of the revolution by enabling other revolutions to profit from our experience.

It was clear to us that, without the support of the world revolution, the victory of the proletarian revolution was impossible. Before the revolution, and even after it, we thought that either revolution will break out in the other countries, in the capitalistically more developed countries, immediately, or at least very quickly, or we must perish. In spite of this conviction, we did all we possibly could to preserve the Soviet system under all circumstances, come what may, because we knew that we were working not only for ourselves, but also for the international revolution. We knew this. We repeatedly expressed this conviction before the October Revolution, immediately after it, and at the time we signed the Brest-Litovsk Peace Treaty. And this was right, of course; it was correct in general.

---

10. In May 1921 counterrevolutionary Russian forces backed by Japanese troops seized control in Vladivostok, then part of the pro-Soviet Far Eastern Republic. In October 1922 Japanese forces were forced to withdraw in face of the Red Army's advance, and Soviet power was re-established the following month.

Actually, however, events did not proceed along as straight a line as we had expected. In the other big, capitalistically most developed countries the revolution has not broken out to this day. True, we can say with satisfaction that the revolution is developing all over the world, and it is only thanks to this that the international bourgeoisie is unable to strangle us, in spite of the fact that, militarily and economically, it is a hundred times stronger than we are. (*Loud applause*)

In point 2 of the theses, I examine the manner in which this situation arose, and the conclusions that must be drawn from it. Let me add that my final conclusion is the following: the development of the international revolution, which we predicted, is proceeding, but not along as straight a line as we had expected. It is clear at the first glance that after the conclusion of peace, bad as it was, it proved impossible to call forth revolution in other capitalist countries, although we know that the signs of revolution were very considerable and numerous, in fact, much more considerable and numerous than we thought at the time. Pamphlets are now beginning to appear which tell us that during the past few years and months these revolutionary symptoms in Europe have been much more serious than we had suspected.

What, in that case, must we do now? We must now thoroughly prepare for revolution and make a deep study of its concrete development in the advanced capitalist countries. This is the first lesson we must draw from the international situation. As for our Russian republic, we must take advantage of this brief respite in order to adapt our tactics to this zigzag line of history. This equilibrium is very important politically, because we clearly see that in many Western European countries, where the broad mass of the working class, and possibly the overwhelming majority of the population, is organised, the main bulwark of the bourgeoisie consists of the hostile working-class organisations affiliated to the Second and Two-and-a-Half Internationals.

I speak of this in point 2 of the theses, and in this connection I think that I need deal with only two points, which were discussed during the debate on the question of tactics and strategy. First, winning over the majority of the proletariat. The more organised the proletariat is in a capitalistically developed country, the greater is the thoroughness that history demands of us in preparing for revolution, and the more thoroughly must we win over the majority of the working class. Second, the main bulwark of capitalism in the industrially developed capitalist countries is the part of the working class that is organised in the Second and Two-and-a-Half Internationals. Without the support of this section of the workers, these counterrevolutionary elements within the working class, the international bourgeoisie would be altogether unable to retain its position. (*Loud applause*)

## The movement in the colonies

Here I would also like to emphasise the significance of the movement in the colonies. In this respect we see in all the old parties, in all the bourgeois and petty-bourgeois workers' parties affiliated to the Second and Two-and-a Half Internationals, survivals of the old sentimental views: they are in full sympathy with oppressed colonial and semi-colonial peoples. The movement in the colonial countries is still regarded as an insignificant national and peaceful movement. But this is not so. It has undergone a great change since the beginning of the twentieth century: millions and hundreds of millions, in fact the overwhelming majority of the population of the globe, are now coming forward as independent, active, and revolutionary factors. It is perfectly clear that in the impending decisive battles in the world revolution, the movement of the majority of the population of the globe, initially directed towards national liberation, will turn against capitalism and imperialism and will, perhaps, play a much more revolutionary part than we expect. It is important to emphasise the fact that, for the first time in our International, we have taken up the question of preparing for this struggle. Of course, there are many more difficulties in this enormous sphere than in any other, but at all events the movement is advancing. And in spite of the fact that the masses of toilers – the peasants in the colonial countries – are still backward, they will play a very important revolutionary part in the coming phases of the world revolution. (*Loud applause*)

## The internal situation in Soviet Russia

As regards the internal political position of our republic, I must start with a close examination of class relationships. During the past few months changes have taken place in this sphere, and we have witnessed the formation of new organisations of the exploiting class directed against us. The aim of socialism is to abolish classes. In the front ranks of the exploiting class we find the big landowners and the industrial capitalists. In regard to them, the work of destruction is fairly easy; it can be completed within a few months, and sometimes even a few weeks or days. We in Russia have expropriated our exploiters, the big landowners as well as the capitalists. They had no organisations of their own during the War and operated merely as appendages of the military forces and of the international bourgeoisie. Now, after we have repulsed the attacks of the international counterrevolution, organisations of the Russian bourgeoisie and of all the Russian counterrevolutionary parties have been formed abroad.

The number of Russian émigrés scattered in all foreign countries may be estimated at one and a half to two million. In nearly every country they publish daily newspapers, and all the parties, landowner and petty-bourgeois, not excluding the Social Revolutionaries and Mensheviks, have numerous ties with foreign bourgeois elements, that is to say, they obtain enough money to run their own press. We find the collaboration abroad of absolutely all the political parties that formerly existed in Russia, and we see how the 'free' Russian press abroad, from the Social Revolutionary and Menshevik press to the most reactionary monarchist press, is championing the great landed interests. This, to a certain extent, facilitates our task, because we can more easily observe the forces of the enemy, his state of organisation, and the political trends in his camp. On the other hand, of course, it hinders our work, because these Russian counterrevolutionary émigrés use every means at their disposal to prepare for a fight against us.

This fight again shows that, taken as a whole, the class instinct and class consciousness of the ruling classes are still superior to those of the oppressed classes, notwithstanding the fact that the Russian Revolution has done more than any previous revolution in this respect. In Russia, there is hardly a village in which the people, the oppressed, have not been roused. Nevertheless, if we take a cool look at the state of organisation and political clarity of views of the Russian counterrevolutionary émigrés, we shall find that the class consciousness of the bourgeoisie is still superior to that of the exploited and the oppressed. These people make every possible attempt and skilfully take advantage of every opportunity to attack Soviet Russia in one way or another and to destroy it. It would be very instructive – and I think the comrades from abroad will do it – to watch systematically the most important aspirations, the most important tactical moves, and the most important trends of this Russian counterrevolution. It operates chiefly abroad, and it will not be very difficult for the foreign comrades to watch it. In some respects, we must learn from this enemy. These counterrevolutionary émigrés are very well informed, excellently organised, and are good strategists. And I think that a systematic comparison and study of the manner in which they are organised and take advantage of every opportunity may have a powerful propaganda effect upon the working class. This is not general theory, it is practical politics; here we can see what the enemy has learned.

During the past few years, the Russian bourgeoisie has suffered a terrible defeat. There is an old saying that a beaten army can learn a great deal. The beaten reactionary army has learned a great deal, and has learned it thoroughly. It is learning with great avidity, and has really made much headway. When we took power at one swoop, the Russian bourgeoisie was unorganised and politically undeveloped. Now, I think, its development is on a par with modern, Western European development. We must take this into account, we must improve our own organisation and methods, and we shall do our utmost to achieve this. It was relatively easy for us, and I think it will be equally easy for other revolutions, to cope with these two exploiting classes.

*The relationship between the proletariat and the peasantry*

However, in addition to this class of exploiters, there is in nearly all capitalist countries, with the exception, perhaps, of Britain, a class of small producers and small farmers. The main problem of the revolution now is how to fight these two classes. In order to be rid of them, we must adopt methods different from those employed against the big landowners and capitalists. We could simply expropriate and expel both of these classes, and that is what we did. But we cannot do the same thing with the remaining capitalist classes, the small producers and the petty bourgeoisie, which are found in all countries. In most capitalist countries, these classes constitute a very considerable minority, approximately 30% to 45% of the population. Add to them the petty-bourgeois elements of the working class, and you get even more than 50%. These cannot be expropriated or expelled; other methods of struggle must be adopted in their case.

From the international standpoint, if we regard the international revolution as one process, the significance of the period into which we are now entering in Russia is, in essence, that we must now find a practical solution for the problem of the relations the proletariat should establish with this last capitalist class in Russia. All Marxists have a correct and ready solution for this problem in theory. But theory and practice are two different things, and the practical solution of this problem is by no means the same as the theoretical solution. We know definitely that we have made serious mistakes, but it is a challenging problem. From the international standpoint, it is a sign of great progress that we are now trying to determine the attitude that the proletariat in power should adopt towards the last capitalist class – the rock-bottom of capitalism – small private property, the small producer. This problem now confronts us in a practical way. I think we can solve it. At all events, the experiences we are having will be useful for future proletarian revolutions, and they will be able to make better technical preparations for solving it.

In my theses, I tried to analyse the problem of the relations between the proletariat and the peasantry. For the first time in history there is a state with only two classes, the proletariat and the peasantry. The latter constitutes the overwhelming majority of the population. It is, of course, very backward. How do the relations between the peasantry and the proletariat, which holds political power, find practical expression in the development of the revolution? The first form is alliance, close alliance. This is a very difficult task, but at any rate it is economically and politically feasible.

How did we approach this problem practically? We concluded an alliance with the peasantry. We interpret this alliance in the following way: the proletariat emancipates the peasantry from the exploitation of the bourgeoisie, from its leadership and influence, and wins it over to its own side in order to jointly defeat the exploiters.

The Menshevik argument runs like this: the peasantry constitutes a majority; we are pure democrats, therefore, the majority should decide. But as the peasantry cannot operate on its own, this, in practice, means nothing more nor less than the restoration of capitalism. The slogan is the same: alliance with the peasantry. When we say that, we mean strengthening and consolidating the proletariat. We have tried to give effect to this alliance between the proletariat and the peasantry, and the first stage was a military alliance. The three years of the Civil War created enormous difficulties, but in certain respects they facilitated our task. This may sound odd, but it is true. The war was not something new for the peasants; a war against the exploiters, against the big landowners, was something they quite understood. The overwhelming majority of the peasants were on our side. In spite of the enormous distances, and the fact that the overwhelming majority of our peasants are unable to read or write, they assimilated our propaganda very easily. This proves that the broad masses – and this applies also to the most advanced countries – learn faster from their own practical experience than from books. In Russia, moreover, learning from practical experience was facilitated for the peasantry by the fact that the country is so exceptionally large that in the same period different parts of it were passing through different stages of development.

In Siberia and in the Ukraine, the counterrevolution was able to gain a temporary victory because there the bourgeoisie had the peasantry on its side, because the peasants were against us. The peasants frequently said, 'We are Bolsheviks, but not Communists. We are for the Bolsheviks because they drove out the landowners; but we are not for the Communists because they are opposed to individual farming.' And for a time, the counterrevolution managed to win out in Siberia and in the Ukraine because the bourgeoisie made headway in the struggle for influence over the peasantry. But it took only a very short time to open the peasants' eyes. They quickly acquired practical experience and soon said, 'Yes, the Bolsheviks are rather unpleasant people, we don't like them, but still they are better than the White Guards and the Constituent Assembly.' 'Constituent Assembly' is a term of abuse not only among the educated Communists, but also among the peasants. They know from practical experience that the Constituent Assembly and the White Guards stand for the same thing, that the former is inevitably followed by the latter.[11] The Mensheviks also resort to a military alliance with the peasantry, but they fail to understand that a military alliance alone is inadequate. There can be no military alliance without an economic alliance. It takes more than air to keep a man alive; our alliance with the peasantry could not possibly have lasted any length of time without the economic foundation, which was the basis of our victory in the war against our bourgeoisie. After all, our bourgeoisie has united with the whole of the international bourgeoisie.

The basis of our economic alliance with the peasantry was, of course, very simple, and even crude. The peasant obtained from us all the land and support against the big landowners. In return for this, we were to obtain food. This alliance was something entirely new and did not rest on the ordinary relations between commodity producers and consumers. Our peasants had a much better understanding of this than the heroes of the Second and Two-and-a-Half Internationals. The peasants said to themselves, 'These Bolsheviks are stern leaders, but after all they are our own people.' Be that as it may, we created in this way the foundations of a new economic alliance. The peasants gave their produce to the Red Army and received from the latter assistance in protecting their possessions. This is always forgotten by the heroes of the Second International, who, like Otto Bauer, totally fail to understand the actual situation. We confess that the initial form of this alliance was very primitive, and that we made very many mistakes. But we were obliged to act as quickly as possible, we had to organise supplies for the army at all costs. During the Civil War we were cut off from all the grain districts of Russia. We were in a terrible position, and it was a true miracle that the Russian people and the working class were able to endure such suffering, want, and privation, sustained by nothing more than a deep urge for victory. (*Loud applause and cheers*)

When the Civil War came to an end, however, we faced a different problem. If the country had not been so laid waste after seven years of incessant war, it would, perhaps, have been possible to find an easier transition to the new form of alliance between the proletariat and the peasantry. But bad as

---

11. Elections to the Constituent Assembly were held several weeks after the November 1917 victory of Soviet power. While the Bolsheviks won a majority in the cities and working-class centres, the Socialist-Revolutionaries took an overall majority in the country as a whole. The Assembly met 18 January 1918, but was dispersed by Soviet troops that same day when it refused to acknowledge Soviet authority. During the Civil War, some of the counterrevolutionary white forces raised the Constituent Assembly as a banner in their fight against the Soviet republic.

conditions in the country were, they were still further aggravated by the crop failure, the fodder shortage, and so on. In consequence, the sufferings of the peasants became unbearable. We had to undertake something immediately in order to show the broad masses of the peasants that we were prepared to change our policy, while holding to our revolutionary path, so that they could say, 'The Bolsheviks want to improve our intolerable condition immediately, and at all costs.'

*The change in economic policy*

And so, our economic policy was changed; the tax in kind superseded the (grain) requisitions. This was not invented at one stroke. You will find a number of proposals in the Bolshevik press over a period of months, but no plan that really promised success. But this is not important. The important thing is that we changed our economic policy, yielding to exclusively practical considerations, and impelled by necessity. A bad harvest, fodder shortage, and lack of fuel – all, of course, have a decisive influence on the economy as a whole, including the peasant economy. If the peasantry goes on strike, we get no firewood; and if we get no firewood, the factories will stand idle. Thus, in the spring of 1921, the economic crisis resulting from the terrible crop failure and the fodder shortage assumed gigantic proportions. All that was the aftermath of the three years of Civil War. We had to show the peasantry that we could and would quickly change our policy in order immediately to alleviate their distress.

We have always said – and it was also said at the Second Congress – that revolution demands sacrifices.[12] Some comrades in their propaganda argue in the following way: we are prepared to stage a revolution, but it must not be too severe. Unless I am mistaken, this thesis was put forward by Comrade Šmeral in his speech at the congress of the Communist Party of Czechoslovakia. I read about it in the report published in the Reichenberg [Liberec] *Vorwärts*.[13] There is evidently a leftist wing there; hence this source cannot be regarded as being totally impartial. At all events, I must say that if Šmeral did say that, he was wrong. Some comrades who spoke after Šmeral at this congress said, 'Yes, we shall go along with Šmeral because in this way we shall avoid civil war.' (*Laughter*) If these reports are true, I must say that such

---

12. In his speech at the Comintern's Second Congress, Lenin stated, 'The workers' victory cannot be achieved without sacrifices, without a temporary deterioration of their conditions.' Riddell (ed.) 1991, 2WC, 1, p. 383.
13. For Šmeral's report to the Czechoslovak CP congress, see p. 221, n. 72.

agitation is neither communistic nor revolutionary. Naturally, every revolution entails enormous sacrifice on the part of the class making it. Revolution differs from ordinary struggle in that ten and even a hundred times more people take part in it. Hence every revolution entails sacrifices not only for individuals, but for a whole class. The dictatorship of the proletariat in Russia has entailed for the ruling class – the proletariat – sacrifices, want, and privation unprecedented in history, and this will, in all probability, be the case in every other country.

## Distributing the burdens

The question arises: how are we to distribute this burden of privation? We are the state power. We are able to distribute the burden of privation to a certain extent, and to impose it upon several classes, thereby relatively alleviating the condition of certain strata of the population. But what is to be our principle? Is it to be that of fairness, or of majority? No. We must act in a practical manner. We must distribute the burdens in such a way as to preserve the power of the proletariat. This is our only principle. In the beginning of the revolution the working class was compelled to suffer incredible privations. Let me state that from year to year our food policy has been achieving increasing success. And the situation as a whole has undoubtedly improved. But the peasantry in Russia has certainly gained more from the revolution than the working class. There is no doubt about that at all.

From the standpoint of theory, this shows, of course, that our revolution was to some degree a bourgeois revolution. When Kautsky used this as an argument against us, we laughed. Naturally, a revolution which does not expropriate the big landed estates, expel the big landowners, or divide the land is only a bourgeois revolution and not a socialist one. But we were the only party to carry the bourgeois revolution to its conclusion and to facilitate the struggle for the socialist revolution. The Soviet power and the Soviet system are institutions of the socialist state. We have already established these institutions, but we have not yet solved the problem of economic relations between the peasantry and the proletariat. Much remains to be done, and the outcome of this struggle depends upon whether we solve this problem or not. Thus, the distribution of the burden of privation is one of the most difficult practical problems. On the whole, the condition of the peasants has improved, but dire suffering has fallen to the lot of the working class, precisely because it is exercising its dictatorship.

I have already said that in the spring of 1921 the most appalling want caused by the fodder shortage and the crop failure prevailed among the peasantry, which constitutes the majority of our population. We cannot possibly exist unless we have good relations with the peasant masses. Hence, our task was to render them immediate assistance. The condition of the working class is extremely hard. It is suffering horribly. Those who have more political understanding, however, realise that in the interest of the dictatorship of the working class we must make tremendous efforts to help the peasants at any price. The vanguard of the working class has realised this, but in that vanguard there are still people who cannot understand it, and who are too weary to understand it. They regarded it as a mistake and began to use the word 'opportunism'. They said, 'The Bolsheviks are helping the peasants. The peasants, who are exploiting us, are getting everything they please, while the workers are starving.'

But is that opportunism? We are helping the peasants because without an alliance with them the political power of the proletariat is impossible, its preservation is inconceivable. It was this consideration of expediency and not that of fair distribution that was decisive for us. We are assisting the peasants because it is absolutely necessary to do so in order that we may retain political power. The supreme principle of the dictatorship is the maintenance of the alliance between the proletariat and the peasantry in order that the proletariat may retain its leading role and its political power.

*The tax in kind*

The only means we found for this was the adoption of the tax in kind, which was the inevitable consequence of the struggle. This year, we shall introduce this tax for the first time. This principle has not yet been tried in practice. From the military alliance we must pass to an economic alliance, and, theoretically, the only basis for the latter is the introduction of the tax in kind. It provides the only theoretical possibility for laying a really solid economic foundation for socialist society. The socialised factory gives the peasant its manufactures and in return the peasant gives his grain. This is the only possible form of existence of socialist society, the only form of socialist development in a country in which the small peasants constitute the majority, or at all events a very considerable minority. The peasants will give one part of their produce in the form of tax and another either in exchange for the manufactures of socialist factories, or through the exchange of commodities.

*Freedom of trade*

This brings us to the most difficult problem. It goes without saying that the tax in kind means freedom to trade. After having paid the tax in kind, the peasant will have the right freely to exchange the remainder of his grain. This freedom of exchange implies freedom for capitalism. We say this openly and emphasise it. We do not conceal it. Things would go very hard with us if we attempted to conceal it. Freedom to trade means freedom for capitalism, but it also means a new form of capitalism. It means that, to a certain extent, we are re-creating capitalism. We are doing this quite openly. It is state capitalism. But state capitalism in a society where power belongs to capital, and state capitalism in a proletarian state, are two different concepts. In a capitalist state, state capitalism means that it is recognised by the state and controlled by it for the benefit of the bourgeoisie and to the detriment of the proletariat. In the proletarian state, the same thing is done for the benefit of the working class, for the purpose of withstanding the as yet strong bourgeoisie, and of fighting it. It goes without saying that we must grant concessions to the foreign bourgeoisie, to foreign capital.[14] Without the slightest denationalisation, we shall lease mines, forests, and oilfields to foreign capitalists, and receive in exchange manufactured goods, machinery, etc., and thus restore our own industry.

*State capitalism*

Of course, we did not all agree on the question of state capitalism at once. But we are very pleased to note in this connection that our peasantry has been developing, that it has fully realised the historical significance of the struggle we are waging at the present time. Ordinary peasants from the most remote districts have come to us and said: 'What! We have expelled our capitalists, the capitalists who speak Russian, and now foreign capitalists are coming!' Does not this show that our peasants have developed? There is no need to explain to a worker who is versed in economics why this is necessary. We have been so ruined by seven years of war that it will take many years to restore our industry. We must pay for our backwardness and weakness, and for the lessons we are now learning and must learn. Those who want to learn must pay for the tuition. We must explain this to one and all, and if we prove it in practice, the vast masses of the peasants and workers will agree with us, because in this way their condition will be immediately improved, and because it will ensure the possibility of restoring our industry.

What compels us to do this? We are not alone in the world. We exist in a system of capitalist states, as a component of the world economy. On one side, there are the colonial countries, but they cannot help us yet. On the other

---

14. 'Concessions' here refers to Soviet Russia's willingness, under the New Economic Policy, to permit limited foreign investment projects, subject to government control.

side, there are the capitalist countries, but they are our enemies. The result is a certain equilibrium, a very poor one, it is true. Nevertheless, we must reckon with the fact. We must not shut our eyes to it if we want to exist. Either we score an immediate victory over the whole bourgeoisie, or we pay the tribute.

We admit quite openly, and do not conceal the fact that concessions in the system of state capitalism mean paying tribute to capitalism. But we gain time, and gaining time means gaining everything, particularly in the period of equilibrium, when our foreign comrades are preparing thoroughly for their revolution. The more thorough their preparations, the more certain will the victory be. Meanwhile, however, we shall have to pay the tribute.

## Electrification of Russia

A few words about our food policy. Undoubtedly, it was a bad and primitive policy. But we can also point to some achievements. In this connection I must once again emphasise that the only possible economic foundation of socialism is large-scale machine industry. Whoever forgets this is no Communist. We must analyse this problem concretely. We must pose problems not in the manner of the theoreticians of the old school of socialism, but in a practical manner.

What is modern large-scale industry? It is the electrification of the whole of Russia. Sweden, Germany, and the United States are on the road to achieving this, although they are still bourgeois. A Swedish comrade told me that in Sweden a large part of industry and 30 per cent of agriculture are electrified. In Germany and America, which are even more developed capitalistically, we see the same thing on a larger scale. Large-scale machine industry is synonymous with electrification of the whole country. We have already appointed a special commission consisting of the country's best economists and engineers. It is true that nearly all of them are hostile to the Soviet power. All these specialists will come over to communism, but not our way, not by way of twenty years of underground work, during which we unceasingly studied and repeated over and over again the ABC of communism.

Nearly all the Soviet government bodies were in favour of inviting the specialists. The expert engineers will come to us when we give them practical proof that this will increase the country's productive forces. It is not enough to prove it to them in theory; we must prove it to them in practice, and we shall win these people over to our side if we present the problem differently, not from the standpoint of the theoretical propaganda of communism. We say: large-scale industry is the only means of saving the peasantry from want and starvation. Everyone agrees with this. But how can it be done? The restoration of industry on the old basis will entail too much labour and time. We must give industry a more modern form, that is, we must adopt electrification. This will take much less time. We have already drawn up the plans for electrification. More than two hundred specialists worked on it with keen interest, although they are not Communists. From the standpoint of technical science, however, they had to admit that this was the only correct way.

Of course, we have a long way to go before the plan is achieved. The cautious specialists say that the first series of works will take at least ten years. Professor Ballod has estimated that it would take only three to four years to electrify Germany. But for us even ten years is not enough. In my theses, I quote actual figures to show you how little we have been able to do in this sphere up to now. The figures I quote are so modest that it immediately becomes clear that they have more value as propaganda than as science. But we must begin with propaganda. The Russian peasants who fought in the World War and lived in Germany for several years learned how modern farming should be carried on in order to conquer famine. We must carry on extensive propaganda in this direction.

Taken by themselves, these plans are not yet of great practical value, but their impact as propaganda is very large. The peasants realise that something new must be created. They realise that this cannot be done by everybody working separately, but rather only by the state working as a whole. The peasants who were prisoners of war in Germany found out what real cultural life is based on. Twelve thousand kilowatts is a very modest beginning. This may sound funny to the foreigner who is familiar with electrification in America, Germany, or Sweden. But he who laughs last laughs best. It is, indeed, a modest beginning. But the peasants are beginning to understand that new work must be carried out on a grand scale, and that this work has already begun. Enormous difficulties will have to be overcome. We shall try to establish relations with the capitalist countries. We must not regret having to give the capitalists several hundred million kilograms of oil on condition that they help us to electrify our country.

## On 'pure democracy'

And now, in conclusion, a few words about *'pure democracy'*. I will read you a passage from Engels's letter to Bebel of 11 December 1884. He wrote:

> Pure democracy...at the moment of revolution [acquires] a temporary importance as the last sheet-anchor of the bourgeois and, indeed, feudal economy generally.... It was thus that, from March to September 1848, the entire feudal-bureaucratic mass swelled the ranks of the liberals in order to keep down the revolutionary masses.... At all events, on the crucial day

and the day after that, our only adversary will be *collective reaction centred round pure democracy*, and this, I think, ought never to be lost from view.[15]

Our approach must differ from that of the theoreticians. The whole reactionary mass, not only bourgeois, but also feudal, groups itself around 'pure democracy'. The German comrades know better than anyone else what 'pure democracy' means, for Kautsky and the other leaders of the Second and Two-and-a-Half Internationals are defending this 'pure democracy' from the wicked Bolsheviks. If we judge the Russian Social Revolutionaries and Mensheviks, not by what they say, but by what they do, we shall find that they are nothing but representatives of petty-bourgeois 'pure democracy'. In the course of our revolution, they have given us a classic example of what 'pure democracy' means, and again during the recent crisis, in the days of the Kronstadt mutiny.[16] There was serious unrest among the peasantry, and discontent was also rife among the workers. They were weary and exhausted. After all, there is a limit to human endurance. They went hungry for three years, but you cannot go on like that for four or five years. Naturally, hunger has a tremendous influence on political activity.

How did the Social Revolutionaries and Mensheviks behave? They wavered all the time, thereby strengthening the bourgeoisie. The organisation of all the Russian parties abroad shows us the present state of affairs. The shrewdest leaders of the Russian big bourgeoisie said to themselves: 'We cannot achieve victory in Russia immediately. Hence our slogan must be: Soviets without the Bolsheviks.' Milyukov, the leader of the Cadets, defended the Soviet government from the attacks of the Social Revolutionaries. This sounds very strange, but such are the practical dialectics which we, in our revolution, have been studying in a peculiar way, from the practical experience of our struggle and of the struggle of our enemies. The Cadets defend 'Soviets but without the Bolsheviks' because they understand the position very well and hope that a section of the people will rise to the bait. That is what the clever Cadets say. Not all the Cadets are clever, of course, but some of them are, and these ones have learned something from the French Revolution. The present slogan is to fight the Bolsheviks, whatever the price, come what may. The whole of the bourgeoisie is now helping the Mensheviks and Social Revolutionaries, who are now the vanguard of all reaction. In the spring we had a taste of the fruits of this counterrevolutionary cooperation.

That is why we must continue our relentless struggle against these elements. The dictatorship is a state of intense war. We are experiencing such a state of

---

15. See *MECW*, 47, pp. 233–4.
16. For the Kronstadt uprising, see p. 213, n. 61.

intense war. There is no military invasion at present; but we are isolated. On the other hand, however, we are not entirely isolated, since the whole international bourgeoisie is incapable of waging open war against us just now, because the whole working class, even though the majority is not yet communist, is sufficiently class-conscious to prevent intervention. The bourgeoisie is compelled to reckon with the temper of the masses. That is why the bourgeoisie cannot now start an offensive against us, although one is never ruled out.

Until the final issue is decided, this awful state of war will continue. And we say: In conditions of war, take measures of war. We do not promise any freedom, or any democracy. We tell the peasants quite openly that they must choose between the rule of the bourgeoisie and that of the Bolsheviks – and in the latter case we shall make every possible concession within the limits of retaining power, and later we shall lead them to socialism.

It is a difficult road. But everything else is deception and pure demagogy. Ruthless war must be declared against this deception and demagogy. Our point of view is: for the time being, big concessions and the greatest caution, precisely because a certain equilibrium has set in, precisely because we are weaker than our combined enemies, and because our economic basis is too weak and we need a stronger one.

That, comrades, is what I wanted to tell you about our tactics, the tactics of the Russian Communist Party. (*Prolonged, loud applause and cheers*)

**Loriot** (Chair): Comrades, the discussion on Comrade Lenin's report is now open. No one has asked to speak yet. It is extremely important that the report be followed by a vigorous discussion. I ask the delegations to submit their names of delegates who wish to take the floor.

**Sachs** (Schwab, KAPD): Comrades, since no other delegation has asked for the floor, it is my duty to be the first to step into the breach, carry out my delegation's instructions, and assume the thankless task of initiating this discussion.

Comrade Lenin's remarks were of great interest to us because they showed how the Russian Communist Party intends to overcome the difficulties that have arisen from both Russia's backward economic development on the one hand and the halting advance of world revolution on the other. Comrade Lenin spoke decisively at the crucial moment. He said that so long as we, the comrades in the industrially developed countries, are still preparing and laying the groundwork for the revolution, we in Russia will still have to pay tribute. The idea is obvious, and Comrade Lenin expressed it very clearly: under present conditions, to win time is to win everything.

But I must say that we still have some concerns about this situation.

**Shout:** We do too!

**Sachs:** I certainly believe that. I also believe it is proper that these concerns, which are shared not only by Western European comrades but by those of Russia, be expressed openly. In my view, these concerns, which we cannot set aside, are that the Russian party's economic policies both within Russia and in its relations to the capitalist states, must surely have repercussions, not only in strengthening Russia economically at the outset of the Soviet state's economic development, but also, as is inevitable, repercussions that are disquieting and dangerous. As Marxists, we must concede that within Russia, a political party, whichever it may be, and however tightly knit and disciplined it may be, can never remain unaffected by the economic foundation upon which it rests.

The party's activity and political life cannot escape the influences flowing from changes in the economic foundations – for a certain time it can, but not in the long run. So our first concern is that even the strictest unity, the strictest discipline, and the clearest and most ruthless use of force on the part of the Russian Communist Party provides no automatic guarantee that this party will remain unchanged as the economic foundation changes. This affects foreign relations. We already took this up in the debate on the theses of Comrade Trotsky, at least in the commission. In Comrade Trotsky's theses, there is a sentence that says that the resumption of economic relations between Soviet Russia and the capitalist countries will not result in any significant changes in the near term. I disagreed with this sentence in the commission, but I was defeated by the majority.

These theses have been adopted by the congress, but the same question comes up again in this discussion, and since it arises, I feel justified in once more formally posing the issue. I am convinced that the resumption of international capitalist economic relations is possible, firstly, in the form of treaties whose principal goal is the recognition of the Soviet government. Their economic character serves only as a kind of excuse. In this case, there is no gain in economic development. Alternatively – and this is more likely – these treaties may actually serve as the foundation for building concrete, real economic relations, either through concessions, or possibly through a large import trade based on credits.

If the economic provisions of these treaties are observed and thus contribute to Soviet Russia's economic development, it is unavoidable that they will simultaneously contribute to strengthening capitalism in the relevant capitalist countries. The Russian comrades see these repercussions and heed the danger they pose. We must ask, however, insofar as our politics as the Communist International come into question, how this situation affects us as

Communist parties and as the Communist International. It must be said that Russia is now compelled by circumstances to advance along this path. For it must be conceded without hesitation that this compulsion exists. The Communist parties of the industrialised countries and the Communist International as a whole must therefore work all the harder to nullify the strengthening effect this policy will have for capitalism.

However, we have the impression here that the policy of the Communist International, as it has been carried out recently, and as it appears to have been determined by this congress in its decisions to this point, has been inadequate to recognise this danger. It can be readily foreseen – indeed, not merely foreseen but already perceived – that from time to time a certain conflict of interest necessarily arises between the interests of revolutionary workers in the Western countries and those of the Soviet government. Nobody is to be personally criticised for this. These are objective facts. Such a conflict of interest was evident when the British miners' strike actually seriously disrupted implementation of the Russo-British trade agreement, as Krasin stated in an interview in *Die Rote Fahne*.[17] On the other hand, had the miners been expressly told, 'You may not strike because Russia needs the coal and the machines', that would not have helped the revolution in Western Europe. The course that has been attempted seems to me to be a middle path – a middle path that is disastrous for both sides. For I will tell you frankly, the support given to the British miners' strike was absolutely inadequate. True, it was not said that you may not strike because of Russian interests. But even if this has not yet happened, we foresee a great danger that the opportunists will gladly, very gladly seize this opportunity and tell the workers, at the onset of economic struggles, 'Yes, certainly, we are on your side with all our hearts, but think about Russia, don't strike because Soviet Russia is dependent on your deliveries.' Comrade Radek thinks that's a good joke. If that's his view, then he is, I'm sorry to say, insufficiently familiar with our circumstances.

Comrades, our task is to create a safeguard against that. It is the task of the Communist parties and naturally also of this congress. Now this congress, in fact, truly gets its intellectual shape from the Russian comrades, who provide its essential leadership. This is the fault not of the Russian comrades but of the other parties whose conduct and whose inadequate criticism did not contribute to shaping this congress and the Communist International differently, in order to create a counterweight.

---

17. L.B. Krasin, a high official in Soviet economic management, was in Berlin 16 January 1921.

What I have to say in this regard amounts to this: a warning to the Communist parties of the industrialised countries as a whole. The current path is very heavily influenced – indeed, in our view, too heavily influenced – by Russian government policies. These parties must create a counterweight, not through speeches, but rather through practical and real actions and the openness of the criticism that they should express here.

**Radek**: Comrades, I consider it a service by the KAPD that its delegate took the floor here on this question. I also note that the comments we have just heard from Comrade Sachs took a certain measure of courage, with regard to both the facts and the congress. The KAPD's position is useful to us because the Mensheviks cannot appear at a congress of the Communist International, and the KAPD's delegate is only saying what the Mensheviks have written in their press all along regarding the policies of the Soviet government and the International.

I do not want to examine at great length the economic theories underlying Comrade Sachs's comments. I do not want to analyse the glorious notion that Russia's purchases of goods from Western Europe can hold back the global crisis of imperialism, and similar ideas. I want to focus on the following questions: Are the policies of the Communist Party of Russia, both internally and abroad, necessary from the standpoint of the Russian proletariat, not only in terms of the relationship of forces within Russia but also from the standpoint of the international proletariat?

After Comrade Lenin's remarks, I do not believe I still need to demonstrate the impossibility of any policy other than the one we are carrying out, not only in the present conditions of transition from war to peace but, more generally, in a country with a predominantly agricultural population. This policy raises an important point of theory that Communist parties need to grasp. The Mensheviks have been saying for years that the relationship of forces within Russia does not permit any attempt to realise socialism. For this reason it was necessary to orient consciously toward putting the bourgeoisie at the helm, which would then develop the country's economic forces to the point where socialism could finally be achieved. Fifteen years ago, during the first revolution, the Bolsheviks advanced the viewpoint that a proletarian revolution, a victory establishing the dictatorship of the proletarian class, was then impossible. However, they indicated that victory over tsarism was possible only through an alliance of the proletariat with the peasantry.

Comrade Trotsky pointed out that if the working class takes power in an economically undeveloped country, it will be compelled by the logic of the situation to attempt to give expression economically to its power by attempting to implement socialism. He posed a practical question: what will the government – a revolutionary government, resting on an alliance of the peasants and workers – do, if there is unemployment and the capitalists are sabotaging? We must attempt to realise socialism. In the first revolution we did not get to that point, given the economic level at that time and the fact that Western European capitalism was then in a position to sustain Russian tsarism, and the peasant sons, clad in uniform, suppressed the revolution.

During the revolution, at its very outset, the Communist Party very cautiously raised the question of what it would do if it achieved power. Comrade Lenin wrote in his April Theses of 1917 that we would then be able to take only the initial steps toward communism, because communism is not possible, as a general form of social organisation, in a country where the peasants, the petty bourgeoisie, form a majority of the population; a country where the economy is fragmented.[18] We can project no more than the socialisation of large-scale industry, transport, and the banks, along with the monopoly of foreign trade. We actually went beyond this programme. As Comrade Lenin explains in his pamphlet on the tax in kind, when we must unify all the resources of a country in order to wage war, this must apply not only to large-scale industry but also to smaller and medium-sized enterprises.

Our policies may also respond to a deeper necessity. The first task must be to smash the bourgeoisie. But it is still resisting. We had to expropriate the roots of its power, and these roots were lodged in private ownership of the means of production, of goods. And there is yet another cause. In a country marked by acute deprivation, acute poverty, the working class naturally sought to introduce a rough-hewn egalitarian communism. It had to provide some improvement over yesterday. Somewhat more bread, or better clothing – this spurred the working class to promote equalisation. Now we are making the transition from foreign wars to a certain period of peace, which places the economic questions in the forefront. And policy must now orient to what is actually possible. During the War, we were driven, indeed required, to go beyond that point. And now the question is posed of genuine socialisation on the basis of Soviet power and the Communist Party – namely of large-scale industry. As for the other question, it concerns not socialisation but the relationship between socialised large-scale industry and the small bourgeois economy.

That is necessary from the point of view not only of Soviet Russia but also of the world revolution. You do not deny that Soviet Russia is at present the

---

18. Lenin's April Theses of 1917 were issued following his return to Russia after the February Revolution. See 'The Tasks of the Proletariat in the Present Revolution', in *LCW*, 24, pp. 19–26.

strongest outpost of world revolution. It restricts the forces of counterrevolution while making it possible not only to introduce a communist economic order for large-scale industry, but also to utilise the strength of the Russian peasantry, which otherwise would serve only the counterrevolution, for a variety of revolutionary purposes. If that is agreed, it follows that what we are doing is essential for world revolution.

Recall the debate with Laufenberg, Wolffheim, and company, in which you vacillated greatly.[19] They said that, when we have the power (in Germany), we will break with the Versailles Treaty. At the time when we were blockaded, I explained, from the standpoint of the Russian proletariat, that we were then not in a position to foil the Versailles policy. It will perhaps be necessary to win a breathing spell for the German revolution, by recognising the Versailles Treaty. If the policy we are following is essential for the world revolution, then it is only possible with the approval of the Communist International and all its components. The entire Communist International carries responsibility for this. Our policies are carried out in the interests not of the isolated Russian state but of the world proletariat, for whom we must defend this strongpoint.

And now we come to the second question, that of the Communist International's relationship to this policy. I will cite a specific example demonstrating that the assertions made regarding this issue are completely absurd.

Comrade Sachs asked about the British miners' strike: 'Why did you not intervene; why did you not call for support? Because the trade treaty had been signed, and that made you shut your mouth.' Comrades, I can reveal to you the secret of why we did not intervene. It was because we were aware that you cannot help the British miners with words. We could help the British miners only by mobilising the German and American miners to deliver no coal to Britain. In Germany, we had just suffered the March defeat, and if we had called for blocking coal deliveries to Britain, it would have been merely for the record. As for the American miners, unfortunately our relations with them are so limited that an appeal would have had no significance. We are shifting more and more from making general appeals to concrete work by the Communist International. So, after careful consideration, we said there was no point in mere talk. You may well say that this may be true in this case, but we also influence the policies of the Soviet government. To this, we reply that the representatives of non-Russian Communist parties have the majority in the Executive. I note that the Executive has not made any proposal for action.

---

19. For the National Bolshevik current in the KAPD led by Laufenberg and Wolffheim, see p. 333, n. 3. Radek's polemic with this current appeared as a pamphlet, *Die auswärtige Politik des deutschen Kommunismus und der Hamburger nationale Bolschewismus*, Radek 1920.

As for our Russian representatives on the Executive, we have learned to carry out flexible policies, so we will be fully able to carry out our revolutionary duty even in Honolulu and Haiti, even if we have treaties of alliance with these countries.

I will now take up quite briefly the conclusions that flow from this situation. The policies of Soviet Russia are plain to see. These are necessities flowing from the present relationship of forces – not only for Russia but for the international proletariat. As to the question whether these policies contain dangers, we respond that of course they do – great dangers. Comrade Lenin said in his theses that a proletarian government can remain isolated only for a certain period.

We are carrying out a lively discussion of these dangers at our congresses. There is only one remedy for these dangers: to speed up the world revolution.

Now I come to what is logically the most contradictory point in the criticisms by Comrade Sachs and his co-thinkers. They say, 'You are isolated; your policies pose great dangers for you, as you yourselves recognise.' What conclusions do you draw from this, in terms of Russian state policy? We need only consider that, if it was really a question of Russian state policy for us, we would then be putschists, as we are always portrayed. I remember when I was released from jail in Germany (1919),[20] I was visited by the editor in chief of *Vorwärts*, Stampfer, who said, 'When I saw your file, I was amazed. I thought that you, with your country quite devastated, had come to Germany in order to force the Entente to occupy this country.' That is the position that you are actually adopting when Gorter and Pannekoek criticise us, saying that the March Action was a putsch. And simultaneously you tell us that we are trying to make the party as opportunistic as possible. The contradiction is obvious. But we are not putschists, and not opportunists either. We are of the opinion that Soviet Russia will be poorly placed if the working class is defeated. In face of the dangers, we have the courage to say that, while we stand ready to shed blood in defence of our positions, you should not lose battles but rather broaden out your struggles so that you can really win.

**Seemann**: Revolutions don't come with guarantees.

**Radek**: Revolutions don't come with guarantees. Very true! But a revolution with a certificate of certain defeat – that will not be accepted even by

---

20. In December 1918 Radek travelled to Berlin illegally as Bolshevik and Soviet emissary to Germany and to attend the founding congress of the Communist Party of Germany. On 12 February 1919 he was arrested. Initially imprisoned, Radek was released a few weeks later and put under house arrest, where he was able to meet with many political figures. He was finally able to leave Germany in January 1920.

a dimwit, and we do not want you to be dimwits! (*Loud applause*) That is how things stood in 1919, when you carried out a fierce struggle against us in the Spartacus League. At that time, you said that conditions were ripe for revolution, but the Spartacus League did not recognise this fact. It turned out that we were not then on the threshold of revolution; conditions were not yet ripe. Two years have passed, and we are not yet on its threshold, but on the threshold of its antechamber. We are only now forming up in struggle, and the enemy has an interest in destroying us in this process. Our words to you are: do not evade struggles that are necessary, but understand this: the broader their foundation, the more certain is our victory.

The conclusion that I draw from this, therefore, is that the concessions we are making here, the policy of compromises we are carrying out – we are making compromises with hard facts, and anyone who does not see this will stumble – this policy is in the interest of the International. And that interest lies in mobilising the parties with all their strength, attention, and energy, and preparing them for decisive struggles. They should not seek out a decisive struggle without a chance for victory – no insurance policy, no guarantee, but a chance for victory.

In this regard, the policies of the Communist International and the Soviet Russian party are instructive, as Comrade Lenin pointed out. We learned that insufficient examination of the relationship of forces can only cause damage. We propose that you proceed just as we do: assemble your forces, and then strike at a moment of your choosing, when you have a chance of victory.

We began the struggle under very unfavourable conditions. We began it at the end of 1918, when the Entente intervention began, and Trotsky, who spoke here in a spirit of caution, carried out the task of a revolutionary, organising the Red Army with the party's help, when the army was still weak and in an unfavourable situation. But simultaneously the government was able to tell Wilson to his face, 'How many pounds of flesh do you want from our body?'[21] We were trying to buy time. And when that proved impossible, we fought empowered by our confidence in world revolution and with the strength born of desperation, because we knew that Russia would stand or fall as the strongest pillar of world revolution. But we were also trying to win time, and we are still in such a period. One conclusion flowing from this is that the Soviet government and the International must have a policy that adapts to changing

---

21. Presumably a reference to the March 1919 visit to Moscow of William Bullitt. A junior US diplomat, Bullitt was sent by President Woodrow Wilson and British Prime Minister David Lloyd George on a confidential mission to Moscow to ascertain Soviet peace objectives. Bullitt met with Lenin and obtained written Soviet proposals, but these received no response from the Entente powers.

situations. Our slogan is to buy time in order to organise victory. Organising as Lenin said, not only by reading books but by drawing the lessons of life in the struggles that life lays on us. (*Loud applause and cheers*)

**Alexandra Kollontai** (Russia): Comrades, I am not taking the floor on behalf of the Russian delegation; I am rather speaking on behalf of a small minority in the Russian Communist Party.[22] We believe that as Communists we have a higher duty than that laid on us by party discipline, namely the discipline and responsibilities we owe to the entire Communist International. I have also taken the floor so that comrades from other countries will know that there are a number of comrades in the ranks of the Communist Party of Russia who harbour great reservations regarding the present policies of Russia, and we consider it our duty to inform comrades from other countries about this.

The first and principal question is whether this turn and these policies will really serve to secure and promote a new communist system of production in Russia. As Marxists, comrades, we are aware that only through a new communist system of production will it truly be possible to promote the development of the productive forces and ease this process. As long as the old system survives, with its various levels and various divisions – that is, as long as the capitalist system exists – it will not be possible to expand the forces of production or wait for their further expansion. Comrades, we base ourselves on the fact that the capitalist economic system is obsolete on a world scale. We also know that social revolution is shaped by the fact that either humankind as a whole will perish or the rising new class will invent a new productive system that expands production.

Looking at Russia today and observing how relationships are taking shape, we must pose the question whether this turn in domestic politics is leading to the restoration of the old system of production, on a capitalist basis. We do not want to deny that the New Economic Policy in Russia creates the possibility that capitalism will once again strike root, and that the capitalist system might be restored in Russia. The question is whether we are encouraging the development of productive forces and the flourishing of Russia's entire economic system by facilitating the restoration of capitalism. Will this restoration

---

22. Kollontai spoke for the Workers' Opposition, a group within the Russian CP that she led together with Aleksandr Shlyapnikov, S.P. Medvedev, and others. Formed in September 1920, it called for trade-union control of industrial production and greater autonomy for CP fractions in the unions. After its position was rejected by the Tenth CP Congress in March 1921, the Workers Opposition subsequently raised criticisms of measures adopted introducing the NEP. Following its censure at the party's Eleventh Congress in March–April 1922, the Workers' Opposition ceased organised activity.

make it possible to emerge from economic collapse? We believe this view is incorrect.

Restoration of private property in Russia is made possible by freedom of trade. It is facilitated by the establishment and authorisation of small enterprises in Russia, which exist alongside the apparatus of our central economic agencies. This alone indicates the possibility of a number of concessions to capital. We understand, comrades, that Russia does not yet have a homogeneous population. Three social layers are acting on our political system. The majority of the population consists of peasants, then there is the moribund bourgeoisie, which survives in the form of our bureaucracy. This layer also includes specialists who have a link to foreign capital, not materially of course but ideologically. Thirdly, there is the working class, as a social layer and a social power.

Is it truly the working class that promotes the restoration, by and large, of the old system of production and the possibility that capitalism will be restored? Is it really the proletariat that is calling for this new turn in economic policy? Or is it rather the petty bourgeoisie, the peasantry, imbued with its old traditions, its concept of private property, its love for a small plot of land, which the peasant regards as if it were his property? Is it not also the power of the foreign capitalists, who after all have what one might call their ideological agents in Russia influencing our politics?

Comrade Lenin also does not deny that we are now making an alliance with the Russian peasantry. But what is this alliance? Does not our entire economic policy represent, in fact, a gigantic concession to the Russian petty bourgeoisie? We must respond sincerely that it is indeed such a concession. Comrade Lenin and other comrades say this is true, but there is no other alternative. We need the concessions in order to stick it out; it is a way of winning time until our comrades in other countries carry out the social revolution. But so long as the comrades in other countries have not carried out the social revolution, these concessions pose an urgent danger for Russia, particularly if this period lasts for many years, if the social revolution does not break out in other countries soon enough.

I am convinced it will come more quickly, but what if it does not happen quickly enough: what will then be the result of these concessions? They convey a recognition that the Communist principles on which our policies were built were not capable of accomplishing what we had hoped of them. This discourages the workers. On the other hand, the concessions encourage among the peasants the conviction that it is they, the peasants, who are the layer sustaining all our economic gains and that, as a result, they have a tangible capacity to influence politics, which they will exert.

Thirdly, these concessions rob the working masses of their confidence in communism. They eliminate confidence that the workers can achieve something through their self-activity, that they can create a new system, a communist economic system in Russia. And I am very much afraid that if we continue further with all these concessions, we will reach a situation where, when social revolution breaks out in other countries, it will be too late. I fear that the upright, solid, proletarian, class-conscious nucleus of workers, upon which the revolution can rely, will be absent. It may be that by then the peasantry and also the bourgeoisie will be so entrenched that it will actually be necessary for the proletarians to carry out another revolution in Russia against these alien social forces, in order to achieve communism. A great many of our comrades share this concern, and that is why I am obliged to impose on your patience for a few minutes.

Comrade Lenin said here that there is no alternative. I am aware that many of our comrades share this point of view. But why do we always forget, comrades, when we look for a solution, that there is still a great force in Russia that has not been fully utilised? This force is the creative power of our working class. Comrades will say that the proletarian class has every possibility of expressing itself. Comrades, you yourselves know that during the most recent period this creative power has been insufficiently utilised. In the first years of the revolution, the broad masses of the proletariat were genuinely and creatively active. But now workers are more and more pushed back by a whole array of alien social forces, which are winning more and more influence over our social life.

It is indicative that Comrade Lenin's theses, in describing the revival of production, place so much weight on mechanical factors and their development, and that not a single passage of his theses mentions how the creative working class, a living new force, acts on production, creates new methods of production, and thereby promotes it. Not a word on how workers should be educated, how they should be encouraged to create a new system of production. That receives no emphasis. But it is precisely the living, creative force of the proletariat that creates new methods of production and new forces of production. But for the proletariat to be creative, it must have scope, it must have the possibility of giving expression to its initiative. And this initiative is more and more crippled by our present system.

We should be considering how to alter this system, not only on paper but in practice, in order to develop the new spirit of the masses. So long as we do not do this, we will always be required to search for alien forces to help us out of our plight.

Comrades, the stance we take toward the creative power of the proletariat can be seen in a few examples. We just had an example that shows how little we concern ourselves with truly encouraging and promoting the creative power of the masses. As you know, comrades, there is at present a severe famine in the country. Instead of attempting to draw the workers into assisting the afflicted through free initiative, giving them scope to organise themselves for this, as we ought to do in such a situation, an aid committee for the starving peasantry and proletariat is being formed in Russia right now that is headed by alien and politically hostile forces, including a Mrs. Kuskova, a Russian Beatrice. And we tolerate that, instead of putting all our emphasis on the need for the workers to gain confidence in their own forces and thus strengthen the alliance between workers and peasants.

We also forget that when we took this new turn in our economic policy, at that moment, in a single stroke we cancelled out all our previous work. We must not forget that the workers had already grown accustomed to the new system, based not on taxes but on a guarantee that they receive everything from the state. They already have this system firmly in mind. Their psychology, their outlook changed and became aligned with communism. The workers said, 'If I must engage in speculation, it is really a crime, and I do it only because we do not yet receive enough from our state supply system, because our rations are still insufficient.' But they were already beginning to understand the concept of common property, the common good, and that is a great achievement, which our revolution has truly fought for and won.

This new creative force of the proletariat will educate the new human being who will really help us in implementing a new social order. Today we are forgetting this task. We are abandoning it, by carrying out this turn in our policies. This turn may make it possible, comrades, to expand the productive forces in Russia for a time, but only within certain limits. The capitalist social order does not provide much scope for that. But even if we achieve that, if we salvage production in Russia for a time, there is still a great danger that we will thereby lose the trust of the working masses in our party. Our conclusion is that it is wrong to support this policy, as many comrades do. On the contrary, we should react critically to this policy, so that comrades in all the other countries that are still capitalist can learn lessons from this. The only thing that can save us is for our party to have a strong nucleus that stands by our old and firm principles and that will be present at the moment when revolution breaks out in your countries. If the turn in Soviet policy as a whole continues, and our communist republic develops not into communism but into solely a Soviet republic, this nucleus of firm Communists will be present to grasp the red flag of revolution and aid in the victory of communism around the world.

**Trotsky**: Comrades, I don't get the opportunity to regularly read *Die Neue Zeit*, the theoretical organ of the so-called Social Democracy, edited by Heinrich Cunow, but from time to time an issue falls into my hands. I have just read an article by Heinrich Cunow on the decomposition of Bolshevism, in which he deals with the question we are now discussing.[23] He formulates the question as follows: how can one avoid a complete economic collapse, raise industrial and agricultural production, assure more or less adequate food rations to urban workers, employees, and intellectuals, and eliminate the growing dissatisfaction among these circles?

The polemical barb of this formulation is aimed at us, but it is in essence correct. Then he lists the tendencies which presumably exist in our party and goes on to say: 'Trotsky is supported by Bukharin, Rakovsky, Pyatakov, Larin, Sholnikov...'

I have no idea who this Sholnikov is, unless, perhaps, it is a synthesis of Sokolnikov and Shlyapnikov. Comrade Kollontai is not mentioned, I don't know why. The author continues: 'and other Left Communists.' Do you hear, Comrade Béla Kun – Left Communists! (*Laughter*)

> ...and other Left Communists, in analysing this question, came to the conclusion that the only way out lies through a more rigid application of the communist labour system. Both factories and agricultural enterprises must be placed under even stricter control; economic organisations still retaining their independence must be likewise be nationalised; the peasants must be compelled to deliver their surpluses to the needy cities; and the laws against illicit trading and speculation in foodstuffs must be made more severe. In general, it is necessary to energetically discipline and centralise the economic enterprises.
>
> But this goal can be achieved only when an end is put to the election of the supervisory personnel by the workers, since the workers frequently elect absolutely illiterate individuals. It is necessary to replace these functionaries by people appointed by the Soviet authorities. In order to raise productivity, Trotsky also wants to harness the trade unions, which are predominantly non-Communist and to politicise them, that is, place them under the supervision of the political organisations. Moreover, labour conscription must be introduced among the peasantry, the cultivation of the land must be decreed a 'state duty', and the peasants compelled under pain of stringent penalties to cultivate and deliver fixed amounts of the most essential food

---

23. Cunow's article, 'Der Bankrott des Bolschewismus' [The Bankruptcy of Bolshevism], was published in *Die Neue Zeit*, 22 and 29 April 1921 (2, 4, pp. 73–80 and 2, 5, pp. 97–102).

products. In addition to all this, Trotsky is conducting a fight against leasing large areas to exploitative foreign capitalist companies, which he considers as anti-Communist.

In a word, this article paints a political portrait of our friend Kollontai – but under the pseudonym of Trotsky. In general this article, like everything concocted by its author, is a rehash of trite Bernsteinism of the nineties. And these ideas now appear as the modern postwar doctrine, the spiritual sustenance of German Social Democracy. Bernstein put all this together far more systematically, consistently, and methodically than does Heinrich Cunow. But this does not affect the essence of the matter.

Let us return to the Russian question. It is not solely Cunow's personal opinion that we have great differences of views among us, and that I personally belong to the opposition on the question of concessions and on the question of changing our economic policy. Not only the Social-Democratic press but also the capitalist newspapers harp on this. Every comrade who is in the least acquainted with our internal affairs is well aware that there are no serious differences among us, in the party, over these questions, except for a very small group whose representative you heard today. If this question ever did come up among us, in the Central Committee, it was discussed only from the standpoint of whether this or that area, this or that concession should be granted or not, that is, from a purely practical standpoint. And it was precisely in these practical aspects that I happened to be in agreement with Lenin. Neither Comrade Bukharin nor Comrade Rakovsky, nor any of the comrades mentioned in Cunow's article has opposed concessions and the new agricultural or peasant policy in principle.

This is an excellent illustration of the intellectual level of German Social Democracy. For indeed, insofar as an individual really belongs to the International – as was also the case with the Second International in its best days – he is always greatly concerned in honestly following and understanding what takes place within a sister party, even if he has differences with it. When some lie was spread about tsarism, it was a common saying that tsarism had broad shoulders and could bear up under anything. But from a theoretical representative of a party who is obliged to analyse events calmly, one could demand – not that he should understand and vindicate us, God forbid! – but that he should at least have some comprehension of the things about which he writes. But he lacks even this.

Well, the fact is, there are no differences among us over this question. The figure of 99 per cent would be a conservative estimate of the party majority on this issue. But how do matters stand with regard to the danger which the representatives of the Communist Workers' Party and Comrade Kollontai depicted before us from two different sides – one from the side of Western European capitalism, and the other from the side of Russian communism? This question also came up for discussion among us in the Economic Commission. One comrade set out to prove that to enable capitalism to unfold its activities 'on the great Russian steppes' is to provide it with a road to salvation, with a way out from a difficult situation. But capitalism can move around only within limits offered it by our railroad network, our transport facilities, our open spaces, generally our entire economic culture. We have in mind not a business firm like Gerngross of Vienna which might very well be able to save itself at the expense of the Soviet republic by becoming its supplier; we are talking of capitalism.

If capitalism could, by basing itself on Russia, gain an equilibrium during the coming decades, then this would signify that we have no need whatever of turning to Western European capitalism; for this would signify that we are powerful and strong enough to brush aside the cooperation of Western European and American capitalism. But this is not the situation. We are not strong and powerful enough to be able to renounce capitalist technology, which is as yet available only in its capitalist form; we are certainly not strong and powerful enough to enable capitalism to heal all its wounds with Russia's assistance. This is the inner logic of the situation. In any case, comrades who fear that capitalism may become strengthened by obtaining here a field for its activity must take into consideration that in between this developing capitalism in Russia and the world revolution stands Soviet Russia. Long before Russian capitalism could start relaxing and regaining its strength 'in the Russian steppes', it would have to crush the budding communist economy. The first victim would be our budding socialist organisation. In the Economic Commission, I said that the key factor is still that the power in our country belongs to the vanguard of the proletariat; that in our country the working class rules, represented in political and state relations by this vanguard; and that is why we ought to grant concessions only to the extent that it benefits our cause. That is the obvious prerequisite.

If capitalism had conquered militarily, the question of concessions would have never arisen. Capitalism would have resolved it on its own, and we would not then have had a tactical question. But we do have this question today. Why? Because the power in our country belongs to the working class. It conducts negotiations with capitalism; it has the possibility of granting concessions to some while refusing others; it has the opportunity to make combinations; to weigh the overall state of its own economic development and that of the world revolution; to reflect and seek advice; and then make its decision. That is how things stand.

I then drew the conclusion that those Western European and American comrades, who really fear that capitalism may regain its health in Russia, show thereby that they overestimate our technological and transport facilities and underestimate our Communist powers of judgement. As I said, Comrade Kollontai, who belongs among comrades usually called Left Communists, was not mentioned in connection with the concessions question. But she has done so herself. She has the full right to do it. She puts the discipline of the International above the discipline of the party. I do not know, perhaps it also pertains to the question of concessions, but she wants to display the spirit of knighthood – I don't know how to put it in German – she wants to conduct herself like an Amazon –

**Radek**: Like a Valkyrie!

**Trotsky**: Like a Valkyrie. I place the responsibility for this expression on Comrade Radek. (*Laughter*) That is how Comrade Kollontai conducted herself in placing her name on the speakers' list, although it is customary among us to first take up the question with the delegation, with the Presidium, and with the Central Committee. I merely ask the comrades who are present here and for whom Comrade Kollontai is the spokesperson how they regard the fact that no one raised any objections to it at the session of the Central Committee?[24] We deemed it wholly natural for a politically insignificant and hardly noticeable minority on this question to acquaint the World Congress with its own views and its own tendency.

Let us now pass on to the substance of Comrade Kollontai's speech. Her main idea is that the capitalist system is outlived and that therefore it is impermissible, so to speak, to derive any benefits from it. That is her basic idea. Everything else is for her superfluous. This gives us an entirely adequate idea of Comrade Kollontai's historical and politico-economic approach. In the language of philosophy, this is a purely metaphysical outlook, which operates with immutable, non-historical, dogmatic concepts. Capitalism has outlived itself, and it is therefore not possible to get anything from it that can be of use to us. But, comrades, if it were actually true that capitalism has outlived itself, and we were then attacked by a British or French army, say, on the shores of the Black Sea, I could say that capitalism has outlived itself and then sit down with arms folded. (*Loud applause*) I believe that we would then all be sent to hell, with the permission of Comrade Kollontai. (*Loud applause*)

---

24. This sentence is not found in the German text.

Capitalism will not stop to inquire whether or not it has outlived itself in line with Comrade Kollontai's dogmatic conceptions. It will run us through with bayonets manufactured in its capitalist factories; it will kill and bury us with soldiers rigidly trained under its capitalist discipline. But the fact that an outlived capitalism is capable of slaughtering and murdering us shows that it has plenty of power left. And the very fact that Comrade Kollontai, who belongs to an opposition in the Russian party, is compelled to present her oppositional views to a world congress that must convene in Moscow is itself a scrap of evidence that while capitalism is outlived in the great historical sense and cannot open up any new possibilities for mankind, it still remains powerful enough to prevent us from convening our congresses in Paris or Berlin. (*Applause*) That is a significant fact. Or let us take capitalist technology, for example. What does Comrade Kollontai think of a good locomotive, an honest-to-goodness German capitalist locomotive? This is an interesting question. I am afraid that the German proletariat, even after its conquest of power, will have to travel across the country for a couple of years or so using genuine capitalist locomotives. At least for another two years. After all, it will be very busy and I hardly believe that it will be able immediately in the very first months to begin building new locomotives.

But comrades, is it permissible – from the standpoint of the ten commandments of Comrade Kollontai – to buy a new German locomotive from the firm of Ebert and company? That is the first question. I believe that in answering this point-blank question Comrade Kollontai will not deny us the right to buy a locomotive from Ebert. But if we buy a locomotive there, we must also pay for it there, and, what is more, with gold. And, comrades, gold that flows from Russia into capitalist coffers strengthens them. Of course the amount is far too small to pay the German debts. Fortunately, we do not have such a quantity of gold. (*Laughter*) But if we want to remain steadfast in principle, we must not pay gold to capitalists.

Or suppose we pay with lumber instead of gold. Comrade Kollontai will perhaps then say: I agree to permit trade between Soviet Russia and Germany or Britain, but concessions are out. What are concessions? To get locomotives, we must sell lumber. But we lack enough saws and other mechanical appliances and so we say: 'There is the wood, growing in a forest; let the British capitalist come with his machines and technical equipment, chop himself some trees and logs, and give us locomotives in return.' In short, I should very much like to know where Comrade Kollontai's principled opposition begins and where it ends. Is it with the purchase of locomotives, with the payment in gold, or with payment in lumber in the shape of forests? I am afraid that the opposition begins only with the chopping of trees. (*Loud laughter*)

Comrade Kollontai furthermore asserts that we, in general, want to replace the working class with specialists and with experts, such as technicians.

**Kollontai**: I didn't say that.

**Trotsky**: You said that the initiative of the working class is being replaced by other forces, that the vanguard of the working class is being compelled to cede its place to other forces. And these other forces are on the one hand the so-called technical intelligentsia, and on the other – the peasantry. Of course replacing the peasantry is excluded. But the class that holds the power in its hands negotiates with the peasantry. As regards the technicians, on this question, too, we had a controversy in our party. The echoes of it still reverberate to this day.[25] And perhaps we have heard – if not the last – then the next to the last echo from the lips of Comrade Kollontai.

In a general sense, comrades, the proletariat obviously has considerable power and initiative, and we hope that the power of the working class will considerably alter the face of humankind as a whole. But we never claimed that the working class possesses from its birth the capacities needed to build a new society. All it can do is create the necessary social and political preconditions for this society. What is more, by taking direct control of state power, it can find all the necessary assistants; place them, wherever necessary, in the service of communist economy; and thereby set the entire machine in motion. But we never said that an ordinary worker, by becoming a Communist, acquires the ability to perform the work of a technician, astronomer, or engineer. And now these technical forces are designated simply as 'other social forces', and the fact that these forces have been placed in the service of our cause is characterised as a lack of confidence in the working class. I must state that such reasoning has absolutely nothing in common with Marxism and communism.

Comrades, in the extremely simple field in which I have had to work up to now, the military field, we were compelled from the beginning to resort to the aid of alien technical forces. A good deal of friction arose over this among us. The Central Committee committed quite a few errors, and our military organisation encountered opposition on more than one occasion. We were told: 'You are placing alien technical forces (the reference here was to the officers) in the service of the proletariat.' Yet it later became obvious that if we

---

25. A reference to the debate in the Russian Communist Party over the Red Army's use of thousands of officers and military specialists from the old tsarist army. Trotsky had instituted this policy, over the objections of a military opposition led by Kliment Voroshilov and Joseph Stalin. Lenin declared his support for Trotsky's position, and the RCP's Eighth Congress in March 1919 ratified that stance.

had based ourselves solely on the energy and self-sacrifice of our own comrades, who were certainly carrying out their duty to the fullest extent, and had failed to utilise alien military forces, we would have perished long ago. This is absolutely clear. The Russian working class with its abilities and its capacity for self-sacrifice achieved wonders. It also displayed great initiative after it seized power through its capacity – even though it was backward and was living in a peasant country – to draw officers into its service, sometimes utilising force and sometimes propaganda. (*Loud applause*) We had to have an army. But the working class did not possess sufficient experience and knowledge, and we could not place officers from among the workers immediately and everywhere. Today we already have a great many red officers drawn from the working class. They occupy the highest posts, and their number is increasing daily.

The very same thing applies to the technical field as well. The fact that we are still encircled by a capitalist world forces us to the concessions that we must carry out in the field of technology, too. But we have complete faith that our working class, which feels itself more and more as a member of the great International, will also be able to withstand this breathing spell of capitalism and the unstable equilibrium that now prevails and that will last a while yet. During this pause it will borrow alien forces and alien means, and place them in the service of its own cause. We say to the Russian workers: 'We are conducting negotiations with foreign capitalists, but we shall take all the necessary measures to stand on our own feet.' We want the working class to survey this entire field of activity and say: 'I can offer this or that concession to the German and American capitalists, but I want machinery in return.' Does this betray a lack of faith in the power of the Russian working class, of the Russian proletariat? If anyone is to be reproached with lacking faith in the power of the working class, it is not us but the little group in whose name Comrade Kollontai has spoken here today. (*Loud applause and cheers*)

**F.L. Kerran** (Britain): Comrades, I am surprised that there are so few requests to speak about the political situation in Russia. In today's session, only a single German has taken part in the debate. Personally, I consider that the economic situation in Russia is considerably more important than the political situation. I fear that many delegates will return home with the impression that everything here is in great shape and that nothing is lacking. However, I can assure you that we have certainly not achieved abundance. If that is delegates' impression of conditions in Russia, they are making a mistake. If you want to learn about the real conditions in Russia, you must not limit yourself to superficial observations. I am fortunate in being able to understand not only English but also other languages, and it has been possible for me to gain a more profound knowledge of conditions in this country. I can assure delegates that there is an exceptionally acute crisis here. The worst aspect of the situation is that this crisis will probably last for a considerable time.

From what I have heard, projections for the harvest this year in some of the most important grain-growing districts of Russia are exceptionally bad, such that the economic crisis will endure at least two years. But it is not just a matter of the harvest. Industrial life in Russia is also virtually at a standstill.

As for Russia's possibilities of obtaining goods from abroad, in my opinion – and our Russian comrades will agree with me, based on their practical experience – Russia is not capable of purchasing with gold even a thousandth of the goods that it needs. The gold reserves of the entire world would not be sufficient to pay for everything that Russia needs. Russia thus faces immense difficulties in concluding agreements and in receiving concessions from the capitalists or in granting them. In this regard, we Communists could provide Russia with a significant service by becoming active in the cooperatives in our own countries. Just before I left Britain, there was a conference of cooperatives. The executive committee of the wholesale purchasing cooperative was asked by delegates why it had not yet conducted any business with Russia. The committee responded that it would be glad to have business relations with Russia but it had not yet been able to come to agreement with the Russians. If these people could be contacted in the right way and offered concessions, the British cooperatives could doubtless be readily persuaded to invest quite significant sums in Russia. I am convinced of this.

Comrade Kollontai told us today that the concessions to foreign capitalists harboured dangers. However, I must say that I am in complete agreement on this point with the majority of the Russian comrades. Necessity knows no law. If you are able to induce the foreign capitalists to help you in some way, in my opinion you must do it whatever the cost. I for one would summon the devil if he could provide me with any service. We have to keep a firm grip on reality here. I will therefore certainly not reproach our Russian comrades in any way for having offered concessions to the foreign capitalists, all the more in that we have not yet got to the point where we could help them ourselves.

In Germany, I had a discussion with Wiegand, among others. He said that the experiment with communism in Russia had lost its fiery red hue and had now taken on a pink shading such that respectable people now had every possibility of travelling to Russia. When I passed through Belgium and Germany and had contact with capitalists there, I noticed that all of them were casting longing glances toward Russia. They believed that they would find their only salvation in Russia. Every one of them said, 'Oh, if only I could do business with Russia.' I observed the same thing in Britain, Belgium, and Germany.

A certain multi-millionaire in Germany – I must concede that he is something of an idealist – expressed his desire to travel with me to Russia, because he is so interested in what is being done here. I believe he meant it quite sincerely. He said that he would make available all his capital, all his factories, if he could see that the experiment had prospects of success.

In conclusion, I wish to say that in our capacity as delegates we must get to the bottom of this matter. If we are able to come to an understanding with our Russian comrades to send experts from Germany, Britain, France, and other countries, these workers, in my opinion, should receive special advantages. If I were in the Russians' shoes, and if I could recruit a hundred thousand specialists, I would give them everything that they needed, even if this had to be done at the cost of hundreds of thousands of others. It is extremely important that the entire technical experience of workers in other countries be utilised for Russia's welfare. For if the Russian experiment ends in failure, if Russia proves to be incapable of developing its economic and industrial life, all our ideals will be dashed, and we will be unable to break the resistance of the bourgeoisie. We must demonstrate, first, that we can make a revolution, and, second, construct an economic and industrial system that assures the entire population of food, clothing, and shelter.

Since I am keenly interested in Russia and the Russians, I would very much like to know what we foreigners can do to assist Russia in restoring its economic apparatus. Through some research I have determined that most of the industrial enterprises in Russia before the War were in the hands of foreigners. About four million foreigners lived in Russia, managing the Russian factories. Most of them have left Russia. This is obviously the cause of the present economic paralysis in Russia. The Russians, to be sure, are the best propagandists in the world, but they have not yet fully proved their worth as organisers. I therefore believe that it is absolutely necessary for Communist parties in other countries to get to the bottom of this matter and seek ways and means to help our Russian comrades in reconstructing their industrial life. I do not reproach the Russians in any way, but I do believe that there have been foreigners who came here and wanted to help the Russians in reconstructing their industry.

**Hempel** (Appel, KAPD): Comrades, first I must make a remark to Comrade Radek, who is apparently not here –

**Shout**: He is present.

**Hempel**: My remark is this: Comrade Radek should spare us the jokes identifying us with the Mensheviks. When such jokes are repeated so often, it becomes absurd.

Comrade Radek then asked us a question, calling on us to say whether the Russian policies are right for Russia and the International. Our answer is simply this: it is the Russian comrades themselves who should decide whether the internal policy of the Russian Communist Party is correct. We were always of the opinion that the course of action pursued by the Russian comrades in their own country has been correct. Now we hear in Comrade Kollontai's speech today that more emphasis should be placed on heightening initiative in the working class, so as not to be obliged to give so many concessions to the capitalists. If Comrade Kollontai has really portrayed conditions accurately, we must say that this represents an error in Russian policy. We say this because we have a different conception of party dictatorship of the proletariat for Germany and Western Europe. Certainly our opinion was that the dictatorship in Russia was correct for Russian conditions, because the forces of the proletariat were insufficiently developed, and the dictatorship must therefore be exerted more from above. But now we see that efforts are being made inside the Russian proletariat to help out and share in responsibility for this development. Such strivings from below to above must be supported and taken into account. This is a power that sustains the proletarian dictatorship better than foreign capital. If we utilise this power as fully as possible, we will not have to make as many concessions to the capitalists.

Secondly, we need to investigate how Russian policy affects the International. Here we must say, however, that it is not yet clear at this moment whether this policy is completely wrong. However, we see that the preparations being made are wrong, and that needs to be examined.

The question is whether the comrades in Russia are supermen, people who can rise above circumstances, or will their actions be shaped by their surroundings? That is something we will have to observe. We are not influenced by a desire to voice criticisms, but we see the error and also that it is growing and will continue to grow. Comrade Trotsky said it clearly, and he is right; we are all in agreement: we must win time. Everything depends on whether the vanguard survives, on getting through what Comrade Lenin calls this state of unstable equilibrium, on the arrival of help from the world revolution or a revolution in some country.

Will this vanguard, this state power be able to survive the unstable equilibrium? That is the question. Trotsky responded to one aspect of it by saying that we will perish if we do not follow this simple path of making concessions to the petty bourgeoisie, that is, to small-scale capitalism, to foreign capital, to state capitalism. That is necessary. Who would oppose doing something when there is simply no other option? But can one do this and simultaneously remain a Communist? Are we that tough? Well, I want to direct our attention to the heart of the matter, namely, whether the Communist Party will be able to survive this activity, whether it lasts one year or many years? Will the Communist Party remain what it is today? Will it not then develop a stronger interest, for this or that reason, in not expanding the revolution abroad? That means renewed misery.

If the revolution breaks out abroad, in Germany, and it lasts for a year or even longer, we will not be able to help Russia. We must consider that the entire population, and the Russian party along with it, has become accustomed to reconstruction, to a rest period, to a certain stability. This is so obvious! If things fall once again into disorder, if trade relations break off, if poverty returns, the population will rage against the government. That is the question. And this is evidence that the broad masses have a revolutionary need for a pause, a pause after the revolution. That has already become evident. This will have an impact on the Communist Party, and it must take this into account. I must ask if it is strong enough to do so.

There is something else I want to raise. As we know, in every country – we are now experiencing it again in Germany – if the economy is ruined, if capitalism is engaged in reconstruction, this generates an enormous amount of corruption. We see the black market, which is also here. We have heard about many things that penetrate into the Communist Party, and against such things even people as able as Lenin and Trotsky are powerless. That is the greatest danger, and we should keep it in view. That is why we say it is in the interests of the Russian Revolution, the world revolution, and communism that this unstable equilibrium does not last too long.

We will come, to be sure. We will unite in this process. We will find ways to speed things up. The Russian comrades lack an understanding of the prevailing situation in Western Europe. The Russian comrades think in terms of a population like that of Russia. The Russians endured long years of tsarist rule, and they are solid and firm, while our proletariat has experienced parliamentarism and become fully contaminated. Something different must be done. The task is to bar the road to opportunism.

**Shout**: Scheidemann's theory.

**Hempel**: Nonsense. It is not Scheidemann's theory. Since when does Scheidemann want to bar the road to opportunism? The task is to bar the road to opportunism for the fighting proletariat and the Communist parties, which must lead the way. And in our country opportunism is making use of parliament, making use of bourgeois economic institutions. And also the attempt to transform cooperatives into instruments of struggle that could possibly provide help to Russia, not in a revolutionary fashion but by using capitalist methods, to the degree that the proletariat has access to them.

Well, comrades, what does it mean to influence the international proletariat? If you persuade your consumer cooperatives to engage in trade relations with Russia, does that help Russia? Not in the slightest. The cooperatives must deal in terms of capital, just like any other entrepreneur. They will be even more expensive. That diverts us from the correct path. That is the key issue here. The Third International has to ensure that Russia is not supported from abroad by capitalist methods, but rather by the proletariat, using revolutionary methods. That's what is at issue. And this cannot be done by adopting the policy followed by the Third International. We demand a tougher policy. That's the catch. (*Laughter*) Comrades may well laugh. Even Comrade Lenin is laughing; well, we can't help that. This is our conviction.

**Shout**: Comrade Bukharin will explain why we are laughing.

**Hempel**: Anyone can laugh. I must point out once more something common to Germany and to every country in the world with many long years of experience with democracy, which is not revolutionary at all. The working class and along with it the big Communist mass party, which harbours many opportunist elements, are very prone to take the path of not using tough methods but utilising parliament and trade unions and other such methods to help Russia. That is not support at all, but rather an evasion of any form of struggle.

Now Trotsky says that we must get out of this unstable equilibrium as quickly as possible. That brings me to my next point: There are great dangers if every effort is not made to give the foreign capitalists as little scope as possible here to extend their influence. We have to be extremely alert, and proletarians must watch closely, in order to keep control. Otherwise, I believe, we will live to see Soviet Russia become something quite different from what Comrade Trotsky projects. It will become a territory where – while the international proletariat is groaning – international capitalism rises up once again – not to the degree that it can regain complete health but sufficiently to stumble along for a lengthy period. The policies of the Third International must aim at rendering impossible this period of time, this course of capitalist development. This can be done through sabotage in the factories, sabotage in production, which by no means signifies destroying the means of production but aims rather at making the business unprofitable for the capitalists. That is the task of proletarians around the world, in order to drive the revolution forward as quickly as possible. For revolution will surely arise from the plight of the working population.

Thus, comrades, our message to the Third International is that the Russian party should be more aware of the dangers and should state them openly; this will reduce the dangers. In addition, the Russian party should also be aware that it is the foundation of the Third International, and that the other parties are not in a position to match it either intellectually or materially. That is evident in the fact that no opinions critical of the Russian comrades can be expressed here. The Russian comrades should also take note and recognise that if they are not to be forced more and more – let us say it – to steer Russian state policy to the right, and given that they are not supermen, they need to have a counterweight in the Third International, one that has broken with all compromising policies, with parliamentarism, and with the old trade unions.

**Roland-Holst**: Comrades, I had not intended to take the floor on this question. But since the discussion has taken on this character, I asked to speak because I consider it my duty to demonstrate that opinions in the so-called Left of the Third International are divided on Russian policy. I would like to speak briefly on three of the points touched on here. The first of these is that of initiative by the masses and the measures taken by the Russian party to draw strength from the masses' initiative and creative activity. I cannot judge exactly how things stand as regards momentary difficulties and the new laws and governmental measures, which have evidently been taken under the direct pressure of these difficulties. I would therefore like to stress that the past years have provided us, by and large, with magnificent and unprecedented examples of how to awaken the initiative and creative power of the working masses, and how such initiatives can be kept alive. If this were not the case, clearly the Soviet republic would simply no longer exist. If the creative power of Russian proletarians had not fertilised the fields of the revolution again and again, all that has been done to organise life, education, and military strength would not have been possible. (*Applause*)

Second, we have the question of whether the Russians, the Russian party, is genuinely interested in maintaining European capitalism in a certain equilibrium, and in stabilising it. If that were truly the case, obviously it would be a terrible and tragic conflict, from which there would be no escape. However, I view the matter differently. The Russian party is not interested in safeguarding an equilibrium but is strongly committed to the development of revolution in Europe and the world. The Russian comrades have repeatedly assured us of this, and we can give full credit to their statements, because they coincide with what we can grasp and understand from our own reasoning, if only we attempt to survey the situation calmly and without prejudice. It is certain that Soviet Russia will attempt strenuously to extract goods from capitalist

Europe and the United States by means of concessions. On the other hand, the danger remains that Soviet Russia will be attacked by capitalist Europe. There is thus still a need for Soviet Russia to ward off this danger and to maintain a military organisation, perhaps not to the same extent as earlier, but nonetheless a quite extensive one. We were well aware when we came here – indeed we have often read and also heard from the lips of Comrade Trotsky – that military activity, while indispensable, saps the energies of Soviet Russia at this moment of history, when the economy is so ruined, poverty is so dreadful, and Russia has lived beyond its means in order to maintain its position and defend the world revolution as its most advanced outpost. That is why it is extremely important for Soviet Russia that the revolution grow in strength in other countries. It may be that for some time Russia will receive fewer industrial goods. Nonetheless, we hope and are confident that peace will make it possible to demobilise the army and for all energies to be fully devoted to building up the communist economy.

And now just a few more words on the third point, the attitude of the Russian party to the Third International. One could get the impression that Russia now wants to slow down revolutionary developments somewhat. However, I am convinced that this is a false impression, which will be rapidly refuted by the facts. Before I came, I too was somewhat uncertain, but I have heard and seen a great deal here. I have tried to examine things more profoundly, and I have come to the conclusion that I was perhaps mistaken. The great leaders of the revolution have spoken to us of the necessity to prepare the revolution well and thoroughly, as Comrade Lenin too stressed repeatedly in his speech today. They have spoken out against dangers from the left, against the dangers of putschism, against launching the revolution prematurely. Why are they doing this? Is it for the same reasons as the Western European opportunists, who do not want a revolution? We all know that they do this because they have confidence in the revolution, they do it because they are firmly and unshakeably convinced that capitalism, although it may flare up again, cannot achieve new and genuine viability.

We witnessed that in the discussion over the world situation. In the commission, it was the Russian comrades who took a clear stand on the basis that capitalism may go up or down, but it is overall tending downwards, that is, we are experiencing the development of revolution. We must never lose that from our sight. Only when we judge Russian policies and the policies of the Third International from this angle can we arrive at correct conclusions. Our conclusion can only be that the Russians are not on the right, they are on the left; they are always on the left. I have become convinced of this here in Russia, and I regard it as my duty to express this conviction here publicly.

The Russians are on the left, by and large, because they have great and unshakeable trust in the revolution. In Western Europe and Central Europe, we live under different conditions. We are perhaps less imbued with this thought, because we do not have the revolution yet. We have capitalism, and we live and struggle under the pressure and the immense power of Western European capitalism. When our revisionists and opportunists say the same thing, 'Be cautious, do not move too quickly,' they do so because they do not want the revolution. When the Russians say that, it is simply because they want the revolution, have confidence in it, and know the power that resides in the working-class masses. They know that the working class will carry out a revolution – if not today, in this unfavourable period, one possibly marked by increased prosperity, then certainly tomorrow, or the day after tomorrow. The Third International cannot at present perceive a revolutionary counterweight to Russia in Western Europe, because revolutionary forces are too limited there. The Russians are still the firm pillar of world revolution. (*Loud applause and cheers*)

**Bukharin**: Comrades, I would like to make some comments here about the speeches of two different comrades representing the KAPD, Comrades Sachs and Hempel. Comrade Sachs offered as his best argument against us the following: our concessions and different trade relationships to the capitalist states are buttressing capitalism in the Western European countries and are thus holding back the cause of revolution. In my opinion, this is not accurate for the following reasons: first, the amount of our aid is completely inadequate for Western European capitalism. The quantity of goods that we receive from Western European countries comes directly to us. On the other hand, the goods that we export are divided among all the different countries of the capitalist world. Naturally, the statistical relationship is more favourable for us than for capitalism.

The second counterargument is that this economic reality is accompanied by another reality: the heightening of political competition among the different capitalist states. We must not overlook this argument. To the extent that we conclude genuine concessions, we thereby disorganise the entire political structure of world capitalism as a whole, and this has economic consequences. Political disorganisation always has a crippling effect on economic activity.

Thirdly, we must draw a balance sheet here. When we give something, we simultaneously receive something. And if you undertake to evaluate this fact, you must compare all its components, and then you will immediately note that we strengthen ourselves more than the aid we provide to capitalism. These three arguments are completely adequate to destroy Comrade Sachs's line of reasoning.

Now as to the speech of Comrade Kollontai. It is quite understandable that all the old Menshevik memories of Comrade Kollontai are being regenerated in the present period of her intellectual development. (*Laughter*) That is of course why we come across things that have an almost completely Menshevik ring, and there is also a noticeable link to the KAPD. Yet Comrade Kollontai's line of argument is somewhat humorous. She begins with a diagnosis and a prognosis: a new class of specialists, bureaucrats, and bourgeois is in formation here. This is a new class; it will constantly grow in strength; and we will need to carry out a third revolution against it. But if we have a close look at this so-called third revolution, then we wind up with the same third revolution that the Mensheviks and Social Revolutionaries talk of.

But their understanding of it is more logical. They regard the October Revolution as a counterrevolution, and in their opinion the third revolution is the real revolution, which will restore the suppressed February Revolution. But Comrade Kollontai's third, future revolution is a proletarian revolution. What does Comrade Kollontai say to this? Already, the class that really rules is almost the former bourgeoisie. Then comes a sudden leap from the realm of necessity to that of freedom, with quite a different assertion, that it is really not the proletariat that is ruling in our country, and not this new bureaucracy either, but the peasantry. That is quite a different thesis advanced by Comrade Kollontai.

Let us examine the substance of this second thesis. What is it based on? On the fact that we have made substantial economic concessions to the peasantry. Comrades, permit me to make an analogy here. Imagine that you have a capitalist factory director, and the workforce goes on strike. Under the pressure of the workers, the factory director doubles their wages and makes substantial economic concessions. Now Comrade Kollontai comes along, saying, what is going on here? The factory director has made substantial concessions to the workforce, and he has thereby ceased to be a capitalist. The same argumentation. What does that signify? It signifies a truly revisionist theory. Consider a bourgeois government, which makes major concessions to workers during a war, and even sets up figures from the ranks of the working class as ministers. It is as if one were to regard such a government as no longer bourgeois but as suspended above the classes. The line of reasoning is the same, and it has nothing to do with Marxism. (*Applause*)

Now the third point: the question of state capitalism. When Comrade Lenin uses the term state capitalism here, it is different from the term 'state capitalism' as used in Western Europe, which is something quite different. In Western Europe, state capitalism is quite correctly understood as capital in the form of a state monopoly, exerted by the bourgeois state. That is the concept of state capitalism in its pure form. That is something quite different. In genuine state capitalism, the means of production are actually owned by the bourgeoisie, represented by the state. Here the relations of production are different. Even in the case of concessions, the real proprietor is the proletariat, which leases out its property to the capitalist holding the concession. The property relations and corresponding productive relations are quite different. This is a distinctive economic structure, and in terms of theory, it should not be confused with 'state capitalism' in the usual sense of the word.

Comrade Kollontai – and this is what is striking with all these critics – says that we are menaced by great dangers. She has a striking formulation: I am very frightened. What conclusions flow from that? Big fears do not lead to big deeds.

**Radek**: But they did result in a big speech.

**Bukharin**: What did she propose to us? For example, we replaced the system of grain requisitioning with the tax in kind. That was the first step in our new orientation. Now has Comrade Kollontai proposed that we go back again to the requisitioning system? Not at all! At our party congress, the Workers' Opposition did not say a single word against it, not a single word. I do not know what group it is that Comrade Kollontai is representing here. It seems to me that the group is quite monolithic, and consists of Comrade Kollontai alone. (*Laughter*) I must point out that no arguments have been advanced against our policies. Intellectual manipulation carried out in a mechanistic spirit: that is not a genuine argument; we cannot be satisfied with that.

Comrades, Gorter says in his much-renowned pamphlet that the world is headed for ruin because the Russian comrades do not hold to a historical-materialist point of view. Now let us understand what historical materialism is. We have the historical materialism of Comrade Kollontai, who had much to say about the spirit of creation and things like that, a spirit that could not care less about base material conditions and mechanical considerations of the type invoked here by Comrade Lenin.

In my view, the most inadequate aspect of Comrade Kollontai's entire speech is that no one can understand what exactly she is proposing. Much can be said about how prevalent corruption is here, how we are poor organisers, how we have made this and that error. All this is true. But, comrades, tell me what we should do? We are striving with every means to overcome these deficiencies. But if you have a magical formula, do not be bashful, tell us what it is, and we will be very grateful. (*Laughter*)

As for the speech by Comrade Kerran, he said quite rightly that we should utilise the cooperatives in Western Europe. And here Comrade Hempel was quite correct to say that cooperatives in Western Europe are organised along capitalist lines. But everything Kerran says applies not to the line of the Communist International but to that of the Soviet government. Comrade Kerran's speech would be excellent if it had been delivered not to the congress of the Communist International but in the Commissariat of Foreign Trade. It can be said that we want to conduct trade with the social patriots but carry out revolution with the Communists. These two things are by no means mutually exclusive.

Then Comrade Hempel told us that he does not need to judge whether or not this policy is good for Soviet Russia; that is for the Russian comrades to decide. And it is precisely on these grounds that his entire speech criticises our position. But, in our opinion, every Communist Party ought to concern itself with the affairs of every other Communist Party in order to generalise our experiences. That is an entirely routine internationalist approach.

Comrade Hempel said that he gained more wisdom about Russian politics than ever before in his life by what Comrade Kollontai said in this session. And he added: we must increase initiative. Well, comrades, we can cry out for initiative a thousand times, but tell us please how this initiative is to be generated? We have tried conferences of non-party people, various institutions, inspections on the job – please make us a specific proposal. And if you do not propose anything, then we must say, comrades, that this criticism has no substance. Propose something specific, and we will adopt it gratefully, but do not just make a noise about increasing initiative. If you do not take up the topic from a practical point of view, it's simply futile. (*Loud applause*)

Comrade Hempel also said that when social layers are pressing up from below, then you have a power. And given this power, there is no need to make concessions to capitalism. If by this pressure from below you are thinking of the process of education and development of our workers, we must certainly clear the road for this new and growing power. That is our highest duty. But sometimes this pressure from below to above is confused with what we experienced in Kronstadt. For that too was from below to above.

**Trotsky**: But its goals were directed from above to below. (*Loud applause*)

**Bukharin**: As for the class character of the struggle with the peasantry, I have spoken of that on another occasion.[26] Hempel talks about concessions from an international point of view. He said that we have acquired a stake in maintaining the functioning of economic life in the West, which

---

26. This may be a reference to Bukharin's 1920 work, *Economics of the Transformation Period* (Bukharin 1971). The question is taken up in the chapter, 'City and Country in the Process of Social Transformation'.

is important to us, and for this reason the policy of economic relations and concessions is unacceptable. Let me make an analogy here, one that was used by Karl Renner. He said that the terms 'worker' and 'capitalist' are mutually related. Capital cannot exist without workers, and workers cannot exist without capital. There is therefore a common interest shared by capital and the proletariat. And that is why revolution is impossible. But of course this common interest, at any given moment, is relative. There are also much greater and more enduring interests of the working class that break up this common interest. The situation here is identical. It would be good if we could obtain something from Britain, but we are well aware that the development of the workers' movement provides us with a far greater and more definitive guarantee. The interests of the Russian Revolution are fundamentally those of the world revolution. That is why we are the most active component of the Communist International.

Of course I will not refute the argument advanced by Comrade Hempel that borders on slandering the German working class, by saying that German workers are completely contaminated. If the entire German working class is contaminated, what is this revolution that you in the KAPD want to make, dear comrades? If this is the case, you will only be able to make a contaminated revolution. I don't know what to make of that. But when Comrade Hempel argues in favour of sabotage, that is really quite humorous. He says we must make the factories unprofitable. The train of thought here is obvious. The proletariat must worsen economic conditions, so that it can then rise in revolution against these bad conditions. Thus, a general boycott against preservation of wages. Then all the workers will be discontented. They will be hungry, they will revolt, and they will do away with capitalist society as a whole.

Comrade Hempel also says that if you initiate trade relationships with the different capitalist states, you cannot be a Communist. Comrades, we heard the same things said about the Brest-Litovsk Treaty. It was said that we were sitting at the same table as generals, and that is why we suddenly turned into generals. But you know that we are in a much more favourable position, for capitalism and capitalist society fear that we are infecting their society with Bolshevism. There are perhaps dangers running the other way, but they are not as great. We have already achieved a certain immunity. Now it is a question of time: can we hold on or not? There is no way to answer this question with absolute certainty. But for us, the main task right now is to gain time. If we perish, that does not mean the Western European revolution will perish. They will take our experiences to heart. But we have not yet perished.

Now as for the speech by Comrade Hempel, I really do not know whether or not he is against trade relations. He did not answer the question whether he is against concessions. But those are precisely the crucial issues. His criticism is marked by the same clichés as that of Comrade Kollontai. Comrade Hempel says that the Russian party must see the dangers. Well, we see them all right. All the Russians who have come to the podium say that class relations are such and such, and that, in order to preserve the power of the proletariat, we are compelled to make major concessions to the peasantry. What does that tell you? It tells you that we see these dangers. The struggle has already begun to cleanse our party of bureaucrats.[27] The Central Committee has just decided to expel many thousands, perhaps more than one hundred thousand members from the party, under strict supervision by the commissars. That tells you that we see the danger. So Comrade Hempel's advice is very good, but it has been made rather too late. What he has said is just another expression of the 'Russian diktat', a campaign of theoretical abuse mounted by the KAPD to the effect that delegations cannot act independently because they are under our orders. This abuse will not succeed.

As for the notion that the Third International is a counterweight to the Soviet government, that concept of Comrade Hempel is completely illogical, because the Third International is actually counterposed to the League of Nations. But what is important here is to see that there is a division of labour between our organs of government, on the one hand, and the Third International as an independent revolutionary organisation of the working class.

By and large, I must say that the entirety of the criticism directed against us is not criticism at all, but rather consists only of empty words. (*Loud applause*)

**Kolarov** (Chair): No one else has asked to speak. The debate is therefore closed. Comrade Lenin has the floor for his summary.

**Lenin**: Comrades, I am in complete agreement with what my friend Bukharin has said. I have nothing to add, and I therefore waive my summary. (*Loud laughter*)

---

27. The Tenth Congress of the Russian Communist Party in March 1921 passed a resolution, 'The Issues of Party Building' that stated: 'There is the absolute necessity for the party to make a decisive shift towards attracting workers and cleansing itself of non-Communist elements.' It called for carrying out a cleansing campaign during August and September 1921. By the time of the Eleventh Congress in 1922, more than one hundred thousand members had been expelled from the party. Bosić et al. (eds.) 1981, p. 784, n. 265.

Here and elsewhere, 'cleansing' translates the Russian word *ochistka*, which is also sometimes rendered as 'purge'. The latter word, however, has been avoided because it has since acquired a pejorative connotation due to its association with Stalinist repression in the 1930s.

**Kolarov** (Chair): The Presidium has received a resolution on the Russian question for presentation to the congress. Comrade Koenen will read out the resolution.

**Koenen**: (*Reads the resolution*)

[*For text of resolution, see p. 977.*]

[*signed*] *Thalheimer, Friesland* (for the Communist Party of Germany)

*Michalak, Glinski* (for the Communist Party of Poland)

*W. Münzenberg* (for the Youth International)

*Roland-Holst, J.C. Ceton* (for the Communist Party of the Netherlands)

*Kolarov* (for the Communist Party of Bulgaria)

*Kreibich* (for the Communist Workers' Party of Czechoslovakia, German Section)

Italy: (*signature*)

Belgium: (*signature*)

**Kolarov** (Chair): We will proceed to the vote on this resolution. I wish to inform you that the Czechoslovak delegation has also handed in its written endorsement.

**Delagrange**: On behalf of the French delegation, I declare that it too endorses this resolution.

**Kolarov** (Chair): Is there any opposition to this resolution? The resolution is unanimously adopted. (*Prolonged loud applause and cheers*) I would like to inform you that our next session will take place tomorrow, Wednesday afternoon, at 6:00 p.m. On the agenda will be continued discussion of the trade-union question.

(*The session is adjourned at 7:00 p.m.*)

# Session 18 – 6 July 1921, 8 p.m.
## Trade Unions – Discussion

*Continuation of the discussion on the trade-union question. Speakers: Malzahn, Misiano, Rwal, Haywood, Brand, Lozovsky, Marshall.*

**Kolarov** (Chair): Comrade Malzahn is the first speaker. He has the floor.

**Malzahn**: Comrades, Comrade Zinoviev quite rightly declared in his report on the trade-union question that the Amsterdam trade-union International is the main buttress of the bourgeoisie. He also said that the struggle against the Amsterdam International is not one between tendencies but a class struggle in the true sense of the word, and that our task is to break through the nodal point represented by this organisation. We are in complete agreement with Comrade Zinoviev, including with regard to the way we should handle our relationship with the Red International of Labour Unions and to putting an end to political neutrality in the unions.

But the most important point, comrades, is that the congress must clarify how this struggle should be conducted in order to win over the trade unions and make them into instruments of revolution. And here we must look backward. The Second Congress of the Communist International resolved that Communists were duty-bound to win over the trade unions by carrying out a struggle within the unions. It is our task to counter every tendency that stands in the way of our carrying out this task. Every split by revolutionary forces from the trade unions, from the economic mass organisations, necessarily signifies a weakening of our struggle, and thereby a weakening of our preparation for proletarian revolution.

Comrades, the futility of such breakaways can be best demonstrated with reference to the German trade-union movement. In the spring of 1919, information from the General German Trade Union Federation [ADGB] indicated that the free trade unions had a total membership of three million.[1] Subsequently, the reported membership total rose rapidly, *from three million to nine million members* for the year 1920. If we take together the Gelsenkirchen Free Workers' Union, the syndicalist group, and the General Workers' Union, we must register the fact that despite all their propaganda, these breakaway groups have not succeeded in surpassing a total membership of three hundred thousand. So we have on the one hand the nine million members of the free trade unions and, on the other, despite the trade-union betrayals, the three hundred thousand in the Free Workers, the General Workers, and the syndicalist groups in Germany, all taken together.

Comrades, we have felt very keenly the impact of this splintering in our trade-union activity in Germany. First of all, these revolutionary forces are not united. Instead, because of this splintered struggle, the revolutionary forces do not stand together in struggle – which benefits and profits only the Amsterdam trade-union International, the ADGB, and the counterrevolutionary trade-union bureaucracy. Moreover, the slogan raised by these groups, 'Out of the trade unions!', is pinned on our party in a very clever manner. The KAPD, which is known as a sympathising party of the Communist International, constantly issues the call 'Out of the trade unions!', giving this trade-union bureaucracy a wonderful opening for propaganda that erects a barrier against Communist trade-union work. We therefore welcome the decision that the congress has taken on the KAPD question.

In addition, our previous experience in the different districts of Germany, even in districts where the syndicalist unions play a relatively decisive role and have consolidated their strength to some degree – above all with the miners in Westphalia – demonstrates that they are not capable of carrying out the necessary economic struggles. When challenged by this or that measure, they fail completely, once more handing the miners' federation telling arguments against the Communists.

The German trade-union movement is undergoing a crisis. Membership is declining in almost every federation. Thus the strongest organisation, the German metalworkers' federation, has lost one hundred thousand members in the course of the last year. The membership loss of the free trade unions as a

---

1. 'Free trade unions' was a commonly used term referring to the Social-Democratic-led ADGB, Germany's largest union federation.

whole amounts to one million. This shrinkage is evident not only in Germany but in the entire international trade-union movement as well. I would have liked to have had this problem taken up in detail in the report. Without any doubt, this decline in membership represents a danger for the revolution. That is why our task is to examine the causes of this loss of trade-union members.

After the November [1918] revolution, the masses streamed into the trade unions. Instinctively they expected an improvement in their standard of living. They believed that by joining the unions they had accomplished their revolutionary duty, and that the unions would lead the struggle on their behalf. But we have had to recognise that the unions are not carrying out policies of active struggle. They do not educate the masses into a consciously revolutionary fighting force. Instead, their policy of collaboration with the employers compels them to betray every revolutionary struggle, whether economic or political. The masses, still imprisoned by bourgeois ideology, became disappointed. The trade unions sabotage revolutionary struggle while collaborating with the employers and pursuing social reform. Communists, as a force pressing forward, want to counter these policies, regardless of circumstances. The trade-union bureaucracy therefore undertakes to drive them, and above all the Communist leaders, out of the federations.

Rather than explaining their real reasons, they claim that the Communists want to split, defeat, and destroy the unions. The propaganda of the syndicalist unions and the KAPD creates ideal conditions for the union bureaucracy to carry out this policy. Undoubtedly, the KAPD's view that the decline of the trade unions is advantageous for the revolution is fundamentally wrong. These masses who are streaming out of the trade unions are not joining the syndicalist unions but sinking back into the swamp of indifference. That is a danger for the trade-union movement, and that is why the task of Communists in the trade unions is to exert all their strength to revolutionise them. That makes the trade-union issue a life-and-death question for the revolution. Revolutionising the unions is a precondition for carrying out a revolution.

Bergmann says that the syndicalist unions are necessary, after the taking of power, to maintain the economy. He would have done better to use his report to grasp the essence of the trade-union movement and to recognise that the unions must be put to the task of taking political power. It is wrong to think that winning the trade unions is a statistical process, in which Communists must take all the functionary-level positions or occupy at least 60 per cent of them. As you know, only a certain percentage of trade-union members are politically active. It is this segment, which dominates the meetings and the activity of functionaries, that we must win. When the employers launch attacks aimed at suppressing the workers, it is not difficult to expose the trade-union bureaucracy on the basis of their calls for collaboration with the employers. If the KAPD comrades shy away from winning the trade unions, we would like to know how they expect to arrive at a revolution. The World Congress and the Red International of Labour Unions must set down a clear basic line for the activity for Communists in the trade unions of every country. (*Loud applause*)

**Francesco Misiano** (Communist Party of Italy): We must pay very close attention to the question now under discussion. In a battle, there must be a general staff with a clear overview of the situation, familiarity with the battlefield, and knowledge of which weapons to use against the enemy. There must also be a unified and disciplined army that is equal to all the requirements of battle, at all times. We need to think clearly in our international political organisation, the Third International. Even more, we need an army, the trade unions, which will heed our call when the time comes to plunge into battle.

The slogans and programme of the Third International on the trade-union question must therefore be clarified to everyone as much as possible.

We have not yet received the theses developed by the Executive. It is thus a difficult task, at this point, to present specific views on the different points. Only tomorrow will we be able to go through each point in detail. So our discussion must draw on our experience, first of all, and also on the theses of the Second Congress of the Third International. The Second Congress presented us with the fundamental points of our programme on the question now before us. By and large, we are in complete agreement with the Second Congress theses, including the point saying that economic and trade-union organisations should be subordinate to the political party and that the task of Communists is to win the leading posts in the trade unions.[2] Obviously the question must be posed in these terms: trade unions must enjoy a certain autonomy; we must reckon with the necessity for a certain degree of formal, superficial autonomy. However, the very nature of the unions demands that they be fully and completely subordinated to the political movement. To achieve this discipline, we must rely principally on the Communist Party members to penetrate the leading bodies and the heart of the unions.

We must strive to achieve complete unity between the trade-union and political organisations. The moment an order is issued by the political organisation, the general staff of our army, we must be capable of bringing a unified disciplined army into the field at once.

---

2. A reference to the 'Theses on the Trade Union Movement, Factory Committees, and the Communist International' (Riddell (ed.) 1991, 2WC, 2, pp. 625–34). Point 4 includes the call for Communist leadership of the unions; point 13 calls for subordinating factory committees and unions to the CP's leadership.

Our congress must therefore explain our programme of formal autonomy once and for all. The workers must be led to understand that from now on there is only a single struggle, the final struggle for revolution by the working masses, for the victory of communism.

We must not limit ourselves to small skirmishes like those of the prewar period. We must make it clear that small struggles only delay the final battle.

We will not be able to avoid these small struggles, but during these limited encounters we must always keep in mind and direct the workers' attention to the inevitability of the great, final battle. Only the revolutionary overthrow of the capitalist class will enable us to resolve all the problems – great and small – of the working class. There is thus no basis for the slightest doubt regarding Communist policy in the trade unions.

In the coming skirmishes as well – the wage struggles, the strikes to achieve a shorter working day – we must clearly formulate our programme, counterposing it to that of the reformists and Social Democrats. It has transpired often in Italy (and also, I believe, in other countries) that the Communists, lacking in clarity, have conducted themselves in action in a fashion similar to the reformists. Our party was forced several times to point out to certain Communists the errors they had made. We now ask all comrades, both in Russia and abroad, to assist us in formulating our theses, so that we can determine, for the future, the difference between how Communists and Social Democrats conduct trade-union struggles.

We must now raise the question of factory councils, both in Italy and in other countries.[3] We have collected rich experiences on this question in Italy, in the city of Turin. We created factory councils in Turin and also in other cities, but we did not succeed in bringing into being an organisation of this type for Italy as a whole. The Second Congress theses take a clear position on this point. However, the idea of organising factory councils must not remain just on paper. The delegates present at this congress must do everything they can, after they return home, to form factory councils in the factories and everywhere that the working masses are to be found. These factory councils are extremely important for the struggle against the bureaucratism of the old Social Democrats, which has taken root in the economic organisations. We cannot accept the VKPD's view that the trade unions are the main thing. Rather we are of the view that the factory councils are the most appropriate

---

3. Factory councils began emerging in Britain, Germany, Italy, and other countries during the latter stages of World War I. Unlike most trade unions bodies at the time, these councils were chosen by all workers in a given workplace. The resolution on factory councils adopted by the Comintern's Second Congress focused on their role in the fight for workers' control of industry.

means with which to fight the trade unions. We must win the trade unions to our side, and in order to achieve this goal we must have the factory councils standing by us vigorously.

With the factories as our starting point, we can take up the struggle against the Social Democrats and drive them from the leading posts in the economic organisations.

We must not limit ourselves to talk about the factory councils. We must see to it that they are established in every country, in every field. I will not spend more time on this, the first question posed in the theses, since we will discuss them in more detail tomorrow. Moreover there is no point in going over this matter a second time for the delegates who voted for the resolution on this question at the Second Congress of the Third International.

I ask you to excuse me if I speak for a moment about the situation in Italy. We must develop an understanding of the state of our unified struggle around the world, and we must lead this struggle in unified fashion in different arenas.

We have Communist groups in Italy that work in political organisations. They are active among the workers in the factories and have the task of leading in agitation and in trade-union struggles. We have founded Communist groups everywhere, and we have quite a bit of work left to do in this arena. I ask the congress to utilise the authority of our world organisation to promote consolidation of the Communist groups and to instil in them the determination needed to continue our work.

As you know, the Italian General Confederation of Labour is led by reformists and Social Democrats. You saw our D'Aragona and others who head the big organisations within the Confederation of Labour at the Second Congress. We, the Communists of Italy, have begun a bitter struggle to overturn the reformists, and we have defeated them. We still have a great question left to resolve, namely the state of the political parties, in order for the Italian Communists to be able to take control of the Confederation of Labour. In order to enable the revolutionary masses of Italy to take the path of the Communist International, we must expose once and for all the ambiguous policy of the Italian social patriots and Social Democrats, who waver back and forth between Turati and Serrati.

We must impress on the working masses of Italy that the Third International is a genuinely revolutionary world organisation, and that all those who are still outside this organisation are not revolutionaries, or are merely revolutionaries of the sort who must be exposed, since their deeds are counter-revolutionary. They imagine themselves to be revolutionaries while sitting at their desks. The Confederation of Labour was a strong bulwark of the bourgeoisie against our Communist movement. We must say here that the Italian

Communists are equal to their task and will never permit the adoption of a position – as was the case at Livorno and at the Second Congress of the Third International – that leaves much to be desired with regard to clarity and firmness. In order to win the working masses in the trade unions for revolutionary struggle, we must break with the deceitful reformists and bogus Maximalists, who are the worst enemies of the world proletariat's cause.

We must tell you, comrades, that we considered it necessary at the Livorno Congress to go with the Third International from this point forward. The reformists, however, are afraid that the Socialist Party of Italy might stay in the Third International. Since they had the majority, they began to work toward the organisation of a labour party (*partito di lavoro*). They abandoned this intention when they saw that a large majority of the Italian Socialists stayed outside the Third International. The Confederation of Labour began a bitter struggle against the Communists in order to drive them out of the factories and trade-union secretary posts. Now the confederation is working hand in hand with the bourgeoisie and the factory directors to exclude the Communists, who are doing the organisational work.

I must also mention that, at the last congress of the Confederation of Labour, a resolution on this burning issue was adopted, stating that the confederation is staying in the Amsterdam trade-union bureau, but is nonetheless coming to this congress to see if it would join the Red International of Labour Unions, which works hand in hand with the Third International. The Russian comrades, who are responsible for leading the workers' movement, as well as the comrades from abroad, who will discuss this matter at the trade-union congress, must not forget that the leaders of the Confederation of Labour, who have come here in order to discuss the state of red trade unions internationally, are atrocious reformists who bitterly attack revolutionary Communist organisations around the world. We must take care not to fall into the trap that they are trying to set for our Communist comrades. Italian revolutionaries are imbued with solidarity toward the Italian comrades and Soviet Russia. That is precisely why the Italian reformists and the bogus Maximalists are trying to establish contact with Moscow and with the Communist International, in order to protect their leadership over the working masses. We must head off this attempt, which is truly counterrevolutionary in nature. We must deal with these people as they deserve to be treated.

And now, comrades, since my time is up, I would like to make a short statement. The Italian Confederation of Labour is responsible for the fact that counterrevolutionary organisations such as the Fascists have sprung up. The reformists are to blame, because they have stood on the defensive against the attack of the bourgeoisie and the White Guards. The reformists are responsible for the fact that Communists were persecuted and did not have the strength to carry the struggle against the bourgeoisie through to the end. We read today in the newspapers that yet another fifteen Communist workers were murdered by Fascists and bourgeois in Grosseto. I am sure that I express the feelings of the congress as a whole in expressing our regret and our sympathy for these victims.

I ask the congress to excuse the fact that I will take a few extra minutes to direct your attention to the efforts of the Italian reformists to transform the trade unions from organisations of resistance to cooperative societies. This is a phenomenon that could well be transplanted from Italy to other countries. The trade unions can readily change over into organisations whose entire activity consists of purchasing clothing, hats, and boots in order to sell them to workers at low prices. Thus we see that the Italian confederation of textile workers, for example, has busied itself for months with nothing more than the purchase of clothing for the workers. Instead of combating the bourgeoisie, they limit themselves to competing in this field with the Fascists.

Consider, comrades, that Amsterdam organisations are thereby acquiring new weapons of struggle against the revolutionary movement of our political organisations inside the trade unions.

In addition, in Italy we also have the Unione Syndicale, a supposed trade-union federation that stands outside the Confederation of Labour. We have done all we could to induce this trade-union federation to join the Confederation of Labour, so that all workers would be joined together in the same organisation. We received a rejection from the anarchists and syndicalists leading this federation. They are against the dictatorship of the proletariat and communism and do not want to join our organisation. We must have no illusions about this organisation. It is merely a barren and powerless expression of certain working-class forces.

I must now close, comrades. Our ideas on this issue must be clear. We must advance a specific programme that takes into account the decisions of the Communist International's Second Congress and the experiences we have gained. That will give us the strength and the clarity of vision needed to take up the final struggle and lead the working class to the International and to communism.

**Rwal** (Gustaw Reicher, Upper Silesia):[4] I would like to point out that work in the trade unions is especially difficult in an area like Upper Silesia or

---

4. The Upper Silesia industrial region, rich in coal and iron ore, had mostly been part of Germany prior to World War I. Under the Versailles Treaty the region was divided primarily between Poland and Germany, with some land going to Czechoslovakia.

many parts of Czechoslovakia where a united front of the proletariat cannot be built, where the proletariat is mixed in composition. This is obviously utilised by the bourgeoisie and the entire counterrevolution. We have had many experiences that convince us that we must be particularly active in the trade unions in such regions. We cannot split up our work in these trade unions, both Polish and German, that exist in Upper Silesia. We must unify them around a common outlook and make every effort, straining all our forces, to win them over and thus establish a unified front of class struggle.

Comrades, we have acquired a great many experiences of trade-union struggle in Germany. It is difficult to win over the trade unions there, given that the trade-union bureaucracy is today a pillar of capitalism as a whole. But it is not as difficult to win the trade unions there as in Upper Silesia. As regards the role of the trade-union bureaucracy, the so-called trade-union bosses, let me stress that people like Noske, the former trade-union leader, after they leave the trade unions, take leading posts in the social-bourgeois government in order to murder the working class. In Germany, people like Noske stand condemned for all time. Still, that is not as bad as with us, where the trade-union leaders, still at the head of the unions, simultaneously head up the counterrevolution. During the recent events, we saw the leaders of these, our strongest Polish trade unions, join the executive committee of the Polish uprising and co-sign along with Korfanty, leader of the uprising, a decree that was a sentence of death for the striking workers. The Polish union federation alone includes more than 120,000 organised workers; the so-called class-conscious unions have more than 60,000 members. That is what the Polish unions are doing. But on the other hand the German unions, the colleagues of Noske, are doing the same thing. So at the very moment that the Polish trade unions descended on the working class, the leaders of the German trade unions joined a so-called executive committee set up in Upper Silesia on the other side of the Oder, which together with the German Orgesch acted against the working class as a whole. Some German trade-union leaders united with General Höfer and took part in the mobilisation of the Orgesch. During the entire period of the plebiscite, both the German and the Polish

---

It became the scene of fighting between German and Polish nationalist forces. The treaty also provided for a plebiscite on whether the population wished to remain in Germany or join Poland. In the plebiscite, held 20 March 1921, 60 per cent of residents voted to remain within Germany.

In early May 1921 Polish nationalists in Upper Silesia, led by Wojciech Korfanty, staged an uprising. An agreement was negotiated by the League of Nations in October 1921 that gave most of the territory and population to Germany, but gave Poland three-quarters of the region's coal-producing area and two-thirds of its steel plants.

trade unions not only sabotaged the workers' movement but acted as direct agents of German and Polish imperialism.

Comrades, we also have revolutionary trade unions in Upper Silesia, and I would like to mention in particular a syndicalist union that has about 20,000 members. Needless to say, these 20,000 workers are revolutionaries. They are the only class-conscious proletarians who have stood firm for class struggle and have not joined the Orgesch army. The question now arises whether the syndicalist union will be necessary for the struggle and to develop the revolution further. It already exists in Germany and has a foothold there. Based on the experiences we have had in our region, I would say it is superfluous. Obviously, given the weakness of our forces there, we cannot divide them up among all the trade unions. That means, we cannot scatter our revolutionary trade-union forces in the General German Trade Union Federation, the Polish trade unions, the unions of the Polish Socialist Party, and in syndicalist trade unions, all of which exist there.

We must affirm, finally, that we are going to organise the workers in the trade unions and the factories. That is how we have resolved the question so far, because there was no alternative. We in Upper Silesia have concluded that it was a mistake two years ago to issue the slogan, 'Out of the trade unions!'. This error resulted in the best forces actually walking out and then having absolutely no influence on subsequent developments in the struggle. They remained isolated.

We cannot foresee future developments. Comrade Malzahn says that during recent years we have seen a million trade-union members leave the unions. The fact that this did not result in another revolutionary movement, that the million did not come to us and did not join the syndicalist unions, is evidence that the trade-union movement as a whole is now in overall decline. And experience teaches us that *we must win over the trade unions*, for we know full well that without winning the trade unions we cannot lead decisive struggles. Without the trade unions the working class is not capable of moving against the capitalist order once and for all. That is why we have to go into the unions and build our organisations within them.

We can see evidence in the present strength of the trade unions in the fact, which I will now repeat, that during the entire time of the plebiscite – that is, a year and a half – *both the German and the Polish unions acted as agents not of revolutionary struggle but of the imperialist policy of bourgeois Poland and bourgeois Germany.* The Polish and German trade-union leaders and organisations failed to carry out the class struggle. They failed to struggle against wage reduction and the so-called seventh shift.[5] Instead, they all concerned them-

---

5. Presumably reference to imposition of a seven-day work week.

selves exclusively with nationalist struggles, not just on a conceptual plane but in life. The Polish trade unions organised military workers' organisations not just for a possible putsch but even more for a daily struggle against the revolutionary workers. The German unions did the same. During this entire period they were strong supporters of the Orgesch.

In this regard, I would like to condemn in particular the great leaders of the Amsterdam trade unions. Recently, it seemed possible that the movement in Upper Silesia might turn in a revolutionary direction. In a number of mines where the workers had organised themselves along nationalist lines, they became disillusioned with this after a few weeks and raised the red flag. Simultaneously, the trade-union bosses, the bureaucracy, and the bourgeoisie ended the uprising. What is more, the president of the Amsterdam federation, Jouhaux, and his colleagues came specially to us in order to pacify the workers, who had taken a revolutionary stand, with the lie that the Upper Silesian question would supposedly be resolved in a manner favourable for the working class. All workers should lay down their weapons and go back to the mine, they said.

I would like to stress once again: *go into the unions and win over the unions through revolutionary factory councils.* (*Loud applause*)

**William D. Haywood** (United States):[6] First of all, I would like to correct the theses of Comrade Zinoviev with regard to the passage saying that since the end of the War the membership of trade unions has risen in the United States. In reading the theses, one could conclude that it was bad times and unemployment that drove the workers of the United States into the unions. That was not the case. In fact, the total membership of the American Federation of Labor dropped significantly. The federation cannot grow in bad times. It grew because of the War and many of the conditions created by the War. The greatest increase in membership in recent years came during the War, when the government called on all workers on the docks, in the munitions factories, and in war industries to join the American Federation of Labor.

I wish I could show the congress, in the ten minutes at my disposal, what the Federation of Labor represents. Every bit of mortar used in its construction was squeezed from the blood of the Haymarket martyrs.[7] I hope in the

---

6. William 'Big Bill' Haywood was the founding leader of the IWW. Convicted and sentenced to twenty years' imprisonment in 1918 as part of a mass trial of IWW members, Haywood had been out on bail since July 1919 as his case was being appealed. Faced with the likelihood of returning to prison, Haywood jumped bail and went to the Soviet Union, arriving in April 1921. One of his fellow defendants in the same trial, Leo Laukki (Pivio) (also a delegate to the Third Congress) did the same.
7. Following a rally at Haymarket Square in Chicago on 4 May 1886 to support striking workers, a bomb was thrown at police officers by an unknown person.

future to have the opportunity to relate the history of this so-called workers' organisation, which is nothing more than a partner and a tool of the government and the capitalist class. The American Federation of Labor's executive committee, meeting in Denver last month, adopted the following curious document:

> The organised workers of the United States may not take any action which could be construed as an assistance to, or approval of, the Soviet government of Russia. The Executive Council of the American Federation of Labor warned against the Soviet government in its annual report, which will be expanded here for presentation to the federation in a longer declaration at its annual convention in Denver. This regime cannot be considered to represent the Russian people and is hostile to the trade-union movement.[8]

There are two passages in the theses of Comrade Zinoviev that urgently need discussion and that this conference must seriously consider. They are paragraphs 5 and 6 in Section 1,[9] which take up the need for work in revolutionary organisations and for support of small revolutionary cells in every country. Here we must mention the Industrial Workers of the World (IWW) in the United States of America. I stress this point because I know that there are some in the American delegation who favour the American Federation of Labor and harbour the wish to liquidate the IWW. Comrades, in the United States they have been trying to liquidate the IWW for fifteen years. Every single capitalist institution, and all these institutions in concert, have joined with the country's press in an attempt to achieve this. Now these federation people have taken another tack: they have come to Moscow in order to get the Red International, when possible, to issue instructions to the bureau of the Communist Party to liquidate the IWW. And why? Because we do not have as many members as is needed. They point to the growth of the American Federation of Labor as evidence and tell us, the members of the IWW: 'You don't amount to anything. You are just a handful.'

They are lying. They do not know anything about the IWW. The IWW is an organisation of immense importance for the revolutionary workers of

---

The incident was used to stage a frame-up against the workers' leaders, who were anarchists. Eight were tried and convicted of murder. Four were hanged and one committed suicide before his scheduled execution. The Haymarket martyrs were defended and honoured by the workers' movement throughout the world, and they became associated with the establishment in 1890 of May Day as an international workers' holiday.

8. Text from American Federation of Labor Records: The Samuel Gompers Era, Columbia University Libraries.

9. These paragraphs are in Section 3 of the finished text; see pp. 956–7.

the United States. It was born from the womb of the Western Federation of Miners, and we can trace its origins still further back, to the Knights of Labor, which was crushed by the American Federation of Labor in connection with the Haymarket affair, when the capitalist press wanted to destroy this organisation. The old drunkard and lecher Sam Gompers used the occasion to push the workers of the United States into the American Federation of Labor.

The IWW was accused of saying that workers should leave the trade-union federation. But this is not true. Thousands of IWW members also belong to the American Federation of Labor. But the IWW is a revolutionary organisation. It stresses the need to destroy wage labour as a system. It acknowledges the class struggle. No less than thirty thousand of its members have been arrested and thrown in jail. Many of them were murdered. They have been slandered, cursed, and degraded. There is not a single newspaper in the United States that would dare to speak the truth about the IWW. The IWW consists of men and women who have set the goal of destroying the capitalist order, and it will stand in the front ranks of the class struggle. It has already demonstrated this. It has been attacked and maligned by the American Federation of Labor. Even so, every time the American Federation of Labor has gone on strike, the IWW has supported the striking workers.

Needless to say, I do not hold the entire organisation, the masses who support the American Federation of Labor, responsible for the despicable actions of a Sam Gompers. But we know that people like him are not the only reactionary elements in the American Federation of Labor, and even if we succeed in unmasking the leaders of this organisation, we are not yet rid of the evil. This venality, this willingness to hand out little favours to capitalists on every side, is found not only among the leaders but extends to their contemptible agents. The entire organisation is corrupt.

Communists everywhere recognise the need to organise on an industrial basis. This is needed especially here in Russia. The Russian Revolution was won not by the Communists but by the workers. However, in Russia this class was not organised along industrial lines, with the results that you can see now. They carried through the class struggle; in the Civil War they were triumphant. Even now they continue to struggle under the dictatorship of the proletariat. But because they are not organised along industrial lines, Russian industry is almost entirely paralysed.

I recognise the great achievement of the work to drain the mines of the Don Basin. I take into consideration the four years of war and the three years of multiple conflicts that this country had to traverse. Nonetheless, I am convinced that Russia would have it a great deal easier and would arise once again if the Russian workers were organised according to the same revolutionary economic education as the members of the IWW.

The IWW has issued 800,000 membership cards. Its delegate to the Red International represents 80,000–100,000 members. We are organised in six sections, which are, in turn, divided into industrial federations, so that the IWW embraces every type of labour. Despite the intrigues and machinations of the American Federation and the capitalist class, some of the IWW industrial federations predominate in their field. The IWW endured many severe battles in the United States. It suffered more injuries and greater losses than any other organisation. It carried out the steel strike at McKees Rock and is the only organisation that can claim to have defeated the steel trust. The IWW organised a strike in northern Canada and won better conditions for the workers. It carried out the textile strike in Lawrence, and achieved a 25%–30% wage increase for unskilled workers. No other organisation has done this. It carried out the strike for silk workers in Patterson and strikes for freedom of speech in almost every American city.[10]

We have fought so honourably that every state except one has passed anti-anarchist laws against us. And nonetheless the IWW has retained its strength, even though hundreds of its members are sitting in jail, and I must live here in exile in Russia. I am here for the same reason that Russians, in the past, had to leave their great and renowned homeland, when the tsar sat on his throne in this very room.

The IWW has a large print shop for producing revolutionary literature. We have halls and camps and cooperative hotels in the west of the United States, particularly where Finnish workers are gathered. And now we hear voices in the Red International calling for the IWW to be liquidated. These people do not understand what it means for the revolution when you have a revolutionary group, a nucleus on which you can rely, which has shown through its history that it is ready for revolution, can stand its ground in the class struggle and in civil war, and understands the meaning of the dictatorship of the proletariat. The IWW is such a nucleus. And that is why I hope to convince the Red International's congress not to support any resolution aimed against the IWW.

---

10. In McKees Rocks, Pennsylvania, a strike by 5,000 workers at the Pressed Steel Car Co. took place from July to early September 1909.

In Western (not Northern) Canada, the IWW led strikes in 1912 by over 10,000 railway construction workers in British Columbia and Alberta.

In Lawrence, Massachusetts, a strike by 20,000 textile workers took place from January to March 1912.

In Paterson, New Jersey, the strike by silk workers took place from January to July 1913.

**Brand** (Poland): I would like to address a few words to the syndicalists of France, Spain, and other countries who are present at this congress. Comrades, you came here in order to work together with us for liberation from capitalist rule, liberation of the working class. We know that your views on the question of the relationship of parties to trade unions are different from ours. But none of you have taken the floor in order to present your point of view. We would like to hear the opinion of such authentic representatives. We therefore ask you to make use of your consultative voice and present your views to us here.

**Lozovsky**: Comrades, I am not a revolutionary syndicalist and regret that I cannot present their view. Regarding the question of revolutionary syndicalism that Comrade Brand has just raised, we can refer to a document that was printed in *L'Humanité* of 21 May, the declaration of the Central Committee of the revolutionary trade-union council.[11] The statement begins as follows: 'The Revolutionary Trade Union Committee declares categorically that French unionism is fully independent and autonomous.'

Here we have the philosophy of syndicalism in its entirety: complete independence and autonomy.

Our task is then to inquire: independent of whom? Autonomous from whom? One wonders what this term 'independent' refers to and how the concept of autonomy is to be understood. What is at issue is to compare the concept that excludes Communists from common work to the concept that strives for collaboration of Communists and syndicalists in seeking their common goal. What is at issue is to compare the principles of the Communist movement to another concept, namely that which holds revolutionary syndicalism to be sufficient in itself to carry out the social revolution and construct the future society. That is the essence of revolutionary syndicalism.

So we must know whether it is sufficient for the struggle we are carrying out in Britain, Germany, and France to have a workers' movement independent of communism. Is this possible or not? I will present facts that show the formula stemming from the revered Amiens Charter of 1906 to have become rather obsolete. The time has come for a thorough overhaul. When we announce that the trade-union movement is independent and autonomous, we are saying that there are two movements that are proceeding parallel to each other but do not seek the same goal. We are saying that there is a syndicalism that

---

11. A reference to the Revolutionary Syndicalist Committee (CSR), a grouping of twenty-six left-wing minority unions within the CGT formed in October 1919 with Pierre Monatte as secretary. The CSR was the nucleus around which the future CGTU was organised.

aims to replace communism and another syndicalism that runs parallel to communism – two movements advancing together, which maintain neighbourly relations and exchange greetings, only then to go their separate ways.

But is it possible in the social struggle for the proletariat to be divided into two organisms, to have two souls, one of which is syndicalist and the other Communist? Is it possible that any organisation imbued with communism can be truly autonomous? I have asked our syndicalist comrades why is it, if we have two parallel organisations, that we cannot build a bridge between them? They reply, not a bridge, but only a catwalk, a very weak one so that no one can walk across. If they conceive of a close alliance as nothing more than a catwalk, syndicalism will be defeated, and communism too. The bourgeoisie can be repulsed only if the preconditions for victory and unity – unity in goals, in deeds, in convictions, and in the struggle – are present. The ideas defended by our syndicalist comrades, however, all run counter to the victory of the working class.

The syndicalist comrades are on the wrong road. Within a few months they will see that those who are for the Amiens Charter are against us and are allying in a bloc with people who are reformists. But the Amiens Charter is not just the slogan of the CSR;[12] Merrheim, Jouhaux, and the like also proclaim on every street corner that they are for the Amiens Charter. The syndicalist Communists also ride the same hobby horse. You are well aware that these two currents, reformist syndicalism and revolutionary syndicalism, are counterposed in the workers' movement as class enemies. It is remarkable that the trade-union leaders always talk about the Amiens Charter and do not notice that their enemies, waving the same banner of the Amiens Charter, are trying to strangle the syndicalist movement, while beseeching God to bless the sacred Amiens Charter.

Comrades, in this bitter struggle communism and syndicalism must go hand in hand. If they do not go together, they will clash against each other. That is the choice before us, as you will come to recognise in your own country.

In order to demonstrate that one cannot swing back and forth in international politics between the Second and Third Internationals, I will tell you of a small episode in the negotiations between the Italian Confederation of Labour and the official representative of the Amsterdam trade-union bureau, Oudegeest. Oudegeest travelled to Milan and was given a warm reception by the Confederation of Labour. Oudegeest says that he was greatly moved by the warm reception prepared by the representatives of the Italian Confederation of Labour. Comrades, he said, we must not allow ourselves to be divided by theoretical discrepancies. We must come to agreement in the arena of practice.

---

12. CSR is the Revolutionary Syndicalist Committee; see p. 719, n. 11.

So Oudegeest was deeply moved. I submit this example to demonstrate that the Italian Confederation of Labour and the Amsterdam trade-union bureau are separated only by differences on theory.

Now for a second example. As you know, comrades, Spain is ravaged by white terror. A few days ago, we learned that a number of syndicalists in Spain had been murdered. Every day, revolutionary workers there are brutally assassinated on order of the government. This was too much even for the Amsterdam trade-union bureau, which wrote a letter to the Spanish government, which read, and I quote:

> The International Trade Union Bureau wishes to draw to the attention of the Madrid government that it has subscribed to point 13 of the Versailles Treaty, which solemnly recognises trade-union organisations. Your government was represented at the international conference in Washington and, through your representative, the Viscount de Eza, signed the agreement, which ratified and enacted the principles of the rights and freedom of labour established by the Versailles Treaty and the League of Nations. The Spanish government has a representative – Viscount de Eza – in the administrative council of the Labour Office. The main function of this office is to see to it that the rights of workers are respected and the international agreement is carried out.

This is the cordial tone in which the Amsterdam organisation converses with the Spanish government, which has committed such atrocities. They are told: you have after all signed the celebrated Versailles Treaty, in which the freedom of workers is mentioned. And having addressed such sweet words to the Spanish government, their representative goes to Italy and says to the Italian workers: Let us be done with theoretical disputation; we must come to agreement on economic and other issues.

Let us consider another example. The American Federation of Labour is fully satisfied by the revolutionary conduct of the Amsterdam trade-union bureau. But no, for Gompers even the Amsterdam International is too revolutionary. He reproaches it for having issued a manifesto in which it is stated that this revolutionary International no longer has confidence in Appleton.[13] Jouhaux, Mertens, and others write to Gompers: 'But my dear Gompers, how did you come upon the idea that we are revolutionary?' And as to the question of Appleton, they say, 'But please listen, we are really not responsible for the fact that Appleton had to go. He had a little mishap at the Portsmouth Congress.' The British trade unionists put it this way: 'This did not happen because we are too revolutionary, but because the eight million trade-union

---

13. For Appleton's presidency of the Amsterdam International and his ties to Gompers, see p. 602, n. 5.

members represented in the trade-union assembly of their country withdrew their confidence from him.' So you see, it is only abstract theoretical disagreements that separate Amsterdam from Moscow!

The representatives of Amsterdam went to the Italian Confederation of Labour, where they were received with more than fine speeches of welcome, because Oudegeest surely did not go to Milan only for the sake of the speeches. He went there in order to come to agreement with the Confederation of Labour over questions of practical collaboration. In a word, what we have here is a second edition of the Washington story.[14] The representatives of the Italian Federation of Labour say: 'We want to await the return of our delegates from Moscow.' They do not yet know whether they will stay with Moscow or with Amsterdam. They are suspended between two bales of hay: Moscow and Amsterdam. They do not yet know where their steps will lead them. They send delegates to Moscow while they wait for the door to open so they can negotiate with Oudegeest.

Now I ask you, comrades, does this policy of neutrality represent one of independence, of autonomy? No, of course not. Were the revolutionary syndicalists independent and autonomous in their communist actions? Let us consider the celebrated Amiens Charter, which was drafted in 1906. I now ask the old syndicalists, members of the Italian party: Was the Italian Confederation of Labour acting neutrally, in the spirit of the Amiens Charter and all the supporters of autonomy? No, it followed the anarchists. The anarchist leaders write for all the papers of the Confederation of Labour, which even invited the anarchists to be editors. Do you doubt that? Just look at the *Grido del popolo*, publication of the Confederation of Labour. Look at all the literature of the Italian Confederation of Labour since 1906. I tell you, they have never been neutral, because neutrality is impossible; it simply does not exist. It exists only in the heads of the leaders, who use it to conceal their real opposition to neutrality, against certain concepts, and against true communism. That is the real meaning we discover in this theory of independence and autonomy.

As for the Amiens Charter, the comrades reproach us for falling behind. This surprises me. I ask the revolutionary syndicalists, who want to make the revolution: During the years from 1906 to 1921, apart from the Amiens Charter, did anything else happen? There was the World War, and we have

---

14. A reference to the 29 October–29 November 1919 Washington conference of the International Labour Organisation, which was set up by the League of Nations. Attended by government representatives and leaders of the Amsterdam International, the meeting formulated draft conventions on the eight-hour day, unemployment, employment of women and children, and workers' safety. The Amsterdam leaders hailed the conference as a victory for organised labour.

called into being the social revolution. Did it not change the whole world? But the Amiens Charter stands unshaken for all time! This is inconceivable. There is a policy hiding behind autonomy and independence, a policy consisting simply of fear that some outside force might occupy territory that the trade-union movement has claimed and might destroy the workers' organisation. This shows a lack of confidence in your own strength, in yourselves. And that is the basis of the entire theory.

The Amiens Charter reads, in part:

> The congress assures to all union members the right to take part, outside the union framework, in any form of struggle that corresponds to their philosophic or political conceptions, *reserving only the right to ask, in return, that they not introduce within the union the opinions that they profess on the outside.*[15]

Comrades, this is idiotic. It is an idiotic trifle, as a great Russian writer said.[16] Can you really ask of people that they not bring their opinions along with them? Can you perhaps have two opinions, one outside the trade unions and another inside them; one in the party and one in the trade unions? You have two bags, one to carry your communist opinions, and the other for your socialist ones. If you are in the trade union, you pull the appropriate opinions out of one of the bags, as if you were taking a product off the appropriate shelf. Comrades, to me this is incomprehensible. I wonder how it is that this great syndicalist movement, in the fifteen years of its existence, has not learned from this great revolution that it is impossible to carry on such a double life. Because you cannot tell someone to leave their own opinions outside. Dear God, I cannot go into the unions without opinions. What is that supposed to mean?

In my view, instead of always referring to the Amiens Charter, it is high time to draw up a new charter. We have the documents needed for this, we have the facts, we have revolutions; in a word, we possess all the material necessary to construct a new building.

We cannot draw our nourishment forever from this little Amiens Charter. A new building must be constructed, corresponding to today's requirements. That is why the slogan of the Amiens Charter is in itself erroneous and will not bring about the desired results. The mass movement will compel you to draw up a different charter – not the Amiens Charter, but one that corresponds to today's requirements.

---

15. For the full text of the Amiens Charter, see p. 607.
16. Lozovsky may have been referring to Anton Chekhov, who wrote a short story whose title, translated into German, is 'A Trifle' (*Eine Bagatelle*).

And now we come to the final paragraph of the celebrated, sacred Amiens Charter:

> As for the organisations, the congress declares that, in order to achieve the maximum success, the trade-union movement must carry out action directly against the employers. The confederal organisations, as union bodies, should not concern themselves with parties and sects that, outside and on the side, strive in full freedom for social transformation.

Certain groups are accorded the right to be freely active. How accommodating of the Amiens Charter!

Comrades, is the issue here perhaps whether these groups can be active, or want to be active? No. The issue is the need to unify the efforts of organisations that share the same goal. If you in France now adopt 'independence and autonomy' as the foundation for your organisation, I must tell you that you are taking a step backwards. In chasing out the reformists, throwing them out the windows and doors, you are taking a step forwards. But in proclaiming autonomy and independence, you are taking two steps backwards, because your point of view is erroneous. Jouhaux and his colleagues say to those championing independence and autonomy, 'We already agree regarding the Amiens Charter.'

This reminds me of the time I spent in Germany.[17] When I arrived, I was told of when the government was made up of Independents [USPD] and Majority Socialists [SPD]. For a whole week the Independent and Majority forces cudgelled their brains trying to somehow patch together a programme. Finally they decided, 'Let us form a government with five members on the basis of the [Erfurt] programme of 1891.'[18] I am afraid, comrades, that to continue brooding over the Amiens Charter at this point is an extremely dangerous policy. I tell you as a friend that we recognise all the difficulties that exist in France: the mood of the workers, the betrayal by the [Socialist] party leadership. The party leaders who have betrayed the workers maintain warm relations with the leaders of syndicalism, as if thrown in the same sack. But what is at issue here is not the leaders but the direction the movement is taking. This congress, this initiative that we are leading in every single country, must promote powerful, direct action. Your slogans are unsuitable. What you

---

17. Lozovsky attended the October 1920 USPD congress in Halle, Germany, together with Zinoviev.

18. In the days after the overthrow of the Hohenzollern monarchy in November 1918, a government was established composed of six members (not five): Friedrich Ebert, Philipp Scheidemann, and Otto Landsberg from the SPD; and Wilhelm Dittmann, Hugo Haase, and Emil Barth from the USPD.

For the 1891 Erfurt Programme, see p. 439, n. 37.

are saying leads only to confusion, which we find expressed in the Amiens Charter.

I am now finished with the Amiens Charter, and I hope that you will be finished with it too, quite soon.

Now I would like to take up the question of the trade unions, the Communist International, and the KAPD. The KAPD comrades have their own Amiens Charter. It consists of the demand that all the trade unions should be destroyed. Yes, these trade unions! They are led by bandits, reformists. The house must be burned down and abandoned, so that a new little house can be built, which will be inhabited only by upright folk. It is true that we will then no longer have ten million, but 50,000 will come with us, and they, together with us, will make the revolution.

This point of view is not only wrong but flatly counterrevolutionary. Why is that? Because, by their very nature, trade unions are mass organisations. In Germany there are ten million workers in the trade unions. And there are honest revolutionary workers now who say, 'We do not want to have anything to do with these ten million. We do not want to have them, because we are better than they are.' Our response to them is, 'You will never make the revolution, because you do not smell the gunpowder of revolution. You have no feel for how it must be carried out, and you will never pull it off, because one must be where the workers are. If there are moneychangers in the workers' temple, they must be driven out. But to respond by burning the temple down would be the stupidest thing you could do.'

It is we who created the trade unions. In saying now that we want to win over the unions, our concern is not for the cashboxes or the building but for the masses of workers and their world of thought. So long as you do not have masses in your organisation, you will not carry out the revolution.

In this regard, our French comrades have demonstrated that the programme of the KAPD is completely wrong. Our French comrades now have the support of almost half the organised workers; in a few months, they will have the majority. And this has been possible only because they go with the workers. If they have the workers' support, then they have the unions' support as well, because the unions are made up of the working class.

We must firmly condemn the point of view raised against us. They tell us, 'How can this be? Through many years of effort we have created the trade unions. We sacrificed for decades to construct them. And now bandits have crept in.' Well, we must win the support of the organised masses, drive out the bandits, and thus make an end of the matter.

If the revolutionary masses in Germany were to take up the slogan of destroying the trade unions, this would only prolong Germany's present convulsive evolution. It would cause a tremendous disruption. The split of left forces would be perpetuated, and the revolution would be delayed, not only in Germany but in the world as a whole.

Reviewing our present structures, methods, and goals, we must say: no comrades, we must not have two parallel columns, like in school or on the parade ground. We must advance with our ranks closed up, so that we can achieve our goal more quickly. We must tighten our unity and come to agreement on ideas and policies. Only then will we be able to carry the social revolution through to the end. Autonomy and independence, on the other hand, run counter to the interests of the working class and of revolutionary policy. They delay achieving the revolution and the dictatorship of the proletariat.

**Marshall** (Bedacht, United States): Comrades, on behalf of the American delegation I must explain two concepts on which you may possibly have a misimpression: first, regarding the delegation of the American party to the Second Congress, which has repeatedly been referred to as being infected with a 'radical infantile disorder'; and, second, with regard to the speech made here a few minutes ago by Comrade Haywood.

As far as the first point is concerned, it is true that the delegation of the American party last year displayed some symptoms of such an infection, which resulted from the practice of the revolutionary movement in the United States during the last twenty-six years.[19]

The conception that it is impossible to reform the trade-union federations, that their structures are counterrevolutionary, and that – regardless of their number – the union federations could not possibly provide assistance to revolutionaries in drawing the workers into revolutionary action: all this has become a slogan. Twenty-six years of propaganda on this issue left their mark and have influenced the new Communist movement in the United States. After the Second Congress, even before the theses were brought back to the United States, the American comrades did not close their minds to the need to approach the elections together with the broad working masses and to win over a significant segment of these masses.

What we have witnessed is that twenty-six years of separating the revolutionaries from the trade-union federations has not had good results. The number of revolutionaries who split off was less than ten thousand, and their departure from the union federations made these instruments for class

---

19. At the Second Congress, the US delegation expressed disagreements with the proposed policy of working in the American Federation of Labour and abstained from the vote on the trade-union theses. Riddell (ed.) 1991, 2WC, 2, pp. 606–11. Marshall's mention of 'the last twenty-six years' presumably refers to the 1895 founding of the Socialist Trade and Labor Alliance, formed by the Socialist Labor Party as a left-wing alternative to the American Federation of Labor.

struggle even more reactionary. Another important fact opened the eyes of the American comrades regarding the false position they had taken. This was the slogan advanced by both the revolutionary and the reactionary wings of the trade-union movement. We are referring here to the revolutionary William Haywood and the reactionary Samuel Gompers, who both wanted the same thing, that is, that the revolutionaries leave the trade-union federations. Now obviously when the revolutionary comes to the same conclusion as the reactionary, something is not right.

We now see that something of this spirit is still with us, and it was extolled today by Comrade Haywood. He demanded revolutionary or industrial union federations as the primary condition for revolution, even drawing the conclusion that the revolution in Russia would have been more successful if the IWW – or rather the spirit of the IWW – had been present here. He comes to the even more peculiar conclusion that it was not the Communists who made the revolution and were victorious but the working class as a whole. Now we don't want to dispute this fact, because after all it was the working class in its majority. But it was the Communists who permeated the working class and brought it forwards and upwards in the revolution and to the ultimate founding of the proletarian dictatorship. We and Comrade Haywood of the IWW have come to the conclusion that ultimately it is not the structure but the spirit and understanding of the working masses that makes the revolution. To repeat, it is not the structure that makes the revolution but the revolution that creates the structures.

We are fully aware of the revolutionary potential of the IWW and have acknowledged it. Otherwise, we could have presented a large amount of evidence that this stance of the IWW has not prevented it from being an enemy of Soviet Russia – at least from permitting its editors, not just one but a whole number of them, to criticise the Russian Soviet republic. Let me single out one incident in order to show you the spirit that prevailed among the members of the IWW, a revolutionary organisation. On one occasion an article appeared in *Solidarity* that opposed the dictatorship of the proletariat and maintained that Russia was not a state of the working class.[20] And why? Because the workers were not permitted to travel freely from one spot to another and to seek employment wherever they please, a freedom guaranteed to workers in the United States, provided of course that they can find work somewhere.

Well, we Communists thought that it is not the structure that prevents an organisation from being revolutionary, but rather the revolutionary spirit of

---

20. For Pivio's reply to Marshall on this incident, see p. 759.

the workers that makes them capable of tearing down all existing structures that stand in their path.

Now I come to the question of liquidating the IWW. We, or rather the delegates of the Red International of Labour Unions, have been accused of wanting to carry out the liquidation of the IWW, or at least to assist in this process. Comrade Haywood provided you with some statistics, and I will do so as well. He tried to show you that the AFL is declining and breaking apart, while the forces of the IWW are growing. I would like to cite the figures provided by the AFL in their yearly reports. In 1918, after the War, the AFL had 2,726,478 members. In 1919 the total rose to 3,260,068 members. In 1920 it reached 4,078,740, while in 1921 it fell to 3,906,528. The figures show an increase of 533,000 in the first year after the War, an increase of 818,600 in the second, and a loss of 172,000 in the last of these years. That makes a net increase of 1,280,000.

But this increase in membership should absolutely not be seen as evidence that the revolutionary spirit of the AFL has also grown. We are familiar with the AFL's dark side. We know that it is shot through with corruption. We will cite only the fact that this corruption increased after the War. On the other hand, we have the IWW, which has existed for fifteen or sixteen years and, according to its official reports, counts 15,674 members. I believe I am justified in estimating the number of members on the basis of the dues they pay, and the figure cited above is derived on this basis. Of course these figures cannot be regarded as absolutely precise. They are determined by dividing the total of membership dues received by 25 cents, the amount paid by each member. Unemployment and other causes contributed to a decline in membership dues, which should not mean a decline in membership. Be that as it may, we can certainly assume that the IWW at present has not more than 25,000 members, and probably less.

You have been told that the IWW is an industrial association. Please excuse me if I probe this question more fully. It is not really a question of programme. But since Comrade Haywood touched on it only briefly, speaking only of the IWW and not about unionism, I must take the liberty of speaking to this point.

The IWW is itself divided into industrial organisations. It can be pictured as a wheel in which each spoke represents a particular industry and a particular division.

Now the proposal before us is that in sectors where the IWW does not have substantial influence, revolutionaries should throw all their energies into work in and through the federations and trade unions. In other branches of industry, by contrast, such as mining, lumber, agriculture, and food, the IWW has the greatest influence and other organisations have almost none, and here revolutionaries and Communists must focus all their energy on the IWW divisions. This should be the focus and the foundation of the organisation. That is the programme presented to you by a number of comrades representing trade unions.

I have used up my time and must close. I will wind up by saying only that the Communists of the United States have learned that it is impossible to bring the workers to revolutionary action by creating new organisations that in and of themselves would guarantee the goal of revolution. We have learned that it is not the structure but the spirit and zeal that counts. We must carry it into all the existing organisations, into the mills, the mines, the factories, and make them the foundation for revolutionary action. True revolutionaries and Communists can work much better when they do not divide themselves off from the masses but rather remain inseparably part of them, working in the interests of the revolution. In this way, they can show workers that 'something is rotten in the state of Denmark' and show them the true revolutionary course of action for each organisation.

Down with the barriers posed by the inadequate structures of these organisations! Create new structures that are genuinely helpful in leading the revolution, leading the United States working class forward to the same goal as the workers of Russia, to the dictatorship of the proletariat!

**Kolarov** (Chair): This closes today's session. The next session begins tomorrow evening at 6:00 p.m.

The agenda is: Continuation of the discussion on the trade-union question. Youth organisation. Organisation of the women's secretariat.

*(The session is adjourned at 11:45 p.m.)*

# Session 19 – 7 July 1921, 7:30 p.m.
## Trade Unions – Discussion

*Continuation of the discussion on the trade-union question. Speakers: Landler, Riehs, Rees, Morgan, Hourwich, Torralba Beci, Kolarov, Tommasi, Bell, Leo Pivio, Marković. Statement by the Norwegian delegation.*

**Gennari** (Chair): Thirteen more speakers are on the list for the trade-union question. The Presidium has decided to take first the representatives of parties that have not yet taken part in this debate. It will then be up to the congress to decide whether it wishes to give the floor to the remaining speakers. Comrade Landler has the floor.

**Landler** (Hungary): Comrades, Comrade Zinoviev pointed out in his report that the trade-union question is the most important issue before the International. It might appear that the congress does not share this opinion. Already yesterday and also today the congress has displayed its disinterest through indifference. I would not have mentioned this, except that it leads to further conclusions. This indifference is all the more significant in that Comrade Zinoviev said, in diplomatic fashion, that no single section of the International has succeeded in carrying out the relevant theses of the Third International's Second Congress. Comrades, we are well aware that – as Comrade Loriot said in the Executive, for example – they had built no cells among the syndicalists [CGT]. The reasons for this are secondary; they had not done it. We know from Comrade Radek and also from the British delegate how our British comrades responded to the miners' strike.

Comrades, Comrade Zinoviev also reported briefly on what the Czechoslovak party has done in the trade unions, or, better, has not done. And we have also seen that the Yugoslav sister party, for example, responded when the trade unions were outlawed because of a political strike. They did not carry out any appropriate action in parliament. So some of the parties acted like Modigliani, when he said he would join the Third International, but would do no more than send a postcard. The fractions recognised in theory that we must influence the trade unions, but they did everything to ensure that in reality the trade unions were not influenced by the party. Other fractions simply believed that the mountain must come to Mohammed; they wanted to win the unions through an edict.

Comrades, I ask you: how is it possible to win the trade unions if we act in this way? If we accept that winning the unions is a life-and-death question for revolutionary growth, how should the trade-union issue be dealt with in the party? Comrade Zinoviev was right to note in his report that the unions cannot be influenced mechanically, and he also indicated how this can be accomplished. Not through mechanical work, not through edicts, not through revolutionary routine, but by grappling with the immediate issues facing the organised working class and carrying out this revolutionary detail work in the unions. That is the only way we can win over the unions.

Taking into consideration the indifference evident in this session, we must say frankly that a large segment of the congress shows more understanding for what one might call revolutionary phrase-mongering than for organised, revolutionary detail work. And that is quite curious. There are a great many workers here. The theses say that we should throw the parliamentarians and diplomats out of positions of responsibility, and replace them – if there is no alternative – with inexperienced workers. But this was said, comrades, in the assumption that inexperienced workers were rooted in the masses and lived with the masses. But if such inexperienced workers are placed in responsible posts, comrades, and they then lose their link with the masses and become so-called 'great leaders', then the only gain from this entire switch in leadership consists simply in the fact that in place of experienced and clever diplomats, we obtain leaders whose only virtue is their inexperience. I believe that such comrades, on achieving leadership positions, have to carry out even more revolutionary detail work in order to win the masses.

This is an international phenomenon, and most Communist parties do not keep it in view. Certainly there are many exceptions, but it appears that this is the rule. This reality makes it quite impossible for the party to gain influence in the trade unions. If this is always kept in view, if the work is carried out in this fashion, then the question of destroying the trade union will not arise. It will certainly not be the primary organisational question.

Revolutionary organisational detail work must be carried out not with indifference but with revolutionary devotion. We must understand from the outset that this is an important question that must be attended to. If this is done, then there will no longer be any doubt regarding where, above all, the revolution must be prepared. If decisive social layers are organised, and in Western Europe they are indeed organised; if the unemployed are also organised, and in fact they are organised; then it is obvious that this preparatory work for the revolution must be carried out above all where the decisive layers and also the unemployed are located, that is, in the trade unions. In this context, whether these organisations are syndicalist or Menshevik is not the issue. If we correctly grasp the essence of this question, then whether these trade unions are organisations of struggle or not becomes quite secondary.

In accord with the concepts of the Bebels, Legiens, and the like, these trade unions are oriented to immediate issues. They do not grapple with the final goal; they simply want to improve the workers' living conditions. But in the present crisis, as has been correctly demonstrated here, it is impossible to improve the prospects of life or to push through demands for higher wages. In such conditions, and given that the unions are oriented only to issues of the day, we can indeed influence the class consciousness of the organised masses, through work oriented to immediate issues, through agitation, and also actions along these lines. This is possible precisely because the trade unions cannot achieve anything during this crisis. We should carry out this work in such a fashion as to tear the workers away from both the Mensheviks and also from the syndicalist leaders.

It is self-evident that the Communist parties should not stake everything on this one card. They must also carry out preparatory revolutionary work in other fields. But one thing is quite certain, comrades. When we carry out an action, it is very beneficial – regardless of historical and psychological factors – to prepare the action in such a fashion that, as much as possible, it is initiated from the trade unions. That will give us, to some degree, a guarantee that, when such an initiative is set in motion, the trade unionists, the big shots, the Mensheviks, and the like will not have unlimited power over the masses as the action unfolds. In addition, I consider it necessary to stress, in this regard, that it would be correct to advise the parliamentary fractions and the Communist parties to carry out major Communist actions regarding every issue that affects the trade unions and the organised workers, because this has a very positive impact on the organised masses.

One more point, and then I will conclude.

We are witnessing the reduction of wages as a generalised international phenomenon. I believe that this constitutes a very important issue for the Third International. The Third International itself – and not merely the trade-union

International – must immediately begin broad international agitation with respect to this crisis and must carry it out on a broad scale in every country. In this regard we must educate and arouse the entire global working class. It may be possible, by arousing the working class, to prepare major actions even during this crisis. If that is not possible and prosperity returns for a time, then at least the workers will be more educated and will immediately undertake class-conscious actions because of the reduced wage levels. It will be much easier to escalate such actions if we have already done the educational and preparatory work with energy and purpose. (*Loud applause*)

**Jakob Riehs** (Austria): Comrades, there is no doubt that the congress is sluggish. This is not surprising, given that a large part of what is said here deals with making the revolution only through preparation. Yet the question we are now dealing with is crucial for agitation.

There is therefore no reason why our work here should be boring. There is certainly agreement here with regard to the enemies that we must battle. On the other hand, there are major differences, for example, with the comrades of the KAPD, who believe that we are in a position to contend successfully against an apparatus as powerful as that of the trade unions. Comrades, that is a grave error. These comrades are wrong in their judgement of where the main emphasis of our struggles should be placed. It is not always enough to rail against the social patriots and social pacifists. They hold real power deployed against us, and this power is rooted solely in the trade unions. By lending each other mutual support, they are capable of erecting a protective wall and stationing themselves in front of capitalism, so that whenever we have the opportunity to engage in struggle, we find ourselves in struggle with our own brothers, with workers in the factories and on the streets.

This is a very great mistake. None of us would deny that the comrades of the KAPD are for the cause of revolution with all their hearts. But if you think that the trade unions will play no role, and that we have the capability to found separate unions and to disregard the trade unions' formidable power, we must conclude that the methods they want to apply are simply crazy. Austria is the most developed country in terms of organisation; there are 800,000 workers organised in unions. The political party, Social Democracy, boasts 250,000 members, most of them won through the factory councils or the shop stewards. Nonetheless, it is capable of bringing 200,000 to 400,000 workers who do not belong to the party onto the streets within twenty-four hours. Does this not make it clear that we should be striving with all our energy to win over the uncommitted forces within the unions? And that is not so difficult. As long as we busied ourselves with other issues in the trade unions, the Social Democrats and the trade-union bureaucracy left us pretty much alone.

But the moment we began to form our cells in the factories and trade unions, the struggle flared up, because they suddenly recognised what was at stake.

Our comrades who were active in the factories were immediately driven out. Obviously, comrades, we had touched a sensitive nerve. We will win over the masses not only in meetings but through genuinely agitational work in the trade unions. And that is why we welcome the theses, which tell us that we must expand through complementary work in both the Communist Party and the trade unions, just as Social Democracy expands in both these realms. If we do this, comrades, I believe that in a short time we will reach the point where we can bring workers into struggle in numbers far greater than those of our party.

If it's a matter of theoreticians, who are certainly sincere, this short-sightedness is understandable. But, when workers in the factory talk in these terms, we cannot understand why they are so short-sighted and do not see where this is leading. We must follow our instructions and directives and work in the trade unions for revolution and for communism. (*Applause*)

**Alf Rees** (Australia): I am speaking on behalf of the Australian Communist Party. I would like to refute two assertions of Comrade Earsman.[1] He advanced a point of view that, coming from a Communist, is hard to understand, indeed, is hardly credible. He said that the Communist Party of Australia was founded by leaders of the trade-union federations. During the last four years we have become accustomed to many big surprises, but when a Communist is supposed to accept that the Communist Party was founded by trade-union leaders, that is really too much. I will show you that the Australian Communist Party, as such, originated in 1920, but it was the Socialist Party of Australia that founded it. The importance of this fact will become clear in the course of my speech. When I joined the Australian Socialist Party in 1910, it was already quite a significant revolutionary force.

After the First Congress of the Third International, our party turned to Moscow and asked to join the International. However, we received no reply. After the Second Congress, we took further steps in order to carry through our affiliation, but again we received no reply – although we did manage to determine that our party was already inscribed as a member of the International. The Second Congress of the Third International questioned the Socialist Party of Australia regarding the measures taken against the 'infantile disorder' of radicalism and sectarianism in Australia. In response, the Australian party joined with radical forces in Australia in calling a conference to consider the

---

1. For Earsman's remarks, see pp. 648–50.

question of founding a mass Communist Party. This conference gave birth to our Communist Party.² But disagreements arose during this conference, and the Socialist Party recalled its delegates and changed its name to Communist Party of Australia. The rest of the delegates continued the conference, and as a result, we have two Communist parties in Australia. So as you see, it is not the case that trade-union members founded the Communist Party of Australia.

The other assertion that I want to refute is more and more becoming a focus of the discussion. This regards the relationship of the Communist Party to the trade unions and work that can be carried out within the unions. Comrade Earsman said that no revolutionary agitation or work in Australia was carried out between 1912 and 1920. I must disagree. The Socialist Party of Australia never halted its revolutionary work and has never shied away from calling for struggle for the dictatorship of the proletariat and for unity with the workers of Russia.

I can provide an example that shows how effectively our work in the unions is organised. In 1916 the Australian capitalists resolved to destroy the Industrial Workers of the World (IWW). During 1916 and 1917, many IWW members were thrown in jail with terms of ten to fifteen years. The other members were given a deadline by which they had to quit this organisation, and after this date, all those whose names were still in the IWW membership records would be jailed. Many refused to quit and were jailed.³ The IWW organisation was destroyed, but in the process the Australian capitalists showed the workers the path that we aim to follow here at this congress. The IWW penetrated the trade unions and began, together with the Socialist Party, to carry out intensive propaganda within these workers' organisations. The result of this work was that we were able to register, at the 1920 congress, that the trade unions were functioning better in Australia than in any other country.

The third assertion of Comrade Earsman to which I must respond is his claim that the congress of trade unions, which took place in Australia in June, voted by an 80 per cent majority in favour of affiliation to the Third International. The first page of our theses on the Communist Party, at the end of the first paragraph, states categorically that there is no country in which the Communist Party's influence embraces the majority of workers. But Comrade Earsman says that 80 per cent of the workers of Australia have decided to join the Red International of Labour Unions. If that were true, there would not be

---

2. The founding conference of the Australian Communist Party was held in Sydney 30 October 1920.
3. During September and October 1916, twelve leading members of the Australian IWW were arrested, tried, and convicted for treason and sentenced to up to fifteen years of hard labour. In late 1916 the Unlawful Associations Act was passed banning the IWW, and many of its members were sentenced to six months' imprisonment in 1917.

a single person in Australia condemned to fifteen years of imprisonment. If we were that strong, we would have freed them long ago. If only 51 per cent of the workers – that is, far fewer than 80 per cent – had voted for the Red International, we would have immediately established the dictatorship of the proletariat, and if we had not done that we would not be a Communist Party.

Let me repeat the three points that I have touched on. First, I wanted to show that it was not the Australian trade unions that founded the Communist Party. Second, I want you to know that, from 1917 to 1920, the Communist Party of Australia conducted intensive and successful propaganda together with members of the IWW. Third, I do not want you to believe that we received 80 per cent of the votes within the Australian unions and are nonetheless incapable of establishing the dictatorship of the proletariat.

**Morgan** (Joseph R. Knight, United States):[4] Comrades, the Third Communist International's ties with the trade-union movement are especially important for both the trade-union and Communist movements in the United States and Canada. The truth is that there is no workers' movement in these countries capable of pulling the revolutionary masses along with it. Let me remind you of the facts presented by Comrade Haywood in his talk – facts that are full of meaning. They must be brought home and explained to those who are struggling against the illusion that the organisation portrayed to you [IWW] claims to be a workers' organisation not only of the United States but of the entire world and is proclaimed as a workers' organisation to the four corners of the world.

You should give no credence to Haywood, when he presents such hollow formulations from the platform of the Third Congress. Such empty advertisements for the IWW in the United States have caused us considerable damage. The organisation has claimed it has 800,000 members. That sounds so grand: 800,000 members and fifteen years of activity! And yet the most recent reports of this organisation informs us that they have no more than 15,000–16,000 members. I suggest that KAPD members study the history of the IWW in the United States very closely. This will give them a picture of what the future holds in store for them.

---

4. The country identification here is from the published proceedings. Morgan (Joe Knight) was actually from Canada, where he belonged to a group affiliated to the US-based Communist Party of America. Knight's group joined with other Communists in Canada on 23 May 1921 to form the Communist Party of Canada, section of the Communist International, but by then Knight had almost certainly left the country for Moscow.

Knight also attended the Red International of Labour Unions founding congress as a delegate of One Big Union. There he strongly but unsuccessfully opposed the seating of another Canadian, Gordon Cascadden, a radical journalist influenced by the IWW, who represented a lumber workers' union in Alberta. Tosstorff 2004, pp. 317, 330.

The attempt to found an ideal industrial organisation in the framework of a system of [wage] slavery is in itself childish and absurd. Evidence for this can be seen in the fact that all previous attempts to do this have failed. Is it not somehow preposterous to try to establish a new society 'in the shell of the old'? I recently saw an interesting picture in one of their publications. It was a map of the IWW's affiliates. They were displayed on a map of the world in such a fashion that the centre was located in New York, and there we had the Industrial Workers of the World. As I looked at it, I thought: who should sit in the middle of this? Either Daniel De Leon or William Haywood. The United States and Canada are inundated with the pictures, cards, and drawings from the IWW. But the key slogan of their propaganda is not 'overthrow capitalism' but 'admire the perfection of our organisational forms'. That is the absolute and indisputable truth.

Here is a copy of an official IWW publication, from which I will read you the following passage:

> The IWW has not yet been able to establish direct contact with the Russian unions. Nonetheless, we are convinced that not a single voice will be raised against joining such a trade-union International. On the other hand, however, we believe that only a very few IWW members will be prepared to adhere directly to the political Third International.

Quite true.

> We have always been just a workers' organisation. We still are, and hope to solve the entire social problem on the basis of industrial unionism. We want to build industrial federations as instruments for production and distribution. The central councils of these federations will serve as agencies for local and regional administration. Industrial federations and central councils must be subordinate to the overall administration of the IWW. That is how we propose to solve the social problem. The moment that we include a political party in our plans, whether it is Communist or not, we deviate from our principles and destroy our own independence. If we accept the proposal of the Third International, we give up our leadership position in the world workers' movement, and accept as our masters and leaders the members of a political party who have been recruited from all layers of society. The Industrial Workers of the World have tasted the fruits of intellectual independence and now feel themselves to be masters of their own fate. They will never enter into such a proposal in earnest. Their goal is to achieve workers' rule. For fifteen years they have strived for this, and now they have become a world movement. They will hardly agree to a programme that puts them under the tutelage of a political party.

This excerpt is from an official publication of the Industrial Workers of the World. As you see, they fear the Third International because it challenges the IWW's claim to world leadership. 'World leadership' – with a membership of 15,000–16,000.

Let us take the main principle on which the IWW rests – quitting the old union federations. Based on my experience, I can speak of this with some authority. Someone may well say: 'You yourself belong to a dual union. You belong to the One Big Union in Canada.' That is true. I belong to this union, which does not compete with the IWW. However, the One Big Union does not presume to be a world organisation. It sees itself only as a revolutionary conduit. It was born out of specific conditions, and we had no choice in the matter.

From the very beginning of the War, in 1914–15, the workers of Canada were driven into a corner not only by their government, but by their own reactionary officialdom. They were sacrificed to the military machine. What was the situation of the Socialist Party, the only revolutionary party in America at that time?[5] It either had to go into the trade unions and participate in the struggles of the workers there, or it had to try to continue its old educational and propaganda activity, at the risk of going under without having fulfilled its historic revolutionary role. So, under the pressure of circumstances, we joined the unions of Western Canada. Revolutionaries did not go into the trade unions as individuals in order to bore from within. They did not give up their individuality in order to gain a good position. They were in a sense disciplined by the organisation, which supervised its members.

From Vancouver to Winnipeg, a span of 2,000 miles, revolutionaries conducted continuous correspondence regarding tactics and strategy. They discussed how to build the union, win over the masses, and elect delegates to congresses and conferences. Thanks to the tactic of 'boring from within,' the socialists were present at the Ottawa Congress of 1917 with 51 delegates, representing a powerful fraction. That moment marked the beginning of a new epoch for the Canadian movement.[6]

What was the outcome of this policy? Here certain opponents will take the floor and call out, 'You should not agree to compromises.' But what really happened? We had gained control of the council, that is, the old Winnipeg

---

5. Knight is referring to the Socialist Party of Canada, which stated its revolutionary opposition to the War on 6 August 1914, declared for a Third International in 1916, and supported (if inconsistently) the Soviet government. The SPC's left wing joined the Communist movement in December 1921–January 1922.

6. The Thirty-third Annual Convention of the Trades and Labor Congress was held in Ottawa, 17–22 September 1917.

trade-union council. The various trade unions had elected Socialists as delegates, who actively defended the workers' interests. They were revolutionaries. They did not limit themselves to the parliamentary struggle. Their goal was rather to utilise the movement for revolutionary ends.

Then came the strike, or as some here have put it, 'collective bargaining of the workers with the employers'. Some 'collective bargaining'! The whole Winnipeg strike was actually a matter of tactics and revolution.[7] We used something as routine as collective bargaining to unite the workers. The metalworkers went on strike to obtain better conditions. The employers wanted to negotiate only with separate groupings, like the lead workers, the sewage workers, the boilermakers, and so on. But the metalworkers said, 'No, we are going to unite. We will form a committee, and you will have to negotiate with us collectively.'

The comrades from the [Winnipeg Trades and Labor] council seized on the opportunity right away. 'Collective bargaining on such a small scale? No. We must involve all the workers in the region in the metalworkers' struggle.' Their work was so outstanding, they succeeded so splendidly in forging the workers' unity, that the Winnipeg strike of 1919 has become a milestone in the history of the American workers' movement. The meaning of the strike was understood not only by two or three unions but by all of them. All the workers joined the strike, even the civil servants and the postal and telegraph employees. They all took part in the big general rally and in the strike, which lasted seven weeks. This created a situation in which we were only a step away from taking power. Nothing was done in Winnipeg except by order of the strike committee, which was just as powerful as the state itself. Of course, Winnipeg is not the same thing as Canada as a whole. But had the struggle in Winnipeg embraced all of Canada, we would certainly have had a revolution. We had a reactionary state against us, and the masses did not follow us. Most of our people were thrown in jail, and the strike had to be broken off.

I ask you: do you not think that the policies of the Winnipeg revolutionaries were correct? We had control of the organisation. And if you haven't succeeded in achieving this, you should not blame the organisation's principles, its rigidity, or its functionaries, but rather blame yourselves for not having found the right way to link up with the workers. That is my experience. I am sharing it with you Communists and trade unionists so you can benefit from it in the future.

---

7. The Winnipeg general strike lasted from 15 May until 26 June 1919. It was called by the Winnipeg Trades and Labor Council in solidarity with striking building trades workers. Some 35,000 workers took part, the big majority of the city's working class. Sympathy strikes took place in Calgary, Edmonton, Toronto, and other Canadian cities.

Let me add just one thing. There is also the matter of domination by the Communist Party, which is feared by some. What rubbish! How do Communists propose to take command of the unions? Can they perhaps go to the trade unions and say, 'We have come in order to take control'?

On the contrary, we must work from within, take part in their struggles, win their trust, and then try to get elected by them to the most important posts in the revolutionary movement. So I completely agree that we must go into the trade unions. In addition, we in the trade unions must maintain as close a connection as possible with the Communist Party, because its goal is not to be active as a political/industrial organisation, but to build a great, unified, revolutionary army of the workers of the world to overthrow capitalism.

**Nicholas Hourwich** (United States): I am taking the floor to make a few remarks. In agreement with Comrade Marshall, I would like to refute officially, on behalf of the American delegation, some false assertions made by Comrade William Haywood. Comrade Haywood told us yesterday that in his opinion the Russian working class lacks the scientific structure and revolutionary spirit of the IWW. If the Russian proletariat had possessed these qualities, he said, industry would not have become as disorganised as we now see to be the case in Russia. Such an assertion displays a lack of scientific understanding among even the leaders of the IWW. I think it must surely be clear to everyone that the disorganisation of Russia's industry is caused not by a lack of scientific understanding or scientific organisation, but by the seven years of war and many other factors. With regard to revolutionary spirit, the Russian working class does not deserve such a reproach by the IWW. The Russians have displayed their revolutionary spirit not with words but with deeds. What is more, the American delegates can testify to the fact that all the pretensions to a scientific organisation made by the IWW are empty words, based on the syndicalist theory of the IWW and its co-thinkers.

Their concept is that the unions founded in capitalist society must be the bearers of a new economic foundation. However, the Russian Revolution demonstrates that unions founded before the proletarian revolution are quite different from those founded after it. The unions existing within the capitalist state cannot prepare the ground for the industrial organisation of communist society, since their sole and overriding task is the struggle against capitalist society.

We do not find among the IWW members any particularly marked scientific understanding or scientific preparations for the new organisation of industry. We do not want to dwell excessively on the IWW. We value it as a revolutionary organisation, but we think that, in praising it, Comrade Haywood, as an enthusiastic partisan of this organisation, has stepped beyond the boundaries of obvious fact, while showing little understanding of the fundamentals of communism. He touched on the question of liquidating the IWW. Among some delegates to the Red International of Labour Unions, other than the Communist delegates, there is evidence of a current that is really striving for the IWW's liquidation. We do not agree with them. We believe that liquidation of the IWW in the United States or elsewhere contradicts the theses of the Communist International and, what is more, is just as useless as an attempt to liquidate the American Federation of Labor. The IWW exists, and we must take this into account.

If the IWW did not yet exist, and the American Communist Party were asked whether an organisation of this type should be founded, alongside the American Federation of Labor, the Communist Party would be opposed to that and would favour a unified organisation. But the IWW exists, and we recognise that fact. We have to win it over, just as we must do with the American Federation of Labor. We advise some Communists who belong to the IWW to switch over to the American Federation of Labor. We do this in order to remove them from the anarchist and syndicalist influence that is very pronounced in the IWW. This is why we work at present in both the IWW and the American Federation of Labor, without quitting either the one or the other. We do not want to act as defenders of the IWW. But there is no way around recognising that this organisation is imbued with revolutionary spirit, even if it lacks a revolutionary understanding of communism. The comments of Comrade Haywood confirm what I have said.

The IWW maintains that it is able to embrace the entire spectrum of the revolutionary movement in such a way as to make any other revolutionary organisation superfluous. Comrade Haywood also expressed this idea. It is also true that the IWW calls on Communists to work and struggle in the ranks of its organisation, in order to arouse an understanding for communism among IWW members.

I will now take up the question of neutrality, which Comrade Zinoviev touches on in his theses. I consider it extremely important to pay attention to what Comrade Zinoviev said. Although the IWW claims to be a thoroughly revolutionary organisation, it lacks communist understanding. As regards the other organisations in the United States, there is a notable inclination toward neutrality among the trade unions, including the Communist ones.

We often find that even respected trade-union leaders and Communists advance Communist viewpoints only up to the point where they have reached the door of their union. Once they are in the framework of their union, they take off their Communist garb and put on everyday clothing – that of the trade union. Very often Communists, although union members, avoid involvement in union matters. We must awaken in the unions – especially the American ones – an understanding of the fact that Communist discipline is just as binding for unionists who belong to the party as it is for any other member. In fact, perhaps even more so.

Our effort at boring from within the American Federation of Labour could have been just as successful as our work in the Socialist Party. If we had supervised the activity of our members working within the federation, we would have been able to place our members in the unions under discipline. It must be stressed in particular that all trade-union members who belong to the Communist Party and are active in the union are under the supervision and discipline of the Communist Party. We cannot and do not want to issue direct instructions to the unions, but our members active within them must think of themselves above all as Communists and only secondarily as unionists. In the United States, the opposite is often true. We must imbue unionists with an understanding of communism. They cannot arrive at that on their own, for Communist understanding is on a higher level than the conventional philosophy of trade unions.

I have only a few more remarks. In our opinion, the theses adopted by the congress must give special attention to the relationship between the bureaus of the Red International of Labour Unions in different countries and the Communist parties in each of these countries. This is particularly important in order to avoid division of authority.

The bureau in America will carry out the instructions of the Red International of Labour Unions and, simultaneously, work in complete harmony with the Communist Party of America, in order to prevent frictions. Appropriate rules for collaboration must of course also be drawn up.

Our delegation considers these remarks necessary in order to round out the comments of Comrade Marshall and correct the assertions of Comrade Haywood, who is a member of our delegation with consultative voice but is not an official spokesperson of the delegation.

**Eduardo Torralba Beci** (Spain): The debate now unfolding on the trade-union question is of special interest for the Spanish Communist Party. Relations between the Spanish Communist Party and the unions were initiated only recently, after the [1920] congress of the Communist International. The Second Congress theses made it possible to form cells of Communists in the syndicalist unions and to carry out there truly effective propaganda on behalf of the Third International. However, if theses on the trade-union question adopted at this congress were to differ from those of the Second Congress, that would be harmful for the Communist Party of Spain and the Communist movement as a whole. The syndicalists in Spain have already accustomed themselves to the Second Congress theses, and if these are now modified, they will surely view the Communist movement and the Communist cells with mistrust and turn away from us in the trade unions.

There are two broad currents in Spain. First, the Social-Democratic Party [Spanish Socialist Workers' Party, PSOE], whose chief virtue is that it provides good Marxist education. This party leads the General Union of Workers [UGT] in Spain, which has about 100,000 members. This union, of course, is led in the fashion of Jouhaux and the yellow Amsterdam International. The second strong current in Spain is the syndicalist union [CNT], which is genuinely imbued with the spirit of the Communist International. Its organisational structures are syndicalist and anarchist. However, Communist groups have the task of winning over the anarcho-syndicalist unions. These unions do not have any Marxist foundation, but the Communist groups work to assure that they will acquire one.

Two Communist parties have been formed recently in Spain. The first is a unification of the left wing of the old Social-Democratic Party with the Communist youth organisation of Spain. The second is the Communist Workers' Party. It is possible that these two parties may achieve unity in the coming period. The masses, a powerful factor in Spain, will then be able to lead jointly the trade unions [UGT] and the syndicalists [CNT]. Very few obstacles remain to be overcome. However, the position taken here toward the KAPD and some comrades of the Italian party could prevent us from returning with the same approach. This could obstruct the unification of these two Communist parties, the United Communist Party and the Communist Workers' Party. I hope that we will succeed here in Moscow in obtaining a stretch of time from the Executive within which to resolve this question in Spain. The United Communist Party includes the metalworkers, the miners, and a large majority of the Madrid trade unions. It thus already represents one of the main revolutionary forces in Spain. We are still applying the line of the Second Congress in Spain, and we absolutely must continue to do so for a time, in order not to imperil the unification of the two Communist parties and to be able to carry through successfully the winning over of both the trade unions [UGT] and the syndicalists [CNT]. (*Applause*)

**Kolarov** (Bulgaria): The trade unions in Bulgaria are comparatively young. The Social-Democratic Party arose there much earlier than the unions. This explains the extremely important role that the party has played in the economic organisation of the workers. The Socialists brought the workers together, instructed them in the elementary notions of the trade-union movement, and called on them to organise. Later, the socialists also played an outstanding role in the life of the trade unions.

From the very beginning, the question arose of what should be the character of the trade-union movement, and of how its relations to the Socialist

Party should be structured. The social reformists conceived of the trade unions as nothing more than a cooperative organisation that defended the immediate and purely trade-union interests of the workers. They therefore preached trade-union neutrality. The revolutionary socialists (Tesniaki), on the other hand, started from the position that the economic struggle is only one of the forms of working-class struggle, that the activity of the trade unions must be oriented in terms solely of working-class interests, and that neutrality between the unions and the Socialist Party is therefore out of the question.

Corresponding to these two doctrines, two different trade-union organisations were formed, one of which was neutral, while the other worked hand in hand with the Socialist Party (Tesniaki).[8] What was the fate of these two organisations?

During the early years, the neutral organisation had the upper hand. However, thanks to the stubborn efforts of the Tesniaki, the red trade unions emerged more and more as the focal point of the workers' movement. As the industrial proletariat began to awaken, it joined only the revolutionary trade unions.

Thanks to the conduct of the Socialist Party (Tesniaki) during the War, thanks to their unshakable loyalty to the working class, defending its interests under the most difficult conditions and carrying out vigorous propaganda for socialist ideas in the trade unions, the red trade-union federation soon became the only trade-union organisation in Bulgaria. After the War, the neutral trade-union federation rapidly dissolved. Even the one neutral organisation that displayed a degree of stability, namely the federation of railway workers and of postal and telegraph employees, could not withstand the test of the general strike of 1919.[9] Last year, the remnants of all these neutral organisations joined the red trade-union federation. At present there are only revolutionary unions in Bulgaria.

Our trade-union federation is a red organisation in the truest sense of the word. It is linked to the Communist Party by indissoluble ties. All comrades of the trade-union committee and all trade-union leaders are tested Communists who work simultaneously in both the unions and the party. A large segment of the trade-union members are also members of the party; the rest are party sympathisers, and we are striving to make them into good Communists. The

---

8. The two union federations were the General Labour Federation, led by the right-wing social democrats, and the Free Bulgarian Union Federation, under the influence of the Tesniaki, which became the General Industrial Union.

9. In response to a wave of strikes during the fall of 1919, on 24 December the Bulgarian government declared a state of emergency in Sofia. A protest strike began among transport and communications workers and became a general strike on 27 December. The government responded through repression by police and armed squads. The strike was called off on 3 January.

Communist educational work of the party encompasses the broad masses of trade-union members. The trade unions enjoy the powerful material, moral, and political support of the Communist Party in all their struggles. The party, for its part, is supported by the unions. Everywhere, the unions and the party have common headquarters, the workers' clubs, in which most of their activity takes place.

The trade-union and political movements thus actually form two components of a single broad revolutionary movement, whose third component is the workers' cooperatives. Is each segment equally important? The trade-union and political organisations of the working class are indispensible for the great revolutionary struggles. However, in terms of its character and its means of struggle, the Communist Party alone is called on to lead the revolutionary movement. By its nature, the party stands higher than the trade-unions and unifies all the oppressed social layers into a revolutionary movement. As for the character of the revolutionary struggle, which by its nature aims at the winning of political power by the proletariat, the party cannot be replaced by any other organisation. In similar fashion, the means of struggle possessed by the party, in giving the go-ahead for a strike, call upon all the unified striking power and capacity for struggle of the exploited and oppressed masses.

The Communist Party is the accumulated expression of all the revolutionary forces in the capitalist social order. Historically, through the process of struggle, it necessarily becomes the focus of all revolutionary action. This evolution is historically necessary, and it is being carried out before our eyes. The masses who belong to the yellow unions are breaking from Amsterdam in increasingly large numbers and turning to red Moscow. Nothing can halt this revolutionary tide. Our syndicalist comrades as well have taken this path. They have taken the first step in coming here to the congress of the red trade unions. Now they must take the second step as well, and I am certain they will not hesitate long. They will not resist much longer the revolutionary forces of the entire world that have come together around the Communist International. This evolution will proceed all the more quickly, the faster and more decisively the Communist parties of every country break with the methods of the old opportunist parties and win the trust of the working masses by their revolutionary deeds.

**Joseph Tommasi** (France): Comrades, it was actually supposed to be Comrade Loriot who was to present the French point of view on relations between the Communist Party and the trade unions. Since he is unwell, I am obliged to do this in his place. After dealing with this question, I will ask your indulgence as I attempt to reply to Comrade Lozovsky's remarks, which strike me as a bit tendentious. Yesterday, Comrade Lozovsky called on us to present the viewpoint of the French syndicalists. We certainly agree that it is important for you to understand our viewpoint. It is important for us as well to present our views here completely. It is also important for those who today are not fully on a Communist course and still believe there are grounds to reject the course of action to which they have been summoned.

Comrades, if we consider the question of the trade unions and their relationship to the party from a Communist point of view, we see that this question as a whole and in all its specific features is closely linked to the great challenges of revolution. The trade unions claim to be outside politics and, in principle, neutral organisations, but this is not the case, simply because it is impossible. The principles of syndicalism and, in particular, the concept of syndicalism as expressed in the Amiens Charter – the sacred Amiens Charter, as Comrade Lozovsky put it – say this:

> The CGT includes, independently from every political current, all workers who are aware of the struggle that must be waged to abolish wage labour and the employing class.

In our opinion, comrades, there is an obvious contradiction here. If the assembled working people were conscious of the struggle that must be waged to bring down the employers, then they would also be aware that they cannot do this so long as they cling to political neutrality. They would perceive that every class struggle is a political struggle, and that the employers cannot be brought down without destroying the political apparatus of the capitalist order. There are divergent points of view on this, comrades. I will leave it to my comrades from other syndicalist camps to explain the basis for this divergence. I am certain that they will do this, because it is important that you learn both our and their opinions on the relevant questions. However, I do not believe we are divided by divergent views on tactics and strategy, given that we maintain that even those who say, 'Politics out of the trade unions!' cannot renounce politics. We will now demonstrate this to you.

In reality, concealed behind these unclear forms lies a whole spectrum of different political viewpoints, as bad as they get. The trade union is an open arena for all parties, which contend with each other with varying success – not to mention the yellow trade unions, which encompass a considerable number of workers. The bourgeois parties send their agents into the unions, who come and say, 'The trade union is an organisation that must concern itself with improving the state of the working class. It should not get involved in politics. The trade unions give the masses strength to rise up against power – every type of power – and against politics – every type of politics – in order to satisfy their immediate material needs. A strictly corporative policy is sufficient to achieve the needed results.'

There are also other politicians outside the bourgeois parties and the yellow trade unions who hide behind the mask of political neutrality in order to achieve their goals, since only this neutrality enables them to act. But they do not neutralise the trade unions with regard to the political parties, rather they simply disarm them. In reality, these agents do not express the policies of the bourgeois parties openly. They conceal these policies behind political neutrality. What is neutralised is really simply the class struggle, and the trade unions are left to the mercy of the bourgeoisie.

On the other hand, we deal with comrades with anarchist convictions who strive to impose their doctrine on the trade unions. It is significant that these avid propagandists also recognise the clause of the Amiens Charter, saying: 'The French trade unions do not need to engage in politics at all. They must develop their very own politics. Outside the trade unions, anyone can put forward any conceivable point of view and say whatever one wants, one can adhere to whatever doctrine or party that one wants. But when one goes into the trade union, one must be simply a trade unionist.' Our anarchist comrades have shown us that they are very well capable of carrying out their own politics in the trade unions while they demand political neutrality.

We must concede that the policies of the Socialist Party were a factor in this. Over the last fifty years, this party was nothing more than a laboratory, a forum for preparing election campaigns, and this was the policy they pursued in trying to win control of the trade unions. This gave these comrades some degree of justification in rising up against this policy. Yet the trade union has nonetheless remained a battlefield in which all political currents waged a pitiless struggle against each other. And it cannot be otherwise, because a trade union cannot exist, it cannot act, without pursuing a form of politics. And in reality, as soon as a question is raised in the union, all the political currents assert themselves, whether you want them to or not, and they determine the course of the trade-union movement.

I will refer to just two movements that we experienced in the course of ten years, which took very similar forms.

In 1910, the railway workers' federation launched a strike for a wage of five francs, since the workers could not then survive on less than that amount.[10] Although a claim was made of neutrality toward the political parties, our comrades nonetheless entered the struggle under the influence of politicians. They were defeated, and the reason was simply that these politicians did not summon up the proverbial political honesty. They continued to carry out their

---

10. A reference to the six-day railroad strike of October 1910. The workers were defeated after the government declared that the strike constituted an insurrection and put railway workers under martial law.

own deals, taking very little interest in the trade unions and the movement itself. They drove the movement to defeat, although the people in the leadership claimed to be apolitical. Actually these people were of a certain political tendency, which then predominated. Bidegaray, the secretary and one of the leaders of the trade unions, was controlled by a politician. I am referring to Mr. Rabier; Bidegaray was still his tool in 1920. (*Applause*)

The situation was the same in 1920.[11] The trade union went into struggle with all the forces – Communists, pure syndicalists, and anarchists – joined together in struggle. It was clear right from the start that the movement could be successful only if it abandoned its corporatist framework and adopted one that was outspokenly political. The cowards, those who were no longer resolute revolutionaries, had helped to bring about the Amiens Charter as a response to the Socialist Party's reformist policies. Now they immediately rose up and said, 'Down with politics!' That means one is supposed to remain within a corporative framework. When the task is to seize the enemy by the throat, mobilise all the workers' offensive strength, function in an illegal framework; when the task is to carry out conscious acts of sabotage, they will say 'no'. These are alien elements that penetrate the trade-union movement, attempting to give it another form. We will not permit that. After the strike had lasted a month, the pressure of the Labour Confederation's reformist leaders compelled the railway workers to abandon the struggle.

Revolutionary action, the only option that might have led to success, could not take place, because these people were no longer revolutionaries, because they had forgotten any concept of revolutionary action. We therefore maintain that the trade unions are never outside of politics. And now that we have provided the evidence that politics cannot be banished from the unions, that political forces will penetrate the unions and work there, the next task is to identify these forces. Where France is concerned, comrades, you must not fail to note the strength represented by the syndicalists, how strong each individual tendency is, and how these tendencies look. The French trade-union movement has behind it fifty years of history. It was born from the efforts of people active in a political organisation – people from the Socialist Party – whose goal was to combat the individualistic spirit dominant at the time. However, they did not hold to a course of revolutionary action, did not prepare the masses for decisive action, and did not advance toward the goal of a breach between employers and workers and the seizure of all power in the interests of working people. Instead of that, they remained mired in electoral politics.

---

11. For the French rail strike of May 1920, see p. 105, n. 7.

This is the reason why different currents came into being and took shape. It is wrong to claim that the Amiens Charter exists unchanged and immutable. We can attest that the people who helped establish the Amiens Charter have also evolved and are joining us in increasing numbers. You must not think that the forces that today seem to be most remote from Communist action are really opponents of communism. That is not so. They are demanding merely that the Communist Party act in a truly Communist fashion.

At the time when the party shook off the reformist elements, driving away all the reformist vermin that had held it back from revolutionary action for far too long, we had reason to think that the trade-union members who adhered to pure syndicalism or anarcho-syndicalism would join the Communist Party in order to hasten and better define this evolution. But they did not do this. If this possibility had become reality, it would have provided evidence to sustain the views of those who wanted, in good faith, to fully understand the War and the Russian Revolution. The party has to provide such forces with something more than mere formulas. It must offer something more than mere instructions and congress resolutions. The party must convince them that it is capable of action, and that it alone can lead the workers to freedom.

The workers will then recognise that you cannot use a single criterion to measure all political organisations and parties. They will recognise that there are distinctions between various political parties and their own. They will return to it – or at least, this will be true of the majority of those who understand that political cells are needed in the unions, that the unions must embrace politics, but still doubt whether the Communist Party is the bearer of this indispensable policy.

We must penetrate the trade unions, and whether or not we succeed in this will depend on this congress. The Third International must not say, 'Starting tomorrow you must have nothing more to do with this or that current. Starting tomorrow you must break with those who yesterday were your comrades in the Left.' We are convinced that the left forces in the Confederation of Labour, with a few exceptions, have seen the need for this evolution. The questions that still prevent us from uniting are merely those of tactics, stance, debate, and affiliation – and this is simply the result of bad policies pursued far too long. Certain members of the Socialist Party, indeed, some who now belong to the Communist Party, say, 'It is sufficient that our trade-union members concern themselves with trade-union issues.' But, in fact, we are all engaged in politics. We need only clarify why it is that we are engaged in politics, and I am convinced that we will come to agreement.

In this regard, however, Comrade Lozovsky was exaggerating, when he appeared to say that the sacred Amiens Charter should be cancelled, trampled into the ground, and summarily discarded. We cannot share this point of view. I hope Comrade Lozovsky will forgive us, but we prefer to apply a prudent, flexible policy that makes it possible for us to come to agreement with each other. We know that there is common agreement on one point, that of revolutionary action within the trade unions. With few exceptions, we all agree that revolutionary action must be born in the heart of the trade unions, of the Confederation of Labour.

At the Lille Congress, the representatives of French unions will explain exactly why we wish to avoid any split.[12] They will explain plainly that they want to win over the entire Confederation of Labour. Immediately after the congress, however, we will transform into reality all the actions and policy principles that we have proposed.

We must stop contending with each other. We must clarify what are the reasons and the policy issues that divide us. And I am convinced that the Red International of Labour Unions will then have a unified front for revolutionary action. We must not speak in our country about subordinating trade-union action. Please believe us, however: the Communists, the present members of the Communist organisation, will no longer hide their banner in their pocket. They will go into the union waving banners that display their convictions and their ideas. We will position our comrades to meet the unions eye to eye. It will then no longer be possible for our opponents to bring into play the issue of politics and of neutrality.

We are in agreement with you that these two forces are not simply advancing parallel to each other but must come together in thoroughgoing unity. Collaboration must be established that grows closer with every passing day. Moreover, even those who still have mental reservations do not resist this necessity or seek to evade it. None of those who belong to the far-left or the centre currents, no one in the French [CGT] minority has any concept of pushing the Communist Party to the side. At the time of the grave events surrounding the military call-up, everyone was unanimous on the need to proceed together with the Communist Party. We did not ask the Communist Party whether it intended to subordinate us. Only the weak are subordinated; a powerful force cannot be subordinated. It will also be our task to present our viewpoint precisely, to say that we really do want to carry out politics in the unions – intelligent, clear, precise, and revolutionary politics. And I am not worried about this. People can make as many accusations as they want against our viewpoint, the trade-union organisation, and the Communist Party. There is a certain something that workers value more than formulas,

---

12. For the July 1921 CGT congress in Lille, see p. 102, n. 2.

and that is the deed. The revolutionary trade-union fractions stand ready to move into action.

To conclude this brief overview, I will present the point of view of people who cannot be expelled from the trade-union movement. There are people who have worked in the movement for twenty years and have showed that they understand that the Amiens Charter is merely an element in the life of the trade unions and does not embody their entire life. They understand this. None of them today disagree with this view.

Would you like to know what our metalworker comrades say – those who were the only force supporting Merrheim at the outset of the War? Merrheim was not then what he has become today. Then he praised the Russian Revolution; now he slanders it. Actually the Russian comrades are themselves to blame for Merrheim's transformation. They neglected to get his permission before making the revolution. They forgot even to ask his opinion. To our great shame, we recognise that we respected and followed him for too long. He enjoyed our sympathy to such a degree that we could easily go wrong.

The metalworkers' organisation has now come back to its senses. It occupies an outstanding place in the revolutionary trade-union committee and holds great promise for the future. Now that we have won over the construction and railway workers to our cause, we are sure that the metalworkers will come back to the path from which they momentarily deviated. Side by side, hand in hand with us, they will stride forward to revolutionary action. I ask Comrade Lozovsky and others who share his point of view to bear in mind the following statement from the revolutionary action subcommittee of the metalworkers' federation:

> Joining Zimmerwald expressed our pacifist outlook; joining Moscow must express our revolutionary convictions. To repeat: the revolutionary trade-union committees are not organisations native to Moscow. The question of organising the minority has already been raised in Lyon, and what was projected there will become reality in Orléans.[13] The minority supporters will form study and propaganda groups there. It is also untrue that the revolutionary trade-union committees pursue the goal of placing the trade-union movement under the tutelage of the Communist Party. Neither split nor subordination: that was our slogan and remains so now, all the more in that the minority resolution in Orléans projects collaboration with every party that acts in revolutionary fashion, a collaboration in which the trade-union movement will retain its autonomy.

---

13. A reference to CGT congresses held in Lyon, 15–21 September 1919, and in Orléans, 27 September–2 October 1920.

In calling for affiliation to the Red International of Labour Unions, we remain true to our internationalist convictions. No one could seriously maintain that the Amsterdam International, whose leaders headed the nationalist movement during the entire War, is a genuine International. It is rather a faction with no substance, whose superficial unity will be destroyed by the slightest threat of war. The reason that syndicalists have come together with supporters of political parties on the road to Moscow is that we and they are pursuing common goals. We cannot forbid them from travelling the same road as us, any more than we can prevent certain politicians from working with the Confederation of Labour in the campaign on behalf of war-devastated regions, or any more than we can prevent the well-known Hai Noblemaire, who was responsible for laying off thousands of workers, from singing the praises of the International Labour Office, in which the Confederation of Labour has a delegate.

Whatever the case may be, one thing is certain: despite differences in outlook and ideas, there are only two groups, one of which strives to maintain the present social order, and the other that advances boldly toward revolution. We must no longer tolerate neutral zones to which the vacillators and cowards can flee. Wavering is becoming dangerous. It is high time to take a stand. As for us, we will make every effort to banish from our federation the presently prevailing confusionism, which threatens to divert it completely away from revolutionary syndicalism.

I refer those familiar with the French trade-union movement, those who know the disputes through which it had to develop, to the declaration of our metalworker comrades, which portrays conditions more precisely. The same forces that even yesterday were willing to approve at most a degree of collaboration now recognise that an important point is no longer at issue: departure from the Amsterdam trade-union bureau and affiliation to the Moscow International.

On a national level, there is also a second point that could make a serious rapprochement possible. The statement that one is going to engage in collaboration with a revolutionary political party indicates approval of its other political policies. It is enough for this party to move into action in order for those who are now with us in the [trade-union] opposition to show their readiness to negotiate with us and move together with us into the struggle.

I would like to inform you regarding the viewpoint of a comrade who holds purely syndicalist views, and I ask you to keep this in mind. He belongs to those who have assisted the recovery of the revolutionary movement in our country. I am referring to Comrade Monatte. He is among those who agree that the Amiens Charter had its merit in 1906, but that there are now two important factors that must influence people's thinking and their spirit.

He believes that the War and the Russian Revolution justify the effort to pause before the Amiens Charter, consider it, and withdraw those aspects that no longer correspond to current requirements. Here is what Comrade Monatte said at the congress of a segment of the syndicalist minority in St. Étienne:

> There has never been a more unjustified accusation than the notion that the Central Committee [of the revolutionary trade-union council] is hungry for authority and centralism. One could better reproach the committee for doing the opposite, and that criticism is indeed made. In fact, our revolutionary trade-union committees are all too inactive, which gives the impression that only the centre is speaking, acting, and giving orders. You need only work in the districts and take an interest in all their problems, and this impression will fade away.
>
> As for the delegation to Russia, it consists of comrades representing the most diverse minority currents of opinion. Although participation of comrades from outside Paris is relatively limited, that is because many comrades who were considered have declined. As regards the mandate, two opinions were advanced: some were for an imperative mandate, and others for a firm mandate that nonetheless was open to an organisational structure to which all movements could affiliate, even if they are not completely identical and are united only by a revolutionary spirit.

France is not alone in its demand for independence of the trade-union movement, and Monatte is convinced that the Russian comrades will give way in this regard. The central issue is that our trade unions affiliate to the Red International of Labour Unions, without sacrificing anything of their character.

Comrades assembled here in the Third Congress: merely consider the difficulties that we must still surmount. There is the danger from the Right, and – whatever you think of them – that danger is still quite serious. Do not forget that the French working class believes it possible that victory will yet bring reparations. Four to five years of a bad policy have instilled in our workers a malignant chauvinism and nationalism. Too much egoism has penetrated the workers' hearts and minds. We must put a stop to all this. And we will surely win out – that is certain. To those who have betrayed syndicalism since 1914, we will say: enough! The moment has come. Go on your way; we will not make the slightest concession to you. But there are other forces we must reckon with. We French syndicalists and – I believe I may say – the entire Communist Party ask you to have confidence in us and to enable us to find a point of contact among the different comrades and the different tendencies.

To conclude, I must repeat yet again that there is a point on which there will never be disagreement among us: revolutionary action. In this field we are in complete agreement. Our next task will be to define our outlook more precisely and to take counsel together. I am convinced that the discussions we will have during the coming year will lead to the desired outcome. When we see each other again at the next congress of the red trade unions, we will have joined to present a unified front.

**Bell** (Britain): Comrades, we are by and large in agreement with what Comrade Zinoviev has said, namely that the experiences of the last year have confirmed the correctness of the theses adopted by the previous congress. These theses stated that Communists must remain in extremely close touch with broad segments of the working masses. The trade-union and industrial union movements represent and encompass the most numerous and best forces of the international workers' movement. The task of the Communist Party consists of leading these masses, or at least a large segment of them, to communism and the Communist Party. A proposal was made at our congress to induce workers to leave the trade unions, and the slogan 'Out of the trade unions!' was proposed. I would like to share with you the experience we had in Britain when we attempted to carry out this slogan.

After the conference in Chicago in 1905,[14] the idea of industrial unions spread in Britain, and supporters of this principle agitated for it to be carried out. At that time, we wanted to found entirely new unions, trade unions based on the structure of industry rather than, as before, on craft principles. We had the same idea then that has been expressed at this congress, especially by our comrades from the KAPD, namely, that organising the revolution economically must precede political activity and political victories. This point of view was widespread among us in Britain for a considerable length of time. But our British experience shows the uselessness of trying to achieve even the slightest success with the slogan, 'Out of the trade unions!'

Despite our widespread propaganda, through declarations and lectures, not only to factory workers but also in the different unions, we were never able to shake the old trade unions. Experience showed us that the workers' movement is best educated through the struggle itself. Only in a very few cases, such as in new branches of industry like production of scientific tools or motor cars, were we successful in recruiting members who rejected the old unions and their fundamental principle of division by trade.

I must also warn you that the slogan 'Out of the trade unions!' is very advantageous for the employers. They refer the grievances of these oppositional trade-union locals to the leaders of the old craft unions. That is why

---

14. A reference to the 27 June–8 July 1905 convention in Chicago that founded the Industrial Workers of the World (IWW).

this agitation benefits only the employer. The revolutionary forces are best suited for struggle and best equipped to understand the employers' tricks. If they leave the old unions, this puts a very strong weapon in the hands of the employers. That is why Comrade Zinoviev is right to say that the employers do not rely on force alone but seek to deceive and trick the workers. But they are best able to pull the wool over the workers' eyes when they are aided by the so-called labour leaders that we in Britain call 'labour fakers'. The slogan 'Out of the trade unions!' delivers the unions into the hands of the labour fakers, which can only strengthen the employers.

As for the principle of working within the trade unions, our ten years of experience in Britain before the War shows that a completely new policy must be applied in order to salvage even a minimal remnant of industrial freedom. This was one of the factors that led to the founding of the Workers' Committee Movement, or, as it is now known, the Shop Stewards' Movement.[15] This movement responded to a challenge by the employers, who were robbing the trade unions of their legal rights. The Workers' Committee Movement defended the basic principles of workers' organisations in the factory. But this movement did not propose, as our friends of the KAPD suppose, to found separate trade unions. They sought something quite different. They wanted to awaken workers to the idea and principle of workers' control of the factory. We created the Shop Stewards' Movement to carry this principle into the trade unions, compel them to take part actively in the revolutionary struggle, and prevent the reactionary leaders from obstructing the revolutionary agitational work. We pursue our tireless criticism of the old trade unions, their leaders, and their methods, but it never crossed our minds to leave these unions and thus act in the interests of the labour fakers.

We keep the workers constantly on their toes, clarifying every small event in the life of the factory and directing workers' attention to the most ordinary forms of the daily class struggle. In this way, we explain our point of view to them and win their sympathy. If I had enough time, I could present many facts showing that active propaganda and the work of these workers' committees and the Shop Stewards Movement has succeeded in many cases, banishing the spirit of splintering, bringing together the best trade-union forces, and fusing together different unions.

I would like to refer to a few facts that are worth consideration at this congress. When we were discussing how to define the functions of trade unions, we took up the question of whether the unions can be called schools of communism. I am not entirely sure what that means, but I assume that the trade

---

15. For the Shop Stewards Movement, see p. 448, n. 1.

unions are supposed to smooth the way for Communist agitation and propaganda for the Communist Party. It seems to me that there is only one conclusion we can draw here: If the unions are to be schools of communism, we must be active in these schools. Their effectiveness and the successes achieved through propaganda and agitation depend mainly on the capacities of the Communists who are active as teachers. If the students do not want to come to communism, then the teachers must go to them. This is the point that must be made in reply to the contention that the workers are too apathetic to give any heed to Communists. Communists must go to the workers, if workers do not come to them.

But the workers have a great deal more to learn in these schools of communism – the unions – than in conventional schools, and much more must be done than distributing literature and the usual lectures. We must give special consideration to the fact that the ordinary worker, who is not so well versed in economic theory, history, and so on, is accustomed to dealing with specific concepts. He understands very well when his wage level is at stake; he is aware of when he is mistreated; he has strong opinions on the daily events in his life at the factory. Communists must organise in such a fashion as to be in close contact with the daily interests and needs of the workers. Here is where they will find the best raw material and the best techniques to educate the workers in communism.

But the trade unions must be not only schools of communism but also schools of struggle. And whether you want it or not, the unions will continue to influence this struggle along the lines of their concepts and present it with their own slant. Communists' most important work consists of taking the leadership of these organisations, in order to bring the Communist viewpoint into line with the longings of the workers, or vice versa. I hope it is now clear what I mean in saying that Communists' work in the trade unions does not consist only of assisting the workers in day-to-day struggles. It is mainly a matter of implanting the spirit of communism in these unions and eradicating the old impulse to split these unions into various craft-based divisions. We must oppose the attempts of different craft divisions to proceed on their own. We must transform them until we are finally able to carry out the demand, 'A single union for each entire branch of industry'.

That is the banner under which we must struggle. Communists must learn to understand that the unions' functions are not limited to promoting and leading the struggle, but also extend to the work of founding a new communist society, which we all seek to construct.

That is precisely the cause of the present crisis in Russia. If the workers were organised industrially as they are politically, the industrial life of Soviet Russia would make rapid progress. That is what we are striving for: an effective union in each branch of industry. Communists must keep in mind the slogan, 'One union, one industry'.

As for the proposal that unions be free of politics, our experiences in Britain in this regard are quite interesting. At present, we have a trade-union movement in Britain that does not want to pose industrial issues in a political framework. That is a characteristic weakness of today's union movement. Politics is not conducted in the unions, which are opposed to any political action. This is a significant fact. Communists have the task of showing workers that industrial and political questions cannot be separated even today, and that in every industrial struggle the moment arrives, sooner or later, when it takes on a political character. It is up to the Communists to fuse together these two different forms of struggle.

And now, in conclusion, a word on the relations of the Communist International with the Red International of Labour Unions. As far as the British delegation is concerned, we regard the industrial movement, the Red International of Labour Unions, as a complement to our Communist work.

In our preparations for the communist revolution, we hope that the organised workers will provide us with the forces necessary to support the achievements of the Communist political movement. If that is the case, it is obvious that the Communists should influence and lead the Red International of Labour Unions and have a great interest in controlling it. For that reason there must be a close relationship between the Communist International and the Red International of Labour Unions, a coalition expressed through an exchange of delegates.

As for Amsterdam, we must not forget how dangerous it is to make it into a fetish. That is certainly the case in Britain. We have found that the best method of criticism is not to lay too much weight on criticism itself. The best method is to go into the national unions and attack the Amsterdam International from there by overturning the reactionary leaders, which will make it possible to withdraw this union and its support from the Amsterdam International.

That is what we have to say to the congress, in the hope that it will be given all due attention.

**Gennari** (Chair): There are two more speakers on the list. After them, the debate will be closed. The reporter will not speak until the commission has concluded its work.[16]

---

16. For the report by Heckert from the Trade Union Commission, see Session 24, pp. 883–7.

**Leo Pivio** (Leo Laukki, Finland, United States): Comrades, I do not intend to speak against the theses presented by Comrade Zinoviev. I would also like to say, right from the start, that I agree with what Comrade Bell has said about relations with the trade unions. I must add a few words, however, about the industrial unions and the American IWW.

I have been a member of the IWW since I came to the United States in 1907, and, during all these years, I have taken part actively in the American workers' movement. I consider it my duty to correct the false and inadequate statements made here regarding the IWW. In particular, I must stress that the quotations from IWW publications read out here do not reflect the organisation's position. Most of these quotations are wrong. In reality, not a single voice was raised against Soviet Russia. The statements against the Third International and communism were repudiated by the IWW. Sandgren, who was responsible for this episode, was removed as editor of the largest monthly, *One Big Union*. He appealed to the IWW convention that took place a few weeks ago in Chicago, but the delegates did not give him a hearing.[17] On the contrary, the convention approved the position taken by the Executive Board on the Sandgren case.

In this regard, the proposal that I am going to make here is extremely important. It is true that organisations like the IWW sometimes include individuals who are not in agreement with positions of the organisation. They may even go so far as to reject the organisation's traditions. This was the case in the IWW in 1917. A number of members and functionaries took a position contrary to the traditions and principles of the organisation and harmful to its good name. They wrote slanderous articles against Soviet Russia. They wrote counterrevolutionary articles and published counterrevolutionary literature. As soon as the IWW's components and local units learned of this, they registered protests. They demanded the withdrawal of this literature and these articles. The IWW Executive Board did not neglect to do this. The articles were not only repudiated; they were destroyed. If you hold the organisation to be responsible for the quotations read out here, you are on the wrong track. The organisation is not responsible for them.

Nonetheless, this question must be cleared up, so that the Russian comrades can understand what was going on in the IWW during 1917–19. Some comrades here shook their heads when those quotations were read out. They must have thought, 'What a reactionary organisation it must be!'

---

17. In October 1920 the IWW's Executive Board removed John Sandgren from his position as editor of *One Big Union Monthly* for attacks on the Bolsheviks and Soviet Russia that were published in the October issue. The removal was sustained at the IWW's May 1921 convention in Chicago.

The IWW was a large organisation in 1917, during the War. It was the only organisation to struggle boldly against the War. The IWW declared a general strike in the western states and organised a strike in the mining districts.[18] It aroused the entire West against the War, against the Wilson government, and against the American plutocracy. Nonetheless, it received no support from the ranks of the Socialist Party or the people who now represent the trade unions here. They all left the IWW in the lurch in its struggle against the government. The result was that the American capitalists closed ranks and hurled themselves at the IWW. Three thousand editors, speakers, organisers, and active members were jailed or murdered. The entire organisation was smashed. The capitalist hirelings invaded the IWW headquarters, destroyed and burned books and papers, smashed typewriters, and so on.

Of course, reaction then set in. That resulted from the hard-fought strikes – some of them extremely successful – that the IWW had carried out just before the misdeed of the American government and bourgeoisie. I do not need to explain to the Russian comrades just how important economic strikes are. It is enough to recall the state of the Russian workers' movement in the years from 1896 to 1900. Even the Socialists then issued a manifesto that not a single revolutionary may join the trade unions, because a great many spies were active there. The same was true in 1917 in the IWW. The organisation was smashed, and all its best forces, who had fought for an entire decade in the IWW – teachers, organisers, speakers, and educators – were thrown in prison.

What was then to be expected? The workers believed in economic action, because they had achieved gains in this way. Only young people were left in the organisation, and they were inexperienced and unfamiliar with its traditions and basic principles. As in all other organisations, many spies were at work. In connection with the trial against us in Chicago,[19] the government stated that it had maintained eighty-six spies in the IWW since 1916, with the

---

18. From late June to late August 1917, the IWW led a general strike of workers in the lumber industry of the Pacific Northwest. The strike, which involved 50,000 lumberjacks, paralysed more than 80 per cent of the lumber industry in parts of the region, threatening the manufacture of war materiel. The strike forced the lumber barons to grant workers the eight-hour day.

In June–July 1917 the IWW organised a strike by copper miners against the Phelps Dodge company in Bisbee, Arizona. It ended with the mass deportation of some 1,200 strikers.

19. A reference to the 1918 mass frame-up trial in Chicago of members of the IWW. A total of 93 workers were convicted, including Haywood and the speaker Laukki (Pivio), and sentenced to up to twenty years in prison.

aim of carrying out provocation. It was either fifty-six or eighty-six; I can't remember exactly.

So I must repeat that this record does not provide any grounds for reproaching the organisation. On the contrary, an organisation that fought back against the capitalists and the plutocracy so energetically must have a healthy core. Only a strong organisation could have carried out the very bold attacks on the capitalists that forced the bourgeoisie to concentrate all its forces on beating down the IWW, as was the case in 1917. True, the IWW had its Sandgrens and the like. But our comrades here are blaming Haywood and others, even though all members of the organisation who were not in jail protested vigorously against Sandgren's statements and demanded that they be repudiated. Indeed, the IWW was the first organisation to take a stand for Bolshevism. In 1917 it was the IWW publications that most vigorously defended the Soviet system and Bolshevism. The American Communists gathered the harvest, but the seeds had been sown by the IWW.

In this regard, I must take up another question, that of the relationship between the Communist International and the revolutionary trade unions, particularly as laid down in the current text by Comrade Zinoviev. It would be a major mistake to take a position on revolutionary unions in the United States hostile to the IWW and to industrial unionism. If the American Communists commit this error, as the American Socialists did in the past, if they adopt a hostile stance toward the industrial unions with their thousands and millions of supporters, they will meet the same fate as befell the Socialist Party. They will then remain a small organisation, while the main task is for the Communist Party of America to increase its membership. At present it is more a sect than a party. It is vital that it become a mass party. But where will it find its members if not among the active revolutionary forces? There are hundreds of thousands of active, class-conscious revolutionaries in the United States. They are not Communists, to be sure, but they have the courage of Communists, they apply Communist tactics and work tirelessly for the revolution. They never take the capitalist side of maintaining the present social order.

That is why it is important for the Communist Party of America to recruit its members from these masses, these hundreds of thousands of true revolutionaries, who are active members of the IWW and from the industrial unions outside the IWW. The party must win over these young, strong, militant revolutionaries. This is the task of the American party, and if it does not grasp this, it has no prospects for further development.

The American Communist Party must not fight against industrial unionism, or it will suffer the same fate as the Socialist Party. If this happens, a left wing will form and the party will split, just as the Socialist Party split. If you take a position hostile to this, you will simply hasten a split in the party. Hundreds of IWW members belong to the Communist Party. I know all the Finnish comrades, and they are all industrial unionists. In addition, many American Communists of my acquaintance are for industrial unionism. If you set yourselves against this, you promote division in the Communist Party and contribute to its becoming a doctrinaire sect just like the Socialist Labor Party.

I would now like to refute a statement made with regard to Comrade Haywood. It was said here that he favours some sort of 'dual union'. I have here the theses that he proposes for adoption by the red trade-union congress, and I would like to read a quotation that clarifies his point of view.

> The Communist Party as a revolutionary political movement can have only one goal, namely the forcible overthrow of the capitalist system of production and distribution in the bourgeois state and its replacement by the dictatorship of the proletariat as expressed in the Soviet system. It is therefore historically and tactically indispensable for the workers' unions to subordinate themselves to this goal and to take part in the Communist political movement.

I do not believe I need to add anything to that statement.

**Marković** (Yugoslavia): Comrades, I have taken the floor in order to refute a very thoughtless assertion by Comrade Landler. According to the transcript, Comrade Landler said the following: 'The Yugoslav sister party refrained from organising a political strike when the Yugoslav trade unions were banned. They did not even undertake an initiative in parliament.'[20]

This assertion is completely contradicted by reality. It must originate in a very disreputable source, namely the social-patriotic and centrist press. Here are the facts: when the striking miners were militarised, a political strike was launched, which resulted in banning not only the trade unions but the Yugoslav Communist Party. How did our party respond? The general strike we had proclaimed lasted one, two, or three days. Despite extreme repression, the miners' strike lasted fourteen days. The Communist Party of Yugoslavia focused all our energy on extending and intensifying this general miners' strike. In this we were fully successful. Through this general miners' strike we were able, temporarily, to cause the Yugoslav bourgeoisie very great damage. And I stress that we were completely successful in this. In wide

---

20. See p. 732.

areas of Yugoslavia, the miners' strike turned into open civil war. There were bloody clashes with the police and army in many locations, with dead and many wounded on both sides.[21] That is how the Yugoslav Communist Party responded to this coup d'état.

In this regard, I would like to add that, if the Hungarian trade unions had reacted to the collapse of the council dictatorship in Hungary with at least this vigour, perhaps the situation today in Hungary would be somewhat different. As for parliamentary initiatives, let me point out that what we have in Yugoslavia right now is not an ordinary parliament but a constituent assembly, meeting under special conditions, namely with the specific task of drawing up a constitution as rapidly as possible. This assembly's rules of order almost completely excluded any other form of activity. Nonetheless, through an energetic initiative, our parliamentary fraction succeeded three times in forcing a discussion on the banning of the trade unions and the Communist Party. During these discussions, there were tumultuous disorders and demonstrations in parliament, which found an echo among the broadest proletarian masses on the outside. Those are the facts. As you see, they are quite different from the picture that Comrade Landler tried to present, in a fashion that I cannot explain but consider to be completely tendentious.

**Gennari** (Chair): The Norwegian delegation has submitted a statement, which reads as follows:

> What Comrade Zinoviev said about the movement in Norway did not entirely correspond to reality. He maintained that the leadership of the Norwegian trade unions has remained in the hands of centrists. The situation is as follows: At the most recent trade-union congress, held last year, six Communists and three centrists were elected as members of the General Commission.[22] One of the latter is chair. We did not dare fill every position on the General Commission with Communists, because that ran the danger of blowing apart the national organisation. The centrists and Social Democrats still hold the leadership of a number of not very large craft unions.
>
> In a few months another congress will be held, at the desire of broad masses in the movement. These broad masses are embittered regarding

---

21. On 17 December 1920, 12,000 coal miners went on strike in the Trbovlje Basin in Slovenia, followed five days later by the miners of Bosnia-Herzegovina. With strikebreaking action by the police and local authorities unsuccessful, the government decided on 24 December to militarise the mines. To crush a planned protest general strike, on 29–30 December the government banned the Communist Party and 2,500 trade unions, and conducted mass arrests.
22. The Ninth Norwegian Trade Union Congress met 11–16 July 1920.

the outcome of the great strike in June.[23] This congress will certainly adopt a new national orientation. Many of the old craft unions will probably be dissolved, which will deal a death blow to bureaucratism in the trade-union movement.

**Gennari** (Chair): On Saturday, at 7:00 p.m., the youth congress will convene in the Zimin theatre. All delegates are invited to the opening celebration.

The next session will take place tomorrow evening at 6:00 p.m.

*(The session is adjourned at 12:00 midnight.)*

---

23. For the 1921 Norwegian general strike, see p. 106, n. 9.

Session 20 – 8 July 1921, 8:00 p.m.
# Youth and Women's Movements

*The Communist International and the Communist Youth Movement. Speakers: Münzenberg, Frölich. Resolution on the Communist International and the Communist Youth Movement. Clara Zetkin: Report on the Women's Movement. Speakers: Lucie Colliard, Kollontai. Resolution on the International Communist Women's Movement and the International Communist Women's Secretariat. Resolution on the forms and methods of Communist work among women.*

**Kolarov** (Chair): Comrade Münzenberg has the floor for a report on the youth question.

### Report on Communist Youth Movement

**Münzenberg**: Comrades, Comrade Zinoviev has already noted in his report on the activity of the Executive that the Communist youth movement deserves to receive far more attention and consideration. Comrades, Comrade Zinoviev was quite right to admonish us in this way. Despite the history of the Communist youth movement, there are even today many comrades who regard this movement as something trivial, immature, and childish, while other comrades fear that separate Communist youth leagues could readily develop into parallel Communist parties. Both points of view miss the essence of the Communist youth movement.

For the Communist International, the problem of the youth movement is much greater and more challenging. Through special methods of capitalist production – the introduction of machines, increased specialised work in the factories, and so on – it was possible to draw into the production process large numbers of women and youth. When I speak of youth here and in the rest of this report, I am referring to the layer of the working class whose ages lie between 14 or 15 years (after leaving school) and 19 or 20 years. This is the layer of the working class that we designate as youth when we are thinking of bringing them together in a separate Communist youth organisation.

Even before the War, a rather large number of such youth were drawn into the overall production process as helpers and factory workers. This process has been enormously speeded up by war industry and the rapid evolution of capitalism and imperialism. Through this process, greater and greater numbers of youth, who at an earlier time worked as agricultural labourers and apprentices, were drawn into the large factories as factory workers and helpers. This process is still continuing. Today the army of youth who occupy this position in the process of production already numbers many millions. At the same time, comrades, there has been a complete change in the economic position of youth in the production process. With the increase in direct and active participation by youth in production, there has also been a social shift. The exploitation of craft apprentices, which prevailed in the sixties, seventies, and eighties, has receded more and more. Comrades are by and large well aware of this. But let me provide just a few figures to indicate how rapidly this process has been advancing.

In Switzerland, for example, there were 400,000 wage workers in 1912, of which only 30,000 were apprentices, as against more than 60,000 youth working as helpers. In a particularly capitalist Swiss industry, textiles, there were 97,000 workers, of whom only 1,500 were apprentices, while 22,500 were young factory workers. One and a half thousand apprentices as against 22,000 young helpers. In Vienna, there were 61,500 apprentices in 1913, but only 29,000 in 1916 and only 18,000 in 1917. The number of apprentices learning a trade declines with extraordinary speed as the number of youthful helpers and factory workers grows. These tendencies can be found in every country and every industry.

The decisive factor in this change is that apprentices and journeymen no longer have their previous perspective and hope that after a three-year apprenticeship they will become masters, on their own. The decisive factor is that the youth, when entering the factory, sees before him an entire life as a factory worker until he is an old man. That is decisive in this picture. His interests are fundamentally the same as those of the adult workers. Like them, he can defend his interests only by selling his labour power at the highest possible price. Even so, comrades, the conditions of youth are, in every conceivable respect, worse, and youth are, in economic terms, the most disadvantaged category of worker. If we examine the statistics, we find that the wages of youth in every country have experienced the smallest increases in recent years.

In Germany, there are many categories of apprentices, of young workers, who are receiving the same wages – with only quite minimal increases – as before and during the War, although the cost of living has increased by several hundred per cent. The work performed by young workers is just as important as that of the adults in the factory, but their wages are relatively the worst. They receive the worst wage and the worst treatment from their foremen, and they make up a large proportion of the unemployed. In all these respects, they are economically among the most poverty-stricken category of the working class. This fact alone places them in the same position as the unemployed, who are also in every country the layer of the working class that is most quickly won to Communist ideas.

Not only is their economic situation poor; they also suffer bad conditions politically and culturally. In all capitalist countries, the youth are completely deprived of political rights, not only in terms of active participation in parliament but also through exclusion from any role in any legally established factory council or similar institution. What is more, during the War, special laws were adopted in various capitalist countries against young workers.

On top of that, there is cultural backwardness. Even before the War, the elementary schools were not worth much, but the frenzy of war made them a great deal worse. Then there are the special psychological characteristics of youth – their receptivity to what is new and revolutionary – which makes them more inclined to embrace Communist ideas. Especially in the colonial countries of the East, we have seen that the first layers to be caught up in the Communist movement always come from the younger generation.

In some countries, young workers number in the millions. In Germany, for example, there are about four million. As for the total number of these youth in the capitalist countries, an estimate of twenty million would not be too high. Comrades, I am sure that this cursory overview has shown you that all the economic, political, and cultural characteristics of this layer of twenty million young workers makes them particularly receptive to Communist ideas. For this reason, we believe that the Communist parties should do all in their power to carry out special Communist propaganda among these twenty million young men and women. This work should be intensified and extended, because their overall situation makes it particularly easy to win them over to us. Winning a large number of these twenty million would be a great success for the Communist movement as a whole. The simple fact of adding these youth to the Communist International's array of forces would greatly broaden and deepen our battle line.

But that is not all. The history of the revolutionary movement and, even more, that of the proletarian movement in recent years – in Finland, Hungary, Eastern European states, and Russia – demonstrates that it is above all from the ranks of youth that we can win the most self-sacrificing fighters for proletarian revolution. This factor should not be underestimated in judging why we must win the masses of youth for the movement. The old Social-Democratic leaders were no mean strategists in some respects, but they completely failed to utilise the enthusiasm of young workers. In a discussion of this theme in 1908, Legien and others had nothing but stupid jokes to offer regarding youth's willingness to sacrifice. Hindenburg, Ludendorff, and [Kaiser] Wilhelm utilised youths' enthusiasm and spirit of sacrifice very cleverly during the War. Hundreds of thousands of youth voluntarily signed up for the War.

What is more, in the split of the SPD and later of the USPD in Germany, the old and tested layer of functionaries and activists stayed in the old parties, and the Communist Party was not able to bring over more than a very low percentage of them. By winning youth and systematic education in the youth organisations, it will be possible in a few years to construct a quite good staff of tested functionaries, activists, and leaders.

Indeed, even today a considerable number of youths can be engaged directly in party activity. There are a great many tasks in party life for which youth are particularly well suited. I am thinking of different tasks related to illegal work, for example, courier service, illegal propaganda, and above all anti-militarist propaganda.

There was a short discussion of this task in the Executive, in relationship to France.[1] The French Communist Youth were wrongly criticised for having gone too far and having taken a wrong position when they spoke in favour of refusing military service. But there is something we must consider here. In Central and Western Europe, there are standing armies numbering in the hundreds of thousands – in Czechoslovakia, Italy, France, and the new countries like Poland. We have carried out systematic and continuing work to undermine these armies from within. This is a task for which youth, thanks to their social situation, are particularly well suited, and whose importance must not be underestimated. There are many other such tasks. In Germany, during the Kapp Putsch, we saw how masses of youth were recruited to paste up posters, especially in Berlin. The Communist Party enjoys an enormous advantage here.

These tasks are not ended by the taking of power. The example of Russia and of Russia's Communist Youth League shows that even after power is

---

1. For the expanded ECCI discussion on France, see Appendix 3f on pp. 1108–32.

taken, under the proletarian dictatorship, Communist youth organisations can carry out good and useful work for the Communist movement and the Communist parties – through training and educating proletarian instructors and proletarian leaders in the various commissariats and the Red Army, through appointing instructors and, later, officers. Here, we see the truly broad scope of the Communist Youth, out of whose ranks come all those who will replace the bourgeois intellectuals as proletarian instructors in the new economy.

The Communist International and its parties have all the more reason to focus on winning these twenty million, since all their opponents, of every hue, do everything in their power to win over the new proletarian generation. Let me remind you of what the bourgeois state does through the old organisations, such as schools, churches, press, and youth newspapers. It has done even more. In Germany, France, and Britain, there are bourgeois youth leagues of every variety, ranging from religious to so-called sport leagues. As the proletarian revolution advances, the class character of these institutions becomes more and more blatant. In Germany, a large portion of these associations, led by bourgeois students, have been deployed and have fought against revolutionary workers.

Moreover, the Social-Democratic parties and the Second International are also doing everything in their power to win over the new proletarian generation. A few weeks ago, they undertook to create a new yellow International.[2] There are still numerically strong Social-Democratic youth leagues in a number of countries. In Germany, where the Communist youth league numbers 25,000 members, the Social-Democratic youth wing has more then 70,000. Meanwhile the trade-union youth groups include 250,000 members. In the Netherlands, we have barely 500 members, while the Social-Democratic youth leagues count 10,000 members. A short while ago, the Second International set about unifying these groups and developing its youth movement systematically. You are well aware how important that is and how much attention the Second International has devoted to its youth movement. None other than Fritz Ebert, the current president of the German republic, was for many years chair of the committee for propaganda among youth in Germany.

When the Two-and-a-Half International met in Vienna [in February 1921], Kautsky, that greybeard did all in his power to gather the youth under his protection and sceptre, and a Two-and-a-Half Youth International was founded

---

2. On 12–13 May 1921, a meeting was held in Amsterdam of Second International youth organisations in Germany, Sweden, Denmark, Netherlands, Belgium, and France. The meeting established the Labour Youth International.

then whose Austrian section has 25,000 members, and so on elsewhere.[3] Comrades, we must not underestimate our enemies' exertions and efforts in this field. We know full well that there are limits to what the social patriots and the centrists can achieve by such efforts to win the new proletarian generation, but we must not underestimate our opponents in this regard. The social patriots, the trade-union International, and the centrists are striving to secure the new proletarian generation, prevent it from turning to us, hold it back, and block it from joining the Communist movement. Our task is to confront these efforts and thwart them. The Communist International and its parties are all the better able to do this since the youth themselves are pressing toward the Communist movement.

The youth sense instinctively that their real and true interests are the same as those of the Communist International and will truly be advanced only by the Communist parties. Everywhere the Communist parties have helped in winning the youth – and where it is possible to carry out propaganda openly and freely: in Italy until recently, in Scandinavia, Denmark, and Norway, and in Czechoslovakia, the youth organisations have been able to compete freely with the bourgeois and social-patriotic youth. In all these cases, the overwhelming majority of the youth has fought on the side of the Communists against the social patriots and bourgeois. Only a few days ago, it was reported that in Czechoslovakia – where especially the old social patriots were trying to win over the new proletarian generation through the scouting organisations – the vast majority of these organisations have gone over to the Communist youth movement.

The proletarian youth, who instinctively sensed the correctness of the Communist International's revolutionary policies, were among the first who took up the struggle against the War, under the leadership of Karl Liebknecht, Rosa Luxemburg, Clara Zetkin, and other comrades in Germany, Höglund in Sweden, Koritschoner in Austria, and others. At the time of the Zimmerwald and Kienthal Conferences, the youth had already held their first international congress.[4] The Swedish, Norwegian, and Swiss youth organisations, and the oppositional youth groups in Germany were the first to take a stand

---

3. The Two-and-a Half Youth International (International Working Union of Young Socialists) grouped centrist socialist youth organisations from Austria, Germany, France, Czechoslovakia, Yugoslavia, Lithuania, and Hungary. In May 1923, following the fusion of the Two-and-a-Half International and Second Internationals, the Two-and-a-Half Youth International fused with the Second International's Labour Youth International to create the Socialist Youth International.

For the Vienna congress of the Two-and-a-Half International, see p. 59, n. 2.

4. A reference to the International Socialist Youth Conference in Bern, Switzerland, 5–7 April 1915. That meeting attempted to reconstitute the Socialist Youth International – which had effectively dissolved with the outbreak of World War I –

for Zimmerwald and Kienthal and later for the Zimmerwald Left.[5] None other than Comrade Zinoviev, in a short pamphlet for Russian youth, underlined how important was the impact of the revolutionary youth leaders struggling against the War in the process of assembling all revolutionary forces.

Twelve of these leagues gathered in the autumn of 1919 in a Berlin conference that resolved to reorganise the Youth International as a Communist Youth International.[6] At that time, the Youth International's twelve leagues embraced a little more than three hundred thousand members. As a result of several unfortunate accidents and misfortunes, the Executive Committee set up in Berlin was not able until last summer to undertake wide-ranging and planned agitational and organisational work to broaden and strengthen the International youth movement. Comrades, the correctness of my earlier statement that the twenty million constitute the layers that we can most readily win over is proven by the fact that, although only a few months have passed since the autumn of 1920, the leagues affiliated to the Youth International have grown in number from twelve to fifty, which now embrace significantly more than eight hundred thousand youth – despite the limited resources at our disposal and the limited efforts made during the initial months.

These months were filled with lively propaganda activity to win the leagues that then still stood aside from the Communist Youth International, above all through a struggle against the centrist organisations that, until a few months ago, still dominated the entire proletarian youth movement in Central Europe. Until a few months ago, the entire French youth organisation was controlled by the centrists. The last few months were dedicated to winning these youth, and this has been completely successful. Through its press, its newspapers, the Youth International has attempted to unify the entire Communist youth movement around the consistent programme of the Communist International. Consider *Jugend-Internationale*, which now appears

---

and called for youth to fight for peace through resumption of the class struggle. See Riddell (ed.) 1984, pp. 280–2.

5. The Zimmerwald movement was named after an international conference of socialists opposed to the social-patriotic position of the leading parties of the Second International that took place in Zimmerwald, Switzerland, 5–8 September 1915. Attended by 37 delegates from 12 countries, the conference adopted a resolution and manifesto against the War. Lenin attended the conference and headed the Zimmerwald Left, which favoured responding to the War with class struggle for social revolution. A second conference of the Zimmerwald movement took place in Kienthal, Switzerland, 24–30 April 1916. Excerpts from the debates and resolutions at these two conferences can be found in Riddell (ed.) 1984, pp. 286–322; 519–25 and Gankin and Fisher (eds.) 1940, pp. 320–56; 407–62.

6. The Conference of the International Union of Socialist Youth Organisations, held in Berlin 20–26 November 1919, voted to change its name and became the First Congress of the Communist Youth International.

each month as a journal in French, Russian, Yiddish, English, and Hungarian, with a total press run of 160,000.[7] The leagues themselves, although formed only recently, have carried out very intensive agitational and organisational work. And, during the discussion of both the Czech and the French questions [at the Expanded Executive meeting], there were repeated references to the participation of the Communist youth leagues in all revolutionary work and struggle. The Communist youth organisations conducted themselves with particular vigour in Italy and Eastern Europe, where they are even today the main factor in the Communist parties' underground work.

The importance of the Communist youth movement is evident above all in the respect they are accorded by the bourgeois governments. During the last few days, the French government has set about drawing up a new emergency law against the Communist youth movement, in order to stop its anti-militarist propaganda.[8] We see such persecution of the Communist youth organisations in almost every country. In France, Alsace-Lorraine, and Bavaria, *Jugend-Internationale* has been banned. It sounds like a bad joke, but yet the reports reaching us from Bavaria are absolutely true: the Kahr government there has banned even the Communist paper for children, *Der Junge Genosse*, on grounds of incitement to class hatred. (*Laughter*) That is of course evidence more of the Kahr government's fears than of a class struggle by our young Communists. Our young Communists will of course do everything they can to educate these children.

Comrades, I will not give you more than these few examples. The overriding reason why I took the floor here is to stress that *it is absolutely necessary to expand the scope of the work now under way*. The lion's share of this work must be taken on by the youth themselves, and they will do this. The youth who have so far been the real architects, agitators, and creators of the Communist youth movement must and will remain in future the most active force in this arena. They will be all the more able to do this as the development of the Communist movement as a whole enables and permits them to devote themselves again to their special youth work.

Comrades, as you are aware, the proletarian youth organisations, just like the workers' movement as a whole, has gone through an evolution. Founded before the War, in Central Europe above all, they served as a defensive and auxiliary organisation against capitalist exploitation. When the Social-

---

7. Münzenberg omits mention of the main, German-language edition of *Jugend-Internationale*.

8. The Briand cabinet had proposed to the Chamber of Deputies a law criminalising anti-militarist propaganda. In face of determined opposition by the CP and others, the project was dropped in July.

Democratic parties failed during the War, the youth organisations served as a propaganda army against the War. In this process, they assumed tasks in various countries, and later in the Youth International as well, that properly fall to the adult organisations.

There was a time when the youth organisations stood at the centre of all revolutionary efforts against the War. They carried out the functions of a Communist Party. The proletarian youth have been relieved of this task by the emergence of revolutionary Communist mass parties and the existence of the Communist International. The youth no longer need to carry out these tasks. If, on the contrary, the youth continued to assume these tasks, despite the existence of the Communist parties, this would have harmful results for the Communist movement itself. There would then be two Communist parties in each country, differentiated by the age of the members.

This is the framework in which the theses have been presented to the congress by a three-member commission, with the agreement of all the youth present. Their main point is that in the present phase, given the maturity reached by the international Communist movement as a whole, *the youth ceases to be an independent vanguard political organisation. It rather adheres to the party and accepts the party's political direction.* The Youth International should now be simply the intermediary between the political will of the Communist International and the masses of working youth around the world. That is the decisive aspect of the theses now before you – its central point. Comrades, given that the political tasks that the youth carried out during the War, in a revolutionary upsurge against the War, have now been assumed by the Communist parties, the youth can now turn again to their specific youth tasks, above all, *leading and unleashing youths' economic struggle.* They will attempt to perceive the crucial interests of youth in the factories and mills, and propose demands and slogans for their struggle. In the factories, mills, and workplaces, the Communist youth leagues will advance propaganda slogans, as they go into the youth wings of the trade unions, and the trade unions themselves, to agitate for these demands of economic struggle. During rising conflicts, and as youth take up these struggles, they will attempt to win the Communist parties to an awareness of the economic interests of youth. The Communist Youth International is about to hold its Second Congress. We can already be sure that it will make a decision along these lines, on behalf of all its affiliates.[9]

---

9. The Second Congress of the Communist Youth International held its inaugural session in Moscow on 9 July 1921, and held its formal deliberations 14–23 July. The congress followed on a protracted internal debate in the CYI.

Leaders of the Russian Communist youth, supported by the ECCI, had pressed for the CYI congress to be held in Moscow rather than in Germany, where the CYI

In this way, the youth will establish a link with the large, broad masses of young people, with the twenty million. In step with the parties, it will grow in Germany, the Netherlands, Italy, and France from small circles of conscious, intelligent, and educated young workers into mass movements.

The second great task will be *improved and broadened agitation through the Youth International and the youth leagues*. In many countries that are decisive for capitalist development, there is still no youth organisation, or only an extremely small one. The most important propaganda is carried out among the rural young workers and small peasants. We must also attempt to broaden our range of agitational methods, supplementing the spoken word with pictorial presentations. Given the changed conditions in the workers' movement as a whole, the youth organisations have an important task in carrying out general educational work, with the goal of training young workers to be competent, Marxist-minded revolutionary fighters, who influence the thinking of youth by means of educational work by the youth groups, courses, public meetings, rallies, cinema, and every other possible method.

Comrades, one more word on the forms of agitation. Where and how should these youth be brought together? Our point of view on this is that a special youth organisation is best suited to this. As I said earlier, the youth organisations should be subordinate, politically and tactically, to the leadership of the Communist parties. But this does not deprive the youth of the right to discuss in their own organisations all the political questions of the day and all the current tactical issues, taking positions and making decisions.

As you know, comrades, previously, the youth were always among those in the left wing of the International. Comrade Lenin said once that it is inevitable; the youth will always be on the left. The youth should have the right to continue to take positions within their organisations on all these issues, and to attempt to influence the party along the lines of its decisions, striving

---

was headquartered, with the goal of achieving closer coordination between the CYI and ECCI. Rejecting an appeal from the ECCI, the CYI initially convened its second congress in Jena, Germany, on 3 April 1921, with representatives from twenty-five countries. It debated the March Action, where Münzenberg and some other CYI leaders initially expressed criticisms of the VKPD's conduct. The report on the world situation by Pogány, an ECCI envoy, won the majority to adopt theses aligned with the theory of the offensive.

After four days of deliberations, the congress was dispersed by police; it resumed in Berlin. Delegates then accepted under protest a renewed ECCI request that they adjourn and reconvene in Moscow.

Prior to and during the Third Congress, the youth representatives in Moscow held intensive discussions and also attended a congress of the Russian Communist Youth. Münzenberg and the majority of CYI leaders from abroad then rallied to the proposals of the Russian youth, presented by Münzenberg in this report.

to win a hearing for their positions within the party through their newspapers, delegations, and so on. But as our theses state, the Communist youth organisation must never take a stand opposed to the party and combat it. This is different from the past, when the socialist and revolutionary youth had the right and even the duty to struggle with leaflets and pamphlets against the party's rotten reformism. We consider ourselves to be part of the party as a whole, but within the party, the youth – just like any other wing of the party – should have the right to influence the party by its ideas and points of view. We are in favour of bringing young workers together in their own special youth organisations – particularly for educational purposes. We are against the option of dissolving the youth organisations and recruiting individual youth directly to the party. That would not only compromise its organisational strength but would be very harmful for education of the youth. The independent organisations make it possible for the youth to be active in their own right and to develop early a sense of responsibility and duty in their own organisational work. They will become organisationally competent early on. All these enormous advantages of youth having their own organisational activity can and must be retained in the future, in order to be able to *pass on well-trained, tested, and competent recruits to the Communist Party*. In this way, as I have sketched out all too briefly, we hope that the youth themselves will be active and energetic in agitation and in the winning of the twenty million young workers.

The Communist parties, however, can and must support this work. And here we must note that despite the obligation laid on all parties by the Communist International's Second Congress to do this, very few parties have carried it out in a fashion corresponding to their resources.[10] We must appeal to the parties in this as in other fields not to regard the decisions of the International congress as pieces of paper but to actually act and work to implement them.

Comrades, the Communist parties can express their support for the Communist youth movement in winning the broad masses of young workers for the Communist movement through both political and moral assistance and help. Reciprocal representation should begin at the lowest level, the lowest local bodies, and reach up to the central leadership. The youth groups and leagues delegate a representative to the party, and in return the party chooses a representative to the youth. This enables the party to exert constant supervision and ongoing political influence on the youth, and, on the other hand, assures the youth of contact with the party. In this way, the youth can draw

---

10. See 'Theses on the Youth Movement' in Riddell (ed.) 1991, 2WC, 2, pp. 999–1001. Drafted for the Second Congress, these theses were not discussed there, but were adopted by youth representatives and the ECCI in August 1920.

benefit from the experiences of the adults in the party. Every Communist newspaper should include a special supplement for the youth at least once a week – as has been the case recently in the German party newspapers. The Communist Party can achieve a great deal by establishing schools, by encompassing the youth in party courses, by organising events on the development and character of the youth movement, and by material and financial support. This is above all the case in countries where the party is relatively strong, and the youth movement relatively weak. I think of Germany and the countries where the youth movement is still in embryo, while the parties have already got a firm foothold. Britain and America seem to be countries where we should hurry to the assistance of the youth in the coming period. On the international plane as well, the youth movement can be supported more effectively than in the past, by bringing the full authority of the Communist International and the Executive to bear to assure that the decisions on work among the youth are carried out. The International should make further proposals to the individual parties, including by introducing a special supplement to *Communist International* on the problems of youth, providing help and support in organising international schooling and the training of agitators, and so on. It is absolutely necessary that the parties of the Communist International come to the assistance in this way of the work that the young Communists are themselves carrying out among the masses of young people.

I would like to conclude by once again highlighting the enormous importance for the Communist movement of winning the youth to the Communist International.

Comrade Trotsky was quite right in referring to the fact that long years of war and deprivation have fully exhausted and physically wasted a good portion of the workers in Central Europe, Austria, and parts of Germany, making them unusable for carrying forward the proletarian struggle. It was Comrade Trotsky who pointed out how another portion of the Central European working class has been poisoned over several decades by the Social-Democratic parties and the trade-union bureaucracy and is also lost to the proletarian revolution. And it was Trotsky who explained that there is only one remedy here: *We must win the young generation in time.* This generation has not endured decades of the Social-Democratic school of stupefaction and is physically and intellectually in a position to drive the proletarian revolution forward.

Let us recall that the bourgeoisie, after the War, sought to win over the young generation of workers and turn it against the proletariat. The majority of Noske's army, with which we fought a running battle, was made up of young workers, forced by poverty and hunger temporarily to join up with this army. The volunteer army, which represents a special form of militarism, is even today recruited mostly from young workers.[11] Comrades, the question of young workers is truly a serious one. The response to it must not be to turn away with a smile, seeking to present it as something childish and immature. The task is to truly win these youth, so that they will carry forward the work of revolution and complete it around the world. (*Loud applause*)

I recommend the theses for the attention of the congress.

**Kolarov** (Chair): Comrade Frölich has the floor.

**Frölich**: Comrades, the theses proposed to us here represent an enormous advance in the development of the youth movement. It is a historic advance because the youth movement can now, with good conscience and in the interests of the revolutionary movement, dispense with its political independence. As we take this decisive step, we must recognise that this political independence has been of very great significance for Communists and for the revolutionary movement. The very establishment of the Communist International and the Communist parties was significantly aided by the fact that the youth was prepared to break the old bonds that tied them to the Social-Democratic parties and to become politically active independently, without supervision by any party. During the War and in the first years of the revolution, the political independence of the youth organisation was extremely productive for us. One of the fruits of this work is the very fact that we are now able to decide that this independence of the youth organisation can now be ended. For only this independence made it possible in the most important countries for us to establish large and strong mass Communist parties, carrying out revolutionary Communist politics.

In my opinion, while carrying out this turn inside the youth movement, we must energetically stress *the importance of the youth organisation for each Communist Party and for the Communist International as a whole*. We cannot stress too much that the youth movement takes on a task that is vital to us: the education of our young people for the struggle. The youth organisation has shown itself to be one of the best reservoirs for the forces that we need in the party. It is our experience in Germany that the best party workers come from

---

11. 'Volunteer army' is a reference to the Freikorps, counterrevolutionary forces used to suppress the revolutionary wave that swept Germany in 1918–19. Initiated by Social-Democratic defence minister Gustav Noske and composed largely of war veterans, the Freikorps became known for summary executions of revolutionary workers. They also operated in the Baltic countries and Poland, which had been under German occupation during the War. The Freikorps were formally absorbed into the army in 1920, but many of their members, leaders, and structures continued to function independently in right-wing militias and later in the Nazi SA and SS.

the youth organisation. And we are convinced that, now and in the future, the best forces in other parties as well will come from the youth organisation, having gained their Communist education there in order to devote themselves to the Communist movement as a whole.

We also know, however, that the youth organisation as such is an extremely important factor in our political struggles. This is true not only because it is in a position to educate the broad mass of revolutionary-minded youth and lead them in organised fashion into the struggle, but also because there are certain tasks that can be carried out much better by the youth organisation than by the Communist Party as a whole. It has been the experience of our German Communist movement that certain tasks relating to underground work can be carried out better, with much less danger and much greater success, by the youth organisation than by party members themselves. We also know that one of the most important of our tasks – propaganda among soldiers – can be pursued with much more success and with greater impact by the youth organisation than by the Communist Party. The youth organisation can only accomplish these tasks if it has the most intimate contact with the party itself and with the institutions that the party establishes for these purposes.

The turn that the youth movement is now undertaking – namely its full political subordination to the party – demands that the party adopt a meaningful orientation to the youth organisation. We have two separate organisations that are to take part actively in political struggles. A seriously implemented relationship of subordination between these two organisations demands absolutely that the youth organisation be integrated into party work as a whole and all the important political decisions.

Comrades, I believe we have to put great stress on this, because we have all experienced the fact that the view is still prevalent in the party that the youth organisation and youth in general do not require all that much political attention. Let me say that it is absolutely necessary in this regard to abandon any presumption and prejudice and ensure that the entire party and youth apparatus, despite their organisational separateness, are closely tied together. We must ensure that it is possible for the youth organisation to influence the party's decisions from the party's top leadership on down to the smallest of our cells. In this fashion the entire political thinking within the party will have its effect on the youth organisation, mobilising it and holding it in constant contact with the party's aims and activities. Only on this foundation, in my opinion, will the youth organisation be in a position to hazard this great step and accept full subordination to the party's political leadership. That is the only possible guarantee.

In addition, I believe that a precondition for such subordination is for the youth movement to be strongly supported by each individual party. I would like to say to the parties that have not yet had much experience with revolutionary struggle that they would face much greater difficulties if the organisational apparatus of the youth organisation was not at their disposal in major political battles. They need to cultivate this organisational apparatus by making the best forces they can spare available for this work, and supporting and promoting the youth organisation by every means at their disposal. If the parties do this, then the step that the youth organisation is about to take, and that the congress should approve, will be advantageous for the Communist movement.

## Resolution on the Communist International and the Communist Youth Movement

*[For text of this resolution, see pp. 1030–3.]*

**Kolarov** (Chair): There is no one left on the speakers' list, and the debate is therefore closed. Some amendments have been proposed to the theses distributed by Comrade Münzenberg. The Presidium therefore proposes to form a five-member commission to carry out the necessary changes and report back to the congress tomorrow. The Presidium proposes that the commission consist of Comrades Frölich, Kolarov, Bukharin, Münzenberg, and Shatskin. Are there any objections? Seeing none, the list is accepted. We will now have the report on the women's movement. Comrade Clara Zetkin has the floor.

## Report on Communist Women's Movement

**Clara Zetkin**: Comrades, on behalf of the International Secretariat of the Executive for Communist Work among Women, I am going to give a short overview of the Communist Women's Movement and the Communist women's conference.[12]

Beyond any doubt, we have registered gratifying progress during the last year. This is evident in the development of the Communist Women's Movement in individual countries, where increasing masses of women comrades are resolutely joining the Communist Party. There has also been progress in international coordination of efforts to place the broadest masses of women at the service of proletarian revolution. This applies to the struggles to win political power and establish the dictatorship of the proletariat, and also to

---

12. The Second International Conference of Communist Women was held in Moscow 9–15 June 1921, on the eve of the Third Comintern Congress.

defence of these achievements and Communist construction in countries like Russia, where the proletariat has already taken power.

But, mixed into our pleasure regarding these steps forward is a measure of bitterness. In most countries, the gains of the Communist Women's Movement have been achieved without support from the Communist Party, indeed in some instances against its open or hidden opposition. There is still insufficient understanding of the fact that without the participation in revolutionary struggles of women who are conscious, clear on their goal, certain regarding the path, and prepared to make sacrifices, the proletariat will be able neither to seize power in civil war nor, after establishing its dictatorship, to begin constructing a communist society.

Even before the War, it was almost a truism in the socialist workers' movement that the proletariat could not succeed in its economic and political struggles without the participation of masses of women. To be sure, the actions of the old Social-Democratic parties and the trade unions lagged far behind this lip-service. Women's activity was regarded more or less as that of a servant to the party or union, and its true significance as a meaningful factor in proletarian struggle for liberation was not recognised.

But consider, comrades, how different things are for the proletariat today. The economic struggles of the proletariat now take place under conditions of capitalism's accelerating decay. What does that tell us? It means that these struggles are now more bitter and difficult than before, claiming more victims. And there is more: they ultimately strive for a higher goal. Not merely the alleviation of suffering by reducing the hours of work, increasing wages by a few pennies, or improving working conditions. No, all the economic struggles now ultimately point toward one goal: *the assumption by the revolutionary proletariat of control over production and then of ownership of the means of production*. The political struggles of the proletariat no longer lead to minor reforms and concessions, soup kitchens and formal political rights. In a word, *these struggles head not toward the reform of bourgeois society but toward its destruction*. They put in question the very existence of capitalism, the very existence of communism. These struggles take place in the white-hot atmosphere of capitalist economic collapse and civil war.

Given that proletarian struggles take on this character, there is no way that they can make do without the participation of women. The task is *to throw broader masses of women than before into the revolutionary struggle* to overthrow capitalism and the bourgeois state, mobilise and train them, and make them ready and competent to undertake the construction of communism. (*Loud applause*)

Even before the War, Europe had a surplus of five to six million women. This surplus is now estimated to be about fifteen million. Earlier, this surplus of women existed only in the large industrial states, while there was a surplus of men in the Balkan countries. Now the surplus of women has grown substantially in the larger industrial states, and, even in the Balkan countries, there is no longer a surplus of men; rather, the opposite phenomenon is more and more evident. How, then, is it possible to conceive of the struggle to win political power and the building of a communist society without the conscious, enthusiastic, and intelligent collaboration of women? The figures I cited make one thing clear: larger and larger masses of proletarian women are yoked to capitalist exploitation and are therefore driven by their immediate daily needs to struggle against the bourgeois order. But the figures show us something else: that the number of bourgeois and privileged women, who seem to live in an enchanted garden in their home and family, full of peace and joy, is decreasing. No, today, even the privileged women can no longer remain passive and indifferent toward public life and the struggles of our time. They have taken jobs by the millions, where – so long as capitalism reigns – they will suffer the pain of competition between the sexes, in which men contend against them for the means and the pleasures of life.[13] And the civil war, with all its consequences, cuts so deeply into even bourgeois family life that the surrounding walls of indifference and political mindlessness begin to crumble.

Comrades, I am the last one to overestimate the significance of this evolution in the world of bourgeois families. But we must also not underestimate it. To be sure, the masses of women in the bourgeoisie who are uprooted in the epoch of capitalist decay will hardly be readily transformed into the advancing troops of revolution. We must not expect such a development; to do so would be foolish. The masses of bourgeois women will never pour into the broad ranks of proletarian shock troops, who will fight the decisive battles to establish the dictatorship. We should however not overlook the services they can provide as skirmishers in a time of civil war. Moreover, they can carry unrest, ferment, and discord into the camp of the bourgeoisie, our deadly enemy, and thus weaken it.

That is why, in summary, it does immense damage to the revolution and to activating the masses for this revolution if the Communist parties of every country fail to commit the same energy to the revolutionary mobilisation and training of women for the battles of the proletariat as they do to mobilise the men. As for the comrades who do not gather and train women to be conscious partners in revolution, I call them conscious saboteurs of the revolution.

---

13. This passage is worded differently in the Russian text, which reads: 'They have taken jobs by the millions, where they are forced to withstand competition from men. So long as capitalism reigns, the stronger sex will threaten to deprive the weaker one of earnings and the means of subsistence.'

Comrades, the failings of almost every Communist Party in this regard have been less evident because the Executive has endeavoured in word and deed to promote efforts to assemble the broadest masses of women under the banner of the Third International. The Executive's chair, Comrade Zinoviev, has displayed a full understanding of the fact that Communist work among women is nothing less than half the work of Communists as a whole. After the Second World Congress, the Executive provided moral, political, and financial resources to sustain the efforts in each country to gather the Communist women in the parties and lead them as a cohesive force into the struggle. In this manner, the Executive facilitated, promoted, and successfully structured the passionate struggle of the small vanguard of convinced and trained Communist women in different countries. What we have achieved has brought honour and joy to the small contingent of Communist women in each country that gathered around the banner of the Third International, often with no encouragement and, indeed, even against intense opposition.

So it is that, since last year, the systematic work of Communist women for the revolutionary mobilisation and education of the broadest masses of proletarian women has come into being. Our Russian Communist Party has carried out pioneer, exemplary work in this regard. In Germany, too, the Communist women – in the old Spartacus League and later in the United Communist Party [VKPD], from the moment of its foundation – have worked systematically and energetically to make women inside the organisation into partners in the struggle. In Bulgaria, as well, we have a powerful and purposeful Communist women's movement, a women's movement in the true Communist sense, which engages in common activity of men and women with the goal of winning the broad masses of proletarian and peasant women for the revolutionary struggle. But, in other countries, we have only made a beginning, and in some cases not even that, to develop such systematic work.

We hope that our international women's conference and this congress here will remind all Communist parties of the duty that they have until now neglected or carried out only with gritted teeth, in order to keep up appearances.

Our Second International Women's Conference stands as evidence of the vigour and success with which Communist women in different countries have collaborated with the Executive. The First International Conference of Communist Women in Moscow last year brought together only twenty delegates with decisive vote from sixteen countries, plus some consultative guests.[14]

---

14. The First International Conference of Communist Women was held in Moscow 30 July–2 August 1920, during the Second Comintern Congress. The conference appeal, 'To the Working Women of the World', can be found in Riddell (ed.) 1991, 2WC, 2,

However, this year, comrades, representatives came to the international conference from twenty-eight countries. Eighty-two delegates took part, of which sixty-one had decisive vote and twenty-one had consultative vote only.

Efforts to promote the international revolutionary advance of women in the framework of the Second International have never led to a conference with this measure of success. Surely, quite apart from the number of women delegates, when we consider the large number of countries that have gathered around the banner of the Third International, we can truly say that no international conference of bourgeois women has ever been more inclusive in representation or more far-reaching in its significance than the conference just held here in Moscow. And let us not omit a particularly prominent and historically significant feature of this conference: the participation of women from the Eastern peoples.

Comrades, it would perhaps be tempting and seductive for some to view the appearance of delegations from the Near and Far East simply from an aesthetic viewpoint. But the women delegates personified more than the exotic, unusual, and fairy-tale character of the Orient. The conference experienced a powerful historical moment, unforgettable and undying in its significance. For what was the significance of the appearance of women's delegations from the East? It told us that the Eastern peoples have begun to awaken and enter into struggle. Even the most downtrodden of the downtrodden, women who have lived for centuries and millennia under the spell of age-old religious and social beliefs, rules, customs, and practices, are entering the revolutionary struggle. The appearance at the conference of women from the Near and Far East was an indication of how wide-ranging and profound is the advance of revolution in the East.

And that is exceptionally important for us in the West, for the proletarians in all the capitalist countries. Indeed, the battles to liberate the British and French proletariat will be fought not only on their native land but also in the torrid lands of India and Iran, on the variegated landscape of China, and throughout the Near and Far East. Comrades, the fact that women of the East came to us shows the exceptionally wide-reaching significance of the Third International's revolutionary struggle. It is the first, and until now the only organisation that truly inspires the hopes and the trust of the Eastern peoples; it is the first International to embrace all humankind. 'The International shall

---

pp. 972–6. Detailed theses 'for the Communist Women's Movement' were drawn up for presentation to the World Congress but were considered instead by the ECCI, which published them later in 1920. See 2WC, pp. 977–1001.

be the human race'[15] – the entirety of humanity. That was the significance of the appearance of women of the East at the conference.

Let us take a quick look at the International Conference of Communist Women itself. The goals and tasks of what we call the Communist Women's Movement are identical with the goals, tasks, principles, and policies of the Third International, to which we are proud to belong. The task of the conference was to create the weapons needed to defend these principles and these policies in struggle against the capitalist world and all its supporters. For this reason, the conference devoted a large part of its deliberations to two questions: the *forms* and the *methods* that Communist parties will utilise for Communist work among women; and the *close and firm international ties* that can be established between Communist women of each country and their parties, with the Communist Women's International in Moscow, and, through its intermediary, with the common unified leadership: the Executive of the Third International.

Comrades, in discussing and making decisions on these questions, the conference was guided by an overriding principle: There is no special Communist women's organisation. There is only a movement, an organisation of Communist women inside the Communist Party, together with the Communist men. The tasks and goals of Communists are our tasks and goals. Here there is no spirit of faction or of particularism that would tend in any way to divide and divert the revolutionary forces from their great goals of winning proletarian political power and building a communist society. The Communist Women's Movement signifies simply the systematic deployment and systematic organisation of our forces, both women and men, in the Communist Party in order to win the broadest masses of women for the proletariat's revolutionary class struggle, for the struggle to vanquish capitalism and achieve the construction of communism.

However, comrades, this principle of common organisation and work was also acknowledged by the old Social-Democratic parties. Nonetheless, it was carried out so narrow-mindedly, so pettily, with such a mechanical application of the principle of equality, that it did not unleash and fully engage women's energies in the service of the revolution. We Communists are revolutionaries of the deed, of action. We do not in the slightest lose sight of the common interests and struggle of proletarian men and women. However, we are alert to the given, specific conditions that Communist work among women must deal with. We do not forget the social conditions that still hinder women's

---

15. A reference to a line from Franz Diederich's 1908 German translation of 'The Internationale', the anthem of the world workers' movement.

activity, political awakening, and political struggle in many ways – acting through social institutions, family life, and existing social prejudices. We recognise the impact that thousands of years of servitude has left in women's soul and psychology. That is why, in addition to all that the organisation has in common, it needs special structures, special measures, to link up with the masses of women, bring them together, and educate them as Communists.

We propose that such bodies be created by the leading and governing party committees: committees or commissions for agitation among women, or whatever the parties want to call them. These committees should exist from the leadership of a small local group right up to the top central leadership.

We call these bodies *women's committees*, because they carry out work among women, but not because we consider it important that they consist only of women. On the contrary. We welcome it when the women's committees include men, with their greater political experience and knowledge.

What concerns us is that these committees be systematically and continually active among the masses of women, that they take a stand on all the needs and interests that bear on women's lives, and that they intervene in every field of social life, with practical knowledge and energy, for the welfare of millions and millions of proletarian and semi-proletarian women. These women's committees can and should work, of course, only in close organisational and ideological partnership with the bodies of the party as a whole. But, for them to carry out their tasks, it is also obvious that they must enjoy freedom to take initiatives and have some scope for their activity. The Communist parties of Russia, Germany, and Bulgaria have acted in this spirit, to the best of my knowledge, or are striving to do so. And they certainly have not had a bad experience.

The party bodies for work among women should carry out systematic agitational, organisational, and educational work, speaking, writing, and using all means at their disposal. One thing they must not forget: it is not the spoken and written word, but above all work and struggle that is the most important and indispensible method of gathering and educating the broadest masses. For this reason, the women's committees must direct their efforts to drawing women as an independent and active force into all the Communist Party's actions and all the struggles of the proletarian masses.

Women, who are now often obstacles to revolutionary struggle, must become its driving force. For let us not be deceived, comrades: either the revolution will win the women or the counterrevolution will do it! Do not count on the fact that, as the civil war takes ever more intense forms, this will force women to decide where they stand and what they are fighting for. If you Communists do not see to it that the broadest masses of women are present in the revolutionary camp, the bourgeois parties will make sure they are in the camp of the counterrevolution. The Scheidemanns and Dittmanns – all the half and quarter Internationals – will make every effort to keep women in the border area between revolution and counterrevolution, which is today the most secure defence of counterrevolution and bourgeois society.

In view of this fact, comrades, the Communist parties must strive through the women's committees to draw women workers and women Communists into not only the legal work but also underground activity. That goes without saying. There are underground tasks, beginning with courier duties, which women are particularly well fitted to carry out ably and loyally. It is equally obvious that the Communist parties must strive to integrate the broadest masses of women as an active force into all the struggles of the proletariat: from a strike against lengthening the workday, to a street demonstration, to an uprising, to armed struggle. There is no aspect or form of revolutionary struggle and civil war that is not the business of women seeking their liberation through communism. The resolution we are submitting to you presents in detailed form the principles I have outlined to you here.

As regards international connections among Communist women of each country and with the [women's] secretariat in Moscow, we ask that Communist parties do the following: First of all, elect an international women's correspondent in each country. These correspondents will maintain communications with each other and with the Secretariat in Moscow. Second, establish an auxiliary body in Western Europe that can assist the International Women's Secretariat in Moscow.

In acknowledging the work of our conference, I neglected to refer to a particularly important decision. We must direct the attention of Communist cells in the trade unions to the urgent task of encompassing women workers in their activity, both in the trade-union struggle against the exploiters and also in the struggle against the trade-union bureaucracy. Representing the interests of employed women provides the basis for a broad alliance through which the Communist comrades in the trade unions can contend with the trade-union bureaucracy.

This bureaucracy has triply betrayed the interests of employed women. First, it has abandoned, for the greater good of capitalism, the struggle for the slogan of equal pay for equal work, without distinction between men and women. Second, it has also betrayed by standing by without resistance – indeed even approving – that, when the War ended, the women were the first to be thrown out of the factories and other employment. Why was that? Because starving women are less feared than men, because of women's political backwardness. In addition, they falsely claimed that women's needs were taken care of by the fact that they could, of course, always take to the streets as a prostitute or contract an arranged marriage. The trade-union bureaucracy betrayed the interests of employed women a third time by failing to take up the struggle against the crying injustice that unemployed women are fobbed off with less compensation than unemployed men – if they receive anything at all.[16]

These, in my opinion, are issues that must be taken up and utilised by our Communist trade-union cells, in order to educate women in the factories as revolutionary fighters. We must also recognise the great importance of vocational and trade-union training of women for communist construction after the proletariat has won political power.

Let me continue on what the conference decided – or more properly, what it decided to present to this congress – in order to improve international communications among Communist women in different countries. As I said earlier, the parties are to choose international women correspondents, who are to maintain regular, ongoing correspondence with each other and with the Communist Women's Secretariat in Moscow. But this secretariat itself must be made more efficient. We want it to be more than a mere information bureau for Communist women's work and struggle. It should be a leadership and management body that unifies, intensifies, and increases the activity of proletarian women in proletarian struggles. To this end, it needs an international auxiliary body abroad. The secretariat itself must stay in Moscow, and not merely in order to assure close organisational ties with the Executive, but because of the same objective and historical reasons for which the Executive itself must be based in Moscow. Moscow is the heart of the revolution and the capital of revolutionary Russia. It is here that the experiences of revolutionary struggle converge and can be utilised as the basis for theoretical insights and practical direction. Comrades, we are convinced that a modest auxiliary body in Western Europe will provide useful service to the Moscow Executive, and we ask you, therefore, to approve the relevant resolution.[17]

The conference also considered the duties and capacities of women in the struggle to establish and maintain the proletarian dictatorship, the soviet order. We addressed this question first and above all in terms of its general, fundamental meaning for the revolutionary struggle of the proletariat and thus for the complete liberation of all women. As a result, we examined this in terms of the world economic and political situation, which leaves the proletariat with only the choice between a revolutionary conquest of power or

---

16. For a fuller presentation of demands of the Communist Women's Movement, see Riddell (ed.) 1991, 2WC, 2, pp. 988–92.
17. Following the Second Congress, the Secretariat as a whole moved to Berlin, leaving an auxiliary body in Moscow.

acceptance of intensified exploitation and servitude. Freedom or descent into barbarism: that is the decision history has placed before the proletariat and also the broad masses of women.

We then discussed the question in terms of women's participation in efforts and struggles to defend the [workers'] dictatorship, including their collaboration in reconstruction of economic and social life after the dictatorship has been established. Finally, we took up the question of the proletarian class struggle to win and maintain political power with regard to the struggle for political equality of the female sex before the law and in life.

The conference was unanimous in its conviction that all roads lead to Rome. In other words, all demands that women raise in their employment, as mothers, and as human beings; all demands they must raise in order to become, on the basis of their social labour, members of society fully equal in rights and responsibilities; all the pain and hardship of their lives; all their longing and striving – all this converges in a single call: for active, bold, and devoted participation in revolutionary struggle to win the dictatorship of the proletariat and establish the soviet order. And after achieving this goal: working with self-sacrifice and to the last ounce of energy to defend the soviet order, with not only weapons but shovels in hand, to construct a new social life, which not only justifies the dictatorship of the proletariat, the soviet order, but provides the surest foundation to maintain it.

Comrades, in discussing these questions, we made clear, beyond any doubt, that the Communist Women's Movement does not live and strive in a cloud of political neutrality. True, our conference did not take up all the principled and tactical questions posed for decision by the Third International now and in the past. But it is self-evident that every Communist woman has formed her general principled and tactical convictions along these lines and taken a stand on the problems whose impact on the women's movement concerns us. And something else is obvious: your struggles for these principles and tactics, within every Communist Party, will and must be our struggles as well.

Comrades, as delegates to the International Conference of Communist Women, we want to go out to every country and show women there that Russia is a great historical example. It teaches that without winning political power and establishing a council dictatorship, there is no way to build communism and achieve liberation and women's equality. But it also tells the Communist parties of every country that unless women join in collaboration and struggle, communism cannot be built. In its battles both to surmount capitalism and to achieve communism, the proletariat needs the collaboration of women, and not merely because of the quantitative factors I referred to earlier. No, we tell proletarians who long for freedom and who have achieved it that our collaboration is also indispensable because of the qualities contributed by our achievements. Thank heavens, we are not your ape-like imitators, not failed, inferior copies of yourselves. We inject our distinctive intellectual and moral values, in both revolutionary struggle and revolutionary construction. And that signifies not a threat or a lessening of the revolutionary struggle but rather its intensification and sharpening. It signifies not that life in the new society will be impoverished, or deformed, or superficial, but that it will be richer, more diverse, more profound, and more sophisticated.

So, women in the soviet states: join the decision-making, administrative, supervisory, economic, political, and cultural bodies and organisations! And so, proletarian women, unfree and oppressed in the countries that still languish under capitalist rule, join in all the proletariat's struggles and battles! Let us not forget what one of the best students of Russia's earlier revolutionary movement wrote. In his famous book, *Underground Russia*, Stepniak said that the revolutionary movement in Russia owed the vigour of its high ideals, its almost religious enthusiasm and power, to the collaboration of women in work, in struggle, in life, and in death. That great tradition remains alive in Russia, and it must become the great tradition that leads the way for proletarian struggle in all the capitalist countries and all countries of the East.

Comrades, at this congress we have been told, 'Caution, caution, caution. Do not lose touch with the broad proletarian masses, who will carry out the decisive struggles of the proletarian revolution.' And we know how true and correct that is. But we have learned something else from the history of revolution: 'Audacity, audacity, and yet again audacity', in leading the revolutionary masses to drive forward.[18] And let me assure you: we women, whose souls burn with desire for the land of communism, we who must surely harbour the strongest and most implacable hatred for capitalism, we must strive to combine sober assessment of the situation before us with a bold wager on the great goal of victory.[19]

We are well aware of the dangers that beset us – not only where we are struggling to win power but also where power has already been won and is threatened by counterrevolution from within and without and by all the difficulties of building communism under the most difficult circumstances imaginable. However, we women are not discouraged by what lies behind us,

---

18. The quote is by the French Revolutionary leader, Georges Danton.
19. 'Sober assessment....bold wager': The German text, 'kühle Wägen...kuhne Wagen' is typical of Zetkin's characteristic use of assonance, also found elsewhere in this speech: 'lebt und webt', 'standen und stehen', 'Verarmung, Verpfuschung, Verflachung', 'Mitkämpfen, Mitleben, und Mitsterben.'

nor are we afraid of what threatens us. Our eyes are fixed on the shining goal of communism, which will liberate humanity. We clearly perceive the path to this goal: civil war, revolutionary struggle with its terrors and dangers. And despite everything, we have only one slogan: 'Onward!' (*Prolonged loud applause*)

**Lucie Colliard** (France): Comrades, although I have been chosen by the Communist women to give a report here, I must first concede that I am a delegate from a party that has never done anything to involve women in party work. Nonetheless, there are some female members in France. But we are scattered across the entire country and hardly know each other. Recently, we have recognised that special propaganda is needed for women. But when we asked for party support in this, we received the response that it was enough to appoint a woman for this work, who was, moreover, not only to agitate among women but to organise propaganda as a whole. Nonetheless, we obtained a Central Committee decision to set up a special section for organising women, just as there is a special section for propaganda among peasants.

Women have the same interests as men, and when they join the party, they must carry out the same responsibilities. However, it would be better to first develop their abilities, for example, through the establishment of nurseries that need to be set up in every factory. I will be told that this is the specific task of the trade unions, but I do not believe that the unions should be the only ones to take up this question. The Communist Party, just like the trade unions, must undertake to organise everything related to the interests of women and children.

So far, this has not been recognised in our party. We have been shoved aside. No one believed that women were capable of conducting the struggle shoulder to shoulder with men. You have probably heard it said that women shrank back from their revolutionary duty during the War. I have no patience with men who make this accusation. We must recognise that all of us shamefully failed in our duty. But in this period, preparatory to the revolution, a time of preparation for our war, we must not trade accusations. We must strive for the thoroughgoing education of the masses. It is not enough to organise women in sections or subcommittees, where they can be educated or where they can develop alongside the men. We must instil in them their duty to the working class, so that when the revolution comes they will not fail, as they did during the War.

Men must recognise, however, that they have not fulfilled their duty with regard to drawing women into party work. Now they know that if you do not integrate women into the organisations, you must at least neutralise them, so that they do not obstruct the activity of the men. During the May movement last year,[20] the trade unions had to recognise that the strike was carried out much longer, more energetically, and with more vigour in the places where women workers took part, even if it was only the housewives who supported the Communists and syndicalists. Now the party understands that drawing women into the Communist Party and the trade unions benefits these organisations, not just women and the women's movement as a whole.

We have asked the party to organise women on the model of Russia, Germany, and Bulgaria. We want them to get accustomed, first of all, to discussing in their own circle, so that they develop the self-confidence necessary to discuss when men are present. We must found a newspaper to organise this education. So far, we have no special publication, although the party publishes two daily papers in Paris alone and the youth has its own newspaper. The existing publication, *La Voix des femmes*, is intended only for a few comrades and does not belong to the party. The Third International must charge our Central Committee – which we too have been pressing for action – to develop this work and, with our help, to organise women, draw them into the work, and educate them. This is urgent in order to open the road to the revolution that we all yearn for and have long desired. That is why we must organise both women and men, so that the revolution does not fail, as our revolutionary propaganda failed during the War.

**Kollontai**: Comrades, I believe that Comrade Zetkin's report was so thorough that I need add only a few words. The main issue is how the Communist parties can exert influence on the broad masses and win them to communism. That is one of the chief aspects of our programme and of the Communist Party's overall method of work. There is also a tactical question of how the Communist parties can exert influence on the broad non-party masses, in order to win them to communism.

But what is the composition of these broad layers that do not belong to a party – both in the bourgeois capitalist countries and in Soviet territory? Obviously, they are working women, because the men, the workers, belong to one sort of organisation or another – whether bourgeois or social-patriotic, Two-and-a-Half or Two-and-a-Quarter – to some kind of political organisation or party. There are still many women who are not in organisations. In the bourgeois countries, they are corrupted by bourgeois points of view. This makes it easy for the Communist Party to win over these broad layers who have previously been passive, and to produce the fresh, militant forces that are so urgently needed to achieve our ambitious goals in this time of struggle.

---

20. For the May 1920 railway strike in France, see p. 105, n. 7.

But how can we reach the broad masses of women? The Communist Party, like the Social-Democratic Party before it, has always told us that the doors of the Communist Party stand open for women. So women should come to us, to our party. Unfortunately, we must recognise that we have not yet won women for our goals. That raises the question whether we must not use other means to win over these broad layers of women – methods that take into account women's distinctive role in society. This is true not only in bourgeois society but to a certain degree in the Soviet republic, where women still have a special social situation, including within the family, a situation different from that of men. In order to take this into account, we too have to build a new apparatus. As a result, we also saw how essential it is that every party have such an apparatus, such an organisation. This is not a new decision, comrades. The decision was made last year at our previous International Conference of Communist Women.

But as Comrade Zetkin said, so far only in a few countries have the parties carried out this decision, because it was taken only at our conference and not at the International congress. In our view, if the decision is now successfully adopted here, it will perhaps spur comrades to establish this structure in their own countries, where this is possible. I believe we are now in a position to create this structure, which must be simply a special party organisation. We should minimise as much as possible giving the impression that it represents only women's special interests and that only women will be active there. Its work should not have that character. These are special structures with defined powers to carry out defined tasks. These structures must work not only among women. I would like to point out that here in Russia, for example, it is quite evident that the women we have already reached, the broad masses of working women and peasants, are already sympathetic to us. Unfortunately, however, our own comrades in the party still resist drawing women into active work and into posts where they are chosen by the broad masses and in which they are to carry out important work.

So in my opinion, comrades, you must adopt the goal of creating this structure. It is not intended only for work among women; it must also serve for work among male comrades. We name this structure not a women's committee but a committee for work among our comrades, so that we can finally overcome the previously existing situation. Women are party members. In Soviet Russia they undertake the entire and enormous burden of construction. But when a woman is placed in a responsible post, people always think, 'Well, really a man would be more suitable.' In capitalist countries the task is still posed of drawing women into the organisation itself. In Soviet Russia, however, there is also the task of *training women to undertake active, creative work and placing them in responsible posts.*

I also want to stress, comrades, that our method and practice in work among women leads us to an understanding of the idea of communism, moving from the specific to what is large and broad. Work among women must be shaped by this basic principle. In the process, we stress that all Communist parties have a stake now in drawing women into the ranks of the party not only because women should be trained as fighters, but also because we must always keep our eye on the period after the revolution, the period that we are now traversing in Russia. The big challenge before us is: how can we develop new forces of production? The answer is by drawing on all living forces. Everyone must belong to the creative population, both men and women.

In Soviet Russia, where everyone has the obligation to work, we already face a large, new problem – not just in drawing women into the organisation, but in employing the energies of proletarian and peasant women to create a new system of production and a new social order. All workers are now utilised and registered, and as a result the position of women in society changes. The Soviet republic and the October Revolution have thus launched a revolution perhaps much greater than the winning of equal rights for women. On the other hand, the party faces the question of *educating women to be active as a creative force*.

In all the capitalist countries the Communist parties have a new task. This lies not just in recruiting women into their ranks and spurring them on to struggle, in order to carry out struggles together with the men. Rather, the task is to awaken them to full activity through struggle, through deeds, through involving them in all the tasks and responsibilities that banish their old passivity, while encouraging and securing their new creative power, their activity, and the feeling that they too can achieve something.

Comrade Zetkin is right. She is right to stress that we need the initiative and creative power of working women in order to speed our development and enrich the life of the party. Let me take an example, comrades. In Russia we have our special structure for work among women. Please bear in mind that it is not a separate organisation, it is a structure in which our male and female comrades work together – although unfortunately the men are too few in number. We try to persuade them to see it as their duty to carry out this special party work. These organisations do not merely repeat whatever the party says. No. Not always but very often we bring our own initiatives into the party. A large number of issues are resolved there, as, for example, that of the universal obligation to labour.

We welcome these enormous strides forward in the reform of Russia's social and economic life, but our structures and committees also say: well and good, but the party should and must simultaneously pay heed to the special interests of women workers as mothers. In this regard we set up an array of restrictions, because we must always bear in mind that women have two duties in a communist state. First, they must more and more become a human being, a fighter, and a creative force. On the other hand they remain those who bring forth a new and healthy generation. They are mothers. As mothers they must be protected, collectively, by the entire state and by society.

It was our committees that introduced initiatives in a large number of questions, such as the abolition of the old law banning abortion, the struggle against prostitution, the protection of mothers, the universal people's militia, and other questions. Did any of this weaken our work in Soviet construction? Not at all. We have enriched it, and that is the initiative of which Comrade Zetkin spoke. That is why we believe that these structures, intended to involve the broad masses, require special methods, tactics, and organisational forms. Women receive thereby a certain flexibility for action while remaining integrated into the struggle as a whole. At the same time, in the struggle in bourgeois countries, these structures will enable us to be prepared, at the most difficult moments, to make backward women into Communists and convince them that *the deliverance of women can be achieved only through the dictatorship of the proletariat*. In the soviet countries, where our structures assist the party in the colossal, difficult, and necessary task of construction of a new social system and socialist order, we must encourage male and female workers to continue the great struggle for communism on a world scale. (*Loud applause*)

**Kolarov** (Chair): Since the speakers' list is exhausted, the debate is now closed. We will take the vote. There are two theses and two resolutions on the women's movement.[21] The resolutions read as follows.

## Resolution on International Ties between Communists and the International Communist Women's Secretariat

[For text of this resolution, see pp. 1026–7.]

---

21. The German-language proceedings include two resolutions on work among women ('Resolution on International Ties between Communists and the International Communist Women's Secretariat' and 'Resolution on Forms and Methods of Communist Work among Women'). A set of theses was also published in Comintern-prepared collections of Third Congress resolutions ('Theses on Methods and Forms of Work of the Communist Parties among Women') and is included in the present collection. The second set of theses mentioned by Kolarov could possibly be 'Theses for the Communist Women's Movement', drafted by CWM leaders and adopted by the ECCI in late 1920; see Riddell (ed.) 1991, 2WC, 2, pp. 977–98.

## Resolution on Forms and Methods of Communist Work among Women

*[For text of this resolution, see pp. 1028–9. The text of a set of theses, 'Methods and Forms of Work among Women', will be found on pp. 1009–25.]*

**Kolarov** (Chair): These resolutions and the theses form a unified whole. No resolution contradicts the others. We can therefore vote on them together.

Is anyone opposed to these resolutions? I see no one. Does anyone abstain? No. The resolution and the theses are therefore adopted *unanimously*. (Loud applause)

*(The session is adjourned at 12:15 a.m.)*

Session 21 – 9 July 1921, 8:30 p.m.
# Tactics and Strategy, Germany, Cooperatives

*Radek: Report of the Commission on Tactics and Strategy. Sachs: Statement of the KAPD delegation. Resolution on the situation in the VKPD. Malzahn: Statement by the German opposition on the situation in the VKPD. Statement of the VKPD delegation. Zinoviev: Summary remarks on the resolution. Meshcheriakov: The cooperative movement. Theses on the work of Communists in the cooperative movement.*

**Gennari** (Chair): The first speaker is Comrade Radek, reporting for the Commission on Tactics and Strategy. He has the floor.

## Report from Commission on Tactics and Strategy

**Radek**: Comrades, the Commission on Tactics and Strategy has concluded its work by unanimously adopting all the substantive amendments. I am not going to read the entire list of amendments, most of which are purely editorial in nature. They will be distributed to delegates within the next two to three days. I will only take a moment to explain the most important political changes. These changes bear on the portrayal of the situation in the Communist International. The changes are as follows:

The passage on France was reworked once again, and the characterisation of the tendency to launch attacks prematurely, which as you know was stressed quite strongly in the earlier version, was softened.

As for the situation in Czechoslovakia, you will recall that the Executive of the Communist International adopted a detailed resolution on this question.[1] That resolution called attention to the existence of a centrist current, described as the Šmeral current, and opposed it.

In our resolution, we maintained the characterisation of this current, all the more given that Comrade Šmeral, who in the meantime arrived, did not at all deny in his remarks that centrist qualities can be found in the party. On the contrary, he sought to demonstrate that since the majority of the old party came over to communism without significant breakaways, the existence of centrist tendencies in the party was inevitable.

The Czechoslovak question played a major role in the commission. A special session was devoted to it, in which we heard a presentation by Comrade Šmeral, on the one hand, and by Comrade Kreibich, on the other. And when the discussion ended, we can say that we formed an opinion, namely, that the leading group in the Czechoslovak party ought to take two or three steps to the left, as Comrade Lenin put it. And we simultaneously advised the German-Czech organisation and its leader, Comrade Kreibich, that it should perhaps take a further step in the direction of the main forces of the Czechoslovak party.

Our most important conclusion was that Comrade Šmeral is determined to carry out fully the line of the Executive. For this reason, it was decided that we will write the party leadership a letter taking up in detail the errors of the party and the rightist currents within it. However, we decided to eliminate any reference to Comrade Šmeral. That does not signify any weakening of the struggle against half-centrist tendencies in the party. It means that we are indicating this is not a matter of a struggle against Comrade Šmeral personally.[2]

In the theses on partial actions of a preparatory character, we inserted the idea that anyone who denies in principle that the struggle of the Communist International is offensive in nature, who opposes an offensive in specific circumstances, is violating the principles of the Communist International.

In the theses on the lessons of the March Action we made the following change. Where we say that the March Action is a step forward, we explained specifically what this step forward consists of, so that no one can say that this is just an empty phrase. We say that it is a step forward because: (1) thousands

---

1. A resolution on Czechoslovakia was adopted on 14 July by the pre-congress expanded ECCI meeting. It can be found in Comintern archives, RGASPI 594/1/36/158–9.
2. See Lenin's comments on the Czechoslovak question in Appendix 4b, pp. 1155–7.

of workers struggled courageously; and (2) the party placed itself at the head of the struggle.

Other changes that we made are more editorial in character. For example, it did not cause any difference of opinion when we added a statement, in the passage on the Balkan countries, that building up the Balkan Communist Federation is extremely important for this struggle.[3]

We decided to propose that the congress adopt these theses. We did not adopt them merely as a basis for a position; indeed, we made no change whatsoever in their political line and adopted them unanimously.

The commission proposes the following changes to the original draft of the theses:

Page 2, last paragraph, line 6, left-hand column, delete 'even capitalist, that is, on the basis of exploitation'.

Page 2, right-hand column, line 25, replace 'goes' with 'went'.

Page 2, right-hand column, line 17 from the bottom, after 'Romania' add 'Latvia and Estonia'.

Page 2, right-hand column, line 14 from bottom, after 'law on Communists' add 'France, Switzerland'.

Page 2, right-hand column, line 3 from bottom, replace 'render impossible' with 'obstruct'.

Page 3, right-hand column, line 18, after the dash, add, 'called on them to take part in the trade unions'.

Page 3, left-hand column, line 25, after 'party as a mass party', add 'In Poland in February, we had the railway workers' strike, led by the Communist Party, and following that the general strike, and we are witnessing an ongoing process of disintegration in the social-patriotic Polish Socialist Party'.

Page 4, left-hand column, line 16, after 'the trade-union bureaucracy', add 'frightened by the revolutionary impact of Communist work in the trade unions, expelled many Communists from the unions and held them responsible for the split in the unions. In Czechoslovakia...'.

Page 4, left-hand column, line 29, replace 'lasting increase in its influence' with 'become a leader in mass struggles'.

Page 5, right-hand column, line 31, replace 'centrists' with 'reformists'.

---

3. Socialist parties in Bulgaria (the Tesniaki), Greece, Romania, and Serbia joined in July 1915 in the Balkan Revolutionary Social-Democratic Federation on a platform of internationalist opposition to the War and support for a new, revolutionary International. Their alliance was renamed the Balkan Communist Federation at a conference in Sofia, January 1920, which called for a federation of Balkan socialist republics. It remained a Comintern coordinating body for Balkan parties until 1933.

Page 5, right-hand column, line 34, replace 'centrists' with 'reformists'.

Page 5, right-hand column, line 40, replace 'reinforced' with 'created'.

Page 5, right-hand column, line 40, add 'on the other hand the danger of anarchist influence...'.

Page 5, right-hand column, lines 14, 15, and 16 from the bottom, delete 'in which the masses lead in anticapitalist struggle'.

Page 5, right-hand column, line 14 from bottom, change to 'and the creation of anti-parliamentary verbal-radical...'.

Page 6, left-hand column, last paragraph, and right-hand column; page 7, left-hand column, replace 'in France' with 'to France'.

Conclusion of the first paragraph on page 7, change to:

*[See the text on the French party in the adopted theses, part 4, pp. 931–2.]*

Page 7, right-hand column, line 17, replace 'they' with 'the old and newly recruited members'.

Page 7, right-hand column, lines 17 to 22 from the bottom, delete 'as expressed in the policies of the Šmeral current, if they follow the advice given them by their best imprisoned comrades, Muna, Hula, Zápotocký, and by the Communist International'.

Page 7, right-hand column, line 12, after 'carry out', add 'The congress decides that the Czechoslovak and the German-Bohemian Communist parties are to fuse their organisations into a unified party within a time period to be set by the Executive'.

Page 8, left column, last line, after 'break', add 'and become the leader of the mass movement in the coming struggles of the proletariat'.

Page 8, left column, line 14, after 'of the proletariat', add 'and those before...'.

Page 8, left column, line 20 from the bottom, after 'not counterposed', add 'but if they constantly maintain in their organisation a spirit of readiness for struggle'.

Page 8, right-hand column, line 14, after 'betray', add 'the slogans and principles'.

Page 9, right-hand column, line 27, replace 'that from an illusion' by 'that in obvious'.

Page 9, right-hand column, line 18 from the bottom, replace 'making flans' with 'making plans'.

Page 9, right-hand column, lines 12 and 11 from the bottom, replace 'lead the struggle in doctrinaire fashion down a course of fixed stages' with 'concentrate on a conception worked out in doctrinaire fashion'.

Page 9, right-hand column, lines 6–7 from the bottom, replace 'amount to' with 'form'.

Page 9, right-hand column, line 5 from the bottom, replace 'this struggle' with 'these struggles'.

Page 10, left-hand column, lines 31–2, replace 'the content of the transitional measures as stages in the struggle for the proletarian dictatorship'.[4]

Page 10, left-hand column, 5 lines from the bottom, after 'deepening and unifying', add: 'Every partial action undertaken by the working masses in order to achieve a partial demand, every significant economic strike, also mobilises the entire bourgeoisie, which comes down as a class on the side of the threatened group of employers, aiming to render impossible even a limited victory by the proletariat ('Emergency Technical Assistance',[5] bourgeois strikebreakers in the British railway workers' strike, Fascists). The bourgeoisie mobilises the entire state apparatus for the struggle against the workers (militarisation of the workers in France and Poland, state of emergency during the miners' strike in Britain). The workers who are struggling for partial demands will be automatically forced into a struggle against the bourgeoisie as a whole and its state apparatus.[6]

Page 10, right-hand column, line 23, delete 'factory organisation, only through its'.

Page 12, right-hand column, line 10 from below, after 'are present', add 'Anyone who objects to a policy of offensive against capitalist society is violating the principles of communism.'[7]

Page 13, left-hand column, lines 3–7 from below, delete 'By acting courageously to defend the workers of Central Germany, the VKPD demonstrated that it is the party of the revolutionary proletariat of Germany.'

Page 13, right-hand column, line 12, replace 'as the chief means' with 'as the chief method'.

Page 13, right-hand column, line 19, after 'as a step forward', add 'The March Action was a heroic struggle by hundreds of thousands of proletarians against the bourgeoisie. And by courageously taking the lead in the defence of the workers of Central Germany, the VKPD showed that it is the party of Germany's revolutionary proletariat.'[8]

Page 13, right-hand column, line 30, replace 'voices' by 'facts and considerations'.

---

4. This sentence is incomplete in the original text.
5. Regarding 'Emergency Technical Assistance', see p. 624, n. 15.
6. For the corresponding text in the theses, see p. 937.
7. For the corresponding text in the theses, see p. 940.
8. For the corresponding text in the theses, see p. 941.

Page 13, right-hand column, line 40, add after 'done only in the party organisation'.[9]

Page 14, left-hand column, line 19, replace 'make room for', with 'replace'.

Page 14, right-hand column, line 6, replace 'its' with 'their'.

Page 14, right-hand column, line 29, replace 'organs' with 'organisations'.

Page 15, left-hand column, line 4, after 'most active', add 'forces in the factories and the trade unions'.

Page 15, left-hand column, line 18, replace 'the military bodies' with 'the organs of struggle'.

Page 15, left-hand column, line 19, replace 'the enemy forces and their staffs' with 'the white-guard forces and their staffs'.

Page 15, left-hand column, line 7 from the bottom, after 'the use of weapons and acts of sabotage is justified only when this blocks the transport of troops sent against masses of proletarians in struggle', add 'or captures strategic positions from the enemy in direct combat'.

Page 15, left-hand column, line 3 from the bottom, replace 'evidence' with 'symptom'.

Page 15, left-hand column, line 3 from the bottom, replace 'ferment' with 'uprising'.

Page 15, right-hand column, lines 4–9, after 'raise their readiness for struggle', add 'for they awaken in the masses the illusion that the heroic deeds of individuals can replace the revolutionary struggle of the proletariat'.

Page 15, right-hand column, line 2 from the bottom, after 'circles of commercial and technical employees', add 'of the lower and middle-level civil servants'.

Page 16, left-hand column, line 4, replace 'industry' with 'economic and state administration'.

Page 16, left-hand column, line 17, replace 'organisation' with 'recruitment'.

Page 17, right-hand column, line 4, is to read: 'broaden out the revolution into the most developed neighbouring countries'.

Page 17, right-hand column, paragraph 2, line 28 reads 'not only in demonstrations'.

Page 17, left-hand column, 8 lines from the bottom, after 'make efforts', add 'by strengthening the Balkan Communist Federation, and confronting nationalism'.

**Gennari** (Chair): We will proceed to the vote. Which delegates vote against the unanimous motion of the commission?

---

9. This sentence is incomplete in the original text.

**Sachs** (Schwab, KAPD): The Communist Workers' Party submits the following statement on the Theses on Tactics and Strategy for the record:

## Statement of the KAPD

The Theses on Tactics and Strategy submitted for a vote by the Third Congress represent a consistent, direct continuation of the fundamental line initiated by the Second Congress and carried out since then by the Executive Committee. It provides traitorous opportunist and reformist intellectuals of every country with unlimited scope for their interpretive genius, particularly with regard to the Theses on the World Economic Situation. This is a licence for ambiguity, which contradicts the concept of revolution. Every clear demarcation from the Hilferdings is obliterated; every inner connection with the essence of the modern class struggle is abandoned.

The so-called Left at this congress, impelled by the revolutionary workers who support it, made feeble attempts to correct the Theses on Tactics and Strategy. These efforts were rightly rejected by the majority for their inconsistency, and we did not at all support them. Although they displayed good intentions with regard to increasing revolutionary activity, they lacked any insight into the concrete conditions of struggle. They did not challenge either the bourgeois parliamentary framework of the Twenty-One Points or the corresponding overall drive of the theses. They thus became an obstacle to all further clarification.

Victory of the proletarian revolution in the capitalist countries can be prepared only in the struggles themselves. These struggles arise inevitably out of capitalist economic and political attacks. The Communist Party cannot command these struggles, and it must also not evade them, for that would sabotage preparation for victory. The Communist Party can achieve leadership of these struggles over time by counterposing to the masses' illusions the full clarity of its goal and its methods of struggle. This is the only way it can, through a dialectical process, become a nucleus bringing together the revolutionary militants who will, as the struggle proceeds, win the confidence of the masses.

In line with this statement, we completely oppose the adoption of these Theses on Tactics and Strategy, and propose instead our Theses on the Role of the Party in the Proletarian Revolution.[10]

*Delegation of the KAPD*

---

10. For the KAPD resolutions submitted to the Third Congress, see p. 559, n. 42.

**Gennari** (Chair): Does anyone wish to make any proposals regarding the theses prepared by the commission? We are proceeding to the vote, and we ask if there are any counterproposals.

**Zinoviev**: Delegations that are voting against or abstaining, please so indicate. It is not possible to have a new discussion. I see that no delegation is voting against. The amendments are therefore adopted unanimously. (*Loud applause*)

Comrades, I have a proposal to make on behalf of the Russian delegation. The congress has dealt rather fully with the situation in the VKPD. We propose the following resolution:

## Resolution on the Situation in the VKPD

*[For the text of this resolution, see p. 951.]*

**Zinoviev**: I would like to read the following quotation from a letter, dated 30 June, from our representative in Germany. I received this letter yesterday. The letter says:

> The right wing of the party is consolidating more and more. On 25 June there was yet another meeting of the opposition. About sixty persons were present, including Levi and Däumig. It was decided to hold regular weekly meetings in order to consolidate and firm up the opposition and to be in a position to take a position on the Third Congress. Däumig gave an extensive report. In his opinion, Heidelberg was a victorious battle of revolutionary Marxism against anarcho-syndicalist currents, which made it possible for the revolutionary workers in the USPD to unite with the Spartacus League.[11] After the fusion convention, a KAPD spirit in the VKPD became much more evident. The VKPD evolved backwards to before Heidelberg. The VKPD today has only one goal: to link up organisationally with the KAPD. Levi supplemented Däumig's remarks, recounting Rosa [Luxemburg]'s differences with Lenin and portraying the state of the Russian party, which he claimed was suspended in mid-air.

I regard it as my duty to inform the congress of this so that all comrades can draw conclusions regarding a situation in the VKPD that, in many respects, is quite dangerous. We have spoken quite frankly regarding the errors of our friends in the Zentrale, and the congress has expressed its view. According

---

11. For the KPD's Heidelberg Convention of 1919, see p. 484, n. 2.

to the resolution of the Russian delegation, the congress should call on the Zentrale and the party majority to treat the opposition with great leniency, provided that the opposition carries out the congress decisions. The congress must stress vigorously that, once it has spoken, the Communist International can no longer tolerate factionalism in the German party. If that was possible before the congress, it is absolutely impermissible after the congress. We are firmly convinced – and we say this on the basis of our many discussions with Comrades Zetkin, Neumann, Malzahn, and the other opposition comrades – that the comrades present here will carry out the congress decisions with complete loyalty, and that they have enough influence in Germany to push that through. As for groups or individual comrades who are not prepared to submit to the congress decisions, in my opinion the new Executive must speak very firmly to them and make it clear to them, in advance, that anyone who does not comply with these decisions and continues factional activity in the German party cannot and will not belong to the Communist International. (*Loud applause*)

**Gennari** (Chair): Does anyone wish to speak on the resolution of the Russian delegation?

**Malzahn**: Comrades, we obviously have a great interest in fully resolving the conflicts arising from the March Action in Germany. That has been achieved at this congress and in the Theses on Tactics and Strategy, which take up the March Action. We have every interest in achieving an understanding with the German delegation. Right after the March Action, the Menshevik parties – the SPD and the USPD – launched an assault on the VKPD. In addition, there are acute economic conflicts in Germany, and the political conflicts are also more and more severe. Conditions in Germany are such that we have an interest in the party returning to Germany with full clarity, in order to resolve the party crisis as rapidly as possible. We need to avoid any internal disputes, so that the party's full striking power can be turned outwards to the task of revolutionising the working class.

But I must say that the way the Russian section's proposal is formulated does not contribute to distributing light and darkness equitably. (*Shout: 'Very true!'*) At the very least, this resolution does not add clarity to the line adopted by the congress but through its skilled formulations aims to create the impression that the opposition was put in the wrong here at the congress. We already said that the decisions of the congress are authoritative for us in every respect. As the proletarian representatives of the opposition, we will work with all our energy in Germany to silence the opposition, in the interests of the party. But, on the other hand, it should also be recognised that this resolution must not give rise to a new attack. We have therefore drafted a text that expresses more clearly and precisely what applies to both contending forces. It will undoubtedly help bring an end to the internal disputes and contribute to common work in Germany. We therefore propose the following text:

## Resolution Proposed by the VKPD Opposition

The Third World Congress is pleased to note that the resolutions on Tactics and Strategy and, in particular, the portion dealing with the hotly disputed March Action, have been adopted unanimously.

The congress regards it as the self-evident duty of all supporters of the currents contending for influence to take an energetic stand for the implementation of the congress decisions, to reject any attempt to form factions or act factionally, and to work and struggle together, in a unified and cooperative manner, in the framework of the Communist International's principled and tactical positions, and while observing party discipline.

The economic and political situation in Germany, the struggles taking place on every side, and the attacks on the Communist Party by the SPD and USPD all demand that the party carry out intense activity in every field. It must be constantly armed and prepared for decisive struggles. It must strengthen more and more its ties with the proletarian masses, while exerting increasing political and moral influence on them. An indispensible precondition for this is the party's firm unity and the application of party discipline for all comrades without exception, for all party organs and party bodies, in accord with the Twenty-One Conditions of the Communist International's Second Congress.

The congress charges the Executive to observe closely the German movement's future development and to take all necessary measures for the implementation of the relevant decisions.

*Paul Franken, H. Malzahn, P. Neumann, Clara Zetkin*

**Malzahn**: This resolution speaks generally of the conduct of all the VKPD party members as a whole. The Russian resolution is slanted and formulated in such a way as to awaken feeling against the opposition. If you, the congress, want us in Germany to overcome the crisis rapidly and move rapidly to united work in the interests of the revolution, then we request and ask you to adopt the resolution that we are proposing.

**Thalheimer**: Comrades, I wish to state on behalf of the German delegation that it agrees with the motion by the Russian delegation. We ask you to adopt this motion unanimously and to reject that of the opposition, which speaks all too much in generalities. The Russian delegation's motion is definite and precise, reflecting the situation before us in Germany. The other resolution is vague and indefinite. On these grounds we ask you to adopt the more precise and clear resolution of the Russian delegation.

Zinoviev: The comrades of the opposition group wish to declare that they do not insist that the text read out by Malzahn be brought to a vote. Instead they would like merely to submit it as a statement for the minutes, signed by Malzahn, Neumann, Franken, and Zetkin. So there is no need to speak of it further, and there is clearly only one vote to be taken, namely on the resolution of the Russian delegation.

I would like to say a few words in response to the remarks of Comrade Malzahn. He says that the resolution is excessively sharp. In fact, it is definite and clear, nothing more. And, in my opinion, Neumann and Malzahn may yet take pleasure in this resolution when, in a few weeks, they encounter opposition to the congress decisions from comrades who do not share the views of Neumann, Malzahn, and the other comrades. I just read some relevant facts in the letter from Germany. We have no cause to doubt them.

If it turns out that everyone in Germany is prepared to be done with the old quarrel, all the better. Our resolution does not aggravate the situation. But toward comrades in Germany who wish to carry on with the old factionalism, the resolution provides Comrades Neumann and Malzahn with a very effective weapon. I therefore ask you to adopt our resolution unanimously, so that we may do everything possible, in the name of the Communist International's highest body, the congress, to create genuine unity in the VKPD. (*Loud applause*)

Gennari (Chair): There are still two speakers on the list, Comrades Neumann and Radek. The Presidium proposes to them that the debate be closed. Is there any objection? There is none.

We now come to the vote on the resolution proposed by the Russian delegation. Is there anyone opposed to the resolution? Does anyone wish to abstain? No one does. The resolution is unanimously adopted.

The next point is consideration of the cooperative movement. The reporter is Comrade Meshcheriakov.

## Report on Cooperative Movement

Nikolai L. Meshcheriakov: I ask the comrades to forgive me my poor French. It is fourteen years since I have had the occasion to speak French.

Comrades, before the Revolution the workers' movement consisted of three parts. First, the political work in a political party; second, the trade unions; and third, the cooperative movement. And these three movements functioned quite independently one from another. Before the Revolution, the Communists and the Social Revolutionaries took little part in the work in the cooperatives, which seemed to them to be too dull. The work in cooperatives was therefore left to the reformists, which is the reason why this work is not yet imbued with revolutionary and Communist ideas.

But the Communist parties must no longer permit this state of affairs. The Communist parties must prepare themselves, the proletariat, and the cooperatives for the great role that these organisations will play in the revolution. That is why the World Congress has placed the question of cooperatives on the agenda. I am not going to make a long speech on this question. I am only going to indicate a few key points.

When the Revolution took place, it completely transformed the nature of the cooperatives' work. Until now, the cooperative movement did not have the goal of combating capitalism, but aimed merely at alleviating the suffering that capitalism causes. The cooperative movement had the goal of adapting its organisations to the capitalist environment. Today's cooperatives must fight against capitalism.

Until now, only a portion of the population took part in cooperatives. Now, all Russian subjects, without exception, are members of cooperatives. The revolution made that necessary. I will not give you a lengthy lecture on the situation of the Russian cooperative movement today. We will do that later in the articles published after the cooperative section of the International has been established. Right now I will only read you the theses, drafted by a small commission formed of various congress delegates and proposed to the congress for adoption.

## Theses on the Work of Communists in the Cooperatives

*[For the text of the resolution, see pp. 967–9.]*

**Gennari** (chair): Important committee meetings are taking place right now, and it is therefore not possible to continue the session. The Presidium therefore proposes to end today's sitting. Is there any objection? There is not. The next session will take place tomorrow evening at 6:00 p.m. On the agenda is the Organisational Report and the Report on the East.

*(The session is adjourned at 10:30 p.m.)*

# Session 22 – 10 July 1921, 7:00 p.m.
## Cooperatives, Organisation

*Vote on the theses on work of Communists in cooperatives. Koenen: Report on the organisational structure of Communist parties and the method and content of their work. The organisational structure of the Communist International. Discussion: Schaffner, Zinoviev, Vaillant-Couturier, Delagrange.*

**Kolarov** (Chair): The session is open. The next agenda item is Organisation of the Communist Party and the Communist International. Before we proceed to the agenda, we must complete the translation of the report on cooperatives, which was begun yesterday. I ask the translator to do this now. (*This is done.*) That concludes this task. Does anyone wish to speak on this report? No one. So we will proceed to the vote. Those in favour of adopting the Theses on Cooperatives, please raise your hands. (*This is done.*) Is there anyone opposed to the theses? No one. Are there any abstentions? (*Shouts: 'Yes'*) I therefore declare that the theses are adopted unanimously, with one abstention.

We will now take the discussion of the organisational questions. Comrade Koenen has the floor.

### Report on the Organisational Question

**Koenen:** Comrades, first a small apology. The report on the organisation of the parties and the methods and content of their work was assigned to me only in the course of the last week. This caused a small delay in dealing with it, and the drafting of theses did not take place in a completely orderly manner.[1] You must also excuse the fact that the assignment of this task only in the last week made it impossible to prepare this report in a comprehensive and thorough manner.

The report that I will give is very broad in scope. I have been asked to take up not only our organisational tasks, but also the methods and content of the parties' work, the organisational structure of the Communist International, and its relationship to the individual parties. To deal with this system of questions would require a very comprehensive presentation. I must say right at the start that, given the breadth of my topic, I cannot provide a historical introduction regarding the development of the different parties or of the concept of a Communist Party. To the degree necessary, I will take up the conditions and prerequisites for the party's work at certain points during the course of the report.

Surely it is universally understood in all the Communist parties that the organisation is not an end in itself. Instead, the organisation, and especially the organisational apparatus, is only a means to the greater goal of promoting the cause of revolution, driving the revolution forward, in order to achieve our goal of constructing a communist society. Already in the initial general statutes of the First International Workingmen's Association, Karl Marx declared that every movement is merely a means subordinated to the great goal of economic emancipation of the working class.[2] And in line with these statutes, an organisation can most effectively promote the solution of the social problem if it achieves collaboration of the most advanced groups, both theoretically and in practice. The organisational apparatus of the modern workers' movement must be shaped in such a way as to offer proletarians a weapon for their struggles, so that at any given moment they receive the most effective help possible from other proletarian groups, organised as they are.

In today's turbulent times of latent civil war, it goes without saying that the Communist International seeks to bring about the reciprocal strengthening of organisational and active forces through strict centralism. The organisation's goal is clear. Its immediate aim is to win political power for the proletariat. A militant leadership aiming for that goal must be able to act within the Communist organisation, sure of its forces and armed with a definite plan. The struggle requires concentrated preparation through education and a recruitment campaign. This effort directs the entire attention of the proletariat in

---

1. The theses on the organisational question were drafted primarily by Otto Kuusinen, who sent several drafts to Lenin beginning in early June. Lenin suggested that a German Communist leader be brought in to help in the completion of the theses and to give the report to the congress, and Koenen was assigned. For Lenin's comments on the drafts and the drafting process, see Appendix 3b, pp. 1101–4.
2. Marx, 'Provisional Rules of the Association', in *MECW*, 20, p. 14.

struggle at the great goal shared by the entire class, truly uniting all forces that wish to engage in any way in the struggle. The organisation must therefore be centralised as a unification of forces and held together as a fusion of workers who are not merely conscious but also truly revolutionary in outlook.

Comrade Béla Kun, who was originally assigned to give this report, was quite right in his comments on the organisational lessons of the March Action,[3] when he coined the phrase that the revolution is not, ultimately, an organisational question. However, we must be aware that resolving this question is an important revolutionary task.

When we survey our organisational forms in different countries, we must concede that the International still displays quite a variegated mixture of diverse forms. And we must not think that the Second Congress has already carried out a decisive change in this regard. We must not even expect that the Third Congress can carry out this change. Nonetheless, although we recognise this diversity, we must make every effort toward uniform organisational forms. Despite the varied conditions and organisational forms in each country, we know full well that we must achieve a degree of conformity in methods and content. The goal – winning power – is the same, and so too the enemy, the bourgeoisie, and the forms of struggle it employs against us. This forces us to strive for a degree of uniformity in the Communist parties' methods of struggle and the content of their work.

Many parties still harbour all the weaknesses of the old bureaucratic centralisation, the old Social-Democratic parties. They are still burdened with these old traditions, because their Communist experience is quite brief. One can well say that the large mass parties still haul along remnants of this old Social-Democratic bureaucracy. Other parties were formed through a rebellion against such bureaucratic centralism, against this bureaucratic party structure.

This was the case, for example, with one wing out of which the German party was constituted. The USPD was typical of a party arising from a rebellion of the active forces against the passive central office. In the old Social Democracy during the War, the passivity of this centre evoked the spontaneous rebellion of the active forces. The result was that the rebellious districts unified and the party was built on a foundation that was rather federalist. These forces carted the remnants of this federalism around with them. They had to stress that only this federalism had a right to exist and that the passive Centre had nothing further to offer.

---

3. A reference to Kun's article, 'Organisatorisches zur Märzaktion' [Organisational Issues in the March Action] (written under the pseudonym Franz Richter) in Zentrale der VKPD 1921, pp. 117–36.

Such expressions of federalism must be opposed just as vigorously as the centralist heritage of the old Social-Democratic party.

### [Leadership and centralisation][4]

The parties must increasingly become centres of action and activation. We face the task of how we will shape the party structures in a fashion consistent with the goals set down in the Communist Manifesto. This entails, as the initial task, securing a solid leadership at the head of a centralised organisation. Unfortunately, it is still necessary to stress the need for such a solid leadership – indeed, for the very notion of the dominant role of leadership – given that there are still tendencies in the KAPD that oppose this. Surely that needs no further motivation at this congress. I need only explain that we believe this defined, centralised leadership to be necessary. But an equally urgent requirement in carrying out the tasks before the party's leading bodies is that this leadership have strong ties with the masses. So our tasks take a specific form: beside the centralised, strict, unified, clear, and solid leadership, we must achieve well-developed, extensive, and intricate links with the masses.

The link between the leadership and the masses can be created by building the party in accord with the decisions of the Second Congress, on a foundation of democratic centralism. This democratic centralism is not a bureaucratic formula but can be expressed in other words as centralisation of activity and unification of the party's achievements in work and struggle. That is the only way to conceive of centralisation. In the most recent draft of our theses, we saw a need to express this concept more explicitly. There is an incomprehensible sentence in part 2, point 6, which we have deleted and replaced with a new formulation, which expresses the concept of democratic centralism more clearly. Our new proposal reads as follows:

> Democratic centralism in a Communist Party should be a true synthesis and fusion of centralism and proletarian democracy. This fusion can be achieved only on the foundation of constant and common activity, common and constant struggle of the entire party.
>
> In a Communist Party, centralisation should not be formal and mechanical. It should relate to Communist activity, that is, to the formation of a strong, agile, and also flexible leadership.
>
> A formal or mechanical centralisation would amount to domination over the membership at large or of the revolutionary proletarian masses outside the party. But only enemies of communism could assert that the Communist

---

4. Subheadings in this report have been supplied by the editor.

Party seeks by centralising its leadership function to dominate the proletarian class struggle. That is a lie. Moreover, internal power struggles and efforts to dominate the party are equally incompatible with the fundamentals of democratic centralism adopted by the Communist International.[5]

In a word, this passage aims to stress that we will not permit leadership cliques within the party that might think that, because they have been given control of the leadership of the central apparatus, they are now justified in using it against the expressed will of the party majority, and in transforming this apparatus into an instrument for domination by their narrow circle. There have been many warnings about dangers of this type. It must be stated here that the International has no intention of permitting such leadership domination to arise. Centralisation applies only to activity and the leadership of that activity. That will enable us to initiate and conduct our work and struggles in truly centralised fashion. Achieving true democratic centralism is a lengthy process. The Second Congress theses have already explained that achieving democratic centralism of this nature cannot be done in a short period or in a year.[6]

The theses stressed that achieving concentration and centralisation of the true leadership of the party is a lengthy and difficult process. The theses stress that parties should improve and diligently examine their apparatus, in order to assure that their activity is marked by a centralism that is authentic and not bureaucratic, so that they can genuinely concentrate the leadership of their work. The strongest defence against a bureaucratised apparatus is vigorous ties between the party leadership and all the party's structures. This living relationship must lead the masses of members, through constant contact with the leadership, to recognise and understand that centralisation is objectively justified as a means to strengthen and promote common activity and struggle. The members themselves must feel and experience that the leadership is in no way alien but reinforces their capacity in struggle. If centralism comes to life in this manner, if it does not remain merely a form but pulses with life, this will provide the best protection against the danger of bureaucratism and ossification. Comrade Béla Kun was right to point out, in his article, that, aside from the Russian party and this or that small party, we hardly have a party that has yet achieved the necessary degree of living centralism, that

---

5. In the final text, this amendment was slightly edited; see p. 979.
6. The 'Theses on the Role and Structure of the Communist Party before and after the Taking of Power by the Proletariat' can be found in Riddell (ed.) 1991, 2WC, 1, pp. 190–200.

centralism is too much applied in a purely mechanical way and is really not being applied politically at all.

### [Party activity and organisation]

How do we go about applying this concept in a truly political manner? In order to meet this need, we have added, right after the section on democratic centralism, one on the requirement to be active. Drawing all members into activity will bring them into a close relationship with the leadership. Implementing Communists' responsibility to be active, along with the responsibility to struggle, gives us the certainty that we can overcome bureaucratism. To achieve a living centralism and a vibrant concentration of forces, we must strongly emphasise the requirement of activity. So far, most of the parties have not yet been able to activate all their forces for a goal, a movement, and a struggle. Leadership in the Communist parties must set this goal. They must strive actively to lead the entire party membership not only in its work but in the movements. We have provided a number of instructions along these lines in the theses. The section has been written at length in order to make this clear in detail. It would not do for the congress merely to adopt the requirement of activity; that in itself will not change anything. Our task is to make specific proposals on how this should be done. We found it necessary to provide organisational instructions for the party leaderships: how to involve members, organise them, and develop a division of labour, how branches and cells ought to function. And we said that the party leaderships should themselves set about organising such bodies and putting them to work. That is absolutely necessary, because we know very well that they have barely begun to take hold in the International.

There are a number of parties where such supposed cells exist in the factories and trade unions on paper, along with such commissions or committees, which supposedly take on special work assignments. But, as I said, this exists only on paper. That hardly benefits the Communist movement. Rather the task is to convert such bodies from paper things to solid reality and make the entire party into a working organism.

This advice applies especially to legal parties. True, there is fundamentally no distinction between legal and illegal parties, but in reality they are very different. In an illegal party, the only members are those who are really active. Anyone who was not active would attract attention and arouse suspicions. Freeloaders cannot be tolerated in an illegal party. As a result, there is a distinction between illegal and legal parties, which can be overcome only by giving an assignment to every single member of a legal party. That is the only way to overcome the difference between these types of parties and create a truly distinct form of party organisation. We considered it necessary to provide instructions in this regard.

Yet there are still certain differences that, in my opinion, cannot be conclusively resolved at this congress. This concerns whether the parties should now be definitively organised around factory cells, as their foundation. The Second Congress decided that factory cells should be the organisation's foundation. We also know from reports we have received that a number of parties – illegal parties – really regard these cells as the basis of their organisation. This is far from being the case in the broad mass parties. I will have more to say on this under the heading of party structure.

Since the concept of factory cell does not yet provide the basis for the party as a whole, we have referred rather to the branches. Branches are party institutions that are still formed in residential districts and are responsible for mobilising the party's forces. The regional organisation should set up its branches in such a way that each branch has its task. This is done by tens, so that each ten or twenty comrades are grouped together and assigned special tasks. It is not absolutely necessary to do this in so mechanical a fashion; it is a matter of assigning these tasks objectively so that all members are, in fact, involved in the work.

There are many possible assignments of this type. We mention a number of such tasks: agitation with the newspaper, door-to-door agitation, trade-union work, women's work, agitation among youth, and much more. Such branches should be set up for all the various party tasks, and they must be initiated by the leadership if these tasks are to be carried out at all. It would be quite wrong for the party to say we are dividing up everything on paper and then distributing this schema, and we now anticipate that every district will divide up its members in the same schematic fashion – and then everything will work just fine. Such a schematic division would be bureaucratic centralism. By contrast, the way to begin is to set up only a small number of branches and cells, but these cells must then really be set in motion, in order to then go on and activate other branches. Mobilising branches in this way takes a lot of time, energy, vigour, and persistence. The parties will have to show, in the course of the year, whether they have understood the essence of centralism, and whether they have really undertaken to organise the branches. That is the only way for us to produce properly functioning parties.

It is also necessary to assist these branches in carrying out their tasks, giving them all the special instructions needed so that they can draw the necessary consequences for their work. The lessons and conclusions flowing from this practical work constitute the teachings on specialisation. We will see the branches produce a number of specialists. Specialisation is an absolute necessity. We must have a variety of trained personnel in the different fields of struggle. Without such specialisation, we will not obtain our future forces. We will not encompass the proletariat unless we undertake to train the specialists.

Specialisation must be encouraged, but when we talk of it we must caution against exaggeration. If we have a party consisting only of specialists, each of whom wants to have nothing to do with the others, this will sap the party's vibrant life. And that would be senseless. Therefore, comrades who have become specialists in one branch need to be shifted into another, so they can learn about the life and work of other branches. To be sure, we do not want a constant switching and mixing up of assignments. We need to train certain specialists, but an exchange of assignments is also helpful in order to establish an internal balance among our forces, and in this way to give reality to the party's real working activity.

While emphasising the need not to exaggerate specialisation, it is also necessary to stress the need to institute regular reporting in this organisation of work and struggle. The need for reporting is quite obvious with regard to a number of divisions established for future struggles, such as the courier service, the news service, obtaining safe houses, underground print shops, and the like. In these cases, reporting comes naturally, which is unfortunately not the case in a number of other forms of activity. For example, it may happen that a branch that has to obtain space for a meeting and carry out related preparations will remain closed within itself, so that only this branch knows about the meeting place. That is a big mistake, and there is a danger that if such a branch falls apart, the entire apparatus will be paralysed. Proper reporting by these branches is absolutely essential, and this is emphasised in the theses. We believe it should be a permanent function of all branches, so that the party receives all-sided information and can truly evaluate the experiences of this or that branch. Such reporting will also provide effective instruction for new groups in other cities.

Reporting of this type also enormously aids activating the party. For if the central leadership is receiving activity reports from the most varied branches, it will be able to draw accurate conclusions regarding the degree to which the party's activity can be increased. When no reports are received, this must be rectified. Through this interaction, the true activation of the party can make headway.

[Propaganda and action]

I will now move on to the section on propaganda and action. Here, I must start with an introductory comment: the first sentence was wrongly interpreted, and we therefore corrected the text. The sentence now reads: 'Our most general task prior to the revolutionary uprising is revolutionary propaganda and agitation.' Revolutionary propaganda and agitation is thus termed a general preparatory task. The part of the report dealing with struggles was too brief. A section on organising political struggles, which I will report on later, must be added to this section on organisation and propaganda.

The section on agitation and propaganda is quite extensive because there are a number of smaller parties, such as those in Britain and the United States, that believe they have to apply special principles here. In addition, there are some syndicalist remnants in our party who still think in terms only of a fighting advance guard and do not consider it necessary to conduct propaganda alongside the other struggles.

We must note that, even after the revolution, agitation and propaganda must not stop. The revolution does not sideline propaganda and agitation. On the contrary, as we know, in Russia after the revolution, after political power had been won, when revolutionary activity was at its peak, agitation and propaganda had to be brought to the highest level. Nowhere have we ever seen broader agitation and more comprehensive propaganda than in Russia after the winning of political power. That is precisely why, in cases where there is too much of a tendency to individual struggles, we must emphatically underline the need for revolutionary propaganda. The report describes various methods for this agitation, and I do not believe I need to say more on this point.

It is important for propaganda to have a direct link with every movement that breaks out in the International. Propaganda needs to relate to real conditions. Where the proletariat is engaged in struggle, fighting to eliminate social distress, that is where we should orient our propaganda. The best teacher is the force of example. If we prove our worth as comrades in struggle, people will give credence to our words and ideas. If we prove our worth as good leaders, good strategists, people will believe deeply in our newspaper articles and our theoretical explanations. It is necessary not only to conduct propaganda with words, but to unify it with action, in which we become part of even the smallest movements of workers. We have provided a number of simple examples in order to show clearly that no struggle is too small to merit Communists' involvement. Communists must take up every issue around which workers are really ready to struggle. Linking ourselves up with all movements of this type is the best way to pursue our propaganda and agitation.

Propaganda and agitation linked with work, with activity, and with struggle – this can help propel the Communist Party forward. These close ties should be strongly emphasised. The goal in such small struggles is not merely to address them with our propaganda but to gain benefits by achieving leadership. We are firmly resolved to gain leadership, and we can do it by leading even very small struggles and, in every struggle or movement, by moving to the front ranks. We need to draw advantage systematically from every movement. Examples of this are provided in the theses. Everyone should read them not just as empty words but as urgent requirements for every Communist.

The type of struggle to be conducted in the trade unions is described there in detail, providing a basis for everyone to draw practical conclusions on how to surmount the trade-union bureaucracy and the present form of the unions. These attempts to overcome the trade-union bureaucracy and thrust aside the present leadership layer indeed express the goal of our present propaganda and agitation. These efforts must be carried out in a planned and systematic manner, not just as isolated efforts to annoy and harass the opponent.

Carrying out this task efficiently is the only way to advance from propaganda to genuine leadership of the proletariat. We must also stress that it is appropriate in a number of countries – especially where the party must work underground – to create so-called sympathising organisations that make it possible to carry the Communist Party's propaganda and agitation to broader circles. Such organisations exist in a number of countries. Where they do not exist, we should attempt to form them from those who are organised in a different way or not at all and place them under more or less Communist leadership. They give us an opportunity to go into the truly broad masses. In parties that have until now only been able to work underground, this proposal will truly create a chance to link up with the broad masses.

We alert these parties to the urgent and special task of achieving ties with the masses, whatever the cost. To reach the masses, any organisational means and any form of propaganda is justified. The women's and youth organisations can provide very valuable services, since they are often able to carry out special tasks outside of the legal organisation itself. We have a large number of examples of how the youth organisation has served as a vanguard for the party, in every situation where we are underground and are seeking broader scope, to be used both organisationally and propagandistically.

Propaganda must also be carried out in the milieu of semi-proletarian layers, such as peasants, the middle class, office employees, and so on. Propaganda among such layers is important even though we cannot reckon on winning them as core units for the conquest of political power. However, we can banish the horror of communism prevalent in the outlook of middle layers. Special propaganda is needed for that purpose. Once we have freed them from this nightmare, they will be to some degree neutralised, and it will be much easier, at critical junctures, to conduct our great and decisive battles without having to reckon with too much resistance from these layers, and without having to pay them special attention.

These semi-proletarian layers are found especially in rural areas. The need to neutralise the rural population and win a degree of trust among them has already been cited several times from this podium. I need only remind you that the parties must carry out systematic propaganda in these circles. The parties must turn to the agricultural workers, and also the small peasants, to open their ears to the ideas of communism. To this end, we must also take the necessary organisational steps. It is not enough to have a newspaper lying on a table in the party office; it has to be actually delivered to the houses of the rural population. Rural agitation is quite tedious and sometimes also dangerous. The Junkers are experts at whipping up the rural population against us. Despite this danger, we must reach these layers, in order not to have to face their conscious resistance in periods where we are winning power or have won it. Before then we have to succeed in driving a wedge into their ranks.

That is why we must have an organisation that carries out propaganda in these rural areas. This can be done by assigning rural localities to districts in the cities that have extra forces, who can go to these localities to distribute leaflets and other publications of the Communist Party. Or it can be done if groups that we already have in rural areas undertake to work in nearby villages. Bicyclists or sports groups or youth groups can be drawn into this propaganda and ensure that a Communist spirit is taken into rural communities, preventing the construction there of a thick wall against communism. Destroying this wall is one of the most important tasks before the conquest of political power, so that we will not face a universal Vendée outside the gates of the major cities, from which the counterrevolution can recruit its battalions.[7]

Soldiers represent a no less important field for propaganda, particularly where there are still standing armies. It is hardly appropriate to speak of this in detail. It is vitally important to establish information offices in each country, which ensure the working out, with all due precision and care, of what will have an educational impact among the soldiers. It is dangerous to work from a template or fall into a routine; everything depends on the particular circumstances in a given country. I will make only one general point.

We must sow division and antagonism in the army between the officers and the soldiers. We must explain to the soldiers how the officers are lifted above them not only by their external insignia but by their economic position. On the one hand, the life of an officer is brilliant and secure, while the ordinary

---

7. Vendée is a department in west-central France that was a centre of royalist and peasant insurrection against the French Revolution from 1793 to 1795.

soldier, by contrast, faces a future without any hope. After his discharge from the army, all he can do is work for others, with no perspective of escaping this class contradiction. Constant stress on the class contradiction in the army is the best way to decompose the military order, and every effort should be made to introduce this contradiction in the army. In addition, I believe it is also possible to do this among the armed bands, the irregular volunteer corps, because corruption in these bands is endemic under capitalism, and we must always stress the contradiction and undermine these formations. It is enough for me to emphasise briefly these general concepts.

[*The party press*]

Let me move on to the section on the party press. I do not think it necessary to say a great deal here. This section is extensive, and special points are dealt with in detail, because leading comrades in Russia are convinced that the press represents the best means of organising broad masses of the population for communism. In order to highlight propaganda via the press, this section was written in considerable detail. We do not want any party to complain next year that they have few subscribers or that they do not know how to promote their newspapers. We want no such excuses at the next congress. No party will be able to say that it did not know how to take its newspapers to the masses. The text portrays in detail how the press becomes an organ of struggle, and how the regular collaboration of individual members makes this a living organism in the ranks of the party. I strongly recommend this chapter, which has been written to deprive comrades of any excuse for backwardness in their country's press. Comrades should not tolerate any failure in this very important field.

[*Political struggles*]

Let me move on to the topic of the party's general structure. Wait – no, at this point, after dealing with agitation and propaganda, I will move to the chapter that we wish to add, on political struggles. We considered it necessary to add this chapter because it is possible to draft some theses on organising movements, ranging from very small to the largest actions. Despite the variation in context, some general directives are needed. Flowing from the requirement to be active, we introduce the explanation on organising political struggles by saying that, for the Communist Party, there is never a time in which large movements could not occur. Regardless of the situation, there are always various ways to be politically active. It's a matter of improving our capacity to utilise economic and political situations to the point where it evolves into the art of strategy and tactics. The methods and means will vary, depending on what is objectively possible. They must be carefully selected. But if the party has a resolute will to struggle and works with cautious and intelligent calculation, it will be able to choose the appropriate means for its actions. It is important that each section closely watch what is happening in neighbouring countries, in order to learn from the actions of other sections and put the collective experiences in activation to good use in its own actions. So far almost nothing has been done in this regard.

Weak parties that do not yet possess a sufficient staff of functionaries can still develop revolutionary propaganda that enables workers to understand the Communists' general slogans, provided they link up with economic and political events. To this end, they need to utilise connections made in the factories, in the trade unions, and through the cells and branches. Anywhere that we have such cells, and major movements take shape, we need to intervene with meetings, in order to convey the party's slogans to the masses. In locations where we are unable to hold our own meetings, we can take advantage of those held by our opponents. These too must be carefully organised, so that the result is not a disgrace but a gain for our propaganda. If there is a chance of winning the masses for our slogans through such radical propaganda, these slogans should be summarised skilfully. We should work to advance the same set of slogans – or at least, basically similar ones – in a large number of meetings. We should get them adopted, or at least get a substantial minority vote. That will demonstrate the party's intellectual influence on the masses.

We will also be able to gauge our increasing influence through our growing ranks. We will influence layers of proletarians who feel they have something in common with us. In our ideas they perceive a new leadership. They grasp that something is emerging that will fight for them, and this will strengthen their willingness to struggle and their militant spirit. As a rule, the groups that organise these meetings and take part in them actively need to get together afterwards and draw the lessons. Also, reports should be sent along to the leading party committee, so that lessons can be drawn generally. Such propaganda actions are built by placards, leaflets, and the like, and it is therefore necessary to organise teams that understand how to carry out this work by distributing leaflets in front of factories, railway stations, and employment agencies.

It has proven useful in many districts to locate comrades who are able to combine such leaflet distributions with adroit discussion. What we say will then be passed along among the working masses, as they move forward. In this way, propaganda will spread through the factory on its own. Parallel to this intensified propaganda, we must increase our activity in the trade-union and factory meetings. Where necessary, comrades must organise such factory and trade-union meetings themselves and take care that speakers are available to support their activity. Our party's newspapers must spread the ideas of such actions every day and must make available their best arguments and the greater part of their space for such actions. Overall, the entire organisational apparatus must pitch in to advance the general concept that the party is striving to realise. The point is that when the parties are taking a concept to the masses, they must keep it alive for a lengthy period, for weeks, if necessary for months, so that the proletariat is truly inspired by this propaganda and realises what is at stake.

*[Demonstrations and actions]*

Small parties enjoy other possibilities for activity, if they truly succeed in recognising their historical mission. Their immediate goal should be to win for the party a leading role in the proletariat. That is why they must consider whether or not it is not appropriate to move on from the propaganda phase to that of demonstrations and actions, which can be carried out by both legal and illegal parties. We need only consider the brilliant example of the Spartacus League and the Left USPD during the War. Despite grave dangers they carried out actions around the slogans, 'Down with the war! Down with the government!' We need only remember Rosa Luxemburg and Karl Liebknecht, who became casualties of this propaganda.[8] Another example is the work of the small socialist group in Britain, whose 'Hands Off Russia' movement showed that constantly repeated demonstrations for a concept can ultimately engage the interest of the general public.[9]

Similarly, during the recent Polish-Russian War, the Polish Communist Party conducted a truly comprehensive propaganda campaign for the concept of soviets and the idea of peace with Russia. They attempted to keep this idea on the agenda for weeks and months, working toward the point where it finally did score a breakthrough. On a critical note, the French party would have met this challenge if the party as a whole had been focused on the campaign. They had a chance to do this at the time of the military call-up,

---

8. Karl Liebknecht was arrested in April 1916 for his participation in one of these demonstrations and was sentenced to two-and-a-half years at hard labour. Rosa Luxemburg, who had been in jail from March 1915 to January 1916, was rearrested and imprisoned in July 1916.

9. The Hands Off Russia Committee, set up in November 1919, included leading members of the British unions and Labour Party. Its most effective work came during the 1920 Polish-Soviet War (see p. 90, n. 29).

which was aimed against Germany. But preparations had been inadequate; the demonstrations started too late and, as a result, their impact was limited.

Recent reports from Italy indicate that the mood there against the Fascists has grown to the point that our party, together with other parties, can undertake energetic activity in demonstrations. Gigantic demonstrations have already taken place. The moment appears to have come in which the Fascist mentality is clashing so violently with the thinking of workers that they are now rising up and turning against the Fascist currents in mass actions. I believe that the Italian party stands on the eve of such a movement and, if it intervenes, it has a chance to assume the leading role and enable the proletariat to take a great step forward.

Even countries where action has been followed by a shift to the right provide lessons about action campaigns. The first requirement for an action campaign is an agile and self-sacrificing leadership. The leadership of such a movement must be able to keep its focus on the limited goal of the action or demonstration and keep an overview of the changing situation. It is necessary to have a clear understanding of the movement's forms, constantly checking how the movement can be intensified and whether the time has perhaps come to broaden out the movement into a major action. The peace demonstrations during the War clearly showed that such an action need not necessarily be crushed, and even if it is, that does not necessarily entail the collapse of the movement as a whole. Even when we suffer casualties in such demonstrations, there will be situations where it is impermissible to cut them short. Despite the danger of casualties, such rallies must be held again and again. If preparations for such events are well organised, it not only increases their impact but decreases the number of casualties.

Alongside the self-sacrifice of proletarians, the efficient organisation and truly strict execution of such a demonstration ensures it will be effective. The task is to learn how to carry out such actions in a truly disciplined and well-organised manner. Experience shows that street demonstrations are most effective when based on the larger factories. To be sure, large rallies on holidays can be staged as a parade with banners leading out of the residential districts. However, such demonstrations usually do not have a revolutionary impact but are instead rather festive and propagandistic in character. But to achieve a genuinely revolutionary impact, the workers need to be mobilised for the rally right out of the factory. Preparations by the cells and fractions are crucially important here, including systematic preliminary discussions. The workers must be of one mind. This is absolutely indispensable for carrying out such actions and enabling them to take a step forward.

But this unified mood in the factories must be reinforced by the cells and fractions. The masses need to go into the streets not as an amorphous crowd, influenced by diverse ideas, but as a body of proletarians that knows full well what it is demonstrating for. A structure of factory shop stewards and cell leaders is needed, alongside the political leadership, to give such demonstrations a firm structure. If the time is ripe for such demonstrations, the workers' responsible leaders, the leading functionaries, must meet with the shop stewards in order to discuss out the action in detail. Following such discussions, they can then, the next day, carry out the demonstration in a firmly united, well-organised, and disciplined manner.

On the day of the demonstration, however, a strong instrument is needed that serves as the demonstration's backbone from the moment it steps off to when it disperses, always available wherever it is needed. This is the only way to carry out the demonstration with the fewest casualties and the maximum impact. After the action, its lessons must be critically reviewed by the group of functionaries, shop stewards, and factory council members, so that such initiatives can be renewed and strengthened, escalating into revolutionary mass actions.

There are also other ways to involve the masses in action. In every working-class movement, we have the task of showing ourselves to be genuine leaders of the proletariat. We must set our sights on ending the influence of the social traitors and thrusting these people to the side. In conditions of political and economic stagnation, we must strive to break through this by utilising other methods of agitation, similar to what the VKPD did last year through its Open Letter.[10] I do not think I need to go into that in detail here.

You can read in the text how the concept underlying an action can be effectively expressed through factory fractions, trade-union functionaries, newspapers, and parliamentary fractions. The party must demonstrate that when it has written about an issue, that is not the end of the matter. If it is convinced that the action has merit, the party must be able to continue the actions for weeks and months and intensify them. But, after having perhaps aroused support for some initiative like the Open Letter through numerous meetings, much talk in the newspapers, speeches in parliament, and endorsements, we must not make the mistake of failing to continue this action and instead allow it to wither. Allowing such actions to lapse is the worst error the party could make. If it is not possible to sustain and pursue an action, it is far better not to begin it at all, but to be satisfied with more modest initiatives and with organisational consolidation.

---

10. While the KPD's Open Letter itself was issued in January 1921, not 'the previous year', Koenen may be referring to the initiatives leading up to it, going back to late 1920. See p. 15; Riddell 2011a.

What if the party succeeds in a given industry in establishing its strongest organisations, in achieving broad support for its demands, and in gaining a degree of leadership? In that case, our organisational strength must be utilised propagandistically to win recognition within the trade unions for the party's leading role. Our comrades must then succeed in convening conferences of any local bodies that have come out for our demands, gatherings that can then win recognition for the common demands. It is then necessary to bring the real movements together around these shared demands. All those who take part in such actions must make every effort to bring together the movements that are under way or are likely to break out, so that they become a unified movement.

In this way, the Communist leadership will bring about a new relationship of forces, which will have an impact on the social-traitor leaders. In the face of such struggles, waged in a unified fashion, these leaders will find evasion impossible. They will have to show their colours and say precisely what they want. If we do not succeed in getting them to pull their share of the load, our task is to expose them, not only politically but also in practical, organisational terms, showing that they are completely unwilling to lead unified struggles of the proletariat. In that case, we must act independently.

But, for a Communist Party to make the attempt to take leadership of the masses in a time of severe disruption and economic and political tension, it must use methods other than simply propaganda. The party may even abstain from proposing its own slogans and demands. In such periods, when movements are growing and heading toward explosion, it will address public appeals to the proletarians who are pressing for action because they are close to destitution, and to the organised proletarians who always take the lead in such struggles, in order to demonstrate that there is no way to avoid these struggles. The party must demonstrate that the leadership of these struggles must not be left in the hands of the social traitors, but that a determined leadership is needed, one that is ready for battle, in order to lead these small proletarian struggles and unify them into broad political campaigns. In the course of these struggles, it must be shown that even though the living standards of the proletariat are being undermined, the old organisations seek to avoid and prevent this struggle.

Our factory and trade-union organisations must constantly emphasise in meetings the readiness for battle of the Communist working class, and that there can be no more evasion. If no other party is willing to take the leadership, the Communist Party is the only force that can show the way forward out of this destitution. The main issue, however, is to unify the struggles generated by such a situation. The cells and fractions in the industries and factories drawn into such a movement must maintain close organisational ties not only among themselves but also with the district committees and central leadership. And these bodies must accept the responsibility to send special representatives to all regions where movements are taking place. They should support efforts to take leadership in these districts and to ensure that the concept of unity underlying these struggles is truly developed, so that all workers can recognise their unified character and also sense their political nature.

In the course of generalising such struggles, it is necessary to create unified bodies to lead it. Given the present failure of the bureaucratic trade-union leaders in strike situations, it is appropriate to call for new elections, in which an effort should be made to elect Communists to the strike leadership. Where several wage movements have been successfully combined and linked with various political uprisings – for example in blocking troop transport – it is necessary to establish a common leadership for the action, preferably made up of Communists heading the action. In this way, trade-union fractions, factory councils, and assemblies of factory councils can generate common campaigns that represent the core and basis of the Communist leadership, which makes the necessary preparations.

If the movement takes the desired political form, as a result of involvement by employers' organisations or the local authorities, then we must argue for political workers' councils, moving forward as decisively as needed, even without the trade unions. If Communists intervene in partial actions in this way, with careful, intensive, and thoughtful work, it can win them the leadership of the proletariat in extensive regions while equipping the proletariat for broader struggles.

*[Workplace organisation and ties]*

Parties that are already consolidated, and mass parties in particular, should take organisational measures to prepare for decisive mass political actions. We should always be mindful of the need to use experiences in actions, whether partial or mass in character, to establish closer and closer ties with the broad masses. Our ties with the masses – that's the main issue. In factory conferences, the responsible party leaders must discuss the experiences of mass actions again and again with the shop stewards and the factory and trade-union fractions, in order to strengthen their ties to the stewards. A close relationship of trust with the shop stewards is the best organisational assurance that mass political actions will not break out prematurely and will always be initiated with the scope corresponding to objective conditions and the party's degree of influence.

Such a network of trusted factory stewards has enabled many parties to lead successful movements. Consider the Russian Revolution. We know that in Petersburg it was such a network of factory fractions, factory stewards, and cells, working quite closely with the leadership, which led the decisive struggles. In Germany too we can say that the last decisive struggles – the general strike to end the War in 1917 in Central Germany and, at the beginning of 1918, in Berlin; the November [1918] revolution and the struggles that followed in March [1919], were initiated and carried through only because a solid network of factory shop stewards had developed, which had close ties with the political leaders.[11] These leaders, in alliance with the shop stewards, had a broad influence on the masses. I recall vividly how Karl Liebknecht, among many others, sought to maintain very close ties with the factory stewards.

All parties should work in this way, with all their energy, to establish such ties through the stewards with the factory work force. This will assure great flexibility. We have witnessed in Germany that it is precisely such perfected organisational ties – not at all artificial but arising naturally out of the movement – that enabled the stewards to lead the masses, when necessary even in armed struggle.

In Italy last year, there was a movement that was unquestionably revolutionary and found expression in the occupation of the factories. However, on a critical note, we can say that this movement was betrayed by the trade-union bureaucracy and did not receive sufficient leadership from the party. On the other hand, we can also say that one of the main reasons for the collapse of the movement was that the factories were occupied without giving thought to the need to closely link the factories and the political leadership through the factory shop stewards. So there, too, a truly extensive shop stewards network would have made it possible to extend the activity and drive it forward into a genuine revolutionary mass movement, which would have established close ties among all these components.

In addition, I believe that we could have taken advantage of the big British miners' movement if the British party had been capable of establishing close ties with the masses through the shop stewards in every workplace.

So we see how essential it is to build a truly active network of shop stewards, fractions, and the like, which will be the backbone of all genuine activity by the parties.

Through such factory stewards and fractions, we will make the entire party more active and capable of carrying out actions. What is more, when the working masses see a real leadership, they will develop trust in it. They

---

11. Besides the November 1918 revolution and the March 1919 struggles in Berlin, Koenen is referring to the April 1917 strikes in Saxony and Berlin, and to the strikes in Berlin in January–February 1918.

will develop intense trust in a leadership that shows it has close ties with the factories.

[Party structure]

I will now move on to the section dealing with the party's structure. Like the section on the press, it could be shortened, although you would be justified in asking that the party structure be discussed in detail. But what we are discussing is not the party structure as such but the movement, and how our forces and our branches are set up. We could be content to give some general instructions, which have proved their worth, on the framework of the party apparatus. Here, too, we should bear in mind that the party can be effective only if it extends outwards from the centres of power, the main cities and industrial centres. It would be wrong to go back from Moscow now and say we have to spread out in a network of groups covering the entire country. In some cases, these groups would be so weak that their forces could not be utilised. It is more important to build our forces in the main cities and industrial centres, where the masses are present and the party can have genuine importance and build its strength.

If we have consolidated units in the main locations, then the surplus forces should extend the party's network outward from the centres into the surrounding areas. But local groups and new districts should be formed only when there is a solid core in that locality. This will assure that the group is effective. A party does not excel organisationally by having the largest number of local groups, but rather by having groups that are strong and effective, and that give expression to this effectiveness in their political propaganda and activity. In constructing the organisation, we will also encounter more complicated situations, such as a concentration in large cities; in other cases, we will also have to rely on the rural organisations.

It is also important to establish flexible ties between the districts and the leadership. This does not require a hierarchical structure of local groups, districts, regions, combinations of regions and the central leadership. That could seriously limit the party's flexibility. Our task here is to establish living ties between the party's main centres and the central leadership, by dividing the country into districts composed of a number of cities – separate districts receiving information directly from the party. Overall, mutual exchange of information and instructions is an important task for the organisational apparatus. Béla Kun was quite right on this point when he said, in his pamphlet:

> In general, parties have lacked political correspondence and ongoing, direct, and systematic verbal instructions. The natural basis for instructions is a systematic information service.

Such a thorough and systematic information service, the party's lifeblood, will protect it from falling into routine and bureaucracy. Béla Kun says elsewhere:

> Such an information service, functioning automatically yet free of any spirit of routine, is the only way to develop informational activity that fully unifies the party's work and creates a genuine and solid centralisation.[12]

Such an ongoing, regular, and efficient information service is – together with the obligation to be active – the best way to overcome bureaucratism.

Our theses on structure also give a number of instructions on how the party central leadership should be set up, in order for it to be flexible. I would like to direct the attention of all parties to point 40,[13] which deals with division of labour. We point out that division of labour in the districts must be carried out in a centralised fashion. But, there too, a constant rotation of assignments is needed, and let me say a word on that topic. Comrades who had been active for a long time as political secretaries came to do the work quite bureaucratically. It did them a lot of good to be removed from this post and made editors. On the other hand, editors were inclined to place too little value on the organisational work, and it was very helpful to appoint editors to such organisational posts, and vice versa. This brought the party unquestioned benefits. Former editors were outstanding in organisational roles, while former secretaries functioned well as editors. Such an exchange of roles also proved its worth in campaigns. Functionaries who had sunk roots in the districts, where they formed close friendships and family ties, could not launch a movement, but they excelled once we moved them into another district. Thus this exchange of roles was a way to stimulate the party.

This section contains a number of changes that have been distributed to you.

*[Legal and illegal work]*

I will now take up the final section, dealing with legal and illegal work. The heading here is misleading and will be modified. The text here explains that the illegal and legal parties are not two different things, but constantly grow over into each other. Here we must make a small correction in the theses of the Second Congress. Comrade Béla Kun explained this well in his pamphlet,

---

12. The quotations are from Kun's article, 'Organisatorisches zur Märzaktion', in *Zentrale der VKPD* 1921, pp. 126–27.
13. An apparent reference to point 48 of the finished resolution.

saying, 'The major organisational task is to orient the entire party toward illegal organisational preparations to carry out revolutionary struggles.'

He then gives several examples of how a parallel illegal apparatus in Berlin separated itself off and launched into military operations in Mansfeld.[14] Kun comments, 'The entire party organisation must be so adapted to the shape of the struggles that its organisational understanding prevents any organisational or political separation [of the illegal] from the legal organisation, even if only for a very short time.' Kun then objects to a portion of the theses on party tasks, which reads, 'As a result of the state of siege and the emergency laws, these parties are not in a position to carry out the entirety of their work legally.' He says it is essential to create an underground apparatus, stressing that the entire party apparatus must be equipped to function either legally or illegally. We attempt to clarify this legal and illegal activity, so that everyone will see that the organisation must be trained for both. Now it can be objected that too little is said here. Quite right. Others will say there is too much. We believe we have taken a middle course, in order to indicate and make clear the interrelationship between the two forms.

The party must be truly capable of understanding the organisational principle of the obligation to be active and of democratic centralism. It must carry out agitation and propaganda, take part in political struggles, and edit its press as a genuine community of struggle. It must take note of what we have said regarding the party's structure. Only then will we be able to project that the next congress will present us with parties that can really be awarded the honour of being designated Communist parties.

---

14. When the Comintern addressed the building of a revolutionary party at its Second Congress, several resolutions addressed the issue of preparedness for underground work. The most authoritative passage, from the Conditions for Admission, stated that under existing conditions of incipient civil war, 'it is [Communists'] duty to create everywhere a parallel [underground] organisational apparatus'. Further, 'It is absolutely necessary that legal and illegal activity be combined.' Riddell (ed.) 1991, 2WC, 2, p. 767.

Similar passages are found in the Statutes (p. 698) and the theses on the Comintern's tasks (p. 756) The theses on the Communist Party, however, stated that 'the legal work must be under the actual control of the illegal party at all times'. (p. 199)

Basing himself on a rough paraphrase of the Conditions for Admission, Kun contended that the 'theses' had encouraged a tendency toward parallel legal and illegal structures. In the March struggles, which were centred in the Mansfeld region, the illegal organisations broke free of party leadership control and functioned independently, Kun wrote. 'The March struggles showed that this parallelism of legal and illegal organisations must absolutely be destroyed. The illegal organisation must be fully aligned with the party as a whole so that it cannot separate off, even for a moment.' Zentrale der VKPD 1921, pp. 129–30.

[*Structure of the Communist International*]

Comrades, that brings me to the conclusion of the main portion of this talk. I must add a few words on the second section, which can be much shorter, on the organisational structure of the Communist International and its relationship to the affiliated parties. You will have found in *Moscow* a proposal made by the German Communist Party in its central committee meeting on 5 May.[15] Based on this proposal, discussions took place with representatives of the Executive, and that produced the resolution I will now propose to you for adoption. It encompasses all the significant goals of the German resolution.

What were these goals that we wished to achieve? Some of them have already been cited in the Executive's report on the trade unions. These matters were already dealt with in the resolution submitted at the end of the discussion on the Executive report. This resolution reads:

> The congress expects that the Executive will strive to establish an improved communications apparatus, with strengthened collaboration of the affiliated parties, which in turn will put the Executive in a position to carry out its steadily growing tasks better than before.[16]

The resolution also demands that parties send their best forces to be part of the Executive, as the leadership of the entire international struggle. This political consideration provides the starting point for the resolution that I am presenting to you. I will first read it and then add a few words to motivate it. The resolution reads as follows:

[*For the entire resolution in edited form, see pp. 1007–8.*]

I recommend this resolution for discussion and adoption. It does not need much explanation. I would only like to stress in particular that the parties should definitely decide to make their best forces available to the Executive. In this way we will be able to achieve what the resolution insists on, namely that the individual representatives in the Executive act not only as reporters on their country but as resource persons on defined problems. We need such forces. We can no longer demand of Russia that it provide all these forces.

---

15 Apparently a reference to the 'Theses on Building the Communist International', which was published in *Die Internationale*, 3, 7 (1 June 1921), pp. 244–5. Among the proposals of that resolution were an increase in the number of ECCI members from parties with more than 100,000 members; assignment of four ECCI members, including two Russians, with the task of informing the ECCI of conditions in which parties were struggling; and publication of a correspondence service in several languages to help maintain closer ties among the parties.

16 For the corresponding passage in the resolution, see p. 923.

We must send leading comrades here and thus ensure that the Executive can be more active.

It is all too easy to say that the Executive should inform us about this or that matter. Take the Levi case: given that delegates passed through Germany and spent at least twenty-four hours in Berlin, they could readily have gathered information. Such criticisms are impermissible in an international party that calls itself Communist. We must have closer ties in the International, and the individual sections must do all they can to achieve this. Common actions and mutual support can take very different forms. We must not think that the revolution is developing everywhere at the same pace. There are a great many openings for mutual support in very diverse fields of action and propaganda. For example, if large demonstrations take place in a country, another country can respond through its press and through propaganda about these demonstrations.

If demonstrations in a country around some international question result in severe casualties and battles, other countries can express solidarity with their proletarian neighbours, at least through speeches in parliament. If big economic struggles break out, in which it is not possible to provide direct assistance, the spirit of struggle must penetrate the neighbouring countries. Fraternal support must find expression through appeals, rallies, and collection of funds. So there will be many possibilities to forge stronger links between the national organisations, going beyond those between the Executive and each party.

The bourgeoisie achieves this kind of centralisation. As I said at the congress of the trade-union international, there was recently another discussion in Berlin between the chief of Germany's political spying agency and public prosecutor, Weissmann, and the heads of the French and British secret police, in order to set up an organisation that would serve, if Russia collapses or there are other complications, to block a flood of Communist rabble rousers. They are preparing to deal with every possible contingency, even the most ingenious and sophisticated variants. If the international bourgeoisie is already concluding complex agreements spanning all national frontiers, we must do likewise, not only through resolutions but through practical organisational measures. Only then will the International truly embrace all humanity. (*Loud applause*)

**Schaffner** (Switzerland): Comrades, I move that the theses on organisational questions be referred back to the commission as providing an inadequate basis for discussion. A commission was chosen to draft these theses. Instead of that we have eighteen pages here, written in a questionable journalistic style. These eighteen pages of elaboration certainly include some useful ideas, but it is all so vague, so indistinct, that they hardly deserve the name theses.

If we were to begin making criticisms, we would have to start with points of style and wording. We would have to rewrite the whole thing, and that would make a discussion fruitless. So I request – or rather make a motion – to refer back these theses without discussion, and charge the commission to meet tomorrow, not just at 1:00 p.m. but as early as possible. That will make it possible to draft new theses, perhaps picking up what is good and useful in the present ones, and to present them to the congress. I also move that the extraordinarily important question of reorganising the International and the Executive not be disposed of in a resolution that is quite questionable and is known, I think, to only a very few people in this hall. Instead, this question – so important for the International – should be dealt with in a commission in which all delegates are represented. A commission should be set up for this special question, and it too should meet tomorrow morning and present its conclusions tomorrow evening.

**Zinoviev**: Comrades, it really seems to me that Comrade Schaffner has rejected these theses somewhat too categorically. He has presented a motion to reject this document without discussion. I believe he is completely wrong. The theses were drafted by a number of comrades. Perhaps the German text drawn up by this varied international team is in fact not easy to understand. But the content of the theses, in my opinion, is quite correct and quite good. They offer all our parties a whole number of valuable and important points. Let me cite just one chapter – on the duty of members to be active, for example, or the one on propaganda. In my opinion, comrades, we should and will adopt these theses by and large as they stand.

But obviously this should be done after discussion. If comrades are so tired that discussion is impossible, or if the French text has not yet been distributed, we can hold the discussion later. The next step is for the commission to meet tomorrow, but we should not simply reject the theses. To repeat, those who have read the theses attentively will come to the conclusion that they are, by and large, quite good, quite correct, and quite important for the movement. (*Applause*)

Comrades, I did not hear any motion against Comrade Schaffner's second proposal. I did not hear it. But I am told that Comrade Schaffner proposed a motion to set up a special commission on the composition of the Executive. In my opinion, comrades, all parties had the opportunity – and have it still – to send their representatives to the Organisation Commission. This commission should take up the question. Let me point out that we are all very tired, and it would be difficult to create a special commission. We should ask parties to please send representatives to the Organisation Commission, so that both questions can be dealt with in the same commission. (*Applause*)

**Vaillant-Couturier:**[17] Comrades, the French delegation has discussed the question of organising the International, which was raised by Comrade Koenen. Our delegation meeting yesterday evening voted to ask the congress to create a commission to study this question. Given that a commission on organisational issues has already been chosen, we ask that two sub-commissions now be established, one to take up the organisational question and the other on organising the International. We ask that these commissions be established right away, given that organising the Executive Committee is an exceptionally important issue.

**Kolarov** (Chair): The congress can take the proposal of the French delegation under advisement and refer it to the commission. This is the most practical step.

Since no one else has asked to speak, I close debate on this question, on condition that the commission have a thorough discussion of all these extremely important questions.

Before the session ends, I have a few announcements.

**Vaillant-Couturier**: Obviously, several delegates should be sent from each country.

**Kolarov** (Chair): Several delegates can be sent to the commission, given that there are two sub-commissions.

**Delagrange**: You understand that we cannot debate the proposed theses, because we have not yet received them. This will also be true in the commission session tomorrow, unless the theses are printed [in French]. The French delegation therefore asks that it receive the theses before the start of the commission session.

**Kolarov** (Chair): Measures to do this have already been taken.

*(The session is adjourned at 10:30 p.m.)*

---

17. In the German text, the paragraph that follows is presented as a continuation of Zinoviev's speech. The attribution to Vaillant-Couturier is found in the Russian text and is sustained by the substance of these remarks.

Session 23 – 12 July 1921, 1:00 p.m.
# Eastern Question

*The Eastern Question. Speakers: Tom Mann, Süleyman Nuri, Dimitratos, Aqazadeh, Makhul Bey, Zinoviev, Kasyan, Tskhakaia, Abilov, Roy, Zhang Tailei, Nam Man-ch'un, Taro Yoshihara, Kara-Gadiyev, Julien, Colliard, Kolarov.*

**Zinoviev** (Chair): Today we will take up the Eastern question. Our first speaker is an outstanding representative of the British working class, Comrade Tom Mann.

**Tom Mann** (Britain): Comrades, I am glad for the opportunity to report briefly to the congress on the Eastern question. I happened to hear in a discussion the claim that Britain is not a free country. I want to show you that the opposite is true. In Britain not only the bourgeoisie but the proletariat too is permitted to take up scientific questions. We are permitted to believe what we were told as children, namely, that the earth was created about six thousand years ago, but we may also hold the opinion that it originated 600,000 or millions of years ago. Britain is thus a free country, but despite such freedom of thought, we are not permitted to seriously challenge the privileges of the higher clergy. Everyone has the right to study any field of learning, whether practical or theoretical. Workers can use every opportunity to penetrate even deeper into the riddles of nature.

A short while ago an important event took place in Britain. I am referring to the visit of Professor Einstein from Berlin. He gave lectures in London on the theory of relativity, stressing the fact that science has priority over the principle of nationality.[1] He cited by way of example the very important fact that during the War the British government equipped two expeditions and sent them to different points on the earth's surface to prove, through scientific observation, the correctness of a theory proposed by a German professor. So, as far as science is concerned, the scientists and even the governments rise above all nationalist interests.

Perhaps you are not familiar with this theory of relativity and are not aware of its great significance for workers. To explain this, I will cite only one passage, dealing with the proof of the principle of relativity. It addresses the solution of the well-known and previously unexplained contradiction between the astronomic reckoning of the precession of Mercury and evidence from observation. In addition, this passage tells us that, thanks to the resolution of this contradiction, it was possible to determine the refraction of the light of any star as it passed the sun during a total solar eclipse, which was demonstrated by observations during the solar eclipse of May 1919.

We have complete freedom to study these important issues and others like them because, I believe, study of such questions does not threaten the economic situation of the ruling classes. We are able to devote our time and energy to the study of applied science, and we can help to perfect technology – in fact we are encouraged to do so. We can introduce technical innovations that make it possible to produce more with fewer workers. For that we receive the blessing of the ruling class. We can not only replace the steam locomotive with one powered by oil, we can eliminate boilers and introduce diesel engines, we can even get rid of the boilermakers, because they are no longer called on to make boilers. We are even permitted to eliminate the very possibility of working and earning a living. We are permitted to make advances in this direction.

But there are also one or two forms of activity in which we do not enjoy full freedom. For example, we are permitted to occupy ourselves with sociology, to support social reforms, even to study the relationship of the ruling class with the subjugated. Of course this is with the limitation that we do not plan any specific measures for the liberation of these oppressed classes; for freedom is, after all, somewhat restricted in this regard.

Yet Britain remains a great nation, where the sciences are supported. This country's greatest pride is the freedom of the individual Englishman. I am getting older all the time, but never yet in my entire life have I been able to state

---

1. Albert Einstein visited London in June 1921, lecturing at King's College and elsewhere on 'The Development and Present Position of the Theory of Relativity'.

that the children of this so very free country are adequately fed and clothed or that they live in decent dwellings. We are very regretful about these facts.

But then we are told that the British Empire is so great that everyone speaks of it with respect and we should truly be thankful to belong to such a great empire. We learn how extended and powerful this empire is. As regards the Eastern peoples, we hear that in India two hundred million of the three hundred and twenty million inhabitants live under the immediate and complete rule of Britain – not of Britain as a whole but of a handful of Englishmen. The ruling British bourgeoisie, which holds dictatorial power in this country, uses machine guns and other weapons in an attempt to reinforce and maintain its rule. I deeply deplore the exploitation and servitude that prevail in India. Two hundred and fifty million Indians are under British rule, and 85 per cent of these slaves are peasants, who have every right to demand economic freedom. The British demand the development of Indian industry and, it follows, of the bourgeoisie. British spinning mill owners from Lancashire have founded cotton spinning mills in India, imposing an eleven-hour day instead of the British eight-hour day. And for that they give the workers only a few pence a day in wages, deepening the oppression of the peoples of India.

Industry is growing with tremendous speed, and with it the wealth of the bourgeoisie, but the people are oppressed. We would like you to know that there is another segment of the population that is not at all proud to belong to the British Empire but is doubly shamed by this fact. We are outraged by the tyranny that weighs on us, and doubly outraged by the oppression of other peoples. Anyone who wishes to act in the interests of the Indian population must make efforts to abolish this tyranny. We are too few in number to do this, but we have a clear and objective view of the future and an unclouded understanding. We therefore seek every opportunity and utilise every means to hasten the liberation of the Indian people.

We do the same in Egypt. Here there lives a people possessing not only an ancient civilisation but an evident capacity and desire to rule themselves. But the British bourgeois is alert; British soldiers and guns stand permanently at the ready. Merely consider that the British government has organised its oppression in such a fashion that it dares to burden the Egyptian and Indian population with taxes in order to better subjugate them.

Beyond any doubt, the exploitation of India is enormous. Systematic pillage of Indian production, including through taxes and superprofits, has reached immense proportions. However, the British worker does not receive any part of this wealth and wants nothing to do with it. Every penny of this treasure flows into the pockets of the ruling classes. Moreover, they extract just as much from the population of England, Scotland, Wales, and Ireland.

The bourgeoisie rules all of the United Kingdom. We will turn all our energy to hastening the liberation of the British workers, and we grasp every opportunity to do the same for other peoples.

A purely nationalist movement cannot be strong enough to contend with a plutocracy that has spread across the entire world. This is why we want to support the class struggle in each of these oppressed peoples, so that the revolutionary movement among them can develop its own strength and link up with revolutionary movements of other countries. If this happens, the sun of freedom will rise for all oppressed peoples. In the meantime, we British Communists carry out propaganda in our own country and protest vigorously against the oppression of peoples. All the British comrades who have attended the two congresses in Moscow have told me again and again how vigorously they condemn any attempts at imperialist expansion.

I am convinced that the hour will come when the European countries will be just as aroused as was the case in Russia. Beneath us, in the Kremlin courtyard, is the great bell of Moscow, whose ring can be heard very far away. So too Soviet Russia is for us like a giant bell, announcing the entire world's salvation.

May the day soon arrive in which the world revolution will bring full social, political, and economic freedom.

**Zinoviev** (Chair): Comrades, we have been informed that the Organisational Commission will meet today at 6:00 p.m. All sections are requested to send their delegates to this session.

**Süleyman Nuri** (Turkey): Comrades, on behalf of the Turkish Communist Party, I wish to inform the congress regarding its work and the national movement in Anatolia. The Turkish independence movement is extremely important for the East. Before the World War, Turkey, like the other countries of the East, was under the yoke of imperialism. The Turkish people, the peasants and workers, were driven against their will and desire into this imperialist war by their oppressors, the pashas. During the War, a great many of the Turkish youth – officers and soldiers – were taken prisoner and interned in Russia, Germany, and other countries. There they learned about the meaning and origins of the War, and when they returned home, they brought with them the spirit of the socialist and Communist movement. And when, after the War, the pashas signed the Versailles Treaty, the Anatolian workers and peasants rose up to fight for independence, arms in hand. This independence movement was headed by the same pashas – Kemal Pasha and others.[2] Kemal Pasha's role and policies were the same as under the earlier

---

2. The Turkish war of independence, which began in May 1919, was waged after the Ottoman Empire's defeat in World War I and its subsequent partition by the Entente.

Turkish government. On the one hand, the government in Angora [Ankara] carried out an armed struggle for independence against the Entente, and on the other it sought to repress any Communist movement. The death of our comrades, above all Comrade Subhi, and the imprisonment of many others shows that Kemal is carrying out a bitter struggle against the Communists.[3]

The party organised by Kemal was founded for purposes of provocation, in order to persecute the Communists and to stamp out any Communist influence. Our Communist Workers' Party has nothing in common with this party.[4] But the Anatolian peasants and workers are well aware that as long as the independence movement continues, they – and also we Communists – must support it. The destruction of the Entente and of the imperialists is the basis and the beginning of world revolution, which will destroy every form of slavery. And the Anatolian workers and peasants will therefore support this struggle, as long as it is directed against the Entente. But if Kemal Pasha dares to break off this independence struggle and accept a compromise, the Anatolian workers and peasants will rise up as one man to overthrow Kemal and march over his body to the front, where they will fight alongside the entire East for independence. Our Communist Party, which held its first congress in Baku, Azerbaijan,[5] continues its agitational activity in Turkey, despite all persecution. It expresses the hope that the world revolution, carried out under the banner of the Third International, will be victorious and will liberate the oppressed people and the working class of the entire world.

**Nikolaos Dimitratos** (Greece): Greece was the last power to enter the European war, dragged into it by the pressure of the Entente powers. In this action, Greece served the interests not of its own people but of the Entente capitalists. For the Greek people, this war is not yet over. Greece is now fighting against Turkey.[6] The Greek people have held many rallies to protest the ongoing war in Asia Minor. The proletariat of Greece understands full well that the war benefits only the capitalists of its own country and of the Entente, especially British capitalism. Greece has become a colony of the Entente, or more precisely, of Britain. The Greek people are in an even worse situation than the population of the colonies, because they pay

---

In response to the British occupation of Istanbul, the Grand National Assembly was created in Ankara in April 1920, and Mustafa Kemal Pasha (Atatürk) became prime minister. The Republic of Turkey was proclaimed in October 1923.
 3. For the murder of Subhi, see p. 74, n. 3.
 4. Mustafa Kemal Pasha (Atatürk) had set up a 'Communist Party' in October 1920 as a way of channelling the energies of more radical elements to serve his own nationalist movement.
 5. The Turkish Communist Party was founded at a congress in Baku on 10 September 1920.
 6. For the Greek-Turkish War of 1919–22, see p. 159, n. 18.

not only an economic but a political tribute to world capitalism. They pay a tribute in blood, which they are even today still shedding in Asia Minor for the British capitalists. The people – that is, the proletariat – has protested many times against this war and has made clear many times, through our party, that it refuses to support this slaughter.

The incessant wars that the Greek people have been dragged into since 1912 – beginning with its war against Bulgaria and then against Turkey[7] – and the extent of its national debt, two times greater than the country's wealth, have created an unbearable situation. The degree of mass discontent with the policies of the Greek government is indicated by the fact that an immense number of soldiers have deserted. More than one hundred thousand soldiers have deserted the army, thereby making clear that they no longer wish to support the Greek government in continuing its policies. They no longer want to take part in the slaughter, which is not in the interests of either Turkish or Greek workers.

Beyond any doubt, our party has done its duty. It has not let any opportunity pass to spur on discontented forces against the government. Our party has taken the lead of the discontented many times in opposing the government and is persecuted for this by the authorities. Only two months ago, 160 persons were arrested in a single city for resisting the war. At this moment, about forty persons in different cities face charges of high treason.

The Greek bourgeoisie is combating us with all the means at its disposal. It sees us as its enemy. It knows that we are fighting against it, while opening the people's eyes to the crimes it has committed jointly with the European capitalists and imperialists. The Communist Party of Greece declares to the delegates at this congress that the Greek proletariat, the Greek workers and peasants, do not differentiate between themselves and the people, proletarians, and peasants of Turkey. Our party desires that peace and friendship may reign between the workers and peasants of the two countries. Everything that we seek and desire, our entire party activity, is aimed at forcing the government to halt this war that is devastating the proletariat of both countries.

Our party declares that it will work for the restoration of friendly relations between the two peoples and between the proletariat of Turkey and Greece. It will work to link up with the proletariat of the Balkans as a whole, that is

---

7. The first Balkan War, from October to December 1912 was waged by Serbia, Bulgaria, Greece, and Montenegro against the Ottoman Empire. Under the terms of a May 1913 peace treaty, the Ottoman Empire lost almost all of its remaining European territory. A second Balkan War was waged from June to August 1913 with Serbia and Greece defeating Bulgaria over division of the territory conquered from the Ottoman Empire in Macedonia.

of Bulgaria, Romania, and Serbia – indeed with the proletariat of the entire world. The Communist Party of Greece will exert all its energy to strengthen the bonds of friendship and fraternity with the proletariat of the East. We will combat our own bourgeoisie, which has become a tool of Entente capitalism and the Entente bourgeoisie and tyrannises our peoples. We are convinced that only a close alliance of Communists around the world with the countries of the East can overthrow the power of capitalism, end the slaughter, and free the peoples of the East.

On behalf of the class-conscious proletariat of Greece, we welcome the International's efforts to free the Eastern peoples. We express our conviction that the Eastern peoples, spurred on by the Russian Revolution, will not hesitate to break their chains and throw off the yoke of domestic and foreign imperialism and capitalism.

**Kamran Aqazadeh** (Iranian Communist Party): Comrades, we are in complete agreement that the theses on the national and colonial question adopted by the Second Congress deal with this topic in exhaustive fashion. We would like to refer here only to the experience of the last year in our work in Iran, a country that is economically backward but yet extremely rich. Above all, it must be emphasised that during recent decades Iran became the arena for a struggle between Russian tsarism and the British occupation, which gave decisive support to the most villainous reaction.[8] Only after the October Revolution, when the Russian proletariat renounced the piratical treaties signed by the Russian landlords, did the revolutionary movement expand to even greater dimensions, all the more because the British were engaged in occupying and pillaging Iran. This cynical brigandage enormously reinforced the hatred against British imperialism. The struggle against its brutal tyranny became the most popular revolutionary slogan among broad layers of the population.

During the years 1919–20, the revolutionary movement against the British and the shah grew in many regions of Iran – in Kherson, Mazandaran, Gilan, Azerbaijan, Kurdistan, and other regions – with such power that the Tehran government, despite a flood of British munitions, was unable to suppress the movement.

---

8. In the early twentieth century the Iranian monarchy faced increasing domination by tsarist Russia and the British Empire. In 1907 the two powers agreed between themselves to divide up Iran into spheres of influence, with the north going to Russia and the south to Britain; both sent in troops. Popular outrage at Russian and British domination helped fuel the Constitutional Revolution of 1905–11, which led to the establishment of a parliament.

The national liberation movement took on the greatest dimensions in Gilan, where the British had concentrated all their forces.[9] This struggle had an unfortunate conclusion, caused mostly by the fact that the Gilan nationalists planned to besiege the British with the aid not only of the bourgeoisie and the peasants but also of the princes and landlords, and then to overthrow the shah. That was the greatest error of the Gilan nationalists, since both the British imperialists and the shah's government was based precisely on this landholder aristocracy. The new government, established in Tehran after the February [1921] uprising, appeared to be striving to take this into account. A declaration to the Iranian people, alongside the annulment of the piratical British-Iranian treaty of 9 August 1919, cited the hateful role long played in Iran by the landowning aristocracy.[10]

The British, in fact, could not have maintained themselves in our country for a single day without the participation and support of the Persian landowners. The Iranian Communist Party, during its four years of practical activity, has become convinced that even the bourgeois-democratic revolution in Iran is inconceivable without the liberation of the peasants from a whole range of feudal remnants and an improvement of their economic situation at the cost of the landowners.

The immediate task posed in our programme is not only to drive out the British and overthrow the government of the shah but also to convene a constituent assembly that would do away with all survivals of feudalism and liberate the productive forces from the exceptionally heavy chains that now restrict it. While lending decisive support to the national liberation movement, our party also strives, by creating trade unions of workers and apprentices in the cities and peasant revolution in the countryside, to draw these broad masses into the course of revolutionary struggle. It seeks, by raising their class consciousness, to gradually prepare them for the struggle that will commence after the victory of the bourgeois revolution.

The process through which working people will take power in our country will be very lengthy, and it is closely tied to the proletarian world revolution. Only after the social revolution has triumphed, even if in only a few of the

---

9. In the course of this upsurge, a soviet republic was established in the Iranian province of Gilan, existing from June 1920 until September 1921. The movement was headed by leaders of the Constitutionalist movement and Iranian Communists, and backed by contingents of the Soviet Red Army.

10. On 21 February 1921 the Persian Cossack Brigade led by Reza Khan carried out a coup in Tehran. The new government signed a friendship treaty with Soviet Russia, and on 22 June it formally renounced the 1919 Anglo-Persian Agreement. The new government also carried out a campaign against the Gilan soviet republic, which was overthrown by September.

advanced capitalist countries of Europe, will the Iranian Communists be able, in alliance with the Iranian masses, to pose the question of taking political power and establishing workers' and peasants' councils. And we are firmly convinced that the victory of the international party will come much sooner than we expect. When it does, it will free the oppressed peoples of Iran and the entire world, once and for all, from subjugation and exploitation by the bourgeoisie both at home and abroad.

**Zinoviev** (Chair): Comrades, a revolutionary organisation of Muslims, which is not Communist, has approached the Presidium with a request that it be allowed to present a declaration to the congress. This is the Union of Islamic Revolutionary Societies, founded in 1919.[11] They work in Turkey, Egypt, Tripoli, the French colonies, and India. To repeat, they are not a Communist organisation, but rather an organisation that struggles against the subjugation of Muslims and against imperialism. The Presidium proposes to the congress to hear this declaration. I will therefore ask the congress if it is agreement with this. Is there anyone opposed? No one. The Presidium's proposal is therefore adopted. Makhul Bey has the floor.

## Declaration by the Union of Islamic Revolutionary Societies[12]

**Makhul Bey:** Almost a year has gone by since the congress of the Peoples of the East in Baku.[13] We have followed with great satisfaction the development of the liberation movement among the five hundred million inhabitants of the Eastern countries, from the Atlantic Ocean across North Africa and China to the Pacific, four-fifths of whose population adheres to the same belief, Islam, the basic principle of which is freedom.

---

11. The Union of Islamic Revolutionary Societies (İslâm İhtilal Cemiyetleri İttihadı) was founded by Enver Pasha, a leader of the Young Turk revolution of 1908 and an Ottoman Empire government leader during World War I. By early 1920 Enver, now in exile, declared his solidarity with the Soviet government, and represented the Union of Islamic Revolutionary Societies at the Baku Congress of Peoples of the East. He broke with Soviet Russia in September 1921, however, and joined an anti-Soviet revolt in Central Asia. Enver was killed in battle against the Red Army in 1922.
    According to most accounts, the Union of Islamic Revolutionary Societies led a largely fictitious existence, and it ceased functioning by the end of 1921.
12. The present translation has consulted the Turkish-language version of this report, published in two instalments in the journal *Liva el-Islam* (15 August, 1 September 1921). It has not been possible to establish the identity of Makhul Bey. Thanks to Mete Tunçay for research assistance.
13. The First Congress of the Peoples of the East, organised by the Comintern, was held in Baku, 31 August–7 September 1920. The proceedings can be found in Riddell (ed.) 1993.

Revolutionary organisations affiliated to the Union of Islamic Revolutionary Societies have been active in Morocco, Algeria, Tunisia, Tripolitania [Libya], Syria, Egypt, Albania, Yemen, Mesopotamia [Iraq], Iran, and India. The results of this activity give us firm hope in a decisive victory.

Our comrades in Turkey, the only country that still maintains its freedom and forms a bastion for all revolutionary organisations, are not laying down their arms. This is due to the fact that Soviet Russia has now entered an epoch of peace and reconstruction, while continuing its struggle against the forces of crime and oppression.

Examining the situation in Turkey, we must concede that it is incomparably better this year than last. The imperialist Armenians, the Dashnaks, were overthrown – as you know, they had to cede power to the Communists. This brought an end to the bloody Turkish-Armenian slaughter, which benefited Western imperialism but brought no advantage to the peoples engaged in that struggle. After Turkey had overcome this danger, threatening it from the east, it dealt two tangible blows to Greece, a blind tool of Britain. We are convinced that this danger as well will soon vanish, and that the victory of the Anatolian peoples will soon secure the peace for which they are in such great need.

This successful defence was possible because the peoples of Anatolia were closely united, advancing against the enemy with their united strength. Given the common danger, they set aside all their disagreements and all divergence in their goals. All oppressed peoples can take their liberation struggle as an example.

*Morocco*:[14] The billions that the French have spent on Morocco have not hindered the activity of the Moroccan revolutionaries in the slightest. They have inflicted countless defeats on the French imperialists.

Here we cannot avoid mentioning Abd al Malik, the son of the emir, Abd al Qadir, who is among the most active members of our organisation and fights together with his comrades in eastern Morocco. During the past year we succeeded in unifying leaders of uprisings in different parts of Morocco in a single leading centre. This leads us to hope the best for the future.

*Algeria*:[15] The revolutionary movement in Algeria and Tunisia is in a preparatory phase, but we have unshakable hope for the future.

---

14. Morocco became an object of European colonisation efforts beginning in 1840. In 1904, France and Spain secretly divided the country into spheres of influence. In 1912 most of Morocco formally became a French protectorate. It became independent in 1956.

15. Algeria was militarily seized by France in 1830, ending over three hundred years of Ottoman rule. The entire Mediterranean region of Algeria was administered as an integral part of France. Tunisia became a French protectorate in 1881.

*Tripolitania:*[16] In order to portray the situation in Tripolitania, it is sufficient to say that the struggle that has gone on there for ten years now has cost the Italians billions of lire and taken hundreds of thousands of lives. However, the people have won a decisive victory over the Italians. During the last three years alone, more than seventy thousand rifles were taken from the Italians in eastern Tripolitania. In the process, Italy lost about thirty-five thousand men.

Power is now held fully by a central committee elected by the people. In this country, our organisation has long since gone beyond the preparatory stage. It has moved on to direct action and revolution, securing freedom for the people, and is poised to take governmental power. The Italians felt compelled to retreat to the coastline, where they continue to occupy a stretch of land over one thousand kilometres wide. Nonetheless, they get no benefits from this and must, instead, cover costs of billions of francs a year. The day is no longer distant when they will be completely driven out of the country.

*Egypt:*[17] We do not have a great deal to say about Egypt. Only a short while ago, the population there rose up against the British and moved into action against their oppressors, armed with only sticks and stones. The moment the Egyptian population has arms, it will be quite a different story. The Hizb-al-Wataini (Free Nile) party and the terrorist organisations,[18] all of which belong to our association, are more and more adopting our basic ideas, namely that freedom can be won only through armed struggle, and it is fruitless to wait for the oppressors to do something willingly for the native peoples. This is particularly true after the Zaglul Pasha incident. The Egyptian revolutionaries are taking measures appropriate to these beliefs.

*Albania:*[19] Before taking up the more westerly countries, we must discuss the liberation movement in Albania. This brave people is beset on all sides by

---

16. Tripolitania designates the northwest portion of Libya. In 1911, Italian troops invaded Libya, formerly part of the Ottoman Empire, and it came under Italian control in 1912. A war of resistance by nationalist forces against Italian troops developed, which was not entirely suppressed until 1931. With the defeat of Italy in World War II, control of Libya passed to Britain and France in 1943. The country became independent in 1951.
17. Egypt, which had been under effective British control since the late 1870s, was declared a British protectorate in 1914. In March 1919 a popular uprising took place in response to Britain's deportation of Saad Zaghlul Pasha, leader of the nationalist Wafd Party. The uprising was crushed within a month, with some 4,000 Egyptians killed. Britain declared Egypt formally independent in February 1922 under the rule of a monarchy, but it was not until the military toppling of the monarchy in 1952 that the country was able to throw off British domination.
18. Hizb al-Wataini (National Party) was a revolutionary nationalist movement formed in Egypt as a secret society in 1907 to fight British occupation.
19. An armed rebellion by nationalist forces in Albania in 1910–12 won the country's effective independence from the Ottoman Empire. As a result of efforts by the

the imperialists: Italians to the west; Greeks to the south; Serbians to the north and east. They have emerged victorious from a bitter struggle. The western portion of Albania is now freed of all the invaders. Those who are now vanquished, the country's previous oppressors, are not prepared to give official recognition to independent Albania. Nonetheless, we hope that free Russia will be an example to the imperialists and will prompt them to establish official relations with Albania.

*Thrace*:[20] There is no need to deal with Turkey again. However, we cannot avoid calling to mind that thousands of people have died in Thrace, which is even now continuing its struggle against invasion. In western Anatolia, behind the Greek front, about two hundred thousand men, women, and children have been cut down by the barbarism of Greek imperialism. Many of them were burned alive. Despite this, the struggle continues without letup.

*Iran*: The unfortunate Iranian people cannot expect help from any side. They have no choice but to win their freedom by their own strength. We are glad to note that organisations in Iran are joining our association and growing stronger every day.

*India*:[21] Until recently, our comrades in India, although members of our association, believed that they could achieve freedom through peaceful means. Now they increasingly recognise that force must be answered with force. They have now taken a truly revolutionary path.

The Sarekat Islam association and the other revolutionary groups in Java are working with us. We work harmoniously with the Copts in Egypt, the Christians in Syria, the Hindus in India. We collaborate with all peoples who groan under the same yoke as us.

Comrades, we remain true to the pledge we made in Baku, namely to struggle together with you against the imperialists. We greet you today with the same feelings as we did a year ago. In particular, we thank the French and Italian comrades for the honesty that they have displayed. So long as the Third International remains true to the promises it undertook with respect to

---

Greek, Serbian, and Montenegrin governments, which aimed to partition the country, Albania became a battleground in the first Balkan War. Albania's independence was recognised by the 1913 treaty ending that war. After being occupied during World War I at various points by the armies of several foreign powers, Albania won admission to the League of Nations and recognition as a sovereign state in 1920.

20. Formerly part of the Ottoman Empire, the southeastern part of Thrace – the European portion of present-day Turkey – was occupied by Greek and Entente forces during the Greek-Turkish War of 1919–22.

21. An effective colony of Britain since the early nineteenth century, India in 1921 was in the midst of an upsurge of anticolonial struggle known as the non-cooperation movement. Begun in 1920 under the leadership of Mohandas K. Gandhi, the movement sought to resist British occupation through nonviolent means.

the freedom struggle of Eastern peoples, we will stand with you as true and sincere comrades in struggle. We are convinced that the Communist Party of Russia will hold the cause of liberating the East close to its heart and will exert the necessary pressure on the governments so that the peoples of the old tsarist empire, the Muslim population in particular, will secure their rights and freedom as set down in the principles of communism. This population suffered unspeakable atrocities under the tsarist regime and paid in blood to help establish the soviet order.

In this way the imperialist propaganda among the Eastern peoples will collapse of its own accord.

*Arabia*:[22] As we all know, Arabia was torn from the Ottoman Empire on the pretext of freeing the Arabian population from Turkish barbarism. Arabia was promised full equality. In reality, however, the country fell into the hands of the French and British conquerors. As everyone knows, despite the enormous sums paid for the country by the French and British governments, instead of peace there is oppression and pogroms.

On 24 June, two bullets grazed the cuff of General Gouraud, while striking down his interpreter and Haqqi al-'Azm, whom the French had appointed as head of the Syrian government.[23] This clearly shows what credence can be given to stories spread everywhere by the French that the Syrian population greeted them with delight and enthusiasm. Comrades, Syria will be the grave of French imperialism. The French colonial troops are a danger for you just as for us. But if we recall the Sepoy rebellion in India in 1857,[24] we will understand that these troops can be very useful to us. Meanwhile, France's ally, Britain, has set up a princedom in the eastern part of Jordan, appointing the previous emir of Syria, Faisal, as king of Mesopotamia. They are setting

---

22. At the start of World War I, most of the Arabian Peninsula was in the hands of the Ottoman Empire. Beginning in 1916, with help from British forces, an anti-Ottoman revolt spread throughout the region. With Turkey's defeat in the War, Britain became the dominant power in most of Arabia, with Syria and Lebanon coming under French rule. Arabia is here defined to include Syria and Palestine, mandated respectively to France and Britain.

23. Following dissolution of the Ottoman Empire, an independent kingdom of Syria was established in May 1920. In July, French troops defeated Syrian forces and occupied Damascus. A nationalist uprising began against the French occupation, lasting until 1923, to which the French responded with brutal repression. In June 1921, nationalist forces attempted to assassinate French high commissioner Henri Gouraud and the French-appointed prime minister Haqqi al-'Azm.

24. The Sepoy uprising that broke out in 1857 was a rebellion by Indian troops (sepoys) in the service of the British East India Company. The movement was savagely suppressed by British troops, with hundreds of captured sepoys bayoneted or fired from cannons.

a trap for the French imperialists. Let us hope that conflicts will quickly arise between the French and the British, which will bring us great benefits.

In central Arabia, the emir, Ibn Saud, continues resistance against foreign invasion. The great sheik of the Senussis, Sayyid Ahmad Al-Sharif, is in Mesopotamia. His organisation is active in Africa among a population of twenty million. They have contributed substantially to beating back the Italian conquerors.[25] Around him are other leaders: Ibn Rashid, the emir of Najd; Hajim, leader of the Anayzah; Hougeimi, leader of the Shammar. Together they are developing the revolutionary organisation and offering resistance that the fake kings imposed by the British cannot withstand. The mere fact that the British now maintain 120,000 troops in Mesopotamia and are spending £60 million shows the scope achieved by the revolutionary movement in these countries.[26]

*Yemen*:[27] Imam Yahya, elected by the population of four million, is mounting effective resistance against the foreign oppressors. The revolutionaries in Yemen, working hand in hand with our comrades, recently drove the British out of Hodeida [Al Hudaydah].

Comrades, we are firmly resolved to apply the principles that we adopted last year in Baku. We will always work in close alliance with the oppressed people and are convinced that final victory will be ours.

Comrades, we must now repeat what we said last year. The imperialist war that began in 1914 is not yet over. The insatiable imperialist predators will long continue to throttle each other for domination of the Eastern peoples – only in the end to be overthrown by the oppressed. Let us make all preparations for the world revolution, and at a fitting moment rise up together to win our freedom. Time is on our side. Let us work bravely and with self-sacrifice. Final victory will be ours, because we are the oppressed. Justice is on our side. Nothing can prevail against truth and justice.

Comrades, delegates from each one of the countries mentioned above have already given the [ECCI] Bureau a report on their country. We hope that

---

25. The word 'Italian' does not appear in the Turkish-language original of this report that was published in *Liva el-Islam*. The struggle in Mesopotamia was against the British; Senussi activity against the Italians took place in Libya.

26. Iraq, previously known as Mesopotamia, was carved out of the Ottoman Empire by the British and French following Turkey's defeat in World War I, and it remained under British military occupation. An uprising by nationalist forces began in 1920, lasting into 1922. Iraq was given formal independence in 1932.

27. Prior to World War I control of Yemen was divided between the Ottoman Empire in the north and the British Empire in the south. With Turkey's defeat in the War, the north became independent under the rulership of the imam Yahya Mahmud al-Mutawakkil, who sought to bring the south under his control. A British force occupying Hodeida on the western coast was driven out in January 1921.

unifying all these efforts will make them much more effective. Comrades, we are convinced that this movement to combat imperialism will triumph, speeded to victory by your assistance.

**Zinoviev** (Chair): Comrades, with your permission we will publish this document in the press and include it in the proceedings. It is impossible to translate it right away. I would also like to say the following on behalf of the Bureau. As you know, the Communist International has had a very clear stand on the national question since its founding congress. The Communist International decided to promote the beginnings of the workers' movement, of a Communist movement, in all oppressed, colonial countries. That is the first task of the Communist International.

At the same time, the Communist International resolved to support every genuine revolutionary movement of oppressed peoples and of colonial countries against imperialism. The Communist International is convinced that only the victory of proletarian revolution can genuinely liberate the oppressed peoples. Our slogan is, *Proletarians and oppressed peoples of every country, unite in common struggle against imperialism and for communism!*

We must, of course, combat every form of nationalism. We are well aware that Communists are murdered just as despicably in Kemal's Turkey as in Social-Democratic-bourgeois Germany. It goes without saying that the Communist International will fiercely combat such methods of struggle and the suppression of Communists in general. However, where there is a genuine, broad revolutionary movement – perhaps semi-nationalist, but still genuinely revolutionary, the Communist International will support this movement, to the extent that it is directed against imperialism. The world proletariat will lead all such movements and march in their front ranks. (*Applause*)

**Kolarov** (Chair): Comrades, I give the floor to Comrade Kasyan, representing the Communist Party of Armenia.

The history of the Armenian peoples is among the most tragic recorded in world history. They were always victims of race hatred promoted and utilised by the barbaric despotism of Turkey. In vain did this people appeal to the humanitarian feelings of the so-called civilised nations. The only result of their pleadings was butchery. During the European war, Armenia sought again to achieve its freedom and its right to exist, relying on the Entente, which offered to make its forces available. Armenia sought to achieve its freedom and its right to exist, but once again it was disappointed. It fell victim to a new wave of fanaticism.[28]

---

28. In the years following 1915, hundreds of thousands of Armenians were deported by forces of the Ottoman Empire in conditions of such neglect and brutality that a

After this last wave of slaughter, the Armenian people turned to Russia, resolved to follow the example of the Russian proletariat. Under the leadership of Soviet Russia, the Armenian people rose up against its own bourgeoisie, against its own social patriots, and proclaimed the Soviet Republic of Armenia.[29] (*Applause*)

Comrade Kasyan, who has come here as a representative of the Armenian people, is among the oldest and most courageous members of the Armenian and Russian Communist Party. He shared the experiences and enthusiasm of the Russian proletariat and was able to adapt these ideas to the masses of Armenian proletarians and peasants. I am certain that I express the feelings of the entire congress when I greet, in Comrade Kasyan, the Armenian soviet republic and the revolutionary Armenian people. (*Applause*)

**Sarkis I. Kasyan** (Communist Party of Armenia) Comrades, there is not a corner of the world where the imperialists do not carry out shameful and base deeds under the cover of beautiful and pompous words. One of these corners in the Near East is Armenia. The Entente imperialists, especially Britain, attempted from the time of the October Revolution to create a base in Armenia for their struggle against Soviet Russia and against the Communist and socialist ideas spreading across the East. They sought to establish influence in order to serve their predatory interests. From the beginning this supposedly independent Armenia was a prisoner of the Entente and served as its compliant tool. Armenia was led by a petty-bourgeois party, the Dashnaks, similar to the Mensheviks and Social Revolutionaries. As a true servant of the Entente, this party carried out the Entente's plans fully and completely, harming broad layers of the population. Constant war with the neighbouring peoples, bloody clashes within the country, persecution and reprisals against the workers and peasants who dared to express discontent with the social and agrarian policies of the government, brought the country to the edge of ruin.

In view of a new direction in the shah's governmental policy, the Dashnaks decided to drive back the Turks by armed force. The people, who had experienced three years of administration by the Dashnak Party, were convinced from experience that the orientation to Britain was leading to destruction.

---

high proportion died. Thousands more were summarily massacred. Many estimates put the death toll at well over a million.

29. With the defeat of the Ottoman Empire in World War I and the collapse of Russian tsarism, the Dashnaks, an Armenian nationalist party, became the ruling party in a sovereign Armenia, with recognition from the Entente powers. In September 1920 Turkish forces attacked the country. In November, as Armenian military resistance collapsed, Soviet troops entered the country in support of a rebellion by pro-Soviet forces and ousted the Dashnak government. Armenia was proclaimed a soviet republic on 29 November.

Unable to bear this any longer, they rose up against the leadership of this party and the government, in order to resist imperialism.

With the establishment of soviet power, the national conflicts came to an end. The Armenians and Muslims began to live as brothers, as if they had never been divided by enmity. However, thanks to the intrusion of imperialism, the land was completely ruined and devastated. We were unable to restore the country's economy quickly on our own. Our resources were inadequate to meet the population's urgent needs. Help could not be expected from anywhere, although our great mother, Soviet Russia, and fraternal Azerbaijan made every effort to assist us. We were blockaded. On one side, Menshevik Georgia blocked the railways, and what they let through was stopped by the Turkish high command. The Turkish command did not allow us to send goods to Iran in return for grain. The criminal and counterrevolutionary Dashnak party tried to utilise this hopeless situation in the hopes of help from the Georgian Mensheviks and the exploiting layers in the country itself. They staged a revolt against the soviet government.

We were partly to blame here. Our party failed to carry out the policy dictated by objective conditions in the country.[30] Instead it was impatient, seeking to accelerate the transformation of the bourgeois regime. Nonetheless, we succeeded in defeating the enemy, who fled into the mountains, where they received help from the British imperialists. The effort to put an end to the civil war in our country peacefully did not succeed. However, the overturn in Georgia and the withdrawal of the Turks certainly helped the soviet government in Armenia to stabilise.

The only danger that can threaten us, comrades, is Turkey, which continues to engage in imperialist efforts on our border. Now, after the establishment of the Armenian soviet republic, we have declared that soviet Armenia renounces its treaty[31] and will speak a revolutionary language in seeking a resolution of the disputed questions. We are sincere in seeking peace with Turkey and harbour no animosity against it. But should any real danger threaten us from its side, the workers and peasants will defend their freedom and their homeland with arms in hand, confident of the support of the great Russian Socialist Soviet republic. (*Applause*)

**Kolarov** (Chair): Comrades, I give the floor to Comrade Tskhakaia, representing the Communist Party of Georgia.

---

30. On this, see Lenin's 14 April 1921 letter to the Communists of Azerbaijan, Georgia, Armenia, Dagestan, and the Mountaineer Republic, in *LCW*, 32, pp. 316–18.
31. Presumably a reference to the Treaty of Sèvres, which allocated to Armenia territory in what is now north-east Turkey. See p. 159, n. 18.

The people, the workers and peasants of Georgia, have also followed the glorious example of the Russian proletariat by recently founding a soviet republic.[32]

In greeting Comrade Tskhakaia, I cannot conceal the fact that other representatives of the Georgian peasants and workers are presently active in Europe, seeking to deceive the international proletariat and win it for the cause of counterrevolution. Zhordania, Chkheidze, and other betrayers of the socialist and proletarian cause have turned for support to their brothers, the social traitors of Europe, and to the Second and Two-and-a-Half Internationals. But we can reassure the Georgian people that the efforts of these social traitors will be fruitless. The reception that Comrade Tskhakaia has received from the Communist International congress demonstrates to the entire world that the international revolutionary proletariat stands with the dictatorship of the proletariat and the peasants of Georgia.

Comrade Tskhakaia has the floor.

**Mikhail G. Tskhakaia** (Georgia): (*Tskhakaia mentions the treacherous role of the Georgian Mensheviks during the revolutions of 1905 and 1917 and especially after the October uprising and speaks at greater length about the country's political and economic situation on the eve of the February–March 1921 revolution.*)

The [former Georgian government's] rejection of the Brest-Litovsk Treaty, their breach with Soviet Russia, their independent relations with the imperialists and Turkey, and the subjugation of the country to these powers – all this opened the eyes of the workers and peasants of Georgia. The imperialism of the bourgeoisie and the landowners and the nationalism of the Mensheviks were exposed. While rejecting civil war [in Russia], the Mensheviks carried it out themselves, against their own workers and peasants, in alliance with the imperialists. Indeed, from the end of 1917 to the moment when Georgia was sovietised, that is, February–March 1921, civil war in the country was more or less uninterrupted.

Toward the end of this period, the Mensheviks were fully discredited. Politically and economically bankrupt, they had brought the country to ruin. The people rose up, and there were revolts all across Georgia. In a country where tsarism fought for sixty years, the Red Army organised by the

---

32. On 16 February 1921, Red Army troops entered Georgia in support of a local rebellion by pro-soviet forces against the rule of the Menshevik-led independent republic of Georgia (established in May 1918), and by mid-March had completed their occupation of the country. Georgia became an independent Soviet republic linked by treaty with Russia.

rebellious workers and peasants did not need even half of sixty days. Thanks to the complete bankruptcy of the Mensheviks, Georgia became a soviet state.

The Menshevik claims to the contrary are refuted by the events of the past period and also by what the Mensheviks themselves admitted a few weeks before they were overthrown. Only White Guard ideologues could suspect Soviet Russia of striving for conquest or occupation, when it was fully occupied with restoring its own economy. Chkheidze, Tseretelli, and company are attempting now in Western Europe to distort the historical facts and to show that they had organised an ideal democratic state, a paradise, that even their masters, the heroes of the Second International, came to visit. Why then did Zhordania, in reports made in November–December 1920, almost on the eve of the revolution, admit frankly that the situation was catastrophic? There was no way out, he said, unless some magic potion, some new democratic imperialism could be discovered. But alchemy and astrology will only get you so far. The Georgian Mensheviks condemned themselves to defeat by their treacherous policies toward the workers and peasants of their own country.

The Mensheviks' conduct in the first days after the revolution was particularly shameful. They plundered the entire country and shipped out on French vessels whatever had been left by four years of pillage of the unfortunate country by the German, Turkish, and Entente imperialists. They carried off not only gold, gems, and other valuables, but the last carloads of sugar as well. They ran off with the entire supply of quinine and condemned the workers and peasants of Georgia to death from the malaria prevalent there. The people speeded them on their way with curses. In Batumi, their army melted away from 30,000 to 3,000 men, and even among them, despite a promise of five years' pay and clothing in advance, only twenty men went with them. These gentlemen fled in the dark of the night with the people's property assembled by theft and saved themselves from the anger of the people under protection of French cannon. Disregarding the repeated assurances of amnesty by the central revolutionary committee, the Menshevik leaders decided not to stay in the country, which they had so long and so shamefully betrayed, and where they could expect nothing but contempt and hatred.

Zhordania, Chkheidze, Tseretelli, and company: your hopes are in vain, your efforts are futile. Workers' and peasants' Georgia, which has survived four years of civil war, will not again accept your tutelage. You will not be saved either by distortion of historical fact or by your flight into the arms of Lloyd George, Millerand, Pilsudski, and the like. We are convinced that Georgia, in alliance with the fraternal soviet republics and under the leadership of the Communist International, will earn a rich harvest, both in the wheat fields and in the building of socialism, of communism, of a new communist order. And when the entire East sees Kolkhida rampant,[33] it will in the same fashion sow the seeds of communism and the soviet government.

**Kolarov** (chair): Comrades, there are still eight speakers from different countries of the East on our list. All these comrades must speak. But this discussion must absolutely end in this session, and the Presidium therefore proposes that the speeches not be immediately translated. They will be translated later.

Secondly, the Presidium proposes that the speaking time be reduced to five minutes.

Are there any objections? Since I see no objections, the proposal is accepted.

I now give the floor to Comrade Abilov, delegate of the Communist Party of Azerbaijan, which has also founded a soviet republic.[34]

**Abilov** (Communist Party of Azerbaijan): Comrades, it is of course impossible to say everything that must be said about Azerbaijan in five minutes. I will make an effort to be brief. Many comrades who have come here from Western Europe obviously do not know Azerbaijan. So I will say here, as I did at the trade-union congress, that the party of Azerbaijan, of Baku, began its struggle in the nineties alongside the Russian proletariat and has worked throughout the intervening years toward achieving soviet power. Like Georgia, Armenia, and Ukraine, Azerbaijan formed part of the Russian Empire. After the October Revolution, the proletariat in Baku took power and proclaimed a soviet government, which existed only in Baku and was not able to extend its reach into the rest of the country. As a result of betrayal by the Social Revolutionaries and the Mensheviks, who summoned the British to Baku, the soviet government in Azerbaijan fell in 1918. Twenty-six glorious comrades of ours, the commissars, were shot by the executioners of Denikin and the British.[35]

Once the British had taken the reins, they declared Azerbaijan an independent country, although this existed only on paper. British occupation troops held Azerbaijan and repressed every revolutionary movement, arresting workers along with their representatives and leaders. Nonetheless, the

---

33. Kolkhida is a territory in Georgia on the shore of the Black Sea, named after the ancient kingdom of Colchis.

34. In late April 1920 a rising by Communist forces in Baku overturned a government previously sustained by British troops, founding the Azerbaijan Soviet Socialist Republic.

35. The Baku soviet regime, known also as the Baku Commune, lasted from 11 April to 25 July 1918. Under pressure from invading British and Turkish troops, it was ousted by a government of right-wing SRs, Mensheviks, and Dashnaks. The new government arrested twenty-six soviet leaders, who fell into the hands of Russian anti-soviet forces and were executed the night of 19–20 September 1918.

proletariat carried on its struggle tirelessly. On 27 April it rose up and, with the help of the glorious Red Army, proclaimed the dictatorship of the proletariat. The counterrevolution did not recede and continued its work. But all these attempts were suppressed by the mighty power of the Red Army and the Azerbaijan proletariat. The soviet government was consolidated.

Recently, the first congress of soviets was convened in Azerbaijan. This congress established the central and local soviet governments. There is now a solid soviet government in all the district capitals and in the countrywide, in which the landless peasants and workers take part.

The Communist Party of Azerbaijan, now holding its Fourth Congress, has led the working class of Baku and Azerbaijan from the October Revolution to the present day. The Communist Party of Azerbaijan now counts sixteen thousand members – after four successive re-registrations, which excluded from the party forces who had pushed their way in for egotistic reasons. The Azerbaijan trade unions include 150,000 organised workers, who are led by our party and by the Azerbaijan trade-union council.

Comrades, Azerbaijan has enormous importance for the revolution in the East. Azerbaijan is the only Muslim republic in which the councils hold power. Azerbaijan is the gateway to the East and provides an example for our Eastern comrades. The Azerbaijan proletariat is not only struggling to consolidate its power; it has also fought for the liberation of Georgia and Armenia, and it sends its best party workers to the East. All the revolutionary forces of the East are politically educated and trained in Baku, before being sent back to the East. That is why Azerbaijan is very important for the revolution in the East. That is why, after the Second Congress, the Communist International convened the First Congress of the Peoples of the East in Baku. It organised the Council for Propaganda and Action of the Peoples of the East, which trains party workers for the East, under the leadership of the Communist International, and leads the entire movement in the East.[36] (*Applause*)

**M.N. Roy** (India): I have been given five minutes for my report. Since the topic could not be exhausted even in an hour, I will use these five minutes to launch an energetic protest.

The way that the Eastern question has been handled at this congress is purely opportunistic and more appropriate for a congress of the Second International. It is impossible to reach any specific conclusions in the few comments that delegates from the East are permitted to make.

I protest against this way of dealing with the Eastern question. It was included in the congress agenda by decision of a meeting of the Executive.

---

36. For the Council for Propaganda and Action, see p. 231, n. 93.

But during the entire course of the congress, no attention was paid to this question. Finally, yesterday, there was a session of the commission, but it presented a very pathetic spectacle. Not a single representative of the European and American delegations was present. Because of the confusion attending the congress, the commission had not been constituted.[37] It decided not to adopt any theoretical resolution on the Eastern question. This decision is absolutely incorrect and should not be allowed to stand. I therefore call on the congress to refer the Eastern question to a constituted commission and give it the serious treatment it deserves.

**Zhang Tailei** (China): I had intended to give you a picture of the Communist movement of China and a rough description of the revolutionary forces in struggle against imperialism. But my time is too short for that. I will only touch on the importance of the movement in the Far East.

Japanese imperialism poses an important and urgent problem, demanding solution not only for the Far East but for the entire world proletariat. So long as this problem is not solved, Japan will be a constant danger for Soviet Russia and will bar the road to communism for the peoples of the Far East.

But that is not all. Since the War, Japan has become an imperialist state just as strong as Britain and the United States. If imperialist Japan is able to extend its control over all of China in the way that it already does over the north of the country, the Japanese government will not only have rich revenue and an excellent labour force at its disposal, but will use these resources in a struggle against the proletariat. This is a severe impediment for the world revolution. That is why the Communist International and the Communist parties of the West need to devote much more attention and give more support to the movement in the Far East than they have done in the past. The destruction of Japanese imperialism will signify the collapse of one of the three pillars of world capitalism. Only then can we overthrow world capitalism, and only then will the world revolution complete its work.

The Chinese proletariat and other revolutionary forces in China can be of great assistance to you in this great task, if only you will pay more attention to China's development. For us, this is precisely the time to work for communism. Young students are now rising up against China's old social structure. Many of them are at a crossroads and will follow us, if we provide them with help. We need to lead these forces along the correct path and not leave them to anarchism and reformism. Since the Russian proletarian revolution, the Chinese workers have begun to awaken. There are a great many small-scale

---

37. The decision to establish the Eastern Commission was made in Session 16, p. 635.

strikes in China. We must bring this nascent movement under our red banner and not let it go yellow. Later on it would cost us a great deal of effort to win their sympathies. The lumpenproletariat, a rather large percentage of China's population, is not class-conscious but is revolutionary. If we could encompass them in our party, it would greatly advance our cause. The Chinese proletariat has already demonstrated, through its participation in the war against Kolchak and Denikin, that it is made up of good fighters.[38] But this layer could also become dangerous if we do not pay attention to it and if it is misused in struggle against the proletariat by the capitalists. This was done by the Russian and French imperialists, who utilised them as front-line labourers, and by the Japanese imperialist government in police duties in Manchuria and Shantung [Shandong].

In the coming world revolution, it will depend largely on the Communist Party of China and – above all – on the support of the Communist International whether the rich natural and human resources of China fight with the capitalists against the proletariat or with the proletariat against capitalism.

Long live the world revolution!

Long live the Communist International!

**Nam Man-ch'un** (Communist Party of Korea): Korea, with twenty million inhabitants, was long a vassal of economically backward China and was torn by disturbances. Unable to develop its productive forces, it was locked in conditions of stagnation. It is primarily an agricultural country. Its natural resources became an apple of discord between imperialist Japan and tsarist Russia. Japanese imperialism proved to be stronger and more persistent, and it drove out tsarist Russia. In 1910 it robbed Korea of its independence, converting it into a colony.[39]

From this point on, the land of 'morning tranquillity' became the prey of greedy and predatory Japanese imperialism. Its economic and social conditions changed with dizzying speed.

Japanese imperialism, in its greed, made no efforts to raise the country's economic conditions. Instead, it devoted all its attention to sucking the lifeblood from the country, in order to extract the greatest possible profit from its colony.

The Japanese occupation administration has now been active for ten years in the form of a capitalist colonisation firm, Chek Si Choi Sa (Company for Exploitation of the Colony), which received material and moral support from

---

38. During the Russian Civil War, some 50,000 Chinese immigrants fought in the Red Army.
39. Korea became a protectorate of Japan in 1905 and was effectively annexed in 1910.

the Japanese government.[40] Given the legal right to acquire land on the peninsula, the firm gained possession of all crown land and almost all peasant holdings. Masses of peasants were driven from their land and forced either to emigrate abroad, in Manchuria, or to lease land from Chek Si Choi Sa under usurious conditions. Rent was 50%–70% of the crop in kind or in money. In years of crop failure it was 100% or more of the crop's value. They could also enter service with Chek Si Choi Sa or its agents as day labourers, or work in the mines or pits or factories, where for a working day of twelve to thirteen hours they received only a third of the wages of a Japanese worker. Otherwise they filled the growing ranks of the jobless.

The most recent Japanese statistics, from 1920, report a native population of 16,912,800, of which 7,843,658 work as day labourers and in the lumber industry, while 518,906 work in the mines and factories and in transport and the fishery. The others are the jobless, the tenant farmers (who have either their own piece of land or no land at all), and, finally, a thin layer of the native bourgeoisie, most of whom are in the service of the Japanese capitalists. That is a rough outline of the economic conditions of the population.

However, working people also suffer no small degree of political servitude. Above all, they are deprived of participation in the country's political life. They have no rights; they enjoy no protection in law. The laws introduced by the Japanese government on the peninsula protect only the interests of the Japanese, at the cost of Koreans' interests. Thus a Japanese who has, for example, killed a Korean, gets away with a small fine, while a Korean guilty of the same crime will be condemned to death. The schools are closed, and those that are still open are energetically carrying out Japanisation.

The masses, peace-loving by nature, have been driven to despair by these policies of Japanese imperialism. All the accumulated hatred against the foreign bandits exploded on 1 March 1919 in the form of an uprising.[41] In order to suppress the rebellion, the Japanese government sent in three divisions of police. The horrors and cruelty of Japanese militarism led even the cold and dispassionate British and American journalists to make passionate

---

40. This is apparently a reference to the Oriental Development Company. Subsidised by the Japanese government, this company was set up in 1908. One of its purposes was to force Korean peasants into debt and then drive them off their lands, turning it over to Japanese landlords and opening the way for settlers. By 1918 at least 98,000 such Japanese owner-families had been resettled as proprietors in Korea.

41. On 1 March 1919 Korea's movement of resistance to the Japanese occupation staged mass rallies throughout the country, with an estimated two million participating in peaceful demonstrations. A declaration of independence was announced. Japanese forces responded with brutal repression to suppress the demonstrations, killing 7,500 and arresting 47,000.

appeals. The forms of torture applied to revolutionaries surpassed in cruelty and inhumanity those of the medieval inquisition. When a Japanese spy was killed in Suwon during 1919, all inhabitants of the village were driven into the church, which was barricaded and burnt, with the women and children inside.[42] The atrocities of the Japanese army in Kando are indescribable.[43] In December 1920, seventy villages were literally eradicated from the earth and thousands of peaceful inhabitants, including women and children, were shot. During two years of struggle (1919–20), 80,000 people were killed by the Japanese executioners, while 150,000 were thrown in jail. We must stress here the similarity of Japanese imperialism's methods of struggle in Korea with those in the Russian Far East, where they dealt in the same way with the peaceful population.[44]

Despite all these atrocities and all this torture, the masses are irreconcilable. The Russian proletarian revolution has inspired even more enthusiasm among the proletarian masses, who feel there is no going back. Their slogan is, 'Final victory or death!' It is a tragic situation for the Korean workers and peasants. Left to themselves, as victims of pillage by Japanese imperialism, they are condemned to perish or to bleed to death in an unequal struggle. There is no way out.

The toiling masses of Korea put all their hopes in world social revolution, and their interests lie in supporting it. Who will lead this revolution, now that it is moving into a new phase? During the last two years, the nationalists have shown their utter incapacity to lead the revolutionary struggle, and they are now discredited. There is only one answer to this question: the newly created Communist Party of Korea, formed at a founding conference in Irkutsk in May 1921, with support from the Communists led by the Communist International and from proletarians around the world.

**Taro Yoshihara** (Communist Party of Japan): Comrades, I bring you the revolutionary greetings of the Communist Party that has just been organised in Japan. A few days ago, I received the party's resolutions, statutes, and manifestos.

---

42. On 15 April 1921, Japanese troops entered the Korean town of Suwon. Locking thirty residents inside a Christian church, they set it on fire and burned them alive. Thirty-one other houses in the town were also set on fire, as well as 317 houses in fifteen villages in the vicinity.
43. In the fall of 1920, 15,000 Japanese soldiers were sent to the Korean community of Chientao (Kando in Korean) in Manchuria, a stronghold of the Korean independence movement. Over 3,100 inhabitants were murdered, and the Japanese troops burned 2,404 homes, 31 schools, 10 churches, and over 800,000 bushels of grain.
44. For the Japanese intervention in the Soviet Far East, see p. 657, n. 12.

Since we are speaking of Japan, a country so reactionary that our revolutionary comrades in the West consider it almost impossible to organise the population there, we have all the more reason to congratulate ourselves that the radical movement in Japan has taken its first steps. Our main goal must now be to develop this movement until we finally overthrow the capitalist system and establish the dictatorship of the proletariat.

While the bloody butchery was under way in Europe, the United States and Japan, fishing in murky waters, had a free hand in all the world's markets. America monopolised the entire European market, while Japan gained control in the Far East.

That was not enough to satisfy Japanese imperialism. For years it had set its sights on the limitless natural resources of Siberia and Central Asia, which would enable it to provide the needed raw materials for Japan's constantly growing industries.

After the October Revolution, the Allies organised the Czechoslovaks against Soviet Russia. They used the excuse that they had to fight the German and Hungarian danger in Siberia. The Entente governments sent in their own expeditionary forces, in order to support the Czechs in their bold plan.[45]

Japan, which had always dreamed of the natural resources of Siberia, did not want to be left out of the game. It was not content merely to aid the Allies in their humanitarian mission – lending support to the Czechs. Instead, it exceeded the Entente governments in the number of troops utilised and in the character of the struggle.

The Czechs' game in Siberia collapsed. The Allies withdrew their troops. Kolchak is dead, along with his government. Semyonov has been chased out of his 'kingdom' of Chita by the workers and peasants of the Far East.[46] But

---

45. The Czechoslovak Legions were Czech and Slovak volunteer units formed within the imperial Russian army, beginning in 1914. As the War progressed, the legions became composed primarily of prisoners of war and deserters from the Austro-Hungarian army, growing into a force that peaked at over 60,000. After the October Revolution an agreement was reached to evacuate the legions to France through Vladivostok. But in May 1918 they rebelled against Soviet power and linked up with the White armies. The Czechoslovak Legions were finally evacuated through Vladivostok in early 1920, after which they formed the core of the army of the newly created state of Czechoslovakia. 'German and Hungarian danger' referred to the Austro-Hungarian empire.

46. Gen. G.M. Semyonov was a White Army leader and commander of the so-called Provisional Siberian Government with headquarters in Chita. In early 1919 Semyonov, supported by Japanese troops, declared himself ataman of the Transbaikal Cossack Host. Semyonov's forces were driven out by the Red Army in November 1920, after which he retreated to Primorski Territory on Russia's Pacific Coast, before he was forced to abandon Russia altogether in September 1921. Vladivostok is in Primorski Territory.

the Japanese are still in Siberia. Japanese troops hold the southern part of the Primorski territory. They are holding a territory that belongs to the working masses of the Far East. But they are not satisfied with that. They are also setting in motion counterrevolutionary conspiracies against the workers and peasants of the Far Eastern Republic and Soviet Russia.

An example of this is provided by the recent 'occupation' of Vladivostok by the bloodthirsty gangs of Semyonov, protected by Japanese bayonets. Vladivostok and the southern part of the Primorski region are, however, only one link in the chain of Japanese imperialism's intervention and its counterrevolutionary plans. The Chinese Eastern railroad and the surrounding territory, a strip of land twenty miles wide on either side of the railroad, has been occupied by Japanese troops and is being used by Russian counterrevolutionaries as their base for operations. The railroad also serves as a communications link between the counterrevolutionaries in Manchuria, directly supported by the Japanese, and the counterrevolutionaries led by the bloodthirsty Baron Ungern in Mongolia.[47] Both these forces are supplied by the Japanese with abundant munitions.

During the War, Japan overwhelmed the markets of the Far East (including the Dutch Indies) with its low-quality goods. As soon as the War ended, it was apparent that Japan could not compete with the higher-quality goods coming from the United States. This led to an economic crisis in Japan. Factories shut down, and work halted in the mines. Unemployment grew; banks and businesses large and small went bankrupt; wages were reduced. No wonder that the discontent of workers and social ferment increased more and more.

The American capitalists are not content to control the markets of Europe. They view Europe as unreliable as a field for large and small investments. The revolutionary ferment in the countries of Europe has prompted the American capitalists to turn their eyes to the East, which seems to them to be a secure field for exploitation. They are striving to conquer the markets of the Far East with their surplus goods. At the same time, their appetite is aroused by the natural resources of China. The Japanese imperialists are pursuing the same prize. A clash between these two vultures is therefore inevitable. In the meantime, the workers of China are groaning under not only the yoke of their own landowners, their bourgeoisie and their rulers, but also that of foreign imperialists.

---

47. In 1919 Mongolia was taken over by Russian White Army troops led by Baron Roman von Ungern-Sternberg, who established a regime of murderous brutality. Mongolian revolutionaries approached Soviet Russia for help, and a joint Mongol-Red Army unit captured the Mongolian capital in July 1921.

Korea is Japan's Ireland. It has been nailed to the cross by the Japanese imperialists, aided by Korean estate owners, traitors, and spies. Surely Korea is the most unfortunate country of the world. The Japanese hangmen deny to its population even the most basic political and economic rights. Every attempt of Korean workers and peasants to win even the most minimal measure of freedom is mercilessly suppressed by the Japanese army. Nonetheless, there is quite a strong movement in Korea against Japanese imperialism and for national independence. Although this movement is to some degree nationalist in character, it should be warmly greeted everywhere, and in particular by the Communists. If the Koreans succeed in achieving their national independence, this will significantly weaken Japanese imperialism while greatly strengthening the revolutionary movement in the Far East, particularly in Korea and Japan.

Japan offers fertile soil for Communist propaganda. The scope for our propaganda there cannot be underestimated. The upsurge of large-scale industry and wholesale trade in Japan has resulted in the gradual ruin of small business. This increases the size of the industrial proletariat. The Japanese proletariat is organising in industry, in order to do battle with the capitalists' growing power. The rice disturbances of 1918 taught the Japanese workers the value of mass action. During the strike, all the leaders were jailed, and nonetheless the strike movement grew without interruption.[48]

Recently, sabotage has become a strong weapon in the hands of Japanese workers. In May last year, the striking electricity workers of Osaka were able, through sabotage, to set free their leaders. This was the first experience of this kind in Japan.[49]

Communists of Korea and Japan should utilise the situation to carry out tireless agitation among the broad masses. They should organise and take part, directly or indirectly, in all movements, seeking to increase their effectiveness. The decisive blow against capitalists must be dealt by the revolutionary forces of Japan themselves.

Japan's growing population forces the imperialist government to be on the lookout for new colonies. Expanding its colonial possessions has become an urgent economic necessity for Japan. Japanese imperialism did not suffer from the World War. Its need for territory is now greater than before the War.

---

48. When the price of rice doubled in Japan in 1918, protests and rebellions occurred throughout the country from July to September. An estimated 10 million people participated in 33 cities, 104 towns, and 97 villages. Some 50,000 troops were employed to suppress the uprising. Over 8,000 were arrested, and 5,000 were jailed, with a few sentenced to life imprisonment.

49. The term 'sabotage' referred to work slowdowns in disputes with employers.

Japanese imperialism dates from the sixteenth century, when the feudal lords demanded the extension of Japanese power over Korea and China. However, these countries were capable of defending themselves against Japanese attacks.

During the last fifty years, through methodical and systematic efforts, Japan has succeeded in seizing Korea and part of China. The policies that it carried out in 1894, 1904, 1914, and 1921 mark out definite periods in the life of the Japanese government.[50]

The revolutionary forces in Japan are much weaker than in any other growing industrial country. Japanese capitalists, by contrast, grow stronger and stronger, because they join forces to drive out the smaller capitalists. Korea is now subjugated and quite helpless.

Japan's diplomats are no less cunning than those of other countries. While Japan makes a show of its friendly relations with Great Britain, it is bending every effort to promote a rebellion in India against the British government. Similarly, Japan helped Dr. Sun Yat-sen to chase away the Chinese imperial family. Yet when Sun Yat-sen was at the point of success in establishing a republic, Japan began to support Yuan Shikai, who favoured a monarchy.[51] In this way Japan kept China in conditions of inner division and upheaval.

The power slumbering within the Chinese people is inactive, for now; in times to come it will provide good service in the class struggle. China possesses huge wealth in raw materials of every type. If we should fail to train China's huge population in revolutionary tactics and strategy, the Japanese bourgeoisie could readily convert it into an instrument of foreign capitalists in combating the world revolution.

As we have seen, Japanese imperialism represents a great danger for Communist world revolution. I therefore turn to the Communist International and the Communist parties in the European countries and ask them to come to the

---

50. During the first Sino-Japanese War of 1894–5, fought mainly over control of Korea, Japan was able to gain control over Liaodong Peninsula, Taiwan, and the Penghu Islands.

Japan's victory in the Russo-Japanese War of 1904–5 led to Russia's recognition of Japanese influence in Korea. Russia also signed over leaseholding rights to Port Arthur and ceded Japan the southern half of Sakhalin Island.

After declaring war on German on 29 August 1914, Japan seized all Chinese ports controlled by Germany and, with British help, captured the Pacific Islands that Germany had previously held.

The reference to 1921 is apparently to the Japanese intervention in Siberia.

51. In 1911 Sun Yat-sen led a national revolution in China that overthrew the Qing dynasty. A provisional Republic of China was set up in 1912 with Sun as president, but he was forced to cede power to army commander Yuan Shikai, who, with Japanese support, subsequently sought to proclaim himself emperor.

assistance of comrades in the Far East, who must fight against imperialism in their countries under the most fearful conditions.

Long live the Communist International!

**Kara-Gadiyev** (Turkestan): Comrades, we have heard one of the speakers here describe the Japanese imperialists' mistreatment of the Koreans, subjecting them to oppression and systematic devastation to such a degree that the very description of it makes one's hair stand on end. Another speaker complained that British imperialism oppresses India, where conditions are even worse. Consider Africa, ruled by French imperialism, or – in this or that corner – by Italy, while the Americans conduct systematic destruction on the Atlantic. I will not speak of the past. I will not portray the October Revolution, which is known to all workers and all oppressed peoples. I will just touch on where the root of the evil lies.

Europe has its Eastern question, and so, too, we in Asia have a British question. The British imperialists are the fount of all provocations and the root of evil. If we do not resolve the British question, we cannot resolve the Eastern question. Comrades here said that we must be cautious and begin with preparations, and so on. I can tell you that the Eastern peoples have a distinctive approach, relying entirely on Suvorov's policies.[52] Does it really need a great deal of cogitation to overturn the entire capitalist order in a day and sweep it away? How can this be achieved? If we provide Chinese Turkestan [Xinjiang] with the means of founding the mere beginnings of an underground organisation, using soviet means and under soviet supervision; if we create only small nuclei there, within six months we will see there 100,000 workers with revolutionary convictions.

Comrades, with these 100,000 workers we will accomplish miracles, and induce these fishermen – that's what I call the British – to board their ships and sail away. Then revolution will break out across all Europe, and the British workers – if they do not throw their government in prison – will call it to account. British workers should not fear the revolution in India. Given that the British imperialist government has been able to come to an agreement with India,[53] why would the British workers not be able to reach an accord with the oppressed people of India? And not only the British workers, but those of Germany, France, Austria, and other republics, some of them microscopic.

---

52. The eighteenth-century Russian general A.V. Suvorov was known for his tactics of constant attack.
53. This may be a reference to the Government of India Act that had been adopted by the British Parliament in 1919. That act aimed to transfer certain limited areas of state administration to local Indian authorities.

I see that there has been a minor division among the European delegates, and that there are two currents among the Germans. That is completely impermissible. I am an Asian; I understand little of politics. But still I can see that these two parties are bringing the people to the edge of the abyss. The British, French, and other capitalists will exert themselves to drive a wedge between these parties. That will not only condemn the German people to a century of subjugation; it will possibly put the entire revolution in question. German comrades, you must achieve unity. You must follow the example of the Russian comrades.

Now I will say a few words on the Near East, which is the key to India and to China. Every revolutionary movement in the Near East may well have a purely national character at the start. And in my opinion, we must receive support not only from the Russian workers but from those of Germany, France, Britain, and other countries. The Near East is where the most oppressed workers live, workers who are in the grip of religious prejudices. For example, I was raised to be a mullah. I began studying the Koran when I was twelve years old and I studied it thoroughly – otherwise I would not have been let out of the seminary. However, when I was released from the seminary, I refused to become a mullah.

Comrades, we already have soviet republics in some regions: Azerbaijan, Turkestan. I cannot say that the situation there is all that bad. Conditions are improving, although more effort, more exertion is needed. Some comrades criticise me because I do not belong to the party, and sometimes what I say is not quite right. However, I tell you that I want to see soviet power consolidated, and not only in Turkestan and Azerbaijan. I will be happy to see the day when soviet power exists across the entire surface of the earth. I will be happy to see the day when soviet power around the world does away with the capitalist system.

**Charles-André Julien** (France): Comrades, the French delegation is in principled agreement with the protest by Comrade Roy, who has objected to the way that the Eastern question has been dealt with.

The Executive proposed to include this question on the agenda. In all likelihood, they considered it essential. Nonetheless, consideration of this question was shoved off to the end of the congress, when discussion would necessarily be squeezed to the limit. Moreover the commission, which met here yesterday for the first time, dealt mainly with setting up the list of speakers. In short, we have had a session this evening in which the main role has been played by cinematography.[54]

---

54. The Soviet Commissariat for Public Education's division for cinema and photography was filming portions of the congress, to be featured in a film on 'the entire

Based on the presentations by different comrades, the commission reporter now has the task of determining what are the common features among these different peoples that point toward a single goal, that of combating imperialism. However, these peoples, these different colonies and nations, as we have heard, are for the most part quite different in their inclinations and capacities. The task now is to determine what form imperialism takes and whether the situation in the East is the same today as it was before the War and the Russian Revolution.

All the Eastern peoples are today striving toward a common goal because of the fact that they will not gain liberation from the normal development of capitalism but rather solely and exclusively from that of their own class consciousness. The forms taken by capitalism in the Eastern countries are different from what we see in the West. In the East it did not absorb all the productive forces to the same degree as in the West. It has not transformed relations among the different social classes to the same degree. In the East, capitalism was merely a superstructure, a supplement to the already existing structures, which it for the most part respected. It left untouched the ruling classes and the privileges they enjoyed. It thus did no more than to add foreign rule to the domination existing within each country. This had certain economic consequences that created a commonality or at least a similarity in the problems of all Eastern countries.

Before the War, it was primarily the artisan class that was oppressed. In the West, when an artisan faces ruin, he becomes a proletarian. In the East, by contrast, the artisan becomes an agricultural worker. He returns to the land and becomes a sort of half-slave of the landowner. Moreover, the agricultural system introduced by capitalism in the East is different from ours. There the system is based on maintenance of the large landowner, as is notably the case in India and in Iran. This is not a regime of intensive exploitation, as in the West. The capitalist system in the East is one of extensive production, which does not enable the local farmers to perfect their means of production and always keeps them in a subordinate social status.

Industry, trade, and agriculture are thus carried out differently in the East than in the West. The entire problem of capitalism has a unique character in the East, which is common to all Eastern peoples. This has some consequences that are significant both economically and politically. First, in each country there is a class that has a greater or lesser stake in moving close to the capitalist class. Secondly, there are classes that, despite the disparity in

---

history of the Comintern' to be shown, according to an article in the 25 May 1921 issue of *Moscou*, in 'thirty regional centres and in all the autonomous republics'.

their interests, have one interest in common: the struggle against imperialism, under which they all suffer. That simplifies the problem, but also leads it down a sidetrack.

First of all, there exists in the East a class of large landowners, which has been retained by capitalism in many Eastern countries. It is closely linked to the system established by imperialism and draws advantage from it, just like the foreign exploiter. Secondly, there is an intellectual bourgeoisie, a petty bourgeoisie, for which the existing system has very few advantages. It suffers grievously because its national traditions and strivings, its cultural needs, and its conservatism are violated and trampled underfoot by the feudal aristocracy and by foreign capitalism. This petty bourgeoisie thus has common interests with the factory worker, the ruined artisan, and the farmer, of whom we spoke earlier. Although the endeavours of this class are by their nature democratic rather than communist and differ vastly from the class interests of workers and peasants, we must recognise and take into account that under present conditions the struggle against imperialism unites all these classes. The Communist Party must address the question along these lines.

This challenge was greatly clarified by the Russian Revolution and the War. For the Russian Revolution did not merely proclaim the rights of the people, but also attempted to realise them in life. It created a new organisational form, the soviets, which proved to be much more flexible than they first appeared to be. They are appropriate not only for culturally advanced but also for more primitive peoples. In addition, the War fundamentally reshaped the world economic system. Relationships between Western capitalism and the Eastern countries have shifted. Production in the Western countries declined significantly, and the West was not able to dip into the production of the East as freely as in the past. As a result, in some Eastern countries a new class of artisans took shape, who have pursued their craft or run their little shop since the War – a layer that is becoming more and more significant. The fact that introduction of protective tariffs is now being considered in countries like Turkey shows that in many Eastern countries industrial transformation is more profound than it might seem at first glance.

From all these facts, all these phenomena interacting with one another, there emerges a general spirit of revolt, of independence, a striving for clarity that was not present before the War. Economically, these peoples were more or less isolated by the War, which imposed on them new organisational tasks. They were forced to develop much more initiative in the fields of industry and agriculture. In this way, the Eastern peoples developed an awareness of their own capacities, a need to broaden their scope and achieve independence. This is a dynamic force of enormous value for the struggle against imperialism in the East.

We, the Communist parties, must keep our eyes on these forces. We must not lose sight of a single one of them. We must utilise them all for revolutionary action, to the greatest extent possible. If a struggle against imperialism is unavoidable, if the East cannot achieve its goals without the destruction of imperialism, we must not pull back into presumptuous Communist isolation. We must not limit ourselves to observing rather than acting. Yes, we must extend communism into the East, we must build Communist parties there, we must support all communist aspirations. However, we must not give way in this to false hopes. In the present economic situation, in the struggle against imperialism, the national question inevitably comes to the fore. The question of communism and of the Communist organisation must of necessity take second place.

It is therefore an urgent task to do everything possible to advance to Communist action and, simultaneously, to lead the national aspirations down the right course. Of course, we have principled reasons not to join the national movement. We must always carefully conserve our own point of view, always holding to the position adopted last year by the Second Congress of the Communist International.[55] That is why our commission decided to stand by the principles set down last year, although the French delegation came here with the intention of requesting a modification in the theses. But, quite apart from the theses, we must attend to life, to its daily requirements. There is only one way to approach the people. We must do all we can to win the Eastern proletariat, and to that end we must not fail to link up with the nationalists of the East.

To be sure, this class deceives us in what it says about the people. It deceives the people with respect to what we are saying. Nonetheless, we have a very effective way to draw this deluded people to our side. We need only point out that the nationalists act in exactly the same way as the capitalists and the imperialists. It follows that we must keep a close eye on these nationalist movements, but we do not want to deprive them of their courage right away. We must direct them in a manner favourable to us. Or rather, we must educate the masses, arranging matters and preparing the ground so that when the moment comes, the liberation movement can be taken right out of the hands of these nationalist leaders and turned against them, so that it can pursue its course under Communist leadership. In our view, this should be the position of the Communist Party on the Eastern question.

---

55. A reference to the resolution, 'Theses on the National and Colonial Questions', in Riddell (ed.) 1991, 2WC, 1, pp. 283–90.

What we heard here today is very edifying, comrades. It is a sort of balance sheet of the heinous deeds of capitalism, which are similar in all the Eastern countries. At the same time, it is a proclamation that in all of these countries without exception, whatever form it takes, whatever mistakes may be made, there is an aspiration for freedom, which has an importance for the economic life of the world and even more from a political point of view that must not be underestimated.

We can only regret that the Eastern question was dealt with here so briefly. In our opinion, this is among the most important international issues. We must absolutely not neglect it, and the congress must say clearly and definitely today that it must receive further attention, in a more effective way than was the case today. In our opinion, the Eastern bureau plays a merely Platonic role.[56] Thus, for example, it has not yet established contact with the Communist parties of the West. We are concerned about the Eastern question because of France's colonies, and this situation therefore seems somewhat disconcerting. The congress must decide that the Bureau needs to be more energetic in the future and, moreover, not on its own but in close collaboration with the Western proletariat. It must decide to give this work increasingly greater emphasis and precision. If we act along these lines, then the Eastern question will surely become the most important factor in the world revolution.

Comrades, this evening you will be presented with the Executive's draft on this question. I would like to ask the congress to provisionally support the comments of the commission reporter, to indicate the interest we have in the comrades in the East, and to promise our brothers who have told us of the suffering of Asian peoples that they can count on the effective and prompt support of the Communist International.

**Colliard** (France): With regard to the protest by Comrade Julien, I would like to declare on behalf of a number of members of the French delegation that we do not agree with his statement. He has said that we are in a congress where cinema played the main role. We protest against this statement.

---

56. The reference is presumably to the Council for Propaganda and Action, established in 1920 by the Baku congress and based in that city. It carried out widespread educational activity, mainly in the Near East. In early 1922, the council was wound up and its functions transferred to the Comintern centre in Moscow.

Julien might also have been referring to one of two other bodies established by the Comintern to promote work in central and east Asia. In October 1920 a Central Asian Bureau based in Tashkent was set up by the ECCI, composed of Grigorii Sokolnikov, Georgy Safarov, and M.N. Roy; it was disbanded after the Third Congress in 1921. A second office in Irkutsk was established in July–August 1920, headed by Boris Shumiatsky. In January 1921 it became the Far Eastern Secretariat.

**Kolarov** (chair): On behalf of the Presidium, I support the statement by Comrade Colliard and protest on behalf of the congress against what was said by Comrade Julien. The congress gave all representatives of the Eastern countries an opportunity to come here and make contact with the international proletariat.

There is no cause, I believe, to belittle the great work of the congress. We regret that the congress does not have time to deal with the Eastern question with the thoroughness it deserves. But this misfortune is not great, because the question was already dealt with thoroughly at the Second Congress of the Communist International, which adopted theses on the colonial question. This question was also up for discussion at the Congress of the Peoples of the East, which took place in August last year. I am convinced that it will also be dealt with in future congresses and other gatherings.

For us, the most important aspect on this occasion was to demonstrate international solidarity by the Western proletariat, the oppressed peoples in the colonies, and the other Eastern peoples. The main thing is that this demonstration took place.

The debate is closed. The congress will reconvene at 8:00 p.m. this evening.[57]

---

57. For a speech to Session 23 by a member of the South African delegation not contained in the published proceedings, see Appendix 5d on pp. 1193–6.

## Session 24 – 12 July 1921, 9:00 p.m.
## Closing Session

*Announcements from the Presidium. Frölich: Report of the Youth Commission. Vote. Koenen: Report of the Organisation Commission. Vote. Heckert: Report of the Trade Union Commission. Vote. Election of the chair of the Executive. Koenen: Summary. Zinoviev: Summary.*

**Koenen** (Chair): The final session of the congress is open. Comrades, on the agenda we have, first of all, a number of manifestos that have been submitted or that are to be published by the Executive. In addition, we have the reports of the Youth Commission, the Trade Union Commission, the Organisation Commission, and, finally, the election of a chair.

To begin with, regarding the previous discussion on the Eastern question, we have the draft of a manifesto. The Presidium proposes that the congress refer this draft back to the Executive and instruct it to publish the manifesto on behalf of the congress. I believe there is no objection to that.[1]

Since no objection has been raised, the draft is referred to the Executive.

We also have before us a proposal by the South African delegation to instruct the Executive to take up the Black question, or the proletarian movement among Blacks, as an important part of the Eastern

---

1. No manifesto on revolution in the East was published after the congress, and the draft referred to here is not found in the Comintern archives. However, draft resolutions on this question were submitted by M.N. Roy, Sultanzade, and Zhang Tailei, and their texts are found in Appendices 5a, 5b, and 5c on pp. 1181–93.

question.² The Presidium proposes to refer this matter as well to the Executive for further consideration. Is there any objection to that? No one, so the proposal is adopted.

We have before us a manifesto to the Italian working class, drafted in consultation with the Italian delegation. It attacks the Serrati group, alerts the workers of Italy to the weaknesses and mistakes of this group, and calls on them to rally to communism. We propose that this manifesto, which has been discussed with the Italian delegation, be referred to the Executive for final editing, and for publication in the name of the World Congress.³

In addition, the Presidium has received theses for an appeal of the Third World Congress of the Communist International to the Romanian working class. The theses deal in particular with the terror unleashed by the government against the Second Congress there. We propose, with the agreement of the authors, to refer the theses to the Executive Committee as the basis for a manifesto to the Romanian working class, and to instruct the Executive to publish this manifesto as well in the name of the congress. If there is no objection, this is decided.⁴

In connection with discussion of the first agenda point, the congress approved a motion by Comrade Radek to make an appeal to workers around the world regarding the struggles going on at present. We do not yet have a finished draft. We propose to empower the Executive to publish in the name of the congress such a manifesto to workers around the world on the present situation.⁵

Finally, there are three other resolutions or proposed manifestos: one on pogroms against the Jews, one on the exceptional circumstances in Palestine, and, finally, a proposal to publish a manifesto on the situation in White Russia [Belarus].⁶ The Presidium proposes that these manifestos not be drafted now, but rather that these tasks be referred to the incoming Executive Committee

---

2. A member of the South African delegation, Ivon Jones, addressed Session 23, although his speech is not included in the published proceedings. In his remarks, Jones made a motion 'That this Congress resolves to further the movement among the working masses of Africa as an integral part of the Oriental question, and desires the Executive to take a direct initiative in promoting the awakening of the African Negroes as a necessary step to the world revolution.' For Jones's remarks, see Appendix 5d, pp. 1193–6.
3. The manifesto to Italian workers was adopted by the Small Bureau of the ECCI on 17 July 1921. It can be found in Comintern archives, RGASPI 490/1/159.
4. The appeal to Romanian workers was not published, and its text has not been located for this volume.
5. A reference to 'Forward to New Work and New Struggles', published on pp. 1034–40.
6. The resolutions on anti-Jewish pogroms and on White Russia can be found in Comintern archives, RGASPI, 490/1/178 and 490/1/151 respectively. For the statement on Palestine, see Appendix 5e on pp. 1196–7.

for a decision. There is also a resolution of the Communist Workers' Party of Poland, which also deals with conditions in White Russia. We ask that all this be referred to the Executive.

With regard to this latest proposal, just received, you are asked to decide that this resolution will be published explicitly on behalf of the congress.

Now we have an announcement. The Credentials Commission announced that the Greek mandates have been examined and approved. Greece is now part of the fourth category, with ten votes. The Credentials Commission asks that this belated report be accepted; that the mandates be recognised, as proposed; and that Greece be added to the fourth category.

We now move on to the rest of the agenda. Comrade Frölich has the floor for the report of the Youth Commission.

## Report from Youth Commission

**Frölich** (VKPD): Comrades, the commission assigned to review the Theses on the Youth International and the relationship between it and the Communist parties proposes three amendments.

The first involves only some minor improvements in formulation. In point 2, on page 2 of the draft, the final paragraph presents the vanguard role played by the youth organisation in a number of countries. It says that these youth organisations played the role of the revolutionary Communist Party, which was absent. In fact, there were revolutionary parties in some countries, and there the youth organisation did not have to play that role. In order to avoid any misunderstanding, the words 'given the absence of revolutionary parties' will be followed by 'in most countries'. That is a small matter.

Further, point 4 of the draft explains how economic struggles in which the youth organisation is active should be conducted. Clearly, the youth organisation cannot lead such struggles, so an addition has been made that it will conduct these struggles jointly with the Communist parties and the trade unions.

Finally, an addition has been made to point 5, which explains the relationship of the youth organisation to the Communist parties. The draft states that the youth organisation is politically subordinate to the parties, but that organisationally it remains autonomous. However, there are certain parties in which the youth organisation already has a more intimate organisational relationship with the party than in the countries for which this point is intended.

It is therefore proposed, in cases where the fusion of the youth organisation with the Communist Party has already gone further, not to change this relationship, but rather to recognise it. Assuming there is no objection, the following passage will be added at the end of point 5, page 4:

Successful leadership of the revolutionary struggle requires the strongest possible centralisation and the greatest possible unity. For that reason, in countries where, as a result of historical development, the youth organisation is more dependent, this relationship will, as a rule, be maintained. If there are disagreements between the two organisations, this will be resolved by the Executive Communist of the Communist International together with the Executive Committee of the Communist Youth International.[7]

That concludes the proposed amendments.

**Koenen** (Chair): It appears that there is no desire for a discussion on this report. We come to the vote. We ask that delegates in favour of the commission's proposed amendments of the theses on the relationship of the Youth International to the Communist International and of its affiliated parties to the youth in their country please raise your blue card. (*Vote*) It is adopted unanimously.

## Report from Organisation Commission

**Koenen:** Comrades, the Commission on Organisation had thorough discussions in two sub-commissions and discussed out the entire draft. A large number of minor changes have been made, all of which were unanimously adopted by the commission. In addition, a number of passages have been shortened, and these changes have also been unanimously adopted by the Commission on Organisation. There are also a number of proposed amendments, and I will report on these.

First of all, there is a substantive proposed change and addition to the section on democratic centralism. You already have this amendment in printed form in all languages, and there is no need for me to read it out. This amendment, also unanimously adopted, makes the concept of democratic centralism somewhat more explicit and comprehensible.

The next important addition deals with agitation and propaganda among national minorities. A special request has been added that this agitation and propaganda be carried out vigorously and, where possible, in the language of these minorities.

Formulations relating to the trade-union question and the handling of wage agreements have been improved, so that no principled disagreements can arise over wage agreements.

---

7. For the corresponding passage of the theses, see p. 1032.

The paragraph regarding propaganda in the army and navy has been reformulated. In particular, it now specifies that agitation should take into account that in the countries with a standing army, the future of the soldiers and sailors is closely tied to that of the exploited class. Finally, a separate proposal has been adopted regarding the way to approach officers and student training corps.[8]

The proposed addition regarding the organisation of political struggles, which I proposed in my report and read out almost in its entirety, has been basically adopted. A few deletions were made where these concepts were already encompassed in the Theses on Tactics and Strategy.

An addition has been made regarding the role of the press in carrying out political campaigns, particularly regarding how the editors must be tied more closely to the party's activity. It describes how a uniform approach to revolutionary work should be adopted by the party's press. There is also a proposed addition relating to the magazines, pamphlets, and other theoretical and propagandistic publications of the party. All these publications should be integrated in centralised fashion in accord with the party's campaigns.

An addition has been made relating to the Social-Democratic and Independent Socialist [USPD] press, describing how to carry out subscription work against them. Here too the commission was unanimously in favour of making this addition.

In the section on 'structure of the party', a discussion took place on whether the party leadership is responsible only to the party convention or also to the International Executive Committee. The commission unanimously adopted the latter proposal.

The proposal that the party leadership, including the smaller leadership, be elected only by its convention, was reviewed. It was decided to leave open whether the smaller leadership should be elected directly by the convention or by the elected Central Committee or by some advisory council or other body. The changes were adopted unanimously.

Additions were made in several places to the effect that special working groups and – on occasion, special leaderships – should be established for agitation among women and in rural areas. The same was decided for Red Aid.[9] It was agreed that special auxiliary bodies should be created in each party to assist the victims of white terror.

---

8. See point 30 of the resolution on the organisational structure of Communist parties, p. 989.

9. See p. 1001. Committees for Red Aid were formed in Germany, early in 1921, to aid political prisoners in that country. International Red Aid (Russian acronym: MOPR) was founded on 30 November 1922.

With regard to the subordination of different party bodies, an important aspect was omitted from the theses, namely that parliamentary deputies are also subordinate to the central leadership. This has been rectified by an addition. It was proposed and agreed to recommend to all parties the setting up of a special auditing commission that would supervise the management of party funds and accounting, and would report regularly on its activity and conclusions to the broadened committee or advisory board.

A number of comrades in the commission wished to indicate in the theses that freedom of criticism has its limits. The commission accepted this request and came up with a formulation that I think it appropriate to read out.

> In order to ensure that every party decision will be carried out energetically by all party units and members, the broadest possible range of members should be involved in considering and deciding every question. The party and its leading bodies have the responsibility of deciding whether and to what extent questions raised by individual comrades should be discussed publicly (newspapers, pamphlets).[10]

This proposal was unanimously adopted. Also, a change has been made in the sentence saying that only a bad Communist would forget himself and publicly attack the Communist Party.

The section on 'Illegal and legal work' is now called, 'On the relationship between legal and illegal work'. The goal here is to make clear that there is no contradiction between legal and illegal work, but that each flows over into the other. Some paragraphs in this section have been formulated more cautiously and some deletions have been made so as not to provide too much ammunition for the bourgeois governments. But it was thought necessary to add some wording on the need for caution when new members are recruited. The establishment of a candidate status aims at preventing the recruitment of unreliable members. Nonetheless, it is left for now to individual comrades to apply this rule in their parties to the degree possible. In order to prevent spies and provocateurs from infiltrating the underground work, it is proposed that comrades who wish to be involved in underground work should first be tested in legal activity. Finally, a comment: the words 'before the revolution' met with objections, and they have now been replaced with the words, 'before the open revolutionary uprising'.

These are the significant proposed changes to the present draft on party organisation. It is entitled, 'Theses on the Organisational Structure of the Communist Party and on the Methods and Content of Its Work'.

---

10. For the corresponding passage of the theses, see p. 1002.

I now come to the section that deals with the organisation of the Communist International. Changes have been made in several parts of the resolution. Some unimportant deletions have been made in the introduction, on the basis that the deleted passages were already covered by other resolutions. Similarly, in point 1, first sentence, the sentence saying that the sections of the International should maintain close contact with each other has been replaced by a description of how this is to be done. Significant changes have been made only in the last paragraph, which now reads as follows:[11]

> 5. In order to be able to carry out this much increased activity, the Executive must be substantially expanded. Each section granted forty votes in the congress and the Executive of the Communist Youth International will receive two places; each section granted twenty or thirty votes will receive one place. The Communist Party of Russia will have five places, as before. Representatives of other parties will have consultative vote. The chair of the Executive will be chosen by the congress. The Executive will be instructed to engage three secretaries, drawn if possible from different sections. In addition, members of the Executive sent from the sections are required to take part in carrying out the work of the divisions relating to their country or by serving as reporters responsible for the work of entire topic areas. Members of the administrative Small Bureau will be chosen separately by the Executive.[12]

There were some disagreements on this point. A vote took place regarding which sections should receive two places. Nonetheless, the proposal just read to you was adopted by a large majority.

There was also a discussion on whether the Executive should choose members of the administrative Small Bureau from its own ranks, or whether the Executive was empowered to choose other comrades, who happened not to be among its members, as members of the Small Bureau. It was ultimately decided to word the sentence in such a way as to leave this to the Executive's discretion. Nonetheless, there are still differences of opinion on this point, which have yet to be resolved.

Finally, the commission dealing with international issues raised a number of other proposals, which obviously did not need to be taken up in a public discussion and have therefore, for the most part, been referred to the new Executive for consideration. It was proposed that a Control Commission be established for the Executive's activity and especially its initiatives with

---

11. 'Organisation of the Communist International' was published as a separate resolution, and Point 5 is not its last but its second-to-last section. See pp. 1007–8.
12. For the corresponding text in the resolution, see p. 1008.

parties abroad and their work. It was not possible to present a finished proposal. However, the commission considered this question to be so important that we did not want to leave it over to the next congress. Rather, our opinion was that we should seek a solution now.

The commission unanimously proposes that we begin by establishing a provisional Control Commission. The Executive should come to agreement with the first voting category, that is, with the leaderships of the largest delegations. If these delegations and the Executive come to an agreement, this provisional Control Commission should function for the next year. These two groups and the Executive should determine the interim demarcation of this body's activity. Nonetheless, the commission unanimously proposes to establish at this time that the powers of the Control Commission, in general, will not be greater than those of the Control Commissions of the national organisations, and that they will not, in general, decide on political matters. That is the proposal we are making to the congress on this matter. We ask you all to adopt this proposal, if possible, without a great deal of discussion.[13] (*Loud applause*)

There is a proposal to expand the Executive by one representative in order to give the Indian Communist movement a representative with full rights instead of, as previously, with only consultative vote. The Presidium has no objection to this. We believe that this proposal is agreeable.

There is also an amendment that members of the Small Bureau be chosen only from the ranks of the Executive's members. Is there a speaker on this point?

**Souvarine:** I ask that the vote here be taken by delegations.

**Radek:** Comrades, on behalf of the Russian delegation, I oppose this motion for the following reasons: all political decisions will be taken by the Executive. The Small Bureau's primary duty must be to lead the illegal work, on the basis of the Executive's decisions. In this work we can utilise, in different situations, comrades who could not be elected to the Executive for this or that reason, for example because they were not present at the congress.

Similarly, when we send a representative abroad, we do not want the choice to be limited to members of the Executive, and we have had to send

---

13. At the Comintern's Fourth Congress the following year, a balance sheet was drawn on this proposal: 'Experience has shown that a Control Commission structured in this way is incapable of functioning. It has not been possible even once for all the members of the Control Commission to meet together.... For this reason, we propose that, in future, the choice of members of the Control Commission be carried out by two sections, changing every year.' See Riddell (ed.) 2011b, *4WC*, p. 932.

responsible comrades who are not Executive members. That is how we have always functioned. In the same way, the Executive must be in a position to designate comrades outside its ranks to belong to the Small Bureau. The argument against this is purely formal and schematic in nature; the argument in favour rests on our movement's experiences. The conduct of underground work demands much greater flexibility. It is significant that this motion has been made by representatives of an organisation that has not been required to carry out much underground work. (*Objections*)

I ask that the motion be defeated. It is no big principled question. If the congress decides otherwise, we will follow its instructions. But this proposal would make our work more difficult.

**Koenen:** Does anyone wish to speak?

**Franz Koritschoner** (Austria): We ask that you vote for Comrade Souvarine's proposal. It is not right that comrades who have not been chosen by their country's delegation wind up on the Executive's Small Bureau. The Small Bureau is a committee of the Executive, and as such it must be composed in the same fashion and must develop out of it organically. In other cases, we always favour organic development. I would like to mention that the need to create organisational clarity is inescapable, and this is the only way it can be established. We should also note the fact that this motion has indeed been sponsored by delegations that have been repeatedly forced to carry out underground work.

**Henryk Walecki** (Poland): Comrades, I must speak against the amendment introduced by a group of delegates for the following reason: until now, we have had an Executive that has not been adequate, either numerically or in other ways, to provide candidates for the Small Bureau. We decided at this congress to reinforce the Executive and to call on the parties in other countries to send their best forces as delegates to Moscow. Nonetheless, we cannot predict at this moment to what extent the parties will respond to this appeal. It is impossible for us to know whether in the future we will still have to look for forces outside the Executive Committee who are able to carry out all the functions of the Small Bureau.

We should not tie the hands of the Executive Committee in this way. We must give them the responsibility of making the choice. From a formal point of view, this type of representation is certainly permissible. Different parties delegate members into the Executive who are not directly members of the party leadership. As a rule, the Executive will certainly choose its own members to serve in the Small Bureau. But, in exceptional cases, we should not forbid them, in advance, from drawing in one or two persons who at the given moment are not members of the Executive.

**Vaillant-Couturier**:[14] The French delegation stands by the resolution we presented. Comrade Radek spoke out strongly against it, but he also said that this was not a principled question. Nonetheless, it is worth noting that the Small Bureau, which has special importance and meets on an ongoing basis, needs to be made up of responsible members. In our view, the objection raised by Comrade Radek regarding the Small Bureau's special tasks and the need for it to contain members experienced in underground work is insufficient grounds to reject the amendment. We consider that if necessary, the members of the Executive Committee belonging to the Small Bureau can create a technical auxiliary apparatus for certain special tasks. Finally, Comrade Walecki said that it is hard to find among the thirty members of the broader Executive Committee the seven people needed for the Small Bureau. This comment gives an unflattering picture of the capacities of our comrades for underground work.

The French delegation therefore asks that this amendment be adopted, on the grounds that it will simplify the tasks of the International. The delegation considers that its adoption will make it possible to function more conveniently and productively. We stress that the amendment does not in any way express a lack of confidence, given that the issue here is purely one of the methods of work needed to enable the International to undertake its tasks seriously and fully carry out its revolutionary duty.

**Koenen**: No one else has asked to speak. We must vote on the motion.

**Radek**: Given that the proposal has been sponsored by a number of delegations – Australia, Austria, and so on – we must ask if other delegations support the motion, because raising the cards will not dispose of the question.

**Koenen** (Chair): We will now take the vote by delegations. Delegations that are in favour of restricting membership of the Small Bureau to those who are members of the Executive, please vote 'yes'. Delegations who want to retain the original text, as proposed by the commission, will vote 'no', in rejection of the amendment.

**Pogány**: The question is wrongly formulated. Those in favour of the commission's proposal should vote 'yes'.

---

14. The comments by Vaillant-Couturier are not in the German edition and are translated from the Russian text.

**Koenen** (Chair): In order to clarify the matter still further, let us put it this way: for the Souvarine amendment or for the commission's proposal. I believe that will eliminate any confusion.

**Souvarine**: For us, putting the question that way is unacceptable. We are not altering the commission's text. The vote should be for or against the amendment.

**Vaillant-Couturier**: I ask that the list of all the countries that have signed the amendment be read out.

**Radek**: Comrades, Comrade Souvarine is playing a game of hide-and-seek. The fact is that this motion was defeated twice in the commission. So the motion is counterposed to that of the commission. The commission's motion empowers the Executive to draw comrades from outside its ranks into the needed work. The French comrades reject that. They are therefore proposing a countermotion. That is why the vote must take the form: for the commission or for the motion by Souvarine.

**Koenen** (Chair): The Presidium will not recognise further speakers, but will take the vote instead. The vote will be as follows. Those favouring the commission proposal should state that they are voting for it. Those favouring the amendment should state, for Souvarine's amendment. I will now comply with the request to read out the delegations that have signed the motion: the French, Spanish, Swiss, Yugoslavian, Austrian, and Australian delegations.

We will now take the vote. I ask the delegations to state which motion they are supporting. Russia: for the commission. Germany: commission. France: against the commission. Italy: commission. Czechoslovakia: 30 for Souvarine, 10 for the commission. Youth group: against the commission. Poland: for the commission. Ukraine: commission. Bulgaria: for the amendment. Yugoslavia: amendment. Norway: commission. Britain: commission. United States: commission. Spain: amendment. Finland: commission. Netherlands: commission. Belgium: amendment. Romania: 5 for the commission; 15 for the amendment. Latvia: commission. Switzerland: amendment. Hungary: 10 for the commission, 10 for the amendment. Sweden: already departed. Austria: amendment. Azerbaijan: commission. Georgia: commission. Lithuania: commission. Luxembourg: amendment. Turkey: not present. Estonia: absent. Denmark: commission. Greece: amendment. South Africa: commission. Iceland: commission. Korea: absent. Mexico: absent. Armenia: commission. Argentina: commission. Australia: commission. New Zealand: absent. Dutch Indies: absent.

That concludes the vote.

Comrades, although the vote totals are not yet available, it is nonetheless clear that the commission's motion obtained a large majority. (*Applause*) The majority amounts to approximately 150 votes.[15]

Following the vote, Comrade Zinoviev has the floor.

**Zinoviev**: Comrades, this has been the only roll-call vote during the entire congress, and it actually concerns only a very small matter. So in my opinion we should attempt to find a formula that we could perhaps all agree on. I propose that, following on this brilliant victory (*Laughter*), we make a concession to those who proposed the motion, as follows: the Small Bureau should, as a rule, be made up only of members of the Executive, and only in exceptional cases can another procedure be adopted. For it is really about a matter of an exceptional case. Of course, as a rule only Executive members will belong. The only thing that we require for the needs of the work is that the members of the Executive not have their hands tied. Of course, there is no mistrust here on the part of those moving the motion; it is simply a question of how to conduct the work. And since we now have two years of experience with the Executive's work, we ask you to accept that it will be more expedient to permit such exceptions, but as a rule things will be done as requested by comrades of the French delegation. I believe, if we put it to a vote in this way, we will have a solid majority.[16]

**Koenen** (Chair): So the wording is as follows: members of the administrative Small Bureau will be chosen by the Executive. As a rule, they will be members of the Executive, but, in exceptional cases, this need not be so. That is Comrade Zinoviev's proposal.[17]

There is no opposition to this wording. We will therefore once again take the vote, which will replace the previous vote. I ask that all those in favour of this amendment please raise their green cards. (*Vote*) Adopted, against one vote in opposition.

After this vote, I assume that the entire draft of the Organisation Commission on the methods of work, and also that on the International's organisation,

---

15. While the announced vote does not include all delegations, what was recorded in the proceedings comes to 435 for the commission and 255 for the amendment. For the allocation of votes to delegations, see pp. 177–8.

16. Zinoviev's proposal is incorporated in point 5 of the resolution, p. 1008.

17. At a meeting of the ECCI on 13 July 1921 – the day after adjournment of the Third Congress – a new Small Bureau was elected consisting of Zinoviev (chairman), Radek, Gennari, Bukharin, Kun, Heckert, and Souvarine, with a Secretariat consisting of Kuusinen, Rákosi, and Humbert-Droz.

has been adopted. All those in favour, please raise their cards. (*Vote*) Unanimously adopted.

We now come to the next point on the agenda: Report of the Trade Union Commission. Comrade Heckert has the floor.

## Report from Trade Union Commission

**Heckert**: Comrades, we are at the close of the congress, but we still have to report on the trade-union theses. Only a few minor, factual corrections have been made in the printed text of the Theses that you have before you. However, quite a number of motions were submitted to make changes of substance. Many or, better, most of the amendments result from the fact that the translation into English and French was inadequate. In both texts, a large number of passages have been wrongly translated. As we corrected the translation errors, it was clear that most of the requested amendments were superfluous.

Actually the commission dealt with only two amendments of importance, in fact, really only one. This amendment states that the trade unions must also carry out a struggle against governmental institutions set up to protect capital from the united working-class attack through the trade unions. First, in many countries individual factories or branches of industry have been militarised, in order to protect supposedly essential operations from being shut down. Also, capitalist governments have adopted laws obligating trade unions, before they go on strike, to convene an arbitration court or commission and present their concerns there. The commission considers – and I am sure this is accurate – that both these cases involve merely devices to cripple and inhibit the capacity for working-class struggle.

Third, another amendment was adopted calling for struggle against measures in a number of countries to deduct taxes from wage payments. The capitalists are converted into tax collectors. In several countries, a sum of money – 10 per cent of the wages or even more – is withheld from what the worker receives on payday. In the commission's view, withholding taxes is a method of shifting the entire costs of the war off the shoulders of the capitalists and onto those of the workers. It is thus a measure to reduce workers' wages or income. The commission proposes to oblige the trade unions to make use of all resources for union struggle to oppose the militarisation of the factories, compulsory arbitration, and the withholding of taxes from wages.

Unfortunately, we were not in a position to edit the English, French, and Russian texts. That will have to be done later. I can tell you, though, that all the theses contained in the printed draft before you were adopted by an overwhelming majority, mostly unanimously, with only a very few areas of disagreement.

In the section on the action programme, point 8, the majority of the commission decided to delete one concept. Point 8 contains the concept that the working class needs compensation for its debilitation as a result of the War through shorter working time and improved living conditions, in order to restore its strength. The commission majority considered that this concept should not be included because the demand to compensate workers for debilitation by granting them shortened working hours and better wages was simply a utopia.

However, comrades, a minority of the commission was of the opinion that this concept should be retained. Firstly, it corresponds to the facts. Secondly, calling it utopian is hardly an argument, since from this point of view almost all the other proposals of the action programme are utopian in character. The commission minority therefore proposes to let this passage stand.[18]

At the beginning of the commission's proceedings, the Communist Workers' Party [KAPD], represented here at the congress, proposed that its programme and the theses it has proposed be taken as the basis for discussion. However, the commission – apart from the KAPD representative – considered that the KAPD's train of thought was not that of the overwhelming majority of the congress. The KAPD's amendments or theses could not, therefore, be made the basis for discussion.

That concludes the report on the theses. Now a few words on the question as a whole. In discussion of the trade-union question, specifically with regard to the Communist International's relations with the red trade unions and also to the action programme, everyone who spoke here at the congress, apart from the IWW and KAPD speakers, has accepted the principles laid down in the theses. Through these speakers the congress has made clear that it wants not to destroy the trade unions, as the KAPD would have it, but rather to win them over, as is clearly and unambiguously stated in the Theses.

In addition, the congress – again through the unanimous opinion of every speaker who took the floor – expressed the notion that it is absolutely necessary to have close relations with the red trade unions and to combat any concept of trade-union neutrality or independence. On this point, the range of those who do not agree with us is even narrower than on the issue of destroying the trade unions. Actually, only in the case of a sector of the French syndicalists and one speaker of the IWW did we see an aversion to establishing close ties with the Communist International. In my opinion – and it is also

---

18. For the final text of point 8 of the theses, see p. 962.

that of the commission – the vote of the congress signifies rejecting the notion of destroying the trade unions and adoption of the goal of winning them over; and also rejection of neutrality and approval of close ties with the red trade unions.

However, I would like to throw some light on some of the concepts of comrades who have met with us here and were in opposition. The KAPD told the congress that trade unions were the issue where we had to move closer to them, so they could develop for us the line of thought behind their method and plan of struggle and their entire approach to the revolutionary movement. The remarks by the KAPD comrade have left us puzzled over what exactly the KAPD wants. But some KAPD documents in our possession show us that their position is completely contrary to communism. Their position is also not above criticism with regard to advancing a firm and clear line and dealing with us frankly.

Here at the congress, the KAPD speaker stated that Communists want to build cells in the unions, in order to win them over through this cell policy. All the speakers here except those of the KAPD said that the cell policy was correct. Nonetheless, the KAPD speakers and writings say that this policy destroys the unions. You Communists do not see this, they say, but in reality this is what you do. They have presented comprehensive theses on this cell policy. But, in addition to these theses, they have a so-called theoretical organ, *Der Proletarier*, in which the position of the General Workers' Union [AAUD] regarding the Red International of Labour Unions is expressed in terms of the need to build cells in the Red International, in order to slow it down and change its course, because it does not conform to their thinking. So the idea is that the KAPD is against cells formed by the Communists in the trade unions but in favour of those they themselves succeed in building inside the red trade unions and the Communist International.

In one of its pamphlets, the KAPD explains why the Communists form cells in the trade unions as follows:

> The Moscow forces want to split the trade unions. In forming cells, their goal of winning over the unions simply means a split. When their big-shots call for winning over the trade unions, this is simply the big-shots' demand to get possession of high posts. And these big-shots' campaign against the policy of destroying the unions is merely a cry of rage by swindlers who have been swindled.

Further, the KAPD says that our policy on cells does nothing more than simply cause an uproar in the organisation. You would think that they would be grateful to us for creating an uproar in the workers' movement. But that is not all. They reject working with us in a common framework, explaining that they fundamentally reject this policy. But even so, this is not supposed to prevent the Communist International and the red unions from recognising the Communist Workers' Party and the General Workers' Union.

So they intend to fight us. They reject what we are working for. Nonetheless, in their view, we are obliged to recognise their organisation as Communist and their policies as correct. Comrades, we can best get a picture of this celebrated clear opposition against the general policies that we are adopting here at this congress by reading a KAPD circular, in which we find the following passage:

> Our propaganda is failing completely. The press run of our newspaper is stagnating. Where copies are circulated to non-subscribers, this is done by individual comrades. That is how things are in the organisation as a whole. The rest are apparently chasing after cushy positions.

So no one can criticise the KAPD and its fine notions better than that party itself, which says its organisation is completely falling apart and few members are doing anything. The others are chasing after cushy positions. So the criticism that the congress can make of the KAPD is in fact expressed quite fully by the KAPD itself.

We must also speak to a small organisation that has said a few things here – the IWW. The comrades have spoken passionately here for their organisation. We understand very well why the comrades have this opinion. They are on the right path. A struggle carried out for fifteen years against an enemy as malicious as Samuel Gompers cannot be dismissed just like that. The American comrades decided at their congress that the IWW should be called on to dissolve their organisation. We do not believe that should be done. We cannot ask of these fighters that they now go into the Samuel Gompers organisation. That is too much to ask, just like that.

But, when we look at the IWW and discover that, according to their own accounting, they now have only 15,674 members in thirteen different organisations, we can only conclude that the path followed by these comrades, for which they gave their blood and their freedom, has not led to victory. It has led only to their isolation from the broad masses of the working class, a situation in the American workers' movement where the masses are with Samuel Gompers and they have only a few fighters.

So it is appropriate to tell the comrades: reconsider the position you have taken and come to agreement with the comrades carrying out revolutionary work. Perhaps your joint work will succeed in banishing reactionary ideas among the anarchist workers. You will have more success that way than if you always cry, 'Out of the trade unions!', thereby isolating the courageous revolutionary fighters from the masses.

So we see that in America, where we have fifteen years of experience, the slogan 'Out of the trade unions!' is just as bankrupt as in the German workers' movement with the KAPD. And that is why, comrades, even though it is hard for us to fight in the ranks of the Amsterdamers for our ideas and to destroy the Amsterdamers' ideas, in order to win over the mass organisations of the proletariat and convert them into tools for revolution, that is what we must do. The short history – one year – in which we have been working in cells shows that we have fought victorious battles everywhere, while the slogans of the others create nothing but piles of rubble in the revolutionary working class.

We therefore ask you to adopt the theses with the few changes that have been proposed and to transform the ideas of these theses into living reality in the struggle of all organised proletarians against the bourgeoisie and its accomplices. When we meet again at the next congress, it is quite conceivable that the broad masses of workers who belong to unions will already have joined the ranks of that great encampment of fighters where the Third International has raised its banner. Under this banner the Third International is assembling all the masses of the working class to overthrow capitalism, for the victory of our ideas, for the liberation of proletarians around the world and for the workers' council republic. (*Loud applause and cheers*)

**Koenen** (Chair): You have just heard the report of the Trade Union Commission, together with the proposal regarding amendments and the reporter's summary. We can proceed to the vote.

**Sachs** (Schwab, KAPD): On a point of order, comrades. Comrade Heckert's written and oral report informed you that the KAPD submitted theses to the Trade Union Commission – comprehensive theses dealing with the trade-union question as a whole and everything related to it. In addition, you have heard that the commission declined to review these theses. We therefore propose that our comrade Hempel be given the floor for a short time to explain the theses we have presented. We also move that the theses that we presented to the commission also be put to a vote.

**Koenen** (Chair): Comrades, I note that we have already granted the KAPD representatives ample speaking time to motivate their theses. The KAPD delegates have intervened repeatedly in the plenary discussions and in the commission. As a result, the Presidium is unanimously of the opinion that we should not take further discussion at this time. (*Loud applause*) Does anyone have a different view? No. So the discussion will not be reopened.

We therefore proceed to the vote on the theses as a whole along with the amendments proposed here today by Comrade Heckert. Those in favour of adopting the theses and amendments on the trade-union question, raise your cards. (*Vote*) Those opposed? (*No one*) Are there any abstentions? (*Shouts: 'Yes'*) So I declare that the theses and amendments are adopted unanimously with one abstention. (*Loud applause and cheers*)

We come to the next point on the agenda: election of the chair of the Executive.

**Belloni**: On behalf of a number of delegations – the Italian, German, Bulgarian, Polish, and Hungarian delegations – I move that we elect our Comrade Zinoviev as president.[19] (*Loud applause*)

**Koenen** (Chair): We will proceed to the vote. Those in favour of Comrade Belloni's proposal, please raise your cards. (*Vote*) Those opposed? No one. I declare that the previous president of the Executive, Comrade Zinoviev, is unanimously re-elected. (*Enthusiastic prolonged applause and cheers*)

The Presidium has received a proposal to establish a commission of members of various parties to establish an international auxiliary language. I propose to refer this motion to the Executive for its consideration. (*Agreement*)

## Expressions of Thanks

**Koenen**: Comrades, we have here a large number of dispatches greeting the congress. The number of such dispatches so far is 381. I believe it would take far too long to read all these statements to the congress. I will only inform you that, as you might expect, most of these telegrams have been sent by our Russian brothers, including a considerable number from various units of the Red Army. (*Enthusiastic applause, loud shouts, 'Long live the Red Army!'*) In addition, a large number of telegrams have arrived from units of the Russian party in different cities and villages. (*Loud applause*)

Comrades, it is not possible for the congress to express our thanks individually to each of those who sent telegrams of greetings. I believe the congress will be in unanimous agreement that we instruct the Communist International Secretariat to convey the heartfelt thanks of the congress to all of those who have sent us telegrams and resolutions of greeting. (*Enthusiastic applause*)

---

19. The meaning of the German word 'Präsident' then overlapped the English 'president' and 'chair', but in the Comintern it was usually translated as 'president'.

The Presidium informs you that the new Executive will be constituted tomorrow afternoon at 1:00 p.m. here in the Kremlin. All delegations are instructed that the delegates they want to send to the new Executive should appear at tomorrow's session.

Comrades, permit me to express our profound thanks to those who have organised this congress. I believe that I convey the feelings of all those present, all participants in this Third World Congress of the Communist International, in expressing our warm gratitude to all our Russian party comrades, members of the Russian Communist Party, its Central Committee, and members of the Executive for their efforts in enabling us to meet here again in Moscow, the capital of world revolution, and bring our congress to so successful a conclusion. (*Enthusiastic applause*) Comrades, we all know how to pay heartfelt tribute to the warm and generous hospitality that the Russian people and the Russian Communist Party offered to Communists from around the world during the last few weeks. (*Enthusiastic applause*)

Despite the deep deprivation, suffering, and cares that weigh down on the Russian people and the Russian Communist Party, they have welcomed us with heartfelt hospitality. We held our deliberations in these resplendent halls, gleaming in gold, and we looked with pride at the party that, in a sudden leap forward, was able to forcibly seize the bastions of tsarism and thereby make it possible for representatives of the proletariat in every country to hold its deliberations in such a palace, in such halls. (*Loud applause*)

Comrades, we are actually indebted to our Russian comrades for more than merely this gathering. In a word, they have not only given us a theory but provided us with a tested practice of revolution. We came together here and hurried so gladly to Moscow to meet with our Russian brothers because we all consider ourselves students of these great revolutionary fighters, because we all know that we all have a great deal to learn from our outstanding Russian brothers, not only theory but also practice, and indeed on a human level. (*Loud applause*)

We are deeply moved to think that not only the Russian Communists but the entire Russian people lost not just tens of thousands but hundreds of thousands who fell in the revolutionary struggles. Only the hundreds of thousands who fell made it possible for Communist thinking in the world to take a coherent form and come vigorously alive in a manner that can never ever be extinguished. (*Tumultuous applause*) Only this enormous sacrifice made it at all possible to call into being the Communist International. And just as our Russian brothers stood prepared for sacrifice through all the long years of revolution, so too they stand today. The people that endured suffering, destitution, deprivation, and troubles without measure does not waver and does not yield, holding firmly to the Soviet republic, to its revolutionary achievements, and to the Communist Party.

And, in the party, we do not see only the ordinary party member but also those who are called leaders. They proceed simply through life without deviating, yielding, without being distracted, thinking always only of struggle, struggle, and more struggle. They have no thought and no desire other than to be revolutionary, revolutionary for Russia and the entire world. We see how this and only this fills their entire being, and how they pursue the final revolutionary struggle almost to the point of breakdown, almost to the ruin of their personal being, almost to exhaustion. But again and again they are restored by the great idea. Again and again we see how they express the great ideas, how they breathe new life into the struggle, how they raise it up and carry it forward, how they again and again find the way to lead the first proletarian state, the first example of proletarian power, through every difficulty. (*Loud applause*)

Comrades, that is why we owe our most heartfelt thanks to the Russian party and the Russian leaders. I am sure that we will all join with enthusiasm in the call: Long live Soviet Russia! Long live the Russian Communist Party! Long live its leadership! Long live the Third International! (*Prolonged, loud applause and cheers*)

**Koenen** (Chair): Comrade Zinoviev will now give the closing speech.

## Closing Speech

**Zinoviev** (*Enthusiastic applause*): Comrades, first I must express heartfelt thanks for my unanimous election. I must also stress that this is not a matter of confidence in me as an individual but rather of confidence in the party in which many of us have for decades had the honour of fighting. Over the next year our party will continue doing everything in its power to be deserving of the great trust in us that the Communist International has expressed today.

Comrades, we have reached the end of the Third Congress of the Communist International. When we addressed our first manifesto to Communists of every country at the end of 1917 [1918],[20] calling on them to found a Communist International, we were mocked around the world as a group of

---

20. As indicated in the Serbo-Croatian edition of the Third Congress proceedings (Bosić et al. (eds.) 1981), the allusion to 1917 was a mistake. Zinoviev is presumably referring to the Bolshevik Central Committee appeal of 24 December 1918, calling on revolutionary forces around the world to build a Third, Communist International. The text of that appeal can be found in Riddell (ed.) 1986, pp. 441–3.

dreamers. It was said that if we did actually form such an International it would be a nine-day wonder rather than a solid organisation. But now, comrades, we've had the First Congress, in which truly only a handful of Communist revolutionaries managed to find their way together. Then we had the Second Congress, in which a number of significant parties met here under the banner of the Communist International. And now we have experienced the Third Congress, which has shown us that, despite all inadequacies and all defeats, our workers' association has grown enormously during the last year. We have become a gigantic organisation, the strongest world organisation of the proletariat, at least in Europe and soon, we hope, in the United States.

Comrades, it was not that easy for us to take decisions during this congress on the urgent questions before us. We had to struggle to reach the truth and achieve a correct position. The reason for this, in my opinion, is that we convened our congress in what was quite definitely a transitional period, in which it has become evident that the revolution is unfortunately not developing as rapidly as every honest revolutionary would and should desire. The situation in Europe is varied, and our sister parties face quite disparate conditions.

We in the Executive sensed, as did many in the different parties, that this was precisely the time, at the beginning of a transitional period, to come together and fraternally consider the situation, examining all the difficulties. This was the time to correct the errors we had committed and adopt a clear and precise line for the future. That is why we found it difficult during the congress to resolve the most important questions. Nonetheless, all the key votes were unanimous. And I believe we have the right to say, comrades, that our unanimity is not of the kind that prevailed in the Second International. Ours is no superficial, parade-ground unanimity. If it had turned out during the congress that we were divided by major differences of opinion, we would of course not have concealed this. Instead, we would have had a clear tendency struggle, and that might well have been reflected in the votes.

Our unanimity is not that of a lazy compromise, but the unanimity of an international organisation of struggle, aware that it is surrounded by a world of enemies, that it must forge unity in struggle, and that it must never permit the minor differences of opinion in our ranks to give rise to even a hint of a rift. Our unanimity is the true accord of the global revolutionary proletariat, of the class-conscious proletarians of the entire world.

What we have set down in our resolutions is truly the common opinion of forces in the proletariat that, Communist in thought and feeling, are prepared to struggle for communism. We have discussed three major questions: tactics and strategy, trade unions, and organisation. Our resolution on tactics and strategy did not shy away from talking frankly of our errors. By the way, that is how the Russian Bolshevik Party has acted for decades, without worrying over whether enemies would rub their hands with malicious glee. We have had to criticise many theoretical formulations. We spoke against the theory of the offensive, not because we do not want to conduct a genuine offensive, but rather precisely because we want to better prepare an offensive. We criticised the theory of the offensive during the Third Congress, while during the year to come, before the Fourth Congress, we want to prepare a genuine offensive and, in many countries, carry out a genuine offensive of the revolutionary proletariat against our enemy, the bourgeoisie. (*Loud applause*)

Comrades, the central concept of our resolution on tactics and strategy is to alert all our sister parties, particularly those in Europe, to something that they must already have realised on their own: that they face an enemy of quite a different sort than what the Russian party faced during the October Revolution. In Europe and the United States you face an enemy that is smarter and better organised than what we faced in Russia. You have an enemy armed to the teeth, clever and cunning. They have good strategists, who have also learned something from the Russian Revolution. They are now arming their sons, while making every effort to ensure that the proletariat remains disarmed.

Our sister parties in Europe will therefore have to wage a much more difficult struggle. And for this reason alone – an important reason indeed – we must draw a simple conclusion, namely that the preparation of proletarian struggles in Europe must also be more robust and more painstaking than was the case in Russia or during the last two years in Europe. The enemy is stronger and more cunning, and we must therefore better prepare our struggles. That is the central concept, very plain and simple, but very important for every Communist worker around the world. And we must go out now with this concept to the entire world, to all the parties, and impress it on the mind of every ordinary worker, drawing from it all the necessary practical conclusions.

In my opinion, there are two things that put the stamp on our Third Congress. First, the resolution on tactics and strategy, which explicitly criticises many errors, calls on us to undertake more thorough preparations. It appeals to all parties for greater caution and better preparation of every struggle. Second, our congress is characterised by the answer the congress unanimously gave to the Socialist Party of Italy. Initially, it was the Executive that expelled this party from the Communist International. The Third Congress has ratified this expulsion. Of course, that does not mean that we wanted to calmly and casually break with hundreds of thousands of Italian workers. No, we will struggle passionately to draw into our ranks the workers who belong there.

But the congress stated clearly before the entire world that the things done by the Socialist Party of Italy do not have a place in any way in the Communist International. As you know, this faction calls itself Communist and Unitarian. And we say that it is neither Communist nor Unitarian. For the sake of twelve thousand reformists it broke with sixty thousand Communist workers. What kind of unitary politics is that? They are no Communists, because for the sake of the reformists they walked out of the Communist International.

As you see, these people even call themselves Communist, and yet they are actually more like the last Mohicans in the centrist camp. The Communist International had to say clearly and frankly whether such people can belong to us or not. As you know, some voices were raised before the congress suggesting that we were perhaps in the wrong, and that such people do in fact belong in our ranks. The Third Congress spoke on this question with complete clarity. It said: he who is not with us is against us. The Communist International believes firmly and resolutely that such elements cannot belong to it, and that we must bypass the leaders while struggling to bring these workers into our ranks.

This complex of decisions shows the true face of our congress. We have quite openly criticised various errors – which you may call leftist or whatever – that were harmful to our cause. At the same time we have made clear that half-centrist forces have no place in our ranks. Here is a line that is entirely clear and will, I trust, be understood by every ordinary worker.

We also brought clarity to the trade-union question. It was said quite correctly that the resolution of this congress breathes the same spirit as that of the Second Congress.[21] We want to continue along these lines. We have not limited ourselves to proposing abstract guidelines. Simultaneously with our congress, the first world congress of the trade unions is meeting, and – what is even more significant – during that conference important ties have been established within the largest branches of industry. They will now initiate a decisive and weighty economic struggle against the bourgeoisie and the Amsterdam International.

In addition, comrades, there is the youth congress, which is still meeting and which will obviously contribute a great deal to improving the training and organisation of our dearly beloved youth vanguard for its future struggles. There was also a women's conference, which preceded our congress.

---

21. A reference to the Second Congress resolution, 'Theses on the Trade Union Movement, Factory Committees, and the Communist International'. In Riddell (ed.), 2WC, 2, pp. 625–34.

We adopted today a resolution on the organisation question that, I hope, will aid greatly in strengthening the party. The section on the obligation to be active is of great importance, in my opinion, and must not be overlooked. In the past, our parties were really much too loose and not organised strictly enough. Ordinary workers must know how they are to take part in the party's legal and illegal work. The section on the obligation to be active must be explained everywhere. In all the smaller meetings, it must be brought home to workers that they have to take part in this work. That will signify a great step forward.

Comrades, right in the final days, as our work was coming to an end, we received a great deal of news from Europe that showed us, once more, how acute is the overall situation in Europe and that we must be prepared at any moment for a collapse of the present balance of forces. You need only consider the telegram from Rome, which says that 50,000 or more workers came together, without regard to party distinctions and under Communist leadership, in struggle against the Fascists.[22] Two days earlier, Serrati's party concluded a military pact with the Fascists, one of whose conditions was the disarming of Italian proletarians.[23] And then 50,000 workers rise up in Rome, go onto the streets, form battalions of war veterans, and declare a holy war against the bourgeoisie.

What does that tell us? It tells us that Europe is still in a revolutionary situation. The news from Berlin regarding the outbreak of a strike among municipal workers shows that there is more than enough inflammable material present.[24] It shows that we were right in saying that the situation in Europe remains revolutionary. That is why we must prepare better, in order to strike more effectively. We have said that a revolutionary must possess not only fire in his heart, but a hand that is strong and an eye that is sure, in order to reduce our defeats to the minimum. Every blow against the bourgeoisie must be considered ten times before it is struck. But when we strike the blow, it must find the enemy's heart.

---

22. The anti-fascist demonstration of fifty thousand in Rome on 8 July 1921 was in fact sponsored by the Arditi del Popolo, a fighting organisation for anti-Fascist defence that arose independently of the Communist and Socialist parties. The CP and SP leaderships were not involved in organising the demonstration.

23. In early July 1921 the Socialist Party began negotiations with the Fascists to reach a 'pacification pact', which would be signed on 3 August.

24. In early July 1921 eighty thousand Berlin municipal workers voted to go on strike for higher pay. The strike was averted following negotiations between the workers' representatives and the Berlin Municipal Council.

The organisational unification that we have arrived at here will assist us in achieving a genuine international fraternisation of the revolutionary proletariat. No bombastic phrases here, but nonetheless we must attempt during the coming period to actually achieve a degree of genuine international coordination, rather than just talk about it. We must attempt to knit together the revolutionary parties, and to bring the parties in Central Europe closer together. Central Europe should be defined here in the broadest sense possible, to include Italy and the Balkans, as well as – of course – Czechoslovakia.

The new Executive must do all in its power to bring these parties closer together. These parties must attempt, in every way possible, to strengthen their ties, and to prepare truly common demonstrations and truly decisive struggles. That should be the meaning of our decisions. We will not proceed merely propagandistically. We will also set about – cautiously but also irresistibly, energetically, doggedly, and tenaciously – to truly prepare the struggles that are now approaching.

The congress has honoured our country and our party once again by leaving the headquarters of the Executive here. We hope that this is only provisional. For this year, it will still be in Moscow, but for the following year we earnestly desire that it should be in Berlin, in Paris – and we should be very happy if it is in Milan. We are even prepared, comrades, despite the rather poor air and the very wet climate, to vote for London next year. (*Laughter*)

Comrades, when you take your leave from us in the next few days, the thoughts of us Russian revolutionaries will be turned, deeply moved, to the struggle that you are approaching. Yes, we still have to endure difficult times in Russia, very true, and our people, our working class, endures a great deal. But we are justified in saying, comrades, that the most difficult period is now behind us. It lies in the past, and after only a period of exertion we will lead the proletariat of our country, with firm steps, to complete victory.

But all of you, comrades, are going to countries ruled by the capitalists, under the dictatorship of the bourgeoisie, where thousands of our best brothers are languishing in prison, where hundreds are shot each day. You all run the danger of soon being imprisoned or perhaps suffering even worse for the cause of communism. We must impress on the ordinary worker, who today perhaps does not yet belong to our party but will join it tomorrow, that each of us is determined to give all that he has for the party. (*Loud applause*)

We should educate the youth and the adult workers in the belief that there is nothing higher and more sacred in the world than a Communist Party, a Communist world party, the Communist International. (*Loud applause*) And come what may, comrades, even though destiny may demand even greater sacrifices from us than we have made so far, however trying the struggle may be – and it will be trying – we will live and die with a single call: Long live the Communist International! (*Prolonged loud applause and cheers. The members of the congress rise from their seats and sing the 'Internationale'*)

**Koenen** (Chair): That concludes the Third World Congress of the Communist International.

*(The session is adjourned at 2:30 a.m.)*

# List of Delegations

| Country | Party | Participants |
|---|---|---|
| Argentina | CP | 2 |
| Armenia | CP | 8 |
| Azerbaijan | CP | 6 |
| Austria | CP | 7 |
|  | PZ[1] | 14 |
| Australia | CP | 4 |
| Baku | Youth | 1 |
|  | Eastern Bureau | 2 |
| Bashkiria | CP | 2 |
| Belgium | Socialist Revolutionaries | 2 |
|  | Youth | 1 |
|  | CP | 2 |
| Britain | CP | 14 |
|  | SP | 1 |
|  | Antiparliamentary Group | 1 |
| Bukhara | CP | 7 |
| Bulgaria | CP | 19 |
|  | Youth | 1 |
| Canada | SP | 1 |
| China | CP | 1 |
|  | Youth | 1 |
| Constantinople | CP | 1 |
| Czechoslovakia | CP | 27 |
|  | Youth | 2 |
| Denmark | CP | 6 |
| Egypt | CP | 1 |
| Estonia | CP | 5 |
|  | USP | 2 |
|  | Youth | 1 |

---

1. PZ may stand for Poale Zion.

| | | |
|---|---|---|
| Far Eastern Republic | CP | 2 |
| | Youth | 1 |
| Finland | CP | 30 |
| France | CP | 8 |
| | Syndicalists | 9 |
| | Youth | 3 |
| | Syndicalist Minority | 11 |
| Fünfkirchen[2] | SP | 3 |
| Georgia | CP | 11 |
| | Youth | 1 |
| Germany | KAPD | 5 |
| | VKPD | 25 |
| | Youth | 8 |
| | Women | 1 |
| | VKPD (Opposition) | 2 |
| Greece | CP | 3 |
| Hungary | CP | 12 |
| | Youth | 1 |
| India | CP | 4 |
| | Youth | 1 |
| Iran | CP | 5 |
| Ireland | CP | 2 |
| Italy | CP | 21 |
| | Youth | 4 |
| | SP | 3 |
| Java | CP | 1 |
| Khiva | Youth | 1 |
| Kirghizia | CP | 1 |
| Korea | CP | 2 |
| Latvia | CP | 11 |
| | Youth | 1 |
| Lithuania | CP | 9 |
| | Youth | 2 |
| Luxembourg | CP | 4 |
| | SP | 1 |
| | Youth | 1 |
| Mexico | CP | 1 |
| | Youth | 1 |

---

2. Fünfkirchen (Pécs) is a region south of Budapest that was occupied by Serbian troops until August 1921, after which it became part of Hungary.

| | | |
|---|---|---|
| Mongolia | Rev. Peoples Party | 2 |
| Near East | Youth | 1 |
| Netherlands | CP | 5 |
| | Youth | 1 |
| Norway | Workers' Party | 11 |
| | Youth | 2 |
| | CP | 1 |
| Palestine | CP | 2 |
| Poale Zion | | 3 |
| Poland | CP | 20 |
| | Bund | 3 |
| Romania | CP | 10 |
| | Youth | 4 |
| Russia | CP | 72 |
| | Youth | 2 |
| South Africa | Int. Socialist League | 2 |
| Sweden | CP | 15 |
| | Youth | 3 |
| Switzerland | CP | 13 |
| | Youth | 2 |
| Spain | CP | 5 |
| | Communist Workers' Party | 4 |
| | Syndicalists | 5 |
| Tatar Republic | CP | 1 |
| Turkey | CP | 4 |
| Turkestan | CP | 4 |
| | Revolutionary League | 2 |
| Ukraine | CP | 22 |
| United States | United CP | 10 |
| | Youth | 2 |
| | Japanese Com. Group | 1 |
| White Russia | CP | 2 |
| Yugoslavia | CP | 12 |
| | Youth | 2 |

604

# Theses, Resolutions, and Appeals

## Theses on the World Situation and the Tasks of the Communist International[1]

### I. *The essence of the question*

1.) The revolutionary movement toward the end of the imperialist war and in the postwar period is marked by a momentum never before seen in history. In March 1917 tsarism was overthrown. Beginning in May 1917, a tumultuous strike movement swept Britain. In November 1917, the Russian proletariat won state power. In November 1918, the German and Austro-Hungarian monarchies collapsed. The strike movement gripped a number of European countries and, during the following year, became exceptionally broad in scope. In March 1919, the soviet republic was born in Hungary. At the end of the year, the United States was shaken by turbulent strikes by metalworkers, miners, and railwaymen. In Germany, following the January and March battles in 1919, the movement reached its peak during the Kapp Putsch of March 1920. In France, the moment of greatest internal political tension occurred in May 1920. In Italy, the movement of the industrial and agricultural proletariat, growing continually in strength, led in September 1920 to the workers'

---

1. This resolution, submitted by Trotsky and Varga, was presented and discussed in Sessions 2 and 3, and approved in Session 16.
  The English-language text is best known from a translation in Trotsky's *First Five Years of the Communist International* (Trotsky 1972), also found on: <www.marxists.org>, which is based on a Russian text. The present translation is taken from the German version, which is somewhat different in formulation.

occupation of factories, mills, and estates. In December 1920, the Czech proletariat wielded the weapon of a political mass strike. In March 1921, the workers of Central Germany and the miners of Britain began massive strikes.

The movement was particularly extended and intense in the countries involved in the War, and especially in the defeated countries. However, it also extended to neutral countries. In Asia and Africa, the revolutionary indignation of millions of colonial peoples was awakened or intensified.

This mighty wave, however, did not sweep away either world or European capitalism.

2.) During the year between the Second and Third Congresses of the Communist International, a number of working-class uprisings and struggles ended in partial defeats (the offensive of the Red Army toward Warsaw in August 1920, the movement of the Italian proletariat in September 1920, the uprising of German workers in March 1921).

The initial phase of the postwar revolutionary movement was marked by its elemental power, a lack of definition in its methods and goals, and the extraordinary panic it inspired among the ruling classes. This period now seems to be essentially over. Without a doubt, the bourgeoisie has recovered its self-confidence as a class and its state structure has regained the appearance of solidity. The panicky terror regarding communism has not vanished but has certainly abated. The leaders of the bourgeoisie even boast of the power of state institutions, and everywhere they have launched both an economic and political offensive against the working masses.

3.) Consequently, the Communist International poses both to itself and to the entire working class the following questions: to what extent does the new political stance of the bourgeoisie toward the proletariat express the actual relationship of forces? Is the bourgeoisie really close to restoring the social equilibrium that was disrupted by the War? Are there grounds to project that political tremors and class struggles will now give way to a new and prolonged epoch of capitalist consolidation and growth? Does it therefore follow that the Communist International needs to revise its programme and policies?

II. *The War, the speculative boom, and the crisis. The countries of Europe*

4.) The two decades before the War were a period of particularly forceful capitalist development. The periods of boom were marked by their long duration and high intensity; the periods of depression were brief. In general, the curve sloped decidedly upward, as the capitalist nations enriched themselves.

Those directing the world's fate, having taken a close reading through their trusts, cartels, and consortiums, concluded that the rapidly expanding production could not escape a collision with the limits of the capitalist world market's capacity. They therefore sought to break free of these limits by violent surgery. In place of the imminent period of extended economic depression, they substituted the bloody paroxysm of world war, two methods with a single result: massive destruction of the productive forces.

The War, however, combined the exceptional destructive power of its methods with the unforeseen length of time during which they were applied. In the end, the War not only destroyed the economically 'superfluous' productive forces, but weakened, undermined, and ruined Europe's entire productive apparatus as well. At the same time, the War boosted the mighty capitalist expansion in the United States and the feverish rise of Japan. The world economy's centre of gravity shifted from Europe to the United States.

5.) The bourgeoisie quite rightly considered its most dangerous moment to be the time when the four years of slaughter were brought to an end, the time of demobilisation and transition from wartime to peacetime conditions. Given the exhaustion and chaos resulting from the War, this transition necessarily resulted in crisis. Indeed, the countries devastated by the War did witness mighty proletarian movements during the two years that followed.

The bourgeoisie nonetheless preserved its ruling position. One of the main reasons for this was the fact that what began a few months after the War was the onset – not of the crisis that seemed inevitable – but of an economic upswing. It lasted for about a year and a half. Industry almost completely absorbed the workers released from the army. Although workers' wages did not fully keep pace with the general increase of prices for consumer goods, wages did rise continuously, creating a mirage of economic accomplishment.

It was precisely this boom of 1919–20 that eased the most acute postwar period of liquidating the War, giving a sharp boost to the bourgeoisie's self-confidence and raising the question of whether a new period of organic capitalist development had begun. However, the upswing of 1919–20 was not at bottom the beginning of postwar restoration of the capitalist economy, but rather only a prolongation of the artificial prosperity created by War.

6.) The imperialist war broke out at a time when a crisis, which originated in the United States (1913), had begun to threaten Europe. The normal course of the industrial cycle was then interrupted by the War, which itself became one of the most powerful economic forces. The War created an almost unlimited market for the main branches of industry, which were almost completely protected from any form of competition and acted as a powerful and insatiable purchaser. Production of the means of production was replaced by production of the means of destruction. Objects of personal consumption, whose prices rose without let-up, were consumed by millions of people who did not produce but destroyed, a process that signified ruin. Because of the contradictions of capitalist society, escalated to extremes, this process took on the appearance and form of enrichment. The state floated one loan after another, flooding the market with paper money, reckoned not in millions but in billions. Machines and buildings wore out and were not replaced. The land was poorly cultivated. Important construction projects in the cities and along the transport routes were cancelled. Meanwhile, the quantity of government bonds, credits, banknotes, and treasury notes grew without limit. Fictitious capital grew even as productive capital was destroyed. The system of credit was transformed from a means of circulating commodities to a means of mobilising national wealth for the War, including the wealth of future generations.

Frightened by the danger of catastrophic crisis, the capitalist state's postwar response was just the same as it had been during the conflict: new issues of currency, new loans, regulation of the most important prices, profit guarantees, bread subsidies, and other types of state subsidies for salaries and wages, plus maintenance of wartime censorship and military dictatorship.

7.) At the same time, the end of military operations and the restoration of international relations, even if on a reduced scale, facilitated demand for every type of commodity in every part of the world. The War left behind large stocks of unused goods. Suppliers and speculators laid out the money in their possession wherever they saw the promise of the highest immediate profit. This led to a feverish upswing in commerce. As for industry, although prices rose enormously and dividends reached incredible levels, not a single branch of production reached prewar levels.

8.) The bourgeois governments, together with the banking and industrial trusts, succeeded in postponing the beginning of the economic crisis to the moment when the political crisis, caused by army demobilisation and the initial assessment of the War's consequences, had begun to abate. True, this was done at the cost of further organic disruption of the economic system (growth of fictitious capital, monetary depreciation, speculation rather than healing the economic wounds). Nonetheless, the bourgeoisie received a breathing spell and imagined that the danger of crisis had been postponed indefinitely. It was a moment of exceptional optimism. It seemed that the needs of reconstruction had opened up an extended epoch of expansion of industry, commerce, and especially speculation. These hopes were shattered in 1920.

The crisis began in March 1920, affecting first the financial sector, then commerce, and finally industry. It began in Japan, reached the United States in

April (a slight fall in prices had begun in January), then extended in April to Britain, France, and Italy. It reached Europe's neutral states, appeared in mitigated form in Germany, and, in the second half of 1920, extended over all regions embraced by capitalist relations.

9.) *The crisis of 1920* is thus not a conventional stage in the 'normal' industrial cycle. It is a deeply rooted *reaction against the fictitious upswing during the War and the first two postwar years, which was based on ruin and exhaustion.* This is one of the most important elements in a correct assessment of the world situation.

The normal succession of boom and bust took place along the upward curve of industrial development. During the last seven years, production in Europe has not risen; instead it has fallen significantly.

Destruction of the economic foundation must also find expression in an inner consolidation of the entire superstructure. In the coming years, Europe's economy can only shrink and shrivel, in order to achieve a degree of inner coordination. The curve of development of the productive forces will decline from its present fictitious heights. In such conditions, an upswing can only be brief and primarily speculative in character. Crises will be lengthy and profound. The present crisis in Europe is one of underproduction. This is a reaction of impoverishment in the face of efforts to produce, to trade, and to live on the same broad capitalist scale as formerly.

10.) *Britain* is the country of Europe that is strongest economically and suffered the least through the War. Nonetheless, even here there is no chance of restoring capitalist equilibrium after the War. True, thanks to its all-embracing organisation and its status as victor, Britain achieved certain gains after the War in the fields of *commerce and finance*: it improved its balance of trade, raised the exchange rate of the pound sterling, and achieved a fictitious surplus in its national budget. However, industry in Britain moved backward after the War, not forward. Both labour productivity and national income are considerably lower than before the War. Conditions in the main branch of industry, coal mining, worsen continually, pulling down other branches of industry. The persistent strike wave is not the cause but the result of the decline of Britain's economy.

11.) *France, Belgium, and Italy* were economically ruined by the War beyond any cure. The attempt to restore the French economy at the cost of Germany is crude robbery combined with diplomatic extortion. It intensifies Germany's devastation (coal, machines, cattle, gold) without saving France. The entire economy of continental Europe is severely damaged by this effort. France receives far less than Germany loses. Although French peasants, through a supreme effort, have restored considerable parts of the ruined landscape, and although certain industries (chemical, armaments) experienced new growth during the War, France is headed for economic ruin. The national debt and government expenses (militarism) have reached unbearable heights. At the end of the last upswing, the French currency had lost 60 per cent of its value. Restoration of the French economy is hindered by the severe losses of human life during the War – losses that, given the low rate of population increase, cannot be made good. The economies of Italy and Belgium, with some variations, is in similar condition.

12.) The illusory nature of the upswing is most clearly evident in *Germany*. While prices have increased seven times over during a year and a half, productivity has continued to fall. After the War, Germany appeared to take part in international trade successfully, but for this it paid a double price: national capital was squandered (destruction of the production, transport, and credit systems), and the living standard of the working class continued to fall. The successes of German exporters, viewed in terms of general economic criteria, signify pure loss. The exports actually represent nothing other than a clearance sale of Germany at low prices. Capitalist circles claim a steadily growing part of the national wealth, which is constantly declining. The German workers are becoming the coolies of Europe.

13.) The supposed political independence of the *small neutral countries* is actually maintained only by antagonism among the great powers. These countries subsist in the pores of the world market, whose fundamental character after the War is determined by Britain, Germany, the United States, and France. During the War, the bourgeoisie of Europe's small neutral countries raked in enormous profits. The devastation of the warring countries of Europe, however, also entailed economic devastation in the neutral countries. Their debts increased; their currency sank in value. The crisis dealt them blow after blow.

III. *The United States, Japan, the colonial countries, and Soviet Russia*

14.) The development of the *United States* during the War is, in a certain respect, exactly opposite to that of Europe. The participation of the United States in the War was essentially that of a supplier. It was not subjected to the direct destructive force of the War. The War's indirect destructive force on transportation, agriculture, and the like was much weaker than in Britain, let alone France or Germany. On the other hand, the United States benefited from the elimination or significant weakening of European competition, and brought several important branches of industry (petroleum, shipbuilding, automobiles, coal) to a level of development it had never anticipated. Today most of the countries of Europe are dependent not only on American petroleum and grain but also on American coal.

Before the War, the United States mainly exported agricultural products and raw materials, which made up two-thirds of its exports; now industrial products account for 60 per cent of exports. Before the War, the United States was a debtor; now it is the creditor of the entire world. Approximately half of the world's gold reserves are now located in the United States, and gold continues to pour in. Before the War, the pound sterling played the leading role in world markets; this role has now passed to the dollar.

15.) But American capitalism, too, has been thrown out of equilibrium. Its vigorous industrial upswing was made possible by an unusual coincidence of unusual circumstances in the world situation: the elimination of European competition and, above all, the demands of the European war market. Following the War, devastated Europe is unable to regain its previous role as a competitor of the United States on the world market. Moreover, it is also unable to retain more than a small part of its previous importance as a market for American products. Meanwhile, to a much greater extent than before the War, the United States is an exporting country. The productive system that overdeveloped during the War cannot be fully utilised because of an absence of markets. Certain industries have become seasonal in character, offering employment to the workers during only part of the year. The crisis in the United States is the beginning of its profound and continuing economic dislocation as a result of the European War. This is the result of the destruction of the previous worldwide division of labour.

16.) *Japan* also took advantage of the War to expand into the world market. Its development, however, is incomparably more limited than that of the United States; in several branches of industry it has a hothouse character. When competitors were lacking, its productive forces were sufficient to conquer a market, but they will be inadequate to maintain this market in struggle against the more powerful capitalist countries. That is why the acute crisis began precisely in Japan.

17.) *The overseas countries*, including the purely *colonial countries* (South America, Canada, Australia, China, India, Egypt, etc.), for their part, utilised the breaking off of international relations to develop domestic industry. The world crisis has gripped these countries as well. The development of national industry in these countries, in turn, is also a source of additional trade difficulties for Britain and Europe as a whole.

18.) A survey of production, commerce, and credit not only in Europe but in the world market as a whole provides no grounds to identify even the beginning of a restoration of stable equilibrium.

The economic decline of Europe continues, and the devastation of Europe's economic foundations will be fully felt only in the coming years.

The world market is devastated. Europe needs American products but has nothing of value to offer in exchange. Europe suffers from anaemia; the United States from excessive growth. Gold has been destroyed as a world currency. Devaluation of the currency of European countries (up to 99 per cent) poses very serious obstacles to the exchange of goods on the world market. Incessant and sharp currency fluctuations transform capitalist production into chaotic speculation. The world market is left without a universal equivalent.

Restoration of the gold standard in Europe would be possible only by expanding exports and reducing imports. But that is exactly what devastated Europe is unable to do, while the United States, for its part, protects itself from the dumping of European products by raising its tariffs.

Moreover, Europe is still a madhouse. Most countries are enacting export and import bans and multiplying their tariffs. Britain has introduced tariffs. A gang of Entente speculators, especially in France, has gained control of German exports and its entire economic life. The former territory of Austria-Hungary is now criss-crossed by a web of tariff barriers. The system of peace treaties grows more and more tangled.

19.) The elimination of Soviet Russia as a market for industrial goods and a supplier of raw materials has contributed greatly to the disruption of world economic equilibrium. However, Russia's return to the world market in the near future would not greatly change the situation. Russia's capitalist organism was highly dependent on the productive forces of world industry. This dependency was intensified during the War with regard to the Entente countries. The blockade cut off these vital interrelationships with a single blow. In a country devastated and ravaged during three years of civil war, organising new branches of industry was absolutely excluded. But without them, the old industrial structure was doomed to decay through the wearing out of its capital inventory. What is more, hundreds of thousands of the best and – in large measure – the most skilled proletarian forces were enrolled in the Red Army. Given the historical conditions – blockade, incessant warfare, the heritage of ruin – no other regime would have been able to maintain the country's economic life and create conditions for its centralised direction. Beyond any doubt, the struggle against world imperialism had to be carried out at the cost of further decline of the productive forces in several branches of the economy. Only now, as the blockade weakens and with the re-establishment of appropriate forms of exchange between city and countryside, does the Soviet government achieve the capacity to strengthen, gradually but with increasing firmness, centralised leadership in the country's economic revival.

IV. *The aggravation of social contradictions*

20.) The War, which entailed a historically unprecedented destruction of productive forces, did not halt the process of social differentiation. On the contrary, during the last seven years, in the countries that suffered most from the War, there have been enormous strides forward in the proletarianisation of the broad intermediate layers, including the new middle classes (employees, civil servants, etc.), and in the concentration of property in the hands of small cliques (trusts, combines, etc.). Stinnes has become the central issue of German economic life.[2]

In all the warring European states, prices of all goods have risen, while the currency's value has plunged catastrophically. In itself, this signifies a redistribution of national income to the detriment of the working class, civil servants, employees, small-scale rentiers, and all those with a more or less fixed income.

With respect to its material resources, Europe has been thrown back several decades. Moreover, the aggravation of social antagonisms continues without letup. Far from being halted, it was markedly accelerated. This underlying fact is sufficient to banish any hope for enduring peaceful development in a democratic framework. *On the one hand, we have progressive differentiation and Stinnesisation; on the other, proletarianisation and pauperisation. Economic decline lends the class struggle its intensive, convulsive, and bitter character.* In this regard, the present crisis merely continues the work of the War and the speculative postwar boom.

21.) The increase of prices for agricultural production created an illusion of general enrichment of the village, while bringing the rich peasants a genuine increase in income and property. The peasants succeeded in paying off with depreciated paper money, which they had accumulated in large quantities, the debts they had contracted in undepreciated currency. But agriculture involves more than simply paying off mortgages.

Despite enormous increase in the price of land, despite unscrupulous utilisation of the food monopoly, despite the enrichment of big landowners and rich peasants, the decline of European agriculture is unmistakable. It is seen in the frequent regression to more extensive forms of cultivation: tilled land

---

2. For Stinnes, see p. 630, n. 3.

converted to pasture, disappearance of livestock, three-field crop rotation.[3] This was caused in part by the shortage of labour, the shrinkage of herds, the lack of chemical fertiliser, high prices of manufactured goods. Also, in Central and Eastern Europe, production was deliberately reduced in reprisal against attempts of the government to take possession of agricultural products.

Large and, to some extent, middle peasants are creating strong political and economic organisations to defend themselves against the burdens of reconstruction. Taking advantage of the bourgeoisie's distress, they are imposing on the government, as the price of their support against the proletariat, a one-sided pro-peasant tariff and tax policy that restricts capitalist reconstruction. A division between the bourgeoisie of village and city has arisen that saps the strength of the bourgeois class.

At the same time, a large segment of the poorer peasants are proletarianised and pauperised. The village has become a breeding place for discontent, and class consciousness is growing among the agricultural proletariat.

On the other hand, however, the overall impoverishment of Europe renders it incapable of buying sufficient quantities of American grain, causing a severe crisis of the farm economy on the other side of the Atlantic. We note an economic decline among peasants and small farmers not only in Europe but also in the United States, Canada, Argentina, Australia, and South Africa.

22.) As a rule, the status of *government and private-sector employees* has worsened more severely than that of the proletariat, as a result of inflation. Torn out of their stable conditions of existence, the lower and middle layers of civil servants have become a factor for political unrest, undermining the stability of the state apparatus that they serve. In such a transitional period, the new middle class, which according to the reformists ought to be the pillar of conservatism, can become a force for revolution.

23.) Capitalist Europe has definitively lost its economic primacy, which was the very foundation of equilibrium among its social classes. The efforts of European countries (Britain and, in part, France) to restore previous conditions only reinforce chaos and insecurity.

24.) Property in Europe is further concentrated amid conditions of general impoverishment. In the United States, by contrast, feverish capitalist money-making has brought the concentration and sharpening of class antagonisms

---

3. Three-field cultivation is a method of farming widely used in Europe during the Middle Ages. In this method one-third of the land was planted in the spring, one-third in the fall, and one-third was to lie fallow. By the twentieth century, it had been largely superseded.

to a new peak. Sharp fluctuations of the business cycle, flowing from the overall instability of the world market, lend to class struggles on American soil an extremely tense and revolutionary character. Following a period of historically unprecedented capitalist expansion, revolutionary struggles will flare up with exceptional force.

25.) Emigration of workers and peasants across the ocean always served as a safety valve for the capitalist system in Europe. It increased in periods of extended depression and after the collapse of revolutionary movements. At present, however, the United States and Australia are placing increasing barriers in the path of immigration. The safety valve of emigration has been shut off.

26.) Capitalism's vigorous expansion in the East, especially in India and China, created a new social foundation for revolutionary struggle. The bourgeoisie of these countries clings tightly to foreign capital, which wields it as a significant and compliant tool. Therefore, its struggle against foreign imperialism – as a very weak competitor – is inherently conflicted and feeble. In addition, the expansion of the native proletariat paralyses the national-revolutionary impulses of the capitalist bourgeoisie. Meanwhile, the numerous peasant masses gain a revolutionary leadership: the Communist vanguard of the proletariat.

The combination of national oppression imposed militarily by foreign imperialism, capitalist exploitation by both the foreign and native bourgeoisies, and the survivals of feudal servitude create favourable conditions for the young proletariat of the colonies, in which it will develop quickly and take its place at the head of the revolutionary movement of the broad peasant masses.

The revolutionary people's movement in India and the other colonies has become just as essential a part of the world revolution as the uprising of the proletariat in the capitalist countries of the Old and New World.

V. *International relations*

27.) The general state of the world economy – above all the decline of Europe – causes lengthy periods of great economic difficulties and convulsions and both partial and generalised economic crises. In the wake of the War and the Versailles Treaty, international relations exacerbate the situation even further.

Imperialism arose from the drive of the productive forces to destroy national borders and create a unified European and global economic territory. The clash of hostile imperialist forces, however, has created many new borders in Central and Eastern Europe, with new customs authorities and new armies. In terms of its state and economic structure, Europe has been thrown back into the Middle Ages.

On this debilitated and devastated soil, an army is now being nourished that is half again as large as the army of 1914, the high point of armed peace.

28.) The policies of France, the leading force on the European continent, now combines two tendencies. First, we see the blind rage of a usurer prepared to strangle his insolvent debtor, and the greed of predatory heavy industry, which wants to utilise the coal fields of the Saar, Ruhr, and Upper Silesian districts to replace bankrupt financial imperialism with the preconditions for industrial imperialism.

The second tendency is directed against Britain. Britain's policy is based on separating German coal from French iron, although their unification is one of the most important preconditions for the reconstruction of Europe.

29.) The British Empire now appears to stand at the summit of its power. It retained its old possessions and acquired new ones. However, present conditions demonstrate that the dominant world position of Britain stands in contradiction to its actual economic decline. German capitalism, incomparably more advanced both technologically and organisationally, has been overthrown by force of arms. But the United States, which has now economically subjugated both halves of the hemisphere, stands as a victorious enemy more dangerous than Germany. As a result of superior organisation and technology, productivity of labour in US industry is much higher than in Britain.

The United States now produces 65% to 70% of the world's consumed petroleum, providing the gasoline on which the automobile and tractor economy, the navies, and aviation are dependent. Britain's century-long monopoly in the coal market has finally been broken. The United States has taken first place, and its exports to Europe are increasing menacingly. In the merchant marine, the United States has almost overtaken Britain. The United States no longer tolerates Britain's monopoly of overseas cables. British industry is now on the defensive, and under the pretext of combating competition from German dumping, it is arming itself with protective tariffs against the United States. The British navy, composed in large measure of obsolete ships, is stagnating, while the Harding presidency has taken over from Wilson a construction programme that aims to secure naval predominance within two or three years.

Thus Britain, despite its victory over Germany, will either be reduced automatically to the rank of a second-rate power, or it will be compelled in the near future to put the power accumulated in earlier times to the test in a life-and-death struggle against the United States.

That is why Britain is consolidating its treaty with Japan and making efforts, through concessions, to secure the help of France, or at least its neutrality.

The increased international importance of France during the past years is due not to any gain in its strength but to the weakening of Britain.

Nonetheless, Germany's surrender in May on the reparations question represents a temporary victory for Britain, assuring the further economic decline of Central Europe without, however, excluding France's occupation of the Ruhr region in the immediate future.[4]

30.) The antagonism between Japan and the United States, concealed for a time by their participation in the war against Germany, is now developing with full force. Japan edged closer to American shores during the War by occupying a number of strategically important islands in the Pacific.

The crisis of Japan's rapidly developing industry has aggravated once more the problem of emigration. Japan, densely populated and poor in natural resources, is forced to export either products or people. On either path, it collides with the United States, in California, in China, and on the small island of Yap.[5]

Japan spends more than half of its budget on the army and navy. In the struggle between Britain and the United States, Japan will play the role at sea that fell to France on land in the war with Germany. For now, Japan gains advantage from the antagonism between Britain and the United States, but the final struggle of these giants will be played out to Japan's disadvantage.

31.) In terms of its causes and its main participants, the last great war was a European conflict. The heart of the struggle was the antagonism between Britain and Germany. The entry of the United States broadened the framework of the struggle, to be sure, but its central direction remained unchanged: the European conflict was settled by drawing on the means of the entire world. The War, in its own way, resolved the contradiction between Britain and Germany, and thus also that between the United States and Germany, but it left unresolved the question of the mutual relationship between the United States and Britain. Instead, it posed this question, for the first time, as the focus of world politics. It reduced the question of US-Japanese relations

---

4. On 5 May 1921, the Allies threatened to occupy the Ruhr district unless Germany agreed to pay 132 billion gold marks in reparations including one billion that month. Sixteen days later, Germany accepted this ultimatum.

5. Among the signs of tension between the United States and Japan were California's 1913 and 1920 laws against Japanese immigrant farmers and United States-Japanese competition for economic and commercial opportunities in China.

Yap Island, a Japanese possession in the western Caroline Islands, was a centre for underwater cable communication, a role that made it a point of conflict between Japan and the United States.

to second-rank importance. The recent war was thus a European prelude to a genuine world war to resolve the question of imperialist supremacy.

32.) But this is only one of the axes of world politics. There is a second axis. The recent war resulted in the establishment of the Soviet federation and the Third International. The assembled international revolutionary forces are arrayed in fundamental opposition to every imperialist alliance. From the point of view of the interests of the proletariat and the maintenance of peace, whether the alliance between Britain and France is maintained or broken off is no different from that of whether the British-Japanese agreement is or is not renewed or whether the United States does or does not join the League of Nations: the proletariat sees no guarantees in the transitory, treacherous, predatory, and disloyal combinations of capitalist states.

The conclusion of peace treaties and trade agreements between some capitalist countries and Soviet Russia does not indicate that the world bourgeoisie has abandoned the notion of destroying the Soviet republic. Rather, the struggle has undergone only a temporary change in its methods and forms. The Japanese stroke in the Far East may already signal the onset of a new period of armed intervention.[6]

It is quite clear that the slower the revolutionary movement of the world proletariat develops, the more inevitably will the bourgeoisie be forced by its international economic and political contradictions to seek a new bloody settlement of accounts on a world scale. In this case, the 'restoration of capitalist equilibrium' after a new war would take place amid economic destitution and cultural collapse in comparison to which present conditions in Europe would seem the height of well-being.

33.) Even though the experience of the last war showed with frightening clarity that the War was a miscalculation – this truth is recognised not only by socialist pacifists but by the bourgeoisie – the economic, political, ideological, and technical preparations for a new war are in full swing across the capitalist world. Anti-revolutionary humanitarian pacifism only assists militarism.

Social Democrats of every shading and the Amsterdam trade unionists tell the international proletariat to adapt to the norms of economic life and international law resulting from the War. By this they act as indispensable accomplices of the imperialist bourgeoisie in preparing a new war, which will threaten to destroy human civilisation once and for all.

---

6. For the Japanese intervention in the Soviet Far East, see p. 657, n. 10.

## VI. *The working class after the War*

34.) The prospect of reconstructing capitalism on the foundations outlined above poses basically the following question: Will the working class be prepared to make the sacrifices under these new and incomparably more difficult conditions that are required to re-establish stable conditions for its own slavery, more onerous and cruel even than what existed before the War?

The reconstruction of Europe's economy requires both the replacement of the productive apparatus destroyed in the War and extensive new formation of capital. This would be possible only if the proletariat were willing to labour under sharply reduced living standards. This is what the capitalists insist on, and this is what the traitorous leaders of the yellow Internationals advise workers to accept: first help capitalism to reconstruct, and then struggle for an improvement in the status of workers. But the proletariat of Europe is not prepared to accept this sacrifice; it demands an improvement in its conditions, which is in direct contradiction to what is objectively possible for capitalism.

That is the cause of the interminable strikes and uprisings; that is what makes restoring Europe's economy impossible. Restoring the currency signifies for many European states (Germany, France, Italy, Austria, Hungary, Poland, and the Balkan states) above all ridding themselves of unbearable debts, that is, declaring bankruptcy. But doing so entails enormously escalating the struggle among all the classes for a new distribution of national income. Restoring the currency also means reducing government expenditures at the masses' expense (abandoning regulation of wages and of prices for basic necessities), cutting off access to more inexpensive foreign goods for mass consumption, raising exports through reduction of production costs – that is, above all through renewed intensification of exploitation of the working masses.

Every serious measure to restore capitalist equilibrium damages even more the already devastated class equilibrium, providing new impetus for the class struggle. Whether capitalism can revive to new life becomes a question of the struggle of living forces, of classes and parties. If one of the two fundamental classes, the proletariat, should abandon revolutionary struggle, the bourgeoisie would doubtless establish a new capitalist equilibrium, one of material and intellectual decay – through new crises, new wars, further destitution of entire countries, and the death of yet more millions of working people.

But the present state of the international proletariat gives absolutely no justification for a prognosis of this kind.

35.) *The forces of lethargy, conservatism, and tradition* in social relations have been worn down and have lost most of their power over the consciousness of the working masses. True, Social Democracy and the trade unions, thanks to the organisational machine inherited from the past, still preserve their influence on a good part of the proletariat, but this has already been deeply undermined. The War brought about major changes not only in the proletariat's mood but in its composition, which is completely incompatible with the leisurely organisational progress of prewar times.

In most countries, the proletariat is still dominated by an extraordinarily expanded workers' bureaucracy. Welded tightly together, it has developed habits and methods of rule and is tied by a thousand threads to the institutions and bodies of the capitalist state. The bureaucracy enjoys the backing of:

- The better-off segment of production workers, who occupy administrative positions, or hope to do so, and provide the most reliable pillar of support for the workers' bureaucracy.
- The older generation of Social Democrats and trade unionists, chiefly skilled workers, who are tied to their organisations by decades of struggle and cannot take the decision to break with them, despite their betrayal. In many factories, however, skilled workers have been supplanted by the unskilled, many of whom are women.

Then there are:

- The millions of workers who have just passed through the school of war, are familiar with the use of weapons, and are ready, in large measure, to turn against the class enemy – but subject to a condition: serious preparation and reliable leadership as indispensible preconditions for victory.
- The millions of new workers, both men and – especially – women, drawn into industry during the War, have brought into the proletariat not only their petty-bourgeois prejudices but also their impatient aspirations for better living conditions.
- The millions of young working men and women, who rose up during the thunder of war and revolution, who are the most receptive to the teachings of communism, and who are burning with desire to act.
- The gigantic army of the unemployed, to some extent declassed or partly declassed, whose ebb and flow harshly portrays the decay of the capitalist economy and represents a constant threat to bourgeois order.

These layers of the proletariat, so diverse in their origins and character, were not immediately and homogeneously drawn into the postwar movement, and that remains true today. This accounts for the fluctuations, the ebb and flow, the attacks and retreats that mark the revolutionary struggle. But in their immense majority, the proletarian masses will be rapidly welded together by the shattering of all the old illusions, the fearsome insecurity of existence, the omnipotence of capital united in trusts, and by the bloody techniques of the militarised state. This many-millioned mass is seeking a firm and lucid leadership and a well-defined action programme. It thus provides the foundation on which a firmly united and centralised Communist Party can play a decisive role.

36.) Unquestionably, the conditions of the working class have worsened during the War. Only isolated groups of workers made headway. Families in which many members were able to hold jobs during the War succeeded in maintaining or even improving their living standards. In general, however, workers' wages did not keep pace with inflation.

In Central Europe, starting with the onset of war, the proletariat was subjected to constantly increasing deprivation. In the continental countries belonging to the Entente, the decline in living standards was, until recently, less evident. In Britain, the proletariat succeeded through energetic struggle in the final phase of the War in bringing to a halt the worsening of its living conditions. In the United States, conditions of some layers of the working class improved, while other layers maintained previous standards or suffered a worsening in their conditions.

The crisis hit the proletariat of the entire world with enormous force. Wages declined more quickly than prices. The number of jobless and part-time workers reached a level unprecedented in capitalist history.

Abrupt fluctuations in personal living conditions do not merely restrict the productivity of labour but exclude the possibility of restoring class equilibrium on the most important terrain, that of production. The instability of living conditions, reflecting the general instability of national and world economic conditions, is now one of the most important factors in revolutionary development.

## VII. *Perspectives and tasks*

37.) The War did not lead directly to a proletarian revolution. The bourgeoisie regards this fact, with some justification, as its great victory. Only a petty-bourgeois ignoramus, however, could view the fact that the European proletariat did not overthrow the bourgeoisie during the War or immediately after its end as evidence that the programme of the Communist International was bankrupt. The course of the Communist International is not based on predicting the onset of proletarian revolution at a dogmatically predetermined date on the calendar, or on the intention to mechanically carry out the revolution within a specified period of time. The revolution was and remains a struggle of living forces within given historical conditions. The disruption of capitalist equilibrium on a global scale creates favourable conditions of struggle for social revolution. All efforts of the Communist International have been and remain directed to taking full advantage of this situation.

The difference between the Communist International and both varieties of Social Democrats is not based on the fact that we have determined that the revolution must take place by a specific deadline, while they, by contrast, reject utopianism and putschism. Rather the difference lies in the fact that Social Democrats work against the actual development of the revolution. Whether in opposition or in government, they promote with all their strength restoring the equilibrium of the capitalist state. Communists, by contrast, utilise every path, every method, and every possibility to overturn the capitalist state and destroy it through the dictatorship of the proletariat.

In the course of the two and a half years since the War, the proletariat of several countries has demonstrated more energy, readiness for struggle, and self-sacrifice than would be needed for a victorious revolution, if the working class was headed by a strong, centralised, and battle-ready international Communist Party. However, for historical reasons, the proletariat was headed, during and immediately after the War, by the Second International, which served as an invaluable political tool of the bourgeoisie and still plays that role.

38.) In Germany, power actually rested in the hands of the working class at the end of 1918 and the beginning of 1919. The Social Democrats – Majority and Independent Socialists alike – and the trade unions employed their entire apparatus, their entire traditional influence, in order to hand over power to the bourgeoisie.

In Italy, the tempestuous revolutionary movement flooded over the country for a year and a half. Only the petty-bourgeois spinelessness of the Socialist Party, the treacherous policies of the parliamentary fraction, and the cowardly opportunism of the trade unionists permitted the bourgeoisie to repair its apparatus, mobilise its White Guards, and go over to an offensive against the proletariat, which had been temporarily disheartened by the bankruptcy of its previous leading bodies.

In Britain, the powerful strike movement of the past year was repeatedly repulsed by the government's ruthless imposition of military force and the resulting intimidation of the trade-union leaders. If the leaders had remained loyal to the cause of the working class, the trade-union machinery, despite its defects, could have been utilised for revolutionary struggles. The recent crisis of the Triple Alliance provided the occasion for a revolutionary confrontation with the bourgeoisie, which was prevented by the conservatism, cowardice, and betrayal of the trade-union leaders.[7] If the machinery of the British trade unions would accomplish only half the work in the interests of socialism that they have carried out in the interests of capitalism, the British proletariat could seize power with a minimum of casualties and could move forward to the planned transformation of the national economy.

The same is true, to a greater or lesser extent, in all the capitalist countries.

39.) It is incontestable that there has been a slowing in many countries of the open revolutionary proletarian struggle for power. However, it was not to be expected that the revolutionary postwar offensive, having not led to immediate victory, would continue to develop uninterruptedly in an upward curve. Political movements too have their cycles, their ups and downs. The enemy does not remain passive, but struggles. If the proletarian offensive does not lead to victory, the bourgeoisie seizes the first opportunity to launch a counterattack. The loss of some easily conquered positions induces temporary discouragement in the ranks of the proletariat. Nonetheless, it remains indisputable that the curve of capitalist development is generally – despite temporary upswings – moving downwards, while the curve of revolution, through all its fluctuations, is rising.

The re-establishment of capitalism requires, as a precondition, an enormous increase in exploitation, the destruction of millions of lives, the reduction of the standard of living for millions below the survival level, and the perpetual insecurity of proletarian existence. As a result, the workers are driven again and again to constant strikes and rebellions. These pressures and struggles build the masses' determination to overthrow the capitalist order.

40.) A Communist Party's basic task in the present crisis is and remains to lead, broaden, deepen, and unite the proletariat's present defensive struggles and, in pace with the developing situation, *turn them into decisive political struggles for power*. However, should the pace of these developments slow, and should the present economic crisis be followed in a greater or lesser number of countries by a period of expansion, this would not signify the beginning of an 'organic' epoch. So long as capitalism exists, such cyclical fluctuations are inevitable. They will accompany capitalism's death agony just as they did its youth and maturity.

In the event that the proletariat is thrown back during the present crisis by the capitalist offensive, the beginning of an economic upturn will see it move back to the offensive.

---

7. For the British miners' strike and its betrayal by the leaders of the Triple Alliance, see p. 78, n. 18 and p. 148, n. 10.

In that case, its economic offensive will inevitably raise the slogan of revenge for all the betrayals of the war period and all the robbery and humiliation of the crisis. It would thus display a tendency to turn into open civil war, just as the present defensive struggle does.

41.) Regardless of whether the revolutionary movement in the coming period proceeds at a rapid or slow tempo, the Communist Party must in either case be a *party of action*. It stands at the head of the struggling masses. It formulates clear and direct slogans for the struggle, while exposing the always compliant and compromise-oriented slogans of Social Democracy. Through all the vicissitudes of struggle, the Communist Party strives to consolidate new bases of support, accustom the masses to active manoeuvring, and arm them with new methods, preparing them for a direct encounter with the enemy forces. It utilises every breathing spell to learn the lessons of previous phases of struggle. It strives to deepen and broaden the class conflict and to link it nationally and internationally through unity of action and purpose. In this way, the Communist Party, at the head of the proletariat, aims to break all resistance on the road to its dictatorship and to social revolution.

## Resolution on the Report by the Executive Committee of the Communist International[8]

The congress has heard the Executive report and is satisfied with it. It confirms that the Executive's policies and activity during the past year were directed at carrying out the decisions of the Second Congress. In particular, the congress approves the way the Executive applied in different countries the Twenty-One Conditions established by the Second Congress. It also approves the Executive's work to form large, mass Communist parties and to combat ruthlessly the opportunist tendencies that came to light in these parties.

1.) In *Italy* the conduct of the Serrati leadership immediately following the Second Congress demonstrated that it did not take seriously either the World Congress decisions or the Communist International. Above all, this leadership's role in the September battles, its stance in Livorno, and, even more, its policies since that time clearly show that it wants to use communism only as a mask for its opportunist policies. These circumstances made the split inevitable. The congress welcomes the fact that Executive intervened firmly and decisively in this matter of fundamental importance. It approves the Executive Committee's subsequent decision to immediately recognise the Communist Party of Italy as the only Communist section in this country.

After the Communists left the Livorno Congress, it adopted the following resolution by Bentivoglio: 'Reaffirming fully the party's affiliation to the Communist International, the congress refers the dispute to the upcoming congress of the Communist International, to be dealt with there. The party commits itself now, in advance, to accept the decision of the congress and carry it out.'

The Third Congress of the Communist International is convinced that this decision was forced on the Serrati leadership by the pressure of revolutionary workers. The congress expects that when the Third World Congress decisions are made known, these revolutionary working-class forces will do everything possible to carry out these decisions in life.

In response to the appeal of the Livorno Congress, the Third World Congress issues the following ultimatum:

So long as the Socialist Party of Italy has not expelled those who took part in the reformist conference in Reggio Emilia and their supporters, this party cannot belong to the Communist International.

---

8. Approved in Session 9.

If this necessary precondition is fulfilled, the Third World Congress instructs the Executive to take the necessary steps to fuse the Socialist Party of Italy – cleansed of reformist and centrist forces – with the Communist Party of Italy as a unified section of the International.[9]

2.) In *Germany*, the USPD convention in Halle was the result of the Second World Congress decisions, which drew a balance sheet of the development of the workers' movement. The Executive acted to form a strong Communist Party in Germany, and experience has shown that this policy was correct.

The congress also fully approves the Executive's conduct regarding later developments in the VKPD. The congress voices its expectation that, in the future, the Executive will continue to apply strictly the principles of international revolutionary discipline.

3.) The *KAPD* was admitted as a sympathising party in order to test whether its future development would bring it closer to the Communist International. The elapsed waiting period has been sufficient. Now we must demand of the KAPD that it affiliate to the VKPD in a set time, failing which it will be expelled as a sympathising party of the Communist International.[10]

The congress greets the way that the Executive has applied the Twenty-One Conditions to the *French party*, by drawing away from the influence of Longuet opportunists the broad working masses who seek a road to communism and by speeding up their revolutionary development. The congress expects the Executive to continue in the future to promote the French party's development toward clarity in its principles and capacity for struggle.

4.) Regarding *Czechoslovakia*, the Executive has followed with patience and consideration every aspect of the revolutionary development of the proletariat, which has already given evidence of its will and capacity for struggle. The congress approves the Executive's resolution admitting the Communist Party of Czechoslovakia.

The congress expects the Executive to apply the Twenty-One Conditions fully to the Communist Party of Czechoslovakia. It must insist on the formation as quickly as possible of a unified Communist Party, bringing together the workers of every nation within Czechoslovakia around a clear Communist programme and a firm Communist leadership, with a centralist founda-

---

9. The PSI expelled its reformist faction in October 1922. Meeting the following month, the Comintern's Fourth Congress adopted a 'Resolution on the Italian Question' that called for a fusion of the Communist and Socialist parties. See Riddell (ed.) 2011b, 4WC, pp. 1138–42.

10. At its September 1921 congress, the KAPD formally rejected the Third Congress conditions for the party's continued membership in the Communist International.

tion. This party should rapidly and systematically win the trade unions and unify them across national barriers.

As regards the work in the *Near and Far East*, the congress welcomes the extensive agitation in this field. It is absolutely necessary to undertake a transition to organisational work in these countries.[11]

Finally, the congress rejects the objections that have been raised by open and concealed opponents of communism against a strict international centralisation of the Communist movement. The congress expresses its conviction that parties must make their best forces available to serve on the Executive, in order to achieve an even more effective central political leadership of the Communist parties everywhere, unified in indissoluble alliance.

The lack of a central leadership has been evident, for example, with regard to unemployment and reparations, where the Executive did not intervene with sufficient speed and effectiveness.

The congress expects that the Executive will strive to establish an improved communications apparatus, with strengthened collaboration of the affiliated parties, which in turn will put the Executive in a position to carry out its steadily growing tasks better than before.

---

11. This paragraph was added to the draft text by a decision recorded on p. 401.

# Theses on Tactics and Strategy[12]

### 1.) *Definition of the question*

'The new international workers' association was founded to organise the *common activity* of proletarians of different countries who strive for one single goal: overthrowing capitalism and establishing the dictatorship of the proletariat and an international Soviet republic to completely abolish classes and realise socialism, the first stage of the communist society.'[13]

This definition, set down in the Statutes of the Communist International, *encompasses all the questions of tactics and strategy* that are posed for solution, questions relating to our struggle for the proletarian dictatorship. They relate to how we win the majority of the working class to the principles of communism and how we organise the socially decisive layers of the proletariat for the struggle to achieve them. They relate to our relationship to the proletarianised petty-bourgeois layers, to the ways and means of rapidly undermining and shattering the organs of bourgeois power, and to the final international struggle for the dictatorship.

The question of the dictatorship itself, as the only road to victory, is not part of this discussion. The developing world revolution has shown plainly that there is only one alternative in the present situation: capitalist or proletarian dictatorship. The Third Congress of the Communist International is undertaking its review of tactical questions at a time when the objective conditions are ripe for revolution. A number of mass Communist parties have been formed, but there is not yet a single country in which they have actual leadership of the majority of the working class in genuinely revolutionary struggle.

### 2.) *On the eve of new battles*

The *world revolution* – that is, the decay of capitalism, the accumulation of the proletariat's revolutionary energy, and its organisation into an aggressive and

---

12. Drafted by Radek, this resolution was reported on and discussed in Sessions 10–14. It was approved in Session 21. For Lenin's comments on the drafting of this resolution, see Appendix 3a on pp. 1097–1101.
    This text is known to English-speaking readers mainly from a translation in Adler (ed.) 1980 (Ink Links edition), also found on: <www.marxists.org>, which is based on a Russian text. The present translation is taken from the German version, which is somewhat different in formulation. In the title, as elsewhere in the resolution, the German word *Taktik*, when used to indicate the entirety of the Communist course of action leading to the revolution, has been translated as 'tactics and strategy' or as 'course of action'.
13. The paragraph is taken from the Statutes of the Communist International. See Riddell (ed.) 1991, 2WC, 2, pp. 696–7.

victorious power – will require a *lengthy period* of revolutionary struggles. As a result of variations in the level of antagonisms in different countries, variations in their social structure and in the scope of the obstacles to be overcome, and the high degree of organisation of the bourgeoisie in the developed capitalist countries of Western Europe and North America, the World War was not immediately followed by the victory of world revolution.

The Communists were correct in saying, even during the War, that the *epoch of imperialism* would lead into a time of *social revolution*, that is, a long succession of civil wars within individual capitalist states and of wars between capitalist states on one side and proletarian states and exploited colonial peoples on the other. The world revolution does not develop in a straight line. Instead, periods of chronic capitalist decay and everyday revolutionary preparatory work come to a head and find expression in acute crises.

The pace of world revolution became even slower because of the evolution of workers' organisations and workers' parties formed by the proletariat to lead its struggle against the bourgeoisie. During the War, these organisations – namely the Social-Democratic parties and the trade unions – were transformed into counterrevolutionary tools to mislead and restrict the proletariat, and they retained that character after the end of the War. This made it easy for the world bourgeoisie to overcome the crisis of the demobilisation period. During the apparent prosperity of 1919–20, it was able to awaken new hopes of bettering conditions within a capitalist framework, which led to the defeat of uprisings during 1919 and the slower tempo of revolutionary movements during 1919–20.

The world economic crisis that began in mid-1920 and extended around the world, multiplying unemployment everywhere, shows the international proletariat that the bourgeoisie is not capable of rebuilding the world. The sharpening of all world-political antagonisms – France's plunder campaign against Germany, the British-American and American-Japanese enmity, with the resulting armaments race – all this shows that the dying capitalist world is again hurtling toward world war.

The League of Nations is simply an international trust of victor states for the exploitation of their defeated rivals and the colonial peoples. It has now been broken apart by the British-American rivalry. International Social Democracy and the trade-union bureaucracy held the working masses back from revolutionary struggle through the illusion that, by rejecting the conquest of political power in revolutionary struggle, they could progressively and peacefully achieve economic power and self-government. That illusion is now disappearing.

In *Germany*, the farce of socialisation, which the Scheidemann-Noske government used in March 1919 to hold back the working class from an uprising, is at an end.[14] The phase of socialisation has given way to a genuine Stinnesisation, that is, the subjugation of German industry to a capitalist dictator and a clique of his cronies. The attack of the Prussian government, led by the Social Democrat Severing, against the miners of Central Germany was the prelude to a general offensive by the German bourgeoisie to drive down wages of the German working class.

In *Britain*, plans for nationalisation have been cast aside. Instead of carrying out the Sankey Commission [coal] nationalisation plan,[15] the government calls up the army to support the lockout of British miners.

As for the *French* government, only its campaign of robbery against Germany holds it off from bankruptcy. It gives no thought to any plan to strengthen its economy. Even the reconstruction of devastated northern France, to the extent it is done at all, serves only to enrich private capitalists.

In *Italy*, the bourgeoisie, supported by the Fascist White Guards, have launched an attack on the working class.

Bourgeois democracy has been further exposed everywhere, both in countries where it has long been established and in the new countries resulting from imperialist collapse. White Guards; dictatorial powers for the British government against the miners' strike; Fascists and the Royal Guard in Italy; Pinkertons, expulsion of socialist congressmen,[16] and lynch justice in the United States; white terror in Poland, Yugoslavia, Romania, Latvia, and Estonia; legalisation of the white terror in Finland, Hungary, and the Balkan countries; anti-Communist laws in Switzerland and France; and so on. Everywhere, the bourgeoisie seeks to burden the working class with the results of heightened economic anarchy by lengthening the working day and reducing wages.

Everywhere they are assisted by the leaders of Social Democracy and the Amsterdam trade-union International. However, they can only postpone, not prevent, the awakening of the working masses to new struggles and the approach of a new revolutionary upsurge. Already we see that the German proletariat is preparing for a counterattack. The British miners, despite the betrayal of the trade-union leaders, held out for weeks in heroic struggle against the capitalist mine owners. After the Italian proletariat's experiences

---

14. On 1 March 1919 the SPD fraction in the National Assembly put forward a resolution calling for the socialisation of certain industries. Two days later the government published a scheme to that end.

15. For the Sankey Commission, see p. 91, n. 30.

16. Presumably a reference to the January 1920 expulsion of five SP members from the New York State Assembly on the grounds that the SP 'was not truly a political party' but rather 'a membership organisation admitting within its ranks aliens, enemy aliens, and minors'.

with the Serrati group's vacillation, we see a new will to struggle emerging in its front ranks, expressed in the formation of the Communist Party of Italy.

In France, after the split of the social patriots and centrists, we see the Socialist Party beginning to shift from Communist agitation and propaganda to mass demonstrations against imperialist robbery.[17] In Czechoslovakia, we experienced a political strike in December, in which a million workers took part, despite the lack of a unified leadership. It was followed by the formation of the Czech Communist Party on a mass basis. In Poland in February, we had the railway workers' strike, led by the Communist Party, and following that the general strike, and we are witnessing an ongoing process of disintegration in the social-patriotic Polish Socialist Party.

*Under present circumstances we must not expect an ebb of world revolution or a lessening of its waves. On the contrary, the most likely variant under present circumstances is a rapid aggravation of social antagonisms and social struggles.*

3.) *The most important present task*

The most important task of the Communist International at present is to gain decisive influence over the majority of the working class and to lead its decisive sectors into struggle. The economic and political situation is objectively revolutionary, and can give rise to an acute revolutionary crisis at any moment – be it a mass strike, a colonial uprising, a new war, or even a major parliamentary crisis. However, the majority of the working class is not yet subject to Communist influence. This is especially true in countries where the strength of finance capital makes possible the existence of significant layers of workers corrupted by imperialism (Britain and the United States, for example), and where genuinely revolutionary mass propaganda has hardly begun.

The Communist International does not aim to form small Communist sects seeking to exert influence on the working masses through propaganda and agitation. *Rather, from the earliest days after its formation, it has clearly and unambiguously pursued the goal of taking part in the struggles of the working masses, leading these struggles in a Communist direction, and, through the struggle, forming large, tested, mass revolutionary Communist parties.*

From the very first years of its existence, the Communist International rejected sectarian tendencies by calling on its affiliated parties – no matter how small – to participate in the trade unions, in order to defeat the reactionary bureaucracy from within and to transform the unions into revolutionary

---

17. By 'Socialist Party', the resolution is referring to the Communist Party of France, the name taken by the former Socialist Party majority in December 1920.

mass organisations of the proletariat and agencies for its struggle. Already in its first year of existence, the Communist International called on Communist parties not to close themselves off as propaganda circles but to utilise every opportunity that the bourgeois state is compelled to provide, as a weapon, a platform, a point of assembly for communism. This includes freedom of the press, freedom of assembly, and the bourgeois parliamentary institutions, regardless of how stunted they may be. At its Second Congress, the Communist International openly rejected sectarian tendencies in its resolutions on the trade unions and on utilising parliament.

*The experiences of two years of struggle have fully confirmed the correctness of the Communist International's point of view.* The policies of the Communist International have brought about, in a number of countries, the *separation of the revolutionary workers not only from the open reformists but also from the centrists.* The Centrists have formed the Two-and-a-Half International, which joins publicly with the Scheidemanns, the Jouhauxs, and the Hendersons within the Amsterdam trade-union International. This clarifies the field of battle for the proletarian masses, which can only facilitate the coming struggles.

*German* communism was able to develop from a political current at the time of the January and March struggles of 1919 to a large revolutionary mass party thanks to the Communist International's tactics and strategy: revolutionary work in the trade unions, Open Letter, and so on. The party has won such influence in the trade unions that the union bureaucracy has taken fright at the revolutionary impact of Communist work there. It has expelled many Communists from the unions, taking on itself the odium of splitting the movement.

In *Czechoslovakia*, the Communists succeeded in winning over the majority of the politically organised workers. In *Poland*, the Communist Party has faced severe persecution, which has forced it completely underground. Nonetheless, it has been able, thanks above all to its underground work within the trade unions, not only to maintain its ties with the masses but to lead them in mass struggles. In *France* the Communists have won a majority in the Socialist Party. In *Britain*, the Communist groups are consolidating a fusion carried out on the basis of the Communist International's tactical guidelines. The Communists' growing influence has forced the social traitors to attempt to bar them from entry into the Labour Party.

*By contrast, the sectarian Communist groups (KAPD, etc.) have not gained the slightest success from their policies.* The concept of strengthening communism through pure propaganda and agitation and the formation of separate Communist trade unions has been shipwrecked. Nowhere has an influential Communist Party been built in this fashion.

## 4.) *The situation in the Communist International*

The Communist International is on the road to forming mass Communist parties, but it is far from having gone far enough. Indeed, in two of the most important countries of capitalist triumph, the work has hardly been begun.

In the *United States of North America*, a broad revolutionary movement was lacking before the War, for historical reasons. Here, the Communists still face the initial and most elementary tasks of building a Communist nucleus and linking it up with the working masses. Favourable conditions for this work have now been created by the economic crisis, which has thrown five million workers into unemployment. American capitalism is aware of the threatening danger that the workers' movement may radicalise and fall under Communist influence. It has therefore attempted to crush the young Communist movement through barbaric persecution, to destroy it and drive it underground, where, it believes, the party will lose any connection with the masses, degenerate into a propaganda sect, and wither away.

The Communist International draws the attention of the United Communist Party of America to the fact that the underground organisation can provide the basis only for uniting and educating the most active Communist forces. The party is obligated to seek in every way possible to reach out from its underground organisation and link up with the working-class masses now in ferment. It is obligated to find ways and means to unite these masses in open political activity for the struggle against American capitalism.

The *British* Communist movement too has not yet succeeded in becoming a mass party, even though it has brought its forces together in a unified party.

The British economy remains in disorder; the strike movement is intense as never before; the broad popular masses are increasingly discontented with the Lloyd George government; and the Labour Party and Liberal Party may well win in the coming parliamentary elections. All these factors open up new revolutionary perspectives for Britain and pose extremely important questions to British Communists.

The initial, overriding task of the Communist Party of Britain is to become a party of the masses. The British Communists must strengthen their roots in the already existing and developing mass movement. They must get involved in all the specific forms through which this movement finds expression and take up the workers' individual and partial demands as the starting point for their own tireless and energetic agitation and propaganda.

Through the mighty strike movement, hundreds of thousands and millions of workers are subjecting to close examination the capacity, reliability, steadfastness, and conscientiousness of the trade-union apparatus and leadership. Under these conditions, Communists' work in the unions has taken on decisive importance. No criticisms by the party from the outside can have even a small fraction of the influence on the masses exerted by steadfast daily work by Communist trade-union cells. This work aims to expose and discredit the petty-bourgeois traitors in the trade unions, who have become in Britain, more than anywhere else, the political pawns of the capitalists.

In other countries, where there are mass Communist parties, their task consists largely of seizing the initiative in mass actions. In Britain, by contrast, the task of the Communist Party is above all to show the masses, in the framework of their experience in mass actions that are currently under way, that the Communists courageously and accurately express these masses' interests, needs, and feelings.

The mass Communist parties of Central and Western Europe are in the process of developing the appropriate methods of revolutionary agitation and propaganda and the organisational methods suitable to their character as organisations of struggle. They are making the transition from Communist propaganda and agitation to action. This process is hindered by the fact that, in several countries, the workers embraced revolution and came to communism under the direction of leaders who had not overcome centrist tendencies. They are not capable of carrying out genuinely Communist popular agitation and propaganda and may even fear it, knowing that it will lead the parties into revolutionary struggles.

In *Italy*, these centrist tendencies brought about a split in the party. The party and trade-union leaders associated with Serrati failed to transform the spontaneous movements of the working class and its increasing activity into a conscious struggle for power, for which conditions in Italy were fully ripe. Instead, they let these movements run aground. They did not see communism as a means to arouse and unite the working masses for struggle. And because they feared the struggle, they could only steer Communist propaganda and agitation into a centrist channel. They thereby reinforced the influence of reformists like Turati and Treves in the party and D'Aragona in the trade unions. Because the Serrati forces did not differ from the reformists either in word or deed, they did not want to break with them, preferring to break with the Communists. The policies of the Serrati current, while strengthening reformist influence on one side, created on the other a danger of anarchist and syndicalist influence and the generation of anti-parliamentary and verbally radical tendencies within the party itself.

The split in Livorno and the formation of a Communist Party in Italy united all the genuinely Communist forces on the basis of the decisions of the Communist International's Second Congress. This initiative will make communism a mass force in Italy, provided that the Italian Communist Party, while continually and unrelentingly combating the opportunist policies of Serrati, is also capable of linking up with the proletarian masses in the trade unions, in strikes, and in struggles against the Fascist counterrevolutionary organisations. It must unify their movements and transform their spontaneous actions into carefully prepared struggles.

In *France*, the chauvinist poison of 'national defence' and the subsequent intoxication of victory were stronger than in any other country. Opposition to the War developed more slowly than in other countries. Thanks to the moral influence of the Russian Revolution, the revolutionary struggles in the capitalist countries, and the experiences of the French proletariat betrayed by its leaders, the majority of the French Socialist Party evolved in a Communist direction, even before the course of events placed it before the decisive challenges of revolutionary action. The French Communist Party can utilise this situation all the better and more fully to the degree that it does away with the excessively strong remnants in its own ranks – especially in its leadership – of national-pacifist and parliamentary-reformist ideology.

To a greater extent than now and in the past, the party must move closer to the most oppressed layers in the cities and the countryside, giving full expression to their sufferings and needs. In its struggles in parliament, the party must break decisively with the hypocritical formalities and deceitful courtesies of French parliamentarism, which are deliberately encouraged by the bourgeoisie in order to hypnotise and intimidate leaders of the working class. Communist Party parliamentary deputies must strive through strictly supervised activity to expose the fraud of nationalist democratism and traditional revolutionism and approach every question in terms of class interests and relentless class struggle.

Party agitation must be carried out with much more concentration and energy. It must not dissolve into the changing and varied situations and patterns of day-to-day politics. It must draw basic revolutionary conclusions from every event, large and small, and convey those lessons to the most backward layers of workers. Only such truly revolutionary conduct will show the Communist Party to be something more than the left wing of the radical bloc around Longuet, which offers its services to bourgeois society with increasing energy and increasing success, in order to protect it from the convulsions that are inevitably approaching in France. Regardless of whether these decisive revolutionary events take place sooner or later, a disciplined Communist Party, imbued with revolutionary determination, will find it possible even now, in a preparatory period, to mobilise the masses both economically and politically, broadening and clarifying their struggles.

Impatient and politically inexperienced revolutionary forces attempt to apply extreme methods – more appropriate to a decisive revolutionary proletarian uprising – to individual issues and tasks, such as the proposal to appeal to conscripts in the army's class of 1919 to resist the military call-up. If put into practice, such methods set back for a long time genuine revolutionary preparation of the proletariat for winning power.

The Communist Party of France, like the parties in other countries, has the task of rejecting these extremely dangerous methods. However, this absolutely must not lead the party into inactivity; quite the contrary.

Strengthening the party's links with the masses requires above all closer ties to the trade unions. The party's task is not to subordinate the trade unions mechanically and superficially or to deny them the autonomy necessitated by the character of their work. Rather the task is to give direction to the work of truly revolutionary forces unified and led by the Communist Party within the unions, along lines that express the broad interests of a proletariat struggling to win power.

In this regard, the Communist Party of France is obligated to offer friendly but clear and resolute criticism of anarcho-syndicalist currents that reject the dictatorship of the proletariat and the need to unify the proletarian vanguard in a centralised and leading organisation, that is, the Communist Party. As for syndicalist currents in transition – who barricade themselves behind the Amiens Charter, drafted eight years before the War, and do not want to give a new and forthright answer to the basic questions posed in the new epoch following the War – they must be subjected to criticism in the same fashion.

The prevailing hatred of politicians among French syndicalists is directed chiefly against the traditional 'socialist' parliamentarians, and here it is quite justified. The purely revolutionary character of the Communist Party creates an opportunity to demonstrate convincingly to all revolutionary forces the need for a political movement for the winning of power by the working class.

The revolutionary-syndicalist and Communist organisations need to be fused together, as a necessary condition for any serious struggle by the French proletariat.

French syndicalism displays tendencies to premature action, to vagueness on principles, and to organisational separatism, all of which need to be overcome and removed. But this will be achieved only to the degree that the party itself, as stated, transforms itself into a powerful attractive force for the working masses of France, by dealing in truly revolutionary fashion with every question of daily life and struggle.

In *Czechoslovakia* the working masses have shaken off in two and a half years most reformist and nationalist illusions. In September 1920, the majority of Social-Democratic workers separated from their reformist leaders. In December, about a million of Czechoslovakia's three and a half million industrial workers took part in a revolutionary mass action against the Czechoslovak capitalist government. The Czechoslovak Communist Party was formed this past May with 350,000 members, alongside the Communist Party of German Bohemia [Sudetenland], which had been formed earlier and has 60,000 members. The Communists thus make up a large segment not only of the Czechoslovak proletariat but also of its population as a whole.

The Czechoslovak party now faces the task of attracting broader masses of workers through truly Communist agitation. It must also train its members, both longstanding and newly won, through effective and unremitting Communist propaganda. It must unite the workers of all nations within Czechoslovakia in a solid proletarian front against nationalism, the main weapon of the bourgeoisie in Czechoslovakia. It must strengthen the proletariat's power, created through this process, during all coming struggles against government and capitalist oppression, and convert this strength into an invincible power. The Communist Party of Czechoslovakia will accomplish these tasks all the more quickly if it overcomes centrist traditions and hesitations in clear and determined fashion, pursuing a policy that educates the broad masses of the proletariat in a revolutionary spirit, unites them, and is thus capable of preparing their actions and carrying them through to victory. The congress instructs the Czechoslovak and the German-Bohemian Communist parties to fuse their organisations into a unified party within a period of time to be set by the Executive.

*The United Communist Party of Germany* was formed from the fusion of the Spartacus League with the working masses of the Independent [USPD] left wing. Although already a mass party, it faces the major task of increasing and strengthening its influence on the broad masses; winning the proletarian mass organisations, the trade unions; breaking the hold of the Social-Democratic party and trade-union bureaucracy; and taking the leadership of the proletariat in the mass struggles to come. This central task requires orienting all agitational and organisational work toward winning the support of the working-class majority, without which, given the power of German capitalism, no victory of communism in Germany is possible.

The party has not yet succeeded in this task, with regard either to the scope or the content of its agitation. It has also failed to consistently follow the path it had blazed through the Open Letter, which counterposed the practical interests of the proletariat to the traitorous policy of the Social-Democratic parties and the trade-union bureaucracy. The party's press and organisation is still too marked by the stamp of an association, not an organisation of struggle, expressing centrist tendencies that have not yet been fully overcome. These tendencies led the party, when faced with the requirements of struggle, to jump in too precipitously and without sufficient preparation, and to neglect the need for vital contact with the non-Communist masses. The disintegration of Germany's economy and the capitalist offensive against workers' living standards will soon confront the VKPD with tasks of struggle that cannot be resolved if the party counterposes tasks of agitation and organisation to those of action. The party must keep the spirit of struggle in its ranks always at the ready, while shaping its agitation in a truly popular fashion and building its organisation in such a manner that, through its ties with the masses, it develops the capacity to carefully evaluate challenges to struggle and to carefully prepare for action.

The parties of the Communist International will become mass revolutionary parties only when they overcome the remnants and traditions of opportunism in its ranks. This can be done by seeking close ties with the struggling masses of workers, deducing their tasks from the proletariat's ongoing struggles, rejecting the opportunist policy of covering up and concealing the unbridgeable antagonisms, and also avoiding revolutionary verbiage that obstructs insight into the real relationship of forces and overlooks the difficulties of the struggle.

The Communist parties came into being through a split in the old Social-Democratic parties. The split resulted from the fact that the parties had betrayed the proletariat's interests in the War, and then, after the War, had continued their betrayal through an alliance with the bourgeoisie or through a timid and evasive course that evaded every struggle. The slogans and principles of the Communist parties form the only basis on which the working masses can regain unity. They express the requirements of proletarian struggle.

For that reason, it is now the Social-Democratic and centrist parties and currents that represent the atomisation and division of the proletariat, while the Communist parties are the force promoting unification. In Germany it was the centrists who broke away from the majority of the party, when this majority declared for communism. Fearing the influence of communism as a force for unity, the Social Democrats and the Independent Social Democrats of Germany and the Social-Democratic trade-union bureaucracy have refused to join with Communists in action to defend the elementary interests of the proletariat. In Czechoslovakia, it was the Social Democrats who split the old party, when they saw the approaching victory of communism. In France, the Longuet supporters broke from the majority of French Socialist workers, while the Communist Party sought the unification of socialist and syndicalist workers. In Britain, it is the reformists and centrists who, fearing the Communists' influence, drive them out of the Labour Party, while again and again sabotaging the unification of workers in struggle against the capitalists. The

Communist parties thus become the main force in a process of proletarian unification on the basis of the struggle for its interests. Conscious of this role, they will attract new forces.

## 5.) *Partial struggles and partial demands*

The Communist parties can develop only through struggle. Even the smallest Communist parties cannot limit themselves to mere propaganda and agitation. In all the proletariat's mass organisations they must be a vanguard that, by pressing for struggle for all the proletariat's vital necessities, demonstrates how the struggle should be carried out, thus exposing the traitorous character of the non-Communist parties. Only if the Communists are able to take the lead in and promote all the proletariat's practical struggles will they be able to actually win broad masses of the proletariat for a struggle for its dictatorship.

All the Communist parties' agitation and propaganda, indeed all their work must be imbued with the consciousness that no enduring improvement in the conditions of the masses is possible in a capitalist framework. Steps to improve working-class conditions and to reconstruct an economy devastated by capitalism can be taken only by overthrowing the bourgeoisie and smashing the capitalist state. *But this insight must not lead to any postponement of the struggle for the proletariat's immediate and urgent necessities of life until the time when it is capable of erecting its dictatorship.*

The present period is one of capitalist decay and collapse, a time when capitalism is no longer capable of assuring workers of even the life of a well-fed slave. Social Democracy advances the old Social-Democratic programme of peaceful reforms, carried out on the basis and in the framework of bankrupt capitalism, through peaceful means. This is conscious deception of the working masses. Not only is decaying capitalism incapable of providing the workers with relatively humane living conditions, but the Social Democrats and reformists show every day, in every country, that they do not intend to conduct any type of struggle for even the most modest reforms contained in their programme. The demand for socialisation or nationalisation of the most important industries, advanced by the centrist parties, is equally deceptive. The centrists mislead the masses by seeking to convince them that all the most important branches of industry can be torn out of the grip of capitalism without the defeat of the bourgeoisie. Moreover, they seek to divert the workers from the real, living struggle for their immediate needs through hope that branches of industry can be taken over, one after another, ultimately creating the basis for 'planned' economic construction.

In this fashion, they go back to the Social-Democratic minimum programme for reforming capitalism, which has been transformed into an obvious counterrevolutionary fraud. Some of the centrists advance a programme to nationalise the coal industry, for example, in part as an expression of Lassalle's concept that all the proletariat's energies should be focused on a single demand, in order to convert it into a lever for revolutionary action, whose progress would lead to a struggle for power. What we have here is empty schematism. The working class in all the capitalist states suffers today from so many and such terrible scourges that it is impossible to concentrate the struggle against all these oppressive burdens that weigh it down by focusing on some formula dreamed up in doctrinaire fashion.

The task, by contrast, is to take all the masses' interests as the starting point for revolutionary struggles that only in their unity form the mighty river of revolution. The Communist parties do not propose a minimum programme for these struggles, one designed to reinforce and improve the rickety structure of capitalism. Instead, destruction of this structure remains their guiding goal and their immediate task. But to achieve this task, the Communist parties have to advance demands whose achievement meets an immediate, urgent need of the working class, and fight for these demands regardless of whether they are compatible with the capitalist profit system.

Communist parties direct their concern not to the viability and competitiveness of capitalist industry or the resilience of capitalist finance but to the dimensions of a deprivation that the proletariat cannot bear and should not have to bear. Demands should express the needs experienced by broad proletarian masses, such that they are convinced they cannot survive unless these demands are achieved. If that is the case, the struggles for these demands will become starting points for the struggle for power.

In place of the minimum programme of the centrists and reformists, the Communist International offers a struggle for the specific demands of the proletariat, as part of a system of demands that, in their totality, undermine the power of the bourgeoisie, organise the proletariat, and mark out the different stages of the struggle for proletarian dictatorship. Each of these demands gives expression to the needs of the broad masses, even when they do not yet consciously take a stand for proletarian dictatorship.

The struggle for these demands to meet the masses' essentials of life needs to embrace and mobilise broader and broader numbers. It must be counterposed to defence of the essentials of life for capitalist society. To the extent that this is done, the working class will become aware that for it to live, capitalism must die. This awareness provides the basis for a determination to struggle for [proletarian] dictatorship. Communist parties have the task of broadening, deepening, and unifying the struggles that develop around such specific demands.

Every partial action undertaken by the working masses in order to achieve a partial demand, every significant economic strike, also mobilises the entire bourgeoisie, which comes down as a class on the side of the threatened group of employers, aiming to render impossible even a limited victory by the proletariat ('Emergency Technical Assistance',[18] bourgeois strikebreakers in the British railway workers' strike, Fascists). The bourgeoisie mobilises the entire state apparatus for the struggle against the workers (militarisation of the workers in France and Poland, state of emergency during the miners' strike in Britain). The workers who are struggling for partial demands will be automatically forced into a struggle against the bourgeoisie as a whole and its state apparatus.

To the extent that struggles for partial demands and partial struggles by specific groups of workers broaden into an overall working-class struggle against capitalism, the Communist Party must escalate its slogans and generalise them to the point of calling for the enemy's immediate overthrow. In advancing such partial demands, the Communist parties must take care that these slogans, anchored in the needs of the broad masses, do not merely lead them into struggle but are also inherently demands that organise the masses. All specific slogans that arise from the economic needs of the working masses must be steered toward a struggle for control of production – not as a scheme for bureaucratic organisation of the economy under capitalism, but as a struggle against capitalism through factory councils and revolutionary trade unions. Building such organisations and linking them according to branches and centres of industry is the only way to organisationally unify the struggle of the working masses and resist the splitting of the masses by Social Democracy and the trade-union leaders. The factory councils can carry out these tasks only if they arise from struggle for economic goals shared by the broadest masses of workers, only if they create links among all revolutionary sectors of the proletariat – between the Communist parties, the revolutionary workers, and the trade unions that are evolving in a revolutionary direction.

Objections raised against raising such partial demands and accusations of reformism based on partial struggles express the same incapacity to grasp the living conditions for revolutionary action. This weakness was also expressed when certain Communist groups opposed participation in the trade unions and parliamentary activity. The task is not to summon the proletariat for the final struggle but to intensify the actual struggle, the only factor that can lead the proletariat to the struggle for the final goal. The objections to partial

---

18. For Emergency Technical Assistance, see p. 624, n. 15.

demands are groundless and alien to the requirements of revolutionary activity. This is demonstrated conclusively by the fact that even small organisations formed by the so-called Left Communists as places of refuge for their pure teachings have been required to advance partial slogans in an attempt to attract larger numbers of workers into the struggle than those immediately around them or to take part in the struggle of broader masses in the hopes of influencing them.

The revolutionary essence of the present period consists precisely in the fact that even the most modest subsistence needs of the working masses are incompatible with the existence of capitalist society. It follows that even the struggle for quite modest demands expands into a struggle for communism.

The capitalists utilise the constantly expanding army of the unemployed to pressure organised workers by reducing wages. The cowardly Social Democrats, Independents, and official trade-union leaders hold themselves aloof from the unemployed, regarding them only as recipients of government and trade-union charity, and categorising them politically as the lumpenproletariat. Communists must understand that under present conditions the army of unemployed is a revolutionary factor of immense importance. Communists must take the leadership of this army. Through the pressure of the unemployed on the trade unions, Communists must hasten the unions' renewal and, above all, free them from their traitorous leaders. By uniting the unemployed with the proletarian vanguard in the struggle for socialist revolution, the Communist Party will restrain the most revolutionary and impatient forces of the proletariat from isolated acts of desperation. They will render these forces capable, in favourable conditions, of giving effective support to a sector of the working class that goes on the attack. They will extend these conflicts beyond their initial framework and make them the starting point for a decisive offensive. In short, they will transform the mass of unemployed from a reserve army of industry into an active army of revolution.

By energetically taking up the cause of this layer of workers and stepping down into the depths of the working class, the Communist parties are not acting on behalf of one layer of workers against another but defending the interests of the working class as a whole. The counterrevolutionary leaders betray this cause in order to serve the momentary interests of the labour aristocracy. As the number of jobless and part-time workers grows, their interests become those of the working class as a whole, to which the passing interests of the labour aristocracy must be subordinated. Those who defend the interests of the labour aristocracy, counterposing them to those of the unemployed or simply abandoning them, are tearing the working class apart, to counterrevolutionary effect. The Communist Party, as tribune of the interests of the working class as a whole, cannot limit itself to recognising these interests and asserting them propagandistically. To defend these interests effectively, the party must, under certain conditions, lead the bulk of the most oppressed and destitute workers against the resistance of the labour aristocracy.

## 6.) *Preparing the struggle*

The character of the transitional period makes it the duty of all Communist parties to increase to the utmost their readiness for struggle. Every individual struggle can lead to a contest for power. To heighten this readiness, the party's entire agitation must take the form of an impassioned attack on capitalist society. Through this agitation, it must succeed in linking up with the broadest popular masses, speaking in a language that can convince them they are being led by a vanguard engaged in a genuine struggle for power. We do not need house organs proving theoretically that communism is correct. Rather our newspapers and appeals must sound the alarm for proletarian revolution.

Communists' activity in parliament does not aim to discuss with the enemy or convince him but to ruthlessly and pitilessly expose him and the agents of the bourgeoisie. It must arouse the will to struggle of the working masses and draw the semi-proletarian petty-bourgeois layers to the proletariat. Our organisational work in both the trade unions and the party must not aim to consolidate the structure and increase the membership in mechanical fashion; it must rather be inspired with awareness of the coming struggles. In all its activity and its organisational forms, the party must personify the will to struggle. Only then will it be capable of carrying out its task at the moment when conditions for broader action campaigns are present.

Where the Communist Party represents a mass force, with influence extending beyond its own structures to the broader layers of workers, it has the duty, through its deeds, to awaken the working masses to struggle. Large mass parties cannot rest content with criticising the failings of other parties and with comparing their demands to those of the Communists. As a mass party, they carry the responsibility to develop the revolution. As the conditions of the working masses become more and more unbearable, the Communist parties must do everything necessary to bring the working masses into a struggle for their interests.

In Western Europe and the United States, where the working masses are organised in trade unions and political parties, spontaneous movements are therefore for the time being quite infrequent. Given that fact, Communist parties are obliged to attempt, by mustering their strength in the trade unions and increasing their pressure on other parties based on the working masses, to enable the proletariat's struggle for its immediate interests to unfold on a unified basis. If the non-Communist parties are forced to join the struggle, the Communists have the task of preparing the working masses from the start for the possibility of betrayal by these parties in a subsequent stage of struggle. Communists should seek to intensify the conflict and drive it forward. The VKPD's Open Letter can serve as a model of a starting point for campaigns. If pressure by the Communist Party in the trade unions and the press is not enough to achieve a unified front in the struggle, the Communist Party is duty-bound to seek to lead large sectors of the working masses on its own.

Through this autonomous policy, the most active and class-conscious sector of the proletariat seeks to defend the class's vital interests. For this policy to achieve success in arousing the backward masses, the struggle's goals must grow out of the specific situation and be comprehensible to the masses. They must recognise these goals as their own, even if they are not yet capable of struggling for them.

The Communist Party should not limit itself, however, to defending the proletariat against threatening dangers and the blows raining down on it. In a time of world revolution, the Communist Party is essentially a party of attack, of assault on capitalist society. It is obligated to broaden every defensive struggle of any depth and breadth into an attack on capitalist society. It is also obliged to do everything possible, when conditions are appropriate, to lead the working masses directly into this struggle. Anyone who objects to a policy of offensive against capitalist society is violating the principles of communism.

Taking the offensive depends, first, on an intensification of struggles, both nationally and internationally, within the bourgeois camp itself. When struggles within the bourgeois camp have grown to proportions that make it possible that the working class will be facing divided enemy forces, the party has to seize the initiative, in order, after careful political and – if possible – organisational preparation, to lead the masses into struggle. The second condition for offensive attacks on a broad scale is an intensive ferment in the decisive sectors of the working class that provides grounds for hope that the class will be ready to struggle against the capitalist government in unified fashion. When the movement is growing, the slogans of the struggle should become more comprehensive. Similarly, if the movement is receding, the Communist leadership of the struggle has the duty of leading the masses out of the struggle in as orderly and unified a fashion as possible.

Whether the Communist Party is on the defensive or the offensive depends on the specific circumstances. The most important condition is that the party be imbued with a spirit of readiness for struggle, overcoming through the struggle itself any centrist passivity that would necessarily sidetrack the party's propaganda into semi-reformism. Mass Communist parties must be characterised by a constant readiness for struggle. This is true not only because mass Communist parties, as such, have an obligation to struggle, but because of the entire present situation, one of capitalist decay and increasing destitution of the masses. The task is to shorten the period of decay, so that it does not destroy the material foundations for communism and wear down the energy of the working masses.

### 7.) *The lessons of the March Action*[19]

The March Action was forced on the VKPD by the government's attack on the proletariat of Central Germany.

In this, the VKPD's first great struggle since its foundation, the party made a number of errors. The most serious of these was that it did not clearly stress the defensive character of the struggle. Instead, its call for an offensive was utilised by the unscrupulous enemies of the proletariat – the bourgeoisie, the SPD, and the USPD – to denounce the VKPD to the proletariat for instigating a putsch. This error was compounded by a number of party members who contended that, under present conditions, the offensive represented the VKPD's main method of struggle. The party opposed this error in its newspapers and through its chair, Comrade Brandler.

The Third Congress of the Communist International considers that the March Action was a step forward. The March Action was a heroic struggle by hundreds of thousands of proletarians against the bourgeoisie. And, by courageously taking the lead in the defence of the workers of Central Germany, the VKPD showed that it is the party of Germany's revolutionary proletariat. The congress believes that the VKPD will be all the more successful in carrying out mass actions if, in the future, it better adapts its slogans for the struggle to actual conditions, studies these conditions closely, and carries out the actions in unified fashion.

In order to carefully weigh the possibilities for struggle, the VKPD needs to take into account the facts and considerations that point to the difficulties of a proposed action and work out carefully how they may be countered. But, once the party leadership has decided on an action, all comrades must abide by the party's decisions and carry out this action. Criticism of an action should be voiced only after it has concluded, and then only within the party

---

19. See also 'The March Action and the Situation in the VKPD', p. 951. For a short account of the March Action, see pp. 18–23 of the Editorial Introduction.

structures and in its newspapers, and after taking into consideration the party's situation in relationship to the class enemy. Since Levi disregarded these self-evident requirements of party discipline and conditions for criticism of the party, the congress approves his expulsion from the party and considers any political collaboration with him by members of the Communist International to be impermissible.[20]

## 8.) *Forms and methods of direct struggle*

The forms and methods of struggle, its extent, and questions of offensive or defensive action are all dependent on specific conditions that cannot be created arbitrarily. Previous revolutionary experience indicate that there are different forms of partial actions.

1. Partial actions by specific layers of the working class, such as the actions of miners and railway workers in Germany and Britain, of agricultural workers, and so on.
2. Partial actions by the working class as a whole for limited goals, such as the action during the Kapp Putsch and the action of British miners against military intervention by the British government in the Russian-Polish War.

Such partial struggles may expand to encompass a single district, an entire country, or several countries at once.

In the course of a revolution in a single country, all these forms of struggle will take place, one after another. Although the Communist Party cannot, of course, reject territorially limited partial actions, it should direct its efforts to transforming each major local struggle of the proletariat into a generalised struggle. Just as the party is obliged to defend the workers in struggle in a particular branch of industry by involving, if possible, the entire working class, so too it is obliged, when workers are in struggle in a single locality, to defend them, if possible, by bringing the workers of other industrial centres into struggle. Revolutionary experience shows that broadening the scope of the struggle improves the chances of victory. In countering the developing world revolution, the bourgeoisie relies not only on the White Guards but also on the fact that the working class is atomised and that it is only very gradually forming a unified front. When the proletarian masses engaged in struggle are more numerous, and the field of battle is greater in scope, the enemy is forced to divide and split up his forces. Even if a working-class sector rushing to aid another is, for the moment, not capable of committing all its forces, the mere

---

20. This sentence is omitted from the Russian text.

fact that it moves into action compels the capitalists to divide their military strength, since they cannot know the extent to which the participation of a second proletarian sector will broaden and intensify the struggle.

During the past year, in which the capitalist offensive against labour became more and more shameless, we noted that the bourgeoisie, in every country, was not content with the normal pace of work by its government agencies. It formed legal and semi-legal White Guard organisations, enjoying governmental protection, which came to play a decisive role in every major economic confrontation.

In Germany, there is the government-supported Orgesch, which included a wide range of parties, from Stinnes to Scheidemann.

In Italy, there are the Fascists, whose feats of gangsterism have brought about a sharp shift in the mood of the bourgeoisie, giving the impression that the political relationship of forces has changed completely.

In Britain, the Lloyd George government, faced with a strike danger, turned for protection to volunteers charged with defending property and the 'right to work', first by replacing the strikers and ultimately by destroying their organisation.

In France the leading and semi-official newspaper, *Le Temps*, clearly inspired by the Millerand clique, engages in energetic propaganda to develop the already existing Civic Leagues and to transplant the methods of Fascism onto French soil.

In the United States, the groups of strikebreakers and assassins that have long supplemented the system of American freedom have now received a leadership body – the American Legion – recruited from the riffraff of the War.[21]

The bourgeoisie boasts of its power and stability, yet its leading governments are fully aware that it has received only a breathing spell. Under present circumstances, every massive strike tends to become a civil war and an immediate struggle for power.

In the proletarian struggle against the capitalist offensive, it is the duty of Communists to march in the forefront and promote understanding of the basic revolutionary tasks among those in struggle. In addition, Communists are obliged to rally the best and most active forces in the factories and trade unions to create their own workers' contingents and defence organisations in order to resist the Fascists and deter the *jeunesse dorée* [gilded youth] of the bourgeoisie from harassing strikers.

---

21. Formed in 1919, the American Legion's founding objectives called for maintenance of law and order and 100 per cent Americanism. A resolution passed by its founding convention called for Congress to 'pass a bill for immediately deporting every one of those Bolsheviks or Industrial Workers of the World'.

Given the extraordinary importance of counterrevolutionary gangs, the Communist Party must devote attention – particularly through its trade-union cells – to setting up a special information and communication service to keep a close eye on the White Guard fighting detachments, their staff, their inventory of weapons, and their links with the police, the press, and the political parties. This service must work out a detailed plan for defence and counterattack.

The Communist Party must instil the broadest layers of the proletariat, through word and deed, with an understanding that every economic or political conflict – given the right combination of circumstances – will develop into a civil war, during which the task of the proletariat is to take state power.

Faced with the fury of white terror and white travesties of justice, the Communist Party must ensure that the proletariat understands the futility, during a time of uprising, of appeals to the enemy for clemency. Instead, acts of organised popular and proletarian justice are needed to settle accounts with those persecuting the proletariat. But at times when the proletariat is still only coming together and must be mobilised through agitation, political campaigns, and strikes, the use of weapons and acts of sabotage is justified only when this blocks the transport of troops sent against masses of proletarians in struggle or captures strategic positions from the enemy in direct combat. Acts of individual terror may represent symptoms of revolutionary indignation that must be defended against the lynch justice of the bourgeoisie and its Social-Democratic lackeys. However, they are in no way conducive to raising the proletariat's level of organisation and readiness for struggle, because they awaken in the masses the illusion that the heroic deeds of individuals can replace the revolutionary struggle of the proletariat.

9.) *Relations with the proletarian middle layers*

In Western Europe, there is no other class that could, alongside the proletariat, become the decisive factor in world revolution as happened in Russia with the peasantry, which was destined for that role from the outset by war and hunger for land. But in Western Europe, *sectors of the peasantry, large sectors of the urban petty bourgeoisie, and a broad layer of the so-called new middle class* (office workers, etc.), are subjected to increasingly intolerable living conditions. The pressure of inflation, the lack of housing, and the insecurity of their lives generates a ferment among these masses that jolts them out of political inactivity and draws them into the struggle between revolution and counterrevolution. The bankruptcy of imperialism in the defeated countries and of pacifism and social reformism in the victor countries drives a sector of these middle layers into the camp of open counterrevolution, while another sector rallies to the camp of revolution. The Communist Party is obliged to devote constant attention to these layers.

Winning the small peasantry to the ideas of communism, plus winning and organising the agricultural workers, are among the most important preconditions for the victory of proletarian dictatorship. These tasks enable the revolution to extend out from the industrial centres into the countryside and create bases from which to resolve the question of food – a life-and-death challenge for the revolution.

Winning over substantial layers of the commercial and technical employees, the lower and middle civil servants, and intellectuals would make it much easier for the proletarian dictatorship to master the technical and organisational challenge of economic and government administration during the transition from capitalism to communism. This can sow discord in the ranks of the enemy and break through the isolation of the proletariat in the eyes of public opinion. Communist parties must pay close attention to the ferment among petty-bourgeois layers and find appropriate ways to utilise such forces, even if they are not free of petty-bourgeois illusions. Intellectuals and office employees who are free of such illusions should be recruited to the proletarian front and utilised to draw in the discontented petty-bourgeois masses.

As a result of economic decay and the resulting breakdown of government finances, the bourgeoisie itself is forced to consign the foundation of its state apparatus, the lower and middle civil servants, to increasing destitution. The economic struggles of such layers directly affect the structure of the bourgeois state. These layers may repeatedly be appeased, for a time, but in the long run the bourgeoisie will find it impossible to maintain its organisational foundation, just as it is impossible for capitalism to maintain the physical existence of wage labour while safeguarding its system of exploitation. The Communist parties take up energetically the economic needs of the lower and middle civil service, without regard for the state of public finances. In so doing, they carry out effective preparatory work for the destruction of bourgeois state institutions and take preparatory steps for building the proletarian state.

10.) *Coordinating action internationally*

In order to rally all the forces of the Communist International to break the resistance of the international counterrevolution, and to hasten the revolutionary victory, we must strive with all our energy for unified international leadership of the revolutionary struggle.

The Communist International requires that all Communist parties lend each other energetic mutual support in struggle. The developing economic struggles demand, whenever possible, immediate intervention by the proletariat of other countries. Communists in the trade unions have to make every effort to block not only the shipment of strikebreakers but exports to countries in which an important segment of the proletariat is in struggle. In cases where the capitalist government of one country uses force to plunder or subjugate another, Communist parties must not be satisfied with protests but must do everything possible to obstruct the invasion by its own government.

The Third Congress of the Communist International welcomes the demonstrations by the *French Communists* as a start toward escalating their campaign against the role of French capitalism as a counterrevolutionary exploiter. The congress reminds them of their duty to explain energetically to French soldiers in the occupied territories their role as thugs of French capitalism and encourage them to resist the shameful duties assigned to them. The French Communist Party has the task of making the French people aware that, by tolerating the formation of a French occupation army imbued with nationalist feelings, it is tying its own noose. Troops are being trained in the occupied territories who will then stand ready to drown in blood the revolutionary movement of the French working class. The presence of black troops on French soil and in the occupied territories poses special tasks before the French Communist Party.[22] It gives the French party an opportunity to make contact with these colonial slaves and explain to them that they are serving their oppressors and exploiters. It must call on them to rise up in struggle against the government of the colonisers and seek, through these soldiers, to link up with the peoples of France's colonies.

The *German Communist Party* has to show the German proletariat, through action, that a struggle against exploitation by Entente capitalism is impossible unless the capitalist government is overthrown. This government makes a great outcry against the Entente, while acting as overseer and gang boss for Entente capitalism. The VKPD must demonstrate through impetuous and ruthless struggle against the German government that it is not seeking a way out for German imperialism, but aims rather to sweep away its ruins. This is the only way to heighten the will to struggle among the proletarian masses of France.

Before the world working class, the Communist International denounces the call of Entente capitalism for reparations as a campaign of plunder against the working masses of the defeated countries. As for the attempts of the Longuet current in France and the Independents in Germany to find the form of robbery that would be least painful for the working masses, the Communist International brands this as a cowardly capitulation to the sharks of

---

22. Regarding black troops, see p. 550, n. 35.

Entente finance. It shows the proletariat of France and Germany that the only way to rebuild the devastated regions and compensate widows and orphans is by calling on the proletarians of both countries to struggle jointly against their exploiters.

The German working class can help the Russian workers in their difficult struggle only by hastening, through victorious struggle, the unification of agricultural Russia with industrial Germany. Communist parties of all countries whose troops are taking part in the subjugation and partitioning of *Turkey* must do everything possible to win these troops to revolution. The Communist parties of the *Balkan countries* have the duty of committing the strength of their mass parties to build a Balkan Communist Federation, which will do everything possible to stand up to nationalism in order to hasten the day of victory. The victory of Communist parties in Bulgaria and Yugoslavia will bring with it the collapse of the shameful Horthy government and the elimination of Romania's boyar regime, broadening the base for rural revolution in the most developed neighbouring countries.

The outstanding responsibility of Communists internationally remains, now as before, *consistent support to Soviet Russia*. They must not only react energetically to every attack on Soviet Russia, but also struggle vigorously to eliminate all the barriers erected by capitalist states in the path of Soviet trade with the world market and with all the world's peoples. Only when Soviet Russia succeeds in restoring its economy and lessening the poverty created by three years of imperialist war and three years of civil war, only when it succeeds in raising the working capacity of its people, will it be in a position to assist the victorious proletarian states of the West with foodstuffs and raw materials and protect them from strangulation by US capitalism.

The Communist International's world-political task entails not just holding demonstrations when important events occur but also *steadily increasing international ties among Communists* and conducting extended common struggles as a unified whole. There is no way to predict where the proletariat will achieve a breakthrough. Perhaps it will be in capitalist Germany, where the proletariat is under extreme pressure from the German and Entente bourgeoisies, facing the choice between winning or perishing. Or perhaps it is in the agrarian South-East or in Italy, where the disintegration of the bourgeoisie is very far advanced. That is why the Communist International has the duty of intensifying to the utmost its efforts in all sectors of world proletarian struggle to support the decisive struggles of every section of the International with all available means. When major conflicts break out in a country, this support takes the form above all of heightening and bringing to a head the internal conflicts in all other countries.

11.) *The decline of the Second and Two-and-a-Half Internationals*

During its third year, the Communist International was witness to the further political decline of the Social-Democratic parties and reformist trade-union leadership, in which they were unmasked and exposed. At the same time, however, it was a year of efforts to unite them organisationally and move them into attack against the Communist International.

In *Britain* the leaders of the Labour Party and the trade unions showed during the coal strike that their task is simply to consciously destroy the growing unity of proletarians and to consciously defend the capitalists against the workers. The breakdown of the Triple Alliance provides proof that the reformist trade-union leaders have no intention even of improving the status of the working class in a capitalist framework.

In *Germany*, the Social-Democratic Party showed, after it left the government,[23] that it is incapable of even the type of agitational opposition carried out by the old Social Democracy before the War. Each of its oppositional gestures was accompanied by efforts to avoid unleashing any working-class struggles. Although in supposed opposition on a national level, Social Democracy, ruling in Prussia, organised the military campaign of the White Guards there against the Central German miners, with the conscious aim of provoking them before the Communists had arrayed themselves for battle. Given the German bourgeoisie's capitulation to the Entente, given the evident fact that it can carry out the measures demanded by the Entente only by creating absolutely intolerable living conditions for the German proletariat, German Social Democracy re-entered the government, in order to help the bourgeoisie enslave the German proletarians.

In *Czechoslovakia*, Social Democracy is mobilising the army and police in order to rob Communist workers of their buildings and institutions. The *Polish Socialist Party's* deceptive policies aid Pilsudski in organising his campaign of pillage against Soviet Russia. It helps his government throw thousands of Communists into prison by seeking to drive them out of the trade unions, where – despite all persecution – they can gather the support of growing masses. The *Belgian Social Democrats* remain in the government that is taking part in the complete enslavement of the German people.

The *centrist parties and groups of the Two-and-a-Half International* are no less blatant in showing themselves to be parties of counterrevolution. The German Independents curtly reject the call of the German Communist Party,

---

23. The SPD resigned from the government in June 1920 after an electoral defeat. It re-entered the government in May 1921, joining a coalition cabinet headed by Catholic Centre Party leader Joseph Wirth.

despite differences of principle, to conduct a joint struggle against the worsening of working-class living conditions. During the March struggles, the Independents firmly supported the White Guard government against the Central German workers, helping to assure the victory of white terror and denouncing the proletarian vanguard before bourgeois public opinion as robbers, plunderers, and lumpenproletarians. And, after that, they hypocritically complain about the white terror. Although they pledged at the Halle convention to support Soviet Russia, their newspapers are conducting a slanderous campaign against the Russian Soviet republic. They align themselves with the entire Russian counterrevolution, with Wrangel, Milyukov, and Burtsev, by supporting the Kronstadt uprising against the Soviet republic, a rebellion that represented a new policy of the international counterrevolution against Soviet Russia. By overthrowing the Communist Party of Russia, they seek to destroy the soul, the heart, the skeleton, and the nervous system of the Soviet republic, in order then to be able to easily dispose of its body. The *Longuet group in France* lines up with the German Independents in this campaign and thereby, as we have seen, links up with the French counterrevolution, which has been shown to be the initiator of this new policy against Russia. In *Italy* the policy of the centre group of Serrati and D'Aragona is to evade every struggle. This course has inspired the bourgeoisie to new courage, enabling it to use the Fascist white gangs to dominate the life of the entire country.

Although the centrist and Social-Democratic parties differ only in phraseology, no union of the two groups in a single International has yet taken place. True, the centrist parties came together in February in their own international association with their own political platform and statutes. This Two-and-a-Half International seeks to shuttle verbally between the slogans of democracy and proletarian dictatorship. They provide the capitalist class in each country with much practical assistance by cultivating moods of indecision among the working class. Moreover, despite the devastation carried out by the world bourgeoisie and the subjugation of a large part of the globe by the victorious capitalist countries of the Entente, they pass on to the bourgeoisie blueprints of how to carry out exploitation without unleashing the power of the popular masses.

The Two-and-a-Half International shares with the Second International a common fear of the power of communism. The centrists' difference, however, lies simply in the fact that they also fear that a clear formulation of their point of view would cost them the rest of their influence on masses who may still be confused but have revolutionary sentiments. The political equivalence of the reformists and centrists is expressed through their common defence of the Amsterdam trade-union International, the last bulwark of the world bourgeoisie. Wherever they have influence in the trade unions, the centrists unite with the reformists and the trade-union bureaucracy in struggle against the Communists. They respond to Communist attempts to win the unions to revolution by splitting the unions. This demonstrates that, just like the Social Democrats, they are determined opponents of proletarian struggle and pacesetters for counterrevolution.

The Communist International must carry out, as before, a resolute struggle against not only the Second International and the Amsterdam trade-union International but also the Two-and-a-Half International. This unrelenting struggle shows the masses, every day, that the Social Democrats and centrists are not only unwilling to fight to overthrow capitalism, but that they are also unwilling to fight for the most elementary and urgent needs of the working class. Only in this way can the Communist International overcome the influence of these agents of the bourgeoisie over the working class. The Communist International can bring this struggle to a successful conclusion only by rooting out any centrist tendencies or impulses in its own ranks and demonstrating in its daily practice that it is the International of Communist deeds and not of Communist phrases and theory.

The Communist International is the only organisation of the international proletariat whose principles equip it to lead the struggle against capitalism. The task is to reinforce its inner unity, its international leadership and its activity in such a fashion that it can genuinely carry out the aim stated in its Statutes: 'To organise the common activity of the proletarians of different countries who strive for one single goal: overthrowing capitalism and establishing the dictatorship of the proletariat and an international Soviet republic.'[24]

---

24. In Riddell (ed.) 1991, 2WC, 2, pp. 696–7.

# The March Action and the Situation in the VKPD[25]

The Third World Congress is pleased to note that all important resolutions, and particularly the portion of the resolution on tactics and strategy that takes up the much-disputed March Action, have been adopted unanimously. The representatives of the German opposition, in their resolution on the March Action, share for the most part the point of view of the congress. The congress regards this as evidence that unified and harmonious work inside the VKPD on the basis of the Third Congress decisions is not only desirable but practicable. The congress considers that any further splintering of the forces inside the VKPD, any factional formation – let alone a split – is a grave danger for the movement as a whole.

The congress expects of the Zentrale and the VKPD majority that it will treat the former opposition leniently, provided that it carries out the Third Congress decisions in a loyal fashion. The congress is convinced that the Zentrale will do everything possible to draw together all the forces in the party. The congress instructs the former opposition to immediately dissolve any factional structure within the party, to fully and completely subordinate the parliamentary fraction to the Zentrale, to completely subordinate the press under the relevant party committee, and to immediately cease any political collaboration (in their publications, etc.) with those expelled from the party and the Communist International.

The congress instructs the Executive to closely follow the German movement's further development and, if there is the slightest breach of discipline, to take energetic measures.

---

25. Approved in Session 21. See also 'Theses on Tactics and Strategy', pp. 941–2. For a short account of the March Action, see Editorial Introduction, pp. 18–23.

## Appeal for Max Hoelz[26]

*To the German proletariat*

The German bourgeoisie has sentenced the fighters of the March Days to two thousand years in jails and penitentiaries. To that total, they have now added a sentence of life imprisonment against *Max Hoelz*.[27]

The Communist International is opposed to individual terror and acts of sabotage that do not directly serve the goals of struggle in a civil war. It opposes volunteer contingents operating independently of the political leadership of the revolutionary proletariat. However, the Communist International views Max Hoelz as a courageous rebel against capitalist society, for which reform means reformatories and security means the violent rampages of security forces. His actions were not appropriate. The white terror can be defeated only through an uprising of the workers in their masses, which is the only force that can bring the proletariat to victory. But his actions flowed from love for the proletariat and hatred for the bourgeoisie.

The congress therefore sends Max Hoelz its fraternal greetings and recommends him to the care of the German proletariat. The congress expresses its hope that on the day when the German proletarians break open the gates of his prison, he will fight in the ranks of the Communist Party of Germany for the liberation of German workers.

---

26. Approved in Session 4.
27. Max Hoelz was a KAPD member who organised an armed workers' detachment in Saxony during the Kapp Putsch of 1920. During the March struggles of 1921, Hoelz formed an independent guerrilla force that functioned in Central Germany. Hoelz was subsequently sentenced to life imprisonment for murder. Following an international defence campaign, he was amnestied in 1929. See the report by Radek on pp. 235–6.

# Theses on the Communist International and the Red International of Labour Unions[28]

*The struggle against the yellow Amsterdam trade-union International*

I.

The bourgeoisie holds the working class in slavery not only through brute force but also through quite elaborate deception. The school, the church, parliament, art, literature, the daily press – in the hands of the bourgeoisie, they all serve as a powerful means of beguiling the working masses and of transmitting bourgeois ideas to the proletariat.

Among the bourgeois notions that the ruling classes have succeeded in implanting among the working masses is the concept that trade unions are neutral, apolitical, and non-partisan.

During recent decades, and especially after the imperialist war ended, trade unions in Europe and the Americas have become the most extensive organisations of the proletariat, embracing in some countries nothing less than the entirety of the working class. The bourgeoisie knows full well that the fate of the capitalist system depends on the degree to which the trade unions will be capable, in the near future, of shaking off bourgeois influences. That explains the convulsive efforts of the entire world bourgeoisie and its accomplices, the Social Democrats, to keep the trade unions under the spell of bourgeois-Social-Democratic ideas at all costs.

The bourgeoisie cannot simply tell the trade unions to support the bourgeois parties. So, instead, it calls on them to support no party at all, meaning in reality that the unions should not support the party of communism.

The gospel of neutrality or political abstention already has a long history. Over the years, the bourgeois concept was drummed into the trade unions of Britain, Germany, the United States, and other countries by spokesmen of clerical-Christian unions and bourgeois Hirsch-Duncker unions, by leaders of peaceful British trade unions of the old school, and by representatives of the so-called free trade unions in Germany [ADGB] and of syndicalism. Legien, Gompers, Jouhaux, and Sidney Webb proclaimed for decades the 'neutrality' of unions.

In reality, however, the trade unions were never neutral and could not be, no matter how hard they tried. Not only is trade-union neutrality harmful to the working class; it is also unrealisable. No mass workers' organisation can remain neutral in the struggle between capital and labour. It follows that the

---

28. Reported on and discussed in Sessions 15, 16, 18, and 19; approved in Session 24.

trade unions, too, cannot remain neutral with regard to the bourgeois parties and the party of the proletariat. The leaders of the bourgeoisie understand this full well. However, just as it is absolutely necessary for the bourgeoisie that the masses believe in the life hereafter, they also need the masses to believe that trade unions are apolitical and can remain neutral toward the Communist workers' party. Bourgeois rule and extraction of profits from the workers requires not only priests, police, generals, and informers, but also the trade-union bureaucrats, the 'workers' leaders', who preach trade-union neutrality and abstention from political struggle.

Even before the imperialist war, the most advanced proletarians of Europe and America had begun to see through the false notion of neutrality. Its fallaciousness became more evident as class antagonisms became increasingly acute. When the imperialist slaughter began, the old trade-union leaders were compelled to take off the mask of neutrality and offer open support to their 'own' bourgeoisie.

During the imperialist war, the Social Democrats and syndicalists who had preached for decades that trade unions should avoid any involvement in politics now placed the unions in the service of the bourgeois parties' despicable and murderous policies. Yesterday's preachers of trade-union 'neutrality' had now taken on the role of undisguised agents of specific political parties – not workers' parties but those of the bourgeoisie.

Now that the imperialist war has ended, the same Social-Democratic and syndicalist trade-union leaders once again put on the mask of trade-union neutrality and abstention. Now that the predicament of war is over, these agents of the bourgeoisie seek to adjust to the new conditions and want to remove workers from the path of revolution and put them on a path more advantageous for the bourgeoisie.

Economics and politics are always tied together by indissoluble bonds. This connection is particularly strong in periods like the present one. Every single important question of political life is of interest not only to the workers' party but also to proletarian trade unions. Conversely, every important economic question is of interest not only to the unions but to the workers' party. When the imperialist government of France orders the call-up of specific age categories in order to occupy the Ruhr Basin and, in general, to strangle Germany, can any truly proletarian union in France maintain that this is a purely political issue of no concern to the unions? Can a truly revolutionary syndicalist union in France remain neutral or non-political on this issue?

Let us take another example: the coal strike, a purely economic movement under way in Britain. Can the Communist Party say that this is an exclusively trade-union question and is of no concern to the party? Millions of unemployed today face destitution and are reduced to the status of beggars. The question must be posed of requisitioning the dwellings of the bourgeoisie in order to ease the housing crisis of the proletariat. Broader and broader masses of workers are forced by the realities of life to consider the question of arming the proletariat. Workers in one country after another are organising the occupation of factories and industrial establishments. Under such conditions, the assertion that the unions should not get involved in political struggle and should remain neutral toward all parties amounts in practice to entering the service of the bourgeoisie.

Despite the wide variety of political parties in Europe and America, on the whole they can be categorised under three headings: (1) parties of the bourgeoisie; (2) parties of the petty bourgeoisie (chiefly the Social Democrats); (3) the party of the proletariat. Trade unions that claim to be apolitical and neutral toward the three above-mentioned groups of parties are, in reality, supporting the parties of the petty bourgeoisie and the bourgeoisie.

## II.

The Amsterdam trade-union International is the place where the Second and Two-and-a-Half Internationals met and joined hands. The entire international bourgeoisie regards this organisation with trust and confidence. The central idea inspiring the Amsterdam trade-union International is trade-union neutrality. It is no accident that the bourgeoisie and its servants, the Social Democrats and right-wing syndicalists, seek to rally the broad masses of Western European and American workers around this slogan. While the Second International, which openly went over to the bourgeoisie, has completely collapsed, the Amsterdam trade-union International, which has again assumed the disguise of neutrality, is enjoying a degree of success. While flying the flag of neutrality, the Amsterdam trade-union International undertakes the most challenging and despicable tasks for the bourgeoisie, such as finishing off the coal miners' strike in Britain. This task was carried out by the notorious J.H. Thomas, who is simultaneously chair of the Second International and one of the best-known leaders of the Amsterdam yellow trade-union federation. Other such tasks include driving down wages and the organised plundering of German workers to pay for the sins of the imperialist German bourgeoisie.

Leipart and Grassmann, Wissell and Bauer, Robert Schmidt and J.H. Thomas, Albert Thomas and Jouhaux, Daszynski and Zulawski – they have all divided up their various roles. Some of them, previously trade-union leaders, now serve as ministers, officials, or accomplices of various kinds. Others, however, committed body and soul to these accomplices, occupy the top positions in the Amsterdam trade-union International and urge workers to remain neutral in political struggles.

The Amsterdam trade-union International now stands as a central pillar of international capitalism. No one can successfully challenge this capitalist stronghold unless they have fully grasped the need to contest the false notion of abstention and neutrality. To develop effective methods of struggle against the yellow Amsterdam International, it is necessary above all to determine precisely the mutual relations between party and trade union in each country.

## III.

The Communist Party is the vanguard of the proletariat, a vanguard that fully recognised what was needed to free the proletariat and therefore consciously adopted the Communist programme.

The trade unions, on the other hand, are a mass organisation of the proletariat, which develop toward embracing all the workers of a given branch of industry. They include not only convinced Communists but also intermediate and even quite backward layers of the proletariat, who approach communism only step by step, based on the lessons of life. The role of the trade unions in the period preceding the struggle for power is different in many ways from their role after the taking of power. However, during all these stages – before, during, and after the taking of power – trade unions are broad organisations embracing larger masses than the party. To some degree, they must necessarily play the role, with respect to the party, of a periphery to a centre.

Before the taking of power, truly proletarian and revolutionary trade unions organise workers primarily on an economic basis to win such improvements as are possible before capitalism's complete overthrow. Their attention is chiefly directed, however, at organising proletarian mass struggle against capitalism and for proletarian revolution. During the proletarian revolution, genuinely revolutionary trade unions work together with the party to organise the masses for an immediate assault against the capitalist strongholds and to undertake the basic work of organising the socialist revolution. After proletarian power has been established and consolidated, the work of the trade unions shifts chiefly to the field of economic organisation. They devote their resources almost completely to organising the economy on a socialist basis. In this way, they become a practical school of socialism.

During all three of these phases of struggle, the trade unions must support the proletarian vanguard, the Communist Party, which leads the proletarian struggle at every stage. To achieve this goal, the Communists and their sympathisers must organise Communist cells in the trade unions, units that are fully subordinated to the Communist Party as a whole.

The policy of forming Communist cells in every trade union, adopted by the Communist International's Second Congress, has proved its worth during the last year, leading to good results in Germany, Britain, Italy, and a number of other countries. In Germany, significant numbers of untested and politically inexperienced workers, seeing no immediate advantage in membership in the Free Trade Unions [ADGB], have recently left the ranks of the Social-Democratic unions. This in no way changes the Communist International's principled position regarding the unions. The task of Communists is to explain to proletarians that nothing is to be gained by leaving the old trade unions and remaining unorganised. Rather the solution is to win the trade unions to revolution, rid them of the spirit of reformism and of the traitorous reformist leaders, and thus to transform the unions into genuine strongholds of the revolutionary proletariat.

## IV.

The main task of all Communists in the coming period consists of tenacious, vigorous, and stubborn effort to win the majority of workers in all trade unions. We must not be discouraged by current reactionary moods in the unions, but rather should take part actively in the unions' daily struggles, despite every obstacle, and thus work to win them to communism.

The strength of every Communist Party can be best measured by the degree of influence that it really exerts on the masses of workers in the trade unions. *The party must be able to exert its decisive influence in the trade unions without petty, patronising interference.* Only the Communist cells in the union, not the union as such, are subordinated to the party. Only through consistent, devoted, and perceptive work by Communist trade-union cells can the party achieve a situation where the unions as a whole heed the advice of the party happily and willingly.

In France, there is at present a healthy ferment in the trade unions. The working class is finally recovering from the crisis of the workers' movement and is now learning to reject the betrayal carried out by the reformist socialists and syndicalists.

Many of the revolutionary syndicalists in France are still prejudiced against political struggle and against the idea of a proletarian political party. They pay homage to the concept of neutrality, as expressed in the celebrated Amiens Charter of 1906. The ineffective and incorrect approach of this wing of revolutionary syndicalism holds dangers for the movement. Should this current win the majority, it will not know what to do with it and will be disarmed in the face of the agents of capitalism like Jouhaux and Dumoulins.

The revolutionary syndicalists in France will continue to lack a firm line until such a line is developed by the Communist Party itself. The Communist

Party of France must work toward friendly cooperation with the best forces of revolutionary syndicalism. However, the party must rely above all on its own members, and form cells wherever as few as three Communists are located. The party must begin an educational campaign against neutralism. In a friendly but firm manner, it must point out what is erroneous in the positions of revolutionary syndicalism. Only in this way can the trade-union movement in France become revolutionary, working in close cooperation with the party.

In Italy, there is an unusual situation. Here the bulk of trade-union members are revolutionary in outlook, but the leadership of the [General] Confederation of Labour is held by outright reformists and centrists, whose sympathies are with Amsterdam. The first task of Italian Communists is to organise a stubborn and extended daily struggle in the unions, from bottom to top. They must work methodically and patiently to expose the traitorous and indecisive nature of this leadership and wrest the trade unions from its control.

As regards the revolutionary syndicalist forces in Italy, the Italian Communists face, by and large, the same tasks as the Communists in France.

In Spain, the trade-union movement is strong and revolutionary but lacking in purpose, while the Communist Party is still young and relatively weak. In this situation, the party must do all it can to win a foothold in the unions, it must provide the unions with advice and assistance, playing an educational role and developing friendly relations, in order to join with the unions in organising the entire struggle.

In Britain, an important evolution is under way in the trade-union movement, which is rapidly becoming revolutionary. The mass movement is developing, and the old trade-union leaders are quickly becoming discredited. The party must make every effort to win a foothold in the large unions, such as the miners. Every member of the party must be active in a union, winning support for communism through energetic, persistent organisational work. Nothing should be neglected in seeking closer ties with the masses.

In the United States, the same evolution is proceeding at a somewhat slower pace. By no means should the Communists simply leave the ranks of the reactionary [American] Federation of Labor. On the contrary, they should try by every means to win the old unions to revolution. Cooperation with the best sectors of the IWW is necessary, but it should not preclude an educational effort to counter the IWW's prejudices.

In Japan, a broad trade-union movement is developing spontaneously, without, as yet, a defined leadership. The main task of Communist forces in Japan consists of supporting this movement and influencing it in a Marxist direction.

In Czechoslovakia, our party has the support of the working-class majority, but most of the trade unions remain in the hands of the social patriots and centrists. Moreover, it is split along national lines. This situation is the result of inadequate organisation and a lack of clarity among revolutionary-minded trade unionists. The party must do everything possible to put an end to this situation and win the entire trade-union movement to support a Communist leadership. That requires forming cells and establishing a single Communist trade-union confederation common to all nationalities. We should also work vigorously to unite the nationally divided federations.

In Austria and Belgium, the social patriots have skilfully managed to gain control of the trade-union movement. In these countries the unions are the main arena of struggle. Communists must focus their attention on this task.

In Norway, the party, which enjoys the support of the majority of workers, needs to strengthen its hold in the trade-union movement and oust the centrist forces from the leadership.

In Sweden, the party has to struggle against not only reformism but also a petty-bourgeois socialist current and devote its full energy to that task.

In Germany, the party is well on the way to gradually winning the trade unions. Absolutely no concessions should be made to supporters of the slogan, 'Out of the trade unions!'. That would mean supporting the social patriots. All attempts to expel the Communists must be opposed, while waging a stubborn struggle and exerting every effort to win a majority in the trade unions.

## V.

These considerations should shape mutual relations between the Communist International and the Red International of Labour Unions.

The Communist International has the task of leading not only the political struggle of the proletariat, in the narrow sense of the term, but also its entire liberation struggle, whatever forms that may take. The Communist International must be more than the arithmetical sum of Communist Party leaderships in different countries. The Communist International must inspire and unify the activity of all proletarian organisations, whether they are purely political or are trade-union, cooperative, soviet, or cultural organisations.

The International Trade Union Council cannot follow the yellow International in adopting an apolitical or neutral stance. An organisation that remained neutral with regard to the Second, Two-and-a-Half, and Third Internationals would necessarily become a pawn in the hands of the bourgeoisie. The action programme of the Red International of Labour Unions, included in this resolution, is being submitted by the Communist International to the first congress of red trade unions. In reality, only the Communist parties and the Communist International will defend it. This factor alone indicates that, in order to win the trade-union movements in each country and to carry out honestly and resolutely the unions' new revolutionary tasks, the red trade unions will be required to work hand in hand and in close contact with the Communist Party of each country. They will also have to bring the Red International of Labour Unions, at each stage, into accord with the work of the Communist International.

The bias toward neutrality, 'independence', and an apolitical, non-party approach, which still afflicts some honest revolutionary syndicalists in France, Spain, Italy, and other countries, is objectively nothing other than a tribute paid to bourgeois ideas. To vanquish yellow Amsterdam and, even more, capitalism itself, the red trade unions must renounce once and for all the bourgeois notions of independence and neutrality. The best situation, from the point of view of economising forces and concentrating blows, is to create a unified International that includes in its ranks both political parties and other forms of workers' organisations. Undoubtedly, the future will see such an organisational set-up. However, in the present transitional period, given the diversity and heterogeneity of unions as they presently exist, it is vitally necessary to form an independent international association of red trade unions, which accepts the platform of the Communist International in general terms, but admits members with more flexibility than is the case in the Communist International.

The Third Congress of the Communist International pledges its support to the Red International of Labour Unions being organised on this basis. In the interests of a closer relationship between the Communist International and the Red International of Labour Unions, the Third Congress proposes that the Communist International be represented by three members in the executive of the Red International of Labour Unions and vice versa.

In the opinion of the Communist International, the action programme of the red trade unions should be approximately as follows:

*Action Programme*

1.) An acute economic crisis extends over the entire world. Wholesale prices have fallen catastrophically, and overproduction prevails even amid shortages of goods. The bourgeoisie is pursuing an offensive against the working class, marked by stubborn attempts to reduce wages and to throw workers back decades. As a result, the masses are growing more embittered, while the old methods of the trade unions are shown to be impotent. All these factors pose new tasks to revolutionary trade unions internationally. The disintegration of capitalism demands new methods of economic struggle. The trade unions need aggressive economic policies in order to repel the capitalist attack and, after consolidating their positions, to themselves go over to the attack.

2.) Trade-union policy is based on direct action by the revolutionary masses and their organisations against capitalism. All workers' achievements are closely related to direct action and revolutionary pressure from the masses. Direct action should be understood to encompass every type of pressure exerted by workers on the employers and the state: boycotts, strikes, street protests, demonstrations, occupations of the enterprise, forcible resistance to shipping goods out of the enterprise, armed uprisings, and other forms of revolutionary action that contribute to unifying the working class in struggle for socialism. The task of revolutionary trade unions therefore consists of converting direct action into a tool to educate and prepare the working masses for the struggle for social revolution and the dictatorship of the proletariat.

3.) During the last year of struggle, all the weaknesses of the trade unions were graphically evident. When workers in an enterprise belong to multiple trade unions, this weakens them in struggle. The starting point to exert workers' full strength in struggle is to make the transition from unions organised by trades to unions based on branches of industry. 'One enterprise, one union' must be the slogan for building the movement. Related unions must be fused into a single federation in a revolutionary fashion by posing the question directly to union members in the factories and shops, and then to regional and national congresses.

4.) Every factory and shop must become a bulwark and fortress of revolution.
The previous form of relationships with ordinary union members (treasurer, chair, stewards, and other posts) must be replaced by factory councils, elected by all workers of a given enterprise, regardless of their political persuasion. Members of the Red International of Labour Unions need to ensure that all workers of the enterprise in question take part in the election of the council that is to represent them. All attempts to restrict elections of factory councils to meetings of those sharing a common viewpoint, those supporting a given party, while excluding the broad mass of non-party workers from the elections, must be categorically rejected. Such a structure would be a cell, not a factory council. Through its cells, action committees, and individual members, the revolutionary sector of the workers must exert its influence on the general assembly and on the factory council it elects.

5.) The first demand that the factory and shop committees must consider is that the employer pay for support to laid-off workers. Under no circumstances must we allow the workers to be thrown on the street without any consequences to the enterprise. The employer must be obliged to pay a full wage to the unemployed. This demand serves to organise not so much the jobless but, above all, the workers in various enterprises, who need to understand that the question of unemployment cannot be resolved within the capitalist system and that the best measure against unemployment is social revolution and the dictatorship of the proletariat.

6.) Enterprise shutdowns and reductions in the number of working days are, at present, one of the most important tools used by the bourgeoisie to reduce wages, lengthen the working day, and get rid of collective agreements. Lockouts are increasingly used by the united employers as a form of 'direct action' against large numbers of unionists. A struggle is therefore needed against factory closures, in which workers demand to know the reason for the shutdown. Special control commissions should be formed for this purpose, assigned to check on raw materials, fuel, and orders. They should also conduct an inventory of the raw materials actually available for production and the money reserves deposited in banks. These specially elected control commissions must carefully investigate the financial relations between the enterprise in question and other enterprises. Among the workers' immediate objectives should be abolition of business secrecy.

7.) Among the means of resistance against widespread workplace shutdowns, wage reductions, and worsening of working conditions is workers' occupation of the factory or workplace and the continuation of production against the employers' will. Given the prevailing shortages, continuation of production is necessary, and workers should therefore not permit the deliberate shutdown of factories and workplaces. Depending on local conditions, the nature of production, the political situation, and the level of tension in social struggles, occupations can be supported by other methods of exerting pressure on the employer. When an enterprise is occupied, its management must be taken over by the factory or shop committee alongside a specially chosen representative of the union.

8.) The economic struggle should be waged under the slogan of raising wages and improving working conditions compared to the prewar period. All attempts to drive working conditions down to the prewar level should be rejected decisively and in revolutionary fashion. The War led to the exhaustion of the working class, and this must be countered by better working conditions. No attention should be paid to the capitalists' complaints that they face foreign competition. Revolutionary unions must approach the issues of wages and working conditions from the point of view not of competition among exploiters of different nations but of the need to maintain and protect labour power.

9.) If the capitalists are demanding wage reductions in conditions of national economic crisis, the task of revolutionary trade unions is to prevent wage reductions spreading from one branch of production to another – that is, not to allow themselves to be split into many separate groups. Above all, workers in essential industries (coal miners, railwaymen, electric technicians, gas workers, etc.) must be drawn into the struggle, so that it hits at capitalism's key centres within the country's economic life. It is useful and necessary here to employ every type of resistance, starting with individual walkouts and leading to a national general strike in an important branch of production.

10.) The trade unions must make practical preparations to organise international strikes embracing a given branch of production. Halting coal production or interrupting trade on an international level are important forms of struggle against reactionary attacks by the international bourgeoisie.

The unions must follow the world economic situation attentively, in order to choose the best moment for an attack. They must not overlook the fact that an international action, whatever its form, will be possible only with the formation of truly international revolutionary trade unions, which have nothing in common with the yellow Amsterdam International.

11.) Opportunists everywhere encourage the belief that collective agreements are unrivalled in value. This concept must be decisively refuted by the revolutionary movement. A collective agreement is nothing more than a truce. Employers always violate the collective agreement as soon as the slightest opportunity arises. A religious faith in collective agreements shows that bourgeois ideology is deeply rooted in the leaders of the working class. Revolutionary unions should not reject collective agreements, but rather recognise their limited value, and always consider the possibility of breaking the agreement, if this is advantageous to the working class.

12.) The struggle by workers' organisations against the employers – whether individual or collective – should be shaped not only by national and local circumstances but also by the entire experience of the working-class struggle for liberation. Therefore it is not enough for workers to carefully prepare each important strike. When the strike breaks out, they must also establish special squads for struggle against strikebreakers and resistance to the various provocations of White Guard organisations supported by the bourgeois governments. Italy's Fascists, the Emergency Technical Assistance in Germany, White Guard organisations in France and Britain made up of former officers and NCOs – all these organisations have set the goal of disrupting and destroying every action by workers. They try to do this not only by supplying strikebreakers but also by smashing working-class organisations and killing their leaders. Under such conditions, organising special contingents to defend the strike and the workers is a matter of life and death.

13.) These newly formed struggle organisations should not only fend off attacks by the employers and strikebreaker organisations but also take the initiative in halting shipments of goods intended for the factory in question, as well as its shipments of finished products to other factories and enterprises. In this regard, transport workers play a particularly important role. It is their responsibility to hold up goods in transit, which is only feasible with solid support from all the workers in that locality.

14.) During the coming period, the entire working-class economic struggle should focus on the party's slogan of 'workers' control of production', which must become reality before the government and the ruling classes set up surrogates for workers' control. This will bring positive results only if an uncompromising struggle is launched against every attempt by the ruling classes and reformists to establish parity enterprise committees or parity control commissions. Revolutionary trade unions must decisively oppose socialist deception and knavery promoted by leaders of the old trade unions with assistance from the ruling classes. All the chatter by these gentlemen about peaceful socialisation merely serves the goal of diverting workers from revolutionary action and social revolution.

15.) Ideas of profit-sharing – that is, paying back to workers an insignificant portion of the surplus value they have produced – are being advanced with the aim of diverting workers' attention from their immediate tasks and arousing in them petty-bourgeois aspirations. This slogan leads to workers' demoralisation, and it must be subjected to harsh and pitiless criticism. The slogan of revolutionary class-struggle trade unions is not sharing in the profits but 'destruction of capitalist profits'.

16.) In order to cripple or break workers' capacity for struggle, the bourgeois states have resorted to temporary militarisation of individual factories or entire branches of industry, on the pretext of protecting essential industries. Claiming the need to head off economic dislocation, they have introduced compulsory arbitration and mediation boards. In the interests of capitalism, they also introduced direct deduction of tax payments from workers' paycheques, in order to shift the economic burden of the War entirely onto workers' shoulders, with the employers now taking on the role of tax collectors. The trade unions must conduct an unrelenting struggle against these government measures, which serve only the interests of the capitalist class.

17.) During the struggle for improved working conditions, a higher standard of living, and the introduction of workers' control it must be borne in mind that these problems cannot be resolved within the framework of capitalist relations. The revolutionary trade unions must therefore wrest concessions from the ruling classes step by step, by forcing them to enact socialist legislation. In so doing, they must explain fully to the working masses that the social question can be settled only by the destruction of capitalism and the introduction of the dictatorship of the proletariat. It is in this sense that every partial action by the workers, every partial strike, every conflict, no matter how insignificant, must leave its mark. The revolutionary trade unions should generalise these conflicts and help the workers involved to recognise the necessity and inevitability of social revolution and the dictatorship of the proletariat.

18.) Economic struggle is also political, that is, an expression of the class struggle as a whole. Even if the struggle embraces broad layers of workers across the country, it will become revolutionary and bring real gains for the working class as a whole only if the revolutionary trade unions work hand in hand with the Communist Party in their country, collaborating closely in a tight alliance.

In the present revolutionary situation, dividing the workers' class struggle into two independent parts is extremely harmful, both in theory and in practice. To make headway, strength must be concentrated to the utmost. This can be done only if the revolutionary energy of the working class – that is, of all its Communist and revolutionary components – is exerted to the maximum. Separate campaigns by the Communist Party and the red revolutionary unions are doomed in advance to failure and destruction. Therefore, the precondition for success in anticapitalist struggle is unity in action and organic alliance between the Communist Party and the trade unions.

## Resolution on Work in the Cooperative Movement[29]

The Third Congress of the International instructs the Executive to establish a cooperative division. It will convene international cooperative consultations, conferences, and congresses, as required, with the goal of carrying out internationally the tasks listed in the accompanying theses.

The division should also take on the following practical tasks:

1.) Strengthen cooperative activity among working people in agriculture and commerce by joining together small, semi-proletarian operations in cooperatives. Draw working people into collectively managing and upgrading their operations.
2.) Lead the struggle on a national level for the transfer to the cooperatives of all distribution of foodstuffs and consumer goods.
3.) Conduct propaganda for the principles and methods of revolutionary cooperation, and encourage revolutionary cooperatives to lend material aid to the working class where it is in struggle.
4.) Establish international trade and financial relationships among workers' cooperatives and organise them for joint production projects.

---

29. The German edition of congress resolutions states that this resolution was adopted in Session 22, although there is no record of this in the congress proceedings.

## Theses on the Work of Communists in the Cooperatives[30]

1.) In the epoch of proletarian revolution, proletarian cooperatives face two tasks:

a.) Assist the working masses in their struggle for political power.
b.) Where power has already been won, help them in building a socialist society.

2.) The old cooperatives took the reformist path and sought to avoid revolutionary struggle. They embodied the notion of a gradual 'growing over' into socialism without the aid of a dictatorship of the proletariat.

They preached that cooperatives should be politically neutral. However, behind this pretence, they subordinated the cooperatives to the political goals of the imperialist bourgeoisie.

Their internationalism was purely verbal. In reality they transformed international workers' solidarity into collaboration of the working masses with the bourgeoisie of their country.

The old cooperatives do not promote revolution with these policies; they hold it back. They do not hasten it; they hinder it.

3.) The various forms and varieties of cooperatives cannot serve the proletariat's revolutionary goals.[31] Consumer societies can most readily be adapted to these goals, but even they include many societies composed of bourgeois elements, which will never side with the proletariat in revolutionary struggles. That can be done only by workers' cooperatives in the city or countryside.

4.) Communists in the cooperative movement have the following tasks:

a.) Carry out propaganda for Communist ideas.
b.) Transform the cooperatives into instruments for revolutionary class struggle, without disaffiliation of individual cooperatives from their national federation.

In all cooperatives, it is the duty of Communists to form cells, with the goal of creating a central leadership of Communist cooperatives in a given country.

These cells and their central leadership must maintain constant contact with the Communist Party and its representatives in the cooperatives. The

---

30. Reported on and discussed in Session 21. Approved in Session 22. See also the theses on the cooperative movement by L. Khinchuk ('Richtlinien der internationalen Genossenschaftsbewegung') published on the eve of the congress in *Die Kommunistische Internationale*, 16, pp. 391–4, and the discussion of cooperatives at the subsequent world congress, Riddell (ed.) 2011b, 4WC, pp. 813–36.

31. Based on the context, this sentence presumably refers to producer cooperatives.

central leadership must formulate the fundamentals of Communist policy in the cooperative movement, while leading and organising this movement.

5.) The practical tasks facing the revolutionary cooperatives of the West at this time will stand out more distinctly as work progresses. Some of them, however, are already clearly recognisable:

- a.) Carry out oral and written propaganda and agitation for Communist ideas, and struggle to rid the cooperatives of leadership and influence by bourgeois compromisers.
- b.) Establish ties between the cooperatives and the Communist Party and revolutionary trade unions. Direct and indirect participation by cooperatives in the proletariat's political struggle, demonstrations, and political campaigns. Material support for the Communist Party and its publications. Material support for strikers and for workers suffering from lockouts, and so on.
- c.) Struggle against the imperialist policies of the bourgeoisie and thus also against Entente interference in the affairs of Soviet Russia and other countries.
- d.) Establish ideological, organisational, and also business ties between workers in cooperatives of different countries.
- e.) Struggle for the rapid conclusion of trade treaties and the implementation of trade relations with Soviet Russia and the other soviet republics.
- f.) Conduct as much trade as possible with these republics.
- g.) Participate in developing the natural resources of the soviet states through concessions granted to cooperatives.

6.) The tasks of cooperatives will fully develop only after the proletarian revolution. However, based on the experiences of Soviet Russia, some of the characteristic features of this work can already be identified.

- a.) Consumer societies will have to take charge of distributing products according to the proletarian government's plan. This will result in an unprecedented flowering of the cooperatives.
- b.) The cooperatives will need to develop into an organisation that provides a link between isolated small productive units (peasants and handicraft workers) and the central economic organs of the proletarian state. The assistance of the cooperatives will enable the state to direct the work of isolated small productive units. The consumer cooperatives will serve to collect the foodstuffs and raw materials from small-scale producers and pass them on to members of the cooperative and the state.

c.) In addition, the producers' cooperatives can unify the small producers into workshops or larger enterprises, in which it is possible to utilise scientific and technical methods and machinery. This will provide a technical basis for the small producers that makes it possible to develop socialist enterprises that destroy the individualistic psychology of the small producer and promote development of a collectivist psychology.

7.) Given the important role of the revolutionary cooperatives in the epoch of proletarian revolution, the Third Congress instructs the Communist parties, groups, and organisations to promote the concept of the revolutionary cooperative and the organisation of Communist cells in the cooperatives. The cooperatives need to be transformed into instruments of the class struggle and brought into a unified front with the revolutionary trade unions.

The congress leaves it to the Communist International Executive to organise a cooperative section, which will carry out the tasks outlined here. In addition, this section must convene meetings, conferences, and congresses to carry out our tasks in the cooperatives on an international level.

# Theses on the Report Concerning the Policies of the Communist Party of Russia[32]

### 1.) *The international position of the RSFSR*

The international position of the RSFSR [Russian Soviet Federative Socialist Republic] at present is characterised by a certain equilibrium. Although it is highly unstable, it has nevertheless given rise to a peculiar state of affairs in world politics.

This idiosyncrasy is as follows: on the one hand, the international bourgeoisie is filled with furious hatred of and hostility toward Soviet Russia and is prepared at any moment to attack it in order to strangle it. On the other hand, all attempts at military intervention have ended in complete failure, despite the bourgeoisie's expenditure of hundreds of millions of francs and the fact that the Soviet government was then much weaker than it is now, while the Russian landowners and capitalists then had at their disposal entire armies on RSFSR territory.

Opposition to the war against Soviet Russia has grown considerably in all capitalist countries, adding fuel to the revolutionary movement of the proletariat and extending to very wide sections of the petty-bourgeois democrats. The conflict of interests between the various imperialist countries has become acute, and is growing more acute every day. The revolutionary movement among the hundreds of millions of oppressed peoples of the East is growing with remarkable vigour. The result of all these conditions is that international imperialism has proved unable to strangle Soviet Russia, although it is far stronger. Indeed it has been obliged for the time being to grant Russia recognition, or semi-recognition, and to conclude trade agreements with her.

In this way, we have attained a very insecure and unstable equilibrium that enables the socialist republic to exist – not for long, of course – within the capitalist encirclement.

### 2.) *The international relationship of class forces*

This state of affairs has given rise to the following international alignment of class forces:

The international bourgeoisie, deprived of the opportunity of waging open war against Soviet Russia, is waiting and watching for the moment when circumstances will permit it to resume the war.

---

32. Drafted by Lenin, these theses were reported on and approved in Session 17. Also printed in *LCW*, 32, pp. 453–61.

The proletariat in all the advanced capitalist countries has already formed its vanguard, the Communist parties, which are making steady progress towards winning the majority of the proletariat in each country. They are destroying the influence of the old trade-union bureaucrats and of the upper stratum of the working class of America and Europe, which has been corrupted by imperialist privileges.

The petty-bourgeois democrats in the capitalist countries, whose foremost sectors are represented by the Second and Two-and-a-Half Internationals, serve today as the mainstay of capitalism. They retain an influence over the majority, or a considerable section, of the industrial and commercial workers and office employees who are afraid that if revolution breaks out they will lose the relative petty-bourgeois prosperity created by the privileges of imperialism. But the growing economic crisis is worsening the condition of broad masses everywhere, and this fact, together with the evident inevitability of new imperialist wars if capitalism is preserved, is steadily weakening this mainstay.

The masses of the working people in the colonial and semi-colonial countries, who constitute the overwhelming majority of the population of the globe, were roused to political life at the turn of the twentieth century, particularly by the revolutions in Russia, Turkey, Iran, and China. The imperialist war of 1914–18 and Soviet power in Russia are completing the process of converting these masses into an active factor in world politics and in the revolutionary destruction of imperialism – even though the educated petty bourgeois of Europe and America, including the leaders of the Second and Two-and-a-Half Internationals, stubbornly refuse to see this. British India is at the head of these countries, and there revolution is maturing in proportion, on the one hand, to the growth of the industrial and railway proletariat, and, on the other, to the increase in the brutal terrorism of the British, who resort to massacres (Amritsar[33]), public floggings, and so on.

3.) *The relationship of class forces in Russia*

The internal political situation in Soviet Russia is determined by the fact that here, for the first time in history, there have been, for a number of years, only two classes: the proletariat, trained for decades by a very new, but modern, large-scale machine industry, and the small peasantry, who constitute the overwhelming majority of the population.

---

33. On 13 April 1919, British troops opened fire on an unarmed religious festival in the northern Indian city of Amritsar. More than 1,500 were shot, with over 1,000 killed.

In Russia, the big landowners and capitalists have not vanished, but they have been subjected to total expropriation and crushed politically as a class, whose remnants survive as Soviet government employees. They have preserved their class organisation abroad, as émigrés, numbering probably between one and a half million and two million people, with more than fifty daily newspapers of all the bourgeois and 'socialist' (i.e., petty-bourgeois) parties, the remnants of an army, and numerous connections with the international bourgeoisie. These émigrés are striving, with might and main, to destroy Soviet power and restore capitalism in Russia.

4.) *The proletariat and the peasantry in Russia*

Given this internal situation in Russia, the main task now facing its proletariat, as the ruling class, is to properly determine and carry out the measures necessary to lead the peasantry, establish an enduring alliance with it, and achieve the transition, in a series of gradual stages, to large-scale, socialised, mechanised agriculture. This is a particularly difficult task in Russia, because of both its backwardness and its extreme state of ruin as a result of seven years of imperialist and civil war.

Quite apart from these specific circumstances, this is one of the most difficult tasks of future socialist construction in all the capitalist countries, with, perhaps, the sole exception of Britain. Even in regard to Britain, it must not be forgotten that, while the small tenant farmers there are very few in number, the percentage of workers and office employees who enjoy a petty-bourgeois standard of living is exceptionally high, due to the actual bondage of hundreds of millions of people in Britain's colonial possessions.

As a result, from the standpoint of development of the world proletarian revolution as a single process, the epoch Russia is passing through is significant as a practical test and a verification of the policy of a proletariat in power towards the mass of the petty bourgeoisie.

5.) *The military alliance between the proletariat and the peasantry in the RSFSR*

The basis for proper relations between the proletariat and the peasantry in Soviet Russia was created in the period of 1917–21. The offensive of the capitalists and landowners, supported by the whole world bourgeoisie and all the petty-bourgeois democratic parties (Socialist-Revolutionaries and Mensheviks), caused the proletariat and the peasantry to form, consolidate, and give shape to a military alliance to defend the Soviet power. Civil war is the most intense form of class struggle, but the more intense it is, the more rapidly and clearly does this experience prove to even the most backward strata of the peasantry that only the dictatorship of the proletariat can save it, and that the Socialist-Revolutionaries and Mensheviks are in fact merely the servants of the landowners and capitalists.

But, while the military alliance between the proletariat and the peasantry was – and had to be – the initial form of their firm alliance, it could not have been maintained even for a few weeks without an economic alliance between the two classes. The peasants received from the workers' state all the land and protection against the landowners and the kulaks; the workers received from the peasants loans of food supplies until large-scale industry could be restored.

6.) *The transition to proper economic relations between the proletariat and the peasantry*

The alliance between the small peasants and the proletariat can become a correct and stable one, from the socialist standpoint, only when the complete restoration of transport and large-scale industry enables the proletariat to give the peasants, in exchange for food, all the goods they need for their own use and for the improvement of their farms. With the country in ruins, this could not possibly be achieved all at once. The surplus appropriation system was relatively the most bearable measure available to the insufficiently organised state to maintain itself in the incredibly arduous war against the landowners. The crop failure and the famine in 1920 increased even more the hardships of the peasantry, already severe enough, and made the immediate transition to the tax in kind imperative.

A moderate tax in kind will bring about at once a big improvement in the condition of the peasantry, while also stimulating them to enlarge crop areas and improve farming methods.

The tax in kind signifies a transition from the requisition of all the peasants' surplus grain to regular socialist exchange of products between industry and agriculture.

7.) *The significance of capitalism and concessions under the Soviet government and the conditions governing their existence*

Naturally, the tax in kind means freedom for the peasant to dispose of his after-tax surplus at his own discretion. To the degree that the state cannot provide the peasant with goods from socialist factories in exchange for all his surplus, freedom to trade with this surplus necessarily means freedom for the development of capitalism.

Within these limits, however, this is not at all dangerous for socialism as long as transport and large-scale industry remain in the hands of the proletariat. On the contrary, the development of capitalism, controlled and regulated by the proletarian state (i.e., 'state' capitalism in *this* sense of the term), is advantageous and absolutely necessary in an extremely devastated and backward small-peasant country (within certain limits, of course), inasmuch as it is capable of hastening the *immediate* revival of peasant farming. This applies still more to concessions: without denationalising anything, the workers' state leases out certain mines, forest tracts, oilfields, and so forth, to foreign capitalists in order to obtain from them new equipment and machinery that will enable this state to accelerate the restoration of Soviet large-scale industry.

The payment made to the concessionaires in the form of a share of the highly valuable products obtained is undoubtedly a tribute paid by the workers' state to the world bourgeoisie. Without in any way glossing this over, we must clearly realise that we stand to gain by paying this tribute, so long as it accelerates the restoration of our large-scale industry and substantially improves the condition of the peasants and workers.

8.) *The results of our food policy*

The food policy pursued by Soviet Russia from 1917 to 1921 was undoubtedly very crude and imperfect, and gave rise to many abuses. A number of mistakes were made in its implementation. But as a whole, it was the only possible policy under the conditions prevailing at the time. And it did fulfil its historic mission: it saved the proletarian dictatorship in a ruined and backward country. There can be no doubt that it has gradually become more comprehensive. In the first year that we had full power (1 August 1918 to 1 August 1919) the state collected 110 million poods of grain; in the second year it collected 220 million poods, and in the third year – over 285 million poods.[34]

Now, having acquired practical experience, we have set out, and expect, to collect 400 million poods (the tax in kind is expected to bring in 240 million poods). Only when it is actually in possession of an adequate stock of food will the workers' state be able to stand firmly on its own feet economically, secure the steady, if slow, restoration of large-scale industry, and create a proper financial system.

9.) *The material basis of socialism and the plan for the electrification of Russia*

Only large-scale machine industry capable of reorganising agriculture can provide the material basis for socialism. But we cannot confine ourselves

---

34. A pood is equal to approximately 16.38 kilograms (36.11 pounds).

to this general thesis. It must be made more precise and specific. Large-scale industry based on the latest achievements of technology and capable of reorganising agriculture implies the electrification of the whole country. We had to undertake the scientific work of drawing up such a plan for the electrification of the RSFSR and we have accomplished it. With the cooperation of over two hundred of the best scientists, engineers, and agronomists in Russia, this work has now been completed. It was published in a large volume and was endorsed, in broad outline, by the Eighth All-Russia Congress of Soviets in December 1920. Arrangements have now been made to convene an all-Russian congress of electrical engineers in August 1921 to examine this plan in detail, before it is given final government endorsement. It will take an estimated ten years to carry out the first part of the electrification scheme, which will require about 370 million man-days of work.

In 1918, we had eight newly erected power stations; in 1919, the figure rose to thirty-six, and in 1920, one hundred. Modest as this beginning is for our vast country, a start has been made; work has begun and is making steady progress. In the imperialist war, millions of prisoners of war in Germany became familiar with modern up-to-date technique, and this was followed by the stern but hardening experience of three years of civil war. As a result, the Russian peasant is a different man. With every passing month he sees more clearly and more vividly that only the guidance given by the proletariat is capable of leading the mass of small farmers out of slavery and toward socialism.

10.) *The role of 'pure democracy', the Second and Two-and-a-Half Internationals, the Socialist-Revolutionaries, and Mensheviks as allies of capital*

The dictatorship of the proletariat does not signify a cessation of the class struggle, but its continuation in a new form and with new weapons. This dictatorship is essential so long as classes exist, so long as the bourgeoisie, overthrown in one country, intensifies tenfold its attacks on socialism on an international scale. In the transition period, the small-farmer class is bound to experience certain vacillations. The difficulties of transition, and the influence of the bourgeoisie, inevitably cause the mood of these masses to change from time to time. Upon the proletariat, enfeebled and to a certain extent declassed by the destruction of the large-scale machine industry, which is its vital foundation, devolves the very difficult but paramount historic task of holding out in spite of these vacillations, and of carrying to victory its cause of emancipating labour from the yoke of capital.

The vacillations of the petty bourgeoisie find political expression in the policy pursued by the petty-bourgeois democratic parties, that is, the parties affiliated to the Second and Two-and-a-Half Internationals, represented in Russia by the Socialist-Revolutionary and Menshevik parties. These parties now have their headquarters and newspapers abroad, and are actually in a bloc with the whole of the bourgeois counterrevolution and are serving it loyally.

The shrewd leaders of the Russian big bourgeoisie headed by Milyukov, the leader of the Cadet (Constitutional Democratic) Party, have quite clearly, definitely, and openly appraised this role of the petty-bourgeois democrats, that is, the Socialist-Revolutionaries and Mensheviks. In connection with the Kronstadt mutiny, in which the Mensheviks, Socialist-Revolutionaries, and White Guards joined forces, Milyukov declared in favour of the 'soviets without the Bolsheviks' slogan. Elaborating on the idea, he called for 'honour and recognition to the Socialist-Revolutionaries and Mensheviks, because theirs is the task of first taking power away from the Bolsheviks' (*Pravda* no. 64, 1921, quoted from the Paris *Poslednye novosti*). Milyukov, the leader of the big bourgeoisie, has correctly appraised the lesson taught by all revolutions, namely, that the petty-bourgeois democrats are incapable of holding power, and always serve merely as a screen for the dictatorship of the bourgeoisie, and a stepping stone to its undivided power.

The proletarian revolution in Russia again confirms this lesson of 1789–94 and 1848–9, and also what Frederick Engels said in his letter to Bebel of 11 December 1884:

> Pure democracy...at the moment of revolution [acquires] a temporary importance as the last sheet-anchor of the bourgeois and, indeed, feudal economy generally....It was thus that, from March to September 1848, the entire feudal-bureaucratic mass swelled the ranks of the liberals in order to keep down the revolutionary masses....At all events, on the crucial day and the day after that, our only adversary will be *collective reaction centred round pure democracy*, and this, I think, ought never to be lost from view.[35]

---

35. *MECW*, 47, pp. 233–4.

## Resolution on the Policies of the Communist Party of Russia[36]

After having heard the report of Comrade Lenin on the policies of the Communist Party of Russia and taken note of the relevant theses, the Third World Congress of the Communist International declares:

The Third World Congress of the Communist International views with admiration the nearly four years of struggle by the Russian proletariat to win and maintain its political power. The congress unanimously approves the policies of the Communist Party of Russia, which from the very start has in every situation correctly assessed the threatening dangers. True to the principles of revolutionary Marxism, it has always found ways and means to overcome these dangers. Today open civil war has ended, for the moment. And now too, the Communist Party of Russia's policies toward the peasantry and on the question of concessions and of building up industry serve to focus the energies of the proletariat under its leadership on maintaining the dictatorship of the proletariat in Russia until the proletariat of Western Europe comes to the aid of its brothers.

The World Congress expresses its conviction that only the consistent and purposeful policies of the Communist Party of Russia have enabled Soviet Russia to endure as the first and most important citadel of world revolution. The congress condemns the traitorous conduct of the Menshevik parties, who campaign in every country against Soviet Russia and the policies of the Communist Party of Russia, thus reinforcing capitalist reaction against Russia while seeking to delay social revolution on a world scale.

The World Congress calls on the proletariat of every country to take a stand unanimously on the side of the Russian workers and peasants and to bring into reality the October Days of the entire world.

Long live the struggle for the dictatorship of the proletariat!

Long live the social revolution!

---

36. Adopted in Session 17.

# Theses on the Organisational Structure of the Communist Parties and the Methods and Content of their Work[37]

I. *General principles*

1.) The organisation of the party must correspond both to the purpose of its activity and to the conditions in which it is conducted. The Communist Party aims to be the vanguard of the proletariat, its leading contingent, in every phase of its revolutionary class struggle and during the subsequent period of transition to socialism, the first stage of communist society.

2.) There is no immutable, absolutely correct structure for Communist parties. The conditions of proletarian class struggle are variable and subject to a process of constant change. In line with these changes, the organisation of the proletarian vanguard must also constantly seek appropriate forms. Similarly, the organisation of each party must conform to the historically determined features of its country.

However, there are limits to this differentiation. Despite all peculiarities, there is a similarity in the conditions of proletarian class struggle in different countries and in different phases of the proletarian revolution, and this has fundamental importance for the international Communist movement. This provides a common foundation for the organisation of Communist parties in each country.

The task is to further develop the Communist parties' organisation in an expedient fashion on this foundation, and not to strive for the founding of new model parties to replace those that already exist, or to seek an absolutely correct organisational form or ideal statutes.

3.) Most of the Communist parties, as well as the Communist International as a world party of the revolutionary proletariat, share as a condition of their struggle that they must still struggle against the ruling bourgeoisie. Victory over the bourgeoisie and taking power out of its hands remains the decisive goal, setting our course in the coming period.

The organisational work of the Communist parties in the capitalist countries is thus directed toward building an organisation that can make possible and secure the victory of the proletarian revolution over the possessing classes.

---

37. Drafted by Kuusinen, this resolution was reported on in Session 22 and approved in Session 24. For correspondence relating to this resolution, see Appendix 3b, pp. 1101–4.

4.) To be effective, every joint action needs a leadership. This applies above all to the great struggle of world history. The Communist Party is the organisation of Communist leadership in the proletarian revolution.

To lead effectively, the party itself needs a good leadership. Our basic organisational task is thus to form, organise, and train an active Communist Party with competent leading bodies, as the competent leadership of the revolutionary proletarian movement.

5.) To lead the revolutionary class struggle, the Communist Party and its leading bodies must combine great striking power with great capacity to adjust to the changing conditions of struggle.

Successful leadership also requires close ties with the proletarian masses. Without such ties, the leaders of the masses will not lead them but at best only follow along after.

The Communist Party seeks to achieve such organic ties through democratic centralism.

II. *On democratic centralism*

6.) Democratic centralism in a Communist Party should be a true synthesis and fusion of centralism and proletarian democracy. This fusion can be achieved only on the foundation of constant and common activity and struggle by the entire party.

In a Communist Party, centralisation should not be formal and mechanical. It should relate to Communist activity, that is, to the formation of a strong, agile, and also flexible leadership.

A formal or mechanical centralisation would concentrate 'power' in the hands of a party bureaucracy, lording it over the other members and the revolutionary proletarian masses outside the party. But only enemies of communism could assert that the Communist Party seeks to utilise its leadership function and its centralisation of Communist leadership to dominate the proletarian class struggle. That is a lie. Moreover, internal power struggles and efforts to dominate the party are equally incompatible with the fundamentals of democratic centralism adopted by the Communist International.

In the organisations of the old, non-revolutionary workers' movement, a pervasive dualism developed, similar to that of the bourgeois state, between bureaucracy and 'people'. Under the paralysing influence of the bourgeois environment, functionaries became estranged from members, a vibrant collaboration was replaced by the mere forms of democracy, and the organisations became split between active functionaries and passive masses. Even the revolutionary workers' movement cannot avoid being influenced to some degree by the formalism and dualism of the bourgeois environment.

The Communist Party needs to thoroughly overcome such contradictions through systematic, ongoing political and organisational work, marked by repeated improvements and changes.

7.) During the transformation of a mass socialist party into a Communist Party, care must be taken not to limit the process to gathering instruments of power into the hands of the central leadership, while otherwise leaving the previous setup unchanged. For centralisation not to remain a dead letter but to be carried out in practice, it must be implemented in such a way that the members perceive it as an objectively required strengthening and broadening of their overall work and capacity to struggle. Otherwise the masses will perceive it as a bureaucratisation of the party, which can give rise to opposition to any centralisation, any leadership, any strict discipline. The polar opposite of bureaucratism is anarchism.

The mere forms of democracy cannot rid the organisation either of the tendency toward bureaucratism or of that toward anarchism, which indeed find fertile soil in this type of democracy. It follows that efforts to centralise the organisation, that is, to establish a strong leadership, cannot succeed if limited to the framework of formal democracy. Such a leadership requires above all developing and maintaining living ties and interrelationships both within the party, between its leading bodies and the rest of the membership, and also between the party and the masses of proletarians outside its ranks.

### III. *On Communists' obligation to be active*

8.) The Communist Party should be a working school of revolutionary Marxism. Through daily common work within the party, organisational ties will be established between its different wings and among the individual members.

Even today, in the legal Communist parties, most of the members still are not consistently active in the party's daily work. This is a major failing of these parties and a cause for uncertainty regarding their future development.

9.) Any workers' party taking its first steps toward Communist transformation runs the risk of resting content with adoption of a Communist programme. Communist doctrine replaces previous doctrine in its propaganda, and Communist-oriented functionaries replace those with other views, and that is all. Adoption of a Communist programme, however, is only a statement of intent to become Communist. If there is no Communist activity, and if the passivity of most members in party work remains unchallenged, the party is not carrying out even the minimum of what it has promised the proletariat by adopting a Communist programme. Indeed, the first condition in implementing this programme is to draw all members into ongoing daily collaboration.

The art of Communist organisation is to make use of everything in the proletarian class struggle, to divide up party work effectively among all members, and through the members to draw broader masses of the proletariat into the revolutionary movement. This art also involves maintaining a leadership position in the movement as a whole not by virtue of power but by virtue of authority, energy, and great experience, diversity, and ability.

10.) In its efforts to have a genuinely active membership, a Communist Party should ask of everyone in its ranks to commit their energy and time to the party, to the extent possible under given circumstances, and to always do their best in its service.

Besides commitment to Communist ideas, membership in the Communist Party normally involves formal registration, perhaps initially as a candidate and later as a full member; regular payment of fixed dues; a subscription to the party newspaper; and so on. The most important thing, however, is the participation of every member in daily party work.

11.) In order to take part in daily work, each member should, as a rule, belong to a small working group, be it a committee, collective, fraction, or cell. This is the only way that party work can be properly allocated, led, and carried out.

In addition, of course, members should take part in general meetings of the local organisation. Under conditions of legality, it is not good to replace these periodic assemblies by delegated local bodies. Rather, all members should be obliged to attend these meetings regularly. But that is not adequate. Such meetings need to be properly prepared by the work of smaller groups or of assigned comrades. The same applies to preparations to make effective use of broad assemblies of workers, demonstrations, and workers' mass actions. Only small groups can carefully assess and intensively carry out the varied tasks flowing from such activity. Without such ongoing detailed work by the entire membership, functioning through a great many small working groups, even the most energetic efforts to take part in proletarian struggle will lead only to vain, feeble attempts to gain influence. They will not lead to the necessary unification of all the living, revolutionary proletarian forces in a unified Communist Party capable of action.

12.) Communist nuclei should be formed for day-to-day work in different arenas of party activity: door-to-door agitation, internal education, newspaper circulation, literature sales, information services, communications, and so on.

Communist cells are nuclei carrying out ongoing Communist work in factories and workplaces, trade unions, proletarian cooperatives, military units, and so on – wherever there are at least a few Communist Party members or candidates. If there are many party members in the same workplace, union, etc., the cell expands into a fraction, whose work is led by a nucleus.

If it is appropriate to form a more broadly based opposition formation [in a union] or to take part in one that already exists, the Communists need to strive to lead such formations through their own cells.

Whether a Communist cell should make its presence known to those around it, or declare itself publicly as Communist, must be decided by conscientiously weighing the dangers and advantages present in the specific situation.

13.) Introducing the obligation to party activity and organising these small working groups is particularly difficult for Communist mass parties. It cannot be done overnight. It demands tireless persistence, careful consideration, and much exertion.

It is particularly important that this reorganisation be carried out from the outset with care and balanced consideration. It would be a simple matter to allocate all members in each organisation into small cells and groups according to some formal schema and then simply call on these structures to take on the party's daily work. Starting that way would be worse than not starting at all. It would quickly lead party members to object to this essential reorganisation or to reject it.

The party leadership will do well to begin with intensive discussion with a number of competent organisers who are convinced and enthusiastic Communists, with a detailed grasp of where the movement stands in different areas of struggle. On this basis, a detailed outline can be prepared for the first steps toward this renewal. Next, trained organisers or organisational committees must effectively prepare the plan of work on the local level, choosing the initial group leaders and taking the first steps. The next step is to assign concrete, specific tasks to the organisations, working groups, cells, and individual members, tasks that are clearly useful, desirable, and practicable. Where necessary, practical demonstrations can show how these tasks are to be carried out. It should be explained what errors are to be particularly avoided.

14.) This reorganisation should be carried out one step at a time. At first, not all that many new cells or working groups should be founded in a local organisation. It is first necessary to show through a brief experience that the cells founded in certain important factories and unions are functioning properly. It is also necessary that working groups founded in the other main areas of party activity – such as information gathering, communications, door-to-door work, the women's movement, distributing literature and the paper, work among the jobless – are reasonably well consolidated. It would be wrong to tear down the old organisational framework before the new one has been broken in to some extent.

However, this fundamental task of Communist organisational work must be carried out energetically everywhere. This places great demands not only on legal but also on illegal parties. An extensive and active network of Communist cells, fractions, and working groups is needed in all crucial arenas of the proletarian class struggle. The party must be strong and purposeful, with every member taking part in the daily revolutionary work. The participation must become a self-evident routine. Until all this is reality, the party cannot take any respite from its efforts to carry out this task.

15.) This fundamental organisational task obligates the leading party committees to exert constant, inexhaustible, and direct leadership of the party's work. It requires varied efforts by every comrade active in the party leadership. The leadership of Communist activity must not merely ensure that all comrades are busy; it must assist them and lead their work systematically and expertly. Precise orientation is needed on the specific conditions of work. An effort is needed to identify errors in one's own activity, apply the lessons of experience to improving methods of work, and to never lose sight of the struggle's goal.

16.) The entirety of our party work consists of struggle, whether theoretical or practical, or of preparation for this struggle. In the past, specialisation of this work has mostly been very inadequate. There are important arenas of work in which the party has carried out work only accidentally, at best, such as efforts by legal parties to struggle against the political police. Instruction of party members is usually haphazard, incidental, and so superficial that the majority of the party's most important principled decisions, including its programme and resolutions of the Communist International, remain unknown to broad layers of the membership. Ongoing and systematic instruction is needed throughout the organisation, in all its working groups, in order to achieve a continually rising level of specialisation.

17.) The duty to be active in the Communist organisation also necessarily includes submission of reports. This applies to all party branches and committees as well as to every individual member. General reports must be regular and frequent, while special reports are needed when specific party tasks are carried out. It is important to carry out submission of reports so systematically that it becomes a firmly established tradition of the Communist movement.

18.) Four times a year, a party makes its regular report to the leadership of the Communist International. Each unit within the party reports to the leading body immediately above it – such as monthly reports by the local organisation to the relevant party committee.

Every cell, fraction, or working group should report to the party committee that actually leads its work. Individual members should report – perhaps weekly – to the cell or working group to which they belong. Where special tasks have been carried out, the report should go to the party unit that made the assignment.

Reports should always be made at the first opportunity. They should be given orally, unless the party or the appropriate committee has asked for a written report. Reports should be brief and factual. The recipient of the report must ensure that reports whose publication would cause harm are kept secure, and that important reports are passed on without delay to the relevant party committee.

19.) These reports should not be limited, of course, to what the reporter has done. They should also include information relevant to our struggle on what has been observed during activity, especially observations that could occasion a change or improvement in our future activity. When our activity reveals the need for improvement, this should be passed on.

All Communist cells, fractions, and working groups should, as a rule, discuss the reports they have received as well as those they have to deliver. These discussions must become routine.

All cells and working groups must ensure that individual members or groups of members regularly receive a special assignment to observe and report on enemy organisations, especially on petty-bourgeois workers' organisations and 'socialist' parties.

IV. *On propaganda and agitation*

20.) In the period before an open revolutionary uprising, our universal task is revolutionary propaganda and agitation. This activity is often largely carried out in the old, formal way, by intervening occasionally in mass meetings from the outside, without much care as to the actual revolutionary content of what is written or said.

Communist propaganda and agitation must take root in the very heart of the proletarian milieu. It must arise from the workers' lives, common interests and strivings, and especially from their common struggles.

Revolutionary content is the most important aspect of Communist propaganda. The slogans and positions advanced on specific questions in different situations must be evaluated from this point of view. Not only full-time propagandists and agitators but all party members must receive ongoing and extensive instructions, to enable them to take correct positions.

21.) The main forms of Communist propaganda and agitation are: personal discussions, participation in struggles by the trade-union and political workers' movement, and the impact of the party's press and literature. Every member of both legal and illegal parties should take part regularly in this activity in one way or another.

Oral, person-to-person propaganda must be carried out above all through systematically organised door-to-door agitation by working groups established with that purpose. No dwelling in the reach of local party units should be omitted. In larger centres, good results can be had from specially organised street agitation, utilising posters and leaflets. In addition, cells or fractions must organise regular person-to-person agitation at workplaces, linked to distribution of written materials.

In countries whose population includes national minorities, special attention is needed to agitation and propaganda in the proletarian layers of these minorities. This work is to be carried out, of course, in the language of the national minority in question. Special party publications must be created for this purpose.

22.) In capitalist countries where a large majority of the proletariat still has no conscious inclination to revolution, ways must be sought to improve Communist propaganda. It must be adapted to the understanding of non-revolutionary workers to link up with their incipient revolutionary understanding and open their road to the revolutionary movement. The slogans of Communist propaganda must foster the impulses of such workers toward revolution – even though still germinating, unconscious, incomplete, wavering, and semi-bourgeois – as they undergo an inner struggle against bourgeois traditions and appeals.

Communist propaganda must not rest content with the present limited and unclear demands or hopes of the proletarian masses. The revolutionary seeds of these demands and hopes are no more than the necessary starting point for us to gain influence. Only from such starting points can proletarians be brought closer in understanding to communism.

23.) Communist agitation among the proletarian masses must be such that proletarians in struggle recognise our Communist organisation as a courageous, perceptive, vigorous, and consistently loyal leader of their common movement.

To achieve this, Communists must take part in all elemental working-class struggles and movements and lead the workers in every battle with the capitalists over hours and wages, working conditions, and the like. Communists must closely study specific issues of workers' lives. They must help workers to disentangle these questions, direct their attention to the most important abuses, help them formulate precise and practical demands on the capitalists, strive to develop their consciousness of solidarity, and arouse their awareness of the common interests and goals of workers of all countries, as a unified working class in the world proletarian army.

Only such daily work, detailed but indispensable, and such continual devoted participation in all the proletariat's struggles can enable a 'Communist Party' to become a *Communist* Party. This is the only way it can depart from the outdated model of socialist parties dedicated entirely to propaganda and recruitment, whose activity consists of gathering members, making speeches about reforms, and utilising the opportunities that arise – or, more likely, do not arise – in parliament. The broad masses of party members need to take part, with devotion and a sense of purpose, in the school of daily struggles and conflicts between the exploited and the exploiters. That is the indispensable precondition for winning the dictatorship of the proletariat and, even more, for exercising it. Only leading the working masses in an ongoing guerrilla war against the attacks of capital enables the Communist parties to become a working-class vanguard that can really learn to lead the proletariat and gain the capacity to consciously prepare for elimination of the bourgeoisie.

24.) When strikes, lockouts, or mass layoffs take place, Communists must mobilise in large numbers to take part in the workers' movement.

Communists make an enormous mistake by pointing to the Communist programme or the armed struggle as excuses for passivity, scorn, or even hostility to workers' current struggles for small improvements in their working conditions. No matter how small and modest the demands may be that the workers now pose for struggle against the capitalists, this is never cause for the Communists to stand aloof from the struggle. Of course, our agitation should not give the impression that we Communists blindly instigate unwise strikes or other rash actions. However, among the workers in struggle, the Communists should always earn the reputation of being the most competent comrades-in-arms.

25.) In trade-union activity, the Communist cells and fractions have often been at a loss in face of the simplest daily issues. It is easy to preach only the general principles of communism, and then – faced with a specific challenge – to fall back into the negative approach of vulgar trade unionism. But this is harmful, merely playing into the hands of the yellow leaders of Amsterdam.

Communists, by contrast, should determine their revolutionary position based on the factual content of each question that arises. For example, rather than resting content with principled opposition to all wage contracts, Communists should contest the actual factual content of the contracts proposed by the Amsterdam leaders. Every move to rein in the proletariat's readiness to struggle should be condemned. As is well known, the capitalists and their Amsterdam accomplices try to use every wage agreement to tie the hands of the workers in struggle. Communists must certainly explain this to workers. But as a rule, Communists can best do this by proposing a wage scale that does not shackle the workers.

This same approach applies, for example, to the workers' mutual aid societies and trade-union benefit plans. It is certainly beneficial to provide strike support and pay for costs of the struggle from common funds. It would be quite wrong to oppose such arrangements in principle. However, the type of collections favoured by the Amsterdam leaders and the way they use the funds contradicts the workers' revolutionary class interests. As for trade-union health insurance and similar arrangements, Communists may, for example, propose an end to the requirement to pay special premiums and the removal of restrictive provisions relating to voluntary insurance schemes. But if some of the members still want to secure their health insurance by paying premiums, they will not understand it if we want to simply forbid that out of hand. It is first necessary to carry out intensive personal propaganda to free these members from their petty-bourgeois aspirations.

26.) In the struggle against Social-Democratic and other petty-bourgeois trade-union leaders and the various workers' parties, we cannot hope to achieve anything through persuasion. The struggle against them must be organised with full vigour. However, this can be done successfully only by separating them from their supporters, convincing workers that the social-traitor leaders are simply doing the menial work for capitalism. Where possible, these leaders should be put in a situation where they are compelled to expose themselves – and when that is achieved, vigorously attacked.

It is certainly not enough to curse the Amsterdam leaders as 'yellow'. Practical examples are needed to demonstrate this. We can point to their activity in labour-employer collaborative bodies, in the League of Nations' International Labour Office, in bourgeois ministries and administration. We can cite their traitorous statements in speeches at conferences and in parliaments and the decisive passages of their many appeasing articles in hundreds of newspapers. We can point in particular to their wavering and hesitant conduct in preparing and carrying out even the smallest wage movements and workplace conflicts. In all these ways, we have the opportunity every day to present simple motions, resolutions, and clear speeches exposing and characterising the unreliable and traitorous activity of the Amsterdam leaders as 'yellow'.

The cells and fractions have to strike these blows systematically. The lower-level trade-union bureaucracy should not be exempt. Although their intentions are often good, they hide their weakness behind union bylaws and decisions and instructions of the union top leadership. Communists should not hesitate to act resolutely, always demanding that the lower-level bureaucrats explain clearly what they are doing to remove these supposed obstacles, and whether they are prepared to join with the membership in struggle for this goal.

27.) Communist participation in trade-union meetings and conferences needs to be carefully prepared by the fractions and working groups. Motions should be drafted, reporters and speakers chosen, and competent, experienced, and energetic comrades proposed as candidates.

Communist organisations must prepare just as carefully when parties opposed to them call workers' meetings, election rallies, demonstrations, political festivals, and the like. When the Communists themselves call general meetings of workers, as many Communist working groups as possible must collaborate according to a unified plan both before and at the rallies, in order to draw full advantage for the organisation.

28.) Communists must improve their ability to attract workers who are unorganised and lack consciousness into the party's permanent sphere of influence. Our cells and fractions should convince these workers to join the trade unions and read our party newspaper. Our influence can also be conveyed through other workers' associations (consumer cooperatives, groups of wounded veterans, study circles, sports associations, theatrical groups, etc.). If the Communist Party must work illegally, such workers' associations can be formed outside the party by its members – with the approval and under the supervision of the party's leading bodies (sympathiser organisations).

Communist youth and women's organisations can also awaken the interest of many proletarians uninterested in politics in the activity of collective organisations, through their classes, reading groups, special trips, festivals, Sunday excursions, and so on. In this way, they can be won to permanent participation in the organisation and involved in useful party work (distributing leaflets, newspapers, pamphlets, etc.). Active participation in the common movement is the best way to free them from petty-bourgeois inclinations.

29.) In order to win semi-proletarian layers of the working people to the side of the revolutionary proletariat, Communists must utilise the conflicts of interest that set these layers against large landowners, capitalists, and the capitalist state. Through constant discussion, these intermediate layers must be freed from their suspicion of proletarian revolution. This often demands lengthy contact. Their trust in the Communist movement will be increased by showing sympathetic interest in their day-to-day needs, providing free information in coping with small challenges they cannot deal with on their own, inviting them to special free educational events, and so on. In this process, Communists must cautiously but persistently counter hostile organisations and individuals who have local authority, and influence working peasants, household servants, and other semi-proletarians. Enemies close at hand, whom the exploited know from their experience as oppressors, must be exposed as personifications of the criminal capitalist system as a whole. Every day-to-day event in which the governmental bureaucracy infringes on the ideals of petty-bourgeois democracy and the rule of law must be forcibly explained in simple language in Communist propaganda and agitation.

Every local unit in rural areas must carefully divide up among its members the work of door-to-door agitation, and extend this work to all villages, estates, and individual houses in the area.

30.) To conduct propaganda in the capitalist army and navy, Communists must look into the most appropriate methods for each individual country. Pacifist agitation against militarism is very harmful, since it furthers the bourgeoisie's efforts to disarm workers. The proletariat rejects in principle and combats all the military institutions of the bourgeois state and the bourgeois class. Nonetheless, these institutions (army, rifle clubs, neighbourhood patrols, etc.) can be useful to prepare workers for revolutionary struggle. The target of anti-militarist agitation, therefore, is not military training of the youth and workers, but the militarist system and the despotism of the officers. Every chance for proletarians to hold weapons in hand should be energetically utilised.

Rank-and-file soldiers in the army must be made aware of the class antagonisms expressed in the shabby treatment they receive and officers' material privileges. In addition, it must be explained to soldiers how their whole future is linked to that of the exploited classes. In periods of increasing revolutionary ferment, agitation for the election by soldiers and sailors of all those in command and for the formation of soldiers' councils can be very effective in undermining the pillars of capitalist class rule.

Attentive and vigorous agitation is needed against the bourgeoisie's special class-war contingents, especially their volunteer armed bands. Where their social composition and corrupt practices make this possible, systematic efforts are needed, at the appropriate time, to introduce social discord into their ranks. In cases where they are homogeneous in class character, such as contingents formed entirely of officers, they must be exposed to the contempt and hatred of the entire population, so that they will be undermined internally by social isolation.

## V. *Organising political struggles*

31.) For a Communist Party there is never a situation in which political activity is impossible. The party's strategy and tactics must be built on utilisation of every political and economic conjuncture, in all their variations.

Even if the party is still weak, it can still take advantage of major political events or strikes that shake the entire economy in order to carry out well-prepared radical propaganda initiatives. When the party decides on such an initiative, it must commit all the energy of its branches and sectors to this campaign.

All the connections that the party has acquired through the work of its cells and working groups should be used to hold meetings in the main centres where political organising or a strike movement is under way. At such meetings, party speakers should advance Communist slogans showing how participants can surmount the difficulties of their struggle. Special working groups should meticulously prepare these meetings. If it is not possible to hold our own meetings, suitable comrades should take the lead as speakers in general assemblies of strikers or other proletarians in struggle.

When there is a chance of winning support for our slogans from most or many participants in a meeting or rally, we must try to express these slogans through well-written and well-motivated motions and resolutions. If they are adopted, efforts should be made to pass the same or similar resolutions in every meeting on this issue in that city or region, or at least to win substantial minority support for them. In this way we will draw together layers of the proletariat in the movement on whom we previously had only limited influence and enable them to recognise the new leadership.

After each meeting of this sort, the working groups involved in preparing and conducting it should meet briefly, not only to prepare a report for the leading party committee, but also to draw out the lessons of this experience for future work.

The slogans can also be conveyed to interested layers of workers, as befits the situation, through posters or short handbills. More extensive leaflets can show how these workers are linked to the struggle and present Communist slogans in accessible fashion. A skilled poster campaign requires specially organised groups to identify the best spots and the best times for pasting up the posters. Distributing handbills inside or in front of the factory or in places where travelling workers congregate (traffic junctions, employment offices, railway stations) should be accompanied, where possible, by personal discussions that pass on slogans orally to working masses who are in motion. Detailed leaflets should properly be distributed indoors, in the factories, meeting rooms, or homes, or wherever else they can receive an attentive response.

This intensive propaganda must be accompanied by parallel activity in all trade-union and factory meetings affected by the movement. Our comrades may build or organise such meetings themselves, and then assign members to give presentations or contribute to discussions. Our party's newspapers must give a great deal of space and assign their best writers to respond to such a special movement. Indeed the entire party apparatus must be freed up as long as needed to support unrelentingly the main ideas of this movement.

32.) Demonstrations need a flexible and dedicated leadership that keeps the purpose of the action in view. This leadership must be constantly able to judge whether the demonstration has reached its limit of effectiveness, or whether – in the given situation – the campaign can be brought to the level of a mass action by demonstrative strikes or even mass strikes. The peace demonstrations during the War taught us that even when such an action has been repulsed, if the goal is urgent and overriding and is inherently of continued broad interest to the masses, a genuine proletarian combat party, even if underground and quite small, cannot turn aside or hold back.

Street demonstrations should rely on the largest factories for their main support. Our cells and fractions should carry out systematic preparatory work through discussions and handbills to establish some degree of agreement regarding the situation. Our leading committee should convene our factory shop stewards and cell and fraction leaders to a briefing to decide on measures to rally forces effectively on the appointed day and have them meet punctually. This meeting should determine the nature of the slogans, the prospects for intensifying the action, and the time to break off and disperse the demonstration. A well-trained and experienced staff of energetic functionaries is needed to form the backbone of the demonstration from its outset, when contingents leave the factories, to its dissolution. To enable these functionaries to maintain effective contact with each other and to be supplied throughout with the requisite political instructions, responsible party workers must be integrated into the mass of demonstrators. Such a mobile political and organisational leadership maximises the chances of renewing the action and possibly broadening its scope.

33.) Communist parties that are already somewhat consolidated and have an experienced team of functionaries and significant mass support should do everything possible, through major campaigns, to overcome fully the influence of the social traitors on the working class and bring its majority under Communist leadership. The way campaigns are organised depends on circumstances, such as whether the current struggles enable Communists to take the lead of proletarian forces or whether the movement is temporarily stagnant. The party's composition also influences organisational methods in an action. That is why the VKPD, as a new mass party, resorted to the so-called Open Letter in order to win the socially decisive layers of the proletariat more effectively than had been possible in individual districts. In order to expose the social traitors, the Communist Party approached the other mass organisations of the proletariat, at a time of increasing impoverishment and class antagonisms. The party demanded that they tell the proletariat publicly whether they were willing to commit their supposedly powerful organisations to a struggle together with the Communist Party for very modest demands to counter the evident impoverishment of the proletariat.

When a Communist Party begins a campaign of this type, it needs to prepare organisationally so that its initiative can receive a response among the broadest layers of workers. All the party's factory fractions and trade-union functionaries must, after thorough preparation, effectively present the party's demands as an overall response to the proletariat's most urgent needs in their next factory or trade-union meeting and in all public meetings. Leaflets, handbills, and posters must be effectively distributed wherever our cells or fractions aim to generate and develop support for our demands among the masses. While the campaign is under way, our party press must publish daily articles – sometimes short, sometimes detailed – examining the issues from varied points of view. Party units need to send in a steady stream of materials and be vigilant that the editors do not flag in covering the campaign journalistically. In addition, party fractions in parliament and municipal councils should be placed at the service of such struggles. They must implement party instructions by speaking about the movement and advancing appropriate parliamentary resolutions. The deputies should act consciously as a wing of the masses in struggle, as their spokespersons in the enemy camp, and as responsible functionaries and party workers.

Let us say that the unified activity of every wing of the party leads within a few weeks to a large and growing number of resolutions of support. The party then faces a significant challenge: how to give organisational form to the masses' support for its demands. If the movement is based primarily in the trade unions, the main effort should be to increase our influence in the unions. Our fractions should take well-prepared initiatives against the local trade-union leaderships, in order either to push them aside or to convince them to carry out an organised struggle for our party's demands. If there are factory councils, committees, or similar bodies, our fractions should carry out an orderly intervention to induce a full meeting of these bodies to join in supporting the struggle.

If such a campaign for the proletariat's basic interests has led to formation of local groups under Communist leadership, these must be brought together in conferences, which should also include special delegates from factory meetings that have come out in support of the movement. The new leadership consolidated in this fashion under Communist influence can gain strength through such a unification of active groups of organised workers. This strength can then be utilised to drive forward the leadership of socialist parties and trade unions or to unmask them organisationally.

In branches of the economy where our party is strongest and has won the greatest support for its demands, this exerts pressure on the local trade unions and factory councils. This situation should then be utilised to draw together all the individual economic struggles and budding independent movements into a unified campaign that will now go beyond the concerns of a specific union by raising some basic common demands. All district organisations can then join forces in pushing them through. In such a movement, the Communist Party will prove itself as the genuine leader of the proletariat in struggle. If the trade-union bureaucracy and socialist parties oppose such a unified campaign, they will be thrust aside, not only on the plane of political ideas but organisationally as well.

34.) If the Communist Party is attempting to achieve leadership of the masses at a moment when heightened political and economic tensions provoke new movements and struggles, there is no need to advance special demands. The party can then appeal directly to the members of the socialist parties and trade unions, in a popular style. It can point to the struggles needed to respond to the situation's urgency and to increasing oppression by the employers. It can call on these members to disregard the desires of their bureaucratic leaders by engaging in these struggles, so as to avoid complete collapse. During such a movement, the party publications – and especially the daily newspapers – have to stress and demonstrate that the Communists stand ready to take the lead in impoverished proletarians' struggles, whether impending or under way. In such a situation, the Communists stand prepared to come to the aid of all the oppressed, wherever possible. It must be stressed daily that, although the old organisations seek to evade and obstruct these struggles, without them there is no way to secure a tolerable living standard for the workers.

Factory and trade-union fractions must explain to assembled workers that there is no turning back, while stressing the Communists' dedication and readiness for struggle. The most important factor in such a campaign is to draw together and unify the struggles and movements that arise from a given situation. Cells and fractions have to maintain tight organic ties among the trades and factories drawn into the struggle. In addition, the leadership has to act, through both district committees and the central leadership, to make functionaries and responsible party workers immediately available to join with those in struggle in the process of leading the movement – broadening, building, intensifying, generalising, and linking it together. The party's main task is to highlight what the different struggles have in common and convert that into a general slogan, if necessary advocating political measures.

During the process of building and generalising struggles, it will be necessary to create unified leadership bodies. If bureaucratic strike leaders abandon the struggle prematurely, prompt efforts are needed to replace them with Communists who will assure a firm and determined leadership. If efforts to combine several struggles have succeeded, an attempt should be made to create a common action leadership, which can, if possible, be headed by Communists. Such a unified leadership can often be easily attained, through trade-union and factory fractions, factory councils, factory council general assemblies, and especially through assemblies of all the strikers.

If the movement becomes generalised and intervention by the employers' organisations and government give it a political character, it may be possible and increasingly necessary to elect workers' councils. The party should advocate and prepare organisationally for this step. All party units should insist that only councils arising directly from working-class struggles can act for their liberation with the needed single-mindedness. Such councils should not be weighted down with the trade-union bureaucracy and its Socialist Party satellites.

35.) Already consolidated Communist parties, and especially large mass parties, should take organisational measures to assure ongoing readiness for mass political actions. The organisational lessons of demonstrations, mass economic movements, and all partial actions must always be utilised to resolutely firm up ties with the broad masses. The experiences of all recent and large movements should be thoroughly discussed in broad conferences of leading functionaries and party workers together with the shop stewards of large and mid-sized factories. Energetic efforts are needed to constantly strengthen the network of links among shop stewards. A close relationship of trust linking the leading functionaries and party workers to the shop stewards is the best guarantee that mass political actions will not be launched prematurely and that they assume dimensions appropriate to the conditions and the party's current influence.

The Communist Party cannot carry out mass actions and genuine revolutionary movements unless the party has close ties with the proletarian masses in large and mid-sized factories. Consider how the unquestionably revolutionary uprising in Italy last year, expressed above all in the occupation of the factories, collapsed prematurely. In part, this was because of betrayal by the trade-union bureaucracy and the inadequacies of the party leadership. But it was also caused, in part, by the utter lack of organic ties between the party and the factories, through politically aware shop stewards engaged in party activity. An intensive analysis of the large movement of British miners this year shows that it certainly suffered greatly from this weakness.

## VI. *On the party press*

36.) The party must work tirelessly to develop and improve the Communist press.

No newspaper should be recognised as a party publication unless it accepts the party's instructions. This principle should be applied, by analogy, to all publications, including magazines, books, pamphlets, and so on, while taking into account their theoretical, propagandistic, or other purpose.

The party must focus more on the quality of its newspapers than on their number. Every Communist Party needs above all a strong central organ, appearing if possible on a daily basis.

37.) A Communist newspaper must never become a capitalist business, in the fashion of the bourgeois and often the so-called 'socialist' newspapers. Our papers must guard their independence from capitalist loan-making institutions. Skilled collection of advertising greatly assists the survival of mass legal parties' newspapers, but it must never lead to any kind of dependency on large ads. Instead, our mass parties' newspapers should acquire the necessary authority through their unyielding stance on all proletarian and social questions. Our newspaper should not serve to satisfy the public's varied desires for sensation or amusement. It should not strive to be socially acceptable by providing a platform for criticisms by petty-bourgeois literary figures or journalistic virtuosos.

38.) A Communist newspaper must be concerned above all with the interests of the oppressed workers in struggle. It should be our best propagandist and agitator for proletarian revolution.

Our newspaper has the task of gathering useful experiences from the activity of all party members and presenting them to party comrades as guidance for ongoing correction and improvement of Communist methods of work. These experiences should be exchanged at meetings of editors from the entire country. The exchange of views there will bring about the greatest possible unity in the tone and orientation of the party press as a whole. In this way, the party press and each of its components will be the best organiser of our revolutionary work.

Without the unifying and purposeful organisational work of Communist newspapers, especially the official paper, it will hardly be possible to implement democratic centralism, achieve an effective division of labour within the party, and thus carry out its historic task.

39.) A party newspaper must attempt to be a Communist undertaking. It must be a proletarian organisation of struggle, a working collective of revolutionary workers, including all who write regularly for, typeset, print, administer, distribute, and sell the paper, those who gather local material for it and discuss and prepare this material in the cells, and those active in its distribution.

A number of practical measures are needed to convert the newspaper into a genuine organisation of struggle and a vibrant working collective of this type.

Each Communist acquires a close relationship with his newspaper by making sacrifices for it and working for it. The paper is his daily weapon, which must be steeled and sharpened anew each day in order to be usable. The Communist newspaper can be sustained only by ongoing and substantial material and financial contributions. Party members need to provide continual injections of support for the paper's expansion and improvement until the point where, in the mass legal parties, it achieves such broad distribution and solidity that it begins to contribute materially to the Communist movement.

It is not enough to be an active recruiter and agitator for the newspaper. One must also be a helpful collaborator. Factory fractions and cells need to report as quickly as possible everything that is socially and economically notable, from on-the-job accidents to factory assemblies, from mistreatment of an apprentice to the company's official report. The trade-union fractions must convey all important decisions and measures taken by the committees and secretariats of their union federation. Goings-on at meetings and in the streets often enable an observant party worker to note details of social significance. These can be reported in the newspaper to indicate close ties to the daily needs of those indifferent to politics.

The editorial committee must handle with great care and affection these reports coming from the lives of workers and their organisations. They can be used as short news items that make our newspaper into a living, strong, and vibrant working collective. Alternatively, such reports can be used as practical examples from workers' daily existence – the best way to make the teachings of communism comprehensible to masses of workers. Wherever possible, editorial collectives should be available at times convenient for workers, in order to hear their desires and complaints regarding the hardships of life, take copious notes, and use them to enliven the newspaper.

None of our newspapers, to be sure, can become perfect Communist working collectives under capitalist conditions. But even under such difficult circumstances it is possible to successfully organise a revolutionary workers' newspaper. This is shown by the example of our Russian comrades' *Pravda* in 1913–14. It did in fact serve as an ongoing and active organisation of the conscious, revolutionary workers in the most important centres of the Russian empire. These comrades edited the newspaper collectively, published it, and distributed it, most of them in addition to working for wages and setting aside from their wages the money needed for the newspaper's costs. The newspaper, for its part, could give them what they most needed and what they utilised in the movement – material that is still useful today in work and struggle. Such a publication was capable of becoming viewed as 'our paper' by party members and many other revolutionary workers.

40.) The characteristic feature of a Communist newspaper is direct involvement in campaigns led by the party. When the party focuses its activity for a period of time on a specific campaign, the party newspaper must serve this campaign, not only in its political editorials but in all its departments. The editors must use every type of material to build the campaign, while designing and shaping the entire paper to serve this purpose.

41.) Subscription work for our paper should be based on defined procedures. Every situation should be utilised where a worker is involved in a living movement and his interest in political or social life is stimulated by some political or economic event. Thus, immediately after every significant strike movement or lockout in which the newspaper has energetically defended the interests of the workers in struggle, person-to-person subscription work should be started up among the former strikers. Factory and trade-union fractions in the industrial sector involved in the strike should seek subscriptions among their contacts, using lists and subscription forms. In addition, where possible, they should obtain lists of the addresses of workers who took part in the struggle, so that special working groups building the newspaper can carry out vigorous door-to-door agitation.

In the same way, whenever an election campaign has aroused the interest of the masses, working groups should carry out systematic door-to-door work in the proletarian districts.

When a political or economic crisis is looming, its impact is felt by broad working masses through inflation, joblessness, or other expressions of deprivation. Skilled propaganda regarding these developments should be followed up by attempts by the trade-union fractions to obtain comprehensive lists of union members in different trades. The working group building the newspaper can then pursue fruitful ongoing, planned door-to-door agitation. Experience shows that the best time for this continuing subscription work is the last week before the end of the month. Any local organisation that leaves this last week unutilised for subscription work, even if only for a single month of the year, is guilty of a serious dereliction of duty with regard to expanding the Communist movement. The working group building the newspaper should also be active at every public meeting or large rally of workers, circulating its subscription forms at the start, during the breaks, and after the wrap-up. The trade-union fractions must do this in meetings of their union, as must the cells and factory fractions at factory-wide meetings.

42.) Party members must also consistently defend our newspaper against all enemies.

All party members must campaign strongly against the capitalist press, exposing and condemning its venality, its lies, its suppression of facts, and all its misdeeds.

As for the Social-Democratic and Independent Socialist [centrist] press, it must be defeated through a constant effort, without straying into petty factional polemics. Examples from daily life should be used to expose their traitorous conduct, which conceals class antagonisms. Fractions in the trade unions and elsewhere must strive to free members of the trade unions and other workers' associations from the confusing and crippling influence of these Social-Democratic newspapers. In addition, subscription work for our newspaper, whether door-to-door or, must importantly, in the factory, must be carefully designed to undercut the press of the social traitors.

## VII. *Concerning the party's overall structure*

43.) The party's expansion and consolidation should not take place according to a formal, geographical schema. Instead, it should correspond to real economic and political patterns as well as the communications structure of the given region. The main emphasis should be placed on the capital cities and the centres of large-scale industry.

When a new party is being built, there is often an effort at the start to immediately expand the network of party units across the entire country. Even if the available forces are very limited, they are often scattered about in obscure corners, thereby undercutting the party's capacity to recruit and grow. After a few years, there is usually a comprehensive administrative system, while the party may not yet have struck roots in the country's most important industrial centres.

44.) Optimal centralisation of party activity is not aided by dividing up the party leadership schematically into a hierarchy with many different levels arrayed one above the other. Efforts should be made to equip every large city that is a centre of economic, political, or communications activity with a network of connections into the surrounding hinterland and the economic or political region linked to it. The party committee in the large city that directs this structure and gives political leadership to the district must be in close touch with the worker-members in the main centre.

The district conference or convention should elect full-time organisers, who are to be confirmed by the party central leadership. These organisers are obliged to participate consistently in party activity in the district capital. The district party committee needs to be constantly reinforced by activists from the membership in the district capital, in order to maintain a close contact between this committee, which gives political leadership to the entire district, and the broad membership in the main centre. As forms of party organisation develop, an effort should be made to have the district leadership committee coincide with the political leadership of the district capital. In this way, the leading party committees of the district organisation, together with the Central Committee, will be able to provide effective leadership for the party organisation as a whole.

The reach of a party district is, of course, not limited to the district's boundaries. What is important is that the district committee is capable of giving unified leadership to all the local party units within the district. When that is no longer possible, the district should be divided, and a new district committee established.

In the larger countries, the party also needs coordinating committees that stand between the central leadership and the different district leaderships (provincial or regional leaderships). Such committees will also coordinate between the district leadership and the local units (sub-district or county committees). It may sometimes be appropriate, for example in a large city or one with a large membership, to give one of these intermediate committees a leadership function. However, it is usually better to avoid decentralisation.

45.) The larger party units (districts) are composed of local units: local branches in rural areas or small centres; districts or wards in the various parts of large cities.

When a local party unit has grown to the point that it cannot hold general membership meetings of a size appropriate to legal conditions, it must be divided.

Members of a local party unit should be divided up, for the purposes of daily party work, in different working groups. In larger units, it may be expedient to link working groups in a number of different collectives. A collective, as a rule, includes members who come into contact at the workplace or in some other aspect of their daily lives. A collective has the task of dividing up the party work among the different working groups, receiving reports from the heads of these groups, training candidate members in these groups, and so on.

46.) The party as a whole is under the leadership of the Communist International. The instructions and resolutions of the international leadership concerning an affiliated party will be forwarded either: (a) to the Central Committee of the party; (b) through the Central Committee to the leadership of some special activity; or (c) to all party units.

The instructions and decisions of the International are binding for the party and, of course, for every individual party member.

47.) The central leadership of the party (Central Committee or expanded Central Committee) is responsible to the party's convention and to the leadership of the Communist International. Both the smaller leadership and the broader committee or council are usually elected by the convention. If the convention considers it expedient, it can instruct the central leadership to elect the smaller leading body from its own members; the latter consists of both the Political Bureau and the Organisational Bureau. Both the party's political course and its ongoing work are directed by the smaller leadership through these two bureaus.

The small leadership convenes regular plenums of the party's central leadership in order to make decisions of greater significance and more lengthy applicability. When electing the central party leadership, it is important to take account of the different regions in the country, if possible. That will help provide a thorough grasp of the political situation as a whole and give a vivid image of the party, its level of understanding, and its capacities. For the same reason, when electing the central leadership, minority points of view on significant political issues should not be excluded. On the contrary, they should be encompassed in the leadership as a whole through their best representatives. Whenever possible, however, the small leadership should be homogeneous in outlook. In addition, in order to lead firmly and confidently, it should not have to rely only on its own authority but rather be backed by a numerically clear majority in the leadership as a whole.

Legal mass parties, in particular, will find that a more inclusive central leadership of this type is the most rapid way to achieve a strong basis for firm discipline and unconditional confidence among the membership. In addition, any vacillations or ailments that may crop up among the party's layer of functionaries will be more rapidly evident and thus more readily remedied. This approach can make it possible to head off, to a certain degree, an accumulation of such ailments in the party. Otherwise, such an accumulation can lead, later on, to a drastic remedy at a party convention with possibly catastrophic consequences.

48.) Every leading committee in the party must institute an appropriate division of labour, in order to be able to direct party work effectively in every field. Special leading bodies may be necessary in a number of work areas, such as propaganda, newspaper distribution, trade-union struggles, rural agitation, agitation among women, communications, Red Aid,[38] and so on. Each special leading body is subordinate either to the party's central leadership or to the leading committee of a district.

The district leadership – and, ultimately, the central leadership – must supervise all subordinate committees to ensure that they are functioning properly and are constituted in a sound manner. All the party's full-time staffers and its parliamentary deputies are directly subordinate to the leading party committee. It may be advisable now and then to change the assignments and locations of full-time staffers (editors, propagandists, organisers, and so on), provided that this does not overly disrupt the party's activity. Editors and propagandists must take part in regular party work through one of the working groups.

49.) The central leadership of the party and the Communist International can at any time demand comprehensive reports from all Communist organisations, their leaderships, and from individual members. Representatives and delegates of the central leadership have the right to attend all meetings with consultative voice and the right of veto. The central leadership must always have such delegates (commissars) at its disposal, so that it is able to address district and local leaderships not only through political and organisational circulars but through direct verbal instructions and information. Both the central leadership and each regional leadership needs a control commission, made up of tested and trained comrades, to supervise the administration of funds. They should make regular reports to the broader committee, council, or commission.

Every party unit and committee and every single member has the right to express their wishes and make proposals, comments, and complaints at any time directly to the party central leadership or the International.

---

38. For Red Aid, see p. 875, n. 9.

50.) Instructions and decisions of the party's leading bodies are binding for all subordinate bodies and for individual members.

Leading bodies have the responsibility and duty of guarding against neglect or abuse of their leadership position. This can never be fully assured by formal provisions. Moreover, the smaller the formal obligations – as for example in illegal parties – the greater is the duty to seek the opinion of other party members, obtain frequent and reliable reports, and take their decisions only after thorough and comprehensive consideration.

51.) Party members are obligated always to conduct themselves, in all their public activity, as disciplined members of a combat organisation. When disagreements arise over a course of action, these should, if possible, be settled within the party before acting. In order to ensure that every party decision will be carried out energetically by all party units and members, the broadest possible range of members should be involved in considering and deciding every question. The party and its leading bodies have the responsibility of deciding whether and to what extent questions raised by individual comrades should be discussed publicly (newspapers, lectures, pamphlets). Even when some members consider a decision of the party or its leadership to be wrong, they must bear in mind in their public activity that the worst breach of discipline and the worst mistake in struggle is to disrupt the unity of the common front.

The highest duty of every member is to defend the Communist Party and, above all, the Communist International, against all enemies of communism. Anyone who forgets this and publicly attacks the party or the Communist International must be treated as an enemy of the party.

52.) The party statutes must be drafted so as not to pose any barriers to the leading committees in the steady development of the party organisation and the constant improvement of its work. On the contrary, the statutes should assist this process.

Decisions of the Communist International should be carried out without delay by the affiliated parties, including in cases where the requisite changes in existing statutes and party decisions can be carried out only after the fact.

## VIII. *On combining legal and illegal work*

53.) Every Communist Party modifies its functioning in line with the changing phases of the revolutionary process. This does not, however, change the basic character of the desirable structure of the party, regardless of whether it is functioning legally or is driven underground.

The party must be organised in such a fashion that it is always able to adjust quickly to changes in the conditions of struggle.

The Communist Party must evolve into an organisation of struggle. When the enemy is arrayed for battle with superior forces and with all its strength concentrated at one point, the party must be capable of evasion. On the other hand, when the enemy is clumsy, the party must seize upon this to launch the attack when and where it is least expected. It would be a great mistake for the party to reckon only with the prospect of an uprising and street fighting or, on the other hand, the prospect of severe repression. Communists must carry out their preparations for revolution in every situation, standing always ready for struggle. It is often almost impossible to predict the shifts from periods of uprising to those of quiescence. Even in cases where the shift can be predicted, only rarely does this make possible a corresponding party reorganisation. Usually the shift comes quite fast, indeed, arrives as a total surprise.

54.) Most of the legal Communist parties in the capitalist countries have not sufficiently grasped their task of properly preparing for revolutionary uprisings, armed struggle, or underground existence. The party is built too one-sidedly in expectation of lasting legality and is structured for the needs of legal daily work.

The underground parties, by contrast, often do not understand well enough how to utilise opportunities for legal activity and how to build a party that has living ties with the revolutionary masses. In such conditions, the party tends to lapse into a sterile labour of Sisyphus or impotent conspiratorial work.

Both approaches are erroneous. Every legal Communist Party must be able to maintain the greatest possible readiness for struggle even if forced underground and must, in particular, be prepared for the outbreak of a revolutionary uprising. Every illegal Communist Party must make energetic use of openings afforded by the legal workers' movement in order, through intensive work, to become the organiser and authentic leader of the broad revolutionary masses.

Leadership of both legal and illegal work must always be carried out by the same unified party central committee.

55.) In both legal and illegal parties, the work of an underground Communist organisation is often understood to consist of founding and maintaining a closed-off and exclusively military organisation, isolated from the rest of the party's work and structure. That is quite wrong. On the contrary, during the prerevolutionary period, fighting contingents are formed primarily through the general work of the party. The party as a whole should be trained as a battle organisation for the revolution.

If isolated revolutionary military organisations are formed too far in advance of the revolution, they can easily become demoralised and disintegrate, simply because there is not enough useful party work for them to do.

56.) For an underground party, it is naturally very important, in all its activities, to protect its members and committees from discovery, and not to give them away through carelessness regarding membership records, dues payment, or distribution of printed materials. It cannot utilise open organisational forms for underground work in the same manner as a legal party. Nonetheless, it can learn to do this more and more.

Every precaution must be taken to prevent dubious or unreliable forces from entering the party. The choice of methods for this depends greatly on whether the party is legal or illegal, persecuted or tolerated, growing or stagnating. One method that has brought good results under certain circumstances is the institution of candidate membership. An applicant for membership in the party, proposed by one or two members, is admitted first as a candidate. How they then acquit themselves in party work assigned to them will determine whether they are accepted into full membership.

Inevitably, the bourgeoisie will seek to infiltrate the underground organisation with spies and provocateurs. The struggle against this must be pursued with great caution and persistence. One way to do this is to combine legal and illegal activity. Extended legal revolutionary work is the best way to test who is sufficiently reliable, courageous, conscientious, energetic, skilled, and punctual to be entrusted with important tasks of underground work appropriate to his abilities.

A legal party should constantly improve its defences against surprises – as, for example, by carefully protecting cover addresses, making a habit of destroying correspondence, vigilantly protecting essential documents, training contacts in the arts of underground functioning, and so on.

57.) Our overall party work should be divided up in such a way that, even in the period prior to a revolutionary uprising, the roots of a fighting organisation of the type needed for this phase develop and are consolidated. It is vital that the Communist Party leadership always keep these needs in view and that it attempt, as much as possible, to form a clear idea of these tasks in advance. Of course, this conception can never be sufficiently precise or defined. That is no reason, however, to neglect this important aspect of Communist organisational leadership.

When the time comes for a revolutionary uprising, this produces a great transformation in the functioning of the Communist Party. Even the best-organised party can then face difficult and complicated tasks. It may then be necessary to mobilise our party for military struggle within a few days. And this applies not only to the party but to its reserves, the groups of sympathisers, indeed even the entire Landsturm[39] – that is, the unorganised revolutionary masses. At this stage, it is too early to think of forming a regular Red Army. We must win victory without a previously constituted army, through the masses and under the party's leadership. It follows that even the most heroic struggle will not succeed unless the party is already organisationally prepared in advance.

58.) It has often been the case in revolutionary situations that the revolutionary central leadership showed itself incapable of carrying out its task. During the revolution, the proletariat may score splendid successes in lower-level tasks, while the central leadership is gripped by disorder, helplessness, and chaos. Even the most elementary division of labour may be lacking. In particular, the information service is usually so poor as to cause more harm than good. Communications are unreliable. When secret postal services, secret transport, safe houses, and secret print shops are needed, their availability usually is a matter of sheer chance. Provocations by the organised enemy have good chances of success.

The only way to remedy this is for the leading revolutionary party to set up in advance a special apparatus for these tasks. For example, tracking and exposing the political police requires special training. An apparatus for secret communications can function securely and quickly only if it has been in operation for some time. Every legal Communist Party has to make preparations, no matter how limited, in all these fields of special revolutionary activity.

The apparatus needed in these fields can largely be developed through activity that is entirely legal, provided that this activity is developed in full knowledge of the purpose it is to serve. For example, carefully structured distribution of legal leaflets, publications, and letters can serve in large measure as a vehicle for setting up an apparatus for secret communications, including a courier service, a secret postal service, safe houses, secret transportation, and the like.

59.) A Communist organiser sees in every party member and every revolutionary worker the future soldier in his historic role in the battle organisation at the moment of revolution. It follows that the organiser will direct

---

39. In Germany, the Landsturm consisted of those liable to military service who were not part of the armed forces or the organised reserves. Calling up the Landsturm was the final stage in mobilising for all-out war.

individuals to the nucleus or the task that best corresponds to his future role in combat. His present activity must also be useful and necessary for today's struggle, rather than a mere drill that the activist cannot today understand. Indeed, the present activity is, in part, training for the urgent requirements of tomorrow's final struggle.

# Resolution on Organising the Communist International[40]

The Communist International Executive should be constituted in such a way as to enable it to take a position on all questions posed for action by the proletariat.[41] The Executive must go beyond the general appeals it has been publishing on such critical issues. More and more, it must find the road to practical initiatives that enable its sections to take unified organisational and propagandistic steps on disputed questions of international politics. The Communist International must mature into an International of the deed, an international leadership of the common daily struggle waged by the revolutionary proletariat in every country. The prerequisites for this are:

1.) Parties affiliated to the Communist International must make every effort to maintain close and active ties with the Executive. They must appoint their best representatives to serve on the Executive. What is more, they must exercise judgement and persistence in providing the Executive with good information, so the Executive can take a position based on actual documents and basic materials relating to political problems as they arise. The Executive must establish specialised departments to process this material effectively. In addition, the Executive should establish an international economic and statistical institute for the workers' movement and for communism.

2.) The affiliated parties must maintain intimate informational and organisational ties with each other, especially when they are neighbours with an equal stake in capitalist antagonisms. At present, this common relationship in action can best be initiated through the exchange of delegates to important conferences and of appropriately chosen members. Such an exchange of members must become an ongoing programme of all efficient sections.

---

40. Discussed in Session 22 and approved in Session 24.
41. The draft of this resolution presented in Session 22 began with two sentences, most of which were deleted in the final version. Here is the draft version of these sentences, with subsequently deleted passages italicised:
*The Third World Congress notes that the development of the Communist International has reached the point where it can make the transition from the stage of influencing the masses of the capitalist and colonial countries to that of a more and more tightly organised and genuine political and organisational leadership of the revolutionary proletarian forces around the world.* The Communist International Executive should be constituted in such a way as to enable it to take a position on all questions posed for action by the proletariat, *such as the increasingly urgent problems of mass unemployment; the increasing hostility and violence of political relations among capitalist governments (sanctions threatened and imposed, peace treaties, and the new world armaments race between the United States, Britain, and Japan).*

3.) The Executive will help the national sections fuse, as they must, into a unified international party of proletarian propaganda and action by publishing a political newsletter in Western Europe in all the more important languages. This newsletter must present an increasingly clear and cohesive analysis of Communist ideas and provide reliable, regular information that gives national sections a basis to respond simultaneously and actively.[42]

4.) The Executive can give organisational backing to efforts to forge a genuine International of effective daily struggle by sending representatives with full powers to the sections. The task of such emissaries is to inform the Executive regarding the particular conditions in which the Communist parties of the capitalist and colonial countries are struggling. In addition, they must ensure that the parties remain in close contact with the Executive and with each other, in order to increase effectiveness on both sides. The Executive and the individual affiliated parties should also ensure that communication between them takes place not only personally, through trusted representatives, but also through written correspondence. This should be more frequent and more timely than has been the case in the past, so that a common position can be adopted on all the major political issues.

5.) In order to be able to carry out this much increased activity, the Executive must be substantially expanded. Each section granted forty votes in the congress and the Executive of the Communist Youth International will receive two places; each section granted twenty or thirty votes will receive one place. The Communist Party of Russia will have five places, as before. Representatives of other sections will have consultative vote. The chair of the Executive will be chosen by the congress. The Executive will be instructed to engage three secretaries, drawn if possible from different sections. In addition, members of the Executive sent from the sections are required to take part in carrying out the work of the divisions relating to their country or by serving as reporters responsible for the work of entire topic areas. Members of the administrative Small Bureau will be chosen by the Executive, as a rule from among the Executive's members. Exceptions are permissible in special circumstances.

6.) The Executive will be based in Russia, the first proletarian state. The Executive will, however, seek to widen its influence through conferences organised outside Russia, in order to consolidate and centralise its organisational and political leadership of the International as a whole.

---

42. In September 1921 the Comintern established a German-language newsletter *Inprekorr* (*Internationale Presse-Korrespondenz*), published several times a week. The following month the newsletter began to be published in English as *Inprecorr* (*International Press Correspondence*).

# Theses on Methods and Forms of Work of the Communist Parties among Women[43]

*Basic principles*

1.) The Third Congress of the Communist International, together with the International Conference of Communist Women, confirms once again the decisions of the First and Second Congresses that point to the necessity of strengthening the work of Communist parties of the West and East among the female proletariat.[44] This work aims at educating the broad messes of working women in the ideas of communism and drawing them into the struggle for soviet power and the building of a soviet republic.

Around the world the working class, and thus also working women, face the essential question of the dictatorship of the proletariat.

The capitalist economic system has landed in a dead end. There is no longer scope for the further development of the productive forces within the capitalist framework. The increasing poverty of working people, the bourgeoisie's inability to further expand the productive forces, the prevalence of speculation, the decline of production, unemployment, price fluctuations, the gap between wages and prices: all these factors lead inevitably to a sharpening of class antagonisms in every country. This struggle decides who will determine, lead, administer, and organise the system of production, and whether this leadership will be assumed by a handful of bourgeois and exploiters on the basis of capitalism and private property or by the class of producers on the basis of communism. In accord with the laws of economic development, the new class striving forward – the class of producers – must take control of the productive system in order to create new economic structures. Only in this way will it be possible to maximise the development of productive forces that have previously been held back by the anarchy of the capitalist system of production.

So long as power remains in the hands of the bourgeois class, the proletariat is not able to improve the system of production. So long as power is in the hands of capital, it is not possible to save the situation in a bourgeois country through reforms, whether taken by a democratic or a so-called socialist government. It is not possible to ease the grave and unbearable suffering

---

43. Approved in Session 20.
44. The First Congress 'Resolution on the Need to Draw Women Workers into the Struggle for Socialism' can be found in Riddell (ed.) 1987, *1WC*, pp. 250–1. A draft resolution for the Second Congress, the 'Theses for the Communist Women's Movement', was prepared by Zetkin and approved by the ECCI following the congress. It can be found in Riddell (ed.) 1991, *2WC*, 2, pp. 977–98.

of working women and men that results from the decay of the capitalist economic system. Only the seizure of power by the proletariat makes it possible for this class of producers to take possession of the means of production and promote economic development in the interests of working people. In order to hasten the hour of the proletariat's inevitable decisive struggle against the decayed capitalist world, the working class must hold firmly and without hesitation to the policies laid down by the Third International. The workers' dictatorship of the proletariat is the immediate goal that determines the methods of work and the direction of the struggle by both men and women of the proletariat.

The Third Congress of the Communist International begins with the proposition that proletarians in all capitalist states now face a struggle for the dictatorship of the proletariat. In countries where workers already possess this dictatorship, the immediate task is to build communism. The Third Congress of the Communist International notes that it is not possible either to win power or to achieve communism in a country where capitalism has already been overthrown, without active support by the broad masses of women of the proletariat and semi-proletariat.

At the same time, the congress directs the attention of all women to the fact that every attempt to free women from servitude and achieve their equality will fail unless they enjoy the support of the Communist parties.

2.) Today above all, the interests of the working class urgently require that women be drawn into the organised ranks of the proletariat fighting for communism. As economic dislocation assumes more and more drastic and unbearable forms for the poor people of city and countryside, it becomes increasingly essential for the workers to carry out the social revolution in the capitalist countries. Meanwhile, the workers in Soviet Russia have to rebuild the economy on new communist foundations. Both tasks will be all the easier to carry out to the degree that women take an active, conscious, and determined part in carrying them out.

3.) Wherever the question arises of taking power, the Communist parties must properly evaluate the great danger to the revolution represented by the masses of women workers, housewives, office workers, and peasants who have not been encompassed by the movement. They have not been freed from the grip of a capitalist world outlook, the church, and bourgeois prejudices; they have not encountered, in one way or another, the great Communist movement for freedom. The masses of women of the West and East who have not been brought into the movement are a pillar of support to capitalism and are vulnerable to counterrevolutionary propaganda. The experience of the

Hungarian revolution, in which large numbers of women who lacked class consciousness played such an unfortunate role, must stand as a warning for proletarians in every country who have taken the road of social revolution.

On the other hand, the experience of the Soviet republic shows the important role played by women workers and peasants both in defending the republic and in every arena of Soviet construction. The facts clearly show the importance of the role played by women workers and peasants in organising defence behind the battle lines, in the struggle against desertion and against every form of counterrevolution, sabotage, and so on, in the Soviet republic. The proletariat of other countries must learn from the experience of the proletarian republic.

It follows that the Communist parties face the task of extending the influence of the party and of communism among the broad masses of women in their countries. They must use special, more effective methods that enable them to liberate women from the influence of the capitalist outlook and the compromisers, educating them to be true fighters and, in this way, to achieve their true liberation.

4.) The Third Congress of the Communist International entrusts the Communist parties of the West and East with the special task of strengthening work among the female proletariat. It also points out to the working women of the entire world that only the victory of communism will open the road to their liberation from servitude and oppression. What communism offers women is not offered at all by the capitalist women's movement. So long as capitalist power and private property still prevail in the capitalist countries, the liberation of women from dependency on men cannot get beyond the right to dispose over her earnings and property and to a voice equal to that of the man in raising the children. The efforts of feminists in countries with parliamentary systems to extend the right to vote to women do not resolve the question of achieving real equality, especially for women of the non-propertied classes. Workers have learned this in capitalist countries where the bourgeoisie in recent years introduced formal equality of the sexes. The right to vote cannot destroy the original causes of women's enslavement in the family and society. Introduction of civil marriage in place of indissoluble marriage in the capitalist countries does not grant women equality in marriage and does not resolve the challenge of mutual relations of the sexes so long as conditions persist where women workers are economically dependent on the capitalist and the male wage earner and where there are no laws protecting mothers and youth and women's social education.

Women can achieve genuine, as opposed to formal, equality only in communism. In other words, women of the working masses will be free only when they can take part in ownership of the means of production and distribution and the leadership of society on an equal basis. They must be able to carry out the obligation of labour in the same way as other members of labouring society. In other words, this is possible only when the system of capitalist production has been overturned and replaced by a communist economic structure.

Only communism creates conditions in which women's natural function of motherhood does not conflict with her social obligations and her creative labour on behalf of all society. Communism will promote the harmonious and all-sided development of personality, which is closely and indissolubly linked to the life of the labour collective. All women who strive for women's liberation and the recognition of their rights must adopt communism as their goal.

Communism, however, is simultaneously the goal of the proletariat as a whole. Therefore, the struggle of working women and men must be conducted jointly and in unified fashion, in the interests of both sides.

5.) The Third Congress of the Communist International stresses the basic postulate of revolutionary Marxism that there is no 'special women's question'. For working women to join together with capitalist feminism weakens the struggle of the proletariat. Marxism also stresses that any support by working women to the traitorous policies of the social compromisers and opportunists equally weakens the proletariat's cause. This approach would postpone the social revolution and delay the victory of communism and also the hour of women's liberation.

It is not the united efforts of women of different classes that makes communism possible, but rather the united struggle of all the exploited.

The proletarian masses of women are obliged by their own interests to support the revolutionary tactics and strategy of the Communist parties. They must take part actively and directly in the mass actions and the civil war that is emerging in all its expressions both on a national and an international scale.

6.) Women are doubly oppressed, by capitalism and by their dependency in family life. Their struggle against this oppression must take on an international character in the coming period and become a struggle by proletarians of both sexes for the dictatorship of the proletariat and for Soviet construction, waged under the banner of the Third International.

7.) The Third Congress of the Communist International warns working women against any collaboration or compromise with the bourgeois feminists. It also underlines that support to women of the Second International or opportunist forces close to it will cause enormous harm to women's cause and that of the proletariat. Women must never forget that their slavery is rooted in the capitalist structure. Ending this slavery requires a transition to a new form of society.

Support to the Second and Two-and-a-Half Internationals and similar groups obstructs the development of social revolution and thereby also that of a new form of society. The more decisively that broad masses of women turn away from the Second and Two-and-a-Half Internationals, the more certain is the victory of the social revolution. It is the duty of Communist women to condemn all those who shrink back from the revolutionary policies of the Communist International and to struggle unrelentingly and inexorably to exclude these forces from its united ranks.

Women must bear in mind that the Second International has not made even an attempt to launch a publication dedicated to the struggle for the universal liberation of women. The International Association of Socialist Women, to the extent that it has taken shape at all, was formed outside the framework of the Second International on the independent initiative of working women.[45]

As early as its First Congress, in 1919, the Third International set down specifically its position on the question of drawing women into the struggle for the dictatorship.[46] It was on the initiative of the First Congress that the first conference of women Communists was convened.[47] In 1920 the International Secretariat for Work among Women was founded, with permanent representation in the Executive Committee of the Communist International. It is the duty of all class-conscious women workers everywhere to break without fail from the Second and Two-and-a-Half Internationals and give whole-hearted support to the revolutionary stand of the Communist International.

8.) Women workers, peasants, and employees should give expression to their support for the Communist International by joining the Communist Party in their country.

In countries and parties in which the struggle between the Second and Third Internationals has not yet been brought to a conclusion, women workers should give full support to the party or group that comes out for the Communist International. They should fight ruthlessly against all wavering or openly traitorous forces, without giving heed to any supposed authorities. Class-conscious proletarian women struggling for their genuine liberation

---

45. The First International Conference of Socialist Women, held in Stuttgart 17 August 1907 prior to a congress of the Second International, established an International Socialist Women's Bureau. The original idea for holding this international conference came out of a conference of Socialist Women in Germany held in conjunction with the SPD's September 1906 congress.
46. A reference to First Congress 'Resolution on the Need to Draw Women Workers into the Struggle for Socialism'.
47. The First International Conference of Communist Women was held in Moscow 30 July–2 August 1920, during the Second Comintern Congress.

should not stay in parties outside the Communist International. Any enemy of the Third International is an enemy of women's liberation.

For purposeful working women of the West and East, there is only one place: under the banner of the Communist International, that is, in the ranks of the Communist Party of their country. Any wavering by working women, any evasion of the struggle against the compromising parties and leaders that call themselves socialist, will have a pernicious effect on the proletariat's struggle and will endanger its victory in a struggle that is developing into a national and international civil war.

*The methods and forms of work among women*

On the basis of the principles described above, the Third Congress of the Communist International resolves that the Communist parties in every country are to conduct their work among the female proletariat along the following lines:

1.) Women are to be regarded as members with equal rights of the party and all class organisations (trade unions, cooperatives, factory councils, etc.).
2.) It is necessary to recognise that women active in every field of proletarian struggle, not excluding military self-defence of the proletariat, are to be drawn into the building of new social foundations and the organisation of production and life on a communist basis.
3.) The role of motherhood must receive recognition as a social function. Efforts are needed to institute and realise measures that protect women in their role as mothers.

The Third Congress of the Communist International is strongly opposed to forming separate, special women's associations within the party or the trade unions, or in the form of a special women's organisation. However, it nonetheless recognises the need for the Communist parties to use special methods of work among women. It therefore recognises that it is appropriate to create special organs to carry out this work inside all Communist parties. The congress is guided here by the following considerations:

a.) Women suffer subjugation in the capitalist countries and also are in a difficult position in the soviet countries that are undergoing a transition from capitalism to communism.
b.) A certain passivity and political backwardness is evident among the masses of women, which results from the fact that women have for centuries been excluded from social life and chained to the family.

c.) The special social function – motherhood – and the resulting characteristics that nature assigns to women call for greater protection of women's health and energies in the interests of society.

Based on these considerations, the congress recognises that it is advisable to create special bodies to carry out work among women. These bodies consist of sections and commissions linked to all party committees, from the party Central Committee down to the city or ward committee. This decision is binding on all parties belonging to the Communist International.

The Third Congress of the Communist International considers that the tasks of these sections and commissions are as follows:

1.) Educate the broad masses of women in Communist ideas and integrate them into the ranks of the party.
2.) Struggle against the prejudices linked to women's social role and strengthen the awareness of working men and women that proletarians of both sexes share common interests.
3.) Strengthen the willpower of women. Draw them into all expressions of the civil war in capitalist countries. Arouse women to activity by drawing them into mass actions and into the struggle against capitalist exploitation (lack of housing, inflation, unemployment, the wretched conditions of children). Pursue the same goal in the soviet republics by drawing women into building a communist economy and way of life.
4.) Place on the agenda the questions related to women's equality and protection of the woman as a mother. Direct the attention of the party and, in soviet countries, the legal authorities, to these issues.
5.) Struggle systematically against the power of tradition, bourgeois customs, and religion, in order to promote more healthy and harmonious relations between the sexes, relations capable of assuring the physical and moral vitality of working people.

The party's leadership bodies must directly lead the work of the commissions [for work among women] and take responsibility for their work. The head of each commission should be a member of the leading committee. If possible, several Communist men should be members of such a commission.

The commissions should not act on their own to carry out the necessary measures on issues as they arise.[48] Instead, in soviet countries, this should be done through the appropriate economic or political bodies (soviets,

---

48. The German text of this sentence leaves out the word "not", inverting its meaning. The translation here follows the Russian text, which is consistent with the thrust of the resolution.

commissariats, commissions, trade unions, etc.). In capitalist countries, help should be sought from appropriate bodies of the proletariat (trade unions, councils, etc.). Wherever Communist parties are illegal or semi-legal, they will build an underground apparatus for work among women, subordinated and adapted to the underground apparatus of the party. Just as in a legal organisation, an underground party needs a woman comrade in each local, district, or central committee who is responsible for leading underground propaganda work among women.

The main arena for Communist Party work among women at this time is the trade unions, production collectives, and cooperatives. This is true both in countries where the struggle to overthrow capitalism is under way and in the soviet workers' republics. Work among women must be carried out with respect for the unity of the party as a movement and of its structures, and also with respect for the independent initiatives of the commissions. This applies to all initiatives for complete liberation and equality of women, which are to be carried out fully by the party.

The goal is not to duplicate the party's work but rather to expand it through women's creative self-activity and initiative.

## *The party's work among women in the soviet countries*

The task of the women's sections in a soviet workers' republic is to educate the broad masses of women in Communist ideas and win them to the Communist Party. These sections have to arouse and raise women's self-activity and initiative by drawing women into the work of building communism and educating them as steadfast partisans of the Communist International. The women's sections must strive in every way possible to draw women into every arena of soviet construction, beginning with defence and including their involvement in the republic's diverse economic projects.

The women's sections in the Soviet republic must ensure implementation of the decisions of the Eighth Congress of Soviets [December 1920] regarding drawing women workers and peasants into construction and organisation of the economy and women's involvement in all bodies that deal with the organisation, supervision, and direction of production.

The women's sections must take part, through their representatives and through party bodies, in the drafting of demands for new laws for the economic liberation of women and for modification of existing measures with this purpose. The sections must show particular initiative in drafting laws relating to protection of women and young people at work.

Women's sections are obliged to rally the greatest possible number of women workers and peasants for campaigns around the soviet elections and to ensure that women workers and peasants become members of the soviets and their executive committees.

Women's sections must make efforts to ensure that all the political and economic campaigns undertaken by the party are carried through rapidly and successfully.

Women's sections have the task of improving the quality of women's work by more effective trade-union training and of ensuring that women workers and peasants have access to the appropriate educational institutions.

Women's sections must ensure that women join the commissions for protection of labour in individual enterprises and must help promote the work of commissions for protection of women and youth.

Women's sections must help strengthen the entire network of social institutions (public orphanages, laundries, repair shops, communal residences, institutions for social care) that provide new Communist foundations for everyday life, ease the hardships women experience during this transition period, promote women's economic independence, and transform the slave of the home and family into a free partner in creating new forms of living.

The women's sections must ensure that women trade-union members are educated in the ideas of communism, in which they can draw on the assistance of groups for work among women formed by the Communist fractions in the trade unions.

The women's sections must ensure that women factory workers attend meetings of factory delegates. The sections are responsible to plan the allocation of women delegates – practitioners – to different tasks in the soviets, in economic work, and in the unions.[49]

Women's sections of the party must work above all to develop deep roots among the women workers and closer contact with housewives, office workers, and small-peasant women.

The women's sections convene delegated conferences of women workers in order to strengthen the party's ties with the masses, to spread its influence among the non-party masses, and to pursue systematic education of masses of women in the ideas of communism through independent activity and participation in practical work.

Delegated assemblies are the best means to educate women workers and peasants. Through these delegates, the party's influence can spread among the broad masses of non-party and backward women workers and peasants.

---

49. The following nine paragraphs are not found in the German edition, and are translated from the Russian.

These assemblies are composed of women representatives from factories of a given district, city, or rural area (for delegated meetings of peasant women), or neighbourhood (for delegates of housewives). In Soviet Russia, women delegates are drawn into political and economic campaigns of every description. Women are delegated to take part in commissions of various types in the workplace. They are involved in supervision of Soviet state administration. Finally, by the law adopted in 1921, they take part in the ongoing work of Soviet departments as practitioners delegated for two months.[50]

Women delegates are chosen in general assemblies of a workshop or of housewives, according to a procedure set by the party. The women's sections must carry out propagandistic and agitational work among the women delegates, and the sections meet for this purpose at least twice a month. Delegates, elected for a three-month term, are required to give a report on their activity to their workshop or to neighbourhood meetings.

The second form of agitation among the masses of women is through conferences of non-party women workers and peasants. Delegates to these conferences are elected by meetings of women workers in an enterprise or of women peasants in rural areas.

Women's sections are responsible for calling these conferences and leading them.

In order to reinforce the experiences of women workers in the practical work of the party and its activities, the women's sections conduct systematic and broad propaganda, both through publications and in person. The sections hold assemblies, discussions, and meetings of women workers in the enterprise or of housewives in a neighbourhood. They organise delegated meetings and carry out door-to-door agitation.

Sections for work among women must be formed to develop working women as cadres and to strengthen work in Soviet schools at both the central and local levels.

*In the capitalist countries*

The immediate tasks of commissions for work among women are determined by the objective situation. On the one hand, we have the decay of the world economy, the immense increase in unemployment (expressed particularly in a decline in the demand for women workers), the growth of prostitution,

---

50. The term 'practitioners' referred to women workers, freed up from their responsibilities on the job, who served as delegates for a period of several months while they received their normal wage. The goal was for them to gain experience working in various Soviet institutions.

inflation, the housing shortage, the threat of new imperialist wars. On the other hand, we see incessant economic strikes by workers, repeated attempts by the proletariat at armed insurrection, and the looming prospect of worldwide civil war. All this is the prologue to inevitable world social revolution.

The commissions of working women must stress the tasks posed for proletarian struggle, advance the slogans of the Communist Party as a whole, and draw women into participation in Communist revolutionary activity against the bourgeoisie and the social traitors.

The commissions must ensure that women are integrated into the party, the unions, the cooperatives, and other class organisations as members with equal rights and obligations. They must oppose any separating out of women workers or any special status for them. What is more, the commissions must promote the integration of working women as collaborators with equal rights in the leading bodies of the party, the unions, and the cooperatives.

The commissions need to encourage the broad masses of women in the proletariat and the peasantry to utilise their right to vote in parliamentary and other elections by supporting the Communist Party. In so doing, they need to explain how women's rights are limited with regard to eliminating or easing capitalist exploitation and also to compare the parliamentary system with the soviet order.

The commissions must also ensure that women workers, employees, and peasants take part with energy and class awareness in the elections of worker deputies to revolutionary economic and political councils. They must strive to succeed in arousing the housewife to political activity and popularising the idea of councils among the women peasants in particular. The commissions face a special task in applying the principle of equal pay for equal work. The commissions need to win working men and women for a campaign for free and generally available vocational schooling, in order to increase the skills of women workers.

The commissions must strive to involve Communist women in municipal and all other legislative social agencies – in which women can now participate with voice and vote, thanks to the achievement of suffrage – in order to take their party's revolutionary politics into that arena.

When participating in the municipal and other legislative bodies of the bourgeois state, Communist women must strictly observe the principles and policies of their party. It cannot and should not be their main goal to win reforms within the bourgeois system. Rather, they should utilise the demands of working women in order to point women toward achieving their demands and defending their interests along the path of revolutionary struggle, of struggle to establish the proletarian dictatorship.

The commissions should maintain close contact with the party fractions in parliament and municipal councils, consulting jointly on all issues affecting women.

The commissions must make clear to women that the system of separate home economies is backward and impractical, while capitalist methods of bringing up children are imperfect. They should direct the attention of working women to practical methods of improving workers' home life proposed and supported by the party. The commissions must make every effort to win women trade-union members for the Communist Party. To this end the trade-union fractions should appoint organisers for work among women, functioning under the leadership of the party and the local sections.

The commissions for agitation among women should encourage proletarian women in the cooperatives to spread the ideas of communism, enter their leadership, and influence their functioning, since these organisations will be of great importance in organising distribution of goods during and after the revolution.

The entire work of the commissions must aim to develop the masses' revolutionary activity and thus to hasten the revolution.

*In the economically backward countries of the East*

In countries where industry is little developed, the Communist parties and the women's sections must together seek to achieve recognition of women's equal status, in both rights and duties, by the party, the trade unions, and the other organisations of the working class.

Sections of the commission must conduct a vigorous struggle against all prejudices, customs, and religious practices that bear down on women. This agitation should also be addressed to men.

The Communist Party and the sections of its commissions must apply the principle of women's equal status to the raising of children, family relations, and public life.

The sections must try to win support among the exploited working women engaged in small shops, cottage industries, and rice, cotton, and other plantations. Wherever possible – and this applies mainly to the Eastern peoples living in the territory of Soviet Russia – the sections should seek to establish cooperative workplaces and industries and draw the plantation workers into the trade unions.

The best means of struggle against the backwardness of the country and religious prejudices is to raise the overall cultural level of the population. The commissions must seek to speed the development of schools for adults and children. Women must win admission to these schools. In the capitalist countries, women must wage a struggle against bourgeois influence in the schools.

## Work among Women: Theses

Wherever possible, the women's sections or commissions must conduct their agitation inside the home. Clubs for working women should be established that aim above all to influence the most backward layers of women. The clubs should be centres of cultural enlightenment, showing in life what women can achieve through their self-activity (establishing homes for children, kindergartens, schools, etc.) for their liberation. Mobile clubs should be established for nomadic peoples.

In the soviet countries, sections should work together with the party to promote the transition from a precapitalist economy to a collective mode of production. Working women should be convinced through practical experience that the domestic economy and previous family relationships enslave them, while collective labour will liberate them.

The women's sections working among the peoples of the East in Soviet Russia should see to it that Soviet legislation – which assures women of legal equality with men and protects women's interests – is actually observed. The sections should therefore support the appointment of women as judges and jury members.

The sections must draw women into the soviet elections and work to assure that women become members of soviets and their executive committees. Work among women workers of the East must be carried out on the basis of class principles. The sections have the task of explaining to women the futility of feminist efforts in resolving the woman question. In countries of the Soviet East, women intellectuals, such as teachers, should be drawn into educational work.

The sections or commissions must strictly avoid tactless, inappropriate, or rude attacks on religious beliefs or national traditions, while still resisting the influence of nationalism and religion.

In both the West and East, organisations of working women should not identify with national interests but should rather be instruments for the unification of the international proletariat of both sexes and should carry out tasks shared by the entire class. Given the particular importance of work among women of the East, special instructions are appended to these theses,[51] setting down the guidelines for work among these women while taking into account the specific conditions of everyday life among Eastern peoples.

### Methods of agitation and propaganda

In order to carry out the primary task of the sections – Communist education of the broad masses of proletarian women – and thus to expand the ranks of Communist fighters, it is necessary for all Communist parties of the West

---

51. No text of the appendix referred to here has been located.

and East to adopt the basic principle of work among women: agitation and propaganda through action.

Agitation through action means above all the ability to arouse the self-activity of working women, reinforce their confidence in their own capacities, and – by drawing them into practical work either for construction or struggle – to convince them that every success of the Communist Party, every action against capitalist exploitation, represents a step toward improving the status of women. Practical work and action leads to understanding of communism's ideals and its theoretical principles. That is the spirit in which Communist parties and their sections should approach the broad masses of working women.

To the extent that the sections are vehicles for propaganda not merely of the word but of the deed, they must be based on Communist cells inside the factories and workplaces. They must ensure that every Communist cell has an organiser of work among women in the factory.

The sections must, through their representatives, establish ties with the trade unions, ties sustained by the trade-union fractions and working under the leadership of the sections.

In Soviet Russia, propaganda through deeds for the ideas of communism means drawing women workers and peasants, housewives, and women employees into every area of Soviet construction, from the army and militia to activities for the liberation of women (communal kitchens, institutions of social education, protection of motherhood, etc.). It is particularly important at present to draw working women into all the efforts to rebuild the economy.

In the capitalist countries, propaganda through the deed means drawing women workers into participation in strikes, demonstrations, and uprisings, which consolidate and strengthen revolutionary willpower and consciousness. It also means drawing them into party work of every variety, from underground tasks (especially regarding communications) to the organising of Communist Saturdays or Sundays, through which sympathetic women workers and employees learn to be of use to the party through voluntary work.

The goal of propaganda through the deed is also served by drawing women into all political, economic, and cultural educational campaigns initiated by the Communist Party. Women's committees in the Communist parties must extend their activity to increasingly broad layers of the exploited and socially enslaved women of the capitalist countries. In the soviet countries, this applies to women oppressed by survivals of the old order. The commissions need to respond to all the hardships and evils, all the interests and demands, that display capitalism to women as a deadly enemy to be overcome and communism as a force to be welcomed as their liberator.

To carry out systematic agitation and propaganda work through the spoken word, women's commissions organise meetings in the factory or neighbourhood and public gatherings of women workers, employees, and civil servants, organised by trade or by district, whether through general open meetings of women or in other ways. They have their agitational and organisational representatives in the Communist fractions in the trade unions, cooperatives, factory councils, and in all the working, administrative, supervisory, and leading organs of the soviet system. This applies, in short, to all organisations in the capitalist countries that must be made useful in winning the exploited and oppressed masses to revolution and in their struggle to win political power, and, in the soviet states, all organisations that defend the proletarian dictatorship and pursue the realisation of communism. They choose experienced Communist women to serve as workers or employees in factories and enterprises in which many women are employed. They establish such comrades in large proletarian districts or centres, as has been done successfully in Soviet Russia.

The women's committees of the Communist Party of Soviet Russia have worked to hold the extraordinarily useful delegated meetings and conferences of non-party women. So too, the commissions of Communist women in the capitalist countries hold public meetings of women workers, employed women of every variety, peasant women, and housewives. These meetings take a position on the specific hardships and demands of those present and choose committees on an ad hoc basis that will pursue work on a given question in constant contact with those who elected them and with Communist women's commissions. Each member of these commissions should establish regular contact with no more than ten women in her neighbourhood, to be renewed when the Communist parties and proletarian masses hold major activities.

The women's commissions of the Communist parties are instructed to use the written word in carrying out their agitational, organisational, and educational activity. They should work toward publication of a national Communist women's newspaper, inclusion of women's pages or discussions among women in the Communist newspapers, and articles and contributions in the political and trade-union papers. They should choose women to serve as editors of these publications and recruit and train collaborators for them from the ranks of women on the job and in the struggle. They must create and distribute an appropriate and straightforward array of leaflets and pamphlets that can awaken and attract women.

The commissions should work for women party members to make energetic use of all the educational institutions and materials of the Communist parties.

In order to clarify and deepen the understanding and strengthen the willpower of Communist women who are still backward and timid, as well as employed women who are awakening to consciousness, they should draw these women into the party's general study sessions and discussions. Only where there are compelling reasons should they create their own educational institutions, such as reading circles, evenings of discussion, courses, and lectures.

In order to strengthen solidarity between working women and men, it is desirable not to organise separate courses and schools. Instead, every party school should include a compulsory course on the methods of work among women.

The commission has the right to delegate a number of its members to the party school.

## Structure of the commissions

Every party local unit, regional committee, and central committee will establish commissions for agitation among women. The number of members of the commissions should correspond to the needs of the particular country. The party will also determine the number of paid collaborators. The leader of the women's agitation commission both nationally and in regional and local groups has voice and vote in the corresponding national, regional, and local party leaderships. The leader of such a commission should also be a member of the local party leadership. Where this is not the case, the commission leader should take part in all leadership discussions of questions affecting the women's section with decisive vote, and on all other questions with consultative vote.

In addition to these general tasks, the regional or provincial commissions have the following functions: maintaining a link between the women's agitation commission of a given region and the regional leadership; collecting materials regarding the commission's activity in its region; ensuring that local commissions exchange materials; supplying the region with publications; assigning agitational resources to different parts of the region; mobilising party members for work among women; convening (at least twice a year) regional conferences of Communist women, with one or two delegates from each commission; and holding conferences of non-party women workers and peasants and housewives in the region.

Regional commissions should consist of five to seven members, proposed by the commission leader and confirmed by the chair of the district leadership. The leader and all other members of the district or regional commissions are elected by the respective party conferences.

The members of regional or local commissions are elected by regional, district, or city conferences, or by the relevant commission in consultation with the party leadership. The national commission for work among women consists of two to five members, of which one is paid by the party.

In addition to the functions listed above for the regional commissions, the national commission (national women's committee) has to do the following: supervise the work of commissions; lead and assign the members working among women; supervise the nature and development of work by women, taking into account women's legal and economic conditions; assign authorised representatives of the national commission to take part in special commissions that address issues of improving or altering workers' living conditions, laws, industrial health and safety standards, and the protection of children; publication of the national and women's newspapers and editorship of the women's publications and women's pages; convening women's representatives of all regions at least once a year; organisation of groups to instruct agitators regarding work among women across the country; supervision of the recruitment of women workers and their assignment to commissions taking part in the party's various political and economic campaigns; maintenance of ongoing ties with the International Secretariat of Communist Women; holding an annual International Women's Day.

If the leader of the women's commission of the central committee is not a member of that committee, this comrade has the right to attend all central committee sessions, with decisive vote on all questions affecting the commission, and otherwise with consultative vote. The chair of the commission is chosen by the party central committee or national congress. Decisions and instructions of all commissions must be ratified by the appropriate party committee.

*On international work*

The International Women's Secretariat of the Communist International has the tasks of leading the [women's] work of all Communist parties, rallying working women in struggle for the tasks posed by the Communist International, and drawing working women in every country into the revolutionary struggle for soviet power and the dictatorship of the working class on a world scale.

The number of members of the national commission with decisive and consultative vote will be determined by the party central committee.[52]

---

52. This sentence, which seems misplaced, is not found in the Russian text.

## Resolution on International Ties between Communist Women and the International Communist Women's Secretariat[53]

The Second International Communist Women's Conference calls on Communist parties in every country of the West and East to have their central women's committees elect international women's correspondents, in keeping with the theses of the Third International.[54]

The duty of the correspondent in each Communist Party, as laid down in the guidelines, is to maintain regular relations with the international correspondents in other countries as well as with the International Communist Women's Secretariat in Moscow, which is a working body of the Third International Executive. The Communist parties must help provide their international women's correspondents with the opportunity and the means for international communications with each other and with the secretariat in Moscow.

Once every six months, the international correspondents will meet together with a delegation of the International Women's Secretariat for consultation and an exchange of views. The Secretariat can also convene such consultations at any time if so required.

The International Women's Secretariat in Moscow, in collaboration with the Executive and in close accord with the international correspondents of each country, will carry out the tasks laid down in the guidelines. In particular, it may concern itself with assisting in word and deed the development of the still weak women's movement in each country. It will also provide the Communist Women's Movement of all countries, East and West, with unified direction for their work and struggle. Under Communist leadership and with energetic Communist support, it will lead actions suitable to broadening and sharpening the revolutionary proletarian class struggle through the advance of women.

In order to strengthen and regularise ties with the Communist Women's Movement in every country, the International Women's Secretariat will establish an auxiliary body in Western Europe. This body will carry out preparatory and follow-up work for the International Women's Secretariat. However, its functions lie in implementation, not in decision making; its actions and decisions will follow the directives of the main secretariat in Moscow and the Third International Executive. The Western European auxiliary body will

---

53. Approved in Session 20.
54. The 'Theses for the Communist Women's Movement' submitted by Zetkin to the Comintern Second Congress include a call to elect international correspondents. See Riddell (ed.) 1991, 2WC, 2, p. 996.

always include at least one representative of the main body. To the degree that the composition and scope of the main secretariat is not laid down in the guidelines, these issues – and also the formation, structure, and activity of the auxiliary body – will be settled by the Third International Executive, in collaboration with the International Women's Secretariat.

## Resolution on Forms and Methods of Communist Work among Women[55]

The Second International Conference of Communist Women in Moscow declares:

The disintegration of the capitalist economy and the bourgeois order based on it, along with the advance of the revolutionary power of the proletariat in countries where the bourgeois order still prevails, makes it increasingly and urgently necessary for the proletariat to conduct its revolutionary struggle and establish its dictatorship. This can be achieved only if the broad masses of working women take part in this struggle consciously, resolutely, and with devotion.

In countries where the proletariat has already taken state power and established its dictatorship through a council system – as in Soviet Russia and Ukraine – it is incapable of maintaining its power against the national and international counterrevolution and beginning the construction of a communist order, which will free humankind, unless the broadest masses of working women are imbued with a clear and unshakable determination that they too must take on the tasks of defence and construction.

The Second International Conference of Communist Women in Moscow therefore calls on parties in all countries, in accord with the principles and decisions of the Third International, to commit their full energy to awakening, gathering, training, and recruiting the broadest masses of working women into the Communist parties and for revolutionary struggle and construction. Their determination and capacity for action and struggle must be constantly intensified and strengthened.

In order to achieve this goal, all the parties affiliated to the Third International are obliged to establish women's committees in all their branches and institutions, from the lowest to the highest. These should be headed by a member of the party leadership. The task of these committees is to carry out agitational, organisational, and educational work among the broad masses of working women. These committees will have representation in all the party's leading and governing bodies.

These women's committees are not separate organisations. They are merely working bodies for the particular task before us, that of mobilising and educating the broad masses of working women for the struggle to win political power and for the work of communist construction. They therefore function continuously in every field under the leadership of the party. However, they enjoy the freedom of action needed to carry out the methods and forms of

---

55. Approved in Session 20.

work and to create the institutions that are called for in view of the state of their work, the special role of women, and their still unsurmounted special position in society and the family. The conference refers these committees to its adopted theses, which provide detailed guidance for their work.

The Communist Party's working women's structures must always be aware, in their work, of their double task:

1.) To inspire increasing masses of women to gain a clear understanding of the revolutionary class struggle of the exploited and oppressed against capitalism and for communism, and to make a firm commitment to this cause.
2.) After the victory of the proletarian revolution, to make them into collaborators in communist construction, imbued with deep understanding and a willingness to sacrifice.

The women's structures of the Communist Party must, in their activity, be aware that the spoken and written word is not the only means of agitation and education among the masses of women. Instead, the most important method, which must be fully considered and evaluated, is the collaboration of organised Communist women in every field of activity of the Communist parties – both in the struggle and also in construction. This entails the active participation of working women in all actions and struggles of the revolutionary proletariat, in strikes, street demonstrations, and armed uprisings, while in soviet countries working women must play an active part in all spheres of Communist construction.

## The Communist International and the Communist Youth Movement[56]

1.) The socialist youth movement arose under the pressure of heightened capitalist exploitation of worker youth and their utilisation by bourgeois militarism. The movement was a reaction to attempts at poisoning the worker youth with bourgeois and nationalist ideology. It responded to the neglect by Social-Democratic parties and trade unions in most countries of the economic, political, and cultural demands of worker youth.[57]

Most of the socialist youth organisations were created without assistance from and often against the will of the Social-Democratic parties and trade unions, which were becoming increasingly opportunist and reformist. The reformist Social-Democratic parties and trade unions saw the rise of independent revolutionary socialist youth organisations as a serious threat to their opportunist politics. They sought to place the movement under bureaucratic tutelage and destroy its independence, in order to oppress the movement, change its character, and bring it into line with their politics.

2.) The imperialist war and the response of Social-Democratic parties in most countries could only deepen the discord between the Social-Democratic parties and the international revolutionary youth organisations and drive them into open conflict. The conditions of worker youth deteriorated unbearably during the War because of conscription and war duties, heightened exploitation in war industries, and militarisation behind the front. The best layers of socialist youth took a stand against the War and nationalism. As a result, they broke away from the Social-Democratic parties and took their own political initiatives (international youth conferences in Bern 1915 and in Jena 1916).[58]

In their struggle against the War, the socialist youth organisations, supported by the best revolutionary groups among the adults, became points of assembly for revolutionary forces. Given the absence of revolutionary parties,

---

56. Discussed in Session 20. Approved in Session 24.
57. The international socialist youth movement was formed at a congress of socialist youth organisations in Stuttgart 24–26 August 1907, attended by 21 representatives from socialist youth organisations in 13 countries. The congress established the International Union of Socialist Youth Organisations (*Internationale Verbindung Sozialistischer Jugendorganisationen*, IVSJO) and elected Karl Liebknecht as its first president. The IVSJO fell apart in 1914 at the onset of the War, but was reconstituted in 1915 by left-wing forces led by Willi Münzenberg. See Riddell (ed.) 1984, p. 280–2. These forces went on to found the Communist Youth International in 1919.
58. For the 1915 Bern conference, see p. 770, n. 4.
The Jena Conference was an all-German youth conference, initiated by Karl Liebknecht, held 24–25 April 1916.

the youth organisations took over their functions, becoming politically independent organisations acting as a vanguard in the revolutionary struggle.

3.) When the Communist International was established, along with Communist parties in each country, this changed the role of the revolutionary youth organisation in the proletarian movement as a whole. Both their economic situation and their distinctive psychological profile make the worker youth more receptive to Communist ideas. They display greater enthusiasm in revolutionary struggle than the adult workers. But the role of vanguard, in the sense of independent political activity and leadership, is assumed by the Communist parties. If the Communist youth organisation continued to exist as a politically independent and leading organisation, this would result in the emergence of two Communist parties competing with each other, differing only in the age of their members.

4.) The present role of the Communist youth organisation consists of assembling the masses of young workers, educating them in a Communist spirit, and bringing them into the Communist front of struggle. The time has passed in which a Communist youth organisation could limit itself to the work of a numerically small propaganda circle. In order to win the broad masses of young workers, the Communist youth organisation carries out tenacious agitation, conducted with new methods, and also initiates and leads economic struggles.

In accordance with its new tasks, the Communist youth organisation must broaden and strengthen its educational work. The basis for Communist education in the Communist youth movement is active participation in all revolutionary struggles, which must be closely linked to Marxist training.

The Communist youth organisation has another important task in the coming period: to destroy centrist and social-patriotic ideology among worker youth and to break them away from the Social-Democratic leaders and guardians of youth. At the same time, the Communist youth organisation must do all in its power to promote the movement's rejuvenation, a process driven by its development into a mass movement, by passing on its older members to the Communist Party at a rapid pace.

The Communist youth organisations conduct animated discussion of all political problems, collaborate in building Communist parties, and participate vigorously in revolutionary struggles and actions. This is the main and fundamental difference between them and the centrist and social-patriotic youth leagues.

5.) The relationship of the Communist youth organisation to the Communist Party is fundamentally different from that of the revolutionary youth organisations to the Social-Democratic parties [before and during the War]. The common struggle to carry out rapidly the proletarian revolution requires strong unity and strict centralisation. Political leadership can be exerted only by the Communist International, at the international level, and its national sections in each country. The Communist youth organisation has the duty of subordinating itself to this political leadership, in terms of programme, tactics, and political instructions, and of integrating itself into the common revolutionary front.

There is considerable disparity in the level of revolutionary development among the Communist parties. It is therefore necessary, in exceptional cases, for the application of this principle to be guided by the Executive Committee of the Communist Youth International, taking into account the particular conditions in the relevant country. The Communist youth organisations have begun to organise their own forces according to the rules of strict centralisation. They will conduct themselves with iron discipline with regard to the Communist International, which is the main force and leader of proletarian revolution.

The Communist youth organisations must take up all political and tactical issues that arise within their ranks. They must work within the Communist Party of their country – and never against it – in the spirit of adopted decisions. In the event of a serious disagreement between the Communist Party and the Communist youth organisation, the latter has the right to appeal to the Executive Committee of the Communist International. In giving up its political independence, the youth organisation does not lose its organisational independence, which is indispensable for educational purposes.

Successful leadership of the revolutionary struggle requires the strongest possible centralisation and the greatest possible unity. For that reason, in countries where, as a result of historical development, the youth organisation is more dependent, this relationship will, as a rule, be maintained. If there are disagreements between the two organisations, this will be resolved by the Executive Committee of the Communist International together with the Executive Committee of the Communist Youth International.[59]

6.) One of the most immediate and important tasks of the Communist youth organisation is to vigorously clear away all remnants in its ranks of the ideology of its political leadership role, left over from the time when it was completely autonomous. The youth press and the entire organisational apparatus of the Communist youth organisation must be vigorously utilised to fully

---

59. This paragraph was added as an amendment to the draft text in Session 24.

imbue the youth with the feeling of being a soldier and responsible member of the one Communist Party.

The Communist youth organisation must devote all the more attention, time, and work to this task as it begins to win broader layers of young workers and become a mass movement.

7.) The close political collaboration of the Communist youth organisation with the Communist Party must also find expression in a firm connection between the two organisations. It is absolutely necessary for the party and youth organisations to establish ongoing reciprocal representation at the leadership, regional, district, and local level, right down to the Communist cells in factories and trade unions, and including strong reciprocal representation at all conferences and congresses. This will make it possible for the Communist Party constantly to influence the youth's political line and activity and to support the youth, while the youth, for their part, will be able to exert an effective influence in the party.

The relationship between the Communist Youth International and the Communist International will be even closer. The Communist Youth International's task is to provide centralised leadership of the Communist youth movement; to support and promote the individual affiliates morally and materially; to create new Communist youth organisations, where they do not exist; and to carry out international propaganda for the Communist youth movement and its programme.

The Communist Youth International is a component of the Communist International, and it therefore subordinates itself to the decisions of the Communist International congresses and its Executive Committee. This framework guides all the work of the Youth International, which passes on the Communist International's political will to all its sections. Efficient mutual representation and close, ongoing collaboration will assure that the Communist International can exercise constant supervision and that the Communist Youth International can develop fruitful work in every field of its activity – leadership, agitation, organisation, and the strengthening and support of Communist youth organisations.

# Forward to New Work and New Struggles[60]

*Appeal of the Executive Committee of the Communist International*

*To proletarian men and women of every country:*
The Third Congress of the Communist International is over. The great army of the world Communist proletariat has passed on review. This has shown that communism, in the course of the past year, has grown into a force able to move the masses and threaten capitalism in a number of countries where previously it was still in its beginnings. At its founding congress, the Communist International, outside of Russia, was made up only of small groups. At its Second Congress last year, it was still seeking the path that would lead to mass parties. Today, not only in Russia, but in Germany, Poland, Czechoslovakia, Italy, France, Norway, Yugoslavia, and Bulgaria, broad masses have rallied to the banner of its parties.

The Third Congress calls on Communists in every country to continue down this path and to make every effort to gather many more millions of working men and women in the ranks of the Communist International. The power of capitalism can be broken only if the idea of communism takes shape in the impetuous upsurge of the proletariat's large majority, led by mass Communist parties, which forge indissoluble ties to the fighting proletarian class. 'To the masses!' – that is the call to struggle that the Third Congress transmits to Communists around the world.

*Forward to new and great battles*

These masses are coming to us, flocking to us. World capitalism is showing them more and more clearly and obviously that it can eke out its existence only while it increasingly ruins the entire world, while imposing on the masses increasing chaos, hardship, and slavery. For years, the bourgeois class and the Social-Democratic lackeys of capitalism have cried out to the workers, 'Work! Work!' Now this cry is heard no more. The global economic crisis has thrown millions of workers onto the streets, and the *cry for work is now a fighting slogan of the working class*. And it will be achieved only on the ruins of capitalism, when the proletariat takes control of the means of production it has itself created.

---

60. The decision to prepare this manifesto was taken in Session 3. It was drafted by Trotsky and adopted after the congress by the ECCI.

The capitalist world stands on the edge of the abyss of war. The conflicts between the United States and Japan, Britain and the United States, Britain and France, France and Germany, Poland and Germany, the conflicts in the Near and Far East: all this is driving the capitalists to increased armaments. Alarmed, the capitalists face the question, 'Is Europe once again taking the path to world war?' It is not the prospect of the slaughter of millions that frightens them. Even after the War, through their blockade of Russia, they cold-bloodedly delivered over millions of people to death by starvation. What they fear is that a new war would drive the masses once and for all into the arms of world revolution, that this war would bring the final uprising of the world proletariat.

Just as before the World War, they are trying to bring about an easing of tensions through diplomatic manoeuvres. But moves to decrease tensions at one point only increase them at another. The negotiations between Britain and the United States on restricting the two countries' naval armaments necessarily align them against Japan. The French-British rapprochement delivers Germany over to France, while handing Turkey to the British. The efforts by world capitalism to create some kind of order amidst growing world chaos results not in peace but growing unrest, growing enslavement of the defeated peoples by the victorious capitalists.

World capitalism's newspapers now speak of global political détente and calm, because the German bourgeoisie has submitted to the Allies' ultimatum and, in order to preserve its power, has delivered the German people over to the hyenas of the Paris and London stock markets. But the financial press is also full of reports of mounting economic collapse in Germany, of the unheard-of taxes that will rain down this autumn on the masses, already beset by unemployment, making every bit of food and every scrap of clothing enormously more expensive.

The Communist International bases its policies on a calm and objective examination of the world situation. Only by carefully observing the field of battle, only through sober understanding, can the proletariat achieve victory. In this spirit, the Communist International tells proletarians around the world that capitalism has so far shown itself to be incapable of providing the world with even the degree of stability that existed before the last war. For what it is doing now cannot bring consolidation or stability; it can only prolong your suffering and prolong capitalism's death agony. The world revolution is marching forward. Everywhere the foundations of world capitalism are trembling. The second call that the World Congress of the Communist International addresses to proletarians around the world is: 'We are moving toward new, great struggles! Prepare for new battles!'

*Build the united fighting front of the proletariat*

The world bourgeoisie is incapable of guaranteeing that workers receive jobs, bread, housing, and clothing, but it displays great capacity in organising war against the world proletariat. It has overcome its initial and deep disorientation and its deep fear of the workers returning from war. It has succeeded in herding them back once more into the factories and has suppressed their initial uprisings. It has been able to prolong its alliance with the Social-Democratic and trade-union leaders, who betrayed the workers and thus split the proletariat. It has bent every effort to organise White Guard contingents against the workers and to disarm the proletariat.

Armed to the teeth, the world bourgeoisie stands ready not only to beat back every proletarian uprising, arms in hand, but when necessary to provoke premature uprisings, when the proletariat is still preparing for struggle, and crush them, before the proletariat has established a united and invincible fighting front. Against this strategy of the world bourgeoisie, the Communist International must counterpose its own strategy. In opposing the moneybags of capitalism, who goad their armed bandits against the organised proletariat, the Communist International has an unfailing weapon: the mass of proletarians joined in a single unified front.

If millions and millions move into struggle, with ranks closed, the bourgeoisie's tricks will fail and its violence will be impotent. The railway trains on which the bourgeoisie wishes to send its White Guard troops against the proletariat will stop rolling. Portions of the White Guard will be gripped by panic. The proletariat will seize their weapons and use them to fight against other White Guard formations. If the proletariat succeeds in entering struggle in unity, capitalism and the world bourgeoisie lose the most important precondition for struggle, namely their hope of victory – which they have only regained thanks to the betrayal by Social Democracy and the splintering of the working masses. The road to victory over world capitalism passes through winning over the hearts of the working-class majority.

The Third World Congress of the Communist International calls on Communist parties in every country and Communists in the trade unions to apply all their strength to freeing the broad working masses from the influence of the Social-Democratic parties and the traitors of the trade-union bureaucracy. In this difficult time, in which each day brings the working masses new hardships, such a goal can be achieved only if Communists in every country show that they are vanguard fighters for the everyday needs of the working class. They must lead the struggle to lighten the increasingly unbearable burdens that capitalism loads on the backs of the working masses. The task is to show the greatest possible number of workers that only the Communists are struggling to improve their conditions, while the Social Democrats and the reactionary trade-union bureaucrats, rather than take up the struggle, are quite willing to see the proletarians die of hunger.

The betrayers of the proletariat and the agents of the bourgeoisie will not be defeated through theoretical debates about democracy and dictatorship. Rather, they will be defeated by taking up the questions of bread, of wages, of the workers' clothing and the workers' housing. And the first and most important field of struggle in which they must be defeated is that of the trade-union movement, in the struggle against the Amsterdam trade-union International and for the red trade-union International. This is a struggle to seize the enemy fortresses planted in our own camp. It is a struggle to form a front of struggle against which world capitalism can only fail. Keep your organisations free from centrist currents and build their will to struggle!

Only in the struggle for the most basic essentials of life of the working masses can we establish the unified front of the proletariat against the bourgeoisie and end the splintering of the proletariat, which alone enables the bourgeoisie to continue to exist. But this proletarian front will be strong and militant only if it is held together by Communist parties, unified and strong in spirit and iron in their discipline. The Third World Congress of the Communist International turns to Communists everywhere with the call, 'To the masses!' and 'Establish the unified proletarian front!' But at the same time it also tells them, 'Keep your ranks free from forces capable of disrupting the militant spirit and discipline of the world proletariat's shock troops, the Communist parties.'

The congress of the Communist International approves the expulsion of the Socialist Party of Italy until such a time as it breaks with the reformists and expels them from its ranks. In this decision, the congress expresses its conviction that in order to lead millions and millions of workers into battle, the Communist International must free its ranks from reformists, whose goal is not a victorious proletarian revolution but reconciliation with capitalism and its reform. Armies that tolerate leaders seeking reconciliation with their opponents will be betrayed and sold out to the enemy.

The Communist International also turned its attention to the fact that a number of parties that have expelled the reformists still contain currents that have not definitively overcome reformism's spirit. If they are not seeking reconciliation with the enemy, nonetheless these currents' agitation and propaganda does not prepare the struggle against capitalism energetically enough. They do not pursue with sufficient vigour and determination the work of winning the masses to revolution. Parties that are not capable in their daily activity of breathing the revolutionary spirit of the masses, of working with passion to strengthen the will to struggle of the impetuous masses – such parties will let favourable opportunities for struggle pass them by. They will allow spontaneous proletarian struggles to fizzle out, as was the case with the factory occupations in Italy and the December strike in Czechoslovakia.

The Communist parties must develop a fighting spirit. They must train themselves to be a staff capable of quickly assessing favourable situations for struggle. When there is a spontaneous movement of the proletariat, their prudent and courageous leadership of the struggle must gain every particle of advantage that is to be gained. 'Be the vanguard of the working masses moving into struggle; be their heart and their brain!' That is the call of the Communist International's Third Congress to the Communist parties. Being a vanguard means marching at the head of the masses, as their bravest, most far-sighted, and most level-headed component. Building such a vanguard is the only way these parties can be capable of establishing the proletariat's unified front and, what is more, leading it to victory over the enemy.

*Counterpose the strategy of the proletariat to the strategy of capitalism; prepare your struggles!*

The enemy is strong because he has ruled for centuries, and this has bred in him an awareness of his power and a determination to retain it. The enemy is strong because he has learned over centuries how to split the proletarian masses, hold them down, and vanquish them. The enemy knows how to wage civil war victoriously. The Third World Congress of the Communist International therefore warns Communist parties everywhere to *keep in mind the danger lodged in the fully developed strategy of the ruling and possessing class and the deficient, still only emerging strategy of the working class struggling for power.*

The March events in Germany revealed a great danger: that the front ranks of the working class, the Communist vanguard of the proletariat, may be forced by the enemy into battle before the broad masses of proletarians have mobilised. The Communist International rejoiced that hundreds of thousands of workers across all of Germany, indeed, around the world, hurried to assist the Central German workers who were under attack. For the Communist International, the spirit of solidarity displayed in the uprising of proletarians across the country represents the path to victory. The Communist International welcomed the fact that the United Communist Party of Germany took the leadership of the working masses who rushed to defend their endangered brothers.

But the Communist International also has the duty to tell workers everywhere frankly and emphatically: *even when the vanguard is not in a position to* avoid a struggle, and this struggle has the potential to hasten the mobilisation of the entire working class, the vanguard must still not forget that it must not be drawn into any decisive struggle when it is alone and isolated. When the vanguard of the proletarian army is forced into battle in isolation, it must avoid an armed confrontation with the enemy. For only the masses can enable the proletariat to triumph over the armed White Guards. If the overwhelming majority does not mobilise, the vanguard must not confront the armed foe as an unarmed minority.

The March struggles also offer us another lesson that the Communist International brings to the attention of the world proletariat. The broad masses of workers must be prepared for the coming struggles through ongoing, increasingly intense, and extensive daily revolutionary agitation. Struggles must be begun with slogans that the broad masses of proletarians can grasp and understand. Against the strategy of the enemy, we must counterpose a superior and intelligent strategy of the proletariat. The vanguard's will to struggle, courage, and determination is not enough. The struggle must be prepared and organised in a fashion that engages the broad masses. They must see it as a struggle for their vital interests and mobilise for it.

As world capitalism becomes more and more imperilled, it will increasingly seek to thwart the future victory of the Communist International by striking at its front ranks without engaging the broad masses. This dangerous plan must be countered by comprehensive agitation by the Communist parties to arouse the masses, energetic organisational work to consolidate their influence on the broad masses, and sober evaluation of the field of battle. This enables us to adopt effective tactics: avoiding battle when the enemy forces are superior and attacking when the enemy is divided and the masses are united.

The Third World Congress of the Communist International is well aware that only experience in the struggle will enable the working class to develop Communist parties capable of attacking the enemy with lightning speed, when he is vulnerable, and evading him, when he has the upper hand. That is why proletarians everywhere have to gather all the lessons learned at great cost by the working class in each country, studying and making good use of these lessons internationally.

*Maintain discipline in struggle*

*The working class and the Communist parties of every country must prepare not for a period of quiet agitation and organisation but for major struggles that capitalism will impose on the proletariat, aiming to defeat workers and burden them with all the costs of capitalist policies.* In this struggle, the Communist parties must develop strict discipline in struggle. Their party leaderships must soberly and thoughtfully weigh the lessons of struggle, carefully survey the field of battle, and unite bold plans with cold calculation. They must forge their tactical plans for battle through intellectual labour by the entire party, taking into account criticisms from the membership. But all party units must unhesitatingly carry out the line of the party. Every word and deed of every party unit must be directed to this goal. The parliamentary fractions, the party's publications, and the party's organisations must unwaveringly carry out the orders of the party leadership.

The world review of the Communist vanguard is over. It has shown that communism is a world force. It has shown that the Communist International still has to form and build great proletarian armies. It has shown that great battles await these armies, and that we intend to triumph in these battles. It has shown the world proletariat how to prepare for victory and how to achieve it.

It is now the task of Communist parties in all countries to enable these decisions, representing the experiences of the world proletariat, to become the common understanding of Communists everywhere, so that Communist proletarian men and women can be effective as leaders of hundreds of thousands of non-Communist proletarians in the coming struggles.

Long live the Communist International!

Long live the world revolution!

Onward to the work of preparing and organising our victory!

The Executive of the Communist International: Germany: *Heckert, Frölich.* France: *Souvarine.* Czechoslovakia: *Burian, Kreibich.* Italy: *Terracini, Gennari.* Russia: *Zinoviev, Bukharin, Radek, Lenin, Trotsky.* Ukraine: *Shumsky.* Poland: *Warski.* Bulgaria: *Popov.* Yugoslavia: *Marković.* Norway: *Schefflo.* Britain: *Bell.* United States: *Baldwin.* Spain: *Merino-Gracia.* Finland: *Sirola.* Netherlands: *Jansen.* Belgium: *van Overstraeten.* Sweden: *Kilbom.* Latvia: *Stuchka.* Switzerland: *Arnold.* Austria: *Koritschoner.* Hungary: *Béla Kun.*

The Executive of the Youth International: *Münzenberg, Lékai.*

Moscow, 17 July 1921.

# Addendum: Amendments to Theses on Tactics and Strategy (Not Approved)

*Editor's note: The pages that follow compare proposed amendments to the Theses on Tactics and Strategy with passages in the Theses text that they aimed to modify or replace. The adopted text is in the left-hand column; the amendments are on the right. The passages that the amendments proposed to delete from the text are indicated by words crossed out in the left-hand column.*

*The text of the adopted theses has been abridged to show only paragraphs to which the amendments apply. For the full text of the Theses on Tactics and Strategy, see pp. 924–50. For background to the amendments, see the Editorial Introduction, pp. 33–9. The amendments are translated from the French text in* Moscou, 5 July.

*The amendments, submitted by the German, Austrian, and Italian delegations, were presented to the congress by Terracini (see pp. 457–65). In their speeches to the congress in sessions 11 and 14, Lenin and Trotsky each rejected the amendments as a counterposed political line. The congress adopted the general line of the draft theses as submitted and referred them, together with the amendments, to the commission on tactics and strategy for final editing (see p. 598) The commission adopted only one of the amendments' proposals (see pp. 801 and 1052). The amendments' sponsors then withdrew their other proposals and joined in supporting the commission's revised text of the theses.*

*Two brief amendments (points 10 and 21 in the* Moscou *text) have been omitted from this comparison; the first does not correspond to any identifiable passage in the final text; the second merely signals an editorial slip in the original.*

## Theses as Adopted

1.) *Definition of the question*...
This definition, set down in the Statutes of the Communist International, *encompasses all the questions of tactics and strategy* that are posed for solution, questions relating to our struggle for the proletarian dictatorship. They relate to how we win ~~the majority of~~ the working class to the ~~principles~~ of communism and how we organise the socially decisive layers of the proletariat for the struggle to achieve them....

The question of the dictatorship itself, as the only road to victory, is

## Proposed Amendments

[*Delete*]
[*Substitute*] goals

not part of this discussion. The developing world revolution has shown plainly that there is only one alternative in the present situation: capitalist or proletarian dictatorship. The Third Congress of the Communist International undertakes its review of tactical questions at a time when the objective conditions are ripe for revolution. A number of mass Communist parties have been formed, but there is not yet a single country in which they have actual leadership ~~of the majority~~ of the working class in genuinely revolutionary struggle.... [Delete]

3.) *The most important present task...*
German communism was able to develop from a political current at the time of the January and March struggles of 1919 to a large revolutionary mass party thanks to the Communist International's tactics and strategy: revolutionary work in the trade unions~~, Open Letter, and so on~~. The [Delete] party has won such influence in the trade unions that the union bureaucracy ~~has taken fright at the revolutionary impact of Communist work there. It has expelled many Communists from the unions, taking on itself the odium of splitting the movement.~~ [Substitute] for fear of the revolutionary impact of Communist work there, will expel many Communists from the unions and will have to take on itself the odium of splitting the movement.
....

4.) *The situation in the Communist International*
~~The Communist International is on the road to forming mass Communist parties, but it is far from having gone far enough. Indeed, in two of the~~ [Substitute] Many of the Communist parties have not gone far enough along the road to forming mass parties. On the other hand, forming

~~most important countries of capitalist triumph, the work has hardly been begun.~~ mass Communist parties has become the touchstone for open centrists and semi-centrists who have been forced by mass pressure to enter the Communist International.

In Italy, during the struggle to assert Communist policies, the Serrati group revealed itself to be, in reality, a centrist group for whom a break with the reformists was far more painful than a break with the Communist International. Committed to forming mass parties that are revolutionary and not opportunist, the Communist International preferred breaking for a time with the working masses of Italy who have not yet shed their reformist illusions, until the Serrati group has been exposed. At that point, these forces, aided by the example of the Italian Communist Party, will become Communist, genuinely conscious, and combative.

This policy of the Communist International Executive Committee will assist in the discovery of centrist and semi-centrist tendencies in other mass Communist parties. Once these currents realise that the Communist International intends to form only genuinely revolutionary mass parties, they declare war against the International's degeneration, claiming that it has become sectarian. This has been done by the Levi group in Germany and, to a certain degree, by the Šmeral group in Czechoslovakia. These currents reveal their nature openly and clearly. They are centrist and semi-centrist currents representing political dilution. They do not want the class struggle to become sharper. They limit themselves to agitation and propaganda. They are incapable of linking up with the militant wing of the proletariat. They represent the centrist tendency to political passivity.

The Communist International will support revolutionary workers everywhere in their struggle against efforts to dilute the revolutionary tactics and strategy as they have been developed by the Communist congresses. In this way, it will achieve its goal of forming revolutionary mass parties.

Wherever groups of opportunist leaders are constantly striving to prevent the party and its press from assisting in revolutionary mass mobilisations; wherever they attempt to hold back these masses from making revolutionary gains; wherever parliamentary fractions and trade-union and party bureaucracies or party journalists do not submit to the decisions of the party and its Central Committee: in all these cases the Communist International believes the Communist parties must take a categorical stand against these forces. Every effort by revolutionary workers to discipline and gain authority over their leaders will enjoy the official support of the Communist International.'

[*Insert*] In two of the most important victorious capitalist countries, the work of forming mass Communist parties has barely begun.

In the *United States of North America*, a broad revolutionary movement was lacking before the War, for historical reasons.....

....

The mass Communist parties of Central and Western Europe are in the process of developing the appropriate methods of revolutionary agitation and propaganda and the organisational methods suitable to their character as organisations of struggle. They are making the transition from Communist propaganda and agitation to action. This process is hindered by the fact that, in several countries, the workers embraced revolution and came to communism under the direction of leaders who had not overcome centrist tendencies. They are not capable of carrying out genuinely Communist popular agitation and propaganda and may even fear it, knowing that it will lead the parties into revolutionary struggles.

[*Insert*] In times of action, given the centrist nature of the leadership bodies, the Communist parties did not attempt to take in hand the leadership of the mass action and were weighed down with the burden of centrist and semi-centrist forces (Serrati, Levi).

In *Italy*, these centrist tendencies brought about a split in the party....

In *France*, the chauvinist poison of 'national defence' and the subsequent intoxication of victory were stronger than in any other country. Opposition to the War developed more slowly than in other countries.

Thanks to the moral influence of the Russian Revolution, the revolutionary struggles in the capitalist countries, and the experiences of the French proletariat betrayed by its leaders, the majority of the French Socialist Party evolved in a Communist direction, even before the course of events placed it before the decisive challenges of revolutionary action. The French Communist Party can utilise this situation all the better and more fully to the degree that it does away with the excessively strong remnants in its own ranks – especially in its leadership – of national-pacifist and parliamentary-reformist ideology.

[*Insert*] Leftovers of national-pacifist and reformist ideology were particularly evident during the reparations crisis, when the predatory claims of French financial capital were presented as the claims of justice.

When French troops occupied Luxembourg, disbanding the workers' councils in this country, the French Communist Party failed even to carry out vigorous propaganda. When the class of 1919 was called up, the party did not adequately utilise this situation as the signal for revolutionary propaganda and demonstrations. The Communist parliamentary fraction permitted its spokesperson to advocate an Anglo-French entente, that is, an alliance between predatory imperialism in each of these countries.

# Amendments on Tactics and Strategy • 1047

The most advanced forces within the parties and trade unions must consciously demand that the party undergo a process of freeing itself from centrist and semi-centrist currents, as well as making progress toward activation.

To a greater extent than now and in the past, the party must move closer to the most oppressed layers in the cities and the countryside, giving full expression to their sufferings and needs....

~~Impatient and politically inexperienced revolutionary forces attempt to apply extreme methods – more appropriate to a decisive revolutionary proletarian uprising – to individual issues and tasks, such as the proposal to appeal to conscripts in the army's class of 1919 to resist the military call-up. If put into practice, such methods set back for a long time genuine revolutionary preparation of the proletariat for winning power.~~

~~The Communist Party of France, like the parties in other countries, has the task of rejecting these extremely dangerous methods. However, this absolutely must not lead the party into inactivity; quite the contrary.~~

[*Substitute*] Impatient and politically inexperienced revolutionary forces attempt to apply the technique of a decisive revolutionary insurrection in conditions that are insufficiently developed. They call, first of all, for heightened revolutionary propaganda, demonstrations, and partial actions. Such tendencies will be readily overcome if the party as a whole is capable of fully utilising all the given opportunities to the maximum.

The party must be imbued with clarity and revolutionary activity in order to prevent mass actions from overshooting this mark and to facilitate close attention to the relationship of forces.

Strengthening the party's links with the masses requires above all closer ties to the trade unions. The party's task is not to subordinate the trade unions mechanically and superficially or to deny them the autonomy necessitated by the character of their work. Rather the task is to give direction to the work of truly revolutionary forces unified and led by the Communist Party within the unions, along lines that express the broad interests of a proletariat struggling to win power....

In *Czechoslovakia* the working masses have shaken off in two and a half years most reformist and nationalist illusions. In September 1920, the majority of Social-Democratic workers separated from their reformist leaders. In December, about a million of Czechoslovakia's three and a half million industrial workers took part in a revolutionary mass action against the Czechoslovak capitalist government. The Czechoslovak Communist Party was formed this past May with 350,000 members, alongside the Communist Party of German Bohemia [Sudentenland], which had been formed earlier and has 60,000 members. The Communists thus make up a large segment not only of the Czechoslovak proletariat but also of its population as a whole.

~~The Czechoslovak party now faces the task of attracting broader masses of workers through truly Communist agitation. It must also train its members, both longstanding and newly won, through effective and unremitting Communist propaganda. It must unite the workers of all nations within Czechoslovakia in a solid proletarian front against nationalism, the main weapon of the bourgeoisie in Czechoslovakia. It must strengthen the proletariat's power, created through this process, during all coming struggles~~ [*Substitute*] The Czechoslovak party now faces the challenge of transforming the working masses within its ranks, through propaganda and education, into fully conscious Communists. Through truly Communist action and participation in the pending struggles against capitalist oppression, it must attract broader and broader masses of workers. It must unify workers of every nationality in Czechoslovakia in order to create a united proletarian front against nationalism, which is a bastion of

~~against government and capitalist oppression, and convert this strength into an invincible power.~~

The Communist Party of Czechoslovakia will accomplish these tasks all the more quickly if it overcomes centrist traditions and hesitations....

*The United Communist Party of Germany* was formed from the fusion of the Spartacus League with the working masses of the Independent [USPD] left wing. Although already a mass party, it faces the major task of increasing and strengthening its influence on the broad masses; winning the proletarian mass organisations, the trade unions; breaking the hold of the Social-Democratic party and trade-union bureaucracy; ~~and taking the leadership of the proletariat in the mass struggles to come.~~ This central task requires orienting all agitational and organisational work toward winning the support of the working-class majority, without which, given the power of German capitalism, no victory of communism in Germany is possible.

The party has not yet succeeded in this task, with regard either to the scope or the content of its agitation. ~~It has also failed to consistently follow the path it had blazed through the Open Letter, which counterposed the practical interests of the proletariat to the traitorous policy of the Social-Democratic parties and the trade-union bureaucracy.~~ The party's

bourgeois influence in this country. It must vigorously support the proletarian power created in this fashion in struggle against capitalism and against the bourgeois government.

[*Replace*] and pointing the way for the mass movements in coming proletarian battles.

[*Add after 'majority'*] for the goals of communism.

[*Substitute*] It has not yet found a way to make the transition from propaganda, initiated by the Open Letter, to winning the working masses attracted by Open Letter propaganda to the Communist Party and involving them in partial struggles.

press and organisation is still too marked by the stamp of an association, not an organisation of struggle, expressing centrist tendencies that have not yet been fully overcome. These tendencies led the party, when faced with the requirements of struggle, to jump in too precipitously and without sufficient preparation, ~~and to neglect the need for vital contact with the non-Communist masses. The disintegration of Germany's economy and the capitalist offensive against workers' living standards will soon confront the VKPD with tasks of struggle that cannot be resolved if the party counterposes tasks of agitation and organisation to those of action. The party must keep the spirit of struggle in its ranks always at the ready, while shaping its agitation in a truly popular fashion and building its organisation in such a manner that, through its ties with the masses, it develops the capacity to carefully evaluate challenges to struggle and to carefully prepare for action.~~

[*Substitute*]...and, reacting against the centrist tendency to merge into the masses' state of mind, to neglect the party's role in leading the masses and to give insufficient attention to the need for vital contact with the non-Communist masses.

The disintegration of Germany's economy and the offensive of national and foreign capital against workers' living standards will soon confront the VKPD with tasks of struggle that cannot be resolved unless the party – far from counterposing tasks of agitation and organisation to those of action – maintains the spirit of struggle in its ranks always at the ready, while shaping its agitation in a truly popular fashion, and, through its ties with the masses, it develops in them the capacity to make use of openings for struggle, after careful preparations and assessment of the situation.

The parties of the Communist International will become mass revolutionary parties only when they overcome the remnants and traditions of opportunism in its ranks....

5.) *Partial struggles and partial demands*....

The task, by contrast, is to take all the masses' interests as the starting point for revolutionary struggles that only in their unity form the mighty river of revolution.

[*Insert*] This attitude of the centrists and reformists is also evident in the way they conduct actions. When a partial action takes place, they limit its goal in advance. When there is an explosion of action, they seek to block its extension to broader layers of the proletariat (British miners' strike) and to bring it to an end as quickly as possible through a compromise (German railway workers in December 1920–January 1921).

The Communist parties do not propose a minimum programme for these struggles, one designed to reinforce and improve the rickety structure of capitalism. Instead, destruction of this structure remains their guiding goal and their immediate task. But to achieve this task, the Communist parties have to advance demands whose achievement meets an immediate, urgent need of the working class, and fight for these demands regardless of whether they are compatible with the capitalist profit system....

In place of the minimum programme of the centrists and reformists, the Communist International offers a struggle for the specific demands of the proletariat, as part of a system of demands that, in their totality, undermine the power of the bourgeoisie, organise the proletariat, and mark out the different stages of the struggle for proletarian dictatorship. Each of these demands gives

[*Substitute*]...demolish the bourgeoisie's power, organise the proletariat, and pose the transitional measures between a capitalist and a communist economy. Giving expression to the hopes of the broad masses,

~~expression to the needs of the broad masses, even when they do not yet consciously take a stand for proletarian dictatorship.~~ they mobilise them step by step for the proletarian dictatorship, even if these masses are not yet consciously in favour of this dictatorship.

The struggle for these demands to meet the masses' essentials of life needs to embrace and mobilise broader and broader numbers. It must be counterposed to defence of the essentials of life for capitalist society. To the extent that this is done, the working class will become aware that for it to live, capitalism must die. This awareness provides the basis for a determination to struggle for [proletarian] dictatorship. Communist parties have the task of broadening, deepening, and unifying the struggles that develop around such specific demands.

Every partial action undertaken by the working masses in order to achieve a partial demand, every significant economic strike, mobilises the entire bourgeoisie, which comes down as a class on the side of the threatened group of employers, aiming to render impossible even a limited victory by the proletariat ('Emergency Technical Assistance', bourgeois strikebreakers in the British railway workers' strike, Fascists). The bourgeoisie mobilises the entire state apparatus for the struggle against the workers (militarisation of the workers in France and Poland, state of emergency during the miners' strike in Britain). The workers who are struggling for partial demands will be automatically forced into a

[*Adopted amendment*: The entire paragraph beginning 'Every partial action...' originated as one of the points in the amendments to the Theses on Tactics and Strategy – the only significant point that was adopted. There was one change by the Congress: the word 'immediately' was deleted before 'mobilises the entire bourgeoisie'.]

struggle against the bourgeoisie as a whole and its state apparatus.

To the extent that struggles for partial demands and partial struggles by specific groups of workers broaden into an overall working-class struggle against capitalism,....

*7.) The lessons of the March Action*

The March Action was forced on the VKPD by the government's attack on the proletariat of Central Germany.

~~In this, the VKPD's first great struggle since its foundation, the party made a number of errors. The most serious of these was that it did not clearly stress the defensive character of the struggle. Instead, its call for an offensive was utilised by the unscrupulous enemies of the proletariat – the bourgeoisie, the SPD, and the USPD – to denounce the VKPD to the proletariat for instigating a putsch. This error was compounded by a number of party members who contended that, under present conditions, the offensive represented the VKPD's main method of struggle. The party opposed this error in its newspapers and through its chair, Comrade Brandler.~~

[*Substitute*] The VKPD engaged courageously in action to defend the workers and repulse the initial action of the German bourgeoisie. Its goal was to open the road to clarifying the war reparations issue more effectively to the entire German working class. In this way, it showed that it is a combat party of the first order for the German revolution.

The Third Congress of the Communist International considers that the March Action was a step forward. ~~The March Action was a heroic struggle by hundreds of thousands of proletarians against the bourgeoisie. And by courageously taking the lead in the defence of the workers of~~

[*Substitute*] The strongest mass party of Central Europe made the transition to effective struggle. It marked an initial attempt by the Communist Party to achieve a leading role in

~~Central Germany, the VKPD showed that it is the party of Germany's revolutionary proletariat. The congress believes that the VKPD will be all the more successful in carrying out mass actions if, in the future, it better adapts its slogans for the struggle to actual conditions, studies these conditions closely, and carries out the actions in unified fashion.~~

~~In order to carefully weigh the possibilities for struggle, the VKPD needs to take into account the facts and considerations that point to the difficulties of a proposed action and work out carefully how they may be countered. But once the party leadership has decided on an action, all comrades must abide by the party's decisions and carry out this action. Criticism of an action should be voiced only after it has concluded, and then only within the party structures and in its newspapers, and after taking into consideration the party's situation in relationship to the class enemy. Since Levi disregarded these self-evident requirements of party discipline and conditions for criticism of the party, the congress approves his expulsion from the party and considers any political collaboration with him by members of the Communist International to be impermissible.~~

the struggles of the German proletariat, a role which the party identified in its initial programme. The March Action exposed and defeated the Independent party [USPD] and the centrist forces hidden within the VKPD itself, exposing their plainly counterrevolutionary character.

The March Action made it possible to identify clearly the many errors committed in the March Action and the deficiencies in the party organisation, and enabled the party to take measures for their elimination. The March Action revealed a lack of discipline in the combat party and contributed to firming up this discipline. The March Action attracted working masses still affiliated with the Social Democrats and created a revolutionary ferment within these parties. Far from shaking the party's structures, the March Action strengthened its fighting spirit.

In this, the first major, sustained struggle since its foundation, the VKPD committed a series of errors. One of these was its failure to denounce with sufficient clarity the provocative nature of the attack by the bourgeoisie and its servants. The party did not stress strongly enough that the March Action did not result from a decision by the party to move into action but was rather sparked by Hörsing's offensive against Central Germany. The theory of the offensive advanced after the March Action is not valid.

In the March Action, the party sought to move from the defensive to an offensive. The error in this was that the goal of the struggle was not closely enough tied to the course of the movement. A number of leaders of the party conducted themselves in centrist fashion, with the result that the party's preparation for a defensive struggle was inadequate in terms of agitation and propaganda.

The Third Congress of the Communist International considers that the VKPD can carry out actions with greater success if a will to struggle and strict discipline prevail in every sector of the party. The party needs to align its slogans effectively with the real situation, conduct its actions methodically, establish close ties with the masses, and display the greatest possible unity and flexibility.

In order to gain an accurate estimate of the potential for struggle, the VKPD needs to listen attentively to opinions pointing out the difficulties that an action will encounter and to those giving significant reasons for engaging in it. But as soon as the party's leading bodies have decided to launch an action, all comrades must accept this decision and commit all their energy to carrying it out. The party is obliged to oppose categorically all those who actively or passively sabotage the action while it is under way, removing them from their posts or expelling them, depending on the circumstances. Criticism of the action cannot begin until after it is over. It can take place only within the framework of party discipline. It must take into account the conditions the party faces with regard to its class enemies.

Levi defied these natural requirements of party discipline and these conditions for criticism within the party. He sabotaged the struggle, making common cause with the Social Democrats and centrists and committing betrayal while the struggle was raging. When the struggle was over, he openly took the side of the party's bitter enemies, directly providing the reactionary courts with evidence for the prosecution against victims of the struggle. The Congress therefore approves his expulsion from the party for gross violation of discipline and betrayal. The Congress considers any political collaboration with him by members of the Communist International as incompatible with membership in the International. The conduct of Levi and a group of his friends obstructed carrying out a retreat in good order and consolidating its ranks for struggle. The Third Congress of the Communist International requires that criticism of actions and of the party's leading bodies take place only within the organisation.

8.) *Forms and methods of direct struggle…*

In the proletarian struggle against the capitalist offensive, it is the duty of Communists to march in the forefront and promote understanding of the basic revolutionary tasks among those in struggle. In addition, Communists are obliged to rally the best and most active forces ~~in the factories and trade unions~~ to create their own workers' contingents and defence organisations in order to resist the Fascists and deter the *jeunesse dorée* [gilded youth] of the bourgeoisie from harassing strikers....

[*Substitute*] of the factories and trade unions

9.) *Relations with the proletarian middle layers...*

Winning the small peasantry to the ideas of communism, plus winning and organising the agricultural workers, are among the most important preconditions for the victory of proletarian dictatorship. These tasks enable the revolution to extend out from the industrial centres into the countryside and create bases from which to resolve the question of food – ~~a life-and-death challenge~~ for the revolution.

[*Substitute*] a vital issue

Winning over substantial layers of the commercial and technical employees, the lower and middle civil servants~~, and intellectuals~~ would make it much easier for the proletarian dictatorship to master the technical and organisational challenge of ~~economic and government administration~~ during the transition from capitalism to communism. This can sow discord in the ranks of the enemy and break through the isolation of the proletariat in the eyes of public opinion....

[*Delete*]

[*Substitute*] economic life and government administration

10.) *Coordinating action internationally...*

The Third Congress of the Communist International welcomes the demonstrations by the *French Communists* as a start toward ~~escalating their campaign~~ against the role of French capitalism as a counterrevolutionary exploiter. The congress reminds them of their duty to explain energetically to French soldiers in the occupied territories their role as thugs of French capitalism and encourage them to resist the shameful duties assigned to them....

[*Substitute*] a serious campaign

# Appendices

# Appendix 1
# Before the Congress: The Open Letter

### 1a. Open Letter to German Workers' Organisations[1]

8 January 1921

*To the General German Trade Union Federation [ADGB], the Free Association of Employees, the General Workers' Union, the Free Workers' Union (Syndicalists), the Social-Democratic Party of Germany, the Independent Social-Democratic Party of Germany, the Communist Workers' Party of Germany:*

At a moment so crucial and difficult for the entire German proletariat, the United Communist Party of Germany believes it has the duty to address all socialist parties and trade unions.

Capitalism is progressively disintegrating. Its incipient world crisis is feeding into the national crisis in Germany. The currency is devaluating more and more. Prices for foodstuffs and the necessities of life are escalating. Unemployment is rising and the broad masses are increasingly impoverished.

All these factors make it essential that the proletarian class defend itself as a whole – not just industrial workers but all layers, even those only now awakening and becoming aware of their proletarian character.

---

1. Published in *Die Rote Fahne*, 8 January 1921; the drafters appear to have been Paul Levi and Karl Radek.

Under these unbearable conditions, the proletariat is gripped by escalating reaction, expressed by the Orgesch, by cowardly assassinations, and by the judicial system that covers up for every murder. Reaction counts on the fact that proletarians are disunited, while loading them down with more and more chains.

The VKPD therefore proposes to all socialist parties and trade unions that they come together in action on the following points, proposed as a basis for individual and detailed discussion.

1a.) Begin unified struggles for higher wages, in order to secure the existence of workers, employees, and public servants. Draw together the scattered wage struggles of railway workers, public servants, and miners, along with those of workers in other industries and agricultural workers, into a concerted mobilisation.

b.) Raise all payments to victims of the War and pensioners in line with the demanded wage increases.

c.) Grant the unemployed across the whole country uniform payments, aligned with the income of those with full-time jobs. These payments, made by the state, should be covered entirely by drawing on capitalist property. Special commissions of the unemployed, working together with the trade unions, should supervise care of the unemployed.

2.) *Measures to reduce living costs, such as:*

a.) Distribute foodstuffs at reduced prices to all wage earners and those with low incomes (pensioners, recipients of aid to widows and orphans, etc.). The state will be responsible to gather the resources for distribution by cooperatives under trade-union and factory-council supervision.

b.) Confiscate immediately all available habitable spaces. This includes not only obligatory accommodation of the homeless but also obligatory eviction of small-sized families occupying oversized apartments or entire large houses.

3.) *Measures to ensure the supply of foodstuffs and the essentials of life:*

a.) Supervision of all available raw materials, coal, and fertilisers by factory councils. Restart production in shut-down consumer-goods factories and distribute the products along the lines of point 2a.

b.) Supervision by councils of estate workers and small peasants, in collaboration with farmworkers' unions, of planting and tilling the soil, harvesting, and the sale of the harvest.

4a.) Immediate disarmament and disbandment of bourgeois militias and formation of proletarian defence organisations in every region and community.

b.) Amnesty for all infractions committed for political reasons or because of the prevailing generalised destitution. Free all political prisoners.
c.) Cancel existing bans against strikes.
d.) Establish diplomatic and trade relations with Soviet Russia immediately.

In proposing this as a basis for action, we do not for a moment delude ourselves or the working masses into thinking that the proposed demands can eliminate their poverty. We do not for a moment cease explaining to the working masses that the only road to their deliverance is through struggle and through [their] dictatorship. We do not for a moment cease calling on the working masses, whenever circumstances are favourable, to struggle for this dictatorship; and leading them in this effort. In other words, the United Communist Party of Germany (VKPD), relying on the proletariat, stands ready to move into action for the above-cited tasks on a united basis.

We do not conceal the disagreements that divide us from the other parties. Moreover, we call on the organisations addressed by this letter not to limit themselves to lip-service for the proposed basis for action but to move into action for these demands.

We do not ask the recipients of this letter whether they recognise these demands as justified. We take that for granted. Instead, we ask them whether they are prepared to undertake immediately a determined struggle for these demands.

This clear and unambiguous question requires an equally clear and unambiguous response. Present conditions demand a rapid reply. We therefore await a reply by 13 January 1921.

If the parties and trade unions to whom we make this appeal are not willing to take up the struggle, the VKPD will consider itself obliged to wage the struggle on our own. Starting today, the VKPD calls on all proletarian organisations in Germany and on the working masses who look to them to hold meetings and announce their intention to carry out jointly a common defence of their interests against capitalism.

Zentrale of the United Communist Party of Germany (VKPD)

## 1b. ECCI Debate on Open Letter[2]

[*From the ECCI agenda point on Germany and Levi, 22 February 1921*]

---

2. Comintern archives, RGASPI, 495/1/29, pp. 183–98 (German) and 232–47 (English). A different account of this meeting is reprinted in Goldbach 1973, pp. 135–43. Lenin was not present at this meeting; for his assessment of the Open Letter, see Appendices 2d and 3a, pp. 1086–7 and 1097–1101.

**Zinoviev**: ...I now come to the Open Letter. In my opinion, the letter was quite artificial. One can discuss this matter. I do not propose any official decision on our part. The comrades regarded it as a tactical move in order to establish contact with Scheidemann. A Communist Party has, of course, the right to do that, but under the given circumstances, it could not possibly succeed. I do not believe that one can call on the workers to form an alliance with other workers' parties. I do not think real masses were drawn into this move. It was more a literary fantasy than a mass movement. If the facts show me to be wrong, I am prepared to change my opinion. It seems to me to be the same as the common manifesto signed with the Scheidemann people during the summer. No substance at all; something for the masses...

**Bukharin**: The Open Letter was an invitation to 'all proletarian parties', to all organisations that, like the VKPD, are based on the proletariat. So there are other organisations and parties that are similar in nature to the VKPD. That [approach] flows logically from present circumstances, but it is not revolutionary. After all, we want communism; we want the dictatorship of the proletariat – and we must say that too. But what the letter says is that we want the proletariat to live. That is bizarre. Are we living for a new capitalism? All this points to only one conclusion: that communism means death. But we want the proletariat to live, and that is why we are advancing these demands. There is no other possible interpretation[3]....

I would like to say a few more words about the Open Letter and the new policy. There are factors that can make it permissible to put forward such demands, such as when the proletariat is uniting in action. In such conditions, putting forward such demands is permissible. But they must consist of slogans that can serve as a lever for development. The slogans must be presented from the point of view of proletarian dictatorship.

The [Open Letter] programme does not correspond at all to Communist demands. These demands, taken together, are thrown together from a variety of demands that do not at all focus one's attention on the most important points. These are not partial demands of the type raised earlier by the Russian party. In my opinion, we ought to compare the two resolutions and analyse the differences. There is a principled difference between the ways that the VKPD and the Russian party have put forward partial demands. The Russian partial demands directed attention entirely to the conquest of power, while the German demands are a hodgepodge. This programme fails completely to

---

3. In the German text, Bukharin continues for four and a half sentences on another topic, and the manuscript then breaks off, resuming with the remarks by Bukharin that follow.

present partial demands in terms of the conquest of power. Our programme focuses attention above all on the necessity of a revolutionary uprising. The documentation illustrates this. The Open Letter states:

> In proposing this as a basis for action, we do not for a moment delude ourselves or the working masses into thinking that the proposed demands can eliminate their poverty. We do not for a moment cease explaining to the working masses that the only road to their deliverance is through struggle and through [their] dictatorship. We do not for a moment cease calling on the working masses, whenever circumstances are favourable, to struggle for this dictatorship; and leading them in this effort. In other words, the United Communist Party of Germany (VKPD), relying on the proletariat, stands ready to move into action for the above-cited tasks on a united basis.

And then it says that the VKPD is not playing tricks and is concealing nothing. But there is no emphasis here on the necessity of revolutionary struggle; instead, the main emphasis lies on the partial demands, which have the character of a minimum programme.

Among other things, there is yet another contradiction here. If you advance partial demands, you must also be for partial struggles. Otherwise the partial demands make no sense. And what do we find in the documentation?

> For this reason, we must above all avoid sharpening the struggle at certain points in a way that is out of step with the overall character of the struggle at that moment, leading to the defeat of sectors of the proletariat and making it easier for the party opposed to us to accuse the VKPD of supposed putschism and retreat from the struggle.[4]

There is an undertone here that the struggle should not be carried through to the end. This sentence is found in the resolution of the district secretaries. The most important points are exposing the enemy and the proletarian struggle. We must spread our ideas among the masses who belong to the organisations. We will only have a truly revolutionary course of action if the party understands that what we have here is really only a tactical manoeuvre,[5] that we must not shrink back from Communist tasks, and that Communist unity can be established only in struggle.

---

4. The document Bukharin is reading from, 'the resolution of the district secretaries', is not available.
5. In German: 'Wir werden eine wirklich revolutionäre Taktik haben, wenn die Partei versteht, dass dies wirklich nur ein strategisches Manöver ist.' The German words *Taktik* and *strategisch*, as in some other Communist texts of the period, carry roughly the opposite meaning from their equivalents in present-day English.

The proposal is directed to the yellow organisation. We issue a slogan for a desperate struggle against the Independents [USPD], because we regard them as hangmen. No one will understand us if we say, on the one hand, that these are agents of the bourgeoisie and, on the other hand, that we should not carry out this struggle against them as energetically and communistically as is really necessary. In the Open Letter, we read:

> We do not ask the recipients of this letter whether they recognise these demands as justified. We take that for granted.

If they are agents of the bourgeoisie, how can they recognise these demands as being justified? By its whole conception, the Open Letter addresses itself to the workers' parties and speaks of them in the same way that Kautsky does.[6]

Furthermore, we do not carry on a struggle for the party. What does that mean? It is an opportunistic blabbering of Levi. That is reprinted as the official introduction of the Open Letter.

Then we take the article of Paul Levi headed 'Tactical Questions' (*Die Rote Fahne*).[7] There he talks a lot of nonsense, but the worst bit seems to be the one about the worker who published a letter in *Vorwärts*. And then the sentence where he speaks about the Communists today still being a minority, unable to follow an offensive tactic. They have already more than five hundred thousand members. We [in Russia] only have that many now, and at the time of the October Revolution we had far fewer members. The party fails in the real struggle, and fantastically and artificially works itself into it by making concessions to other parties.

You cannot create a united front through a house of cards; it can only be done in struggle.

**Radek:**[8] ... Now as to the difference on the Open Letter expressed by Zinoviev and Bukharin. The Open Letter is a partial action for transitional demands. The question was: how do we provoke organisations in a way that enables us to take power? It must be stressed that the initiative expressed in the Open Letter was not artificial, as Zinoviev believes. To be sure, he concedes that he is not yet sufficiently familiar with the materials.

---

6. At this point there is a break in the German text. The remaining text of Bukharin's remarks, except for the last sentence, is taken without change from the English translation found in the Comintern archives.
7. A reference to Levi's article, 'Taktische Fragen', published in *Die Rote Fahne*, 4 January 1921.
8. The first three paragraphs of Radek's speech, which do not take up the Open Letter, are omitted.

What was the situation? People were unwilling to undertake any form of action. We faced the railway workers, the civil servants, and the unemployed movement. What should we do? Will the bureaucracy sabotage the cause through negotiations with the government? Will they split the proletariat or unite it? We had to be clear on this. We had to determine quickly whether the bureaucracy would fight. That was the situation in which we wrote the Open Letter.

The KAPD asks, 'How can you turn to Scheidemann? Either you knew that he was useless, or else you had illusions.'

We had no illusions. However, we knew that the broad masses of the proletariat have illusions, and we did not yet know whether the bureaucrats would struggle. There is always a possibility that they will join the struggle in order to botch things up. If we do not ask them, then we are playing into their hands.

I am not going to take up the question whether it is permissible in principle to address a letter to other parties. How did we carry out the initiative? Bukharin quotes from an article by Levi. When I read this article, I asked the editor, 'How can you accept an article that makes such a mess of the situation?' The editor excused himself by saying he was not in the office at the time. In referring to this article, Bukharin was playing a trick. You should not pass judgement on an initiative on the basis of a newspaper article. I ask you: have we ever exposed the bureaucracy in the eyes of the working class? Let me tell you, in localities where we have few supporters, entire trade unions came over to our side. Both Majority Socialists [SPD] and Independents [USPD] took a stand against their leadership on this question.

We were shown to be right in mid-February when Barth, the shrewdest of the 'democrats', went to the shop stewards' council demanding that they sabotage our initiative. He turned to us with the question whether we were prepared to struggle together with the unemployed, subject to the condition that the struggle would not be escalated. He was hoping that we would reject his demand, so that he could discredit us in the eyes of the working class. There was complete agreement in the party on the tactical side of this question.[9]

---

9. Emil Barth, a USPD leader, headed the Berlin council of factory committees. The council proposed a united campaign to ease the poverty of the unemployed and provide meals for needy children in the schools. Barth then conducted negotiations to this end with the ADGB, USPD, SPD, and KPD.

Barth demanded that the VKPD commit itself (1) to join in a united campaign without factional provocations; (2) to accept the discipline of the united leadership; (3) to cease advocating affiliation to the red trade-union International; (4) not to call for separate actions; (5) not to call for a radicalisation of the united movement's demands. The VKPD accepted demands 1, 2, and 4; rejected demand 3; and stated that a decision on demand 5 would depend on the movement's strength.

The USPD and SPD responses were not made known.

By the way, I can reassure Bukharin. Meyer and Frölich were so delighted with this policy that they thought Bukharin must be in Berlin.[10]

It can be said that this is all very well, but when the bureaucracy did not join the movement, why did you not launch your attack? But we can't launch partial actions just like that. We must be able to rely at least on our own comrades. Our comrades said that a Communist partial action was not possible, and that we had to wait. The unemployed did not go on the attack because the others did not do so. Perhaps Bukharin has a recipe in his pocket with which to bring about a revolution in Germany. The result of this initiative was that our strength in the trade unions grew significantly, and if we are expelled, we will draw broader masses with us.

This initiative was in no way artificial. On the contrary, it was well-prepared and can lead to an entire campaign of actions. Bukharin has the recipe for a revolutionary action in Germany, but he has not had any opportunity to utilise it. I hope he never finds this opportunity, because the recipe is poor. The recipe consists of saying that when the Orgesch hurls itself against us, the workers should join in a united front. We must compel the Orgesch to do us good services. The Orgesch is waiting for our partial actions, in order to pounce on us.

Why was it that, during the Kapp days, the workers stood united in support of the Socialist government?[11] They did this because of their democratic illusions. In my opinion, if the Orgesch were to launch an attack today, it is likely that the result would be different. Workers would no longer rise up in support of the government, because it is clearly ruling through Stinnes and the Orgesch. However, if the workers of Germany rise up now in a generalised struggle, and the Orgesch attacks them, the workers will close ranks.

If we rise up in a partial action, and the Orgesch attacks us, we will be beaten down, and neither the Majority Socialists nor the Independents will fight for us. The fate of the German revolution will not be decided by the question of this or that slogan. The question is how we manoeuvre the German workers into the struggle, how we escalate the struggle, how we do away

---

No action was taken on the Berlin council's proposal, but on 26 February, the ADGB published its own list of 10 demands to combat unemployment. The VKPD declared support for the ADGB demands and campaigned for action to achieve them. Reisberg 1970, pp. 65–6. See also p. 1080, n. 12.

10. Meyer and Frölich were leftist VKPD leaders in Berlin.

11. Radek is presumably referring to workers' support for the coalition government led by the SPD, which also included the Centre Party and People's Party. The term 'socialist government' was also used in that period to signify a regime composed of workers' parties (SPD, USPD, KPD) without bourgeois participation.

with the trade-union bureaucracy, and how we conduct the struggle against the Orgesch. That is the question of unity in Germany. Possibly we will suffer major defeats in this or that situation, but these are the decisive questions.

Comrades Zinoviev and Bukharin ask what kind of struggle is it where you make excuses based on the fact that you are a minority. The comrades have fallen victim here to a misreading of the situation. It is said that there is widespread sluggishness among the workers in Germany. There is no discussion, no assemblies, and the masses are narrow-minded and reluctant. What is the reality here? A necessary process of splitting has taken place among the working masses. And the working class takes this very badly, because it has the impression that the enemy is arming and mobilising while our ranks are crumbling. As a result, whatever increases the unity of the working class makes it easier to raise the struggle to a higher level.

When the Open Letter was written, we did not say that these demands signify the dictatorship of the proletariat. It was rather our aim to show workers that they must fight for more than a crust of bread. We did not need to pose the question of whether workers wanted to fight for the dictatorship. We had to show that the trade-union bureaucracy aims to split, while we aim to unite. We said that we are taking a step backward today, in order to take three steps forward tomorrow. The Open Letter was the first vigorous initiative of the party, strengthening its readiness to struggle. If Comrade Zinoviev will examine it more closely, he will perceive that this initiative was not superficial.

There is no need for us to decide this question today. I propose that we elect a commission with the task of writing a confidential letter to both parties. I do not want the KAPD to be dealt with in worse fashion than the VKPD. We must tell both parties confidentially what we think of them.[12] At the same time, we should say publicly what must be said regarding the situation in Germany…

---

12. This sentence is taken from the English text. The German text, which appears garbled, reads: 'Wir wollen einstweilen beiden Parteien die Leviten vertraulich lesen.'

# Appendix 2
# Before the Congress: The March Action

### 2a. Radek to VKPD Leaders in Berlin[1]

14 March 1921

*To Brandler, Thalheimer, Frölich, Meyer, Böttcher, and Felix [Wolff]*

Dear Comrades,

1.) Situation here as follows: greater concessions to peasants essential; this means temporary economic strengthening of capitalist forces. Concessions abroad. Major efforts to maintain army battle-ready. Similar efforts to transform rearguard of exhausted proletarians into vanguard, endow it with courage and will to struggle. Spring and summer will be very hard. Help from abroad very necessary to raise confidence here among masses.

2.) Situation in your party is clear to me. Levi is trying to form faction with slogan: mass party or sect. That is a fraud, since his policies have dispersed the party. Meanwhile we, through activating our politics, can win new masses. No one here thinking of a mechanical split or any split at all in Germany. Task is to clarify differences, to make left wing the dominant force. Levi will go downhill fast. But we must do everything possible so Däumig and Zetkin do not go downhill with him.

---

1. Archiv der sozialen Demokratie, NL Paul Levi 1/PLAA00043.

3.) Everything depends on world political situation. If rift between Entente and Germany widens, if war breaks out with Germany, we will speak. Mere existence of these possibilities means you must make every effort to mobilise party. Action cannot be shot out of a revolver. You must do everything possible to utilise the constant pressure of Communist masses for action in order to imbue them with awareness of how essential they are. If you do not do this, then at the decisive moment you will fail once again. Given the world-political stakes, think less of 'radical' phrases and more of deeds that bring the masses into motion. In case of war, think not of peace or mere protest but of armed struggle.

I am writing all this in a great rush at the party convention.[2] I will say more in an article.

Greetings, Max [Karl Radek]

## 2b. VKPD Theses on March Action[3]

[7 April, 1921]

1.) The London negotiations have been broken off; sanctions are in force; the Upper Silesian question is posed for a decision: these factors mark the start of a new period of heightened crisis for the German bourgeoisie. The peace previously concluded between the bourgeoisie and the social-patriotic parties has once more turned into open struggle: an economic war, a time of hunger. The bourgeoisie had only made a pretence of ending its war; now it has gone back to its starting point. The inherent contradictions of the imperialist war and imperialist peace were now blatantly exposed. Victory and defeat, both bankrupt, clashed against one another.

In the bourgeois camp, the heightened crisis resulted in an evident and rapid advance by the counterrevolution. Kahr banged on the table with his sword.[4] Meanwhile, the parties of social betrayal broadened and deepened their alliance with the bourgeoisie. The Social Democrats and the Independents [USPD] were already closely allied by their joint crusade against the Communist vanguard in the trade unions. They now surrounded the counterrevolution with a protective wall. The counterrevolutionary bloc expanded

---

2. The Tenth Congress of the Russian Communist Party was held 8–16 March 1921.
3. These theses were adopted by the VKPD Central Committee at its meeting of 7–8 April 1921 by a vote of 26 to 14. They are translated from Zentrale der VKPD 1921, pp. 139–46; the version in IML-SED 1966a, 7, part 1, pp. 451–6 has also been consulted.
4. The rightist politician Gustav von Kahr was then prime minister of Bavaria.

to reach from Westarp to Ledebour.[5] The Independent and Social-Democratic parties and the trade-union bureaucracy became transformed into a tool of the bourgeoisie, working both openly and secretly, while making a pretence of opposition. The bourgeoisie uses this tool to blunt the revolutionary class consciousness of the working class and cripple its fighting power. It places the working class in the service of its bankrupt imperialist peace policy, expressed in the Social-Democratic betrayal of 4 August 1914, which harnessed the working class to the wagon of imperialist war.

The 1914 policy of civil peace has been revived in the form of a governmental alliance, both open and concealed, between the bourgeoisie and the Social Democrats and Independents.[6] This has given the German bourgeoisie a free hand to open a path to an agreement with the bourgeoisie of the Entente. Its alliance with the Socialist parties enabled it to impose the costs of the War – both in Germany and elsewhere – on the German working class. This alliance shackled the German workers and delivered them into the hands of the German and Entente bourgeoisie.

2.) This overall situation absolutely demanded of the German working class that it break the bonds that tie it to the broken wagon of the bourgeoisie, which is hauling it to destruction. It required that the working class launch fierce class struggles *through which it seizes the revolutionary initiative*. The hour had struck when the working class has no choice but to act. It had to rally in independent action and take the initiative, striking a mighty counterblow against the counterrevolution.

The German working class had to choose. Either it could passively obey the bourgeoisie's orders and the laws laid down by the counterrevolution, or it could make its own decision and act in revolutionary fashion, using its strength to impose on the counterrevolution the law of action.

3.) In all previous crises (adoption of the Versailles Treaty, punishment of war criminals, the Russian-Polish War), the Communist Party stressed to the proletarian masses the need for them to intensify the crisis and act independently to resolve it in a revolutionary fashion. However, the Communist

---

5. Kuno von Westarp was a leader of the most right-wing major party in Germany, the German National People's Party (DNVP); George Ledebour was among the most radical figures in the USPD.

6. The SPD was formally in opposition when these theses were written. Nevertheless, the SPD (together with the USPD, which did not participate in a governmental coalition), were viewed by many Communists as engaging in a de facto alliance with the bourgeois government. Later, in May 1921, the SPD re-entered the government, joining a coalition cabinet headed by Catholic Centre Party leader Joseph Wirth.

Party of Germany (Spartacus League) was not strong enough to respond to this crisis with more than propaganda.

By contrast, the VKPD's strength obligated it to go beyond mere propaganda and agitation. It was required to advance in action ahead of the working class. This was acknowledged in its founding manifesto.[7] In a situation that demanded proletarian struggle, it had to demonstrate that it was ready and willing to take the initiative.

Relying on its own strength, it had to make the attempt to pull the masses along with it, even at the risk that at first it would draw only a narrow layer of the working class with it into the struggle.

4.) The VKPD responded to the crisis with broad propaganda both within and outside of parliament for an alliance with Soviet Russia. After the London negotiations broke off, its initiative in parliament was blocked by the solid wall of a national front reaching from Westarp to Hilferding. At this point, the initiative in parliament and the propaganda outside it demanded an advance beyond the framework of parliamentary action and mere mass propaganda. It demanded a transition to mass action and a mass attack on the [bourgeoisie's] inner class alliance.

5.) The mass action was triggered by a brazen attack by Hörsing, a tool of the counterrevolution, against the workers of Mansfeld. This attack was the first step in a broad campaign to strike down the revolutionary vanguard. This occupation aimed at freeing the hands of the bourgeoisie to pursue passive resistance,[8] while aiming for ultimate agreement with the bourgeoisie at the workers' expense. The workers' parties had to choose between going with Hörsing against the revolutionary working class or joining with the Central German workers against Hörsing and the counterrevolution. The Independents and the Social Democrats did not delay for a moment in taking the side of Hörsing against the workers. The Communist Party could not delay either in rallying all its strength to lead the working class by defending Central Germany through a counteroffensive. The VKPD called for a general strike across Germany as a whole.

---

7. The reference is probably to the following statement in the VKPD's December 1920 manifesto: 'A party that influences only tens of thousands recruits its supporters mainly through propaganda. But a party that embraces hundreds of thousands, that has the ear of millions, must recruit above all through deeds and through action.... The United Communist Party of Germany is strong enough to move into action on its own, when events make this possible or necessary.' In IML-SED 1966a, 7, 1, pp. 367–8.

8. 'Passive resistance' was the German government's prescription for responding to the French occupation of cities in the Ruhr region.

6.) The counteroffensive to which the VKPD summoned the masses was beaten back, not by open counterrevolution but through its concealed form, that is, by the leaderships of the Independent and Social-Democratic parties and the trade unions.

This attempt to seize the revolutionary initiative antagonised a portion of those influenced by the SPD, USPD, and trade-union bureaucracy. These layers, made up mostly of the more privileged workers, believed it was still possible to wait, without struggle. On the other side, however, there are the growing ranks of the unemployed and short-time workers, of layers of proletarians and petty bourgeois sinking into the proletariat. Their conditions are increasingly wretched, and they cannot wait. The despair of broad layers of workers, their lack of confidence in their own class action, is expressed both in passive acceptance of the bourgeois dictatorship and in desperate acts by individuals and small groups.

This belief in salvation through bourgeois democracy, and, on the other hand, in the liberating power of individual terror, sabotage, and dynamite: these are the two poles of the despairing mistrust in revolutionary class struggle, poles that complement and reinforce each other. Not only the overall political situation but also the state of mind of the working class cried out for mass action. A revolutionary party could not possibly limit itself to mere propaganda; it could not avoid taking action. Such an evasion would mean a clear repudiation of its mission to lead the revolution and a betrayal of the working class at the decisive moment.

Understanding and readiness for serious struggle has grown in the ranks of the revolutionary vanguard. It is impossible to stockpile the strength of this revolutionary vanguard layer and the will to struggle arising from mounting poverty, while the VKPD limits itself to mere propaganda and evades action, until the day when victory appears to be guaranteed. The VKPD cannot wait until mere revolutionary propaganda has broken through the passivity and disinclination to struggle of the economically privileged and ideologically backward layers. Any revolutionary advance will initially be seen by these layers as premature, as a putsch, as a political adventure.

Yet in times of great political tension, such actions – even when they lead to a temporary defeat – are the precondition for future victories. For a revolutionary party, they represent the only possible way to win the masses for the party and for a victorious revolutionary struggle; the only way to awaken the apathetic masses to awareness of the objective political situation. The action has as its preconditions the objective heightening of class antagonisms and also a certain mood among the masses. Moreover, the action is also, in itself, a factor in arousing this revolutionary mood among the masses.

7.) This revolutionary offensive appeared to end with the defeat of the VKPD. The VKPD is temporarily isolated from broad layers of the working class.

In reality, however, this outcome holds fruitful seeds for renewed broad revolutionary actions. It creates new openings for revolutionary propaganda. Its ultimate result will be to strengthen confidence of the working class in the VKPD and thus increase workers' revolutionary striking power.

The struggles of December 1918, of January and March 1919 – all ended in defeat. Yet through these struggles, and as a result of them, communism carried out its advance in Germany. However, the revolutionary vanguard then stood on the defensive; now it is attacking. That represents an enormous step forward. The March Action, as an initial step, is inevitably still flawed. Yet it is through the March Action that the VKPD leads the German working class onward to a revolutionary offensive.

During the Kapp episode, the German working class fought united in a purely defensive struggle. However, the fruits of this defence dissolved before the eyes of the working class. Only a transition to an offensive could have secured these for the workers. The fruits of defence were harvested by the counterrevolution.

The working class can carry out a decisive struggle for power only through a mighty, all-encompassing offensive. This unifying offensive can unfold only if the working class, under Communist leadership, learns how to carry out partial and limited struggles in an offensive fashion.

8.) The following are the revolutionary results of this initial offensive action:

    a.) Overall, it sharpened the class struggle, broke through the wall of passivity and civil peace, and thereby showed the objective necessity for the working class to go over on a broader scale to the attack.

    As a result of working-class passivity, an alliance existed, when the action began, consisting of the bourgeois parties, Social Democracy, the Independent party, and the trade-union leadership. Now, at the end of the action, this alliance takes the form of an open common front in struggle against the resistance of the revolutionary vanguard, against the growing resistance of the working masses. Through the action that they carried out against the revolutionary vanguard, the Independent and Social-Democratic leaders have become prisoners of open counterrevolution.

    b.) The action and its results exposed the USPD and the SPD and their trade-union bureaucracy as counterrevolutionary forces that had, through their actions, openly joined the bourgeois line of battle.

Social Democracy's pretended opposition in parliament and the Independents' verbal revolutionary heroism: both now stand exposed before the broad masses. The March Action has completed an unmasking that began with the Open Letter of the VKPD.

c.) Workers have been aroused out of stagnation and idle submission to bourgeois dictatorship.

d.) The final result has been to deepen and broaden the effectiveness of propaganda for communism, which has shown that it knows how to struggle at the decisive moment.

e.) The March Action gave a new stimulus to the international class struggle, compelling the Menshevik parties to expose themselves by taking the side of the Independents and the Social Democrats, the side of Severing and Hörsing. The March Action finally demonstrated to the working classes of the Entente that the supposed national alliance of bourgeoisie and proletariat is a blatant lie, while the German revolution is a living reality.

f.) Finally, the March Action enabled the United Communist Party itself to identify its persisting organisational weaknesses and deficiencies.

9.) Through this action, the VKPD held true to the methods of revolutionary mass struggle. During the action, it firmly rejected all methods that sought to replace mass struggle by acts of terror and denounced such acts to the working class as deeds of the counterrevolution. And today, following the end of the struggle, it denounces, before the working class as a whole, Social Democracy and the Independent Party, who try to confuse the workers by placing the VKPD in the same category as the Orgesch and its cronies.

10.) The VKPD must rid itself of the organisational and tactical deficiencies displayed in this initial attempt. In order to carry out its historic task, it must hold firm to the line of revolutionary offensive that formed the basis of the March Action. It must continue down this path with confidence and resolution.

11.) From this approach, it flows that the VKPD has the duty of intensifying all conflicts that are suitable for bringing the masses into motion and action. When partial actions break out, whether for economic or political reasons, the party has the task of supporting these struggles with every appropriate means, while intensifying and broadening them.

12.) In light of the above theses, the Central Committee regards the party's March struggles as an action expressing this approach. The struggle began in unfavourable circumstances and ended in defeat. Nonetheless, given the systematic mobilisation of the counterrevolution, both legal and illegal, the party could not be a mere spectator, without engaging in struggle and taking action. Otherwise, it would be a party of revolutionary phrases, not a party of Communist action.

Therefore, the Central Committee approves the political and tactical conduct of the Zentrale. *It harshly condemns the passive and active opposition of individual comrades during the action.* It calls on the Zentrale to imbue the organisation with a great capacity for struggle, and take all the organisational measures needed to this end.

*Organisational measures*[9]

The organisational tasks of a Communist Party in heightening its capacity for revolutionary struggle are set down, in the main, in the decisions of the Second World Congress of the Communist International.[10] These decisions have guided the VKPD in shaping its organisation.

The organisation is constructed on the principle of democratic centralism. It demands iron discipline from every party body and every individual party member.

During the March Action, not only did major organisational shortcomings come to light, but also many comrades did not maintain the necessary discipline, which weakened the party's effectiveness in struggle. Therefore, the Central Committee requests that the Zentrale, through careful selection, achieve a healthy and systematic allocation of the party's forces. The organisational apparatus must be modified so as to make possible a quick mobilisation of all the party's forces and their rapid deployment in a manner corresponding to the party's action plans. Party members must be engaged more effectively in revolutionary detail work, through which the working masses can be won for the struggle.

In addition, the Central Committee requests the Zentrale to implement the organisational principles and statutes of the VKPD more strictly than previously, in order to increase the party's unity and striking power. The Central Committee empowers the Zentrale to immediately expel from the party those members who, during an action, contravene the party's principles and tactics or violate its decisions and directives. Appeal can be made only to the Central Committee.

---

9. The section on organisational measures, appended to the theses in Zentrale der VKPD 1921, does not appear in the version of the resolution reprinted from *Die Rote Fahne* in IML-SED 1966a.

10. See Riddell (ed.) 1991, 2WC, especially 'Basic Tasks' (2, pp. 746–65) and 'Conditions for Admission' (2, pp. 765–71).

## 2c. Resolution by Clara Zetkin on March Action[11]

[7 April 1921]

Regarding the present situation, the VKPD Central Committee states that both the economic conditions as well as domestic and international political relations called for the VKPD to undertake intensified activity as well as for its offensive and action. The possibilities for such an initiative were also there. The preconditions for successfully carrying out what was necessary and possible were as follows:

1.) In its offensive and action, the VKPD needed to have a clear and unrestricted view of the terrain of struggle, giving due weight to all existing tendencies and possibilities, many of which were contradictory. The party needed an accurate perception of the likely response to its advance from the Scheidemanns, Hilferdings, and trade-union bureaucrats, a response that would be a certainty given the pressure of their supporters.

2.) In its offensive, the VKPD needed to maintain very close contact with the broad masses of proletarians and, as their leader, make them conscious, determined, untiring partners, ready to share the burdens of struggle. Indeed, the party needed to integrate into the struggle the most advanced forces from the middle layers between the proletariat and the bourgeoisie. Decaying capitalism deprives these layers of security in either the essentials or the purpose of life. As a result, they come into increasing conflict with the bourgeois state.

3.) As a result, the VKPD needed to conduct its action with reference not to propagandistic slogans but to clearly defined and specific goals of the struggle, goals flowing from the economic situation as well as in domestic and international political relations that the broadest masses of workers, employees, public servants, and others consider to be urgent necessities.

---

11. *Sowjet: Kommunistische Zeitschrift*, 3, 1, pp. 4–9. The resolution was drafted for submission to the VKPD Central Committee meeting of 7–8 April 1921.

'The resolution is my work from beginning to end, *and my work alone,*' Zetkin later wrote. 'I drafted the resolution at a time when Comrade Paul Levi was absent and without the possibility before it was written of having a personal or written exchange of views with him regarding my basic outlook on the questions posed for the party by the March Action.'

The evening before the Central Committee session, Zetkin read her text to Levi and other colleagues. They did not amend the text, she said, but 'the comrades found it quite long. That persuaded me to present to the Central Committee a short extract, which contained many sentences and sections of the original draft without change.' *Sowjet* 3, 3, pp. 55–6. Zetkin's resolution received 6 votes with 44 opposed and 3 abstentions.

The specific goals of struggle had to be those that would necessarily lead to an intensification and broadening of the struggle and to more ambitious goals.

4.) The VKPD's advance needed to be extremely carefully prepared, on the basis not of routine reports about moods but of precise and sober evaluation and supervision of the party's entire apparatus of struggle and its capacities.

Taking into account all these points, it was possible for the VKPD to launch a worthwhile action that would drive the masses and the revolution forward on the basis of the following two specific goals of struggle:

a.) The demands of the VKPD Open Letter or, alternatively, the ten points of the trade-union federation.[12]
b.) Alliance with Soviet Russia or, alternatively, immediate establishment of diplomatic and economic relations.

It goes without saying that an action for the demands of the Open Letter would not take up the individual points of the programme schematically, one at a time, but would link the action to demands whose meaning had become clear as measures to meet urgent needs.

Carrying out the demands of the Open Letter would have been recognised by rapidly growing masses of manual and intellectual workers as a matter of life and death. The alliance between Germany and Soviet Russia was the essential foreign-policy precondition for this. The capacity of these two slogans to awaken, recruit, and gather forces would have been demonstrated in the Prussian state elections, in the heat of struggle with the trade-union bureaucracy. The masses' living conditions and the VKPD's agitation had prepared the ground for both demands to be transformed from slogans to educate and gather forces into specific goals pressing the struggle onward. The demands of the Open Letter had as their result that the masses organised in trade unions drove the union bureaucracy forward. This is substantiated by the ten points of the General German Trade Union Federation [ADGB]. As for the demand for an alliance with Soviet Russia, its significance lay not only in mobilising proletarian masses for the VKPD action but also in gaining active

---

12. Largely in response to the VKPD's campaign around its Open Letter, on 26 February 1921 the executive of the ADGB – the SPD-led trade-union federation – published ten demands 'to combat unemployment', including emergency work projects, increased payments to the jobless, and the mandated rehiring of unemployed in the factories at the employers' expense. The VKPD criticised the ADGB's 'ten demands' as inadequate, but declared it would do everything possible to support them and help achieve their victory.

support from many petty and middle bourgeois.[13] This would introduce an infectious decay into the bourgeois camp, splitting it and weakening its striking power, while redoubling the strength of our party's advance.

The VKPD offensive for these two goals of struggle could be carried out only as an intense proletarian class struggle against the possessing, exploiting, and ruling minority and their political lackeys and protectors: the Ebert republic with its Noske regiments, Hörsing cops, Orgesch gangs, Severing spies, and judges applying military law. This offensive would thus be driven beyond its limits and initial goals and become a struggle against the bourgeois government and the bourgeois state. How far could this go? What successes could it achieve? There was no way to foresee that. It depended on the understanding of the masses, growing in the heat of action, and their strengthening will. The bourgeois government could be overrun and overthrown, or, on the other hand, it could save itself through a compromise. Whatever the case, the outcome and fruit of a revolutionary advance would thus be a strengthening of the proletariat's political power and above all of its awareness of this power and its self-confidence – an important advance toward winning state power.

Partial actions were permissible as part of the urgently needed VKPD offensive. Partial actions take place when the offensive flares up initially in a particular focus of crisis – a centre or a district – but must never be limited to the Communist Party alone. They represent an advance not merely of the party but of the proletarian masses under its leadership, and with strong support of our party as a whole.

The VKPD Central Committee strongly disapproves of the party leadership's failure to carry out action that was historically necessary around the demands of the Open Letter and the alliance with Soviet Russia and to engage the full striking power and energy of our party in a manner appropriate to the situation. The Central Committee thus failed to utilise these extraordinarily favourable circumstances to pull the German proletariat out of its apathy and dull resignation and to imbue it with revolutionary understanding, virile self-confidence, and a self-sacrificing will to action. It failed to dislodge a greater range of proletarian masses than before from the grip of manipulative and cowardly betrayers of the revolution. It failed to make them charge forward against capitalism in unambiguous opposition to opportunism and reformism of every kind. Rejection of this type of action was a grievous sin against

---

13. For the KPD's demand for an alliance with Soviet Russia, see p. 427, n. 25. In Zetkin's view, alliance with Soviet Russia would help shield Germany from the oppressive exactions of the Entente powers under the Versailles Treaty. The demand thus had appeal to layers outside the working class.

the dictates of the moment, namely to drive the revolution forward in Germany and carry out vigorous solidarity with the heroic Russian proletariat.

The VKPD Central Committee also strongly disapproves of the party leadership's conduct in initiating the unfortunate recent action, marked by such severe losses – an action that was not in the spirit of its 17 March decisions.[14]

The offensive that the Zentrale decided on was, in the given circumstances, in blatant contradiction to the conditions enumerated above, through which the VKPD could have pushed the masses of working people forward in a revolutionary advance. It dangled in heady breezes of speculation regarding current tendencies, particularly concerning the international situation, which were prematurely considered as an accomplished fact. Meanwhile, the impact of the economic situation on the effectiveness of the general strike as a weapon of struggle and the position of the trade unions in relation to that weapon were simply disregarded. The offensive took place without contact with the proletarian masses and with no concern for their mood or attitude.

The offensive had no goals whose achievement would have appeared to the proletarian masses as a vital necessity and would, therefore, have aroused and reinforced their revolutionary energy. Instead, it confronted the proletariat with a series of demands and slogans that – however justified they may be in themselves – were not suited at that moment to unleashing a revolutionary will to struggle in the vast majority of workers, employees, civil servants, and others. It lacked comprehensive and thorough mental and organisational preparation – and organisational here is not understood in the Menshevik sense of having the majority of workers organised and paying their dues promptly.

The action arose from the organisational decision of a party committee rather than from an economic and political situation whose meaning was absorbed by the broad proletarian masses. It remained from the outset an isolated action of the party alone. Indeed, it did not even draw in all the members and supporters of the VKPD, deploying its maximum revolutionary potential. All the more was it powerless to induce the proletarian following of the social patriots and social pacifists to rise in rebellion against their treacherous and pampered leaders and take up the struggle and to mobilise the unorganised workers. Incapable of taking on the scope of a mass action, it could

---

14. At the VKPD Central Committee meeting of 16–17 March, there was much talk of the need to go over to the offensive and of the decisive role that could be played by a revolutionary minority. However, as contemporary historian Stefan Weber notes, the meeting 'took no decision. No one made any specific proposals about launching a coordinated confrontational action to overthrow the government at any specific time.' Weber 1991, pp. 79–80. Thus, in Zetkin's view, the meeting provided no basis for the March Action.

not develop into the hoped-for massive assault by the revolutionary masses against the bourgeois exploiters and their state. Instead, it became a struggle of the party against the proletarian masses.

The onset and course of the action, in all its diverse forms, demonstrate that the VKPD has not learned enough from the hard lessons of the past – while it has forgotten a great deal of what it learned previously. This type of offensive signifies a relapse into the 'infantile disorder of radicalism', that is, into Bakuninist putschism. It was an attempt not merely to act without the broad proletarian masses but to act against them. The relapse into putschism is all the more disastrous since it involves not a wretched propagandistic sect without experience in struggle, but rather a large party committed to a serious revolutionary offensive. What is so damaging in this type of action is not the resulting defeat but something else again. The defeat does not result from a monumental error, from the struggle of proletarian masses with a too powerful enemy. No, this shamefully severe defeat was suffered by a revolutionary party that was completely unable to carry out the necessary intensification of its activity and action. Instead of striding confidently forward, the party fled backward to the KAPD's course of action, to an outmoded stage of the proletariat's struggle for emancipation.

The Central Committee considers it enormously dangerous to try to erase the VKPD's defeat from the party's account books through grandiloquence, reinterpretation of the facts, and playing with figures. That may fool a few naïve supporters; it will not fool our deadly enemies. More then ever, speaking the truth is the essence of political wisdom.

The Central Committee concludes that:

The failed offensive has deeply shaken the opinion of counterrevolutionaries regarding the VKPD's insight and capacity as a leading revolutionary party, its ties with the broad proletarian masses, and its influence on them. It has thus diminished their fear of the party's power and facilitated utilising the party as a bogeyman for counterrevolutionary goals and measures. It has led, in particular, to further arming of the bourgeoisie and disarming of the proletariat, providing the counterrevolutionaries with the desired easy pretexts to implore the Entente to allow the Orgesch gangs to carry on,[15] while increasing the power of the bourgeoisie's mercenaries to take weapons from the workers.

The failed action has shaken the confidence of broad proletarian masses in the VKPD, which was achieved so slowly and with such difficulties, and

---

15. The Entente had demanded that armed militias like the Orgesch be dissolved in conformity with the military restrictions imposed on Germany by the Versailles Treaty. See p. 486, n. 8.

blocked them off once more behind a wall of mistrust. This weighs extremely heavily. It led to the expulsion of many hundreds of our active and determined comrades from the factories. In the process, it has undermined the party's influence there – indeed, destroyed it – and has greatly hindered our future activity in the factories and workplaces and, particularly, in the trade unions. It has thereby halted the process through which the working masses gained in understanding and maturity, essentially delivering them over to further deception and misleadership by the trade-union bureaucracy, the Eberts and the Crispiens. It has thus enhanced the power of those who consciously or unconsciously defend capitalism and further strengthened the counterrevolution.

Within the VKPD's own ranks, the failed action generated timidity, unclarity, confusion, and vacillation, while yielding no new enhanced certainty regarding the path and method of struggle. Yes, it brought the party together with the KAPD, but not on the firm ground of its own fundamental positions, but rather on the quicksand of putschism. It thereby brought us into the dubious and dangerous vicinity of senseless acts of individual violence and destruction, which were not symptoms of the broad masses' desperation, not unavoidable requirements of struggle, but rather deeds born of political childishness, of bandit romanticism, expressing the movement's weakness rather than its strength. The action repelled the masses, rather than drawing them to us. The result was a weakening of the VKPD's unity, discipline, capacity for action, and joy in struggle. The party, the most important conscious bearer and vanguard fighter for revolution in Germany and for active solidarity with Soviet Russia, was weakened in impetus and striking power.

All these consequences of the unsuccessful action damaged not only the cause of revolution in Germany but also the interests of revolutionary Russia and the moral and political power of the Third International. It was grist for the mill of slanders and lies operated by Mensheviks of every shade and every country in cosy unity with the Anti-Bolshevik League[16] – lies regarding the Communist International's character, goals, and methods and its supposed imitation of 'Russian methods'. And all this was done in a situation that cries out for a mighty action by the working masses under Communist leadership, an action that could shape the present and future of the German proletariat, Soviet Russia, and the world revolution.

Compared to the manifold damage, the gains from this ruined offensive are less than scanty. Reference is repeatedly made to the brutality of the

---

16. The German Anti-Bolshevik League was organised by Eduard Stadtler in late 1918, financed by capitalist magnate Hugo Stinnes.

bourgeoisie, disguised as democracy; to the malicious betrayal of the proletariat by trade-union bureaucrats, social patriots, and social pacifists, who sacrificed the cause of the workers to the interests of their party saloon; to the KAPD's insignificant influence on the masses; to the weaknesses of the VKPD's organisational apparatus and the need to improve it. This game was not worth the candle.

Given the facts laid out here, the Central Committee's disapproval must also apply to the political editorship of *Die Rote Fahne*. It too lost sight of the long and secure line of march, which is firmly charted for the party, as a leader of mass actions, by the decisions of the Third International. It was just as quick to push for the putsch, without insight or criticism, as it was, after the defeat, meekly and shamefacedly, to call the whole thing off. When the action ended, instead of undertaking the needed critical and objective assessment and clarification, it provided a thoroughly one-sided justification and glorification.

The Central Committee remembers with loyalty and comradeship the many thousands who, confident and trusting, committed their all, their final efforts to the struggle. The Central Committee sends the victims of judicial terror its fraternal greetings and its promise of proletarian solidarity.

The Central Committee declares that, contrary to the joyful assertions of our enemies, the defeat has not destroyed us. The party will rapidly recover and take up the struggle with new and increased strength. The precondition for this is that the party rise above itself in ruthless and relentless self-criticism and, without false inhibitions, lays bare its weaknesses and errors. Such criticism is the essential first step to arming ourselves at once for new actions. It generates the insight, spirit, and willpower that inspire and lead the organisational apparatus, whose improvement is an equally urgent task.

The Central Committee most decidedly rejects the belief that the party can choose only between the USPD's policies, which reject action and evade any revolutionary struggle, and putschism in the style of the recent action. The Central Committee believes that the VKPD's course of action goes directly forward, but certainly not in the style of historical pseudo-Marxism, which decks out immobility with revolutionary phrases. The party's action is not dependent either on the number of members or on the certainty of victory. The Central Committee considers that in the present historical situation, the VKPD must engage in a vigorous offensive. It must commit itself to an action in a manner that will necessarily transform it into mass action. An action by the party can prepare for a mass action and provide it with a goal and leadership, but it is incapable of replacing the masses. The party's offensive acquires real revolutionary significance not as a party action but as the determining force and persevering will within a mass action. Revolutionary gymnastics on the party premises will not generate revolutionary mass struggle.

The Central Committee is convinced that the party's revolutionary offensive must be prepared as an offensive by the masses through greatly increased activity by all comrades in every field of party work. This demands that the party be constantly focused on readiness for struggle, educating the masses and each individual in the virtues of self-sacrifice, heroic courage, and bravery. The party needs to work toward territorially limited partial offensives when conditions make such mass actions under Communist leadership possible. The party must learn not only how to lead the masses into battle under such circumstances but also how to withdraw from them in united fashion and at the right moment. The masses, wiser for these experiences and raised to a higher level of insight and unity, can then be held together for future struggles. The VKPD's revolutionary offensive cannot be guided by the allure of supposed 'positive' successes or the threat of defeat. Its leitmotif is what the *Communist Manifesto* proposes as the greatest success of every revolutionary struggle: welding together the growing masses of proletarians in their understanding and their determination to win state power and establish a proletarian dictatorship.[17]

The Central Committee decides on the immediate convocation of a special party convention, so that the entire body of party comrades can take a position on the issues under debate. The convention will wind up the just-completed action and thus equip the party with clear decisions for its future struggles. The Central Committee calls on party members to close their ranks and to advance along the line of the viewpoints advanced here, loyally offering the proletarian masses both direction and example in their assault on capitalism.

## 2d. Lenin to Zetkin and Levi on Open Letter, Livorno, and VKPD Leadership[18]

16 April 1921

Comrades Zetkin and Levi:

Thank you very much for your letters, dear friends. Unfortunately, I have been so busy and so overworked in the last few weeks that I have had practically no opportunity to read the German press. I have seen only the Open

---

17. Presumably a reference to the *Communist Manifesto*'s statement that 'The real fruit of [workers'] battles lies, not in the immediate result, but in the ever-expanding union of the workers.' In *MECW*, 6, p. 493.

18. Stoljarowa and Schmalfuss (eds.) 1990, pp. 226–7. The letter, written in German, was sent via the ECCI office in Berlin, which declined to forward it. Only after a telegram from Lenin was it finally re-mailed to its addressees on 11 May.

Letter, which I think is *an entirely correct policy* (I have condemned the contrary opinion of our 'Lefts' who were opposed to this letter).

As for the recent strikes and movement for revolt in Germany, I have read absolutely nothing about it. I readily believe that the representative of the Executive Committee defended stupid tactics, that were too leftist – to take immediate action 'to help the Russians': this representative is very often too leftist.[19] I think that in such cases you should not give in but should protest and immediately bring up this question officially at a plenary meeting of the Executive Bureau.

I consider your policy with regard to Serrati erroneous. Any defence or even semi-defence of Serrati was a mistake. But to withdraw from the Central Committee!!??[20] That, in any case, was the biggest mistake! If we tolerate such practices, where responsible members of the Central Committee withdraw from it when they are placed in a minority, the Communist parties will never develop normally or become strong. Instead of withdrawing, it would have been better to discuss the controversial question several times *jointly* with the Executive Committee. Now, Comrade Levi wants to write a pamphlet, that is, to deepen the conflict! What is the point of that?? I am convinced that it is a big mistake.

Why not wait? The [World] Congress opens here on 1 June. Why not have a private discussion here, *before* the congress? Without public polemics, without withdrawals, without pamphlets on differences. We have so few tried and tested forces that I am really indignant when I hear comrades announcing their withdrawal and the like. There is a need to do everything possible, and a few things that are impossible, to avoid withdrawals and aggravation of differences at all costs.

Our position in February and March was grave. A peasant country, a peasant economy – the vast majority of the population. They vacillate; they are ruined; they are disgruntled. But we should not be too pessimistic. We have made some timely concessions. And I am sure that we shall win.

Best regards and good wishes.<br>Yours,<br>*Lenin*

---

19. The reference is to Béla Kun.
20. For the resignations of Levi, Zetkin, and others from the VKPD Zentrale, see p. 206, n. 46.

## 2e. Béla Kun Defends March Action to Lenin[21]

[Berlin], 6 May 1921

Greatly esteemed comrade Vladimir Ilyich,

I do not want to interrupt you with my report. I assume that you have been informed about events in Germany, even if only indirectly, by Karl [Radek]. However, permit me to write you about what might seem to be a personal matter.

There is talk right now in the circles of the German party bureaucracy to the effect that you have expressed an opinion against the tactics of the German Central Committee and in favour of Levi and Zetkin.[22] These rumours have it that you also stated that I had demanded the German party carry out an action of solidarity [with Soviet Russia]. It is also said that you based this statement on a letter from Paul Levi and Clara Zetkin, reporting my supposed statement that Soviet Russia needed help, and therefore an action must be initiated. Levi and Zetkin are utter *hysterics*, and what they are saying in the German party right now consists of nothing but lying gossip. No one can believe it contains even a grain of truth.

I cannot accept that you, my highly esteemed comrade, could make such a statement about me, based on [a report from] a leader like Paul Levi – who is *universally recognised as dangerous* – without first raising this with me. I do not find it pleasurable to be repudiated in this manner. However, as a revolutionary, and in the interests of the revolution, I am able to bear even this. But in this case I deny that this repudiation is of any use to the revolution.

First of all, here is what I actually told Levi: Soviet Russia is in great peril. There is no hope that Russia can continue to exist in isolation for decades. It is true that Soviet Russia can still hold out for two years without genuine aid from the Western European proletariat. You are well aware of Soviet Russia's importance for the world revolution and of what a disaster it would be for the Soviet state to fall. When you consider what it would mean if the absence of the world revolution causes Soviet Russia to fall in two years, you must reorient your line of march in order to break through the counterrevolutionary

---

21. Drabkin et al. (eds.) 1998, pp. 266–9. Drabkin notes that Kun's letter was taken by Frölich to Moscow and delivered to Lenin there. Frölich added a short covering note that confirmed Kun's account of what Kun told the German party leadership on his arrival in Berlin.
Italics indicate words that Lenin underlined three times in the original text.
22. Kun is referring here to the views expressed by Lenin in his 16 April letter to Zetkin and Levi (Appendix 2d).

front. Do not wait, standing on the defensive, while the bourgeoisie strangles the proletariat through capitalist restoration.

I said the same thing to Clara Zetkin. I described the situation in Russia to her more frankly and in stronger terms than I had to Levi. This was because I considered her to be much more revolutionary than Levi. I must admit I was mistaken. If my statement represented a 'stupidity', I am willing to accept responsibility for this before the entire world. But I am strongly convinced that this will not be required. I do not say that you should take me at my word, but I do ask that you have somewhat more trust in me than in Mr. Levi and Mrs. Zetkin.[23]

If you examine closely the history of the German party, you will find that, with reference to both the Serrati case and in the Heidelberg conference,[24] Levi tried to conceal his swinishness and stupidity behind Radek's authority, although in both cases Radek spoke out against Levi's point of view. This did not prevent Levi from long repeating the lie that Radek had only later changed his point of view. As for the statements of the aged comrade Zetkin, I would like to say only this: the old woman is suffering from senile dementia. She provides a living proof that Lafargue and his wife acted entirely correctly.[25] She is completely in the hands of Levi. Despite all my sentimental feelings toward the old fighter, if she says that I demanded an action of solidarity from the German party, I can only term that a *complete lie*.

I am well aware of the errors committed in the German March Action. I do not say that our activity was free from error. Nonetheless, we acted *honestly and in a revolutionary fashion*, even as those who sent you a statement attacking me – Levi and Zetkin – were sabotaging the action in counterrevolutionary fashion. This fact reinforces my hope that you have not made statements like those of Levi and Zetkin – which constitute only a particle of Levi's big lie.

I also hope that I will have the opportunity of speaking with you personally in the near future. Beyond any question, the March Action has brought us great political and organisational successes and will bring us many more in the future.

---

23. The words 'Mr.' and 'Mrs.' (in this case, *gospodin* and *gospozhe*) were used ironically to signify that the persons so named had left the workers' movement and were no longer comrades. Beside this sentence, Lenin added a comment, 'So!'
24. The 'Serrati case' refers to the split between Serrati's current and the Comintern at the January 1921 Livorno Congress. For Levi's actions at the 1919 Heidelberg convention, see p. 484, n. 2.
25. Paul Lafargue and his wife Laura, the daughter of Karl Marx, both leaders of the socialist movement in France, jointly committed suicide in 1911 at the ages of 69 and 66, respectively, fearing the advent of old age and believing they had nothing further to contribute to the workers' movement.

However, I ask that you give no credence to these lies until you have heard my oral report and until full documentation is available.

With Communist greetings,<br>Your devoted adherent,<br>The Spaniard.[26]

## 2f. Paul Levi Appeals to Third Congress[27]

*[The following appeal was addressed to the Presidium of the Third World Congress.]*

Frankfurt am Main, 31 May 1921

Dear Comrades,

In its session of 27 [29] April 1921, the Executive Committee of the Communist International adopted a motion approving my expulsion from the VKPD and thus from the Communist International.[28]

I register my protest against this decision and ask the congress to rescind it.

*Motivation*

A decision like that made by the Executive could be taken for three different reasons.

1.) That the text published by me was not Communist; that its contents violated the principles of the Communist International.

The Executive Committee declined to draw such a conclusion. On the contrary, it explicitly conceded the possibility that my opinion on the March Action was correct. This justification must therefore be ruled out in assessing the Executive Committee's action. Nonetheless, I would like to devote a few words to this question, as it relates to the congress's decision.

No one in the German section contests that the Communist Party's March Action was a break from the party's entire past. In my pamphlet, I published

---

26. Beside this signature, Lenin added the word 'So!'
27. Weber 1991, pp. 303–13.
28. The Executive Committee decision, adopted on 29 April 1921, read, in part: 'With regard to Paul Levi's pamphlet, "Our Path: Against Putschism," the ECCI ratifies the expulsion of Paul Levi from the United Communist Party of Germany and, consequently, from the Third International. Even if Paul Levi were nine-tenths right in his views of the March offensive, he would still have to be expelled because of his outrageous violation of discipline and because, by his action, *in the given circumstances*, he stabbed the party in the back.' *Kommunistische Internationale*, 2, 17, p. 366. See also Degras (ed.) 1971, 1, p. 220.

passages from the 17 March Central Committee session where this was made plain.²⁹

Paul Frölich said:

> What the Zentrale now proposes is *a complete break with the past*. Up till now we had the tactic, or rather the tactic had been forced on us, that we should let things come our way, and as soon as there was a situation of struggle we should make our decision in this situation. What we say now is: we are strong enough, and the situation is so serious, that we must proceed *to force the fate of the party and of the revolution itself*.³⁰

Ernst Meyer said:

> In conclusion, *we have to break with the party's former attitude*, one of avoiding partial actions and refusing to give out slogans that might appear as if we were demanding a final struggle.³¹

Paul Frölich expressed this concept in greater detail in the third issue of *Die Internationale*, Volume 3.

> The decision actually signifies precisely a break with the party's past, a break, moreover, with the past of both its components.³²

A text on the March Action published by the Zentrale of the Communist Party of Germany reads, in part:

> The decisiveness with which the March Action broke with the past of the revolutionary parties in Germany corresponded to the intensity with which the need was felt for a revolutionary offensive in Germany.

Any number of similar passages could be cited. The Communist Party of Germany was admitted to the Communist International on the basis of its previous outlook. In similar fashion, the [USPD] Left was admitted on the basis of political and tactical conceptions developed prior to the Halle convention. If these conceptions were in accord with the principles of the Communist International and of communism in general, it certainly cannot be said that to persist with these principles is anti-Communist or a betrayal. On the contrary, this can only be said of the *conscious break* with these principles that the VKPD Zentrale – through its spokespersons – admits it has made.

---

29. See Levi's 'Our Path: Against Putschism' in Fernbach (ed.) 2011, pp. 119–65.
30. Fernbach (ed.) 2011, p. 140. Emphasis in original.
31. Ibid.
32. The 'components' referred to here are the KPD (Spartacus League) and the USPD Left.

In addition, I believe my pamphlet and my 4 May speech thoroughly demonstrated how these 'new principles' actually represent an abandonment of Communist conceptions.[33] In the entire array of insulting writings published against me, I do not see even an attempt to refute this. In this regard, it is only necessary to refer to two efforts by Karl Radek found in the afterword to his pamphlet, *Should the VKPD Be a Mass Party of Revolutionary Action or a Wait-and-See Centrist Party*.[34] Radek asks:

> Does Levi carry out his critique in the framework of Communist principles? He accuses the Communist Party of sectarianism, Bakuninist putschism, Moscow dictatorship – the very grounds given by the Hilferdings for refusing to join the party. This fact alone demonstrates that his criticism is made from the point of view of an opponent, of centrist conceptions.

It is hard to view these remarks as anything other than conscious deception. Certainly Hilferding and others have combated the Communist International with such arguments. We refuted them most energetically, responding, 'What you say is a distortion that you've cooked up; you've made yourselves a scarecrow.'

And while we combated the Independents in *this* fashion, we simultaneously combated putschism, sectarianism, and talk about the 'dictates of Moscow', and the Executive Committee supported us in this. The question, therefore, is not whether *we* are now employing Hilferding-style arguments, but rather whether the VKPD's March Action corresponds to *our* Communist outlook or, instead, to a Hilferding-style caricature of communism. It is not my fault that the answer to this question is so unambiguous.

Further on, Radek asserts that my entire theory amounts to saying that the Communist Party must not undertake any kind of revolutionary mass actions until it has the support of the majority of workers, because otherwise these actions would represent a struggle against the proletarian majority. One of two things is true. Either the pamphlet is being wrongly criticised for presenting a concept that is, in fact, expressly rejected in its pages, precisely in anticipation of this criticism. Or, on the other hand, this sentence reveals a lack of clarity on the part of the critic that deprives his statement of any validity.

---

33. A translation of Levi's 4 May speech, 'What Is the Crime: The March Action or Criticising it?' see Fernbach (ed.) 2011, pp. 166–205.

34. The afterword to Radek's pamphlet on the March Action (Radek 1921) was published in *Kommunistische Internationale*, 17, pp. 55–78. Excerpts from this afterword can be found in Gruber (ed.) 1967, pp. 341–6.

In the first case, my critic is trying to foist on my pamphlet the view that, as a precondition [for action], the majority of workers must be won to the Communist party. On this, my pamphlet says the following (p. 26):

> I have already explained above what is not a precondition. It is not a precondition that the majority of the German proletariat carry a membership card in the Communist Party. Nor is it a precondition that the proletariat has already gone manfully to the electoral urns and proclaimed its readiness on written or printed ballots.
>
> It is not even a necessary precondition that those middle strata that I referred to above should be Communist or completely in sympathy with the Communists. Certainly, their sympathy means, *in every case*, an extraordinary easing of the task of the proletariat, both *in* and *after* the seizure of power, and circumstances can also be imagined in which the hostility and refusal of these strata makes the seizure of power impossible. These however, are matters that, for the most part, arise only in the course of struggle, so that it is hard to lay down rules in advance; applied mechanically, these would only weaken the offensive spirit.
>
> But, leaving these aside, there are indeed certain preconditions for the seizure of state power. Lenin says in 'The Elections to the Constituent Assembly and the Dictatorship of the Proletariat': 'We can identify three conditions that enabled the Bolsheviks to triumph: (1) an overwhelming majority among the proletariat; (2) [support of] almost half the army; (3) an overwhelming superiority of forces at the decisive moment and in the decisive points, namely in the two capital cities [Petrograd and Moscow] and along the nearby battle lines.'[35]

In that passage, therefore, I laid out my thinking about Communists and the majority with all the clarity one could desire, clear enough for anyone who has any concern for the truth. I would like to add only that the preconditions for the seizure of state power set down there also had to serve as preconditions for the March Action. It was, as I explained in my 4 May speech and in the foreword to the second edition of my pamphlet, an *armed uprising* with the goal of overthrowing the government, which – in Germany at this time – can signify only the proletarian struggle to win power.

Or, in the second case, counterposing the mass action to the majority of the proletariat signifies confusing all concepts of mass, class, and party. I am sure

---

35. Fernbach (ed.) 2011, pp. 134–5. The passage from Lenin has been translated from Levi's German text, which differs slightly from the standard English translation (*LCW*, 30, p. 262).

there is no need for me to demonstrate to a World Congress the frightfulness of this confusion.

Let me summarise: my critique of the Communist Party of Germany's March Action is Communist, and the Executive Committee acted rightly in not challenging this.

2.) The second charge raised against me is that the criticism is slanderous.

This charge was first raised by the Zentrale in its decision of 15 April 1921. It states that the pamphlet contains a number of irresponsible and untrue assertions and grievous accusations 'against' the party leadership and representatives of the Communist International Executive.[36]

The contrary is true. I maintain that every one of the assertions I made is true. I hope that the comrades who share my viewpoint will succeed in furnishing proof of this [to the World Congress].[37] The facts have not been seriously contested by anyone anywhere. Indeed, what I have asserted publicly is far less than the truth. I remained silent on many incidents that, if publicised, could have caused damage to the party without any compelling need. I recall the case of the dynamite attempts.

I also stand by what I said regarding the influence of the Executive, although there are several things that must be said in the Executive's defence that I did not stress sufficiently in what I wrote. In reality, the Executive merely provided a *stimulus*.[38] (This does not apply to their representatives in Germany, who went much further.) The Executive assumed that this stimulus would be reviewed in Germany, and possibly amended or rejected, by independent and competent people capable of reaching their own decision. I concede that the Executive perhaps did not reckon with the possibility that the VKPD Zentrale would *indiscriminately* swallow everything that was offered them in the name of the Executive. But as to the fact that the Executive's representatives exerted an influence of the type that I described, indeed, that they intervened

---

36. In this sentence, Levi presents the wording of the Zentrale statement, adding quotes around 'against'. See Weber 1991, p. 300.

37. On her trip to the Third World Congress, Zetkin took with her a sweeping documentation of provocative actions promoted by VKPD leaders, compiled from VKPD sources. When she reached the frontier, however, German police seized these records. In November 1921 these papers were published by the SPD's *Vorwärts*. The documents, which became known as the *Enthüllungen* (revelations), confirmed Levi's account of the March Action in broad outline and supplied reports on attempted dynamiting and other incidents on which Levi remained silent. See Zentrale der KPD 1922; Angress 1963, pp. 143–6. For a sceptical view of the *Enthüllungen*, see Knatz 2000, pp. 83–4.

38. For a letter that reflected the Executive's role, see Appendix 2a, pp. 1071–2.

independently beside the Zentrale or even behind its back – there is no doubt about that whatsoever.

3.) The third objection that could be raised – and, in fact, the only objection that actually was offered – refers to the point in time when the pamphlet appeared.

a.) It has been said that the pamphlet provided evidence for the prosecution and appeared at a moment when Germany was gripped by the white terror.

As for the first point, not a single case has been cited where the prosecution took action because of the pamphlet. Surely there is no need to demonstrate that it did not cause problems to comrades across the country facing charges. But not even the Zentrale faced charges based on my pamphlet. With the exception of Comrade Brandler, members of the Zentrale were either not arrested or, if arrested, were immediately released. As for Brandler, the accusations against him were based on the Zentrale's own appeals. The prosecution did not need even a single line of my pamphlet.

Furthermore, I must state frankly that the kind of precautions being advocated here cannot be accepted. We have all recognised from the start that the well-being of the party cannot be sacrificed to prevent comrades from losing their freedom or more. This conception guided the Zentrale as well, when it set in motion the March Action, which cost many comrades their freedom and their lives. If it is true that the March Action was a disastrous error and that it was politically essential for the party to correct that error, then that had to be done even at the risk that those responsible would be forced into illegality. I cannot accept any rule for the Communist Party according to which the consequences of disastrous errors are borne *only* by the members and *not* by the leaders who made the errors in the first place.

b.) I did not freely choose the moment when my pamphlet was published.

When the March Action was called off, the German party had far from regained insight into the lunacy of such an action. This insight came only later. At first, the Central Committee was left free to decide to 'hold firm to the line of the revolutionary Left, which formed the basis for the March Action'. There was a danger of renewed follies.

That danger was all the greater because, when the action was called off, organisational reprisals began immediately. Even during the action, the Executive representative said that when it ended, and because of its occurrence, the 'Levi-ites' would then be cleansed out of the party. The representative will not contest that fact, and if he does, I will prove it to be true.

On the direct instructions of another Executive representative, the German party Zentrale made such a decision, had it approved by the Central

Committee, and thereupon set about – the day after the [7–8 April] Central Committee meeting – to implement it. On that day, expulsion proceedings began against two comrades, Richard Müller and [Fritz] Wolff. It was therefore *politically essential* to construct a political basis on which the expulsions could be carried out, before an effort to halt the expulsions took shape. Just how necessary that was became clear when the Zentrale, facing a political challenge, desisted from its criminal undertaking.

Finally, it has also been said that the pamphlet was published 'during the action'. It was not even written, let alone published during the action. The Zentrale issued the order to break off the struggle on 1 April. This instruction had only declarative value, since it was not given until a moment when not even a dog was still stirring. The action had collapsed several days earlier.

For the Zentrale to claim that the pamphlet went to press while the action was still under way is brazen fraud. In the very statement of 15 April where it claims that the pamphlet was published 'while the action was still under way', only a few lines further on, it says that I stabbed the party in the back '*immediately following* the end of the struggle'. In reality, the pamphlet went to press on 9 April and was published on 13 April, that is, fourteen days after the actual ending of the struggle. That was a moment when the party had every reason to give attention to the damage done and the persons responsible.

Finally, I would like to take up one other argument that plays a role in the thinking of some – including Radek, it seems to me – the public nature of the criticism. Yes, criticism can be expressed 'within the party framework'.

If a Zentrale mismanages membership dues, squanders party funds, or – in a word – compromises itself before the members, in such conditions criticism can remain in the party framework. However, the German party's Zentrale and, along with it, the party as a whole were compromised before the German and international proletariat.

And I maintain that if the party had summoned the courage to admit the errors *publicly*, accept all the consequences, and repair the damage done, this would have eliminated a large part of the harm caused by the March Action. This damage can be expressed with statistics but reaches far beyond that. The damage is expressed in a loss in prestige and moral authority among the proletarian masses; a loss suffered by Communists, the Communist Party, and the Communist International – a loss beyond measure or calculation.

How much of the loss can be made good is now up to the congress. It can achieve a great deal, provided that it freely and openly identifies the errors and those responsible, while taking political distance from them. That is why I consider it my duty to present my 'case' as well to the congress.

With Communist greetings,

# Appendix 3
# The Political Struggle at the Congress: June 1921

### 3a. Lenin to Zinoviev on Tasks at Congress[1]

10 June 1921

The crux of the matter is that Levi in very many respects is *right politically*. Unfortunately, he is guilty of a number of breaches of discipline for which the party has expelled him.

Thalheimer's and Béla Kun's theses are politically utterly fallacious. Mere phrases and playing at leftism.

Radek is vacillating and has spoilt his original draft [Resolution on Tactics and Strategy] by a number of concessions to 'leftist' silliness.[2] His first 'concession' is highly characteristic: in #1 of his theses, 'Defining the Question', he first had 'winning the majority of the working class (*to the principles of communism*)' (note this). Amended (absurdly) to: 'winning the *socially decisive sections* of the working class'.

A gem! To weaken here, in such a context, the necessity of winning precisely the *majority* of the working class 'to the principles of communism', is the height of absurdity.

To win power, you need, *under certain conditions* (even when the *majority* of the working class have already been won over *to the principles of communism*) *a blow* dealt at the decisive place by the majority of the socially decisive sections of the working class.

---

1. *LCW*, 42, pp. 319–23; checked against *PSS*, 52, pp. 265–9.
2. For Radek's letter to Lenin presenting his draft theses, see Drabkin et al. (eds.) 1998, pp. 282–5.

This modifies, absurdly, this truth in such a way that point 1 on the general tasks of the Communist International about winning the working class *to the principles of communism, weakens* the idea about the necessity of winning the *majority* of the working class. This is a classic example of Béla Kun's and Thalheimer's ineptitude (it looks all right, damn it, but it's all damned wrong) and – of Radek's *hasty complaisance*.

Radek's theses were much too long and boneless, and lacked a political central point. And Radek diluted them *still* more, completely spoiling them.

What's to be done? I don't know. So much time and effort wasted.

If you don't want an open fight at the congress, then I propose:

1.) That Thalheimer's and B. Kun's theses be rejected by an exact vote this very day (since Bukharin assures me that the basic points have to be settled not later than today; it would be better to postpone this) as being basically erroneous. Have this recorded. You will spoil everything if you don't do this and show indulgence.

2.) That Radek's first draft, 'unimproved' by any corrections, one specimen of which I have quoted, should be adopted as a basis.

3.) That one to three persons be entrusted with cutting down the text and improving it so that it is no longer boneless (if that is possible!) and clearly, precisely, and unequivocally puts into focus as the central ideas the following:

None of the Communist parties anywhere have yet won the majority (of the working class) – not only as regards organisational leadership, but to the principles of communism as well. This is the basis of everything. To 'weaken' this foundation of the only reasonable policy *is criminal irresponsibility*.

Hence: revolutionary explosions are nonetheless possible very soon, considering the abundance of inflammable material in Europe; an easy victory of the working class – in exceptionable cases – is also possible. But it would be absurd to base the present tactics of the Communist International on this possibility. It is absurd and harmful to write and think that the propaganda period has ended and the period of action has started.

The policies of the Communist International should be based on a steady and systematic drive to win the *majority* of the working class, first and foremost *within the old trade unions*. Then we shall win for certain, whatever the course of events. As for 'winning' for a short time in an exceptionally happy turn of events – any fool can do that.

Hence: the tactic of the Open Letter should definitely be applied everywhere. This should be said straight out, clearly and exactly, because wavering in regard to the 'Open Letter' is extremely harmful, extremely shameful, and *extremely widespread*. We may as well admit this. All those who have failed to grasp the necessity of the Open Letter tactic should be *expelled* from the Communist International within a month after its Third Congress. I clearly see my mistake in voting for the admission of the KAPD. It will have to be rectified as quickly and fully as possible.

Instead of spinning a long yarn like Radek, we had better have the whole text of the Open Letter translated (and in German quoted in full), its significance properly brought home and adopted as a model.

I would confine the *general* resolution on tactics to this.

Only then will the *tone* be set. The central idea will be clear. There will be no woolliness. No possibility of everyone reading his own meaning into it (like in Radek's).

Radek's original draft would then be cut down to a quarter, at least.

It is time we stopped writing and voting *brochures* instead of theses. Under this system partial mistakes are inevitable with any of us, even when the matter is indisputable. And when we have something boneless and disputable, we are bound to make *big* mistakes and spoil the whole thing.

And then, if you have the itch for it, you can add a supplement: on the basis of such a policy, specifically by way of example, precisely as an example and not as a principle, we add so-and-so and so-and-so.

Further.

To generalise Serrati and Levi into the same 'opportunism' is stupid. Serrati is guilty; of what? It should be said clearly and precisely – on the *Italian* question, and not on the question of general policy. Of having split with the Communists and not having expelled the reformists, Turati and company. Until you have carried this out, Italian comrades, you are *outside* the Communist International. We are expelling you.

And to the Italian Communists – serious advice and the *demand*: so long as you have not been able by persistence, patience, and skill to *convince* and win over the majority of the Serratian *workers*, don't swagger, don't play at leftism.

'The Levi case' concerns not general tactics but the appraisal of the March Action, the German question. Brandler says it was a defensive action. The government provoked it.

Let us assume this is true, this is a fact.

What deduction is to be drawn from this?

1.) That all the shouting about an offensive was erroneous and absurd.
2.) That it was a tactical *error* to call for a *general* strike once there was provocation on the part of the government, who wanted to draw the *small fortress* of communism into the struggle (the district in the centre where the Communists already had a majority).

3.) Mistakes like this must be avoided in the future, as the situation *in Germany is* a special one after the killing of 20,000 workers in the civil war through the skilful manoeuvres of the Right.[3]

4.) To use the term 'putsch' or, even worse, 'Bakuninist putsch' for a defensive action by hundreds of thousands of workers (Brandler says *a million*. Isn't he mistaken? Isn't he *exaggerating*? Why are there no figures by regions and cities???) is worse than a mistake; it is a breach of revolutionary discipline. Since Levi added to this a number of other breaches (list them very carefully and exactly) he deserves his punishment and has earned his expulsion.

The *term* of expulsion should be fixed, say, at six months at least. He should then be *permitted* to seek readmission to the party, and the Communist International advises that he be readmitted *provided* he has acted loyally during that time.

I have not yet read anything, apart from Brandler's pamphlet, and am writing this on the basis of Levi's and Brandler's pamphlets.[4] Brandler has proved one thing – if he has proved anything – that the March Action was not a 'Bakuninist putsch' (for such *abusive language* Levi ought to be expelled) but a heroic defence by revolutionary workers, hundreds of thousands of them. But however heroic it was, *in the future* such a challenge, provoked by the government, which, since January 1919, has already killed by provocations twenty thousand workers, *should not* be accepted until the Communists have the majority behind them, all over the country, and not just in one small district.

(The July Days of 1917 were not a Bakuninist putsch.[5] For such an appraisal we would have expelled a person from the party. The July Days were an heroic *offensive*. And the deduction we drew was that we would not launch the next heroic offensive *prematurely*. Premature acceptance of a general battle – that is what the March Action really was. Not a putsch, but a *mistake*, mitigated by the heroism of a defensive by hundreds of thousands.)

Concerning Šmeral. Can't we have at least two or three *documents*?

There would be no harm in having at least two documents (two to four pages each) on each country printed for the Comintern.

---

3. Conditions of civil war existed in Germany in early 1919, when the SPD-led government utilised rightist paramilitary formations to crush centres of workers' resistance across the country, and in March 1920, when workers took up arms against the rightist Kapp Putsch and then faced an onslaught by the army.

4. See Brandler 1921 and Levi, 'Our Path: Against Putschism', in Fernbach (ed.) 2011.

5. For the July Days, see p. 594, n. 20.

What are the facts about Šmeral? About Strasser?

Do not forget one of the chief things – to delete from Radek's first theses everything relating to the 'waiting party', to its censure. It must all come out.[6]

Regarding Bulgaria, Serbia (Yugoslavia?) and Czechoslovakia, the question of *these* countries must be put concretely, specially, clearly, and precisely.

If opinion is divided on this, I suggest convening the Politburo.

*Lenin*

## 3b. Lenin on the Theses on Organisation[7]

1. *Letter to Otto Kuusinen, 10 June 1921*

Urgent.

Comrade Kuusinen,

I have read your article (three chapters) and the theses with great pleasure.

I enclose my remarks regarding the theses.

I advise you to immediately find a *German* comrade (a real German) who must *improve* the German text (of the article and the theses). Perhaps this comrade, on your behalf, would read your article as a *report* at the Third Congress (it would be much more convenient for the German delegates to hear a *German*).[8]

My advice is – cross out the end (of the theses).

Re propaganda and agitation – much greater detail – especially on the press, but also on verbal propaganda.

I think you should definitely *take upon yourself* the report at this congress. I shall write to Zinoviev about this today.

Best regards, yours,
*Lenin*

---

6. For the reference to Šmeral in the original draft of the Theses on Tactics and Strategy, see p. 225, n. 78.

7. *LCW*, 42, pp. 316–19; 45, 185–6; compared with *PSS* 44, pp. 13–15, 56. See resolution as approved by the congress on pp. 978–1006.

8. When the report on the organisational structure of the Communist Parties was given to the Third Congress in Session 22, the reporter was the German Communist Koenen.

**Theses:**

(Thesis 6 or) point 6, second part, last sentence should read:

'...will inevitably inherit this tendency to a certain extent from... environment....'

And the next sentence should read:

'...the Communist Party *should overcome* this tendency by systematic and persistent organisational work and *repeated* improvements and corrections...'

(Thesis 7 or) point 7:

It should be stated at greater length that this is exactly what is lacking in most of the legal parties of the West. There is no *everyday* work *(revolutionary work)* by *every member of the party.*

This is the chief drawback.

To change this is the most difficult job of all.

*But this is the most important.*

Point 10.

This needs amplifying.

More details.

Examples.

The role of the newspaper.

'Our' newspaper compared with the *usual* capitalist newspaper.

Work for 'our' newspaper.

Example: Russian newspapers of 1912–13.

The fight against the bourgeois papers. Exposure of their venality, their lies, etc.

Distribution of leaflets.

*Agitation in the home.*

Sunday outings, etc.

Far more details.

Point 11 – Far more details here too.

Point 13 – Presenting reports and *discussion* of reports in the 'cells'.

Reports on hostile and *especially on petty-bourgeois* organisations (the Labour Party, the Socialist parties, etc.).

Greater detail about duties *among the mass* of the unorganised proletariat and of the proletariat organised in the yellow trade unions (including the Second and Two-and-a-Half Internationals) *and the non-proletarian* sections of the *working people.*

Points 26 and 27.

This is irrelevant.

This is not an 'organisational question'.

This subject had better be dealt with in a special article for the *Communist International*, say: 'Organisational Questions in Revolutionary Periods' and so forth.

Or: 'On the Question of Mounting Revolution and Our Corresponding Tasks' (on the basis of Russian and Finnish experience).

Lenin


## 2. *Letter to Grigorii Zinoviev, 11 June 1921*

Urgent, 11 June

Comrade Zinoviev:

I have just read Kuusinen's theses and one-half of the article (the report),
I have returned them to him with my remarks.

I do insist that he *and* he *alone* (i.e., not Béla Kun) should be allowed to give a report at this congress without fail.

This is necessary.

He knows and *thinks* (which is a great rarity among revolutionaries).

What needs to be done right away is to find *one* German, a real one, and give him strict instructions

- to make stylistic corrections at once,
- and dictate the corrected text to a typist.

And at the congress read out for Kuusinen his article-report (tell Kuusinen to complete the second half within three days).

The German [Wilhelm Koenen] will read it out well. The benefit will be enormous.

The question will be *posed*: and this will be very much more than enough for a start.

Greetings,
Lenin

P.S. You have not returned to me the copy of my letter to Levi.[9] *Do so without fail.* If you don't, I will not make up.

---

9. See Appendix 2d, pp. 1086–7.

3. *Letter to Otto Kuusinen and Wilhelm Koenen, 9 July 1921*

Dear Comrades,

I read your draft theses on the organisational question with great pleasure. I think you have done a very good job. May I suggest just two addenda:

1.) Advice – control commissions consisting of the best, tried, and experienced workers to be formed in all parties.
2.) Re spies – a special point in connection with the question of illegal work. Contents roughly as follows: the bourgeoisie is bound to infiltrate spies and provocateurs into the illegal organisations. A thoroughgoing and unremitting struggle should be waged against this, and a method of struggle to be specially recommended is a skilful combination of *legal* with illegal work and verification (of fitness for illegal work) by *means of* prolonged *legal* work.

With communist greetings, yours,
Lenin

## 3c. German Delegation to ECCI on Zetkin's Role[10]

Moscow, 10 June 1921

*To the Executive of the Communist International (copy to attention of the Communist Party of Russia [RCP] Central Committee and Comrade Lenin)*

Dear Comrades,

The German delegation considers it necessary to indicate emphatically to the Executive Committee and the RCP Central Committee that there is absolutely no objective foundation for the consideration that is being given here to the person of Clara Zetkin in deciding the tactical and organisational issues linked to the March Action.

By aligning herself with the Levi clique in the German movement, Comrade Clara Zetkin has lost her influence. That was demonstrated by the results of the recent Central Committee sessions, where only an insignificant minority supported the Levi-Zetkin position. What is more, it is shown by the decisions of every party district. In the Württemberg district, for example, where

---

10. Stoljarowa and Schmalfuss (eds.) 1990, pp. 264–6.

Comrade Zetkin has been active for decades and was granted both a report and a summary, she received only six votes out of approximately two hundred. After her report in the Chemnitz district, one of the best-organised in our party, she received only *one* vote from about 190 district representatives.[11]

At the most recent convention in the mid-Rhine district (Cologne), Clara Zetkin was nominated as a delegate to the party convention, after Comrade Fries, a Reichstag deputy, had withdrawn his candidacy in her favour. She received only two of the thirty-five votes. It should be noted that the Cologne party newspaper was edited in Levi's spirit during the crucial weeks following the March Action.

The German delegation stresses that the entire German party stands on one side, while on the other we find only Comrade Zetkin and a few parliamentary deputies and trade unionists.

Therefore, the German delegation must stress vigorously that any concession to the person of Comrade Clara Zetkin would severely damage the capacity for action and discipline of the Communist movement in Germany. The delegation certainly anticipates that the Executive and the Russian delegation at the Communist International congress will not show any sentimental consideration for the person of Clara Zetkin.

For far too long the German Communist Party carried out such a policy of concessions toward the former comrade Paul Levi. Events showed that this had extremely damaging consequences for the Communist movement and the International. The VKPD is thus firmly resolved not to repeat under any circumstances this type of policy toward the person of Clara Zetkin, and here it is counting absolutely on the support of the Executive and the Russian delegation to the congress.

This statement has been adopted unanimously by all the delegates present in Moscow.

On behalf of the VKPD delegation,
W. Koenen, A. Thalheimer, Paul Frölich.

---

11. For Zetkin's reply on this point, see Appendix 3k, pp. 1151–2.

## 3d. German Delegation Gives Conditional Support to Draft Theses[12]

Strictly confidential

Moscow, 16 June 1921

To the Central Committee of the Communist Party of Russia (RCP)

Dear Comrades,

On the basis of yesterday's discussion with members of the Political Bureau of the RCP Central Committee, the German delegation states the following:

1.) In giving approval to the theses on tactics and strategy, the German delegation was making a concession. The delegation recognised that these theses contained a criticism of the March Action. It made this concession because it was politically desirable for the German delegation to collaborate at the congress with the Russian delegation – but not, however, with delegations like the French.
2.) If it is planned – beyond these theses – to make a special statement on the March Action, the German delegation insists on the following points.
    a.) The March Action was not a 'putsch'.
    b.) Viewed politically, the March Action was a step forward in the development of the German revolution and the party. It clearly demonstrated the party's readiness and capacity for struggle. It enabled the party to gather important experiences in struggle and to gain strength for future battles.
    c.) The delegation considers that the following errors were made in preparing for and carrying out the action: it was presented as an offensive; preparations for it were insufficiently broad and thorough; the goals of the struggle were not formulated with sufficient precision.
3.) Levi's categorical expulsion for base betrayal of the party and violation of party discipline must be confirmed.
4.) Party members must be forbidden to collaborate on *Sowjet* and other publications that have escaped party control. Formation of factions that distribute secret materials without the organisation's knowledge must be forbidden.

---

12. Stoljarowa and Schmalfuss (eds.) 1990, pp. 267–9. The German text is a retranslation from an archival Russian typescript in RGASPI.

5.) The Communist Party commits itself to apply strict party discipline, especially with regard to leading comrades, parliamentary deputies, and editors.

The delegation confirms the statement submitted by Comrade Frölich that it supports the Theses on Tactics and Strategy drafted jointly with the Russian delegation. If the Russian delegation dissociates itself from these theses, the German delegation will submit them as its own.[13]

The points made here are the absolute minimum of what the German delegation is demanding.

On behalf of the German delegation,<br>W. Koenen, A. Thalheimer, Paul Frölich.[14]

### 3e. Lenin Withdraws Harsh Language[15]

16 June 1921

Comrades Koenen, Thalheimer, Frölich

Dear Comrades,

I have received a copy of your letter to our party's Central Committee. Thank you very much. I communicated my answer orally yesterday.[16] I take this opportunity to emphasise that I do most resolutely withdraw the rude and impolite expressions I used, and hereby repeat my oral apology in writing.

With communist greetings,<br>Lenin

---

13. See Lenin's 10 June letter to Zinoviev, Appendix 3a, pp. 1097–1101. The German delegation is apparently protesting changes in the draft theses demanded and obtained by Lenin. This protest ultimately took the form of amendments; see pp. 1041–58.
14. The Russian text identifies the signatories as Thalheimer, Friesland, and a third indecipherable name. The names given here are supplied by Stoljarowa and Schmalfuss, based on their research.
15. Stoljarowa and Schmalfuss (eds.) 1990, p. 271.
16. According to the Russian edition of Lenin's Collected Works, Lenin is referring to remarks made in a meeting of the German delegation with members of the Russian CP Central Committee on 15 June 1921, where he sharply attacked the positions of 'leftists' in the VKPD. *PSS*, 52, p. 434.

## 3f. ECCI Debate on French Communist Party and Leftism

16–17 June 1921[17]

**Edy Reiland**: The Luxembourg delegation must speak out in the debate on France. The Luxembourg Communists have a close-up view from which to assess the French Communist Party's activity, and we are unanimously of the opinion that its politics are ambiguous and anti-Communist. We base this judgement on the fact that when the party joined the Third International, it entrusted the leadership to a pronounced Menshevik. Moreover the press continues virtually unchanged, and the party's activity has not altered. Comrade Jouwel (?)[18] has raised the necessary criticisms regarding the party's position on the mobilisation and the occupation of the Ruhr region.

We need only review the party's position at the time of the mobilisation and the occupation of the Ruhr region.[19] It is scandalous that Comrade Frossard, the party's dominant intellect, has written articles that are plainly anti-Communist and that sabotage the party's revolutionary development. I must tell you, it is entirely wrong to claim that comrades like Frossard have good will toward communism. The available facts flatly contradict this.

Frossard is a very dangerous politician and an outright centrist, whose intentions are absolutely not Communist and who is actually sabotaging the revolutionary movement in France. It is regrettable that even today the party Executive Committee has done nothing to alert French workers to this fact. Luxembourg workers are up in arms over this situation.

At the last [administrative] congress in France, Frossard stated that the agenda of the Third Congress of the Third International could not be discussed, because otherwise the delegation might not be able to leave in time. Comrades, is that a Communist point of view? In the same report, Comrade

---

17. Prior to the Third Congress, a series of expanded meetings of the Comintern Executive Committee took place from 11 to 20 June 1921, to which about seventy congress delegates were invited. The main topics under discussion were the Czechoslovak and French Communist parties.

The text that follows consists of five speeches taken from the debate on the French CP, which was initiated by a report given by Fernand Loriot. Included are contributions by Reiland (Luxembourg) and Laporte (Communist Youth in France), and responses by Trotsky, Kun, and Lenin. The material, previously unpublished, is found in Comintern archives, RGASPI, 495/1/37–8. The base language for translation is French (Laporte and Trotsky) and German (Reiland, Kun, and Lenin), but texts in other languages have been consulted.

The ECCI discussion on France also included a speech by Zinoviev, which he inserted into the proceedings of the Third Congress; see pp. 215–20.

18. The question mark appears in both the German and Russian texts.

19. For the French occupation of cities in the Ruhr Valley in March 1921, see p. 486, n. 9.

[Frossard] contradicted himself by saying that he was well aware that speeches in the old *constituante* were not Communist,[20] and later he said that there is deep harmony between us and these people. If he considers that the discussions were not Communist, then it is his duty to say this openly in France, and we criticise him for not having had the courage to do so.

As for relations between the party and the trade unions, it goes without saying that they remain what they were. Indeed, by and large, the application of party policies remains unchanged. During the Tours Congress, it was evident that the French syndicalists have taken a step toward the party. But they have not gone further, because the party's politics are not revolutionary and because they do not trust Frossard, with good reason. During the May Day celebrations too, the party was not capable of advancing a Communist point of view. Simple political indifference and fear induced them to leave it to the trade unions to organise the May Day events. The party did nothing, thereby handing the Luxembourg Social Democrats and Mensheviks the best argument to use against us. The Social Democrats in Luxembourg always buttress their arguments with references to the politics of the [French] Communist Party.

Here I would like to direct a special question to the French delegates: What have you done to protest French military occupation of Luxembourg?[21] What did you do to protest the invasion by the French police? After the occupation, a member of the Central Committee came to Luxembourg. He noticed the French soldiers and, quite puzzled, asked us: what are they doing here?

By way of a general conclusion, I'd like to stress that we are well aware that there are special conditions in France and that the social and historical environment is quite different. But precisely because there is an eighty-year history of democracy in France, the party there – as nowhere else – must be Communist. A period of passivity is precisely the time when a Communist Party is essential in order to promote revolutionary development. To this end, in the view of the Luxembourg party, it is absolutely necessary for the Executive of the Communist International to declare that it is not in agreement with the past politics and leadership of the party and does not grant this its silent approval. The best way to do this and also to put the International to the test, in our opinion, is to decide right here to decree Frossard's expulsion.

---

20. Both the German and Russian texts record the French word *constituante* and signal it with a question mark. The reference may be to the founding administrative congress of the French Communist Party, held in Marseilles 15–17 May.

21. French troops entered Luxembourg in March 1921 to help crush a strike by coal miners along the border with France.

**Maurice Laporte**: Following on the report by Comrade Loriot on the Communist movement in France, I must tell you something of my personal situation. I am well aware that this session of the Executive Committee is not focusing on our Communist Youth, their situation, and their activity, but I also know that the youth movement in France is closely tied to the party, and that the two cannot be separated.

Comrades, as you know, we fought for several years to separate the youth from the [Socialist] party. At that time, the party was purely a vehicle for parliamentary figures and politicians, and the youth, for their part, wanted to take instead the path of revolutionary action. They were drawn irresistibly to the newly formed Third International, and then to the Communist Youth International founded by the Berlin congress of November 1919. Inevitably, there was a deep antagonism between the youth and the party.

That is why, two or three years ago, we posed the question of the youth movement's autonomy, of its absolute independence vis-à-vis the party. Since then, the situation has changed somewhat: we had the Tours Congress, [the party's] affiliation to the Third International, and we could no longer pose the question so starkly. We could no longer tell the party, 'You are still the old reformist party; you are still the party of parliamentary deputies whose actions were so harmful to the workers' movement; we want to keep our distance from you', because the party had just adopted the principles and line of march of the Third International. Given the acute situation at the Tours Congress, everyone present agreed to refer the issue of youth-party relations to the administrative congress that was to convene within three months of the political congress. Everything remained in abeyance, and we still had no ties with the party.

Comrades, the changes in the party's policies after Tours were quite inadequate. There is a big difference between adopting the principles and theses of the Third International and putting them into practice. Loriot has just told us, 'After the Tours Congress, we experienced the split. The Dissidents stole the party treasury and tried to steal its headquarters and newspaper, and we had to battle against the reformists.'[22] His natural conclusion was that 'in combating the Dissidents we could not combat the bourgeoisie'. It must be stated, however, that there were openings to undertake action and that nothing was done. When taking action, the youth have always been isolated. As for me, at the congress I had spoken specifically on our willingness to work for rapprochement. Following the congress, although we wished to engage in

---

22. 'Dissidents' refers to the minority at the SP's Tours Congress, which opposed the decision to affiliate to the Comintern and rename itself 'Communist Party'. After the split, this minority retained the old Socialist Party name.

struggle in the framework of close ideological unity, we always felt that we were taking a different path, a different road.

So it was that when the class of 1921 was called up in France, the party did not speak out.[23] Its Executive Committee did not publish a single manifesto or protest about the call-up of the class of 1921. You cannot tell us that the Dissidents [SP] prevented the party from making some gesture. The youth were isolated in this action. When the class of 1921 was called up, they undertook a vigorous campaign. This took the form of broad propaganda for Communist demands: disarmament of the bourgeoisie, arming of the proletariat. This campaign reinforced and firmed up the youth cadres, and in addition the youth gained true authority in the French movement. As for the bourgeoisie, they were also not slow in reacting. A considerable proportion of our comrades suffered raids and were arrested.[24] In addition, our headquarters were wrecked. That indicates the scope of our campaign against militarism. On the one hand, we gained undeniable authority, but we also were subjected to repression.

Some time later, our imperialists revealed their intention of occupying the Ruhr by mobilising fourteen levies, of which the first was the class of 1919, which had just been demobilised only a month earlier. Despite the repression, despite our momentary disorganisation, we took a real and effective stand against the mobilisation and the threatened outbreak of war – on our own. And here a little comment is called for. We went to see the party's Executive Committee. We told them that *L'Internationale*, their evening Communist newspaper, was reporting the general mobilisation in its every issue. That in itself is an error, we said, because the general mobilisation has not yet been decreed. You report the general mobilisation, and meanwhile you do nothing, you write nothing against it.

We went to see the Anti-war Action Committee, to which we belong.[25] Because, contrary to what was said, this committee consisted not only of the party and the CSR [Revolutionary Syndicalist Committee] but also the Communist Youth, the Workers' Federation of Disabled War Veterans, the

---

23. On 3 May 1921 the French government called up the conscription class of 1919, some 200,000 men who had reached draft age that year, to meet its manpower needs for occupying the Ruhr Valley, with the goal of forcing Germany to pay war reparations. Laporte misspeaks here and refers to the 'class of 1921'; the confusion over the date is repeated later in the session and corrected during Trotsky's speech.

24. A total of thirty-seven Communist Youth members were arrested for participation in the campaign against the military call-up. Laporte himself was imprisoned in April 1921 for an allegedly subversive article in the anti-war newspaper *Le Conscrit*.

25. On 8 March 1921, the day French troops occupied the Ruhr, the CP helped establish an Anti-war Action Committee, together with the groups Laporte subsequently mentions.

Republican Veterans' Association, and also the Anarchist Federation. We told the Anti-war Action Committee, 'There is only one way to resist the call-up of the class of 1919 and the others and to resist the war danger, and that is to tell the young soldiers who are being instructed to leave for the army, "You must not go. You must stay at home. You must act and resist so that this slogan does not remain mere words."' We also said that it is essential for the CSR Central Committee to launch a movement for an insurrectional general strike in support of this slogan. That was our position.

And we did not take it lightly. We ourselves were at first divided regarding what slogan we should propose. Some of us held that the soldiers should return to their barracks, should not desert, and should undertake revolutionary action in other forms. Others of us said that, on the contrary, we had to propose the slogan that I have just explained to you. In the end, we united in support of this slogan. We told the party, 'Live up to your responsibilities and work together with us in support of this slogan.' We did everything we could in the party Executive Committee to press for action. And that was when we truly realised that there was an enormous gulf between the resolutions adopted at the Tours Congress and the way they were being applied.

We were told, as Louis Sellier put it, 'Mobilisation does not mean war.' We were told, via Cachin, 'We have to wait; there is a conference in London, and its decisions will change the course of events. For us to take action would become futile.' And further, 'We must be very cautious; we must not launch this action regardless of circumstances.' Everything testified to uncertainty, indecision, and above all ineffectiveness. The situation was quite new and we were taken by surprise. The result was universal panic. This indecision was deplorable at a moment when the crisis called for a bold slogan. That is the main thing that we hold against the party – its lack of clarity and of a firm stand toward developments.

Here is a typical example: the party Executive Committee meets regularly every Tuesday evening. The situation was urgent. We considered it revolutionary, but at the very least it was critical and harrowing. Despite this, the Executive Committee continued to meet each Tuesday evening, without taking any decision and without even trying to hold a special meeting.

In view of all this, we threw ourselves into the work of the Anti-war Action Committee. To a considerable degree, we succeeded in securing a victory for our principles in the committee. Within a few days, we secured the adoption of our slogan by the Veterans' Association and also by the CSR Central Committee. On our suggestion, the Action Committee sent a delegation to the party Executive Committee, seeking discussion of what we were to propose to the masses. The party Executive Committee gave the same response to the Anti-war Action Committee that it had given to the Communist Youth.

The war did not break out, and these events now lie in the past. The party showed itself to be ineffective. It did not take a decision. It did not present the masses with the necessary slogan through the voice of its speakers and the pen of its journalists. Granted, it did try to say that the looming war was a new imperialist war and that it did not want to take part, but in practice it did nothing to prevent the war and was not able to gain from the prevailing tumult and ferment.[26]

It was not enough to condemn the war verbally. More had to be done, and we called in vain for more to be done.

The situation was favourable. The state of mind across all France, and especially in Paris, was very favourable. Judge for yourselves: when the class of 1921 was leaving, we published a newspaper called *Le Conscrit* [The Conscript]. As I said, this newspaper was repressed and outlawed. When they set out to call up the class of 1919, we published *Le Conscrit* again, and this issue, too, was banned. In this issue we indicated our own position, our private view, because, after all, we did not want to move into action, taking the necessary initiatives, over the head of the party's Executive Committee. We told our units, 'Go back home. We do not want to launch this action, above all because we will achieve nothing. In order to act, the party's moral authority is needed, and, what is more, we are subject to its discipline. We do not want to rebel in this struggle against the decisions of the party, even if these decisions are bad.'

These are the facts regarding the party's inactivity at that time and the action of the youth. That is why the old antagonism between the youth and the party still exists. Nonetheless, at the party's administrative congress, a month and a half ago, we took a categorical stand. I told the party, 'These events lie in the past. Will they occur again in the future in such a way that the party is once again taken by surprise and will have the same approach as what we have seen? I refuse to believe it. In any case, regardless of our position, we intend to submit to discipline in action – but only in action. We will accept the instructions and decisions of the Communist Party, even if these are bad decisions. Nonetheless, when the action is over, we reserve the right of criticism, on the broadest scale possible, and if the instructions are bad, we reserve the right to appeal them to our international organisation.'

We drew a practical conclusion from all this. We asked the party to add two of our members to its Executive Committee, with vote. In exchange, we asked

---

26. During the two-week-long war crisis, headlines in *L'Humanité* reported Communist-initiated anti-war protest demonstrations in the Paris area with more than 12,000 participants on 5 May and 100,000 on 8 May. Police attacked the 8 May action, killing one protester and wounding fifty, *L'Humanité* stated.

the party to send two of its members, in the same way, to our National Committee, with vote. The party's administrative congress was won over fully to our point of view. As Loriot has indicated, a party commission of Frossard and Louis Sellier will meet with a commission of several youth comrades and will draw up logical and practicable rules that will govern future relations between the youth and the party.

Despite everything, we are anxious to state certain things to the Executive Committee of the Communist International. The party's activity has not always been as it should. Resolutions were adopted but were not always carried out. Regardless of where you look, that is the problem. That's the case with the trade-union question. Loriot does not see this and speaks only of doctrinal disagreements. As for us, we say that there are certainly deep disagreements, and the trade unions want to keep separate from the party and retain their autonomy. But if this attitude is still prevalent, we are partly to blame. Members of the party in the trade unions are not viewed as representing a special kind of politics; they are seen as politicians.

We understand that errors have undoubtedly been made, but we do not see evidence of good will on the part of the Communist Party. Yes, we recognise that a big step to the left has been taken. But the trade unionists, for their part, believe that the party they see still lacks vigour. They still see the same vacuum and conclude that the party, while adopting new formulations, has remained what it was before the War – a party of politicians and parliamentary deputies. We must say that, in our opinion, we will never gain influence in the trade unions unless the party moves into action and proves its worth. It must gain true awareness of its strength, consolidate its strength, and set an example along the road of action. Only then will it speak authoritatively in the name of French workers' organisations. When it has proven its worth in everyday action, it will be able to made demands and take charge.

Until the party has taken this revolutionary path, it will not be a Communist Party and it will not enjoy any real mass influence.

**Trotsky**:[27] I asked to speak in order to comment on the policies of the French Communist Party. But having heard the very eloquent speeches of our young

---

27. The archives contain a French text, which appears to be a direct transcription of Trotsky's speech, plus a quite different German text, and a Russian translation of the German. It is likely that Trotsky gave this speech twice, once in French and once in German. In the German text, he sought to answer views held by Hungarian and German delegates. The present translation is based on the French text.

friend Laporte and the comrades from Luxembourg [Reiland] and Hungary,[28] I must begin by responding to them.

What was it that Comrade Laporte told us in such a spirited manner? He said that we experienced a decisive moment when the class of 1921 was called up, in which the party failed completely to carry out its revolutionary duty. In his view, the party should have demanded that members of the class of 1921 refuse to obey the mobilisation order. Now, Comrade Laporte, what does that mean for the class of 1921 to refuse –

**Interjection**: It was the class of 1919.

**Trotsky**: I do not see how that makes any difference, because in either case this concerns about 150,000 or 200,000 men. Well, you call on them to turn down the order to report to the army. The call-up order, as I understand it, is quite a serious matter. First you get an order written on paper, and then the policeman, the constable, comes to your door. Well, if the party tells a young worker, 'You should not report for duty,' the party should also say, 'When the constable arrives at your door, you should do this or that.' In other words, 'You should equip yourself with a club, a stone, or a revolver and use violence to prevent the order from being carried out.' Or else, the party can say, 'Well, our opposition will merely be nominal. When the constable arrives and puts his hand on your shoulder, you will go along with him.' Now Comrade Laporte has not told us which policy he recommends to the party.

**Laporte**: Provided that the party supports the demand.

**Trotsky**: Well, does this involve, in short, carrying out a revolution against the capitalist state during the call-up? I have learned through study and experience, Comrade Laporte, that making the revolution is the task of the working class, not of the class of 1919. There you have it. You say that when the mobilisation was decreed, the party should have told the class of 1919, 'Given that the working class has not made the revolution so far, it's up to you, my little class of 1919, to make this revolution.' Yes indeed, Comrade Laporte. But you say that the conditions for revolution – not only a revolution of the class of 1919 but one of the working class – were not present. So it was not possible to make the revolution.

You have had three opportunities to make the revolution, because three classes are serving in the military. But the government wants to call up the fourth class. You say that we had to put up with having these three classes in

---

28. The Hungarian delegate is János Lékai. The text of Lékai's remarks to the plenum can be found in RGASPI, 495/1/37, pp. 46–51.

the military, but now that the fourth class is at stake, well then, now we will make the revolution. Not at all, not at all, Comrade Laporte. Not at all. I completely understand your feelings; I understand them very well. But it is not enough to have intense revolutionary feelings. Clear-headed revolutionary thinking is needed. Where that is lacking, you can make attempts at revolution, but you will never achieve victory. And what we want to achieve right now in France is not just revolutionary movements, necessary as they are, but a victory over the French bourgeoisie.

Very well, you say that when the president of France issued the decree for mobilisation, the time had come to tell the workers to make the revolution. It's up to you to demonstrate that to us, to show us that when the president signed the decree mobilising the class of 1919, the moment had come for social revolution in France – a moment determined by the entire economic and political situation, by the state of mind of the working class, by the party's capacities and state of organisation. You say that you are not concerned with any of that. The only relevant fact is the mobilisation decree.

Not at all, not at all! Revolution is not carried out in this fashion. This leads me to wonder what would have happened if the party had actually acted on your appeal. A call goes out to the class of 1919, 150,000 young men. I imagine that perhaps 50,000 of them, perhaps 5,000, perhaps 10,000 – you will agree – perhaps only half of them will not obey the call-up order. They are those with the greatest courage. And 5 per cent of them, the bravest ones, would be executed, and the others would obey the decree – isn't that true? And what would be the result? For the party, the result would be completely disastrous, because it would be shown by this action to be a part of purely verbal demagogy, because – at a critical moment, when it does not have the capacity to make the revolution – it turned to the youth. And in so doing, it indicated to the capitalist state who were the bravest among these youth, saying, 'Kill them.' That would be the outcome. Simply that. I do not see any other results of such an attitude; I do not see them at all.

As for the comrade from Luxembourg, he was even harsher. Indeed, pardon me, but he struck me as even a bit nationalist. What did the French party do when the French troops occupied Luxembourg? To stop the French army from occupying Luxembourg, you would have to carry out the revolution. And do the French workers have only one reason to make the revolution? Why would it be precisely Luxembourg that would lead the French worker to make the revolution? I do not understand this. Walking down the street, the French worker sees the jobless, the prostitutes, and the French cops: three reasons to make the revolution, right there in the street. And when he gets home, he finds a thousand more reasons. I wonder about the French worker – by and large, the French are not so gifted in geography, and particularly not the French workers – I wonder if the French worker knows exactly where Luxembourg is located. I have my doubts. He is told that because the French have just invaded this little country, because they have occupied this country, about which he knows so little, 'You must make the revolution.' Why? Because our comrade Reiland is from Luxembourg. But this motivation is national rather than revolutionary and communist. I could well ask what the French proletariat did when Loriot and Monatte were imprisoned. What did the French proletariat do? Why did it remain unconcerned? For that, too, was a reason to make the revolution.[29]

Why exactly have you come up with this example? Because it affects you. You see the young French soldier in his red trousers, and that bothers you somewhat. And then you ask: why don't they make the revolution? That is no way to promote revolution. The Luxembourg comrade said that the French are afraid of action. If this involves individual action, it may of course involve individual fear, a lack of courage, and such a lack of personal courage is a quite painful situation. But this is not a case of a lack of personal courage. It's a matter of political courage, given the results of such an action. Well, the Luxembourg comrade defended Laporte's proposal without understanding or analysing its results.

On the contrary, the task in France is to prepare for the revolution through propaganda, agitation, and action. However, comrades, when the decree was issued mobilising the class of 1919, preparing for the revolution and making the revolution are two entirely different things. True, I can say that when the mobilisation took place, the [party] Executive Committee perhaps did not do what it should have done. It's necessary to analyse what it did in terms of propaganda, of organising the masses, and of protests in parliament and in the streets. It can be said that the Executive Committee and the party as a whole could have done a great deal more than they actually did.

I concede that this is possible because I am not happy with the French party in its present condition, and Comrade Loriot knows this very well. But in criticising and persuading the French party, via Comrade Frossard, of course, I find the Luxembourg comrade's proposal of expelling Comrade Frossard to be completely out of place. Let me make a parenthetical comment here. When Frossard and Cachin came here, I was just as sceptical as other comrades, and perhaps more so, because I had spent some time in Paris.[30] I had some

---

29. Loriot and Monatte were among a number of Communists and syndicalists arrested in May 1920, charged with breaking the laws against 'anarchist intrigues' and plotting against the security of the state. They were imprisoned for ten months.
30. Frossard and Cachin came to Moscow in 1920. When Trotsky was living in France (1914–16), Cachin was a prominent supporter of the French war effort, while Frossard advanced both pacifist and patriotic views.

knowledge of the socialist parliamentary milieu and a close-up view of the party's stance during the War and at its outset. Many were not pleased, and I was among them. I was quite pessimistic regarding these two comrades.

But I have been quite pleased by what I have seen of their conduct since the Second Congress of the International. During this period they have been of service to the Communist International – that is a fact. They have succeeded – with the help and support of more resolute comrades, of course – in carrying out the split against the centrists. They assisted in launching the Communist Party. That is a fact, a very great fact, and we must now work on this foundation. We must give the party a stance that is more defined, more revolutionary. But to say at this point, when the party is coming into being, during the time between the two [French] congresses, that it's necessary to expel those who aided in launching it – and this is said by those who did not take part in the Second [Comintern] Congress – no, no, not at all. Comrades from Luxembourg, you are getting carried away by your indignation.

We must answer the question whether the situation in France is conducive to revolution. Yes or no?

**Interjection**: No, but it is favourable for action.

**Trotsky**: Favourable for action, but what kind of action? The proposed action is to refuse to obey the military call-up. In other words, an action that is permissible for a proletarian party only when the working class is on the verge of revolution. Only under those conditions can the conscripts called up into the army defy this order. This would have been justified, politically and historically, only in circumstances where the entire class to which the party belongs was drawn into a decisive revolutionary movement.

Tell us that we have now reached that decisive point. Tell us that the party's Executive Committee's stand is obviously wrong. Why? Because the revolution is knocking at the door, and nothing remains to be done but to open it. And here these members stick to their offices, writing leaflets – propagandistic, agitational, organisational – and attending to finances, instead of opening the door to revolution. Be that as it may, I have some knowledge of conditions in France. At this point, conditions across all of Europe and the entire world are destabilised economically. The spirit of the working class is fundamentally revolutionary. Conditions could become revolutionary in a very short time.

But what do we see in France? During this period, France has been the most reactionary country, the country most poisoned by illusions in war, in victory, and in the hopes that victory would bring tangible gains. France is the most poisoned country.

**Shout**: Yes!

**Other voices**: Hear! Hear!

**Trotsky**: Revolutionary France is strong in its spirit, in the resolve of its most advanced forces, and in you – yes! – because you also make up a significant part of the French working class. I have a good picture of that, Comrade Laporte. I have some knowledge of the French proletariat, of its spirit, the resolve it shows at the decisive moment. I understand that very well. But you cannot deny that Jouhaux's General Confederation of Labour (CGT)....[31] And the party, with Loriot, carried out the split only a few months ago. And now I see that the party is not decisive in its approach. What does that tell us? Of course the party has an apparatus, one that can become independent, quite independent – as in the CGT. But independent as it is, this apparatus reflects the thinking and spirit of the class – a clear inadequacy of the will needed to make the revolution....[32]

So the situation in France is as follows. Victory went to the chauvinists, who emerged triumphant. Hopes had not yet been quelled because of the continuous pillage of Germany, which of course paid a good deal less than had been hoped – a great deal less. Still, this booty nonetheless represented a partial payment of the enormous sum that the bourgeois class hopes to receive. The anticipation of this payment still governs the spirit of the bourgeois class. It makes concessions to the working class in the hope of receiving compensation extracted from the German nation.

That is the situation in France. Dominant following the War, it is the most reactionary country. We saw revolutions in Germany and Austria-Hungary; we saw quite revolutionary situations in Italy, when the police and the capitalist bourgeois state were demoralised. Nothing like this took place in France. Its government was by far the most stable and was led forcefully by the will of the ruling class, which even now feels that it is triumphant. Only now do we begin to notice a certain decline, reflected in the fluctuating results of Radicals and Radical-Socialists in the by-elections. This shows that the opposition has taken a very uncertain path via these Radicals and Radical-Socialists. This means that the political evolution of the masses in France, as I conceive of it, displays a wave of Radicalism and Longuetism, heading toward a Radical-Longuet bloc. If entirely unexpected events take place – a war, a revolution – so much the better!

---

31. Several words have here been erased from the French transcript.
32. The ellipsis is in the original text.

We must prepare for a situation that will be less than ideal. Still, if events head in this direction, it is no misfortune for us. In a situation where the Radicals and Longuetists form the government, we will be the only party of revolutionary opposition. Our situation will be clearly defined. We will criticise and unmask the Longuetists, who represent the most extreme wing of the bourgeoisie in power. We will draw the masses into increasingly energetic action corresponding to their class needs as defined by conditions. We cannot foresee everything. That's how I conceive of the situation in France. I believe that conditions there are fundamentally revolutionary, because the French economy has been thrown completely off balance. The society's material foundations are off balance. France is very impoverished in terms of its productive forces, just as impoverished as a defeated county, yet it has a lifestyle that could be that of the most powerful and richest country in the world.

This contradiction is quite evident in the decline of the French franc. You know this from personal experience. The French franc has lost part of its purchasing power. The fact that this victorious franc retains only a small fraction of its value demonstrates the contradiction between the lifestyle of bourgeois society in its entirety and the poverty of this society's foundations. This contradiction will also assert itself and find expression in the thinking of the working class. In other words, it is headed for ruin.

So conditions are excellent. We need a French honesty in fully utilising them. But in such conditions, it would be suicidal to let ourselves be drawn into partial actions whose scope and method lead to a showdown. I know this and understand it well. Defying the decree calling up the class of 1919 would have been a partial action created by entirely partial conditions that had no immediate and close relationship with the evolution of French politics – conditions, however, that would have required recourse to the most decisive methods, those of social revolution. Here we have a contradiction that could destroy us.

I do not say that I am happy with the conduct of the French Socialist Party.[33] Far from it, because what you need in a partial situation is clarity. Before you make the revolution, you need the will to do so. You have to understand what makes it possible and make yourself ready to carry it out.

I have noticed that the comrades making criticisms, while imbued with a desire to make the revolution, have not gained a full understanding of the conditions that make it possible. But if we consider the party at its outset, its Executive Committee and its parliamentary caucus, we note that the will to

---

33. Trotsky means the French Communist Party, the name adopted by the Socialist Party majority several months earlier.

make the revolution is quite indistinct. Comrade Laporte has a great advantage in that this will, in his case, is quite defined.

I tell you truly, Comrade Laporte, without any irony, this is how things stand. If you had told us that the party's Executive Committee lacked a well-defined will to make the revolution, that it could have done much more than it did in certain critical situations, you would have been correct. But that does not apply to the appeal that you proposed to us.

Let me give you an example from the pages of *Le Temps*. I see there some articles expressing a point of view from outside Paris, signed by initials that are not identifiable, but as far as I can see they reflect the views of Millerand and his extremely reactionary coterie. These articles express a fascist mentality that influences the country's political and social life. You in France should be preparing for a quite crucial situation, because the bourgeois layers are now aware of their class situation. The bourgeois newspaper states:

> We will experience difficult and quite dangerous conditions, and we have to create the appropriate state of mind right away. We must organise this and induce a universal awareness of this crucial fact: everyone must understand well his duty, his role, standing ready to struggle and when the signal is given, annihilating the anarchist-like forces led by agents of Moscow.

That's the gist of one such article, well written with well worked-out ideas. I expected, of course, to find the next day in *L'Humanité* three responses to this article, to be reprinted in full. 'Workers, an attack on you is being organised. The French bourgeois class is forming a combat organisation along fascist lines, equipped with arms, revolvers, rifles. Workers, we have to build our own combat organisation. We need a secret intelligence service, able to inform us regarding the enemy's weaponry, combat organisations, and so on.' That would be an initial, serious step. Not a vague and unprepared appeal to the class. A small beginning. I searched in vain through the pages of *L'Humanité*; I found nothing. No note was taken of this article in *Le Temps*.

Does this show a failure to direct all our attention to the most essential aspects of preparing for civil war? Attention to revolution is superficial; there you have it. Well, it is highly dangerous for the revolutionary will to be superficial. And it is just as dangerous if the party's political thinking is superficial. And that can be seen every day in *L'Humanité*. I cannot give additional examples, but I have a collection of newspapers dealing with the congress. I can give quite a number of examples to anyone who is interested. The accounts of parliamentary debates report the positions of various parties, among which there is one that bears the name 'Communist'. This is done with some shading, of course. The Communist speeches are presented as being more eloquent than those of the Longuet people. That is not always factually true, of course, but it provides shading.

We do not see here the abyss that our press and our language ought to create between the Communist Party and the entirety of bourgeois society. It is not visible. As for the workers who support *L'Humanité*, they have very good reasons to do so. But now these workers should be coming and telling you, 'But what are you up to? Why don't you speak like Communists? We see very indistinct shadings in what you write, hardly more distinct than among the Longuet people, in fact fundamentally the same.'

Of course, the revolutionary situation is not going to evolve more quickly because of our activity and influence or because of the voice of this congress. However, we must recognise and understand another fact: The party's attitude to the trade unions, in my opinion, is completely wrong. This is the most important question posed in France – that of relations between the parties and the unions. There are the unions [*syndicats*], and then there are the French syndicalists.

The French syndicalists are a party without knowing it. They do not consider themselves a party and are confused because they use the same name as the unions. The unions are workers' organisations that include all working people, without regard to their points of view or affiliations – workers who are socialist, communist, or unaffiliated – people organised for the economic struggle. Yet the unions have a certain leaning and a certain programme. Around this programme and certain comrades who advocate it, a party comes together that treats the unions as a territory subject to its influence. Two questions arise here: first, relations between the parties and the unions; and, second, relations between the Communist Party and this syndicalist party within the unions.

Small groups within the unions assert with regard to this socialist-syndicalist party that they do not want to be mixed up with the Communist Party for various reasons. These reasons were false and remain so. Wishing to avoid such contact, they hide behind trade-union autonomy. But we do not want to subordinate the unions to the party. What they are really saying is that they do not want their party to unite with another. I want to defend trade-union independence, but this is a camouflage – sincere, to be true – but a camouflage that must be removed, in the most friendly fashion, given that there are outstanding revolutionary forces among the French syndicalists. And then there are the French workers in their trade unions. We have to act with adroitness, but we must say openly what we are doing.

Well, in my view the French Communist Party does not always show courage in its conduct toward the syndicalists. It still preserves the practice of

Jaurès, who managed the unions without speaking about it. Just as you do not speak of the rope in the house of the hanged. You do not speak of the union's strengths or weaknesses; you just say that it is a workers' organisation with which you have fraternal relations – and let it go at that.

In the time of Jaurès, the party was quite reformist, opportunist, and nationalist, while the syndicalists represented a really revolutionary current. So the diplomatic management employed by the Jaurès current aroused legitimate fears. Any time the Jaurès current told the syndicalists that they had made such and such errors, the syndicalists could respond with a much longer list of errors by the Jaurès people. We are not required now to offer any apologies to the working class regarding our approach to the syndicalists. But I never see a word of criticism in *L'Humanité* regarding syndicalist doctrine. As for the syndicalists, I find only the Amiens Charter.

It was not their spirit or their willpower that led them to support reconstruction [of the International],[34] but intellectual subservience. I very well remember my old friend Bourderon, who said with regard to resuming international relations, 'Avoid above all seeking a Third International'. What Bourderon wanted was a return to the International as it had existed before 31 July 1914.[35] As for the syndicalists, they tell us, 'You talk about the dictatorship of the proletariat, you talk about soviets, but what we want is to go back to the Amiens Charter.' But my god! After the Amiens Charter there was that little war! There was the revolution in Russia and half a revolution, or a third of one, in Germany! A great upsurge in Italy! Does the Amiens Charter take these events into account? Not in the slightest. But didn't we, as Marxists, make many corrections and changes in our programme? We made corrections, we made changes, while the syndicalists in France always insist on going back to the Amiens Charter. It's like in the old song of Béranger.[36] In my opinion, the Socialist Party will do well to initiate in its press a fraternal and open discussion with the syndicalists. Our friend Monatte, for whom I have the greatest respect and affection, does not have a fixed position on these issues. He has been silent, and our comrade Loriot helps him remain silent on these issues.

---

34. A reference to the Committee for the Reconstruction of the International (CRI). In January 1916 a number of prominent socialists and syndicalists formed the Committee for the Resumption of International Relations, to oppose the pro-war stance of the leaderships of the SP and CGT. In March 1917 that committee split into pacifist and revolutionary wings, with the revolutionary minority founding the Committee for the Defence of International Socialism. In December 1919 the CDSI became the CRI.
35. This is the date of the murder of SP leader Jean Jaurès by a chauvinist assassin on the eve of the War.
36. Pierre-Jean de Béranger was a celebrated French songwriter of the early nineteenth century.

He did this in prison. It's true that you have to exercise tact in maintaining relations, because discussions in prison can end up badly; you can get too worked up there. But when you get out and rejoin, in your case, the party, and in his case, the trade union, you must open up a discussion. And I am confident that when comrades such as Monatte – and there are many others among the syndicalists – enter the party, this will result in a strong revolutionary impulse, an impulse very favourable both to the party and the unions. Well, this question is still pending. Not only is it unresolved, but nothing has been set in motion to resolve it. And here I think we see a lack of courage.

Comrades, I could present many more facts on the condition of the party, indicating that it is not yet equal to its job. Yet I must also say that at this time the Communist Party is more favourably situated in France than, perhaps, in any other country of Europe. Why is this? Events in France are developing much more slowly but in a fashion that is much more instructive for the working class. The great illusions in the War and in victory and the evolution of the Longuet forces are like preparatory lessons – a first, then a second and third – that they pass through gradually. The Communist Party that has been formed is strong in the context of conditions in France, where parties are not usually very large. Not usually. But they have very broad political influence. And for a party to have 120,000 members in France means a great deal indeed.

We see the rising wave of radical, Longuetist opposition. But this will position us, tomorrow, as the only opposition party. There was a similar revolutionary period in Italy where ideas were much less clear and the Communist International much less understood. In Germany, during the revolutionary period, the Communist Party was almost non-existent. There were the large Social-Democratic and Independent parties. The German Communist Party was formed, and it developed after great struggles and great decisions by the German working class. Already the will to revolution there is very strong, but there is also a certain scepticism and a certain weariness among some forces in the German working class. These are obstacles faced by the German Communist Party.

In France, we have not seen revolutionary struggles, but there is increasing discontent. Current conditions are more and more sharply defined. We have a Communist Party launched in France on the eve of the first great revolutionary event there, a party based on all the experience gained by the Communist International during the first three years after the War. That is a very favourable situation for the French Communist Party, and that is why I am confident, of course, that Comrade Reiland will not counterpose to the motion before us his proposal to expel Comrade Frossard. Of course, if anyone were to make a motion along these lines, it would be rejected, I trust, by a unanimous vote.

But we need to say the following to the Communist Party of France, in a friendly but emphatic manner. We do not ask that it undertake revolutionary actions without sizing up whether or not the situation is favourable. Of course, conditions must be analysed. Rather what we are asking of you is that you break with your previous attitudes, your previous relationships, your previous links with capitalist society and its parliament – with this parliamentary courtesy, which reveals simply a lack of revolutionary determination and clarity. We ask that you make this break not only in a formal sense but rather in your ideas, your feelings, your overall attitude, and that this break be categorical, total, and absolute.

What we ask of you is that your revolutionary resolve find expression in your press, in your parliamentary activity, in the unions – anywhere and everywhere, and that it ultimately find its highest expression on the Paris barricades. That is what we ask of you, without posing precise conditions or saying it must all be done tomorrow.

We do not say that you must make the French revolution tomorrow, but we do say that tomorrow the French party must have the determination to carry it out.

**Béla Kun**: Comrades, first of all, an episode from the experiences of a Turkestaner[37] (*Laughter*) that includes mention of a French comrade. It was during the March Action. The machine guns jumped into action. The Turkestaner was sitting in a room in Berlin with a friend from the German party, talking to a French comrade. The Turkestaner was not addressing the French comrade in the spirit of a Moscow diktat. He was not demanding that the revolution be carried out at once. He was merely asking quite unassumingly that if the Rhineland was occupied, could they please carry out a small amount of propaganda in the French army. The French comrade, a member of the party leadership, answered this quite unassuming question as follows: 'Dear comrade Turkestaner, how do you imagine that we could carry out propaganda in the French army? Dear Turkestaner, that would be high treason.' (*Laughter*)

This statement typifies the outlook of the French so-called Communist Party. This incident shows that the revolutionary outlook of the French party after Tours is the same as before Tours. What you could call a mechanical division is made between the periods before and after Tours, but there is very little actual difference between the two periods. The state of the French party is best indicated by the fact that Serrati's statements in his defence have repeatedly referred to the stance of the French party. After the Livorno

---

37. For Kun's status as a 'Turkestaner', see p. 197, n. 30.

Congress he even declared that in the French party he would be part of the left wing. As for *L'Humanité*, the [USPD's] *Freiheit* is by comparison a revolutionary newspaper. Certainly no one can maintain that I cherish great sympathy for *Freiheit*, but *L'Humanité* is not even able to speak to the masses in as revolutionary a spirit as *Freiheit*. No one, not a single Communist, could claim in good conscience that *L'Humanité* is a revolutionary Communist newspaper.

The way that *L'Humanité* speaks to the French comrades is very important because, while we do not expect the French party to make the revolution instantly, we do ask that it carry out revolutionary propaganda. The politics of the party is a somewhat different matter. Perhaps the party's politics need not be as Communist as its propaganda. In reality, the party's politics are not revolutionary and not Communist. The proof of this is the party's conduct on the questions of reparations, sanctions, and the call-up into the army.

Reparations are just another way of demanding indemnities. Every pacifist writes and agitates against annexations and indemnities. Every pacifist takes a rather clear position on this. But what has the French party done? I'm not going to speculate here; I will simply refer to what Comrade Rappoport, a long-time Marxist and leader of the French party, wrote in an article in *Die Rote Fahne*. The French party has declared its policy on this awkward and important question. For the French party, and above all Comrade Cachin, reparations are viewed as a justified demand on the Germans, he said.

And when the military call-up took place, and the French bourgeoisie mobilised its troops to occupy the Rhineland, what did the French party do? *L'Humanité* said very little about the response of the working class and its prevailing mood. However, we can conclude from *L'Humanité* that the working class did not at all approve of the leadership's position on this question. Thus we read daily reports in *L'Humanité* from Tours, Nancy, Troyes, and other cities that the called-up soldiers sang the 'Internationale', demonstrated against the war, often threw away the [...], and so on. The party took no initiatives before and during this period of the call-up, although it knew very well from the outset that mobilisation was coming and that new levies would be called up. Only on 4 May did the party publish a statement, which provides most convincing proof that the French party is not a Communist Party. This declaration reads:

> The party will not delay a single day in raising its protest against the call-up decreed by the government. The present difficulties arise out of the Versailles Treaty, which the party condemns as imperialist, unworkable, and tending toward generalised war. They flow from the brutal policies of the National Bloc, which the party combats unrelentingly. The government's resort to violent measures will not resolve these difficulties but only aggravate them.

This passage reveals that there is no difference between the party's position and that of Longuet. Further on, we read:

> The party reiterates that the government is being guided by sinister reaction and by heavy industry's thirst for annexations, while doing absolutely nothing regarding reconstruction of the devastated areas and *reparation*.[38] The party regards this as a hoax perpetrated against the French nation. The party believes that the young men, torn from homes, jobs, and personal freedom, do not have any duty toward the handful of profiteers who compelled the government to decree the call-up.

Absent here is any serious argument against indemnities, against reparations. The appeal also speaks passionately of revolution, just as *Freiheit* does in addressing the masses.

Yesterday, Comrade Trotsky thoroughly pummelled the French youth.

**Radek**: In a fatherly manner.

**Kun**: Trotsky spoke of the youth with much irony and asserted that the young comrades had presented foolish demands to the party leadership. That may be true. But if they made foolish demands, that is simply a result of the French party leadership's immobility, impotence, and anti-Communist outlook. (*Hear! Hear!*) More could be said about the blunders of the French youth comrades, but they result from the opportunist conduct of the French party. However, Comrade Trotsky has thoroughly studied all the documentation concerning the French party. Yet he said not a word about the fact that the Communist municipal councillors in France, with two or three exceptions, all signed the call-up decree, and that the party said not a single word against that and did nothing to call these Communist municipal councillors to account. It stands to reason that in such circumstances the youth can only conclude that it is the vanguard and that it must absolutely advance and not go backward like the party. That is what causes the youth's blunders. The party has committed much greater blunders, opportunist blunders. This can be shown by a few quotations from *L'Humanité*. On 5 May, Comrade Frossard wrote an article entitled 'Sangfroid and Discipline', which reads:

> There are times in the life of a party activist in which he cannot remain silent and bears a duty to speak out. We are now in such a situation. The party's sections in Paris are in a feverish condition, in which they impatiently desire

---

38. The German word used by Kun, *Reparation*, means 'reparations' or, less frequently, 'repairs'. The French text he is quoting probably used the same word, which in French means 'repairs' or, less frequently, 'compensation'.

to test their young forces in the hard battles of class struggles and urge us on to action. They know that the country is being led into war. Our rulers do not even take the trouble to conceal their imperialist policies.

And after this introduction, Frossard comes to the remarkable conclusion that the [call-up] orders should nonetheless be obeyed.

It is easy to comprehend why the youth under such conditions would commit blunders. When I consider the fact that the French party did nothing in this situation except to write pretty articles like that of Comrade Frossard, in his article 'Sangfroid and Discipline', I can easily grasp why the youth would not feel so bound by this discipline. No discipline can be maintained in a party that calls itself revolutionary but does not act in a revolutionary manner.

**Lenin** arrives in the meeting room.

**Kun**: All the regions and all party organisations took a clear position against indemnities; only the party itself failed to do so. Let me stress again that we are not expecting the French party to carry out a revolution, only revolutionary propaganda and revolutionary Communist agitation. If *L'Humanité* continues to be edited in this manner, if the French party continues to issue protests written with this kind of tone, not only will the French working class be repelled by communism, but it will also forget the revolutionary language of France. In that case, the French working class must recall the French Revolution of long ago in order to learn the French revolutionary language of old. I propose that the [Communist International] Executive Committee dispatch a commission to thoroughly investigate the situation in France and pose a series of conditions that must absolutely be fulfilled in a very brief time period, before the party is finally admitted by the world congress. (*Loud applause*)

**Lenin**:[39] I arrived at just the right moment, during the speech by Béla Kun. I came here precisely in order to oppose the remarks by Béla Kun. I suspected that if Béla Kun opened his mouth, it could only be to defend the leftists,

---

39. Victor Serge is probably referring to this speech when he recalls:
Lenin spoke in French, briskly and harshly. Ten or more times, he used the phrase 'Béla Kun's stupid mistakes': little words that turned his listeners to stone. My wife took down the speech in shorthand, and afterwards we had to edit it somewhat: after all it was out of the question for the symbolic figure of the Hungarian Revolution to be called an imbecile ten times over in a written record. (Serge 2012, p. 163)

Serge presents Lenin's speech as taking place during an ECCI debate on Germany. However, Lenin's comments at such a debate would have been delivered in German, not French, and the stenographic transcript would not likely have been compiled by Serge's wife (Liuba Russakova Kibalchich).

and so I wanted to find out on whose behalf he would speak. In Comrade Béla Kun's opinion, communism means defending the leftists. He is wrong, and this error must be most energetically opposed.

It must be stated openly that if there are still opportunists in the French party (and I am convinced that this is true) if they are not Marxists (and that is quite accurate), the leftists, for their part, have also committed an error, in trying to appear as leftists in the mould of my friend Comrade Béla Kun and some of the French comrades. Comrade Béla Kun thinks that there are only opportunist errors, but leftist errors exist as well.

According to the stenographic record of Comrade Trotsky's remarks, he said that if the leftist comrades continue to act in this manner, they will be digging the grave of the Communist and workers' movement in France. (*Applause*) I am strongly convinced of that as well. I have come here in order to protest the speech by Comrade Béla Kun in which he attacked Comrade Trotsky instead of defending him, as he was obligated to do if he was a real Marxist.

Marxism consists of determining what policy should be adopted in different types of circumstances. However, when Comrade Béla Kun comes here and talks of sangfroid and discipline, and of what was said about that in an article in *L'Humanité* with that title, it is he who understands nothing and is clearly in error. During a crisis such as that created by the mobilisation of French troops in the Ruhr, a party cannot launch slogans of that type. Anyone who does not understand that is not a Marxist.

Comrade Béla Kun believes that being revolutionary is a matter of defending the leftists, everywhere and under all circumstances. Preparing the revolution in France, one of the largest countries in Europe, cannot be done by a party on its own. What gives me the greatest pleasure is the fact that the French Communists have won over the trade unions. When I pick up this or that French newspaper – and I must frankly admit that I do this only rarely, because I do not have time to read newspapers – I notice the word 'cell' (*noyau*). I don't think you will find this word in any dictionary, because it is a purely Russian expression, which emerged from our long struggle against tsarism, against the Mensheviks, against opportunism and the bourgeois-democratic republic. It is our experience that gave rise to this organisational form. Cells act in concerted fashion, whether in the parliamentary fraction, in the trade unions, or in other organisations. And when Communists commit this or that error, even if less serious than the blunder committed by Béla Kun, we do not give it our approval.

When I regard this outstanding work by the French party, these cells in the unions and other organisations, I must say that the victory of revolution in France is assured, provided that the leftists do not commit blunders. If people say, like Comrade Béla Kun, that sangfroid and discipline cannot be justified, that is a leftist blunder. And I have come here to tell the leftist comrades that if you follow that advice, you will dig the grave of the revolutionary movement, just as Marat did.[40] I am not trying to defend the Communist Party of France. I do not claim that it is a thoroughly Communist Party. Not at all. Comrade Zalewski quotes a passage from *L'Humanité*, saying that the demand is justified; it may well be that he is quite right, from his point of view.[41] But we must not tolerate such a view.

Let us take another example, that of Marcel Cachin and others who defended the foreign policy of the Franco-British alliance in the French legislature and said it was a guarantee of peace, when in fact this alliance is nothing more than a gang of robbers. That is opportunism, and a party that tolerates its parliamentary representative taking such a political position is not a Communist Party. We have certainly referred in our resolution to various facts that must be emphasised, and to various actions that cannot be tolerated and are not Communist. But criticism must be specific in character. The task is to condemn opportunism. But the pronounced opportunism expressed in Cachin's speech has not been criticised. Instead, criticism has been directed at this formulation and new advice has been proposed. Comrade Trotsky said the following in his speech: (*Lenin quotes a passage from the German stenographic transcript of Comrade Trotsky's speech.*)

In addition, Comrade Laporte is quite wrong and Comrade Trotsky absolutely right in protesting against this statement. I am prepared to concede that the conduct of the French party is perhaps not fully Communist. But in that given situation, a blunder of this type would destroy the Communist movement in France and Britain. The revolution cannot be carried out by the class of 1919. And Comrade Trotsky was a thousand times right to emphasise this repeatedly. The same holds true for the Luxembourg comrade [Reiland] who charged the French party with having failed to sabotage the occupation of Luxembourg. He thinks this is a geographical question, as does Comrade Béla

---

40. The comment on Marat attributed here to Lenin is at odds with other writings of his that express respect for Jacobin revolutionaries of 1793. Marxists of his time generally evaluated Marat positively. The name index of Lenin's *Collected Works* (Lenin 1960–71) includes no mention of Marat. The present translation is based on an uncorrected archival record that is not free from anomalies; the reference to Marat may represent a slip by either Lenin or the stenographer. Lenin may have been thinking of Maximilien Robespierre, whom many Marxists outside France held responsible for having begun the repression of the popular movement. Thanks to Jean-Numa Ducange for research assistance on this point.

41. The 'demand' referred to here and subsequently is the French Communist youth's slogan that youth drafted for military duty refuse to report for service, explained earlier in this discussion by Laporte.

Kun. That's way off the mark. It is a political question. And Comrade Trotsky was absolutely right to protest against this. Yes indeed, it is an entirely leftist blunder, in which you appear to be very revolutionary, but which is in fact very harmful for the French movement.

The only thing that can prevent the victory of communism in France, Britain, and Germany is leftist blunders of this sort. If we pursue our campaign against opportunism without exaggeration, our victory is certain. We should openly criticise the French party. We should say that they are not a Communist Party. We should say bluntly that the policy advanced by Marcel Cachin regarding the alliance of France and Britain to exploit the working masses – and here, if I may use a word in an unofficial sense, they are robbers, and not only that, but robbers on a huge scale – we should state emphatically and entirely openly that the policy advanced by Cachin in this or that speech, in this or that article is not Communist but opportunist. The Central Committee of the Communist Party and, I hope, the Communist International congress as well will not approve this policy. Nonetheless we will not tolerate the even greater blunders committed by Comrade Béla Kun, or the blunders in the speech by the comrade from Luxembourg, or those of Comrade Laporte – even though he speaks so eloquently. I know that there are true revolutionaries among the Communist youth. Criticise the opportunists in a specific fashion; demonstrate the errors of official French communism – but do not commit such blunders!

Now, as the masses are approaching you more and more closely and as you are advancing toward victory, you must win over the trade unions. Preparations are under way in outstanding fashion to win a majority in the unions. And when you win them over, it will be an enormous victory. The bourgeois bureaucracy is powerless. It is the bureaucratic leaders of the Two-and-a-Half International that have the upper hand in the unions. Our task is to win a firm Marxist majority and then we will begin to make the revolution. But not with the class of 1919 and similar blunders, in which Béla Kun excels, but through the struggle against opportunism, and against the leftist blunders now coming to light.

Perhaps, in that case, there will be no need for a struggle, but only a warning against Marcel Cachin's speech. An open struggle against traditions and opportunism, but only a warning against leftist blunders. That is why I have considered it my duty to support Comrade Trotsky's position, by and large. The position advanced by Comrade Béla Kun is not worthy to be expressed by any Marxist, by any Communist comrade. It must be actively opposed. And I hope, comrades, that after the commission proposed here has done its work (and setting it up is a sensible move), and after an investigation of the

French party's conduct, it will come to a conclusion that does justice to this idea.[42]

## 3g. Zetkin on March Action Resolution[43]

Moscow, 18 June 1921

Lenin, my dear and esteemed friend,

In order to avoid any possible misunderstandings that could result in unpleasant surprises for either side and could harm the project we discussed, I will summarise my opinion as follows:

1.) The congress must immediately deliver an unambiguous and principled condemnation of the March Action, with respect both to its putschist character and its harmful results. This can be expressed in gentle fashion. However, a principled condemnation is indispensable to prevent its prolongation and repetition.

In the Central Committee's collection, *Tactics and Organisation of the Revolutionary Offensive: Lessons of the March Events*, the following was formally stated:

> Only the decisiveness of the March Action could break from the past of the revolutionary party in Germany, etc.... If this idea penetrates deeply into the masses' consciousness, the March Action will not be the final episode. The March Action as an isolated initiative by the party – for our opponents are right about that – would be a crime against the proletariat. The March offensive as a prelude to a series of self-reinforcing actions – that is a liberating act.[44]

---

42. In a 29 June 1921 letter to the Italian CP leadership, Umberto Terracini described the impact of this speech: 'I will not conceal the impression created among all congress participants during the commission and Executive discussions, ...namely, that these comrades have leaned enormously to the right. Lenin gave a speech on the French party...[i]n which he laid out tactical principles, but did so using terms that were so crude and expressing himself so curtly that it was quite clear...he was trying to prepare the delegates for even coarser statements in his speech to the congress. The content of his speech was markedly toward the right, as against what he explicitly terms 'les bêtises de gauche' [leftist stupidities]. Nor did he find more genial terms to describe the factions at the extreme [left] in all the International's parties.' Natoli 1982, p. 131.
43. Translated from a Russian rendering of the German original text. Drabkin et al. (eds.) 1998, pp. 290–3.
44. Translated from VKPD Zentrale 1921. The first sentence of the quotation appears to be a summary of the VKPD collection's introduction, while the remainder is translated from page 6.

I hope you will find the time to read this collection or a fully objective summary of it. It is a mirror of the Central Committee's confusion as to principle and of its political bankruptcy. The fact that the CC does not wish to publish it is quite understandable.[45] I could not give my agreement to any resolution that would mean taking my distance politically from Comrade Levi or repudiating him. I could not make any statement along those lines.

I can only repeat what I said to tens of thousands of workers in public meetings, during which there was not a single protest, and no one condemned my stand.

I am in agreement with Comrade Paul Levi's principled political assessment and criticism of the March Action, but I do not put my name to every word in his pamphlet and do not share every aspect of his conclusions.

I continue to believe that it was essential and helpful that Comrade Levi's criticism was expressed right after the end of the March Action, because there was a danger that the action would be continued.

I am convinced that Comrade Levi, in writing his pamphlet, was guided by passionate concern for the party's present and future.

Continuation of the March Action policy would have meant the party's full political, moral, and organisational collapse, repelling the proletarian masses from it for a long time. And this in conditions that actually do call out for action, for activity. In my view, the greatest crime of the CC lies in the fact that its one-sided political position ignored crucial aspects of reality. It refused to see that, caught up with theoretical speculation born of office discussions and carried away by the lust for action, it was destroying and paralysing the forces who could and should have been the effective moving forces – if they had been called to action by political means rather than by terrorist and bandit romanticism.

Zinoviev visited me yesterday evening. Unfortunately, I was not able to discuss everything with him. He informed me that the Russian CP is proposing a resolution along the following lines: the March Action is not a putsch but a defensive action with many errors. It is an isolated action, rather than the starting point of a new era of revolutionary tactics and offensives.

For us, this resolution is unacceptable. The word 'putsch' refers not to its small size, as Zinoviev says, but to its *essence*. That consists of using terrorist means to force the pace of history and seeking though such means to push the masses into action. In practice, this leads to a struggle by the minority against the proletarian masses. It is not enough to note that many errors were

---

45. The VKPD collection was published 4–5 April 1921 but was rapidly withdrawn from circulation when the Zentrale majority began to adjust its line.

made in carrying out the action. What's at stake here is understanding that such errors are inevitable as a result of a political position that was wrong in principle, and of erroneous leadership in the struggle. In our view, there is no need to formally repudiate the CC; it has been sufficiently repudiated and condemned by the events themselves. But we reject any ambiguity that could and would be utilised politically by an incompetent and frivolous CC to justify its dangerous stupidity. The CC compensates for its political incompetence through vanity, capriciousness, and malice.

The Russian comrades should take into account that the party's decay cannot be prevented solely by a resolution on paper – even one adopted by the Third International – but rather only through joint struggle and harmonious fraternal collaboration. But it must be made impossible for one of the forces in the party to seize on a formulation for use against the other side. In that case the struggle would continue rather than coming to an end. It will not destroy the CC to recognise that the March Action was neither a revolutionary offensive nor a transition to a 'new tactic'. Surely even the one-eyed king in the land of the blind would recognise that the action was not an offensive. Moreover, in light of Brandler's defence before the court, I must ask whether this represents a stance of revolutionary heroism and consciousness. It was legalistic chicanery of the most vulgar sort, rather than fiery revolutionary propaganda. A comrade who was here yesterday said that the report on this in the [USPD] newspaper *Freiheit* was completely accurate. The trial made an extremely depressing impression.[46]

I would like you to talk privately to Comrade Neumann, a member of the trade-union commission, and with Comrade Franken, chair of the Rhineland-Westphalia district, our strongest and most important industrial region. Despite stupid harassment by the CC and its supporters in the region, he was elected by the base organisation by an extremely large margin.

---

46. Brandler was condemned in June 1921 to five years imprisonment for his role in the March Action. In November 1921, he succeeded in escaping and making his way to Soviet Russia. According to his biographer, during his trial Brandler utilised every legal device to undercut the charge of high treason. He denied that the VKPD had engaged in terrorist actions, invoking the passage in the KPD's founding programme that repudiated individual terrorism and set its goal as winning a working-class majority. He dismissed the VKPD's call to overthrow the government as no more treasonous than a parliamentary vote of non-confidence. He called in personalities from the SPD and bourgeois public life to testify as to his character.

Brandler's conduct in court aroused protests from many VKPD leaders, like Eberlein and Meyer, who held he should have taken a more aggressive stance in court. Becker 2001, pp. 139–41.

Before the congress begins, I would like to talk to you about *one important point*. Could you please tell me where and when this would be possible? I send my greetings to you and to our dear comrade Krupskaya.

Yours truly,<br>Clara Zetkin

## 3h. Radek on Differences among Bolshevik Leaders[47]

*Report by Radek to meeting of Russian Delegation, 21 June 1921 (Extract)*

**Radek:** ...Now I will turn to the differences of opinion that developed among members of the Central Committee involved in the work of this international movement.[48] Here I must note that the main and basic disagreement arose because only a portion of the comrades were in a position to be closely involved in this work. Neither Vladimir Ilyich [Lenin] nor Comrade Trotsky was in a position to follow the course of this work; only in recent weeks were they able to become acquainted with it.

We proposed theses drafted by the group working in the Comintern. Comrades Zinoviev, Bukharin, and myself drafted theses that had a political thrust as follows: The revolution is not headed into decline. Instead, we are headed into growing struggles. However, nowhere do we have support from the majority in the workers' movement, and winning this majority is our most important task. This task is obstructed above all by opportunist forces within the Comintern, who are not able to show a capacity to attract the masses, the strength possessed by revolutionaries who are linked to the masses and strongly articulate their demands and who also possess organisational skills. Based on experience in Italy, Germany, and Czechoslovakia, we came to conclusions opposed to the rightist tendencies within the Comintern.

As for the leftist dangers, we always took them into account. At the Second [Comintern] Congress we struggled against the Communist Workers' Party of Germany [KAPD], with their rhetoric about pure communism in the party, about recruiting only pure communists, and about how the trade unions can ruin the workers' movement. We also spoke against every opportunist tendency, and if you measure these failings on a European scale, you can

---

47. Radek's report concerned 'the situation of Communist parties when the Third Congress was convened.' The portion reproduced here takes up issues flowing from the March Action in Germany, and then breaks off abruptly. Comintern archives, RGASPI 490/1/36a, pp. 16–19.

48. The members of the Russian Communist Party Central Committee assigned to international work were Bukharin, Lenin, Radek, Trotsky, and Zinoviev.

certainly say that the weakness on the left is much less serious than that on the right.

What is this rightist tendency? The centrist forces in the German Communist Party must be seen against the background of the million-strong Scheidemann party [SPD], the Independents [USPD] with their half-million members, and the trade unions with their bureaucracy. Although more refined and disguised by Communist rhetoric, [the centrists in the VKPD] carry out the same politics as these other groups. In Britain, we have to the right of the party the huge trade-unionist movement, and on the left only small grouplets. In France, the danger on the right is ten times greater than that posed by leftist deviations. Thus we consider that, in general, the left deviation is less dangerous.

Now, Comrades Trotsky and Lenin have been alarmed by the March movement in Germany, demanding that we pay more attention to the left danger and struggle on both fronts, given that the workers' movement in Germany is maturing and new battles could break out at any moment. In Bavaria, which is ravaged by [white] terror, there was a strike in which the Scheidemann people took part together with the Communists. Comrade Trotsky fears that the comrades on the left have come up with bad theories that may lead to defeat.

When the German comrades arrived here, they showed us theses in which this theory was presented very distinctly.[49] We asked them whether they wanted to proceed on their own or together with us. They said they wanted to work with us. In the course of discussions, we persuaded these comrades to withdraw their draft, and they joined in support of our theses, which clearly outlined the left danger in its entirety.

This theory is now – how shall I put it? – somewhat wobbly. We do not want a situation where the Russian delegation argues for one position, while Comrades Zinoviev, Bukharin, and I argue in defence of the March theory. In such a situation, in the heat of battle, the other side would begin to beat up on left adventurism in such a fashion as to discredit a revolutionary group of comrades with whom we have ties. So we made concessions, namely adding another paragraph for clarity, and we corrected some obvious errors. But there is a point in the resolution that refers not to ourselves but to an adventurist left wing, saying that a party in Germany is advancing ridiculous slogans.

By some mischance, Comrade Trotsky arrived at the session precisely at the moment when Comrade Laporte was criticising the [French] party.[50] Comrade Trotsky struck back at him with a reprimand. The next day, Comrade Lenin

---

49. Radek is referring to the 'theory of the offensive'; see p. 208, n. 49.
50. The reference is to the expanded ECCI discussion on France; see Appendix 3f, pp. 1108–32.

arrived at just the moment when Comrade Kun made some exaggerated statement that Communist immunity [to bourgeois pressure] is not strong enough. Comrade Lenin, too, struck out against the left wing.

The German comrades said, with regard to various formulations in the theses, that they could be discussed out in the commission.

### 3i. Zetkin on Discussions with Lenin[51]

On the occasion of the Third Congress of our International and the Second International Conference of Communist Women, I made my second lengthy visit to Moscow. It was muggy. But this was not so much because the sessions took place in late June and early July, when the sun pours down its glowing rays on the golden and beautifully coloured domes of the city, as because of the atmosphere in the parties of the Communist International. In the Communist Party of Germany, in particular, the air was charged with electricity, with storms, lightning, and thunder breaking out every day. Pessimists among us, who are enthusiastic only when they believe they sniff the scent of disaster, foretold the party's disintegration and collapse. The Communists organised in the Third International would have been poor internationalists indeed if the passionate debates on theory and practice in the German party had not inflamed the spirits of comrades in the other countries. 'The German question' was in reality an international question, and indeed – at that moment – the overriding issue in the Communist International itself.

The 'March Action' and the so-called theory of the offensive that underlay it forced the entire International to investigate thoroughly the world economic and political situation. (Although sharply and clearly formulated only afterwards, in order to justify the March Action, the theory of the offensive cannot be separated from its starting point.) Only this analysis of the world situation could provide a firm basis for the International's fundamental and tactical orientation, that is, for its immediate tasks, for the revolutionary mobilisation and activation of the proletariat, of the productive masses.[52]

---

51. Zetkin wrote the following account of her discussions with Lenin before and during the Third Congress in the month of Lenin's death, January 1924. The text is translated from Zetkin 1985, pp. 32–53. An earlier translation (Zetkin 1934, pp. 21–35) has also been consulted. Subheadings have been added.

52. 'Productive' translates the German word *Schaffende*, which means both 'producers' and 'creators'. The term was often used by Zetkin, who defined it in a 1923 speech as referring to 'all those whose labour, be it with hand or brain, increases the material and cultural heritage of humankind, without exploiting the labour of others'. Puschnerat 2003, p. 346.

As is known, I was among the sharpest critics of the March Action, insofar as it was not a proletarian struggle but rather a party action that was wrong in its conception, and lacking in preparation, organisation, leadership, and execution. I vigorously contested the theory of the offensive, which had been conjured up with such strenuous exertion. In addition, I had a personal debt to settle. The German party leadership had veered back and forth in its position on the congress of Italian Social Democrats in Livorno and the Executive's policy [there]. This had led me to a sudden, demonstrative resignation from the Zentrale. I was painfully and sadly aware that this 'breach of discipline' had brought me into sharp disagreement with those who stood closest to me, both politically and personally – my friends in Russia.

There was no small number of fanatical partisans of the March Action in the Executive, the Russian party, and other sections of the Communist International. They celebrated it as a revolutionary mass struggle carried out by hundreds of thousands of resolute proletarians. The theory of the offensive was praised like a new gospel of revolution. I was well aware of the bitter struggle that lay in store for me and firmly resolved to undertake it and fight through the fundamental line of Communist politics, whether this brought me victory or defeat.

What was Lenin's opinion on this tangle of problems? Like none other, he knew how to translate the revolutionary fundamentals of Marxism into action, to conceive of individuals and things as they are united by history, and to judge the relationship of forces. Did he adhere to the 'Left' or the 'Right'? Anyone who did not unconditionally rejoice at the March Action and the theory of the offensive would, of course, be branded as a 'rightist' or 'opportunist'. Trembling with impatience, I awaited unambiguous answers to these questions. These answers would be decisive in setting the International's goals and determining its striking power – indeed, for its very existence. When I resigned from the German party's Zentrale, this cut the threads of my correspondence with my Russian friends. So I had heard only rumours and conjectures – some doubtful, some emphatic – regarding Lenin's assessment of the March Action and the theory of the offensive. A few days after my arrival, I had a lengthy discussion with him, which provided me with an unequivocal answer.

Above all, Lenin wanted to hear a report on conditions in Germany as a whole and within the party. I tried hard to respond as clearly and objectively as possible, citing facts and figures. Now and then, Lenin threw in a question, in order to dot all the i's, while making brief notes. I did not conceal my concern over the dangers that in my view threatened the German party and the Communist International, if the World Congress were to adopt the theory of the offensive.

Lenin laughed heartily and self-confidently. 'Since when have you become one of the doomsayers?' he asked. 'Don't worry, the theoreticians of the offensive will not see their trees take root at the congress. We, too, will be present there. Do people think we 'made' the revolution without learning from it? And we want you all to learn from it too. Can you really call that a theory? Beware, it is an illusion, romanticism, sheer romanticism. That is why it was cooked up in the 'land of poets and theorists', with the help of my dear Béla [Kun], who also belongs to a poetically gifted nation and feels an obligation to always be more left-wing than the leftists. We must not fall into poetry and dreaming. We must assess the world economic and political situation soberly – quite soberly – if we are to undertake the struggle against the bourgeoisie and triumph. And we want to triumph; we must triumph. The congress decision on tactics and strategy of the Communist International and all the other disputed issues must be perceived and examined in conjunction with the international economic situation. It must be dealt with as a whole. In the meantime, we must pay more attention to Marx than to Thalheimer and Béla, although Thalheimer is a skilled, trained theoretician and Béla is an outstanding and true revolutionary. At any rate, there is more to be learned from the Russian Revolution than from the German March Action. As I said, I am not worried about the position the congress will take.'

I interrupted Lenin: 'The congress must also take a position on the March Action, which is the result of the theory of the offensive, putting it into practice and providing a historical test,' I said. 'Can theory and practices be separated? Yet I see that many comrades here, while they reject the theory of the offensive, nonetheless passionately defend the March Action. For me, there is no logic in that. Certainly all of us feel a sincere sympathy with the proletarians who fought because they felt provoked by the thuggish actions of Hörsing and wanted to defend their rights. We will all declare our solidarity with them, regardless of whether they numbered in the hundreds of thousands, as in the fairy tales some are telling us, or only in the thousands. But our Zentrale's fundamental and tactical attitude to the March Action was quite different. The March Action was a putschist transgression, and no theoretical, political, or literary soap will whitewash the reality of that fact.'

Lenin responded quickly and decisively. 'To be sure, the defensive actions of battle-ready proletarians must be judged differently from the ill-advised offensive push of the party – or, more correctly, of its leadership,' he said. 'You who opposed the March Action were partly to blame that this distinction was not made. You saw only the erroneous policy of the Zentrale and its bad results and not the combative workers of Central Germany. In addition, Paul Levi's completely negative criticism lacks any sense of adherence to the party; it embittered comrades perhaps more by its tone than its content.

This distracted comrades' attention from the most important aspects of the problem.

'With regard to the position the congress is likely to take on the March Action, please take into account that we must absolutely prepare the ground for a compromise. Now don't give me that puzzled and reproachful look. You and your friends will have to accept a compromise. You must rest content with taking home the lion's share of the congress laurels. Your fundamental political line will triumph, and triumph brilliantly. That will prevent any repetition of the March Action. The congress decisions must be strictly carried out. The Executive will make sure of that. I have no doubts in that matter.

'The congress will wring the neck of the celebrated theory of the offensive and will adopt a course of action corresponding to your ideas. In return, however, it must grant the supporters of the offensive theory some crumbs of consolation. To do this, in passing judgement on the March Action, we will focus attention on the way that proletarians, provoked, fought back against the lackeys of the bourgeoisie. Beyond that, we let a somewhat fatherly leniency prevail.

'Clara, you will resist this as representing a cover-up and worse. But that will get you nowhere. We want the policy adopted by the congress to become law for the Communist parties' activity as quickly and with as little friction as possible. To that end, our dear leftists must be able to return home without being too humbled and embittered. We must also, first of all and above all, focus on the moods of the genuinely revolutionary workers both within the party and outside it. You once wrote that we Russians should learn to understand something of Western psychology and not thrust in the face right away with our harsh, bristly broom.'[53] Lenin smiled at me contentedly. 'Well then, we are not going to shove our broom in the leftists' face; indeed we will pour some balm on their wounds. Soon they will join with you happily in energetically carrying out the Third Congress policies. And that means gathering the broad proletarian masses around your political line, mobilising them, and bringing them into struggle, under Communist leadership, against the bourgeoisie and for the conquest of power.

'By the way, the principles of this policy are clearly expressed in the resolution that you placed before the German party's Central Committee,' he

---

53. Lenin is presumably referring to Zetkin's letter of 25 January 1921, which says, with regard to the Comintern Executive's letter to the French SP's 1920 congress in Tours, 'I must strongly request that you influence the Executive to exercise more caution in its letters and appeals. They sometimes take the form of a blunt and imperious intervention lacking in knowledge of the real circumstances in question.' Stoljarowa and Schmalfuss (eds.) 1990, p. 211.

added.⁵⁴ 'The resolution was not at all negative, like Paul Levi's pamphlet. Despite all its criticism, its tone was positive. How can it be that it was rejected, and not only that, but with that kind of discussion and motivation! What is more, it is so apolitical not to utilise the difference between positive and negative criticism to separate you from Levi. Instead, they battered you almost over to his side.'

I interrupted him: 'My dear Comrade Lenin, do you really think that you must also provide me with some crumbs of consolation, because I am to swallow this compromise? You don't need to apply balm in my case.'

'No,' Lenin said, fending me off. 'I do not mean it that way. To prove that, I will right away give you a sound thrashing. Tell me, how could you have committed such a first-class blunder – yes, a first-class blunder – as to run away from the Zentrale? Did you take leave of your senses? I was angry about that, truly angry. Such a panicky way to act, without considering the effects of such a step and without sending a single word to inform us and to obtain our opinion! Why did you not write to Zinoviev? Why did you not write me? At the very least you could have sent a telegram.'

I explained to Lenin the reasons that had led me to that decision, which had been taken suddenly on the basis of the situation I faced at that moment. Lenin did not accept my reasoning.

'What nonsense,' he cried sharply. 'You were not elected to the Zentrale from the comrades there but by the party as a whole. You should not have cast aside the confidence they placed in you.' Seeing that I was still unrepentant, Lenin pursued his strong criticism of my resignation from the Zentrale and then immediately added, 'Perhaps we should view it as well-earned punishment that yesterday, at the women's conference, you were subjected to nothing less than a well-organised attack on you as the embodiment of the worst type of opportunism. And this was led by our good Reuter (Friesland), who thus participated, for the first time as far as I know, in Communist work among women.⁵⁵ That was simply stupid, quite stupid. Imagine: he thought

---

54. For Zetkin's resolution see Appendix 2c, pp. 1079–86.
55. During the opening ceremonies of the Second International Conference of Communist Women, held in Moscow 9–15 June 1921, Kollontai introduced a resolution stating, in part, that 'the German proletariat has emerged even stronger from the difficult March struggles'. Zetkin responded in the first session with a written statement protesting against this passage. A counterstatement was made by Bertha Braunthal, Hertha Sturm, and other women of the VKPD delegation, who said that Zetkin's data on this question consisted of 'falsifications or delusional exaggerations'. Neither statement was read out, and the conference continued its business. Friesland thereupon took the floor and delivered an attack on Zetkin, obtaining adoption of a resolution condemning her stand on VKPD policies during the March Action. Reisberg 1971, pp. 170–1. See also Appendix 3j, pp. 1048–51.

he could rescue the theory of the offensive by launching a sneak attack on you at the women's conference. Of course, other conjectures and hopes were at stake.' Lenin regretted that he had learned of this 'sneak attack' only too late and recounted how it was prepared and what it aimed at, making funny and sarcastic remarks about various people, and in particular about 'great men busying themselves with backdoor and petty female politics'.

He then continued, 'I hope you will consider this incident politically and in a humorous spirit, although in a personal sense it leaves quite a bad taste. We need only focus on the workers, on the masses, dear Clara, and always think of them and on the goal that we will achieve, and such trivialities fade away to nothing. None of us are spared this kind of thing. Believe me, I have had to swallow my share of it. Do you perhaps think that the Bolshevik Party you so admire was created as a finished product at one blow? Even friends have sometimes done the most unwise things. But let's get back to your transgressions. You must promise me never again to engage in such pranks – otherwise that will be the end of our friendship.'

After this digression, our conversation returned to the main issue. Lenin laid out the outlines of Communist International tactics and strategy that he later presented to the congress in his splendid and luminous speech, ideas that he had previously presented more polemically and categorically in the sessions of the commission.[56] 'The first wave of world revolution has ebbed,' he said. 'The second wave has not yet arisen. It would be dangerous for us to entertain illusions. We are not Xerxes, who had the ocean whipped with chains.[57] Is it somehow passive to determine the facts and analyse? Not at all! Learn, learn, learn! Act, act, act! Be prepared, fully and well prepared, in order to make full use, consciously, with all your strength, of the next, approaching revolutionary wave. That is our job. Tireless party agitation and propaganda, culminating in party action, free from the delusion that it can set loose mass action. Think how we Bolsheviks worked among the masses, up to the point where we were able to say, "The time has come. Now let's go!" That's why we say: To the masses! Win over the masses as a precondition to winning power. You critics have every cause for satisfaction with the congress adopting this position.'

---

56. Zetkin is referring to Lenin's 6 July speech to the Commission on Tactics and Strategy. No transcript of that speech was located for this volume, although excerpts related to Czechoslovakia can be found in Appendix 4b, on pp. 1155–7.

57. Xerxes was king of Persia from 486 to 465 BCE. Seeking to invade Greece, he built pontoon bridges across the Hellespont (Dardanelles) using flax and papyrus cables; these were destroyed in a storm. Enraged, he ordered his workmen to punish the sea by scourging it with a large whip, as a show of his defiance and his determination to subject it to his will.

'And Paul Levi,' I asked. 'What's your view of him? What position will your friends and the congress take on him?' For a long time, this question had been on the tip of my tongue.

'Paul Levi: unfortunately, that has become a separate matter, Lenin replied. 'It is mainly Paul himself who is to blame for this. He distanced himself from us and, stubbornly, ran into a blind alley. You must have seen this while carrying out such intensive agitation among the delegations. With me, you don't need to press your case in this way. You know how greatly I value Paul Levi and his capability. I got to know him in Switzerland and placed great hopes on him. He proved himself in a time of severe persecution; he was brave, clever, unselfish. I thought he had close ties with the proletariat, even though there was a certain coolness in his relationship to workers – sort of a "wanting to keep one's distance". Since his pamphlet came out, I have had doubts about him. I fear that he has a strong inclination to go his own way, like a lone wolf, and also a touch of literary vanity.

'Ruthless criticism of the March Action was necessary. But what did Paul Levi give us? He cruelly tore the party to pieces. His criticism was highly one-sided, exaggerated, even spiteful, and he gave the party nothing on which it could get its bearings. Missing is any feeling of solidarity with the party. That is what so infuriated comrades of the rank and file, making them unable to see or hear all that was correct in Levi's criticisms – particularly his correct fundamental political orientation. So a mood arose – and it extended to the non-German comrades as well – in which the quarrel over the pamphlet and especially over Levi's personal role became the sole subject of debate, rather than the false theory and bad actions of the "theoreticians of the offensive" and the "leftists". They should thank Paul Levi for the fact that up to now they have come through it all so well, far too well. Paul Levi is his own worst enemy.'

I had to admit the truth of his last sentences, but I strenuously objected to other statements by Lenin. 'Paul Levi is no vain, complacent litterateur,' I said. 'He is not an ambitious political climber. It was his fate, not his desire, to take leadership of the party when he was young, lacking political experience and a thorough theoretical education. After the murder of Rosa, Karl, and Leo [Jogiches], he had to take on the leadership, despite his often expressed resistance. Those are the facts. It is true that he is not very warm in his dealings with our comrades and is a lone wolf. Nonetheless, I am convinced that he is one with the party and the workers in every fibre of his being. He was shaken to the roots by this unfortunate March Action. He firmly believed that they thoughtlessly put at risk the very existence of the party for which Karl, Rosa, Leo, and many others gave their lives. He cried – literally cried – with pain at the thought that the party was lost. He believed it could be saved only through the use of stern remedies. He wrote his pamphlet in the spirit of the legendary Roman who willingly threw himself into the abyss in order, by sacrificing his life, to save his fatherland.[58] Paul Levi's intentions were entirely noble and selfless.'

'I won't dispute that,' Lenin responded. 'You are a better advocate for Levi than he is himself. However, as you know, what counts in politics is not intentions but outcome. Don't you Germans have a saying that goes, "The road to hell is paved with good intentions"? The congress will be severe with Paul Levi and will condemn him – there is no avoiding that. Nonetheless, Paul will be condemned only for his breach of discipline, not because of his basic political point of view. And how could it be otherwise in a situation where his point of view, in reality, is being recognised as correct. And so the road is open for Paul Levi to find his way back to us, provided that he himself does not block off this road. He himself will determine his political fate. He must obey the congress decision as a disciplined Communist and disappear for a time from political life. Granted, he will find that very aggravating. I sympathise with him, and I am truly sorry about it – you can be sure of that. But I cannot spare him this difficult testing period.

'Paul must accept this as we Russians accepted exile or jail time under tsarism. It can be a time of energetic study and calm self-understanding. He is still young in years and new in the party. There are many gaps in his grasp of theory, and in economics, as a Marxist he is still learning his ABCs. Fortified by intensive study, he will come back to us as a better and wiser party leader. We must not lose Levi, both for his own sake and for that of our cause. We are not over-blessed with talent, and we must strive to hold on to what we have. And if your opinion of Levi is correct, then his definitive separation from the revolutionary proletarian vanguard would inflict on him a wound that will not heal. Talk to him as a friend, help him to see things as they are, in terms of the overall situation and not of his personal certainty in his own correctness. I will support you in this. If Levi submits to discipline and conducts himself well – he could for example contribute anonymously for the party press and write some good pamphlets – after three or four months I will write an open letter calling for his rehabilitation. He must endure a trial by fire. Let us hope that he can withstand it.'

---

58. According to Roman legend, when a huge rift appeared in the ground of the Roman Forum, soothsayers warned that the city could be saved only by throwing into the chasm the one thing upon which its strength depended. Mounted on horseback, the soldier Marcus Curtius then leapt into the abyss, which closed over him, saving the city from ruin. Livy, *History of Rome*, 7, chapter 5.

I sighed. My soul was gripped by a cold sensation that I was confronted by the inevitable, whose consequences could not be foreseen. 'Dear Lenin,' I said, 'do what you can. You Russians always stand ready to strike out, and your arms stand ready to embrace in friendship. I know from your party history that among you curses and blessings come and go like fleeting winds across the steppes. We Westerners are phlegmatic. We are weighed down by the nightmare of history of which Marx spoke.[59] I implore you once more to do what you can to see that we do not lose Paul Levi.'

'Have no fear,' Lenin replied. 'I have made you a promise and will keep it. If only Paul himself stands firm.' Lenin reached for his cap, a simple and rather worn peaked cap, and departed with calm, vigorous steps.

*Lenin meets with opposition leaders*

Understandably, the oppositionists within the German delegation – Comrades Malzahn, Neumann, Franken, and Müller – were very anxious to meet with Lenin, in order to report on the character and results of the March Action as they had experienced it. Comrade Franken had been in a district along the Rhine, while the other three were trade unionists. Quite rightly, they thought it extremely important that the Communist International's unchallenged foremost leader hear a portrayal of the mood of broad circles of class-conscious proletarians with strong revolutionary convictions. They also wanted to express their view regarding the theory of the offensive and the policies that they considered correct. They were also anxious to hear Lenin's personal views on the questions that concerned them. Lenin considered it a matter of course to respond to the comrades' request. The day and hour were arranged when he would meet them at my place. The comrades arrived a good deal sooner than he did, because we had to work out how we would intervene in the congress debates.

Lenin was always punctual. Almost to the minute he entered the room, quietly as usual, so that he was hardly noticed by the comrades, who were deep in discussion. 'Good day, comrades,' he said. He shook hands with them all and took his seat among them, so as to take part in the discussion at once.

I was quite familiar with his ways, and I thought it the most obvious thing in the world that every comrade must be acquainted with Lenin. So it did not occur to me to introduce him to the comrades. After about ten minutes

---

59. 'The tradition of all the dead generations weighs like a nightmare on the brain of the living.' Marx, *The Eighteenth Brumaire of Louis Bonaparte*, in *MECW*, 11, p. 103.

of general discussion, one of them drew me aside and asked softly, 'Tell me, Comrade Clara, just who is this comrade?'

'What, you did not recognise him?' I responded. 'This is Comrade Lenin.'

'Imagine that!' my friend said. 'I thought that, like some great man, he would keep us waiting for him. The simplest comrade could not be simpler or more cordial. You should just see how ceremoniously our former comrade Hermann Müller walks through the Reichstag in tails, now that he has been chancellor.'

It seemed to me that the 'opposition' comrades and Lenin were engaged in a mutual examination. Lenin was clearly more concerned to listen, to compare, to learn the facts, to inform himself, rather than sounding off like an editorial, although he did not conceal his point of view. He was tireless with his questions, following the comrades' explanations with intense interest, often asking them to explain or expand on their comments. He strongly emphasised the importance of planned organised work among the broad masses of workers and the need for centralisation and strict discipline.

Lenin told me later that the meeting had pleased him greatly. 'Wonderful fellows, these German proletarians of the type of Malzahn and his friends. I admit that they may never win the trophy for radical oratory. I don't know if they would make good shock troops. But I am sure of one thing: people like them form the broad and firmly anchored pillars of the revolutionary proletarian army. They serve as the basis and mainstay in the factories and trade unions. We must attract such forces and make them active. They bind us to the masses.'

Let me make an apolitical digression. When Lenin came to visit me, it was a day of great celebration for everyone in the house: from the Red Army soldiers standing watch at the front entrance to the young kitchen aide, not to mention the delegations from the Near and Far East, who like me were put up in the quite spacious villa, transformed by the revolution from property of a rich manufacturer to that of the Moscow Commune. 'Vladimir Ilyich has arrived.' The news flew from person to person. Everyone was on the lookout, coming to stand in the front hallway or at the gate to greet Lenin and wave to him. Their faces glowed with intense joy when he walked over to those who were waiting, greeted them with his warm smile, and spoke a few words to one or the other. There was no trace of humility – let alone servility – on the one side, and no hint of condescension or affectation on the other. The Red Army soldiers, workers, employees, and congress delegates in their beautiful clothes – from Dagestan, Iran, and the 'Turkestaners', made so famous by Paul Levi – all of them loved Lenin as one of their own, and he, for his part, felt himself as one of them. Feelings of cordial brotherhood made them one.

*Lenin addresses the congress*

Trotsky gave a profound and brilliant report entitled, 'The Economic Situation and the New Tasks of the Communist International.' The theoreticians of the offensive gained no ground in the debates on this report in either the commissions or the plenary session. Nonetheless, they hoped to win victory for their viewpoint through amendments and additions to the theses on the International's tactics and strategy. The amendments were submitted by the German, Austrian, and Italian delegations. Comrade Terracini spoke in their favour, and there was a passionate agitation for them to be adopted.[60] What would be the decision? In the high and vast Kremlin hall, where the brilliant red of the Communist People's House outshines the sparkling and coldly ostentatious gold of the former royal palace, the atmosphere was very tense. Everyone's nerves were strained to the limit, as hundreds of delegates and the closely packed audience followed the proceedings.

Lenin took the floor. His speech was a masterpiece of his eloquence, free of any rhetorical flourishes. Its impact lay in the force and clarity of his thought, the relentless logic of his argument, and the firm consistency of his line. His sentences, hurled like rough-cut blocks of granite, fused into a unified whole. Lenin did not try to dazzle or enthral but to convince us. He convinced us and also captivated us, not through the intoxication of fine ringing words, but rather through a luminous spirit, which comprehends the world of social developments without self-deception and speaks the truth in its dreadful reality. Like lashes of the whip, then like blows of the club, Lenin's words pour down on those 'who make a sport of hunting down right-wingers' and do not understand what it is that leads to victory. 'Only when, through the struggle itself, we win to our side the majority of the working class, and not of the workers alone, but of all the oppressed and exploited – only then can we truly conquer.'[61]

Everyone felt that the decisive battle had been joined. When I shook Lenin's hand in great enthusiasm, I could not restrain myself from saying, 'You know, Lenin, where I come from, a speaker in the most obscure place would be loath to speak so simply and plainly as you do. He would be afraid of seeming not educated enough. I know of only one equivalent of your way of speaking: that is Tolstoy's great art. Like him, you have a sense for the great, unified, firm line and for inexorable truth. That is beauty. Is this perhaps a specifically Slavic characteristic?'

---

60. Terracini's speech introducing the amendments in Session 11 can be found on pp. 457–65. For the amendments themselves, see pp. 1141–58.
61. Lenin's speech in Session 11 can be found on pp. 465–73.

'I don't know,' said Lenin. 'I only know that when I became a speaker, as they say, I always thought of the workers and peasants in my audience. I wanted them to understand me. Whenever a Communist speaks, he must think of the masses and speak to them. By the way, it is just as well that no one overheard your hypothesis about national psychology. Otherwise it could be said, "Look, look! The old man lets himself get entrapped by compliments." We must be careful that we do not arouse a suspicion that we two old folks are hatching a plot against the Left. Of course, the Left does not engage in intrigues and plots!' Laughing heartily, Lenin left the hall and went to his work.

## 3j. Zetkin Sends Levi a Congress Update[62]

22 June 1921

Dear Paul,

I have no idea of the extent to which you in Germany have been informed of happenings here, and above all whether you have received *accurate* information. So I do not know what aspects I should emphasise in order to give you an objective picture of where things stand and where they are headed. Events are certainly racing forward. What seemed yesterday to be an unshakeable fact, is today brushed aside as a mere mood, an unfortunate attempt, or as nothing whatsoever. And what will happen tomorrow? But I will not lapse into portraying moods, however seductive that might be. I have much to do.

My arrival here was overdue. The worthy and respectable representatives of the worthy and respectable Germans, mostly under Radek's leadership, had done everything possible to agitate and stir up hatred against us. Not without success. The clique then tried to make life impossible for me at the women's conference or to so provoke me that I would just take off.[63] Given that the holy geese of Rome once saved the Capitol,[64] common German geese were supposed to salvage the prestige of the German Zentrale. I've known for some time that Comrades [Bertha] Braunthal and Hertha Sturm were models of political narrowness. I only now learned how indescribably nasty they can be.

---

62. Archiv der sozialen Democratie, NL Paul Levi 1/PLAA000197. In the original text, all names are indicated by initials and abbreviations; full names have been substituted in this translation.
63. Regarding the incident at the women's conference, see 1141, n. 55.
64. According to legend, during the Gauls' attempted conquest of Rome around 387 B.C., Gallic troops tried to sneak up the Capitoline Hill during the night. But the Gauls disturbed a flock of geese, whose loud honking alerted the Roman guards and enabled them to repel the invaders.

Comrade Braunthal was won over by the promise that she would replace me as International [Women's] Secretary.[65] Who knows, perhaps luck will smile on her. Frankly, I would not make a fuss or be envious. Even without that post, I have more than enough to do, and I would be happy to be able at last to focus on work that pleases me rather than on what is demanded by the political conjuncture. The goal of this shabby intrigue was to prevent me from speaking with Lenin – who had gone to the country, exceptionally exhausted and in need of relaxation – and then to keep me outside the congress.

I was close to nervous collapse. The voyage with all its commotion and then the food and other conditions here have not made me any healthier or stronger. But despite all the abuse, I was able to get a firm grip on myself and hope to hold out to the end.

It seems that a page has been turned. At first we were treated like dead dogs, but now they wag their tails at us as if we are living creatures. I have spoken at length, very frankly, and without restraint with Trotsky and with Lenin, who came to me after his return along with Comrade Kamenev and has since then discussed the situation with me again. Trotsky and Lenin share our evaluation of the March Action, but they strongly reject your pamphlet in terms of their sense of party discipline and the party's character. As for the delegations, where the pamphlet is concerned, we're running into a brick wall that we cannot break through. It will crumble away gradually, though, partly through the pressure of events and partly because of your personal conduct, which refutes all the nonsense and slander about your criticism having despicable motivations and plans for future treachery. It has already been asserted here as a fact that you are on friendly terms with the Russian Menshevik leaders, are inspired and assisted by them, and that you will soon take your place as a leader of the USPD. Needless to say, I have said what is necessary on that score and countered the attempt to use the 'Levi Case' as a shield to protect the Zentrale's policies and their March Action.

At the moment, it seems that the official German delegation is not only in retreat but, more precisely, is suffering a complete rout. The day before yesterday, Radek negotiated with the 'oppositional' delegates. We could not refuse

---

65. In a meeting held 7 June 1921, the German delegation discussed a proposal to replace Zetkin as head of the Communist Women's Movement at its conference, which was held 9–15 June. The minutes of the delegation meeting read: '*Point 6*: Report by Comrade Braunthal on the international women's conference. The question was raised whether Comrade Zetkin would be elected as general secretary of the women. After several discussions, the question remains open and will not be settled until Comrade Zetkin arrives. It was decided that all German delegates should attend the women's conference.' Zetkin was subsequently confirmed in her post. Thanks to Bernhard Bayerlein for these minutes, which are published in Bayerlein et al. (eds.) 2013. See also Appendix 3i, pp. 1141–2.

that without formally putting ourselves in the wrong. He shared our opinion of the matter so completely that we are astounded and wonder: why then all his raucous writings during recent months? The Russian section wants to introduce a resolution on the German question that does not formally condemn the March Action but nonetheless corresponds to our viewpoint in every essential feature and thus, in reality, justifies our criticisms. The March Action is treated as a 'defensive', moreover, as one falsely conceived and carried out. The entire theory of the 'revolutionary offensive' is abandoned. We stated that we could determine our position on the theses when we have them in hand and can discuss them. Secondly, we said we will vote against the intended approval of your expulsion.

Clearly, the Executive wants the German question to be dealt with, as much as possible, as dirty laundry within the German delegation. We were advised that, when we receive the theses and take a position on them, we should then discuss with the German delegation. We will do that in order, as much as possible, to prevent those 'loyal to the action' from hiding behind formal pretexts. We can then insist all the more emphatically that the question come before the so-called 'Expanded Executive', consisting of about seventy members of all delegations, and then before the congress as a whole.

It is said that the Germans, while grumbling, have withdrawn their own theses, which demanded the expulsion of the 'right-wing leadership clique around Levi', in order to support the Russian draft. The heroic wire-pullers said that if they did not do this, they would lose the support of their last friends among the Russians, Radek and Bukharin. The worthy and naïve Paul Frölich is said to have cried out that now the party is truly destroyed, because these theses will put the right wing in charge. It is the height of self-deception that this politically incompetent central grouping considers itself to be left-wing and radical. In a word, unless the situation changes once more, members of the Zentrale will return home defeated. But the most distressing and despicable thing is that the decision will not be based on political insight and conviction by the many, but rather on the fundamental clarity and firmness, the insight and political intelligence of Trotsky and Lenin, especially of Lenin alone. Truly, even given all the unspeakable dirty tricks they use against us, Thalheimer and company have never been so contemptible as when they cringe. And that is called theoretical firmness and loyalty to their convictions.

The two upstanding members of our little troop have now received valued reinforcement from Comrades Franken, Malzahn, and Richard Müller.[66] The facts cited by the trade unionists in our support are extremely important and

---

66. The other delegates in Moscow supporting Zetkin were Otto Brass and Paul Neumann.

have decisive weight. And they are all holding firm and acting with wisdom. Zinoviev sent a message by radio that Comrade Anna [Geyer] should not be permitted to travel [to Moscow]. We do not know if he succeeded in this. Her presence would be very useful, particularly in informing other delegations. I am doing what I can in this regard.

So things are not going at all badly for us. On the other hand, your case is 'hopeless', for now. Of course I will strongly oppose your expulsion in the Expanded Executive and the congress as a whole.[67] Our friends will support me. But I must not sow any illusions on the chances of success. I urge you to assess the situation in all its seriousness but also with insight into the fact that it will change, as demanded by the interests of the party. Lenin and Trotsky hold you in high esteem and are convinced that the door must be left open for you to become a leader of the party once again, as soon as possible. A rumour is going around that your expulsion will be upheld only for form's sake and for a brief period. I have reason to believe that this is more than mere talk. I implore you, in the interests of our cause, not to slam the door of the party violently and unwisely. You should keep a low profile for now, at least until I return with more precise information. I know this is a difficult sacrifice, but you must do this for the cause. After having jumped so bravely into the abyss, because you wanted to save the party, you must also now summon up the self-control to wait for a time and be silent, although there is nothing more dreadful than waiting.

With cordial greetings to my friends, especially Mathilde [Jacob] and yourself.

Heartfelt greetings and a warm handshake,<br>
*Clara*

Please bring this letter to the attention of my son Kostia.

### 3k. Zetkin to Lenin on Personal Attacks[68]

Moscow, 28 June 1921

Dear Lenin, my honoured friend,

Enclosed is a comprehensive document that was sent to me by the Württemberg district executive for my information and to be forwarded to

---

67. The German original refers here to Levi's 'Anschluss' (adhesion) instead of 'Ausschluss' (expulsion), an apparent typing error.
68. Stoljarowa and Schmalfuss (eds.) 1990, pp. 272–4.

you. All the important passages are sidelined with blue. This document is interesting from several points of view.

1.) It makes clear that the Zentrale is engaging in lies and falsification in order to defend its policies.
2.) It confirms that Comrade Brandler, acting on behalf of the Zentrale, issued the slogan for a struggle to overthrow the government.
3.) It demonstrates that members of the Zentrale tried to impose the strike not through political means but through those of a putsch.
4.) In addition, it shows that – contrary to gossip by Friesland and company and to the vote of confidence of the Zentrale – the Württemberg party has more confidence in me than in the Zentrale. That is significant only because one of the strongest arguments of Koenen and company is that we lack any support.[69]

These people are fortunate that the international congress is taking place so early. If it had been held later, the mass withdrawal from support for them and the gathering of workers around the opposition would be much more evident than it has been up to this point.

I do not want to trouble you, but it seems to me to be urgently necessary for you to intervene in the debate, to prevent it from going wrong. The tactics and strategy of these bankrupt offensive types has the obvious purpose of driving me out of the International through base personal attacks and lies. I am always ready to accept the consequences of disagreements of substance, but I am wholly incapable of battling against base personal attacks carried out with contemptible means. It would be good to put an end to this battle and for the discussion to focus on the serious material issues.

No one can contribute as much as you to achieve an objective discussion. If this proves impossible, we will face a split in the German party and its certain disintegration. There is no doubt about that.

With cordial greetings for you and Comrade Krupskaya,
Yours, *Clara Zetkin*

---

69. See Appendix 3c, pp. 1104–5.

# Appendix 4
# The Political Struggle at the Congress: July 1921

### 4a. Trotsky Reports to Lenin on Congress Debate[1]

Moscow, 3 July 1921

Comrade Lenin:

The discussion yesterday was extremely instructive in terms of clarifying the position of the congress.[2] One German delegate after another spoke, in an increasingly offensive tone. The last of them, Thälmann, a worker from Hamburg, said the following, word for word:

> Not only your theses, but even your theses modified by our amendments will create great difficulties for us in Germany. Indeed, the moment we arrive in Germany, we will be confronted with different attitudes and will have to carry out a full reversal (*Umstellung*).[3]

On the other hand, Béla Kun announced to all and sundry (including me) that he agreed with Lenin, Zinoviev, and Bukharin but not with me. He said this even before my speech. Bukharin was quoted by several speakers, including Thälmann, who interpreted his remarks as being fully acceptable.[4]

---

1. Meijer 1964, 2, pp. 470–4.
2. Trotsky is referring to Sessions 13 and 14 of the congress, which took up the Theses on Tactics and Strategy.
3. See conclusion of Thälmann's speech, p. 571.
4. The reference to Bukharin is not found in the German transcript of Thälmann's speech.

Brand [Poland] spoke along German lines, accusing us of being scaremongers. Zinoviev spoke in a conciliatory vein, cautiously and in a fully loyal spirit. But the political content of his speech was that there were no serious differences between our theses and the amendments, and that we would ensure complete unity.

In my speech,[5] I expressed agreement with Zinoviev's remarks, but I counterposed our theses categorically to the amendments. I hope you will receive the transcript along with this letter. Explaining that we were not able to tone down the theses, I referred to Thälmann's speech, which had quite correctly reminded everyone that the attitude of the primary and secondary party leaders who stayed in Germany fully coincides with that of Béla Kun and Thalheimer when the theory of the offensive was formulated.

After I had given my speech, Zinoviev and Radek told me privately that I had thrown a 'bomb' and even sent me a brief note to the effect that I had broken the agreement and that they declined responsibility for the consequences. In fact I had stated agreement with Zinoviev's speech and had not carried out either an open or covert polemic with him. I had energetically defended the theses. However, in terms that were – so far as I can judge – quite comradely and moderate, I spoke against the amendments and against the trends hidden behind them. Thus I believe that I not only did not break the agreement but fully carried out the Politburo's decision. My reply was in this spirit.

They tried to scare us with the prospect that our theses would not be accepted as a working draft. Not for a moment did I give that any credence. After a ten-minute pause for the delegates to discuss the theses, Comrade Zinoviev proposed that the session be ended.

Béla Kun and other leftists had submitted their names to speak against me. Zinoviev did not want them to take the floor, and the session was ended. The theses were unanimously adopted. But the Germans, Hungarians, Poles, and Italians made a written statement, protesting against the way the theses were interpreted in my speech. The Italians made a separate statement expressing opposition to the supposed characterisation of their party by Lenin and Trotsky as 'putschist'. In this way, Béla Kun, with the help of his backers, attempted to unite the German delegation, Radek, Zinoviev, and Lenin in a common interpretation of the general approach of the theses. He thus 'isolated' Trotsky as the only one insisting in this session that our theses were incompatible with the German amendments.

In his summary, Radek engaged in a slightly disguised polemic with me with reference to the French, Germans, and Czechoslovaks. The idea was that

---

5. See pp. 571–81.

if anyone claimed the theses to be a compromise making a number of concessions to the Left, we, by contrast, will say they make a great many concessions to the Right. As for the March Action, we must not issue commands to the working class, as if it were the Red Army, but the error of the German Zentrale consisted precisely in trying to bring the working class into struggle by issuing orders, and so on and so forth.

It would be desirable that you acquaint yourself at least with my speech, since you will have to take a 'position' on it in the commission [on strategy and tactics]. It would also be desirable to do so in a plenary session, in one or another form.

With comradely greetings,
Trotsky

The commission on the theses will not be meeting today because of a joint session of the trade-union and political congresses.

## 4b. Lenin on Šmeral and the Czechoslovak Party[6]

[6 July 1921]

### 1. *Comments to the Commission on Tactics and Strategy*

[*The following notes, taken by the Czechoslovak Communist leader Karl Kreibich, summarise comments by Lenin regarding the Czechoslovak Communist movement. Kreibich typed up his transcript on 28 January 1924, seven days after Lenin's death, and submitted it to the Comintern headquarters in Moscow, where it was filed with records of the congress.*

[*According to Kreibich, the comments formed part of a speech given by Lenin on 6 July 1921 to the Third Congress's Commission on Tactics and Strategy. According to accounts of that speech, Lenin also took up the March Action and the theory of the offensive. No full transcript of the speech has been located for this volume. Kreibich's notes are in German, almost certainly the language in which Lenin delivered his speech.*]

**Lenin**: It is hard to establish the facts. Did the Czech Communists fail to publish the resolution of the Second World Congress – yes or no? I belong to the right wing of the congress, because a line is being advanced here that does not represent a correct policy. Our Hungarian friends have behaved in

---

6. Comintern archives, RGASPI, 490/1/183.

a harmful manner in Central Europe and have pursued a harmful policy – I am completely convinced of that.

I recently said that Šmeral must take three steps to the left and Kreibich must take a step to right. Today I would like to say that Šmeral should take somewhat less than three steps –

**Radek**: Two and a half! (*Laughter*)

**Lenin**: – to the left, and Kreibich should take at least a step to the right. I say that *cum grano salis* [with a grain of salt] – indeed, several grains.

It was easier for us in Russia in 1917 than it is today in Europe, including Czechoslovakia. Nonetheless, when we returned to Russia, our first words were caution and patience.

A single word can indicate an incorrect method. Regarding Šmeral's speech, all I have read is a report in the Reichenberg [Liberec] *Vorwärts*.[7] The Reichenberg comrades should have pulled together all relevant materials. A report should be drawn up in somewhat of a party spirit, that is, it should be objective. As for what Šmeral said, there is much that is incorrect.

If the agricultural workers are the most revolutionary, there is something wrong, because the industrial workers should be the most revolutionary.[8] It is bad for the agricultural workers to be out in the lead.

Šmeral is quite wrong to say that, because he is an opportunist, he should not speak out against the opportunists.[9] It is precisely because of this fact that he should confront them and speak out against them.

After I read the speech, I thought, 'This is centrist or half-centrist; it is not a Communist speech.' The portions reprinted in *Vorwärts* indicate that Šmeral's line of political argument is incorrect. What is wrong is not that he wants to be cautious – especially given that leftist Vienna people and other friends are working in Czechoslovakia.[10]

---

7. *Note by Kreibich*: 'Šmeral's speech' refers to an address given at the convention of the Czech [SDP] left wing in May 1921. The reference to a 'single word' indicating an incorrect method refers to a critical remark by Kreibich regarding Šmeral's emphasis on the need for caution.

8. *Note by Kreibich*: The agricultural workers receive special mention here because they were the first who, at that time, declared for the red trade-union International and broke away from the Amsterdam people.

9. Šmeral had belonged to the opportunist wing of Czech socialism and had supported Austria-Hungary's war effort during 1914–18. Only after the War did he rally to a revolutionary policy.

10. Many leading Hungarian Communist exiles who held leftist views lived in Vienna. They were a leading force in *Kommunismus* (February 1920–September 1921), published in Vienna as the main international voice of the Comintern's leftist current. The Austrian CP formed part of the leftist current at the Third Congress led by the German CP and Comintern Executive Committee members in Moscow.

I support the motion by Zinoviev to delete the sentence that refers to Šmeral personally and counterposes him to Muna.[11] A detailed letter should be sent to Šmeral and the party, telling them that their entire propaganda and the party itself is not really Communist. The sentence on Šmeral stands in contradiction to Kreibich's statement regarding the Reichenberg party convention,[12] where – he says – the sentences attacking Šmeral in Hula's letters to the convention were deleted.

2. *Motion on the Draft Theses on Tactics*[13]

[Written by Lenin between 6 July and 9 July 1921.]

1.) Delete the mention of Šmeral and the whole end of the paragraph.
2.) Direct the Commission (or the Executive) to draw up a detailed *letter* to the Czech party containing a practical, lucid, and *documented* criticism of what is *incorrect* in Šmeral's stand and what the editors of the *Reichenberger Vorwärts* have to be more careful of.

## 4c. Lenin Reassures Hungarian Delegates[14]

7 July 1921

To Comrade Zinoviev, with a request to communicate the following to the members of yesterday's commission meeting:

Dear Comrades:

I have been informed that what I said in the commission yesterday against – rather, against some – Hungarian Communists has aroused dissatisfaction.[15] I hasten therefore to inform you in writing: when I was an émigré myself

---

11. For the deleted sentence referring to Šmeral, see p. 225, n. 78. However, there is no reference to Muna in it.
12. On 12 March 1921 the congress of the German section of the Communist Party in Czechoslovakia, meeting in Reichenberg, voted to affiliate to the Comintern. In October–November, it fused with the Communist Party of Czechoslovakia.
13. *LCW*, 42, p. 324; compared with *PSS*, 44, p. 55.
14. *LCW*, 45, p. 203; compared with *PSS*, 53, p. 14. No transcript of Lenin's speech the previous day has come to light, although a portion is summarised in Appendix 4b.
15. Béla Kun had written a letter to Lenin, summarised as follows by Kun's biographer, György Borsányi. The letter began with a quote from the Bible, 'You too were strangers in Egypt at one time.' Lenin's remarks 'had "sanctioned the campaign against the Hungarian exiles"', Kun continued.
'People who refer to themselves as Communists have turned on these exiles,' Kun wrote, 'denouncing them in public, in the press, in circulars, confident that these denunciations would fall into the hand of the police.' Here the reference is clearly

(for more than 15 years), I took 'too leftist' a stand several times (as I now realise). In August 1917, I was also an émigré and moved in our Party Central Committee a much too 'leftist' proposal which, happily, was flatly rejected.[16]

It is quite natural for émigrés frequently to adopt attitudes that are 'too leftist'. It has never entered my mind, now or in the past, to impute this to such fine, loyal, dedicated, and worthy revolutionaries as the Hungarian émigrés, who are so much respected by all of us, and by the whole Communist International.

With communist greetings,<br>Lenin

*Postscript by Zinoviev*[17]

The Hungarian comrades concerned have done a great deal on behalf of the Communist International in 1920–1. I am convinced that the Hungarian comrades deserve the trust of the Communist International, in spite of our present differences of opinion.

## 4d. German Delegation Meets with Bolshevik Leaders[18]

9 July 1921

Proceedings of a meeting of the German delegation at the Third World Congress with comrades of the opposition – Clara Zetkin, Paul Neumann, and Heinrich Malzahn – and the comrades of the Russian Central Committee – Lenin, Trotsky, Zinoviev, Radek, Bukharin – on 9 July 1921 at the Kremlin.[19]

---

to Paul Levi and his defenders. Kun's letter then made a barbed reference to Lenin's years in exile. 'You certainly are unaware of this, that is why you have committed yourself, in spite of yourself, against the Hungarian exiles, forgetting that others had been forced to live on foreign land as well.'

Alluding to his own time as a prisoner of war in Russia 1916–18, Kun added, 'I who spent most of my life in exile in Russia have the hospitality of the Russian proletariat to thank for that, not yours; I fought for this right to live by my work, since I have empathised with this proletariat in the course of tough battles, even before the victorious revolution.' Borsányi 1993, pp. 264–5.

16. Lenin was in hiding in Finland from 10 August to 17 September 1917. No text by him from this period matches the description in this letter. He may have been referring to his article, 'On Slogans', written three weeks before his stay in Finland, while he was hiding in Petrograd. Thanks to Lars Lih for research assistance.

17. Borsányi 1993, pp. 265–6.

18. Comintern archives, RGASPI, 490/1/162.

19. Note by the meeting's secretary.

**Chair:** Comrade Lenin.

**Thalheimer:** The Zentrale looked into the situation and came to quite specific conclusions, which by and large coincide with what is found in the adopted resolution.[20]

All party members are called on to work within the line laid down by the congress. Secondly, members of the former opposition are to cease collaboration on *Sowjet* or its continuator.[21] Third, members of the parliamentary fraction are to conform to decisions of the Zentrale. Fourth, formation of factions within the party must stop. Fifth, members of parliament who formerly belonged to the opposition should state their opinion on Levi's deputy status.[22] These points are to constitute the basis for further [joint] work. In the opinion of the Zentrale, this provides a sufficient basis for future collaboration, without any further inquiry. It will refrain from limiting former opposition comrades' freedom of discussion in the party press, in the customary framework. In order to heal wounds from the past, the Zentrale members present here are prepared to go even further and to propose in the next Central Committee session that Malzahn become a member of the national trade-union commission and that Clara Zetkin be added to the Central Committee as international secretary. Further, if there is a proposal in the next convention for Comrades Malzahn and Clara Zetkin to be members of the Zentrale, the Zentrale would have no objection.

**Malzahn:** Thalheimer expects a declaration that the parliamentary fraction will take a position on the question of Levi's status as deputy. It is not possible to make such a declaration. It makes no sense to ask that, given that Levi was expelled from the party. As you have stated, we will conform to the decisions taken here, and now the Zentrale must act. The Levi case is settled by decision of the congress.

As for the demand that there should be no formation of factions and also that collaboration with *Sowjet* should cease, we are in complete agreement and have already indicated that in our statement.[23] We will refrain from any special efforts, and this matter is thereby settled for us. We anticipate that

---

20. The reference is to the 'The March Action and the Situation in the VKPD' introduced by the Russian delegation in Session 21. See p. 951.
21. The original text reads 'take up collaboration' (*Anstellung*) instead of 'cease collaboration' (*Einstellung*), an apparent typing error. *Sowjet* was published on 1 July 1921 under a new name: *Unser Weg (Sowjet)*.
22. After Levi's expulsion, the Zentrale had called upon him to give up his seat in the Reichstag, which he had won as a candidate of the Communist Party; Levi declined to do so.
23. A reference to the VKPD opposition statement on p. 806.

all members of the VKPD will carry out their activity in the framework of congress decisions. We must all act in unified fashion throughout the party, whether in the press or in the organisation.

We anticipate that the formation of factions will cease on both sides. We will exert pressure to prevent it in order to make unified work possible. As for Thalheimer's proposal that we join the Central Committee and later, in the convention, rise up higher, we prefer not to go into details on such things. We must clarify how the party's reorientation will take place. The new political line will cause a crisis in the party, and the USPD and SPD will use every means to work against us. How will we surmount this crisis, and how do we orient the party apparatus on this basis? How will reports [from the congress] be organised – in order to avoid having counterposed reports, as was the case after the March Action? We must turn the party's entire striking power outwards.

**Heckert**: There is nothing the German Zentrale wants less than to prolong the dispute after the congress. It is therefore out of place to ask whether we are going to give an objective report on the line that has been adopted here. We have never been in opposition to the decisions of international congresses and have always carried out our duty. Orienting the German Communist Party to carry out the congress decisions will not cause any crisis in the party. In our view, there was a crisis because the International's usual practices were not observed. Given the opposition's statement that they intend to carry out the congress decisions, we believe that no special efforts will be needed in Germany in order to battle with the USPD and SPD.

A faction was once formed within the party, the 'cremation' faction, to which the chairman of the Gelsenkirchen miners belonged, and this faction has left the party.[24] Levi claimed something of that sort, but he was never able to provide evidence.

We are glad to hear the comrades say that they will oppose the formation of factions and collaboration with *Sowjet*. As for Levi's status as parliamentary deputy, there is more involved. Levi said he would resign his seat, which was granted him by the Central Committee and by the district in which he was elected, if his eight friends who issued a statement of support on his behalf were in agreement with that.[25] Since Comrades Zetkin, Malzahn, and

---

24. Probably a reference to the Gelsenkirchen Free Workers' Union, a locally influential wing of the syndicalist movement.
25. On 16 April eight party leaders – Ernst Däumig, Clara Zetkin, Otto Brass, Adolph Hoffman, Curt Geyer, Paul Neumann, Heinrich Malzahn, and Paul Eckert – had declared their solidarity with Levi.

Neumann are present, we are quite right to ask that they exert their influence on Levi so that he will resign his seat.

**Lenin**: In my opinion, the Zentrale is quite right to pose specific demands. But how can we influence someone who is outside the party? Members of the party say they share the framework of the congress. What are they being asked to declare? [No] collaboration with *Sowjet*, an end to setting up factions. The undertakings of the Zentrale should also be recorded. The Zentrale says that the opposition will have the right of free criticism and that the [congress] decisions will be carried out. That says it all.

We meet here as members of the Communist International and demand that discipline be maintained within the Communist International framework. With regard to Levi, it was said that there is a crisis in the party. We have often had such crises in our party, in which we have publicly censured our comrades. I recall such an incident in the history of the Russian party, which came to mind while going through *Pravda*. The Mensheviks seized on it to attack us, and we responded, 'Dear opponents, you may be rejoicing, but the party must exercise discipline and should have no fears that its weaknesses may come to light. It is dangerous for us to conceal our weaknesses.' In this spirit, it would be helpful to avoid talking of a crisis. Instead, let us decide that all of us will together say in response to the enemy that we have a genuine International, which corrects our errors; please show us your International.

**Georg Stelzer**: Now that Comrades Malzahn, Zetkin, and Neumann have stated that they accept party discipline, there is no way to avoid talking of these things. The comrades who are with Levi in parliament should call on him not to sit as a Communist deputy.

**Thälmann**: I question whether individual comrades are in a position to report on how all the events took place. We must clarify how we will give our reports. The March Action caused a crisis in the Communist Party that was expressed publicly. This demonstrated the weaknesses of the Communist Party, because a small group of persons within it made an attempt to create chaos. I think of the Italian question. Many comrades were not aware of the implications of the discipline question. There will be a crisis in the party. We must adopt a new attitude everywhere, including among the membership, because these decisions are not the continuation of those of the Second Congress. There is a possibility for us to work in France and Czechoslovakia according to the guidelines of these theses on tactics and strategy. In Germany, the situation is more intense. It will therefore be extraordinarily difficult to orient the membership to these theses. But just as the membership came through the

March Action in good shape, so they will be able to weather this as well. The opposition comrades who should exert influence on Levi can only do this as Levi's friends. Comrade Lenin wants to assure freedom of discussion. We wish to pose a question: what are the limits of this freedom of discussion? The Zentrale must have the right to reject articles that are harmful for the party. A Communist Party must be based on discipline, and freedom of discussion must be held within certain limits.

**Friesland**: A discussion has no point if it consists simply of exchanging diplomatic notes. It's not a matter of determining who is right but of judging the political situation in Germany. The party cannot endure a new split. No one is going to try seriously to contradict the congress decisions, not even those who are unhappy with many aspects of these decisions. They will carry out the decisions loyally and lead the party in unified fashion to undertake the tasks now posed before it. Only those comrades who are serious about carrying out this line will come together in the party. I put no weight on formal statements; only actually carrying out the decisions is of value. The right-wing comrades will not be able to carry out the congress decisions, and the right-wing comrades present here will admit that I am correct in this. I believe the mood of crisis that will certainly grip the party can be overcome much more readily if comrades present here are determined not to permit the outbreak of crisis.

As for giving the reports, let's not get into a philological inquiry here. The point is that we must show we are carrying out these decisions. So far the statements submitted by various comrades have not achieved this goal. They say they will carry out the congress decisions, but they evade formulating this in specific terms. If there are currents that say the March Action has been repudiated, we will undergo a severe crisis. I propose not to discuss formal issues – rather could the comrades please tell us how they propose to act in Germany and what political line they will follow.

**Neumann**: Friesland has the right approach. The initial demands presented by Thalheimer are obviously demands that have been established by the congress. In the declaration we made for the proceedings, we said how we envisage freedom of criticism, such that the party does not suffer any damage in the process. The party's existence is the main issue; criticism must be expressed only to serve the party's interests. Friesland claims that there is no evidence that the right wing will carry out what it is promising here. My view is that we cannot be sure that some members of the Zentrale can carry out the decisions, given the ideas they hold. What guarantee is there that the Zentrale members will implement the decisions? After this congress there will be meetings of the Central Committee and the party's leading bodies, in which it will be clearly stated how reports will be given.

The Zentrale must be reorganised through the addition of several new members who represent the decisions of the congress and who will remain in the Zentrale until the next convention, when regular elections will take place. These elections will reflect the political situation in which the Communist Party finds itself.

**Lenin**: I cannot consent to the use of such language. It is absolutely impermissible to cast doubt on the ability of anyone here present to carry out the congress decisions. We must censure this kind of talk.

**Radek**: During the transitional period, indications of crisis have come to light in the party's leading bodies. Regarding the line theoretically justifying the new offensive, the question now is how deeply has this line penetrated into the party's structures? This line was picked up by a thin upper layer of comrades who come to meetings. After the March defeat, the masses will not be impatient to launch into new struggles. The question now is whether the congress decisions will be carried out with a sure hand. Given the decisions taken here, and the discussion and its influence on the German party, I am convinced this will happen.

As for giving reports, a battle will flare up as to who won and who lost. The new [Comintern] Executive will send a letter to the German party expressing the line of the congress regarding Germany in clear terms. Now we come to the question of who within the party will carry out the congress decisions. Anyone who assumes that the masses are going to spend months discussing what happened in March is overestimating the hunger of the proletarian masses in Germany for discussion.

On the question of Levi, Comrade Lenin asks just what kind of statement is being called for here. Levi remains in parliament not because he is stubbornly clinging to his seat as deputy, but in an atmosphere of approval from a segment of the members of parliament. The party will state that Levi has been expelled from the Communist International. Levi will be called on to resign as deputy. The question will then be posed how the parliamentary fraction acts toward Levi. It is the fraction's duty to tell him that he has no right to continue as a deputy. A few days ago, four opposition comrades joined with Levi in putting a question in parliament. Given that the comrades have demonstrated for Levi for months, the party is duty-bound to demand a clear answer. It must demand that the fraction insist on Levi's resigning his parliamentary seat.

What facts are there to sustain Neumann's demand for a change in the Zentrale's membership? According to the statutes, only a convention can appoint the Zentrale. Formally speaking, there is no way for comrades who oppose the March Action to become members of the Zentrale. Thalheimer made a statement that Malzahn and Zetkin should be members of the Central Committee. Based on my knowledge of the German Zentrale, I do not say that its composition is ideal, but I do not know any comrades in the German party that could do a better job of leading the party. There are no grounds for making this demand.

**Koenen**: As regards Levi's deputy status. The Zentrale has received a letter that says, 'I am not resigning as deputy because a number of comrades are in agreement with me that I should not do it.' We are now asking these comrades to write the Zentrale that they are no longer in agreement. We will challenge Levi once again to resign as deputy. That is what we ask. And by the way, we can also demonstrate against him.

Previously, freedom of criticism could not be [...], but now, of course, we can take up the question that publishing articles in *Die Rote Fahne* has its limitations in terms of time and space. Discussion will not lead to chaos but to intellectual clarification. These discussions have shown that comrades who have submitted many statements hold certain specific views. Given that they have advanced these quite fixed specific views in one statement after another, we must anticipate that they will make certain formal statements. They have spoken out so often against the party; now they must speak out for the party. If they had not engaged in such a proliferation of statements, we would not demand this of them. We must bring things to a conclusion.

In addition, the Zentrale will not consist of sergeant-majors but of political comrades. Your demand that some members of the Zentrale resign, on the other hand, testifies to a sergeant-major attitude. No one has the right to say that so-and-so has to be got rid of because he does not suit me. I'm in favour of integrating all comrades in the work in a tolerant fashion. As for giving the reports, we have attempted to provide comrades returning to Germany with a certain framework for giving reports. The report should be given to a conference organised on a very broad basis, including the secretaries and the editors.

**Trotsky**: With regard to Levi, it is wrong to contend that the situation can be considered as the opposition's responsibility. Levi could appeal to the comrades for support because the opposition did not regard his case as having yet been settled. The opposition wanted to appeal to the international congress, and they could therefore undertake in good conscience to wait for the congress decision. Now that the opposition regards the case as settled, the comrades that have private relations with Levi...[can say] that for them the matter has been settled by the party as a whole and that Levi does not have the right to retain a seat in parliament that he acquired with the party's support.

I do not understand at all why Neumann says that the Zentrale must be reorganised. That indicates he regards the party's structures as non-existent. It would bring about the worst crisis that you could imagine. I believe that the international congress, which has harshly criticised the Zentrale's actions, will decisively reject the concept that the situation of the Zentrale should be made more difficult. Anyone who draws such a conclusion from the criticisms will encounter the most emphatic protest from the Executive and the comrades in question.

Friesland says that we should not negotiate diplomatically. He wanted a statement to be made that everyone was determined to save the party. Thalheimer's statement was more realistic. The question is simply one of deciding on what basis to concretise this call. On the whole, what has been proposed offers a way forward. When the theses are explained, there will be discussion, and the Zentrale will have the final decision on how it should be ended. It is therefore of great value for the comrades belonging to the opposition to be authoritatively represented in the Zentrale. Malzahn says that they do not consider it so important that Clara Zetkin or Malzahn belong to the Central Committee. This is wrong. In this way, these bodies would lose contact with the opposition, causing great problems.

**Maslow**: There is a weak point in the arguments of Malzahn. On the one hand, he says that the Zentrale has the last word and, on the other, that the right wing is always correct. Malzahn was a skilled diplomat, while Neumann acted more aggressively by putting in question whether certain persons would be capable of carrying out the decisions. Both have received a thrashing. The Levi case must be handled more specifically. Some comrades say that it's not possible to influence comrades who are outside the party. Comrades who have worked with [Levi] should make a statement in the press that they dissociate themselves from him, when he claims that he can count on their support.

**Frölich**: I must object to what Trotsky has said about the Levi case. If his view is implemented in the party it leads to uncontrollable consequences, because any group in the party can sabotage the party's decisions and appeal to the [world] congress. Meanwhile, they continue to function on the basis of a line that the party has condemned. That makes it impossible to maintain the organisation. Such a viewpoint is completely impossible in a centralised party.

**Malzahn**: I have no knowledge of this written statement. Levi said he would retain his seat until the decision of the congress. We must wait to see what happens. We question whether it will be possible to give an objective report. After the March Action, genuine criticism of it was amalgamated with the Levi case. Our main concern is to be able to speak on behalf of the congress decisions. We will not fall into personal obstinacy. Many functionaries that were thinking of quitting were persuaded by our conduct to stay. Both sides must now put a stop to criticisms and personal attacks. The comrades who were disciplined must be reintegrated into the work. That is the best way to overcome all this.

**Thalheimer**: All those who loyally accept the framework of the decisions are to be integrated in the work. That is the only way to interpret it. There will be more discussion about freedom of discussion within the party. After the congress, a rather thorough discussion will begin, so the party can orient itself to the line adopted by the congress. Such a discussion would have been necessary in any case, even if there had not been such sharp disagreements. It is in the party's interests to place as few restrictions as possible on this discussion. The only limit is posed by action.

As for the matter of Levi's Reichstag seat, it cannot be demanded of anyone that they exert influence on someone outside the party. In order to undermine Levi's influence in the party, we must demand that when he claims to have support of opposition comrades for retaining his parliamentary seat, they declare this to be no longer true. This can be done quite smoothly. That will ease the situation for the party and also for the comrades within the party. That is what they must do.

**Lenin**: Thalheimer's statement is quite clear. Koenen spoke of a letter from Levi to the Zentrale. Malzahn claims that Levi will obey the decision of the congress. Perhaps it would be possible to persuade him to step aside on his own. Those who expressed support for Levi must absolutely take a stand against him. If this stands as a barrier to collaboration, why insist on the point?

There were severe conflicts in the Russian Bolshevik Party in the past, and I cannot recall that we ever dealt with it in so formal a manner. Yes, we must halt all these statements, but first comrades must state that they accept Thalheimer's proposal as a basis for agreement. We have an Executive that exercises supervision and that can take organisational measures. Is it advisable to make an immediate written statement against Levi? I believe that we all have good will, and so we will soon find the right way to do this. We can wait a bit and not insist in a way that could make matters more difficult. The Zentrale is quite right to say that Malzahn and Zetkin should become members of the Central Committee. That will promote collaboration.

**Koenen**: What's at issue here is that the Zentrale makes the decisions on what is right or wrong between congresses. The Theses on Tactics and Strategy were adopted by the entire German delegation, a fact that no one can deny. We accept the framework of the theses and thereby assume the obligation to present the theses in the spirit in which they were dealt with here. When the Russian delegation brought in its resolution today, only Neumann and Malzahn tried to evade this clear position. Franken acted contrary to the discipline of the fraction. It must be established that Neumann had no right to cast doubt on the capacity of those who accept congress decisions to give an objective report of it. Neumann and Malzahn must explain how they will act toward their friends if they engage in factional activity.

**Peter Mieves**: The present discussion will not clarify relationships in the party. That will depend on us. I don't think it is appropriate to permit counter-reports. We have to report what was decided at the congress, and everyone will draw his own conclusions from this. We cannot say that the Zentrale was the winner or Levi was the winner. The Zentrale has the last word, since it will carry out the decisions of the congress. Under no circumstances should we give a report to the trade-union delegates. They have quite confused points of view. The comrades who expressed support for Levi must make a statement regarding his parliamentary seat; that will take care of this matter.

**Herbert von Mayenburg**: The issue that must be settled is the opposition's relationship to Levi. Even members of the parliamentary fraction have said that the fraction takes upon itself the task of holding the Zentrale within limits. Given this attitude by the fraction, a body subordinate to the Zentrale, the conduct toward Levi makes perfect sense. The fraction must now pull back from Levi and state that he can no longer sit in parliament as representative of any group within the party. Comrades of the German party would find it totally incomprehensible if they heard that someone advanced the viewpoint that a member of the parliamentary fraction can wait for the decision of the international congress and, during this period, retain his parliamentary seat.

**Neumann**: As regards Levi's seat in parliament, we proceed from the standpoint that the Zentrale and the Central Committee always made their decision on the March Action alone. We did not raise any objection to [Levi] resigning the seat before the congress. Now our statement and the decisions of the congress have settled the matter that Levi is no longer a member of the Communist Party. We will now wait to see what happens.

According to a message I have received, Frölich said that we conducted ourselves in a cowardly manner at the congress, and that the struggle will now open up in Germany. We therefore harbour some doubts as to whether the Zentrale is capable of carrying out the congress decisions, and we are not alone in this. We therefore agree with Lenin that the question of Levi's resignation as a parliamentary deputy should be disposed of after the congress, and we will carry out the congress decisions.

**Heckert**: We cannot agree with the remarks by Trotsky to the effect that a group that has disagreements with the party has the possibility of conducting a factional battle until the next congress. In addition, we intend to discuss objectively. We too would have had relevant criticisms of the March Action, except that Levi, before the theory of the offensive was thought up, published his pamphlet. We must also declare that Frölich did not make any such statement. The comrade who sent the report contests that he said any such thing. We can adopt Comrade Lenin's motion and then wait. Our demand is based on the overwhelming majority of the party. Members who give any support to Levi will face the opposition of the whole party.

**Zinoviev**: I propose that Thalheimer's statement and the contrary statements of the opposition be written down and signed by the delegation.

**Malzahn**: I propose that we not write any statement, since we have the resolution adopted by the congress. The worth of the agreement lies in the inner feelings and determination, which carry much more weight than statements. We will commit all our energy to induce the opposition to work in the interests of the party.

**Lenin**: It is better to have a document in order to set down a formulation of what has been discussed during the last hour and a half. I ask for the adoption of Zinoviev's motion.

**Koenen**: Members of the Executive [*Vorstand*] already took a position on the situation on 6 July and drafted a series of decisions regarding the opposition's conduct. We stand by this text, which we give to the comrades of the Executive, and we decline to make any further statement.[26]

**Maslow**: I call on the comrades of the opposition present here to appeal to their co-thinkers to accept the decisions of the congress.

---

26. The first 'executive' (*Vorstand*) mentioned by Koenen is apparently a body of the German delegation; the second (*Exekutive*) is the Comintern's leading body.

**Neumann**: We are prepared to sign what is submitted to us.

**Lenin**: I ask for a vote on whether the outcome of this discussion will be set down in writing. (*The motion is adopted, with two abstentions. Zinoviev's proposal is thus adopted.*)

**Neumann**: (*Proposes that the Executive draft the statement and then collect the signatures.*)

**Maslow**: (*Opposes the proposal.*)

**Friesland**: I propose that Comrade Zinoviev meet with representatives of the Zentrale and a representative of the opposition in order to draft a text.

**Neumann**: I propose that a representative of the Russian Central Committee be added to the commission. (*Rejected, with two in favour.*)
(*Another proposal that Zinoviev alone draw up the text is likewise rejected.*)
(*The meeting then adopts Comrade Friesland's proposal. The text is to be presented for signatures the next day.*)

## The 'Peace Treaty' within the German CP[27]

1.) All comrades recognise the [world] congress decisions as binding for their activity inside and outside the party and undertake to intervene energetically to implement them.
2.) All sides will refrain from the formation of factions and particularist efforts.
3.) All comrades have the obvious duty of collaborating only with publications controlled by the party.
4.) Parliamentary fractions are subject to the supervision and discipline of duly empowered party bodies.
5.) Wide freedom of discussion of disputed questions will be permitted in the party press and structures, to the extent consistent with the movement's interests.
6.) All members sincerely committed to carrying out the Third Congress decisions will be drawn into party work. Obviously, their earlier positions on issues clarified by the congress decisions will play no role in this process.

---

27. The text that follows, drafted on the basis of the 9 July discussion, was printed in the German party press following the congress. See Weber 1991, pp. 234–5; also Reisberg 1971, p. 726–7, n. 111; and *Die Rote Fahne*, 4 August 1921.

## 4e. Lenin Speaks to Central European Delegates[28]

*Remarks made at a meeting of members of the German, Polish, Czechoslovak, Hungarian, and Italian delegations, 11 July 1921*

1.

I read certain reports yesterday in *Pravda* which have persuaded me that the moment for an offensive is perhaps nearer than our view at the congress, for which the young comrades came down on us so hard. I shall deal with these reports later, however. Just now I want to say that the nearer the general offensive is, the more 'opportunistically' must we act. You will now all return home and tell the workers that we have become more reasonable than we were before the Third Congress. You should not be put out by this; you will say that we made mistakes and now wish to act more carefully. By doing so we shall win the masses over from the Social-Democratic and Independent Social-Democratic parties, masses who, objectively, by the whole course of events, are being pushed towards us, but who are afraid of us. I want to cite our own example to show you that we must act more carefully.

At the beginning of the War, we Bolsheviks adhered to a single slogan – that of civil war, and a ruthless one at that. We branded as a traitor everyone who did not support the idea of civil war. But when we came back to Russia in March 1917 we changed our position entirely. When we returned to Russia and spoke to the peasants and workers, we saw that they all stood for defence of the homeland, of course in quite a different sense from the Mensheviks, and we could not call these ordinary workers and peasants scoundrels and traitors. We described this as 'honest defencism'. I intend to write a big article about this and publish all the material.

On 7 April, I published my theses, in which I called for caution and patience.[29] Our original stand at the beginning of the War was correct: it was important then to form a definite and resolute core. Our subsequent stand was correct too. It proceeded from the assumption that the masses had to be won over. At that time we already rejected the idea of the immediate overthrow of the Provisional Government. I wrote: 'It should be overthrown, for it is an oligarchic, and not a people's government, and is unable to provide peace or bread. But it cannot be overthrown just now, for it is being kept in power by the workers' soviets and so far enjoys the confidence of the workers. We are

---

28. *LCW*, 42, pp. 324–8; compared with *PSS*, 44, 57–62.
29. A reference to Lenin's April Theses of 1917. See *LCW*, 24, pp. 19–26.

not Blanquists, we do not want to rule with a minority of the working class against the majority.'

The Cadets, who are shrewd politicians, immediately noticed the contradiction between our former position and the new one, and called us hypocrites. But as in the same breath they had called us spies, traitors, scoundrels, and German agents, the former epithet made no impression. The first crisis occurred on 20 April. Milyukov's note on the Dardanelles showed the government up for what it was: an imperialist government. After this, the armed masses of the soldiery moved against the building of the government and overthrew Milyukov. They were led by a non-party man named Linde. This movement had not been organised by the Party. We characterised that movement at the time as follows: something more than an armed demonstration, and something less than an armed uprising. At our conference on 22 April, the left tendency demanded the immediate overthrow of the government. The Central Committee, on the contrary, declared against the slogan of civil war, and we instructed all agitators in the provinces to deny the outrageous lie about the Bolsheviks wanting civil war. On 22 April I wrote that the slogan 'Down with the Provisional Government!' was incorrect, since if we did not have the majority of the people behind us this slogan would be either an empty phrase or adventurism.[30]

We did not hesitate in face of our enemies to call our leftists 'adventurists'. The Mensheviks crowed over this and talked about our bankruptcy. But we said that any attempt to be slightly, if only a little bit, left of the Central Committee was folly, and those who stood left of the Central Committee had lost ordinary common sense. We refuse to be intimidated by the fact that our enemies rejoice at our slips.

Our sole strategy now is to become stronger, hence cleverer, more sensible, more 'opportunistic', and that is what we must tell the masses. But after we have won over the masses by our reasonableness, we shall use the tactic of offensive in the strictest sense of that word.

Now about the three reports:

1) The strike of Berlin's municipal workers. Municipal workers are mostly conservative people, who belong to the Social Democrats of the majority and to the Independent Social-Democratic Party; they are well off, but are compelled to strike.[31]

---

30. See 'Resolution of the Central Committee of the R.S.D.L.P. (Bolsheviks)', in *LCW*, 24, pp. 210–11.
31. For the Berlin municipal workers' strike of July 1921, see p. 894, n. 24.

2) The strike of the textile workers in Lille.[32]
3) The third fact is the most important. A meeting was held in Rome to organise the struggle against the Fascists, in which 50,000 workers took part – representing all parties – Communists, Socialists, and also Republicans. Five thousand ex-servicemen came to the meeting in their uniforms and not a single Fascist dared to appear on the street. This shows that there is more inflammable material in Europe than we thought.[33] Lazzari praised our resolution on tactics. It is an important achievement of our congress. If Lazzari admits it, then the thousands of workers who back him are bound to come to us, and their leaders will not be able to scare them away from us. *'Il faut reculer, pour mieux sauter'* (you have to step back to make a better jump). This jump is inevitable, since the situation, objectively, is becoming insufferable.

So we are beginning to apply our new tactic. We mustn't get the jitters, we cannot be late, rather we may start too early. If you ask whether Russia will be able to hold out so long, we answer that we are now fighting a war with the petty bourgeoisie, with the peasantry, an economic war, which is much more dangerous for us than the last war. But as Clausewitz said, the essence of war is danger, and we have never been out of that danger for a moment. I am sure that if we act more cautiously, if we make concessions in time, we shall win this war too, even if it lasts more than three years.

Summing up:

1.) All of us, unanimously throughout Europe, shall say that we are applying the new tactic, and in this way we shall win the masses.
2.) Coordination of the offensive in the most important countries: Germany, Czechoslovakia, Italy. We need here preparation, constant coordination. Europe is pregnant with revolution, but it is impossible to make up a calendar of revolution beforehand. We in Russia will hold out, not only five years, but more. The only correct strategy is the one we have adopted. I am confident that we shall win positions for the revolution that the Entente will have nothing to put up against, and that will be the beginning of victory on a world scale.

---

32. Cotton-mill workers in Lille, France, went on strike in early July 1921, and the walkout spread to a number of departments in northern France. In early September the battle turned into a general strike in the Lille area, involving eighty thousand workers, to which the government responded by sending troops. In mid-October, textile workers began returning to work, accepting demands for a 10 per cent wage cut.

33. For the 8 July 1921 anti-Fascist demonstration in Rome, see p. 894, n. 22.

2.

Šmeral seemed to be pleased with my speech, but he interprets it one-sidedly. I said in the commission that in order to find the correct line, Šmeral had to make three steps to the left, and Kreibich one step to the right.[34] Šmeral, unfortunately, said nothing about taking these steps. Nor did he say anything about his views on the situation. Concerning the difficulties, Šmeral merely repeated the old arguments and said nothing new.

Šmeral said that I had dispelled his fears. In the spring he was afraid that the Communist leadership would demand of him untimely action, but events dispelled these fears. But what worries us now is this: will things really come to the stage of preparation for the offensive in Czechoslovakia, or will they be confined merely to talk about difficulties? The left mistake is simply a mistake, it isn't big and is easily rectified. But if the mistake pertains to determination to act, then this is by no means a small mistake, it is a betrayal. These mistakes are not comparable. The theory that we shall make a revolution, but only after others have acted first, is utterly fallacious.

3.

The retreat made at this congress can, I think, be compared with our actions in 1917 in Russia, which therefore proves that this retreat must serve as preparation for the offensive. Our opponents will maintain that we are not saying today what we said before. It will do them little good, but the working-class masses will understand us if we tell them in what sense the March Action is to be considered a success and why we criticise its mistakes and say that we should make better preparations in the future. I agree with Terracini when he says that the interpretations of Šmeral and Burian are wrong. If coordination is to be understood as our having to wait until another country has started, a country that is richer and has a bigger population, then this is not a Communist interpretation, but downright deception. Coordination should consist in comrades from other countries knowing exactly what factors are significant. The really important interpretation of coordination is this: the best and quickest imitation of a good example. The workers of Rome are a good example.

---

34. See Appendix 4b on pp. 1155–7.

## 4f. Zetkin on Taking Leave from Lenin[35]

On the day of my departure, Lenin came to say good-bye and give me 'good advice', which he believed I 'badly needed'.[36] 'Of course you are not fully satisfied with the outcome of the congress,' he said. 'You make no secret of the fact that you believe the congress acted illogically by aligning itself with Paul Levi in terms of fundamentals and course of action and nonetheless expelling him. But he must be punished. I say this not merely because of Levi's errors, of which I spoke before. I am thinking particularly of how difficult he has made it for us to carry through the policy of winning the masses. He too must recognise and admit his mistakes, in order to learn from them. If he does, and given his political capabilities, he will soon lead the party once again.'

'I believe there is a way in which Paul could submit to the discipline of the Communist International,' I answered, 'without abandoning his personal point of view. He could resign his parliamentary seat and conclude publication of his journal with an issue evaluating the work of our Third World Congress objectively and in broad historical terms. Naturally, that would not exclude criticism of this work but encompass it. He could state that he considers the decision of the congress against him to be wrong and illogical, but despite that, for the sake of the cause, he will submit to it. Through such an act of resolute willpower, Paul Levi would not lose as an individual and political figure, but only gain. He would refute the base suspicions of his opponents and demonstrate that for him, communism comes first.'

'Your proposal is excellent,' Lenin said. 'But will the expelled comrade accept it? Anyhow, I hope that your good-hearted optimism in assessing Levi proves to be correct, as opposed to the pessimism of many others. I promise you again that I will write an open letter proposing Levi's readmission to the party, unless he himself makes that impossible.

'But now to the main thing. Taken as a whole, the decisions of our Third Congress must fill us with satisfaction. They have far-reaching historical significance and, in fact, mark a turning point for the Communist International.

---

35. This is the second part of Zetkin's account, written in January 1924, of her discussions with Lenin at the Third Congress. The text is translated from Zetkin 1985, pp. 49–53. The editor has also consulted an earlier English translation in Zetkin 1934, pp. 32–5. For part 1, see Appendix 3i, pp. 1137–48.

36. On 22 July Zetkin had written Lenin, 'Given the situation in Germany, I need to return as quickly as possible. First, however, I must talk to you. Please tell me when and where this will be possible.' They met on the day of her departure, 27 July. Stoljarowa and Schmalfuss (eds.) 1990, p. 283. For Lenin's account of this discussion, see Appendix 4g, pp. 1176–8.

These decisions close the initial period in which the International developed revolutionary mass parties. That is why the congress had to clear away the leftist illusions: that the world revolution was going to rush forward without interruption at the speedy pace of its initial phase; that we will be carried forward by a second revolutionary wave; and that the determination and action of the party is in itself sufficient to secure victory for our cause. Of course it is easy, on paper and in the congress hall, from which all objective circumstances have been banished, to "make" the revolution as "a glorious act of the party itself", without the masses. In the final analysis, this approach is not revolutionary at all but narrow-minded and conventional. The "leftist blunders" found concrete and clear expression in the German March Action and the theory of the offensive. And so they had to be done away with at your expense, and you became the whipping boys. But in reality it was an international settlement of accounts.

'Now you in Germany must, as a unified and resolute party, carry out the policies decided here. The so-called peace treaty patched up among you is not in itself a firm basis for this.[37] It is no more than a scrap of paper, unless it is backed up by the sincere good will of those on the left and on the right to act as a single party on a clear and defined political line. Despite your aversion and reluctance, you must therefore join the Zentrale. And you must not desert it again, even when that seems to you to be your right and duty. You have no other right but to serve the party and thus the proletariat in this difficult time. Your duty right now is to hold the party together. I make you personally responsible for preventing a split, or, at most, limiting it to a small splintering off. You must be firm with the young comrades who still lack thorough theoretical training and have little practical experience, and you must also be very patient with them. I ask you, in particular, to look after Comrade Reuter (Friesland). He collaborated with us here eagerly and well for several years.[38] As the leader of the "radical" Berliners, he should join the Zentrale. That is the only way to establish a better relationship between them and the Zentrale. If I know Reuter, he will feel obligated by the "peace treaty" to collaborate with the so-called right wing as well in comradely fashion. During the congress, I noticed that he was acting in a rigid and narrow manner that is inappropriate in a leader, and if this leads to slipping and sliding there is usually no holding it back.'

---

37. For the text of the 'peace treaty' see Appendix 4d, p. 1169.
38. Reuter had been won to communism while a prisoner of war in Russia.

At this point, I interrupted Lenin's 'wise advice' with a surprised question, 'Do you have any suspicions in his regard?'

My teacher laughed. 'No, but I have experience,' he said. 'It is particularly important that you keep the allegiance of able comrades who won their spurs in the workers' movement in the past. I am thinking of comrades like Adolph Hoffman, Fritz Geyer, Däumig, Fries, and others. You must have patience with them, too, and not jump to the conclusion that Communist purity is endangered and destroyed if now and then they do not succeed in formulating Communist ideas in a clear and incisive manner. These comrades have every intention of being good Communists, and you must help them to become good Communists.

'Of course, you must not make any concessions to leftovers of reformist thinking. Reformism must not be smuggled in under any kind of false colours. But you must put comrades of this sort in positions where they cannot speak and act in any way other than as Communists. Perhaps you will experience disappointments nonetheless – in fact, it is likely. If you lose a backsliding comrade, nonetheless, if you act with firmness and wisdom, you will hold two or three or ten other comrades who came to you along with him and have really become Communists. Comrades like Adolph Hoffman, Däumig, and others bring experience and much specialised knowledge to the party. Above all, they are a living link between you and the broad working masses, who have trust in them. It's the masses that count. We must not make them nervous either through leftist blunders or rightist timidity. And if we act consistently as Communists in both large and small matters, we will win the masses. You in Germany must now pass your examination in the tactics of winning the masses. Do not disappoint us by beginning this process with a split in the party. Always think of the masses, Clara, and you will come to the revolution as we did, with and through the masses.'

### 4g. Lenin on His Final Meeting with Zetkin[39]

*28 July 1921*

Comrade Zinoviev:

I regard the conversation I had with Zetkin yesterday, before her departure, to be so important, in view of a number of statements she made, that I must inform you of it.

---

39. *LCW*, 45, p. 231; compared with *PSS*, 53, pp. 74–5.

She wants to set Levi two conditions:

1.) Resign his parliamentary seat.
2.) Close down his organ (*Sowjet* or *Unser Weg*, as I believe it is now called), issuing a statement of loyalty in respect to the decisions of the Third Congress of the Communist International.

Furthermore, she is afraid that it could occur to some friend of Levi's to publish Rosa Luxemburg's manuscript against the Bolsheviks (which I think she wrote in prison in 1918). If anyone should do this, she intends to make a statement in the press that she is quite sure such an act is disloyal. She would say that she had known Rosa Luxemburg best of all, and is sure that Luxemburg herself admitted these views to be erroneous, admitting, upon her release from prison, that she had been insufficiently informed.

In addition, Leo Jogiches, Rosa Luxemburg's closest friend, in a detailed talk with Zetkin, two days before he died, told her about this manuscript of Rosa Luxemburg's, and about Rosa Luxemburg herself admitting that it was wrong. Zetkin is going to write you about this at my request.[40]

If she has done so, please send me her letter.

Another interesting point, according to her, is that there is a wave of unification of *all* workers (both SDP and USPD people) in the struggle against *Lohnabbau* (wage reductions), etc. Of course, Zetkin was *quite right* in saying that the Communists should *back* this unification *in the struggle against the capitalists*. If the 'Lefts' should object, they should be made to see reason.

With communist greetings,
Lenin

P.S. Lozovsky *has already published* the congress resolutions of the Red International of Trade Unions. Well done![41]

---

40. While she was in prison in 1918, Rosa Luxemburg drafted a manuscript on the Russian Revolution. Written from the standpoint of solidarity with the Bolsheviks, the unfinished manuscript also contained criticisms of aspects of Bolshevik policy. Following his break from the KPD, Paul Levi published the manuscripts in 1922 under the title, *Die Revolution in Russland*.

An English-language translation can be found in Luxemburg 2004, pp. 282–310, and at: <http://www.marxists.org>.

In response to Levi's foreword to this work, Zetkin wrote a pamphlet replying to Luxemburg's criticisms of Bolshevik policy; see Zetkin 1922. She also addressed some of Luxemburg's criticisms in a speech to the Comintern's 1922 congress; for this see Riddell (ed.) 2011b, *4WC*, pp. 305–37.

41. For an English-language collection of RILU resolutions, see RILU 1921.

What about you?? Appoint *a person to be responsible* for editing, and get *Lozovsky* to publish the resolutions of the Third Congress of the Communist International.

## 4h. Lenin on the Outcome of the Levi Initiative[42]

*[Excerpt from letter of 14 August to German Communists on the eve of their convention in Jena, which took place 22–26 August 1921.]*

I must explain to the German comrades why I defended Paul Levi so long at the Third Congress. Firstly, because I made Levi's acquaintance through Radek in Switzerland in 1915 or 1916. At that time Levi was already a Bolshevik. I cannot help entertaining a certain amount of distrust towards those who accepted Bolshevism *only after* its victory in Russia, and after it had scored a number of victories in the international arena. But, of course, this reason is relatively unimportant, for, after all, my personal knowledge of Paul Levi is very small. Incomparably more important was the second reason, namely, that much of Levi's criticism of the March Action in Germany in 1921 was *essentially correct* (not, of course, when he said that the uprising was a 'putsch'; that assertion of his was absurd).

It is true that Levi did all he possibly could, and much besides, to weaken and spoil his criticism, and make it difficult for himself and others to understand the *essence* of the matter, by bringing in a mass of details in which he was obviously wrong. Levi couched his criticism in an impermissible and harmful form. While urging others to pursue a cautious and well-considered strategy, Levi himself committed worse blunders than a schoolboy, by rushing into battle so prematurely, so unprepared, so absurdly and wildly that he was certain to lose any 'battle' (spoiling or hampering his work for many years), although the 'battle' could and should have been won. Levi behaved like an 'anarchist intellectual' (if I am not mistaken, the German term is *Edelanarchist*), instead of behaving like an organised member of the proletarian Communist International. Levi committed a breach of discipline.

By this series of incredibly stupid blunders, Levi made it difficult to concentrate attention on the essence of the matter. And the essence of the matter, that is, the appraisal *and correction* of the innumerable mistakes made by the United Communist Party of Germany during the March Action of 1921, has been and continues to be of enormous importance. In order to explain and

---

42. *LCW*, 32, pp. 516–19 and Lenin *PSS*, 44, 88–100. For a subsequent comment on Levi, written in February 1922, see 'Notes of a Publicist', *LCW*, 33, pp. 207–11.

correct these mistakes (which some people enshrined as gems of Marxist tactics) *it was necessary* to have been on the *right* wing during the Third Congress of the Communist International. Otherwise the *line* of the Communist International would have been a *wrong* one.

I defended Levi, and had to do so, insofar as I saw before me opponents of his who merely shouted about 'Menshevism' and 'Centrism' and refused to see the mistakes of the March Action and the need to explain and correct them. These people made a caricature of revolutionary Marxism and a pastime of the struggle against 'Centrism'. They might have done the greatest harm to the whole cause, for 'no one in the world can compromise the revolutionary Marxists, if they do not compromise themselves'.

I said to these people: Let us assume that Levi has become a Menshevik.[43] As I have scant knowledge of him personally, I will not insist, if the point is proved to me. But it has not yet been proved. All that has been proved till now is that he *has lost his head*. It is childishly stupid to declare a man a Menshevik merely on these grounds. The training of experienced and influential party leaders is a long and difficult job. And without it, the dictatorship of the proletariat and its 'unity of will' remain a phrase. In Russia, it took us fifteen years (1903–17) to produce a group of leaders – fifteen years of fighting Menshevism, fifteen years of tsarist persecution, fifteen years, which included the years of the first revolution (1905), a great and mighty revolution. Yet we have had our sad cases, when even fine comrades have 'lost their heads'. If the West-European comrades imagine that they are insured against such 'sad cases' it is sheer childishness, and we cannot but combat it.

Levi had to be expelled for breach of discipline. Tactics had to be determined *on the basis* of a most detailed explanation and correction of the mistakes made during the March 1921 action. If, *after* this, Levi wants to behave in the old way, he will show that his expulsion was justified; and the wavering or hesitant workers will be given all the more forceful and convincing proof of the absolute correctness of the Third Congress decisions concerning Paul Levi.

Having made a cautious approach at the congress to the appraisal of Levi's mistakes, I can now say with all the more assurance that Levi has hastened to confirm the worst expectations. I have before me no. 6 of his magazine *Unser Weg* (15 July 1921). It is evident from the editorial note printed at the head of the magazine that the decisions of the Third Congress are known to Paul Levi. What is his reply to them? Menshevik catchwords such as

---

43. For 'let us assume,' Lenin's *Collected Works* has 'granted'. The Russian word is *dopustim*.

'a great excommunication' (*grosser Bann*), 'canon law' (*kanonisches Recht*), and that he will 'quite freely' (*in vollständiger Freiheit*) 'discuss' these decisions. What greater freedom can a man have if he has been freed of the title of party member and member of the Communist International! And please note that he expects party members to write for him, for Levi, anonymously!

First – he plays a dirty trick on the party, hits it in the back, and sabotages its work.

Then – he discusses the essence of the congress decisions.

That is magnificent.

But by doing this Levi puts paid to himself.

Paul Levi wants to continue the fight.

It will be a great strategic error to satisfy his desire. I would advise the German comrades to prohibit all controversy with Levi and his magazine in the columns of the daily party press. He must not be given publicity. He must not be allowed to divert the fighting party's attention from important matters to unimportant ones. In cases of extreme necessity, the controversy could be conducted in weekly or monthly magazines, or in pamphlets, and as far as possible care must be taken not to afford the KAPD-ists and Paul Levi the pleasure they feel when they are mentioned by name; reference should simply be made to 'certain not very clever critics who at all costs want to regard themselves as Communists'.

# Appendix 5
# The Colonial Question

### 5a. M.N. Roy: Theses on the Eastern Question[1]

*Presented to the Third Congress of the Communist International*

I.

1.) The fact that, in spite of its general bankruptcy, European capitalism is still holding its own against the increasingly powerful attack of the proletariat in the Western countries proves that capitalism, as a world-domineering factor, has not yet reached such a state of decay that its immediate downfall is inevitable. Since the time that capitalism entered into its last and most highly developed phase – imperialism – its stronghold was no longer kept confined only in the industrially advanced countries of Western Europe. The innate contradictions of the capitalist system inevitably led to overproduction and its consequence, the recurring commercial and financial crisis; in imperialism was found a way out of this entanglement. Of course, it was a temporary solution bound to prove ineffective for saving the capitalist mode of production from collapse under its own contradictions. But the fact is that till today imperial expansion and exploitation do render strength to capitalism to maintain its position in Europe.

---

1. The text, 'Draft Theses on the Oriental Question Presented to the Third Congress of the Communist International', is taken from an English original found in Comintern archives, RGASPI, 490/1/6. Minor corrections have been made on the basis of a comparison with the Russian text in *Narody Dal'nogo Vostoka* (1921), columns 337–42.

The great imperialist war shook the very foundation of the capitalist order in European countries, and had not these states had other sources to draw strength from, they would not be able to continue defending the right of capital till today as they are actually doing. These sources of strength lie in the imperialist character of present-day capitalism, which holds in its hands the entire economic, political, and military control of the whole world, and thus finds itself in a position to put up a stiff and continued resistance against the proletariat in its home countries. The existence and power of the European bourgeoisie do not depend wholly and exclusively on its ability to wring the greatest amount of surplus value out of the labour power of the workers in the home countries. The imperial right of exploiting the vast non-European markets and peoples has supplied and still supplies it with additional modus vivendi and a weapon to defend its position at home in spite of the apparent precariousness and impossibility of maintaining its power there for any length of time.

2.) As a result of the War, the world finds itself divided today into two great colonial empires, belonging to two powerful capitalist states. The United States of America endeavours to assume supreme and exclusive right of exploiting and ruling the entire New World, while Great Britain has annexed to its empire practically the entire continents of Asia and Africa. Then, continental Europe, owing to its utter economic bankruptcy and industrial dislocation, is bound to be an economic dependency of either of these two great imperialist states, which are preparing for another giant struggle for world domination. As far as the power of the American bourgeoisie is concerned, the European war has not affected it very much. On the contrary, the control of world finance, which has been for a century the monopoly of the British capitalists, had been to a great extent transferred to the hands of the American capitalists, who cannot be considered to have reached the period of decay and disintegration as yet. In order to consolidate its newly acquired world power, the American capitalist class inclines towards keeping temporarily away from the infectious ruins of Europe. Thus, the British bourgeoisie is the supreme ruler of the Old World and the backbone of the capitalist order.

Now, where lies the source of strength of the British bourgeoisie? Judging from the industrial conditions obtaining in the British Isles at the present moment, it would appear that if its resources were limited to the productivity of those islands and the power of consumption of continental Europe, the capitalist order in Britain would certainly stand on the very brink of collapse. But despite all its chronic contradictions and the difficulties it is having in reconstructing the industrial fabric of the home country on the prewar basis, the capitalist class of Britain proves to be quite firm in its power. It still succeeds in deceiving a part and coercing another part of the proletariat. The possession of the vast non-European empire, and the control over the newly created economic dependency to which continental Europe has been reduced, afford British capital a very wide scope of action, thus enabling it to maintain its position at home and incidentally securing its international power. Economic and industrial development of the rich and thickly populated countries of the East would supply new vigour to Western capital. There are great possibilities in these countries which will provide cheap labour power and new markets not to be exhausted very soon. Therefore the destruction of its monopolist right of exploitation in the vast Eastern colonial empire is a vital factor in the final and successful overthrow of the capitalist order in Europe.

3.) In view of the fact that the power of international capital is rooted all through the globe, anything less than a worldwide revolution would not bring about the end of the capitalist order and the triumph of the proletariat in Europe. The struggle of the European proletariat must be aided by the revolutionary action of the toiling masses of other lands subjugated by the same power, that is, capitalist imperialism. In its struggle to get out of the inevitable vicious circle, capitalism developed itself into imperialism, thus bringing extensive markets and huge armies of colonial workers under its domination. By converting the peasants and artisans of the subject countries into an agricultural and industrial proletariat, imperialism brought into existence another force which is destined to contribute to its destruction. This being the case, the overthrow of the capitalist order in Europe, which to a great extent rests on its imperial extension, will be achieved not alone by the advanced proletariat of Europe, but with the conscious cooperation of the workers and other revolutionary elements in those colonial and subject countries, which afford the greatest economic and military support to the imperial capital and which are the most developed economically, industrially, and politically.

4.) Therefore, the Communist International, in its task of mobilising the forces of world revolution, should not limit its field of activity only to the countries of Europe and the United States of America. While undoubtedly it is the proletariat of the industrial countries of Europe and America which stands at the vanguard of the armies of the world revolution, the historical phenomenon should not be overlooked that the toiling masses of the most advanced non-European countries are also destined to play a role in the act of freeing the world from the domination of imperialist capital. This historic role of the masses of the most advanced non-European countries consists of: (1) raising the standard of revolt against foreign imperialism simultaneously with the revolutionary action of the Western proletariat; and (2) fighting the native landowning class and bourgeoisie. Thus attacked from both sides, imperialism will have no possible way out of the vicious circle of its own creation. Deprived of the possibility of creating new markets by economically developing countries like China, India, etc., it will not be able to recover from the effects of overproduction in the home countries.

The great countries of the East have become an integral part of the capitalist world; battles against capitalism have begun and are going to be fought there. This is the result of the historic development of imperialism.

## II.

5.) The point of view that the peoples of the East – given that, in general, they are not on the same economic and political level with those of the West – can be conceived of as something uniform, with identical problems to solve, is erroneous, since it lacks the foundation of fact. It is a mistake to think that a uniform policy can be formulated to guide the activities of the Communist International in all the countries beyond a given geographical limit. The Eastern countries vary greatly in their political, economic, industrial, and social conditions. Consequently, the different Oriental peoples have different problems to solve. Therefore, a certain definite line of policy and tactics cannot be laid down to be followed rigidly in all Eastern countries. The conditions obtaining in the various countries should be carefully studied in order to ascertain which social class is historically and circumstantially destined to be revolutionary in the present moment as well as in the immediate future, since in such a revolutionary social class is to be found the natural ally of the Western proletariat in its fight for the overthrow of the capitalist order of society. Or, in other words, in order to mobilise the anti-imperialist forces effectually in the Oriental countries, the Communist International has to look for and base its activities on that social class which historically does belong or is destined to belong to its own ranks.

6.) Whereas, in the Muslim countries of the Near and Middle East, the religious fanaticism of the ignorant masses and the anti-foreign sentiments of the landowning middle-class counterrevolution can be counted upon as a force for the undermining of imperialism, these elements no longer possess the same significance in a country like India, owing to the radical economic and industrial transformation that has taken place there in the last two decades. Imperial capital has just touched the surface of the Near and Middle Eastern countries. The economic structure of the society is still predominantly feudal and the influence of the clergy is strong. But in India, which a considerable time ago was brought fully under the control and exploitation of capital, mainly imperial and partly native (the latter has been growing very fast in the last years), feudalism has been destroyed not by means of a violent revolution but by its long contact with modern political and economic institutions, which are the reflex of the most highly developed capitalist state. There has come into existence in India a native bourgeoisie, which more than thirty years ago began its historical struggle for the conquest of political power from the foreign ruler, and a proletariat, including a huge landless peasantry, which is growing in number and class consciousness in proportion to the rapid industrialisation of the country.

Consequently, the revolutionary movement in India today does not rest on the religious fanaticism of the ignorant masses, which is fast losing its potentiality owing to the economic transformation of the society. Nor does it rest on petty-bourgeois sentimental nationalism, which is built on the imaginary unity of interest of the entire people, not taking into consideration the class division which is becoming more and more clearly defined every day. In India and other countries of the same political and economic condition, the liberal bourgeoisie, which stands at the front of the national-democratic movement, is a revolutionary factor insofar as it carries on its historic struggle against the imperial ruler for the right of exploiting native resources and native labour. But this revolutionary character of the bourgeoisie is temporary, since as soon as foreign political domination is overthrown by a mass revolt, it will turn against the working class and will use all violent measures in order to thwart the further march of the revolution in the name of representative government and national defence. It is also possible that the weak native bourgeoisie will find it more profitable to sell itself out to its imperialist peer in return for such change in the political administration of the country as will provide it with wider scope and opportunity for developing as a class. Thus, the rapidly growing proletariat including the masses of landless peasantry is the principal social class which constitutes the foundation of the revolution in an Oriental country like India.

Therefore, the activities of the Communist International in the economically and industrially advanced countries of the East should consist of the formation of such political parties as are capable of developing and directing the revolutionary movement according to the objective conditions. Such parties will be the apparatus of the Communist International – through them, the peoples of the East will be unified in their respective countries to fight against foreign imperialism, and they will lead the fight further on for economic and social emancipation of the working class against the native bourgeoisie, as soon as it takes the place of the foreign exploiter.

7.) The bourgeoisie of the subjected and dominated countries will serve temporarily the purpose of a weapon against imperialism, but it cannot be relied upon. In the East the forces of world revolution – the forces on which the activities of the Communist International should be based – are to be found in the poor peasantry in those countries where feudalism still exists and among the proletariat and agrarian workers in those where machine industry has been introduced and the major portion of the population has been brought directly under the domination of modern capitalism, either foreign or native. The first stages of the revolution all over the East are bound to be a great upheaval against foreign imperialism, but it will be headed by the most revolutionary social class according to the economic development of the respective countries. Therefore, in organising this upheaval, different tactics will have to be adopted in different countries.

For instance, in India, a country directly ruled by foreign imperialism and needing political independence for free social development, it has not been practicable to unify the entire people, or at least a sufficiently large portion of it, in a movement for political liberation on the basis of bourgeois nationalism. Foreign imperialism exploits the masses through the agency of the native bourgeoisie and the impotent relics of feudalism. Therefore, a movement led by the bourgeoisie and actuated by bourgeois economic and political ideology naturally fails to attract the masses to its standard, since it cannot inspire confidence among them. It does not show them a way out of their present miserable existence. But until and unless the masses of the subject population take an active and conscious part in the revolutionary movement, foreign imperialism cannot and will not be overthrown only by the action of the bourgeoisie, even if it may succeed in rallying a certain section of the people behind it temporarily fired by sentimental enthusiasm. And it is only the historic struggle for economic emancipation which will unify the exploited class to which belongs the great majority of the people in the subject countries, including even the lower strata of the bourgeoisie.

8.) Religious-political movements like pan-Islamism cannot any longer be counted upon as a force against imperialism. Today, under the domination of imperialist capital and thanks to the progressiveness of the rising native bourgeoisie, the so-called Muslim world has become a thing of the past – it has ceased to be a social unit. It exists only in the imagination of fanatics, and the idea serves the ambition of the ruling dynasties and classes of the Muslim countries. Thus, pan-Islamism, which once had a certain revolutionary character, insofar as it could foment a mass upheaval, finds itself resting today only on the most reactionary and counterrevolutionary elements. The khans, mullahs, and even the progressive Muslim merchants and capitalists of the East find in the bankrupt idea of pan-Islamism a very convenient means of exploiting the ignorant masses. Such being its character at the present moment, pan-Islamism stands more on the side of imperialism than for the cause of liberation. In the economically and industrially backward countries of the Near and Middle East, the poor peasantry and handicraft workers should be organised to fight against imperialism and its henchmen, the native landlords and the merchant class.

## 5b. Ahmed Sultanzade: Theses on the Eastern Question[2]

*Presented to the Third Congress of the Communist International*

1.) The 'League of Nations' launched in Paris set up three categories: sovereign states, vassals, and wards under trusteeship [mandates]. In the 'trusteeship' category are almost all the countries of the East, including: Syria, Mesopotamia [Iraq], Arabia, India, Egypt, Korea, and China – proletarian states mercilessly exploited by mandatory states. So we see a classification of states within world imperialism in terms of their relative political weight, corresponding to the class divisions in capitalist society. The dominant states relate to dependencies in a manner quite similar to how an industrialist relates to his workers in bourgeois society. But there is a very significant difference: a portion of the surplus value extracted by the entrepreneurs of the dominant power falls into the hands of the local bourgeoisie. If the entrepreneur realises this surplus value outside the markets of these 'proletarian' states, he retains it in its entirety.

2.) This rather sketchy comparison gives only a rough indication of the place of colonial countries of the East in the world imperialist system. For a more accurate picture, it is necessary to divide these countries into the following categories:

a.) Colonies that have experienced considerable industrialisation and are strongly linked to the colonising country through its financial capital.
b.) Colonies whose industrialisation took place mainly during the War and that are only weakly linked with the colonising country.
c.) Colonies that serve only to supply raw materials to the advanced capitalist countries.

In the East, there are hardly any countries in the first category. It includes countries such as Australia and Canada, where the upper layers of the bourgeoisie have been drawn into the orbit of the imperialist syndicates and trusts.

---

2. Translated from 'Proekt tezisov po vostochnomu voprosu' in *Narody Dal'nogo Vostoka* (1921), columns 343–6. The text has also been compared with 'Theses on the Oriental Question by Sultan Zade' in Comintern archives, RGASPI, 490/1/6.

Thus the Canadian stockholders or owners of steel mills have been absorbed into the reigning imperialist steel trust, thus gaining a stake not only in the exploitation of their own country but in the policies of financial capital in the colonising country, which aim at territorial expansion. This type of colony is normally granted substantial autonomy, given that it does not endanger the interests of trusts in the colonising country.

3.) In the East, this process of incorporation began before the War, although only in India and to some extent in China and only to a very limited extent. However, the War speeded up the industrialisation of these countries enormously, giving the local bourgeoisie a firm foundation and a chance to stand on its own feet. This led them to make efforts to gain a stronger position on a national level. A process of industrialisation is evident in Turkey. The fact that the Indian and Turkish bourgeoisie has carried out some protectionist propaganda reflects the rise of a whole range of branches of production. The local capitalists are seriously engaged in carrying out protectionist policies to defend emerging industry from the competition of highly developed capitalist countries.

At the same time, the new property relations have given rise to the bourgeoisie as a defined class, separate from the big capitalist trusts, and impelled toward taking political power and using it to its own benefit. But in their struggle for power, the local capitalists come into conflict, first, with the feudal aristocracy that still holds political power in many countries of the East, and, second, with the American and European imperialists, who, with the aid of these feudalists, carry out the economic exploitation of these countries. Here the struggle becomes quite fierce, and world imperialism does everything in its power to prevent the local bourgeoisie from fully taking power.

4.) The War not only reinforced and strengthened the national bourgeoisie, which does not wish to share surplus value with capitalism in the colonising country, but it also brought onto the stage a new revolutionary force, which had previously been in decline and disintegration: handicraft and artisanal industry. Imports of cheap manufactured goods from the industrialised centres of Europe and America subjected this layer to an extended period of profound crisis. Thousands were forced to leave their homelands and emigrate to other countries in order to survive, or to endure miserable conditions of semi-starvation in their own country.

The War aroused in them a new spirit, a new soul – enabling them to expand production to meet enormous market demand.

The enormous crisis of the capitalist economy that broke out two years after the War has further increased the weight of handicraft manufacture in the colonial and semi-colonial countries of the East. The artisans and handicraftsmen, ruined before the War, have come back to life, doing everything in their power to hold off their doom. Their contest with world capitalism is becoming a life-and-death struggle. The young native bourgeoisie, which they do not yet recognise as their enemy, takes advantage of this situation to draw them into the struggle to break the yoke of European capitalists. This alone explains the broad support that rallied to the boycott of British goods in India and of Japanese goods in China.

5.) As for the peasant movement, here it is necessary to distinguish countries such as India and Iran, where a feudal bourgeoisie gained possession of huge landed property, from those such as China and in part Turkey, where small landholdings prevail. In the former two countries, the peasant movement is growing day by day, especially in India, where it gives rise to periodic uprisings and disorders, pitilessly repressed by the British administration. So long as world capitalism maintains its grip in the colonies and semi-colonies, the peasants cannot possibly win freedom from bondage to the landlords, given that the imperialists rely for the most part on the landed aristocracy, all the more in countries where the trusts have not yet succeeded in acquiring a firm base among the native capitalists. As a result, the peasant movement is inevitably directed against the rule of the foreign invaders.

The destruction of imperialist rule will also bring benefits to the working class, which greatly expanded in numbers during and after the War, especially in India. It suffers from a double exploitation by both its own and the foreign bourgeoisie. It is unable to free itself simultaneously from both its exploiters, if only because the organised working class is very small and has not yet acquired the necessary skills of the class struggle. Every unconscious step in this direction will tend to reconcile its enemies, who, until this point, were ready to cut each other's throats.

6.) In this fashion, the four strongest classes (bourgeoisie, artisans/petty-bourgeoisie, workers, and peasants) are inevitably driven by their economic interests into a desperate struggle against exploitation by world capitalism and for full national liberation. Even the most reactionary pan-Islamic movement, led by the upper layers of the Islamic clergy, have been led by the course of events into a struggle against British capitalism. The fact that pan-Islamic congresses were convened simultaneously in Ankara (by the Turkish nationalists) and in Mecca (by the British) shows that even in this camp a struggle is unfolding against the rule of world imperialism.

The Communist International must take all these forces into account and direct them against colonial rule by the world bourgeoisie, and above all against British imperialism, whose destruction is a precondition for world revolution. The victory of the national movement in the countries of the East will signal the beginning of the end for the ruling classes of Europe and America.

Even if the native bourgeoisie of some countries, after winning a full or partial victory, concludes an agreement with the great powers, this should not discourage us. Such an event is quite natural and will not halt the revolutionary movement. If the European bourgeoisie is forced in every colonial and semi-colonial country to relinquish even a portion of its political and economic privileges, the power of world capitalism will then be buried by the international proletariat before it is able to strike roots in the East.

7.) Because of the predominant influence of petty-bourgeois forces in the East, who are united in hatred of world capitalism's violent outrages, which Communists as well are fighting against, these forces are often portrayed as being Communist in character. Thus we have the formation in some countries of various groups with a communist tinge – nationalist or Islamic communists. This fact was taken up at the Second Congress in Thesis 11, point (e) of the Theses on the National and Colonial Questions, which reads:

> A resolute struggle is necessary against the attempt to portray as communist the revolutionary liberation movements in the backward countries that are not truly Communist. The Communist International has the duty to support the revolutionary movement in the colonies and the backward countries only on condition that the components are gathered in all backward countries for future proletarian parties – Communist in fact and not only in name – and that they are educated to be conscious of their particular tasks, that is, the tasks of struggling against the bourgeois-democratic movement in their own nation. The Communist International should arrive at temporary agreements and, yes, even establish an alliance with the revolutionary movement in the colonies and backward countries. But it cannot merge with this movement.[3]

This position is still correct today, and we must act decisively to transform it into reality. This is the only road leading to the destruction of world capitalism's power. We must strengthen in the East the idea of international proletarian solidarity; this will lead to decisive victory.

---

3. Riddell (ed.) 1991, 2WC, 1, p. 288.

## 5c. Zhang Tailei: Theses on the Colonial Question[4]

*Presented to the Third Congress of the Communist International*

1.) It is quite wrong to imagine that all the countries of the East present completely uniform tasks to their revolutionary organisations and demand common methods of leadership of their national revolutionary movements. Within the category of oppressed countries of the East we find:

   a.) Countries that have already experienced industrial development.

   b.) Countries that are encompassed only through international commerce, and then only in initial forms.

   c.) Countries that as yet stand completely outside the capitalist relations of the imperialist world – countries that are still primitive.

2.) For each type of country, Communists need a special course of action, which takes into account the specific peculiarities of these countries' position in the world. Flowing from this, they must consider the role of the different classes in each of these countries – whether one of mediation or fundamental antagonism – with regard to its exploitation by imperialism. Each of these three categories of Eastern countries requires a distinct programme of action and revolutionary organisation. Each needs its own strategic plan; each calls for a distinct form of leadership by the Communist International.

3.) It would be a gross error to deny that the peoples of countries in the three categories above have common revolutionary tasks, above all with regard to the struggle against imperialist oppression. Indeed, it is quite obvious that imperialism in its current form (export of capital, import of raw materials, and the problem – still far from resolved for many capitalist countries – of securing markets for their industrial products) imposes the decisive forms of its economy on backward countries. This results in a radical break in the entire economic system of the given colonial country and of them all taken together.

This break does not promote a strengthening of the basis of the national bourgeoisie's 'domestic' industry and finance in a given country. Rather, in the best of cases, it transforms this bourgeoisie and even the new forms of its economy (factories, mines, banks, maritime transport, etc.) into appendages of the imperialist capitalism ruling that colony or semi-colony. As a result, capitalist development among the more 'advanced' colonial countries proceeds in a direction that undermines the independence of their own

---

4. Translated from 'Tezisy po kolonial'nomy voprosy', *Revoliutsionnyi Vostok*, 4–5 (1928), pp. 220–2. Original translation into Russian by Boris Shumiatsky.

national economies. A process of levelling out takes place among the different countries, affecting colonies of different types and expressed in the complete absence of an independent role with regard to their paths for economic and political development.

4.) Despite these general features, which shape imperialist capital accumulation in the economy of Eastern countries, it remains important for the international proletariat to direct its efforts to the national 'peculiarities' of working people's struggle in each of the Eastern countries, which are so varied in their form of development. The international tasks of the proletarian movement have always been and will always be resolved only on the basis of a correct application of the international proletarian party's programme and methods to the specific features of each particular country. This involves examining the relationship not only of forces on a global level but also of those contending within each given country. These may be the feudalists, promoting the cause of counterrevolution and alliance with imperialism; the petty bourgeoisie and oppressed millions of peasants, who may press the bourgeois-democratic revolution through to a victorious conclusion, to its agrarian consummation; or, finally, the young national bourgeoisie, which is fearful, as a rule, of both 'Bolshevik' revolutionary extremism and of oppression by and competition from the enormously more powerful imperialist capitalism.

5.) The role of the bourgeoisie of oppressed countries is only a question of tactics. This is true, first, because it does not determine the course and outcome of the national-revolutionary struggle, and, second, because its participation in this struggle as part of a so-called 'united national front' can only be temporary. The national bourgeoisie takes this path only in circumstances where it cannot establish its role in the form of 'an independent state with economic and financial autonomy' (customs, banking, transport, etc.) or where it does not find the national revolutionary movement standing in contradiction to its efforts to drive out the imperialists so as to be able to take their place in the exploitation of its country's population.

However, the national-revolutionary movement, during its initial phase, gains both tactically and strategically from drawing on the strength of the 'united national front'. Comrade Roy is thus quite wrong to assert that the peasantry and handicraft workers in the economically backward countries of the Near and Middle East should immediately launch a struggle on two fronts – against the imperialists and their own bourgeoisie. This conception of tactical tasks is wrong not only for the economically backward countries of the Near and Middle East but also for China, which Comrade Roy assigns, with some justification, to the grouping of 'advanced' Eastern countries.

6.) Communists in the colonial and semi-colonial countries of the East, while maintaining their programmatic and organisational independence, must therefore set themselves the task of winning over the national-revolutionary movement in each of these countries, freeing the masses participating in this movement from the hegemony of the national bourgeoisie. Moreover, where possible, they must press these masses to go beyond this movement. While urging them to struggle under the slogans 'Down with imperialism!' and 'Long live national independence!', Communists must, at the necessary movement, cut them free from the national movement.

## 5d. Ivon Jones: The Black Question[5]

[12 July 1921]

**Ivon Jones** (South Africa): Comrades, I can see from your expressions that you are surprised to see a white comrade from South Africa, a country so generally associated with the Negro.[6] And indeed I think the Comintern photographer was also dismayed to find the South African delegates white. I have seen a Negro brother in the corridor; I think he has been captured by main force for the photographer (*Laughter*). I have been asked to deal with the Negro question in general. I hope that the fact that we are dealing with this vast question in the closing hours of this congress is no indication of our sense of responsibility.

It is now fifty years since Karl Marx told us that the open slavery of the colonies is the pedestal on which is built up the veiled slavery of European wage labour.[7] And he threw out the warning then, which is as serious a warning to us today, when he said that labour cannot emancipate itself in the white so long as in the black it is branded. I trust that in spite of the hurried notice given to the Oriental question at this congress, that warning of our master Marx will not be forgotten by the Communist International.

---

5. This speech was delivered in Session 23 but its text is not found in the congress proceedings. This omission may have resulted from the decision during this session not to translate speeches, resulting in the absence of a German-language transcript. The English-language text printed here is found in the Comintern archives, RGASPI, 490/1/135 – a file devoted to transcripts of Session 23.

6. In recent decades, the term 'Negro' has acquired a pejorative connotation and has fallen out of use. However, since the Ivon Jones speech is not translated but taken from an English original, the term 'Negro' has been left unchanged.

7. Marx, '[T]he veiled slavery of the wage workers in Europe needed, for its pedestal, slavery pure and simple in the new world.' In *Capital* volume 1, chapter 31.

I agree that last year's theses left nothing to be said on the colonial question. We marvelled, in fact, at the comprehension of matters contained in it which we had only learnt by close association with the facts for years. We agree that these theses now need only local application on the part of the sections, and direct action on the part of the Comintern. This has been lacking so far.

Comrade Radek admitted in committee that they know very little of the state of the movement among vast working masses of India and China so far as definite Communist parties were concerned. We must not be misled into inactivity by the number of interesting and picturesque personalities from the East here who are of such interest to our photographers. We in Africa call for a more direct initiative in the Negro question particularly. The Negro has been the Ishmael of the human race. He must become the Benjamin of the Communist International.[8]

In South Africa we have a replica of the world problem in miniature. Almost in the same proportions as on the world scale, you have there a mass of native workers side by side with a select white skilled class of workers. How is it that just here, where there is a mass of natives side by side with a labour aristocracy you have perhaps the largest Communist Party in the British colonies? The reasons for this form an interesting study. But we are only allowed five minutes and I cannot enter into details.

The Negro question manifests itself also in America, where it takes on a very acute form. There you have the proportion of the Negro in the ratio of one to ten of the whites, and it is just there that you have colony prejudices in its most frenzied form. It is only the other day that we read of the burning of 150 Negro worshippers in a Negro church by the mobs of lynch law.[9] As the disintegration of the bourgeoisie proceeds apace, we can expect more and more violent forms of this frenzy in America, which is today not only confined to Negro states like Georgia, but is spreading to the North as well, fanned as it is by the flames of economic competition between Negroes and whites.

In South Africa, on the other hand, you have the proportion of Negroes to whites in the reverse degree. The natives outnumber the whites by about ten

---

8. In the Bible, Benjamin, the youngest of Jacob's twelve sons, epitomises the righteous child, while Ishmael, first son of Abraham, was disinherited and cast out.
9. This is presumably a reference to the race riot in Tulsa, Oklahoma, although the details of Jones's story are unclear. On 31 May 1921, white racist lynch mobs attacked the city's black community. In the face of armed resistance, the National Guard was sent in to suppress the black community, including with the use of air power. By the following day most of the black community, including many churches and the only hospital, was burned to the ground. Up to 300 people, primarily black, are estimated to have been killed.

to one. In America the problem will come more and more within the scope of the Communist Party there, as the party grows in strength, and as the workers become too oppressed by their economic oppression to be misled by colony prejudice any more. But in Africa we have a relatively small labour aristocracy, from which it is difficult to recruit militant workers for the Communist Party. So that as the natives outnumber the whites by ten to one, the task is beyond the small Communist Party to the same extent. We say nothing now of the vast native populations, working masses outside the Union [of South Africa] proper. Here is a strong case for the direct initiative of the Communist International.

While on this phase of the subject, I should like to mention India. India has nothing to do with the Negro question proper. But insofar as the subject is one of the relations between white and native workers, you have an interesting fact in the case of India, and it is this: There is also a thin upper crust of white skilled workers, much smaller than in Africa, but still it is there. One would have thought that this small labour aristocracy could easily be bought out by the capitalist class. But what do we see? We see white workers coming out on strike on the railways side by side with the Indian workers. Now, here is a good chance for Communist propaganda to get a purchase hold among the white workers. There must be fine opportunities there of bringing out white skilled leaders for the Indian working masses in the difficult early stages of the movement.

As for Africa, I would like to say in conclusion that although there are no brilliant examples of Negro Communists here in Moscow yet, I can assure you that the native working mass as a whole is going to be a brilliant example for communism. They are ripe for communism. They are absolutely propertyless. They are stripped of every vestige of property and caste prejudice. The African natives are a labouring race, still fresh from ancestral communal traditions. I will not say that the native workers are well organised, or have a general conception of communism or even of trade unionism, as yet. But they have made several attempts at liberation by way of industrial solidarity. They only need awakening. They know they are slaves, but lack the knowledge how to free themselves. I should like to say the same regarding colony prejudice. Although colony prejudice is there, I am glad to say that never has it taken on the form of mob lynching and the frenzy of the American outbreaks against the Negroes.

The solution of the problem, the whole world problem is being worked out in South Africa on the field of the working-class movement. In conclusion, I would like to admit this motion for the congress to endorse as a sentiment of solidarity with Africa:

That this congress resolves to further the movement among the working masses of Africa as an integral part of the Oriental question, and desires the Executive to take a direct initiative in promoting the awakening of the African Negroes as a necessary step to the world revolution.[10]

(*Applause*)

## 5e. Against Repression in Palestine[11]

*Motion Submitted to Third Congress by the Communist Party of Palestine*

The inhuman persecution of Communists in all the countries of Central and Western Europe has now been compounded by persecution of the young and growing Communist movement of the Near East. In Palestine, where the atmosphere is poisoned by religious fanaticism and national hatred of British colonial domination, the Communist Party of Palestine has taken the initiative and leads the Arab and Jewish workers in common revolutionary unions and a single international Communist Party. It leads them in struggle against the British invaders, against Arab effendis and sheiks in the pay of Britain and France, and against the nationalist Jewish bourgeoisie, which serves British capitalism.

The third anniversary of the Russian October Revolution and this year's May Day were marked by celebrations under the banner of the Communist International. This gave rise to savage persecution against the Communists.[12] All the workers suspected of being Communist were immediately fired and, in large measure, thrown in prison. And now the British rulers threaten the

---

10. In Session 24, the congress referred Jones's proposal for consideration by the ECCI (see pp. 871–2). While no action was taken at that time, an agenda item on the black question was included in the Fourth Comintern Congress in 1922. Following reports on this point, the congress adopted 'Theses on the Black Question.' See Riddell (ed.) 2011b, *4WC*, pp. 800–11, 947–51.

11. Translated from the French text in Comintern archives, RGASPI 490/1/181a.

12. On 7 November 1920, the Socialist Workers' Party (MPS) – predecessor of the Palestine Communist Party – organised a demonstration with 30–40 participants to mark the anniversary of the October Revolution, as they attempted to organise a strike that day. The police responded by raiding the MPS headquarters.

On 1 May 1921 the MPS organised a demonstration of several dozen around slogans such as, 'Long live the international solidarity of the Jewish and Arab proletariat!' and 'All power to the workers' and peasants' council of Palestine!' Clashes surrounding this action sparked widespread communal violence between Arabs and Jews in which close to a hundred were killed. In the wake of these events, the British authorities arrested dozens of MPS members, deporting fifteen of them.

prisoners with very severe punishment including, in some cases, the death penalty.

The congress expresses its fullest sympathy with the brave comrades of Palestine, who are struggling under such difficult conditions.

We will surely triumph in our struggle for the Communist cause!

*Saar, Arie*

# Chronology

**1917**

*7 November* – Bolshevik-led seizure of power by soviets in Russia.

**1918**

*25–28 January* – Civil war in Finland begins between Red Guard and counterrevolutionary white forces. By mid-May workers are defeated. Ensuing white terror claims tens of thousands of victims.

*3 March* – Brest-Litovsk Treaty signed between Russia and Germany.

*Summer* – Onset of Russian Civil War, as Soviet republic confronts counterrevolutionary white armies and invasion by Western powers.

*30 October* – Revolutionary uprisings in Vienna and Budapest.

*9 November* – Revolution in Germany overthrows Hohenzollern monarchy.

*11 November* – Armistice ends World War I.

*30 December–1 January 1919* – German CP (KPD) holds founding congress.

**1919**

*15 January* – Karl Liebknecht and Rosa Luxemburg are arrested and murdered by German officers.

*3–10 February* – Bern conference seeks to reconstitute Second International.

*1 March* – Uprising in Korea against Japanese occupation.

*2–6 March* – First Congress of Communist International in Moscow.

*8 March* – British exiling of leader of anticolonial movement in Egypt leads to popular uprising.

*21 March* – Proclamation of Hungarian soviet republic.

*7 April* – Soviet republic proclaimed in Bavaria, led by pacifists, centrists, and anarchists.

*13–27 April* – Communists assume leadership of Bavarian soviet republic. Counterrevolutionary forces enter Munich 1 May, and consolidate control by 3 May. Hundreds of workers are executed, with many more imprisoned.

*28 June* – Treaty of Versailles signed.

*28 July–2 August* – Founding Congress of International Federation of Trade Unions (IFTU) in Amsterdam; body becomes known as Amsterdam International.

*1 August* – Hungarian soviet regime is toppled. White terror ensues, with thousands executed, imprisoned, and exiled.

*31 August–7 September* – Communist movement in US founded out of split in SP. It is divided at birth, as Communist Party of America and Communist Labor Party hold rival conventions.

*20–24 October* – German KPD holds Second Congress in Heidelberg. It expels ultraleft forces that will form KAPD.

*20–26 November* – Conference of International Union of Socialist Youth Organisations in Berlin votes to change name to Communist Youth International. Meeting becomes First Congress of CYI.

**1920**

*10 January* – League of Nations begins operations.

*13–17 March* – Kapp Putsch in Germany.

*25 April* – Polish army launches offensive against Soviet forces in Ukraine; takes capital, Kiev, on 7 May.

*1–28 May* – French railway strike. Some 1.5 million are involved, as industrial workers throughout France go out in support.

*Late May* – US Communist Labor Party fuses with a wing of Communist Party to form United Communist Party.

*5 June* – Gilan soviet government proclaimed in northern Iran; it lasts until October 1921.

*Mid-June* – Red Army counteroffensive forces Polish-Ukrainian army into retreat.

*July* – Uprising against British rule in Mesopotamia (Iraq).

*5–16 July* – Conference of Entente powers in Spa, Belgium, discusses war reparations and world economy.

*15 July* – Founding of International Council of Trade and Industrial Unions, forerunner of Red International of Labour Unions (RILU, Profintern).

*19 July–7 August* – Comintern Second Congress held in Moscow.

*30 July–2 August* – First International Conference of Communist Women held in Moscow.

*31 July–1 August* – CP of Britain founded at convention in London, uniting a number of groups in England, Scotland, and Wales.

*31 July–6 August* – Congress of reformist Social-Democratic parties in Geneva reconstitutes Second International as 'Labour and Socialist International'.

*16 August* – Red Army close to Warsaw forced to retreat by Polish counteroffensive.

*30 August–30 September* – With metalworkers in the lead, industrial workers throughout Italy occupy their factories, and many peasants seize land.

*31 August–7 September* – Comintern organises First Congress of the Peoples of the East, held in Baku.

*12 October* – Armistice is signed ending Polish-Soviet War.

*12–17 October* – USPD holds congress in Halle. Majority votes to join Comintern and fuse with KPD, resulting in formation of United Communist Party of Germany (VKPD). Minority splits and retains USPD name.

*14 November* – Effective end of Russian Civil War as Wrangel's white army abandons Crimea.

*9–15 December* – General strike in Czechoslovakia involves 1 million industrial and agricultural workers.

*25–30 December* – Tours Congress of the French SP votes by a 75 per cent majority to accept the Twenty-One Conditions and affiliate to the Comintern, giving birth to the CP of France. The minority ('Dissidents') splits away, preserving the old SP's formal name: French Section of the Workers' International (SFIO).

*29–30 December* – During a massive strike wave in Yugoslavia, the Communist Party and trade unions are banned.

**1921**

*8 January* – VKPD publishes Open Letter addressed to workers' organisations in Germany, calling for united proletarian action against capitalist offensive.

*15–21 January* – Congress of Italian SP in Livorno results in split, as left wing withdraws from party to form Italian CP.

*29–30 January* – British CP holds Second Convention in Leeds, completing unification of pro-Communist forces.

*22 February* – VKPD Central Committee repudiates Paul Levi's criticisms of Comintern intervention at Italian SP Livorno Congress. Levi, Clara Zetkin, and three others then resign from the Zentrale.

*22–27 February* – Congress in Vienna of centrist socialist parties founds International Working Union of Socialist Parties. It is known as the Vienna Union; the Communist movement labels it the 'Two-and-a-Half International'.

*24–28 February* – Conference of Balkan Communist Federation.
*25 February* – Establishment of Georgian Soviet Socialist Republic.
*28 February–18 March* – Kronstadt uprising against Soviet government.
*5–6 March* – CP of Switzerland founded by fusion of former left wing of Social-Democratic Party with members of Swiss CP formed in 1918.
*8 March* – French army occupies Dusseldorf, Duisburg, and Ruhrort on Rhine after Germany fails to meet French reparations ultimatum. French troops withdraw in September.
*8–16 March* – Tenth Congress of Russian CP adopts New Economic Policy (NEP).
*16 March* – Soviet government establishes relations with Turkey.
*16 March* – Otto Hörsing, Social-Democratic governor of Prussian Saxony, announces police occupation of region to repress strikes and militant workers' actions.
*17 March* – VKPD Central Committee calls for offensive action.
*19 March* (Saturday) – Police enter Mansfeld region in Prussian Saxony.
*20 March* – Under provisions of Versailles Treaty, a plebiscite is held in Upper Silesia on whether the territory will become part of Germany or Poland. Majority votes to remain in Germany.
*21 March* (Monday) – Strikes begin to spread in Central Germany.
*22–23 March* (Tuesday–Wednesday) – Max Hoelz forms armed detachment in Eisleben, disarms policemen and seizes arms depot.
*24 March* (Thursday) – On the day before Easter Holiday begins, government declares state of siege; VKPD calls nationwide general strike and unsuccessfully seeks to provoke one.
*25–28 March* – Two months after exit of right-wing minority, congress of Norwegian Labour Party adopts Comintern's Twenty-One Points.
*31 March* – British miners strike to protest owners' intention to cut wages. More than a million workers participate. The strike lasts until 27 June.
*1 April* (Friday) – After all major resistance in Germany has ceased, the VKPD Central Bureau gives order to end strike action.
*3–11 April* – Communist Youth International Second Congress meets in Jena, Germany. Meeting is adjourned to Berlin and eventually rescheduled in Moscow several months later, on proposal of ECCI.
*15 April* – Leaders of transport and rail unions in UK refuse to call for promised strike action in support of embattled coal miners. Militant workers label this betrayal as 'Black Friday'.
*15 April* – VKPD Central Bureau expels Paul Levi from party for breach of discipline in his criticism of March Action. The Central Committee endorses the decision on 5 May.
*29 April–5 May* – Entente powers hold London conference on reparations. The conference sends an ultimatum to Germany demanding 1 billion gold marks by the end of the month, threatening to occupy the Ruhr. Germany then borrows money and accepts payment schedule.
*2 May* – Uprising by Polish nationalist forces against German rule in Upper Silesia.
*8–12 May* – Congress of Romanian SP votes to become Communist Party; minority splits off to form Social-Democratic party.
*14–16 May* – Congress of Czechoslovak Left Socialist Party votes to form CP and join Comintern.
*15–28 May* – Joint Unity Convention of United Communist Party and Communist Party of America unites US Communists into Communist Party of America (Section of the Communist International).
*26 May* – Norway general strike involving 120,000 workers, called over employer attempts to cut wages. Lasts until 6 June.
*9–15 June* – Communist Women's Movement holds second international conference in Moscow.

*11–20 June* – Comintern Executive Committee (ECCI) holds expanded meetings to prepare for Third Congress.

*22 June–12 July* – Third Congress of Communist International in Moscow.

*3–19 July* – First congress of Red International of Labour Unions held in Moscow.

*9–23 July* – Second Congress of Communist Youth International meets in Moscow.

# Glossary

**Abd al Malik** – grandson of Abd al-Qadir; born in Damascus, went to Morocco 1902; declared war against French rule during World War I with support from Germany; later collaborated with Spanish in Morocco against French.

**Abd al-Qadir** [1808–83] – Algerian Islamic scholar; from 1832 leader of guerrilla struggle against French invasion of Algeria; forced to surrender 1847 and exiled.

**Abilov** – This may refer to **Ibrahim Manarramoghh Abilov** [1881–1923], member of Azerbaijani Hümmet [Equality] party and RSDLP from 1905; emigrated to Persia 1908; editor of *Baki hayati* 1912; deputy to Azerbaijani Parliament 1918–20; joined Azerbaijan CP 1920; appointed diplomatic representative of soviet Azerbaijan in Turkey 1921.

**Adler, Friedrich** [1879–1960] – leader of Austrian Social Democracy from early years of century; pacifist during War; jailed 1917–18 for assassination of Austrian prime minister; organiser and president of Two-and-a-Half International 1921–3; secretary of Socialist International 1923–46; in exile during Nazi occupation; settled in Switzerland 1947.

**Alessandri, Cesare** [1869–1929] – worked as journalist for Italian SP from 1894; correspondent for *Avanti* in Paris from 1912; worked with Serrati on *Communismo* 1919–22, then with Turati; subsequently favourable to Fascism.

**Alexakis, Orion** [d. 1920] – Greek Communist from Balaklava; killed by pirates at sea while returning to Greece from Russia October 1920.

**American Federation of Labor** [AFL] – US craft union organisation founded 1881; 3.9 million members in 1921; split 1935–6 with formation of Congress of Industrial Organizations; reunited 1955.

**Amiens Charter** – adopted by French CGT in 1906; a programmatic platform for revolutionary syndicalism.

**Amsterdam International.** See International Federation of Trade Unions.

**Angell, Norman** [1872–1967] – English writer; winner of Nobel Peace Prize 1933.

**Anseele, Edward** [1856–1938] – a founder and leader of Belgian Workers' Party from 1885; aimed to break capitalist economic control through cooperatives; Belgian minister of public works 1918–21, of railways, post and telegraph 1925–7, and of state 1930.

**Appel, Jan** [Hempel] [1890–1985] – joined SPD 1908; active in radical left in Hamburg during War; member KPD 1919, supported its ultraleft wing; founding member of KAPD; Third World Congress delegate; in prison 1923–5; lived in Holland from 1926 as member of Internationalist Communist Group; from 1948 a member of Spartacusbund.

**Appleton, William A.** [1859–1940] – secretary of British General Federation of Trade Unions 1907–38; elected president of Amsterdam International July–August 1920; resigned November 1920 because of opposition of British Trades Union Congress.

**Aqazadeh, Kamran** [1891–193?] – born in Ardebil province of Iran; joined Bolsheviks 1912; a founding leader of Adalat [Iran Justice] Party; elected secretary of CP Central Committee June

1920; head of Iranian CP delegation to Third World Congress.

**Argentina Regional Workers' Federation [FORA]** – main union federation split into anarchist and syndicalist wings; anarchist wing initially sympathetic to Comintern and applied for RILU membership, but broke with it by 1922; syndicalist wing included a pro-communist current in which members of CP participated.

**Armand, Inessa** [1874–1920] – joined RSDLP 1904; Bolshevik; in emigration from 1909; delegate to Zimmerwald Conference 1915; returned to Russia 1917; head of Bolshevik Women's Department [Zhenotdel] from 1918; organised international Communist women's conference 1920; died of cholera.

**Arnold, Emil** [1897–1974] – joined Swiss SP Youth 1912; its secretary 1917–21; founding member of CP 1921; Third World Congress delegate; editor-in-chief of Basel *Vorwärts* 1926–39 and from 1947; broke with CP 1956 on eve of Hungarian Revolution.

**Australian Labor Party** – founded 1891 by trade unionists; won control of Parliament and formed first Labor ministry 1904; member of Second International; chauvinist position during War.

**Australian Socialist Party** – formed 1910; declared support for Comintern December 1919; participated in founding CP of Australia [CPA] October 1920, but split off in December over opposition to stance on Labor Party; sent representatives to Third World Congress; following Comintern recognition of CPA in August 1922 most ASP members joined CPA.

***Avanti!*** [Forward] – central daily organ of Italian SP; began publication 1896.

**Azimonti, Carlo** [1888–1958] – factory worker in youth; socialist from 1904; trade-union staffer from 1911; member CGL National Council 1912; supported its reformist wing; mayor of Busto Arsizio 1919–21; CGL delegate to RILU founding congress 1921; forced out of trade-union activity under Fascist rule.

**Bacci, Giovanni** [1857–1928] – joined Italian SP 1903; became editor of *Avanti* 1912; elected to national party leadership 1914; supported Maximalist faction at 1921 Livorno Congress; took part in SP's parliamentary resistance to Fascism 1924–6.

**Badulescu, Alexandru** [Ghitza Moscu] [1895–1938] – leader of commercial employees' union; joined Romanian SP before War; Romanian CP delegate to Third World Congress, becoming its representative on ECCI; given high position in Moldavia Autonomous Soviet Republic while living in USSR; arrested and executed during Stalin purges.

**Bakunin, Mikhail** [1814–76] – Russian anarchist; leader of split with Marxist forces in First International.

**Baldesi, Gino** [1879–1934] – self-educated worker; SP journalist; assistant secretary of Italian union federation (CGL) 1918; a leader of reformist wing of Italian SP and trade unions 1920–1; left SP with reformist forces October 1921; vainly sought accommodation between CGL unions and Fascists; withdrew from political activity 1927.

**Baldwin**. See Tywerousky, Oscar.

**Balfour, Arthur James** [1848–1930] – Conservative Party prime minister of United Kingdom 1902–5; foreign secretary 1916–19.

**Balkan Communist Federation** – coordinating body for Communist parties of Balkans; formed 1915 as Balkan Revolutionary Social-Democratic Federation, an alliance of Socialist parties opposed to imperialist war; renamed Balkan Communist Federation 1920.

**Ballister**. See Minor, Robert.

**Ballod, Karl** [Kärlis Balodis] [1864–1931] – Latvian economist and statistician; economics professor in Berlin from 1905 and in Riga from 1919.

**Baratono, Adelchi** [1875–1947] – founding member of Italian SP 1892; member of Intransigent wing of PSI that polemicised with reformists; co-opted to national leadership 1919; supported Maximalist faction at Livorno; elected deputy to parliament 1921; joined reformist PSU 1923; rejoined PSI 1925.

**Barbusse, Henri** [1873–1935] – French novelist; wrote about experiences in French army during War; joined CP 1923.

**Barth, Emil** [1879–1941] – joined SPD 1908, USPD 1917; chair of Revolutionary Shop Stewards in Berlin; February–November 1918; member of SPD-USPD government November–December 1918; remained in rump USPD after Halle Congress 1920; chairman of factory councils 1921; rejoined SPD in 1922 fusion.

**Bauer, Gustav** [1870–1944] – deputy chairman of General Commission of ADGB union federation 1908–18; supporter of SPD right wing; German chancellor 1919–20; left SPD in disgrace for corruption scandal 1925.

**Bauer, Otto** [1881–1938] – leader and theoretician of Austrian Social Democracy; secretary of its parliamentary fraction 1907–14; prisoner of war in Russia 1914–17; Austrian minister of foreign affairs 1918–19; opponent of October Revolution and Comintern; leader of Two-and-a-Half International 1921–3; member of Bureau and Executive of Socialist International from 1923; forced into exile 1934.

**Bebel, August** [1840–1913] – a founder of German socialist movement 1869; collaborator of Marx and Engels; SPD co-chairman from 1892 until his death; opposed revisionism in SPD and Second International but came to adopt centrist position.

**Bedacht, Max** [Marshall] [1883–1972] – born in Germany; barber, journalist; joined Swiss SP 1905; moved to US and joined SP 1908; supported its left wing during War; joined CP 1919; a leader of 'Liquidator' wing of CP that favoured functioning openly; Third World Congress delegate; expelled for 'leftism' 1948; later reinstated.

**Belgian Workers' Party** – formed 1885 when SP of Belgium merged with trade unions and cooperatives; chauvinist position during War; 700,000 members 1921, including affiliated unionists and cooperativists.

**Bell, Thomas** [1882–1944] – Scottish foundry worker; joined ILP 1900; a founder and leader of Socialist Labour Party from 1903; leading figure in wartime shop stewards' movement; a founder of British CP 1920 and head of its propaganda department to 1925; Third World Congress delegate; remained leading member of CP until his death.

**Belloni, Ambrogio** [1864–1950] – lawyer; joined Italian SP 1897; elected to national leadership 1907; founding member of Communist Faction 1919 and of CP 1921; Third World Congress delegate; sentenced to five years imprisonment by Fascist regime 1926.

**Bentivoglio, Giorgio** – member of Maximalist wing of Italian SP; maker of its motion at 1921 Livorno Congress defining PSI relations to Comintern.

**Berce, Augusts** [1890–1921] – joined Latvian SDP 1905; elected to CC of Latvian CP 1919; soviet Latvia people's commissar for social welfare; returned to Riga 1920 to work in Communist underground; arrested 1921 and executed.

**Bergmann.** See Meyer, Fritz.

**Berkman, Alexander** [1870–1936] – born in Russian Empire; emigrated to US about 1888; anarchist; imprisoned fourteen years for attempted assassination of notorious capitalist; partner of Emma Goldman; jailed for opposition to War and subsequently deported to Russia; first supported, then opposed Bolshevik rule; emigrated 1921; continued anarchist activity in Western Europe.

**Bernstein, Eduard** [1850–1932] – German socialist; collaborator of Engels; theorist of revisionist current in SPD from 1898; member of USPD during War; opponent of Comintern; rejoined SPD 1919; Reichstag deputy 1902–7, 1912–18, 1920–8.

**Bianchi, Giuseppe** [1888–1921] – born in Italy; printer; became socialist during extended stay in Germany; returned to Italy 1914; edited PSI newspapers; administrator in CGL from end of War; CGL delegate to Moscow 1920; elected to CGL leadership 1921; CGL delegate to RILU founding congress 1921.

**Bidegaray, Marcel** [1875–1944] – general secretary of French railway union from 1909 and member of CGT confederal executive; member of French SP; went with dissidents in 1921 SP split; supported CGT majority; part of reformist split from SP 1933; died in internment during World War II.

**Bissolati, Leonida** [1857–1920] – founding member of Italian SP 1892; editor of *Avanti* 1896–1903, 1908–10; saw British Labour Party as model; expelled from SP 1912 for supporting Italy's war in Libya; founded Reformist Socialist Party, which supported Italy's entry into War; government minister 1916–18.

**Blum, Léon** [1872–1950] – joined French SP 1904; led dissident party after its break with Communists in December 1920; premier of Popular Front government 1936–7 and 1938; jailed by Vichy regime 1940–5.

**Bolsheviks** – formed 1903 following split with Mensheviks in RSDLP; led October Revolution 1917; became Communist Party of Russia (Bolsheviks) March 1918.

**Bombacci, Nicola** [1879–1945] – teacher; union activist from about 1900; elected to CGL national council 1911; member of Italian SP; jailed for stand against War October–November 1918; CP leader after Livorno split 1921; delegate to Second and Fourth World Congresses; expelled from CP for Fascist sympathies 1927; supported Mussolini from 1930s; became Mussolini advisor toward close of World War II; was captured and executed with him by partisans.

**Bonomi, Ivanoe** [1873–1951] – joined Italian SP 1893; expelled 1912 for support of Libya war; minister of war 1920; prime minister July 1921–February 1922; retired from politics after Mussolini's triumph; helped forge bourgeois anti-Fascist coalition 1942; prime minister 1944–5.

**Bordiga, Amadeo** [1889–1970] – joined Italian SP 1910; led Communist-Abstentionist faction after War; central leader of CP from its formation in 1921 to 1926; opposed Comintern's united front policy; member ECCI 1922–8; jailed 1926–30; defended Trotsky 1928; expelled 1930; led small anti-Stalinist Communist current until death.

**Borodin, Mikhail** [1884–1951] – joined RSDLP 1903, became Bolshevik; emigrated to US 1906; member of American SP during War; returned to Russia July 1918, and worked in Commissariat of Foreign Affairs; became Comintern emissary 1919, traveling to US, Mexico, Spain, Germany, and Britain; adviser to Sun Yat-sen and Chiang Kai-shek 1923–7; arrested 1949; died in Siberian labour camp.

**Borojević, Svetozar** [1856–1920] – Austro-Hungarian field marshal during War.

**Böttcher, Paul** [1891–1975] – joined SPD 1908; leader of USPD after 1917; joined CP in 1920 fusion; added to Zentrale to represent radical Left February 1921; lead editor of CP Berlin daily 1921; alternate member ECCI 1922; minister in Saxony SPD-CP coalition government 1923; removed from leadership posts as 'rightist' 1924; expelled with Brandler current 1929; fled to Switzerland 1933; worked with pro-Soviet and anti-Nazi resistance during World War II; returned to East Germany 1945; taken to USSR 1946 and jailed for nine years; subsequently rejoined German CP.

**Bourderon, Albert** [1858–1930] – French syndicalist and SP member; secretary of Coopers' Federation 1903–29 and prominent figure in CGT; pacifist position during War, opposing CGT majority's support for Sacred Union with capitalists; attended Zimmerwald Conference 1915; after War he supported CGT majority and its expulsion of left-wing minority.

**Brand, Henryk** [1890–1937] – joined Swiss SDP as Polish student in Zurich during War; returned to Warsaw 1919 and joined Polish CP; elected to its CC 1920; Third World Congress delegate; ECCI member 1923–7; denounced by Comintern as 'right-winger' 1927; worked for Gosplan in Moscow 1931–7; arrested 1937 and executed.

**Brandler, Heinrich** [1881–1967] – joined SPD 1902; central figure in Chemnitz labour movement from 1914; early member of Spartacus League; co-founder of German CP; convicted and imprisoned for role during March Action; escaped and went to Moscow November 1921; worked for RILU; central leader of CP 1921–3; made scapegoat for defeat of German workers in

1923; expelled as 'rightist' 1929; led Communist Party (Opposition) [KPO] 1929–33; in exile 1933–49; active in Arbeiterpolitik [Workers' Politics], successor group of KPO, from 1949.

**Branting, Karl Hjalmar** [1860–1925] – founding member of Swedish SDP 1889; party leader 1907; headed party's reformist majority; government minister 1917; opponent of October Revolution; chairman of 1919 congress of Socialist International; three times prime minister 1920–5.

**Brass, Otto** [1875–1950] – joined SPD 1895; active in trade-union and cooperative movements; member USPD CC 1917–20; part of USPD-KPD fusion December 1920 and elected to CC; in Moscow March 1921 for discussions with Lenin and Comintern leaders; in April signed declaration of solidarity with Paul Levi; expelled from KPD January 1922; joined KAG and its fusions with USPD and SPD; arrested by Nazis 1938 and sentenced to twelve years imprisonment; became member of SED in East Germany 1945.

**Braunthal, Bertha** [1881–1967] – member of USPD secretariat 1919–20, and secretary for its propaganda work among women; joined VKPD in 1920 fusion, and member of its Women's Secretariat; supported VKPD majority in March Action dispute; delegate to Third World Congress; moved to London 1933; member of British CP until her death.

**Breitscheid, Rudolf** [1874–1944] – initially a Liberal politician, joined German SPD 1912; joined USPD 1917; Prussian minister of the interior 1918–19; after reunification with SPD in 1922 became party's foreign policy spokesperson; emigrated 1933; captured by Vichy in southern France and delivered to Gestapo; died in Buchenwald concentration camp.

**Briand, Aristide** [1862–1932] – French politician; member of SP until he accepted ministerial post 1906; premier of France eleven times, including 1921–2.

**British Labour Party** – formed 1906 by trade-union federation and Independent Labour Party; member of Second International; voted to oppose affiliation of CP 1920; 4.5 million members in 1921.

**Brouckère, Louis de** [1870–1951] – joined Belgian Workers' Party early 1890s; criticised leadership's reformist stance before 1914; adopted social-chauvinist stance during War and joined government; member government council 1919–21; leader of party until his death.

**Bukharin, Nikolai** [1888–1938] – joined Russian Bolsheviks 1906; in exile 1911–17; member Bolshevik CC 1917–30; one of central Bolshevik leaders within Comintern from 1919; delegate to first six Comintern congresses; chairman of Comintern 1926–9; opposed Stalinist forced collectivisation and led Right Opposition in Soviet CP 1928; deprived of leadership posts 1929; executed after Stalin frame-up trial 1938.

**Bund** – General Union of Jewish Workers in Lithuania, Poland, and Russia; founded in tsarist Russia 1897; affiliated to RSDLP 1898–1903 and from 1906, siding with Mensheviks; opposed October Revolution; left-wing split 1919 and became Communist Bund, with most joining Russian CP 1920; social-democratic wing functioned as separate organisation outside Soviet Union.

**Buozzi, Bruno** [1881–1944] – joined Italian SP 1905; general secretary of metalworkers union from 1909; member of CGL directing council 1912 and executive commission 1918–21; joined reformist PSU 1922; secretary of CGL from 1925; member of anti-Fascist resistance during World War II; murdered by Nazi SS.

**Burian, Edmund** [1878–1935] – joined Czechoslovak SDP 1897; editor of Social-Democratic journals; Third World Congress delegate; member of CP executive committee 1921–9; expelled from CP 1929 for 'right-wing opportunism' and rejoined SDP.

**Burtsev, Vladimir Lyovich** [1862–1942] – active in revolutionary student movement from early 1880s; arrested and exiled to Siberia 1885; escaped 1888 and went into exile; close to SRs during

1905 revolution; left Soviet Russia 1918 and became leader of White counter-revolutionaries in exile.

**Cabrini, Angiolo** [1869–1937] – joined Italian socialist movement about 1886; active in union confederation and cooperative movement; expelled from SP 1912 for supporting Italy's war against Libya; a founder of Reformist Socialist Party [PSRI] and supporter of Italy's entry into War; International Labour Office correspondent in Rome from 1919 until his death; collaborated with Fascist regime on labour issues.

**Cachin, Marcel** [1869–1958] – joined Guesde's French Workers' Party 1892; member French SP 1905; social patriot during War; with Frossard, leader of Centre current in SP and, from 1920, in CP; director of *L'Humanité* 1918–58; prominent CP leader until his death.

**Cadets** [Constitutional Democratic Party, Russia] – bourgeois liberal party in tsarist Russia founded 1905; advocated constitutional monarchy; opposed October Revolution and supported Whites in civil war.

**Caldara, Emilio** [1867–1942] – a founder of Italian SP 1892; first socialist mayor of Milan 1914–20; favoured Italy's intervention in War; joined reformist PSU 1922; attempted a reconciliation with Mussolini 1934.

***The Call*** – newspaper published in London by members of British Socialist Party 1916–20; merged with *Communist* August 1920.

**Calwer, Richard** [1868–1927] – German economist; joined SPD 1891; member of reformist wing of party; expelled 1909; worked in ADGB trade-union federation.

**CC** – Central Committee.

**Černý, Jan** [1874–1959] – premier of Czechoslovakia September 1920–September 1921, and in 1926.

***Červen*** [Red] – weekly Communist periodical published in Prague 1918–21.

**Ceton, Jan Cornelis** [1875–1943] – teacher; joined Dutch Social-Democratic Workers' Party [SDAP] late 1890s; secretary of Social-Democratic Teachers Association 1901–5, 1907–8; founding member of left-wing SDP 1909; became party secretary-treasurer and editor of *De Tribune* 1910; founding member of Dutch CP; Third World Congress delegate; expelled from CP 1926 with Rotterdam branch, which formed separate CP; two parties reunited in 1930, but Ceton withdrew from politics soon afterward.

**CGL.** See General Confederation of Labour, Italy.

**CGT.** See General Confederation of Labour, France.

**Chavenon, Léon** [b. 1872] – French journalist and economist; founded financial magazine *L'Information* 1899; longtime editor in chief.

**Chicherin, Georgy Vasilievich** [1872–1936] – joined RSDLP 1904; lived in exile 1905–17; Menshevik before 1914; internationalist during War; joined Bolsheviks on return to Russia 1918; Soviet foreign affairs commissar 1918–30.

**Chkheidze, Nikolai Semyonovich** [1864–1926] – joined Social-Democratic movement in Georgia 1892; spokesperson for Mensheviks in tsarist duma 1907–17; chairman of Petrograd Soviet after February Revolution; opponent of October Revolution; chairman of Menshevik government in Georgia until its Soviet ouster 1918–21; fled to France.

**Churchill, Winston** [1874–1965] – British Conservative Party politician; organiser of intervention against Soviet government 1919–20; colonial secretary 1921–2; prime minister 1940–5 and 1951–5.

**Ciccotti, Ettore** [1863–1939] – founding member of Italian SP 1892; history professor and translator of Marx and Engels into Italian; supporter of SP reformist wing; as deputy in parliament supported Italian entry in War; later broke with workers' movement, expressed sympathy with Fascism, then moved toward liberalism.

**Clausewitz, Karl von** [1780–1831] – Prussian general and military theorist; author of *On War*.

**Clemenceau, Georges** [1841–1929] – French politician; premier 1906–9 and 1917–20; helped shape Versailles Treaty.

**CNT**. See National Confederation of Labour, Spain.

**Colliard, Lucie** [1877–1961] – French schoolteacher and militant unionist; joined SP 1912; pacifist and internationalist during War; supported Comintern affiliation at Tours Congress 1920; became member of CP directing committee January 1921; Third World Congress delegate; elected to international secretariat of Communist Women's Movement 1921; collaborator of Trotskyist *Contre le courant* 1927–9; expelled from CP 1929; rejoined SP 1936.

*The Communist* – weekly newspaper of British CP founded July 1920 and published until 1923; 15,000 circulation in 1921.

*Communist International / Kommunistische International* – journal published by ECCI in English, French, German, and Russian; founded 1 May 1919.

**Communist Party–Argentina** – formed by left-wing socialists as Internationalist Socialist Party in January 1918; voted to affiliate to Comintern April 1919; changed name to CP December 1920.

**Communist Party–Armenia** – originated in Russian Social-Democratic movement; CP founded 1920; headed Armenian soviet republic from December 1920; 3,000 members 1920.

**Communist Party–Australia** – formed October 1920 with 1,000 members; former Australian SP members split off over attitude toward Labor Party December 1920; both ASP and CPA were represented at Third World Congress; following Comintern recognition of CPA in August 1922, most ASP members joined CPA.

**Communist Party–Austria** – founded November 1918; fused with left-wing SDP split-off (Socialist Labour Party) January 1921; 14,000 members 1921.

**Communist Party–Azerbaijan** – originated in Bolshevik wing of RSDLP; CP founded February 1920 with 4,000 members; led soviet regime in Baku November 1917 to July 1918; went underground when soviet regime fell; soviet power re-established April 1920.

**Communist Party–Belgium** – original nucleus formed October–November 1920; joined by left-wing split off from Belgian Workers' Party at September 1921 unification congress; 1,000 members late 1921.

**Communist Party–Britain** – formed from unity conventions in July 1920 (merging British Socialist Party, 22 Communist Unity Groups, South Wales Socialist Society, and other organisations), and January 1921 (Workers' Socialist Federation, Communist Labour Party, ILP members, and others); claimed 1921 membership of 10,000.

**Communist Party–Bukhara** – founded November 1918; leading party in Bukhara soviet republic established October 1920; merged with Russian CP February 1922; led in formation of Tadzhik soviet republic 1924.

**Communist Party–Bulgaria** – name adopted by Tesniaki [See Tesniaki] May 1919; 40,000 members in April 1921, with three-quarters in countryside.

**Communist Party–Canada** [Communist group] – communist groups in Toronto and other cities formed 1919; initially functioned as branches of US CP; CP of Canada founded May 1921; 4,800 members in 1922.

**Communist Party–China** – founded 1 July 1921 at congress bringing together communist groups in Shanghai and other cities; 195 members in 1922.

**Communist Party–Cuba** [Communist group] – Socialist Group of Havana formed 1905; split over Russian Revolution in 1917; left wing went on to form Communist Group of Havana; communist groups formed in other cities; CP founded 1925.

**Communist Party–Czechoslovakia** – originated as Marxist Left of SDP, which won party leadership September 1920; founded CP May 1921; claimed 350,000 members 1921; CP in German Czechoslovakia and other national groups joined united party October–November 1921.

**Communist Party–Czechoslovakia** [German Section] – formed March 1921 by left wing of SDP of German Czechoslovakia at congress held in Reichenberg;

60,000 members; fused with CP of Czechoslovakia October–November 1921.

**Communist Party–Denmark** – formed November 1919 as Socialist Labour Party; changed name to CP November 1920; membership of 2,500 in mid-1921.

**Communist Party–East Galicia** [Communist Party of Galicia and Bukovina] – originated out of International Revolutionary Social Democracy; CP formed February 1919; headed Galician soviet republic July–August 1920; affiliated to Ukrainian and then Polish CPs late 1920; 1,500 members 1923; became CP of West Ukraine 1923.

**Communist Party–East Indies** [Communist Party of the Indies] – born from Indian Social-Democratic Union, formed 1914; became CP May 1920; 200 members 1921; 13,000 members December 1922.

**Communist Party–Estonia** – formed November 1920; originated as Estonian section of Bolshevik Party, which led Estonian soviet government November 1917–February 1918 and November 1918–January 1919; forced underground after its overthrow; 700 members November 1920, 700 members November 1920; 2,800 members 1922.

**Communist Party–Finland** – originated in left wing of Finnish SDP; led revolutionary forces in civil war January–May 1918; CP founded August 1918; illegal in Finland 1918–44; 25,000 members 1922; Communists in country functioned within legal Socialist Workers' Party founded May 1920.

**Communist Party–France** [French Communist Party] – formed by French SP majority at Tours Congress December 1920; 120,000 members in March 1921.

**Communist Party–Georgia** – originated in Russian Social-Democratic movement 1890s; founded as component of Russian CP May 1920; 9,000 members early 1921; became leading party following formation of soviet republic February 1921.

**Communist Party–Germany** [KPD, VKPD] – founded December 1918 by Spartacus League and other Communists; fused with USPD majority December 1920 and became briefly known as United CP [VKPD] claiming 350,000 members; 157,000 dues-paying members summer 1921.

**Communist Party–Greece** – founded November 1918 as Socialist Workers' Party of Greece; voted to affiliate to Comintern 1920, leading to split of minority; 1,300 members in 1920; renamed CP 1924.

**Communist Party–Hungary** – founded November 1918 by left social democrats and former war prisoners in Soviet Russia; fused with SDP to form Socialist Party March 1919 and lead Hungarian soviet republic; disintegrated after August 1919 downfall of government; functioned in exile until 1925.

**Communist Party–Iceland** – pro-Communist faction inside SDP during 1921; 450 members 1922; CP organised 1930.

**Communist Party–India** – founded in exile October 1920 with groups in several countries; groups were functioning in India by 1922; CP established inside India 1925.

**Communist Party–Iran** – formed June 1920 by Enzeli Congress of Adalat [Justice] Party; a leading party in soviet Republic of Gilan 1920–1; 4,500 members in 1921.

**Communist Party–Ireland** [Communist group] – formed 1920 as underground organisation during Irish war of independence; CP founded late October 1921 by SP of Ireland, with claimed membership of 120; dissolved 1924; refounded 1933.

**Communist Party–Italy** [PCI] – formed January 1921 following split from Italian SP at Livorno Congress; 58,000 members at time of split; 43,000 by end of 1921.

**Communist Party–Japan** – originated among Japanese cadres in US CP in early 1920 who returned to Japan; inspired founding of Socialist League in Tokyo December 1920 with 1,400 members; CP founded July 1922.

**Communist Party–Khiva/Khorezm** – formed April 1920; led Khorezm People's Soviet Republic 1920–4; affiliated to CP of Russia in early 1922; dissolved 1924 when boundaries in Soviet Central Asia were redrawn.

**Communist Party–Korea** – organised among Korean exiles in Siberia 1918–19; divided into rival groups in Irkutsk and Shanghai; first Communist groups established inside Korea 1921; first Korean CP organised in Seoul 1925.

**Communist Party–Latvia** – originated in Latvian Social-Democratic Workers' Party, founded 1904; affiliated to RSDLP; changed name to CP March 1919; led Latvian soviet republic in 1918–20 civil war; forced underground after its defeat; 1,500 members 1922.

**Communist Party–Lithuania** – established October 1918 as part of Russian CP; led Lithuanian soviet republic December 1918–April 1919; following its defeat party functioned underground until 1940.

**Communist Party–Luxembourg** – formed January 1921 by left-wing split from Luxembourg SDP; 500 members in 1921.

**Communist Party–Mexico** [Mexican Communist Party] – Mexican SP changed name to CP November 1919 and voted to join Comintern; 1,500 members late 1922.

**Communist Party–Netherlands** – originated 1909 as SDP, formed by expelled members of Dutch Social-Democratic Workers' Party [SDAP]; changed name to CP November 1918; joined Comintern April 1919; 2,000 members late 1921.

**Communist Party–Palestine** – emerged out of Poale Zion left, with one wing forming Socialist Workers' Party [MPS] 1919; 300 members in 1920; after party outlawed in 1921, its members formed clandestine CP; divided into pro- and anti-Zionist wings 1922; merged into Palestinian CP 1923.

**Communist Party–Poland** [Communist Workers' Party] – formed December 1918 through fusion of SDKPiL and Polish Socialist Party–Left; 6,000 members July 1919; functioned in illegality.

**Communist Party–Portugal** [Communist group] – originated out of anarcho-syndicalist movement; decided to join Comintern October 1920; CP founded March 1921 with 1,000 members.

**Communist Party–Romania** – formed May 1921 when majority of Romanian SP voted to affiliate to Comintern; 2,000 members 1921; minority split off and formed separate Social-Democratic party.

**Communist Party–Russia** [Communist Party of Russia (Bolsheviks)] – name adopted March 1918 by Bolshevik Party, which originated 1903 as faction in RSDLP; led October Revolution; ruling party in Soviet republic from 1917; 730,000 members in 1921.

**Communist Party–South Africa** – formed July 1921 by International Socialist League; 200 members in 1922.

**Communist Party–Spain** [Communist Workers' Party, PCO] – formed April 1921 from split in Spanish SP [PSOE]; 4,000–5,000 members in 1921; fused with Communist Party of Spain [PCE] November 1921 to form united CP.

**Communist Party–Spain** [PCE] – formed April 1920 out of socialist youth federation; published *El Comunista*; 1,000–2,000 members in 1921; fused with PCO November 1921 to form united CP.

**Communist Party–Sweden** – name adopted at 1921 congress of Left Social-Democratic Party of Sweden, formed 1917 by expelled left wing from SDP; affiliated to Comintern June 1919; 14,000 members in 1921; majority split from party 1929.

**Communist Party–Switzerland** – founded 5–6 March 1921, uniting members of SDP left who had split from party in December 1920 and Communist groups functioning since October 1918; about 6,000 members March 1921.

**Communist Party–Turkestan** – formed June 1918; became regional unit of Russian CP March 1920; 20,000 members in early 1921; dissolved 1924 as boundaries of USSR were redrawn.

**Communist Party–Turkey** – founded in Baku September 1920, grouping together working-class cadres, left-wing sectors of national movement, and former Turkish POWs won to communism in Soviet Russia; party banned and repressed by Turkish government, with its leadership killed in January 1921.

**Communist Party–Ukraine** [Communist Party (Bolshevik) of Ukraine] – established December 1917 as autonomous component of Russian CP, holding first congress July 1918; 75,000 members 1920.

**Communist Party–US** [United Communist Party] – Communist movement formed September 1919 as Communist Party of America and Communist Labor Party; CLP and minority of CPA of America fused May 1920 to create United CP; CPA majority fused with United CP May 1921; 10,000 dues-paying members July 1921.

**Communist Party–Yugoslavia** – name adopted June 1920 by Socialist Workers' Party of Yugoslavia, formed 1919 from several Balkan socialist parties; 80,000 members early 1921.

**Communist Women's Movement** – established by ECCI April 1920, headed by International Communist Women's Secretariat with Clara Zetkin as secretary; published *Die Kommunistische Fraueninternationale* 1921–5 and coordinated work of women's committees and bureaus in each CP; secretariat dissolved 1926.

**Communist Workers' Federation of Argentina.** See Argentina Regional Workers' Federation.

**Communist Workers' Party of Bulgaria** – ultraleft organisation formed January 1921, looking to German KAPD; sent delegates to Third World Congress, were not seated.

**Communist Workers' Party of Germany** [KAPD] – formed April 1920 by ultraleft current expelled from CP with over 40,000 members; official sympathising member of Comintern 1920–1; 8,000 members by early 1921.

**Communist Working Group** [KAG] – formed by Paul Levi and other expelled members of KPD; held founding conference November 1921; most adherents fused into USPD in early 1922.

**Communist Youth International** – grew out of Socialist Youth International, reconstituted under left-wing leadership 1915; worked with Zimmerwald Left during War; CYI formed November 1919 with seat in Berlin; affiliated to Comintern; moved to Moscow 1921; fifty member organisations and 800,000 members in 1921.

**Communist Youth–France** [Federation of Communist Youth] – formed 1920 out of split in Socialist Youth; known for anti-militarist work; 4,000 members in May 1923.

**Communist Youth–Italy** [Italian Communist Youth Federation] – formed January 1921 when majority of Socialist Youth went with CP after Livorno SP split; 40,000 members at founding.

**Communist Youth–Russia** [Communist Youth League, Komsomol] – founded October 1918; 482,000 members October 1920.

**Confederation of Labour** [Spain]. See National Confederation of Labour [CNT].

**Cosgrove, Pascal** [Crosby] – a leader of US SP left wing; elected member of CP of America Central Executive Committee 1920; organiser for shoe workers union in Massachusetts; delegate in 1921 to Third World Congress and RILU First Congress; sent to China on Comintern mission 1929; a vice-president of National Council for Protection of Foreign Born Workers in 1940s.

**CP** – Communist Party.

**Crispien, Artur** [1875–1946] – German socialist journalist; joined SPD 1894; member Spartacus current 1915; leader of USPD 1917–22; attended Second World Congress 1920 but opposed affiliation to Comintern and remained in rump USPD after split; returned to SPD in 1922 fusion; SPD co-chairman until 1933; in Swiss exile from 1933.

**Cristescu, Gheorghe** [1882–1973] – joined Romanian socialist movement 1898; leader of SDP (later SP) at its formation 1910; supported SP affiliation to Comintern 1921; CP general secretary 1922–4; elected to ECCI 1924; expelled 1926; in 1928 joined Socialist Workers' Party, which eventually merged with SP; imprisoned under Romanian Stalinist regime 1950–4.

*Critica sociale* [Social Criticism] – bimonthly journal of Italian SP right wing; published in Milan 1891–1926; edited by Turati.

**Crosby, John.** See Cosgrove, Pascal.

**Cunow, Heinrich** [1862–1936] – joined SPD early 1890s; became an editor of

*Die Neue Zeit* 1898; social chauvinist during War; replaced Kautsky as main editor of *Die Neue Zeit* 1917–23; opponent of October Revolution; professor at Berlin University 1919; persecuted by Nazis from 1933.

**CYI.** See Communist Youth International.

**D'Aragona, Ludovico** [1876–1961] – joined Italian SP 1892; a founder of metalworkers union; general secretary of CGL union federation 1918–25; SP parliamentary deputy 1919–24; headed trade-union delegation to Soviet Russia and was consultative delegate to Second World Congress 1920; opposed founding CP 1921 and remained in SP; joined reformist PSU 1922; government minister 1946–51.

**Dahlmann, Friedrich** [1785–1860] – German liberal historian; author of *The History of the English Revolution*.

***Daily Herald*** – daily newspaper of Labour Party published in London 1912–64.

**Danton, Georges Jacques** [1759–94] – a leader of French Revolution, promoting overthrow of monarchy and establishment of first French republic; executed following break with Jacobin leaders.

**Dashnak Party** [Dashnaktsutyun] – Armenian nationalist party founded 1890; fought oppression by both tsarist Russia and Ottoman Empire; affiliated to Second International; opposed October Revolution and headed Armenian anti-Soviet government 1918–20.

**Daszyński, Ignacy** [1866–1936] – a founding leader of Polish Socialist Party in Galicia 1892; right-wing Social Democrat; briefly served as head of first Polish government 1918; joined Government of National Defence during war with Soviet Russia 1920.

**Däumig, Ernst** [1866–1922] – joined German SPD 1898; an editor of *Vorwärts* 1911–16; founding member USPD 1917; worked with Revolutionary Shop Stewards in Berlin 1918; as USPD co-chairman supported affiliation to Comintern; co-chairman of united CP 1920–1; left CP September 1921 and joined Levi's KAG, participating in its fusions with USPD and then SPD.

**De Leon, Daniel** [1852–1914] – central leader of US Socialist Labor Party; participated in founding of IWW 1905; led split from it 1908.

**Delagrange, Marcel Émile** [1883–1964] – member of French SP and Committee for the Third International; secretary of railway union and participant in 1920 strikes; in CP after Tours Congress; Third World Congress delegate; joined Faisceau nationalist organisation 1925, calling for reconciliation of nationalism and socialism; expelled from CP 1926.

**Denikin, Anton Ivanovich** [1872–1947] – Russian tsarist general; a leader of White Army during civil war; emigrated 1920.

**Dimitratos, Nikolaos** – secretary 1919–22 of Greek Socialist Workers' Party, which later became CP; Third World Congress delegate; ousted and expelled as opportunist 1922.

**Dimitrov, Georgi** [1882–1949] – joined Bulgarian SDP 1902; CC member from 1909 of left-wing Tesniaki faction, which became CP; Third World Congress delegate; secretary of Balkan Communist Federation 1926–7; directed West European Bureau of Comintern 1929–33; arrested in Germany March 1933 and charged with responsibility for Reichstag fire; acquitted and went to Russia; general secretary of Comintern 1935–43; prime minister of Bulgaria 1946–9.

**Dissidents** – A reference to the French Socialist Party minority that opposed the majority's decision in 1920 to join the Communist International and change the party's name to Communist Party. The minority retained the old party's name.

**Dissmann, Robert** [1878–1926] – joined SPD 1897; on staff of German metalworkers' union from 1900; critical of SPD vote for war credits 1914; joined USPD 1917; chair of metalworkers union 1919; remained in rump USPD after 1920 split; rejoined SPD 1922.

**Dittmann, Wilhelm** [1874–1954] – joined SPD 1894; Reichstag deputy 1912–33; opposed war credits 1915; founding member USPD 1917 and of its Executive Committee; jailed for anti-war activity 1918; member of SPD-USPD provisional government established by November 1918 revolution; attended Second World Congress; opposed affiliation to Third International 1920 and remained in rump USPD as co-chairman, fusing with SPD 1922; in Swiss emigration 1933–51.

**Düwell, Bernhard** [b. 1891] – joined SPD youth movement around 1910; conscripted into army 1914–18; joined USPD 1917; commissar of councils in Merseburg during 1918–19 revolutionary upsurge; part of KPD-USPD fusion 1920; supported Levi and was expelled from CP August 1921; joined KAG and its fusions with USPD and SPD.

**Dugoni, Enrico** [1874–1945] – joined Italian SP mid-1890s; a leader of Italian SP and CGL union federation; delegate to Kienthal Conference 1916; in SP right wing after War; took part in labour/SP delegation to Soviet Russia 1920; opposed formation of CP in 1921 split; victim of several Fascist attacks; left SP in split that founded reformist PSU; arrested for anti-Fascist activities 1930 and 1932.

**Dumoulin, Georges** [1877–1963] – became CGT national treasurer 1910; supported Zimmerwald movement during War, but joined CGT right-wing majority afterward; an official for International Labour Office 1924–32; collaborator of Vichy regime during World War II.

**Earsman, William** [1884–1965] – born in Scotland; lathe operator; moved to Australia 1910; member SP 1911; leader of metalworkers' union 1915; influenced by IWW; co-founder of CP 1920; Third World Congress delegate; refused readmission to Australia 1923; moved to England; left CP about 1927; joined British Labour Party 1934.

**Eberlein, Hugo** [1887–1941] – joined SPD 1906; internationalist and co-founder of Spartacus League during War; member German CP CC 1918; initially opposed, then abstained on Comintern formation at its founding congress 1919; a leader of adventurist wing of CP majority that led March Action 1921; supported Centre current of 'conciliators' 1924–8; stripped of leadership posts for opposing ultraleft turn 1928; fled Germany 1933; arrested in USSR during Stalin purges 1937; executed.

**Ebert, Friedrich** [1871–1925] – joined SPD 1889; member of party executive committee 1905–19; succeeded Bebel as party co-chairman 1913; supported German war effort; as a leader of provisional government coming out of 1918 revolution, he joined with monarchists to defeat workers uprisings 1919–20; German president 1919–25.

**ECCI** – Executive Committee of the Communist International.

**Einstein, Albert** [1879–1955] – German-born physicist; originator of theory of relativity.

**Emergency Technical Assistance** [Technische Nothilfe] – organisation of strikebreakers formed by German government decree of 30 September 1919, signed by Noske, with stated purpose of maintaining essential services.

**Engels, Frederick** [1820–95] – lifelong collaborator of Karl Marx; co-author of *Communist Manifesto* 1848; a leader of revolutionary democratic forces in 1848 German revolution; lived in England 1842–4 and from 1849; political and theoretical leader of revolutionary workers movement after death of Marx.

**Entente** [Triple Entente] – military alliance of Britain, France, and tsarist Russia during War; established 1907; term sometimes applied to all Allied powers in War.

**Enver Pasha** [1881–1922] – Turkish general; a leader of 'Young Turk' revolution of 1908, government leader 1913–18; went to Moscow and declared solidarity with Soviet government 1920, founding Union of Islamic Revolutionary Societies; attended Baku Congress 1920; joined anti-Soviet revolt in Central Asia 1921; killed in action against Red Army.

**Escherich, Georg** [1870–1941] – German right-wing politician; founder of Orgesch proto-fascist military organisation 1920; after its banning in 1921, his private military ventures continued until Nazis took power 1933.

**Estonian Independent Socialist Workers' Party** – organised March 1920 by members of SDP and SRs; entered into negotiations with Comintern; left-wing majority supported Comintern and split 1922 to form Estonian Working People's Party; right wing fused with SDP 1925.

**Faisal I** [Faisal ibn Husayn] [1885–1933] – born in Saudi Arabia; led Arab forces allied with Britain in War; declared king of Greater Syria after Arab military force occupied Damascus 1918; forced into exile by French invasion 1920; crowned king of Iraq in August 1921 under British auspices.

**Faure, Paul** [1878–1960] – joined French socialist movement 1901; supporter of pacifist wing during War; opposed 1920 decision to join Comintern and became general secretary of dissident SP; expelled 1944 for links to Vichy regime.

**Fimmen, Eduard** ['Edo'] [1881–1942] – leader of Dutch trade-union federation from 1907; co-secretary of Amsterdam International 1919–23.

**Flueras, Ioan** [1882–1953] – joined Hungarian SDP 1901 and became a leader of its Romanian section; member of provisional government of Transylvania 1918–20; member of Romanian socialist delegation in Moscow 1921 for discussions on Comintern affiliation, but was part of party minority that did not affiliate and became Romanian SDP 1921; president of General Confederation of Labour 1926–38; supported royalist dictatorship 1938–40; arrested by Stalinist regime 1948; died in prison.

**Franken, Paul** [1894–1944] – joined SPD 1911, USPD 1917; participant in November 1918 revolution in Solingen; part of fusion with KPD 1920; represented KPD opposition at Third World Congress; left KPD 1922; joined KAG and its fusions with USPD and SPD; emigrated 1934; settled in Soviet Union; arrested 1937; died in Siberia.

**Free Association of Employees** [Allgemeiner freier Angestelltenbund] – established 1920 through amalgamation of socialist-oriented trade unions of technical and administrative employees; dissolved 1933 by Nazi regime.

**Free Workers Union of Germany** [Freie Arbeiter-Union Deutschland, FAUD] – anarcho-syndicalist trade union; founded 1919; 150,000 members at its peak; rejected dictatorship of proletariat and degenerated into sect; disbanded by Nazis 1933.

*Freiheit* [Freedom] – daily organ of USPD published in Berlin; began publication 15 November 1918; published until September 1922.

**Frey, Josef** [1882–1957] – joined Austrian socialist students' association at University of Vienna; staff member of SDP daily newspaper; president of council of soldiers at Vienna garrison during November 1918 revolution; leader of SDP left wing; expelled in 1920; joined Austrian CP January 1921; Third World Congress delegate; supported Trotsky-Zinoviev opposition 1926; expelled from CP 1927; in Trotskyist movement until 1932; emigrated to Switzerland 1938.

**Fries, Philipp** [1882–1950] – joined SPD 1900; worked with Karl Liebknecht during War; part of split that formed USPD 1917; joined CP as part of 1920 fusion; member of Levi's KAG 1921, participating in its fusions with USPD and then SPD; imprisoned by Nazis 1933 and 1944; helped re-establish SPD in Cologne after War.

**Friesland**. See Reuter, Ernst.

**Friis, Jacob** [1883–1956] – member of Norwegian Labour Party and socialist journalist from 1909; internationalist and pacifist during War; joined Comintern 1919 together with party; delegate to Comintern Second and Third World Congresses; member ECCI 1920–1; supported Norwegian LP withdrawal from Comintern 1923; joined CP 1928 and remained a member until 1933; rejoined LP and was active in its left wing.

**Frölich, Paul** [1884–1953] – joined SPD 1902; worked as journalist for party papers in Leipzig, Hamburg, and Bremen; a supporter of Zimmerwald Left during War; led International Communists of Germany [IKD], which became part of CP at 1918 founding congress; participant in Bavarian soviet republic 1919; member of CC 1919–23; Third World Congress delegate; expelled from CP 1928, joining Communist Party Opposition [KPO] and later Socialist Workers' Party [SAP].

**Frossard, Louis-Oscar** [1889–1946] – joined French SP 1905; pacifist during War; CP general secretary and leader of its Centre current 1920–2; quit CP January 1923; led 'Socialist-Communist' formation, then member SP 1927–35; several times minister; voted for dictatorial powers to Pétain 1940.

**Gareis, Karl** [1889–1921] – joined USPD 1917, becoming its leader in Bavarian state parliament; assassinated by right-wingers June 1921.

**Gelsenkirchen Free Workers' Union** – members of anarcho-syndicalist FAUD in Gelsenkirchen who left it November 1920 with 110,000 members; strongest in Rhineland-Westphalia coal district; CP members played leading role; joined RILU; in November 1921 fused with two other unions to form Manual and Intellectual Workers syndicalist union of Germany; dissolved into mainstream unions 1925.

**General Confederation of Greek Workers** [GSEE] – trade-union federation founded 1918; voted to affiliate to RILU 1920; 60,000 members October 1920; under Communist leadership 1920–6.

**General Confederation of Workers** [CGL, Italy] – formed 1906; allied with Socialist Party until late 1922; 2 million members September 1920, dropping to 1.1 million in 1921; expressed sympathy with RILU but remained affiliated to Amsterdam International; suppressed under Fascism.

**General Confederation of Labour** [CGT, France] – founded 1895; initially syndicalist in orientation; leadership followed reformist course from 1914; left wing driven out in 1921; 600,000 members in spring 1921; split became definitive December 1921 with expelled left forming CGTU [Unitary CGT]; CGT membership declined to 250,000 following split.

**General German Trade Union Federation** [ADGB] – founded 1919 to replace earlier Social-Democratic union federation; largest federation in Germany; aligned with SPD; over 7 million members in 1921; dissolved by Nazis 1933.

**General Trade Union League, Greece**. See General Confederation of Greek Workers.

**General Union of Labour** [UGT, Spain] – union federation formed 1888; close relationship with SP; over 200,000 members in October 1920.

**General Workers' Union of Germany** [Allgemeine Arbeiter-Union Deutschlands, AAUD] – union federation founded February 1920 by ultraleft current that became KAPD; advocated factory committees to replace trade unions; 150,000 members in 1920–1, declining to 10,000 by end of 1921; maintained existence as sect until banned in 1933.

**Gennari, Egidio** [1876–1942] – teacher; joined Italian SP 1897; a leader of its left wing; internationalist during War; SP political secretary 1920; supported Communists in 1921 Livorno split; a vice chairman of Presidium of Third World Congress; favoured fusion with SP 1922; elected to ECCI 1921; wounded several times by Fascists; forced into emigration 1926; carried out many Comintern assignments; died in USSR.

**Geyer, Anna** [1893–1973] – joined USPD 1917; part of KPD-USPD merger; member of CC; supported Levi and expelled from CP August 1921; joined KAG 1922, participating in its fusions with USPD and SPD; fled Germany 1933.

**Geyer, Curt** [1891–1967] – joined SPD 1911 and became socialist journalist; leader of USPD from 1917; president of Leipzig Workers' Council 1918–19; participated in USPD-KPD fusion 1920; member German CP Zentrale; KPD representative on ECCI February–March 1921; opposed March Action with Levi; expelled August 1921; joined KAG and its fusions with USPD and SPD; exiled 1933; served on SPD executive in exile; left SPD 1941; settled in London.

**Geyer, Friedrich** [1853–1937] – joined German Social Democracy 1871; editor of *Leipziger Volkszeitung* 1890–4; part of split that formed USPD 1917; joined CP as part of 1920 fusion; member of Levi's

KAG 1921, participating in its fusions with USPD and then SPD.

**Giolitti, Giovanni** [1842–1928] – Italian prime minister five times during 1892–1921, including during 1920–1921; tolerated violent attacks by Fascist bands 1921 and initially supported Fascist regime 1922–4.

*Die Gleichheit* [Equality] – bimonthly magazine of proletarian women's movement in Germany 1890–1925; edited by Clara Zetkin 1892–1917.

**Goldman, Emma** [1860–1940] – born in Russian Empire; lived in New York from 1885; anarchist from 1889; leading anarchist educator; jailed several times, including for opposing war 1917; deported to Soviet Russia 1919; first supported, then opposed Bolshevik rule; left Russia 1921; subsequently lived mostly in Western Europe; continued anarchist activity until death.

**Gompers, Samuel** [1850–1924] – president of American Federation of Labor 1886–1924 (except for 1895); advocated collaboration with employers, counterposing 'pure-and-simple unionism' to industrial unionism; supported US entry into War; member of labour commission at Versailles conference.

**Gorky, Maxim** [1868–1936] – Russian novelist; Bolshevik supporter and financial backer during struggle against tsarism; tense relationship with Soviet Russia under Lenin; lived abroad 1921–8.

**Gorter, Herman** [1864–1927] – writer and poet; joined Dutch Social-Democratic Workers' Party [SDAP] 1897; founder of *De Tribune* 1907; a leader of left-wing SDP after 1909 split; internationalist during War; supporter of Zimmerwald Left; CP founding member 1918; criticised Comintern policies from ultraleft standpoint; member of German KAPD 1921; left Comintern with it 1921.

**Gouraud, Henri** [1867–1946] – French general; headed French army in Syria 1919–23; led brutal suppression of popular uprising in Syria; military governor of Paris 1923–37.

**Gramsci, Antonio** [1891–1937] – joined Italian SP 1913; secretary of its Turin section 1917; co-founder of SP weekly *L'Ordine nuovo* 1919; advocate of workers' councils 1920–1; co-founder of CP 1921; represented party in Moscow 1922–3; Fourth World Congress delegate; as advocate of united front against Fascism, headed CP 1924–6; objected to campaign against Trotsky 1926; jailed by Fascists 1926; wrote celebrated *Prison Notebooks*; sickened by prison conditions, he died shortly after release.

**Grassmann, Peter** [1873–1939] – joined SPD 1893; supported reformist wing; held leadership posts in printers' union from 1894 and German trade-union federation 1919–33; briefly arrested by Nazis 1933.

**Graziadei, Antonio** [1873–1953] – economist, joined Italian SP 1893; initially reformist, but radicalised during War, supporting Maximalist current; supported Communists in 1921 Livorno Congress while seeking compromise with forces in Serrati current; delegate to Second and Fourth World Congresses; expelled for 'revisionism' 1928; readmitted to CP after fall of Fascism.

*Grido del popolo* [People's Voice] – Italian syndicalist newspaper published in Turin; founded 1892.

**Griffuelhes, Victor** [1874–1922] – French anarcho-syndicalist; elected general secretary of CGT 1901; drafted Charter of Amiens 1906; resigned 1909 under accusation of financial mismanagement; continued as trade-union journalist; later supported Zimmerwald movement and October Revolution.

**Grimm, Robert** [1881–1958] – joined Swiss SDP 1899; editor-in-chief of *Berner Tagwacht* 1909–18; member of SDP Executive 1915–17, 1919–36; Swiss delegate to International Socialist Bureau from 1912; main organiser of Zimmerwald and Kienthal Conferences 1915–16; rejected entry into Comintern and helped organise Two-and-a-Half International.

**Grimm, Rosa** [1875–1955] – participant in Russian Revolution of 1905; active in student movement in Bern; founding member Swiss CP 1921; Third World Congress delegate; expressed oppositional opinions in 1920s; member of ECCI 1930–1; later joined SDP.

**Gruber, Max von** [1853–1927] – Austrian scientist; head of Hygienic Institute in Munich 1902–23; author of socio-political studies of birth rate and population; held that War was unavoidable as 'biological necessity'.

**Guesde, Jules** [1845–1922] – veteran of Paris Commune; among France's first Marxists; from 1882 leader of French Workers' Party, then SP; opponent of reformism until 1914; social patriot and minister of state without portfolio during War; opposed Comintern.

**Guralsky, August** [1890–1960] – joined Jewish Bund in Kiev 1904; joined Bolsheviks 1918; Comintern emissary to KPD, together with Béla Kun and others, during March Action; member of Russian delegation to Third World Congress with consultative vote; returned to Berlin as ECCI representative 1922–4; supported Zinoviev opposition in Soviet CP 1926–8; jailed 1936–8; arrested 1950 and jailed in Siberia; died soon after release.

**Hajdú, Gyula** [1886–1973] – lawyer; joined Hungarian SDP 1907; commissar during Hungarian soviet republic 1919; lived in exile after its fall; Third World Congress delegate; worked in Hungarian judiciary 1946–50; became professor in Budapest 1950.

**Hajim ibn Muhayd, Fid'an Shaykh** – a leader of fight to set up Kingdom of Syria, 1920–1.

**Halle Congress** – gathering of Independent Social-Democratic Party of Germany [USPD] held 12–17 October 1920; majority voted to accept Comintern's Twenty-One Conditions and affiliate to it, fusing with KPD; right-wing minority split off and kept USPD name.

**Handlíř, Jaroslav** [1888–1942] – member of Austro-Hungarian army in War, taken prisoner on Russian front; won to Bolshevism after October Revolution; helped found Czechoslovak communist group in Russia and represented it at First World Congress; returned to Czechoslovakia and became a leader of CP; briefly imprisoned for role in December 1920 strike; Third World Congress delegate; expelled from CP as rightist 1929; joined SDP; died at Auschwitz.

**Haqqi al-'Azm** [1864–1955] – French-installed governor of Damascus 1920–2; prime minister of Syria 1932–4.

**Harding, Warren** [1865–1923] – Republican Party president of US 1921–3.

**Hauth, Wilhelm** [1895–1968] – member of KPD National Trade Union Commission; aligned with Friesland-led KPD opposition in late 1921 and early 1922; member of Berlin city administration for SED in East Germany 1946–8.

**Haywood, William D.** ['Big Bill'] [1869–1928] – elected secretary-treasurer of Western Federation of Miners 1900; founding member and first chairman of IWW 1905; member of SP National Executive Committee, excluded in 1912 for his syndicalist outlook; became IWW secretary-treasurer 1913; arrested 1917 on frame-up charges of treason and sabotage, convicted and sentenced to twenty years' imprisonment; jumped bail in 1921 and went to Soviet Russia, where he lived until his death; delegate to Third World Congress and first RILU congress 1921.

**Heckert, Fritz** [1884–1936] – construction worker; joined SPD 1902; member Swiss socialist movement 1908–11; head of construction workers union in Chemnitz 1912–18; member Spartacus League during War; chaired workers' and soldiers' council in Chemnitz during November 1918 revolution; CP founding member; CC alternate 1919, full member from 1920; delegate to Third World Congress and elected to ECCI 1921; briefly minister in Saxony government 1923; represented German CP in Moscow 1932–4; member of RILU executive board from 1920; died in USSR before great Stalin purges.

**Helfferich, Karl** [1872–1924] – German financier, politician, and economist; treasury secretary 1915–16; secretary of the interior 1916–17, serving as acting vice-chancellor; became German ambassador to Russia 1918.

**Hempel.** See Appel, Jan.

**Henderson, Arthur** [1863–1935] – British Labour Party chairman 1908–10 and 1914–17, party secretary 1911–34; elected president of Second International 1920; chief party whip in House of Commons 1914, 1921–3, 1925–7;

secretary of state for foreign affairs 1929–31.

**Hervé, Gustave** [1871–1944] – joined French socialist movement 1899; led ultraleft tendency in SP before War, calling for rebellion and draft resistance to halt threat of war; became pro-war ultra-nationalist in 1914; expelled from SP 1916; sympathetic to fascism in 1920s; initial supporter of Vichy regime during World War II.

**Hewlett, William J.** [d. 1921] – originally from South Wales Socialist Society delegate to founding congress of British CP 1920 as member of Communist Unity Group; delegate to Third World Congress and first RILU congress; died in train accident in Soviet Russia.

**Hilferding, Rudolf** [1877–1941] – joined socialist movement as student 1893; based in Germany from 1906; author of *Finance Capital* 1910; opposed SPD support of war credits after 1914; joined USPD 1918; opposed Comintern, remaining in rump USPD 1920; rejoined SPD in 1922 fusion; government minister of finance 1923, 1928–9; forced into exile 1933; arrested by French Vichy regime 1941; tortured and killed by Gestapo.

**Hillquit, Morris** [1869–1933] – founder and central leader of US SP from 1901; supporter of centrist current within international Social Democracy; prominent figure in Two-and-a-Half International 1921–3.

**Hindenburg, Paul von** [1847–1934] – German field marshal during War; German president 1925–34; appointed Hitler as chancellor 1933.

**Hirossik, Janos** [1887–1950] – secretary of hotel workers' union from 1912; founding member Hungarian CP 1918; commissar in Slovakia during Hungarian soviet republic, emigrating after its defeat; Third World Congress delegate; CC member 1926–33; participant in resistance during World War II; withdrew from political activity after 1945.

**Hirsch-Duncker unions** – German trade unions founded by Max Hirsch and Franz Duncker in 1868; asserted identity of interests between workers and employers and advocated class peace; membership of around 225,000 in 1921.

**Hizb al-Watani party** [National Party] – Egyptian revolutionary nationalist organisation formed as secret society to fight British occupation 1907; right wing split off to join Wafd party in 1919–20; left wing oriented to popular masses but was unable to present revolutionary alternative.

**Hoelz, Max** [1889–1933] – joined USPD during War; joined German CP 1919; led workers' armed detachments in Saxony 1920–1 during Kapp Putsch and March Action; expelled from CP for indiscipline and joined KAPD 1920; jailed in frame-up for murder 1921 and sentenced to life imprisonment; freed after international defence campaign; rejoined CP; emigrated to USSR 1929; developed criticisms of Stalin regime; targeted by Stalin's secret police; drowned under mysterious circumstances.

**Hoetzsch, Otto** [1876–1946] – German academic and politician; member of Reichstag during 1920s for right-wing German National People's Party.

**Höfer, Karl** [1862–1939] – German officer during War; commander of Freikorps in suppression of Polish insurgents in Upper Silesia 1921; later became officer in Nazi SS.

**Hoffman, Adolph** [1858–1930] – joined German Social Democracy 1876; delegate to founding congress of Second International 1889; elected to Reichstag 1904 and to Prussian parliament 1908; attended Zimmerwald and Kienthal Conferences during War; part of split that formed USPD 1917; joined CP as part of 1920 fusion; joined Levi's KAG 1921, participating in its fusions with USPD and then SPD.

**Höglund, Karl Zeth** [1884–1956] – journalist; joined Swedish SDP 1904; campaigned for Norway's right to independence 1905; internationalist and supporter of Zimmerwald Left during War; supporter of October Revolution; helped found Left Social-Democratic Party 1917 and led it into Comintern; Third World Congress delegate; elected to ECCI 1922; criticised

Moscow control and left Comintern 1924, forming independent socialist faction; rejoined SDP 1926; mayor of Stockholm 1940–50.

**Hörsing, Friedrich Otto** [1874–1937] – joined SPD 1894; governor in Prussian Saxony 1919–27; led suppression of workers during March Action 1921; expelled from SPD and founded German Social-Republican Party 1932.

**Horthy, Miklós** [1868–1957] – Austro-Hungarian naval commander during War; a leader of counterrevolutionary forces that crushed Hungarian soviet republic 1919 and carried out white terror; regent and dictator of Hungary 1920–44.

**Hourwich, Nicholas** [1882–1934] – member of American SP's Russian socialist federation 1917; rallied to communism after October Revolution; a founder of CP of America; delegate to Second and Third World Congresses, opposing attempt to build legal CP; remained in Soviet Russia.

**Hubin, Georges** [1863–1947] – a leader of Belgian Workers' Party; member of parliament for forty-seven years; Belgian minister of state 1945.

**Hughes, Charles Evans** [1862–1948] – US secretary of state 1921–5; chief justice of Supreme Court 1930–41.

**Hula, Břetislav** [1894–1937] – joined Bolsheviks 1917 as Czech living in Russia; returning to Czechoslovakia, he became editor of *Svoboda*; delegate to Second World Congress and elected to ECCI 1920; imprisoned for communist activities 1921; expelled 1925 as right opportunist.

***L'Humanité*** [Humanity] – daily Paris newspaper of French SP and then CP; began publication 1904; 200,000 circulation in 1921.

**Humbert-Droz, Jules** [1891–1971] – clergyman; joined Swiss SDP 1911; internationalist during War; founding member CP 1921; helped lead Comintern work in Latin countries of Europe and Latin America; delegate to Second through Fourth World Congresses; elected to ECCI 1921; aligned with Bukharin in late 1920s; removed from Comintern posts 1928; in disfavour with Stalin leadership until 1935; leader of Swiss CP 1935–41; expelled 1943; joined SDP and became its secretary 1947–58; leader of dissident SP from 1959; in final years, supporter of Algerian freedom struggle and anti-war activist.

**Huysmans, Camille** [1871–1968] – joined Belgian Workers' Party 1887; journalist; secretary of International Socialist Bureau of Second International from 1905; secretary of Socialist International 1939–44; chairman of Belgian House of Representatives 1936–9, 1954–8; Belgian premier 1946–7.

**Ibn Saud, Abd al Aziz** [1880–1953] – from 1901 worked to revive ruling family dynasty in Arabia; allied with British during War; founder and king of Saudi Arabia 1932, ruling until his death.

**ILP.** See Independent Labour Party.

**Independent Labour Party** [ILP] – British Social-Democratic party formed 1893; played leading role in formation of Labour Party, affiliating to it 1906–32; majority took pacifist position during War; 45,000 members April 1920; affiliated to Two-and-a-Half International 1921; minority split to join CP.

**Independent Social Democracy of Estonia.** See Estonian Independent Socialist Workers' Party.

**Independent Social-Democratic Party of Germany** [USPD] – formed 1917 by left critics of SPD majority leadership; 800,000 members end of 1920; majority fused with CP December 1920; minority retained name until merger with SPD 1922.

**Independents** – A reference to the German USPD specifically, and to the Two-and-a-Half International more generally.

**Industrial Workers of the World** [IWW, Australia] – established in Australia 1907; participated in 1916 miners' strike against War and conscription; declared illegal during War, with principal leaders convicted of 'high treason'; many members joined CP after 1920.

**Industrial Workers of the World** [IWW, United States] – founded 1905 as revolutionary syndicalist union; opposed US participation in War; suffered severe repression 1917–18; sent delegates to founding RILU congress 1921, but rejected affiliation to it; many militants joined CP; went into rapid decline in 1920s.

**Inkpin, Albert** [1884–1944] – joined Social-Democratic Federation 1906; general secretary of British SP 1913–20, leading it to fusion that created CP; general secretary of CP 1920–2, 1923–9; jailed for Communist propaganda activities 1921; elected honorary president of Third World Congress; secretary-general of Friends of the Soviet Union 1930–44.

**International Council of Trade and Industrial Unions** [Mezhsoprof] – founded 15 July 1920 at meeting of revolutionary unions called on initiative of the ECCI and All-Russia Central Trade Union Councils; became RILU in 1921.

**International Federation of Trade Unions** [IFTU, Amsterdam International] – founded by reformist-led unions at July 1919 congress in Amsterdam; viewed as continuation of federation founded in 1901 (adopting IFTU name in 1913) and destroyed by War; 24 million members in 1921.

**International Labour Organisation** – founded in 1919 as agency of League of Nations concerned with labour conditions, with International Labour Office in Geneva; now a United Nations agency.

**International Socialist Bureau** – executive committee of Second International formed 1900 with headquarters in Brussels; last meeting held July 1914.

**International Socialist League** [South Africa] – founded 1915; internationalist position during War; supported October Revolution; adopted Comintern conditions of membership January 1921; founded CP July 1921.

*L'Internationale du travail* [Revue internationale du travail] – monthly publication published in Geneva by bureau of Amsterdam International; began 1921; published in English as *International Labour Review*.

*Die Internationale* – bimonthly theoretical journal of KPD; founded 1915 as underground organ of Spartacus current; 5,000 circulation in 1921.

**Internationalist Socialist Party of the Ruthenian People** – founded March 1920 by former members of Hungarian soviet republic and returning war prisoners from Soviet Russia; merged with left wing of SDP of Slovakia January 1921; joined in creation of Czechoslovak CP May 1921.

**Italian Socialist Party** [PSI] – founded 1892; participated in Zimmerwald movement during War; affiliated to Comintern 1919; refused to expel reformist right wing; left wing split off at January 1921 Livorno Congress to form CP; 200,000 members before Livorno Congress, dropping to 112,000 by October 1921 and 65,000 a year later; sent representatives to Third World Congress; expelled Turati and right wing 1922; pro-Comintern minority subsequently joined CP.

**Itschner, Hans Heinrich** [1887–1962] – anarcho-syndicalist before War; became one of first Swiss Communists after 1917; first representatives of Swiss CP on ECCI 1919–20; expelled for indiscipline 1932; subsequently became anarchist.

**IWW.** See Industrial Workers of the World.

**Jacob, Mathilde** [1873–1943] – SPD member who worked as secretary to Rosa Luxemburg; joined KPD; collaborator of Paul Levi; followed him into SPD; died in concentration camp.

**Jacquemotte, Joseph** [1883–1936] – joined Belgian Workers' Party 1906; permanent secretary of Union of Socialist Employees 1910–24; moved to left during War; leader of left-wing faction of Workers' Party; expelled 1921; Third World Congress delegate; his group fused with CP in September 1921 and he was elected to CC; became general secretary 1934.

**Jansen, I.** See Proost, Jan.

**Jaurès, Jean** [1859–1914] – central leader of French SP from its foundation 1905; advocated reformist positions; resisted imperialist war; assassinated at outbreak of War.

**Javadzadeh, Mir Ja'far** [Ja'far Pishevari] [1892–1947] – born in Iran; joined RSDLP in Baku and helped found Adalat [Iran Justice] Party 1917; returned to Iran and became founding member of CP; Third World Congress delegate; member of CC until his arrest in 1930; imprisoned in Iran until 1941; prime minister of Autonomous Government of (Iranian) Azerbaijan 1945–6.

**Jewish Workers League.** See Bund.

**Jogiches, Leo** [1867–1919] – a central leader of SDKPiL 1893–1914; close collaborator of Rosa Luxemburg; moved to Berlin 1900 and from then on was active in both German and Polish movements; central organiser of Spartacus League and leader of German CP; murdered by government troops March 1919.

**Jones, David Ivon** [1883–1924] – born in Wales, moved to South Africa 1910; joined South African Labour Party 1911; founding member of International Socialist League 1915, becoming its first secretary-editor; attended Second and Third World Congresses; one of first English-language translators of Lenin's works; died of tuberculosis.

**Jouhaux, Léon** [1879–1954] – French unionist; general secretary of CGT from 1909; social patriot during War; pushed split in CGT against left-wing unionists 1921–2; supporter of Popular Front 1936; in concentration camp during Nazi occupation; in 1948 broke with then-CP-led CGT and founded Force Ouvrière union federation.

*Jugend-Internationale* [Youth International] – monthly magazine of Communist Youth International; published 1919–28; 160,000 press run in 1921.

**Julien, Charles-André** [1891–1991] – university professor; joined French SP 1911 in Algeria; became president of Federation of the League for the Rights of Man in North Africa 1917–18; became CP member after Tours Congress 1920; CP permanent delegate for propaganda in North Africa from 1921; Third World Congress delegate; left CP 1926; later rejoined SP; French secretary-general of High Committee of North Africa under Popular Front government; left SP 1958 and joined predecessor of Unified Socialist Party [PSU]; supporter of Algerian independence struggle.

*Der Junge Genosse* [The Young Comrade] – children's paper published twice monthly in Berlin by executive committee of Communist Youth International; founded 1 January 1921.

**Kabakchiev, Khristo** [1878–1940] – joined Bulgarian SDP 1897; member of left-wing Tesniaki wing from 1905; editor-in-chief of its central organ 1908; member Bulgarian CP and its CC from 1919; represented ECCI at Halle and Livorno congresses 1920–1; jailed for three years after 1923 insurrection; lived in Moscow from 1926; lost leadership posts in Bulgarian CP and ECCI 1928; jailed during Stalin purges 1937–8.

**KAG.** See Communist Working Group.

**Kahr, Gustav Ritter von** [1862–1934] – right-wing German politician; prime minister of Bavaria March 1920–September 1921; first endorsed and then opposed Nazis' Munich putsch; abducted and murdered during Nazis' 'Night of the Long Knives'.

**Kamenev, Lev Borisovich** [1883–1936] – joined RSDLP 1901; became Bolshevik 1903; Bolshevik leader in St. Petersburg 1906–7; went to Geneva 1908; arrested and exiled to Siberia 1914–17; in Petrograd 1917; elected to CC at 1917 conference; elected president of Moscow Soviet 1918; member of RCP politburo; elected to ECCI at Third World Congress; allied with Stalin and Zinoviev against Trotsky 1923–5; member of joint opposition with Trotsky 1926–7; expelled 1927; recanted and reinstated 1928; expelled again 1932; condemned to death and executed in first Moscow Trial.

**Kamocki.** See Rydygier, Aleksander Juliusz.

**KAPD.** See Communist Workers' Party of Germany.

**Kapp, Wolfgang** [1858–1922] – reactionary Prussian politician; led attempted coup March 1920 to overthrow German republic and establish right-wing dictatorship; defeated by general strike and armed workers' resistance.

**Kara-Gadiyev** – The delegate lists of the Third World Congress in the Comintern archives show no one by this name. The reference could possibly be to **Karim Hakimov** [1892–1938] – raised as Muslim, he joined revolutionary movement as student; in 1918–19, a Red Army commander and member of Orenburg Muslim Revolutionary Military Committee; secretary of Central Committee of Turkestan CP 1920–1; later Soviet ambassador to Saudi Arabia; arrested and shot during Stalin purges.

**Karl I** [1887–1922] – last ruling member of Hapsburg dynasty in Austria-Hungary; emperor of Austria and king of Hungary 1916–18; overthrown by November 1918 revolution.

**Kasian, Sarkis Ivanovich** [Ter-Kasparian] [1876–1937] – joined Bolsheviks 1905 in Armenia; leader of Tbilisi Bolsheviks 1912–14; chairman of Armenian Committee of Russian CP 1919–20; delegate to Third World Congress; chairman of Armenian SSR Central Executive Committee 1928–30; arrested 1937 and shot.

**Kautsky, Karl** [1854–1938] – born in Prague; joined Austrian Social Democracy 1874; collaborator of Engels; co-founder and leading editor of *Die Neue Zeit* 1883–1917; prominent Marxist theorist and opponent of revisionism before 1914; centrist apologist for social chauvinism during War; joined USPD 1917; opponent of October Revolution; supporter of Two-and-a-Half International 1921–3; rejoined SPD in 1922 fusion; moved to Vienna 1924; fled Nazis 1938 and died in exile.

**Kemal Pasha, Mustafa** [Atatürk] [1881–1938] – Turkish general; led independence struggle 1918–23; founder of Turkish republic and its president, 1923–38.

**Kerensky, Alexander** [1881–1970] – Russian Socialist-Revolutionary; prime minister of Russian Provisional Government July–November 1917; overthrown by October Revolution; emigrated 1918.

**Kerran, F.L.** [1883–1949] – joined ILP 1906; British SP 1908; imprisoned four years without charge during War; founding member CP and member of its Executive 1920; Third World Congress delegate; left CP 1923; subsequently active in Labour Party.

**Khinchuk, Lev Mikhailovich** [1868–1944] – socialist from 1890; Menshevik 1903; chair of Moscow Soviet March–September 1917; joined Bolsheviks 1920; Third World Congress delegate and chair of commission on cooperatives; held posts in Soviet administration of diplomacy, cooperatives, commerce; arrested 1938; died in prison.

**Kibalchich, Liuba Russakova** [1898–1984] – grew up in Rostov; family forced to flee Russia; Liuba returned after revolution and became companion of Victor Serge 1919; stenographer and typist for Comintern; suffered Stalinist repression from 1929; fell victim to severe mental illness; left Soviet Union with Serge 1936; died in French mental hospital.

**Kilbom, Karl** [1885–1961] – metalworker; joined Swedish socialist movement 1903; secretary of Young Social-Democratic Union 1914–17; internationalist and pacifist stance during War; founding member of Left Social-Democratic Party 1917 and its transformation to CP in 1921; elected to ECCI at Third World Congress; expelled 1929 for 'rightist deviation'; founded dissident Communist party that changed its name to Swedish Socialist Party in 1934; rejoined SDP 1938.

**Király, Albert** [1883–1939] – member Hungarian SDP 1900–19 and CP 1919–21, Third World Congress delegate; worked in Moscow for Red Sports International 1921; worked in Peasants' International [Krestintern] 1924–32; arrested and died during Stalin purges.

**Knight, Joseph R.** [Morgan] – main organiser of One Big Union in Ontario and member of Canadian SP; sympathiser of CP; attended Third World Congress and founding RILU congress; joined CP on his return and became CC member.

**Knights of Labor** – first national US labour federation; founded 1869; reached peak membership of 700,000 in 1886; largely disappeared with creation of American Federation of Labor.

**Kobetsky, Mikhail** [1881–1937] – member RSDLP 1903; Bolshevik; often arrested; in exile 1908–17; worked in Comintern apparatus 1919–24; member of ECCI and its Small Bureau 1920; worked in commissariat of foreign affairs from 1924; arrested and executed during Stalin purges.

**Koenen, Wilhelm** [1886–1963] – joined German SPD 1904 and USPD 1917; and member of USPD Central Committee from 1919; commissar of workers' and soldiers' councils in Halle-Merseburg 1918; helped lead KPD-USPD merger 1920; a vice chairman of Presidium of Third World Congress; in exile 1933–45; member of East German CP [SED] CC from 1946; criticised after 1953 workers' rebellion for 'lack of vigilance'.

**Köhler, Bruno** [1900–89] – member of Sudetenland SDP in Austrian empire; became member of Sudetenland CP, which unified with Czechoslovak CP 1921; Third World Congress delegate from Czechoslovak Communist Youth; CC member from 1929; member of ECCI 1933–5; in exile 1938–47; member of CC 1952–64; expelled 1966 for having participated in repression during 1950s.

**Kolarov, Vasil** [1877–1950] – school teacher; joined Bulgarian SDP 1897 and its revolutionary Tesniak wing 1903; member of Tesniaki CC 1905; represented it at Zimmerwald Conference 1915; secretary of Bulgarian CP 1919–23; a vice chairman of Presidium of Third World Congress; ECCI member from 1921; a leader of failed Bulgarian uprising 1923; lived in USSR 1923–45; president of Peasant International 1928–39; signed declaration dissolving Comintern 1943; returned to Bulgaria 1944; prime minister 1949–50.

**Kolchak, Aleksandr Vasilievich** [1874–1920] – tsarist admiral; head of White armies in Siberia and the Whites' 'supreme ruler' of Russia 1918–20; defeated by Red Army; captured and executed.

**Kollontai, Alexandra Mikhailovna** [1872–1952] – joined RSDLP 1899; cooperated with Mensheviks from 1906; specialised in work among proletarian women; lived in emigration 1908–17; joined Bolsheviks 1915; returned to Russia 1917 and became member of Bolshevik CC and editor of its women's journal; commissar of social welfare after October Revolution; head of Women's Section of Central Committee 1920–2; leader of Workers' Opposition 1921–2, giving report on its behalf to Third World Congress; subsequently worked in Soviet diplomatic service until her death.

*Kommunistische Arbeiter-Zeitung* [KAZ, Communist Workers' Gazette] – organ of KAPD published in Berlin; appeared semiweekly 1919–28, weekly 1928–33.

*Die Kommunistische Fraueninternationale* [Communist Women's International] – monthly journal published in Germany by Communist Women's Movement 1921–5; editor Clara Zetkin.

*Kommunistischer Gewerkschafter* [Communist Trade Unionist] – weekly newspaper for communist propaganda in trade unions and factory councils; founded 8 January 1921; edited by Fritz Heckert.

**Korfanty, Wojciech** [1873–1939] – Polish nationalist leader in Upper Silesia; served in German Reichstag from 1903; led rebellion May 1921 that helped induce Allies to set German-Polish border favourable to Poland.

**Koritschoner, Franz** [1892–1941] – bank employee; joined Austrian SPD youth 1914, supporter of Zimmerwald Left during War; founding member of CP 1918; CC member and editor-in-chief of CP daily newspaper; delegate to Third World Congress and elected to ECCI 1921; moved to Moscow 1929; arrested 1937 during Stalin purges; handed over to Gestapo after Hitler-Stalin pact; executed at Auschwitz.

**KPD.** See Communist Party–Germany.

**Krasin, Leonid Borisovich** [1870–1926] – Russian Social Democrat from 1890; elected to RSDLP CC 1903; Bolshevik CC 1905; prominent role in 1905 revolution; became Soviet commissar for Trade and for Transport in 1919; Soviet ambassador to France 1924; Britain 1925.

**Kreibich, Karl** [1883–1966] – Social Democrat from 1902; supporter of Lenin's stand against War 1914; organiser of revolutionary Left in Sudetenland SP; founded Sudeten German section of Czechoslovak CP and represented it

Glossary • 1225

at Third World Congress; member of Czechoslovak CP political bureau 1921-4, 1927-9; part of Comintern staff 1924-7 and 1929-33; moved to London 1938; worked with Beneš exile government during World War II; Czechoslovak ambassador to USSR 1950-2.

**Królikowski, Stefan** [Gliński] [1881-1937] – member Polish Socialist Party [PPS] 1900-6, PPS-Left 1911-18; exiled to Siberia 1915-17; participated in October Revolution in Petrograd; returned to Warsaw and elected to Polish CP CC 1918; Third World Congress delegate; worked in Soviet Union from 1929; arrested and shot during Stalin purges.

**Krupskaya, Nadezhda** [1869-1939] – joined Marxist movement in Russia 1890; co-founder RSDLP 1898; Bolshevik; collaborator and wife of Lenin; leader in Soviet educational administration; target of insults by Stalin 1922-3; briefly supported United Opposition led by Trotsky and Zinoviev 1926; ostracised due to efforts to defend victims of Stalin purges in 1930s.

**Kuliscioff, Anna** [1854-1925] – joined revolutionary movement in Russia during 1870s; fled to Italy; founding member of Italian SP 1892; part of split that formed reformist PSU 1922; companion of Turati.

**Kun, Béla** [1886-1938 or 1939] – Hungarian journalist; joined SP 1903; joined Bolsheviks while war prisoner in Russia; organised Hungarian CP 1918; head of Hungarian soviet government March-July 1919; forced into exile; lived in USSR from 1920; supported ultraleft 'theory of the offensive'; as ECCI emissary to Germany, helped instigate March Action 1921; Third World Congress delegate; ECCI member 1921-2, 1926-36; supported Stalin against left and right oppositions; arrested, tortured, and executed during Stalin purges.

**Kuskova, Yekaterina Dmitrievna** [1869-1958] – leading Russian liberal and member of Cadet Party; opponent of October Revolution; active in Public Committee for Famine Relief 1921, accused of anti-Soviet propaganda; deported from Russia 1922.

**Kuusinen, Otto** [1881-1964] – member Finnish SP 1904; its chairman 1911-17; people's commissar in soviet government of Finland 1918; based in Russia from 1918; a founder of Finnish CP 1918; attended all seven Comintern congresses; leading figure in Comintern ECCI until its dissolution 1943; president of Finno-Karelian Republic 1940-56; member of Soviet politburo at time of his death.

**Labour Party.** See British Labour Party; Australian Labor Party; Norwegian Labour Party; Belgian Workers' Party.

**Lafont, Ernest** [1879-1946] – French lawyer and Freemason; as SP parliamentary deputy gave conditional support to national defence during War; joined French CP 1921; expelled from CP for opposition to Fourth World Congress decisions January 1923; helped found independent socialist group 1923; rejoined SP 1928; split from SP to the right 1933; government minister 1935-6.

**Landler, Jenő** [1875-1928] – lawyer and journalist; joined Hungarian SP 1904; became leader of railwaymen's union; member of Hungarian soviet government and commander of its army 1919; emigrated 1919; led CP faction opposed to Béla Kun; delegate to Third through Fifth World Congresses; carried out assignments for ECCI in 1920s, died in France.

**Lapčević, Dragiša** [1867-1939] – central leader of Serbian SDP from its founding 1903; as parliamentary deputy 1905-8 and 1912-19 made anti-war declarations against Balkan Wars and World War I; joined Yugoslav CP at its founding in 1919 but left December 1920; helped found Yugoslav SP 1922.

**Laporte, Maurice** [1901-87] – French metalworker, journalist; active in Socialist Youth from 1919; advocated its affiliation to Communist Youth International; general secretary of Socialist, then Communist youth 1920-3; delegate to Third and Fourth World Congresses; jailed for anti-militarist activity 1923; left Communist movement in mid-1920s; became prominent writer against communism and Soviet Union, including during

Nazi occupation; after 1945 fled to Switzerland; sentenced in absentia to life imprisonment.

**Larin, Yuri Aleksandrovich** [1882–1932] – joined RSDLP 1900, becoming Menshevik 1904; joined Bolshevik Party August 1917; worked in Soviet government and economic bodies after 1917; during 1920–2 deputy chairman of Supreme Council for Transportation, and member of state Planning Commission and its Presidium; appointed Soviet adviser on Jewish affairs 1925.

**Lassalle, Ferdinand** [1825–1864] – participant in 1848–9 revolution in Germany; founder and first president of General German Workers' Association 1863; campaigner for suffrage and workers' rights; killed in duel; followers joined with Marxists in 1875 to form Socialist German Workers' Party, predecessor of SPD.

**Laufenberg, Heinrich** [1872–1932] – joined SPD 1904; a leader of left wing within SPD in Hamburg; elected chairman of workers' and soldiers' council there January 1919; a leader of National Bolshevism tendency; expelled from KPD 1920; joined KAPD but was expelled from it later that year; co-founder of Communist League; refused all contact with Nazis, unlike collaborator Wolffheim.

**Laukki, Leo** [Pivio] [1880–1938] – joined workers' movement during 1905–6 revolution in Russian Finland; moved to US 1907 and became part of Finnish Socialist Federation; became revolutionary syndicalist and joined IWW 1910; arrested 1918 and condemned to twenty years for espionage and conspiracy; member US CP 1921; out on bail, he fled to Soviet Russia; elected to Finnish CP CC 1921, representing it at Third World Congress; elected to ECCI 1921; remained on CC until 1925; subsequently university professor in Soviet Union; arrested and shot during Stalin purges.

**Lazzari, Costantino** [1857–1927] – joined Italian workers' movement 1883; a founding CC member of Italian SP 1892; SP political secretary 1912–19; supporter of Maximalist wing; attended Zimmerwald and Kienthal Conferences; imprisoned for anti-war propaganda February–November 1918; opposed Communist split at 1921 Livorno Congress; attended Third World Congress as SP representative; remained in SP after Serrati joined CP in 1924.

**League of Peace and Freedom** – international pacifist and democratic organisation founded 1867; watchwords were 'Universal brotherhood of peoples' and 'United States of Europe'.

**Ledebour, Georg** [1850–1947] – joined SPD 1891; Reichstag member 1900–18; in SPD's left wing before 1914; attended Zimmerwald and Kienthal Conferences; opposed social chauvinism; co-chair of USPD 1917–19; opposed affiliation to Comintern 1920 and remained in rump USPD; refused to rejoin SPD in 1922 fusion; led a small socialist group through 1920s; member of Socialist Workers' Party [SAP] 1931; fled to Switzerland 1933; continued anti-Nazi and socialist activity until death.

**Lefebvre, Raymond** [1891–1920] – War veteran wounded at Verdun; joined SP 1916 and drawn to its left wing; founded Republican Association of Veterans; delegate of Committee for the Third International to Second World Congress; on his return trip, he and two others died at sea.

**Left Social-Democratic Party of Sweden.** See Communist Party–Sweden.

**Left Socialist Party** [Levice, Czechoslovakia] – a reference to SDP after Marxist Left Faction (organised December 1919) won leadership of it in September 1920; became CP May 1921.

**Left Socialist Party of Belgium** – a reference to left-wing current expelled from Belgian Workers' Party early 1921, led by Joseph Jacquemotte; fused with CP September 1921.

**Left Socialist Revolutionary Party** [Russia] – split from Russian Socialist Revolutionary Party 1917; participated in October Revolution and Soviet government, but broke with it July 1918 and launched uprising; minority of party eventually joined Russian CP.

**Legien, Carl** [1861–1920] – joined SPD 1885; chairman of lathe operators' union 1887 and of confederation of pro-socialist unions 1890; member of Reichstag from 1893; supported government war effort 1914–18 and SPD right-wing majority; as chairman of main German union federation, called general strike that defeated Kapp Putsch 1920.

**Leipart, Theodor** [1867–1947] – vice president of German Union of Woodworkers 1893–1908 and its president 1908–19; president of Federation of German Trade Unions [ADGB] 1921–33; vice president of Amsterdam International 1922–3; inactive during World War II; joined SED 1946.

*Die Leipziger Volkszeitung* [Leipzig People's Gazette] – German Social-Democratic daily published in Leipzig 1894–1933; became organ of USPD following 1917 SPD split.

**Lékai, János** [1895–1925] – Union of Young Workers chairman during Hungarian soviet republic 1919; member Hungarian CP; emigrated to Vienna and worked on staff of CYI's journal *Jugend-Internationale*; member CYI executive committee 1919–22; delegate to Second and Third World Congresses from CYI; moved to US 1922 and became active in Hungarian Federation of US CP as John Lassen.

**Lenin, Vladimir Ilyich** [1870–1924] – became active in Russian Social-Democratic movement 1892–3; founded *Iskra* 1900; central leader of Bolsheviks from 1903; called for new International 1914; organised Zimmerwald Left to fight for this goal 1915–17; leader of October Revolution; chair of Soviet government 1917–24; founder and leader of Comintern, attending its first four congresses.

**Lepetit, Jules** [1889–1920] – French anarcho-syndicalist; jailed 1917–19; founding member Committee of Syndicalist Defence; observer at Second World Congress; died at sea while returning.

**Levi, Paul** [1883–1930] – joined SPD 1909; collaborator of Rosa Luxemburg; joined Spartacus group during War; co-founder of German CP 1918; chair of CP 1919–21; attended Italian SP Livorno Congress 1921 and opposed Comintern intervention there; led struggle against ultraleftism and for unification with revolutionary majority in USPD; resigned as CP chair February 1921; expelled from CP as result of his public denunciation of March Action and 'strategy of offensive'; founded Communist Working Group [KAG], which joined USPD and was part of SPD-USPD fusion 1922; a leader of SPD left wing until his death.

**Liebknecht, Karl** [1871–1919] – joined German SPD 1900; first president of Socialist Youth International 1907–10; first member of German Reichstag to vote against war credits December 1914; co-founder of Spartacus current; imprisoned for anti-war propaganda 1916; freed by 1918 revolution; a founding leader of German CP December 1918; murdered by rightist officers during Berlin workers' uprising January 1919.

**Liebknecht, Wilhelm** [1826–1900] – participant in 1848 revolution in Germany; collaborator of Marx and Engels; co-founder of German Social Democracy 1869 and, with Bebel, leader of SPD until his death; chief editor of *Vorwärts* 1876–8, 1891–1900.

**Lindhagen, Carl** [1860–1946] – mayor of Stockholm 1903–30; joined SPD 1909; founding member 1917 of Left Social-Democratic Party, which became CP; expelled 1921 for opposing decisions of Second World Congress; rejoined Social Democrats 1923.

**Livorno Congress** – Italian Socialist Party [PSI] gathering held 15–21 January 1921; Unitary Communists [Centre] led by Serrati received 92,028 votes; Communist Faction [Left] led by Bordiga, 58,173; Socialist Concentration [Right] led by Turati, 14,695; Left walked out and formed Communist Party of Italy, which was recognised as section of Comintern.

**Lloyd George, David** [1863–1945] – British Liberal Party leader; prime minister 1916–22.

**Longuet, Jean** [1876–1938] – joined French socialist movement 1890s;

leader of centrists in SP during and after War; opposed affiliation to Comintern; remained with dissident SP after 1920 split; parliamentary deputy 1914–19; 1932–6; leading figure in Two-and-a-Half International; Karl Marx's grandson.

**Loriot, Fernand** [1870–1932] – teacher; joined French SP 1901; treasurer of teachers' union 1912; a leader of internationalist forces in France during War; secretary of Committee for the Third International in France; became part of CP at Tours Congress; jailed 1920–1; elected CP international secretary January 1921; a vice chairman of Presidium of Third World Congress; withdrew from leadership 1922; opposed 'Bolshevisation' 1925–6; quit party 1926; later collaborated with Left Opposition led by Trotsky.

**Loucheur, Louis** [1872–1931] – French politician; owner of arms-making company; minister of armaments 1917–18; parliamentary deputy 1919–31; negotiated with Rathenau on reparations 1921; held various ministerial posts until his death.

**Louis, Paul** [1872–1955] – French socialist, author and journalist; joined socialist movement 1898; became member of SP national leadership prior to War; member CP following 1920 Tours Congress, elected to its directing committee; criticised as bourgeois journalist, he was expelled from CP January 1923; joined Socialist Communist Union led by Frossard, becoming its general secretary; in 1930 it fused into United Proletarian Party [PUP], and then SP in 1936; abandoned political activity during World War II.

**Lozovsky, Solomon Abramovich** [1878–1952] – joined RSDLP 1901; lived in Geneva and Paris 1909–17; active in French revolutionary labour movement during War; returned to Russia and joined Bolsheviks 1917; became secretary of All-Russian Union of Railway Workers 1918; general secretary of RILU 1921–37; Third World Congress delegate; deputy minister of foreign affairs 1939–45; arrested during repression of Jewish writers 1949; shot in prison.

**Ludendorff, Erich** [1865–1937] – German general; shaped German military policy in latter years of War; subsequently a leader of reactionary and fascist political movements; Nazi member of Reichstag 1924–8.

**Lüttwitz, Walther von** [1859–1942] – German baron and general; appointed by Social Democrats to lead crushing of workers' uprising in Berlin 1919; with Kapp, led attempted putsch against German republic 1920.

**Lukács, György** [1885–1971] – joined Hungarian CP 1918; commissar for education and culture in Hungarian soviet republic 1919; emigrated after its defeat; member of CP faction opposed to Béla Kun; Third World Congress delegate; lived in Moscow for most of 1930–45 period; returned to Budapest 1945 and joined Hungarian Academy of Sciences; participated in 1956 revolution, becoming minister of culture in Imre Nagy government; expelled from CP and briefly deported; readmitted to party 1967; author of *History and Class Consciousness*.

**Lunacharsky, Anatoly Vasilievich** [1875–1933] – joined Russian social-democratic movement in early 1890s; became Bolshevik after 1903; broke with Bolsheviks with *Vperyod* group after 1905 revolution; rejoined 1917; people's commissar of education 1917–29; then chairman of Academic Committee under Central Executive Committee of USSR.

**Luxemburg, Rosa** [1871–1919] – born in Poland; co-founder of SDKPiL 1893; later lived in Germany; led SPD left wing against revisionist right and, after 1910, against 'Marxist Centre' led by Kautsky; Marxist theorist and author of *The Accumulation of Capital* 1913; leader of Spartacus current during War; imprisoned 1916–18; founding leader of German CP December 1918; arrested and murdered during workers' uprising in Berlin January 1919.

**MacDonald, Ramsay** [1866–1937] – leader of British Labour Party 1911–14 and 1922–31; opposed British entry into War 1914; opposed October Revolution; member of Second International executive committee; prime minister

1924 and 1929–35; split from Labour Party 1931.

**Maffi, Fabrizio** [1868–1955] – joined Italian socialist movement around 1890; SP parliamentary deputy from 1913; close to Maximalist current; remained in SP following 1921 Livorno split; member of PSI delegation to Third and Fourth World Congresses; supported SP's pro-Comintern current; joined CP 1924; close collaborator of Gramsci 1924–6; jailed 1926–8; active again in CP after fall of Fascism.

**Malthus, Thomas** [1766–1834] – English economist and demographer; known for theory that human population growth will outstrip food supply.

**Malzahn, Heinrich** [1884–1957] – mechanic; active in metalworkers union; joined SPD 1906, USPD 1917; member of revolutionary shop stewards during War; member Executive of Workers' and Soldiers' Councils November 1918; chairman of Berlin Committee of Factory Councils; joined CP in KPD-USPD fusion 1920; opposed March Action but organised strike in Ruhr; supported KPD opposition to March Action, representing it at Third World Congress; continued to voice public opposition to KPD policy; expelled January 1922 and joined KAG; rejoined CP 1923–4; rejoined SPD 1930; imprisoned by Nazis 1940; joined East German SED 1946.

**Mann, Tom** [1856–1941] – toolmaker; joined British Social Democratic Federation 1884; first president of Dockers Union after 1889; founding member and secretary of Independent Labour Party from 1894; lived in Australia and continued trade union work 1901–10; joined British SP 1917; secretary of Amalgamated Engineering Union 1919–21; founding member of CP 1920; Third World Congress delegate; chairman National Minority Movement 1924–9; remained in CP until his death.

**Manner, Kullervo** [1880–1939] – joined Finnish SP 1905; chairman of party 1917–18; headed Finnish soviet government 1918; after its fall, lived in Russia; general secretary Finnish CP 1918–29; arrested as Trotskyist 1935; died in prison.

**Manuilsky, Dmitry Zakharovich** [1883–1959] – member RSDLP 1903; emigrated 1907; co-editor with Trotsky of *Nashe Slovo* in Paris during War; joined Bolsheviks with Mezhrayontsi 1917; participant in October Revolution; member of Ukrainian soviet government 1920–2; delegate to Third World Congress from Ukrainian CP; member Presidium ECCI from 1924 and its secretary from 1928 until Comintern dissolution 1943; ideologist of Stalinism; continued to hold high posts in Ukraine through 1953.

**Marat, Jean-Paul** [1743–93] – radical Jacobin leader during French Revolution.

**March Action** – a general strike called by the VKPD on 24 March 1921 in an unsuccessful attempt to broaden struggles against police occupation of workers' strongholds in Central Germany; the term is also sometimes used to refer to the cycle of VKPD action initiatives from 16 March to the end of the month.

**Marković, Sima** [1888–1939] – joined Serbian SDP 1907 and became member of anarcho-syndicalist current within it; co-secretary of Yugoslav CP 1919 and its general secretary 1920–8; Third World Congress delegate; elected to ECCI 1924; expelled 1929; went to Soviet Union 1934 after being jailed in Yugoslavia; readmitted to CP 1935; arrested and executed during Stalin purges.

**Marshall**. See Bedacht, Max.

**Martov, Julius** [1873–1923] – joined Russian social-democratic movement early 1890s; leader of Mensheviks from 1903; pacifist during War; in left wing of Mensheviks during 1917 revolution; opponent of October Revolution; left Russia 1920; prominent member of Two-and-a-Half International.

**Marx, Karl** [1818–83] – co-founder with Engels of modern communist workers' movement; leader of Communist League 1847–52; co-author of *Communist Manifesto*; editor of *Neue Rheinische Zeitung* in 1848–9 German revolution; central leader of International Workingmen's Association [First International] 1864–76; published first volume of *Capital* 1867.

**Marxist Left Wing of the Czech Socialists.** See Left Socialist Party [Levice, Czechoslovakia].

**Maslow, Arkadi** [1891–1941] – emigrated to Germany from Russia as child; joined German CP 1919; party leader in Berlin, elected to CC November 1920; a leader of party's extreme left wing from 1921; Third World Congress delegate; co-leader of party with Ruth Fischer 1924–6; denounced as ultraleft; expelled 1926; a founder of Leninbund; emigrated 1933.

**Maximalists** – current led by Serrati in Italian SP that stressed importance of 'maximum' demands in party programme relating to achievement of socialism; in 1921–2 favourable to Comintern but unwilling to apply Twenty-One Conditions.

**Mayenburg, Herbert von** [1883–1954] – joined SPD 1906; German army 1914–18; USPD member from 1917, becoming regional party secretary; participated in 1920 fusion with KPD; editor of Rostok CP newspaper 1920–2; delegate to Third World Congress; later left KPD, demoralised by inner-party conflicts; moved to Hungary 1941 and West Germany 1947.

**Mazzoni, Nino** [1874–1954] – joined Italian SP around 1895; worked for agricultural workers union; opposed Italy's entry into War; joined reformist faction of PSI led by Turati 1919; member executive council of CGL 1921; joined Unitary Socialist Party [PSU] 1922; social-democratic deputy and senator after World War II.

**Mehring, Franz** [1846–1919] – became German radical democrat in 1870s, sympathetic to Lassalleanism; won to Marxism and joined SPD 1891; chief editor of *Leipziger Volkszeitung* 1902–7; a leading contributor to *Die Neue Zeit*; author of *History of German Social Democracy* and biography of Marx; close collaborator of Rosa Luxemburg from 1912; founding member of Spartacus current 1914–15, and CP 1918.

**Mensheviks** – originally minority ('Mensheviki') of RSDLP at its 1903 congress; opposed October Revolution; subsequently an opposition force to Soviet government.

**Merges, August** [1870–1945] – leader of Brunswick Workers' and Soldiers' Council 1918–19; delegated to represent KAPD at Comintern Second Congress but left as congress opened; joined KPD 1921; jailed several times by Nazis; died shortly after release from prison.

**Merino-Gracia, Ramón** [b. 1894] – schoolteacher; vice-president of Spanish Federation of Socialist Youth, expelled from Spanish SP April 1920; first general secretary of CP of Spain [PCE]; delegate to Second and Third World Congresses; elected to ECCI 1921; arrested 1924 for Communist activities; made deal with Spanish regime in order to gain freedom; later aligned with fascist-led trade unions under Franco regime.

**Merrheim, Alphonse** [1871–1925] – French syndicalist; leader of metalworkers union; led internationalist current in CGT during War; supported Zimmerwald movement until 1917, then allied with reformist forces in CGT; forced by illness to withdraw from union activity 1923.

**Mertens, Corneille** [1879–1951] – secretary of Belgian Federation of Labour from 1911; vice president of Amsterdam Federation 1919; president of International Labour Conference 1924 and 1936.

**Meshcheriakov, Nikolai Leonidovich** [1865–1942] – joined People's Will 1885; became Marxist 1894 after emigrating to Belgium; active in Russian Social-Democratic movement from 1901; Bolshevik leader in Moscow; exiled to Siberia 1906–17; from 1918 to 1924 a member of *Pravda* editorial board and of board of Tsentrosoiuz [Central Union of Consumers' Cooperatives]; reported on cooperative movement to Third World Congress; organisational secretary of Peasants' International [Krestintern] 1924–7; subsequently chairman of state publishing house [Gosizdat].

**Mesnil, Jacques** [1872–1940] – member of Belgian Workers' Party who became anarchist in 1890s; lived in Italy 1899–1914, then moving to France; became left-wing socialist 1918 and founding member of CP 1920; wrote for

*L'Humanité*; expelled from CP 1924; later collaborated with left syndicalists.

**Meyer, Ernst** [1887–1930] – joined SPD 1908; leader of Spartacus League during War; founding member of CP 1918; member of its Central Committee 1918–23 and 1926–9; party chair 1921–2; removed from central leadership by leftist majority 1924; reintegrated 1926; removed again for opposing Comintern's ultraleft line 1929.

**Meyer, Fritz** – German metal worker; member of Spartacus group during War; left CP with KAPD split 1919; one of its delegates to Third World Congress 1921.

**Michalak.** See Warszawski, Adolf.

**Michelis, Giuseppe de** [1875–1951] – Italian professor and ambassador of king of Italy; Italian representative to governing board of International Labour Organisation 1921–37 and was its chairman 1934–5.

**Mieves, Peter** [1897–1939] – joined KPD 1919, becoming a leader in Middle Rhine district; a leader of German railway union; delegate to Third World Congress; expelled from KPD 1926, accused of being police informer; active in anti-fascist activities, he reapplied for membership 1932; imprisoned by Nazis 1933–4; died of cancer.

**Milkić, Ilija** [1882–1968] – salesman; founding member of Serbian SDP 1903; elected to secretariat of Serbian Central Trade Union 1905; lived in France and Switzerland during war; attended Kienthal Conference as supporter of Zimmerwald Left 1916; supported October Revolution and moved to Soviet Russia 1919; joined Yugoslav Communist group in Russia; attended first three Comintern congresses; moved to Vienna 1922; returned to Yugoslavia 1926 and ceased political activity.

**Millerand, Alexandre** [1859–1943] – initially a leader of French SP; took ministerial post in cabinet 1899 and then moved to right of bourgeois political spectrum; French premier 1920; president 1920–4.

**Milyukov, Pavel Nikolaevich** [1859–1943] – Russian liberal politician and historian; leader of Cadet party under tsar; as foreign minister under Provisional Government, favoured continuation of War March–May 1917; political adviser to Whites in Civil War, then emigrated.

**Minor, Robert** [Ballister] [1884–1952] – political cartoonist; joined American SP 1907; moved toward anarcho-syndicalism by 1912; went to Soviet Russia 1918 and was won to communism; joined US CP 1920; Third World Congress delegate; elected to CC 1922; editor of *Daily Worker*; remained a leader of CP until his death.

**Misiano, Francesco** [1884–1936] – joined Italian SP 1907; active in railway union; internationalist during War; jailed in Berlin for work with Spartacists 1919; worked with Bordiga to create CP in Italy; member of CP executive 1921; Third World Congress delegate; forced into exile November 1921; leader of International Workers' Aid 1922–36; accused of Trotskyism 1935–6; died in Moscow.

**Modigliani, Giuseppe** [1872–1947] – joined Italian SP 1894; organised national federation of glass workers; parliamentary deputy 1913–26; attended Zimmerwald and Kienthal Conferences 1915–16; opposed formation of CP 1921; joined reformist Unitary Socialist Party [PSU] 1922; a leader of social democrats until death.

**Monatte, Pierre** [1881–1960] – French revolutionary syndicalist; member of CGT directing committee 1904; founded *La Vie ouvrière* 1909; worked with Trotsky in internationalist opposition to War; won to communism 1919 and became a secretary of Committee for the Third International; imprisoned nine months 1920; joined CP 1923; expelled for opposing anti-Trotsky campaign 1924; founder and editor of *La Révolution prolétarienne* 1925–39 and 1945–7; active in resistance to Nazi occupation.

**Morgan.** See Knight, Joseph R.

**Moscow-Moskau-Moscou** – daily organ of Third World Congress published in English, German, and French, 25 May–14 July 1921.

**Müller, Hermann** [1876–1931] – joined SPD 1893; member party executive committee 1906–31; chauvinist position during War; SPD co-chairman 1919; as German foreign minister in 1919–20 was one of German signatories to Versailles Treaty; chancellor, 1920, 1928–30.

**Müller, Richard** [1880–1943] – joined SPD 1906 and USPD 1917; metalworker; organised Berlin revolutionary stewards; leader of workers' and soldiers' councils during November 1918 revolution; joined CP in fusion 1920; member of CC; supported Levi 1921; left KPD 1922 and joined KAG but did not rejoin SPD; later withdrew from political activity.

**Muna, Alois** [1886–1943] – joined Czech SDP 1903; a leader of Czech Communist group formed among prisoners of war in Russia; leader of Czechoslovak CP in Kladno from 1919; arrested for Communist activities 1921 and elected honorary president of Third World Congress; alternate member ECCI 1922; full member 1924; expelled as 'rightist' 1929; subsequently led 'Leninist Opposition'.

**Münnich, Ferenc** [1886–1967] – Hungarian prisoner in Russia 1915–18; commander in Hungarian red army 1919; subsequently in CP exile leadership in Vienna; carried out Comintern assignments, including in Germany March 1921; based in Russia 1922–45; fought in International Brigades in Spain 1936–9 and in Soviet Red Army 1941–5; held high government posts in Hungary from 1945, including president 1958–61.

**Münzenberg, Willi** [1889–1940] – factory worker; joined Socialist Youth of Germany 1906 and (from 1910) Switzerland; secretary of left-wing Socialist Youth International 1915–19; member of Zimmerwald Left during War; founding member German CP 1918; secretary of Communist Youth International 1919–21; Third World Congress delegate; leader of International Workers' Aid and of vast Communist cultural enterprise from 1921; opposed Stalin ultra-left course 1932; refused to go to USSR during Stalin purges; expelled from CP 1937; organised anti-Stalinist communists in France 1939; victim of political assassination, with probable Stalinist involvement.

**Mussolini, Benito** [1883–1945] – former leader of Italian SP left wing and editor of *Avanti*; took chauvinist, pro-war position and was expelled from SP 1915; founded Fascist movement 1919; Fascist dictator of Italy 1922–43; executed by Resistance forces.

**Nam Man-ch'un** [b. 1892] – Korean living in Russia before 1917 revolution; fought in Red Army during civil war; formed first Korean Communist Party in Irkutsk, Siberia, 1920; Third World Congress delegate from Irkutsk faction of Korean CP; member ECCI 1921–2; in Shanghai branch 1926.

**Napoleon Bonaparte** [Napoleon I] [1769–1821] – French general; military dictator 1799–1804; emperor 1804–15.

**National Confederation of Labour** [CNT, Spain] – anarcho-syndicalist federation founded 1911; 800,000 members by end of 1920; affiliated to Comintern 1919 and to RILU 1921–2, banned 1923.

**National Labour Secretariat** [NAS, Netherlands] – founded 1893 as small left-wing rival to major Dutch union federation; 36,000 members in 1921; attended RILU founding congress 1921; affiliated to it 1925–7.

**Nationalist Party** [Australia] – formed in 1917 from a merger between the right-wing Commonwealth Liberal Party, which had ruled twice since 1908, and a pro-conscription breakaway from the Labour Party; the Nationalists held office 1917–23.

**Němec, Antonín** [1858–1926] – joined workers' movement 1876; Czech SDP party chairman and editor in chief of daily *Právo lidu* from 1897; leading figure in Second International; helped lead struggle against Marxist wing of party that became CP; honorary SDP chairman at time of death.

*Die Neue Zeit* [New Times] – theoretical journal of SPD published in Stuttgart, monthly 1883–90, weekly 1890–1923; edited by Kautsky up to 1917.

**Neumann, Paul** [1888–1934?] – metalworker; SPD member when very young; joined USPD 1917; leader of revolutionary shop stewards 1918;

delegate to first All-German Congress of Workers' and Soldiers' Councils December 1918; joined KPD in 1920 fusion; opposed March Action 1921; attended Third World Congress as representative of KPD opposition; signed appeal opposing Comintern policies in party; expelled January 1922 and joined KAG, participating in its fusions with USPD and SPD.

**Nikolaeva, Klavdiia Ivanovna** [1893–1944] – Bolshevik from 1909; became editor of *Rabotnitsa* [Working Woman] after February Revolution; a leader of First All-Russian Congress of Women Workers and Peasants 1918; Third World Congress delegate; head of women workers' section of CP CC 1924–6; demoted for supporting Leningrad and United Oppositions 1925–7; led agitation section of CC 1930–3; became member of Presidium of Supreme Soviet 1937.

**Noblemaire, Gustave** [1832–1924] – longtime general manager of Paris, Lyon, & Mediterranean Railway.

**Nobs, Ernst** [1886–1957] – member of Swiss SDP left wing during War; active in Zimmerwald movement; opponent of Comintern, active in SDP right wing during 1920s; editor of *Volksrecht* Zurich 1915–35; president of Switzerland 1949.

**Norwegian Labour Party** – founded 1887; left wing won majority 1918; affiliated to Comintern 1919; 97,000 members end of 1920, including union and individual affiliation; majority left Comintern in 1923, with minority founding CP.

**Noske, Gustav** [1868–1946] – a leader of SPD right wing; minister responsible for German armed forces 1919–20; organised violent suppression of workers' uprisings in Berlin and central Germany in early months of 1919; president of province of Hanover 1920–33; jailed by Nazis 1944–5.

**Olberg, Oda** [1872–1955] – German-born journalist and socialist activist; moved to Italy 1896; correspondent in Rome for German *Vorwärts*.

**One Big Union** [Australia] – industrial union concept spread in Australia by IWW from 1908; picked up broadly by militant unionists; Workers' Industrial Union of Australia formed 1918; Australasian Workers' Union formed 1921.

**One Big Union** [Canada] – militant union formed in Western Canada 1919; membership reached 40,000–70,000 by late 1919; 5,000 members 1921; joined Canadian Labor Congress 1956.

*One Big Union Monthly* – published in Chicago by IWW 1919–21; succeeded by *Industrial Pioneer* February 1921.

*L'Ordine nuovo* [New order] – Italian Communist newspaper in Turin founded 1919; led by Gramsci, Tasca, Terracini, and Togliatti; published until 1925.

**Orgesch** [Organisation Escherich] – armed counterrevolutionary group founded in Munich in August 1920 by Georg Escherich, with claimed membership of 300,000; officially disbanded June 1921, although many of its units remained active, especially in Bavaria.

**Oudegeest, Jan** [1870–1950] – leader of Dutch railroad workers' union from 1898; secretary of Amsterdam International 1919–27; chairman Dutch Social-Democratic Workers' Party [SDAP] 1927–34; member of ILO Governing Board 1919–28.

*L'Ouvrier communiste* [The Communist Worker] – bimonthly newspaper of Belgian CP; founded 1 March 1920.

**Overstraeten, Edouard** ['War'] **van** [1891–1981] – painter, founding member Belgian CP; its general secretary and member of ECCI 1921; delegate to Third and Fourth World Congresses; jailed for opposing French/Belgian occupation of Ruhr 1923; led Belgian CC majority in opposing expulsion of Trotsky and Zinoviev 1927; expelled 1928; joined Left Opposition but soon withdrew from political activity.

**Paish, George** [1867–1957] – British liberal economist and author; assistant editor (1894–1900) and then co-editor (1900–16) of *The Statist*; adviser to Ministry of Finance; author of numerous books.

**Pannekoek, Anton** [1873–1960] – joined Dutch Social-Democratic Workers' Party [SDAP] 1899; helped found *De*

*Tribune* 1907; expelled from SDAP and was founding member of left-wing SDP 1909, which became CP in 1918; theoretician of left-wing communism and of German KAPD; his current broke from Comintern 1921; worked with ultraleft groups in Netherlands and US; prominent astronomer.

**People's Party** [Germany] – party formed 1865, advocating federative German state and opposing Prussian hegemony; lost influence to SPD after the latter's formation in 1869.

**Pétain, Philippe** [1856–1951] – French general; pro-Nazi dictator of French state 1940–4; convicted of treason and jailed 1945.

*Le Peuple* [The People] – founded 1848; became daily organ of Belgian Workers' Party.

**Pieck, Wilhelm** [1876–1960] – joined SPD 1895, becoming a leader in Bremen; a secretary of central party school in Berlin 1910–14; joined USPD 1917 and Spartacus League 1918; member of CP CC 1919–46; member of ECCI 1928–43; fled Germany 1933; elected chairman of CP Central Committee 1935; lived in Moscow until 1945; president of German Democratic Republic 1949–60.

**Pilsudski, Józef** [1867–1935] – a leader of Polish SP [PPS] 1893–1916 and of fight for Polish independence; president of Poland 1918–22; launched war against Soviet Russia 1920; led coup d'état 1926; played leading role in Polish government 1926–35.

**Pirelli, Alberto** [1882–1971] – Italian industrialist; delegate to International Labour Office in Geneva 1920–2; member League of Nations economic committee 1923–7; minister of state under Mussolini 1938.

**Pivio, Leo.** See Laukki, Leo.

**Plekhanov, Georgy Valentinovich** [1856–1918] – pioneer of Marxism in Russia; founder of Emancipation of Labour group 1883; influential Marxist theorist; supported Mensheviks after 1903; took chauvinist position during War; opposed October Revolution 1917.

**Poale Zion** [Workers of Zion] – socialist Zionist organisation formed beginning 1897, with branches in eastern Europe, Austria, Palestine, and elsewhere; in Russia majority opposed October Revolution; left wing split in 1919 and formed Jewish CP–Poale Zion, some of whose members joined Russian CP 1922; right-wing Poale Zion later became integrated into Israeli politics.

**Podrecca, Guido** [1864–1923] – joined Italian socialist movement early 1890s; prominent socialist journalist and editor; elected municipal councillor in Rome and parliamentary deputy 1907; supported Italian war in Libya; expelled from SP 1912; Mussolini collaborator and active Fascist from 1919.

**Pogány, József** [1886–1937] – Hungarian teacher and journalist; joined SDP 1905; joined CP in March 1919 merger; president of Soldiers' Council in Budapest during Hungarian soviet regime 1919; emigrated 1919 to Vienna, then Moscow; became ECCI functionary; part of ECCI mission to Germany led by Béla Kun that helped instigate March Action 1921; Third World Congress delegate; became de facto leader of US party as John Pepper 1922; held high posts in ECCI 1925–9; arrested and executed during Stalin frame-up purges.

**Polano, Luigi** [1897–1984] – joined Italian socialist youth 1914, becoming its secretary 1917; participated in founding congress of Communist Youth International 1918; member of its leadership committee 1919–21; founding member of CP and elected to its CC; delegate to Second and Third World Congresses; left Italy 1925 and moved to Soviet Russia; returned to Italy 1945 and became Communist deputy.

**Polish Socialist Party** [PPS] – founded 1892–3; nationalist in orientation; right-wing faction adopted chauvinist position during War and supported Pilsudski dictatorship in 1926; left-wing faction split in 1906, joining in creating CP in 1918.

*Politiken* [*Folkets Dagblad Politiken*] [People's Political Daily] – daily organ of Swedish CP published in Stockholm; edited by Zeth Höglund; became organ of SP after 1929 CP split.

**Popov, Dimitri** [1878–1924] – active in socialist student movement; became leader of Bulgarian Tesniaki Party, which became CP in 1919; delegate to Third World Congress and elected to ECCI 1921; participated in 1923 Bulgaria insurrection, escaping to Vienna.

*Le Populaire* [The People] – Paris daily reflecting views of SP right wing; published 1918–37.

*Poslednye novosti* [Latest News] – daily paper published by Cadet Party in exile in Paris 1920–40; edited by P.N. Milyukov.

*Pravda* [Truth] – central daily organ of Russian CP, published in Moscow; 250,000 circulation in 1921; began publication as Bolshevik newspaper 1912.

*Právo lidu* [People's Right] – Czech Social-Democratic newspaper published 1893–1938, 1945–8; became organ of right-wing Social-Democratic party after 1920 split.

**Pressemane, Adrien** [1879–1929] – joined French socialist movement 1897; SP parliamentary deputy 1914–28; centrist position during War; voiced support for October Revolution but opposed affiliation to Comintern at Tours and became member of dissident SP.

*Der Proletarier* [The Proletarian] – theoretical monthly of KAPD 1920–7; published in Berlin.

**Proost, Jan** [I. Jansen] [1882–1942] – artist; helped smuggle Marxist literature into Germany during War; founding member Dutch CP 1918; CP's representative in Moscow 1920–3; Third World Congress delegate; left CP with Wijnkoop/Van Ravesteyn group 1926; shot by Nazi troops during occupation.

**PSI**. See Italian Socialist Party.

**PSU** – Unitary Socialist Party (Italy).

**Pyatakov, Yuri Leonidovich** [1890–1937] – joined RSDLP 1910; lived in Switzerland and then Sweden 1914–17; after October Revolution member of government of soviet Ukraine; became deputy head of State Planning Commission 1922 and then deputy chairman of Supreme Council of National Economy; member Left Opposition 1923–7; capitulated 1927; condemned at Moscow frame-up trial and executed.

**Quelch, Thomas** [1886–1954] – member of Social-Democratic Federation and then British SP; founding member of CP; delegate to Second and Third World Congresses; elected to ECCI 1920; member of CP CC 1923–5; *Communist International* editorial staff 1920–31; official in construction workers' union 1924–53; withdrew from CP toward end of life.

**Rabier, Fernand** [1855–1933] – French Radical; parliamentary deputy 1888–1919; senator 1920–33.

**Radek, Karl** [1885–1939] – joined revolutionary movement in Austrian Poland before 1905; a leader of left wing of Polish and German workers' movement; internationalist during War, collaborator of Lenin and supporter of Zimmerwald Left during War; joined Bolsheviks 1917; member of Bolshevik CC 1917–24; vice-commissar for foreign affairs 1918; Bolshevik and Soviet emissary to Germany 1918–19; member ECCI 1920–4 and its Presidium 1921–4; reporter at Third World Congress; with Trotsky, a leader of Left Opposition in Russian CP and Comintern from 1923; expelled and exiled 1927; capitulated 1929; Soviet journalist 1930–7; arrested 1936; convicted in Moscow trial 1937; killed by police agent in prison.

**Radical Socialist Party** [France] – major left bourgeois party of France, formed 1901.

**Rahja, Eino A.** [1886–1936] – joined RSDLP 1903; participant in revolutionary movement in Russia and Finland; commanded Red Guard detachment during Finnish revolution 1918; became member of Finnish CP CC 1918; attended First World Congress; opposed Kuusinen leadership and was removed from CC 1927; expelled from party 1930; died of illnesses.

**Rahja, Jukka A.** [1887–1920] – Finnish Bolshevik; participated in 1905 revolution in Russia; member of Petrograd Bolshevik committee 1917; sent to Finland to organise Red Guard during 1918 revolution; returned to Soviet Russia after its defeat; attended First and Second World Congresses; assassinated in Petrograd August 1920 by rival group of Finnish Communist exiles.

**Railroad Workers' Association** [SFI] – Italian union founded 1907; led by anarchist-socialist coalition; joined CGL 1925.

**Rákosi, Mátyás** [1892–1971] – joined Hungarian SP 1910; became Communist while prisoner of war in Russia 1918; member of Hungarian soviet government 1919, forced into exile after its fall; member of ECCI secretariat 1921–4; ECCI representative at Livorno Congress of Italian SP 1921; Third World Congress delegate; captured during mission in Hungary and jailed 1925–40; lived in Russia 1940–4; head of Hungarian CP and a central leader of government 1945–56; organised Stalin purges in Hungary; expelled from CP 1962 for his association with Stalinism; died in USSR.

**Rakovsky, Christian** [1873–1941] – born in Bulgaria; driven into exile 1890; doctor; active in socialist movement in several European countries; cofounder of Romanian SP; took part in Zimmerwald Conference 1915; joined Bolsheviks in Russia 1917; leader of Ukrainian soviet government 1919–23; attended first four Comintern congresses; with Trotsky, leader of Left Opposition in Russian CP 1923–34; expelled and exiled 1927; capitulated 1934; rearrested 1937; convicted with Bukharin in frame-up trial 1938; executed.

**Rathenau, Walter** [1867–1922] – German capitalist and political leader; organiser of Germany's economy during War; became minister of reconstruction May 1921; foreign minister January 1922; advocated collaboration with Entente powers but also negotiated Treaty of Rapallo with Soviet Russia; targeted as Jew by right-wing forces; assassinated 24 June 1922.

**Red Aid** – formed early 1921 as German committees to aid political prisoners; International Red Aid [MOPR] formed November 1922.

**Red International of Labour Unions** [RILU, Profintern] – founded at 1921 congress attended by Communist and syndicalist forces, representing more than 18 million members; formally dissolved 1937.

**Reed, John** [1887–1920] – journalist; covered labour struggles and Mexican Revolution; in Russia during October Revolution; wrote *Ten Days That Shook the World*; after his return became active in left wing of American SP and was founding member of Communist Labor Party; returned to Russia to represent CLP at Second World Congress; became member of ECCI; attended Baku Congress of Peoples of the East; died of typhus contracted during trip.

**Rees, Alf G.** [b. 1884] – railway unionist; Third World Congress and RILU congress delegate from Australia.

**Reich, Yakov** (Thomas) [1886–1956] – born in Galicia; active in 1905 Russian revolution; in Switzerland from about 1914; edited Soviet information bulletin there 1918–19; headed Comintern Western European secretariat in Berlin from 1919; withdrew from Comintern work 1925; supported Brandler opposition; exiled from Germany 1933; settled in New York 1938.

**Reichenbach, Bernhard** [Seemann] [1888–1975] – socialist student leader in Germany; conscripted during War; joined USPD and Spartacus League 1917; founding member of CP; expelled with ultraleft 1919, became leader of KAPD and editor of *Kommunistische Arbeiterzeitung*; KAPD representative at ECCI and Third World Congress 1921; part of split from KAPD March 1922; rejoined SPD 1925; joined Socialist Workers' Party [SAP] in 1931–2; escaped to Britain following Hitler's rise to power.

**Reicher, Gustaw** [Rwal] [1900–38] – joined SDKPiL 1917; member of Polish CP 1918; member of its Political Bureau in Moscow 1920; worked in Poland and Germany; Third World Congress delegate; imprisoned in Poland 1925–8; worked for ECCI in USSR 1928–9; member of International Brigade in Spanish Civil War; recalled to Moscow, arrested, and shot.

**Reiland, Edy** [1896–1967] – member of Luxembourg SP during War; elected to national leadership of Socialist Youth December 1919; organised 1921 founding of CP; became CP general secretary January 1921 and its delegate to Comintern; Third World Congress delegate; accused of financial mismanagement of Comintern funds, excluded from leadership February 1922; resigned from CP; supported Trotskyist movement 1929; later abandoned political activity.

**Renaudel, Pierre** [1871–1935] – leader of right wing of French SP; social patriot during War; parliamentary deputy 1914–19, 1924–35; opposed SP affiliation to Comintern and became part of dissident SP; led 'neo-socialist' split from SP 1933.

**Renner, Karl** [1870–1950] – right-wing leader of Austrian SDP; Austrian chancellor 1918–20, 1945; president 1945–50.

**Renoult, Daniel** [1880–1958] – joined French SP 1906, member CP directing committee 1920–2; editor *L'Internationale* 1921–2; led independent 'Centre-Right' current in party 1922; imprisoned by republican government February 1940 and held in jail by Vichy regime until freed by anti-Nazi resistance July 1944; active in CP until his death.

**Reuter, Ernst** [Friesland] [1889–1953] – teacher; joined SPD 1912; won to communism while prisoner of war in Russia; leader of pro-Soviet prisoners and of Volga German workers' commune; member of German CP Zentrale 1919; became CP general secretary after Levi's expulsion; Third World Congress delegate; during late 1921 moved toward Levi's position; expelled January 1922; rejoined SPD; jailed by Nazis 1933, in emigration 1935–46; mayor of West Berlin 1948–53.

**Revolutionary Union Minority** [France] – reference to left-wing minority in CGT; split consummated December 1921; minority founded Unitary CGT [CGTU], which affiliated to RILU and had 350,000 members by mid-1922.

**Riboldi, Ezio** [1878–1965] – joined Italian SP 1898; supported Maximalist wing of party at Livorno; PSI representative at Third World Congress; a leader of pro-Comintern faction of PSI October 1921; joined CP in 1924 fusion; imprisoned by Fascist regime 1926–33; expelled from CP 1934 for his pardon request; interned 1940 in concentration camp; collaborated with Fascist newspaper *La Verità* edited by Bombacci 1940–3.

**Riehs, Jakob** [b. 1882] – metalworker; founding member of Austrian CP November 1918; Third World Congress delegate; worked in Soviet Union during 1920s; expelled from Austrian CP 1929; joined SP after 1945.

**Rigola, Rinaldo** [1868–1954] – joined Italian Workers' Party 1886 and SP 1893, becoming part of its reformist wing; general secretary of CGL union federation from its founding in 1906; a founder of reformist Unitary Socialist Party [PSU] 1922.

**RILU.** See Red International of Labour Unions.

**Ríos, Fernando de los** [1879–1949] – university teacher; joined Spanish Socialist Workers' Party 1919; elected to its executive 1920; visited Soviet Russia 1920; opposed affiliation to Comintern; opposed Primo de Rivera dictatorship 1923–30; jailed 1930–1; minister 1931 and 1933; ambassador for Spanish republic in Paris and New York during Civil War; taught in New York after fall of republic.

**Robespierre, Maximilien** [1758–94] – Jacobin leader of French revolutionary government 1793–4; overthrown and executed in Thermidorean Reaction.

**Roland-Holst, Henriette** [1869–1952] – Dutch poet and writer; joined Dutch socialist movement 1897; belonged to left wing of Social-Democratic Workers' Party [SDAP]; joined left-wing SDP 1916; member of Zimmerwald Left during War; founding member of Dutch CP 1918; Third World Congress delegate; left CP 1927; continued to write as socialist; active in resistance during Nazi occupation; advocate of colonial freedom until last years.

**Rosenfeld, Kurt** [1877–1943] – left-wing member of SPD; Berlin city councilman 1910–20; founding member USPD 1917; member of Reichstag 1920–33; opposed Comintern affiliation and remained in rump USPD; an opponent of 1922 USPD-SPD merger, but joined SPD on his own; expelled 1931 as part of left-wing split; founding member Socialist Workers' Party [SAP]; resigned 1932; emigrated to US 1933.

**Rosmer, Alfred** [1877–1964] – proofreader; French revolutionary syndicalist; leader in France of internationalist opposition to War; represented Committee for the Third International at Second World Congress; member ECCI in Moscow 1920–1; Third World Congress delegate; played leading role in founding of RILU; expelled from French CP for opposition to anti-Trotsky campaign 1924; organiser of Left Opposition in France 1929–31; broke with Trotsky 1931 but collaborated with him and with Movement for Fourth International after 1936.

*Die Rote Fahne* [The Red Flag] – daily newspaper of German CP; began publication 9 November 1918; founded by Karl Liebknecht and Rosa Luxemburg.

**Roy, Manabendra Nath** [1887–1954] – active in Indian independence movement from 1910; went abroad 1915 on mission for independence movement; won to Marxism in US 1917; participated in founding Mexican CP 1919; worked in Comintern Far Eastern Bureau and founded CP of India in exile in Tashkent 1920; delegate to Second through Sixth World Congresses; member ECCI 1922–7; Comintern representative to China 1927; expelled for 'opportunism' 1929; worked with anti-Stalinist opposition led by Brandler; returned to India 1930; led current critical of Comintern sectarianism on national question; jailed 1931–6; joined Congress Party 1936; founded Radical Democratic Party 1940.

**RSDLP.** See Russian Social-Democratic Labour Party.

*Rudé právo* [Red Rights] – daily organ of Czechoslovak CP published in Prague; began publication 21 September 1920.

**Rudnyánszky, Endre** [1885–1943] – lawyer; won to Bolshevism as Austro-Hungarian prisoner in Russia; took part in formation of Hungarian Communist group in Russia; representative of Hungarian soviet republic in Moscow 1919; took part in First and Second World Congresses; disappeared from Soviet Russia with Comintern funds; expelled from Hungarian CP 1921; returned to USSR 1926 and served fifteen years in prison.

**Rühle, Otto** [1874–1943] – joined German SPD 1896; Reichstag deputy 1912–18; second deputy to oppose war credits after Liebknecht; a founder of Spartacus group and of CP; part of October 1919 split that established KAPD; represented it in Moscow summer 1920; expelled late October 1920 and founded General Workers' Union; rejoined SPD 1923; helped defend Trotsky against Stalin frame-up.

**Russian Social-Democratic Labour Party** [RSDLP] – founded 1898; split into Bolshevik and Menshevik wings 1903.

**Russian Workers' Federation of South America** – communist-anarchist organisation based among Russian immigrants in Argentina.

**Rydygier, Aleksander Juliusz** [Kamocki] [1892–1942] – teacher; originally member of Polish SP [PPS], then joined SDKPiL 1914; founding member Polish CP; Third World Congress delegate; CP member of Parliament 1930–5; helped refound Polish CP after its dissolution by Stalin 1942; died at Auschwitz.

**Sachs.** See Schwab, Alexander.

**Samoilova, Konkordia Nikolaevna** [1876–1921] – born in Irkutsk, Russia; active in revolutionary movement 1897; joined RSDLP 1903; co-editor of *Pravda* and *Rabotnitsa* [Woman Worker] 1912; co-editor *Kommunistka* [Communist Woman] 1918; chair of Petersburg commission for work among women after 1917.

**Sandgren, John** – Swedish immigrant to US; anarcho-syndicalist; editor of Swedish-language IWW newspaper *Nya Världen* 1919; editor of *One Big Union Monthly* 1919–20, dismissed from it by IWW leadership because of attacks on Soviet Russia.

**Sankey John** [1866–1948] – British politician and jurist; Conservative, later with Labour Party; headed official commission of inquiry into conditions in coal mines 1919; recommended their nationalisation.

**Sarekat Islam** [Islamic Association] – first mass nationalist political party in Indonesia; founded 1912; 350,000 members by 1916; Communist forces participated until their exclusion in March 1921; organisation declined after left-wing departure.

**Schaffner, Erwin** [1883–1942] – member of Swiss SDP 1907–20; a founding leader of Swiss CP 1921; editor of *Basler Vörwarts* 1920–2; Third World Congress delegate; member ECCI 1926–8; moved to Soviet Union 1926 and worked for Comintern; sympathised with Left Opposition 1926–8; suffered political harassment but escaped purges in 1930s; died in USSR.

**Scheflo, Olav** [1883–1943] – joined Norwegian Labour Party 1905; a leader of left opposition in unions 1911; became editor-in-chief of central party organ *Social Democrat* 1918; supported Labour Party affiliation to Comintern; delegate to Third and Fourth World Congresses; member ECCI 1921–7; stayed with Comintern when Labour Party split from it 1923; criticised CP's stance toward Labour Party and quit CP 1928; rejoined Labour Party 1929; defended Trotsky during his stay in Norway 1935–6.

**Scheidemann, Philipp** [1865–1939] – joined German Social Democracy 1883; member SPD executive 1911; co-chair of Reichstag fraction 1913; social chauvinist during War; led in suppressing workers' revolution 1918–19; German prime minister February–June 1919; forced by Nazis into emigration 1933.

**Schmidt, Robert** [1864–1943] joined German Social Democracy 1883; a *Vorwärts* editor 1893–1903; member of General Commission of German Trade Unions 1902–19; supported German war effort 1914–18; minister of food 1919; economics minister 1919–20, 1921–2, and 1929–30; vice-chancellor and minister of reconstruction 1923.

**Schober, Johann** [1874–1932] – president of imperial police in Austria 1918; Austrian prime minister 1921–2, 1929–30.

**Schulze, Ernst** [1855–1932] – official in German trade-union federation [ADGB]; SPD member.

**Schwab, Alexander** [Sachs] [1887–1943] – printer; joined German SPD 1907; member of Spartacus League and founder of CP; a founder of KAPD 1920; Third World Congress delegate; left KAPD 1922 and later rejoined SPD.

**SDKPiL** [Social Democracy of the Kingdom of Poland and Lithuania] – founded 1893; best-known leader was Rosa Luxemburg; merged into Polish CP December 1918.

**SDP** – Social-Democratic Party.

**SED** [Socialist Unity Party of Germany] – formed by fusion of KPD and SPD in Soviet-occupied East Germany 1926; governing party of German Democratic Republic 1949–1989.

**Second International** – founded 1889 as international association of workers parties; collapsed at outbreak of World War I; pro-capitalist right wing reconstituted as Bern International 1919; merged with centrist Two-and-a-Half International 1923 and became Labour and Socialist International.

**Seemann.** See Reichenbach, Bernhard.

**Sellier, Louis** [1885–1978] – joined French SP 1909; member CP executive 1921; supported centre current; CP general secretary 1923–4; expelled as 'rightist' 1929; led dissident-communist current 1930–7; rejoined SP 1937; voted powers to Pétain 1940; served in municipal offices during German occupation; expelled from SP 1944.

**Sembat, Marcel** [1862–1922] – elected French socialist deputy 1893, becoming leading figure in parliamentary group; member of SP National Council from 1905; supported French war effort, becoming minister of public works 1914–16; opposed SP affiliation to Comintern and remained in Dissident party after 1920 split.

**Semyonov, Grigorii Mikhailovich** [1890–1946] – Russian officer in World War I; leader of White Armies in civil war in Trans-Baikal region 1918–20; driven into exile 1921; during World War II worked with Japanese in north China; captured by Soviet army in Manchuria and executed.

**Serbian Socialist Party.** See Social-Democratic Party of Serbia.

**Serge, Victor** [1890–1947] – born in Belgium to Russian revolutionary exiles; wrote for anarchist press from 1908; jailed in France 1912–17; arrived in Russia late 1918 and joined Bolsheviks; translated, wrote, and published for Comintern from 1919; in Germany 1922–3; supported Left Opposition led by Trotsky from 1923; expelled from

CP 1928; jailed 1933; lived in Belgium and France from 1936 and Mexico from 1941.

**Serrati, Giacinto Menotti** [1872–1926] – joined Italian socialist movement 1892; leader of Maximalist left wing of Italian SP; internationalist during War; led SP in affiliation to Comintern 1919; opposed break with reformists and remained head of SP after CP formation 1921; led SP's pro-Comintern current into fusion with CP 1924.

**Severing, Carl** [1875–1952] – joined SPD 1893; Prussian SPD member of Reichstag 1907–11; supported German war effort 1914–18; Prussian minister of interior 1920–6, 1930–2.

**Shablin, Nikolai** [1881–1925] – member of Bulgarian Tesniaki Party, which became CP in 1919; member of its CC; Second World Congress delegate; elected to ECCI 1920; carried out underground work in Bulgaria after 1923; assassinated by police.

**al-Sharif, Sayyid Ahmad** [1875–1933] – Senussi leader of struggle to drive French out of Chad and Italians out of Libya; fought British forces in Egypt during War; left Libya 1918 and took refugee in Turkey and later Arabia.

**Shatskin, Lazar Abramovich** [1902–1937] – joined Bolshevik Party 1917; Communist Youth League first secretary 1919–22; first secretary of CYI 1919–21; delegate to Second through Fifth World Congresses; supported Stalin in late 1920s; barred from political activity for oppositional views 1931; expelled from CP and arrested 1935; tortured and shot.

**Shlyapnikov, Aleksandr Gavrilovich** [1885–1937] – joined RSDLP 1901; active in European labour movement in exile 1908–14; in 1915–16 organised Bolsheviks' Russian Bureau and travelled abroad on political assignment; member of Petrograd Bolshevik Committee during 1917; Soviet commissar of labour 1917–18; leader of Workers' Opposition 1920–2; expelled from party 1933; arrested 1935 and later executed.

**Shop Stewards** [Britain] – originated in Scotland 1915; grew during wartime strike wave; advanced revolutionary demands opposed to official trade-union leadership's no-strike policy; declined after 1918, with many militants joining CP.

**Shumiatsky, Boris Zakharovich** [1886–1938] – railway worker; joined Bolsheviks after 1905 revolution; helped organise Comintern Secretariat for the Far East in Irkutsk 1920–1, representing it at Third World Congress; Soviet ambassador to Iran 1922–5; head of Soviet film industry 1930–7; executed during Stalin purges.

**Shumsky, Oleksander** [1890–1946] – member of Ukrainian Socialist Revolutionary Party 1908; a leader of its left wing that formed Borotbist Party 1918; member of Ukrainian military revolutionary committee during Civil War; joined Russian CP 1920; Third World Congress delegate; Ukrainian commissar of education 1924–7; expelled in 1933 and jailed; released 1946 but died under mysterious circumstances.

**Sievers, Max** [1887–1944] – USPD member and editor of *Freiheit* 1918; joined German CP in 1920 fusion; became an editor of *Rote Fahne* and a secretary for Zentrale; relieved from position for criticising March Action April 1921; left CP April 1921; rejoined SPD and became president of Society for Free Thought; living underground in northern France from 1940, he was captured by Gestapo and executed.

**Šilfs, Janis** [1891–1921] – member of Latvian Bolsheviks from 1908; CC member of Latvian SDP from 1914, renamed CP 1919; a secretary of soviet Latvian government January 1919; following its overthrow later that year he was CP secretary and editor of its newspaper *Cina*; arrested by secret police and shot.

**Sirola, Yrjö E.** [1876–1936] – joined Finnish SDP 1903; SDP general secretary 1905–6; parliamentary deputy 1907–9, 1917; in charge of foreign affairs for soviet Finnish government 1918; fled to Russia after its fall; helped found Finnish CP 1918; Third World Congress delegate; elected to ECCI 1921; Comintern representative in US 1925–7; commissar for education in Karelian SSR 1928–31; member of nationalities committee of Comintern 1931–6.

**Skalák, Josef** [1874–1968] – Czech socialist from 1890s; founding member of Czechoslovak CP 1921; editor of *Rudé právo* from 1920; member of CP executive committee 1921–5; Third World Congress delegate; expelled from CP 1929.

**Small Bureau** [Engeres Büro] – body elected by ECCI following Second World Congress; became ECCI Presidium in September 1921.

**Šmeral, Bohumir** [1880–1941] – member of Czech Social Democracy from 1897; elected to its Central Executive Committee 1909; held chauvinist positions during the war; SDP chairman 1914–17; leader of Marxist Left from 1919; head of Czechoslovak CP 1921; attended Third World Congress; member ECCI 1921–35; in Moscow 1926–35; member International Control Commission 1935–41.

**Smillie, Robert** [1857–1940] – president of Scottish Miners' Federation 1894–1918 and 1922–8; founding member Independent Labour Party 1893; president of Miners' Federation of Great Britain 1912–21; leading figure in campaign for nationalisation of coal industry; Labour Party member of Parliament 1923–9.

**Smythe, Norah** [1874–1963] – worked with Sylvia Pankhurst in women's suffrage movement; treasurer of Workers' Socialist Federation 1916; member British CP; elected to Women's Secretariat of Communist Women's Movement at its Second Conference 1921; Third World Congress delegate; left CP later in year.

**Social-Democratic Party of Finland** – formed 1899 as Finnish Labour Party; became SDP 1903; internationalist position during War; after working-class defeat in 1918 civil war, left wing in exile founded CP; within Finland left-wing split established Socialist Workers' Party May 1920.

**Social-Democratic Party of Germany** [SPD] – founded 1875 from fusion of Marxists and Lassalleans; central party of Second International; majority leadership backed German imperialist war effort 1914; left-wing oppositionists formed Spartacus League 1916 and USPD 1917; headed restabilisation of German capitalist rule after November 1918 revolution.

**Social-Democratic Party of Hungary** – formed 1890; chauvinist position during War; fused with CP and helped lead Hungarian soviet republic May–August 1919; re-established 1921; functioned as legal reformist opposition under Horthy dictatorship.

**Social-Democratic Party of Serbia** – founded 1903; internationalist position during War; predecessor of Socialist Workers' [Communist] Party of Yugoslavia 1919; 80,000 members 1921; minority split to become Yugoslav SDP, with 10,000 members.

**Social-Democratic Party of Slovakia** – founded 1919 by Hungarian, German, and Slovak sections of Slovakian socialist movement; adopted programme of Comintern October 1920; left wing merged with International Socialist Party of Ruthenia January 1921; joined with SDP of Czechoslovakia in creation of Czechoslovak CP May 1921; right-wing minority split off and eventually became Hungarian section of Czechoslovak SDP.

**Social-Democratic Party of Sweden** – constituted 1889; chauvinist position during War; left wing expelled 1917; member of coalition governments 1917–20, 1921–3, 1924–6.

**Social-Democratic Party of Switzerland** – formed 1888; during War took centrist position and helped lead Zimmerwald movement; withdrew from Second International 1919; left wing split and joined CP 1921; 40,000 members in mid-1921; founding member of Two-and-a-Half International 1921.

**Social-Democratic Workers' Party of Austria** – founded 1888–9 as federation of national parties within Austro-Hungarian Empire; broke apart along national lines by 1912; chauvinist position during War; led governmental coalition 1918–20; leading party in Two-and-a-Half International; 336,000 members in November 1920.

**Socialist Concentration** – Reformist faction in the Italian Socialist Party led by Filippo Turati; won 14,695 votes at the party's January 1921 Livorno Congress.

**Socialist Labor Party** [SLP, US] – founded 1876; in 1890 Daniel De Leon assumed leadership and party adopted sectarian stance; initially sympathetic to October Revolution but soon broke with it and rejected Comintern; 5,000 members in 1920.

**Socialist Party of America** – founded 1901; communist left wing expelled 1919; membership referendum voted for conditional Comintern affiliation 1920, which was rejected; joined centrist Two-and-a-Half International 1922; 13,000 members in 1921.

**Socialist Party of Slovakia.** See Social-Democratic Party of Slovakia.

**Socialist Party of Uruguay** – founded 1910; 500 members 1916; joined Comintern and changed name to CP September 1920.

**Socialist Party–Australia.** See Australian Socialist Party.

**Socialist Party–French Section of the Workers' International** [SFIO] – formed 1905 as fusion of parties led by Guesde and Jaurès; took chauvinist position during War; centrists won majority 1918; 180,000 members at time of December 1920 Tours Congress, which voted to join Comintern and change name to CP; minority ('Dissidents') split off and retained old name, with 30,000 members.

**Socialist Party–Italy.** See Italian Socialist Party.

**Socialist Revolutionary Party** [SRs] – Russian party formed 1901, coming out of populist Narodnik tradition; member of Second International; during War contained chauvinist and internationalist wings; split in 1917, majority supported Provisional Government and opposed October Revolution; Left SRs briefly joined Soviet government but took up arms against it in 1918; Left SR minority joined CP.

**Socialist Workers' Party** [Chile] – founded 1912; voted to join Comintern February 1921; changed name to CP January 1922.

**Socialist Workers' Party** [Finland]. See Communist Party–Finland.

**Socialist Workers' Party of Spain** [PSOE] – founded 1879; chauvinist position during War; voted for Comintern affiliation 1920, but reversed position the following year; left wing split April 1921 to form Communist Workers' Party; 42,000 members in 1919.

**Soglia, Giuseppe** [1871–1926] – joined Italian SP 1892; member of its reformist wing; parliamentary deputy; elected president of National Teachers Union 1913; adopted position of patriotic neutralism on War; forced to resign from union post and replaced by more openly chauvinist leadership 1916.

**Sokolnikov, Grigorii Yakovlevich** [1888–1939] – joined Bolsheviks 1905; lived abroad 1909–17; Bolshevik leader in Moscow during 1917; member Central Committee 1917–19, 1922–30; commissar of finance 1922–6; supported United Opposition 1926; Soviet ambassador to London 1929–32; expelled 1936 and arrested; killed in prison by inmates orchestrated by Stalin's secret police.

**Solidarity** – weekly organ of IWW published in Chicago 1920–1.

**Sombart, Werner** [1863–1941] – German economist and author; initially influenced by Marxism, he later adopted Nazi ideology.

**Soukup, František** [1871–1940] – joined Czech SDP 1896; co-founder and member of editorial board of daily *Právo lidu* 1897–1939; minister of justice in first Czechoslovak government 1918–19; vice-president (1920–9) and president (1929–39) of Senate; imprisoned by Nazis 1939.

**Souvarine, Boris** [1895–1984] – jewellery worker; joined French SP around 1914; internationalist during War; international affairs secretary for French Committee for the Third International; leader of left wing of SP and then of CP; delegate to Third and Fourth World Congresses; became member ECCI 1921; expelled for defence of Left Opposition led by Trotsky 1924; a leader of Left Opposition in France 1925–9; broke with Trotskyists and moved toward reformism.

**Sowjet** [Soviet] – Communist journal published in Berlin from May 1919; edited by Paul Levi; became voice of opposition in VKPD May 1921; later organ of KAG as *Unser Weg* until 1922.

**Der Sozialist** [The Socialist] – weekly newspaper published in Berlin 1915–22, edited by Breitscheid; after 1917 reflected views of USPD.

**SP** – Socialist Party.

**Spartacus** – revolutionary socialist current in Germany headed by Luxemburg and Liebknecht 1914–18; functioned as public faction within USPD 1917–18; Spartacus League founded November 1918; helped found German CP December 1918.

**SPD.** See Social-Democratic Party of Germany.

**SRs.** See Socialist Revolutionary Party.

**Stam, Jan Cornelis** [Varkel] [1884–1943] – founding member of left-wing Dutch SDP 1909; moved to Dutch East Indies, where he was a founding leader of Indonesian CP in 1920; returned to Netherlands in 1930s and became secretary of Friends of the Soviet Union; died in Nazi concentration camp.

**Stampfer, Friedrich** [1874–1957] – leader of right wing of SDP in Austria, then Germany; social chauvinist during War; opposed Germany's signing of Versailles Treaty; editor of SPD's *Vorwärts* 1916–33 and its continuation in exile 1933–40; returned to Germany 1948; taught in university and continued to write for SPD.

**Steinhardt, Karl** [1875–1963] – joined Austrian SDP 1891; expelled as left-winger 1916; a founder of Austrian CP 1918; delegate to first three congresses of Comintern; member of ECCI 1921–2; arrested twice under Nazi regime in Vienna.

**Stepniak, Sergey Mikhailovich** [Kravchinsky] [1851–95] – joined Russian revolutionary movement early 1870s; member of Land and Liberty; assassinated head of secret police 1878; went into exile; author of *Underground Russia* (1882).

**Stinnes, Hugo** [1870–1924] – German industrialist; built vast economic empire after World War I, starting from coal and steel industry, moving to media, public utilities, banks, and other areas; during 1918 revolution, negotiated concessions to trade unions; later campaigned against eight-hour day and nationalisation; had ties to far-right; opposed Versailles treaty.

**Stoecker, Walter** [1891–1939] – joined German SDP 1908; a leader of its youth organisation in Cologne; army conscript 1915–18; joined USPD 1917; leading member of workers' and soldiers' council in Cologne during 1918 revolution; USPD secretary 1919; participated in USPD-KPD fusion 1920; delegate to Third and Fourth World Congresses; elected to ECCI Secretariat 1922; member of CP Zentrale 1920–1 and 1923–4; of CC 1927–33; chair of CP fraction in Reichstag 1924–32; arrested 1933; died in Buchenwald concentration camp.

**Strasser, Josef** [1870–1935] – joined Austrian SPD while a student in Vienna; moved to Reichenberg 1905 as editor of *Freigeist* (later *Vorwärts*); supported SPD left wing; returned to Vienna 1913; joined Austrian CP early 1919; editor of *Die Rote Fahne*; critic of ultraleft current in CP; defended Levi in 1921; worked in Soviet Union as editor of *Die Internationale* 1923–8; returned to Austria 1928 and elected to Central Committee; later expelled under accusation of Trotskyism.

**Striemer, Alfred** [b. 1879] – German union official; economist for ADGB trade-union federation; wrote for *Vorwärts*; published academic work under Nazi regime.

**Stuchka, Peter I.** [1865–1932] – joined Latvian Social-Democratic movement 1895, which later aligned to RSDLP; supported Bolsheviks; elected to Latvian CC 1904; member of Petrograd Bolshevik committee 1917; Soviet commissar of justice 1917–18; head of Latvian soviet government 1918–20; fled when it collapsed; elected ECCI member 1920; Third World Congress delegate; president of Supreme Court of Soviet Union 1923–32; chairman of Comintern Control Commission 1924–32.

**Sturm, Hertha** [1886–1945?] – joined SPD 1911 and KPD January 1919; jailed two months for role in Bavarian workers' republic 1919; delegate to Third World Congress; member International Women's Secretariat in Berlin 1921–4; removed from leading posts in KPD as rightist 1924; worked with Zetkin in Moscow 1924–8; returned to Germany, again removed from party staff as rightist; worked with left socialists of 'New Beginning' in Germany 1934–5; arrested, tortured, and jailed for many years under Nazis; believed to have been killed in Allied air strike.

**Subhi, Mustafa** [1883–1921] – joined Ottoman SP 1910; joined Bolsheviks during exile in Russia 1915, organised Communist group among Turkish prisoners of war; elected president of Turkish CP at its founding congress in Baku 1920; returned to take part in Turkish independence war and was murdered by police with fourteen other CC members.

**Süleyman Nuri** [1895–1966] – Turkish Communist; elected to Council for Action and Propaganda at 1920 Congress of the Peoples of the East in Baku; member military-revolutionary committee and people's commissar of justice in soviet Armenia; delegate to Third World Congress.

**Sült, Wilhelm** [1888–1921] – chairman of shop stewards among electrical workers in Berlin and member of German CP; organised strike during March Action; arrested by police 1 April 1921 and shot while 'trying to escape'.

**Sukhomlin, Vasilii** [1885–1963] – a leader of Russian Socialist Revolutionary Party and its representative to Second International; war correspondent for *Avanti*; opponent of October Revolution; in 1920s became editor of Russian-language section of Belgian Socialist *Le Peuple* and a leader of International Socialist Press Bureau.

**Sultanzade, Ahmed** [Avetis Mikailian] [1889–1938] – born in Maraghah, Iran; moved to tsarist Russia 1907 and joined RSDLP; joined Bolsheviks by 1912, working in Caucasus and then Central Asia; organised founding of Iranian CP 1920; CC member 1920–3, 1927–32; elected to ECCI 1920 and 1928; delegate to Second, Third, Fourth, and Sixth World Congresses; worked for Soviet government 1923–7 and after 1932; expelled from Iranian CP 1932, accused of 'leftist deviation'; arrested and shot during Stalin purges.

**Sun Yat-sen** [1866–1925] – leader of Chinese national revolution that overthrew Qing dynasty in 1911; founder and leader of Kuomintang Party from 1912; headed government in Guangdong 1921–2 and from 1923; accepted help of Soviet Russia from 1923.

**Suvorov, Alexander Vasilievich** [1729–1800] – Russian generalissimo; known for tactics of constant attack.

***Der Syndikalist*** [The Syndicalist] – weekly paper of German syndicalists published in Berlin; began publication 14 December 1918.

**Szántó, Béla** [1881–1951] – office clerk; member of Hungarian SDP 1904–8; commissar of war in Hungarian soviet government 1919; member of CP CC 1919–20, 1922; Third World Congress delegate; worked for Comintern in Vienna 1921–2; head of CP in exile 1926–9; moved to Moscow and worked for many years in Comintern apparatus; after World War II worked for Hungarian Stalinist regime on agrarian questions and as ambassador to Poland.

**Taguchi Unzo** [1892–1933] – lived in US 1914–21; helped organise Socialist Circle for Japanese in US November 1919 together with Sen Katayama; member of US CP; attended Third World Congress and RILU congress as representative of Japan Communist movement; lived in Soviet Union 1921–3; moved to Japan 1923 as secretary for Soviet diplomat Adolf Joffe.

**Taussig, Herman** [1878–1951] – sales clerk; member of Czechoslovak SDP from 1919; founding member of CP and a leader in Slovakia; Third World Congress delegate; active in sports movement; regional chairman of EC of Slovakian section of CP; left CP 1927 and rejoined SDP; imprisoned in Buchenwald and Dachau concentration camps during World War II; rejoined CP after war; charged with Trotskyism and arrested 1951; died in prison.

**Terracini, Umberto** [1895–1983] – joined Italian SP 1916; internationalist during War; a leader of *Ordine nuovo* current; member of CP and its executive 1921; elected to ECCI 1921; member ECCI 1921–2; parliamentary deputy 1922–4; jailed by Fascists 1926–43; opposed Stalinist policy on World War II and was expelled from CP 1943; active in anti-Fascist resistance 1943–5; rejoined CP and its leadership after war.

**Tesniaki** – originated as left wing majority of Bulgarian SDP; split from opportunist wing 1903; won mass support during War; became Bulgarian CP May 1919.

**Thalheimer, August** [1884–1948] – writer; joined SPD 1904; director of SPD paper in Göppingen 1909; member of Spartacus group during War; conscripted into army 1916–18; played prominent role in 1918 revolution in Stuttgart; member of CC of German CP 1919–24; defended 'theory of the offensive' at Third World Congress 1921, but subsequently opposed ultraleft Fischer-Maslow wing in German CP; held responsible, with Brandler, for workers' defeat in 1923; taught philosophy in Moscow 1924–8; opposed Stalin's ultraleft course 1928; expelled as 'rightist' 1929; co-founder with Brandler of CP (Opposition); emigrated 1933; Allied powers refused his re-entry into Germany after 1945; died in Cuba.

**Thälmann, Ernst** [1886–1944] – German docker and seaman; joined SPD 1903 and USPD in 1917; army conscript 1915–18; chairman of USPD in Hamburg 1919; participated in USPD-KPD fusion; elected to CC 1920; Third World Congress delegate; member of Reichstag 1924–33 and KPD candidate for president 1925 and 1932; became chairman of KPD 1925; arrested by Nazis 1933; executed in Buchenwald concentration camp.

**Thiers, Adolphe** [1797–1877] – French journalist, historian, and politician; president of Third Republic 1871–3; presided over suppression of Paris Commune.

**Thomas, Albert** [1878–1932] – joined French SP 1902; became leader of its right wing; deputy in parliament from 1910; supported French war effort and became minister for munitions 1916–17; first director of International Labour Organisation 1919–32.

**Thomas, James Henry** [1874–1949] – British railway union president 1905–6 and organising secretary from 1906; Labour Party member of parliament 1910; social chauvinist during War; elected treasurer of Second International 1920; head of Amsterdam International 1920–4; withdrew rail union's support for miners' strike, leading to its defeat 1921; cabinet minister 1924 and 1929–36; broke with Labour Party 1931.

**Thyssen, August** [1842–1926] – German industrialist; established iron, steel, and coal family empire; succeeded by son Fritz [1873–1951], who helped finance Nazis from 1923.

**Tolstoy, Leo** [1828–1910] – Russian author; developed religious doctrine based on Christian anarchism and pacifism.

**Tommasi, Joseph** [1886–1926] – cabinetmaker, mechanic; joined French SP 1904; union activist; supporter of CGT left wing during War; member of CGT administrative committee 1919; supported SP affiliation to Comintern; member of CP executive committee 1921–2; Third World Congress delegate; supporter of Left current in CP; forced into exile by French police 1924; became supporter of Left Opposition led by Trotsky; lived in Moscow 1924–6.

**Torralba Beci, Eduardo** [1881–1929] – journalist; leader of Spanish Socialist Youth from 1904; editor of *El Socialista*; jailed 1906 for 'mocking religion'; elected to UGT executive committee 1914, 1916; favoured Entente side in War; founding leader of Communist Workers' Party [PCO] April 1921 and its delegate to Third World Congress.

**Tours Congress** – French Socialist Party gathering held 25–30 December 1920; voted by a 75 per cent majority to accept Twenty-One Conditions and affiliate to Comintern, giving birth to the CP of France. The minority ('Dissidents') split away, preserving SP's name.

**Tranquilli, Romolo** [1904–32] – press operator; Italian CP delegate to Third World Congress 1921; functionary of Communist youth organisation; worked in CP underground; arrested 1928; died in prison of tuberculosis.

**Treves, Claudio** [1869–1933] – founding member of Italian SP 1892; colleague of Turati; editor of *Avanti* 1910–12; parliamentary deputy 1906–26; in 1917 became supporter of Italy's national defence during War; helped found reformist Unitary Socialist Party [PSU] in split from SP 1922.

*De Tribune* [The Tribune] – daily organ of Dutch CP; began publication as paper of Social-Democratic left 1907.

**Trotsky, Leon** [1879–1940] – born in Ukraine; joined socialist movement 1897; supported Mensheviks at RSDLP congress 1903; internationalist and supporter of Zimmerwald movement during War; joined Bolsheviks and elected to CC 1917; people's commissar of foreign affairs 1917–18 and of war 1918–25; a leader of Comintern; gave major report at Third World Congress; leader of Left Opposition in Russian CP and Comintern from 1923; expelled 1927; exiled abroad 1929; called for new International 1933; main target of 1936–8 Stalin frame-up trials; founding leader of Fourth International 1938; murdered by agent of Stalin.

**Tsereteli, Irakli Georgievich** [1881–1959] – born in Georgia; joined RSDLP 1902; sided with Mensheviks 1903; headed Petrograd Soviet after February Revolution, minister in Provisional Government; opponent of October Revolution; member of Menshevik-led government in Georgia 1918–21; emigrated to France after its fall, becoming Menshevik representative to Socialist International.

**Tskhakaia, Mikhail Grigorievich** [1865–1950] – native of Georgia; joined RSDLP 1898; member of Bolshevik faction from 1903; lived in Switzerland 1907–17; headed Bolshevik committee in Tiflis 1917–20; elected to ECCI 1920; after 1921 chairman of central executive committee of soviet republic of Georgia and member of Georgian CP CC; delegate to Second through Seventh World Congresses.

**Turati, Filippo** [1857–1932] – founding member Italian SP 1892; leader of its reformist right wing; founder and editor of *Critica sociale* 1891–1926; parliamentary deputy 1896–1926; opposed Italy's entry into War but supported national defence as War went on; opponent of October Revolution and Comintern; expelled from SP 1922, forming reformist PSU; emigrated to France 1926.

**Twenty-One Conditions** – resolution adopted by the Second Comintern Congress, defining conditions for admission of new parties to the International and duties for its affiliates.

**Two-and-a-Half International** – term used by Communists for International Working Union of Socialist Parties, or Vienna Union, an alliance of centrist social-democratic parties formed February 1921; merged with right wing Bern International to become Labour and Socialist International 1923.

**Tywerousky, Oscar** [Baldwin] [b. 1893] – Russian immigrant to US and a leader of Russian Federation in SP and then CP; elected to central executive committee at CP founding congress 1919, representing Russian federation; Third World Congress delegate representing US and elected to ECCI; executed in Moscow during Stalin purges.

**Ungern von Sternberg, Roman** [1886–1921] – Russian-German from Baltics; fought in War; White Army commander during civil war; dictator of Mongolia March–August 1921; taken prisoner by Red Army and executed.

**Union of Islamic Revolutionary Societies** [İslâm İhtilal Cemiyetleri İttihadı] – international organisation founded in 1920 by Enver Pasha with branches in several countries; called for liberating Muslims from imperialist oppression; fell apart by late 1921.

**Union of Oppositional Trade Unions** [Fagoppositionens Sammenslutning, Denmark] – syndicalist organisation founded 1910; 4,000 members in 1919;

allied to CP early 1921 in Communist Federation of Denmark, which lasted until January 1922.

**Unione Syndicale Italiana** [USI] – Italian anarcho-syndicalist union federation; founded 1912 out of split in CGL; sent representatives to RILU congress 1921, but did not affiliate; contained both anarchist and syndicalist wings; 800,000 members summer 1920, declining to 150,000 members in 1921.

**Unitary Communist Faction** [Unitarians] – Centrist grouping led by Serrati within Italian SP prior to 1921 Livorno Congress.

**USPD.** See Independent Social-Democratic Party of Germany.

**Vaillant-Couturier, Paul** [1892–1937] – lawyer; joined French SP as soldier 1916; jailed for anti-war articles 1918; SP parliamentary deputy 1919; a leader of CP Left current 1921–2; Third World Congress delegate; member of CP executive 1920–4 and CC 1925–37; lead editor of *L'Humanité* 1926–9 and 1935–7; worked in Comintern headquarters in Moscow 1931–2.

**Van Overstraeten, Edouard.** See Overstraeten, Edouard van.

**Vandervelde, Émile** [1866–1938] – leader of Belgian Workers' Party; chairman of Brussels office of Second International 1900–14; member of Belgian council of ministers 1916–21, 1925–7, 1936–7; chairman of Belgian Workers' Party 1933–8; president of Socialist International 1929–36.

**Vaněk, Miloš** [1897–1967] – joined Czech SDP during War and became member of CP 1921; delegate to Second World Congress; editor *Rudé právo* 1921; assigned by CP to Comintern 1921; rejoined SDP 1926; went to West Germany after CP takeover of Czechoslovakia 1948; worked for Radio Free Europe from 1951.

**Varga, Eugen** [Jenő] [1879–1964] – economist; joined Hungarian Social Democracy 1906, CP 1919; people's commissar for finance in Hungarian soviet government 1919; emigrated to Soviet Russia after its fall; worked for ECCI; delegate to Third and subsequent world congresses; prominent Soviet economist until criticised by Stalin 1947; later partially rehabilitated; died in USSR.

**Varkel.** See Stam, Jan Cornelis.

**Vaughan, Joseph J.** [b. 1878] – electrical worker; Labour Party elected councilor in London 1914–24; member of London Labour Party Executive; founding member CP 1920; Third World Congress delegate; elected Communist mayor of Bethnal Green in London 1919, 1920, 1921; president of Bethnal Green Trades' Council.

**Vergeat, Marcel** [1891–1920] – leader of French syndicalist youth movement from before War; supported Zimmerwald; co-secretary of Committee for the Third International 1919; went to Moscow July 1920 for meeting of revolutionary unionists; died at sea on return journey.

**Versailles Treaty** – peace treaty signed 28 June 1919 between Allied powers and Germany.

*La Vie ouvrière* [Workers' Life] – syndicalist weekly published in Paris 1909–14 and from 1919.

**Viscount de Eza** [Luis Marichalar y Monreal] [1872–1945] – Spanish Conservative politician; director general of agriculture 1907; mayor of Madrid 1913–14; minister of public works 1917; minister of war 1921.

**VKPD.** See Communist Party–Germany.

**Vodovosov, M. H.** – Soviet trade representative in Italy and aide to Krasin, following Soviet-Italy treaty of 1920.

*La Voix des femmes* [Women's Voice] – French feminist and socialist journal founded 1917; adopted Communist standpoint; edited by Madeleine Pelletier.

**Vorovsky, Vatslav Vatslavovich** [1871–1923] – joined Russian socialist movement 1894; Bolshevik from 1903; worked in Bolshevik underground in St. Petersburg 1905–7, and Odessa 1907–12; Soviet diplomatic representative to Scandinavia 1917–19; secretary of First World Congress 1919; Soviet representative in Italy 1921–3; assassinated in Lausanne by White émigré.

*Vorwärts* [Forward, Berlin] – central daily organ of German SPD founded in Leipzig 1876: moved to Berlin 1891; published in exile during Nazi regime.

*Vorwärts* [Forward, Reichenberg] – daily newspaper published by Social Democrats in Reichenberg [Liberec] beginning 1911; in 1921 became organ of Czechoslovak Communist Party (German section); remained organ of Czechoslovak CP until 1934.

**Walcher, Jakob** [1887–1970] – joined SPD 1906; opposed SPD pro-war policy 1914 and joined Spartacus group in Stuttgart; arrested 1915 and conscripted into army; CP founding member 1918; member Zentrale 1919–24; secretary to CC, responsible for trade-union work; worked for RILU 1924–6; expelled from CP 1928 as rightist; moved to Paris after 1933; a leader of German Socialist Workers' Party [SAP]; moved to East Germany 1946 and joined CP; demoted from all positions 1949; expelled 1951; readmitted 1956.

**Walecki, Henryk** [1877–1937] – university graduate in mathematics and physics; member Polish SP from 1899; internationalist during War; took part in Zimmerwald Conference 1915; founding member Polish CP 1919; delegate to Third through Fifth World Congresses; member ECCI 1921–4; attacked as 'opportunist' 1924; moved to USSR 1925; assistant secretary to Comintern Balkan Secretariat 1928–35; editor-in-chief of *Communist International* 1935–7; arrested and executed during Stalin purges.

**Warski.** See Warszawski, Adolf.

**Warszawski, Adolf** [Warski, Michalak] [1868–1937] – pioneer of early Polish socialist movement; co-founder of SDKPiL; a leader of RSDLP after 1905 revolution; attended Zimmerwald and Kienthal Conferences during War; a founding leader of Polish CP 1918; delegate to Third through Sixth World Congresses; ousted from Polish CP leadership for opposition to Stalin course 1929; lived in USSR from 1929; arrested and executed during Stalin purges.

**Webb, Sidney** [1859–1947] – a leader of liberal-reformist English Fabian Society; prominent members of Labour Party after 1914; co-author of *The History of Trade Unionism* and *Industrial Democracy*.

**Westarp, Kuno von** [1864–1945] – leader of German Conservative Party fraction in Reichstag to 1918; in 1920 joined right-wing German National People's Party [DNVP].

**Western Federation of Miners** – militant union of hard rock miners and smelter workers in western US and Canada; founded 1893; joined in creation of IWW 1905 but broke with it and joined AFL 1911; became International Union of Mine, Mill, and Smelter Workers 1916; merged with United Steelworkers of America 1967.

**White Guards** – Counterrevolutionary armies in 1918–20 Russian Civil War.

**Wilhelm II** [1859–1941] – emperor of Germany 1888–1918; fled to Netherlands following November 1918 revolution.

**Williams, Robert** [1881–1936] – secretary of National Transport Workers' Federation 1912–22; member of Labour Party Executive; part of British union delegation to Moscow 1920 to discuss founding new trade-union International; joined CP 1920; expelled 1921, accused of having betrayed miners strike after Black Friday.

**Wilson, Woodrow** [1856–1924] – Democratic Party president of US 1913–21; led US into War 1917; issued Fourteen Points 1918, which promised liberal non-punitive peace and a League of Nations.

**Wirth, Joseph** [1879–1956] – German politician; a leader of Catholic Centre Party; German minister of finance 1920–1; chancellor in government that encompassed SPD May 1921–November 1922; in exile as an opponent of Nazi rule 1933–49; subsequently favoured reunited, neutral Germany.

**Wissell, Rudolf** [1869–1962] – joined German Social Democracy 1888; member of trade-union central secretariat from 1908; became deputy chairman of ADGB union federation 1918; member of Council of People's Representatives 1918–19; German economics minister 1919; head of ADGB's Social Affairs

Department 1919–24; jailed for two months under Nazis; helped rebuild Berlin SPD after 1945.

**Wolf, Felix** [1893–1936] – born to German family in present-day Estonia; moved to Germany 1900; to Russia 1914; joined Bolsheviks 1917; KPD member and ECCI collaborator from 1919; active in Hamburg during March Action; lived in Russia 1924–5 and from 1927; close to anti-Stalinist opposition currents; arrested several times during Stalin purges; executed.

**Wolff, Fritz** [1897–1946] – joined USPD 1917; part of KPD-USPD fusion 1920; graphic artist for *Die Rote Fahne*; expelled from CP for support to Levi 1921; briefly a member of Socialist Workers' Party [SAP] in 1930s; lived in London from 1942, where he took part in German anti-Nazi movement.

**Wolffheim, Fritz** [1888–1942] – joined SPD 1909; worked with ultraleft in Hamburg SPD during War; joined CP 1918; leader of National Bolshevism tendency together with Lauffenberg; expelled 1920; joined KAPD but then expelled August 1920; attempted to continue nationalist-socialist activity but evolved to right; in close contact with left wing of Nazi Party led by Strasser; arrested 1934 during Nazi purge of Strasser current; died in concentration camp.

**Wrangel, Pyotr Nikolaevich** [1878–1928] – Russian general; commander of White forces in southern Russia 1919–20; emigrated to Yugoslavia 1920; subsequently led White exile army.

**Yahya, Imam Muhamed Hamid ed-Din** [1867–1948] – imam of Yemen 1904–48.

**Yoshihara, Taro** [Gentaro Yoshiwara] [b. 1890] – Japanese immigrant in US; member of US IWW and Japanese Socialist Group; moved to Japan 1919 with Japanese Communist Group; delegate to Third World Congress and RILU congress; later returned to Japan and was imprisoned.

**Yuan Shikai** [1859–1916] – Chinese army leader; first president of Republic of China 1912–16; with Japanese support he attempted to proclaim himself emperor.

**Zaglul Pasha, Saad** [1857–1927] – leader of Egyptian nationalist movement and Wafd Party; Britain's deportation of him in March 1919 helped spark revolutionary upsurge; prime minister of Egypt 1924.

**Zalewski, Alexandre** [b. 1888] – pseudonym for Alexandre E. Abramovich; joined Bolsheviks in Russia 1908; lived in Switzerland 1911–17, returning to Russia with Lenin; sent to France November 1919 as member of Comintern Secretariat for Western Europe; arrested in France 1921 and sent back to Russia; worked for Comintern in Latvia and then Vienna; worked for Comintern Department of Organisation 1925–31; taught at Institute of Marxism-Leninism in Tomsk in 1934–49; retired in 1961.

**Zápotocký Antonín** [1884–1957] – member of Czech SP 1902 and of its left wing 1919; an organiser of December 1920 political strikes and chairman of revolutionary committee in Kladno; arrested along with 3,000 other participants in the strike and imprisoned for nine months; member of Czechoslovak CP CC 1921; CC secretary 1922–9; general secretary of Czechoslovak red unions 1929–39; held in Nazi concentration camp 1939–45; prime minister of Czechoslovakia 1948–53 and president 1953–7.

**Zentrale** – Central Bureau of German Communist Party; subcommittee of party Central Committee.

**Zetkin, Clara** [1857–1933] – joined German socialist movement 1878; driven into exile by Bismarck's Anti-Socialist Laws 1882–90; co-founder of Second International 1889; a leader of its Marxist wing; campaigner for women's emancipation; close associate of Rosa Luxemburg in SPD left wing; organised internationalist conference of socialist women 1915; joined German CP 1919; opposed ultraleftism in CP during March Action 1921 and thereafter; member ECCI from 1922; attended Second through Sixth World Congresses; headed Communist Women's Movement 1921–6; opposed 'Bolshevisation' campaign 1924–5 and Stalin's ultraleft turn from 1928; remained prominent figure in German CP and Comintern, without recanting, until her death in Moscow.

**Zhang Tailei** [1898–1927] – won to communism as Chinese student activist 1920; went to Irkutsk 1921 to establish Chinese CP contact with Far Eastern Secretariat; Third World Congress delegate; elected secretary-general of Chinese Communist youth February 1925; elected to party CC 1927; helped lead December 1927 Canton insurrection; executed after it was crushed.

**Zhordania, Noé Nikolaevich** [1868–1953] – joined Georgian Social-Democratic movement 1890s; Menshevik by 1905; chairman of Tiflis soviet 1917; opponent of October Revolution; president of Georgian Menshevik government 1918–21; exiled in France from 1921.

**Zibordi, Giovanni** [1870–1943] – joined Italian socialist movement 1892; journalist living in Reggio Emilia and member of reformist wing of SP; parliamentary deputy 1914–21; joined reformist Unitary Socialist Party [PSU] 1922.

**Zietz, Louise** [1865–1922] – joined German SDP in 1892; member of Executive of Social-Democratic Women's Movement after its founding in 1908; women's secretary on SPD national executive 1908–17; expelled from SPD Executive 1917 and joined USPD; member of USPD Executive; opposed merger with KPD and stayed with rump USPD 1920.

**Zimmerwald** – reference to movement formed at 1915 conference in Zimmerwald, Switzerland, attended by left-wing and centrist socialist parties and currents, following collapse of Second International in 1914; a second conference was held in Kienthal, Switzerland, in 1916.

**Zimmerwald Left** – formed September 1915 by Lenin and left-wing forces at socialist conference in Zimmerwald, Switzerland; a forerunner of Third International.

**Zinoviev, Grigorii** [1883–1936] – joined RSDLP 1901; Bolshevik; elected to CC 1907; internationalist and collaborator of Lenin during War; chair of Petrograd Soviet 1917–26; chairman of Comintern 1919–26; chairman of Presidium of Third World Congress; on death of Lenin, collaborated with Stalin to isolate Trotsky from central leadership 1923–4; broke with Stalin 1925; with Trotsky, led United Opposition to bureaucratic degeneration 1926–7; expelled 1927; recanted and was readmitted 1928; re-expelled 1932 and 1934; convicted in Moscow frame-up trial and shot.

**Zulawski, Zygmunt** [1880–1949] – joined Polish SDP of Galicia 1904; member of its executive committee 1911–18; after Polish independence in 1919 was a member of the Socialist Party [PPS] and its national leadership 1919–39; president of Polish trade-union federation 1919–22; worked in PPS underground during World War II; leader of Polish Social Democracy until his death.

# Selected Bibliography

## Documents of the Communist Movement in Lenin's Time

Riddell, John (ed.) 1984, *Lenin's Struggle for a Revolutionary International 1907–1916*, New York: Pathfinder Press.

—— 1986, *The German Revolution and the Debate on Soviet Power*, New York: Pathfinder Press.

—— 1987, *Founding the Communist International: Proceedings and Documents of the First Congress, March 1919* (1WC), New York: Pathfinder Press.

—— 1991, *Workers of the World and Oppressed Peoples, Unite! Proceedings and Documents of the Second Congress, 1920* (2WC), 2 volumes, New York: Pathfinder Press.

—— 1993, *To See the Dawn: Baku, 1920 – First Congress of the Peoples of the East*, New York: Pathfinder Press.

—— 2011b, *Toward the United Front: Proceedings of the Fourth Congress of the Communist International* (4WC), Historical Materialism Book Series, Leiden: Brill.

*In preparation:*

Taber, Mike (ed.), *The Communist Movement at a Crossroads: Plenums of the Communist International's Executive Committee 1922–1923*, Historical Materialism Book Series, Leiden: Brill.

## Editions of the Third Comintern Congress and Its Resolutions

Adler, Alan (ed.) 1980, *Theses, Resolutions and Manifestos of the First Four Congresses of the Third International*, London: Ink Links.

Comintern 1921c, *Protokoll des III. Kongresses der Kommunistischen Internationale*, Hamburg: Verlag der Kommunistischen Internationale.

—— 1921d, *Thesen und Resolutionen des III. Weltkongresses der Kommunistischen Internationale*, Hamburg: Verlag der Kommunistischen Internationale.

—— 1921e, *Third Congress of the Communist International: Report of Meetings Held at Moscow, June 22nd–July 12th 1921*, London: Communist Party of Great Britain.

—— 1922b, *III vsemirnyi kongress Kommunisticheskogo internatsionala*, Petersburg: Gosizdat.

—— 1934, *Thèses, manifestes et résolutions adoptés par les I$^{er}$, II$^e$, III$^e$, et IV$^e$ congrès de l'Internationale communiste (1919–1923) Textes complets*, Paris: Librairie du Travail.

—— 1988, *Gongchan guoji di 3 ci daibiao dahui wenjian, 1921 nian 6 yue–7 yue* [Documents of the Third Congress of the Communist International, June–July 1921], Beijing: China Renmin University Press.

—— 1994, *The Comintern Archive*, Leiden: IDC.

Kun, Béla 1933, *Kommunisticheskii internatsional v dokumentakh*, Moscow: Partiinoe Izdatel'stvo.

Bosić, Milovan et al. (eds.) 1981, *Treći kongres Komunističke internacionale*, in *Komunistička Internacionale: Stenogrami i documenti kongresa*, Volume 3, Gornji Milanovac: Kulturni centar.

## Comintern Periodicals

*Bulletin des III. Kongresses der Kommunistischen Internationale*, nos. 1–24, 24 June–20 July 1921.
*Inprecorr: International Press Correspondence*, news bulletin of the Communist International from October 1921.
*Inprekorr: Internationale Presse-Korrespondenz*, German-language Comintern news bulletin from September 1921.
*Die Kommunistische Fraueninternationale*, magazine of the Communist Women's Movement.
*Die Kommunistische Internationale*, journal of the Communist International, also published in English, French, and Russian.
*Moscou, organe du 3e congrès de l'Internationale communiste*, 25 May–7 July 1921. Also published in English and German.

## Bibliographies

Herting, Günter 1960, *Bibliographie zur Geschichte der Kommunistischen Internationale (1919–1943)*, Berlin: Institut für Marxismus-Leninismus.
Kahan, Vilém 1990, *Bibliography of the Communist International (1919–1979)*, Leiden: Brill.
Procacci, Giuliano 1958, 'L'Internazionale comunista dal I al VII congresso 1919–1935', *Annali dell'Istituto Giangiacomo Feltrinelli*, 1: 283–315.
Sworakowski, Witold S. (ed.) 1965, *The Communist International and Its Front Organizations*, Stanford: Hoover Institution Press.
See also Broué 1997 and Buckmiller and Meschkat (eds.) 2007.

## Biographical Resources

Andreucci, Franco and Tommaso Detti (eds.) 1975–9, *Il movimento operaio italiano: Dizionario biografico 1853–1943*, 6 volumes, Rome: Editori Riuniti.
Bartke, Wolfgang (ed.) 1990, *Biographical Dictionary and Analysis of China's Party Leadership 1922–1988*, Munich: K.G. Saur.
Buckmiller, Michael and Klaus Meschkat (eds.) 2007, *Biographisches Handbuch zur Geschichte der Kommunistischen Internationale*, Berlin: Akademie Verlag.
Chase, William J. 2001, *Enemies Within the Gates? The Comintern and the Stalinist Repression, 1934–1939*, New Haven: Yale University Press.
Gotovitch, José and Mikhail Narinski (eds.) 2001, *Komintern: L'histoire et les hommes: Dictionnaire biographique de l'Internationale communiste en France, en Belgique, au Luxembourg, en Suisse, et à Moscou (1919–1943)*, Paris: Éditions de l'Atelier.
Jeifets, Lazar, Victor Jeifets, and Peter Huber (eds.) 2004, *La Internacional comunista y América latina, 1919–1943: Diccionario biográfico*, Moscow: Latin America Institute.
Kahan, Vilém 1976, 'The Communist International, 1919–43: The Personnel of its Highest Bodies', *International Review of Social History*, 21, 2: 151–85
Lane, A. Thomas (ed.) (1995), *Biographical Dictionary of European Labor Leaders*, Westport: Greenwood Press.
Lazitch, Branko (ed.) 1986, *Biographical Dictionary of the Comintern*, Stanford: Hoover Institution Press.
Lorwin, Lewis L. 1929, *Labor and Internationalism*, New York: Macmillan
Maitron, Jean (ed.) 1964–97, *Dictionnaire biographique du mouvement ouvrier français*, 44 volumes, Paris: Éditions Ouvrières.
Maitron, Jean and Georges Haupt (eds.) 1971–, *Dictionnaire biographique du mouvement ouvrier international*, 11 volumes, Paris: Éditions Ouvrières.
Morgan, Kevin, Gidon Cohen, and Andrew Flinn (eds.) 2005, *Agents of the Revolution: New Biographical Approaches to the History of International Communism in the Age of Lenin and Stalin*, Oxford: Peter Lang Publishing.
Schneider, Dieter Marc et al. (eds.) 1980, *Biographisches Handbuch der deutschsprachigen Emigration nach 1933*, 2 volumes, Munich: K.G. Saur.
Tych, Feliks (ed.) 1985, *Słownik biograficzny działaczu polskiego ruchu robotniczego*, 3 volumes, Warsaw: Książka i Wiedza.

Weber, Hermann and Andreas Herbst (eds.) 2004, *Deutsche Kommunisten: Biographisches Handbuch 1918 bis 1945*, Berlin: Dietz Verlag.

And the following Web resources:
International Institute of Social History: <http://www.iisg.nl/archives/en/>
Smolny: Collectif d'édition des introuvables du mouvement ouvrier: <http://www.collectif-smolny.org/rubrique.php3?id_rubrique=19>
Friedrich Ebert Stiftung: <http://library.fes.de/fulltext/bibliothek/chronik/persreg_index.html>
Gauche Allemande: <http://troploino.free.fr/biblio/biograph/>
Graham Stevenson: <http://grahamstevenson.me.uk/>
In addition, significant biographical appendices are found in Agosti (ed.) 1974, Bock 1969, Broué 1997, Broué 2005, Bosić et al. (eds.) 1981, Chase 2001, Piatnitskii and Taras 2004, Reviakina et al. (eds.) 2005, Riddell (ed.) 1991, Riddell (ed.) 1993, Riddell (ed.) 2011b, Serge 2012, and Tosstorff 2004.

## Third Congress-Related Comintern Documents

Adhikari, Gangadhar M. (ed.) 1971, *Documents of the History of the Communist Party of India*, 8 volumes, New Delhi: People's Publishing House.
Adibekov, Grant and Kharuki Vada (eds.) 2001, *VKP(b), Komintern i Iaponiia 1917–1941*, Moscow: ROSSPEN.
Agosti, Aldo (ed.) 1974, *La Terza Internazionale: Storia documentaria*, Volume 1 (1919–23), Rome: Editori Riuniti.
Bahne, Siegfried (ed.) 1970, *Archives de Jules Humbert-Droz*, Volume 1, Dordrecht: D. Reidel.
Bosić, Milovan, et al. (eds.) 1981, *Komunistička internacionala: stenogrami i dokumenti kongresa*, 7 volumes, Gornji Milanovac: Kulturni centar.
Broué, Pierre (ed.) 1974, *Les congrès de l'Internationale communiste: Le premier congrès, 2–6 mars, 1919*, Paris: Études et documentation internationales.
—— 1979, *Du premier au deuxième congrès de l'Internationale communiste, mars 1919–juillet 1920*, Paris: Études et documentation internationales.
Chaqueri, Cosroe (ed.) 1969–94, *Asnād-i tārīkhī-i junbish-i kārgarī, sūsyāl dimūkrāsī va kumūnīstī-i Īrān* [Historical Documents: The Workers', Social Democratic, and Communist Movement in Iran], 23 volumes, Tehran: Intishārāt-i Pādzahr.
Comintern 1920, *Der zweite Kongress der Kommunistischen Internationale*, Vienna: Arbeiter Buchhandlung.
—— 1921a, *Ital'ianskaia sotsialisticheskaia partiia i Kommunisticheskii internatsional (sbornik materialov)*, Petrograd: Comintern.
—— 1921b, *Le parti socialiste italien et l'Internationale: recueil de documents*, Petrograd: Éditions de l'Internationale communiste.
—— 1921f, *Der zweite Kongress der Kommunistischen Internationale*, Hamburg: Verlag der Kommunistischen Internationale.
—— 1922a, *Die Tätigkeit der Exekutive und des Präsidiums des E.K. der Kommunistischen Internationale vom 13. Juli 1921 bis 1. Februar 1922*, Petrograd: Verlag der Kommunistischen Internationale.
—— 1923, *Veröffentlichungen des Verlages der Kommunistischen Internationale 1920 bis 1922*, Hamburg: Carl Hoym Nachf.
—— 1988, *Gongchan guoji disanci daibiao dahui wenjian* [Documents of the Third Congress of the Communist International], Beijing: Zhongguo renmin daxue chuban she.
Davidson, Apollon et al. (eds.) 2003, *Socialist Pilgrims to Bolshevik Footsoldiers, 1919–1930*, in *South Africa and the Communist International: A Documentary History*, Volume 1, London: Frank Cass.
Degras, Jane (ed.) 1971, *The Communist International 1919–1943 Documents*, 3 volumes, New York: Frank Cass.
Drabkin, Ia.S., L.G. Babichenko, and K.K. Shirinia (eds.) 1998, *Komintern i ideia mirovoi revoliutsii*, Moscow: Nauka.
Gankin, Olga Hess, and H.H. Fisher (eds.) 1940, *The Bolsheviks and the World War*, Stanford: Stanford University Press.

Gruber, Helmut (ed.) 1967, *International Communism in the Era of Lenin*, Ithaca: Cornell University Press.

Hedeler, Wladislaw and Alexander Vatlin (eds.) 2008, *Die Weltpartei aus Moskau: Der Gründungskongress der Kommunistischen Internationale 1919*, Berlin: Akademie Verlag.

IML-SED (Institut für Marxismus-Leninismus beim ZK der SED) 1966a *Dokumente und Materialien der deutschen Arbeiterbewegung, Bd. VII/1 1919–1921*, Berlin: Dietz Verlag.

—— 1966b. *Geschichte der deutschen Arbeiterbewegung, Band 3. Von 1917 bis 1923*, Berlin: Dietz Verlag.

Joshi, Puran Chandra and K. Damodaran (eds.) 2007, *A Documented History of the Communist Movement in India*, 2 volumes, New Delhi: Sunrise Publications.

Kalmykov, N.P. (ed.) 1998, *Komintern i Latinskaia Amerika: Sbornik dokumentov*, Moscow: Nauka.

Kuo Heng-yü and M.L. Titarenko (eds.) 1996, *RKP(B), Komintern und die national-revolutionäre Bewegung in China: Dokumente*, Volume 1 (1920–5), Paderborn: F. Schöningh.

Meijer, Jan (ed.) 1964, *The Trotsky Papers, 1917–1922*, 2 volumes, The Hague: Mouton.

PCI (Communist Party of Italy) 1921, *La questione italiana al terzo congresso della Internazionale Comunista*, Rome: Libreria Editrice del Partito Comunista d'Italia.

—— 1922, *Manifesti ed altri documenti politici*, Rome: Libreria Editrice del Partito Comunista d'Italia.

Parti socialiste 1921, *18ème congrès national tenu à Tours. Compte rendu sténographique*, Paris.

Prometheus Research Library 1988, *Guidelines on the Organizational Structure of Communist Parties, on the Methods and Content of Their Work*, New York.

Radek, Karl 1924, *Piat' let Kominterna*, 2 volumes, Moscow: Krasnaia Nov'.

Reviakina, Luiza et al. (eds.) 2005, *Kominternut i Bulgariia*, 2 volumes, Sofia: Glavo upravlenie na archivite.

RILU 1921, *Resolutions and Decisions of the First International Congress of Revolutionary Trade and Industrial Unions*, Chicago: The Voice of Labor.

Saich, Tony (ed.) 1991, *The Origins of the First United Front in China: The Role of Sneevliet (Alias Maring)*, 2 volumes, Leiden: Brill.

—— 1996, *The Rise to Power of the Chinese Communist Party: Documents and Analysis*, Armonk: M.E. Sharpe.

Shirinia, K.K. (ed.) 1970, *V. I. Lenin i Kommunisticheskii internatsional*, Moscow: Politizdat.

—— and Kharuki Vada (eds.) 2007, *VKP(b), Komintern i Koreia, 1918–1941*, Moscow: ROSSPEN.

Stoljarowa, Ruth and Peter Schmalfuss (eds.) 1990, *Briefe Deutscher an Lenin, 1917–1923*, Berlin: Dietz Verlag.

Titarenko, M.L. (ed.) 1986, *Kommunisticheskii internatsional i kitaiskaia revoliutsiia: dokumenty i materialy*, Moscow: Nauka.

—— et al. (eds.) 1994, *VKP(b), Komintern, i natsional'no-revoliutsionnoe dvizhenie v Kitae: Dokumenty*, Volume 1 (1920–5), Moscow: ROSSPEN.

Trotsky, Leon 1967, *Le Mouvement communiste en France (1919–1939)*, Paris: Minuit.

—— 1972a, *The First Five Years of the Communist International*, 2 volumes, New York: Pathfinder Press.

Weber, Hermann (ed.) 1966, *Die Kommunistische Internationale: Eine Dokumentation*, Hanover: J.H.W. Dietz Nachf.

Zentrale der KPD 1922, *Die Enthüllungen zu den Märzkämpfen. Enthülltes und Verschwiegenes*.

Zentrale der VKPD 1921, *Taktik und Organisation der revolutionären Offensive: Die Lehren der März-Aktion*, Leipzig-Berlin.

## Selected Bibliography of Third Congress–Related Literature

Abrahamian, Ervand 1982, *Iran Between Two Revolutions*, Princeton: Princeton University Press.

Adibekov, G.M., E.N. Shakhnazarova, and K.K. Shirinia 1997, *Organizatsionnaia struktura Kominterna: 1919–1943*, Moscow: ROSSPEN.

Agosti, Aldo 2009, *Il Partito mondiale della rivoluzione : Saggi sul comunismo e l'Internazionale*, Milan: Unicopli.

Alba, Victor 1983, *The Communist Party in Spain*, New Brunswick: Transaction Books.

Amendola, Giorgio 1978, *Storia del Partito comunista italiano*, Rome: Editori Riuniti.

Andreu, Maurice 2003, *L'Internationale communiste contre le capital, 1919–1924; ou comment empoigner l'adversaire capitaliste?* Paris: Presses Universitaires de France.

Angell, Norman 1913, *The Great Illusion: A Study of the Relation of Military Power to National Advantage*, London: Heinemann.

Angress, Werner T. 1963, *Stillborn Revolution: The Communist Bid for Power in Germany, 1921–1923*, Princeton: Princeton University Press.

Angus, Ian 1981, *Canadian Bolsheviks: The Early Years of the Communist Party of Canada*, Montreal: Vanguard.

Artemov, V.A. 2000, *Karl Radek: Ideia i sud'ba*, Voronezh: Voronezh State University.

Avakumović, Ivan 1967, *History of the Communist Party of Yugoslavia*, Aberdeen: Aberdeen University Press.

Badia, Gilbert 1993, *Clara Zetkin, féministe sans frontières*, Paris: Éditions Ouvrières.

Balsamini, Luigi 2002, *Gli Arditi del Popolo: Dalla guerra alla difesa del popolo contro le violenze fasciste*, Salerno: Galzerano Editore.

Bauer, Otto 1919, *Der Weg zum Sozialismus* [The Road to Socialism], Vienna: Volksbuchhandlung.

Bayerlein, Bernhard 2003, *Deutscher Oktober 1923: ein Revolutionsplan und sein Scheitern*, Berlin: Aufbau-Verlag.

—— et al. (eds.) 2013, *Deutschland, Russland, Komintern – Überblicke, Analysen, Diskussionen: Neue Perspektiven auf die Geschichte der KPD und die deutsch-russischen Beziehungen (1918–1943)*, Berlin: De Gruyter.

Becker, Jens 2001, *Heinrich Brandler: Eine politische Biographie*, Hamburg: VSA-Verlag.

Beckmann, George M. and Genji Okubo 1969, *The Japanese Communist Party 1922–1945*, Stanford: Stanford University Press.

Behan, Tom 2003, *The Resistible Rise of Benito Mussolini*, London: Bookmarks.

Bell, John D. 1986, *The Bulgarian Communist Party from Blagoev to Zhivkov*, Stanford: Hoover Institution Press.

Beradt, Charlotte 1969, *Paul Levi: ein demokratischer Sozialist in der Weimarer Republik*, Frankfurt am Main: Europäische Verlagsanstalt.

Bezvesel'nyi, S.F. and D.E. Grinberg (eds.) 1968, *They Knew Lenin: Reminiscences of Foreign Contemporaries*, Moscow: Progress Publishers.

Bock, Hans Manfred 1969, *Syndikalismus und Linkskommunismus von 1918–1923*, Meisenheim am Glan: A. Hain.

Bois, Marcel and Florian Wilde 2007, 'Modell für den künftigen Umgang mit innerparteilicher Discussion? Der Heidelberger Parteitag der KPD 1919', *Jahrbuch für Forschungen zur Geschichte der Arbeiterbewegung*, 6, 2: 33–46.

*Il Bolscevismo: giudicato dai Socialisti Italiani*, 1921, Rome: Tipografia Soc. Editrice Urbs.

Borkenau, Franz 1962, *World Communism: A History of the Communist International*, Ann Arbor: University of Michigan Press.

Borsányi, György 1993, *The Life of a Communist Revolutionary, Béla Kun*, New York: Columbia University Press.

Brackman, Arnold C. 1963, *Indonesian Communism: A History*, New York: Praeger.

Brandler, Heinrich 1921a, *Der Hochverratsprozess gegen Heinrich Brandler vor dem Gericht ausserordentlich, am 6. Juni 1921 in Berlin*, Leipzig-Berlin.

Brandler, Heinrich 1921b, *War die Märzaktion ein Putsch?* Berlin, Leipzig: Franke.

Brandt, Willi and Richard Lowenthal 1957, *Ernst Reuter, ein Leben für die Freiheit*, Munich: Kindler.

Braunthal, Julius 1967, *History of the International*, Volume 2, London: Nelson.

Broué, Pierre 1988, *Trotsky*, Paris: Fayard.

—— 1997, *Histoire de l'Internationale communiste 1919–43*, Paris: Fayard.

——— 2005, *The German Revolution 1917–1923*, London: Merlin Press.

Brown, W.J. 1986, *The Communist Movement and Australia: An Historical Outline – 1890s to 1980s*, Haymarket, Australia: Australian Labor Movement History Publications.

Buber-Neumann, Margarete 1967, *Kriegsschauplätze der Weltrevolution: Ein Bericht aus der Praxis der Komintern 1919–1943*, Stuttgart: Seewald.

Bukharin, Nikolai 1971 [1920], *Economics of the Transformation Period*, New York: Bergman Publishers.

Calwer, Richard 1921, *Staatsbankrott: Darstellung seiner Ursachem und Wirkungen*, Berlin: Wirtschaftsstatist. Bureau.

Cammett, John M. 1967, *Antonio Gramsci and the Origins of Italian Communism*, Stanford: Stanford University Press.

Campione, Daniel (ed.) 2007, *Buenos Aires – Moscú – Buenos Aires: Los comunistas argentinos y la Tercera internacional, primera parte (1921–1926)*, Buenos Aires: Ediciones CCC Floreal Gorini.

Cannon, James P. 1973, *The First Ten Years of American Communism*, New York: Pathfinder Press.

Carr, E.H. 1966, *The Bolshevik Revolution 1917–1923*, Harmondsworth: Penguin Books.

Chaqueri, Cosroe 1995, *The Soviet Socialist Republic of Iran, 1920-1921: Birth of the Trauma*. Pittsburgh, University of Pittsburgh Press.

——— 2010, *The Left in Iran 1905–1940*, London: Merlin Press

Chesneaux, Jean 1968, *The Chinese Labor Movement, 1919–1927*, Stanford: Stanford University Press.

Claudín, Fernando 1975, *The Communist Movement: From Comintern to Cominform*, 2 volumes, New York: Monthly Review Press.

Cliff, Tony 1979, *The Bolsheviks and World Communism*, in *Lenin*, Volume 4, London: Pluto Press.

Cohen, Stephen 1973, *Bukharin and the Bolshevik Revolution: A Political Biography 1888–1938*, New York: Knopf.

Comintern 1970 [1922], *The First Congress of the Toilers of the Far East*, London: Hammersmith.

Communist Party of India (Marxist) History Commission 2005, *History of the Communist Movement in India*, New Delhi: CPI(M) Publications.

Communist Party of Italy 1922, *Manifesti ed altri documenti politici*, Roma: Libreria Editrice del Partito Comunista d'Italia.

Cornell, Richard 1982, *Revolutionary Vanguard: The Early Years of the Communist Youth International 1914–1924*, Toronto: University of Toronto Press.

Cortesi, Luigi 1999, *Le Origini del PCI*, Milan: FrancoAngeli.

——— 2010, *Storia del comunismo: Da utopia al Termidoro sovietico*, Rome: Manifestolibri.

Courtois, Stéphane 1995, *Histoire du Parti communiste français*, Paris: Presses Universitaires de France.

Cvetković, Slavoljub 1985, *Idejne borbe u Komunističkoi partiji Jugoslavije (1919–1928)*, Belgrade: Institut za Savremenu Istoriju.

Dahlmann, F.E. 1844, *The History of the English Revolution*, London: Longman.

Datta Gupta, Sobhanlal 1980, *Comintern, India and the Colonial Question*, Calcutta: Centre for Studies in Social Sciences.

——— 2006, *Comintern and the Destiny of Communism in India: 1919–1943: Dialectics of Real and a Possible History*, Calcutta: Sreejoni.

Day, Richard B. 1973, *Leon Trotsky and the Politics of Economic Isolation*, Cambridge: Cambridge University Press.

De Weydenthal, Jan B. 1978, *The Communists of Poland: An Historical Outline*, Stanford: Hoover Institution Press.

Degras, Jane 1951, *Soviet Documents on Foreign Policy*, Oxford: Oxford University Press.

Di Biagio, Anna 2004, *Coesistenza e isolazionismo: Mosca, il Komintern e l'Europa di Versailles (1918–1928)*, Rome: Carocci Editore.

Digby, Margaret 1982, *The World Co-operative Movement*, London: Hutchinson's University Library.

Dirlik, Arif 1989, *The Origins of Chinese Communism*, Oxford: Oxford University Press.

Dobbs, Farrell 1983, *Revolutionary Continuity: Birth of the Communist Movement 1918–1922*, New York: Monad Press.

Dornemann, Luise 1973, *Clara Zetkin: Leben und Wirken*, Berlin: Dietz Verlag.

Drachkovitch, Milorad M. and Branko M. Lazić (eds.) 1966, *The Comintern; Historical Highlights, Essays, Recollections, Documents*, New York: Praeger.

Draper, Theodore 1957, *The Roots of American Communism*, New York: Viking Press.

Dreyfus, Michel et al. 2000, *Le Siècle des communismes*, Paris: Éditions Ouvrières.

Droz, Jacques 1977, *Histoire générale du socialisme*, Volume 3, Paris: Presses Universitaires de France.

Ducoulombier, Romain 2010, *Camarades! La naissance du Parti communiste en France*, Paris: Perrin.

Dulles, John W.F. 1973, *Anarchists and Communists in Brazil, 1900–1935*, Austin: University of Texas Press.

Dziewanowski, M.K. 1976, *The Communist Party of Poland: An Outline of History*, Cambridge, MA: Harvard University Press.

Fayet, Jean-François 2004, *Karl Radek (1885–1939): Biographie politique*, Bern: P. Lang.

—— 2008, 'Paul Levi and the Turning Point of 1921', in *Bolshevism, Stalinism and the Comintern*, edited by Norman LaPorte, Matthew Worley, and Kevin Morgan, Basingstoke: Palgrave Macmillan.

Feigon, Lee 1983, *Chen Duxiu, Founder of the Chinese Communist Party*, Princeton: Princeton University Press.

Fernbach, David (ed.) 2011, *In the Steps of Rosa Luxemburg: Selected Writings of Paul Levi*, Historical Materialism Book Series, Leiden: Brill.

Fiori, Giuseppe 1971, *Antonio Gramsci: Life of a Revolutionary*, New York: Dutton.

Firsov, F.I. 1975, *Tretii kongress Kominterna: Razvitie kongressom politicheskoi linii kommunisticheskogo dvizheniia, kommunisty i massy*, Moscow: Politizdat.

—— 2007, *Sekretnye kody istorii Kominterna 1919–1943*, Moscow: AIRO-XXI.

Fischer, Ruth 1948, *Stalin and German Communism*, Cambridge, MA: Harvard University Press.

Flechtheim, Ossip Kurt 1969, *Die KPD in der Weimarer Republik*, Frankfurt: Europäische Verlagsanstalt.

Frank, Pierre 1979, *Histoire de l'Internationale communiste, 1919–1943*, Paris: La Brèche.

Frölich, Paul 2012 [1921], *Autobiographie 1890-1921: Parcours d'un militant internationaliste allemand*, Montreuil: Science Marxiste.

—— 2013, *Im radikalen Lager: Politische Autobiograhie 1890–1921*, Berlin: Basis-Druck.

Fuhrer, Armin 2011, *Ernst Thälmann: Soldat des Proletariats*, München: Olzog.

Galli, Giorgio 1980, *Storia del socialismo italiano*, Rome: Laterza.

—— 1993, *Storia del PCI: Livorno 1921, Rimini 1991*, Milan: Kaos Edizioni.

Geyer, Curt 1976, *Die revolutionäre Illusion: Zur Geschichte des linken Flügels der USPD*, Stuttgart: Deutsche Verlags-Anstalt.

Gilberg, Trond 1973, *The Soviet Communist Party and Scandinavian Communism: The Norwegian Case*, Oslo: Universitetsforlaget.

Goldbach, Marie-Luise 1973, *Karl Radek und die deutsch-sowjetischen Beziehungen 1918–1923*, Bonn: Verlag Neue Gesellschaft.

Gollan, Robin 1975, *Revolutionaries and Reformists: Communism and the Australian Labour Movement 1920–1955*, Surrey: Richmond Publishing.

Gorter, Herman 1920, *Open Letter to Comrade Lenin: A Reply to 'Left Wing' Communism, an Infantile Disorder*, London: Wildcat, 1992. Also available at: <http://www.marxists.org/archive/gorter/1920/open-letter/index.htm>.

—— 1921, *Die Klassenkampf-Organisation des Proletariats*, Berlin: KAPD.

Gramsci, Antonio 1974, *Socialismo e fascismo: L'Ordine nuovo 1921–1922*, Turin: Einaudi.

Gras, Christian 1971, *Alfred Rosmer (1877–1964) et le mouvement révolutionnaire international*, Paris: François Maspero.

Gross, Babette 1991, *Willi Münzenberg: eine politische Biografie*, Leipzig: Forum.

Gruber, Helmut and Pamela Graves 1998, *Women and Socialism, Socialism and Women: Europe Between the Two World Wars*, New York: Berghahn Books.

Gutjahr, Wolf-Dietrich 2012, *Revolution muss sein: Karl Radek – Die Biographie*, Cologne: Böhlau Verlag.

Hájek, Miloš 1969, *Storia dell'Internazionale comunista (1921–1935): la política del fronte unico*, Rome: Editori Riuniti.

Hájek, Miloš and Hana Mejdrová 1997, *Die Entstehung der III. Internationale*, Bremen: Edition Temmen.
Hallas, Duncan 1985, *The Comintern*, London: Bookmarks.
Harman, Chris 1997, *The Lost Revolution: Germany 1918 to 1923*, London: Bookmarks.
Harris, George S. 1967, *The Origins of Communism in Turkey*, Stanford: Hoover Institution Press.
Haywood, William 1929, *Bill Haywood's Book*, New York: International Publishers.
Held, Walter 1942, 'Why the German Revolution Failed', *Fourth International*, December 1942: 3: 12: 377–82.
Hilferding, Rudolf 1919, *Der Weg zum Sozialismus*, Vienna: Volksbuchhandlung.
Hodgson, John H. 1967, *Communism in Finland: A History and Interpretation*, Princeton: Princeton University Press.
Hoelz, Max, 1930, *From White Cross to Red Flag*, London: Jonathan Cape.
Horowitz, Daniel L. 1963, *The Italian Labor Movement*, Cambridge, MA: Harvard University Press.
Howe, Irving and Lewis Coser 1957, *The American Communist Party: A Critical History, 1919–1957*, Boston: Beacon Press.
International Labour Office 1921: *First Special International Trade Union Congress*, Geneva: ILO.
International Socialist Congress 1967, *The Second and Third Internationals and the Vienna Union: Official Report of the Conference between the Executives, held at the Reichstag, Berlin, on the 2nd April, 1922, and the Following Days*, Milan: Feltrinelli.
International Working Union of Socialist Parties 1921, *Protokoll der internationaler sozialistischen Konferenz in Wien von 22. bis 27. Februar 1921*. Vienna: Wiener Volksbuchhandlung.
Ismael, Tareq Y. and Rifat Saïd 1990, *The Communist Movement in Egypt, 1920–1988*, Syracuse: Syracuse University Press.
Izquierdo, Manuel 1995, *La Tercera Internacional en España: 1914–1923*, Madrid: Ediciones Endymión.
Jackson, George D. 1966, *Comintern and Peasant in East Europe, 1919–1930*, New York: Columbia University Press.

Jentsch, Harald 1993, *Die politische Theorie August Thalheimers, 1919–1923*, Mainz: Decaton.
Kalmykov, N.P. 1998, *Komintern i Latinskaia Amerika: sbornik dokumentov*, Moscow: Nauka.
KAPD 1921, *Der Weg des Dr Levi – der Weg der VKPD*, Berlin: KAPD.
Kessler, Mario 2013, *Ruth Fischer: Ein Leben mit und gegen Kommunisten (1895–1961)*, Vienna: Böhlau Verlag.
King, Robert R. 1980, *A History of the Romanian Communist Party*, Stanford: Hoover Institution Press.
Kinner, Klaus and Elke Reuter 1999, *Der deutsche Kommunismus: Selbstverständnis und Realität*, Berlin: Dietz Verlag.
Klugmann, James 1968, *History of the Communist Party of Great Britain*, Volume 1: *Formation and Early Years 1919–1924*, London: Lawrence & Wishart.
Knatz, C. 2000, *Ein Heer im grünen Rock? Der Mitteldeutsche Aufstand 1921*, Berlin: Duncker & Humblot.
Koch-Baumgarten, Sigrid 1986, *Aufstand der Avantgarde: Die Märzaktion der KPD 1921*, Frankfurt: Campus Verlag.
König, Helmut 1967, *Lenin und der italienische Sozialismus 1915–1921*, Tübingen: Böhlau Verlag.
Kopeček, Michal and Zdeněk Kárník 2003, *Bolševismus, komunismus a radikální socialismus v Československu*, Prague: Ústav pro soudobé dějiny AV ČR.
Kössler, Reinhart 1982, *Dritte Internationale und Bauernrevolution: Die Herausbildung des sowjetischen Marxismus in der Debatte um die "asiatische" Produktionsweise*, Frankfurt: Campus Verlag.
Kovrig, Bennett 1979, *Communism in Hungary from Kun to Kádár*, Stanford: Hoover Institution Press.
Krause, Hartfrid 1975, *USPD: Zur Geschichte der Unabhängigen Sozialdemokratischen Partei Deutschlands*, Frankfurt am Main: Europäische Verlagsanstalt.
Kublin, Hyman 1964, *Asian Revolutionary: The Life of Sen Katayama*, Princeton: Princeton University Press.
Kuo Heng-yü and M.L. Titarenko (eds.) 1996, *RKP(B), Komintern und die national-revolutionäre Bewegung in China: dokumente*, Volume 1 (1920–1925), Paderborn: F. Schöningh.

Kurella, Alfred 1970 [1929–31], *Der Kampf um die Massen*, in Schüller, R. et al., *Geschichte der Kommunistischen Jugendinternationale*, Volume 2, Nördlingen: Trikont.

Labour and Socialist International 1920, *The Congress of the Labour and Socialist International (Geneva, July 31st–August 6th, 1920)*, Geneva: International Labour Office.

Langer, Bernd 2009, *Revolution und bewaffnete Aufstände in Deutschland 1919–1923*, Göttingen: AktivDruck.

LaPorte, Norman, Matthew Worley, and Kevin Morgan (eds.) 2008, *Bolshevism, Stalinism and the Comintern*, Basingstoke: Palgrave Macmillan.

Lazitch, Branko and Milorad Drachkovitch 1972, *Lenin and the Comintern*, Stanford: Hoover Institution Press.

Lebedeva, N.S., Kimmo Rentola, and T. Saarela (eds.) 2003, *Komintern i Finlandia: 1919–1943*, Moscow: Nauka.

Lenin, V.I. 1958–65, *Polnoe sobranie sochinenii* (PSS), Moscow: Gosizdat.

—— 1960–71, *Collected Works* (LCW), 45 volumes, Moscow: Progress Publishers.

Leonhard, Wolfgang 1981, *Völker hört die Signale: Die Anfänge des Weltkommunismus 1919–1924*, Munich: Bertelsmann.

Lerner, Warren 1970, *Karl Radek, the Last Internationalist*, Stanford: Stanford University Press.

Levi, Paul 1921a, *Der Beginn der Krise in der Kommunistischen Partei und Internationale. Rede von Paul Levi auf der Sitzung des Zentralauschusses der V.K.P.D. am 24. Februar 1921*, Remscheid: Volksstimme.

—— 1921b, *Unser Weg: Wider den Putschismus*, Berlin: A. Seehof. [For translation see Fernbach (ed.) 2011.]

—— 1921c, *Was ist das Verbrechen? Die Märzaktion oder die Kritik daran?* Berlin: A. Seehof. [For translation see Fernbach (ed.) 2011.]

—— Selected writings, see Fernbach (ed.), 2011.

Leviné-Meyer, Rosa 1977, *Inside German Communism: Memoirs of Party Life in the Weimar Republic*, London: Pluto Press.

Lewis, Ben, and Lars T. Lih (eds.) 2011, *Zinoviev and Martov: Head to Head in Halle*, London: November Publications.

Li Yuzhen and Du Weihua (eds.) 1989, *Malin yu diyici guogong hezuo* [Maring (Sneevliet) and the first period of cooperation between the Guomindang and the Communists], Beijing: Guangming Ribao Chubanshe.

Lorenz, Einhart 1978, *Norwegische Arbeiterbewegung und Kommunistische Internationale 1919–1930*, Oslo: Pax Forlag.

Löwy, Michael (ed.) 1980, *Le Marxisme en Amérique Latine de 1909 à nos jours*, Paris: François Maspero.

Luks, Leonid 1985, *Entstehung der kommunistischen Faschismustheorie: die Auseindersetzung der Komintern mit Faschismus und Nationalsozialismus 1921–1935*, Stuttgart: Deutsche Verlagsanstalt.

Luxemburg, Rosa 2004, *The Rosa Luxemburg Reader*, edited by Peter Hudis and Kevin B. Anderson, New York: Monthly Review Press.

MacFarlane, L.J. 1966, *The British Communist Party: Its Origin and Development until 1929*, Worcester: MacGibbon and Kee.

Malatesta, Alberto 1926, *I socialisti italiani durante la Guerra*, Milan: Mondadori.

Mallmann, Klaus-Michael, *Kommunisten in der Weimarer Republik: Sozialgeschichte einer revolutionären Bewegung*, Darmstadt: Wissenschaftliche Buchgesellschaft.

Mamaeva, N.L., 1999, *Komintern i Gomin'dan: 1919–1929*, Moscow: ROSSPEN.

Martinelli, Renzo, 1977, *Il Partito comunista d'Italia, 1921–1926: Politica e organizzazione*, Rome: Editori Riuniti.

Marx, Karl 1977–81, *Capital*, 3 volumes, New York: Vintage Books.

—— and Frederick Engels 1975–2004, *Collected Works* (MECW), Moscow: Progress Publishers.

Maurseth, Per 1972, *Fra moskvateser til Kristiania-forslag: Det norske Arbeiderparti og Komintern fra 1921 til februar 1923*, Oslo: Pax Forlag.

Mayenburg, Ruth von 1991, *Hotel Lux: das Absteigequartier der Weltrevolution*, Munich: Piper.

McDermott, Kevin 1988, *The Czech Red Unions, 1918–1929*, Boulder: East European Monographs.

―――― and Jeremy Agnew 1996, *The Comintern: A History of International Communism from Lenin to Stalin*, Basingstoke: Palgrave Macmillan.

McVey, Ruth T. 1965, *The Rise of Indonesian Communism*, Ithaca: Cornell University Press.

Meaker, Gerald H. 1974, *The Revolutionary Left in Spain, 1914–23*, Stanford: Stanford University Press.

Mehring, Franz 1960, *Geschichte der deutschen Sozial-demokratie*, Berlin: Dietz Verlag.

Möller, Dietrich 1976, *Revolutionär, Intrigant, Diplomat: Karl Radek in Deutschland*, Cologne: Verlag Wissenschaft und Politik.

Molnár, Miklós 1990, *From Béla Kun to János Kádár: Seventy Years of Hungarian Communism*, New York: Berg.

Morgan, David W. 1975, *The Socialist Left and the German Revolution: A History of the German Independent Social Democratic Party, 1917–1922*, Ithaca: Cornell University Press.

Mortimer, Edward 1984, *The Rise of the French Communist Party 1920–1947*, London: Faber & Faber.

Münzenberg, Willi 1931, *Solidarität: Zehn Jahre Internationale Arbeiterhilfe, 1921–1931*, Berlin: Neuer Deutscher Verlag.

―――― 1978 [1930], *Die dritte Front: Aufzeichnungen aus 15 Jahren proletarischer Jugendbewegung*, Berlin: LitPol.

Mujbegović, Vera 1968, *Komunistička partija Nemačke u periodu posleratne krize 1918–1923*, Belgrade: Institut za Izučavanje Radničkog Pokreta.

Narinsky, Mikhail and Jürgen Rojahn (eds.) 1996, *Centre and Periphery: The History of the Comintern in the Light of New Documents*, Amsterdam: International Institute of Social History.

Natoli, Claudio 1982, *La Terza Internationale e il fascismo, 1919–1923: Proletariato di fabbrica e reazione industriale nel primo dopoguerra*, Rome: Editori Riuniti.

Nofri, Gregorio and Fernando Pozzani 1921, *La Russia com'è*, Florence: Ben Parad.

O'Connor, Emmet 2005, *Reds and the Green: Ireland, Russia, and the Communist Internationals, 1919–43*, Dublin: University College Press.

Palmer, Bryan 2007, *James P. Cannon and the Origins of the American Revolutionary Left 1890–1928*, Urbana: University of Illinois Press.

Pannekoek, Anton 1920, *Die Entwicklung der Weltrevolution und die Taktik des Communismus*, Petrograd. English edition available at: <http://www.marxists.org/archive/pannekoe/tactics>.

Pantsov, Alexander 2000, *The Bolsheviks and the Chinese Revolution, 1919–1927*, Richmond: Curzon Press.

Peng Shu-tse 1983, *L'envol du communisme en Chine: mémoires de Peng Shuzhi*, Paris: Gallimard.

Peterson, Larry 1993, *German Communism, Workers' Protest, and Labor Unions: The Politics of the United Front in Rhineland-Westphalia 1920–1924*, Dordrecht: Kluwer.

Piatnitskii, V.I. and A.E. Taras 2004, *Osip Piatnitskii i Komintern na vesakh istorii*, Minsk: Kharvest.

Plener, Ulla (ed.) 2008, *Clara Zetkin in ihrer Zeit: Neue Fakten, Erkenntnisse, Wertungen*, Berlin: Dietz Verlag.

Porter, Cathy 2013, *Alexandra Kollontai: A Biography*, (revised ed.), Chicago: Haymarket Books.

Post, Kenneth William John 1997, *Revolution's Other World: Communism and the Periphery, 1917–39*, Basingstoke: Macmillan.

Prager, Eugen 1980 [1921], *Das Gebot der Stunde: Geschichte der USPD*, Berlin: Dietz.

Privalov, V.V. 1971, *The Young Communist International and Its Origins*, Moscow: Progress Publishers.

PSI (Socialist Party of Italy) 1962 [1921], *Resoconto stenografico del XVII Congresso Nazionale del Partito Socialista Italiano*, Milan: Edizioni Avanti.

Puschnerat, Tânia 2003, *Clara Zetkin: Bürgerlichkeit und Marxismus*, Essen: Klartext Verlag.

Racine, Nicole and Louis Bodin 1972, *Le Parti communiste français pendant l'entre-deux-guerres*, Paris: A. Colin.

Radek, Karl 1920, *Die auswärtige Politik des deutschen Kommunismus und der Hamburger nationale Bolschewismus*, Vienna: KPD.

——— 1921, *Die taktischen Differenzen in der V.K.P.D.: Soll die V.K.P.D. eine Massenpartei der revolutionären Aktion oder eine zentristische Partei des Wartens sein?* Moscow: Verlag der Kommunistischen Internationale.

Rees, Tim and Andrew Thorpe (eds.) 1999, *International Communism and the Communist International 1919–1943*, Manchester: Manchester University Press.

Reisberg, Arnold 1964, *Lenin und die Aktionseinheit in Deutschland*, Berlin: Dietz Verlag.

——— 1971, *An den Quellen der Einheitsfrontpolitik*, Berlin: Dietz Verlag.

Rentola, Kimmi and Tauno Saarela 1998, *Communism: National and International*, Helsinki: Finnish Literature Society.

Richardson, Al (ed.) 2000, *From Syndicalism to Trotskyism: Writings of Alfred and Marguerite Rosmer*, London: Porcupine Press.

Riddell, John 2011a, 'The Origins of the United Front Policy', *International Socialism*, 130 (Spring): 113–40. Also available at: <http://www.isj.org.uk/index.php4?id=724>.

Riddell, John: For documentary volumes on the Comintern, see opening section of this bibliography.

Robrieux, Philippe 1980, *Histoire intérieure du parti communiste*, Paris: Fayard.

Rosmer, Alfred 1971, *Lenin's Moscow*, London: Pluto Press.

Rothschild, Joseph 1959, *The Communist Party of Bulgaria: Origins and Development, 1883–1936*, New York: Columbia University Press.

Roy, Manabendra Nath 1964, *M.N. Roy's Memoirs*, Bombay: Allied Publishers.

Roy, Samaren 1986, *The Twice-Born Heretic: M.N. Roy and Comintern*, Calcutta: Firma KLM.

Rubenstein, Sondra Miller 1985, *The Communist Movement in Palestine and Israel, 1919-1984*, Boulder: Westview Press.

Rudolf L. Tőkés 1967, *Béla Kun and the Hungarian Soviet Republic*, New York: Praeger.

Scalapino, Robert A. and Chong-Sik Lee 1972, *Communism in Korea*, Berkeley: University of California Press.

Schlesinger, Rudolf 1970, *Die Kolonialfrage in der Kommunistischen Internationale*, Frankfurt: Europäische Verlagsanstalt.

Schröder, Joachim 2008, *Internationalismus nach dem Krieg: Die Beziehungen zwischen deutschen und französischen Kommunisten 1918–1923*, Essen: Klartext.

Schumacher, Horst and Feliks Tych 1966, *Julian Marchlewski-Karski: Eine Biographie*, Berlin: Dietz Verlag.

Serge, Victor 2012 [1951], *Memoirs of a Revolutionary*, New York: New York Review Books.

Simoncini, Gabriele 1993, *The Communist Party of Poland, 1918–1929: A Study in Political Ideology*, Lewiston: E. Mellen Press.

Sivan, Emmanuel 1976, *Communisme et nationalisme en Algérie 1920–1962*, Paris: Fondation Nationale des Sciences Politiques.

Socialist Party of France 1921, *Parti socialiste, 18ème congrès national tenu à Tours. Compte-rendu sténographique*, Paris: Courbevoie.

Spriano, Paolo 1967, *Storia del Partito comunista italiano*, 7 volumes, Turin: Einaudi.

——— 1975, *The Occupation of the Factories*, London: Pluto.

Suda, Zdeněk L. 1980, *Zealots and Rebels: A History of the Communist Party of Czechoslovakia*, Stanford: Hoover Institution Press.

Suh, Dae-sook 1967, *The Korean Communist Movement, 1918–1948*, Princeton: Princeton University Press.

Surmann, Rolf 1983, *Die Münzenberg-Legende: zur Publizistik der revolutionären deutschen Arbeitsbewegung 1921–1933*, Cologne: Prometheus.

Svátek, Frantisék 1977, 'Gli organi dirigenti dell'Internazionale comunista: Loro sviluppo e composizione (1919–1943)', *Movimento operaio e socialista*, (January–March): 89–132; and (April–September): 289–342.

Tasca, Angelo [A.Rossi, pseud.] 1966 [1941], *The Rise of Italian Fascism 1918–1922*, New York: Howard Fertig.

Ter Minassian, Taline 1997, *Colporteurs du Komintern: l'Union soviétique et les minorités du Moyen-Orient*, Paris: Presses des Sciences politiques.

Thalheimer, August 1994, 'The Struggle for the United Front in Germany', *Revolutionary History*, 5, 2 (Spring): 74–91.

Thorpe, Andrew 2000, *The British Communist Party and Moscow, 1920–43*, Manchester: Manchester University Press.

Tismaneanu, Vladimir 2003, *Stalinism for All Seasons: A Political History of Romanian Communism*, Berkeley: University of California Press.

Tivel', A. 1924, *Piat' let Kominterna v resheniiakh i tsifrakh*, Moscow: Kommunisticheskiy Internatsional.

Tosstorff, Reiner 2004, *Profintern: Die Rote Gewerkschaftsinternationale 1920–37*, Paderborn: F. Schöningh.

Trotsky, Leon 1936, *The Third International After Lenin*, New York: Pioneer Publishers.

——— 1972b, *The Stalin School of Falsification*, New York: Pathfinder Press.

——— and Eugen Varga 1921, *Thesen zur Weltlage und die Aufgaben der Kommunistischen Internationale*. Moscow: Verlag der Kommunistischen Internationale.

Tunçay, Mete 1967, *Türkiye'de sol akımlar, 1908–1925*, Ankara: Sevinç Matbaası.

Turati, Filippo 1953, *Da Pelloux a Mussolini: Dai discorsi parlamentari 1896–1923*, Turin: Francesco de Silva.

Ulunian, A. 1997, *Komintern i geopolitika: Balkanskii rubezh, 1919–1938 gg.*, Moscow: Institut vseobshchei istorii.

Upton, A.F. 1973, *Communism in Scandinavia and Finland: Politics of Opportunity*, Garden City: Anchor Press.

Vaksberg, A.I. 1993, *Hôtel Lux: Les partis frères au service de l'Internationale communiste*, Paris: Fayard.

Varga, Eugen 1921, *Die wirtschaftspolitischen Probleme der proletarischen Diktatur*, Hamburg: Carl Hoym Nachf.

Vatlin, A.Iu. 1993, *Komintern: pervye desiat let*, Moscow: Rossiia Molodaia.

——— 2009, *Komintern: idei, resheniia, sudby*, Moscow: ROSSPEN.

Voerman, Gerrit 2001, *De meridiaan van Moskou: De CPN en de Communistische Internationale, 1919–1930*, Amsterdam: L.J. Veen.

Waters, Elizabeth 1989, 'In the Shadow of the Comintern: The Communist Women's Movement, 1920–43', in *Promissory Notes: Women in the Transition to Socialism*, edited by Sonia Kruks, Rayna Rapp, and Marilyn B. Young, New York: Monthly Review Press.

Watlin, Alexander 1993, *Die Komintern 1919–1929: Historische Studien*, Mainz: Decaton (*a translation of* Vatlin 1993).

Weber, Hermann 1969, *Die Wandlung des deutschen Kommunismus: Die Stalinisierung der KPD in der Weimarer Republik*, Hamburg: Europäische Verlagsanstalt.

Weber, Stefan 1991, *Ein kommunistischer Putsch? Märzaktion 1921 in Mitteldeutschland*, Berlin: Dietz Verlag.

Weitz, Eric D. 1997, *Creating German Communism, 1890–1990*, Princeton: Princeton University Press.

Wheaton, Bernard 1986, *Radical Socialism in Czechoslovakia: Bohumir Šmeral, the Czech Road to Socialism and the Origins of the Czechoslovak Communist Party (1917–1921)*, Boulder: East European Monographs.

Wheeler, Robert F. 1975, *The Independent Social Democratic Party and the Internationals: An Examination of Socialist Internationalism in Germany 1915 to 1923*, Pittsburgh: University of Pittsburgh.

Wilde, Florian 2011, 'Ernst Meyer (1887–1930) – vergessene Führungsfigur des deutschen Kommunismus: Eine politische Biographie', PhD thesis, Hamburg University, Hamburg.

Williams, George 1921, *The First Congress of the Red Trade Union International at Moscow, 1921: A Report of the Proceedings by Geo. Williams, Delegate from the I.W.W.*, Chicago: Industrial Workers of the World

Williams, Gwyn A. 1975, *Proletarian Order: Antonio Gramsci, Factory Councils and the Origins of Communism in Italy 1911–1921*, London: Pluto Press.

Winkler, Heinrich August 1984, *Von der Revolution zur Stabilisierung: Arbeiter und Arbeiterbewegung in der Weimarer Republik 1918 bis 1924*, Berlin: J.H.W. Dietz Nachf.

Wohl, Robert 1966, *French Communism in the Making, 1914–1924*, Stanford: Stanford University Press.

Wolikow, Serge 2010, *L'Internationale communiste, 1919–1943*, Ivry-sur-Seine: Éditions de l'Atelier.

Zabih, Sepehr 1966, *The Communist Movement in Iran*, Berkeley: University of California Press.

Zagladin, V.V. et al. (eds.) 1984, *The Socialist Revolution in Russia and the International Working Class (1917–1923)*, in *The International Working-Class Movement*, Volume 4, Moscow: Progress Publishers.

Zetkin, Clara 1922, *Um Rosa Luxemburgs Stellung zur russischen Revolution*, Hamburg: Verlag der Kommunistischen Internationale.

—— 1934, *Reminiscences of Lenin*, New York: International Publishers.

—— 1985, *Erinnerungen an Lenin*, Berlin: Dietz Verlag.

Zheng Chaolin 1997, *An Oppositionist for Life: Memoirs of the Chinese Revolutionary Zheng Chaolin*, Atlantic Highlands: Humanities Press.

# Index

Page numbers in italics refer to individuals' reports and significant contributions during congress proceedings.

AAUD (General Workers' Union of Germany), 19, 643, 885, 886, 1216
Abd al Malik, 844, 1203
Abd al-Qadir, 844, 1203
Abilov, 1203; in Eastern question discussion, *854–5*
ADGB (General German Trade Union Federation), 706, 953, 957, 1216; and VKPD Open Letter, 1061, 1080–1
Adler, Friedrich, *407–8*, 1203
agitation. *See* propaganda and agitation
agriculture, 107, 110, 112, 114, 115, 131
Albania, 845–6
Alessandri, Cesare, 201, 382, 1203
Alexakis, Orion, *74*, 1203
Algeria, 844
Alpári, Gyula, 14
Alsace-Lorraine, 112
Amendments to Tactics Theses, 2, 30, 31, 34–5; Brand on, *526–8*; as counterposed political line, 35, 466, 573, 1154; Heckert on, 35, *481–3*; Hungarian minority on, 536; Lenin on, *465–73*; Münzenberg on, *533–5*; statements in support of, 476, 515, 517; Terracini motivation of, *457–65*; text of, 1041–58; Thalheimer on, *540–2*; Thälmann on, *571*; Trotsky on, *573–81*, 1154; Zinoviev on, *563*
American Federation of Labor (AFL), 711, 958; Communist work in, 742, 743; Haywood on, *715–16, 717*; membership of, 728, 1203
American Legion, 943
Amiens Charter, 932, 957, 1203; Lozovsky on, *719, 720, 722–5*; text of, 607; Tomassi on, *747, 748, 749–51, 752*, 753–4; Trotsky on, 1123; Zinoviev on, 606, 609–11
Amsterdam International (International Federation of Trade Unions), 62, 97, 562, 563, 584, 914, 1221; fight against, 40, 233, 603, 758, 1037; and Hungarian boycott, 601; and International Labour Organisation, 722n; and Italian CGL, 199–200, 258, 372, 383–4, 385, 601–2, 711, 720–1, 722; London Congress of (1920), 258; need for Communist work within, 887; Second and Two-and-a-Half Internationals united by, 80, 928; service to bourgeoisie by, 600–1, 602–3, 621, 705, 926, 949–50; support for trade-union neutrality by, 610; trade-union report and theses on, 600–3, 955–6; and unemployment question, 618–19; and union splits, 706, 950; and Upper Silesia, 715; Versailles Treaty supported by, 601, 621, 721; yellow character of, 600, 987
anarchism and anarchists, 352, 456, 458–9, 748, 1112. *See also* syndicalists and syndicalism
Ancona events (1919), 359
Angell, Norman, 151, 1203
Anseele, Edward, 273, 1203
Anti-Bolshevik League, 1084
anti-militarist work, 768, 772, 989, 1111–13
Appel, Jan. *See* Hempel
Appleton, William A., 602, 721, 1203
April Theses (Lenin), 675, 1170–1
Aqazadeh, Kamran, 1203–4; in Eastern question discussion, *841–3*
Arabia, 847–8

*Arbeitsgemeinschaft*, 501
Arditi del Popolo, 13, 894n
Argentina, 604
Argentina Regional Workers Federation, 68, 1204
Arie, 1196–7
Armand, Inessa, 74, 1204
armed forces: Communist work within, 819–20, 875, 946, 989
Armenia, 844, 849–51, 850
arming the proletariat: Organisation Theses on, 989; Swedish CP and, 228, 404; as transitional demand, 441. *See also* self-defence, workers'
Arnold, Emil, 1040, 1204
Australia, 1187; repression in, 649, 736; trade unions in, 604, 648–50, 735–7
Australian Labor Party, 649, 650, 1204
Australian Socialist Party, 735, 1204
Austria, 155, 412; trade unions in, 604, 734–5, 959; youth movement in, 766, 770. *See also* Communist Party of Austria
Austria-Hungary, 105, 129, 136n, 254, 908
Austrian delegation, 31, 399, 457, 897, 1041
*Avanti*, 258, 259, 367, 375, 518, 1204; on Amsterdam International, 383–4; debate on Twenty-One Conditions in, 317; and factory occupations, 374; Serrati articles in, 186, 192, 196, 197, 199, 206; Serrati as editor of, 190, 196–7
Azerbaijan, 854–5, 865
Azimonti, Carlo, 602n, 1204

Bacci, Giovanni, 348, 1204
Badulescu, Alexandru, 387, 1204
Baku Commune, 854
Baku Congress (1920), 7, 82, 870; Council for Propaganda and Action established by, 231, 855, 869; Union of Islamic Revolutionary Societies on, 843, 846, 848
Bakunin, Mikhail, 22, 1204
Bakuninism, 22, 265, 267, 493, 523, 570. *See also* putsches and putschism
Baldesi, Gino, 190n, 1204
Baldwin. *See* Tywerousky, Oscar
Balfour, Arthur James, 90, 1204
Balkan Communist Federation, 799, 947, 1204
Balkans, 95, 278, 840–1
Balkan Wars, 840
Ballister. *See* Minor, Robert
Ballod, Karl, 669, 1204

Baltic states, 152–3, 777n
Baratono, Adelchi, 190, 202, 1204
Barbusse, Henri, 231, 1204
Barth, Emil, 591, 724n, 1067, 1205
Bauer, Gustav, 955, 1205
Bauer, Otto, 410, 1205; *Dictatorship and Democracy*, 348; political perspective of, 61, 106, 411, 412, 663
Bavaria, 78, 772; disarmament question in, 486, 575; Soviet republic and white terror in, 93
Bebel, August, 367, 733, 1205
Bedacht, Max (Marshall), 101, 582, 1205; in trade-union discussion, 726–9
Belgian Workers' Party, 948; about, 273–4, 308, 1205; left-wing split from, 229, 273, 308
Belgium, 310, 905, 959; working class in, 309–10, 604. *See also* Communist Party of Belgium
Bell, Thomas, 66, 567, 1040, 1205; in tactics and strategy discussion, 551–5; in trade-union discussion, 755–8; in world economic discussion, 151–4
Bellini, 345
Belloni, Ambrogio, 888, 1205
Belori, 346
Bentivoglio, Giorgio, 1205
Bentivoglio resolution, 198, 365, 403, 921
Béranger, Pierre-Jean de, 1123
Berce, Augusts, 74, 1205
Bergmann (Fritz Meyer), 331, 797, 1231; in trade-union discussion, 637–48
Berkman, Alexander, 40, 1205
Bernstein, Eduard, 201, 349, 652, 684, 1205
Bern women's conference (1915), 655
Bern youth conference (1916), 369
Bianchi, Giuseppe, 602n, 1205
Bidegaray, Marcel, 749, 1205
Bissolati, Leonida, 346, 357–8, 362, 367, 1206
Black question: Jones on, 1193–6; South African resolution on, 871–2, 1196
Blum, Léon, 381, 1206
Bologna events (1920), 359, 419
Bolshevik Party, 1166, 1206; during 1917, 295, 352–3, 467, 1170; strategy of, 674. *See also* Russian Communist Party
Bombacci, Nicola, 324, 339–40n, 362, 519, 1206
Bonomi, Ivanoe, 357–8, 1206
Bordiga, Amadeo, 9, 13, 314, 324, 1206; anti-parliamentarism of, 182, 309;

Communist Abstentionist current of, 8, 204, 340n
Borodin, Mikhail, 416, 1206
Borojević, Svetozar, 254, 1206
Böttcher, Paul, 314, 1206
Bourderon, Albert, 1123, 1206
bourgeoisie: American, 94; attempts to split proletariat by, 622, 623; British, 91, 94, 153, 552, 837–8, 1182; and capitalist equilibrium, 162, 915; centralisation of, 832, 925; class instinct and consciousness of, 660; in colonial and semi-colonial countries, 858, 911, 1185–6, 1188–90, 1191, 1192; Czechoslovak, 96, 933; destruction of means of production by, 140–1, 620; as formerly revolutionary class, 93; French, 94, 111; German, 89, 94–5, 205, 486–7, 532, 620, 926, 948, 1035; in immediate postwar period, 118–19, 131, 151, 164, 902, 903, 904, 925; Italian, 105, 193, 366, 371, 420, 926; middle classes and, 132–3, 845; monopolised vs. non-monopolised, 131, 133; offensive against working class by, 105, 127, 148–9, 366, 532, 603, 926, 960, 962; recovery of self-confidence following War, 103–4, 902, 903; rule through deception by, 608–9, 638, 953; Russian, 659, 660–1, 663, 670, 680, 976; Social Democracy and Amsterdam International as tool of, 138–9, 233, 600–2, 621, 658, 914, 918, 926, 948, 955, 971, 1073; and Soviet Russia, 656–8, 667, 671, 970, 972; and state capitalism, 699; struggle within, 132–3; use of repression and white terror by, 73–4, 89, 93–5, 147, 408, 937; women in, 781; and World War I, 610, 914; and youth, 776–7; Yugoslav, 276–7, 278, 762. *See also* capitalism
Brand, Henryk, 597, 1206; in tactics and strategy discussion, 526–8, 1154; in trade-union discussion, 719; Trotsky replies to, 168–9, 573–4; in world economic discussion, 135–9, 142
Brandler, Heinrich, 326, 500, 556, 1206–7; during March Action, 18, 422, 429, 491, 503, 522, 530, 531, 539–40, 941, 1152; on March Action, 208, 588, 1099, 1100; support for VKPD Left by, 10, 16; trial and imprisonment of, 83, 299, 1095, 1134
Branting, Karl Hjalmar, 228, 405, 1207

Brass, Otto, 427, 528–9, 1207; and March Action, 207, 491; resignation from Zentrale by, 206n, 486
Braunthal, Bertha, 1141n, 1148–9, 1207
Breitscheid, Rudolf, 256, 1207
Brest-Litovsk Treaty, 167; Lenin on, 444, 508–9, 657
Briand, Aristide, 166–7, 772n, 1207
Britain: in Arabia, 847–8; Bell on, 153–4, 551–5; coal industry in, 114, 438, 439, 622, 926; colonial empire of, 91–2, 136, 156–7, 835–8, 1182–3, 1189–90; economy of, 113–15, 126, 157; and France, 129, 912, 913; and Germany, 156; Hands Off Russia movement in, 90, 822; and Ireland, 94, 136; and Japan, 863; oppression of India by, 136, 837, 971; repression in, 75, 92, 94, 412, 632, 943; shop stewards in, 756, 827, 1240; and Soviet Russia, 90, 192, 196; strike wave of 1917 in, 104, 901; tenant farmers in, 972; trade unions in, 148, 153, 604, 631–2, 755–6, 758, 948, 958; and Turkestan, 864; and United States, 115, 129–30, 151, 158, 166, 912, 913; and World War I, 91, 156, 905. *See also* Communist Party of Great Britain
British Labour Party. *See* Labour Party (Britain)
British miners' strike (1921), 92, 608, 623, 926, 954; Hewlett on, 91; Pogány on, 148; Radek tactics report on, 415–17; revolutionary potential of, 918–19; Soviet Russia and, 89, 673, 676; Vaughan reply to Radek on, 476–9; Zinoviev on, 77–8
Brouckère, Louis de, 273, 1207
Broué, Pierre, 18
Brussels financial conference (1920), 136, 137–8
Bukharin, Nikolai, 24, 66, 230, 580, 684, 779, 1040, 1207; and differences among Russian CP leaders, 28, 1135–6; at expanded ECCI meeting, 31, 224; on Gorter, 512–14; on KAPD, 512–15, 697; on Levi, 509–11; as member of Small Bureau, 39, 181n, 882n; on Open Letter, 15, 1064–6; on policy of the offensive, 6–7, 468n; Radek reply to on Open Letter, 1066–9; in Soviet Russia discussion, 697–702; support for leftist current by, 15, 1150; in tactics and strategy discussion, 508–15, 526, 551, 559–60, 594

Bulgaria: general strike in, 745; trade unions in, 604, 744–6. *See also* Communist Party of Bulgaria

Bullitt, William, 678n

Bund (General Union of Jewish Workers in Lithuania, Poland, and Russia), 67, 1207; Credentials Commission report on, 175, 177; and Zionism, 321–2

Buozzi, Bruno, 320, 1207

Burian, Edmund, 31, 32, 220, 405–6, 512, 1040, 1173, 1207; at opening session, 96; replies to, 533, 534, 535, 567–8, 584; in tactics and strategy discussion, 494–9

Burtsev, Vladimir Lyovich, 949, 1207–8

Cabrini, Angiolo, 357–8, 1208

Cachin, Marcel, 10, 219, 292, 1208; Lenin criticisms of, 1130, 1131; trip to Moscow by, 216, 370, 1117–18

Cadet Party (Russia), 670, 976, 1171, 1208

Caldara, Emilio, 347, 1208

*The Call*, 416, 1208

Calwer, Richard, 110–11, 1208

campaigns, 822–6, 991–3, 997

Canada, 1187–8; IWW in, 718; trade unions in, 739–40; Winnipeg general strike in, 740

Cannon, Edwin, 119n

capitalism: and artificial postwar prosperity, 103–4, 118–19, 151, 163, 164, 903, 925; Black Friday crisis of (1907), 127; in colonial countries, 866–7, 911, 1184–5; concentration process in, 144, 630n, 909, 910; contradictions of, 904, 1181; crisis beginning in 1920 of, 77, 93–4, 117, 122, 135–8, 147, 156, 163, 904–5, 925, 960; curve of development of, 120–2, 123, 139–40; death agony of, 95, 919, 1035; decline of, 107–9, 122–3, 126–7, 140, 442, 910; downfall not automatic, 124, 155, 160; equilibrium of, 116, 124–7, 130, 161–2, 164–5, 508, 656, 692–3, 908; and European reconstruction, 136, 137, 143, 152–3, 451, 693, 912, 915, 926; illusions in, 124, 163; and imperialism, 128–9, 911, 1182–3, 1187–8; and international interdependency, 143–4, 151–2; no solution for women under, 1009–10; offensive against working class by, 125, 127, 137, 138, 143, 149, 163, 532, 960; in pre-revolutionary Russia, 117; prewar expansion of, 123, 132, 902–3; and primitive accumulation, 147,
536–7; Social Democracy as bulwark of, 138–9, 658, 914, 926, 948, 971, 1073; and working-class division, 451. *See also* interimperialist conflicts

Caporetto, Battle of, 345, 362, 367

Cascadden, Gordon, 737n

Central America Communist groups, 69

centralisation, 226, 244, 832; of bourgeoisie, 832, 925; in Comintern, 63, 234, 281, 923; in Communist parties, 810–11, 812–14, 830, 874, 979–80, 996; Communist Youth International and, 233, 1032; trade-union, 616–17

centrism: Comintern split with, 59–60; influences of in Communist movement, 81, 206, 217, 222, 227, 230, 563; presented as main target for Third Congress, 81, 268, 327–8, 460–1, 465, 526, 548–9, 1179; and programme, 436, 438, 936; as target of Second Comintern Congress, 182, 183, 470, 569. *See also* Two-and-a-Half International

Černý, Jan, 420, 1208

Červen, 496–7, 1208

Ceton, Jan Cornelis, 268, 703, 1208; in discussion of Executive Committee report, 249–50

CGL (General Confederation of Labour, Italy), 70, 369, 382, 1216; and Amsterdam International, 199–200, 258, 372, 383–4, 385, 601–2, 711, 720–1, 722; Communist tasks in, 958; during factory occupations, 8, 76, 203, 319–20, 321, 359, 418, 419; membership of, 605; Misiano on, 710–12; and RILU, 382–3, 384–5, 601–2, 711

CGT (General Confederation of Labour, France), 67, 1119, 1216; Amiens Charter of, 606–7, 609–11, 719, 720, 722–5, 747, 748, 749–51, 752, 753–4, 1123; and International Labour Office, 753; Left-Right struggle in, 78, 97–8, 725, 750; Lille Congress of (1921), 102, 751

chairpersons, Third Congress: Gennari in Sessions 19, 21; Koenen in Sessions 3, 5, 10, 11, 12, 13, 15, 24; Kolarov in Sessions 3, 8, 9, 16, 18, 20, 22; Loriot in Sessions 6, 17; Zinoviev in Sessions 1, 2, 23

Chartists, 433

Chavenon, Léon, 113, 126, 1208

Cheka, 265

Chicherin, Georgy Vasilievich, 196, 1208

China: capitalist expansion in, 911; and Japan, 863; Zhang Tailei on, 856–7
Chkheidze, Nikolai Semyonovich, 852, 853, 1208
Churchill, Winston, 90, 1208
Ciccotti, Ettore, 345, 1208
civil servants, 740, 910, 945
civil war, 147, 149, 944, 1170. *See also* Russian Civil War
class of 1919, 11, 115–16, 460, 534, 549, 577–8, 580, 822–3, 931–2, 954, 1046, 1111–13, 1115–16
class struggle, 127, 621, 978; and capitalist equilibrium, 124–7, 161–2, 164–5, 915; and civil war, 127; under conditions of economic decline, 909; dictatorship of proletariat as continuation of, 975; political aspects of, 747, 965; struggle against Amsterdam International as, 603, 705
Clausewitz, Karl von, 433, 1172, 1208
cleansing (purges), 189
Clemenceau, Georges, 252, 1208
CNT (National Confederation of Labour, Spain), 36, 68, 604, 744, 1232
coal industry: nationalisation scheme in Britain for, 91, 438, 926; production statistics, 107, 112, 114, 115, 116
collective bargaining, 963
Colliard, Lucie, 42, 869, 1209; report on Communist Women's Movement by, 790–1
colonial and semi-colonial countries: capitalism in, 866–7, 911, 1184–5; categories of, 1187–8, 1191; class structure in, 866–7, 1191–2; Communist work in, 82, 231, 323, 401, 868, 923, 1184, 1193; impact of economic crisis on, 907; industrial development in, 157, 1188; Javadzadeh on, 322–3; Lenin on, 656, 659; Marx on, 1193; national bourgeoisie in, 1185–6, 1188–90, 1191, 1192; national liberation movements in, 7, 659, 842, 1189, 1190, 1191–3; Roy theses on, 1181–7; Russian Revolution and, 867, 971; Second Comintern Congress on, 322, 870; Sultanzade theses on, 1187–90; women in, 783–4, 1020–1; workers and toilers in, 1183–4, 1185, 1192, 1195; and world revolution, 168, 1183; Zhang Tailei theses on, 1191–3; Zinoviev on, 849. *See also* Baku Congress; Eastern question
commissions, Third Congress:
— Cooperatives Commission, 134, 635
— Credentials Commission, 99, 134, 321–2, 873; report by Radek for, 175–9
— Eastern Question Commission, 635, 856, 1194
— Economic Commission, 169, 170; debate in, 146, 171–2, 633–4, 672, 696; Radek on discussion in, 169–70, 171; report by, 627–33
— Organisation Commission, 832–4, 838; report by, 874–8
— Tactics and Strategy Commission, 391, 626, 634; Lenin speech to, 1142, 1155–7; Radek on tasks of, 388–9; report by, 797–802
— Trade Union Commission, 625, 635, 887; report by, 883–7
— Youth Commission, 779; report by, 873–4
Committee for the Reconstruction of the International (CRI, France), 1123
Communist Group (Cuba), 69, 1209
Communist Group (Ireland), 69, 1210
Communist Group (Portugal), 69, 1211
Communist groups (India), 69, 1210
Communist International (Comintern): Communist parties' relationship to, 63, 983, 1000, 1002; as 'fashionable', 5, 185; and international action, 234, 550–1, 832, 1007; international discipline in, 65, 244, 247, 357, 396, 589; left danger in, 23, 25, 157–8, 561–3, 578–9, 581, 593, 595, 696; massive growth of, 3, 891; need for centralisation in, 63, 234, 281, 923; RILU relationship to, 62, 612–13, 758, 884–5, 959–60; Russian CP and, 213–14, 676–7, 692, 696, 890; Soviet Russia and, 242, 252, 378–9, 692, 702; Statutes of, 59, 82, 180, 357, 924, 950. *See also* First Comintern Congress; Second Comintern Congress
Communist International – organisation and structure, 43, 170n, 878–80, 881–2, 888; Control Commission, 877–8; ECCI composition, 676–7, 1008; organisation report and theses on, 831, 877–8; resolution on, 1007–8; Small Bureau, 15, 24, 38, 39, 181, 879–80, 882, 1008, 1241; Zinoviev elected chair, 888
Communist Manifesto, 812
Communist parties (general): basic task in economic crisis, 633, 919; centralisation in, 810–11, 812–14, 830,

874, 979–80, 996; cleansing (purges) in, 189; in colonial and semi-colonial countries, 82, 231, 323, 401, 868, 923, 1184, 1193; Communist Women's Movement relationship to, 780, 784, 788; criticism and discussion in, 546–7, 590–1, 876, 941–2, 1096, 1162, 1164, 1166; international collaboration and actions by, 234, 274, 405–6, 550, 945–7; KAPD conception of, 455–6; legal and illegal, 814–15, 829–30, 876, 894, 983, 988, 1002–4; as mass parties, 146–7, 222, 267, 292–3, 370, 473, 592, 934, 982; name of, 350; need for women's committees in, 785, 786, 792, 1014–25, 1028–9; as organisations of struggle, 127, 132, 139, 163, 820–2, 875, 920, 928, 940, 985–7, 990–5, 1003; preparatory work by, 425–6, 733; recruitment and integration of women by, 790–1, 1013–14; relationship to Comintern, 63, 983, 1000, 1002; sending representatives to ECCI, 179, 235, 550, 923, 1007; special methods of work toward women, 1014–16, 1028–9; trade unions' relationship to, 611–12, 751, 761–2, 956–7; as tribunes of working class, 938–9; as vanguard of working class, 1038; youth movement relationship to, 772–3, 775, 778–9, 1031–3. See also party organisation

Communist Party of Argentina, 68, 1209

Communist Party of Armenia, 68, 850, 851, 1209

Communist Party of Australia, 69, 735–6, 1209

Communist Party of Austria, 68, 399, 959, 1209; Executive Committee report on, 229

Communist Party of Azerbaijan, 68, 855, 1209

Communist Party of Belgium, 68, 309, 959, 1209; and French CP, 310; and Jacquemotte group, 229, 274–5, 308–9

Communist Party of Bukhara, 69, 1209

Communist Party of Bulgaria, 67, 93, 1209; and trade unions, 745–6; Executive Committee report on, 231

Communist Party of Canada, 69, 737n, 1209

Communist Party of China, 69, 857, 1209

Communist Party of Czechoslovakia, 31–2, 259, 1209; Amendments to Tactics Theses on, 541, 1043–4, 1048–9; Burian on, 494–9; centrist influences in, 222, 567–8; Commission on Tactics and Strategy on, 798, 1155–7; and December 1920 strike, 14, 420–2; discipline in, 496; discussion at expanded ECCI on, 31, 221–7, 494–5n; federal structure of, 226; founding congress of, 13, 221, 224, 225, 409, 664; Gennari on, 254–5; German Section of, 14, 68, 517, 798, 1209–10; Lenin on, 1155–7; as mass party, 462, 534, 927, 928; membership of, 78, 96, 222, 462, 467, 498, 933; Radek on, 420–2, 584; tasks of, 933; Terracini on, 461–2; Third Congress resolutions on, 922–3, 932–3, 959; and trade unions, 959; and Twenty-One Conditions, 14, 224–5, 922; Zinoviev on, 220–7, 567–8

Communist Party of Denmark, 69, 229, 1210

Communist Party of Eastern Galicia, 67, 1210

Communist Party of Estonia, 69, 1210

Communist Party of Far Eastern Republic, 68, 898

Communist Party of Finland, 68, 1210; Executive Committee report on, 231

Communist Party of France, 67, 1210; agitation by, 927, 931; antimilitarist campaign by, 822–3, 946; Comintern concessions to, 32, 33, 195, 215–18; ECCI telegrams to, 217–18; greetings to opening session from, 86–7; and international work, 310, 946; and Italian question, 325; Kolarov criticisms of, 282–3; Kun criticisms of, 1125–8; Laporte criticisms of, 459, 1110–11, 1113–14; Lenin on, 1130–2; membership of, 78, 219, 1124; and military call-up, 822–3, 1126–8; and occupation of Ruhr, 1111–13, 1126; parliamentary fraction of, 218–19, 282, 1046, 1121–2, 1130; press of, 282–3; Radek on, 585; Reiland criticism of, 1108–9; social-democratic traditions of, 219–20, 548–9, 922; Third Congress resolutions on, 922, 927, 928, 931–2; and trade unions, 219, 283, 590, 611–12, 731, 750, 751–2, 957–8, 1122–4, 1129–30; Trotsky on, 580–1, 1118–25; and Twenty-One Conditions, 10, 922; work among women by, 795–6; Zinoviev on, 32, 33, 195, 215–20, 611–12

Communist Party of Georgia, 68, 1210

Communist Party of Germany (KPD, VKPD), 14–18, 67, 585–6, 1210; Amendments to Tactics Theses on tasks of, 1050; call for alliance with Soviet Russia by, 282, 427–8, 431, 1080–1; Comintern organisation proposal by, 831; development of, 423, 483, 1124; electoral results of, 336, 502; during electrical workers' strike, 240, 556; Executive Committee report on, 204–9; founding manifesto of, 10, 424–5, 1074; greetings to opening session from, 87–9; Heidelberg Congress of (1919), 484, 1089; and international action, 946–7; Italian question debated within, 257–9, 288–93, 314–15, 326, 396; Jena Congress of (1921), 37; during Kapp Putsch, 4–5, 205, 311, 423–4, 484, 557, 563; KPD-USPD fusion, 9, 204–5, 483, 501; leftist faction of, 4, 18, 427; Levi leadership of, 5, 206, 311–12, 500; March Action impact on, 21, 148, 464, 504, 524, 1076–7; as mass party, 464, 487, 928; membership of, 21, 183, 424, 487, 524, 1210; preparatory work by, 425–6, 443; press and propaganda of, 253, 425, 524, 993; resignations from Zentrale, 16, 206–7, 266, 294–5, 313, 486, 503; resolutions on March Action adopted by, 21, 489–90, 587; and Russian army advance on Warsaw, 240, 556; Spartacus League and, 183, 204–5, 240, 423, 485, 541, 642, 653, 678; structure of, 933; *Tactics and Organisation of the Revolutionary Offensive* collection of, 530, 546, 1132–3; tactics and strategy theses on tasks of, 933–4; and trade unions, 524, 539, 642, 959; ultraleft split from, 484, 678; and unemployed movement, 539; work among women by, 782. *See also* Levi, Paul; March Action; Open Letter

Communist Party of Germany – internal situation: faction dissolution called for, 591–2, 1106, 1161; Levi parliamentary seat as issue in, 493–4, 1160–1, 1163, 1166, 1167–8, 1177; Malzahn on, 805–6; meeting with Russian delegation on, 1158–69; Neumann on, 532–3; Opposition resolution on, 806; 'Peace Treaty', 39, 1168–9, 1175; *Sowjet* collaboration as issue in, 200, 591, 1106, 1159, 1160, 1161; Third Comintern Congress resolution on, 804, 806, 951; and Zentrale membership, 1159, 1160, 1163–4, 1165, 1166–7; Zetkin on, 547–8, 1150; Zinoviev on, 565–7, 804–5

Communist Party of Germany – Opposition, 34, 65, 570–1; accused of sabotaging March Action, 490–1, 492, 506, 508; amendments on March Action proposed by, 31, 35, 522, 564–5, 590–1; Lenin meeting with, 1145–6; meeting with VKPD majority and RCP leadership, 1158–69; Radek negotiations with, 1149–50; Radek replies to, 265–7, 272–3, 393–4; resolution on March Action by, 21–2, 266, 1079–86; statement on Levi case by, 399–400; support for Tactics and Strategy report by, 523, 532; Third Congress delegation of, 501, 528–9, 539, 1145, 1150–1; Zinoviev on, 398–9

Communist Party of Great Britain, 68, 551, 1209; arrests of leaders, 75, 92; central task of, 929–30; Executive Committee report on, 228–9; and fight against sectarianism, 551–2, 553, 555; and Labour Party, 181–2, 183–4, 928; membership of, 78, 554, 585; and miners' strike, 415–17, 476–9; opening session greetings from, 89–92; press of, 584–5; and trade unions, 929–30, 958; unification of, 78, 228, 553, 928

Communist Party of Greece, 68, 873, 1210; Dimitratos on, 840–1

Communist Party of Hungary, 14–15, 68, 517, 535, 1157–8, 1210

Communist Party of Iceland, 69, 1210

Communist Party of Iran, 69, 323, 842–3, 1210

Communist Party of Italy (PCI), 67, 459, 1210; Comintern recognition of, 325; during factory occupations, 284–5; and fight against fascism, 13, 894; founding of, 12, 60; greetings to opening session by, 97; in Italian elections, 200, 395; leftist tendency of, 30, 540, 596–7; membership of, 13, 1210; and PSI fusion possibility, 30, 370–2, 403–4; tasks of, 930–1; and trade unions, 958; Trotsky on prospects of, 376; Zinoviev on, 79, 564

Communist Party of Japan, 68, 98–9, 859, 1210

Communist Party of Khiva/Khorezm, 69, 1210

Communist Party of Korea, 70, 859, 1211

1272 • Index

Communist Party of Latvia, 69, 1211
Communist Party of Lithuania, 69, 1211
Communist Party of Luxembourg, 69, 1108–9, 1211
Communist Party of Palestine, 69, 1196–7, 1211
Communist Party of Poland. *See* Communist Workers' Party of Poland
Communist Party of Romania, 69, 176, 1211; Credentials Commission report on, 176–7; Executive Committee report on, 230
Communist Party of South Africa, 1195, 1211
Communist Party of Spain (PCE), 68, 230, 1211
Communist Party of Sweden, 68, 959, 1211; Executive Committee report on, 227–8; Höglund statement on, 404–5
Communist Party of Switzerland, 69, 1211; Executive Committee report on, 229
Communist Party of the Indies (Java), 69, 1210
Communist Party of the Netherlands, 36, 68, 247n, 1211. *See also* Dutch school
Communist Party of the United States (United Communist Party), 68, 519–22, 1212; Executive Committee report on, 228–9; and legality question, 79, 229, 520, 521; tasks of, 929, 958; and trade unions, 528–9, 761–2, 958; unification of, 78–9, 228, 520
Communist Party of Turkestan, 865, 899, 1211
Communist Party of Turkey, 69, 323, 839, 849, 1211
Communist Party of Ukraine, 68, 1211–12
Communist Party of Yugoslavia, 68, 399, 1212; defence of Hungarian soviet republic by, 276–7; and general strike of 1920, 762–3; Marković reply to Zinoviev on, 275–8; outlawing of, 79, 277–8; Zinoviev on, 230, 397
*The Communist*, 416, 477, 1209
Communist Women's Movement, 232n, 785, 1015, 1029, 1211; agitation and propaganda by, 1021–4; Colliard report on, 790–1; Communist parties' relationship to, 780, 784, 788; Congress approval of resolutions on, 794–5; in Eastern countries, 1020–1; ECCI support for, 782; First International Conference of, 782; functioning of, 1028–9; identical goals with Comintern of, 784, 1028; International Secretariat of, 786, 787, 1013, 1025, 1026–7; international work of, 1025, 1026–7; Kollontai report on, 791–4; Second International Conference of, 42, 232, 779n, 782–3 , 893, 1028–9, 1141–2, 1148–9; Smythe on, 328; in soviet countries, 1016–18, 1023; structure of, 1024–5; tasks of, 784, 988, 1018–20, 1029; and women's committees within CPs, 785, 786, 792, 1014–25, 1028–9; Zetkin as general secretary of, 232n, 1149; Zetkin report on, 779–90; Zinoviev on, 232. *See also* women
Communist Workers' Federation of Argentina. *See* Argentina Regional Workers Federation
Communist Workers' Party (PCO, Spain), 230, 743–4, 1211
Communist Workers' Party of Bulgaria, 36, 175–6, 1212
Communist Workers' Party of Germany. *See* KAPD
Communist Workers' Party of Poland, 67, 873, 1211; election participation by, 104; during Polish-Soviet War, 251, 528, 822; and trade unions, 250–1, 527; as underground party, 252, 928
Communist Youth International (CYI), 30, 41, 597, 771, 1212; and centralisation, 233, 1032; and Comintern, 264, 1031–2, 1033; headquarters moved to Moscow, 232–3; organisational and agitational work by, 771–2; Second Congress of, 764, 773–4, 893; Zinoviev on, 232–3
Communist youth movement, 41; anti-militarist work by, 772, 1111–13; Communist parties' relationship to, 772–3, 775, 778–9, 1031–3; Frölich report on, 777–9; Münzenberg discussion on, 264; Münzenberg report on, 765–77; report from commission on, 873–4; resolution on, 1030–3; role and tasks of, 774, 988, 1031; Third Congress vote on, 874; Trotsky on, 1115–17; and youth vanguardism, 773, 1032–3; Zinoviev on, 232–3. *See also* youth
Communist Youth of France (Federation of Communist Youth), 460, 534, 768, 772, 1212; Laporte defence of, 1110–14; Trotsky criticism of, 1115–17

Communist Youth of Germany
  (Communist Youth League), 769
Communist Youth of Italy (Italian
  Communist Youth Federation), 263,
  1212
Communist Youth of Russia
  (Communist Youth League;
  Komsomol), 768–9, 1212
compromise, Third Congress, 3, 35, 37–9,
  45, 541, 633; Lenin on, 37, 465–6, 1140,
  1173; Radek on, 593, 1150; Trotsky on,
  572; Zinoviev on, 891
compulsory arbitration, 964
*Comunismo*, 186–9
Confederation of Labour (Spain). *See*
  CNT
*Le Conscrit*, 1111n, 1113
Constituent Assembly (Russia), 470,
  662–3
contracts, labour, 986–9
Control Commission, international,
  877–8
cooperative movement, 42; commission
  on, 134, 635; Communist propaganda
  and agitation in, 967, 968;
  Meshcheriakov report on, 807–8; in
  Soviet Russia, 693–4; Third Congress
  resolutions on, 809, 966, 967–9; and
  trade unions, 712, 968
*Corriere della sera*, 349–50
Cortesi, Luigi, 46
Cosgrove, Pascal (Crosby), 66, 1212
Council for Propaganda and Action, 231,
  855, 869
Credentials Commission, 99, 134, 321–2,
  873; report by Radek for, 175–9
Crispien, Artur, 80n, 182–3, 193, 311, 410,
  591, 1212
Cristescu, Gheorghe, 230, 1212
*Critica sociale*, 65, 361, 367, 1212
criticism, public, 941–2, 1162, 1164, 1166;
  Levi on, 1096; organisation resolution
  on, 876; Radek on, 590–1; Zetkin on,
  546–7
Crosby, John. *See* Cosgrove, Pascal
CSR (Revolutionary Syndicalist
  Committee, France), 719n, 720, 1111–12
Cunow, Heinrich, 124, 1212–13; on Soviet
  Russia, 683–4
currency, 112–13, 114–15, 126;
  fluctuations in value of, 125, 629–30,
  908; and paper money circulation, 118,
  162, 904; statistics on, 108–9
curve of capitalist development, 139–40,
  905; Trotsky on, 120–2, 123

CYI. *See* Communist Youth International
Czechoslovak delegation, 254, 517, 597–8,
  703, 897; declaration on Little Entente
  by, 405–6; protests condemnation of
  Šmeral, 32, 494–9
Czechoslovakia: formation of, 13, 96,
  221; and Little Entente, 405–6; Social
  Democracy in, 498, 934, 948; trade
  unions in, 604, 958–9; working class in,
  409, 497–8. *See also* Communist Party
  of Czechoslovakia
Czechoslovakia – December 1920 events,
  76, 96, 106, 902, 927; account of events,
  13–14, 76n; lessons of, 421–2; Radek
  tactics report on, 420–2; repression
  following, 14, 75; statistics on
  participation in, 498; Theses on Tactics
  and Strategy on, 932–3; Zinoviev on,
  225
Czechoslovak Legion, 860

Dahlmann, Friedrich, 437, 1213
*Daily Herald*, 192, 196, 1213
Danton, Georges Jacques, 87, 789n, 1213
D'Aragona, Ludovico, 64, 196, 284, 369,
  370, 930, 949, 1213; and Amsterdam
  International, 258, 601; during factory
  occupations, 319–20; on RILU, 384–5;
  at Second Comintern Congress, 183;
  and Socialist Concentration faction,
  190–1
Dashnak Party (Armenia), 844, 850, 1213
Daszyński, Ignacy, 955, 1213
Däumig, Ernst, 80n, 305, 532, 1176, 1213;
  factional activity by, 567, 570, 592,
  804; during March Action, 272–3, 306,
  312, 491, 595; Radek on, 592, 1071;
  resignation from Zentrale by, 206n,
  486
debt, 110, 111, 114, 116, 840, 906
defensive struggles, 139, 149, 150, 163,
  632–3, 1076; March Action and, 148,
  208, 530; Third Congress resolutions
  on, 919, 920, 940
Delagrange, Marcel Émile, 308, 703, 834,
  1213
De Leon, Daniel, 738, 1213
demands and slogans, 436–42; partial
  demands, 61, 452, 935–9, 1064–5;
  transitional demands, 2, 26, 440–2,
  936–8, 1066
democracy: Bauer on, 411–12; bourgeois,
  278, 451, 453, 926, 1075; within party,
  980; proletarian dictatorship and, 510,
  511; 'pure', 669–71, 975–6

democratic centralism, 812–13, 830, 874; Organisation Theses on, 979–80; and party press, 996. *See also* centralisation
demonstrations, 822–4, 991
Denikin, Anton Ivanovich, 854, 857, 1213
Denmark, 604
dictatorship of proletariat, 84, 155–6, 950, 965; as continuation of class struggle, 975; Dutch school on, 413; KAPD view of, 692; Lenin on, 670–1; Marx on, 437; and of party, 510–11, 512–14; and women, 787–8, 794
Dimitratos, Nikolaos, 1213; in Eastern question discussion, 839–41
Dimitrov, Georgi, 66, 1213
direct action, 724, 961
disarmament, 486, 502, 575
discipline, 376–7, 496, 1039–40, 1107, 1161; in Comintern, 65, 244, 247, 357, 396, 589; obedience to binding decisions, 1002
Dissidents. *See* Socialist Party of France (SFIO)
Dissmann, Robert, 504, 505, 1213
Dittmann, Wilhelm, 193, 212, 252, 268, 507, 610, 724n, 1213–14; at Second Comintern Congress, 80n, 182–3
dollar, US, 94, 116, 907
dual unionism, 739, 762
Dugoni, Enrico, 201, 320, 1214
Dumoulin, Georges, 957, 1214
Dutch school: Ceton on, 249–50; Radek on, 268–9, 331, 412–15; Roland-Holst and, 211, 245–6; Zinoviev on, 211, 214. *See also* Gorter, Herman
Düwell, Bernhard, 306, 312, 490, 506, 1214

Earsman, William, 1214; Rees reply to, 736–7; in trade-union discussion, 648–50
Eastern bureaus, 869. *See also* Council for Propaganda and Action; Near and Far East Bureau
Eastern Commission, 635, 856, 1194
Eastern question, 43–4, 63; Abilov on, 854–5; Aqazadeh on, 841–3; Dimitratos on, 839–41; Jones on, 1193–6; Julien on, 865–9; Kara-Gadiyev on, 864–5; Kasyan in, 850–1; Kolarov on, 870; Mann on, 835–8; Nam Man-ch'un on, 857–9; protests about discussion on, 44, 855–6, 865; resolutions on, 43–4, 871; Roy on, 855–6; Roy theses on, 1181–7; Süleyman Nuri on, 838–9; Sultanzade theses on, 1187–90; Tskhakaia on, 852–4; Vaillant-Couturier on, 550; Yoshihara on, 859–64; Zhang Tailei on, 856–7; Zhang Tailei theses on, 1191–3; Zinoviev on, 849. *See also* colonial and semi-colonial countries
Eberlein, Hugo, 9, 16, 1214; during March Action, 19, 539
Ebert, Friedrich, 212, 307, 687, 724n, 769, 1214
ECCI. *See* Executive Committee of the Communist International
Economic Commission, 169, 170; debate in, 146, 171–2, 633–4, 672, 696; Radek on discussion in, 169–70, 171; report by, 627–33
Egypt, 136, 837, 845
Eichhorn, Emil, 502–3
eight-hour day, 126, 137, 138, 837
Einstein, Albert, 115, 835–6, 1214
electrification, 668–9, 974–5
Emergency Technical Assistance (Germany), 624–5, 937, 963, 1214
emigration, 911
Engels, Frederick, 1214; on crises and revolution, 119, 121, 629; on 'pure democracy', 669–70, 976
Enver Pasha, 843n, 1214
equilibrium, capitalist, 116, 130, 508, 908; and class struggle, 124–7, 161–2, 164–5, 915; Soviet Russia and, 656, 692–3
Erfurt Programme, 439, 724
Erzberger, Matthias, 205n
Escherich, Georg, 95n, 147, 1214
Estonian Independent Socialist Workers' Party, 177, 1215
European reconstruction, 136, 137, 143, 152–3, 451, 693, 912, 915, 926
Executive Committee of the Communist International (ECCI), 11, 23, 60, 784, 922; Communist parties' sending representatives to, 179, 235, 550, 923, 1007; composition of, 676–7, 1008; as general staff of proletarian revolution, 235; internationalism of, 180–1, 195; lack of discussion around record of, 26, 38, 39; Moscow as headquarters of, 895, 1008; 'Moscow orders' by, 225–6, 234, 281, 378–9, 579–80; Open Letter debated in, 1063–9; organisational work by, 180, 327; proposal to expand size of, 878; and publication of Inprecorr, 1008; Small Bureau of, 15, 24, 38, 39, 181, 879–80, 882, 1008, 1241; telegrams to French CP by, 217–18; telegram to Livorno by, 325

Executive Committee of the Communist International – emissaries: Hungarian exiles as, 14, 226, 1156; at Livorno Congress, 12, 14, 194, 292, 296–7, 304, 318–19, 323–5, 327, 365; Loriot on, 34, 387; during March Action, 16–18, 19, 30, 32, 34, 38, 487, 1094–5; Radek on, 878–9; resolution on Comintern organisation about, 1008; selection of, 550; Serrati on, 197, 198–9; Zetkin on, 38, 292–3, 297, 298, 397–8; Zinoviev on, 397–8

Executive Committee of the Communist International – expanded meeting (June 1921): 33, 338, 578–9, 768, 1108–31, 1150; Bukharin speech at, 31, 224; discussion on Czechoslovakia at, 31, 494–5n; discussion on Italian question at, 208–9, 318, 1132n; Kun speech at, 33, 218, 1125–8; Laporte speech at, 33, 459, 1110–14; Lenin speech at, 33, 219, 220, 461, 476, 1128–32, 1136–7; Loriot report at, 218–19, 1108n; Münzenberg on, 534–5; Radek on, 1136–7; Reiland speech at, 1108–9; Terracini on, 459–60; Trotsky speech at, 209, 577–8, 1115–16; Zinoviev on Czechoslovak question at, 221–7; Zinoviev on French question at, 23, 33, 215–20, 611–12

Executive Committee report and discussion, 34, 60–1; Ceton in, 249–50; Friesland (Reuter) in, 303–7; Frölich in, 242–5; Gennari in, 254–5; Heckert in, 256–9; Hempel in, 239–42; Jacquemotte in, 273–5; Javadzadeh in, 322–3; Koenen in, 310–16; Kolarov in, 281–3; Malzahn in, 260–2; Marković in, 275–81; Michalak (Warszawski) in, 250–2; Münzenberg in, 262–5; Neumann in, 247–9; Overstraten in, 308–10; Radek in, 265–9; Rákosi in, 323–8; resolution on, 34, 921–3; Roland-Holst in, 245–7; Seemann in, 252–3; Smythe in, 328; statements in, 399–400, 403–5; Terracini in, 316–22; vote on, 401; Zetkin in, 283–301; Zinoviev report, 179–235; Zinoviev summary, 395–9

factory councils, 487, 709–10; KAPD and, 248–9, 450, 455, 457, 643–54; theses on tactics on, 937; trade-union theses on, 961

factory occupations, 620–1, 962. *See also* Italy factory occupations
Faisal I (Faisal ibn Husayn), 847, 1215
fascism: attacks on Italian working class by, 12–13, 30, 95, 193, 359, 386, 419, 519, 711–12, 926, 943; PSI view of fighting, 13, 295–6, 349, 386; Rome demonstration against, 823, 894, 1172
Faure, Paul, 381, 1215
Federation of Oppositional Trade Unions of Denmark. *See* Union of Oppositional Trade Unions
feminists, bourgeois, 1011, 1012
feudal relics, 842, 1185, 1186
fictitious capital, 108–9, 119, 137, 904
Fimmen, Eduard, 258, 601, 1215
Finland, 604; white terror in, 75, 93, 231. *See also* Communist Party of Finland
First Comintern Congress (1919), 5, 221–2, 358, 891, 1034; centrism and opportunism as targets of, 470, 586; resolution on women of, 1009, 1013; on winning broad masses to communism, 415
First International (International Workingmen's Association), 810
Fischer, Ruth, 15, 18, 25, 427
Flueras, Ioan, 230, 1215
Fourth Comintern Congress, 43, 878n
fractions and cells, workplace, 102, 612, 641–3, 732, 735, 814–5, 825–6, 886, 957, 981–2, 988, 992, 996–7
France: black troops in, 550, 946; and Britain, 129, 912, 913; class of 1919 call-up in, 11, 115–16, 460, 534, 549, 577–8, 580, 822–3, 931–2, 954, 1046, 1111–13, 1115–16; as colonial power, 550, 847; economy of, 111–13, 123, 126, 905–6, 1120; and Germany, 151, 154–5, 166, 908, 926; international policies of, 912; Lille textile workers' strike in, 1172; Luxembourg occupation by, 460, 1046, 1109, 1116–17; occupation of Ruhr Basin by, 11, 17, 486, 502, 1074, 1111–12, 1126; parliamentary activity in, 282, 548; political parties in, 609; rail strike of 1910 in, 748; rail strike of 1920 in, 105, 749, 791, 901; repression in, 94, 551, 772, 943; revolutionary traditions of, 87; Trotsky on situation in, 1115–16, 1118–20; and World War I, 86, 129. *See also* Communist Party of France; General Confederation of Labour

Franken, Paul, 1134, 1215; during March Action, 506, 531; as VKPD Opposition delegate, 522, 564–5, 590, 806, 1145, 1150
Free Association of Employees (Germany), 1061, 1215
Freemasons, 189, 191, 195, 356, 358
Free Workers Union of Germany (FAUD), 1061, 1215
*Freiheit*, 452, 529, 539, 542, 1134, 1215; *L'Humanité* compared to, 218, 1126
Freikorps, 776–7
French delegation, 11, 32, 102, 703, 898; amendments to economic theses by, 158, 629; on Comintern organisation question, 24, 834, 880; and Eastern question, 865, 868, 869; on ECCI role in March Action, 34, 387; greetings to Congress from, 86–7; on Italian question, 379–80; on tactics and strategy theses, 548–51. *See also* Communist Party of France
French Revolution, 670
Frey, Josef, 229n, 399, 1215
Fries, Philipp, 1105, 1176, 1215
Friesland (Ernst Reuter), 507, 703, 1175, 1237; attacks on Zetkin by, 27, 1141–2; in discussion of Executive Committee report, 303–7; interjections by, 502, 506, 529; as leader of VKPD leftist wing, 9, 18, 427n, 523n; on Levi case, 304–5, 306–7; on March Action, 303–4, 522–4; on procedure, 457, 583; in tactics and strategy discussion, 522–5, 529; on VKPD internal situation, 1162, 1169
Friis, Jacob, 66, 101, 1215
Frölich, Paul, 83, 387, 507, 1040, 1107, 1150, 1215–16; in discussion of Executive Committee report, 242–5, 253; on economic commission debate, 633–4; as leader of VKPD Left, 4, 1068; during March Action, 18, 19, 312n, 429, 545, 1091; at opening session, 87–9; on procedure, 169, 170–1, 582; reports on Communist youth movement by, 777–9, 873–4; on VKPD Opposition, 1165, 1168; on Zetkin, 1104–5
Frossard, Louis-Oscar, 10, 202, 351, 580, 1114, 1216; calls for expulsion of, 220, 1108–9, 1124; on military call-up, 1127–8; on relations with Comintern, 341; trip to Moscow by, 216, 370, 1117–18

Gandhi, Mohandas K., 846n
Gareis, Karl, 205n, 524, 1216

Gelsenkirchen Free Workers' Union, 706, 1160, 1216
General Confederation of Greek Workers, 70, 1216
General Confederation of Labour (France). *See* CGT
General Confederation of Labour (Italy). *See* CGL
General German Trade Union Federation. *See* ADGB
general strike, 453, 570, 615; called during March Action, 20, 491, 503, 505, 1074
General Union of Workers (Spain). *See* UGT
Gennari, Egidio, 362, 1040, 1216; elected vice-chair of Presidium, 83; in Italian question discussion, 29, 344–9; Maffi reply to, 361–3; at opening session, 97; and Small Bureau, 39, 882n; statement in reply to Maffi, 517–22; in tactics and strategy discussion, on Czechoslovak question, 32, 254–5. *See also* chairpersons, Third Congress
Georgia, 851–4
German delegation, 23, 30–1, 898; greetings to Congress from, 87–9; and March Action, 576, 579, 805; protest of Trotsky's remarks by, 597, 1154; rout of, 1149–50; Russian CP meeting with, 30–1, 1158–69; and tactics and strategy thesis, 523, 549, 569, 572, 577, 593, 1106–7, 1150, 1167; on VKPD internal situation motion, 806–7; and world economic theses, 632–4; on Zetkin, 652–3, 1104–5, 1149
Germany: agricultural workers' movement in, 502; Anti-Socialist Law in, 652; approach of Red Army toward, 240, 244, 452, 485, 556; Berlin electrical workers' strike, 240, 556, 557; Berlin municipal workers' strike, 894, 1171; and Britain, 156; calls for alliance with Soviet Russia in, 282, 427–8, 431, 947, 1080–1; capitalist offensive in, 501, 532; coal miners in, 486–7, 502, 622; disarmament demands on, 486, 502, 575; economy of, 109–11, 122–3, 137, 569–70, 906; Emergency Technical Assistance in, 624–5, 937, 963, 1214; Entente occupation of Ruhr, 11, 17, 486, 502, 1074, 1111–12, 1126; factory shop stewards in, 827; Flensburg events in, 588; and France, 151, 154–5, 166, 908, 926; Freikorps in, 776–7; Hoelz activities in, 19, 235–8, 469,

952; Lichtenberg events in, 105n, 297; postwar revolutionary wave in, 105, 502–3, 901, 918; reparations demands on, 110, 111, 136, 152, 165–7, 243, 532, 616, 622n, 913, 1126; repression in, 21, 74–5, 89, 94–5, 943; socialisation schemes in, 438, 925–6; syndicalists in, 453, 605–6, 643, 706; trade-union movement in, 88–9, 149, 501, 507, 575–6, 604, 641–2, 706–8, 713, 953, 959; unemployed workers in, 155, 426–7, 570, 575; workers' councils in, 440, 639–40; working class of, 585, 701; and World War I, 129; youth in, 767, 769. *See also* Communist Party of Germany; Kapp Putsch; March Action; Open Letter; Social-Democratic Party of Germany; USPD
Geyer, Anna, 1216; exclusion from Third Congress of, 528–9, 539, 1151; during March Action, 312, 491
Geyer, Curt, 16, 290, 427, 1216; article on Italy by, 200, 395; and March Action, 207, 506, 595
Geyer, Friedrich, 1176, 1216–17
Gilan, 843
Giolitti, Giovanni, 192, 259, 377, 1217; and factory occupations, 193, 418
*Die Gleichheit*, 652, 1217
Gliński. *See* Królikowski, Stefan
Goldbach, Marie-Luise, 18
Goldman, Emma, 40, 1217
gold standard, 125, 908
Gompers, Samuel, 116, 602n, 640, 717, 721, 727, 886, 953, 1217
Gorky, Maxim, 231, 1217
Gorter, Herman, 187, 268, 448, 1217; Bukharin on, 512–14; Ceton criticisms of, 249–50; on Kronstadt and Soviet Russia, 213, 334–5, 512, 559–60, 699; on March Action as putsch, 244, 299, 677; Radek on, 413; Roland-Holst defence of, 245–6, 338; Zinoviev on, 210–12, 213 — works: *Class Struggle and the Organisation of the Proletariat*, 512–14; *Open Letter to Lenin*, 246, 413; *The Path of Dr. Levi – the Path of the VKPD*, 210–12, 213, 240, 244
Gota, 635
Gotha Programme, 437
Gouraud, Henri, 847, 1217
Gramsci, Antonio, 8, 14, 340n, 1217
Grassmann, Peter, 504, 505, 955, 1217

Graziadei, Antonio, 11, 12, 287, 324, 362, 1217
Greece, 839–40; and Thrace, 846; trade unions in, 70, 604, 1216; and war with Turkey, 159, 839–40
*Grido del popolo*, 722, 1217
Griffuelhes, Victor, 606, 1217
Grimm, Robert, 410, 1217
Grimm, Rosa, 387, 1217
Group of Left Communists (Bulgaria), 175–6
Gruber, Max von, 619, 1218
Guesde, Jules, 342, 1218
guild socialism, 412
Guralsky, August, 16, 19, 298, 1218

Haase, Hugo, 724n
Hajdú, Gyula, 101, 1218
Hajim ibn Muhayd, Fid'an Shaykh, 848, 1218
Halle Congress (1920), 9–10, 185, 268, 398, 483, 1218; Executive Committee report and resolution on, 204–5, 922; Zinoviev at, 396, 600
Handlíř, Jaroslav, 101, 405–6, 1218
Hands Off Russia movement, 90, 822
Haqqi al-'Azm, 847, 1218
Harding, Warren, 912, 1218
Hauth, Wilhelm, 595, 1218
Haymarket affair and martyrs, 715–16, 717
Haywood, William D., 66, 1218; replies to, 726–8, 737, 741–2, 743; theses for RILU congress by, 762; in trade-union discussion, 715–18
Heckert, Fritz, 99, 500, 597, 635, 1040, 1218; on Amendments to Tactics Theses, 35, 481–3; attacks on Zetkin by, 493–4, 500; in discussion of Executive Committee report, 256–9; interjections by, 285, 289, 299, 300, 506, 640; Malzahn replies to, 392, 499–508; on March Action, 38, 486–94, 531; as member of Small Bureau, 39, 882n; Neumann reply to, 528; on procedure, 389, 392; Sachs reply to, 556–7; in tactics and strategy discussion, 481–94; trade-union reports by, 613–25, 883–7; Trotsky reply to, 572, 575, 576; on VKPD internal situation, 1160–1, 1168; Zetkin birthday tribute by, 27, 651n, 652–3; Zetkin reply to, 542, 595–6; Zinoviev reply to, 565, 566

Helfferich, Karl, 111, 1218
Hempel (Jan Appel), 244, 1203; in discussion of Executive Committee report, 239–42; on Hoelz, 237; in Soviet Russia discussion, 691–5, 697, 699–702; statement to Presidium submitted by, 330; in tactics and strategy discussion, 448–57, 467
Henderson, Arthur, 183, 1218–19
Hervé, Gustave, 590, 1219
Hewlett, William J., 1219; at opening session, 89–92
Hilferding, Rudolf, 61, 160, 268, 296, 432, 438, 1074, 1219; on capitalist equilibrium, 124
Hillquit, Morris, 182, 1219
Hindenburg, Paul von, 768, 1219
Hirossik, Janos, 535–6, 1219
Hirsch-Duncker unions, 953, 1219
historical materialism, 699
Hizb al-Watani party (Egypt), 845, 1219
Hoelz, Max, 19, 235–8, 469, 952, 1219
Hoetzsch, Otto, 124–5, 126, 1219
Höfer, Karl, 713, 1219
Hoffman, Adolph, 206n, 1160n, 1176, 1219
Hoffmann, Paul, 588n
Höglund, Karl Zeth, 770, 1219–20; statement on Swedish CP by, 404–5
Hörsing, Friedrich Otto, 262, 1220; and March Action, 18, 19, 212, 280, 312, 429–30, 451, 487, 502, 530, 1074; as trade-union leader, 603, 610
Horthy, Miklós, 405, 1220
Hourwich, Nicholas, 1220; in trade-union discussion, 741–3
housing, 109, 137, 944, 955
Hubin, Georges, 273, 1220
Hughes, Charles Evans, 116–17, 1220
Hula, Břetislav, 75, 223n, 495, 496, 1157, 1220
L'Humanité, 10, 719, 1130, 1220; criticisms of, 218–19, 283, 310, 580, 1121–2, 1126, 1128
Humbert-Droz, Jules, 24, 882n, 1220
Hungarian delegation, 598, 888, 898; and amendments to tactics theses, 515, 517; Lenin reassurances to, 1157–8; minority of, 535–6
Hungarian soviet republic, 276n, 430, 901; women in, 1010–11; Yugoslavia and, 276–7
Hungary, 405; white terror in, 75, 93, 146, 601; workers' movement in, 146, 763. See also Communist Party of Hungary
Huysmans, Camille, 273, 369, 1220

Ibn Rashid, 848
Ibn Saud, Abd al Aziz, 848, 1220
imperialism, 128–9, 911, 925, 1182–3, 1187–8, 1191. See also interimperialist conflicts
Independent Labour Party (ILP, Britain), 68, 438, 1220
Independent Social Democracy of Estonia, 69, 1220
Independent Social-Democratic Party of Germany. See USPD
India: anticolonial struggle in, 846, 1185; British oppression of, 136, 837, 971; capitalism in, 911, 1184–5; national bourgeoisie in, 1185–6; peasant movement in, 1189; working class in, 1185, 1195
Industrial Workers of the World (IWW, Australia), 650, 736, 1220
Industrial Workers of the World (IWW, US), 638, 755 1220–1; Haywood on, 716–18; Hourwich on, 741–2; influence of, 728–9; KAPD and, 36, 646; Marshall (Bedacht) on, 727–9; Morgan (Knight) on, 737–9; membership of, 718, 728, 737, 886; need for Communist work in, 742, 761–2; Pivio (Laukki) on, 759–61; repression and slanders against, 717, 760–1; and Soviet Russia, 727, 738, 759, 761; strikes led by, 718, 760; structure of, 728; at Third World Congress, 36, 68, 884; trade-union theses on, 958
inflation, 113, 118–19, 126, 151, 910, 917, 944
L'Information, 113
Inkpin, Albert, 75n, 83, 1221
interimperialist conflicts, 128–31, 911–14, 1035; France-Britain, 129, 912, 913; France-Germany, 151, 154–5, 166, 908, 926; US-Britain, 115, 129–30, 151, 158, 166, 912, 913; US-Japan, 861, 913. See also World War I
international actions, 234, 550–1, 945–7
International Association of Socialist Women, 1013
International Council of Trade and Industrial Unions, 62, 80, 1221. See also Red International of Labour Unions
Die Internationale, 537, 1221
L'Internationale, 1111
L'Internationale du travail, 600, 1221
International Federation of Trade Unions. See Amsterdam International
Internationalist Socialist Party of the Ruthenian People, 67, 1221

International Labour Office/ Organisation, 200, 601, 722n, 753, 987, 1221
International Socialist Bureau, 180, 369, 1221
International Socialist League (South Africa), 69, 1221
International Women's Day, 1025
Iran, 323, 841–3, 846
Ireland, 94, 136
Islam, 843, 865, 1184, 1186–7, 1189
Italian delegation, 185, 872, 898; and amendments to tactics theses, 31, 34, 457, 596–7, 1041; statement on Czechoslovak question by, 32, 254–5
Italian Socialist Party. *See* PSI
Italy, 371, 590; anarchists and syndicalists in, 458–9, 712, 718; anti-Fascist demonstration in, 823, 894, 1172; elections in, 200–1, 395; fascist attacks against working class in, 12–13, 30, 95, 193, 359, 386, 419, 519, 711–12, 926, 943; in Libya war, 845; postwar revolutionary wave in, 8–9, 193, 901–2, 918; renewed struggles in, 78, 927; Third Congress manifesto on, 872; trade unions in, 360, 604, 605, 710–12; during World War I, 345–6, 905. *See also* Communist Party of Italy (PCI); General Confederation of Labour (CGL)
Italy factory occupations (1920): about, 8, 76n; CGL union federation during, 8, 76, 203, 319–20, 321, 359, 418, 419; Communist Faction during, 340, 359; Lenin on, 352; PSI and, 8, 105, 193, 319, 359, 374–5, 419–20; Radek on, 417–20; revolutionary possibilities of, 193, 203, 284–5, 417, 620; role of shop stewards network in, 827, 994–5; Serrati on, 203, 417–18; Trotsky on, 374–5; Turati and, 105, 319, 376; world situation theses on, 901–2; Zinoviev on, 193, 203
Itschner, Hans Heinrich, 66, 1221
IWW. *See* Industrial Workers of the World

Jacob, Mathilde, 1151, 1221
Jacquemotte, Joseph, 229, 273–5, 1221; in discussion of Executive Committee report, 273–5; Overstraeten reply to, 308–9
Jansen, I. *See* Proost, Jan
Japan, 859–64; and Britain, 912; and China, 856, 863; compared to Russia in 1905, 232; economy of, 116, 156, 907; and Korea, 857–9, 862; and Soviet Russia, 99, 860–1; and United States, 861, 913; working-class struggle in, 131, 862, 958
Japanese Communist group, 68, 98–9, 1210. *See also* Communist Party of Japan
Jaurès, Jean, 10, 1122–3, 1221
Javadzadeh, Mir Ja'far, 1221–2; in discussion of Executive Committee report, 322–3
Jewish Workers League. *See* Bund
Jews, 321–2, 872
Jogiches, Leo, 595–6, 642, 1143, 1222
Jones, Ivon, 44, 872n, 1222; in Eastern question discussion, 1193–6
Jouhaux, Léon, 562, 715, 721, 953, 955, 1119, 1222; as syndicalist, 605, 720; trade-union neutrality advocated by, 97, 610; at Versailles Conference, 601
*Jugend-Internationale*, 771–2, 1222
Julien, Charles-André, 44, 869, 1222; in Eastern question discussion, 865–9
*Der Junge Genosse*, 772, 1222

Kabakchiev, Khristo, 1222; at Livorno, 12, 194, 292, 296–7, 319, 365
Kahr, Gustav Ritter von, 428, 772, 1072, 1222
Kamenev, Lev Borisovich, 28, 196, 295, 1149, 1222; welcoming speech by, 83–5
Kamocki. *See* Rydygier, Aleksander Juliusz
KAPD (Communist Workers' Party of Germany), 67, 1212; adventurism of, 335, 490; Bukharin on, 512–15, 697; and Comintern membership, 36, 214, 396–7; as Comintern sympathising party, 36, 199, 209–10, 242–3, 247, 249, 334–5, 922; declining influence of, 886; in discussion of Executive Committee report, 239–42, 252–3; formation of, 4, 484; Frölich on, 242–5; Hoelz and, 236, 237; during Kapp Putsch, 240, 557; Lozovsky on, 725–6; during March Action, 20, 36, 243–4, 490; on March Action, 451–4, 556–7, 640; membership of, 36, 1212; Münzenberg on, 263–4; National Bolshevik wing of, 333–4; Neumann on, 247–8; and Open Letter, 15, 243, 335, 440, 452–3, 467, 558–9, 1061, 1067; on parliamentarism, 333; *The Path of Dr. Levi* pamphlet of, 210–12, 213, 240, 334; procedural

discussion over, 329–32, 387–8; Radek on, 330–1, 332–6, 389, 414, 592, 674; relations with international leftist currents, 36, 388; Roland-Holst on, 246–7, 336–8; at Second Comintern Congress, 209, 333, 1135; sectarianism of, 242–3, 245, 334; on Soviet Russia, 144, 241–2, 252, 334–5, 671–5, 691–5; in tactics and strategy discussion, 448–57, 556–60; on Theses on Tactics and Strategy by, 803; Third Congress agenda point on, 36, 65, 329–39; Third Congress resolutions and motions on, 329–30, 400–1, 922, 928; on trade-union question, 333; on trade unions, 212, 248, 453, 456, 513–14, 637–48, 706, 725–6, 734, 884, 885–6, 887; Trotsky on, 210, 246, 247; and Velbert/Köthen uprisings, 240, 244, 452; in world economic discussion, 139–45; Zinoviev on, 209–15, 329–30, 331–4, 396–7

Kapp, Wolfgang, 4, 1222

Kapp Putsch: about, 4, 105n; KAPD during, 240, 557; KPD during, 4–5, 205, 311, 423–4, 484, 557, 563; working-class response to, 563, 768, 901, 1068, 1076

Kara-Gadiyev, 1222–3; in Eastern question discussion, 864–5

Karl I, 254, 1223

Kasian, Sarkis Ivanovich, 1223; in Eastern question discussion, 850–1

Kautsky, Karl, 61, 176, 652, 769, 1066, 1223; on historical process, 160, 193; on Soviet Russia, 570, 665, 670; on strategy of attrition, 474; on trade-union neutrality, 608

Kemal Pasha, Mustafa (Atatürk), 159n, 838–9, 849, 1223

Kerensky, Alexander, 278, 1223

Kerran, F. L., 1223; Bukharin reply to, 699–700; in Soviet Russia discussion, 689–91

Khan, Reza, 842n

Khinchuk, Lev Mikhailovich, 635, 967n, 1223

Kibalchich, Liuba Russakova, 1128n, 1223

Kienthal Conference (1916), 87, 341, 352, 369, 770–1

Kilbom, Karl, 1040, 1223

Király, Albert, 535–6, 1223

Knight, Joseph R. (Morgan), 1223; in trade-union discussion, 737–41

Knights of Labor, 717, 1223

Kobetsky, Mikhail V., 181n, 1223–4

Koch-Baumgarten, Sigrid, 19

Koenen, Wilhelm, 35, 181n, 529, 1224; in discussion of Executive Committee report, 310–16; elected vice-chair of Presidium, 83; expressions of Third Congress thanks by, 888–90; and March Action, 207, 312–13, 490; procedural proposals by, 271, 447, 582, 1168; report from Organisation Commission by, 874–8; report on party organisation by, 43, 809–32, 1103; on status of Congress resolutions, 44, 871–3; on Theses on Tactics and Strategy, 1106–7; Trotsky replies to, 166, 576; on VKPD internal situation, 1164, 1167, 1168; in world economic discussion, 157–9, 166; on Zetkin, 313–15, 1104–5. See also chairpersons, Third Congress

Köhler, Bruno, 597, 598, 1224

Kolarov, Vasil, 387, 703, 779, 1224; in discussion of Executive Committee report, 281–3; in Eastern question discussion, 44, 849–50, 851–2, 870; elected vice-chair of Presidium, 83; on Lenin's role at Congress, 25; speech to opening session, 93–5; in trade-union discussion, 744–6. See also chairpersons, Third Congress

Kolchak, Aleksandr Vasilievich, 430, 857, 860, 1224

Kollontai, Alexandra, 688, 692, 1141n, 1224; Bukharin reply to, 698–9; report on Communist Women's Movement by, 42, 791–4; in Soviet Russia discussion, 41, 679–82; Trotsky reply to, 686–9

*Kommunismus*, 14–15

*Kommunistische Arbeiter-Zeitung (KAZ)*, 213, 241, 334, 1224

*Die Kommunistische Fraueninternationale*, 232, 1224

*Kommunistische Internationale*, 246, 776, 1209

*Kommunistischer Gewerkschafter*, 507, 1224

Korea, 323, 857–9, 862

Korfanty, Wojciech, 713, 1224

Koritschoner, Franz, 101, 399, 598, 770, 879, 1040, 1224

KPD. *See* Communist Party of Germany

Krasin, Leonid Borisovich, 673, 1224

Kreibich, Karl, 387, 598, 703, 1040, 1173, 1224–5; and Commission on Tactics

and Strategy, 798, 1155–7; on Šmeral, 226, 1156n
Królikowski, Stefan (Gliński), 703, 1225
Kronstadt, 213n, 700, 949; Gorter on, 213, 334–5, 512, 559–60; Lenin on, 670, 976
Krupskaya, Nadezhda, 1135, 1152, 1225
Kuliscioff, Anna, 367, 1225
Kun, Béla, 27–8, 1225; defence of March Action by, 1088–90; in ECCI debate on France and Leftism, 33, 218, 1125–8; as ECCI emissary, 14, 16–18, 297, 298; and Hungarian CP factions, 535; Lenin criticisms of, 22, 27–8, 1087, 1097, 1098, 1128–32, 1139; letters to Lenin by, 27, 1088–90, 1157–8n; during March Action, 19, 312n, 428; as member of Small Bureau, 39, 181n, 882n; mentioned, 43, 66, 101, 588, 1040; opposition to Trotsky by, 27, 582, 598, 1127, 1153, 1154; opposition to workers' government demand by, 4; on organisational lessons of March Action, 811, 813–14, 828–30; Trotsky on, 683; as 'Turkestaner', 197n, 1125
Kuskova, Yekaterina Dmitrievna, 682, 1225
Kuusinen, Otto, 66, 882n, 1225; organisational theses drafted by, 810n, 978n, 1101, 1103

labour party: Italian CGL moves toward creation of, 711. See also Australian Labor Party
Labour Party (Britain), 552, 929, 1207; Communists barred from, 183–4, 928, 934; debate over Communist participation in, 181–2, 196, 368; as mass party, 222, 554
Lafargue, Paul and Laura, 1089
Lafont, Ernest, 292, 382, 1225
Landler, Jenő, 40, 535–6, 763, 1225; in trade-union discussion, 731–4
Landsberg, Otto, 724n
Lapčević, Dragisa, 277, 1225
Laporte, Maurice, 597, 1115, 1225–6; in ECCI discussion on French Communist Youth, 33, 459, 1110–14; Lenin reply to, 1130, 1131; Trotsky reply to, 577–8, 1115–16
Larin, Yuri Aleksandrovich, 683, 1226
Lassalle, Ferdinand, 438, 936, 1226
Latvia, 74, 604
Laufenberg, Heinrich, 333, 676, 1226
Laukki, Leo (Pivio), 715n, 1226; in trade-union discussion, 759–62

Lazzari, Costantino, 258, 369, 403–4, 519, 1226; Gennari reply to, 345–9; imprisonment of, 339–40, 346; in Italian question discussion, 339–44; Lenin reply to, 349–51; Loriot reply to, 379–82; support for theses on tactics by, 344, 583, 584, 1172; Trotsky reply to, 376–7, 379; during World War I, 201, 339, 346, 347, 363, 380; and Zimmerwald movement, 341n, 369, 380
leadership: in Communist parties, 315–16, 828, 875, 979, 983, 999–1001; of masses, 285, 311, 313–14, 553, 812, 818, 825–6, 993–4
League of Nations, 112n, 925, 1187
League of Peace and Freedom, 437, 1226
Ledebour, Georg, 205, 311, 1073, 1226
Lefebvre, Raymond, 74, 1226
left/right danger question, 182, 183; Brand on, 526; Lenin on, 470, 696, 1136–7; Münzenberg on, 533, 534–5; Radek on, 268, 593, 595, 1135–7; Rákosi on, 327–8; Roland-Holst on, 337, 338, 696; Terracini on, 460–1, 465; Thalheimer on, 540; Thälmann on, 569; Trotsky on, 338, 578–9, 581, 1136–7; Vaillant-Couturier on, 548–9; Zinoviev on, 23, 26, 233–4, 561–4
Left Social-Democratic Party of Sweden. See Communist Party of Sweden
Left Socialist Party (China), 69
Left Socialist Party (Czechoslovakia), 13–14, 68, 420–2, 1226. See also Communist Party of Czechoslovakia
Left Socialist Party of Belgium, 70, 1226
Left Socialist-Revolutionaries (Russia), 468, 1226
legal and illegal work, 814–15, 829–30, 876, 894, 983, 988, 1002–4
Legien, Carl, 733, 953, 1227
Leipart, Theodor, 539, 955, 1227
Die Leipziger Volkszeitung, 529, 596, 1227
Lékai, János, 1040, 1227
Lenin, Vladimir Ilyich, 25, 1227; on Amendments to Tactics Theses, 35, 465–73, 590, 1147–8; April Theses of, 675, 1170–1; on Czechoslovak question and Šmeral, 31, 1100–1, 1155–7, 1173; and differences within Russian CP leadership, 28, 1135–7; disagreements with on Leftism, 482–3, 526, 527, 533, 534, 535, 540–1, 597; in expanded ECCI discussion on France and Leftism, 33, 219, 220, 461, 476, 1128–32, 1136–7;

harsh language withdrawn by, 25, 31, 1107; as honorary chair of Third Congress, 83; in Italian question discussion, 349–53; on Kapp Putsch response, 5, 484; Kun criticised by, 22, 27–8, 1087, 1097, 1098, 1128–32, 1139; Kun letters to, 27, 1088–90, 1157–8n; on leftist danger in Comintern, 23, 25, 28, 564, 1097–8, 1128–32; *Left-Wing Communism: An Infantile Disorder*, 309; letter to Levi and Zetkin, 1087–8; on Levi as correct politically, 1097, 1178; Levi assessment by, 1099, 1143–4, 1151, 1178, 1179; Levi initiative by, 27, 1099, 1100, 1144–5, 1151, 1166, 1174, 1178–80; on Levi's pamphlet, 22–3, 1139–41, 1143, 1149; on 'majority of working class' concept, 35, 466–7, 470–1, 472, 557, 1097–8, 1131; on March Action, 2, 469, 473, 1087, 1099–100, 1139–40, 1149, 1173; mentioned, 40, 66, 83, 106n, 1040; Open Letter supported by, 15, 25, 467, 1087–8, 1098–9; on organisational resolution, 43, 810n, 1101–3; reassurances to Hungarian delegates by, 1157–8; report on policies of Russian CP, 656–71, 702; resignations from Zentrale criticised by, 1087, 1141; in 'right wing' of Third Congress, 2, 25, 476, 1132n, 1179; on Russian Revolution, 475–6, 1158; on Serrati, 192, 350, 351, 353; speech to Central European delegates, 1170–3; speech to Commission on Tactics and Strategy, 1142, 1155–7; tactical flexibility of, 444, 508–9; on tasks of Third Congress, 1097–101; on theory of the offensive, 468–9, 1139, 1140; on Theses on Tactics and Strategy, 25, 28, 34, 466, 1098–9, 1101; Third Congress assessment by, 1173, 1174–5; on Third Congress compromise, 37, 465–6, 1140; Trotsky letter to, 1153–5; on VKPD internal situation, 39, 1161, 1163, 1166–7, 1168, 1169; VKPD Opposition meeting with, 1145–6; on youth, 774; and Zetkin birthday tribute, 651n; Zetkin discussions with, 1137–48, 1150, 1174–8

Lepetit, Jules, 74, 1227

Levi, Paul, 27, 1227; Amendments to Tactics Theses on, 1056; appeal to Third Congress by, 27, 1090–6; Bukharin on, 509–11; continued factional activity of, 804; on ECCI envoys, 16, 397; expulsion of, 27, 65, 215, 307, 392–3, 398, 400n, 579, 942, 1090, 1151; Friesland (Reuter) on, 304–5, 306–7; and Italian question in VKPD, 326, 327; Koenen on, 311–13, 315; as KPD chairman, 5, 311–12, 500; Kun on, 1088, 1089; Lenin agreement with position of, 1097, 1178; Lenin assessment of, 1099, 1143–4, 1151, 1178, 1179; Lenin initiative toward, 27, 1099, 1100, 1144–5, 1151, 1166, 1174, 1178–80; Lenin on pamphlet by, 22–3, 1139–41, 1143, 1149; at Livorno Congress, 11–12, 16, 206, 257, 324–5; on lumpenproletariat, 487; Malzahn on, 392, 399–400, 1159, 1166; during March Action, 491–2; on March Action, 17, 267, 298, 300, 422, 432, 435, 595, 1090–6; Marković on, 280–1; Neumann on, 34, 393, 399–400; 'Our Path: Against Putschism' pamphlet by, 22–3, 280, 312–13, 422, 432, 475–6, 492, 494, 1087, 1090, 1093, 1095, 1133, 1139–41, 1143, 1149; ouster from VKPD leadership of, 16, 17; parliamentary seat of, 493–4, 1160–1, 1163, 1166, 1167–8, 1177; on putschism, 22, 205–6, 432, 435, 484–5; Radek on, 9–10, 16, 23, 26, 266, 394, 590, 1071, 1092; resignation from Zentrale by, 16, 206n, 486; revolutionary record of, 297, 1143–4, 1178; at Second Comintern Congress, 6, 253, 509–10; and Serrati, 197–9, 258, 324, 1099; on Soviet Russia, 427, 510–11; and *Sowjet*, 200, 202, 232, 591; Trotsky on, 577, 1149, 1151, 1164–5; 'Turkestaner' term coined by, 197, 215, 305, 306, 397; Zetkin Congress update sent to, 1148–51; Zetkin initiative to save, 27, 542, 1174, 1177; Zetkin on, 293–4, 296–9, 297, 542, 1133, 1143–4, 1151; Zinoviev on, 197–9, 215, 392–3

Liberal Party (Britain), 553–4, 585, 929

Libya, 845

Liebknecht, Karl, 252, 379, 655, 1030n, 1227; during German Revolution, 827; murder of, 73, 200, 395, 642, 1143; and struggle against War, 770, 822

Liebknecht, Wilhelm, 367, 1227

Linde, Feodor F., 1171

Lindhagen, Carl, 404, 1227

Little Entente, 405–6

Livorno Congress (1921), 11–13, 223, 340, 366, 1227; Baratono resolution at, 365; Bentivoglio resolution at, 198, 365, 403,

921; cries of 'Out, out!' at, 365, 370; ECCI representatives at, 12, 14, 194, 292, 296–7, 304, 318–19, 324–5, 327, 365; ECCI telegram to, 325; Lenin on, 352–3; Levi at, 11–12, 16, 206, 257, 324–5; resolution on Comintern approved by, 356–7; Serrati and, 11–12, 194–5; vote at, 12, 64, 352, 353, 366; Zetkin on, 287–8, 296
Lloyd George, David, 90, 136, 585, 678n, 853, 929, 943, 1227
London *Times*, 120
Longuet, Jean, 290–1, 381, 580, 922, 946, 1227–8; and Twenty-One Conditions, 216–17
Loriot, Fernand, 83, 342, 1119, 1228; on ECCI emissaries, 34, 387; on German questions at Congress, 387; imprisonment of, 1117; in Italian question discussion, 379–82; report to expanded ECCI, 218–19, 1108n; and trade-union work, 731, 1123; during War, 380; Zetkin tribute by, 654–5. *See also* chairpersons, Third Congress
Loucheur, Louis, 616, 1228
Louis, Paul, 283, 1228
Lozovsky, Solomon Abramovich, 233, 1177, 1178, 1228; in Italian question discussion, 382–6; Tomassi reply to, 746–7, 750–1; in trade-union discussion, 719–26
Ludendorff, Erich, 147, 768, 1228
Lukács, Georg (György), 535–6, 1228; in tactics and strategy discussion, 536–9
lumpenproletariat, 487
Lüttwitz, Walther von, 105n, 1228
Luxembourg: French occupation of, 460, 1046, 1109, 1116–17
Luxemburg, Rosa, 106n, 136, 379, 531, 804, 1228; murder of, 73, 200, 395, 642, 1143; polemic with Kautsky by, 474; on programme, 436–7, 439–40; on Russian Revolution, 1177; and struggle against War, 770, 822; and Zetkin, 595–6, 652, 654, 655, 1177

MacDonald, Ramsay, 92, 183, 1228–9
Maffi, Fabrizio, 201, 258, 403–4, 1229; Gennari reply to, 517–19; in Italian question discussion, 360–6
majority of proletariat, 2; Amendments to Tactics Theses deletion of, 461–3, 482–3, 525, 541, 1041, 1042; Lenin on, 35, 466–7, 470–1, 472, 557, 1097–8, 1131; theses on tactics and strategy on, 927; Trotsky on, 133
Makhul Bey, *843–9*
Malthus, Thomas, 619, 1229
Malzahn, Heinrich, 1145, 1150, 1229; in discussion of Executive Committee report, 34, 260–2, 303–4; interjections by, 266, 493; on Levi case, 392, 399–400, 1159, 1166; on March Action, 20, 260–2, 272, 391, 392, 502–6; Radek replies to, 265–7, 272–3, 393–4; revolutionary record of, 505, 591; statement in reply to Radek, 271–2; in tactics and strategy discussion, 499–508, 522, 528, 565; in trade-union discussion, 705–8; and VKPD internal situation, 805–6, 1159–60, 1165, 1166, 1167, 1168; and VKPD Opposition's amendments to tactics theses, 522, 564–5, 590
*Manchester Guardian*, 119, 602
Mann, Tom, 1229; in Eastern question discussion, 835–8
Manner, Kullervo, 66, 1229
Manuilsky, Dmitry, 101, 1229
Marabini, Anselmo, 11, 287n
Marat, Jean-Paul, 87, 1130, 1229
March Action, 1229; account of events, 18–20; Amendments to Tactics Theses on, 1053–6; Burian on, 498–9; decision to end, 20, 492; ECCI emissaries and, 16–18, 19, 30, 32, 34, 38, 487, 1094–5; and ECCI responsibility question, 17–18, 388, 579–80; events in Germany leading up to, 486–7, 502; fratricidal clashes during, 20; Friesland (Reuter) on, 303–4, 522–4; general strike declared during, 20, 491, 503, 505, 1074; Gorter on, 244, 299, 677; Heckert on, 38, 486–94, 531; impact on VKPD of, 21, 148, 464, 504, 524, 1076–7; KAPD during, 20, 36, 243–4, 490; KAPD position on, 451–4, 556–7, 640; Koenen on, 312–13; Kun defence of, 1088–90; Lenin on, 2, 469, 473, 1087, 1099–100, 1139–40, 1149, 1173; lessons of, 434–6, 941–2; Levi on, 17, 267, 298, 300, 422, 432, 435, 595, 1090–6; Lukács on, 536, 538–9; Malzahn on, 20, 260–2, 272, 391, 392, 502–6; Marković on, 280–1, 299; mentioned, 65, 77; Münzenberg on, 265; Neumann on, 529–32; as not a putsch, 208, 431, 587, 1100, 1106; offensive / defensive nature of, 529–30; as putsch, 244, 298, 299, 394,

432, 435, 493, 530, 536, 677; Radek on, 23, 207–8, 335–6, 428–31, 434–6, 586, 587–9, 798–9, 1071–2; reaction in Moscow to, 22–23; repression following, 21, 74–5, 89; statistics on scope of, 20, 260–2, 430, 503–4; as step forward, 208, 280, 436, 469, 569, 941, 1106; *Taktik und Organisation* book on, 530, 546, 1132; Terracini on, 464; Thalheimer on, 539–40; Thälmann on, 569–71, 1161–2; Third Congress manifesto on, 1038–9; Third Congress resolutions on, 31, 951; Trotsky on, 25, 573–7, 1149; USPD during, 949; Vaillant-Couturier on, 549–50; VKPD majority statement on, 1106; VKPD majority resolutions on, 21, 436, 489–90, 587, 1072–9; VKPD Opposition and, 490–1, 492, 506, 508, 564–5; Zetkin on, 21–2, 27, 298–9, 300–1, 431, 544–6, 595, 1079–86, 1132–5, 1137–8; Zinoviev on, 207–8, 566

Marković, Sima, 399, 1040, 1229; in discussion of Executive Committee report, 38, 275–81; Friesland reply to, 305; on Italian question, 279–80; on Levi case, 280–1; on March Action, 280–1, 299; Terracini reply to, 316, 317; in trade-union discussion, 762–3; Zinoviev reply to, 397

Marshall. *See* Bedacht, Max

Martov, Julius, 106n, 348, 380, 1229; on lack of revolutionary prospects, 407

Marx, Karl, 149, 475, 810, 1145, 1229; on colonial slavery, 1193; on crises and revolution, 119, 121, 629; on programme, 437

Marxist Left Wing of the Czech Socialists. *See* Left Socialist Party

Maslow, Arkadi, 18, 529, 1230; as leader of leftist faction, 4, 15, 427, 532; on VKPD internal situation, 1165, 1168, 1169

mass Communist parties, 146–7, 473, 592, 934; Communist reorganisation required in, 982; Czechoslovak CP as, 462, 534, 927; German CP as, 464, 487, 928; leftists' fear of, 552–3, 557–8; necessity of, 222, 267, 292–3, 370

masses: creating links to, 184–5, 417, 426–7, 442, 506, 818, 826, 932; Lenin on concept of, 471–2, 1172; as path to world revolution, 444–5; Radek on, 267–8, 417, 426–7, 442; Terracini on,

461–2; 'To the masses' watchword, 1, 2, 34, 39, 45, 269, 585, 1037, 1142; winning leadership of, 285, 311, 313–14, 553, 812, 818, 825–6, 927–8, 993–4

Maximalists, 285, 345, 346, 518, 711, 1230. *See also* Unitary Communist faction

Mayenburg, Herbert von, 1167, 1230–1

Mazzoni, Nino, 346, 1230

Medvedev, S. P., 679n

Mehring, Franz, 575, 652, 1230

membership responsibilities and norms: activity as requirement, 814, 894, 980–4; assignments, 815–16, 829, 999–1000; finances, 981; meetings, 981, 999; obeying binding decisions, 1002; subscription work, 875, 997–8

Mensheviks, 1230; in Georgia, 851, 852–3; opposition to Soviet regime by, 510, 660, 670, 674, 698, 854, 972, 976; on peasantry, 662; during Russian Revolution, 352, 1171; and trade unions, 611

Merges, August, 209n, 1230

Merino-Gracia, Ramón, 1040, 1230

Merrheim, Alphonse, 380, 382, 720, 752, 1230

Mertens, Corneille, 721, 1230

Meshcheriakov, Nikolai Leonidovich, 1230; report on cooperative movement by, *807–8*

Mesnil, Jacques, 325, 1230–1

Mesopotamia, 136, 847–8

Mexican Communist Party, 69, 1211

Mexico, 604

Meyer, Ernst, 181n, 1231; as leader of VKPD Left, 9, 16, 1068; and March Action, 19, 312n, 1091

Meyer, Fritz. *See* Bergmann

Michalak. *See* Warszawski, Adolf

Michelis, Giuseppe de, 383, 1231

Mičoh, M., 223n

middle classes, 131, 132, 910, 944–55, 988–9

Mieves, Peter, 1167, 1231

militarism, 114, 129, 157; Communist work in opposition to, 768, 772, 989, 1111–13; pacifism and, 914, 989

Milkić, Ilija, 101, 1231

Millerand, Alexandre, 853, 943, 1121, 1231

Milyukov, Pavel Nikolaevich, 670, 949, 976, 1171, 1231

minimum and maximum programmes: Luxemburg on, 439–40; Radek on, 436;

Theses on Tactics and Strategy on, 935–6
Minor, Robert (Ballister), 1231; in tactics and strategy discussion, 519–22
Misiano, Francesco, 1231; in trade-union discussion, 708–12
Modigliani, Giuseppe, 64, 326, 352, 380, 518, 732, 1231
Monatte, Pierre, 1117, 1231; movement toward communism by, 753–4; Trotsky on, 1123–4
Mongolia, 861
Morgan. *See* Knight, Joseph R.
Morocco, 844
*Moscow*, 339, 458, 490–1, 831; about, 47, 102, 1231
'Moscow orders', 225–6, 234, 281, 378–9, 579–80
Müller, Hermann, 1146, 1231–2
Müller, Richard, 294, 1096, 1232; and March Action, 272, 312, 491n, 506; and VKPD Opposition delegation, 1145, 1150
Muna, Alois, 222, 1232; current supposedly led by, 495, 496, 1157; in prison, 75, 83, 223
Münnich, Ferenc, 298n, 1232–3
Münzenberg, Willi, 101, 387, 703, 779, 1040, 1232; in discussion of Executive Committee report, 262–5; report on Communist Youth Movement by, 765–77; and Soviet aid campaign, 41; in tactics and strategy discussion, 533–5
Mussolini, Benito, 12, 358n, 1232

Nam Man-ch'un, 1232; in Eastern question discussion, 857–9
Napoleon Bonaparte, 169–70, 1232
Napoleonic Wars, 137
national bankruptcy, 110–11, 126, 141–2, 159
National Bolshevism, 333–4, 676
National Confederation of Labour (Spain). *See* CNT
national income, 108, 109, 111, 114, 117, 905, 909, 915
nationalisation schemes, 438–9, 623–4, 926, 935, 936
nationalism, 421, 868, 933, 1185, 1186; Communist opposition to, 368, 754, 849, 933, 947, 1021
Nationalist Party (Australia), 649, 1232
National Labour Secretariat (Netherlands), 70, 1232

national liberation movements, 7, 659, 842, 1189, 1190, 1191–3
national property, 108, 109, 125, 126
naval competition, 130
Near and Far East Bureau, 175, 231–2
Němec, Antonín, 584, 1232
Netherlands, 70, 769; trade unions in, 70, 604, 1232. *See also* Communist Party of the Netherlands; Dutch school
Netherlands Alliance of Anarcho-Communists, 70
*Die Neue Zeit*, 443, 683–4, 1232
*Neue Zürcher Zeitung*, 103–4
Neumann, Paul, 394, 505, 1134, 1145, 1232–3; in discussion of Executive Committee report, 247–9; on Levi case, 34, 393, 399–400; and March Action, 272, 506, 523, 529–32; Radek reply to, 265, 393–4; in tactics and strategy discussion, 528–33, 539–40; and VKPD internal situation, 806, 1162–3, 1165, 1167–8, 1169; and VKPD Opposition amendments, 31, 522, 564–5, 590
neutrality, trade-union, 650, 722, 742–3, 747–9, 885; trade-union report on, 607–10; trade-union theses on, 953–5, 960
New Economic Policy (NEP), 24, 41, 664–8, 679–80, 973–4
Nikolaeva, Klavdiia Ivanovna, 101, 1233
Noblemaire, Gustave, 753, 1233
Nobs, Ernst, 229, 284, 1233
Noffri, Gregorio, 367n
Norway: general strike in, 106, 763–4; trade unions in, 604, 605, 763–4, 959
Norwegian Labour Party, 68, 1233; and trade unions, 959; Zinoviev on, 228
Noske, Gustav, 212, 307, 713, 776–7, 1081, 1233

objective and subjective factors, 161
offensive, theory of the. *See* revolutionary offensive
Olberg, Oda, 420, 1233
One Big Union (Australia), 649, 1233
One Big Union (Canada), 739, 1233
*One Big Union Monthly*, 759, 1233
Open Letter, 22, 824; Amendments on Tactics Theses on, 482, 527, 1042, 1049; as campaign, 992; ECCI debate on, 15, 1063–9; impact of, 1080–1; KAPD opposition to, 15, 243, 335, 440, 452–3, 467, 558–9, 1067; Lenin support for, 15, 25, 467, 1087–8, 1098–9; origins of, 15,

426–7, 501; Radek support for, 15, 26, 426–7, 1066–9; text of, 1061–3; Theses on Tactics on, 928, 933, 940
*L'Ordine nuovo*, 8, 317, 1233
organisational question. *See* party organisation
Organisation Commission, 832–4, 838; report by, 874–8
Organisation Theses, 42–3, 62–3; approval of, 882–3; drafting of, 809–10, 833; Koenen report on, 43, 809–32, 1103; Lenin on, 43, 810n, 1101–4; report from Organisation Commission on, 874–8; Schaffner on, 832–3; text of, 978–1006; Zinoviev on, 833, 894
organisers, 982, 999, 1005–6
Orgesch, 95, 147, 713–14, 715, 943, 1068, 1081, 1233
Oudegeest, Jan, 601, 602, 720–1, 722, 1233
'Our Path: Against Putschism' (Levi), 280, 312–13, 422, 475–6, 492, 494, 1087, 1090, 1093, 1095; Lenin on, 432, 1139–41, 1143, 1149; Zetkin on, 1133
*L'Ouvrier communiste*, 274–5, 1233
overproduction, 157, 960, 1181
Overstraeten, Edouard van, 1040, 1233; in discussion of Executive Committee report, *308–10*

pacifism, 914, 944, 989
Paish, George, 124, 1233
Palestine, 872, 1196–7
Palmer, A. Mitchell, 75n
pan-Islamism, 1186–7, 1189
Pannekoek, Anton, 211, 246, 268, 677, 1233–4; Ceton on, 249–50; Radek on, 413; Roland-Holst on, 245–6
Paris Commune, 93, 475
Paris Conference (1921), 502
parliamentary activity, 184, 548, 1107; KAPD rejection of, 333, 456; parliamentary fraction's subordination to party leadership, 184, 876; Second Comintern Congress debate on, 182, 308–9; Theses on Strategy and Tactics on, 939; Zetkin on, 294
partial actions and demands, 61, 432, 798; Bukharin on, 1064–5; KAPD on, 452, 453; Lukács on, 538; Radek on, 436, 1066, 1068; Theses on Tactics and Strategy on, 935–9, 942–3
party organisation: activity as requirement, 814, 894, 980–4; assignments, 815–16, 829, 999–1000;

campaigns, 822–6, 991–3, 997; candidate membership, 1004; centralisation, 810–11, 812–14, 980; class-struggle participation, 985–7; criticism and discussion, 546–7, 876, 941–2, 1162, 1164, 1166; decision making, 1002; democratic centralism, 812–13, 830, 874, 979–80, 996; demonstrations and actions, 822–6, 991; districts, 828, 998, 999–1000; division of labour, 829, 981, 1001, 1004; factory stewards, 826–8; finances, 981; functionaries, 829, 979, 991–2; general principles, 978–9; information service, 828–9; leadership, 828, 875, 979, 983, 999–1001; legal and illegal work, 814–15, 829–30, 876, 894, 983, 988, 1002–4; membership meetings, 981, 999; obedience to binding decisions, 1002; organisers, 999, 1005–6; parliamentary fractions' subordination, 184, 876; party structure, 828–9, 875, 998–1002; political struggle participation, 820–2, 875, 990–5; press, 820, 822, 875, 991, 995–8; propaganda and agitation, 816–20, 874, 984–9; relationship to Comintern, 43, 983, 1000, 1002; reports, 816, 983–4, 1001; during revolutionary situations, 1004–5; specialisation, 815–16, 983; statutes, 1002; subscription work, 875, 997–8; winning leadership of masses, 993–4; workplace fractions and cells, 814, 815, 825–6, 981–2. *See also* Communist parties (general)
*The Path of Dr. Levi – the Path of the VKPD (KAPD)*, 210–12, 213, 240, 334
PCI. *See* Communist Party of Italy
'Peace Treaty', VKPD, 39, 1168–9, 1175
peasantry, 211, 909–10; Bukharin on, 700–1; in colonial and Eastern countries, 1186, 1189, 1192; Communist propaganda among, 819, 989; social differentiation among, 910, 944–5; in Soviet Russia, 661–4, 669, 972–3; during World War I, 131, 631, 909
People's Party (Germany), 437, 1234
*Le Peuple*, 310, 1234; polemic with *Vorwärts*, 166–7
phrase-mongering, 212, 371, 579, 732
Pieck, Wilhelm, 267, 1234
Pilsudski, Józef, 853, 948, 1234
Pinkertons, 624, 625, 926
Pirelli, Alberto, 383, 1234

Pivio, Leo. *See* Laukki, Leo
Plekhanov, Georgy Valentinovich, 475, 1234
Poale Zion, 175, 321–2, 1234
Podrecca, Guido, 357–8, 1234
Pogány, Jószef, 537, 880, 1234; amendments to economic theses by, 632–3; and March Action, 16, 19, 298, 536–7; Trotsky reply to, 162–4; in world economic discussion, 145–50
Poland, 138, 405; general strike in, 927; Jewish organisations in, 321–2; and Soviet Russia, 251–2; trade unions in, 250–1, 527, 604, 713–14; workers' councils in, 104, 251. *See also* Communist Workers' Party of Poland; Polish-Soviet War
Polano, Luigi, 597, 1234
Polish delegation, 476, 481–2, 597–8, 899
Polish Socialist Party (PPS), 104, 714, 927, 948, 1234
Polish-Soviet War, 6–7, 105, 902; disagreements in Russian CP over, 591; Hands Off Russia campaign during, 90, 822; impact in Germany of, 240, 244, 452, 485; Lenin on, 444; Polish CP and, 251, 528, 822; Radek on, 589
*Politiken*, 228, 404, 1234
Popov, Dimitri, 66, 1040, 1234–5
*Le Populaire*, 201, 381–2, 1235
popular justice, 944
Portugal, 604
*Poslednye novosti*, 976, 1235
postwar revolutionary wave: receding of, 3, 106, 919, 1142; Trotsky on, 104–6; world theses on, 901–2, 918–19
power, conquest of: as Communist goal, 155–6, 780, 811, 950; directing propaganda and agitation toward, 552, 935; and transitional demands and struggles, 415, 624, 919, 939; and winning the masses, 444–5
Pozzani, Fernando, 367n
*Pravda*, 976, 1161, 1170, 1235; role before revolution of, 425, 997
*Právo lidu*, 221, 1235
press, Communist: factory fractions and cells and, 996–7; nature and tasks of, 995–6; and party campaigns, 824, 997; polemics in, 998; and political struggles, 991; subscription work for, 875, 997–8; and work among women, 1023

Pressemane, Adrien, 381, 1235
prices, 125; deflation, 107, 110, 904, 960; inflation, 113, 118–19, 126, 151, 910, 917, 944
primitive accumulation, 147, 536–7
principles and goals, 466, 482–3, 1041
Profintern. *See* Red International of Labour Unions
profit-sharing, 964
proletariat: in Belgium, 309–10, 604; bureaucracy within, 165, 916; capitalist offensive against, 125, 127, 137, 138, 143, 148, 149, 163, 532, 960; in colonial East, 1183–4, 1185, 1192, 1195; Communist Party as vanguard and tribune of, 938–9, 1038; condition of during World War I, 917; condition of after War, 131–2, 140–1, 915–17; in Czechoslovakia, 409, 497–8; divisions and stratifications within, 450–1, 616, 916–17, 934–5; fascist attacks on, 12–13, 30, 95, 193, 359, 386, 419, 519, 711–12, 926, 943; in Germany, 486–7, 502, 585, 622, 701; illusions of, 163, 421, 558, 803; majority of, 2, 35, 133, 461–3, 466–7, 470–1, 472, 482–3, 525, 541, 557, 927, 1041, 1042, 1097–8, 1131; in Soviet Russia, 661–4, 665–6, 680–2, 688, 689, 694, 972–3; sowing divisions among, 622, 623; and unemployment, 536–7, 916; youth in, 766–7. *See also* class struggle; trade unions
*Der Proletarier*, 211, 246, 268, 885, 1235
Proost, Jan (Jansen), 66, 336, 1040, 1235
propaganda and agitation: among peasantry and semi-proletarian layers, 818–9, 989; among women, 1021–4; in armed forces, 819–20, 875, 946, 989; during British miners' strike, 478; in cooperative movement, 967, 968; by German CP, 253, 425, 524, 993; organisation report and theses on, 816–20, 874, 984–9; party press and, 996–7; person-to-person, 985; and political struggles, 442, 538–9, 821–2, 991; during preparatory period, 443, 939; and struggle for power, 552, 935; through deeds, 533, 1021–2; in trade unions, 818
prosperity, 126–7, 146–7, 149–50, 442, 569–70; artificial postwar, 118–19, 163, 164, 903, 925; and revolutionary prospects, 120, 121–2, 128, 162, 164, 165–6, 629, 634

PSI (Italian Socialist Party), 11–13, 29–30, 1221; Amendments to Tactics Theses on, 458–9, 1043; and Amsterdam International, 199–200, 258, 372, 383–4; Baratono-Serrati rift in, 202; Bentivoglio resolution of, 198, 365, 403, 921; Bologna Congress of (1919), 347, 518; CGL ties to, 382; Comintern conditions set for, 64–5, 921–2; Communist Faction of, 8–9, 11, 12, 317, 324, 340, 358, 359–60, 519, 540–1n; door held open to, 29, 370–4; early affiliation to Comintern of, 340–1, 348, 359–60; ECCI book on, 186, 340, 343–4; electoral participation of, 200, 362, 395, 518; evasion of struggle by, 343, 918, 949; expulsion from Comintern of, 564, 892–3, 1037; expulsion of reformist faction from (1922), 30, 922n; during factory occupations, 8, 105, 193, 319, 359, 374–5, 419–20; and fascism, 13, 295–6, 349, 386, 894; and fight for fusion with Communists, 30, 370–2, 403–4; Gennari on, 344–9; Heckert on, 256–7; Lazzari on, 339–44; Lenin on, 349–53; Loriot on, 379–82; Maffi, on, 360–6; manifesto of after Livorno, 343–4; Marković on, 279–80; parliamentary group of, 201, 346, 362, 367; Rákosi on, 324–5, 346, 362, 367; Rakovsky on, 366–71; and reformism, 357–8, 366–7, 922n; resolution on relations with Third International by, 356–7; rightward evolution of, 295–6, 349, 375, 381, 386; Rome Congress of (1918), 347, 518; and Russian Revolution, 341, 359–60; Socialist Concentration faction of, 11, 12, 190–1, 375–6, 1241; and Soviet Russia, 342, 347–8; Terracini on, 316–21; Theses on Tactics and Strategy on, 930–1; Third Comintern Congress delegation from, 29, 67, 186, 258–9, 339–44, 340, 355–60, 360–6, 403–4; Trotsky on, 374–9, 579; and Twenty-One Conditions, 8, 11, 188–90, 317, 356, 357, 358; Unitary Communist faction of, 8, 11, 12, 286, 296, 318, 371–2, 893, 1247; during war in Libya, 379–80; during World War I, 342, 345–7, 360, 363, 367, 379–80; Zetkin on, 284–8, 371–4; and Zimmerwald movement, 341, 359–60, 369; Zinoviev on, 185–204, 395–6, 892–3. See also Livorno Congress; Serrati, Giacinto Menotti; Turati, Filippo
putsches and putschism, 527, 596–7, 1075; Lenin on, 1100, 1139; Levi on, 22, 205–6, 432, 435, 484–5; Lukács on, 536–7; Zetkin on, 1083, 1085, 1133–4
Pyatakov, Yuri Leonidovich, 683, 1235

Quelch, Thomas, 66, 1235

Rabier, Fernand, 749, 1235
Radek, Karl, 26, 1235; on British miners' strike, 415–17, 476–9; on Comintern organisation and structure, 878–9; and congress commissions, 134, 322, 634; Credentials Commission report by, 175–9; on Czechoslovakia, 420–2, 584; on differences among Russian CP leadership, 28–9, 1135–7; in discussion of Executive Committee report, 265–9; drafting of tactics theses by, 25, 34, 1097–9; on economics report and commission, 169–70, 171–2; on Hoelz, 235–8, 469; interjections by, 207, 213, 253, 272, 280, 281, 290, 295, 296, 297, 298, 299, 469, 500, 504, 505, 514, 531, 537, 540, 575, 686, 699, 1127, 1156; on Italian factory occupations, 417–20; on Italian question, 11, 16; on KAPD, 330–1, 332–6, 389, 414, 592, 674; on Levi, 9–10, 16, 23, 26, 266, 394, 590, 1071, 1092; on Malzahn, 265–7, 272–3, 393–4, 504–5; on March Action, 23, 207–8, 335–6, 428–31, 434–6, 586, 587–9, 798–9, 1071–2; as member of Small Bureau, 39, 181n, 882n; mentioned, 4, 25, 66, 83, 240, 691–2; on offensive theory, 431, 433–4, 587, 1136; on Open Letter, 15, 26, 426–7, 1066–9; on Polish-Soviet War, 6, 591; procedural proposals by, 168–9, 275, 279, 307, 330–1, 388–9, 635, 636–7, 880, 881; in Soviet Russia discussion, 674–9; and Third Congress manifesto, 168, 1040; tactics and strategy report by, 34, 406–45; tactics and strategy report from Commission by, 797–802; tactics and strategy summary by, 583–95; ties to German Left faction of, 9–10, 15, 530, 1150; on transitional demands, 26, 440–2, 1066; veiled polemic with Trotsky by, 589, 1154–5; on VKPD internal situation, 1163–4;

and VKPD Opposition, 272–3, 393–4, 532, 1148, 1149–50; Zetkin criticised by, 431, 473–4, 590–1, 1071
Radical Socialist Party (France), 1119, 1235
Rahja, Eino A., 66, 1235
Rahja, Jukka A., 74, 1235
Railroad Workers' Association (Italy), 67, 1235
Rákosi, Mátyás, 882n, 1236; in discussion of Executive Committee report, 323–8; as ECCI emissary at Livorno, 12, 14, 194, 304, 318–19, 324–5, 327; in VKPD leadership debate, 16, 38, 292–3, 296, 315, 325–7, 326
Rakovsky, Christian, 29, 684, 1236; in Italian question discussion, 366–71; on procedure, 386, 390
Rappoport, Charles, 1126
Rathenau, Walter, 616, 1236
Red Aid, 43, 875, 1236
Red Army, 6, 430; in Caucasus, 852–3, 855; during Civil War, 117, 663, 908; Lenin on tasks of, 657; Third Congress thanks to, 890
Red International of Labour Unions (RILU, Profintern), 233, 646–7, 737n, 753, 1236; Action Programme for, 960–5; Australian unions and, 648, 736–7; Comintern relationship to, 62, 612–13, 758, 884–5, 959–60; founding congress of, 40, 626, 646, 650, 893; Haywood theses for, 762; international bureaus of, 743; and Italian CGL, 382–3, 384–5, 601–2, 711; and IWW, 718; membership statistics on, 604; and syndicalists, 605–11, 746
Reed, John, 1236; at Second Comintern Congress, 181, 562; tributes to, 73, 626
Rees, Alf G., 1236; in trade-union discussion, 735–7
reformism, 207, 276, 373, 1037, 1081, 1176; characteristics of, 124; in Italy, 351, 366–7, 369, 385, 519; Leftist charges of, 274, 413, 449, 937; and middle layers, 944. See also Second International
reforms, 437, 780, 935, 1009–10, 1019
Reggio Emilia conference (1920), 190–1, 349–50
Reich, Yakov, 298n, 1236
Reichenbach, Bernhard. See Seemann
Reicher, Gustaw (Rwal), 1236; in trade-union discussion, 712–15

Reiland, Edy, 33, 1236–7; in ECCI debate on French CP, 1108–9; Lenin reply to, 1130–1; Trotsky reply to, 1116–17
Renaudel, Pierre, 369, 1237
Renner, Karl, 412, 701, 1237
Renoult, Daniel, 216, 1237
reparations, 110, 111, 136, 152, 165–7, 243, 532, 616, 622n, 913, 1126; conflict between Second and Two-and-a-Half Internationals over, 166–7
Reuter, Ernst. See Friesland
revolutionary offensive, 22, 260, 262; about theory of, 7, 208n; Amendments to Tactics Theses on, 1054; Bukharin on, 6–7, 468n; Lenin on, 468–9, 1139, 1140; Lukács on, 537; March Action and, 504, 529–30, 544–5; and offence vs. defence, 433, 474–5; Radek on, 431, 433–4, 587, 1136; Terracini on, 464–5; Theses on Tactics and Strategy on, 34, 940–1; Trotsky on, 133, 578; VKPD theses on, 23, 1076; world economic discussion on, 628–9, 919–20; Zetkin on, 266–7, 299–300, 431, 473–4, 543–4, 546, 1137–8, 1150; Zinoviev on, 208, 892
revolutionary prospects: in colonial countries, 168; and economic crisis/prosperity, 119–20, 121–2, 127–8, 146, 162, 164, 165–6, 442, 629, 634; in Europe, 167; Lenin on, 1170, 1172, 1173; as not automatic, 124, 155, 160; Radek on, 406–12; Šmeral on, 14, 221n, 224, 225, 409; Social Democracy on lack of, 407–8, 918; and subjective factor, 160–1, 168, 309, 310; Trotsky on, 33, 131–2, 133, 150; in United States, 167–8, 910–11; world economic theses on, 917–18
Revolutionary Syndicalist Committee (France). See CSR
Revolutionary Union Minority (France), 67, 1237. See also CSR
revolutionary wave. See postwar revolutionary wave
Revolutions of 1848, 119, 120, 669
Riboldi, Ezio, 258, 403–4, 1237
Riehs, Jakob, 1237; in trade-union discussion, 40, 734–5
right/left danger. See left/right danger question
Rigola, Rinaldo, 234, 369, 370, 1237
RILU. See Red International of Labour Unions

Ríos, Fernando de los, 230n, 1237
*Risorgimento*, 367
Robespierre, Maximilien, 87, 1237
Rogalski, 557
Roland-Holst, Henriette, 1237; Ceton reply to, 249–50; defence of Left by, 337, 338, 564, 696; in discussion of Executive Committee report, 245–7; on Dutch school and Gorter, 211, 245–6, 338; in KAPD question discussion, 336–8, 390–1; Radek replies to, 268, 391–2; in Soviet Russia discussion, 695–7, 703
Romania, 604, 872. *See also* Communist Party of Romania
Rosenfeld, Kurt, 525, 1237
Rosmer, Alfred, 66, 181n, 635, 1237–8; on debate at Third Congress, 25, 33, 40
ROSTA, 568
*Die Rote Fahne*, 452, 486, 542, 575, 673, 1126, 1238; circulation of, 524; editorial staff rebellion within, 38, 312; internal discussion in, 1164; on Italy, 325, 327; March Action articles in, 18, 19, 299, 300, 428, 429, 488–9, 504, 523, 529, 546, 1085
Roy, M. N., 134n, 167, 869n, 1238; in Eastern question discussion, 44, 855–6; theses on colonial question by, 44, 1181–7; in world economic discussion, 156–7; Zuang Tailei reply to, 1192
*Rudé právo*, 421, 1238
Rudnyánszky, Endre, 66, 181n, 1238
Rühle, Otto, 209, 253, 333, 617, 1238
Russia, pre-revolutionary, 117, 127–8, 146
Russian Civil War, 85, 117, 662–3, 857; alliance of proletariat and peasantry during, 972–3
Russian Communist Party (RCP), 67, 1211; cleansing campaign by, 702; and Comintern, 213–14, 676–7, 692, 696, 890; debates within, 290, 591, 688; leadership divisions at Third Congress, 23, 24, 28–9, 39, 1135–7, 1154–5; Lenin report on policies of, 656–71; meeting with German delegation by, 30–1, 1158–69; press of, 425; Tenth Congress of (1921), 1072; Third Congress resolutions on, 970–6, 977; Third Congress thanks to, 889–90; welcoming speech from, 83–5; and work among women, 781, 792–4; Workers' Opposition within, 36, 41, 510, 679; and world revolution, 264–5, 594, 693, 695–6. *See also* Bolshevik Party; Soviet Russia
Russian Revolution, 341, 508, 585, 867, 1177; Bolshevik strategy during, 674–5; factory fractions and stewards during, 826–7; July Days during, 594, 1100; Lenin on, 475–6, 1158; Lenin on reasons for victory of, 469–71; size of Bolshevik Party during, 352, 467; and world revolution, 657–8
Russian Workers' Federation of South America, 70, 1238
Rwal. *See* Reicher, Gustaw
Rydygier, Aleksander Juliusz (Kamocki), 101, 1238

Saar (German region), 112, 912
Saar (Palestinian delegate), 1196–7
sabotage, 521, 862, 944
Sachs (Alexander Schwab), 219, 887, 1239; in discussion of Executive Committee report, 387–8; in Soviet Russia discussion, 671–5; in tactics and strategy discussion, 556–60, 592; in world economic discussion, 139–42, 161
Safarov, Georgy, 869n
Samoilova, Konkordia Nikolaevna, 74, 1238
Sandgren, John, 759, 761, 1238
Sankey, John, and Sankey Commission, 91, 926, 1238
Sarekat Islam, 846, 1238
Schaffner, Erwin, 171, 1239; in party organisation discussion, 832–3
Scheflo, Olav, 387, 1040, 1239
Scheidemann, Philipp, 212, 285, 296, 307, 395, 412, 693, 724n, 943, 1064, 1239
Schmidt, Robert, 955, 1239
Schober, Johann, 412, 1239
Schulz, 646
Schulze, Ernst, 294, 619, 1239
Schwab, Alexander. *See* Sachs
Seamen's Union (Italy), 67
Second Comintern Congress, 88, 185, 193, 574, 664, 735, 891, 1034; adoption of basic positions by, 82, 415, 473; D'Aragona at, 183; debate on parliamentarism at, 182, 308–9; on illegal and legal work, 829, 830n; and KAPD, 209, 333, 559, 1135; Labour Party debate at, 181–2, 184; and Left danger, 561–2, 569; Levi at, 6, 253, 509–10; national and colonial questions

at, 322, 550, 870, 1190; as real founding congress, 5, 181; resolution on women of, 1009; Right as main target of, 5, 182, 233, 321, 470, 586; Serrati articles on, 186–90; Serrati at, 184, 253, 256, 284, 289, 563; trade-union debate at, 562, 599, 709, 726; trade-union theses of, 705, 708, 709, 731, 743–4, 755; Twenty-One Conditions adopted by, 60, 182, 183, 316; USPD at, 5, 79–80, 182–3

Second International, 152, 273, 349, 976, 1239; 1914 betrayal by, 610, 1073; as bulwark of capitalism, 138–9, 658, 914, 926, 948, 971, 1073; and colonial question, 659; Copenhagen Congress of (1910), 655; as divisive force in working class, 934–5; and Georgian Mensheviks, 853; International Socialist Bureau of, 180, 369, 1221; minimum programme of, 436–7; and reparations controversy, 166–7; Stuttgart Congress of (1907), 106, 655; and trade-union movement, 80, 610, 954; and Two-and-a-Half International, 104, 949–50; unity-at-all costs tradition of, 568; and work among women, 783, 1013; and youth movement, 769, 1030; Zurich Congress of (1893), 366–7

Second International Conference of Communist Women, 42, 232, 779n, 782–3, 893; attack on Zetkin at, 1141–2, 1148–9; resolution of, 1028–9

sectarianism, 182, 562, 927, 928; in Britain and US, 551–2, 553, 555; KAPD and, 242–3, 245, 334

Seemann (Bernhard Reichenbach), 244, 677, 1236; in discussion of Executive Committee report, 252–3; on procedure, 239, 637; Trotsky reply to, 160, 161; in world economic discussion, 142–5

self-defence, workers', 624–5, 963, 1062. *See also* arming the proletariat

Sellier, Louis, 1112, 1114, 1239

Sembat, Marcel, 342, 1239

Semyonov, Grigorii Mikhailovich, 860, 1239

Serbian Socialist Party. *See* Social-Democratic Party of Serbia

Serge, Victor, 6, 24, 25, 40, 1128n, 1239–40

Serrati, Giacinto Menotti, 341n, 949, 1240; articles on Second Comintern Congress by, 186–9; Baratono rift with, 202; on ECCI emissaries, 197, 198–9, 397; as editor of *Avanti*, 190, 196–7; on French CP, 195, 215–16; on Italian factory occupations, 203, 417–18; Lenin on, 192, 350, 351, 353; and Levi, 197–9, 258, 324, 1099; and Livorno Congress, 11–12, 194–5, 459; Marković on, 279–80; open letter to Lenin by, 192, 203; opposes break with reformists, 256–7, 318; Rakovsky on, 368; reformist evolution of, 207, 373; at Second Comintern Congress, 184, 253, 256, 284, 289, 563; and Šmeral, 254, 255, 259; on Soviet Russia, 196, 202, 256, 347; trip to Germany by, 206, 290–1, 314; Trotsky on, 579; and Twenty-One Conditions, 8, 188–90; Zetkin on, 284, 286–8, 290–1, 324, 373; Zinoviev on, 185–204, 317

Severing, Carl, 502, 926, 1081, 1240

Shablin, Nikolai, 66, 1240

al-Sharif, Sayyid Ahmad, 848, 1240

Shatskin, Lazar Abramovich, 66, 779, 1240

Shlyapnikov, Aleksandr, 679n, 1240

shop stewards, 826–7, 994–5

Shop Stewards' Movement (Britain), 756, 827, 1240; KAPD on, 448, 638, 644

Shumiatsky, Boris Zakharovich, 101, 869, 1240

Shumsky, Oleksander, 1040, 1240

Siberia, 661

Sievers, Max, 312, 1240

Šilfs, Janis, 74, 1240

Sirola, Yrjö E., 101, 281, 1040, 1240

Skalák, Josef, 496, 1241

Small Bureau, 15, 38, 181, 1241; composition of, 181n, 882n; organisational resolution on, 877; selection of, 24, 39, 879–80, 1008

Šmeral, Bohumir, 13, 1241; attendance at Third Congress by, 220, 221; debate over public condemnation of, 31–2, 225n, 495–7, 798; Lenin on, 1100–1, 1156–7, 1173; Münzenberg on, 534, 535; report to Czechoslovak CP founding congress, 221, 224, 225, 409, 664; on revolutionary prospects, 14, 221n, 224, 225, 409; Serrati compared to, 254, 255, 259; during World War I, 226, 254, 1156; Zinoviev on, 222–3, 224–6, 567–8

Smillie, Robert, 439, 1241

Smythe, Norah, 42, 101, 1241; in discussion of Executive Committee report, 328

Social Democracy. *See* Second International

1292 • Index

Social-Democratic Party (Britain), 554
Social-Democratic Party of Czechoslovakia, 498, 934, 948
Social-Democratic Party of Germany (SPD), 285, 768, 948, 1241; in German government, 575, 724, 1073; as mass party, 222; and VKPD Open Letter, 1061, 1067; youth wing of, 769
Social-Democratic Party of Hungary, 276, 1241
Social-Democratic Party of Serbia, 276, 277, 1241
Social-Democratic Party of Slovakia, 68, 1241
Social-Democratic Party of Sweden, 404, 1241
Social-Democratic Party of Switzerland, 229, 367n, 1241
Social-Democratic Workers' Party of Austria, 229, 734, 1241
socialisation demand, 438–9, 623–4, 925–6, 935
Socialist Concentration faction (Italy), 11, 12, 190–1, 375–6, 1241
Socialist Labor Party (US), 726n, 762, 1242
Socialist Labour Party (Britain), 554
Socialist Party of America, 182, 743, 760, 926
Socialist Party of Canada, 739
Socialist Party of France (SFIO), 380, 931, 946, 1242; Dissident Longuet wing of, 61, 217, 381–2, 934, 949, 1213; as electoral party, 748; and Second Comintern Congress, 5, 574; Tours Congress of, 10–11, 217, 251, 261, 655, 1245; and trade unions, 749, 750; during War, 196, 342. *See also* Communist Party of France
Socialist Party of Italy. *See* PSI
Socialist Party of Slovakia. *See* Social-Democratic Party of Slovakia
Socialist Party of the autonomous region of Fünfkirchen, 68
Socialist Party of Uruguay, 69, 1242
Socialist-Revolutionary Party (SRs, Russia), 161, 1242; adventurism of, 589–90; Left SRs, 468, 1226; opposition to Soviet regime by, 510, 660, 670, 698, 854, 972, 976; during Russian Revolution, 469–70
socialist society, 615, 974–5
Socialist Trade and Labor Alliance (US), 726

Socialist Workers' Party (Chile), 69, 1242
Socialist Workers' Party of Finland, 70. *See also* Communist Party of Finland
Socialist Workers' Party of Spain (PSOE), 230, 744, 1242
Socialist Youth Federation of Italy, 263
Social-Revolutionaries (Russia). *See* Socialist-Revolutionary Party
Social-Revolutionary Party (Korea), 70
Soglia, Giuseppe, 345, 346, 1242
Sokolnikov, Grigorii Yakovlevich, 869n, 1242
*Solidarity*, 727, 1242
Sombart, Werner, 437, 1242
Soukup, František, 584, 1242
South Africa, 1193, 1194–5
Souvarine, Boris, 40, 1040, 1242; as member of Small Bureau, 39, 882n; on procedure, 308, 387, 878, 881
Soviet Russia: as agenda point at Third Congress, 41, 65, 81, 656–703; blockade against, 90n, 117, 183, 851, 908; and Britain, 90, 192, 196; and British miners' strike, 89, 673, 676; Bukharin on, 697–702; buying time by, 678–9, 692; and Comintern, 242, 252, 378–9, 692, 702; concessions by, 202, 510, 678, 680, 683–4, 685, 687, 690, 692–3, 974, 1087; dangers facing, 677, 694–5; defence of proletarian dictatorship in, 84–5, 947; and Eastern countries, 7, 838, 841, 844, 846, 850–3, 856, 859, 865, 867; electrification of, 668–9, 974–5; émigrés from, 660, 972; food policy of, 974; freedom of trade in, 666–7; German CP call for alliance with, 282, 427–8, 431, 1063, 1080–1; Gorter on, 213, 334–5, 512, 559–60, 699; Hempel on, 691–5, 697, 699–702; imperialist intervention in, 85, 657; internal situation in, 659–61; and international politics, 656–8, 914; international position of, 970; IWW and, 727, 738, 759, 761; and Japan, 99, 860–1; Jewish workers in, 322; KAPD on, 144, 241–2, 252, 334–5, 671–5, 691–5; Kautsky on, 570, 665, 670; Kerran on, 689–91; Kollontai on, 41, 679–82; Kronstadt revolt in, 213, 334–5, 512, 559–60, 670, 700, 949, 976; Lenin report on, 656–71, 702; Levi on, 427, 510–11; New Economic Policy adopted by, 24, 41, 664–5, 679–80, 973–4; peasantry in, 661–4, 665, 669, 972–3; PSI and, 342, 347–8;

Radek on, 674–9; relationship of class forces in, 971–3; and revolutionary defeats, 430; Roland-Holst on, 695–7; Sachs on, 671–5; Serrati on, 196, 202, 256, 347; and state capitalism, 667–8, 698–9, 974; tax in kind in, 666, 699, 973; technicians and specialists used by, 688–9; Third Congress resolutions on, 41, 703, 970–6, 977; trade unions in, 604, 611, 717, 741; trade with capitalist states by, 701–2; and transition to socialism, 85, 412; Trotsky on, 41, 683–9; Two-and-a-Half International on, 411–12, 976; and United States, 116–17, 678; and Versailles Treaty, 676; war communism policies in, 675; and women, 792–4, 1011, 1016–18, 1022, 1023; work for emergency aid for, 41; working class in, 661–4, 665–6, 680–2, 688, 689, 694, 972–3; and world capitalism, 116–17, 144, 162, 672, 685, 690–1, 908; and world revolution, 657–8, 673, 675–6, 695–6, 697; youth work by, 768–9. *See also* Polish-Soviet War; Russian Civil War; Russian Communist Party; Russian Revolution

*Sowjet*, 202, 232, 313, 395, 492, 1242–3; VKPD members' collaboration with, 200, 591, 1106, 1159, 1160, 1161; Zetkin on, 1177

*Der Sozialist*, 256, 1243

Spa Conference (1920), 622

Spain: repression in, 98, 721; trade unions in, 604–5, 743–4, 958. *See also* Communist Party of Spain (PCE); Communist Workers' Party (PCO)

Spartacus League, 183, 541, 822, 1243; KPD and, 204–5, 240, 423, 485, 642, 653, 678. *See also* Communist Party of Germany

SPD. *See* Social-Democratic Party of Germany

specialists, 368–70

speculation, 118, 125, 904, 908

SRs. *See* Socialist-Revolutionary Party

Stadnik, B., 223n

Stadtler, Eduard, 1084n

Stalin Joseph, 688n

Stam, Jan Cornelis (Varkel), 336, 1243

*La Stampa*, 349–50

Stampfer, Friedrich, 677, 1243

state capitalism, 412, 692; Bukharin on, 698–9; Lenin on, 667–8, 974

Statutes, Comintern, 357, 924, 950

Steinhardt, Karl, 66, 1243

Stelzer, Georg, 1161

Stepniak, Sergey Mikhailovich, 789, 1243

Stern, 588

Stinnes, Hugo, and Stinnesiation, 140, 245, 615–16, 630, 909, 926, 943, 1084n, 1243

Stoecker, Walter, 80n, 1243; and March Action, 531, 588; and Thalheimer-Stoecker resolution on Italy, 288–90, 291

Strasser, Josef, 1101, 1243

strategy, 39, 579, 1038–9; definition of, 924; tactics' relationship to, 368; Third Congress as school of, 2, 45–6. *See also* Tactics and Strategy agenda point; Tactics and Strategy Theses

strategy of attrition, 474

Striemer, Alfred, 618, 1243

Stuchka, Peter I., 66, 101, 1040, 1243

Sturm, Hertha, 1141n, 1148, 1243–4

Subhi, Mustafa, 74, 1244

suffrage: universal, 438; women's, 1011, 1019

Sukhomlin, Vasilii V., 348, 1244

Süleyman Nuri, 1244; in Eastern question discussion, 838–9

Sült, Wilhelm, 73, 1244

Sultanzade, Ahmed, 66, 101, 1244; theses on colonial question by, 44, 1187–90

Sun Yat-sen, 863, 1244

Suvorov, Alexander Vasilievich, 864, 1244

Sweden, 604, 606, 959. *See also* Communist Party of Sweden

Switzerland, 604, 766. *See also* Communist Party of Switzerland

syndicalists and syndicalism, 954; communism and, 720, 753–4; in France, 97–8, 282, 580–1, 590, 746–55, 749, 932, 957–8, 1122–4; in Germany, 453, 605–6, 643, 706; in Italy, 458–9, 712, 718; KAPD on, 456, 638–9; Lozovsky on, 719–25; RILU and, 605–11, 746; in Spain, 604, 744; at Third Comintern Congress, 40, 97–8, 719, 746–55; three varieties of, 605–6; Trotsky on, 1122–4. *See also* Industrial Workers of the World (IWW)

Syndicalist Union (Italy), 67

syndicalist unions, 453, 706

*Der Syndikalist*, 605, 1244

Syria, 847–8

Szántó, Béla, 387, 1244

Tactics and Strategy Commission, 391, 626, 634; Lenin speech to, 1142, 1155–7; Radek on tasks of, 388–9; report by, 797–802

Tactics and Strategy report and discussion, 28–9, 34–5, 61, 1153–5; Ballister (Minor) in, 519–22; Bell in, 551–5; Brand in, 526–8; Bukharin in, 508–15; Burian in, 494–9; Friesland in, 522–5; Heckert in, 481–94; Hempel in, 448–57; Lenin in, 465–73; Lukács in, 536–9; Malzahn in, 499–508; Michalak (Warszawski) in, 473–6; Münzenberg in, 533–5; Neumann in, 528–33; procedural debate, 582–3; Radek report, 406–45; Radek report from Commission, 797–802; Radek summary, 583–95; Sachs in, 556–60; statements on, 596–8; Terracini in, 457–65; Thalheimer in, 539–42; Thälmann in, 569–71; as tied to world economy report, 169, 406–7, 442, 457–8, 500, 547, 628; Trotsky in, 571–81; Vaillant-Couturier in, 548–51; Vaughan in, 476–9; vote, 598; Zetkin in, 542–8; Zinoviev in, 561–9. *See also* strategy

Tactics and Strategy Theses, 28, 30, 34; British delegation on, 551; as compromise, 572, 593; French delegation on, 548; German delegation support for, 1106–7, 1150, 1167; Hungarian minority on, 536; Lenin on preparation of, 28, 465–6, 1098–9; text of, 924–50; VKPD majority amendments to, 523, 549; VKPD Opposition amendments to, 522; Zetkin on, 547; Zinoviev closing speech on, 892. *See also* Amendments to Tactics Theses

Taguchi Unzo, 1244; at opening session, 98–9

*Taktik und Organisation der revolutionären Offensive*, 530, 546, 1132–3

Taussig, Herman, 223–4, 1244

taxes, 141, 883

tax in kind, 666, 699, 973

*Le Temps*, 103, 110, 943, 1121

Terracini, Umberto, 387, 1040, 1173, 1245; Amendments to Tactics Theses motivated by, 35, 457–65, 563; on Czechoslovak question, 255n; in discussion of Executive Committee report, 316–22; at expanded ECCI meeting, 208–9, 1132n; and Italy factory occupations, 285; as leader of PSI Communist faction, 8, 190; Lenin reply, 35, 464–73, 590, 1147–8; on Zionist organisations, 321–2

terrorism, individual, 335, 490, 944

Tesniaki, 745–6, 1245

Thalheimer, August, 297, 387, 507, 703, 1245; defends Amendments to Tactics Theses, 540–2; and exclusion of VKPD Oppositionists from Third Congress, 528–9, 539; interjections by, 531, 546, 577; Lenin on, 1097, 1098, 1139; and March Action, 21, 530, 531, 539–40, 574; resolution on Italy by, 288–90, 291; support of VKPD Left by, 10, 16; in tactics and strategy discussion, 539–42; *Taktik und Organisation* anthology by, 530, 546, 1132; on Theses on Tactics and Strategy, 597, 1106–7; theses presented to Third Congress by, 588, 1097, 1098; Trotsky reply to on world economy, 164–5; on VKPD internal situation, 806–7, 1159, 1166; in world economic discussion, 150–1; on Zetkin role, 1104–5

Thälmann, Ernst, 504, 576, 1245; Radek reply to, 588, 589; in tactics and strategy discussion, 569–71, 1153; Trotsky reply to, 571–2, 576; on VKPD internal situation, 1161–2

Thiers, Adolphe, 94, 1245

Third Comintern Congress organisation: agenda, 57–8, 60–4, 101–2; call, 59–66; delegations: Credentials Commission report on, 175–7; criteria for choosing, 65; listing of, 897–9; invitation to, 67–70; preparation of proceedings, 47; Presidium, 83; scheduling of, 23; secretariat of, 101; translation at, 47, 86n; voting basis and procedures, 170, 177–9, 881–2

Third Comintern Congress political characteristics:
— assessments: by Lenin, 1173, 1174–5; by Trotsky, 46; by Zinoviev, 891–6
— compromise, 3, 35, 37–9, 45, 541, 633; Lenin on, 37, 465–6, 1140, 1173; Radek on, 593, 1150; Trotsky on, 572; Zinoviev on, 891
— divisions within Russian CP leadership, 23, 24, 28–9, 39, 1135–7, 1154–5
— free and open atmosphere, 38, 45

— lies and slanders about, 81–2
— main debates, 33–6
— as school of strategy, 2, 45–6
— trends and tendencies, 2; Lenin on, 35, 466; Trotsky on, 573, 579, 1154
Thomas, Albert, 342, 600, 955, 1245; and ILO, 200, 601
Thomas, James Henry, 1245; as Amsterdam International leader, 80, 258, 602, 955; as British trade-union leader, 80, 92, 602
Thrace, 846
Thyssen, August, 140, 1245
Tolstoy, Leo, 386, 1147, 1245
Tommasi, Joseph, 102, 1245; at opening session, 97–8; in trade-union discussion, 746–55
Torralba Beci, Eduardo, 1245; in trade-union discussion, 743–4
'To the masses' watchword, 1, 2, 34, 39, 45, 269, 585, 1037, 1142
Tours Congress (1920), 10–11, 251, 1245; ECCI telegram to, 217; Zetkin at, 251, 655
trade balance, 112, 115–16, 905
Trade Union Commission, 625, 635, 887; report by, 883–7
trade-union reports and discussion: Bell in, 755–8; Bergmann in, 637–48; Brand in, 719; Earsmann in, 648–50; Haywood in, 715–18; Heckert report on, 613–25; Hourwich in, 741–3; Kolarov in, 744–6; Landler in, 731–4; Lozovsky in, 719–26; Lukács in, 537–8; Malzahn in, 705–8; Marković in, 762–3; Marshall (Bedacht) in, 726–9; Misiano in, 708–12; Morgan (Knight) in, 737–41; Pivio (Laukki) in, 759–62; Rees in, 735–7; report from Trade Union Commission on, 883–7; Riehs in, 734–5; Rwal (Reicher) in, 712–15; theses on, 953–65; Tomassi in, 746–55; Toralba Beci in, 743–4; Zinoviev in, 599–613, 893
trade unions, 40, 61–2; action programme for, 884, 960–5; and anti-labour laws, 148–9, 883; in Australia, 604, 648–50, 735–7; in Austria, 604, 734–5, 959; autonomy of, 612–13, 708–9, 726, 752; benefit plans of, 987; in Britain, 148, 153, 604, 631–2, 755–6, 758, 948, 958; in Bulgaria, 604, 744–6; in Canada, 739–40; and collective bargaining, 963; Communist fractions and cells in, 102, 612, 641–2, 643, 732, 735, 886, 957, 988, 992; Communist participation in, 986–9, 988; Communist parties' relationship to, 611–12, 751, 761–2, 956–7; Communist propaganda in, 818; Communist tasks in, 957–9; and compulsory arbitration, 964; and contracts, 986–7; and cooperative societies, 712, 968; in Czechoslovakia, 604, 958–9; exposure of bureaucracy in, 707–8, 987; expulsion of Communists from, 599, 797; fight for wages and working conditions by, 614, 617, 621, 709, 733, 962; in France, 67, 78, 97–8, 102, 604, 606–7, 725, 750, 751, 753, 1119, 1216; in Germany, 88–9, 604, 706, 953, 957, 1061, 1080–1; in Greece, 70, 604, 1216; in Hungary, 763; industrial, 616, 755, 757–8, 961; international collaboration and solidarity by, 622–3, 963; in Italy, 8, 70, 76, 199–200, 203, 258, 319–20, 321, 359, 369, 372, 382–5, 418, 419, 601–2, 604, 605, 710–12, 720–1, 722, 958; in Japan, 958; KAPD position on, 212, 248, 453, 456, 513–14, 637–48, 706, 725–6, 734, 884, 885–6, 887; loss of membership by, 714; lower-level bureaucracy in, 988; need for centralisation of, 616–17; need for unity of, 624, 625, 705–6; need for winning of, 612, 613, 707, 714, 732, 744, 825, 885, 957; in Netherlands, 70, 604, 1232; and neutrality question, 607–10, 650, 722, 742–3, 747–9, 885, 953–5, 960; in Norway, 604, 605, 763–4, 959; 'Out of the trade unions!' slogan, 642, 706, 755–6, 886–7, 959; in Poland, 250–1, 604, 713–14; and politics, 624, 747–9, 965; and profit-sharing schemes, 964; proposal to smash, 248, 639, 643; and revolutionary struggle, 614–15, 927–8, 964–5; role of, 613–15, 956; as schools of communism, 756–7; in Soviet Russia, 604, 611, 717, 741; in Spain, 604–5, 743–4, 958; and unemployed, 617–20, 723, 961–2; in United States, 640, 715–18, 726–9, 741–2, 958; and unorganised workers, 988; in Upper Silesia, 712–14; and women, 786–7, 1020; and workers' self-defence, 625, 963; in Yugoslavia, 604, 732
Tranquilli, Romolo, 597, 1246
transitional demands, 2; Radek on, 26, 440–2, 1066; theses on tactics on, 936–8

Treves, Claudio, 64, 65, 191, 257, 326, 367, 370, 930, 1246; during World War I, 345–6, 347n
*De Tribune*, 247n, 250, 1246
Triple Alliance, 148, 477, 918, 1214
Tripolitania, 845
Trotsky, Leon, 25–6, 1246; on Amendments to Tactics Theses, 573–81, 1154; assessment of Third Congress by, 46; as author of Third Congress manifesto, 169, 1034n, 1040; on Comintern-Soviet Russia relationship, 378–9; and differences within Russian CP leadership, 23, 28–9, 1135–7, 1154–5; in ECCI debate on France and Leftism, 209, 218, 577–8, *1114–25*, 1136; and economic theses, 169, 170, 632–3, 634; as honorary chair of Third Congress, 83; interjections by, 338, 464, 482, 508, 525, 526, 527, 551, 700; in Italian question discussion, 374–9; on KAPD, 210, 246, 247; Lenin solidarity with, 1129, 1130–1; letter to Lenin on Congress debate, 1153–5; on Levi, 577, 1149, 1151, 1164–5; on March Action, 25, 573–7, 1149; mentioned, 40, 66; on opportunism and verbal radicalism, 443; opposition at Third Congress to, 26, 27, 476, 527, 582, 597–8, 1127, 1153, 1154, 1165; permanent revolution perspective of, 674–5; on Polish-Soviet War, 6, 105; as Red Army commander, 139, 160, 320, 1155; in Soviet Russia discussion, 41, *683–9*; support to Zetkin by, 1149, 1150; in tactics and strategy discussion, 26, 35, *571–81*, 1153–5; on two trends at Third Congress, 573, 579, 1154; on VKPD internal situation, 1164–5, 1168; world economic crisis report by, 26, 33–4, *102–33*; world economic crisis summary by, *159–68*; on youth, 132, 232, 776, 1115–17
Tsereteli, Irakli Georgievich, 853, 1246
Tskhakaia, Mikhail Grigorievich, 66, 1246; in Eastern question discussion, 852–4
Turati, Filippo, 64, 284, 349, 370, 930, 1246; attacks on Soviet Russia and Bolshevism by, 256, 348, 367–8; Bissolati embrace of, 346, 362, 367; demands for expulsion of, 8, 11, 65, 184, 196, 287, 326; as early revisionist, 366–7; and factory occupations, 105, 319, 376; Lazzari on, 343; Lenin on, 349–50; Maffi on, 361–2; and party discipline, 376–7; and Socialist Concentration faction, 190–1; as Socialist Party candidate, 362, 518; and State Postwar Commission, 347; Trotsky on, 376–8, 379; urges restraint by workers, 201–2; during War, 345–6, 347, 362, 367
Turkestan, 864–5
'Turkestaners', 197–8, 215, 305, 306, 393, 397, 584, 1125, 1146
Turkey, 604, 844, 947; and Armenia, 849–50, 851; Greek war with, 839–40; industrialization in, 1188; repression of Communists in, 839, 849; several Communist parties in, 323, 839; Süleyman Nuri report on, 838–9
Twenty-One Conditions, 60, 65, 1246; Czechoslovak CP and, 14, 224–5, 922; French SP/CP and, 10, 216–17, 922; KAPD and, 388; and parliamentary fractions, 184; PSI and, 8, 11, 188–90, 317, 356, 357, 358; Second Comintern Congress adoption of, 60, 182, 183, 316; Socialist Concentration faction on, 191; Swedish CP and, 404; Zetkin on, 296
Two-and-a-Half International, 59, 59n, 80, 928, 1246; approach to programme by, 436, 438; as bulwark of capitalism, 658, 971; and colonial question, 659; and reparations controversy, 166–7; and Second International, 104, 949–50; and Soviet Russia, 411–12, 976; theses on tactics on, 948–50; Vienna Congress of (1921), 408; on world situation, 61, 407–8, 409–11; Youth International of, 769–70
Tywerousky, Oscar (Baldwin), 1040, 1246

UGT (General Union of Workers, Spain), 604, 744, 1216
Ukraine, 662
unemployment/unemployed, 124, 155, 502; capitalism and, 141, 619; KAPD on, 141, 451; as revolutionary factor, 938; trade unions and, 604, 617–20, 723, 961–2; women and, 1018; and working class, 536–7, 916
Ungern von Sternberg, Roman, 861, 1246
Unione Syndicale Italiana (USI), 605, 712, 1247
Union of Islamic Revolutionary Societies: about, 843n, 1246; report to Congress from, 843–9; Zinoviev on, 843, 849

Union of Oppositional Trade Unions (Fagoppositionens Sammenslutning, Denmark), 70, 229, 1246–7
Unitary Communist faction (Italy), 8, 11, 12, 286, 296, 371–2, 893, 1247
United Communist Party (US). *See* Communist Party of the United States
united front, 2, 501, 1036–8, 1192. *See also* Open Letter
United States: Black question in, 1194, 1195; and Britain, 115, 129–30, 151, 158, 166, 912, 913; economy of, 115–16, 122, 126, 167–8, 906–8; and Europe, 152, 159; impact of World War I on, 156, 906–7; as imperialist power, 156, 1182; and Japan, 816, 913; repression in, 75, 94, 520, 521, 926, 943; revolutionary prospects in, 167–8, 910–11; and Soviet Russia, 116–17, 678; strikebreaking in, 624, 625, 926; strikes and labour battles in, 105, 718, 760; trade unions in, 640, 715–18, 726–9, 741–2, 958; unemployment in, 124. *See also* Communist Party of the United States
*Unser Weg*, 1177, 1179
Upper Silesia, 158, 575; dispute over referendum in, 486, 712–13n; trade unions in, 712–14
USPD (Independent Social-Democratic Party of Germany), 148, 596, 768, 946, 1220; action programme of, 438; attacks on Soviet Russia by, 949; formation of, 485, 811, 822; and German government, 88, 575, 724; Halle Congress of, 9–10, 185, 204–5, 268, 396, 398, 483, 600, 922, 1218; during March Action, 949; rightward turn of, 61, 104; at Second Comintern Congress, 5, 79–80, 182–3; and VKPD Open Letter, 1061, 1067

Vaillant-Couturier, Paul, 274, 834, 880, 1247; at opening session, 86–7; in tactics and strategy discussion, 548–51
Vandervelde, Émile, 273, 310, 369, 610, 1247
Vaněk, Miloš, 496, 1247
Van Overstraeten, Edouard. *See* Overstraeten, Edouard van
Varga, Eugen, 34, 66, 113, 163, 1247; Economic Commission report by, 627–33
Varkel. *See* Stam, Jan Cornelis

Vaughan, Joseph J., 545, 1247; in tactics and strategy discussion, 476–9
Velbert and Köthen uprisings (1920), 240n, 244, 452
Vergeat, Marcel, 74, 1247
Versailles Treaty, 135, 156, 616, 838, 1247; Amsterdam International support of, 601, 621, 721; provisions of, 112n, 135–6n, 486n, 711n; Soviet Russia and, 676
*La Vie ouvrière*, 201–2, 310, 1247
Viscount de Eza, 721, 1247
VKPD. *See* Communist Party of Germany
Vladivostok, 657n, 860n, 861
Vodovosov, M. H., 192, 1247
*La Voix des femmes*, 791, 1247
Voroshilov, Kliment, 688n
Vorovsky, Vatslav Vatslavovich, 342, 1247
*Vorwärts* (Berlin), 105, 288n, 1066, 1248; *Le Peuple* polemic with, 166–7
*Vorwärts* (Reichenberg), 664, 1156, 1157, 1248

wages and working conditions: broadening of struggle for, 127; capitalist offensive against, 125, 127, 137, 138, 149, 163, 532, 960; Open Letter on, 1062; trade unions and fight for, 614, 617, 621, 709, 733–4, 962
Walcher, Jakob, 507, 595, 1248
Walecki, Henryk, 66, 527, 879–80, 1248
Warski. *See* Warszawski, Adolf
Warszawski, Adolf (Warski, Michalak), 387, 544, 703, 1040, 1248; in discussion of Executive Committee report, 250–2; Heckert on, 481–2; in tactics and strategy discussion, 473–6
Webb, Sidney, 953, 1248
Westarp, Kuno von, 1073, 1074, 1248
Western Federation of Miners, 717, 1248
White Guards, 295, 493, 625, 662–3, 711, 919, 926, 943–4, 1248
White Russia (Belarus), 872–3
white terror, 75, 89, 93, 149, 408, 926
Wiegand, 690
Wilhelm II, 768, 1248
Williams, Robert, 92, 1248
Wilson, Woodrow, 678n, 1248
Winnipeg general strike (1919), 740
Wirth, Joseph, 412, 948n, 1073n, 1248
Wissell, Rudolf, 955, 1248–9
Wolf, Felix, 298n, 312, 1249
Wolff, Fritz, 1096, 1249
Wolffheim, Fritz, 333, 676, 1249

women, 42; agitation and propaganda among, 1021–4; bourgeois, 781; and bourgeois feminists, 1011, 1012; capitalism and oppression of, 1009–10, 1012; communism as only road to liberation for, 1011–12; in Communist parties, 788–9, 790–1, 1014–16; Communist parties' failings toward, 781–2; double oppression of, 1012; drawing into proletarian struggle of, 780–1, 785–6, 788–9, 790–1, 793, 1010, 1012; in the East, 783–4, 1020–1; equal pay for equal work, 1019; forms and methods of work among, 1009–25, 1028–9; housewives, 1019; and marriage, 1011; and motherhood, 1014, 1015; no interests separate from proletariat, 790, 1012; political backwardness of, 1010–11, 1014; and proletarian dictatorship, 787–8, 794, 1029; recruitment into Communist parties of, 791, 1013–14; and right to vote, 1011, 1019; social conditions and prejudices of, 784–5; in Soviet Russia, 792–4, 1011, 1016–18, 1022, 1023; and trade unions, 786–7; unemployment among, 1018; and wage-labour, 132. *See also* Communist Women's Movement

workers' control, 145, 419–20, 625; RILU action programme on, 962, 963; as transitional demand, 441

workers' councils, 411, 440, 448, 639–40

workers' government, 4–5, 423–4n

Workers' League of Swiss Cities, 69

Workers' Opposition (Russia), 36, 41, 510, 679n; Kollontai speech on behalf of, 679–82

working class. *See* proletariat

world economic situation report and discussion, 34, 61; Bell in, 151–4; Brand in, 135–9; Koenen in, 157–9; Pogány in, 145–50; procedural discussion around vote for, 168–72; Roy in, 156–7; Sachs in, 139–42; Seemann in, 142–5; statements on, 633–4; Thalheimer in, 150–1; Trotsky report on, 33–4, 102–33; Trotsky summary on, 159–68; Zetkin in, 154–6

world economic theses, 34, 142, 143, 145–6; adoption of, 634; amendments to, 150, 158, 627–8; report from Economic Commission on, 627–33; tactics and strategy theses linked to, 169, 406–7, 442, 457–8, 500, 547, 628; text of, 901–20; voting procedure on, 172

world revolution: colonial countries and, 168, 1183; Lenin on, 657–8, 661; pace of, 924–5; and postwar revolutionary wave, 3, 104–6, 901–2, 918–19, 1142; Soviet Russia and, 657–8, 673, 675–6, 695–6, 697; winning masses as path to, 444–5

World War I, 98, 254; and Britain, 91, 156, 905; causes of, 129; economic impact of, 107–8, 123, 137, 903–4; France in, 86, 129; impact on colonial world of, 188–1189; peasants during, 131, 631, 909; PSI during, 201, 339, 342, 345–7, 360, 363, 367, 379–80; and United States, 156, 906–7; working-class struggle against, 770, 822, 1030–1; world bourgeoisie and, 610, 914; and world capitalist order, 128–9, 1182; youth during, 768, 770–1

Wrangel, Pyotr Nikolaevich, 949, 1249

Yahya, Imam Muhamed Hamid ed-Din, 848, 1249
Yap Island, 913
Yemen, 848
Yoshihara, Taro, 1249; in Eastern question discussion, 859–64
youth: bourgeois youth leagues, 769; Lenin on, 774; Trotsky on, 132, 232, 776, 1115–17; winning of to communism, 767, 768, 770; in working class, 766–7; during World War I, 1030–1; and youth vanguardism, 773, 1032–3. *See also* Communist Youth International; Communist youth movement
Youth Commission, 779; report by, 873–4
Yuan Shikai, 863, 1249
Yugoslav delegation, 399, 899
Yugoslavia: formation of, 276; general strike in, 762–3; and Hungarian soviet republic, 276–7; outlawing of CP and unions in, 277–8, 732. *See also* Communist Party of Yugoslavia

Zaglul Pasha, Saad, 845, 1249
Zalewski, Alexandre, 1130, 1249
Zápotocký Antonín, 75, 222, 223, 495, 496, 1249
Zetkin, Clara, 26–7, 1249–50; attacks on at Congress, 26–7, 303, 306, 307,

313–15, 474, 494, 542, 571, 1088, 1089, 1104–5, 1148–9, 1151–2; attacks on at International Women's Conference, 1141–2, 1148–9; birthday tribute for, 27, 651–5; Congress update to Levi, 1148–51; on ECCI envoys, 38, 292–3, 297, 298, 397–8; in discussion of Executive Committee report, *283–301*; on Italian question, 29, 284–8, 296, *371–4*, 459; on Italian question in VKPD, 287, 288–93; and Lenin, 27, 1137–48, 1151–2, 1174–8; on Levi, 293–4, 296–9, 297, 542, 1133, 1143–4, 1151; Levi initiative by, 27, 542, 1174, 1177; and Levi pamphlet, 492, 595, 1133; and Luxemburg, 595–6, 652, 654, 655, 1177; during March Action, 272, 493, 506; on March Action, 21–2, 27, 298–9, 300–1, 431, 544–6, 595, 1079–86, 1132–4, 1137–8; and Nobs, 229, 284; and 'offensive', 266–7, 299–300, 431, 473–4, 543–4, 546, 1137–8, 1150; police seizure of papers of, 288, 1094n; on public criticism of party errors, 546–7; Radek criticism of, 431, 590–1, 1071; report on Communist Women's Movement by, 42, *779–90*; resignation from Zentrale by, 16, 206, 294–5, 313, 396, 486, 1141; revolutionary history of, 493, *595–6*, 652–4; on Serrati, 284, 286–8, 290–1, 324, 373; struggle against War by, 652–3, 655, 770; support for Belgian CP by, 274; in tactics and strategy discussion, *542–8*; Terracini reply to, 316–17, 318–21; and Theses on Tactics and Strategy, 31, 522, 547, 564–5, 590; at Tours Congress, 251, 655; and Trotsky, 1149, 1150; and VKPD factional reconciliation, 547–8, 806, 1159, 1167, 1175; on winning masses, 2, 292–3; on world economic situation, *154–6*

Zhang Tailei, 1250; in Eastern question discussion, *856–7*; theses on colonial question by, 44, 1191–3

Zhordania, Noé Nikolaevich, 852, 853, 1250
Zibordi, Giovanni, 346, 358n, 1250
Zietz, Louise, 311, 1250
Zimmerwald conference and movement, 87, 341, 352, 369, 380, 770–1, 1250
Zimmerwald Left, 771, 1250
Zinoviev, Grigorii, 26, 1250; and Anna Geyer, 529, 1151; change of position at Third Congress, 26, 35, 562; closing speech by, *890–6*; on congress agenda, 101–2; Congress Call by, *59–66*; on Czechoslovak question, 220–7, 567–8, 1157; and differences within Russian CP leadership, 28–9, 1135–6, 1154; and ECCI emissaries, 15, 17, 1158; elected chair of Comintern, 888; elected chair of Presidium, 83; Executive Committee report by, 34, *179–235*; Executive Committee summary by, *395–9*; on French CP, 32, 33, 215–20; at Halle Congress, 396, 600; on Italian question, 29, 185–204, 317, 395–6, 562–3, 892–3; on KAPD, 209–15, 329–30, 331–2, 396–7; on Levi, 197–9, 215, 392–3; on March Action, 207–8, 566; on national and colonial question, 7, 849; on Open Letter, 15, 1064, 1066–9; on Organisation Theses, 833, 894; procedural motions by, 279, 331–2, 389–90, 545, 583, 804, 1168; on roll-call vote, 23, 882; and Small Bureau, 39, 181n, 882n; in tactics and strategy discussion, *561–9*, 1154; trade-union report by, *599–613*; on Union of Islamic Revolutionary Societies, 843, 849; on VKPD internal situation, 204–7, 804–5, 807, 1168; welcoming speech by, *73–82*; on youth movement, 765, 771; and Zetkin, 284, 295, 396, 1133. *See also* chairpersons, Third Congress
Zionism, 321–2
Zulawski, Zygmunt, 955, 1250